PRINCIPLE OF ECONOMICS
10E

ROGER A. ARNOLD

California State University
San Marcos

SOUTH-WESTERN

Australia • Brazil • Canada • . . . . Kingdom • United States

SOUTH-WESTERN
CENGAGE Learning™

Principles of Economics, 10E
Roger A. Arnold

Vice President of Editorial, Business:
  Jack W. Calhoun

Publisher: Joe Sabatino

Executive Editor: Mike Worls

Sr. Developmental Editors: Jennifer Thomas
  and Laura Bofinger Ansara

Sr. Marketing Manager: John Carey

Associate Marketing Manager: Betty Jung

Sr. Marketing Communications Manager:
  Sarah Greber

Sr. Content Project Manager: Cliff Kallemeyn

Sr. Media Editor: Deepak Kumar

Sr. Frontlist Buyer, Manufacturing:
  Sandee Milewski

Print Buyer: Arethea Thomas

Compositor: MPS Limited, a Macmillan Company

Sr. Art Director: Michelle Kunkler

Sr. Rights Specialist: Mardell Glinski Schultz

Internal Designer: Diane Gliebe/Design Matters

Cover Design: Patti Hudepohl

Photo Credits:

B/W Image: Comstock Images

Cover Image: iStockphoto/Jelica Videnovic

ExamView® is a registered trademark of eInstruction Corp. Windows is a registered trademark of the Microsoft Corporation used herein under license. Macintosh and Power Macintosh are registered trademarks of Apple Computer, Inc. used herein under license.

© 2011 Cengage Learning. All Rights Reserved.

Cengage Learning WebTutor™ is a trademark of Cengage Learning.

Library of Congress Control Number: 2010934474

International Edition ISBN 13: 978-0-538-47073-5
International Edition ISBN 10: 0-538-47073-9

Cengage Learning International Offices

Asia
www.cengageasia.com
tel: (65) 6410 1200

Brazil
www.cengage.com.br
tel: (55) 11 3665 9900

Latin America
www.cengage.com.mx
tel: (52) 55 1500 6000

Represented in Canada by Nelson Education, Ltd.
tel: (416) 752 9100/(800) 668 0671
www.nelson.com

Australia/New Zealand
www.cengage.com.au
tel: (61) 3 9685 4111

India
www.cengage.co.in
tel: (91) 11 4364 1111

UK/Europe/Middle East/Africa
www.cengage.co.uk
tel: (44) 0 1264 332 424

Cengage Learning is a leading provider of customized learning solutions with office locations around the globe, including Singapore, the United Kingdom, Australia, Mexico, Brazil, and Japan. Locate your local office at:
cengage.com/global

For product information: **www.cengage.com/international**
Visit your local office: **www.cengage.com/global**
Visit our corporate website: **www.cengage.com**

Printed in China
1 2 3 4 5 6 7 13 12 11 10

BRIEF CONTENTS

CONTENTS

AN INTRODUCTION TO ECONOMICS
PART 1 ECONOMICS: THE SCIENCE OF SCARCITY

OFFICE HOURS
"I Don't Believe That Every Time a Person Does Something, He Compares the Marginal Benefits and Costs." **18**

MACROECONOMICS

PART 2 MACROECONOMIC FUNDAMENTALS

PART 3 MACROECONIMIC STABILITY, INSTABILITY, AND FISCAL POLICY

CHAPTER 11: FISCAL POLICY AND THE FEDERAL BUDGET 232

PART 4   MONEY, THE ECONOMY, AND MONETARY POLICY

CHAPTER 12: MONEY, BANKING, AND THE FINANCIAL SYSTEM 252

CHAPTER 13: THE FEDERAL RESERVE SYSTEM 269

APPENDIX C: THE MARKET FOR RESERVES (OR THE FEDERAL FUNDS MARKET) 285

CHAPTER 14: MONEY AND THE ECONOMY 289

CHAPTER 15: MONETARY POLICY 314

PART 5 EXPECTATIONS AND GROWTH

MICROECONOMICS

PART 8 MICROECONOMIC FUNDAMENTALS

PART 9 PRODUCT MARKETS AND POLICIES

CHAPTER 25: MONOPOLISTIC COMPETITION, OLIGOPOLY, AND GAME THEORY 543

CHAPTER 26: GOVERNMENT AND PRODUCT MARKETS: ANTITRUST AND REGULATION 565

PART 10 FACTOR MARKETS AND RELATED ISSUES

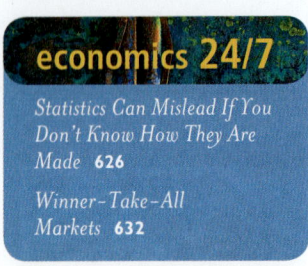

PART 11   MARKET FAILURE, PUBLIC CHOICE, AND SPECIAL-INTEREST-GROUP POLITICS

CHAPTER 31: MARKET FAILURE: EXTERNALITIES, PUBLIC GOODS, AND ASYMMETRIC INFORMATION 657

PART 12 GOVERNMENT AND MARKETS

The Global Economy

PART 13 INTERNATIONAL ECONOMICS AND GLOBALIZATION

CHAPTER 34: INTERNATIONAL TRADE 722

CHAPTER 35: INTERNATIONAL FINANCE 740

PRACTICAL ECONOMICS

PART 14 FINANCIAL MATTERS

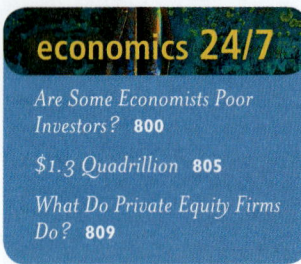

WEB CHAPTER

PART 15   WEB CHAPTER

CHAPTER 38: AGRICULTURE: PROBLEMS, POLICIES, AND UNINTENDED EFFECTS

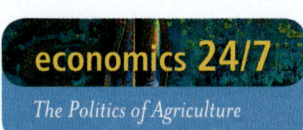

Roger Arnold

THE ECONOMY IS TOUGH— ECONOMICS DOESN'T HAVE TO BE!

Ever wonder what economic factors might determine your first job after college or if a tax on soda would reduce obesity? *Principles of Economics* answers these questions and many more. Using intriguing pop culture examples, Arnold's tenth edition is revised to include the most comprehensive coverage of the financial and economic crisis available. Self-tests help determine how well you're grasping concepts, a traditional study guide prepares you for tests, and **Economics CourseMate** offers a graphing tutorial, quizzes, videos and more. It's all carefully designed to help you get the best economics grade possible!

Features for Student Understanding

Office Hours

Emulating common questions asked by economics students, just like you, replace the need to wait in line for office hours with your instructor.

Enhanced "Thinking Like an Economist"

This classic feature now rotates with Finding Economics throughout the text to illustrate that economics is all around us.

Economics 24/7

Illustrates the practical relevance of key concepts by exploring anything that can be explained through economic analysis.

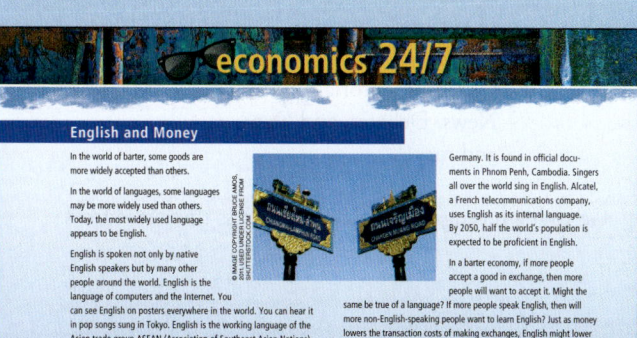

Make the Grade with Economics CourseMate.

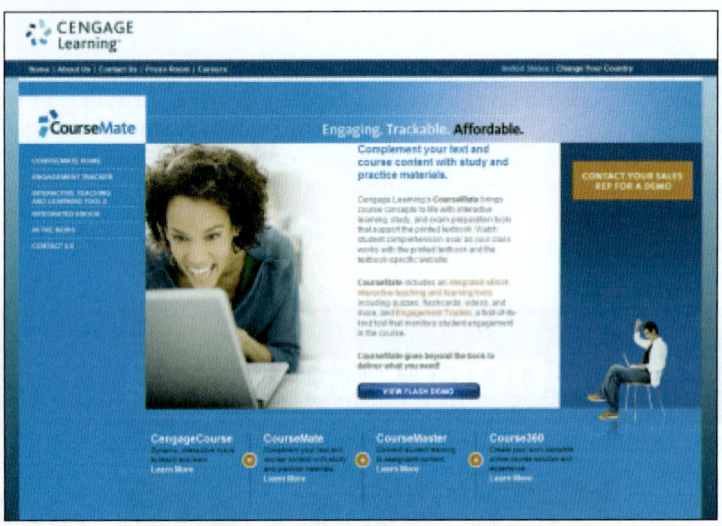

Complement your text and course content with study and practice materials.
Economics CourseMate brings course concepts to life with interactive learning, study, and exam preparation tools that support the printed textbook. Use Economics CourseMate to make the grade!

Economics CourseMate includes:

- an interactive eBook, with highlighting, note taking and search capabilities
- interactive learning tools including:
  - Quizzes
  - Flashcards
  - Videos
  - Graphing Tutorials
  - News, Debates, and Data
  - and more!

Go to login.cengagebrain.com to access these resources.

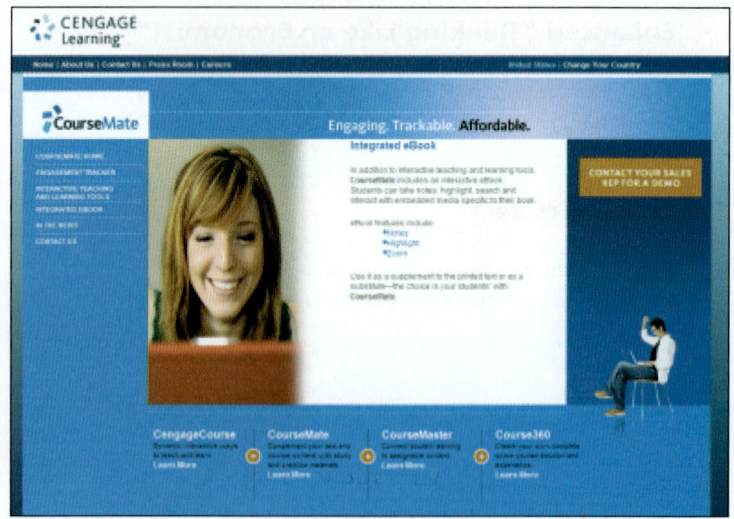

Make Learning Economics Easier!

Video Office Hours with Roger Arnold

New Video Lectures! Roger Arnold takes you through key concepts and graphs in each chapter—just like you were in the classroom with him. Using innovative video, he provides both short concept pieces and longer lectures for each chapter, talking through the concepts just as he would in class, while displaying lecture points and demonstrating graphs visually. For your convenience, you can play and replay these video lectures as often as is needed to review concepts.

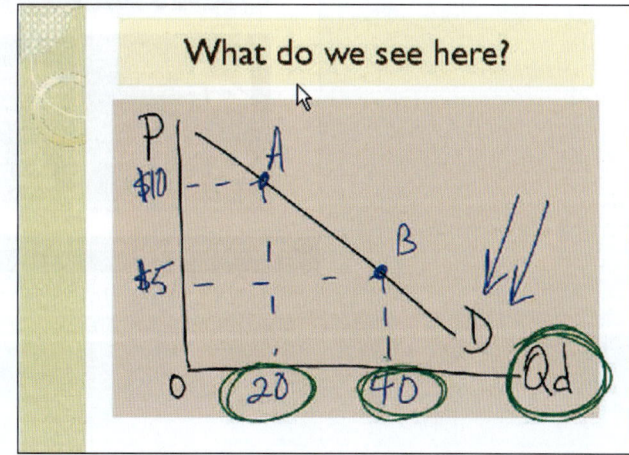

The Global Economic Watch

Cengage Learning's Global Economic Watch: Lessons from real life right now! Cengage Learning's Global Economic Watch adds current events into your studies—through a powerful, continuously updated online suite of content, discussion forums, and more.

The Watch will help you thoroughly understand the global economic downturn. Benefit from these specific features:

- A content-rich blog of breaking news, expert analysis and commentary—updated multiple times each day—plus links to many other blogs.

- A powerful real-time database of hundreds of relevant and vetted journal, newspaper, and periodical articles and videos and podcasts—updated four times every day.

- A thorough overview and timeline of events leading up to the global economic crisis.

- Forums for sharing questions, ideas, and opinions.

History is happening now. Benefit from this resource by learning all the details. **Learn more at www.cengage.com/thewatch.**

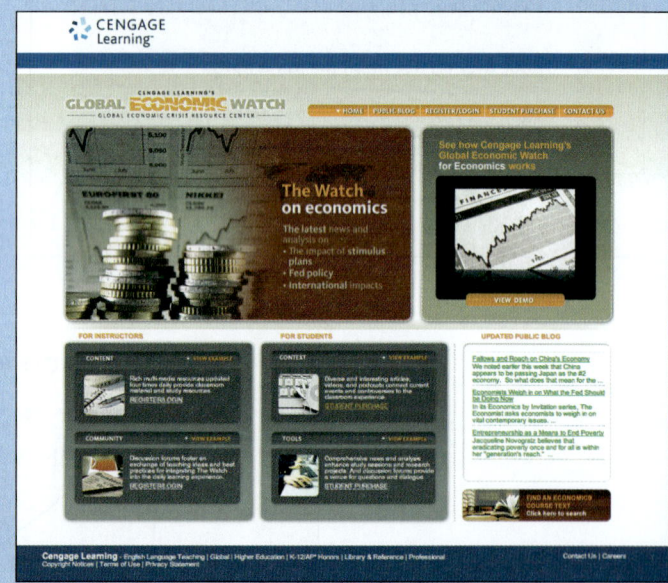

Arnold + Aplia Deliver

Aplia

Aplia is an online interactive learning solution that improves comprehension and outcomes by increasing student effort and engagement. Created by economist, Paul Romer, for his classroom, Aplia provides automatically graded assignments that were written to make the most of the web medium and contain detailed immediate explanations on every question. A digital edition of the complete Arnold textbook is embedded in the Aplia course.

Aplia has been used by more than 1,000,000 students at over 1,800 institutions making it the best selling online solution for principles of economics by far.

For complete details or to access a demonstration, visit: **www.aplia.com.**

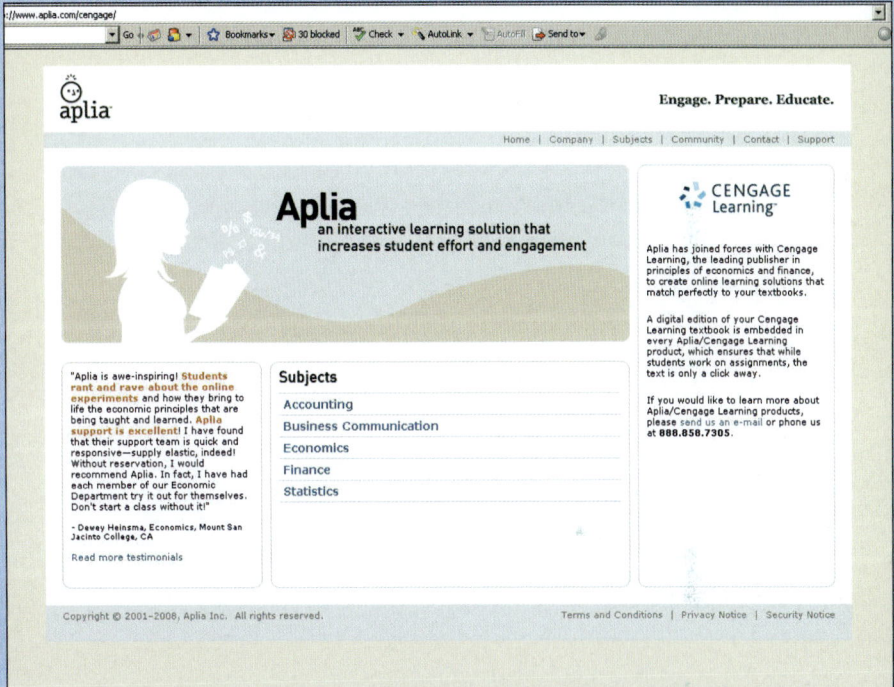

To
Sheila, Daniel,
and David

This book could not have been written and published without the generous expert assistance of many people. A deep debt of gratitude is owed to the reviewers of the first through ninth editions and to the reviewers of this edition, the tenth.

First Edition Reviewers

Jack Adams
University of Arkansas, Little Rock

William Askwig
University of Southern Colorado

Michael Babcock
Kansas State University

Dan Barszcz
College of DuPage, Illinois

Robert Berry
Miami University, Ohio

George Bohler
Florida Junior College

Tom Bonsor
Eastern Washington University

Michael D. Brendler
Louisiana State University

Baird Brock
Central Missouri State University

Kathleen Bromley
Monroe Community College, New York

Douglas Brown
Georgetown University

Ernest Buchholz
Santa Monica Community College, California

Gary Burbridge
Grand Rapids Junior College, Michigan

Maureen Burton
California Polytechnic University, Pomona

Carol Carnes
Kansas State University

Paul Coomes
University of Louisville, Kentucky

Eleanor Craig
University of Delaware

Wilford Cummings
Grosmont College, California

Diane Cunningham
Glendale Community College, California

Douglas C. Darran
University of South Carolina

Edward Day
University of Southern Florida

Johan Deprez
University of Tennessee

James Dietz
California State University, Fullerton

Stuart Dorsey
University of West Virginia

Natalia Drury
Northern Virginia Community College

Lu Ann Duffus
California State University, Hayward

John Eckalbar
California State University, Chico

John Elliot
University of Southern California

Charles Fischer
Pittsburg State University, Kansas

John Gemello
San Francisco State University

Carl Guelzo
Cantonsville Community College, Maryland

Jan Hansen
University of Wisconsin, Eau Claire

John Henderson
Georgia State University

Ken Howard
East Texas Baptist University

Mark Karscig
Central Missouri State University

Stanley Keil
Ball State University, Indiana

Richard Kieffer
State University of New York, Buffalo

Gene Kimmett
William Rainey Harper College, Illinois

Luther Lawson
University of North Carolina

Frank Leori
College of San Mateo, California

Kenneth Long
New River Community College, Virginia

Michael Magura
University of Toledo, Ohio

Bruce McCrea
Lansing Community College, Michigan

Gerald McDougall
Wichita State University, Kansas

Kevin McGee
University of Wisconsin, Oshkosh

Francois Melese
Auburn University, Alabama

Herbert Miliken
American River College, California

Richard Miller
Pennsylvania State University

Ernest Moser
Northeast Louisiana University

Farhang Niroomand
University of Southern Mississippi

Eliot Orton
New Mexico State University

Marty Perline
Wichita State University, Kansas

Harold Petersen
Boston College

Douglas Poe
University of Texas, Austin

Joseph Rezney
St. Louis Community College, Missouri

Terry Ridgway
University of Nevada, Las Vegas

Thomas Romans
State University of New York, Buffalo

Robert Ross
Bloomsburg State College, Pennsylvania

Keith A. Rowley
Baylor University, Texas

Anandi Sahu
Oakland University, Michigan

Richard Scoggins
California State University, Long Beach

Paul Seidenstat
Temple University, Pennsylvania

Shahram Shafiee
North Harris County College, Texas

Alan Sleeman
Western Washington University

John Sondey
University of Idaho

Robert W. Thomas
Iowa State University

Richard L. Tontz
California State University, Northridge

Roger Trenary
Kansas State University

Bruce Vanderporten
Loyola University, Illinois

Thomas Weiss
University of Kansas

Richard O. Welch
University of Texas at San Antonio

Donald A. Wells
University of Arizona

John Wight
University of Richmond, Virginia

Thomas Wyrick
Southwest Missouri State University

Second Edition Reviewers

Scott Bloom
North Dakota State University

Thomas Carroll
University of Nevada, Las Vegas

Larry Cox
Southwest Missouri State University

Diane Cunningham
Los Angeles Valley College

Emit Deal
Macon College

Michael Fabritius
University of Mary Hardin Baylor

Frederick Fagal
Marywood College

Ralph Fowler
Diablo Valley College

Bob Gilette
Texas A&M University

Lynn Gillette
Indiana University, Indianapolis

Simon Hakim
Temple University

Lewis Karstensson
University of Nevada, Las Vegas

Abraham Kidane
California State University, Dominguez Hills

W. Barbara Killen
University of Minnesota

J. David Lages
Southwest Missouri State University

Anthony Lee
Austin Community College

Marjory Mabery
Delaware County Community College

Bernard Malamud
University of Nevada, Las Vegas

Michael Marlow
California Polytechnic State University, San Luis Obispo

Phil J. McLewin
Ramapo College of New Jersey

Tina Quinn
Arkansas State University

Terry Ridgway
University of Nevada, Las Vegas

Paul Snoonian
University of Lowell

Paul Taube
Pan American University

Roger Trenary
Kansas State University

Charles Van Eaton
Hillsdale College

Mark Wheeler
Bowling Green State University

Thomas Wyrick
Southwest Missouri State University

Third Edition Reviewers

Carlos Aguilar
University of Texas, El Paso

Rebecca Ann Benakis
New Mexico State University

Scott Bloom
North Dakota State University

Howard Erdman
Southwest Texas Junior College

Arthur Friedberg
Mohawk Valley Community College

Nancy A. Jianakoplos
Colorado State University

Lewis Karstensson
University of Nevada, Las Vegas

Rose Kilburn
Modesto Junior College

Ruby P. Kishan
Southeastern Community College

Duane Kline
Southeastern Community College

Charles A. Roberts
Western Kentucky University

Bill Robinson
University of Nevada, Las Vegas

Susan C. Stephenson
Drake University

Charles Van Eaton
Hillsdale College

Richard O. Welch
The University of Texas at San Antonio

Calla Wiemer
University of Hawaii at Manoa

Fourth Edition Reviewers

Uzo Agulefo
North Lake College

Kari Battaglia
University of North Texas

Scott Bloom
North Dakota State University

Harry Ellis, Jr.
University of North Texas

Mary Ann Hendryson
Western Washington University

Eugene Jones
Ohio State University

Ki Hoon Him
Central Connecticut State University

James McBrearty
University of Arizona

John A. Panagakis
Onondaga Community College

Bill Robinson
University of Nevada, Las Vegas

George E. Samuels
Sam Houston State University

Ed Scahill
University of Scranton

Charles Van Eaton
Hillsdale College

Thomas Wyrick
Southwest Missouri State University

Fifth Edition Reviewers

Kari Battaglia
University of North Texas

Douglas A. Conway
Mesa Community College

Lee A. Craig
North Carolina State University

Harry Ellis, Jr.
University of North Texas

Joe W. Essuman
University of Wisconsin, Waukesha

Dipak Ghosh
Emporia State University

Shirley J. Gideon
The University of Vermont

Mary Ann Hendryson
Western Washington University

Calvin A. Hoerneman
Delta College

George H. Jones
University of Wisconsin, Rock County

Donald R. Morgan
Monterey Peninsula College

John A. Panagakis
Onondaga Community College

Bill Robinson
University of Nevada, Las Vegas

Steve Robinson
The University of North Carolina at Wilmington

David W. Yoskowitz
Texas Tech University

Sixth Edition Reviewers

Hendrikus J.E.M. Brand
Albion College

Curtis Clarke
Dallas County Community College

Andrea Gorospe
Kent State University, Trumbull

Mehrdad Madresehee
Lycoming College

L. Wayne Plumly
Valdosta State University

Craig Rogers
Canisius College

Uri Simonsohn
Carnegie Mellon University

Philip Sprunger
Lycoming College

Lea Templer
College of the Canyons

Soumya Tohamy
Berry College

Lee Van Scyoc
University of Wisconsin, Oshkosh

Seventh Edition Reviewers

Pam Coates
San Diego Mesa College

Peggy F. Crane
Southwestern College

Richard Croxdale
Austin Community College

Harry Ellis, Jr.
University of North Texas

Craig Gallet
California State University, Sacramento

Kelly George
Embry-Riddle Aeronautical University

Anne-Marie Gilliam
Central Piedmont Community College

Richard C. Schiming
Minnesota State University, Mankato

Lea Templer
College of the Canyons

Jennifer VanGilder
California State University, Bakersfield

William W. Wilkes
Athens State University

Janice Yee
Wartburg College

Eighth Edition Reviewers

Dr. Clive R. Belfied
Queens College, City University of New York

Barry Bomboy
J. Sargeant Reynolds Community College

James Bryan
North Harris Montgomery Community College

Peggy F. Crane
Southwestern College

Richard Croxdale
Austin Community College

Harry Ellis, Jr.
University of North Texas

Kelly George
Embry Riddle Aeronautical University

Alan Kessler
Providence College

Denny Myers
Oklahoma City Community College

Charles Newton
Houston Community College

Ahmad Saranjam
Northeastern University

Jennifer VanGilder, PhD
*California State University
Bakersfield*

Janice Yee
Wartburg College

Ninth Edition Reviewers

Bart Allen
Northern Oklahoma College

Nand Arora
Cleary University

Fathollah Bagheri
University of North Dakota

Mohammad Bajwa
Northampton Community College

Atin Basuchoudhary
Virginia Military Institute

Susan Bell
Seminole Community College

Douglas Campbell
University of Memphis

Franny Chan
Mt. San Antonio College

Stephen B. Davis
Southwest Minnesota State University

William L. Davis
University of Tennessee, Martin

James Dulgeroff
California State University, San Bernandino

Dr. J. Pat Fuller
Brevard Community College

Dr. Robert Garnett
Texas Christian University

Lynde Gilliam
Metropolitan State College of Denver

Judith A. Grenkowicz
Kirtland Community College

Pablo Hernandez
Hollins University

Philip L. Hersch
Wichita State University

Michael Heslop
*Northern Virginia Community College
(NOVA)*

Chandrea Hopkins
College of Lake County

Brian K. Jackson
Oklahoma Wesleyan University

Bun Song Lee
Northwestern State University

Joanne Leoni
Johnson & Wales University

Michael L. Marlow
*California Polytechnic State
University*

Peter Mavrokordatos
*Tarrant County Community
College*

Dominic F. Minadeo
Troy University

Dr. Barbara B. Murray
Baltimore City Community College

Bernard J. Sharkey, Jr.
Louisiana State University

Joe Silverman
MiraCosta College

Martha Stuffler
Irvine Valley College

Vicky Tucker
Lewis University

Mary Louis White
Albright University

Tenth Edition Reviewers

Ercument Aksoy
Los Angeles Valley College

Carol Decker
Tennessee Wesleyan College

Stephen Elliott
*Northwestern State
University*

Kelly Whealan George
*Embry Riddle Aeronautical
University*

Aubrey P. Haynes
Southwest Texas Junior College

Tori Knight
Carson-Newman College

Bun Song Lee
Northwestern State University

Lucy Malakar
*Lorain County Community
College*

Lea Templer
College of the Canyons

Jan Wyatt
Hesser College

I would like to thank Peggy Crane of Southwestern College, who revised the Test Bank, and Jane Himarios of the University of Texas at Arlington, who revised the Instructor's Manual. I would also like to thank Paul Schneiderman of Southern New Hampshire University for creating the PowerPoint slides that accompany this text. I owe a dept of gratitude to all the fine and creative people I worked with at South-Western/Cengage Learning. These persons include Jack Calhoun; Michael Worls, Executive Editor for Economics; Jennifer Thomas and Laura Ansara, Senior Developmental Editors; Cliff Kallemeyn, Senior Content Project Manager; John Carey, Senior Marketing Manager; Michelle Kunkler, Senior Art Director; and Sandee Milewski, Senior Frontlist Buyer.

My deepest debt of gratitude goes to my wife, Sheila, and to my two sons, David, twenty years old, and Daniel, twenty-three years old. They continue to make all my days happy ones.

Roger A. Arnold

CHAPTER 1

WHAT ECONOMICS IS ABOUT

© PHILIP SCALIA / ALAMY

Introduction You are about to begin your study of economics. Before discussing particular topics in economics, we think it best to give you an overview of what economics is and of some of the key concepts. The key concepts can be compared to musical notes: Just as musical notes are repeated in any song (you hear the musical note G over and over again), so are the key concepts in economics repeated. Some of these concepts are scarcity, opportunity cost, efficiency, marginal decision making, incentives, and exchange.

A DEFINITION OF ECONOMICS

In this section, we discuss a few key economic concepts; then we incorporate knowledge of these concepts into a definition of economics.

Goods and Bads

Economists talk about *goods* and *bads*. A good is anything that gives a person utility, or satisfaction. Here is a partial list of some goods: a computer, a car, a watch, a television set, friendship, and love. You will notice from our list that a good can be either tangible or intangible. A computer is a tangible good; friendship is an intangible good. Simply put, for something to be a good (whether tangible or intangible), it only has to give someone utility or satisfaction.

A bad is something that gives a person disutility, or dissatisfaction. If the flu gives you disutility or dissatisfaction, then it is a bad. If the constant nagging of an acquaintance is something that gives you disutility or dissatisfaction, then it is a bad.

People want goods, and they do not want bads. In fact, they will pay to get goods ("Here is $1,000 for the computer"), and they will pay to get rid of bads ("I'd be willing to pay you, doctor, if you can prescribe something that will shorten the time I have the flu").

Can something be a *good* for one person and a *bad* for another person? Smoking cigarettes gives some people utility; it gives others disutility. We conclude that smoking cigarettes can be a *good* for some people and a *bad* for others. This must be why the wife tells her husband, "If you want to smoke, you should do it outside." In other words, "Get those *bads* away from me."

Good
Anything from which individuals receive utility or satisfaction.

Utility
The satisfaction one receives from a good.

Bad
Anything from which individuals receive disutility or dissatisfaction.

Disutility
The dissatisfaction one receives from a bad.

Resources

Goods do not just appear before us when we snap our fingers. It takes resources to produce goods. (Sometimes *resources* are referred to as *inputs* or *factors of production*.)

Generally, economists divide resources into four broad categories: *land, labor, capital,* and *entrepreneurship*.

- **Land** includes natural resources, such as minerals, forests, water, and unimproved land. For example, oil, wood, and animals fall into this category. (Sometimes economists refer to this category simply as *natural resources*.)

- **Labor** consists of the physical and mental talents that people contribute to the production process. For example, a person building a house is using his or her own labor.

- **Capital** consists of produced goods that can be used as inputs for further production. Factories, machinery, tools, computers, and buildings are examples of capital. One country might have more capital than another; that is, it has more factories, machinery, tools, and the like.

- **Entrepreneurship** refers to the talent that some people have for organizing the resources of land, labor, and capital to produce goods, seek new business opportunities, and develop new ways of doing things.

Scarcity and a Definition of Economics

We are now ready to define a key concept in economics: *scarcity*. Scarcity is the condition in which our wants (for goods) are greater than the limited resources (land, labor, capital, and entrepreneurship) available to satisfy those wants. In other words, we want goods, but not enough resources are available to provide us with all the goods we want.

Look at it this way: Our wants (for goods) are infinite, but our resources (which we need to produce the goods) are finite. Scarcity is the result of our infinite wants hitting up against finite resources.

Many economists say that if scarcity didn't exist, neither would economics. In other words, if our wants weren't greater than the limited resources available to satisfy them, there would be no field of study called economics. This is similar to saying that if matter and motion didn't exist, neither would physics or that if living things didn't exist, neither would biology. For this reason, we define economics in this text as the science of scarcity. More completely, *economics is the science of how individuals and societies deal with the fact that wants are greater than the limited resources available to satisfy those wants.*

ⓣhinking like AN ECONOMIST

Scarcity Affects Everyone Everyone in the world has to face scarcity, even billionaires. Billionaires may be able to satisfy more of their wants for tangible goods (houses, cars) than most people, but they still may not have the resources to satisfy all their wants. Their wants might include more time with their children, more friendship, no disease in the world, peace on earth, and a hundred other things that they don't have the resources to "produce." ● ● ●

THINKING IN TERMS OF SCARCITY'S EFFECTS Scarcity has effects. Here are three: (1) the need to make choices, (2) the need for a rationing device, and (3) competition.

Choices People have to make choices because of scarcity. Because our unlimited wants are greater than our limited resources, some wants must go unsatisfied. We must choose which wants we will satisfy and which we will not. Jeremy asks, "Do I go to

---

Land
All natural resources, such as minerals, forests, water, and unimproved land.

Labor
The physical and mental talents people contribute to the production process.

Capital
Produced goods that can be used as inputs for further production, such as factories, machinery, tools, computers, and buildings.

Entrepreneurship
The talent that some people have for organizing the resources of land, labor, and capital to produce goods, seek new business opportunities, and develop new ways of doing things.

Scarcity
The condition in which our wants are greater than the limited resources available to satisfy those wants.

Economics
The science of scarcity; the science of how individuals and societies deal with the fact that wants are greater than the limited resources available to satisfy those wants.

Hawaii, or do I pay off my car loan earlier?" Ellen asks, " Do I buy the new sweater or two new shirts?"

Need for a Rationing Device A rationing device is a means of deciding who gets what of available resources and goods. Scarcity implies the need for a rationing device. If people have infinite wants for goods and if only limited resources are available to produce the goods, then a rationing device is needed to decide who gets the available quantity of goods. Dollar price is a rationing device. For example, 100 cars are on the lot, and everyone wants a new car. How do we decide who gets what quantity of the new cars? The answer is to use the rationing device called *dollar price*. The people who pay the dollar price for a new car end up with one.

Rationing Device

A means for deciding who gets what of available resources and goods.

Scarcity and Competition Do you see competition in the world? Are people competing for jobs? Are states and cities competing for businesses? Are students competing for grades? The answer to all these questions is yes. The economist wants to know why this competition exists and what form it takes. First, the economist concludes, *competition exists because of scarcity.* If there were enough resources to satisfy all our seemingly unlimited wants, people would not have to compete for the available but limited resources.

Second, the economist sees that competition takes the form of people trying to get more of the rationing device. If dollar price is the rationing device, people compete to earn dollars. Look at your own case. You are a college student working for a degree. One reason (but perhaps not the only reason) you are attending college is to earn a higher income after graduation. But why do you want a higher income? You want it because it will allow you to satisfy more of your wants.

Suppose muscular strength (measured by lifting weights) were the rationing device instead of dollar price. People with more muscular strength would receive more resources and goods than people with less muscular strength. In that case, people would compete for muscular strength. (Would they spend more time at the gym lifting weights?) The lesson is simple: *Whatever the rationing device is, people will compete for it.*

finding ECONOMICS

At the Campus Book Store To learn economics well, you must practice what you learn. One of the ways to practice economics is to find it in everyday life. Consider the following scene: You are in the campus bookstore buying a book for your computer science course, and you are handing over $85 to the cashier. Can you find the economics in this simple scene? Before you read on, think about it for a minute.

Let's work backward to find the economics. You are currently handing the cashier $85. We know that dollar price is a rationing device. But let's now ask ourselves why we would need a rationing device to get the book. The answer is scarcity. In other words, scarcity is casting its long shadow there in the bookstore as you buy a book. We have found one of the key economic concepts—scarcity—in the campus bookstore. (If you also said that a book is a good, then you have found even more economics in the bookstore. Can you find more than scarcity and a good?) ▲▲▲

SELF-TEST

(Answers to Self-Test questions are in Answers to Self-Test Questions at the back of the book.)

1. True or false? Scarcity is the condition of finite resources. Explain your answer.

2. How does competition arise out of scarcity?

3. How does choice arise out of scarcity?

Low Admission Rates at Yale

Each year Yale University receives more applications for admission to the freshmen class than spots available. In most years, for every 100 applications for admission that Yale receives, it can accept only seven applicants for admission. What Yale has to do, then, is ration its available admission spots.

How does it ration its available spots? One way is simply to use money as a rationing device. In other words, raise the dollar amount of attending Yale to a high enough level so that the number of spots equals the number of students willing and available to pay for admission. To illustrate, think of Yale as auctioning off spots in its freshman class. It calls out a price of $50,000 a year, and at this price more people wish to be admitted to Yale than there are spots available. Yale keeps on raising the price until the number of students who are willing and able to pay the tuition are equal to the number of available spots. Maybe this price is, say, $200,000.

As we know, Yale does not ration its available spots this way. In fact, it uses numerous rationing devices in an attempt to whittle down the number of applicants to the number of available spots. For example, it might use the rationing device of high school grades. Anyone with a GPA in high school of less than, say, 3.50 is not going to be admitted. If, after doing this, Yale still has too many applicants, it might then make use of the rationing device of standardized test scores. Anyone with an SAT score of under, say, 2100 is eliminated from the pool of applicants. If there are still too many applicants, then perhaps other rationing devices will be used, such as academic achievements, community service, degree of interest in attending Yale, and so on.

Yale might also decide that it wants to admit certain students over others, even if the two categories of students have the same academic credentials. For example, suppose Yale wants at least one student from each state in the country, and only 10 students from Wyoming have applied to go to Yale whereas 300 students from California have applied. Yale could very well use the rationing device of state diversity to decide in favor of the student from Wyoming instead of the applicant from California.

In the first week of April each year, Yale sends out many more rejection letters than acceptance letters. No doubt some students who are rejected by Yale feel that some of the students who were accepted might not be as academically strong as they are. No doubt the student with a 4.00 GPA and a perfect SAT score of 2400 feels that he might have been slighted by Yale when he learns that a student in his high school with a 3.86 GPA and SAT score of 2180 was chosen over him. What did

the 3.86–2180 student have that he didn't have? What rationing device benchmark did the rejected student score lower on?

In life, you will often see arguing over what the rationing device for certain things should be. Should high school grades and standardized test scores be the only two rationing devices for college admission? What role should money play as a rationing device when applying to college? What role should ethnic or racial diversity, or state diversity, or income diversity play in the application process? Our point is a simple one: With scarcity comes the need for a rationing device. More people want a spot at Yale than there are spots available. Yale has to use one or more rationing devices to decide who will be accepted and who will be rejected.

KEY CONCEPTS IN ECONOMICS

A number of key concepts in economics define the field. We discuss a few of these concepts next.

Opportunity Cost

So far we have established that people must make choices because scarcity exists. In other words, because our seemingly unlimited wants push up against limited resources, some wants must go unsatisfied. We must therefore *choose* which wants we will satisfy and which we will not. The most highly valued opportunity or alternative forfeited when we make a choice is known as opportunity cost. Every time you make a choice, you incur an opportunity cost. For example, you have chosen to read this chapter. In making this choice, you denied yourself the benefits of doing something else. You could have watched television, written a text message to a friend, taken a nap, eaten a few slices of pizza, read a novel, shopped for a new computer, and so on. Whatever you *would have chosen* to do is the opportunity cost of your reading this chapter. For example, if you would have watched television instead of reading this chapter—if this was your next best alternative—then the opportunity cost of reading this chapter is watching television.

THERE IS NO SUCH THING AS A FREE LUNCH Economists are fond of saying that *there is no such thing as a free lunch*. This catchy phrase expresses the idea that opportunity costs are incurred whenever choices are made. Perhaps this is an obvious point, but consider how often people mistakenly assume that there is a free lunch. For example, some parents think education is free because they do not pay tuition for their children to attend public elementary school. That's a misconception. "Free" implies no sacrifice and no opportunities forfeited, but an elementary school education requires resources that could be used for other things.

Consider the people who speak about free medical care, free housing, free bridges ("there's no charge to cross it"), and free parks. Again, free medical care, free housing, free bridges, and free parks are misconceptions. The resources that provide medical care, housing, bridges, and parks could have been used in other ways.

ⓣhinking like AN ECONOMIST

Zero Price Doesn't Mean Zero Cost A friend gives you a ticket to an upcoming concert for zero price (you pay nothing). Does it follow that zero price means zero cost? No. There is still an opportunity cost of attending the concert. Whatever you would be doing if you don't go to the concert is the opportunity cost of attending. To illustrate, if you don't attend the concert, you would hang out with friends. The value you place on hanging out with friends is the opportunity cost of your attending the concert. ▲▲▲

Opportunity Cost and Behavior

Economists believe that a change in opportunity cost can change a person's behavior. For example, Ryan, who is a sophomore at college, attends classes Monday through Thursday of every week. Every time he chooses to go to class, he gives up the opportunity to do something else, such as earn $12 an hour working at a job. The opportunity cost of Ryan's spending an hour in class is $12.

Now let's raise the opportunity cost of attending class. On Tuesday, we offer Ryan $70 to skip his economics class. He knows that if he attends his economics class, he will forfeit $70. What will Ryan do? An economist would predict that as the opportunity cost of attending class increases relative to its benefits, Ryan is less likely to go to class.

This is how economists think about behavior: *The higher the opportunity cost of doing something is, the less likely it will be done.* This is part of the economic way of thinking.

Look at Exhibit 1, which summarizes some of the things about scarcity, choice, and opportunity cost up to this point.

Opportunity Cost
The most highly valued opportunity or alternative forfeited when a choice is made.

EXHIBIT 1

Scarcity and Related Concepts

Scarcity

Because of scarcity, a rationing device is needed.

Whatever the rationing device, people will compete for it. Scarcity and competition are linked.

Because of scarcity, people must make choices.

When choices are made, opportunity costs are incurred.

Changes in opportunity cost affect behavior.

finding ECONOMICS

In Being Late to Class John is often a few minutes late to his biology class The class starts at 10 a.m., but John usually walks into the class at 10:03 a.m. The instructor has asked John to be on time, but John usually excuses his behavior by saying the traffic getting to college was bad or that his alarm didn't go off at the right time or something else happened to delay him. One thing the instructor observes, though, is that John is never late when it comes to test day. He is usually in class a few minutes before the test begins. Where is the economics?

We would expect behavior to change as opportunity cost changes. When a test is being given in class, the opportunity cost of being late to class is higher than when a test is not being given and the instructor is simply lecturing. If John is late to class on test day, he then has fewer minutes to complete the test, and having less time can adversely affect his grade. In short, the higher the opportunity cost of being late to class, the less likely John will be late. ▲ ▲ ▲

Benefits and Costs

If we could eliminate air pollution completely, should we do it? If your answer is yes, then you are probably focusing on the *benefits* of eliminating air pollution. For example, one benefit might be healthier individuals. Certainly, individuals who do not breathe polluted air have fewer lung disorders than people who do breathe polluted air.

But benefits rarely come without costs. The economist reminds us that although eliminating pollution has its benefits, it has costs too. To illustrate, one way to eliminate all car pollution tomorrow is to pass a law stating that anyone caught driving a car will go to prison for 40 years. With such a law in place and enforced, very few people would drive cars, and all car pollution would be a thing of the past. Presto! Cleaner air! However, many people would think that the cost of obtaining that cleaner air is too high. Someone might say, "I want cleaner air, but not if I have to completely give up driving my car. How will I get to work?"

What distinguishes the economist from the noneconomist is that the economist thinks in terms of *both* costs *and* benefits. Often, the noneconomist thinks in terms of one or the other. Studying has its benefits, but it has costs too. Coming to class has benefits, but it has costs too. Getting up early each morning and exercising has its costs, but let's not forget that there are benefits too.

Decisions Made at the Margin

It is late at night, and you have already studied three hours for your biology test tomorrow. You look at the clock and wonder if you should study another hour. How would

Why Did the British Soldiers Wear Red Uniforms?

When George Washington and the colonists fought the British, the colonists were dressed in rags, whereas the British troops were clad in fine bright red uniforms. Commenting on this difference, people often say, "The British were foolish to have worn bright red uniforms. You could see them coming for miles."

Economists would not be so quick to label the British as foolish. Instead, they would ask why the British troops wore bright red. For instance, David Friedman, an economist, thinks it is odd that the British, who at the time were the greatest fighting force in the world, would make such a seemingly obvious mistake. He has an alternative explanation, an economics explanation.

Friedman reasons that the British generals did not want their men to break ranks and desert because winning the war would be hard, if not impossible, if a lot of men deserted. Thus, the generals had to think up a way to make the opportunity cost of desertion high for their soldiers. The generals reasoned that the higher the cost of desertion was, the fewer deserters there would be. The British generals effectively told their soldiers that if they deserted, they would have to forfeit their freedom or their lives.

Of course, the problem is that a stiff penalty is not effective if deserters cannot be found. Therefore, the generals had to make it easy to find deserters, and they did so by dressing them in bright red uniforms. Certainly, a deserter could throw off his uniform and walk through the countryside in his underwear alone, but in the harsh winters of New England, doing so would guarantee death. He had almost no choice but to wear the bright red uniform.

NORTH WIND PICTURES/PHOTOLIBRARY

you summarize your thinking process? What question or questions do you ask yourself to decide whether to study another hour?

Perhaps without knowing it, you think in terms of the costs and benefits of further study. You probably realize that studying an additional hour has certain benefits (you may be able to raise your grade a few points), but it has costs too (you will get less sleep or have less time to watch television or talk on the phone with a friend). That you think in terms of costs and benefits, however, doesn't tell us *how* you think in terms of costs and benefits. For example, when deciding what to do, do you look at the total costs and total benefits of the proposed action, or do you look at something less than the total costs and benefits? According to economists, for most decisions, you think in terms of *additional,* or *marginal,* costs and benefits, not *total* costs and benefits. That's because most decisions deal with making a small, or additional, change.

To illustrate, suppose you just finished eating a hamburger and drinking a soda for lunch. You are still a little hungry and are considering whether to order another hamburger. An economist would say that in deciding whether to order another hamburger, you compare the additional benefits of the second hamburger to its additional costs. In economics, the word *marginal* is a synonym for *additional.* So we say that you compare the marginal benefits (*MB*) of the (next) hamburger to its marginal costs (*MC*). If the marginal benefits are greater than the marginal costs, you obviously expect a net benefit to ordering the next hamburger, and therefore you order another. If, however, the marginal benefits are less than the marginal costs, you obviously expect a net cost to ordering the next hamburger, and therefore you do not order another.

Condition	Action
MB of next hamburger > *MC* of next hamburger	Buy next hamburger
MB of next hamburger < *MC* of next hamburger	Do not buy next hamburger

What you don't consider when making this decision are the total benefits and total costs of hamburgers. That's because the benefits and costs connected with the first hamburger (the one you have already eaten) are no longer relevant to the current decision. You are not deciding between eating two hamburgers or eating no hamburgers; your decision is whether to eat a second hamburger after you have already eaten one.

According to economists, when individuals make decisions by comparing marginal benefits to marginal costs, they are making decisions at the margin. The employee makes a decision at the margin when deciding whether to work two hours overtime; the economics professor makes a decision at the margin when deciding whether to put an additional question on the final exam.

Efficiency

What is the right amount of time to study for a test? In economics, the *right amount* of anything is the *optimal* or *efficient* amount—the amount for which the marginal benefits equal the marginal costs. Stated differently, you have achieved efficiency when the marginal benefits equal the marginal costs.

Suppose you are studying for an economics test, and for the first hour of studying, the marginal benefits (*MB*) are greater than the marginal costs (*MC*):

$$MB \text{ studying first hour} > MC \text{ studying first hour}$$

Given this condition, you will certainly study for the first hour because it is worth it: The additional benefits are greater than the additional costs; so there is a net benefit to studying.

Marginal Benefits
Additional benefits; the benefits connected with consuming an additional unit of a good or undertaking one more unit of an activity.

Marginal Costs
Additional costs; the costs connected with consuming an additional unit of a good or undertaking one more unit of an activity.

Decisions at the Margin
Decision making characterized by weighing the additional (marginal) benefits of a change against the additional (marginal) costs of a change with respect to current conditions.

Efficiency
Exists when marginal benefits equal marginal costs.

Suppose for the second hour of studying, the marginal benefits are still greater than the marginal costs:

$$MB \text{ studying second hour} > MC \text{ studying second hour}$$

You will study for the second hour because the additional benefits are still greater than the additional costs. In other words, studying the second hour is worthwhile. In fact, you will continue to study as long as the marginal benefits are greater than the marginal costs. Exhibit 2 graphically illustrates this discussion.

The marginal benefit (MB) curve of studying is downward sloping because we have assumed that the benefits of studying for the first hour are greater than the benefits of studying for the second hour and so on. The marginal cost (MC) curve of studying is upward sloping because we assume that studying the second hour costs a person more (in terms of goods forfeited) than the first, the third costs more than the second, and so on. (If we assume the additional costs of studying are constant over time, the MC curve is horizontal.)

In the exhibit, the marginal benefits of studying equal the marginal costs at three hours. So three hours is the *efficient* length of time to study in this situation. At fewer than three hours, the marginal benefits of studying are greater than the marginal costs; thus, at all these hours, studying has net benefits. At more than three hours, the marginal costs of studying are greater than the marginal benefits, and so studying beyond three hours is not worthwhile.

MAXIMIZING NET BENEFITS Take another look at Exhibit 2. Suppose you had stopped studying after the first hour (or after the 60th minute). Would you have given up

---

EXHIBIT 2

Efficiency

MB = marginal benefits and MC = marginal costs. In the exhibit, the MB curve of studying is downward sloping and the MC curve of studying is upward sloping. As long as $MB > MC$, the person will study. The person stops studying when $MB = MC$. This is where efficiency is achieved.

anything? Yes, you would have given up the *net benefits* of studying longer. To illustrate, notice that between the first and the second hour, the marginal benefits (*MB*) curve lies above the marginal costs (*MC*). This means studying the second hour has net benefits. But if you hadn't studied that second hour—if you had stopped after the first hour—then you would have given up the opportunity to collect those net benefits. The same analysis holds for the third hour. We conclude that by studying three hours (but not one minute longer), you have maximized net benefits. In short, efficiency, which is consistent with *MB* = *MC*, is also consistent with maximizing net benefits.

ⓣhinking like AN ECONOMIST

No $10 Bills on the Sidewalk An economist says that people try to maximize their net benefits. You ask for proof. The economist says, "You don't find any $10 bills on the sidewalk." What is the economist getting at by making this statement? Keep in mind that you don't find any $10 bills on the sidewalk because if there were a $10 bill on the sidewalk, the first person to see it would pick it up; when you came along, it wouldn't be there. But why would the first person to find the $10 bill pick it up? The reason is that people don't pass by net benefits, and picking up the $10 bill comes with net benefits. The *benefits* of having an additional $10 are obvious; the *costs* of obtaining the additional $10 bill are simply what you give up during the time you are stooping down to pick it up. In short, the marginal benefits are likely to be greater than the marginal costs (giving us net benefits), and that is why the $10 bill is picked up. Saying there are no $10 bills on the sidewalk is the same as saying no one leaves net benefits on the sidewalk. In other words, people try to maximize net benefits. ▪▪▪

Economics Is About Incentives

Incentive

Something that encourages or motivates a person to undertake an action.

An incentive is something that encourages or motivates a person to undertake an action.

Often what motivates a person to undertake an action is the belief that by taking that action she can make herself better off. For example, if we say that Jane has an incentive to study for the upcoming exam, we imply that by studying Jane can make herself better off, probably in terms of receiving a higher grade on the exam than if she didn't study.

Incentives are closely related to benefits and costs. Individuals have an incentive to undertake actions for which the benefits are greater than the costs or, stated differently, for which they expect to receive net benefits (benefits greater than costs).

Economists are interested in what motivates behavior. Why does the person buy more of good *X* when its price falls? Why might a person work longer hours when income tax rates decline? Why might a person buy more of a particular good today if he expects the price of that good will go up next week? The general answer to many of these questions is that people do what they have an incentive to do. Economists then hunt for what the incentive is. For example, if a person buys more of good *X* when its price goes down, what specifically is the incentive? How, specifically, does the person make himself better off by buying a good when its price declines. Does he get more utility or satisfaction? Or how does a person make herself better off if she buys a good today that she expects will go up in price next week?

Unintended Effects

Economists think in terms of unintended effects. For example, Andres, 16 years old, currently works after school at a grocery store. He earns $6.50 an hour.

Suppose the state legislature passes a law specifying that the minimum dollar wage a person can be paid to do a job is $9.50 an hour. The legislators' intention in passing the law is to help people like Andres earn more income.

Will the $9.50 an hour legislation have the intended effect? Perhaps not. The manager of the grocery store may not find it worthwhile to continue employing Andres if she has to pay him $9.50 an hour. In other words, Andres may have a job at $6.50 an hour but not at $9.50 an hour. If the law specifies that no one may earn less than $9.50 an hour and the manager of the grocery store decides to fire Andres rather than pay this amount, then an unintended effect of the legislation is Andres' losing his job.

As another example, let's analyze mandatory seatbelt laws to see whether they have any unintended effects. States have laws that require drivers to wear seatbelts. The intended effect is to reduce the number of car fatalities by making it more likely that drivers will survive accidents.

Could these laws have an unintended effect? Some economists think so. They look at accident fatalities in terms of this equation:

$$\text{Total number of fatalities} = \text{Number of accidents} \times \text{Fatalities per accident}$$

For example, if there are 200,000 accidents and 0.10 fatalities per accident, the total number of fatalities is 20,000.

The objective of a mandatory seatbelt program is to reduce the total number of fatalities by reducing the fatalities per accident. Many studies have found that wearing seatbelts does just this. If you are in an accident, you have a better chance of not being killed if you are wearing a seatbelt.

Let's assume that with seatbelts, there are 0.08 instead of 0.10 fatalities per accident. If there are still 200,000 accidents, the total number of fatalities falls from 20,000 to 16,000. Thus, the total number of fatalities drops if fatalities per accident are reduced and the number of accidents is constant.

Number of Accidents	Fatalities per Accident	Total Number of Fatalities
200,000	0.10	20,000
200,000	0.08	16,000

However, some economists wonder whether the number of accidents stays constant. Specifically, they suggest that seatbelts may have an unintended effect: *The number of accidents may increase* because wearing seatbelts may make drivers feel safer. Feeling safer may cause them to take chances that they wouldn't ordinarily take, such as driving faster or more aggressively, or concentrating less on their driving and more on the music on the radio. For example, if the number of accidents rises to 250,000, then the total number of fatalities is 20,000.

Number of Accidents	Fatalities per Accident	Total Number of Fatalities
200,000	0.10	20,000
250,000	0.08	20,000

We conclude the following: If a mandatory seatbelt law reduces the number of fatalities per accident (intended effect) but increases the number of accidents (unintended effect), it may not, contrary to popular belief, reduce the total number of fatalities. In fact, some economics studies show just this.

What does all this mean for you? You may be safer if you know that this unintended effect exists and you adjust accordingly. To be specific, when you wear your seatbelt, your chances of getting hurt in a car accident are less than if you don't wear your seatbelt. But if this added sense of protection causes you to drive less carefully than you would otherwise, then you could unintentionally offset the measure of protection your seatbelt provides. To reduce the probability of hurting yourself and others in a car accident, *the best policy is to wear a seatbelt and to drive as carefully as you would if you weren't wearing a seatbelt.* Knowing about the unintended effect of wearing your seatbelt could save your life.

Exchange

Exchange, or **trade,** is the giving up of one thing for something else. Economics is some-times called the "science of exchange" because so much that is discussed in economics has to do with exchange.

We start with a basic question: Why do people enter into exchanges? The answer is that they do so to make themselves better off. When a person voluntarily trades $100 for a jacket, she is saying, "I prefer to have the jacket instead of the $100." And, of course, when the seller of the jacket voluntarily sells the jacket for $100, he is saying, "I prefer to have the $100 instead of the jacket." In short, through trade or exchange, each person gives up something he values less for something he values more.

You can think of trade in terms of utility or satisfaction. Imagine a utility scale that goes from 1 to 10, with 10 being the highest utility you can achieve. Now suppose you currently have $40 in your wallet and you are at 7 on the utility scale. A few minutes later, you are in a store looking at some new CDs. The price of each is $10, and you end up buying four CDs for $40.

After you traded your $40 for the four CDs, are you still at 7 on the utility scale? The likely answer is no. If you expected to have the same utility after the trade as you did before, you proba-bly would not have traded your $40 for the four CDs. The only reason you entered into the trade is that you *expected* to be better off after the trade than you were before it. In other words, you thought trading your $40 for the four CDs would move you up the utility scale from 7 to, say, 8.

SELF-TEST

1. Give an example to illustrate how a change in opportunity cost can affect behavior.

2. Studying has both costs and benefits. If you continue to study (say, for a test) as long as the marginal benefits of studying are greater than the marginal costs and stop studying when the two are equal, will your action be consistent with having maximized the net benefits of studying? Explain your answer.

3. You stay up an additional hour to study for a test. The intended effect is to raise your test grade. What might be an unintended effect of staying up another hour to study?

THE MARKET AND GOVERNMENT

In recent years, major economic problems and issues have plagued the United States, such as:

- Financial problems in the banking sector
- The economic effects of falling real estate prices
- Growing federal budget deficits
- A fall in economic activity, as measured by the total output of goods and services produced in the country
- Rising unemployment
- The looming crisis in Social Security
- Health-care issues
- Issues related to climate change and the environment
- The proper role of monetary policy
- The proper role of government regulatory policy in the economy, and much more

When it comes to economic problems, the national debate usually proceeds along these lines:

- First, the problem is *identified* and *defined* or *described*.
- Second, individuals attempt to identify the *cause* of the problem.
- Third, individuals propose *solutions* to the problem.

This three-step process was evident in recent discussions of the U.S. financial crisis of 2007–2009 and in discussions of health care. After first *identifying* the financial crisis and describing it, individuals turned to identifying its *cause(s)* and proposing *solutions*.

In this process, there is little debate about identifying the problem. Most of the debate focuses on the cause(s) of the problem and the proposed solutions. With respect to both the cause and the solution, we often hear two words mentioned: the "market" and "government." For example:

- *Either:* The *market* (or capitalism) is the *cause* of the problem.
- *Or:* The *government* is the *cause* of the problem.
- *Either:* The *market* (or capitalism) is the solution to the problem.
- *Or:* The *government* is the solution to the problem.

The market-versus-government debate is an important one to know about, but it takes time to learn the particulars. Much of this book will help you learn those particulars, including:

- How a market system works.
- What markets are and are not capable of doing.
- How government operates.
- How government actions and policies can affect the market system.

At this point, you may be wondering why we don't simply tell you the "right" way to think. Your thinking might be, "Well, which is it? Did the market or government *cause* the problem? Is the market or government the *solution*?" If these are your questions, we sympathize with your frustration over not getting straight answers. We resist telling you the "right" answer for two reasons: First, not all economists agree on what the "right" answer is in a given case. Second, knowing the "right" answer without first understanding how markets and how governments work will leave you feeling unsatisfied because you will have little foundation on which to understand the answer. After all, no matter which "right" answer we give you now, you are going to want it explained, and this book is part of that explanation.

CETERIS PARIBUS AND THEORY

We cover two important topics in this section: (1) *ceteris paribus* and (2) theory.

Ceteris Paribus Thinking

Wilson has eaten regular ice cream for years, and for years his weight has been 170 pounds. One day Wilson decides he wants to lose weight. With this in mind, he buys a new fat-free ice cream at the grocery store. The fat-free ice cream has half the calories of regular ice cream.

Wilson eats the fat-free ice cream for the next few months. He then weighs himself and finds that he has gained two pounds. Does this mean that fat-free ice cream causes people to gain weight and regular ice cream does not? The answer is no. Why, then, did Wilson gain weight when he substituted fat-free ice cream for regular ice cream? Perhaps Wilson ate three times as much fat-free ice cream as regular ice cream. Or perhaps during the time he was eating fat-free ice cream, he wasn't exercising, and during the time he was eating regular ice cream, he was exercising. In other words, a number of factors—such as eating more ice cream or exercising less—may have offset the weight loss that Wilson would have experienced had these other factors not changed.

Now suppose you want to make the point that Wilson would have lost weight by substituting fat-free ice cream for regular ice cream had these other factors not changed.

Ceteris Paribus
A Latin term meaning "all other things constant" or "nothing else changes."

What would you say? A scientist would say, "If Wilson has been eating regular ice cream and his weight has stabilized at 170 pounds, then substituting fat-free ice cream for regular ice cream will lead to a decline in weight, *ceteris paribus.*"

The term *ceteris paribus* means "all other things constant" or "nothing else changes." In our ice cream example, if nothing else changes—such as how much ice cream Wilson eats, how much exercise he gets, and so on—then switching to fat-free ice cream will result in weight loss. This expectation is based on the theory that a reduction in calorie consumption will result in weight loss and an increase in calorie consumption will result in weight gain.

Using the *ceteris paribus* assumption is important because, with it, we can clearly designate what we believe is the correct relationship between two variables. In the ice cream example, we can designate the correct relationship between calorie intake and weight gain.

Economists don't often talk about ice cream, but they will often make use of the *ceteris paribus* assumption. An economist might say, "If the price of a good decreases, the quantity of it consumed increases, *ceteris paribus.*" For example, if the price of Pepsi-Cola decreases, people will buy more of it, assuming that nothing else changes.

But some people ask, "Why would economists want to assume that when the price of Pepsi-Cola falls, nothing else changes? Don't other things change in the real world? Why make assumptions that we know are not true?"

Of course, economists do not specify *ceteris paribus* because they want to say something false about the world. They specify it because they want to clearly define what they believe to be the real-world relationship between two variables. Look at it this way. If you drop a ball off the roof of a house, it will fall to the ground unless someone catches it. This statement is true, and probably everyone would willingly accept it as true. But here is another true statement: If you drop a ball off the roof of a house, it will fall to the ground, *ceteris paribus.* In fact, the two statements are identical in meaning. This is because adding the phrase "unless someone catches it" in the first sentence is the same as saying "*ceteris paribus*" in the second sentence. If one statement is acceptable to us, the other should be too.

What Is a Theory?

Almost everyone, including you, builds and tests theories or models on a regular basis. (In this text, the words *theory* and *model* are used interchangeably.) Perhaps you thought only scientists and others with high-level mathematics at their fingertips built and tested theories. However, theory building and testing is not the domain of only the highly educated and mathematically proficient. Almost everyone builds and test theories.

People build theories any time they do not know the answer to a question. Someone asks, "Why is the crime rate higher in the United States than in Belgium?" Or, "Why did Aaron's girlfriend break up with him?" Or, "Why does Professor Avalos give easier final exams than Professor Shaw even though they teach the same subject?" If you don't know the answer to a question, you are likely to build a theory so that you can provide an answer.

Theory
An abstract representation of the real world designed with the intent to better understand it.

Abstract
The process (used in building a theory) of focusing on a limited number of variables to explain or predict an event.

What exactly is a theory? To an economist, a theory is an abstract representation of the world. In this context, abstract means to omit certain variables or factors when trying to explain or understand something. For example, suppose you were to draw a map for a friend, showing him how to get from his house to yours. Would you draw a map that showed every single thing your friend would see on the trip, or would you simply draw the main roads and one or two landmarks? If you'd do the latter, you would be abstracting from reality; you would be omitting certain things.

You would abstract for two reasons. First, to get your friend from his house to yours, you don't need to include everything on your map. Simply noting main roads may be enough. Second, if you did note everything on your map, your friend might get confused. Giving too much detail could be as bad as giving too little.

When economists build a theory or model, they do the same thing you do in drawing a map. They abstract from reality; they leave out certain things. They focus on the major factors or variables that they believe will explain the phenomenon they are trying to understand.

Suppose a criminologist's objective is to explain why some people turn to crime. Before actually building the theory, he considers a number of variables that may explain why some people become criminals: (1) the ease of getting a gun, (2) childrearing practices, (3) the neighborhood a person grew up in, (4) whether a person was abused as a child, (5) family education, (6) the type of friends a person has, (7) a person's IQ, (8) climate, and (9) a person's diet.

The criminologist may think that some of these variables greatly affect the chance that a person will become a criminal, some affect it only slightly, and others do not affect it at all. For example, a person's diet may have only a 0.0001 percent effect on the person becoming a criminal, whereas whether a person was abused as a child may have a 30 percent effect.

A theory emphasizes only the variables that the theorist believes are the main or critical ones that explain an activity or event. Thus, if the criminologist in our example thinks that parental childrearing practices and family education are likely to explain much more about criminal behavior than the other variables, then his (abstract) theory will focus on these two variables and ignore the others.

All theories are abstractions from reality. But it doesn't follow that (abstract) theories cannot explain reality. The objective in theory building is to ignore the variables that are essentially irrelevant to the case at hand, making it easier to isolate the important variables that the untrained observer would probably miss.

In the course of reading this text, you will come across numerous theories. Some of these theories are explained in words, and others are graphically represented. For example, Chapter 3 presents the theory of supply and demand. First, the parts of the theory are explained. Then the theory is represented graphically in terms of a supply curve and a demand curve.

WHAT TO ASK A THEORIST Physicists, chemists, and economists aren't the only persons who build and test theories. Historians, sociologists, anthropologists, and many others build and test theories. In fact, as suggested earlier in this section, almost everyone builds theories (although not everyone tests theories).

Anytime you listen to someone expound on a theory, you should always ask a key question: *"If your theory is correct, what do you predict we will see in the world?"* To illustrate, let's consider a very simple example. Suppose your history professor comes to class each day clean-shaven and dressed in slacks, shirt, tie, and sports jacket. One day he comes to class unshaven and dressed in jeans and a somewhat wrinkled T-shirt. The difference in appearance is obvious. You turn to your friend who sits next to you in class and ask, "What do you think explains the difference in his appearance and dress?"

Notice that you have asked a question that does not have an obvious answer. Such questions are ripe for theory building. Your friend proposes an explanation. She says, "I think the professor forgot to set his alarm clock last night. He got up late this morning and didn't have time to shave or to dress the way he usually does. He just threw on the first clothes he found and rushed to class."

Your friend has advanced a theory of sorts. She has implicitly assumed that the professor wants to shave and dress in slacks, shirt, tie, and sports jacket but that some unusual event prevented him from doing so today.

Somehow, you don't think your friend's theory is correct. Instead, you think your history professor has decided to make a life change of some sort. He has decided to look more casual, to take life a little easier, to be less formal. You tell your friend what you think explains your professor's new behavior.

You, like your friend, have advanced a theory of sorts. Whose theory, if either, is correct? Now is the time for you to ask your friend, and your friend to ask you, *"If your theory is correct, what do you predict we will see in the world?*

When Are People the Most Likely to "Lose" Library Books? The Case of Alchian and Allen's *University Economics*

Do all the theories that economists build and test have to be "big" theories—theories about prices, unemployment, interest rates, economic growth, and so on. Not at all. An economist can build a theory about almost anything, such as why some library books have a higher probability of not being returned than others.

Start with the obvious: Every day, individuals borrow books from public and college libraries, but not every book borrowed is returned. If a book is not returned, it is because either (1) the book borrower misplaced or lost the book, (2) the book borrower forgot to return the book, or (3) the book borrower decided to keep the book.

Does every book in a library (such as your college library) have an equal chance of not being returned? Most persons say no because not every book has the same probability of being borrowed. Before a book is not returned, it has to be borrowed; so books with a higher probability of being borrowed have a higher probability of not being returned.

But why do some books have a higher probability of being borrowed? One answer is that that people either want to read (for pleasure) or have to read (say, for a class) some books more than others. Books are also borrowed if the borrower intends to sell the borrowed book, which brings us to a well-known economics text, *University Economics: Elements of Inquiry* by Armen A. Alchian and William R. Allen.

University Economics was published in the mid-1960s to early-1970s. Economists often say that it is one of the best introductory economics books ever written. Although the book has been out of print for years, you can still buy a copy of it. On one particular day in September 2009, the book could be purchased from half.com (an

eBay company) from various private sellers. The price of the book (in very good condition) ranged from about $172 to $252.

What does the $252 price mean for the copies of *University Economics* that sit on library bookshelves in college and public libraries all over the country? It means that those copies have a high probability of being checked out of the libraries and never returned. In other words, they have a high probability of being checked out and "lost."

But don't the libraries charge book borrowers for the books they lose and never return? Sure they do, and the price they charge will have much to do with whether the book borrower lost the book in the first place. If the library charges the borrower the purchase price of the book instead of the replacement price, the borrower has a stronger incentive to lose the book. To illustrate, suppose the library purchased *University Economics* ten years ago for $20. If it charges this price, the borrower is more likely to lose the book than if the library charges the price it has to pay to replace the book ($252). In short, library policies will influence how many copies of *University Economics* end up not being returned.

Photo: Inside the stacks of a library

Your friend's answer should be, "If my theory is correct, then the next time the professor comes to class, he will be clean-shaven and dressed in his old way—slacks, shirt, tie, and sports jacket." Your answer should be, "If my theory is correct, then the next time the professor comes to class, he will be unshaven and dressed as he is today—in jeans, T-shirt, and the like."

The question—If your theory is correct, what do you predict we will see in the world?—gives us a way to figure out who might be closer to the truth when people disagree. It minimizes talk and maximizes the chances of establishing who is correct and who is incorrect.

SELF-TEST

1. What is the purpose of building a theory?

2. How might a theory of the economy differ from a description of it?

3. Why is it important to test a theory? Why not simply accept a theory if it sounds right?

4. Your economics instructor says, "If the price of going to the movies goes down, people will go to the movies more often." A student in class says, "Not if the quality of the movies goes down." Who is right, the economics instructor or the student?

ECONOMIC CATEGORIES

Economics is sometimes broken down into different categories according to the type of questions asked. Four common economic categories are positive economics, normative economics, microeconomics, and macroeconomics.

Positive and Normative Economics

Positive economics attempts to determine *what is*. Normative economics addresses *what should be*. Essentially, positive economics deals with cause–effect relationships that can be tested. Normative economics deals with value judgments and opinions that cannot be tested.

Many topics in economics can be discussed in both a positive and a normative framework. Consider a proposed cut in federal income taxes. An economist practicing positive economics would want to know the *effect* of a cut in income taxes. For example, she may want to know how a tax cut will affect the unemployment rate, economic growth, inflation, and so on. An economist practicing normative economics would address issues that directly or indirectly relate to whether the federal income tax *should* be cut. For example, he may say that federal income taxes should be cut because the income tax burden on many taxpayers is currently high.

This book deals mainly with positive economics. For the most part, we discuss the economic world as it is, not the way someone might think it should be. Keep in mind, too, that no matter what your normative objectives are, positive economics can shed some light on how they might be accomplished. For example, suppose you believe that absolute poverty should be eliminated and that the unemployment rate should be lowered. No doubt you have ideas as to how these goals can be accomplished. But will your ideas work? For example, will a greater redistribution of income eliminate absolute poverty? Will lowering taxes lower the unemployment rate? There is no guarantee that the means you think will bring about certain ends will do so. This is where sound positive economics can help us see what is. As someone once said, "It is not enough to want to do good; it is important also to know how to do good."

Positive Economics
The study of "what is" in economics.

Normative Economics
The study of "what should be" in economics.

Microeconomics and Macroeconomics

It has been said that the tools of microeconomics are microscopes, and the tools of macroeconomics are telescopes. Macroeconomics stands back from the trees to see the forest. Microeconomics gets up close and examines the tree itself, its bark, its limbs, and its roots.

Microeconomics
The branch of economics that deals with human behavior and choices as they relate to relatively small units: an individual, a firm, an industry, a single market.

Macroeconomics
The branch of economics that deals with human behavior and choices as they relate to highly aggregate markets (e.g., the goods and services market) or the entire economy.

Microeconomics is the branch of economics that deals with human behavior and choices as they relate to relatively small units: an individual, a firm, an industry, a single market. **Macroeconomics** is the branch of economics that deals with human behavior and choices as they relate to an entire economy. In microeconomics, economists discuss a single price; in macroeconomics, they discuss the price level. Microeconomics deals with the demand for a particular good or service; macroeconomics deals with aggregate, or total, demand for goods and services. Microeconomics examines how a tax change affects a single firm's output; macroeconomics looks at how a tax change affects an entire economy's output.

Microeconomists and macroeconomists ask different types of questions. A microeconomist might be interested in answering such questions as:

- How does a market work?
- What level of output does a firm produce?
- What price does a firm charge for the good it produces?
- How does a consumer determine how much of a good to buy?

OFFICE HOURS

"I Don't Believe That Every Time a Person Does Something, He Compares the Marginal Benefits and Costs"

STUDENT:

In class yesterday you said that individuals compare the marginal benefits (*MB*) of doing something (say, exercising) with the marginal costs (*MC*). If the marginal benefits are greater than the marginal costs, they exercise; if the marginal costs are greater than the marginal benefits, they don't. Here is what I am having a problem with: I don't believe that every time people do something, they compare the marginal benefits and costs. I think people do some things without thinking of benefits and costs; they do some things instinctively or because they have always done them.

INSTRUCTOR:

Can you give an example?

STUDENT:

I don't think of the benefits and costs of eating breakfast in the morning; I just eat breakfast. I don't think of the benefits and costs of doing my homework; I just do the homework before it is due. For me, many activities are automatic; I do them without thinking.

INSTRUCTOR:

It doesn't necessarily follow that you are not considering benefits and costs when you do something automatically. All you have to do is sense whether doing something comes with net benefits (benefits greater than costs) or net costs (costs greater than benefits). All you have to do is sense whether something is likely to make you better off or worse off. You eat breakfast in the morning because you have "decided" that it makes you better off. But making you better off is no different from saying that you receive net benefits from eating breakfast, which is no different from saying that the benefits of eating breakfast are greater than the costs. In other words, better off equals net benefits equals benefits greater than costs.

- Can government policy affect business behavior?
- Can government policy affect consumer behavior?

On the other hand, a macroeconomist might be interested in answering such questions as:

- How does the economy work?
- Why is the unemployment rate sometimes high and sometimes low?
- What causes inflation?
- Why do some national economies grow faster than others?
- What might cause interest rates to be low one year and high the next?
- How do changes in the money supply affect the economy?
- How do changes in government spending and taxes affect the economy?

STUDENT:

I see what you're saying. But then how would you explain the fact that Smith smokes cigarettes and Jones does not. If both Smith and Jones consider the benefits and costs of smoking cigarettes, then it seems that either both would have to smoke or both would have to not smoke. The fact that different people do different things tells me that not everyone is considering the costs and benefits of their actions. If everyone did, they would all do the same thing.

INSTRUCTOR:

I disagree. Not everyone sees the costs and benefits of the same thing the same way. Smith and Jones may not see the benefits or costs of smoking the same way. For Smith, the benefits of smoking may be high, but for Jones they may be low. It is no different from saying different people estimate the benefits of playing chess or eating a doughnut or riding a bicycle differently. The same holds for costs. Not everyone will estimate the costs of playing chess or eating a doughnut or riding a bicycle the same way. The costs of a person with diabetes eating a doughnut are much higher than the costs of a person without diabetes eating a doughnut.

STUDENT:

Let me see if I have this right. You are making two points. First, not everyone has the same benefits and costs of, say, running a mile. Second, everyone who does run a mile believes the benefits are greater than the costs, and everyone who does not run a mile believes the costs are greater than the benefits.

INSTRUCTOR:

Yes, that's it. Everybody is trying to make himself better off (reap net benefits), but not everybody will do *X* because not everybody will be made better off by doing *X*.

POINTS TO REMEMBER

1. If you undertake those actions for which you expect to receive net benefits, then you are "thinking" in terms of costs and benefits. Specifically, you expect the marginal benefits to be greater than the marginal costs.
2. The costs and benefits of doing any activity are not necessarily the same for everybody. Smith may expect higher benefits than Jones when it comes to doing *X*; Jones may expect higher costs than Smith when it comes to doing *X*.

CHAPTER SUMMARY

GOODS, BADS, AND RESOURCES

- A good is anything that gives a person utility or satisfaction.
- A bad is anything that gives a person disutility or dissatisfaction.
- Economists divide resources into four categories: land, labor, capital, and entrepreneurship.
- Land includes natural resources, such as minerals, forests, water, and unimproved land.
- Labor refers to the physical and mental talents that people contribute to the production process.
- Capital consists of produced goods that can be used as inputs for further production, such as machinery, tools, computers, trucks, buildings, and factories.
- Entrepreneurship refers to the talent that some people have for organizing the resources of land, labor, and capital to produce goods, seek new business opportunities, and develop new ways of doing things.

SCARCITY

- Scarcity is the condition in which our wants are greater than the limited resources available to satisfy them.
- Scarcity implies choice. In a world of limited resources, we must choose which wants will be satisfied and which will go unsatisfied.
- Because of scarcity, there is a need for a rationing device. A rationing device is a means of deciding who gets what quantities of the available resources and goods.
- Scarcity implies competition. If resources were ample enough to satisfy all our seemingly unlimited wants, people would not have to compete for the available but limited resources.

OPPORTUNITY COST

- Everytime a person makes a choice, he or she incurs an opportunity cost. Opportunity cost is the most highly valued opportunity or alternative forfeited when a choice is made. The higher the opportunity cost of doing something is, the less likely it will be done.

COSTS AND BENEFITS

- What distinguishes the economist from the noneconomist is that the economist thinks in terms of *both* costs and benefits. Asked what the benefits of taking a walk may be, an economist will also mention the related costs. Asked what the costs of studying are, an economist will also point out its benefits.

DECISIONS MADE AT THE MARGIN

- Marginal benefits and costs are not the same as total benefits and costs. When deciding whether to talk on the phone one more minute, an individual would not consider the total benefits and total costs of speaking on the phone. Instead, the person would compare only the marginal benefits (additional benefits) of talking on the phone one more minute to the marginal costs (additional costs) of talking on the phone one more minute.

INCENTIVES

- An incentive is something that encourages or motivates a person to undertake an action. Incentives are closely related to benefits and costs. Individuals have an incentive to undertake actions for which the benefits are greater than the costs or, stated differently, for which they expect to receive some net benefits (benefits greater than costs).

EFFICIENCY

- As long as the marginal benefits of an activity are greater than its marginal costs, a person gains by continuing to do the activity—whether the activity is studying, running, eating, or watching television. The net benefits of an activity are maximized when the marginal benefits of the activity equal its marginal costs. Efficiency exists at this point.

UNINTENDED EFFECTS

- Economists often think in terms of causes and effects. Effects may be both intended and unintended. Economists want to denote both types of effects when speaking of effects in general.

EXCHANGE

- Exchange, or trade, is the process of giving up one thing for something else. People enter into exchanges to make themselves better off.

CETERIS PARIBUS

- *Ceteris paribus* is a Latin term that means "all other things constant" or "nothing else changes." *Ceteris paribus* is used to designate what we believe is the correct relationship between two variables.

THE MARKET AND THE GOVERNMENT

- When it comes to economic problems and issues, we often see the following three-step process: (1)The problem is identified, and then it is defined or described. (2) Next, the causes of the problem are identified. (3) Finally, proposed solutions to the problem are put forth. With respect to both the cause(s) of the problem and the proposed solutions to the problem, we often hear individuals speaking about the market and the government. Opinions differ as to whether the market or the government is the cause of the problem. Similarly, opinions differ as to whether the market or the government is the solution to the problem. Much of this text will focus on the market-versus-government debate that lies beneath the surface of many economic problems and issues.

THEORY

- Economists build theories to explain and predict real-world events. Theories are necessarily abstractions from, as opposed to descriptions of, the real world.

- All theories abstract from reality; they focus on the critical variables that the theorist believes explain and predict the phenomenon in question.

ECONOMIC CATEGORIES

- Positive economics attempts to determine what is; normative economics addresses what should be.
- Microeconomics deals with human behavior and choices as they relate to relatively small units: an individual, a firm, an industry, a single market. Macroeconomics deals with human behavior and choices as they relate to an entire economy.

KEY TERMS AND CONCEPTS

Good	Entrepreneurship	Decisions at the Margin	Positive Economics
Utility	Scarcity	Efficiency	Normative Economics
Bad	Economics	Incentive	Microeconomics
Disutility	Rationing Device	Exchange (Trade)	Macroeconomics
Land	Opportunity Cost	*Ceteris Paribus*	
Labor	Marginal Benefits	Theory	
Capital	Marginal Costs	Abstract	

QUESTIONS AND PROBLEMS

1. A friend pays for your lunch. Is this an example of a free lunch? Why or why not?

2. The United States is considered a rich country because Americans can choose from an abundance of goods and services. How can there be scarcity in a land of abundance?

3. Smith says that we should eliminate all pollution in the world. Jones disagrees. Who is more likely to be an economist, Smith or Jones? Explain your answer.

4. What is the difference between positive economics and normative economics? Between microeconomics and macroeconomics?

5. Explain the relationship between changes in opportunity cost and changes in behavior.

6. When two individuals enter into an exchange, you can be sure that one person benefits and the other person loses. Do you agree or disagree with this statement? Explain your answer.

7. Discuss the opportunity costs of attending college for four years. Is college more or less costly than you thought it was? Explain.

8. Why do people enter into exchanges?

9. Is it possible for a person to incur an opportunity cost without spending any money? Explain.

10. A change in X will lead to a change in Y. The predicted change is desirable; so we should change X. Do you agree or disagree? Explain.

11. Explain the link between scarcity and each of the following: (a) choice, (b) opportunity cost, (c) the need for a rationing device, (d) competition.

12. What does an economist mean if she says there are no $10 bills on the sidewalk?

13. Can either scarcity or one of the effects of scarcity be found in a car dealership? Explain your answer.

14. Ivan stops studying before the point at which his marginal benefits of studying equal his marginal costs. Is Ivan forfeiting any net benefits? Explain your answer.

15. What is the difference between the resource labor and the resource entrepreneurship?

16. How would an economist define the efficient amount of time spent playing tennis?

17. Give an example of something that is a good for one person and a bad for someone else.

18. Economists say that individuals make decisions at the margin. What does this mean?

19. Give two examples for each of the following: (a) an intangible good, (b) a tangible good, (c) a bad.

20. A layperson says that a proposed government project simply costs too much and therefore shouldn't be undertaken. How might an economist's evaluation be different?

21. A theory is an abstraction from reality. What does this mean?

22. Janice decides to go out on a date with Kyle instead of Robert. Do you think Janice is using some kind of rationing device to decide whom she dates? If so, what might that rationing device be?

23. The person who smokes cigarettes cannot possibly be thinking in terms of costs and benefits because it has been proven that cigarette smoking increases one's chances of getting lung cancer. Do you agree or disagree with the part of the statement that reads "the person who smokes cigarettes cannot possibly be thinking in terms of costs and benefits"? Explain your answer.

24. If you found $10 bills on the sidewalk regularly, we might conclude that individuals don't try to maximize net benefits. Do you agree or disagree with this statement. Explain your answer.

25. Jackie's alarm clock buzzes. She reaches over to the small table next to her bed and turns it off. As she pulls the covers back up, Jackie thinks about her 8:30 American history class. Should she go to the class today or sleep a little longer? She worked late last night and really hasn't had enough sleep. Besides, she's fairly sure her professor will be discussing a subject she already knows well. Maybe it would be okay to miss class today. Is Jackie more likely to miss some classes than she is to miss other classes? What determines which classes Jackie will attend and which classes she won't?

26. Would there be a need for a rationing device if scarcity did not exist? Explain your answer.

WORKING WITH DIAGRAMS

A picture is worth a thousand words. With this familiar saying in mind, economists construct their diagrams or graphs. With a few lines and a few points, much can be conveyed.

TWO-VARIABLE DIAGRAMS

Most of the diagrams in this book represent the relationship between two variables. Economists compare two variables to see how a change in one variable affects the other.

Suppose our two variables of interest are *consumption* and *income.* We want to show how consumption changes as income changes. We collect the data in Table 1. Simply by looking at the data in the first two columns, we can see that as income rises (column 1), consumption rises (column 2). If we wanted to show the relationship between income and consumption on a graph, we could place *income* on the horizontal axis, as in Exhibit 1, and *consumption* on the vertical axis. Point *A* represents income of $0 and consumption of $60, point *B* represents income of $100 and consumption of $120, and so on. If we draw a straight line through the points we have plotted, we have a picture of the relationship between income and consumption, based on the data we collected.

Notice that the line in Exhibit 1 slopes upward from left to right. As income rises, so does consumption. For example, as you move from point *A* to point *B*, income rises from $0 to $100 and consumption rises from $60 to $120. The line in Exhibit 1 also shows that as income falls, so does consumption. For example, as you move from point *C* to point *B*, income falls from $200 to $100 and consumption falls from $180 to $120. When two variables—such as consumption and income—change in the same way, they are said to be directly related.

EXHIBIT 1

A Two-Variable Diagram Representing a Direct Relationship

In this exhibit, we have plotted the data in Table 1 and then connected the points with a straight line. The data represent a direct relationship: as one variable (say, income) rises, the other variable (consumption) rises too.

The variables income and consumption are directly related.

Directly Related
Two variables are directly related if they change in the same way.

TABLE 1

(1) When Income Is:	(2) Consumption Is:	(3) Point
$ 0	$ 60	A
100	120	B
200	180	C
300	240	D
400	300	E
500	360	F

TABLE 2

(1) When Price of CDs Is:	(2) Quantity Demanded of CDs Is:	(3) Point
$20	100	A
18	120	B
16	140	C
14	160	D
12	180	E

EXHIBIT 2

A Two-Variable Diagram Representing an Inverse Relationship

In this exhibit, we have plotted the data in Table 2 and then connected the points with a straight line. The data represent an inverse relationship: as one variable (price) falls, the other variable (quantity demanded) rises.

The variables price and quantity demanded are inversely related.

Now let's take a look at the data in Table 2. Our two variables are the *price of compact discs (CDs)* and the quantity demanded of CDs. Just by looking at the data in the first two columns, we see that as price falls (column 1), quantity demanded rises (column 2). Suppose we want to plot these data. We could place *price of CDs* on the vertical axis, as in Exhibit 2, and *quantity demanded of CDs* on the horizontal axis. Point *A* represents a price of $20 and a quantity demanded of 100, point *B* represents a price of $18 and a quantity demanded of 120, and so on. If we draw a straight line through the plotted points, we have a picture of the relationship between price and quantity demanded, based on the data in Table 2.

Notice:

- As price falls, the quantity demanded rises. For example, as price falls from $20 to $18, the quantity demanded rises from 100 to 120.

- As price rises, the quantity demanded falls. For example, when price rises from $12 to $14, quantity demanded falls from 180 to 160.

When two variables—such as price and quantity demanded—change in opposite ways, they are said to be inversely related.

As you have seen so far, variables may be directly related (when one increases, the other also increases) or inversely related (when one increases, the other decreases). Variables can also be independent of each other if, as one variable changes, the other does not.

In Exhibit 3(a), as the *X* variable rises, the *Y* variable remains the same (at 20). Obviously, the *X* and *Y* variables are independent of each other: As one changes, the other does not.

In Exhibit 3(b), as the *Y* variable rises, the *X* variable remains the same (at 30). Again, we conclude that the *X* and *Y* variables are independent of each other: As one changes, the other does not.

Inversely Related
Two variables are inversely related if they change in opposite ways.

Independent
Two variables are independent if, as one changes, the other does not.

Slope
The ratio of the change in the variable on the vertical axis to the change in the variable on the horizontal axis.

SLOPE OF A LINE

In addition to knowing *how* two variables are related, we also often need to know *how much* one variable changes as the other changes. To find out, we need only calculate the slope of the line. The slope is the ratio of the change in the variable on the vertical axis

EXHIBIT 3

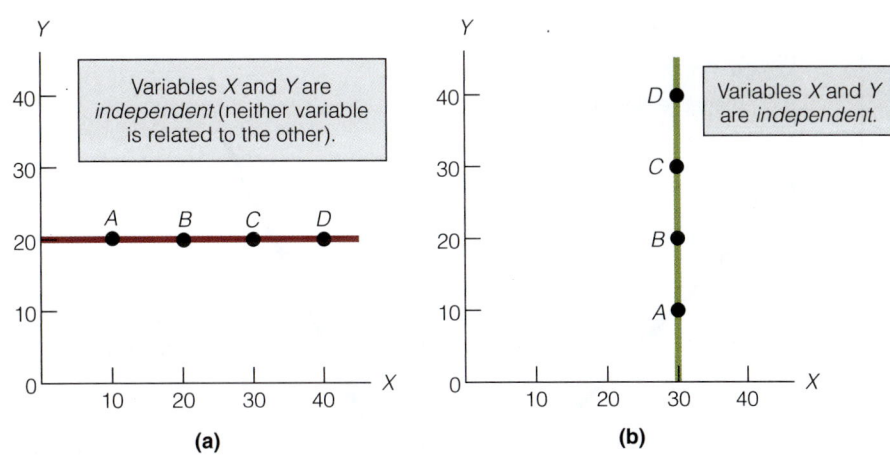

Two Diagrams Representing Independence Between Two Variables

In (a) and (b), the variables X and Y are independent: as one changes, the other does not.

to the change in the variable on the horizontal axis. For example, if *Y* is on the vertical axis and *X* is on the horizontal axis, the slope is equal to $\Delta Y / \Delta X$. (The symbol "Δ" means "change in.")

$$\text{Slope} = \frac{\Delta Y}{\Delta X}$$

Exhibit 4 shows four lines. In each case, the slope is calculated. After studying (a)–(d), see if you understand why the slopes are negative, positive, zero, and infinite.

SLOPE OF A LINE IS CONSTANT

Look again at the line in Exhibit 4(a). The slope between points *A* and *B* is computed to be –1. If we had computed the slope between points *B* and *C* or between points *C* and *D*, would it still be –1? Let's compute the slope between points *B* and *C*. Moving from point *B* to point *C*, the change in *Y* is –10 and the change in *X* is +10. So the slope is –1, as it was between points *A* and *B*. Now let's compute the slope between points *A* and *D*. Moving from point *A* to point *D*, the change in *Y* is –30 and the change in *X* is +30. Again the slope is –1. Our conclusion is that the slope between any two points on a straight line is always the same as the slope between any other two points. To see this for yourself, compute the slope between points *A* and *B* and between points *A* and *C* using the line in Exhibit 4(b).

SLOPE OF A CURVE

In addition to straight lines, economics graphs use curves. The slope of a curve is not constant throughout, as it is for a straight line. The slope of a curve varies from one point to another. Calculating the slope of a curve at a given point requires two steps, as illustrated for point *A* in Exhibit 5. First, draw a line tangent to the curve at the point (a tangent line is one that just touches the curve but does not cross it). Second, pick any two points on the tangent line and determine the slope. In Exhibit 5, the slope of the line between points *B* and *C* is 0.67. The slope of the curve at point *A* (and only at point *A*) is therefore 0.67.

EXHIBIT 4

Calculating Slopes

The slope of a line is the ratio of the change in the variable on the vertical axis to the change in the variable on the horizontal axis. In (a)–(d), we have calculated the slope.

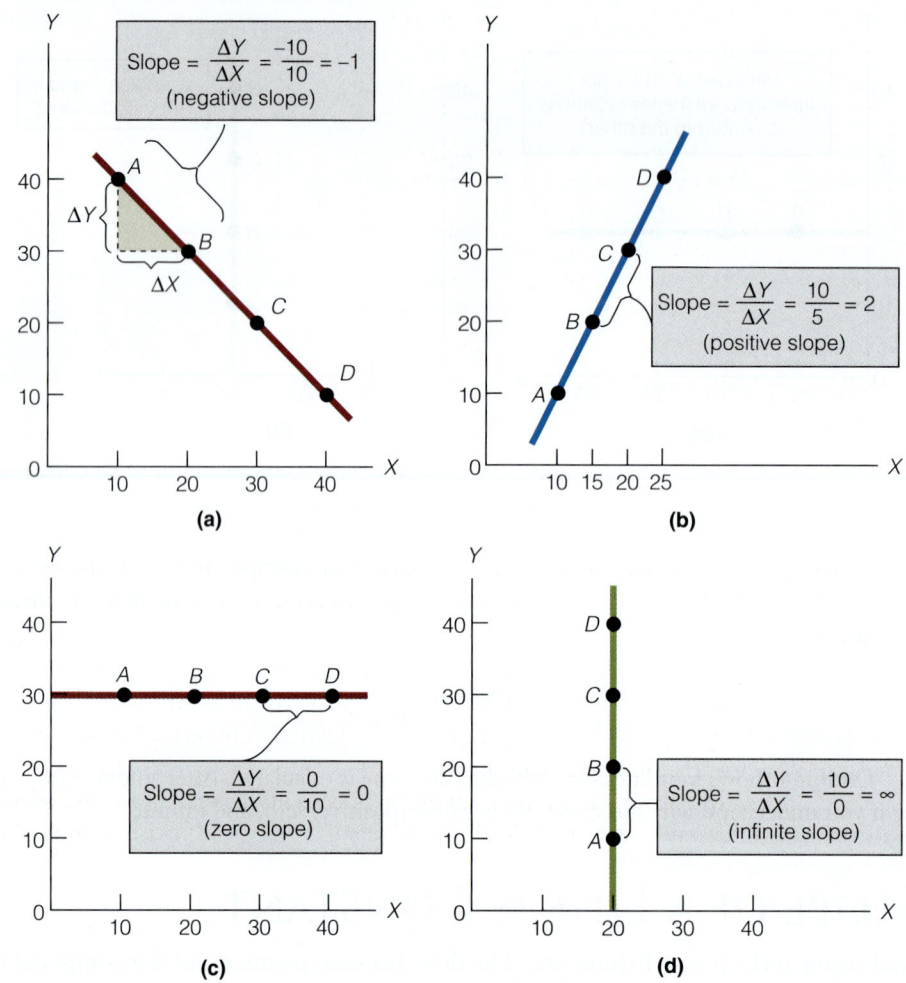

EXHIBIT 5

Calculating the Slope of a Curve at a Particular Point

The slope of the curve at point A is 0.67. This is calculated by drawing a line tangent to the curve at point A and then determining the slope of the line.

THE 45-DEGREE LINE

Economists sometimes use a *45-degree line* to represent data. This is a straight line that bisects the right angle formed by the intersection of the vertical and horizontal axes (see Exhibit 6). As a result, the 45-degree line divides the space enclosed by the two axes into *two equal parts*, as shown in the exhibit by the shading in different colors.

The major characteristic of the 45-degree line is that any point on it is equidistant from both the horizontal and vertical axes. For example, point *A* is exactly as far from the horizontal axis as it is from the vertical axis. Thus, point *A* represents as much *X* as it does *Y*. Specifically, in the exhibit, point *A* represents 20 units of *X* and 20 units of *Y*.

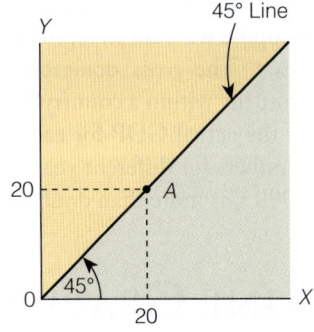

EXHIBIT 6

The 45-Degree Line

Any point on the 45-degree line is equidistant from each axis. For example, point A is the same distance from the vertical axis as it is from the horizontal axis.

PIE CHARTS

Pie charts appear in numerous places throughout this text. A pie chart is a convenient way to represent the different parts of something that when added together equal the whole. Let's consider a typical 24-hour weekday for Charles Myers. On a typical weekday, Charles spends 8 hours sleeping, 4 hours taking classes at the university, 4 hours working at his part-time job, 2 hours doing homework, 1 hour eating, 2 hours watching television, and 3 hours doing nothing in particular ("hanging around"). Exhibit 7 shows the breakdown of a typical weekday for Charles in pie chart form.

Pie charts send a quick visual message about rough percentage breakdowns and relative relationships. For example, Exhibit 7 clearly shows that Charles spends twice as much time working as doing homework.

EXHIBIT 7

A Pie Chart

The breakdown of activities for Charles Myers during a typical 24-hour weekday is represented in pie chart form.

Hanging Around
3 hours a day

Watching TV
2 hours a day

Eating 1 hour
a day

Homework
2 hours a day

Working
4 hours a day

Classes
4 hours a day

Sleeping
8 hours a day

BAR GRAPHS

Gross Domestic Product (GDP)
The value of the entire output produced annually within a country's borders.

The *bar graph* is another visual aid that economists use to convey relative relationships. Suppose we want to represent the gross domestic product for the United States in different years. The gross domestic product (GDP) is the value of the entire output produced annually within a country's borders. The bar graph in Exhibit 8 is a quick picture not only of the actual GDP for each year, but also of the relative relationships between the GDP numbers for different years. For example, the graph makes it easy to see that the GDP in 1990 was more than double what it was in 1980.

LINE GRAPHS

Sometimes information is best and most easily displayed in a *line graph*, which is particularly useful for illustrating changes in a variable over a time period. Suppose we want to illustrate the variations in average points per game for a college basketball team over a number of years. The line graph in Exhibit 9(a) shows that the basketball team was on a roller coaster during the years 1997–2010. Perhaps the visual message is that the team's performance has not been consistent from one year to the next.

Suppose we plot the same data again, except this time using a different measurement scale on the vertical axis. As you can see in Exhibit 9(b), the variation in the team's

---

EXHIBIT 8

A Bar Graph

U.S. gross domestic product for different years is illustrated in bar graph form. Source: Bureau of Economic Analysis

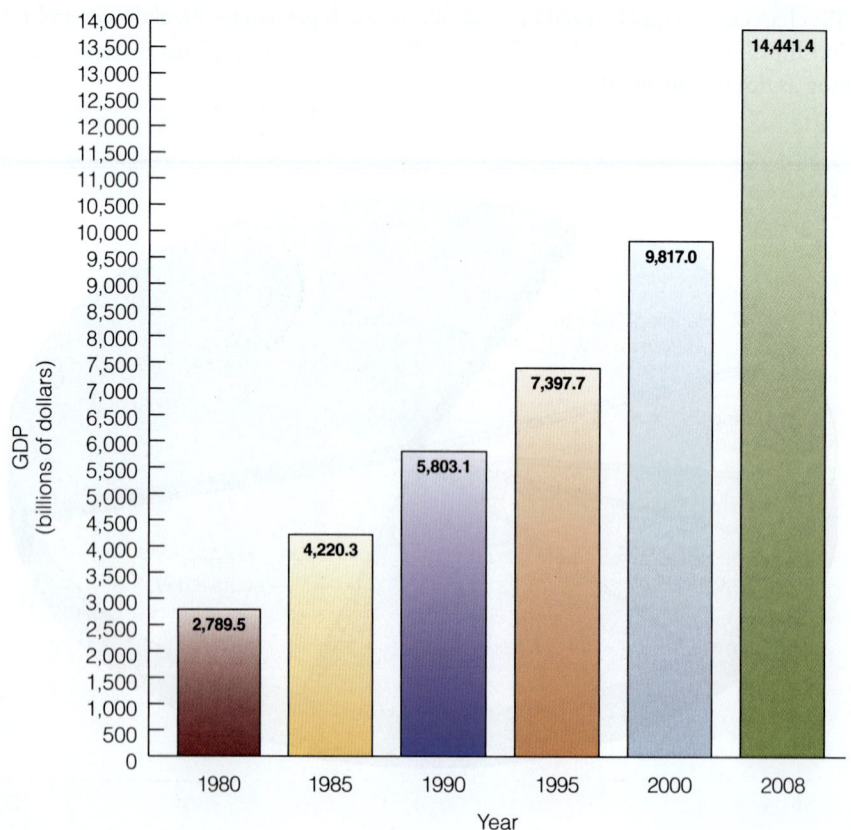

EXHIBIT 9

The Two Line Graphs Plot the Same Data

In (a) we plotted the average number of points per game for a college basketball team in different years. The variation between the years is pronounced. In (b) we plotted the same data as in (a), but the variation in the performance of the team appears much less pronounced than in (a).

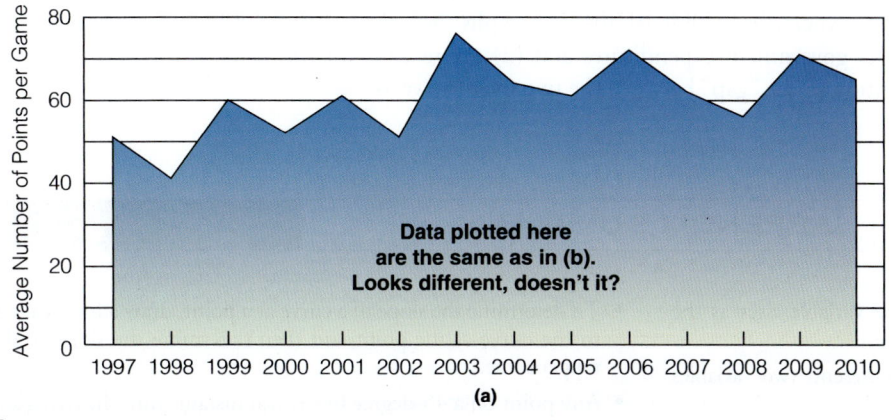

(a)

Data plotted here are the same as in (b). Looks different, doesn't it?

(b)

Data plotted here are the same as in (a). Looks different, doesn't it?

Year	Average Number of Points per Game
1997	50
1998	40
1999	59
2000	51
2001	60
2002	50
2003	75
2004	63
2005	60
2006	71
2007	61
2008	55
2009	70
2010	64

EXHIBIT 10

Projected Federal Government Expenditures and Tax Receipts, 2010–2014

Projected federal government expenditures and tax receipts are shown in line graph form for the period 2010–2014.

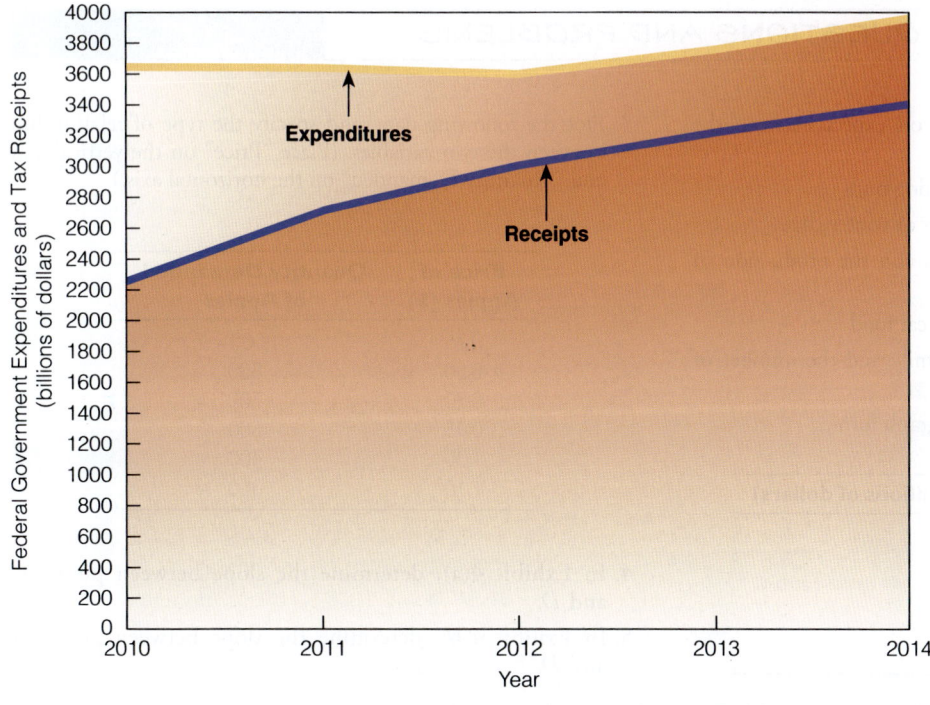

Expenditures

Receipts

Year	Expenditures	Receipts
2010	3,644	2,264
2011	3,638	2,717
2012	3,600	3,010
2013	3,759	3,221
2014	3,961	3,404

Source: Congressional Budget Office

performance appears much less pronounced than in part (a). In fact, we could choose a scale that, if we were to plot the data, would give us something close to a straight line. The point is simple: Data plotted in a line graph may convey different messages depending on the measurement scale used.

Sometimes economists show two line graphs on the same axes. Usually, the purpose is to draw attention to either (1) the *relationship* between two variables or (2) the *difference* between them. In Exhibit 10, the line graphs show the variation and trend in (1) projected federal government expenditures and (2) tax receipts for the years 2010–2014, drawing attention to the "gap" between the two over the years.

APPENDIX SUMMARY

- Two variables are directly related if one variable rises as the other rises.
- An upward-sloping line (left to right) represents two variables that are directly related.
- Two variables are inversely related if one variable rises as the other falls.
- A downward-sloping line (left to right) represents two variables that are inversely related.
- Two variables are independent if one variable rises as the other remains constant.
- The slope of a line is the ratio of the change in the variable on the vertical axis to the change in the variable on the horizontal axis. The slope of a straight line is the same between any two points on the line.

- To determine the slope of a curve at a point, draw a line tangent to the curve at the point and then determine the slope of the tangent line.
- Any point on a 45-degree line is equidistant from the two axes.
- A pie chart is a convenient way to represent the different parts of something that when added together equal the whole. A pie chart visually shows rough percentage breakdowns and relative relationships.
- A bar graph is a convenient way to represent relative relationships.
- Line graphs are particularly useful for illustrating changes in one or more variables over time.

QUESTIONS AND PROBLEMS

1. What type of relationship would you expect between the following?
   a. Sales of hot dogs and sales of hot dog buns
   b. The price of winter coats and sales of winter coats
   c. The price of personal computers and the production of personal computers
   d. Sales of toothbrushes and sales of cat food
   e. The number of children in a family and the number of toys in a family

2. Represent the following data in bar graph form.

Year	U.S. Money Supply (billions of dollars)
2005	1,374
2006	1,365
2007	1,373
2008	1,595
2009	1,689

3. Plot the following data, and specify the type of relationship between the two variables. (Place "Price" on the vertical axis and "Quantity Demanded" on the horizontal axis.)

Price of Apples ($)	Quantity Demanded of Apples
0.25	1,000
0.50	800
0.70	700
0.95	500
1.00	400
1.10	350

4. In Exhibit 4(a), determine the slope between points C and D.

5. In Exhibit 4(b), determine the slope between points A and D.

6. What is the special characteristic of a 45-degree line?

7. What is the slope of a 45-degree line?

8. When is a pie chart better than a bar graph for illustrating data?

9. Plot the following data, and specify the type of relationship between the two variables. (Place "Price" on the vertical axis and "Quantity Supplied" on the horizontal axis.)

Price of Apples ($)	Quantity Supplied of Apples
0.25	350
0.50	400
0.70	500
0.95	700
1.00	800
1.10	1,000

SHOULD YOU MAJOR IN ECONOMICS?

You are probably reading this textbook as part of your first college course in economics. You may be taking the course to satisfy a requirement in your major. Economics courses are sometimes required for students who plan to major in business, history, liberal studies, social science, or computer science.

Of course, you may also be planning to major in economics. If you are like many college students, you may complain that not enough information is available about the various majors at your college or university. For example, students who major in business sometimes say they are not quite certain what a business major is all about, but then they add that majoring in business is a safe bet. "After all," they assert," you're pretty sure of getting a job if you have a business degree. That's not always the case with other degrees."

Many college students choose their majors based on their high school courses. History majors, for example, might say that they decided to major in history because they "liked history in high school." Similarly, chemistry, biology, and math students say they chose their majors based on their experiences in high school. If a student found both math and economics easy and interesting in high school, then she is likely to major in math or economics. Conversely, if a student had a hard time with chemistry in high school and found it boring, then he doesn't usually want to major in chemistry in college.

Students also often look to the dollars at the end of the college degree. A student may enjoy history and want to learn more of it in college but tell herself that she will earn a higher starting salary after graduation if she majors in computer science or engineering.

Thus, when choosing a major, students often consider (1) how much they enjoy studying a particular subject, (2) what they would like to see themselves doing in the future, and (3) income prospects.

People may weight these three factors differently, but, regardless of the weighting, having more information is better than having, *ceteris paribus*. We note *"ceteris paribus"* because having more information is not necessarily better if you have to pay more for it than it is worth. Who wants to pay $10 for information that only provides $1 in benefits? This appendix is therefore a low-cost way of providing you with more information about an economics major.

We start by dispelling some of the misinformation about an economics major. Stated bluntly, some perceptions about an economics major and about a career in economics are just not true. For example, some people think that economics majors almost never study social relationships, but rather only such things as inflation, interest rates, and unemployment. Not true. Economics majors study some of the same things that sociologists, historians, psychologists, and political scientists study.

In addition to myth busting, the appendix also provides you with information about economics as a major: what courses you study, how many courses you are likely to have to take, and more.

Finally, we tell you something about a career in economics. If you have opted to become an economics major, the day will come when you have your degree in hand. What's next? What is your starting salary likely to be? What will you be doing? Are you going to be happy doing what economists do? (If you never thought economics was about happiness, you already have some misinformation about the field. Contrary to what most laypeople think, economics is not just about money. It is about happiness too.)

FIVE MYTHS ABOUT ECONOMICS AND BEING AN ECONOMICS MAJOR

Myth 1: Economics Is All Mathematics and Statistics. Some students choose not to major in economics because they think economics is all mathematics and statistics. Math and statistics are used in economics, but certainly not overwhelmingly at the undergraduate degree level. Economics majors are usually required to take one statistics course and one math course (usually an introductory calculus course). Even students who say, "Math isn't my subject" are sometimes happy with the amount of math they need in economics. The fact is that at the undergraduate level at many colleges and universities, economics is not a very math-intensive course of study. Economics uses many diagrams, but not a large amount of math.

A proviso: The amount of math in the economics curriculum varies across colleges and universities. Some economics departments do not require their students to learn much math or statistics; others do. The majority of economics departments do not require much math or statistics at the undergraduate level. The graduate level is a different story.

If you are thinking of pursuing economics at the graduate level, you should enroll in numerous mathematics and statistics courses as an undergraduate.

Myth 2: Economics Is Only About Inflation, Interest Rates, Unemployment, and Other Such Things. If you study economics at college and then go on to become a practicing economist, no doubt people will ask you certain questions when they learn your chosen profession. Here are some:

- Do you think the economy is going to pick up?
- Do you think the economy is going to slow down?
- What stocks would you recommend?
- Do you think interest rates are going to fall?
- Do you think interest rates are going to rise?
- What do you think about buying bonds right now? Is it a good idea?

People ask these kinds of questions because most believe that economists study only stocks, bonds, interest rates, inflation, unemployment, and so on. Although economists do study these topics, they are only a tiny part of what economists study. It is not hard to find many economists today, both inside and outside academia, who spend most of their time studying anything but inflation, unemployment, stocks, bonds, and the like.

In fact, much of what economists study may surprise you. Some economists use their economic tools and methods to study crime, marriage, divorce, sex, obesity, addiction, sports, voting behavior, bureaucracies, presidential elections, and much more. In short, today's economics is not your grandfather's economics. Many more topics are studied today in economics than were studied in years past.

Myth 3: People Become Economists Only If They Want to "Make Money." Awhile back we asked a few well-respected and well-known economists what got them interested in economics. Here is what some of them had to say:[1]

---

1. See various interviews in Roger A. Arnold, *Economics*, 2nd ed. (St. Paul, MN: West Publishing Company, 1992).

Gary Becker, the 1992 winner of the Nobel Prize in Economics, said:

I got interested in economics when I was an undergraduate in college. I came into college with a strong interest in mathematics, and at the same time with a strong commitment to do something to help society. I learned in the first economics course I took that economics could deal rigorously, àla mathematics, with social problems. That stimulated me because in economics I saw that I could combine both the mathematics and my desire to do something to help society.

Vernon Smith, the 2002 winner of the Nobel Prize in Economics, said:

My father's influence started me in science and engineering at Cal Tech, but my mother, who was active in socialist politics, probably accounts for the great interest I found in economics when I took my first introductory course.

Alice Rivlin, an economist and former member of the Federal Reserve Board, said:

My interest in economics grew out of concern for improving public policy, both domestic and international. I was a teenager in the tremendously idealistic period after World War II when it seemed terribly important to get nations working together to solve the world's problems peacefully.

Allan Meltzer said:

Economics is a social science. At its best it is concerned with ways (1) to improve well-being by allowing individuals the freedom to achieve their personal aims or goals and (2) to harmonize their individual interests. I find working on such issues challenging, and progress is personally rewarding.

Robert Solow, the 1987 winner of the Nobel Prize in Economics, said:

I grew up in the 1930s and it was very hard not to be interested in economics. If you were a high school student in the 1930s, you were conscious of the fact that our economy was in deep trouble and no one knew what to do about it.

Charles Plosser said:

I was an engineer as an undergraduate with little knowledge of economics. I went to the University of Chicago Graduate School of Business to get an MBA and there became fascinated with economics. I was impressed with the seriousness with which economics was viewed as a way of organizing one's thoughts about the world to address interesting questions and problems.

Walter Williams said:

I was a major in sociology in 1963 and I concluded that it was not very rigorous. Over the summer I was reading a book by W.E.B. DuBois, Black Reconstruction, *and somewhere in the book it said something along the lines that blacks could not melt into the mainstream of American society until they understood economics, and that was something that got me interested in economics.*

Murray Weidenbaum said:

A specific professor got me interested in economics. He was very prescient: He correctly noted that while lawyers dominated the policy-making process up until the 1940s, in the future economics would be an important tool for developing public policy. And he was right.

Irma Adelman said:

"I hesitate to say because it sounds arrogant. My reason [for getting into economics] was that I wanted to benefit humanity. And my perception at the time was that economic problems were the most important problems that humanity has to face. That is what got me into economics and into economic development.

Lester Thurow said:

[I got interested in economics because of] the belief, some would see it as naïve belief, that economics was a profession where it would be possible to help make the world better.

Myth 4: Economics Wasn't Very Interesting in High School, So It's Not Going to Be Very Interesting in College. A typical high school economics course emphasizes and spends much time discussing consumer economics. Students learn about credit cards, mortgage loans, budgets, buying insurance, renting an apartment, and other such things. These are important topics because not knowing their ins and outs can make your life much harder. Still, many students come away from high school thinking that economics is always and everywhere about consumer topics.

However, a high school economics course and a college economics course are usually as different as day and night. Simply leaf through this book and look at the variety of topics covered compared to those you might have covered in high school economics. Go on to look at texts used in other economics courses—ranging from law and economics to the history of economic thought to international economics to sports economics—and you will see what we mean.

Myth 5: Economics Is a Lot Like Business, But Business Is More Marketable. Although business and economics have some common topics, much that one learns in economics is not taught in business and much that one learns in business is not taught in economics. The area of intersection between business and economics is not large.

Still, many people think otherwise. Regarding business and economics as pretty much the same thing, they often choose to major in the subject that they believe has greater marketability—which they believe is business.

Well, consider the following:

1. A few years ago, *BusinessWeek* magazine asked the chief executive officers (CEOs) of major companies what they thought was the best undergraduate degree. Their first choice was engineering. Their second was economics. Economics scored higher than business administration.

2. Often the starting median salary and midcareer median salary are higher in economics than in other areas (even business-related areas). Table 1 is the list of the top 30 undergraduate college degrees by salary. Economics is ranked number 5.

TABLE 1

Top 30 Undergraduate degrees by salary

	Starting Median Salary	Midcareer Median Salary
Aerospace engineering	$59,600	$109,000
Chemical engineering	$65,700	$107,000
Computer engineering	$61,700	$105,000
Electrical engineering	$60,200	$102,000
Economics	**$50,200**	**$101,000**
Physics	$51,100	$98,800
Mechanical engineering	$58,900	$98,300
Computer science	$56,400	$97,400
Industrial engineering	$57,100	$95,000
Environmental engineering	$53,400	$94,500
Statistics	$48,600	$94,500
Biochemistry	$41,700	$94,200
Mathematics	$47,000	$93,600
Civil engineering	$55,100	$93,000
Construction management	$53,400	$89,600

continued

Finance	$48,500	$89,400
Management information systems	$51,900	$87,200
Computing and information systems	$50,900	$86,700
Geology	$45,100	$84,200
Chemistry	$42,900	$82,300
Marketing	$41,500	$81,500
International relations	$41,400	$80,500
Industrial technology	$49,500	$79,600
Environmental science	$43,300	$78,700
Architecture	$42,900	$78,300
International business	$41,900	$77,800
Accounting	$46,500	$77,600
Political science	$41,300	$77,300
Urban planning	$43,300	$77,000
Philosophy	$40,000	$76,700

Source: PayScale.com

WHAT AWAITS YOU AS AN ECONOMICS MAJOR?

If you become an economics major, what courses will you take? What are you going to study?

At the lower-division level, economics majors must take the principles of macroeconomics and the principles of microeconomics courses. They usually also take a statistics and a math course (usually calculus).

At the upper-division level, they must take intermediate microeconomics and intermediate macroeconomics, along with a certain number of electives. Some of the elective courses, among many others, are:

- Money and banking
- Law and economics
- History of economic thought
- Public finance
- Labor economics
- International economics
- Antitrust and regulation
- Health economics
- Economics of development
- Urban and regional economics
- Econometrics
- Mathematical economics
- Environmental economics
- Public choice

- Global managerial economics
- Economic approach to politics and sociology
- Sports economics

Most economics majors take between 12 and 15 economics courses.

One of the attractive things about studying economics is that you will acquire many of the skills employers highly value. First, you will have the quantitative skills that are important in many business and government positions. Second, you will acquire the writing skills necessary in almost all lines of work. Third, and perhaps most importantly, you will develop the thinking skills that almost all employers agree are critical to success.

A study published in the 1998 edition of the *Journal of Economic Education* ranked economics majors as having the highest average scores on the Law School Admission Test (LSAT). Also, consider the words of the Royal Economic Society:

> One of the things that makes economics graduates so employable is that the subject teaches you to think in a careful and precise way. The fundamental economic issue is how society decides to allocate its resources: how the costs and benefits of a course of action can be evaluated and compared, and how appropriate choices can be made. A degree in economics gives a training in decision making principles, providing a skill applicable in a very wide range of careers.

Keep in mind, too, that economics is one of the most popular majors at some of the most respected universities in the country. As of this writing, economics is the top major at Harvard, Princeton, Columbia, Stanford, University of Pennsylvania, and University of Chicago. It is the second most popular major at Brown, Yale, and the University of California at Berkeley. It is the third most popular major at Cornell and Dartmouth.

WHAT DO ECONOMISTS DO?

The employment of economists is expected to grow 6 percent from 2008 to 2018. According to the *Occupational Outlook Handbook:*

> Employment growth [in economics] should be fastest in private industry, especially in management, scientific, and technical consulting services. Rising demand for economic analysis in virtually every industry should stem from the growing complexity of the global economy, the effects of competition on businesses, and increased reliance on quantitative methods for analyzing and forecasting business, sales, and other economic trends. Some corporations choose to hire economic consultants to fill these needs, rather than keeping an economist on staff. This practice should result in more economists being employed in consulting services.

Today, economists work in many varied fields. Here are some of the fields and some of the positions that economists hold in those fields:

Education

  College professor

  Researcher

  High school teacher

Journalism

  Researcher

  Industry analyst

  Economic analyst

Accounting

   Analyst

   Auditor

   Researcher

   Consultant

General Business

   Chief executive officer

   Business analyst

   Marketing analyst

   Business forecaster

   Competitive analyst

Government

   Researcher

   Analyst

   Speechwriter

   Forecaster

Financial Services

   Business journalist

   International analyst

   Newsletter editor

   Broker

   Investment banker

Banking

   Credit analyst

   Loan officer

   Investment analyst

   Financial manager

Other

   Business consultant

   Independent forecaster

   Freelance analyst

   Think tank analyst

   Entrepreneur

Economists do a myriad of things. For example:

- In business, economists often analyze economic conditions, make forecasts, offer strategic planning initiatives, collect and analyze data, predict exchange rate movements, and review regulatory policies, among other things.

- In government, economists collect and analyze data, analyze international economic situations, research monetary conditions, advise on policy, and do much more.

- As private consultants, economists work with accountants, business executives, government officials, educators, financial firms, labor unions, state and local governments, and others.

In May 2008, the median annual wage and salary earnings of economists were $83,590. The middle 50 percent earned between $59,390 and $113,590. The lowest 10 percent earned less than $44,050, and the highest 10 percent earned more than $149,110.

In March 2009, the average annual salary for economists employed by the federal government was $108,010. Starting salaries were higher in selected geographical areas where the prevailing local pay was higher.

PLACES TO FIND MORE INFORMATION

If you are interested in a major and perhaps a career in economics, here are some places you can go and people you can speak with to acquire more information:

- To learn about the economics curriculum, speak with the economics professors at your college or university. Ask them what courses you would have to take as an economics major and what elective courses are available. In addition, ask them why they chose to study economics: What is it about economics that interested them?

- For more information about salaries and what economists do, you may want to visit the *Occupational Outlook Handbook* website (http://www.bls.gov/oco/).

CONCLUDING REMARKS

Choosing a major is a big decision and therefore should not be made quickly and without much thought. This short appendix has provided you with some information about an economics major and a career in economics. Economics may not be for everyone (in fact, economists would say that if it were, many of the benefits of specialization would be lost), but it may be right for you. A major in economics trains you in today's most marketable skills: good writing, quantitative analysis, and thinking. It is a major in which professors and students daily ask and answer some very interesting and relevant questions. It is a major that is highly regarded by employers. It may just be the right major for you. Give it some thought.

CHAPTER 2

PhotoAlto/James Hardy/Getty Images

PRODUCTION POSSIBILITIES FRONTIER FRAMEWORK

Introduction In the last chapter you learned about various economic concepts, such as scarcity, choice, and opportunity cost. In this chapter we develop a graphical framework of analysis for understanding these concepts and others. Specifically, we develop the production possibilities frontier.

THE PRODUCTION POSSIBILITIES FRONTIER

Think of yourself alone on an island. You can produce two goods and only two goods: coconuts and pineapples. Because your resources are limited, producing more of one good means producing less of the other. That type of thinking is the intuition behind the *production possibilities frontier* (PPF). Now keep that intuition in mind as we proceed.

The Straight-Line PPF: Constant Opportunity Costs

In Exhibit 1(a), we have identified five combinations of books and shirts that can be produced in an economy. For example, combination *A* is 4 books and 0 shirts, combination *B* is 3 books and 1 shirt, and so on. Next, we plotted these five combinations of books and shirts in Exhibit 1(b), with each combination representing a different point. For example, the combination of 4 books and 0 shirts is represented by point *A*. The line that connects points *A–E* is the production possibilities frontier. A production possibilities frontier (PPF) is the combination of two goods that can be produced in a certain period of time under the conditions of a given state of technology and fully employed resources.

Notice that the production possibilities frontier is a straight line. This is because the opportunity cost of books and shirts (in our example) is constant.

Straight-line PPF = Constant opportunity costs

To illustrate what *constant opportunity costs* means, suppose the economy were to move from point *A* to point *B*. At point *A*, 4 books are produced and 0 shirts; at point *B*, 3 books are produced and 1 shirt.

Production Possibilities Frontier (PPF)

The possible combinations of two goods that can be produced in a certain period of time under the conditions of a given state of technology and fully employed resources.

- Point *A*: 4 books and 0 shirts
- Point *B*: 3 books and 1 shirt

What does the economy have to forfeit (in terms of books) to get 1 shirt? The answer is 1 book. We conclude that moving from point *A* to point *B*, the opportunity cost of 1 shirt is 1 book.

Now let's move from point *B* to point *C*. At point *B*, 3 books and 1 shirt are produced; at point *C*, 2 books and 2 shirts are produced.

- Point *B*: 3 books and 1 shirt
- Point *C*: 2 books and 2 shirts

What does the economy have to forfeit (in terms of books) to get another shirt? The answer is 1 book. We conclude that moving from point *B* to *C*, the opportunity cost of 1 shirt is 1 book.

In fact, when we move from *C* to *D* or from *D* to *E*, we also notice that the opportunity cost

EXHIBIT 1

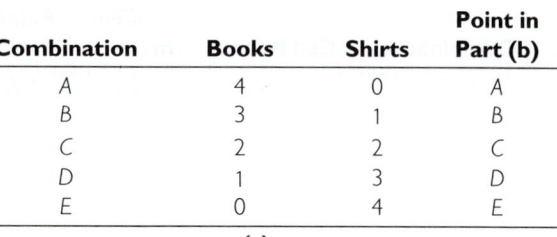

Combination	Books	Shirts	Point in Part (b)
A	4	0	A
B	3	1	B
C	2	2	C
D	1	3	D
E	0	4	E

(a)

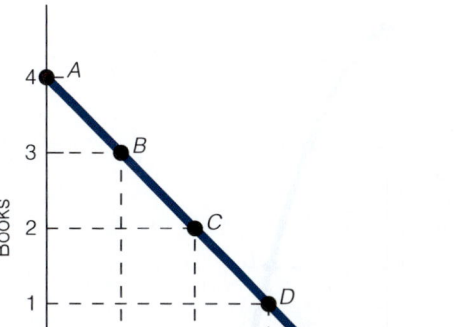

(b)

Production Possibilities Frontier (Constant Opportunity Costs)

The economy can produce any of the five combinations of books and shirts in part (a). We have plotted these combinations in part (b). The production possibilities frontier (PPF) in part (b) is a straight line because the opportunity cost of producing either good is constant.

of 1 shirt is 1 book. This is what we mean when we speak of constant opportunity costs: The opportunity cost of 1 shirt is *always* 1 book. And because of constant opportunity costs, the PPF in Exhibit 1(b) is a straight line. When opportunity costs are not constant, the PPF will not be a straight line, as you will see next.

The Bowed-Outward (Concave-Downward) PPF: Increasing Opportunity Costs

In Exhibit 2(a), we have identified five combinations of cell phones and coffee makers that can be produced in an economy. For example, combination *A* is 10 cell phones and 0 coffee makers, combination *B* is 9 cell phones and 1 coffee maker, and so on. We plotted these five combinations of cell phones and coffee makers in Exhibit 2(b), again with each combination representing a different point. The curved line that connects points *A–E* is the production possibilities frontier. In this case, the production possibilities frontier is bowed outward (concave downward) because the opportunity cost of coffee makers increases as more coffee makers are produced.

Bowed-outward PPF = Increasing opportunity costs

To illustrate, let's start at point *A*, where the economy is producing 10 cell phones and 0 coffee makers and move to point *B*, where the economy is producing 9 cell phones and 1 coffee maker.

- Point *A*: 10 cell phones and 0 coffee makers
- Point *B*: 9 cell phones and 1 coffee maker

EXHIBIT 2

Production Possibilities Frontier (Increasing Opportunity Costs)

The economy can produce any of the five combinations of cell phones and coffee makers in part (a). We have plotted these combinations in part (b). The production possibilities frontier in part (b) is bowed outward because the opportunity cost of producing coffee makers increases as more coffee makers are produced.

Combination	Cell Phones	Coffee makers	Point in Part (b)
A	10	0	A
B	9	1	B
C	7	2	C
D	4	3	D
E	0	4	E

(a)

(b)

What is the opportunity cost of a coffee maker moving from point *A* to point *B*? Stated differently, what does the economy have to forfeit (in terms of cell phones) to get 1 coffee maker? The answer is 1 cell phone.

Now let's move from point *B* to point *C*. At point *B*, the economy is producing 9 cell phones and 1 coffee maker; at point *C*, the economy is producing 7 cell phones and 2 coffee makers:

- Point *B*: 9 cell phones and 1 coffee maker

- Point *C*: 7 cell phones and 2 coffee makers

What does the economy have to forfeit (in terms of cell phones) to get 1 additional coffee maker? The answer this time is 2 cell phones. We conclude that moving from point *A* to *B*, the opportunity cost of 1 coffee maker was 1 cell phone, but that moving from point *B* to *C*, the opportunity cost of 1 (additional) coffee maker is 2 cell phones. If we were to continue producing additional coffee makers, we would see that we would have to give up increasingly more cell phones. You can see this easily if you consider the economy moving from point *C* to *D* (where the opportunity cost of producing an additional coffee maker is 3 cell phones) or moving from point to *D* to *E* (where the opportunity cost of producing an additional coffee maker is 4 cell phones). We end with a question: Why is the PPF in Exhibit 2(b) bowed outward? The reason is the increasing opportunity costs of producing coffee makers.

Law of Increasing Opportunity Costs

We know that the shape of the production possibilities frontier depends on whether opportunity costs (1) are constant or (2) increase as more of a good is produced. In Exhibit 1(b), the production possibilities frontier is a straight line; in Exhibit 2(b), it is bowed outward (curved). In the real world, most production possibilities frontiers are bowed outward. In other words, for most goods, the opportunity costs *increase* as more of a good is produced. This is referred to as the law of increasing opportunity costs.

Law of Increasing Opportunity Costs

As more of a good is produced, the opportunity costs of producing that good increase.

The opportunity costs increase as more of most goods is produced because people have varying abilities. For example, some individuals are better suited to building houses than others are. When a construction company first starts building houses, it employs the people most skilled at house building. The most skilled persons can build houses at lower opportunity costs than others can. But as the construction company builds more houses, it finds that it has already employed the most skilled builders; so it must employ those who are less skilled at house building. The less skilled people build houses at higher

EXHIBIT 3

A Summary Statement About Increasing Opportunity Costs and a Production Possibilities Frontier That Is Bowed Outward (Concave Downward)

Many of the points about increasing opportunity costs and a production possibilities frontier that is bowed outward are summarized here.

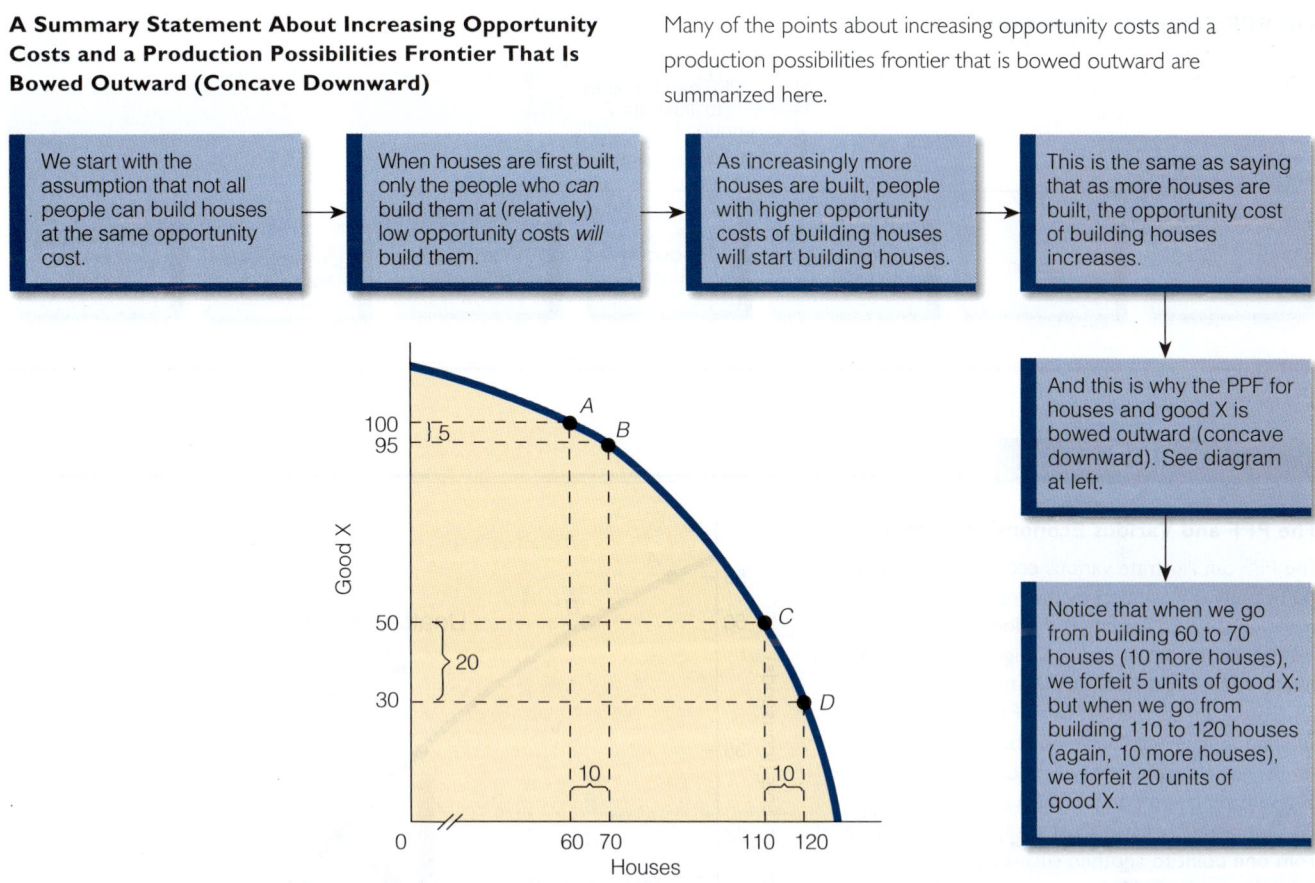

We start with the assumption that not all people can build houses at the same opportunity cost.

When houses are first built, only the people who *can* build them at (relatively) low opportunity costs *will* build them.

As increasingly more houses are built, people with higher opportunity costs of building houses will start building houses.

This is the same as saying that as more houses are built, the opportunity cost of building houses increases.

And this is why the PPF for houses and good X is bowed outward (concave downward). See diagram at left.

Notice that when we go from building 60 to 70 houses (10 more houses), we forfeit 5 units of good X; but when we go from building 110 to 120 houses (again, 10 more houses), we forfeit 20 units of good X.

opportunity costs. Whereas three skilled house builders could build a house in a month, as many as seven unskilled builders may be required to build one as fast. Exhibit 3 summarizes the points in this section.

Economic Concepts in a PPF Framework

The PPF framework is useful for illustrating and working with economic concepts. This section discusses seven economic concepts in terms of the PPF framework (see Exhibit 4).

SCARCITY Recall that scarcity is the condition where the wants (for goods) are greater than the resources available to satisfy them. The finiteness of resources is graphically portrayed by the PPF in Exhibit 5. If the frontier could speak it would tell us: "At this point in time, that's as far as you can go. You cannot go any farther. You are limited to choosing any combination of the two goods on the frontier or below it."

The PPF separates the production possibilities of an economy into two regions: (1) an attainable region, which consists of the points on the PPF itself and all points below it (this region includes points *A−F*), and (2) an unattainable region, which consists of the points above and beyond the PPF (such as point *G*). Recall that scarcity implies that some things are attainable and others are unattainable. Point *A* on the PPF is attainable, as is point *F*; point *G* is not.

The PPF Economic Framework

EXHIBIT 5

The PPF and Various Economic Concepts

The PPF can illustrate various economic concepts:
(1) Scarcity is illustrated by the frontier itself. Implicit in the concept of scarcity is the idea that we can have some things but not all things. The PPF separates an attainable region from an unattainable region.
(2) Choice is represented by our having to decide among the many attainable combinations of the two goods. For example, will we choose the combination of goods represented by point A or by point B?
(3) Opportunity cost is most easily seen as movement from one point to another, such as movement from point A to point B. More cars are available at point B than at point A, but fewer television sets are available. In short, the opportunity cost of more cars is fewer television sets. (4) Productive efficiency is represented by the points on the PPF (such as A−E), while productive inefficiency is represented by any point below the PPF (such as F). (5) Unemployment (in terms of resources being unemployed) exists at any productive inefficient point (such as F), whereas resources are fully employed at any productive efficient point (such as A−E).

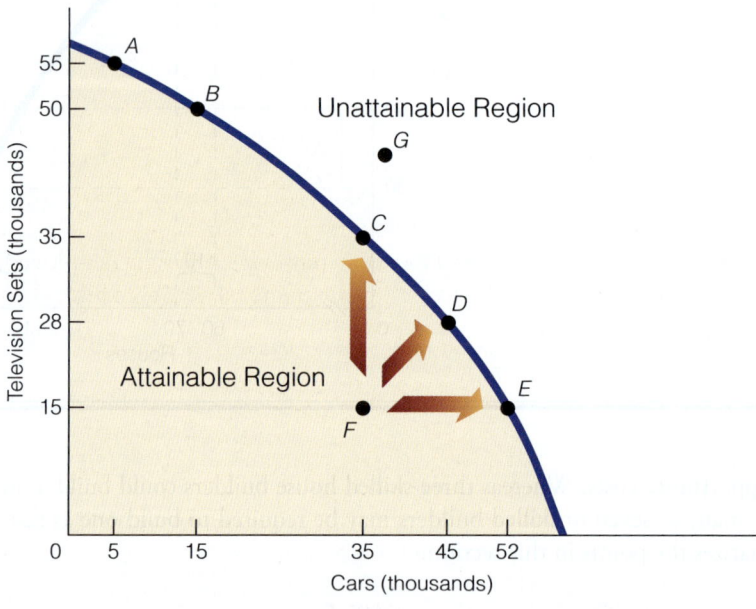

Choice and opportunity cost are also shown in Exhibit 5. Note that within the attainable region, individuals must choose the combination of the two goods they want to produce. Obviously, hundreds of combinations exist, but let's consider only two, represented by points A and B. Which of the two will individuals choose? They can't be at both points; they must make a choice.

Opportunity cost is illustrated as we move from one point to another on the PPF in Exhibit 5. Suppose we are at point A and choose to move to point B. At A, we have 55,000 television sets and 5,000 cars; at point B, we have 50,000 television sets and 15,000 cars. What is the opportunity cost of a car? Because 10,000 *more* cars come at a cost of 5,000 *fewer* television sets, the opportunity cost of 1 car is 1/2 television set.

PRODUCTIVE EFFICIENCY Economists often say that an economy is productive efficient if it is producing the maximum output with the given resources and technology. In Exhibit 5, points *A*, *B*, *C*, *D*, and *E* are all productive-efficient points. Notice that all these points lie on the production possibilities frontier. In other words, we are getting the most (in terms of output) from what we have (in terms of available resources and technology).

It follows that an economy is productive inefficient if it is producing less than the maximum output with given resources and technology. In Exhibit 5, point *F* is a productive inefficient point. It lies below the production possibilities frontier; it is below the outer limit of what is possible. In other words, we can produce more goods with the available resources, or we can get more of one good without getting less of another.

To illustrate, suppose we move from inefficient point *F* to efficient point *C*. We produce more television sets and no fewer cars. What if we move from *F* to *D*? We produce more television sets and more cars. Finally, if we move from *F* to *E*, we produce more cars and no fewer television sets. Thus, moving from *F* can give us more of at least one good and no less of another good. In short, productive inefficiency implies that gains are possible in one area without losses in another.

UNEMPLOYED RESOURCES When the economy exhibits productive inefficiency, it is not producing the maximum output with the available resources and technology. One reason may be that the economy is not using all its resources; that is, some of its resources are unemployed, as at point *F* in Exhibit 5.

When the economy exhibits productive efficiency, it is producing the maximum output with the available resources and technology. In other words, it is using all its resources to produce goods; its resources are fully employed, and none are unemployed. At the productive-efficient points *A−E* in Exhibit 5, no resources are unemployed.

ECONOMIC GROWTH Economic growth refers to the increased productive capabilities of an economy. It is illustrated by a shift outward in the production possibilities frontier. Two major factors that affect economic growth are (1) an increase in the quantity of resources and (2) an advance in technology.

An increase in the quantity of resources (e.g., through a discovery of new resources) makes a greater quantity of output possible. In Exhibit 6, an increase in the quantity of resources makes it possible to produce both more military goods and more civilian goods. Thus, the PPF shifts outward from PPF_1 to PPF_2.

Technology refers to the body of skills and knowledge involved in the use of resources in production. An advance in technology commonly increases the ability to produce more output with a fixed quantity of resources or the ability to produce the same output with a smaller quantity of resources. For example, suppose an advance in technology allows the production of more of *both* military goods and civilian goods with the same quantity of resources. As a result, the PPF in Exhibit 6(a) shifts outward from PPF_1 to PPF_2. The outcome is the same as when the quantity of resources is increased.

If the advance in technology allows only more of *one good* (instead of both goods) to be produced with the same quantity of resources, then the PPF shifts outward, but not in the same way as shown in Exhibit 6(a). To illustrate, suppose an advance in technology allows only more civilian goods to be produced but not more military goods. Therefore, the maximum amount of military goods that can be produced does not change, but the maximum amount of civilian goods rises. This gives us the shift from PPF_1 to PPF_2 shown in Exhibit 6(b).

Productive Efficient
The condition where the maximum output is produced with the given resources and technology.

Productive Inefficient
The condition where less than the maximum output is produced with the given resources and technology. Productive inefficiency implies that more of one good can be produced without any less of another being produced.

Technology
The body of skills and knowledge involved in the use of resources in production. An advance in technology commonly increases the ability to produce more output with a fixed amount of resources or the ability to produce the same output with fewer resources.

EXHIBIT 6

Economic Growth Within a PPF Framework

An increase in resources or an advance in technology (that can lead to more of both goods being produced) can increase the production capabilities of an economy, leading to economic growth and a shift outward in the production

possibilities frontier, as shown in part (a). If the advance in technology leads to the greater production of only one good (such as civilian goods in our exhibit), then the PPF shifts outward, as shown in (b).

(a)

(b)

finding ECONOMICS

In an Attorney's Office An attorney is sitting in his office working. Where is the economics?

Let's first talk about farmers and a change in technology. During the twentieth century, many farmers left farming because it experienced major technological advances. Where farmers once farmed with minimal capital equipment, today they use computers, tractors, pesticides, cellular phones, and much more. In 1910, the United States had 32.1 million farmers; today there are around 4.8 million farmers. Where did all the farmers go?

Because of technological advancements, fewer farmers were needed to produce food, and so many of them left the farms for the cities, where they entered the manufacturing and service industries. In other words, people who were once farmers (or whose parents and grandparents were farmers) began to produce cars, airplanes, television sets, and computers. They became attorneys, accountants, and police officers.

What we learn from this is that a technological advancement in one sector of the economy can have ripple effects throughout the economy. We also learn that a technological advancement can affect the composition of employment. ▲▲▲

SELF-TEST

(Answers to Self-Test questions are in Answers to Self-Test Questions at the back of the book.)

1. What does a straight-line production possibilities frontier (PPF) represent? What does a bowed-outward PPF represent?

2. What does the law of increasing costs have to do with a bowed-outward PPF? ·

3. A politician says, "If you elect me, we can get more of everything we want." Under what conditions is the politician telling the truth?

4. In an economy, only one combination of goods is productive efficient. True or false? Explain your answer.

economics 24/7

The PPF and Your Grades

You have your own PPF; you just may not know it. Suppose you are studying for two upcoming exams. You have only a total of six hours before you have to take the first exam, after which you will immediately proceed to take the second exam. Time spent studying for the first exam (in economics) takes away from time that could be spent studying for the second exam (in math), and vice versa. Also, *time studying* is a resource in the production of a good grade: Less time studying for the economics exam and more time spent studying for the math exam means a higher grade in math and a lower grade in economics. For you, the situation may look as it does in Exhibit 7(a). We have identified four points in the exhibit (1–4) corresponding to the four combinations of two grades (one grade in economics and one grade in English).

Also notice that each grade comes with a certain amount of time studying. This time is specified under the grade.

Given the resources you currently have (your labor and time), you can achieve any of the four combinations. For example, you can spend six hours studying for economics and get a *B* (point 1), but this means you study math for zero hours and get an F in that course. Or you can spend four hours studying for economics and get a *C* (point 2), leaving you two hours to study for math, in which you get a *D*.

What do you need to get a higher grade in one course without getting a lower grade in the other course? You need more resources, which in this case is more time. If you have eight hours to study, your PPF shifts rightward, as in Exhibit 7(b). Now point 5 is possible (whereas it was not possible before you got more time). At point 5, you can get a C in economics and in math, which was an impossible combination of grades when you had less time (a PPF closer to the origin).

Pixland/Getty Images/Jupiter Images

EXHIBIT 7

(a)

Grade in Economics and Time Spent to Earn the Grade

A —
B (6 hrs.) 1
C (4 hrs.)   2
D (2 hrs.)   3   PPF₁
F (0 hr.)   4

F (0 hr.) D (2 hrs.) C (4 hrs.) B (6 hrs.) A

Grade in Math and Time Spent to Earn the Grade

(b)

Grade in Economics and Time Spent to Earn the Grade

A (8 hrs.)
B (6 hrs.) 1
C (4 hrs.)   2   5
D (2 hrs.)   3   PPF₁   PPF₂
F (0 hr.)   4

F (0 hr.) D (2 hrs.) C (4 hrs.) B (6 hrs.) A (8 hrs.)

Grade in Math and Time Spent to Earn the Grade

SPECIALIZATION AND TRADE CAN MOVE US BEYOND OUR PPF

In this section we explain how a country that specializes in the production of certain goods, and then trades those goods to countries for other goods, can make itself better off. In terms of its PPF, it can consume at a level *beyond* its PPF.

A Simple Two-Person PPF Model

Two individuals, Elizabeth and Brian, live near each other, and each engages in two activities: baking bread and growing apples. Let's suppose that within a certain period of time, Elizabeth can produce 20 loaves of bread and no apples, or 10 loaves of bread and 10 apples, or no bread and 20 apples. See Exhibit 8. In other words, three points on Elizabeth's production possibilities frontier correspond to 20 loaves of bread and no apples, 10 loaves of bread and 10 apples, and no bread and 20 apples. As a consumer, Elizabeth likes to eat both bread and apples; so she decides to produce (and consume) 10 loaves of bread and 10 apples. This is represented by point *B* in Exhibit 8(a).

In the same time period, Brian can produce 10 loaves of bread and no apples, or 5 loaves of bread and 15 apples, or no bread and 30 apples. In other words, these three combinations correspond to three points on Brian's production possibilities frontier. Brian, like Elizabeth, likes to eat both bread and apples; so he decides to produce and consume 5 loaves of bread and 15 apples. This is represented by point *F* in Exhibit 8(b).

EXHIBIT 8

Elizabeth's PPF, Brian's PPF | In (a) we show the combination of the two goods that Elizabeth can produce, first in terms of a table and next in terms of a PPF. Because Elizabeth wants to consume some of both goods, she chooses to produce the combination of the two goods represented by point *B*.

In (b) we show the combination of the two goods that Brian can produce, first in terms of a table and next in terms of a PPF. Because Brian wants to consume some of both goods, he chooses to produce the combination of the two goods represented by point *F*.

Elizabeth

Bread	Apples
20	0
10	10
0	20

Brian

Bread	Apples
10	0
5	15
0	30

Elizabeth produces and consumes this combination of bread and apples.

(a)

Brian produces and consumes this combination of bread and apples.

(b)

Elizabeth thinks that both she and Brian may be better off if each specializes in producing only one of the two goods and trading it for the other. In other words, Elizabeth should produce either bread or apples but not both. Brian thinks this may be a good idea but is not sure which good each person should specialize in producing.

An economist would advise each to produce the good that he or she can produce at a lower cost. In economics, a person who can produce a good at a lower cost than another person is said to have a comparative advantage in the production of the good.

Exhibit 8 shows that for every 10 units of bread Elizabeth does not produce, she can produce 10 apples. In other words, the opportunity cost of producing 1 loaf of bread *(B)* is 1 apple *(A)*:

Comparative Advantage
The situation where someone can produce a good at lower opportunity cost than someone else can.

$$\text{Opportunity costs for Elizabeth: } 1B = 1A$$

$$1A = 1B$$

For every 5 loaves of bread that Brian does not produce, he can produce 15 apples. So, for every 1 loaf of bread he does not produce, he can produce 3 apples. Therefore, for every 1 apple he chooses to produce, he forfeits 1/3 loaf of bread.

$$\text{Opportunity costs for Brian: } 1B = 3A$$

$$1A = \frac{1}{3}B$$

Comparing opportunity costs, we see that Elizabeth can produce bread at a lower opportunity cost than Brian can. (Elizabeth forfeits 1 apple when she produces 1 loaf of bread, whereas Brian forfeits 3 apples for 1 loaf of bread.) On the other hand, Brian can produce apples at a lower opportunity cost than Elizabeth can. We conclude that Elizabeth has a comparative advantage in the production of bread, and Brian has a comparative advantage in the production of apples.

Suppose both specialize in the production of the good in which they have a comparative advantage. Elizabeth produces only bread and makes 20 loaves. Brian produces only apples and grows 30 of them.

Now suppose that Elizabeth and Brian decide to trade 8 loaves of bread for 12 apples. In other words, Elizabeth produces 20 loaves of bread and then trades 8 of them for

EXHIBIT 9

Consumption for Elizabeth and Brian With and Without Specialization and Trade

A comparison of the consumption of bread and apples before and after specialization and trade shows that both Elizabeth and Brian benefit from producing the good in which each has a comparative advantage and trading for the other good.

(a)

(b)

economics 24/7

Political Debates Explained in Terms of the PPF

Strictly speaking, the PPF is simply a curve that represents the combination of two goods that a country can produce under certain conditions (a given amount of resources and a certain technology). But the PPF is not only a curve; it is a framework of analysis. With it, we can often gain insights into what is happening in the real world. Specifically, the PPF, used as a framework of analysis, can give us some idea what is behind political battles.

AP Photo/Al Goldis, file

In Exhibit 10 we show the PPF for a country. We assume that the country is currently located at point A, producing 30 units of good X and 35 units of good Y. Notice also that the country is efficient in its production: It is located at a point *on* its PPF instead of below it.

Now let's suppose that there are two major political parties in this country: the X and Y parties. Party X represents people who would like to move the country in the direction of producing more X. Party X would prefer the country locate at point B instead of at point A on the PPF.

Party Y, on the other hand, represents people who would like to move the country in the direction of producing more Y. Party Y would prefer the country located at point C on the PPF instead of at point A.

Will political parties X and Y do battle? Will they be involved in a political tug-of-war, each trying to move the country in a different direction? Probably so.

Now consider what happens when the country falls below its PPF and moves to a point like D in the exhibit. Point D is representative of a country that has unemployed resources; it is likely to be a representative of an economy in a recession, producing far less than it could be producing. At point D, both parties are less content than they were

at point A for the simple reason that less of both goods is being produced at point D than at A. One thing we ought to observe, then, is that both political parties will want to move the country out of the recession. But might the ways they propose to move the country be different? Since political party Y prefers point C to point A, and political party X prefers point B to point A, might each party's proposal for "solving the recession" be geared toward its preferred point on the country's PPF? To illustrate, if each political party is proposing federal monies or tax cuts to stimulate output production, might political party X's specific proposal be geared toward producing more of good X while political party Y's specific proposal is geared toward producing more of good Y?

EXHIBIT 10

Politics and the PPF

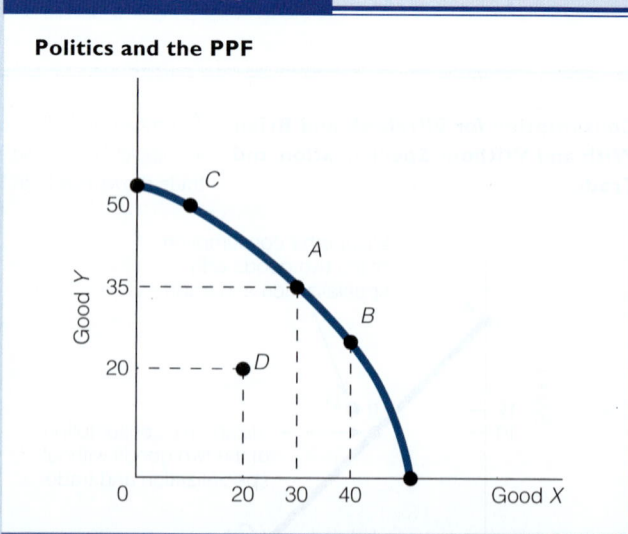

12 apples. After the trade, Elizabeth consumes 12 loaves of bread and 12 apples. Compare this situation with what she consumed when she didn't specialize and didn't trade. In that situation, she consumed 10 loaves of bread and 10 apples. Clearly, Elizabeth is better off when she specializes and trades than when she does not.

But what about Brian? He produces 30 apples and trades 12 of them to Elizabeth for 8 loaves of bread. In other words, he consumes 8 loaves of bread and 18 apples. Compare this situation with what he consumed when he didn't specialize and didn't trade. In that situation, he consumed 5 loaves of bread and 15 apples. Thus, Brian is also better off when he specializes and trades than when he does not.

On or Beyond the PPF?

In Exhibit 9(a) we show the PPF for Elizabeth. When she was not specializing and not trading, she consumed the combination of bread and apples represented by point *B* (10 loaves of bread and 10 apples). When she did specialize and trade, her consumption of both goods increased, moving her to point *D* (12 loaves of bread and 12 apples). Lesson learned: Through specialization and trade, Elizabeth's consumption moved beyond her PPF. It is easy to see the benefits of specialization of trade.

In Exhibit 9(b) we show the PPF for Brian. When he was not specializing and not trading, he consumed the combination of bread and apples represented by point *F* (5 loaves of bread and 15 apples). When he did specialize and trade, his consumption of both goods increased, moving him to point *H* (8 loaves of bread and 18 apples). Lesson learned: Through specialization and trade, Brian's consumption moved beyond his PPF.

What holds for Elizabeth and Brian through specialization and trade holds for countries too. For example, if both Americans and Brazilians specialize in producing those goods for which they have a comparative advantage and then trade some of those goods for the others' goods, both Americans and Brazilians can consume more of both goods than if they don't specialize and don't trade.

finding ECONOMICS

At the Airport You wake up in the morning and drive to the airport. You have your bags checked curbside at the airport. You tip the person who checks your luggage. You then line up to go through security. Once on the plane you hear the pilot telling you the flying time for today's flight. Later in the flight, the flight attendant brings you a soft drink and a snack. What you see at the airport and on board the plane is different people performing different tasks. The pilot is flying the plane and the customer service person at the check-in counter is receiving your luggage, and so on. Can you find the economics? Think about it for a minute before you read on.

What you see at the airport and on board the plane is specialization. The pilot isn't flying the plane and checking your luggage too. He is only flying the plane. The flight attendant isn't serving you food and checking you through security too. He is only serving you food. Why do people specialize? Largely, it's because individuals have found that they are better off specializing than not specializing. And usually what people specialize in is that activity in which they have a comparative advantage. ▲ ▲ ▲

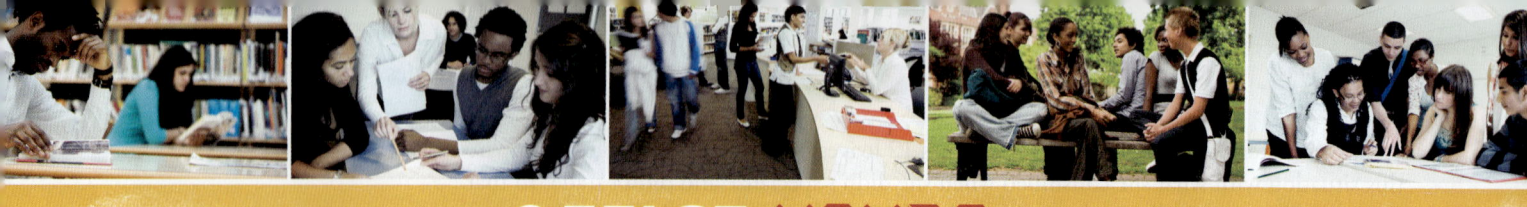

OFFICE HOURS

"What Purpose Does the PPF Serve?"

STUDENT:

Economists seem to have many uses for the production possibilities frontier (PPF). For example, they can talk about scarcity, choice, opportunity costs, and many other topics in terms of the PPF. Beyond this, what purpose does the PPF serve?

INSTRUCTOR:

One purpose is to ground us in reality. For example, the frontier (or boundary) of the PPF represents scarcity, which is a fact of life. In other words, the frontier of the PPF is essentially saying, "Here is scarcity. Work with it." One of the important effects of acknowledging this fact is that we come to understand what *is* and what *is not* possible. For example, if the economy is currently on the frontier of its PPF, producing 100 units of X and 200 units of Y, then getting more of X is possible, but not without getting less of Y. In other words, the frontier of the PPF grounds us in reality: More of one thing means less of something else.

STUDENT:

But isn't this something we already knew?

INSTRUCTOR:

We understand that more of X means less of Y once someone makes this point, but think of how often we might act as if we don't know it. John thinks he can work more hours at his job and get a good grade on his upcoming chemistry test. Well, he might be able to get a good grade (say, a 90), but this ignores how much higher the grade could have been (say, five points higher) if he hadn't worked more hours at his job. The frontier of the PPF reminds us that there are trade-offs in life. That is an important reality to be aware of. We ignore it at our own peril.

STUDENT:

I've also heard that the PPF can show us what is necessary before the so-called average person in a country can become richer? Is this true? And how much richer do we mean here?

INSTRUCTOR:

We are talking about becoming richer in terms of having more goods and services. It's possible for the average person to become richer through economic growth. In other words, the average person in society becomes richer if the PPF shifts rightward by more than the population grows. To illustrate, suppose that a 100-person economy

CHAPTER SUMMARY

AN ECONOMY'S PRODUCTION POSSIBILITIES FRONTIER

- An economy's production possibilities frontier (PPF) represents the possible combinations of two goods that the economy can produce in a certain period of time under the conditions of a given state of technology and fully employed resources.

INCREASING AND CONSTANT OPPORTUNITY COSTS

- A straight-line PPF represents constant opportunity costs: Increased production of one good comes at a constant opportunity cost.

- A bowed-outward (concave-downward) PPF represents the law of increasing opportunity costs: Increased production of one good comes at an increasing opportunity cost.

THE PRODUCTION POSSIBILITIES FRONTIER AND VARIOUS ECONOMIC CONCEPTS

- The PPF can be used to illustrate various economic concepts. Scarcity is illustrated by the frontier itself. Choice is illustrated by the fact that we have to find a point either on or below the frontier. In short, of the many attainable positions, one must be chosen. Opportunity cost is illustrated by a movement from one point to another on the PPF. Unemployed resources and productive inefficiency are illustrated by a point below the PPF. Productive efficiency and fully employed resources are is currently producing 100 units of X and 200 units of Y. The average person can then have 1 unit of X and 2 units of Y. Now suppose there is economic growth (shifting the PPF to the right), and the economy can now produce more of both goods, X and Y. It produces 200 units of X and 400 units of Y. If the population has not changed (if it is still 100 people), then the average person can now have 2 units of X and 4 units of Y. The average person is richer in terms of both goods. If we change things, and let the population grow from 100 persons to, say, 125 persons, it is still possible for the average person to have more through economic growth. With a population of 125 people, the average person now has 1.6 units of X and 3.2 units of good Y. In other words, as long as the productive capability of the economy grows by a greater percentage than the population, the average person can become richer (in terms of goods and services).

STUDENT:

Even if the economy is producing more of both goods (X and Y), the average person isn't necessarily better off in terms of goods and services, right? Can't all the extra output end up in the hands of only a few people instead of being evenly distributed across the entire population.

INSTRUCTOR:

That's correct. What we are assuming when we say that the average person can be better off is that if we took the extra output and divided it evenly across the population, then the average person would be better off in terms of having more goods and services. By the way, this is what economists mean when they say that the output (goods and services) per capita in a population has risen.

POINTS TO REMEMBER

1. The production possibilities frontier (PPF) grounds us in reality. It tells us what *is* and what *is not* possible in terms of producing various combinations of goods and services.

2. The PPF tells us that when we have efficiency (we are at a point on the frontier itself), more of one thing means less of something else. In other words, the PPF tells us life has its trade-offs.

3. If the PPF shifts rightward and the population does not change, then output per capita rises.

illustrated by a point on the PPF. Economic growth is illustrated by a shift outward in the PPF.

SPECIALIZATION, TRADE, AND THE PPF

- Individuals can make themselves better off by specializing in the production of the good in which they have a comparative advantage and then trading some of that good for other goods.

Someone who can produce the good at a lower opportunity cost than another person can has a comparative advantage in the production of the good.

- By specializing in the production of the good for which they have a comparative advantage and then trading it for other goods, people can move beyond their production possibilities frontier.

KEY TERMS AND CONCEPTS

Production Possibilities Frontier (PPF)	Law of Increasing Opportunity Costs	Productive Efficiency Productive Inefficiency	Technology Comparative Advantage

QUESTIONS AND PROBLEMS

1. Why are most production possibilities frontiers for goods bowed outward (concave downward)?

2. Can a technological advancement in sector X of the economy affect the number of people who work in sector Y of the economy? Explain your answer.

3. Give an example to illustrate each of the following: (a) constant opportunity costs and (b) increasing opportunity costs.

4. Suppose a nation's PPF shifts inward as its population grows. What happens, on average, to the material standard of living of the people? Explain your answer.

5. What condition must hold for the production possibilities frontier to be bowed outward (concave downward)? To be a straight line?

6. If the slope of the production possibilities frontier is the same between any two points, what does this imply about costs? Explain your answer.

7. Explain how the following can be represented in a PPF framework: (a) the finiteness of resources implicit in the scarcity condition, (b) choice, (c) opportunity cost, (d) productive efficiency, and (e) unemployed resources.

8. Explain how to derive a production possibilities frontier. For instance, how is the extreme point on the vertical axis identified? How is the extreme point on the horizontal axis identified?

9. Describe how each of the following would affect the U.S. production possibilities frontier: (a) an increase in the number of illegal immigrants entering the country, (b) a war that takes place on U.S. soil, (c) the discovery of a new oil field, (d) a decrease in the unemployment rate, and (e) a law that requires individuals to enter lines of work for which they are not suited.

10. Within a PPF framework, explain each of the following: (a) a disagreement between a person who favors more domestic welfare spending and one who favors more national defense spending, (b) an increase in the population, and (c) a technological change that makes resources less specialized.

11. What exactly allows individuals to consume more if they specialize and trade than if they don't?

12. Use the PPF framework to explain something in your everyday life that was not mentioned in the chapter.

WORKING WITH NUMBERS AND GRAPHS

1. Illustrate constant opportunity costs in a table similar to the one in Exhibit 1(a). Next, draw a PPF based on the data in the table.

2. Illustrate increasing opportunity costs (for one good) in a table similar to the one in Exhibit 2(a). Next, draw a PPF based on the data in the table.

3. Draw a PPF that represents the production possibilities for goods X and Y if there are constant opportunity costs. Next, represent an advance in technology that makes it possible to produce more of X, but not more of Y. Finally, represent an advance in technology that makes it possible to produce more of Y, but not more of X.

4. In the following figure, which graph depicts a technological breakthrough in the production of good X only?

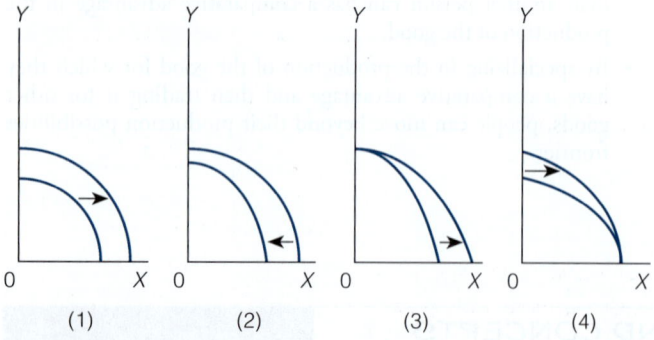

(1)   (2)   (3)   (4)

5. In the preceding figure, which graph depicts a change in the PPF that is a likely consequence of war?

6. If PPF₂ in the following graph is the relevant production possibilities frontier, then which points are unattainable? Explain your answer.

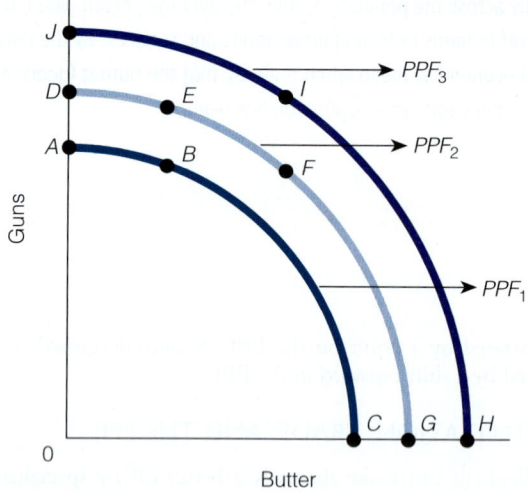

7. If PPF_1 in the preceding figure is the relevant production possibilities frontier, then which point(s) represent productive efficiency? Explain your answer.

8. Tina can produce any of the following combinations of goods X and Y: (a) 100 X and 0 Y, (b) 50 X and 25 Y, (c) 0 X and 50 Y. David can produce any of the following combinations of X and Y: (a) 50 X and 0 Y, (b) 25 X and 40 Y, and (c) 0 X and 80 Y. Who has the comparative advantage in the production of good X ? Of good Y ? Explain your answer.

9. Using the data in problem 8, prove that both Tina and David can be made better off through specialization and trade.

CHAPTER 3

SUPPLY AND DEMAND: THEORY

DON EMMERT/AFP/GETTY IMAGES

Introduction Psychologists sometimes use a technique called "word association" to learn more about their patients. The psychologist says a word, then the patient says the first word that comes into his or her head: morning, night; boy, girl; sunrise, sunset. If a psychologist ever happened to say "supply" to an economist, the response would undoubtedly be "demand." To economists, supply and demand go together. (Thomas Carlyle, the historian and philosopher, said that "it is easy to train economists. Just teach a parrot to say Supply and Demand."

Not funny, Carlyle.) Supply and demand have been called the "bread and butter" of economics. In this chapter, we discuss them, first separately and then together.

A market is any place people come together to trade. Economists often say that every market has *two* sides: a buying side and a selling side. The buying side of the market is usually referred to as the *demand* side; the selling side is usually referred to as the *supply* side. Let's begin with a discussion of *demand*.

WHAT IS DEMAND?

The word demand has a precise meaning in economics. It refers to:

1. the willingness and ability of buyers to purchase different quantities of a good
2. at different prices
3. during a specific time period (per day, week, etc.).[1]

For example, we can express part of John's demand for magazines by saying that he is willing and able to buy 10 magazines a month at $4 per magazine and that he is willing and able to buy 15 magazines a month at $3 per magazine.

Market
Any place people come together to trade.

Demand
The willingness and ability of buyers to purchase different quantities of a good at different prices during a specific time period.

---

1. Demand takes into account *services* as well as goods. A few examples of goods are shirts, books, and television sets. A few examples of services are dental care, medical care, and an economics lecture. To simplify the discussion, we refer only to goods.

Remember this important point about demand: Unless both willingness and ability to buy are present, there is no demand, and a person is not a buyer. For example, Josie may be willing to buy a computer but be unable to pay the price; Tanya may be able to buy a computer but be unwilling to do so. Neither Josie nor Tanya demands a computer, and neither is a buyer of a computer.

The Law of Demand

Law of Demand

As the price of a good rises, the quantity demanded of the good falls, and as the price of a good falls, the quantity demanded of the good rises, *ceteris paribus*.

Will people buy more units of a good at lower prices than at higher prices? For example, will people buy more shirts at $10 apiece than at $70 apiece? If your answer is yes, you instinctively understand the law of demand. The law of demand states that as the price of a good rises, the quantity demanded of the good falls and that as the price of a good falls, the quantity demanded of the good rises, *ceteris paribus*. Simply put, the law of demand states that the price of a good and the quantity demanded of it are inversely related, *ceteris paribus*:

$$P \uparrow Q_d \downarrow$$

$$P \downarrow Q_d \uparrow \text{ ceteris paribus}$$

where P = price and Q_d = quantity demanded.

Quantity demanded is the number of units of a good that individuals are willing and able to buy at a particular price during a time period. For example, suppose individuals are willing and able to buy 100 TV dinners per week at a price of $4 per dinner. Therefore, 100 units is the quantity demanded of TV dinners at $4.

A warning: We know that the words "demand" and "quantity demanded" sound alike, but keep in mind that they do not describe the same thing. Demand is different from quantity demanded. Keep that in mind as you continue to read this chapter. For now, remind yourself that demand speaks to the willingness and ability of buyers to buy different quantities of a good at different prices. Quantity demanded speaks to the willingness and ability of buyers to buy a specific quantity (say, 100 units of a good) at a specific price (say, $10 per unit).

Four Ways to Represent the Law of Demand

Here are four ways to represent the law of demand.

- *In Words.* We can represent the law of demand in words; we have done so already. Earlier we said that as the price of a good rises, quantity demanded falls, and as price falls, quantity demanded rises, *ceteris paribus*. That was the statement (in words) of the law of demand.

- *In Symbols.* We can also represent the law of demand in symbols, which we have also already done. In symbols, the law of demand is:

$$P \uparrow Q_d \downarrow$$

$$P \downarrow Q_d \uparrow \text{ ceteris paribus}$$

Demand Schedule

The numerical tabulation of the quantity demanded of a good at different prices. A demand schedule is the numerical representation of the law of demand.

Demand Curve

The graphical representation of the law of demand.

- *In a Demand Schedule.* A demand schedule is the numerical representation of the law of demand. A demand schedule for good X is illustrated in Exhibit 1(a).

- *As a Demand Curve.* In Exhibit 1(b), the four price–quantity combinations in part (a) are plotted and the points connected, giving us a (downward-sloping) demand curve. A (downward-sloping) demand curve is the graphical representation of the inverse relationship between price and quantity demanded specified by the law of demand. In short, a demand curve is a picture of the law of demand.

EXHIBIT 1

Demand Schedule and Demand Curve

Part (a) shows a demand schedule for good X. Part (b) shows a demand curve, obtained by plotting the different price-quantity combinations in part (a) and connecting the points. On a demand curve, the price (in dollars) represents price per unit of the good. The quantity demanded, on the horizontal axis, is always relevant for a specific time period (a week, a month, and so on).

Demand Schedule for Good X

Price (dollars)	Quantity Demanded	Point in Part (b)
4	10	A
3	20	B
2	30	C
1	40	D

(a)

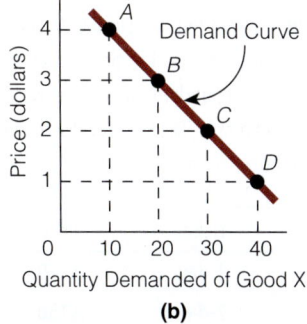

(b)

finding ECONOMICS

In a Visit Home to See Mom A friend tells you that she flies home to see her mother only once a year. You ask why. She says, "Because the price of the ticket to fly home is $1,100." She then adds, "If the price were, say, $600 instead of $1,100, I'd fly home twice a year instead of once." Can you find any economics in what she is telling you? If you listen closely to what she says, she has identified two points about her demand curve for air travel home: One point corresponds to $1,100 and buying one ticket (home), and the other point corresponds to $600 and buying two tickets home. ▲ ▲ ▲

Why Does Quantity Demanded Go Down as Price Goes Up?

The law of demand states that price and quantity demanded are inversely related. This much you know. But do you know *why* quantity demanded moves in the opposite direction of price? We identify two reasons:

The first reason is that *people substitute lower priced goods for higher priced goods*. Often, many goods serve the same purpose. Many different goods will satisfy hunger, and many different drinks will satisfy thirst. For example, both orange juice and grapefruit juice will satisfy thirst. On Monday, the price of orange juice equals the price of grapefruit juice, but on Tuesday the price of orange juice rises. As a result, people will choose to buy less of the relatively higher priced orange juice and more of the relatively lower priced grapefruit juice. In other words, a rise in the price of orange juice will lead to a decrease in the quantity demanded of it.

The second reason for the inverse relationship between price and quantity demanded has to do with the law of diminishing marginal utility, which states that for a given time period, the marginal (or additional) utility or satisfaction gained by consuming equal successive units of a good will decline as the amount consumed increases. For example, you may receive more utility, or satisfaction, from eating your first hamburger at lunch than from eating your second and, if you continue, more utility from your second hamburger than from your third.

What does this have to do with the law of demand? Economists state that the more utility you receive from a unit of a good, the higher the price you are willing to pay for it; the less utility you receive from a unit of a good, the lower the price you are willing to pay for it. According to the law of diminishing marginal utility, individuals obtain less utility from additional units of a good. Therefore, they will buy larger quantities of a good only at lower prices, and this is the law of demand.

Law of Diminishing Marginal Utility

For a given time period, the marginal (or additional) utility or satisfaction gained by consuming equal successive units of a good will decline as the amount consumed increases.

Disney World Ticket Prices

The Walt Disney Company operates two major theme parks in the United States: Disneyland in California and Disney World in Florida. Every year, millions of people visit each site. The ticket price for visiting Disneyland or Disney World differs depending on how many days a person visits the theme park. For example, Disney World sells one- to ten-day tickets. Here are the ticket prices for each of 5 days:

Ticket	Price
1-day	$ 79
2-day	$156
3-day	$219
4-day	$225
5-day	$228

Now if we take the price of a one-day ticket and multiply it by 2, we get $158, but oddly enough, the price of a two-day ticket is not $158 but $156. Of course, if we take the price of a one-day ticket and multiply it by 5, we get $395, but Disney World doesn't charge $395 for a five-day ticket;, it charges $228, which is $167 less than $395.

Disney World is effectively telling visitors that if they want to visit the theme park for one day, they have to pay $79. But if they want to visit the theme park for additional days, they don't have to pay $79 for each additional day. They pay less for additional days. But why? Why does Disney World charge less than double the price of a one-day ticket for a two-day ticket, and why does it charge less than 5 times the price of a one-day ticket for a five-day ticket?

An economic concept, the law of diminishing marginal utility, is the reason. The law of diminishing marginal utility states that as a person consumes additional units of a good, eventually the utility from each additional unit of the good decreases. Assuming that the law of

GINO SANTA MARIA / DREAMSTIME.COM

diminishing marginal utility holds for Disney World, individuals will get more utility from the first day at Disney World than from, say, the second, third, or fifth day. The less utility or satisfaction people get from something, the lower the dollar amount they are willing to pay for it. Thus, people would not be willing to pay as much for the second day at Disney World as for the first, and they would not be willing to pay as much for the fifth as for the fourth and so on. Disney World knows this and therefore prices its ticket prices differently depending on how many days one wants to visit Disney World.

Individual Demand Curve and Market Demand Curve

There is a difference between an individual demand curve and a market demand curve.

An individual demand curve represents the price–quantity combinations of a particular good for a *single buyer*. For example, an individual demand curve could show Jones's demand for CDs. A market demand curve represents the price–quantity combinations of a good for *all buyers*. In this case, the demand curve would show all buyers' demand for CDs.

A market demand curve is derived by "adding up" individual demand curves, as shown in Exhibit 2. The demand schedules for Jones, Smith, and other buyers are shown in part (a). The market demand schedule is obtained by adding the quantities demanded at each price.

For example, at $12, the quantities demanded are 4 units for Jones, 5 units for Smith, and 100 units for other buyers. Thus, a total of 109 units are demanded at $12. In part (b), the data points for the demand schedules are plotted and added to produce a market demand curve. The market demand curve could also be drawn directly from the market demand schedule.

A Change in Quantity Demanded Versus a Change in Demand

Economists often talk about (1) a change in quantity demanded and (2) a change in demand. As stated earlier, although the phrase "quantity demanded" may sound like "demand," the two are not the same. In short, a change in quantity demanded *is not* the same as a change in demand. (Read the last sentence at least two more times.) We use Exhibit 1 to illustrate the difference between a change in quantity demanded and a change in demand.

A CHANGE IN QUANTITY DEMANDED Look at the horizontal axis in Exhibit 1, which is labeled "Quantity Demanded of Good X." Notice that quantity demanded is a *number*—such as 10, 20, 30, 40, and so on. More specifically, it is the number of units of a good that individuals are willing and able to buy at a particular price during some time period. In Exhibit 1, if the price is $4, then quantity demanded is 10 units of good X; if the price is $3, then quantity demanded is 20 units of good X.

> Quantity demanded = The *number* of units of a good that individuals are willing and able to buy at a particular price

EXHIBIT 2

	Quantity Demanded			
Price	Jones	Smith	Other Buyers	All Buyers
$15	1	2	20	23
14	2	3	45	50
13	3	4	70	77
12	4 +	5 +	100 =	109
11	5 +	6 +	130 =	141
10	6	7	160	173

(a)

Deriving a Market Demand Schedule and a Market Demand Curve

Part (a) shows four demand schedules combined into one table. The market demand schedule is derived by adding the quantities demanded at each price. In (b), the data points from the demand schedule are plotted to show how a market demand curve is derived. Only two points on the market demand curve are noted.

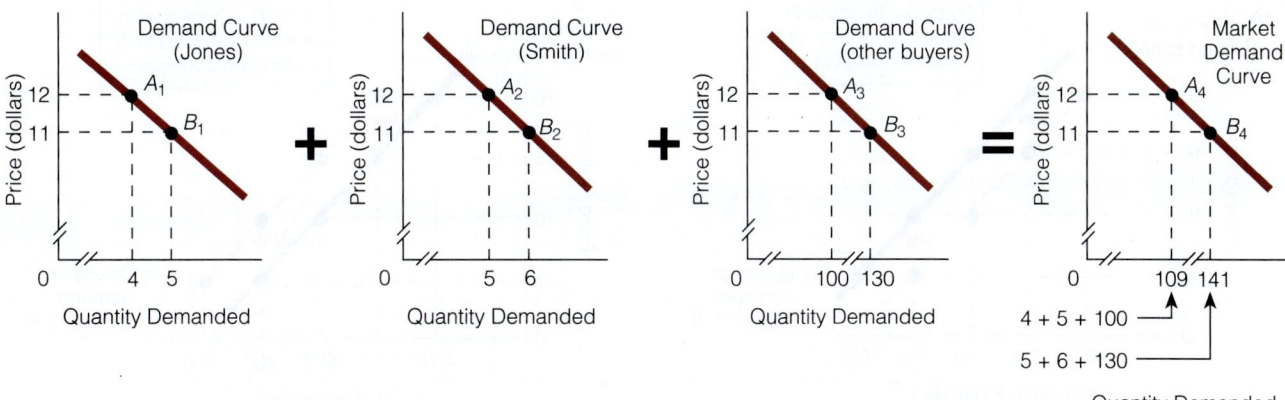

(b)

Own Price

The price of a good. For example, if the price of oranges is $1, this is its own price.

Now, again looking at Exhibit 1, what can change quantity demanded from 10 (which it is at point *A*) to 20 (which it is at point *B*)? Or what has to change before quantity demanded will change? The answer is on the vertical axis of Exhibit 1. The only thing that can change the quantity demanded of a good is its price, which is called **own price.**

> Change in quantity demanded = A *movement* from one point to another point on the same demand curve *caused* by a change in the price of the good

A CHANGE IN DEMAND Look again at Exhibit 1, this time focusing on the demand curve. Demand is represented by the *entire* curve. When talking about a change in demand, an economist is actually talking about a change—or shift—in the entire demand curve.

> Change in demand = Shift in demand curve

Demand can change in two ways: Demand can increase, and demand can decrease. Let's look first at an *increase* in demand. Suppose we have the following demand schedule:

Demand Schedule A

Price	Quantity Demanded
$20	500
$15	600
$10	700
$ 5	800

The demand curve for this demand schedule will look like the demand curve labeled D_A in Exhibit 3(a).

EXHIBIT 3

Shifts in the Demand Curve

In part (a), the demand curve shifts rightward from D_A to D_B. This shift represents an increase in demand. At each price, the quantity demanded is greater than it was before. For example, the quantity demanded at $20 increases from 500 units to 600 units. In part (b), the demand curve shifts leftward from D_A to D_C. This shift represents a decrease in demand. At each price, the quantity demanded is less. For example, the quantity demand at $20 decreases from 500 units to 400 units.

(a)   (b)

What does an increase in demand mean? It means that individuals are willing and able to buy more units of the good at each and every price. In other words, demand schedule *A* will change as follows:

Demand Schedule B (increase in demand)

Price	Quantity Demanded
$20	~~500~~ 600
$15	~~600~~ 700
$10	~~700~~ 800
$ 5	~~800~~ 900

Whereas individuals were willing and able to buy 500 units of the good at $20, now they are willing and able to buy 600 units of the good at $20; whereas individuals were willing and able to buy 600 units of the good at $15, now they are willing and able to buy 700 units of the good at $15; and so on.

As shown in Exhibit 3(a), the demand curve that represents demand schedule *B* (D_B) lies to the right of the demand curve that represents demand schedule *A* (D_A) . We conclude that *an increase in demand is represented by a rightward shift in the demand curve and means that individuals are willing and able to buy more of a good at each and every price.*

Increase in demand = Rightward shift in the demand curve

Now let's look at a decrease in demand. A decrease in demand means that individuals are willing and able to buy less of a good at each and every price. In this case, demand schedule *A* will change as follows:

Demand Schedule C (decrease in demand)

Price	Quantity Demanded
$20	~~500~~ 400
$15	~~600~~ 500
$10	~~700~~ 600
$ 5	~~800~~ 700

As shown in Exhibit 3(b), the demand curve that represents demand schedule *C* (D_C) obviously lies to the left of the demand curve that represents demand schedule *A* (D_A). We conclude that a *decrease in demand is represented by a leftward shift in the demand curve and means that individuals are willing and able to buy less of a good at each and every price.*

Decrease in demand = Leftward shift in the demand curve

What Factors Cause the Demand Curve to Shift?

We know what an increase and decrease in demand mean: An increase in demand means consumers are willing and able to buy *more* of a good at every price. A decrease in demand means consumers are willing and able to buy *less* of a good at every price. We also know that an increase in demand is graphically portrayed as a rightward shift in a demand curve and that a decrease in demand is graphically portrayed as a leftward shift in a demand curve.

iPods and the Law of Demand

The law of demand holds that the price of a good and the quantity demanded of the good are inversely related. But does the law of demand hold for an individual when it comes to a good like an iPod? Will the individual buy more iPods at $10 than at $200? Perhaps she will, if only to give some iPods to friends.

But suppose we assume that the person doesn't want to give away any iPods as gifts. She wants only an iPod for herself. How many more than one iPod does she need? Probably none, since there is little use in buying two iPods if one iPod holds all the songs she wants. In other words, instead of having a downward-sloping demand curve for iPods, an individual's demand curve might look like the one in Exhibit 4(a). This curve says that the individual will buy one iPod no matter what the price is between zero and $300. But if the price is above $300, she will not buy an iPod because the demand curve doesn't extend that high.

Suppose no person has a downward-sloping demand curve. Is it still possible for the *market demand curve* to be downward sloping? The answer is yes.

AP PHOTO/PAUL SAKUMA

To understand why, suppose another person's demand curve for an iPod is shown in Exhibit 4(b). This demand curve says she is willing and able to buy one iPod if the price is anywhere between zero and $200, but she won't buy an iPod if the price is higher than $200.

If we horizontally sum the two demand curves in parts (a) and (b) to get the market demand curve, we see that at a price of $300, one iPod will be purchased and at $200, two iPods will be purchased. See Exhibit 4(c). Notice that this gives us a downward-sloping demand curve: More iPods are bought at a lower price than at a higher price.

EXHIBIT 4

(a)   (b)   (c)

But what factors or variables can increase or decrease demand? What factors or variables can shift demand curves? They are (1) income, (2) preferences, (3) prices of related goods, (4) the number of buyers, and (5) expectations of future prices.

INCOME As a person's income changes (increases or decreases), that individual's demand for a particular good may rise, fall, or remain constant.

For example, suppose Jack's income rises. As a consequence, his demand for CDs rises. For Jack, CDs are a normal good. For a normal good, demand rises as income rises, and demand falls as income falls.

Normal Good
A good for which demand rises (falls) as income rises (falls).

X is a normal good: If income ↑ then D_x ↑

If income↓ then D_x ↓

Now suppose Marie's income rises. As a consequence, her demand for canned baked beans falls. For Marie, canned baked beans are an inferior good. For an inferior good, demand falls as income rises, and demand rises as income falls.

$$Y \text{ is an inferior good: If income} \uparrow \text{ then } D_Y \downarrow$$

$$\text{If income} \downarrow \text{ then } D_Y \uparrow$$

Finally, suppose when George's income rises, his demand for toothpaste neither rises nor falls. For George, toothpaste is neither a normal good nor an inferior good. Instead, it is a neutral good. For a neutral good, demand does not change as income rises or falls.

PREFERENCES People's preferences affect the amount of a good they are willing to buy at a particular price. A change in preferences in favor of a good shifts the demand curve rightward. A change in preferences away from the good shifts the demand curve leftward. For example, if people begin to favor Elmore Leonard novels to a greater degree than previously, the demand for his novels increases, and the demand curve shifts rightward.

PRICES OF RELATED GOODS There are two types of related goods: substitutes and complements. Two goods are substitutes if they satisfy similar needs or desires. For many people, Coca-Cola and Pepsi-Cola are substitutes. If two goods are substitutes, as the price of one rises (falls), the demand for the other rises (falls). For instance, higher Coca-Cola prices will increase the demand for Pepsi-Cola as people substitute Pepsi for the higher priced Coke [Exhibit 5(a)]. Other examples of substitutes are coffee and tea, corn chips and potato chips, two brands of margarine, and foreign and domestic cars.

$$X \text{ and } Y \text{ are substitutes: If } P_X \uparrow \text{ then } D_Y \uparrow$$

$$\text{If } P_X \downarrow \text{ then } D_Y \downarrow$$

Two goods are complements if they are consumed jointly. For example, tennis rackets and tennis balls are used together to play tennis. If two goods are complements, as the price of one rises (falls), the demand for the other falls (rises). For example, higher tennis racket prices will decrease the demand for tennis balls, as Exhibit 5(b) shows. Other examples of complements are cars and tires, lightbulbs and lamps, and golf clubs and golf balls.

NUMBER OF BUYERS The demand for a good in a particular market area is related to the number of buyers in the area: more buyers, higher demand; fewer buyers, lower demand. The number of buyers may increase owing to a heightened birthrate, increased immigration, the migration of people from one region of the country to another, and so on. The number of buyers may decrease owing to an increased death rate, war, the migration of people from one region of the country to another, and so on.

EXPECTATIONS OF FUTURE PRICE Buyers who expect the price of a good to be higher next month may buy it now, thus increasing the current (or present) demand for the good. Buyers who expect the price of a good to be lower next month may wait until next month to buy it, thus decreasing the current (or present) demand for the good.

For example, suppose you are planning to buy a house. One day, you hear that house prices are expected to go down in a few months. Consequently, you decide to delay your purchase for a while. Alternatively, if you hear that prices are expected to rise in a few months, you might go ahead and make your purchase now.

Inferior Good
A good for which demand falls (rises) as income rises (falls).

Neutral Good
A good for which demand does not change as income rises or falls.

Substitutes
Two goods that satisfy similar needs or desires. If two goods are substitutes, the demand for one rises as the price of the other rises (or the demand for one falls as the price of the other falls).

Complements
Two goods that are used jointly in consumption. If two goods are complements, the demand for one rises as the price of the other falls (or the demand for one falls as the price of the other rises).

EXHIBIT 5

Substitutes and Complements

(a) Coca-Cola and Pepsi-Cola are substitutes: The price of one and the demand for the other are directly related. As the price of Coca-Cola rises, the demand for Pepsi-Cola increases. (b) Tennis rackets and tennis balls are complements: The price of one and the demand for the other are inversely related. As the price of tennis rackets rises, the demand for tennis balls decreases.

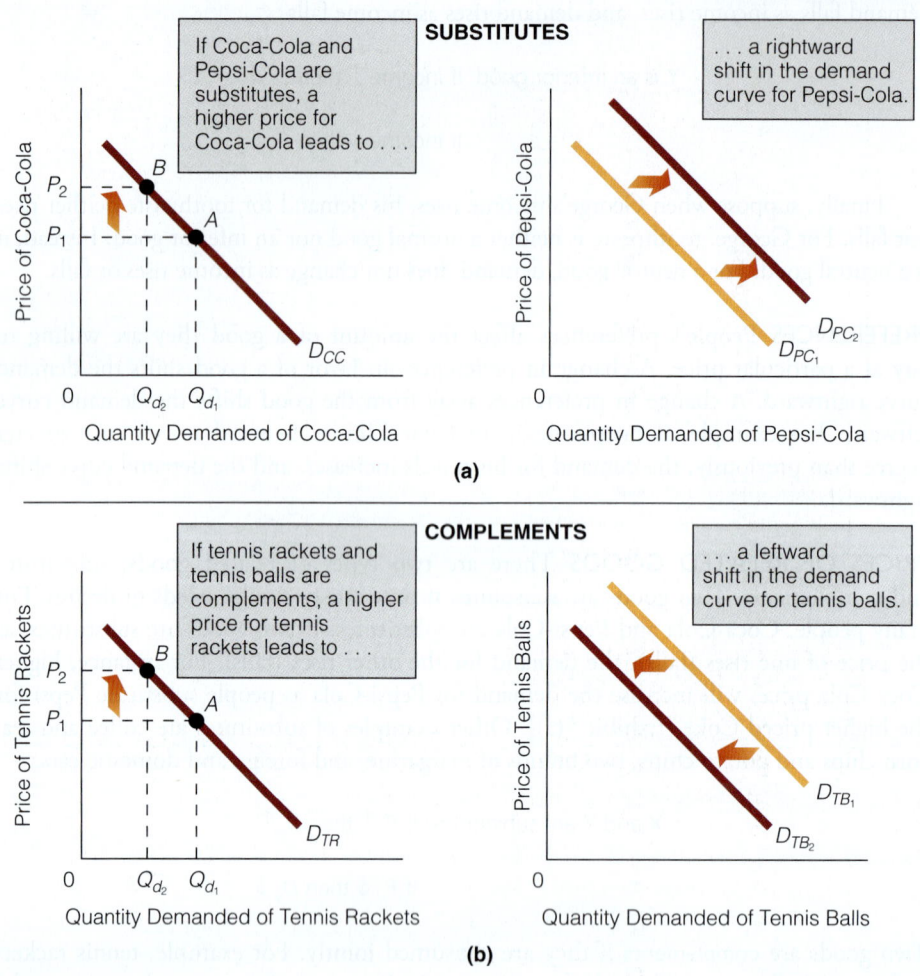

Movement Factors and Shift Factors

Economists often distinguish between (1) factors that can bring about movement along curves and (2) factors that can shift curves.

The factors that cause movement along curves are sometimes called *movement* factors. In many economic diagrams, such as the demand curve in Exhibit 1, the movement factor (price) is on the vertical axis.

The factors that actually shift the curves are sometimes called *shift* factors. The shift factors for the demand curve are income, preferences, the price of related goods, and so on. Often, shift factors do not appear in the economic diagrams. For example, although in Exhibit 1 the movement factor—price—is on the vertical axis, the shift factors do not appear anywhere in the diagram. We just know what they are and that they can shift the demand curve.

When you see a curve in this book, first ask which factor will move us along the curve. In other words, what is the movement factor? Second, ask which factors will shift the curve. In other words, what are the shift factors? Exhibit 6 summarizes the shift factors that can change demand and the movement factors that can change quantity demanded.

EXHIBIT 6

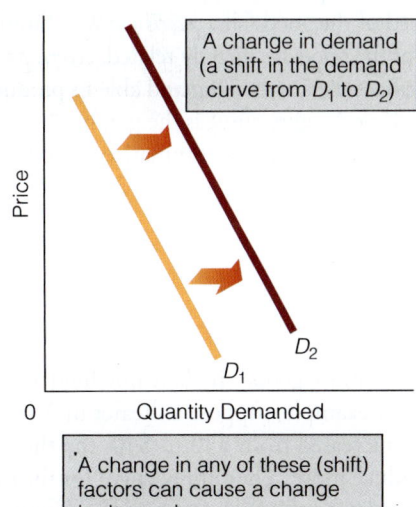

A change in demand (a shift in the demand curve from D_1 to D_2)

A change in any of these (shift) factors can cause a change in demand:

1. Income
2. Preferences
3. Prices of related goods
4. Number of buyers
5. Expectations of future price

(a)

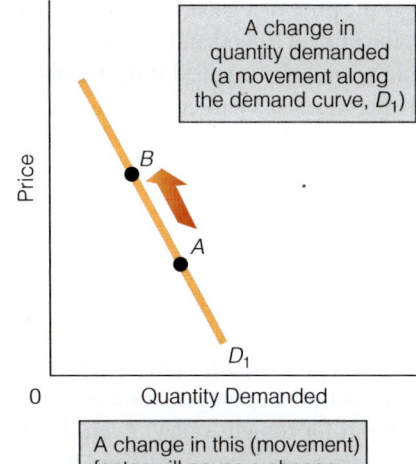

A change in quantity demanded (a movement along the demand curve, D_1)

A change in this (movement) factor will cause a change in quantity demanded:

1. (A good's) own price

(b)

A Change in Demand Versus a Change in Quantity Demanded

(a) A change in demand refers to a shift in the demand curve. A change in demand can be brought about by a number of factors (see the exhibit and text). (b) A change in quantity demanded refers to a movement along a given demand curve. A change in quantity demanded is brought about only by a change in (a good's) own price.

finding ECONOMICS

Soft Drinks Go on Sale Karen buys more soft drinks when they go on sale. Two people interpret this action differently. John says that if Karen buys more soft drinks when they go on sale, Karen's demand curve has shifted to the right. Laura says that if Karen buys more soft drinks when they go on sale, Karen is simply moving down on her individual demand curve. "Karen's quantity demanded of soft drinks," says Laura, "has increased." Who is right? Laura is. Saying that soft drinks went on sale is no more than saying that the price of soft drinks declined. As price declines, quantity demanded (not demand) increases. ▲ ▲ ▲

SELF-TEST

(Answers to Self-Test questions are in Answers to Self-Test Questions at the back of the book.)

1. As Sandi's income rises, her demand for popcorn rises. As Mark's income falls, his demand for prepaid telephone cards rises. What kinds of goods are popcorn and telephone cards for Sandi and Mark?

2. Why are demand curves downward sloping?

3. Give an example that illustrates how to derive a market demand curve.

4. What factors can change demand? What factors can change quantity demanded?

SUPPLY

Just as the word "demand" has a specific meaning in economics, so does the word "supply." Supply refers to

1. the willingness and ability of sellers to produce and offer to sell different quantities of a good

2. at different prices

3. during a specific time period (per day, week, etc.).

Supply
The willingness and ability of sellers to produce and offer to sell different quantities of a good at different prices during a specific time period.

The Law of Supply

Law of Supply
As the price of a good rises, the quantity supplied of the good rises, and as the price of a good falls, the quantity supplied of the good falls, *ceteris paribus.*

The law of supply states that as the price of a good rises, the quantity supplied of the good rises, and as the price of a good falls, the quantity supplied of the good falls, *ceteris paribus.* Simply put, the price of a good and the quantity supplied of the good are directly related, *ceteris paribus.* (The quantity supplied is the number of units that sellers are willing and able to produce and offer to sell at a particular price.) The (upward-sloping) supply curve is the graphical representation of the law of supply (see Exhibit 7). The law of supply can be summarized as follows:

$$P\uparrow \; Q_s\uparrow$$

$$P\downarrow \; Q_s\downarrow \; ceteris \; paribus$$

(Upward-Sloping) Supply Curve
The graphical representation of the law of supply.

where P = price and Q_s = quantity supplied.

The law of supply holds for the production of most goods. It does not hold when there is no time to produce more units of a good. For example, suppose a theater in Atlanta is sold out for tonight's play. Even if ticket prices increased from $30 to $40, the theater would have no additional seats and no time to produce more. The supply curve for theater seats is illustrated in Exhibit 8(a). It is fixed at the number of seats in the theater, 500.[2]

The law of supply also does not hold for goods that cannot be produced over any period of time. For example, the violin maker Antonio Stradivari died in 1737. A rise in the price of Stradivarius violins does not affect the number of Stradivarius violins supplied, as Exhibit 8(b) illustrates.

Why Most Supply Curves Are Upward Sloping

Most supply curves are upward sloping. The fundamental reason for this involves the *law of diminishing marginal returns*, discussed in a later chapter. Here, suffice it to say that an upward-sloping supply curve reflects the fact that, under certain conditions, a higher

EXHIBIT 7

A Supply Curve

The upward sloping supply curve is the graphical representation of the law of supply, which states that price and quantity supplied are directly related, *ceteris paribus.* On a supply curve, the price (in dollars) represents price per unit of the good. The quantity supplied, on the horizontal axis, is always relevant for a specific time period (a week, a month, and so on).

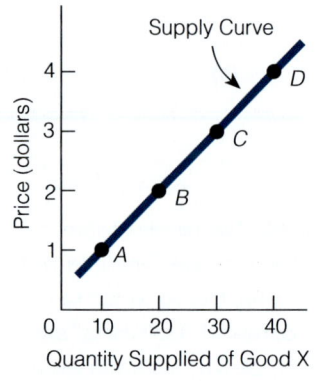

EXHIBIT 8

Supply Curves When There Is No Time to Produce More or No More Can Be Produced

The supply curve is not upward sloping when there is no time to produce additional units or when additional units cannot be produced. In those cases, the supply curve is vertical.

2 The vertical supply curve is said to be *perfectly inelastic.*

price is an incentive to producers to produce more of the good. The incentive comes in the form of higher profits. For example, suppose the price of good X rises, and nothing else changes (such as the per-unit costs of producing good X). In that case, the producers of good X will earn higher profits per unit and are thus encouraged to increase the quantity of good X that they supply to the market.

Generally, though, producing more of a good does not come with constant per-unit costs. As we learned in Chapter 2, the law of increasing costs is usually at work. In other words, the increased production of a good comes at increased opportunity costs. An upward-sloping supply curve simply reflects the fact that costs rise when more units of a good are produced.

THE MARKET SUPPLY CURVE An individual supply curve represents the price-quantity combinations for a single seller. The market supply curve represents the price–quantity combinations for all sellers of a particular good. Exhibit 9 shows how a market supply curve can be derived by "adding" individual supply curves. In part (a), a supply schedule, the numerical tabulation of the quantity supplied of a good at different prices, is given for Brown, Alberts, and other suppliers. The market supply schedule is obtained by adding the quantities supplied at each price, *ceteris paribus*. For example, at $11, the quantities supplied are 2 units for Brown, 3 units for Alberts, and 98 units for other suppliers. Thus, a total of 103 units are supplied at $11. In part (b), the data points for the supply schedules are plotted and added to produce a market supply curve (which could also be drawn directly from the market supply schedule).

Supply Schedule
The numerical tabulation of the quantity supplied of a good at different prices. A supply schedule is the numerical representation of the law of supply.

EXHIBIT 9

Deriving a Market Supply Schedule and a Market Supply Curve

Part (a) shows four supply schedules combined into one table. The market supply schedule is derived by adding the quantities supplied at each price. In (b), the data points from the supply schedules are plotted to show how a market supply curve is derived. Only two points on the market supply curve are noted.

| Price | | Quantity Supplied | | | |
	Brown		Alberts		Other Suppliers		All Suppliers
$10	1		2		96		99
11	2	+	3	+	98	=	103
12	3	+	4	+	102	=	109
13	4		5		106		115
14	5		6		108		119
15	6		7		110		123

(a)

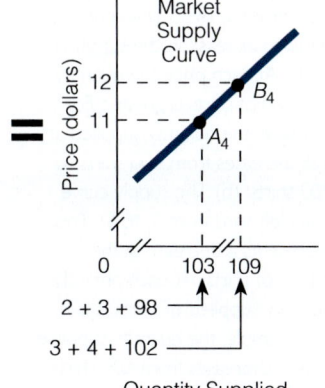

(b)

Changes in Supply Mean Shifts in Supply Curves

Just as demand can change, so can supply. The supply of a good can rise or fall. An increase in the supply of a good means that suppliers are willing and able to produce and offer to sell more of the good at all prices. For example, suppose that in January sellers are willing and able to produce and offer for sale 600 shirts at $25 each and that in February they are willing and able to produce and sell 900 shirts at $25 each. An increase in supply shifts the entire supply curve to the right, as shown in Exhibit 10(a).

The supply of a good decreases if sellers are willing and able to produce and offer to sell less of the good at all prices. For example, suppose that in January sellers are willing and able to produce and offer for sale 600 shirts at $25 each and that in February they are willing and able to produce and sell only 300 shirts at $25 each. A decrease in supply shifts the entire supply curve to the left, as shown in Exhibit 10(b).

What Factors Cause the Supply Curve to Shift?

We know the supply of any good can change, but what causes supply to change? What causes supply curves to shift? The factors that can change supply include (1) the prices of relevant resources, (2) technology, (3) the prices of other goods, (4) the number of sellers, (5) expectations of future price, (6) taxes and subsidies, and (7) government restrictions.

PRICES OF RELEVANT RESOURCES Resources are needed to produce goods. For example, wood is needed to produce doors. If the price of wood falls, producing doors becomes less costly. How will door producers respond? Will they produce more doors, the same number, or fewer? With lower costs and prices unchanged, the profit from producing and selling doors has increased; as a result, the (monetary) incentive to produce doors is increased. Door producers will produce and offer to sell more doors at each and every price. Thus, the supply of doors will increase, and the supply curve of doors will shift rightward. If the price of wood rises, producing doors becomes more costly. Consequently, the supply of doors will decrease, and the supply curve of doors will shift leftward.

TECHNOLOGY In Chapter 2, technology was defined as the body of skills and knowledge concerning the use of resources in production. Also, an advance in technology was said to refer to the ability to produce more output with a fixed amount of resources,

EXHIBIT 10

Shifts in the Supply Curve

(a) The supply curve shifts rightward from S₁ to S₂. This represents an increase in the supply of shirts: At each price the quantity supplied of shirts is greater. For example, the quantity supplied at $25 increases from 600 shirts to 900 shirts. (b) The supply curve shifts leftward from S₁ to S₂. This represents a decrease in the supply of shirts: At each price the quantity supplied of shirts is less. For example, the quantity supplied at $25 decreases from 600 shirts to 300 shirts.

reducing per-unit production costs. To illustrate, suppose it takes $100 to produce 40 units of a good. The per-unit cost is therefore $2.50. If an advance in technology makes it possible to produce 50 units at a cost of $100, then the per-unit cost falls to $2.00.

If the per-unit production costs of a good decline, we expect the quantity supplied of the good at each price to increase. Why? Lower per-unit costs increase profitability and therefore provide producers with an incentive to produce more. For example, if corn growers develop a way to grow more corn using the same amount of water and other resources, then per-unit production costs will fall, profitability will increase, and growers will want to grow and sell more corn at each price. The supply curve of corn will shift rightward.

PRICES OF OTHER GOODS Think of a farmer who is producing wheat. Suddenly, the price of something he is not producing (say, corn) rises relative to wheat. The farmer might shift his farming away from wheat to corn. In other words, as the price of corn rises relative to wheat, the farmer switches from wheat to corn production. We conclude that a change in the price of one good can lead to a change in the supply of another good.

NUMBER OF SELLERS If more sellers begin producing a good, perhaps because of high profits, the supply curve will shift rightward. If some sellers stop producing a good, perhaps because of losses, the supply curve will shift leftward.

EXPECTATIONS OF FUTURE PRICE If the price of a good is expected to be higher in the future, producers may hold back some of the product today (if possible—perishables cannot be held back). Then they will have more to sell at the higher future price. Therefore, the *current* supply curve will shift leftward. For example, if oil producers expect the price of oil to be higher next year, some may hold oil off the market this year to be able to sell it next year. Similarly, if they expect the price of oil to be lower next year, they might pump more oil this year than previously planned.

TAXES AND SUBSIDIES Some taxes increase per-unit costs. Suppose a shoe manufacturer must pay a $2 tax per pair of shoes produced. This tax leads to a leftward shift in the supply curve, indicating that the manufacturer wants to produce and offer to sell fewer pairs of shoes at each price. If the tax is eliminated, the supply curve shifts rightward.

Subsidies have the opposite effect. Suppose the government subsidizes the production of corn by paying corn farmers $2 for every bushel of corn they produce. Because of the subsidy, the quantity supplied of corn is greater at each price, and the supply curve of corn shifts rightward. The removal of the subsidy shifts the supply curve of corn leftward. A rough rule of thumb is that we get more of what we subsidize and less of what we tax.

Subsidy
A monetary payment by government to a producer of a good or service.

GOVERNMENT RESTRICTIONS Sometimes government acts to reduce supply. Consider a U.S. import quota on Japanese television sets. An import quota, or a quantitative restriction on foreign goods, reduces the supply of Japanese television sets in the United States. It shifts the supply curve leftward. The elimination of the import quota allows the supply of Japanese television sets in the United States to shift rightward.

Licensure has a similar effect. With licensure, individuals must meet certain requirements before they can legally carry out a task. For example, owner-operators of day-care centers must meet certain requirements before they are allowed to sell their services. No doubt this requirement reduces the number of day-care centers and shifts the supply curve of day-care centers leftward.

A Change in Supply Versus a Change in Quantity Supplied

A change in *supply* is not the same as a change in *quantity supplied*. A change in supply refers to a shift in the supply curve, as illustrated in Exhibit 11(a). For example, saying that

EXHIBIT 11

A Change in Supply Versus a Change in Quantity Supplied

(a) A change in supply refers to a shift in the supply curve. A change in supply can be brought about by a number of factors (see the exhibit and text). (b) A change in quantity supplied refers to a movement along a given supply curve. A change in quantity supplied is brought about only by a change in (a good's) own price.

A change in supply (a shift in the supply curve from S_1 to S_2)

A change in quantity supplied (a movement along the supply curve, S_1)

A change in any of these (shift) factors can cause a change in supply:

1. Prices of relevant resources
2. Technology
3. Prices of other goods
4. Number of sellers
5. Expectations of future price
6. Taxes and subsidies
7. Government restrictions

(a)

A change in this (movement) factor will cause a change in quantity supplied:

1. (A good's) own price

(b)

the supply of oranges has increased is the same as saying that the supply curve for oranges has shifted rightward. The factors that can change supply (i.e., shift the supply curve) are prices of relevant resources, technology, prices of other goods, the number of sellers, expectations of future prices, taxes and subsidies, and government restrictions.

A change in quantity supplied refers to a movement along a supply curve, as in Exhibit 11(b). The only factor that can directly cause a change in the quantity supplied of a good is a change in the price of the good, or own price.

SELF-TEST

1. What would the supply curve for houses (in a given city) look like for a time period of (a) the next ten hours and (b) the next three months?

2. What happens to the supply curve if each of the following occurs?

   a. The number of sellers decreases.

   b. A per-unit tax is placed on the production of a good.

   c. The price of a relevant resource falls.

3. "If the price of apples rises, the supply of apples will rise." True or false? Explain your answer.

THE MARKET: PUTTING SUPPLY AND DEMAND TOGETHER

In this section, we put supply and demand together and discuss the market. The purpose of the discussion is to gain some understanding about how prices are determined.

Supply and Demand at Work at an Auction

In Exhibit 12, the supply curve of corn is vertical. It intersects the horizontal axis at 40,000 bushels; that is, the quantity supplied is 40,000 bushels. The demand curve for corn is downward sloping.

Now suppose you are at a computerized auction where bushels of corn are bought and sold. At this auction, the auctioneer will adjust the corn price to sell all the corn offered for sale. Each potential buyer of corn is sitting in front of a computer and can immediately input the number of bushels he or she wants to buy. For example, if Nancy wants to buy 5,000 bushels of corn, she simply keys "5,000" into her computer. The total number of bushels that all potential buyers are willing and able to buy appears on the auctioneer's computer screen.

The auction begins. Follow along in Exhibit 12 as it develops. The auctioneer announces the price on the computer screens:

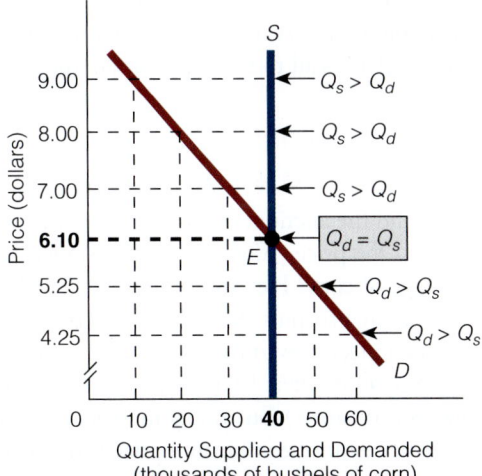

EXHIBIT 12

Supply and Demand at Work at an Auction

Q_d = quantity demanded; Q_s = quantity supplied. The auctioneer calls out different prices, and buyers record how much they are willing and able to buy. At prices of $9.00, $8.00, and $7.00, quantity supplied is greater than quantity demanded. At prices of $4.25 and $5.25, quantity demanded is greater than quantity supplied. At a price of $6.10, quantity demanded equals quantity supplied.

- *$9.00!* The potential buyers think for a second and then register the numbers of bushels they are willing and able to buy at that price. On the auctioneer's screen, the total is 10,000 bushels, which is the quantity demanded of corn at $9.00. The auctioneer, realizing that 30,000 bushels of corn (40,000 − 10,000 = 30,000) will go unsold at this price, decides to lower the price per bushel.

- *$8.00!* The quantity demanded increases to 20,000 bushels, but still the quantity supplied of corn at this price is greater than the quantity demanded. The auctioneer tries again.

- *$7.00!* The quantity demanded increases to 30,000 bushels, but the quantity supplied at $7.00 is still greater than the quantity demanded. The auctioneer drops the price further.

- $4.25! At this price, the quantity demanded jumps to 60,000 bushels, but that is 20,000 bushels more than the quantity supplied. The auctioneer calls out a higher price.

- *$5.25!* The quantity demanded drops to 50,000 bushels, but buyers still want to buy more corn at this price than there is corn to be sold. The auctioneer calls out one more time.

- *$6.10!* At this price, the quantity demanded of corn is 40,000 bushels and the quantity supplied of corn is 40,000 bushels. The auction stops. Sold! The 40,000 bushels of corn are bought and sold at $6.10 per bushel.

The Language of Supply and Demand: A Few Important Terms

If the quantity supplied is greater than the quantity demanded, a surplus, or excess supply, exists. If the quantity demanded is greater than the quantity supplied, a shortage, or excess demand, exists. In Exhibit 12, a surplus exists at $9.00, $8.00, and $7.00. A shortage exists at $4.25 and $5.25. The price at which the quantity demanded equals the quantity supplied is the equilibrium price, or market-clearing price. In our example, $6.10 is the equilibrium price. The quantity that corresponds to the equilibrium price is the equilibrium quantity.

Surplus (Excess Supply)
A condition in which the quantity supplied is greater than the quantity demanded. Surpluses occur only at prices above equilibrium price.

Shortage (Excess Demand)
A condition in which the quantity demanded is greater than the quantity supplied. Shortages occur only at prices below equilibrium price.

Equilibrium Price (Market-Clearing Price)
The price at which the quantity demanded of the good equals the quantity supplied.

Equilibrium Quantity
The quantity that corresponds to equilibrium price. The quantity at which the amount of the good that buyers are willing and able to buy equals the amount that sellers are willing and able to sell, and both equal the amount actually bought and sold.

Disequilibrium Price

A price other than equilibrium price. A price at which the quantity demanded does not equal the quantity supplied.

Disequilibrium

A state of either surplus or shortage in a market.

Equilibrium

Equilibrium means "at rest." Equilibrium in a market is the price–quantity combination from which buyers or sellers do not tend to move away. Graphically, equilibrium is the intersection point of the supply and demand curves.

In our example, it is 40,000 bushels of corn. Any price at which quantity demanded is not equal to quantity supplied is a disequilibrium price.

A market that exhibits either a surplus ($Q_s > Q_d$) or a shortage ($Q_d > Q_s$) is said to be in disequilibrium. A market in which the quantity demanded equals the quantity supplied ($Q_d = Q_s$) is said to be in equilibrium (point E in Exhibit 12).

Moving to Equilibrium: What Happens to Price When There Is a Surplus or a Shortage?

What did the auctioneer do when the price was $9.00 and there was a surplus of corn? He lowered the price. What did the auctioneer do when the price was $5.25 and there was a shortage of corn? He raised the price. The behavior of the auctioneer can be summarized this way: If a surplus exists, lower the price; if a shortage exists, raise the price. This is how the auctioneer moved the corn market into equilibrium.

Not all markets have auctioneers. (When was the last time you saw an auctioneer in the grocery store?) But many markets act *as if* an auctioneer were calling out higher and lower prices until equilibrium price is reached. In many real-world auctioneer less markets, prices fall when there is a surplus and rise when there is a shortage. Why?

WHY DOES PRICE FALL WHEN THERE IS A SURPLUS? In Exhibit 13, there is a surplus at a price of $15: The quantity supplied (150 units) is greater than the quantity demanded (50 units). Suppliers will not be able to sell all they had hoped to sell at $15. As a result, their inventories will grow beyond the level they hold in preparation for demand changes. Sellers will want to reduce their inventories. Some will lower prices to do so, some will cut back on production, others will do a little of both. As shown in the exhibit, price and output tend to fall until equilibrium is achieved.

WHY DOES PRICE RISE WHEN THERE IS A SHORTAGE In Exhibit 13, there is a shortage at a price of $5: The quantity demanded (150 units) is greater than the quantity supplied (50 units). Buyers will not be able to buy all they had hoped to buy at $5. Some buyers will bid up the price to get sellers to sell to them instead of to other buyers.

EXHIBIT 13

Moving to Equilibrium

If there is a surplus, sellers' inventories rise above the level they hold in preparation for demand changes. Sellers will want to reduce their inventories. As a result, price and output fall until equilibrium is achieved. If there is a shortage, some buyers will bid up price to get sellers to sell to them instead of to other buyers. Some sellers will realize they can raise the price of the goods they have for sale. Higher prices will call forth added output. Price and output rise until equilibrium is achieved. (Note: Recall that price, on the vertical axis, is price per unit of the good, and quantity, on the horizontal axis, is for a specific time period. In this text, we do not specify this on the axes themselves, but consider it to be understood.)

Price	Q_s	Q_d	Condition
$15	150	50	Surplus
10	100	100	Equilibrium
5	50	150	Shortage

Some sellers, seeing buyers clamor for the goods, will realize that they can raise the price of the goods they have for sale. Higher prices will also call forth added output. Thus, price and output tend to rise until equilibrium is achieved.

Exhibit 14 brings together much of what we have discussed about supply and demand.

Speed of Moving to Equilibrium

On April 16, 2010, at 10:09 a.m. (Eastern time), the price of a share of IBM stock was $131.50. A few minutes later, the price had risen to $132.00. Obviously, the stock market equilibrates quickly. If demand rises, then initially there is a shortage of the stock at the current equilibrium price. The price is bid up, and there is no longer a shortage. All this happens in seconds.

Now consider a house offered for sale in any city in the United States. The sale price of a house may remain the same even though the house does not sell for months. For example, a person offers to sell her house for $400,000. One month passes, no sale; two months pass, no sale; three months pass, no sale; and so on. Ten months later, the house is still not sold, and the price is still $400,000.

Is $400,000 the equilibrium price of the house? Obviously not. At the equilibrium price, there would be a buyer for the house and a seller of the house: The quantity demanded would equal the quantity supplied. At a price of $400,000, there is a seller but no buyer. The $400,000 price is above the equilibrium price. At $400,000, the housing market has a surplus; equilibrium has not been achieved.

Some people may be tempted to argue that supply and demand are at work in the stock market but not in the housing market. A better explanation, though, is that *not all markets equilibrate at the same speed.* Although the stock market may take only seconds to go from surplus or shortage to equilibrium, the housing market may take months to do so.

Moving to Equilibrium: Maximum and Minimum Prices

There is another way to demonstrate how a market moves to equilibrium. Exhibit 15 shows the market for good X. Look at the first unit of good X. What is the *maximum*

EXHIBIT 14

A Summary Exhibit of a Market (Supply and Demand)

This exhibit ties together the topics discussed so far in this chapter. A market is composed of both supply and demand, as shown. Also shown are the factors that affect supply and demand and therefore indirectly affect the equilibrium price and quantity of a good.

The Dowry and Marriage Market Disequilibrium

Men and women generally accept that monogamy is the ideal marriage practice. In other words, polygyny (the practice of one man being able to have more than one wife) is not the ideal marriage practice and therefore should be illegal. Some anthropologists and evolutionary biologists challenge orthodoxy by arguing that polygyny gives women greater choice. Here is how they structure their argument. Suppose there are 1,000 men and 1,000 women. Suppose each man and each woman is given a ranking of between 1 and 1,000 in terms of a variety of characteristics. The number 1 man is ranked higher than the number 2 man (and so on). Women are also so ranked.

The woman marries the man with whom she shares the same ranking. The number 1 man is matched up with the number 1 woman, the number 2 man with the number 2 woman, and so on. Now suppose the 404th-ranked woman (who is scheduled to marry the 404th-ranked man) prefers to be the second wife of the 40th-ranked man than the only wife of the 404th man. If polygyny is allowed, the 404th-ranked woman could marry the 40th-ranked man and share him with another wife. If polygyny is outlawed, she can't.

Now let's put that argument into economic terms. We know that a shortage exists if the quantity demanded of a good is greater than the quantity supplied. In the event that two women might want to marry the same man, the quantity supplied of the man is one, but the quantity demanded (of him) is two. This sounds like a shortage of the man, unless polygyny is permitted, because in that case the two women can be married to the same man.

But suppose polygyny is not permitted, even though the two women still want to be married to the same man. Now we have the problem of a shortage (of this particular man) that cannot be eliminated through the adoption of polygyny. What other way remains to eliminate the shortage? Normally we think of money as eliminating a shortage, and this is exactly what might be the purpose of the dowry. A dowry is a transfer of assets from the bride's family to the groom's family (usually) before the marriage takes place. If two women want to be married to the same man but only one can be legally married to him, then the dowry may effectively take the place of polygyny in eliminating the shortage of the man. All other things being equal, the prospective bride's family that offers the better dowry to the groom's family ends up with the groom as their son-in-law. This is consistent with the findings of anthropologists Steven J. C. Gaulin and James S. Boster who have shown that the dowry is almost exclusively found in societies where monogamy has been imposed (and polygyny outlawed).

EXHIBIT 15

Moving to Equilibrium in Terms of Maximum and Minimum Prices

As long as the maximum buying price is greater than the minimum selling price, an exchange will occur. This condition is met for units 1–4. The market converges on equilibrium through a process of mutually beneficial exchanges.

Units of Good X	Maximum Buying Price	Minimum Selling Price	Result
1st	$70	$10	Exchange
2nd	60	20	Exchange
3rd	50	30	Exchange
4th	40	40	Exchange
5th	30	50	No Exchange

price buyers are willing to pay for it? The answer is $70. Just follow the dotted line up from the first unit of the good to the demand curve. What is the *minimum price sellers need to receive before they are willing to sell* this unit of good X? It is $10. Follow the dotted line up from the first unit to the supply curve. Because the maximum buying price is greater than the minimum selling price, the first unit of good X will be exchanged.

What about the second unit? For the second unit, buyers are willing to pay a maximum price of $60, and sellers need to receive a minimum price of $20. The second unit of good X will be exchanged. In fact, exchange will occur as long as the maximum buying price is greater than the minimum selling price. The exhibit shows that a total of four units of good X will be exchanged. The fifth unit will not be exchanged because the maximum buying price ($30) is less than the minimum selling price ($50).

In this process, buyers and sellers trade money for goods as long as both benefit from the trade. The market converges on a quantity of 4 units of good X and a price of $40 per unit. This is equilibrium. In other words, mutually beneficial trade drives the market to equilibrium.

Equilibrium in Terms of Consumers' and Producers' Surplus

Equilibrium can be viewed in terms of two important economic concepts: consumers' surplus and producers' (or sellers') surplus. Consumers' surplus is the difference between the maximum buying price and the price paid by the buyer.

Consumers' Surplus (CS)
The difference between the maximum price a buyer is willing and able to pay for a good or service and the price actually paid. CS = Maximum buying price − Price paid

$$\text{Consumers' surplus} = \text{Maximum buying price} - \text{Price paid}$$

For example, if the highest price you would pay to see a movie is $10 and you pay $7 to see it, then you have received a $3 consumers' surplus. Obviously, the more consumers' surplus that consumers receive, the better off they are. Wouldn't you have preferred to pay, say, $4 to see the movie instead of $7? If you had paid only $4, your consumers' surplus would have been $6 instead of $3.

Producers' (or sellers') surplus is the difference between the price received by the producer or seller and the minimum selling price.

Producers' (Sellers') Surplus (PS)
The difference between the price sellers receive for a good and the minimum or lowest price for which they would have sold the good. PS = Price received − Minimum selling price

$$\text{Producers' (sellers') surplus} = \text{Price received} - \text{Minimum selling price}$$

Suppose the minimum price the owner of the movie theater would have accepted for admission is $5. But she sells admission for $7, not $5. Her producers' or sellers' surplus is $2. A seller prefers a large producers' surplus to a small one. The theater owner would have preferred to sell admission to the movie for $8 instead of $7 because then she would have received a $3 producers' surplus.

Total surplus is the sum of the consumers' surplus and producers' surplus.

Total Surplus (TS)
The sum of consumers' surplus and producers' surplus. TS = CS + PS

$$\text{Total surplus} = \text{Consumers' surplus} + \text{Producers' surplus}$$

In Exhibit 16(a), consumers' surplus is represented by the shaded triangle. This triangle includes the area under the demand curve and above the equilibrium price. According to the definition, consumers' surplus is the highest price buyers are willing to pay (maximum buying price) minus the price they pay. For example, the window in part (a) shows that buyers are willing to pay as high as $7 for the 50th unit but pay only $5. Thus, the consumers' surplus on the 50th unit of the good is $2. If we add the consumers' surplus on each unit of the good between and including the first and the 100th units (the equilibrium quantity), we obtain the shaded consumers' surplus triangle.

EXHIBIT 16

Consumers' and Producers' Surplus

(a) Consumers' surplus. As the shaded area indicates, the difference between the maximum or highest amount buyers would be

willing to pay and the price they actually pay is consumers' surplus. (b) Producers' surplus. As the shaded area indicates, the difference between the price sellers receive for the good

and the minimum or lowest price they would be willing to sell the good for is producers' surplus.

(a)

Consumers' Surplus (CS)

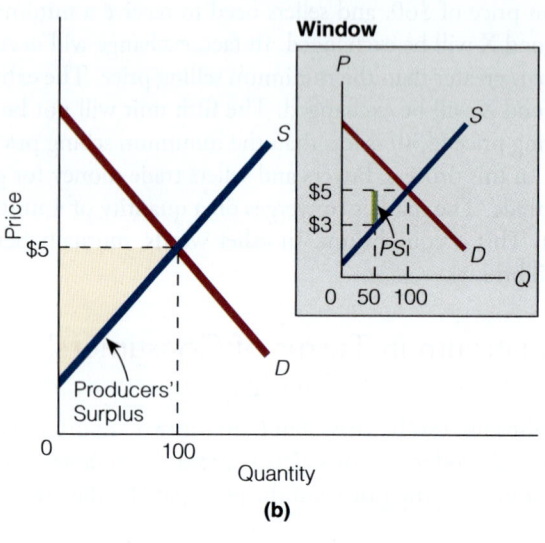

(b)

Producers' Surplus (PS)

In Exhibit 16(b), producers' surplus is also represented by a shaded triangle. This triangle includes the area above the supply curve and under the equilibrium price. Keep in mind the definition of producers' surplus: the price received by the seller minus the lowest price the seller would accept for the good. For example, the window in part (b) shows that sellers would have sold the 50th unit for as low as $3 but actually sold it for $5. Thus, the producers' surplus on the 50th unit of the good is $2. If we add the producers' surplus on each unit of the good between and including the first and the 100th, we obtain the shaded producers' surplus triangle.

Now consider consumers' surplus and producers' surplus at the equilibrium quantity. Exhibit 17 shows that the consumers' surplus at equilibrium is equal to areas $A + B + C + D$, and the producers' surplus at equilibrium is equal to areas $E + F + G + H$. At any other exchangeable quantity, such as at 25, 50, or 75 units, both consumers' surplus and producers' surplus are less. For example, at 25 units, consumers' surplus is equal to area A, and producers' surplus is equal to area E. At 50 units, the consumers' surplus is equal to areas $A + B$, and the producers' surplus is equal to areas $E + F$.

Equilibrium has a special property: At equilibrium, both consumers' surplus and producers' surplus are maximized. In short, total surplus is maximized.

What Can Change Equilibrium Price and Quantity?

Equilibrium price and quantity are determined by supply and demand. Whenever demand changes, supply changes, or both change, equilibrium price and quantity change. Exhibit 18 illustrates eight different cases where this occurs. Cases (a)−(d) illustrate the four basic changes in supply and demand, where either supply or demand changes. Cases (e)−(h) illustrate changes in both supply and demand.

EXHIBIT 17

Quantity (units)	Consumers' Surplus	Producers' Surplus
25	A	E
50	A + B	E + F
75	A + B + C	E + F + G
100 (Equilibrium)	A + B + C + D	E + F + G + H

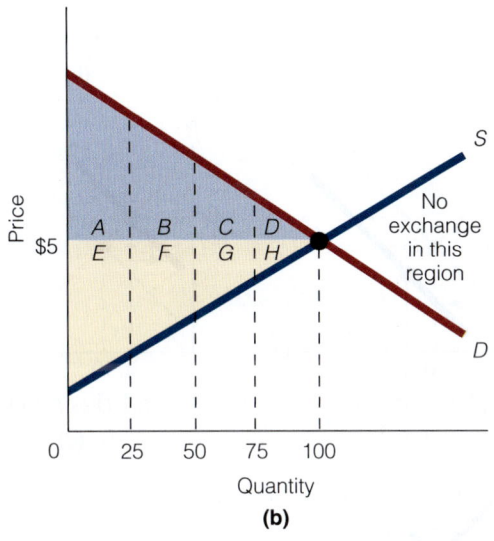

(b)

Equilibrium, Consumers' Surplus, and Producers' Surplus

Consumers' surplus is greater at equilibrium quantity (100 units) than at any other exchangeable quantity. Producers' surplus is greater at equilibrium quantity than at any other exchangeable quantity. For example, consumers' surplus is areas A + B + C at 75 units, but areas A + B + C + D at 100 units. Producers' surplus is areas E + F + G at 75 units, but areas E + F + G + H at 100 units.

- *Case (a):* Demand rises (the demand curve shifts rightward from D_1 to D_2), and supply is constant (the supply curve does not move). As a result of demand rising and supply remaining constant, the equilibrium price rises from P_1 to P_2, and the equilibrium quantity rises from 10 to 12 units. Now let's see if you can identify what has happened to quantity supplied (not supply) as price has risen from P_1 to P_2. (Remember, quantity supplied changes if *price* changes.) As price rises from P_1 to P_2, quantity supplied rises from 10 to 12 units. We see this as a movement up the supply curve from point 1 to point 2, which corresponds (on the horizontal axis) as a change from 10 to 12 units.

- *Case (b):* Demand falls (the demand curve shifts leftward from D_1 to D_2), and supply is constant. As a result, the equilibrium price falls from P_1 to P_2, and the equilibrium quantity falls from 10 to 8 units . Now ask, has the quantity supplied (not supply) changed? Yes, it has. As a result of price falling from P_1 to P_2, we move down the supply curve from point 1 to point 2, and the quantity supplied falls from 10 to 8 units.

- *Case (c):* Supply rises (the supply curve shifts rightward from S_1 to S_2), and demand is constant. As a result, the equilibrium price falls from P_1 to P_2, and the equilibrium quantity rises from 10 to 12 units. Now ask, has the quantity demanded (not demand) changed? Yes, it has. As a result of price falling from P_1 to P_2, we move down the demand curve from point 1 to point 2, and the quantity demanded rises from 10 to 12 units.

- *Case (d):* Supply falls (the supply curve shifts leftward from S_1 to S_2), and demand is constant. As a result, the equilibrium price rises from P_1 to P_2, and the equilibrium

EXHIBIT 18

Equilibrium Price and Quantity Effects of Supply Curve Shifts and Demand Curve Shifts

The exhibit illustrates the effects on equilibrium price and quantity of a change in demand, a change in supply, or change in both. Below each diagram, the condition leading to the effects is noted, using the following symbols: (1) a bar over a letter means *constant* (thus, $\bar{S}$ means that supply is constant); (2) a downward-pointing arrow ($\downarrow$) indicates a fall; (3) an upward-pointing arrow ($\uparrow$) indicates a rise. A rise (fall) in demand is the same as a rightward (leftward) shift in the demand curve. A rise (fall) in supply is the same as a rightward (leftward) shift in the supply curve.

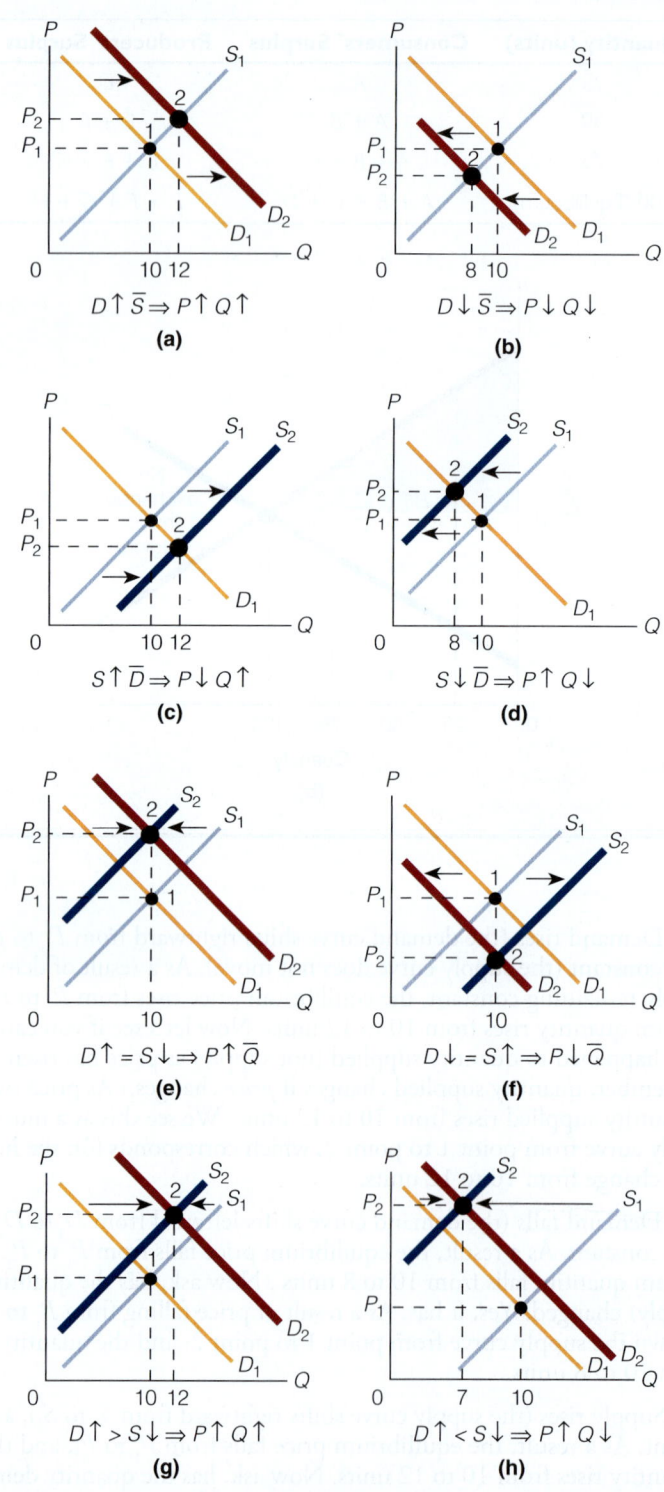

$D\uparrow\bar{S}\Rightarrow P\uparrow Q\uparrow$

(a)

$D\downarrow\bar{S}\Rightarrow P\downarrow Q\downarrow$

(b)

$S\uparrow\bar{D}\Rightarrow P\downarrow Q\uparrow$

(c)

$S\downarrow\bar{D}\Rightarrow P\uparrow Q\downarrow$

(d)

$D\uparrow=S\downarrow\Rightarrow P\uparrow\bar{Q}$

(e)

$D\downarrow=S\uparrow\Rightarrow P\downarrow\bar{Q}$

(f)

$D\uparrow>S\downarrow\Rightarrow P\uparrow Q\uparrow$

(g)

$D\uparrow<S\downarrow\Rightarrow P\uparrow Q\downarrow$

(h)

"Sorry, but This Flight Has Been Overbooked"

Airlines often overbook flights; that is, they accept more reservations than they have seats available on a flight. Airlines know that a certain (usually small) percentage of individuals with reservations will not show up. An empty seat means that the airline's cost per actual passenger on board is higher than it would be if the seat were occupied by a paying passenger. So airlines try to make sure to have few empty seats. One way to reduce the number of empty seats is to overbook.

In the past, when more people with reservations showed up for a flight than there were seats available, the airline simply "bumped" passengers. In other words, the airline would tell some passengers that they could not fly on that flight. Understandably, the bumped passengers were disappointed and angry.

One day while shaving, economist Julian Simon (1932–1998) came up with a better way to deal with overbooking. He argued that the airline should enter into a market transaction with the ticket holders who had reserved seats for an overbooked flight. Instead of bumping people randomly, an airline should ask passengers to sell their seats back to the airline. Passengers who absolutely had to get from one city to another would not sell their seats, but passengers who did not have to fly right away might be willing to sell their tickets for, say, first class on a later flight or some other compensation.

Simon wrote the executives of various airlines and outlined the details of his plan. He even told them that the first airline that enacted the

plan would likely reap larger sales. The airline could, after all, guarantee its passengers that they would not get bumped. Most airline executives wrote back and told him it was a reasonably good idea but unworkable.

Simon then contacted various economists asking them to support his idea publicly. Some did; some didn't. For years, Simon pushed his idea with airline executives and government officials.

Then Alfred Kahn, an economist, was appointed chairman of the Civil Aeronautics Board. Simon contacted Kahn with his plan, and Kahn liked it. According to Simon, "Kahn announced something like the scheme in his first press conference. He also had the great persuasive skill to repackage it as a 'voluntary' bumping plan, and at the same time to increase the penalties that airlines must pay to involuntary bumpees, a nice carrot-and-stick combination."

The rest, as people say, is history. Simon's plan has been in operation since 1978. Simon wrote, "The volunteer system for handling airline oversales exemplifies how markets can improve life for all concerned parties. In case of an oversale, the airline agent proceeds from lowest bidder upwards until the required number of bumpees is achieved. Low bidders take the next flight, happy about it. All other passengers fly as scheduled, also happy. The airlines can overbook more, making them happy too."

quantity falls from 10 to 8 units. One last time: Has quantity demanded (not demand) changed? Yes, it has. As a result of price rising from P_1 to P_2, we move up the demand curve from point 1 to point 2, and quantity demanded falls from 10 to 8 units.

- *Case (e):* Demand rises (the demand curve shifts from D_1 to D_2), and supply falls (the supply curve shifts leftward from S_1 to S_2) by an equal amount. As a result, the equilibrium price rises from P_1 to P_2, and the equilibrium quantity remains constant at 10 units.

- *Case (f):* Demand falls (the demand curve shifts leftward from D_1 to D_2), and supply rises (the supply curve shifts rightward from S_1 to S_2) by an equal amount. As a result, the equilibrium price falls from P_1 to P_2, and the equilibrium quantity is constant at 10 units.

- *Case (g):* Demand rises (the demand curve shifts rightward from D_1 to D_2) by a greater amount than supply falls (the supply curve shifts leftward from S_1 to S_2). As a result, the equilibrium price rises from P_1 to P_2, and the equilibrium quantity rises from 10 to 12 units.

- *Case (h):* Demand rises (the demand curve shifts rightward from D_1 to D_2) by a smaller amount than supply falls (the supply curve shifts leftward from S_1 to S_2). The equilibrium price rises from P_1 to P_2 and the equilibrium quantity falls from 10 to 7 units.

SELF-TEST

1. When a person goes to the grocery store to buy food, there is no auctioneer calling out prices for bread, milk, and other items. Therefore, supply and demand cannot be operative. Do you agree or disagree? Explain your answer.

2. The price of a given-quality personal computer is lower today than it was five years ago. Is this necessarily the result of a lower demand for computers? Explain your answer.

3. What is the effect on equilibrium price and quantity of the following?

   a. A decrease in demand that is greater than the increase in supply

   b. An increase in supply

   c. A decrease in supply that is greater than the increase in demand

   d. A decrease in demand

4. At equilibrium quantity, what is the relationship between the maximum buying price and the minimum selling price?

5. If the price paid is $40 and the consumers' surplus is $4, then what is the maximum buying price? If the minimum selling price is $30 and the producers' surplus is $4, then what is the price received by the seller?

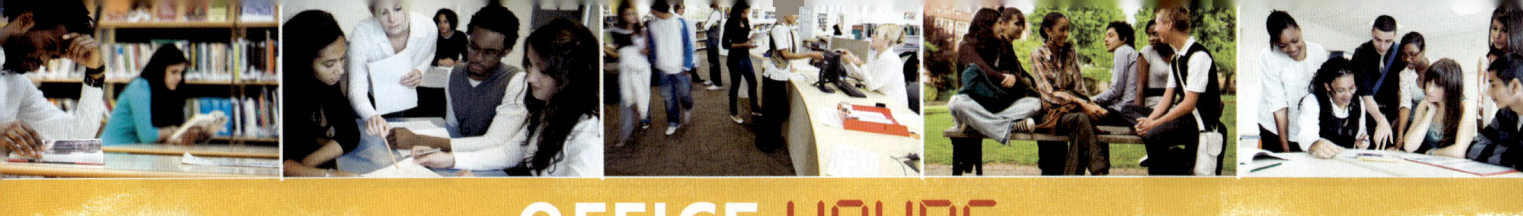

OFFICE HOURS

"I Thought Prices Equaled Costs Plus 10 Percent"

STUDENT:

My uncle produces and sells lamps. I asked him once how he determines the price he sells his lamps for. He said he takes his costs and adds 10 percent. In other words, if it cost him $200 to make a lamp, he sells it for a price of $220. If all sellers do the same thing, then prices aren't being determined by supply and demand, are they?

INSTRUCTOR:

Supply and demand could still be at work even given what your uncle said. For example, the $220 could be the supply-and-demand-determined equilibrium price for the type of lamps your uncle is producing and selling. Look at it this way: If your uncle could sell the lamps for, say, $250 each, then he would have told you that he takes his cost (of $200) and adds on 25 percent ($50) to get "his price" of $250.

STUDENT:

Is the point that what looks like *cost plus 10 percent* to me could really be supply and demand?

INSTRUCTOR:

Yes, that's the point. But we can add something else to make the point stronger. Think of the housing market for a minute. Are the prices of houses determined by *cost plus 10 percent* or by supply and demand? Let's see if we can think through an example together. Suppose you buy a house for $400,000 in one year and then decide to sell it ten years later. What price do you charge for the house? Do you charge the (market) equilibrium price for that house, or do you charge what you paid for the house ($400,000) plus 10 percent (plus $40,000) for a total of $440,000?

STUDENT:

Oh, I think I see what you mean. You mean that if the equilibrium price for the house happened to be $650,000, I wouldn't charge only $440,000.

INSTRUCTOR:

Exactly. In other words, the supply-and-demand-determined price would take precedence over the cost-plus-10-percent price. Now going back to your uncle, he might have just thought that he was charging a price of cost plus 10 percent because the equilibrium price for the good he produced and sold happened to be 10 percent higher than his cost. But as stated before, if that equilibrium price had been 25 percent higher, your uncle would have told you his price was determined by his taking his costs and adding 25 percent. The equilibrium price was determining the percentage your uncle said he added to costs, not simply his picking a percentage out of thin air.

POINTS TO REMEMBER

1. What looks like cost plus 10 percent (cost plus some markup) could instead be supply and demand at work.
2. Supply and demand are obviously determining prices at, say, an auction. A single good is for sale (say, a painting), and numerous buyers bid on it. The bidding stops when only one buyer is left. At the price the last bidder bid, the quantity demanded (of the painting) equals the quantity supplied, and both equal one. Even if you do not see supply and demand at work in nonauction settings, supply and demand are still at work determining prices.

CHAPTER SUMMARY

DEMAND

- The law of demand states that as the price of a good rises, the quantity demanded of it falls and that as the price of a good falls, the quantity demanded of it rises, *ceteris paribus*. The law of demand holds that price and quantity demanded are inversely related.

- Quantity demanded is the total number of units of a good that buyers are willing and able to buy at a particular price.

- A (downward-sloping) demand curve is the graphical representation of the law of demand.

- Factors that can change demand and cause the demand curve to shift are income, preferences, the prices of related goods (substitutes and complements), the number of buyers, and expectations of future price.

- The only factor that can directly cause a change in the quantity demanded of a good is a change in the good's own price.

SUPPLY

- The law of supply states that as the price of a good rises, the quantity supplied of the good rises and that as the price of a good falls, the quantity supplied of the good falls, *ceteris paribus*. The law of supply asserts that price and quantity supplied are directly related.

- The law of supply does not hold when there is no time to produce more units of a good or when goods cannot be produced at all (i.e., over any period of time).

- The upward-sloping supply curve is the graphical representation of the law of supply. More generally, a supply curve (no matter how it slopes) represents the relationship between the price and quantity supplied.

- Factors that can change supply and cause the supply curve to shift are the prices of relevant resources, technology, the prices of other goods, the number of sellers, expectations of future price, taxes and subsidies, and government restrictions.

- The only factor that can directly cause a change in the quantity supplied of a good is a change in the good's own price.

THE MARKET

- Demand and supply together establish the equilibrium price and equilibrium quantity.

- A surplus exists in a market if, at some price, the quantity supplied is greater than the quantity demanded. A shortage exists if, at some price, the quantity demanded is greater than the quantity supplied.

- Mutually beneficial trade between buyers and sellers drives the market to equilibrium.

CONSUMERS' SURPLUS, PRODUCERS' SURPLUS, AND TOTAL SURPLUS

- Consumers' surplus is the difference between the maximum buying price and the price paid by the buyer.

  Consumers' surplus = Maximum buying price − Price paid

- Producers' (or sellers') surplus is the difference between the price the seller receives and the minimum selling price.

  Producers' surplus = Price received − Minimum selling price

- The more consumers' surplus that buyers receive, the better off they are. The more producers' surplus that sellers receive, the better off they are. Total surplus is the sum of consumers' surplus and producers' surplus.

- Total surplus (the sum of consumers' surplus and producers' surplus) is maximized at equilibrium.

KEY TERMS AND CONCEPTS

Market	Normal Good	Supply Schedule	Disequilibrium
Demand	Inferior Good	Subsidy	Equilibrium
Law of Demand	Neutral Good	Surplus (Excess Supply)	Consumers' Surplus
Demand Schedule	Substitutes	Shortage (Excess Demand)	Producers' (Sellers')
Demand Curve	Complements	Equilibrium Price (Market-	Surplus
Law of Diminishing	Supply	Clearing Price)	Total Surplus
Marginal Utility	Law of Supply	Equilibrium Quantity	
Own Price	Supply Curve	Disequilibrium Price	

QUESTIONS AND PROBLEMS

1. Compare the ratings for television shows with prices for goods. How are ratings like prices? How are ratings different from prices? (Hint: How does rising demand for a particular television manifest itself?)

2. Predict what would happen to the equilibrium price of marijuana if it were legalized.

3. At equilibrium in a market, the maximum price buyers would be willing to pay for the good is equal to the minimum price sellers need to receive before they are willing to sell the good. Do you agree or disagree with this statement? Explain your answer.

4. What is the difference between supply and quantity supplied?

5. Must consumers' surplus equal producers' surplus at equilibrium price? Explain your answer.

6. How might the price of corn affect the supply of wheat?

7. Many movie theaters charge a lower admission price for the first show on weekday afternoons than they do for a weeknight or weekend show. Explain why.

8. In the previous chapter you learned about the law of increasing opportunity costs. What does this law have to do with an upward-sloping supply curve?

9. A Dell computer is a substitute for a Hewlett-Packard computer. What happens to the demand for Hewlett-Packard computers and the quantity demanded of Dell computers as the price of a Dell falls?

10. What is wrong with this statement: As the price of a good falls, the supply of that good falls, *ceteris paribus*.

11. Describe how each of the following will affect the demand for personal computers:
    a. A rise in income (assuming computers are a normal good)
    b. A lower expected price for computers
    c. Cheaper software
    d. Simpler-to-operate computers

12. What does a sale on shirts have to do with the law of demand (as applied to shirts)?

13. Describe how each of the following will affect the supply of personal computers:
    a. A rise in wage rates
    b. An increase in the number of sellers of computers
    c. A tax placed on the production of computers
    d. A subsidy placed on the production of computers

14. With respect to each of the following changes, identify whether the demand curve will shift rightward of leftward:
    a. An increase in income (the good under consideration is a normal good)
    b. A rise in the price of a substitute good
    c. A fall in the price of a complementary good
    d. A fall in the number of buyers

15. Use the law of diminishing marginal utility to explain why demand curves slope downward.

16. "The price of T-shirts keeps rising and rising, and people keep buying more and more. T-shirts must have an upward-sloping demand curve." Identify the error.

17. Explain how the market moves to equilibrium in terms of shortages and surpluses and in terms of maximum buying prices and minimum selling prices.

18. Some goods are bought largely because they have 'snob appeal.' For example, the residents of Beverly Hills gain prestige by buying expensive items. In fact, they won't buy some items unless they are expensive. The law of demand, which holds that people buy more at lower prices than higher prices, obviously doesn't hold for the residents of Beverly Hills. The following rules apply in Beverly Hills: high prices, buy; low prices, don't buy. Discuss.

19. Identify what happens to equilibrium price and quantity in each of the following cases:
    a. Demand rises and supply is constant
    b. Demand falls and supply is constant
    c. Supply rises and demand is constant
    d. Supply falls and demand is constant
    e. Demand rises by the same amount that supply falls
    f. Demand falls by the same amount that supply rises
    g. Demand falls less than supply rises
    h. Demand rises more than supply rises
    i. Demand rises less than supply rises
    j. Demand falls more than supply falls
    k. Demand falls less than supply falls

20. "The price of a bushel of wheat, which was $3.00 last month, is $3.70 today. The demand curve for wheat must have shifted rightward between last month and today." Discuss.

21. Suppose the demand curve for a good is downward sloping and the supply curve is upward sloping. Now suppose demand rises. Will producers' surplus rise or fall? Explain your answers.

22. True or false? As the price of oranges rises, the demand for oranges falls, *ceteris paribus.* Explain your answer.

23. When speeding tickets were $100, usually 500 speeders were on the roads each month in a given city; when ticket prices were raised to $250, usually 215 speeders were on the roads in the city each month. Can you find any economics in this observation?

24. What is the difference between *demand* and *quantity demanded*?

25. On most days, more people want to see the taping of *The Tonight Show with Jay Leno* (in Burbank, California) than there are seats in the taping studio. What might explain this shortage?

26. What is wrong with this statement? Demand refers to the willingness of buyers to purchase different quantities of a good at different prices during a specific time period.

WORKING WITH NUMBERS AND GRAPHS

1. Price is $10, the quantity supplied is 50 units, and the quantity demanded is 100 units. For every $1 rise in price, the quantity supplied rises by 5 units and the quantity demanded falls by 5 units. What is the equilibrium price and quantity?

2. Using numbers, explain how a market demand curve is derived from two individual demand curves.

3. Draw a diagram that shows a larger increase in demand than the decrease in supply.

4. Draw a diagram that shows a smaller increase in supply than the increase in demand.

5. At equilibrium in the following figure, what area(s) does the consumers' surplus equal the producers' surplus?

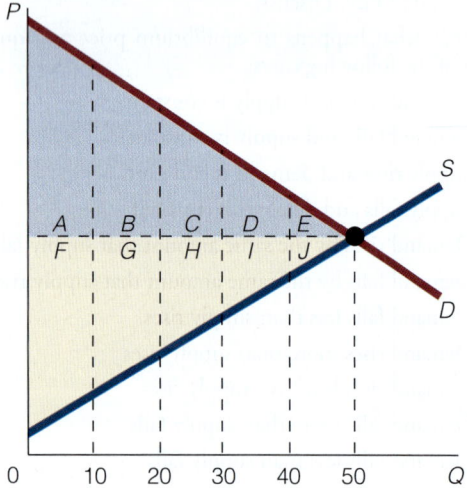

6. At what quantity in the preceding figure is the maximum buying price equal to the minimum selling price?

7. In the following figure, can the movement from point 1 to point 2 be explained by a combination of an increase in the price of a substitute and a decrease in the price of nonlabor resources? Explain your answer.

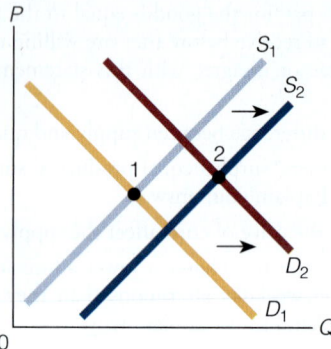

8. The demand curve is downward sloping, the supply curve is upward sloping, and the equilibrium quantity is 50 units. Show on a graph that the difference between the maximum buying price and minimum selling price is greater at 25 units than at 33 units.

CHAPTER 4

PRICES: FREE, CONTROLLED, AND RELATIVE

KCPHOTOS / DREAMSTIME.COM

Introduction In the last chapter we discussed supply and demand. Mainly, we saw how supply and demand work together to determine prices. In this chapter we discuss prices at greater length. First, we discuss two of the key "jobs" that price performs: (1) rationing resources and goods and (2) transmitting information. Second, we discuss government controls that can be imposed on price. Specifically, we discuss both price ceilings and price floors. Third, we discuss two types of price: absolute (or money) price and relative price.

PRICE

To most people, price is a number with a dollar sign in front of it, such as $10. But price is much more. Price performs two major jobs: It acts (1) as a rationing device and (2) as a transmitter of information.

Price as a Rationing Device

In Chapter 1 we said that wants (for goods) are unlimited and resources are limited; so scarcity exists. As a result of scarcity, a rationing device is needed to determine who gets what of the available limited resources and goods. (Because resources are limited, goods are also because the production of goods requires resources.) Price serves as a rationing device. It rations resources to the producers who pay the price for the resources. It rations goods to those buyers who pay the price for the goods. The process is as simple as this: Pay the price, and the resources or goods are yours. Don't pay the price, and they aren't.

Is dollar price a fair rationing device? Doesn't it discriminate against the poor? After all, the poor have fewer dollars than the rich; so the rich can get more of what they want than can the poor. True, dollar price does discriminate against the poor. But then, as economists know, every rationing device discriminates against someone. To illustrate, suppose for some reason that tomorrow dollar price could not be used as a rationing device. Some rationing device would still be necessary because scarcity would still exist. How would we ration gas at the gasoline station, food in the grocery store, or tickets for the Super Bowl? Let's consider some alternatives to dollar price as a rationing device.

Suppose *first-come-first-served* is the rationing device. For example, suppose only 40,000 Super Bowl tickets are available. If you are one of the first 40,000 in line for a Super Bowl ticket, you get a ticket. If you are person number 40,001 in line, you don't. Such a method discriminates against those who can't get in line quickly enough. What about slow walkers or people with disabilities? What about people without cars who can't drive to where the tickets are distributed?

Or suppose *brute force* is the rationing device. For example, of the 40,000 Super Bowl tickets, you get one as long as you can take it away from someone else. Against whom does this rationing method discriminate? Obviously, it discriminates against the weak and nonaggressive.

Or suppose *beauty* is the rationing device. The more beautiful you are, the better your chances are of getting a Super Bowl ticket. Again, the rationing device discriminates against someone.

These and many other alternatives to dollar price could be used as rationing devices. However, each discriminates against someone, and none is clearly superior to dollar price.

In addition, if first-come-first-served, brute force, beauty, or another alternative to dollar price is the rationing device, what incentive would the producer of a good have to produce the good? With dollar price as a rationing device, a person produces computers and sells them for money. He then takes the money and buys what he wants. But if the rationing device were, say, brute force, he would not have an incentive to produce. Why produce anything when someone will end up taking it away from you? In short, in a world where dollar price isn't the rationing device, people are likely to produce much less than in a world where dollar price is the rationing device.

Price as a Transmitter of Information

Rationing isn't the only job that price performs. Price also transmits information. That may sound odd. Consider the following story. On Saturday, Noelle walks into a local grocery store and purchases a half gallon of orange juice for $2.50. On Sunday, unknown to her, a cold spell hits Florida and wipes out half the orange crop. The cold spell ends up shifting the supply curve of oranges leftward, which drives up the price of oranges. Because oranges are a resource in the production of orange juice, the supply curve of orange juice shifts leftward, and the price of orange juice rises.

Noelle returns to the grocery store in a week. She notices the half gallon of orange juice she bought last week for $2.50 has now risen to $3.50. Because Noelle has a downward-sloping demand curve for orange juice, she ends up buying less orange juice. She buys only a quart of orange juice instead of a half gallon.

What role did price play in Noelle's decision to cut back on the consumption of orange juice? It played a major role. If the price hadn't risen, Noelle probably wouldn't have reduced her purchases and consumption of orange juice. Noelle reacted to the price rise, but what the price rise was "saying"—if we had ears to hear it—is this: "The relative scarcity of a good has risen because of a cold spell in Florida. In other words, the gap between people's wants for orange juice and the amount of orange juice available to satisfy those wants has widened."

Now we know that Noelle might not have "heard" price saying this. But if you understand economics, this is what price is saying. In other words, price is a transmitter of information that often relates to the relative scarcity of a good. A market system, oddly enough, is powerful enough to have people respond in appropriate ways to the information that price is transmitting, even if the people do not fully hear or understand it. In the case of Noelle, her cutting back on the consumption of orange juice conserves orange juice in the face of an act of nature that ended up making orange juice relatively scarcer.

Think of how this reaction is similar to what people who tell you to conserve water want. For example, in California in the summer of 2009, advertisements on television asked people to cut back on their consumption of water because water in the state was in short supply. The appropriate behavior to take was to cut back on the consumption of water because it had become relatively scarcer. You were being civic minded if you did so. Well, movements in price can get you to be civic minded too. When the price of orange juice rises due to a cold spell in Florida, you might automatically cut back on your consumption, thus conserving on the consumption of a good that has become relatively more scarce.

PRICE CONTROLS

A rationing device—such as dollar price—is needed because scarcity exists. But price is not always allowed to be a rationing device. Sometimes price is controlled. There are two types of price controls: price ceilings and price floors. In the discussion of price controls, the word "price" is used in the generic sense. It refers to the price of an apple, for example, the price of labor (a wage), the price of credit (the interest rate), and so on.

Price Ceiling

DEFINITION AND EFFECTS A price ceiling is a government-mandated maximum price above which legal trades cannot be made. For example, suppose the government mandates that the maximum price at which good X can be bought and sold is $8. Therefore, $8 is a price ceiling. If $8 is below the equilibrium price of good X, as in Exhibit 1, any or all of the following effects may arise:[1] shortages, fewer exchanges, nonprice-rationing devices, buying and selling at prohibited prices, and tie-in sales.

Shortages At the $12 equilibrium price in Exhibit 1, the quantity demanded of good X (150) is equal to the quantity supplied (150). At the $8 price ceiling, a shortage exists. The quantity demanded (190) is greater than the quantity supplied (100). When a shortage exists, price and output tend to rise to equilibrium. But when a price ceiling exists, they cannot rise because it is unlawful to trade at the equilibrium price.

EXHIBIT 1

A Price Ceiling

The price ceiling is $8 and the equilibrium price is $12. At $12, quantity demanded = quantity supplied. At $8 quantity demanded > quantity supplied. (Recall that price, on the vertical axis, always represents price per unit. Quantity, on the horizontal axis, always holds for a specific time period.)

---

1. If the price ceiling is above the equilibrium price (say, $8 is the price ceiling and $4 is the equilibrium price), it has no effect. Usually, however, a price ceiling is below the equilibrium price.

Fewer Exchanges   At the equilibrium price of $12 in Exhibit 1, 150 units of good X are bought and sold. At the price ceiling of $8, 100 units of good X are bought and sold. (Buyers would prefer to buy 190 units, but only 100 are supplied.) We conclude that price ceilings cause fewer exchanges to be made.

Notice in Exhibit 1 that the demand curve is above the supply curve for all quantities less than 150 units. (At 150 units, the demand curve and the supply curve intersect and thus share the same point in the two-dimensional space.) Thus the maximum buying price is greater than the minimum selling price for all units less than 150. In particular, the maximum buying price is greater than the minimum selling price for units 101 to 149. For example, buyers might be willing to pay $17 for the 110th unit, and sellers might be willing to sell the 110th unit for $10. But no unit after the 100th unit (not the 110th unit, not the 114th unit, not the 130th unit) will be produced and sold because of the price ceiling. In short, the price ceiling prevents mutually advantageous trades from being realized.

Nonprice-Rationing Devices   If the equilibrium price $12 fully rations good X before the price ceiling is imposed, then a lower price of $8 only partly rations this good. In short, price ceilings prevent price from rising to the level sufficient to ration goods fully. But if price is responsible for only part of the rationing, what accounts for the rest?

The answer is that some other (nonprice) rationing device, such as first-come-first-served (FCFS). In Exhibit 1, 100 units of good X will be sold at $8, although buyers are willing to buy 190 units at this price. What happens? Possibly, good X will be sold on an FCFS basis for $8 per unit. In other words, to buy good X, a person must not only pay $8 per unit but also be one of the first people in line.

Buying and Selling at a Prohibited Price   Buyers and sellers may regularly circumvent a price ceiling by making their exchanges under the table. For example, some buyers may offer some sellers more than $8 per unit for good X. No doubt, some sellers will accept the offers. But why would some buyers offer more than $8 per unit when they can buy good X for $8? Because not all buyers can buy the amount of good X they want at $8. As Exhibit 1 shows, there is a shortage. Buyers are willing to buy 190 units at $8, but sellers are willing to sell only 100 units. In short, 90 fewer units will be sold than buyers would like to buy. Some buyers will go unsatisfied. How, then, does any one buyer make it more likely that sellers will sell to him or her instead of to someone else? The answer is by offering to pay a higher price. Because it is illegal to pay a higher price, the transaction must be made under the table.

Tie-In Sale
A sale whereby one good can be purchased only if another good is also purchased.

Tie-In Sales   In Exhibit 1, the maximum price buyers would be willing and able to pay per unit for 100 units of good X is $18. (This is the price on the demand curve at a quantity of 100 units.) The maximum legal price, however, is $8. This difference between the two prices often prompts a tie-in sale, a sale whereby one good can be purchased only if another good is also purchased. For example, if Ralph's Gas Station sells gasoline to customers only if they buy a car wash, the two goods are linked in a tie-in sale.

Suppose that the sellers of good X in Exhibit 1 also sell good Y. They might offer to sell buyers good X at $8 only if the buyers agree to buy good Y at, say, $10. We choose $10 as the price for good Y because $10 is the difference between the maximum per-unit price buyers are willing and able to pay for 100 units of good X ($18) and the maximum legal price ($8).

In New York City and other communities with rent-control laws, tie-in sales sometimes result from rent ceilings on apartments. Occasionally, to rent an apartment, an individual must agree to buy the furniture in the apartment.

Price Ceiling
A government-mandated maximum price above which legal trades cannot be made.

BUYERS AND HIGHER AND LOWER PRICES   Do buyers prefer lower to higher prices? "Of course," you might say, "buyers prefer lower prices to higher prices. What buyer would want to pay a higher price for anything?" Even though price ceilings are often lower than equilibrium prices, does it follow that buyers prefer price ceilings to equilibrium prices? Not necessarily. Price ceilings have effects that equilibrium prices do not: shortages, use of first-come-first-served as a rationing device, tie-in sales, and so on. A buyer could prefer to pay a higher price (an equilibrium price) than to pay a lower price and have to deal with the effects of a price ceiling. All we can say for certain is that buyers prefer lower prices to higher prices, *ceteris paribus*. As in many cases, the *ceteris paribus* condition makes all the difference.

PRICE CEILINGS AND FALSE INFORMATION   Let's go back to the orange juice example in the first section of this chapter. In that example, a cold spell destroys part of the orange crop, leading to a higher price for oranges and orange juice. The market price of orange juice rose from $2.50 to $3.50 a half gallon.

Now let's change things. Suppose that instead of letting the new, lower supply of orange juice and demand for orange juice determine the market price of orange juice at $3.50 a half gallon, government imposes a price ceiling on orange juice at $2.50 a half gallon. Think about what the price ceiling does to prevent price from transmitting information. Specifically, the price ceiling prevents the correct information about the increased relative scarcity of orange juice (due to the cold spell) from getting through to consumers. It's as if price is a radio signal, and the price ceiling jams the signal. Because of the jammed price signal, consumers mistakenly believe that nothing has changed. As far as they are concerned, they can continue buying orange juice at the same rate of consumption they did earlier. But, of course, they can't: There are fewer oranges and less orange juice in the world. One way or another, some people are going to have to curtail their consumption of orange juice.

The lesson is simple. Price ceilings (that are below the equilibrium price) distort the flow of accurate information to buyers. Buyers get a false view of reality; they then base their buying behavior on incorrect information. Problems follow, and the unintended, unexpected, and undesirable effects of price ceilings soon occur.

ⓣhinking like **AN ECONOMIST**

Look for the Unintended Effects   Economists think in terms of unintended effects. For example, a price ceiling policy intended to lower prices for the poor may cause shortages, the use of nonprice rationing devices, illegal market transactions, and tie-in sales. When we consider both the price ceiling and its effects, whether the poor have been helped is not so clear. The economist knows that wanting to do good (for others) is not sufficient. Knowing how to do good is important too. ▰▰▰

Price Floor: Definition and Effects

A price floor is a government-mandated minimum price below which legal trades cannot be made. For example, suppose the government mandates that the minimum price at which good X can be sold is $20. The $20 minimum is a price floor (see Exhibit 3).

EFFECTS OF A PRICE FLOOR   If the price floor is above the equilibrium price, the following two effects arise:[2] surpluses and fewer exchanges.

Surpluses   At the $15 equilibrium price in Exhibit 3, the quantity demanded of good X (130) is equal to the quantity supplied (130). At the $20 price floor, a surplus exists.

The quantity supplied (180) is greater than the quantity demanded (90). Usually, a surplus is temporary. When a surplus exists, price and output tend to fall to equilibrium. But when a price floor exists, they cannot because it is unlawful to trade at the equilibrium price.

Price Floor
A government-mandated minimum price below which legal trades cannot be made.

---

2. If the price floor is below the equilibrium price (say, $20 is the price floor and $25 is the equilibrium price), it has no effects. Usually, however, a price floor is above the equilibrium price.

A Price Ceiling in the Kidney Market

Just as some people want to buy houses, computers, and books, others want to buy kidneys. These people have kidney failure, and they will either die without a new kidney or have to endure years of costly and painful dialysis. This demand for kidneys is shown as D_K in Exhibit 2, and the supply of kidneys is shown as S_K.

Notice that at $0 price, the quantity supplied of kidneys is 350. These kidneys are from people who donate their kidneys to others, asking nothing in return. They may donate upon their death, or they may donate one of their two kidneys while living. We have drawn the supply curve as upward sloping because we assume that some people who today are unwilling to donate a kidney for $0 might be willing to do so for some positive dollar amount. Specifically, we assume that as the price of a kidney rises, the quantity supplied of kidneys will rise.

GALINA BARSKAYA, 2009. USED UNDER LICENSE FROM SHUTTERSTOCK.COM

If there were a free market in kidneys, the price of a kidney would be P_1 in Exhibit 2. At this price, 1,000 kidneys would be purchased and sold; that is, 1,000 kidney transplants would occur.

Today, there is no free market in kidneys. Buying or selling kidneys is illegal at any dollar amount. In essence, then, there is a price ceiling in the kidney market, and the ceiling is set at $0. What is the effect of the ceiling?

If the demand curve for kidneys and the supply curve of kidneys intersected at $0, there would be neither a surplus nor a shortage of kidneys. But there is evidence that the demand and supply curves do not intersect at $0; they look more like those shown in Exhibit 2. In other words, there is a shortage of kidneys at $0: The quantity supplied of kidneys is 350, and the quantity demanded is 1,500. (Although these are not the actual numbers of kidneys demanded and supplied at $0, they are representative of the current situation in the kidney market.)

This chapter has described the possible effects of a price ceiling set below equilibrium price: shortages, nonprice-rationing devices, fewer exchanges, tie-in sales, and buying and selling at prohibited prices (in other words, illegal trades). Are any of these effects occurring in the kidney market?

First, there is evidence of a shortage. In almost every country in the world, more people on national lists want a kidney than there are kidneys available. Some of these people die waiting for a transplant.

EXHIBIT 2

The Market for Kidneys

We have identified the demand for kidneys as D_K and the supply of kidneys as S_K. Given the demand for and supply of kidneys, the equilibrium price of a kidney is P_1. It does not follow, though, that simply because there is an equilibrium price, people will be allowed to trade at this price. Today, it is unlawful to buy and sell kidneys at any positive price. In short, there is a price ceiling in the kidney market and the ceiling is $0. At the price ceiling, there is a shortage of kidneys, a nonprice rationing device for kidneys (first-come-first-served), fewer kidney transplants (than there would be at P_1), and illegal purchases and sales of kidneys.

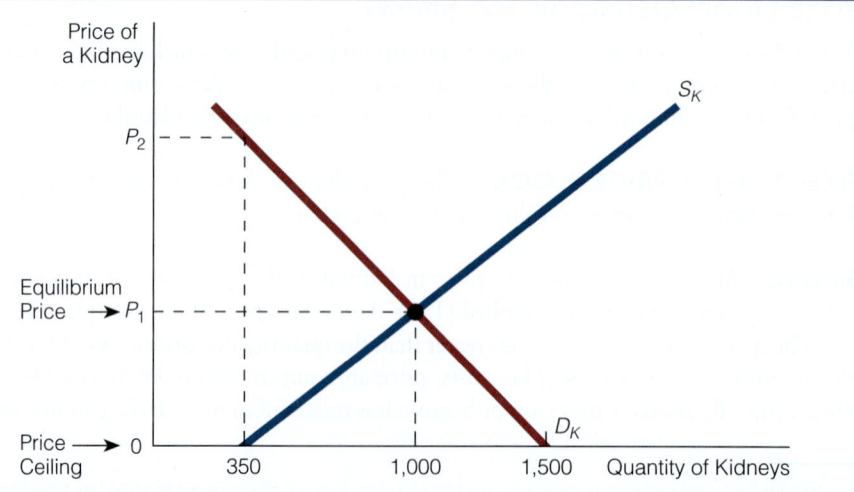

Second, as just indicated, the nonprice rationing device used in the kidney market is (largely) first-come-first-served. A person who wants a kidney registers on a national waiting list. How long people wait is a function of how far down the list their names appear.

Third, there are fewer exchanges; not everyone who needs a kidney gets one. With a price ceiling of $0, only 350 kidneys are supplied. All these kidneys are from people who freely donate their kidneys. If P_1 were permitted, some people who are unwilling to supply a kidney (at $0) would be willing to do so. In short, monetary payment would provide the incentive for some people to supply a kidney. At P_1, 1,000 kidneys are demanded and supplied; so more people would get kidney transplants when the price of a kidney is P_1 (1,000 in all) than when the price of a kidney is $0 (350 in total). More transplants, of course, means fewer people die waiting for a kidney.

Fourth, kidneys are bought and sold at prohibited prices. People buy and sell kidneys today; they just do so illegally. People are reported to have paid between $25,000 and $200,000 for a kidney.

Some people argue that a free market in kidneys would be wrong. Such a system would place the poor at a disadvantage. Think of it: A rich person who needed a kidney could buy one, but a poor person could not. The rich person would get a second chance at life, whereas the poor person would not. No one enjoys contemplating this stark reality.

But consider another stark reality. If it is unlawful to pay someone for a kidney, fewer kidneys will be forthcoming. In other words, the quantity supplied of kidneys is less at $0 than at, say, $20,000. Fewer kidneys supplied means fewer kidney transplants. And fewer kidney transplants means more people will die from kidney failure.

Fewer Exchanges At the equilibrium price in Exhibit 3, 130 units of good X are bought and sold. At the price floor, 90 units are bought and sold. (Sellers want to sell 180 units, but buyers buy only 90.) Thus price floors cause fewer exchanges to be made.

THE MINIMUM WAGE If a price floor is a legislated minimum price below which trades cannot legally be made, then the *minimum wage* is a price floor—a government-mandated minimum price for labor. It affects the market for unskilled labor. In Exhibit 4, we assume the minimum wage is W_M and the equilibrium wage is W_E. At the equilibrium wage, N_1 workers are employed. At the higher minimum wage, N_3 workers want to work, but only N_2 actually do work. There is a surplus of workers equal to $N_3 - N_2$ in this unskilled labor market. In addition, fewer workers are working at the minimum wage (N_2) than at the equilibrium wage (N_1). Overall, the effects of the minimum wage are (1) a surplus of unskilled workers and (2) fewer workers employed.

Suppose two economists decide to test the theory that as the minimum wage rises, some unskilled workers will lose their jobs. They look at the number of unskilled workers before and after the minimum wage is raised, and surprisingly they find that the number of unskilled workers is the same. Is this sufficient evidence to conclude that an increase in the minimum wage does not cause some workers to lose their jobs?

The answer to that question depends on whether the economists

EXHIBIT 3

A Price Floor

The price floor is $20 and the equilibrium price is $15. At $15, quantity demanded = quantity supplied. At $20, quantity supplied > quantity demanded.

A price floor creates a surplus.

EXHIBIT 4

Effects of the Minimum Wage

At a minimum wage of W_M an hour, there is a surplus of workers and fewer workers are employed than would be at the equilibrium wage W_E.

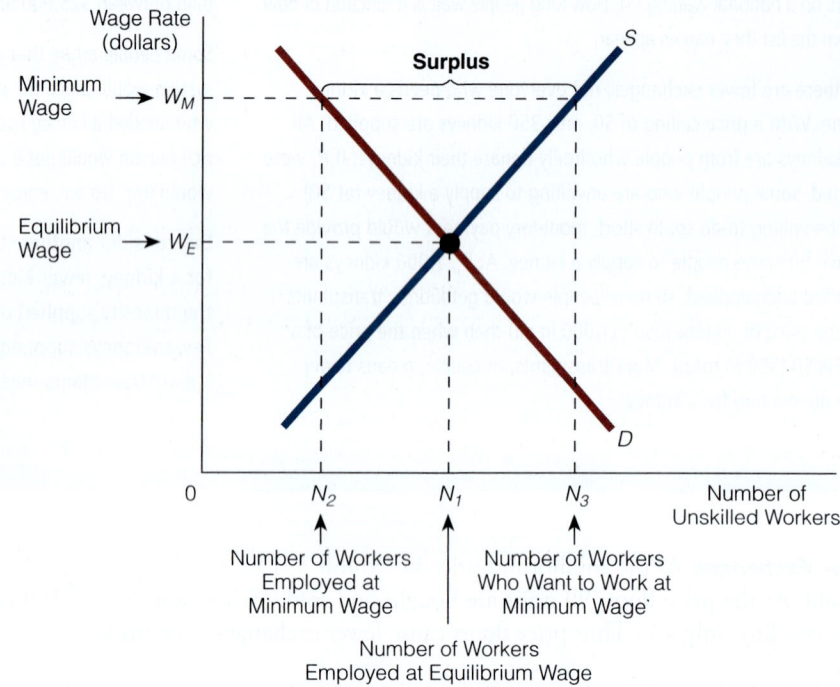

have adequately tested their theory. Instead of focusing on the number of people who lose their jobs, suppose they look at the number of people who keep their jobs but have their hours reduced as a result of the higher minimum wage. Let's look at an example. Suppose a local hardware store currently employs David and Francesca to work after school cleaning up and stocking shelves. The owner of the store pays each of them the minimum wage of, say, $7.25 an hour. Then the minimum wage is raised to $8.75 an hour. Will either David or Francesca lose their jobs as a result? Not necessarily. Instead, the owner of the store could reduce the number of hours he employs the two workers. For example, instead of having each of them work 20 hours a week, he might ask each to work only 14 hours a week.

Now let's reconsider our original question: Has the higher minimum wage eliminated jobs? In a way, no. It has, however, reduced the number of hours a person works in a job. (Of course, if we define a job as including both a particular task and a certain number of hours completing that task, then the minimum wage increase has eliminated "part" of the job.) This discussion argues for changing the label on the horizontal axis in Exhibit 4 from "Number of Unskilled Workers" to "Number of Unskilled Labor Hours."

thinking like AN ECONOMIST

Direction Versus Magnitude In economics, some questions relate to direction and some to magnitude. For example, suppose someone asks, "If the demand for labor is downward sloping and the labor market is competitive, how will a minimum wage that is above the equilibrium wage affect employment?" This person is asking a question that relates to the direction of the change in employment. Usually, these types of questions can be answered by applying a theory. Applying the theory of demand, an economist might say, "At higher wages, the quantity demanded of labor, or the employment level, will be lower than at lower wages." The word "lower" speaks to the *directional change* in employment.

(continued)

ⓣhinking like AN ECONOMIST (continued)

Now suppose someone asks, "How much will employment decline?" This question relates to *magnitude*. Usually, questions that deal with magnitude can be answered only through some kind of empirical (data-collecting and analyzing) work. In other words, we would have to collect employment figures at the equilibrium wage and at the minimum wage and then find the difference. ●●●

PRICE FLOORS, CHANGES IN CONSUMERS' AND PRODUCERS' SURPLUS, AND DEADWEIGHT LOSSES We now turn to a discussion of consumers' surplus, producers' surplus, and price floors in terms of a specific example: a price floor on an agricultural foodstuff.

Exhibit 5 shows the demand for and supply of an agricultural foodstuff (corn, wheat, soybeans, etc.). If the market is allowed to move to equilibrium, the equilibrium price will be P_1, and the equilibrium quantity will be Q_1. Consumers' surplus will equal the area under the demand curve and above the equilibrium price: areas 1 + 2 + 3. Producers' surplus will equal the area under the equilibrium price and above the supply curve: areas 4 + 5. Total surplus, of course, is the sum of consumers' surplus and producers' surplus: areas 1 + 2 + 3 + 4 + 5.

Now suppose that the suppliers of the foodstuff argue for (and receive) a price floor, P_F. At this higher price, consumers do not buy as much as they once did. They now buy Q_2, whereas they used to buy Q_1. In addition, consumers' surplus is now only area 1, and producers' surplus is areas 2 + 4.

Obviously, consumers have been hurt by the increased (government-mandated) price of P_F; specifically, they have lost consumers' surplus equal to areas 2 + 3.

How have suppliers fared? Whereas their producers' surplus was equal to areas 4 + 5 at P_1, it is now equal to areas 2 + 4. (Area 2, which used to be part of consumers' surplus, has been transferred to producers and is now part of producers' surplus.) Whether producers are better off depends on whether area 2 (what they gain from P_F) is larger than area 5 (what they lose from P_F). Visually, we can tell that area 2 is larger than area 5; so producers are better off.

What is the overall effect of the price floor? Have producers gained more than consumers have lost, or have consumers lost more than producers have gained? To answer this question, we note that consumers lose areas 2 + 3 in consumers' surplus; producers gain area 2 in producers' surplus and lose area 5 in producers' surplus. So the gains and losses are:

Losses to consumers: areas 2 + 3

Gains to producers: area 2

Losses to producers: area 5

Part of the loss to consumers is offset by the gain to producers (area 2); so net losses amount to areas 3 + 5. In other words, the total surplus—the sum of consumers' surplus and producers' surplus—is lower than it was. Whereas it used to be areas 1 + 2 + 3 + 4 + 5, it now is areas 1 + 2 + 4. The total surplus lost is in areas 3 + 5. In short, (1) consumers lose, (2) producers gain, and (3) society (which is the sum of consumers and producers) loses.

You can think of this example in terms of a pie. Initially, the pie was made up of areas 1 + 2 + 3 + 4 + 5.

EXHIBIT 5

Agricultural Price Floors

The demand for and supply of an agricultural foodstuff are shown in this exhibit. The equilibrium price is P_1; consumers' surplus (CS) is areas 1 + 2 + 3; producers' surplus is areas 4 + 5. A price floor of P_F effectively transfers some of the consumers' surplus to producers in the form of a gain in producers' surplus. Specifically, at P_F, consumers' surplus is area 1 and producers' surplus is areas 2 + 4. Consumers are net losers because consumers' surplus has decreased by areas 2 + 3. Producers are net gainers because producers' surplus has increased from areas 4 + 5 to areas 2 + 4 and area 2 is larger than area 5. Overall, the economic pie of CS + PS has decreased from areas 1 + 2 + 3 + 4 + 5 to areas 1 + 2 + 4.

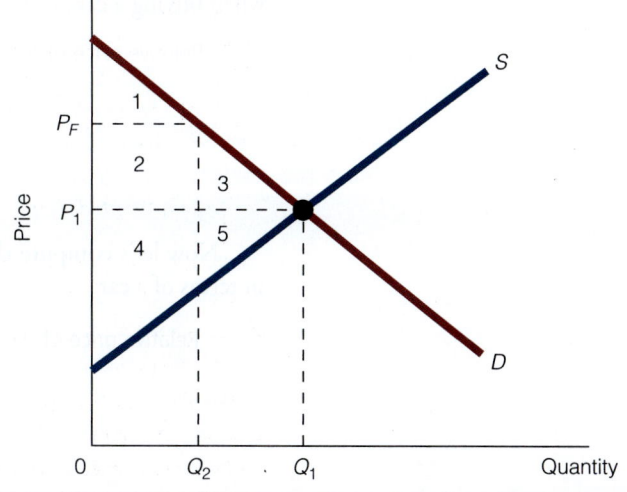

Deadweight Loss.
The loss to society of not producing the competitive, or supply-and-demand-determined, level of output.

This rather large pie registered all the gains of consumers and producers. After the price floor of P_F was imposed, the pie shrank to areas $1 + 2 + 4$; in other words, the pie was smaller by areas $3 + 5$.

A loss in total surplus—in our example, areas $3 + 5$—is sometimes called a deadweight loss. This is the loss to society of not producing the competitive, or supply-and-demand-determined, level of output. In terms of Exhibit 5, it is the loss to society of producing Q_2 instead of producing Q_1.

WHAT SOME PEOPLE GET WRONG In closing, some persons argue that a price floor creates a situation in which (1) someone wins and someone loses and (2) the gains for the winner are equal to the losses for the loser (e.g., one person loses $5, and another person wins $5). A quick look at Exhibit 5 tells us that (2) is not true. The losses (for consumers) are not offset by the gains (for producers). A price ceiling ends with a *net loss,* or *deadweight loss,* of areas $3 + 5$. Now think of how hard it would have been to identify this deadweight loss without the tools of supply, demand, consumers' surplus, and producers' surplus. Economic tools often have the ability to make what is invisible visible.

SELF-TEST

1. Do buyers prefer lower prices to higher prices?

2. "When there are long-lasting shortages, there are long lines of people waiting to buy goods. It follows that the shortages cause the long lines." Do you agree or disagree? Explain your answer.

3. Who might argue for a price ceiling? A price floor?

TWO PRICES: ABSOLUTE AND RELATIVE

In everyday language, we often use the word "price" without specifying the kind of price. Economists often distinguish the *absolute,* or *money, price* of a good from the *relative price* of a good.

Absolute (Money) Price and Relative Price

Absolute (Money) Price
The price of a good in money terms.

Relative Price
The price of a good in terms of another good.

The absolute (money) price is the price of the good in money terms. For example, the absolute price of a car might be $30,000. The relative price is the price of the good *in terms of another good.* To illustrate, suppose the absolute price of a car is $30,000 and the absolute price of a computer is $2,000. The relative price of the car—that is, the price of the car *in terms of computers*—is 15 computers. A person gives up the opportunity to buy 15 computers when buying a car.

$$\text{Relative price of a car (in terms of computers)} = \frac{\text{Absolute price of a car}}{\text{Absolute price of a computer}}$$

$$= \frac{\$30,000}{\$2,000}$$

$$= 15$$

Now let's compute the relative price of a computer—that is, the price of a computer in terms of a car:

$$\text{Relative price of a computer (in terms of cars)} = \frac{\text{Absolute price of a computer}}{\text{Absolute price of a car}}$$

$$= \frac{\$2,000}{\$30,000}$$

$$= \frac{1}{15}$$

Will a Soda Tax Reduce Obesity?

The percentage of the U.S. population that is deemed obese today is higher than it was 20 years ago. Obesity is a health problem; so often we hear proposals directed at trying to reduce the obesity rate in the country. One proposal is to place a tax on high-fat, high-calorie so-called junk food. A similar proposal is to place a tax on soda.

We now know that a tax placed on one good (but not on another) will change the relative prices of the two goods. Placing a tax on good X, but not on good Y, will make good X relatively more expensive and Y relatively cheaper, prompting consumers to purchase relatively less X and relatively more Y.

PAUL BURNS/SHANNON FAGAN/JUPITER IMAGES

Consider a tax placed on soda. We would expect the absolute (money) price of soda to rise. And if the tax is placed only on soda, its relative price will rise too. As soda becomes relatively more expensive, we would expect fewer sodas to be consumed and obesity to decline. Right? Well, fewer sodas might be purchased and consumed, but whether obesity will decline is not so clear. Consider soda and sugared iced tea. Both soda and sugared iced tea are sweet drinks. They might even be substitutes. With this in

mind, suppose the absolute price of a soda is $1 and the absolute price of an iced tea (with sugar) is 50¢. It follows that the relative prices are:

1 soda = 2 sugared iced teas
1 sugared iced tea = ½ soda

Now let's place a tax on soda that drives its price up to $2. The new relative prices for soda and iced tea are:

1 soda = 4 sugared iced teas
1 sugared iced tea = ¼ soda

As a result of the tax on soda, its relative price has risen, but the relative price of sugared iced tea has fallen. We would expect people to consume relatively less soda and relatively more sugared iced tea.

Obesity is lessened by ingesting fewer calories, not the same number or more calories. Simply put, the soda tax might reduce the consumption of sodas, but it doesn't necessarily reduce obesity. The soda tax, although it makes soda relatively more expensive, makes its substitutes (such as sugared iced tea) relatively less expensive and thus makes a rise in the consumption of sugared iced tea likely.

Thus, the relative price of a computer in this example is 1/15 of a car. A person gives up the opportunity to buy 1/15 of a car when buying a computer.

Now consider this question: What happens to the relative price of a good if its absolute price rises and nothing else changes? For example, if the absolute price of a car rises from $30,000 to $40,000, what happens to its relative price? Obviously, the relative price rises from 15 computers to 20 computers. In short, if the absolute price of a good rises and nothing else changes, then its relative price rises too.

ⓣhinking like AN ECONOMIST

Higher Absolute Price Can Sometimes Mean Lower Relative Price Economists know that a good can go up in price at the same time as it becomes relatively cheaper. How can this happen? Suppose the absolute price of a pen is $1, and the absolute price of a pencil is 10¢. The relative price of 1 pen, then, is 10 pencils.

(continued)

thinking like AN ECONOMIST (continued)

Now let the absolute price of a pen rise to $1.20 at the same time that the absolute price of a pencil rises to 20¢. As a result, the relative price of 1 pen falls to 6 pencils. In other words, the absolute price of pens rises (from $1 to $1.20) at the same time as pens become relatively cheaper (in terms of how many pencils you have to give up to buy a pen).

How does this happen? The absolute price of pen went up by 20 percent (from $1 to $1.20) at the same time as the absolute price of pencils doubled (from 10¢ to 20¢). Because the absolute price of a pen went up by *less than* the absolute price increase of a pencil, the relative price of a pen fell. ● ● ●

Taxes on Specific Goods and Relative Price Changes

Suppose that the equilibrium price of good X is $10 and that the equilibrium price of good Y is $20. The relative price of good X is therefore ½ unit of good Y, and the relative price of good Y is 2 units of good X.

$$1X = \tfrac{1}{2}Y$$

$$1Y = 2X$$

Given these relative prices of X and Y, consumers will buy some combination of the two goods. For example, a given consumer might end up buying 10 units of X each week and 12 units of Y.

Now suppose that the government imposes a tax only on the purchase of good X. The tax effectively raises the price the consumer pays for the good from $10 to $15. Because no tax is placed on good Y, its price remains at $20.

The tax thus changes the relative prices of the two goods. The after-tax relative prices are:

$$1X = \tfrac{3}{4}Y$$

$$1Y = 1.33X$$

Comparing the new relative prices with the old relative prices, we recognize that the tax makes X relatively more expensive (going from ½Y to ¾Y) and makes Y relatively cheaper (going from 2X to 1.33X). In other words, a tax placed only on X ends up making X relatively more expensive and Y relatively cheaper. As a result, we would expect consumers to buy relatively less X and relatively more Y. Think in terms of two familiar goods: Coke and Pepsi. A tax placed on Coke, but not on Pepsi, will induce consumers to buy relatively less Coke and relatively more Pepsi.

SELF-TEST

1. If the absolute (or money) price of good A is $40 and the absolute price of good B is $60, what is the relative price of each good?

2. Someone says, "The price of good X has risen; so good X is more expensive than it used to be." In what sense is this statement correct? In what sense is this statement either incorrect or misleading?

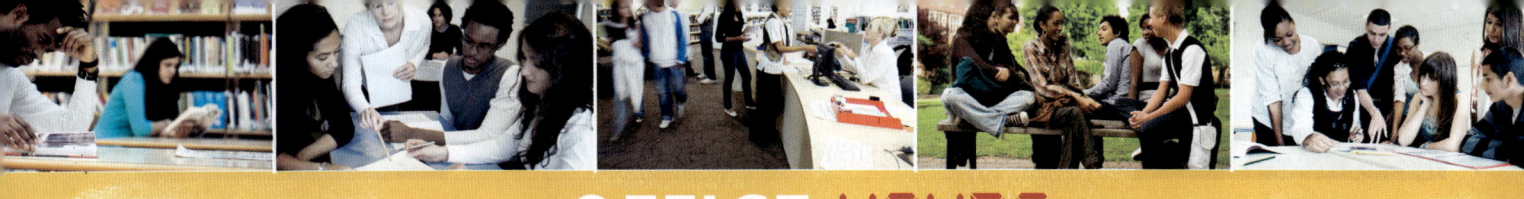

OFFICE HOURS

"I Thought Price Ceilings Were Good for Consumers"

STUDENT:

I still don't quite understand how a price ceiling can hurt consumers. After all, a price ceiling is usually set below the equilibrium price of a good, and everyone knows that consumers prefer lower prices to higher prices.

INSTRUCTOR:

The problem is that when a price ceiling is imposed on a good, certain things happen that don't benefit consumers. Look at it this way: Consumers like the lower price that goes along with the price ceiling, but what they don't like are some of the effects of the price ceiling.

STUDENT:

But it seems to me that if you picked 100 consumers at random and asked them whether they preferred the price of bread to be $1 a loaf as opposed to $2, all 100 consumers would say they prefer the lower price. Because a price ceiling is usually lower than the equilibrium price, doesn't this example prove that consumers benefit from price ceilings? After all, why would they say they prefer paying $1 than $2 for a loaf of bread if they didn't see it benefiting them?

INSTRUCTOR:

A couple of things could be going on here. First, consumers might intuitively take the question to mean do they prefer the *$1 supply-and-demand-determined price* to the *$2 supply-and-demand-determined price*. If this is how they understand the question, then it certainly seems reasonable for them to say they prefer the lower price to the higher price. You might not get the same response from consumers, though, if you asked them this question:

Which of the following two options do you prefer?

Option A:
 $2 (equilibrium) price of bread

Option B:
 $1 (price ceiling) price of bread +
 shortages of bread +
 lines of people waiting to buy bread, and so on.

STUDENT:

In other words, your point is that consumers prefer lower to higher prices, assuming that nothing else changes but the price of the good. But if lower prices as the result of price ceilings come with shortages and long lines of people waiting to buy bread, then they may not prefer lower to higher prices.

INSTRUCTOR:

Yes, that is the point.

STUDENT:

A slightly different question: Do you think all consumers know the adverse effects of price ceilings?

INSTRUCTOR:

Probably not. In fact, even after government imposes a price ceiling and certain adverse effects set in (shortages, long lines, etc.), consumers may fail to relate the cause to the effects of the price ceiling. In other words, X causes Y, but individuals either don't understand how (so they don't connect the two), or they believe that something else—Z—causes Y.

POINTS TO REMEMBER

1. Consumers may prefer a lower to higher price, *ceteris paribus*, but not a lower price with shortages to a higher price without shortages.
2. X may cause Y, but it doesn't necessarily follow that everyone will understand that X causes Y.

CHAPTER SUMMARY

PRICE

- As a result of scarcity, a rationing device is needed to determine who gets what of the available limited resources and goods. Price serves as a rationing device.

- Price acts as a transmitter of information relating to the change in the relative scarcity of a good.

PRICE CEILINGS

- A price ceiling is a government-mandated maximum price. If a price ceiling is below the equilibrium price, some or all of the following effects arise: shortages, fewer exchanges, nonprice-rationing devices, buying and selling at prohibited prices, and tie-in sales.

- Consumers do not necessarily prefer (lower) price ceilings to (higher) equilibrium prices. They may prefer higher prices and none of the effects of price ceilings to lower prices and some of the effects of price ceilings. All we can say for sure is that consumers prefer lower prices to higher prices, *ceteris paribus*.

PRICE FLOORS

- A price floor is a government-mandated minimum price. If a price floor is above the equilibrium price, the following effects arise: surpluses and fewer exchanges.

ABSOLUTE PRICE AND RELATIVE PRICE

- The absolute price of a good is the price of the good in terms of money.

- The relative price of a good is the price of the good in terms of another good.

KEY TERMS AND CONCEPTS

Price Ceiling
Tie-in Sale

Price Floor
Deadweight Loss

Absolute (Money) Price

Relative Price

QUESTIONS AND PROBLEMS

1. Should grades in an economics class be "rationed" according to dollar price instead of how well a student does on the exams? If they were and prospective employers learned of this, what effect might this have on the value of your college degree?

2. Think of ticket scalpers at a rock concert, a baseball game, and an opera. Might they exist because the tickets to these events were originally sold for less than the equilibrium price? Why or why not? In what way is a ticket scalper like and unlike your retail grocer, who buys food from a wholesaler and then sells it to you?

3. What kind of information does price transmit?

4. Many of the proponents of price ceilings argue that government-mandated maximum prices simply reduce producers' profits and do not affect the quantity supplied of a good on the market. What must the supply curve look like if the price ceiling does not affect the quantity supplied?

5. "If price were outlawed as the rationing device (used in markets), there would be no need for another rationing device to take its place. We would have reached utopia." Discuss.

6. Buyers always prefer lower prices to higher prices. Do you agree or disagree with this statement? Explain your answer.

7. Give a numerical example that illustrates how a tax placed on the purchase of good X can change the relative price of good X in terms of Y.

8. Explain why fewer exchanges are made when a disequilibrium price (below equilibrium price) exists than when the equilibrium price exists.

9. If the absolute price of good X is $10 and the absolute price of good Y is $14, then what is (a) the relative price of good X in terms of good Y and (b) the relative price of good Y in terms of good X?

10. James lives in a rent-controlled apartment and has for the past few weeks been trying to get the supervisor to fix his shower. What does waiting to get one's shower fixed have to do with a rent-controlled apartment?

11. What is the difference between a price ceiling and a price floor? What effect is the same for both a price ceiling and a price floor?

1. In the diagram, what areas represent the deadweight loss due to the price ceiling (P_C)?

2. In the preceding diagram, what areas represent consumers' surplus at the equilibrium price of P_E? At P_C? (Keep in mind that the equilibrium quantity is not produced and sold at P_C.)

CHAPTER 5

CPHOTO | DREAMSTIME.COM

SUPPLY, DEMAND, AND PRICE: APPLICATIONS

Introduction In the previous two chapters, we discussed supply, demand, and price. In this chapter, we work with supply, demand, and price. The theory of supply and demand is not very useful to you unless you can use it to explain some of the things you see around you in everyday life. In this chapter, we discuss medical care, changing house prices, college classes at 10 a.m., driving on a freeway, standardized tests (such as the SAT), college athletes, and more—all in the general framework of supply and demand.

APPLICATION 1: WHY IS IT SO HARD TO GET TICKETS TO THE TAPING OF *THE BIG BANG THEORY*

If you go to tvtickets.com, you can request tickets to view the taping of television shows. There is no charge for the ticket; the ticket price is zero. Now ask yourself whether a zero price is the market equilibrium price. Given some degree of positive demand to see the show, you would think that the market equilibrium price would be positive. You would also expect the market equilibrium ticket price to be higher for some shows than for others.

To illustrate, suppose the supply of seats in a TV studio is 200 seats. Three shows are taped in the studio. Will the market equilibrium price for the three shows be the same—say, $20? It could be, but more probably it is not because the demand for each of the three shows is likely to be different. The equilibrium price might be $100 for one show, $70 for another show, and $20 for the third show.

But the market equilibrium price is not charged for any of the three shows. Instead, the price of a ticket is zero for all of them. What follows, then, is that there will be a shortage of tickets for each show, with the shortage being larger for some shows than for others. See Exhibit 1.

SONJA FLEMMING/CBS VIA GETTY IMAGES

How will the shortage for each show manifest itself? And how will we know whether the shortage is different for each show? The answer has to do with how easy or hard it is to get a ticket to a show. At the tvtickets.com site, the tickets for some shows are sold out and some are not. For example, getting tickets for *The Big Bang Theory* (CBS) is very difficult. When tickets become available for that show, the first people to place their requests for the show get the tickets. In other words, tickets are rationed on a first-come-first-served basis (with the exception of persons who might know someone in the cast of the show). Because of the popularity of *The Big Bang Theory*, tickets go quickly.

Of course, tickets don't go as quickly for all other shows. For instance, the demand for new-show tickets is sometimes less than the supply. When this happens, the market equilibrium price might actually be negative. For example, in Exhibit 2, the demand for seats to a new show and the supply of seats for it intersect at a negative price (–$20). The producers of the show would actually have to pay people to watch a taping, specifically, $20. More often than not, however, producers don't pay people.

How, then, do they deal with the surplus of seats that would exist at the zero price (see Exhibit 2). Often they ask friends and family members to do them a favor and come to the taping of the show. As the show gains real fans, the demand to see the show rises, and there may no longer be any surplus seats at a zero ticket price. Of course, if the problem of surplus seats doesn't go away, you can bet that the TV show will.

EXHIBIT 1

The Supply and Demand for Viewing the Taping of Different TV Shows

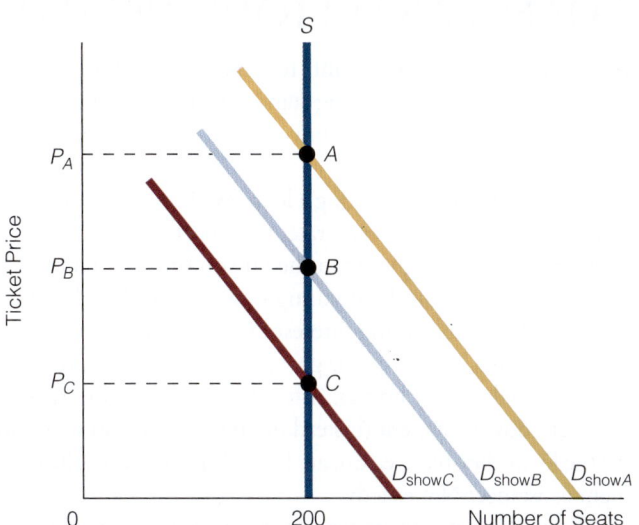

We show the demand to view the taping of three TV shows: *A*, *B*, and *C*. We also show the supply of seats for each show. If the ticket price for each show is $0, then the shortage will be greater for show *A* than for *B*, and greater for *B* than for *C*. Also, if an equilibrium price were charged for each show, the equilibrium price for show *A* would be greater than for show *B* and greater for *B* than *C*.

EXHIBIT 2

A Negative Price: We'll Pay You to View the Taping of the Show

We have assumed that the demand for seats for the taping of a new TV show is low enough that it intersects the supply of seats at a negative price (–$20). At this point, the producers of the show would have to pay people to view the taping of the show.

SELF-TEST

(Answers to Self-Test questions are in Answers to Self-Test Questions at the back of the book.)

1. How can a television network that produces a number of television shows gauge the popularity of each show from ticket requests and the rate at which tickets sell out?

2. Could television networks charge a positive ticket price for the taping of their shows if they wanted to? Explain your answer.

APPLICATION 2: GOVERNMENT, EASIER LOANS, AND HOUSING PRICES

If the federal government wants to make it easier for people to buy houses, one thing it can do is push for lowered lending standards. For example, suppose lenders require individuals who want a mortgage loan to buy a house to make a down payment of 20 percent of the sale price. The government passes a law stating that no lender can require more than a 5 percent down payment before granting a loan. Will this make it easier for individuals to buy homes? Not necessarily. The interest rate on a mortgage loan that requires only a 5 percent down payment might be higher than the rate on one that requires a 20 percent down payment.

Can government do anything now? It could undertake specific monetary actions that have the effect of lowering interest rates (we will discuss this in detail in a later chapter).

Then what happens? The government seems to have met its objective of making it easier for individuals to buy houses. After all, prospective buyers now have only to come up with a 5 percent down payment (instead of 20 percent), and they end up paying lower interest rates for the loans they receive. So, are home buyers necessarily better off with this kind of government assistance? Not exactly.

By making mortgage loans easier to get, the government has indirectly increased the demand for houses. As the demand for houses rises, so do house prices. In short, making it easier to get home mortgage loans (as described) results in rising home prices, which makes buying a house all the harder.

Lower down payments + Lower interest rates → Easier-to-obtain loans → Higher demand for houses → Higher house prices

The main point is simply this: Government set out to make buying a home easier for more people by passing laws that forced lenders to accept lower down payments and by undertaking actions to put downward pressure on interest rates. But making it easier for individuals to get loans had the effect of raising the demand for and the prices of houses. Higher house prices made it harder for people to buy homes.

Continuing on with the story, suppose government now states that individuals need even more help now to get a home because housing prices have risen. In its attempt to help people to buy a house, it pushes for even lower lending standards (maybe requiring only a 1 percent down payment) and lower interest rates. Will that do the trick? Not likely. The lower lending standards and interest rates are likely to stimulate greater demand for housing, leading to even higher housing prices.

SELF-TEST

1. If lowering lending standards can indirectly raise housing prices, can increasing lending standards lower housing prices? Explain.

2. Suppose anyone who buys a house in year 1 gets to pay $1,000 less in income taxes (assuming the tax owed is greater than $1,000). Would the tax credit affect house prices? Explain your answer.

APPLICATION 3: SOUTHWEST AIRLINES AND THE PRICE OF AN AISLE SEAT

Most airlines will reserve an assigned seat for you when you buy a ticket. For example, if you want to buy an airline ticket from U.S. Airways, you can go online, purchase the ticket, and then look at a graphic that shows unreserved seats. If seat 13A is the one you want and no one has chosen it, then it is yours if you click it.

Southwest Airlines does things differently. You do not reserve a seat when you book a flight. You choose a seat when you board the plane. If you are one of the first to board, you have your pick of many seats; if you are one of the last, you have your pick of very few seats.

Keep in mind that aisle seats are more popular than middle seats. Usually, for every aisle seat there is a middle seat (assuming that the row of seats on each side of the plane consists of 3 seats: window, middle, and aisle). So, if the plane has 50 aisle seats, it also has 50 middle seats. In other words, the supply of middle seats equals the supply of aisle seats.

However, the demand for aisle seats is higher than the demand for middle seats. If price were to equilibrate the middle seats market and the aisle seats market, we would expect the price of an aisle seat to be higher than that of a middle seat. See Exhibit 3.

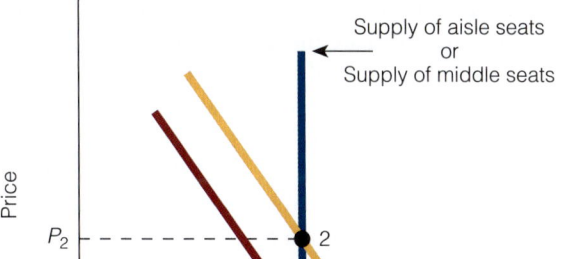

EXHIBIT 3

The Market for Middle and Aisle Seats on Airline Flights

We have assumed that the supply of aisle seats is equal to the supply of middle seats. Because the demand for aisle seats is higher than the demand for middle seats, we conclude that the equilibrium price for an aisle seat is higher than the equilibrium price for a middle seat. In the diagram, P_2 is *the equilibrium price for an aisle seat, and P_1 is the equilibrium price for a middle seat.*

Does Southwest charge more for an aisle seat than a middle seat? Perhaps if you asked the airline this question, its answer would be no. But Southwest does charge more for priority boarding. If you want to board before others, you must choose the Business Select option when purchasing a ticket. If you board before others, you obviously have a larger selection of seats to choose from than later boarders do. Because most people prefer aisle to middle seats, persons who board the plane first will probably choose the aisle seats.

So does Business Select come with an additional charge? Yes. On the day we checked, the added charge was $20. In effect, Southwest was charging $20 more for an aisle seat than a middle seat, as we would expect, because the demand for aisle seats is higher than the demand for middle seats, whereas the supply of each is the same.

SELF-TEST

1. If the equilibrium price is $400 for an aisle seat and $350 for a middle seat but an airlines company charges $350 for each seat, we would expect a shortage to appear in the aisle seat market. (More people will want aisle seats than there are aisle seats available.) How will the airlines decide who gets an aisle seat?

2. Suppose the supply of aisle, middle, and window seats is each 100 seats but the demand for aisle seats is greater than the demand for window seats, which, in turn, is greater than the demand for middle seats. If the equilibrium price of an aisle seat is $300, where do the equilibrium prices of middle and window seats stand in relation to this price?

APPLICATION 4: WHY IS MEDICAL CARE SO EXPENSIVE?

Think of how you buy groceries. You go to the store, place certain products in your basket, and then pay for them at the cash register.

Now think of how you buy medical care. You go to the doctor or hospital, give the doctor's office or hospital your health insurance card, perhaps pay a copayment of $10 or $20, and then receive medical care. Your doctor or the hospital bills your insurance company for the bulk of your expenses.

What is the difference between how you buy groceries and how you buy medical care? In the grocery store, only two parties are involved in the transaction: you (the buyer) and the grocery store (the seller). In the medical care example, three parties are involved: you, the doctor or hospital, and the insurance company. The insurance company is often referred to as the "third party." So no third party is involved in the grocery store transaction, but one is involved in purchasing medical care.

The existence of a third party separates the buying of something from the paying for something. In the grocery store, the person who buys the groceries and the person who pays for them are the same (you). In the medical care example, the person who buys and receives the medical care (you) is different from the person or entity that pays for the medical care (the insurance company).

"Wait a minute," you say. "You indirectly pay for your medical care by paying monthly insurance premiums to the medical insurance company." That is partly true, but what happens is like being at a buffet. You pay a set dollar price for the buffet, and then you can eat all you want. Our guess is that at a buffet you eat more than you would if you had to pay for each plateful.

The same often happens with medical care. You pay a set premium to the insurance company (let's say $250 a month), and then you enter the health-care buffet line. Might you end up buying more health care than you would if each doctor visit and lab test at the health-care buffet were priced separately?

Before we continue, let's consider two objections to this analogy.

First, you might say, "But I don't buy medical care as I buy food in the food buffet line. I like shrimp, steak, salads, and desserts, but who likes being x-rayed, being prodded and poked by doctors, and taking medicine? No one buys MRIs as if they were shrimp cocktails."

That objection is true, of course, but it begs the point: Once you get sick and go to the doctor or hospital, the existence of a third party (who pays for your medical care) makes it easier for your doctor and/or the hospital to opt for more medical examinations/procedures and care than you need. For example, a conversation in your doctor's office may go like this:

Doctor: I think you have condition X, but just to be sure let's order some blood tests and get an MRI too.

You: Whatever you think is best.

Now ask yourself how you might respond if you had to pay—out of pocket—for the blood test and MRI. The dialogue might change:

Doctor: I think you have condition X, but just to be sure let's order some blood tests and get an MRI too.

You: How much is this going to cost me, doctor? And is all this really necessary?

The point is simple: Once you have paid your insurance premium, the price you pay for medical care amounts only to your copayment (which is usually minimal). For all practical purposes, the dollar amount you pay for medical care, out of pocket, is close to zero—a fairly low price for health care. We can expect that the quantity demanded of medical care would be greater at zero than at some positive dollar amount.

Second, let's link the *quantity demanded* for medical care in general (which is high if the price of medical care is zero) with the *demand for specific items* that make up medical care. (In our food buffet example, we would link the *quantity demanded* of food with the *demand* for specific food items—shrimp, chocolate ice cream, a Caesar's salad, and the like.)

If the quantity demanded of medical care is higher at a zero price than at some positive price, then we would expect the demand for the *specific items* that make up medical care to be higher than it would be if the quantity demanded of medical care were lower. This is shown diagrammatically in Exhibit 4. In Exhibit 4(a), the demand for medical care is downward sloping. If the price is zero for health care, then the quantity demanded of medical care is 100 units. But if the price is some positive dollar amount (such as P_1), then the quantity demanded of medical care is 50 units.

Exhibit 4(b) does not show the demand for medical care in general, just the demand for a specific item of medical care—x-rays. Of the two demand curves in panel (b), the first (D_1) is the demand that exists for x-rays if the *quantity demanded of medical care* is

EXHIBIT 4

The Price of Medical Care and the Demand for X-rays

(a) If the price of medical care is low (say, zero), the quantity demanded of medical care is 100

units. If the price of medical care for you is P_1, the quantity demanded of medical care is 50 units. (b) The lower the price of medical care and the higher the quantity demanded of

medical care in panel (a), then the higher the demand curve for x-rays in (b). (c) The higher the demand for x-rays, the higher the price of x-rays.

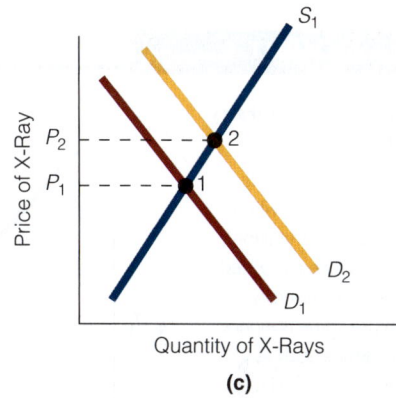

(a)   (b)   (c)

50 units in panel (a); it is the demand for x-rays if the price for medical care (shown in panel a) is P_1. The second demand curve (D_2) is the demand curve for x-rays if the *quantity demanded of medical care* is 100 units in panel (a); it is the demand for x-rays if the price for medical care (shown in panel a) is zero.

Here is the point in a nutshell:

- The *lower* the price of medical care, the higher the quantity demanded of medical care and the higher the demand for x-rays.

Price of medical care is low → Quantity demanded of medical care is high → Demand for x-rays is high

- The *higher* the price of medical care, the lower the quantity demanded of medical care and the lower the demand for x-rays.

Price of medical care is high → Quantity demanded of medical care is low → Demand for x-rays is low

Now the question is what does a high demand for x-rays do to the price of an x-ray? Obviously, it pushes the price upward. See Exhibit 4(c).

As a result, the health insurance company finds itself paying more for the x-rays you receive. Can you see what will happen next? The health insurance company makes the argument that with rising medical costs, the premiums for your coverage need to rise too.

Why is health insurance as expensive as it is? You now have a large part of the answer. Think buffet.

SELF-TEST

1. Suppose food insurance exists. You pay the food insurance company a certain dollar amount each month and then you purchase all the food you want from your local grocery store. The grocery store sends the bill to your food insurance company. What will happen to

the price of food and to the premium you pay for food insurance?

2. In Exhibit 4(a), suppose that the price a person has to pay for medical care is between P_1 and zero. Where would the demand for x-rays in panel (b) be in relationship to D_1 and D_2?

APPLICATION 5: WHY DO COLLEGES USE GPAS, ACTS, AND SATS FOR PURPOSES OF ADMISSION?

At many colleges and universities, students pay part of the price of their education (in the form of tuition payments), and taxpayers and private donors pay part (by way of tax payments and charitable donations, respectively). Thus, the tuition that students pay to attend colleges and universities is usually less than the equilibrium tuition. To illustrate, suppose a student pays tuition T_1 at a given college or university. As shown in Exhibit 5, T_1 is below the equilibrium tuition, T_E. At T_1, the number of students who want to attend the university (N_1) is greater than the number of openings at the university (N_2); that is, quantity demanded is greater than quantity supplied. The university receives more applications for admission than there are places available. Something has to be done. But what?

The college or university is likely to ration its available space by a combination of money price and some nonprice-rationing devices. The student must pay the tuition, T_1, *and* meet the standards of the nonprice-rationing devices. Colleges and universities typically use such things as GPAs (grade point averages), ACT scores, and SAT scores as rationing devices.

EXHIBIT 5

College and University Admissions

If the college or university charges T_1 in tuition (when T_E is the equilibrium tuition), a shortage will be generated. The college or university will then use some nonprice rationing device, such as GPAs, ACTs, and SATs, as admission criteria.

thinking like AN ECONOMIST

Identifying Rationing Devices The layperson sees a GPA of 3.8 and an SAT score of 1,900 or better as requirements for admission. Economists see them as a rationing device. Economists then go on to ask why this particular nonprice-rationing device is used. They reason that a nonprice-rationing device would not be needed if (dollar) price were fully rationing the good or service. ● ● ●

SELF-TEST

1. The demand rises for admission to a university, but both the tuition and the number of openings in the entering class remain the same. Will this change affect the admission standards of the university? Explain your answer.

2. Administrators and faculty at state colleges and universities often say that their standards of admission are independent of whether there is a shortage or surplus of openings at the university. Do you think this is true? Do you think that faculty and administrators ignore surpluses and shortages of openings when setting admission standards? Explain your answer.

APPLICATION 6 : SUPPLY AND DEMAND ON A FREEWAY

What does a traffic jam on a busy freeway in any large city have to do with supply and demand? Actually, it has quite a bit to do with supply and demand. Look at the question this way: There is a demand for driving on the freeway and a supply of freeway space. The supply of freeway space is fixed (roadways do not expand and contract over a day, week, or month). The demand, however, fluctuates; it is higher at some times than at others. For example, we would expect the demand for driving on the freeway to be higher at 8 a.m. (the rush hour) than at 11 p.m. But even though the demand may vary, the money price for driving on the freeway is always the same: zero. A zero money price means that motorists do not pay tolls to drive on the freeway.

Exhibit 6 shows two demand curves for driving on the freeway: $D_{8\ a.m.}$ and $D_{11\ p.m.}$ We have assumed the demand at 8 a.m. to be greater than at 11 p.m. We have also assumed that at $D_{11\ p.m.}$ and zero money price the freeway market clears: The quantity demanded of freeway space equals the quantity supplied. At the higher demand, $D_{8\ a.m.}$, this is not the case. At zero money price, a shortage of freeway space exists:

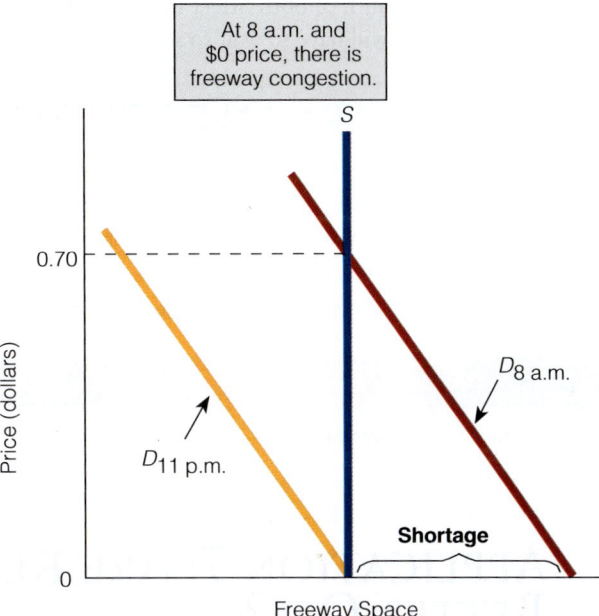

At 8 a.m. and $0 price, there is freeway congestion.

EXHIBIT 6

Freeway Congestion and Supply and Demand

The demand for driving on the freeway is higher at 8 a.m. than at 11 p.m. At zero money price and D_{11} p.m., the freeway market clears. At zero money price and D_8 a.m., there is a shortage of freeway space, which shows up as freeway congestion. At a price (toll) of 70 cents, the shortage is eliminated and freeway congestion disappears.

The quantity demanded of freeway space is greater than the quantity supplied. The shortage appears as freeway congestion and bumper-to-bumper traffic. One way to eliminate the shortage is through an increase in the money price of driving on the freeway at 8 a.m. For example, as Exhibit 6 shows, a toll of 70¢ would clear the freeway market at 8 a.m.

If charging different prices (tolls) depending on the time of day on freeways sounds like an unusual idea, consider how Miami Beach hotels price their rooms. They charge different prices for their rooms depending on time of year. During the winter months, when the demand for vacationing in Miami Beach is high, the hotels charge higher prices than when the demand is (relatively) low. If different prices were charged for freeway space depending on time of day, freeway space would be rationed the same way Miami Beach hotel rooms are rationed.

Finally, consider three alternatives usually proposed to counter freeway congestion:

- *Tolls:* Tolls deal with the congestion problem by adjusting price to its equilibrium level, as shown in Exhibit 6.

- *Building more freeways:* Building more freeways deals with the problem by increasing supply. In Exhibit 6, the supply curve of freeway space would have to be shifted to the right so that there is no longer any shortage of space at 8 a.m.

- *Encouraging carpooling:* More carpooling deals with the problem by decreasing demand. Two people in one car take up less space on a freeway than two people in two cars. In Exhibit 6, if, through carpooling, the demand at 8 a.m. begins to look like the demand at 11 p.m., then there is no longer a shortage of freeway space at 8 a.m.

A final note: A fee to drive in the Central London area was introduced in 2003. Anyone going into or out of the Central London area between 7:00 a.m. and 6:30 p.m., Monday through Friday, must pay a fee of approximately $15. (Not everyone has to pay the fee. For example, taxi drivers, ambulance drivers, police vehicles, motorcycle drivers, and bicyclists are exempt. The residents who live in the area receive a 90 percent discount.) Many people have claimed the fee a success because it has cut down on traffic and travel times and reduced pollution in the area.

Some people have urged New York City to institute a fee program to drive on certain streets in the city. On any given day in New York City, approximately 800,000 cars are on the streets south of 60th Street in Manhattan. According to many, the city is "choking in traffic." We will have to wait to see whether New York City goes the way of London.

ⓣhinking like AN ECONOMIST

It's One of Three The economist knows that when there are buyers and sellers of anything (bread, cars, or freeway space), only three conditions are possible: equilibrium, shortage, or surplus. When the economist sees traffic congestion, the first thing that comes to mind is the shortage of road space. Buy why is there a shortage? The economist knows that shortages occur at prices below equilibrium price. In other words, the price is too low. ▰▰▰

SELF-TEST

1. In Exhibit 6, at what price is there a surplus of freeway space at 8 a.m.?

2. If the driving population increases in an area and the supply of freeway space remains constant, what will happen to freeway congestion? Explain your answer.

APPLICATION 7: ARE RENTERS BETTER OFF?

We begin with an analysis of two laws related to the eviction of a renter.

- Under law 1, a renter has 30 days to vacate an apartment after being served with an eviction notice.

- Under law 2, the renter has 90 days to vacate.

Landlords will find it less expensive to rent apartments under law 1 than under law 2. Under law 1, the most money a landlord can lose after serving an eviction notice is 30 days' rent. Under law 2, a landlord can lose up to 90 days' rent. Obviously, losing 90 days' rent is more costly than losing 30 days' rent.

A different supply curve of apartments exists under each law. The supply curve under law 1 (S_1 in Exhibit 7) lies to the right of the supply curve under law 2 (S_2). It is less expensive to supply apartments under law 1 than under law 2.

If the supply curve is different under the two laws, the equilibrium rent will be different too. As shown in Exhibit 7, the equilibrium rent will be lower under law 1 (R_1) than under law 2 (R_2).

So:

- Under law 1, a renter pays lower rent (good) and has fewer days to vacate the apartment (bad).

- Under law 2, a renter pays a higher rent (bad) and has more days to vacate the apartment (good).

EXHIBIT 7

Apartment Rent and the Law

Under law 1, a renter has 30 days to leave an apartment after receiving an eviction notice from his or her landlord. Under law 2, a renter has 90 days to leave an apartment after receiving an eviction notice from his or her landlord. The cost to the landlord of renting an apartment is higher under law 2 than law 1, and so the supply curve of apartments under law 1 lies to the right of the supply curve of apartments under law 2. Different supply curves mean different rents. Apartment rent is higher under law 2 (R_2) than under law 1 (R_1).

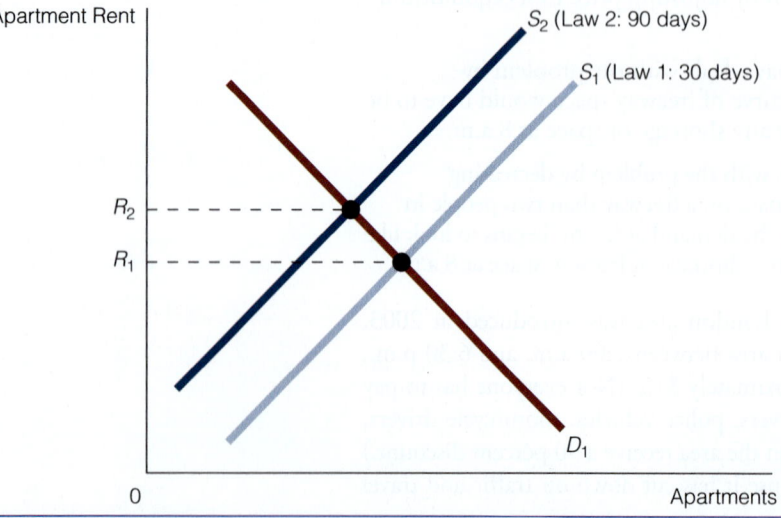

Who pays for the additional days to vacate the apartment under law 2? The renter pays for them by paying a higher rent.

finding ECONOMICS

In an HMO You may frequently hear people complain about their health maintenance organizations (HMOs). Of the diverse and wide-ranging complaints, a common one is that patients cannot sue their HMOs in state courts for denial of benefits and poor-quality care. Some people argue that patients should have the right to sue their HMOs.

Let's consider two settings: one in which patients cannot sue their HMOs and one in which they can. If patients cannot sue, an HMO's liability cost is lower than if patients can sue. A difference in liability costs is then reflected in different supply curves.

To illustrate, recall that any single point on a supply curve is the minimum price sellers need to receive for them to be willing and able to sell that unit of a good. Suppose that when patients cannot sue, an HMO is willing and able to provide health care to John for $300 a month. If patients can sue, is the HMO still willing and able to provide the service for $300 a month? Not likely. Because of the higher liability cost due to patients' ability to sue, the HMO is still willing and able to provide health care to John, but for, say, $350 month, not $300.

Saying that a seller's minimum price for providing a good or service rises is the same as saying the seller's supply curve has shifted upward and to the left. In other words, the supply curve of HMO-provided health-care will shift upward and to the left if patients have the right to sue. This is how the supply curve of apartments moved in Exhibit 7. So, will a difference in supply curves affect the price patients pay for their HMO-provided health-care coverage? Yes. One effect of moving from a setting where patients do not have the right to sue to one where they do is that patients will have to pay more for their HMO-provided health-care coverage.

Economists don't determine whether a patient having the right to sue is good or bad or right or wrong. Economists use their tools (in this instance, supply and demand) to point out that the things people want, such as the right to sue their HMOs, often come with price tags. Individuals must decide whether the price they pay is worth what they receive in return. ▲ ▲ ▲

SELF-TEST

1. Economists often say, "There is no such thing as a free lunch." How is this saying related to patients moving from a system where they cannot sue their HMOs to one where they can?

2. A professor tells her students that they can have an extra week to complete their research papers. Under what condition are the students better off with the extra week? Can you think of a case where the students would actually be worse off with the extra week?

APPLICATION 8: DO YOU PAY FOR GOOD WEATHER?

Some places in the country are considered to have better weather than others. For example, most people would say the weather in San Diego, California, is better than the weather in Fargo, North Dakota. Often, a person in San Diego will say, "You can't beat the weather today. And the good thing about it is that you don't have to pay a thing for it. It's free."

In one sense, the San Diegan is correct: There is no weather market. Specifically, no one comes around each day and asks San Diegans to pay a certain dollar amount for the weather.

But in another sense, the San Diegan is incorrect: San Diegans indirectly do pay for their good weather. How do they pay? To enjoy the weather in San Diego on a regular basis,

EXHIBIT 8

The Price of Weather and Housing Prices

We show two demand curves, D_1 and D_2. D_1 represents the demand for housing in San Diego if the weather were not so good. The higher demand curve D_2 shows the demand for housing in San Diego if the weather is good. Notice that the price of housing in San Diego is higher if the weather is good than not so good. Lesson learned: You pay for good weather (in San Diego) in terms of higher house prices.

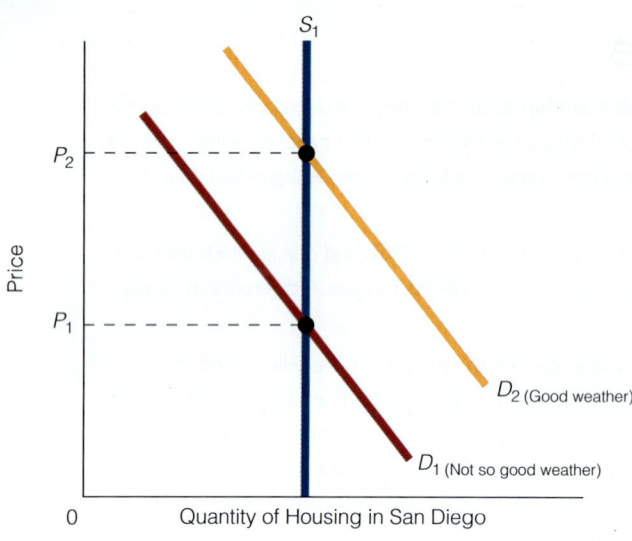

you have to live there; you need to have housing. There is a demand for housing in San Diego just as there is a demand for housing in other places. Is the demand for housing in San Diego higher than it would be if the weather were not so good? Without the good weather, living in San Diego would not be as pleasurable, and therefore the demand to live there would be lower.

See Exhibit 8. In short, the demand for housing in San Diego is higher because the city enjoys good weather. It follows that the price of housing is higher too (P_2 as opposed to P_1 in Exhibit 8). Thus, San Diegans indirectly pay for their good weather because they pay higher housing prices than they would if area had bad weather.

Was our representative San Diegan right when he said the good weather was free?

finding ECONOMICS

Good Schools and House Prices There are two neighborhoods, A and B. The kids who live in neighborhood A go to school A, and the kids who live in neighborhood B go to school B. Currently, school A has a much better academic reputation than school B. Can you find the economics?

This case is really no more than a disguised version of our good weather example. If school A is better than school B, then the equilibrium price of houses in neighborhood A is likely to be higher than the equilibrium price of similar houses in neighborhood B. Just as we pay for good weather in terms of house prices, we pay for good schools in terms of house prices too. ▲▲▲

SELF-TEST

1. Give an example to illustrate that someone may "pay" for clean air in much the same way as she "pays" for good weather.

2. If people pay for good weather, who ultimately receives the "good-weather payment"?

APPLICATION 9: COLLEGE SUPERATHLETES

A young man, 17 years old, is one of the best high school football players in the country. As a superathlete, the young man will be recruited by many college and university football coaches. Every one of those schools will likely want its coach to be successful at signing up the young athlete; after all, at many universities, athletics is a moneymaker.

Our superathlete decides to attend college A, where he receives a "full ride"—a full scholarship. How should this full scholarship be viewed? One way is to say the superathlete is charged zero tuition to attend the college. (In other words, whereas some students pay a price of $30,000 a year to attend, the superathlete pays nothing.)

Another way to view the full scholarship is as a two-step process. First, the college pays the superathlete a dollar amount equal to the full tuition. Second, it charges the superathlete the full tuition. (In other words, the college gives the athlete $30,000 with one hand and then collects it with the other.)

Either way we view the scholarship, the effect is the same for the athlete. For purposes of our analysis, let's view it the second way: as a payment to the athlete combined with full price being charged. This view leads to two important questions:

1. Can the college pay the athlete more than the full tuition? In other words, if the full tuition is $30,000 a year, can the college pay the athlete, say, $35,000 a year?

2. Is the superathlete being paid what he is worth?

Because of NCAA rules, the answer to the first question is essentially no. The NCAA states that a college or university cannot pay a student to attend, and for all practical purposes the NCAA views payment as anything more than a full scholarship. The NCAA position is that college athletes are amateurs, and amateurs cannot be paid to play their sport.

How does the NCAA rule affect the second question? What if the athlete's worth to the college or university is greater than the dollar amount of the full tuition? For example, suppose the athlete will increase the revenues of the college by $100,000 a year, and the full tuition is $30,000 a year. In this case, the NCAA rule is actually a price ceiling (a below-equilibrium imposed price) on what the college may pay an athlete.

What is the effect of this price ceiling? Let's consider the demand (on the part of various colleges) for a single superathlete and the supply of this single superathlete (see Exhibit 9). We assume that the supply curve for athletic services is vertical at 1. If the representative college charges $30,000 in tuition, because of the NCAA rule, this dollar amount is the effective price ceiling (or wage ceiling). If the single athlete's market equilibrium wage is $35,000 and the NCAA rule did not exist, the athlete's wage would rise to $35,000. This dollar amount is equal to areas $B + C$ in Exhibit 9. The consumers' surplus for the college that buys the athlete's services for $35,000 is obviously equal to area A.

However, the NCAA rule stipulates that the college cannot pay the athlete more than $30,000 (full tuition). So the athlete's payment falls from $35,000 to $30,000, or from areas $B + C$ to simply area C. The college's consumers' surplus increases to areas $A + B$. Essentially, the NCAA rule transfers part of the athlete's income—area B—to the college in the form of greater consumers' surplus.

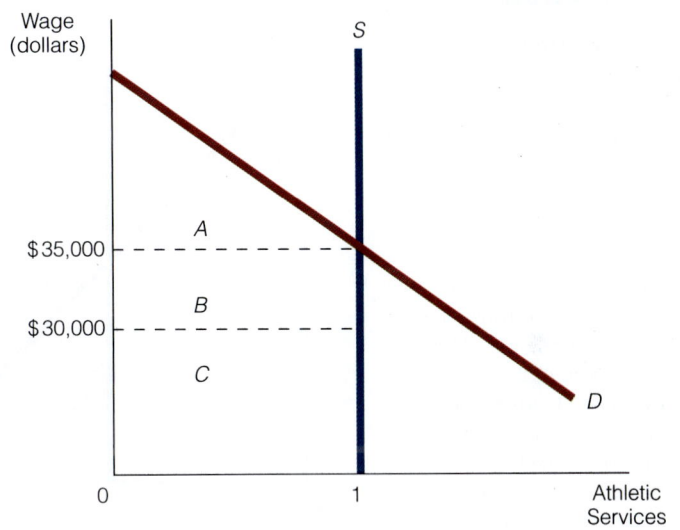

EXHIBIT 9

The College Athlete

The exhibit shows the demand for and supply of a college athlete. If the market wage for the college athlete is $35,000, then the buyer of the athlete—in this case, the college—receives consumers' surplus equal to area A. If the wage can be held down to the tuition cost of attending the college—$30,000 in this example—then the college receives consumers' surplus of areas A + B.

1. University X is a large school with a major football team. A new field house and track were just added to the campus. How is this related to the discussion in this application?

2. Sometimes it is argued that if colleges paid student athletes, the demand for college sports would decline. In other words, the demand for college sports is as high as it is because student athletes are not paid (in the same way as professional athletes are paid). How would the analysis in this application change if we assume this argument to be true?

APPLICATION 10: 10 A.M. CLASSES IN COLLEGE

Suppose an economics class is offered in the same classroom twice in a day: at 10 a.m. in the morning and at 8 p.m. at night. Most students would prefer the 10 a.m. class to the 8 p.m. class. So, in Exhibit 10, the supply of seats in the class is the same at each time, but the demand to occupy those seats is not. Because the demand is greater for the 10 a.m. class than for the 8 p.m. class, the equilibrium price for the morning class is higher than the equilibrium price for the evening class.

But the university or college charges the same tuition no matter what time students choose to take the class. The university doesn't charge students a higher tuition if they enroll in 10 a.m. classes than if they enroll in 8 p.m. classes.

Suppose that tuition T_1 is charged for all classes and that T_1 is the equilibrium tuition for 8 p.m. classes (see Exhibit 10). T_1 is therefore below the equilibrium tuition for 10 a.m. classes. At T_1, the quantity demanded of seats for the morning classes will be greater than the quantity supplied; more students will want the earlier class than there is space available.

How will the university allocate the available seats? It may do it in the same way as airlines ration aisle seats: on a first-come-first-served basis. Students who are first to register get the 10 a.m. class; the latecomers have to take the 8 p.m. class. Or the university could ration the high-demand classes by giving their upper-class students (seniors) first priority.

EXHIBIT 10

The Supply and Demand for College Classes at Different Times

A given class is offered at two times, 10 a.m. and 8 p.m. The supply of seats in the classroom is the same at both times; however, the student demand for the 10 a.m. class is higher than the demand for the 8 p.m. class. The university charges the same tuition, T_1, regardless of which class a student takes. At this tuition, there is a shortage of seats for the 10 a.m. class. Seats are likely to be rationed on a first-come-first-served (first to register) basis or on seniority (seniors take precedence over juniors, etc.).

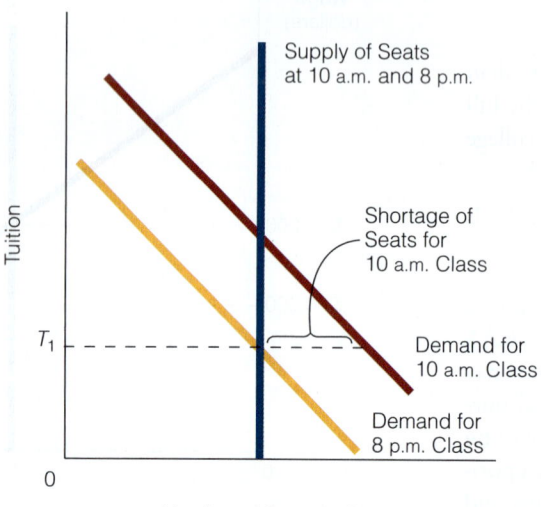

Supply of Seats at 10 a.m. and 8 p.m.

Shortage of Seats for 10 a.m. Class

Demand for 10 a.m. Class

Demand for 8 p.m. Class

Tuition

Number of Seats in Class

thinking like AN ECONOMIST

Remembering Price Laypersons see students clamoring to get 10 a.m. classes and conclude that the demand is high for early classes. They then wonder why the university doesn't schedule more 10 a.m. classes. The economist knows that what laypeople see is as much an effect of price as of demand. The demand for 10 a.m. classes may be high, but the quantity demanded may not be if the price is high enough. In fact, even though the demand for classes at certain times may vary, some set of prices will make the quantity demanded of each class the same. ● ● ●

1. Suppose college students are given two options. With option A, the price a student pays for a class is always the equilibrium price. For example, if the equilibrium price to take Economics 101 is $600 at 10 a.m. and $400 at 4 p.m., then students pay more for the early class than they do for the later class. With option B, the price a student pays for a class is the same regardless of the time the class is taken. When given the choice between options A and B, many students would say they prefer option B to option A. Is this the case for you? If so, why would this be your choice?

2. How is the analysis of the 10 a.m. class similar to the analysis of a price ceiling in a market?

APPLICATION 11: WHAT WILL HAPPEN TO THE PRICE OF MARIJUANA IF THE PURCHASE AND SALE OF MARIJUANA ARE LEGALIZED?

In the United States, the purchase or sale of marijuana is unlawful, but there is still a demand for it and a supply of it. There is also an equilibrium price of marijuana. Let's say that price is P_1. If tomorrow the purchase and sale of marijuana become legal, would P_1 rise, fall, or remain the same?

The answer, of course, depends on what we think will happen to the demand for and supply of marijuana. If the purchase and sale of marijuana are legal, then some people currently producing corn and wheat will likely choose instead to produce and sell marijuana. So the supply of marijuana will rise. If nothing else changes, its price will fall.

But something else is likely to change. If marijuana consumption is no longer illegal, then the number of people who want to buy and consume it will likely rise. In other words, more people will buy marijuana, thus increasing demand.

So decriminalizing the purchase and sale of marijuana is likely to shift both the marijuana demand and supply curves to the right. What happens to the price of marijuana depends on how much the curves shift. Three possibilities exist:

1. The demand curve shifts to the right by the same amount as the supply curve shifts to the right. In this case, the price of marijuana will not change. (Try to visualize the demand and supply curves shifting.)

2. The demand curve shift to the right is greater than the supply curve shift to the right. In this case, the price of marijuana will rise. (Try to visualize the demand curve shifting to the right more than the supply curve does. Can you see the higher price on the vertical axis?)

3. The supply curve shift to the right is greater than the demand curve shift to the right. In this case, the price of marijuana will fall.

If you can't visualize the shifts of the demand and supply curves for these three possibilities, draw the original demand and supply curves, then draw the shift in each curve, and identify the new equilibrium price.

SELF-TEST

1. What will happen to the price of marijuana if the supply increases by more than the demand for it?

2. What will happen to the quantity of marijuana (purchased and sold) if the demand for it rises more than its supply falls.

OFFICE HOURS

"Doesn't High Demand Mean High Quantity Demanded?"

STUDENT:

The other day in class you said, "The demand for 10 a.m. classes may be high, but the quantity demanded may not be if the price is high enough." In other words, you were saying that high demand doesn't necessarily mean high quantity demanded. But I thought it did. Could you explain?

INSTRUCTOR:

Let me explain what's going on by first showing you the demand schedule for two goods, A and B.

Good A Demand Schedule		Good B Demand Schedule	
Price	**Quantity Demanded**	**Price**	**Quantity Demanded**
$6	100	$6	200
7	80	7	150
8	60	8	125
9	40	9	90

As you can see from the two demand schedules, the demand for good B is greater than the demand for good A. In other words, if we were to derive a demand curve for each good (based on its demand schedule), the demand curve for good B would lie farther to the right than the demand curve for good A.

Now suppose we look at quantity demanded for each good at the price of $6. The quantity demanded of good A (the low-demand good) is 100 units and the quantity demanded of good B (the high-demand good) is 200 units. What can we conclude? At the same price for each good ($6), the quantity demanded is higher when demand is higher.

But now let's consider quantity demanded for each good when the price of good A is $6 and the price of good B is $9. The quantity demanded of good A (the low-demand good) is 100 units and the quantity demanded of good B (the high-demand good) is 90 units. In other words, if price is high enough for good B (the high-demand good), the quantity demanded of good B may be lower than the quantity demanded of good A (the low-demand good).

Now let's go back and repeat the statement I made in class: "The demand for 10 a.m. classes may be high, but the quantity demanded may not be if the price is high enough." Now do you understand what I was saying?

STUDENT:

Yes, I think I do. You were saying that high demand doesn't necessarily mean high quantity demanded if we are dealing with different prices.

INSTRUCTOR:

Yes, that's it.

POINTS TO REMEMBER

1. High demand means high quantity demanded, but only if the prices for the high-demand good and the low-demand good are the same. From our example, at a price of $6, the quantity demanded for the high-demand good B is greater than quantity demanded for the low-demand good A.

2. The quantity demanded for the low-demand good can be higher than the quantity demanded for the high-demand good if the prices for the two goods are not the same and the price for the high-demand good is high enough. From our example, at a price of $9 for good B (the high-demand good), the quantity demanded is lower than quantity demanded for good A (the low-demand good) at a price of $6.

114

CHAPTER SUMMARY

TICKET PRICES AT THE TAPING OF A TV SHOW

- The ticket price to the taping of a TV show is usually zero, which usually leads to a shortage of tickets. The greater the demand for the show is, the greater the shortage of tickets will be. Because tickets are (mainly) rationed on a first-come-first-served basis, we would expect that tickets for the most popular shows (those with the greatest demand and the largest shortages at a zero ticket price) would sell out faster than tickets for less popular shows.

GOVERNMENT, LOANS, AND HOUSING PRICES

- Lower lending standards and lower interest rates make it easier to get a mortgage loan. But as the ease of getting a mortgage loan increases, so does the demand for housing rise. As the demand for housing rises, house prices rise.

THE PRICE OF AN AISLE SEAT

- If the supply of aisle and middle-of-the-row seats is the same, but the demand for aisle seats is greater, then the equilibrium price for aisle seats will be greater than the equilibrium price of middle-of-the-row seats.

WHY IS MEDICAL CARE SO EXPENSIVE?

- When it comes to medical care, often three parties are involved: the person who sells medical care, the person who buys medical care, and the person who (directly) pays for the medical care (the third party).
- Once a person has paid her medical insurance premium, the price paid thereafter for medical care may amount to no more than a copayment (usually minimal). For all practical purposes, then, the dollar amount she has to pay out of pocket to get medical care is zero. We expect the quantity demanded of medical care to be greater than at some positive dollar amount.

WHY DO COLLEGES USE GPAs, ACTs, AND SATs FOR PURPOSES OF ADMISSION?

- Colleges and universities charging students less than the equilibrium tuition for admission create a shortage of spaces at their schools. Consequently, colleges and universities have to impose some non-price-rationing device, such as GPAs or ACT or SAT scores.

SUPPLY AND DEMAND ON A FREEWAY

- The effect of a disequilibrium price (below equilibrium price) for driving on a freeway is a traffic jam. If the price to drive on a freeway is $0 and at this price the quantity demanded of freeway space is greater than the quantity supplied, then a shortage of freeway space will result in the form of freeway congestion.

ARE WE REALLY MAKING RENTERS BETTER OFF?

- If renters have 90 days instead of 30 days to vacate an apartment, the supply curve of apartments will shift upward and to the left. As a result, renters will pay higher rents when they have 90 days to vacate an apartment.

DO YOU PAY FOR GOOD WEATHER?

- If good weather gives people utility, then the demand for and the price of housing will be higher in a city with good weather than in a city with bad weather. People who buy houses in good-weather locations indirectly pay for the good weather.

COLLEGE SUPERATHLETES

- A college superathlete may receive a full scholarship to play a sport at a university, but the full scholarship may be less than the equilibrium wage for the superathlete (because of a mandate that the athlete cannot be paid the difference between his higher equilibrium wage and the dollar amount of his full scholarship). In such a case, the university gains at the expense of the athlete.

10 A.M. CLASSES IN COLLEGE

- Colleges usually charge the same tuition for a class no matter when it is taken. The supply of seats in the class may be the same for each time slot, but the demand for the class may be different. At least for some classes, the quantity demanded of seats (in the class) will be greater than the quantity supplied. Thus, some non-price-rationing device will have to be used to achieve equilibrium.

LEGALIZATION OF MARIJUANA

- If the purchase and sale of marijuana are legalized, the price of marijuana may rise, fall, or remain the same. The price will depend on whether the rise in the demand for marijuana is more than, less than, or equal to the rise in the supply of marijuana.

QUESTIONS AND PROBLEMS

1. Application 8 explains that even though no one directly and explicitly pays for good weather ("Here is $100 for the good weather"), you may pay for good weather indirectly, such as through housing prices. Identify three other things (besides good weather) that you believe people pay for indirectly.

2. Samantha is flying from San Diego, California, to Arlington, Texas, on a commercial airliner. She asks for an aisle seat, but only middle-of-the-row seats are left. Why aren't any aisle seats left? (*Hint:* The airline charges the same price for an aisle seat as a middle-of-the-row seat.)

3. In the discussion of health care and the right to sue your HMO, we state, "Saying that a seller's minimum price for providing a good or service rises is the same as saying the seller's supply curve has shifted upward and to the left." Does it follow that if a seller's minimum price falls, the supply curve shifts downward and to the right? Explain your answer.

4. What is the relationship between the probability of a person being admitted to the college of his choice and the tuition the college charges?

5. Economics has been called the "dismal science" because it sometimes "tells us" that things are true when we would prefer they were false. For example, although there are no free lunches, might we prefer that there were? Was there anything in this chapter that you learned was true that you would have preferred to be false? If so, identify it. Then explain why you would have preferred it to be false.

6. Consider the theater in which a Broadway play is performed. If tickets for all seats are the same price (say, $70), what economic effect might arise?

7. What do the applications about freeway congestion and 10 a.m.. classes have in common?

8. Suppose the equilibrium wage for a college athlete is $40,000, but, because of NCAA rules, the university can offer him only $22,000 (full tuition). How might the university administrators, coaches, or university alumni lure the college athlete to choose their school over others?

9. Suppose the purchase and sale of marijuana are legalized and the price of marijuana falls. What is the explanation?

10. University A charges more for a class for which there is high demand than for a class for which there is low demand. University B charges the same for all classes. All other things being equal between the two universities, which university would you prefer to attend? Explain your answer.

11. Harvard, Yale, and Princeton all charge relatively high tuition. Still, each uses ACT and SAT scores as admission criteria. Are charging a relatively high tuition and using standardized test scores as admission criteria inconsistent? Explain your answer.

12. Wilson walks into his economics class ten minutes late because he couldn't find a place to park. Because of his tardiness, he doesn't hear the professor tell the class there will be a quiz at the next session. At the next session, Wilson is unprepared for the quiz and ends up failing it. Might Wilson's failing the quiz have anything to do with the price of parking?

13. If there were no third parties in medical care, medical care prices would be lower. Do you agree or disagree? Explain your answer.

14. Suppose there exists a costless way to charge drivers on the freeway. Under this costless system, tolls on the freeway would be adjusted according to traffic conditions. For example, when traffic is usually heavy, such as from 6:30 a.m. to 9:00 a.m. on a weekday, the toll to drive on the freeway would be higher than when traffic is light. In other words, freeway tolls would be used to equate the demand for freeway space with its supply. Would you be in favor of such a system to replace our current (largely zero-price) system? Explain your answer.

15. Explain how lower lending standards and lower interest rates can lead to higher house prices.

WORKING WITH NUMBERS AND GRAPHS

1. The price to drive on a freeway is $0 at all times of the day. This price establishes equilibrium at 3 a.m. but is too low to establish equilibrium at 5 p.m. There is a shortage of freeway space at 5 p.m.

    a. Graphically show and explain how carpooling may eliminate the shortage.

    b. Graphically show and explain how building more freeways may eliminate the shortage.

2. Diagrammatically show and explain why there is a shortage of classroom space for some college classes and a surplus for others.

3. Smith has been trying to sell his house for six months, but so far he has had no buyers. Draw the market for Smith's house.

CHAPTER 6

MACROECONOMIC MEASUREMENTS, PART I: PRICES AND UNEMPLOYMENT

©ROBERT SHAFER/BRAND X PICTURES/JUPITER IMAGES

Introduction Government economists often collect and analyze the latest economic data. Their analysis includes computing important economic measurements such as the inflation rate and the unemployment rate. Our elected representatives and certain government officials then use these measurements in formulating economic policy. The structure and timing of that economic policy often affects you in your roles as buyer, seller, taxpayer, and employee.

MEASURING THE PRICE LEVEL

There is a difference between *price* and the *price level*. The word *price* refers to a single price, such the price of apples or the price of oranges. Price level is a weighted average of the prices of all goods and services. The key phrase in that definition is "a weighted average of all prices." Here is a rough way of thinking about a price level. Suppose an economy consists of three goods: apples, oranges, and pears. The prices of apples, oranges, and pears, respectively, are 50¢, 60¢, and 80¢ cents, respectively. The average price (of these three goods) is 63¢. That is also the price level.

Price Level
A weighted average of the prices of all good and services.

Computing the Price Level Using the CPI

Economists measure the price level by constructing a price index. One major price index is the Consumer Price Index (CPI).[1] The CPI is based on a representative group of goods and services, called the *market basket,* purchased by a typical household. The market basket includes eight major categories of goods and services: (1) food and beverages, (2) housing, (3) apparel, (4) transportation, (5) medical care, (6) recreation, (7) education and communication, and (8) other goods and services.

Price Index
A measure of the price level.

Consumer Price Index (CPI)
The weighted average of prices of a specific set of goods and services purchased by a typical household; a widely cited index number for the price level.

---

1. Although changes in the CPI are often used to compute the change in the so-called cost of living, one's cost of living usually involves more than what is measured by the CPI. For example, the CPI does not include income taxes, yet income taxes are a part of the cost of living for most people.

Base Year
The year chosen as a point of reference or basis of comparison for prices in other years; a benchmark year.

To simplify our discussion, we assume the market basket includes only three goods instead of the many goods it actually contains. Our market basket consists of 10 pens, 5 shirts, and 3 pairs of shoes.

To calculate the CPI, first calculate the total dollar expenditure on the market basket in two years: the current year and the base year. The base year is a benchmark year that serves as a basis of comparison for prices in other years.

In Exhibit 1, we multiply the quantity of each good in the market basket (column 1) by its current-year price (column 2) to compute the current-year expenditure on each good (column 3). By adding the dollar amounts in column 3, we obtain the total dollar expenditure on the market basket in the current year. This amount is $167.

To find the total expenditure on the market basket in the base year, we multiply the quantity of each good in the market basket (column 1A) by its base-year price (column 2A) and then add these products (column 3A). This gives us $67.

To find the CPI, we use the formula:

$$CPI = \left(\frac{\text{Total dollar expenditure on market basket in current year}}{\text{Total dollar expenditure on market basket in base year}} \right) \times 100$$

As shown in Exhibit 1, the CPI for our tiny economy is 249.

The consumer price index for the United States for the years 1959 to 2009 is shown in Exhibit 2.

MORE ABOUT THE BASE YEAR Recall that the base year is a benchmark year that serves as a basis of comparison for prices in other years. The CPI in the base year is 100.

EXHIBIT 1

Computing the Consumer Price Index

The exhibit uses hypothetical data to show how the CPI is computed. To find the "total dollar expenditure on market basket in current year," we multiply the quantities of goods in the market basket times their current-year prices and add these products. This gives us $167. To find the "total dollar expenditure on market basket in base year," we multiply the quantities of goods in the market basket times their base-year prices and add these products. This gives us $67. We then divide $167 by $67 and multiply the quotient by 100.

(1) Market Basket		(2) Current-Year Prices (per item)		(3) Current-Year Expenditures	(1A) Market Basket		(2A) Base-Year Prices (per item)		(3A) Base-Year Expenditures
10 pens	×	$ .70	=	$ 7.00	10 pens	×	$ .20	=	$ 2.00
5 shirts	×	14.00	=	70.00	5 shirts	×	7.00	=	35.00
3 pairs of shoes	×	30.00	=	90.00	3 pairs of shoes	×	10.00	=	30.00
				$167.00 ↗ Total dollar expenditure on market basket in current year					**$67.00** ↗ Total dollar expenditure on market basket in base year

$$CPI = \left(\frac{\text{Total dollar expenditure on market basket in current year}}{\text{Total dollar expenditure on market basket in base year}} \right) \times 100$$

$$= \left(\frac{\$167}{\$67} \right) \times 100$$

$$= 249$$

How do we know this? Look again at the formula for calculating the CPI: The numerator is the "Total dollar expenditure on market basket in current year," and the denominator is the "Total dollar expenditure on market basket in base year." In the base year, the current year *is* the base year; so the numerator and denominator are the same. The ratio is 1, and 1 × 100 = 100.

In Exhibit 2, however, notice that there is no year in which the CPI is 100. This does not mean that there is no base year. The base year has been defined by the government to be the period 1982–1984. Look at the CPI in each of the years 1982, 1983, and 1984. If we add the CPIs for the three years and divide by 3, we get 100: (96.5 + 99.6 + 103.9) ÷ 3 = 100.

WHEN WE KNOW THE CPI FOR VARIOUS YEARS, WE CAN COMPUTE THE PERCENTAGE CHANGE IN PRICES

To find the percentage change in prices between any two years, use the following formula:

$$\text{Percentage change in prices} = \left(\frac{\text{CPI}_{\text{later year}} - \text{CPI}_{\text{earlier year}}}{\text{CPI}_{\text{earlier year}}} \right) \times 100$$

For example, Exhibit 2 shows that the CPI in 1990 was 130.7, and the CPI in 2005 was 195.3. The percentage change in prices over this period of time was 49.43 percent:

$$\text{Percentage change} = \left(\frac{195.3 - 130.7}{130.7} \right) \times 100 = 49.43$$

This means that from 1990 to 2005 prices increased 49.43 percent. You can think of the percentage change in prices this way: What cost $1 in 1990 cost approximately $1.49 in 2005.

Inflation and the CPI

Inflation is an increase in the price level and is usually measured on an annual basis. The *inflation rate* is the positive percentage change in the price level on an annual basis. When you know the inflation rate, you can find out whether your income is (1) keeping up with, (2) not keeping up with, or (3) more than keeping up with inflation. How you are doing depends on whether your income is rising by (1) the same percentage as, (2) a smaller percentage than, or (3) a greater percentage than the inflation rate, respectively. When you make this computation and comparison, you are determining your real income for different years. Real income is a person's nominal income (or current dollar amount of income) adjusted for any change in prices. Real income is computed as follows:

$$\text{Real income} = \left(\frac{\text{Nominal income}}{\text{CPI}} \right) \times 100$$

CASE 1. KEEPING UP WITH INFLATION: REAL INCOME STAYS CONSTANT

Jim earns $50,000 in year 1 and $55,000 in year 2. The CPI is 100 in year 1 and 110 in year 2; so the inflation rate is 10 percent: [(110 − 100)/100] × 100 = 10. Jim's income has risen by 10 percent: [($55,000 − $50,000)/$50,000] × 100 = 10. Jim's income has risen by the same percentage as the inflation rate; so he has kept up with

EXHIBIT 2

CPI, 1959–2009

Source: The data were reported at the website for the U.S. Department of Labor, Bureau of Labor Statistics. Site address: http://www.bls.gov/home.htm. Beginning in 2007, the Bureau of Labor Statistics began reporting the CPI to three decimal points.

Year	CPI	Year	CPI
1959	29.1	1985	107.6
1960	29.6	1986	109.6
1961	29.9	1987	113.6
1962	30.2	1988	118.3
1963	30.6	1989	124.0
1964	31.0	1990	130.7
1965	31.5	1991	136.2
1966	32.4	1992	140.3
1967	33.4	1993	144.5
1968	34.8	1994	148.2
1969	36.7	1995	152.4
1970	38.8	1996	156.9
1971	40.5	1997	160.5
1972	41.8	1998	163.0
1973	44.4	1999	166.6
1974	49.3	2000	172.2
1975	53.8	2001	177.1
1976	56.9	2002	179.9
1977	60.6	2003	184.0
1978	65.2	2004	188.9
1979	72.6	2005	195.3
1980	82.4	2006	201.6
1981	90.9	2007	207.342
1982	96.5	2008	215.303
1983	99.6	2009	214.537
1984	103.9		

Inflation
An increase in the price level.

Real Income
Nominal income adjusted for price changes.

Nominal Income
The current dollar amount of a person's income.

inflation. This is evident when we see that Jim's real income is the same in both years. In year 1 it is $50,000, and in year 2 it is $50,000 too.

$$\text{Real income year 1} = \left(\frac{\$50,000}{100}\right) \times 100 = \$50,000$$

$$\text{Real income year 2} = \left(\frac{\$55,000}{110}\right) \times 100 = \$50,000$$

CASE 2. NOT KEEPING UP WITH INFLATION: REAL INCOME FALLS Karen earns $50,000 in year 1 and $52,000 in year 2. The CPI is 100 in year 1 and 110 in year 2. Karen's income has risen by 4 percent, and the inflation rate is 10 percent. Her income has risen by a smaller percentage than the inflation rate; so she has not kept up with inflation. Karen's real income has fallen from $50,000 in year 1 to $47,273 in year 2.

$$\text{Real income year 1} = \left(\frac{\$50,000}{100}\right) \times 100 = \$50,000$$

$$\text{Real income year 2} = \left(\frac{\$52,000}{110}\right) \times 100 = \$47,273$$

CASE 3. MORE THAN KEEPING UP WITH INFLATION: REAL INCOME RISES Carl earns $50,000 in year 1 and $60,000 in year 2. The CPI is 100 in year 1 and 110 in year 2. Carl's income has risen by 20 percent, and the inflation rate is 10 percent. His income has risen by a greater percentage than the inflation rate; so he has more than kept up with inflation. Carl's real income has risen from $50,000 in year 1 to $54,545 in year 2.

$$\text{Real income year 1} = \left(\frac{\$50,000}{100}\right) \times 100 = \$50,000$$

$$\text{Real income year 2} = \left(\frac{\$60,000}{110}\right) \times 100 = \$54,545$$

finding ECONOMICS

In Your Paycheck Sharon comments to a friend that she recently received a $5-an-hour raise at work. Her friend congratulates her and then goes on to talk about how prices have been rising lately. Where is the economics?

Obviously, if Sharon's nominal (or money) income has risen, and prices have risen too, then Sharon's real income might have changed. Has her real income risen, fallen, or stayed the same? The answer depends on how much her nominal income has risen relative to how much prices have gone up. Let's say her nominal income has risen by 5 percent and prices have increased by 2 percent. In that case, Sharon's real income has gone up. ▲▲▲

thinking like AN ECONOMIST

Comparing One Thing with Another Comparing one thing with something else can be extremely useful. For example, in each of the three cases just discussed, we compared the percentage change in a person's nominal income with the inflation rate. Through this comparison, we learned something that we could not have learned by looking at either factor alone: how a person fared under inflation. Making comparisons is part of the economic way of thinking. ▲▲▲

GDP Implicit Price Deflator

Besides the CPI, another price index is often cited: the *GDP deflator* or the *GDP implicit price deflator*. Obviously, an economy produces more goods and services than find their

Economics at the Movies

Some movies do better at the box office than others. For example, *Spider-Man 3*, released in 2007, earned higher gross receipts than *The Bourne Ultimatum,* another movie released in 2007. As of February 2010, the following list ranks the all-time top 10 movies in the United States in terms of domestic gross receipts:

1. Avatar (2009)
2. Titanic (1997)
3. The Dark Knight (2008)
4. Star Wars (1977)
5. Shrek 2 (2004)
6. E.T.: The Extra-Terrestrial (1982)
7. Star Wars: Episode I—The Phantom Menace (1999)
8. Pirates of the Caribbean: Dead Man's Chest (2006)
9. Spider-Man (2002)
10. Transformers: Revenge of the Fallen (2009)

Avatar, first on the list, earned gross receipts in the United States of $689 million (as of February 2009) , and *Star Wars*, in second place, earned $461 million. Comparing these two dollar amounts, it is easy to conclude that *Avatar* did better at the box office than *Star Wars*.

But *Avatar* was released in 2009, and *Star Wars* was released 32 years earlier in 1977. In other words, the receipts for *Avatar* are in 2009 dollars, and those for *Star Wars* are in 1977 dollars. To accurately compare the receipts of the two movies, we need to put them on an even footing. We need to change each movie's receipts into today's dollars (let today's dollars be 2009 dollars). When we do this, *Star Wars* earned more than *Avatar*. Specifically, *Star Wars* earned $1.6 billion and *Avatar* (as of February 2010) had earned $689 million.

COPYRIGHT © 20TH CENTURY FOX LICENSING/MERCHANDISING/EVERETT COLLECTION

What is the top grossing film of all time in today's dollars? It is *Gone with the Wind*, released in 1939. In today's dollars, it earned approximately $3 billion.

way into the CPI's representative market basket. The GDP implicit price deflator, unlike the CPI, is based on all goods and services produced in an economy.

Converting Dollars from One Year to Another

Suppose someone says, "Back in 1960, I had an annual salary of $10,000 a year. That sure isn't much these days." Of course, the person is right in one sense: An annual salary of $10,000 doesn't buy much these days, but was it a good salary back in 1960? It certainly could have been, because prices in 1960 weren't as high as they are today. For example, the CPI was 29.6 in 1960 and 214.537 in 2009. In other words, one of the

Woodstock, 1969

Actin' funny, but I don't know why
'scuse me while I kiss the sky
—Purple Haze, Jimi Hendrix

Officially called the Woodstock Music and Art Fair, it took place at Max Yasgur's 600-acre dairy farm in Bethel, New York (about 43 miles from Woodstock), for a period of three days: August 15, 16, and 17 of 1969. It was advertised as three days of peace and music. To many, it came to represent the counterculture and hippie era of the 1960s. It is simply known as Woodstock.

© CORBIS

As for the performers, there were many. Here is a partial list:

Richie Havens
John Sebastian
Sweetwater
Ravi Shankar
Arlo Guthrie
Joan Baez
Santana

Canned Heat
Janis Joplin
Sly & the Family Stone
Grateful Dead
Creedence Clearwater Revival
The Who
Jefferson Airplane
Joe Cocker
The Band
Blood, Sweat & Tears
Crosby, Stills, Nash & Young
Jimi Hendrix

The price of a one-day ticket to Woodstock was $8 in 1969. That sounds like a cheap ticket nowadays. But how much is $8 in 1969 comparable to in 2009? We use the following formula:

$$\text{Ticket in 2009 dollars} = \$8 \times \frac{214.537}{36.7}$$
$$= \$46.77$$

Buying a one-day ticket at Woodstock was the same as buying a $46.77 ticket in 2009. Not a bad price at all, especially for all the groups you could see on any given day.

EXHIBIT 3

C-CPI, 2000–2009

Here we show the Chained CPI (C-CPI) for the years 2000–2009. The Chained CPI is yet another price index.

Year	C-CPI
2000	102.0
2001	104.3
2002	105.6
2003	107.8
2004	110.5
2005	113.7
2006	117.0
2007	119.957
2008	124.433
2009	124.353

things that make a salary good or not so good is what the salary can buy.

Now suppose someone tells you that a $10,000 salary in 1960 is the same as a $68,000 salary today. Would you then be better able to say whether the 1960 $10,000 salary was good or not so good? Of course you would because you understand what it means to earn $68,000 today. Economists convert a past salary into today's salary by using this formula:

$$\text{Salary in today's (current) dollars} = \text{Salary}_{\text{earlier year}} \times \left(\frac{\text{CPI}_{\text{current year}}}{\text{CPI}_{\text{earlier year}}}\right)$$

Assume the CPI today is the same as the most recent CPI in Exhibit 3 (which is the CPI for 2009). Using the formula, we get:

$$\text{Salary in 2009 dollars} = \$10,000 \times \frac{214.537}{29.6}$$
$$= \$72,479$$

finding ECONOMICS

In What Grandfather Says Ursula, who is 25, told her grandfather that she just got a job that pays $67,000 a year. Her grandfather said, "That's a lot of money. When I got my first real job I earned only $18,000 a year. You're earning a whole lot more than I did." Where is the economics?

Income earned in one time period cannot always be adequately compared to income earned in another time period. To do so, we need to convert the dollars earned in one period into dollars earned in the other period. Ursula is earning $67,000 today, but her grandfather earned $18,000 (in his first job) many years ago. Obviously, earning $18,000 many years ago is not the same as earning $18,000 today; so Ursula's grandfather's statement that she is earning a whole lot more than he did might not be accurate. ▲ ▲ ▲

SELF-TEST

(Answers to Self-Test questions are in Answers to Self-Test Questions at the back of the book.)

1. Explain how the CPI is calculated.

2. What is a base year?

3. In year 1, your annual income is $45,000 and the CPI is 143.6; in year 2, your annual income is $51,232 and the CPI is 150.7. Has your real income risen, fallen, or remained constant? Explain your answer.

MEASURING UNEMPLOYMENT

Every month, the government surveys thousands of households to gather information about labor market activities. It uses the information from the survey to derive the number of Americans unemployed.

Who Are the Unemployed?

The total population of the United States can be divided into two broad groups (Exhibit 4). One group consists of persons who are (1) under 16 years of age, (2) in the armed forces, or (3) institutionalized (in a prison, mental institution, or home for the aged). The second group, which consists of all others in the total population, is called the *civilian noninstitutional population*.

EXHIBIT 4

Breakdown of the U.S. Population and the Labor Force

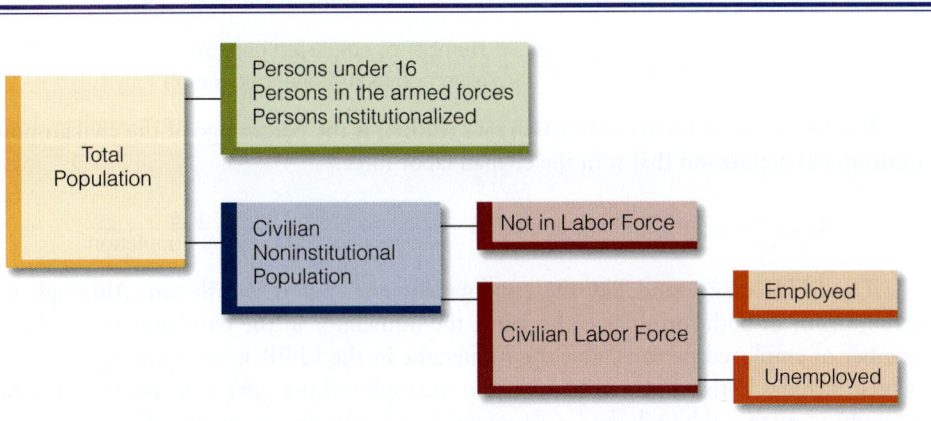

The civilian noninstitutional population, in turn, can be divided into two groups: persons *not in the labor force* and persons in the *civilian labor force.* (Economists often refer to this group as the labor force instead of the civilian labor force.)

$$\text{Civilian noninstitutional population} = \text{Persons not in the labor force} + \text{Persons in the labor force}$$

- Persons not in the labor force are neither working nor looking for work. In this category, for example, are people who are retired, who are engaged in own-home housework, or who choose not to work.
- Persons in the civilian labor force fall into one of two categories: *employed* or *unemployed.*

$$\text{Civilian labor force} = \text{Employed persons} + \text{Unemployed persons}$$

According to the Bureau of Labor Statistics (BLS), employed persons consist of:

- All persons who did any work for pay or profit during the survey reference week.
- All persons who did at least 15 hours of unpaid work in a family-operated enterprise.
- All persons who were temporarily absent from their regular jobs because of illness, vacation, bad weather, industrial dispute, or various personal reasons.

According to the BLS, unemployed persons consist of:

- All persons who did not have jobs, who made specific active efforts to find a job during the prior four weeks, and who were available for work.
- All persons who were not working and who were waiting to be called back to a job from which they had been temporarily laid off.

The Unemployment and Employment Rates

Unemployment Rate
The percentage of the civilian force that is unemployed: Unemployment rate = Number of unemployed persons ÷ Civilian labor force.

The unemployment rate is the percentage of the civilian labor force that is unemployed. It is equal to the number of unemployed persons divided by the civilian labor force.

$$\text{Unemployment rate } (U) = \frac{\text{Number of unemployed persons}}{\text{Civilian labor force}}$$

Employment Rate
The percentage of the civilian noninstitutional population that is employed: Employment rate = Number of employed persons ÷ Civilian noninstitutional population.

The employment rate (sometimes referred to as the *employment/population ratio*) is the percentage of the civilian noninstitutional population that is employed. It is equal to the number of employed persons divided by the civilian noninstitutional population:

$$\text{Employment rate } (E) = \frac{\text{Number of employed persons}}{\text{Civilian noninstitutional population}}$$

Labor Force Participation Rate
The percentage of the civilian noninstitutional population that is in the civilian labor force: Labor force participation rate = Civilian labor force ÷ Civilian noninstitutional population.

Finally, the labor force participation rate (LFPR) is the percentage of the civilian noninstitutional population that is in the civilian labor force.

$$\text{Labor force participation rate (LFPR)} = \frac{\text{Civilian labor force}}{\text{Civilian noninstitutional population}}$$

The LFPR may sound like the employment rate, but it is different. Although the denominator in both formulas is the same, the numerator in the employment rate is the number of employed persons, and the numerator in the LFPR is the civilian labor force (which includes both employed persons and unemployed persons). For this reason, some economists say that although the employment rate gives us the percentage of the population that is working, the LFPR gives us the percentage of the population that is *willing to work.*

economics 24/7

What Was a Penny Worth?

You are walking and you look down and see a penny on the sidewalk. Do you stop and pick it up? Many people will say no, explaining that the penny isn't worth their time. After all, a penny is not worth very much, they say.

You buy a magazine at the campus store. The total price (including tax) comes to $6.02. You hand the cashier a $10 bill. Instead of giving you $3.98 in change, she reaches into the cup next to the cash register and pulls out two pennies; she gives you $4 in change. It is easier for her to get the two pennies from the cup than it is to count out $3.98 in change. You say, "Thank you" and go on your way.

The next day, you buy something for $5.99. You hand the cashier $6. When the cashier gives you back one penny in change, you drop it into the cup next to the cash register. One day you take from the cup; another day you give to the cup.

Twenty years ago, there were no penny cups next to cash registers. Why were there no penny cups then, but penny cups now? The reason is that 20 years ago, a penny had more purchasing power than it does today. If a penny today had greater purchasing power than it does, you'd be less likely to drop the penny into the cup; instead, you'd drop it into your pocket.

So what was a penny worth in, say, 1900? A different way of asking the question is, "What coin today is equal to the purchasing power a penny had in 1900?" The answer is a quarter. In other words, having a penny in 1900 was equivalent of having a quarter (25¢) today. So having four pennies in 1900 was the equivalent of having $1 today.

Imagine the year is 1900 and you are walking down the street. You look down and see a penny. Do you stop and pick it up?

Common Misconceptions About the Unemployment and Employment Rates

Many people mistakenly think that if the unemployment rate is, say, 7 percent, the employment rate must be 93 percent. Their assumption is that the unemployment rate plus the employment rate must equal 100 percent. But the unemployment and employment rates do not add up 100 percent, because the denominator of the unemployment rate is not the same as the denominator of the employment rate. The unemployment rate is a *percentage of the civilian labor force*. The employment rate is a *percentage of the civilian noninstitutional population*, which is a larger number than the civilian labor force.

Reasons for Unemployment

Usually, we think of an unemployed person as someone who has been fired or laid off from his or her job. Certainly, some unemployed persons fit this description, but not all of them do. According to the BLS, an unemployed person may fall into one of four categories.

1. *Job loser.* This person was employed in the civilian labor force and was either fired or laid off. Most unemployed persons fall into this category.

2. *Job leaver.* This person was employed in the civilian labor force and quit the job. For example, if Jim quit his job with company X and is looking for a better job, he is a job leaver.

3. *Reentrant.* This person was previously employed, hasn't worked for some time, and is currently reentering the labor force.

4. *New entrant.* This person has never held a full-time job for two weeks or longer and is now in the civilian labor force looking for a job.

Unemployed persons = Job losers + Job leavers + Reentrants + New entrants

Discouraged Workers

Adam is fired from his job at company A in September, and he looks for a job for about six months. During this time, he is considered an unemployed person and is counted in the unemployment rate. At the end of the sixth month, Adam is very discouraged; he doesn't think he will ever find a job, and he stops looking. A month passes and he still is not looking for a job. Is Adam considered an unemployed person? The answer is no. To be an unemployed person, you have to meet certain conditions, one of which is that you have to be actively looking for work. But Adam isn't actively looking for work, and he isn't waiting to be called back to a job or to report to a job. So Adam isn't unemployed, and for that reason he does not get counted in the unemployment rate.

The BLS considers Adam a *discouraged worker.* You may think that for all practical purposes, a discouraged worker is the same as an unemployed person because neither has a job. But they aren't the same for calculating the unemployment rate. The unemployed person gets counted, but the discouraged worker does not.

Some economists think that because discouraged workers are not considered unemployed, the unemployment rate is biased downward. Consequently, it doesn't really give us a good fix on the "real" unemployment problem in society.

Types of Unemployment

This section describes a few types of unemployment.

FRICTIONAL UNEMPLOYMENT Every day, demand conditions change in some markets, causing qualified individuals with transferable skills to leave some jobs and move to others. To illustrate, suppose there are two computer firms, A and B. For some reason, the demand falls for firm A's computers and rises for firm B's computers. Consequently, firm A produces fewer computers. With fewer computers being produced, firm A doesn't need as many employees; so it fires some employees. On the other hand, firm B is producing more computers. With more computers being produced, firm B hires additional employees. The employees fired from firm A have skills that they can transfer to firm B; after all, both firms produce computers. However, it takes time for people to make the transfer. During this time, they are said to be frictionally unemployed.

Frictional Unemployment
Unemployment that is due to the natural so-called frictions in the economy and that is caused by changing market conditions and represented by qualified individuals with transferable skills who change jobs.

Frictional unemployment is unemployment that is due to the natural so-called frictions in the economy and that is caused by changing market conditions and represented by qualified individuals with transferable skills who change jobs. The frictional unemployment rate (U_F) is the percentage of the labor force that is frictionally unemployed.

$$U_F = \frac{\text{Number of frictionally unemployed persons}}{\text{Civilian labor force}}$$

A dynamic, changing economy like that of the United States always has frictional unemployment. Many economists believe that the basic cause of frictional unemployment is imperfect or incomplete information, which prevents individuals from leaving one job and finding another instantly. For example, imagine an economy with 1,000 job vacancies and 1,000 persons qualified to fill the jobs. Some unemployment is likely because not every one of the 1,000 job seekers will know where the available job are. Nor will all employers give the job to the first applicant who knocks on the door. Employers don't know whether better applicants are around the corner. Matching qualified workers with the available jobs takes time.

STRUCTURAL UNEMPLOYMENT Structural unemployment is unemployment due to structural changes in the economy that eliminate some jobs and create others for which the unemployed are unqualified. Most economists argue that structural unemployment is largely the consequence of automation (labor-saving devices) and long-lasting shifts in demand. The structurally unemployed differ from the frictionally unemployed mainly in that they do not have transferable skills. Their choice is between prolonged unemployment and retraining. For example, suppose automobile workers are being laid off and the demand for computer analysts is rising. If the automobile workers do not currently have the skills needed to become computer analysts, they are structurally unemployed. The structural unemployment rate (U_S) is the percentage of the labor force that is structurally unemployed.

$$U_S = \frac{\text{Number of structurally unemployed persons}}{\text{Civilian labor force}}$$

Structural Unemployment
Unemployment due to structural changes in the economy that eliminate some jobs and create others for which the unemployed are unqualified.

NATURAL UNEMPLOYMENT Adding the frictional unemployment rate and the structural unemployment rate gives the natural unemployment rate (or natural rate of unemployment, U_N). Currently, most economists estimate the natural unemployment rate at between 4 and 6.5 percent.

$$\text{Natural unemployment rate } (U_N) = \text{Frictional unemployment rate } (U_F) + \text{Structural unemployment rate } (U_S)$$

Natural Unemployment
Unemployment caused by frictional and structural factors in the economy: Natural unemployment rate = Frictional unemployment rate + Structural unemployment rate.

The Natural Unemployment Rate and Full Employment

What do you think of when you hear the term "full employment"? Most people think *full employment* means that the actual or reported unemployment rate is zero. But a dynamic, changing economy can never have full employment of this type due to the frictional and structural changes that continually occur. In fact, it is natural for some unemployment to exist—some natural unemployment, that is. For this reason, economists *do not* equate full employment with a zero unemployment rate. Instead, full employment exists *when the economy is operating at its natural unemployment rate.* For example, if the natural unemployment rate is 5 percent, then full employment exists when the unemployment rate (in the economy) is 5 percent. In other words, the economy can be operating at full employment, and some people will be unemployed.

Full Employment
The condition that exists when the unemployment rate is equal to the natural unemployment rate.

Cyclical Unemployment

The unemployment rate in the economy is not always the natural rate. The difference between the existing unemployment rate and the natural unemployment rate is the cyclical unemployment rate (U_C).

$$\text{Cyclical unemployment rate } (U_C) = \text{Unemployment rate } (U) - \text{Natural unemployment rate } (U_N)$$

Cyclical Unemployment Rate
The difference between the unemployment rate and the natural unemployment rate

When the existing unemployment rate (U) is greater than the natural unemployment rate (U_N), the cyclical unemployment rate (U_C) is positive. For example, if $U = 8$ percent and $U_N = 5$ percent, then $U_C = 3$ percent. When the unemployment rate is less than the natural unemployment rate, the cyclical unemployment rate is negative. For example, if $U = 4$ percent and $U_N = 5$ percent, then $U_C = -1$ percent.

A review of variety of unemployment rates can be seen in Exhibit 5.

EXHIBIT 5

Various Unemployment Rates

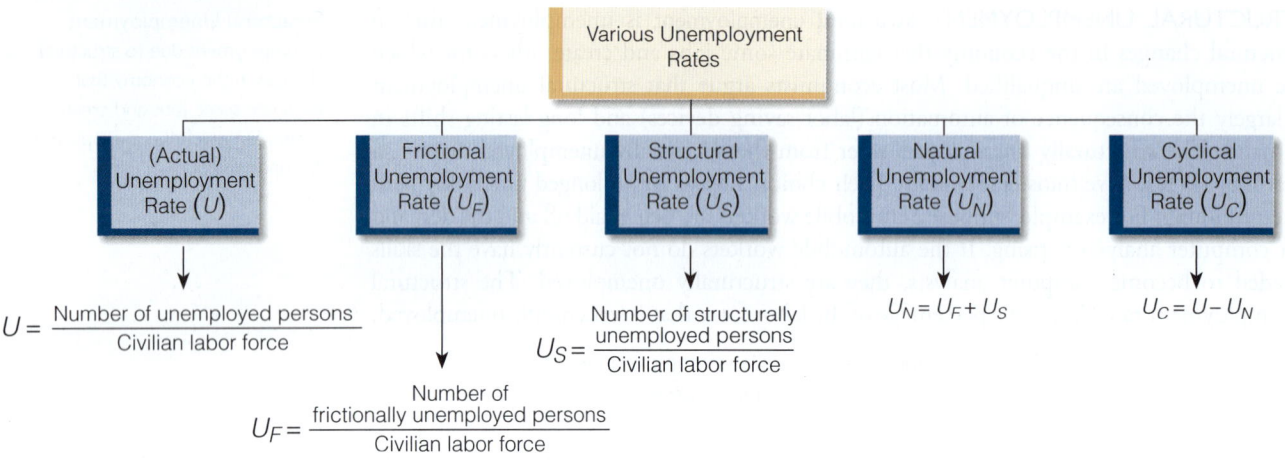

$$U = \frac{\text{Number of unemployed persons}}{\text{Civilian labor force}}$$

$$U_F = \frac{\text{Number of frictionally unemployed persons}}{\text{Civilian labor force}}$$

$$U_S = \frac{\text{Number of structurally unemployed persons}}{\text{Civilian labor force}}$$

$$U_N = U_F + U_S$$

$$U_C = U - U_N$$

OFFICE HOURS

"Is There More Than One Reason the Unemployment Rate Will Fall?"

STUDENT:

If the unemployment rate drops, does it follow that some of the people who were once unemployed are now employed?

INSTRUCTOR:

Not always. To see why, recall that the unemployment rate is equal to the number of unemployed persons divided by the civilian labor force.

$$\text{Unemployment rate} = \frac{\text{Number of unemployed persons}}{\text{Civilian labor force}}$$

Now let's say there are 100 unemployed persons and the civilian labor force consists of 1,000 persons. The unemployment rate is 10 percent. Suppose the number of unemployed persons rises to 105 (a 5 percent increase) at the same time that the civilian labor force rises to 1,120 (a 12 percent increase). The new unemployment rate is 9.4 percent, even

though the number of unemployed persons has not decreased. In fact, it has increased from 100 to 105.

STUDENT:

In other words, if the number of unemployed persons rises by a smaller percentage than the civilian labor force rises, the unemployment rate will decline—even though the number of unemployed persons has risen.

INSTRUCTOR:

Yes, that's correct. Now consider something else. Again suppose 100 unemployed persons and a civilian labor force of 1,000 persons. These numbers give us an unemployment rate of 10 percent. Now suppose 10 of the unemployed persons become discouraged workers and stop looking for work. The number of unemployed falls to 90, and

1. What is the major difference between a person who is frictionally unemployed and one who is structurally unemployed?

2. What does a positive cyclical unemployment rate imply?

the civilian labor force (which consists of employed plus unemployed persons) falls to 990. The unemployment rate now is 9.09 percent. The unemployment rate has dropped, but not for the reason most people think. It hasn't dropped because some of the unemployed persons found jobs. It has dropped because some of the unemployed became so discouraged that they stopped looking for jobs.

STUDENT:

In other words, we might think that the unemployment rate has dropped because 10 of the 100 unemployed persons found work, but in reality those 10 persons did not find work. They just became so discouraged that they left the civilian labor force.

INSTRUCTOR:

Yes, that's correct.

STUDENT:

Does the government do anything to take these discouraged workers into account?

INSTRUCTOR:

The Bureau of Labor Statistics computes an alternative unemployment rate that includes discouraged workers in the ranks of both the unemployed and the civilian labor force. In short, it computes what it calls "total unemployed plus discouraged workers, as a percent of the civilian labor force plus discouraged workers."

$$\text{Alternative Unemployment rate} = \frac{\text{Number of unemployed persons} + \text{Discouraged workers}}{\text{Civilian labor force} + \text{Discouraged workers}}$$

This alternative unemployment rate tells us what the unemployment rate would look like if we include discouraged workers in our calculation.

POINTS TO REMEMBER

1. The unemployment rate can decline even if the number of unemployed persons has not declined. For example, if the number of unemployed persons rises by a smaller percentage than that of the civilian labor force, the unemployment rate will decline (even though more, not fewer, persons are unemployed).

2. The alternative unemployment rate is defined as:

$$\text{Alternative Unemployment rate} = \frac{\text{Number of unemployed persons} + \text{Discouraged workers}}{\text{Civilian labor force} + \text{Discouraged workers}}$$

CHAPTER SUMMARY

MEASURING PRICES

- A major price index is the consumer price index (CPI).
- Inflation is an increase in the price level or price index.
- A given dollar amount in an earlier year does not have the same purchasing power in a later year (or current year) if prices are different in the two years. To convert a dollar amount of an earlier year into today's (or current) dollars, we use the formula:

$$\text{Dollar amount in today's (current) dollars} =$$
$$\text{Dollar amount}_{\text{earlier year}} \times \left(\frac{\text{CPI}_{\text{current year}}}{\text{CPI}_{\text{earlier year}}} \right)$$

UNEMPLOYMENT AND EMPLOYMENT

- An unemployed person may be a job loser, a job leaver, a reentrant, or a new entrant.

- The unemployment rate may be biased downward because discouraged workers are not considered unemployed.
- Frictional unemployment, due to the natural so-called frictions of the economy, is caused by changing market conditions and is represented by qualified individuals with transferable skills who change jobs.
- Structural unemployment is due to structural changes in the economy that eliminate some jobs and create others for which the unemployed are unqualified.
- Natural unemployment is caused by frictional and structural factors in the economy. The natural unemployment rate equals the sum of the frictional unemployment rate and the structural unemployment rate.
- Full employment exists when the unemployment rate is equal to the natural unemployment rate.
- The cyclical unemployment rate is the difference between the existing unemployment rate and the natural unemployment rate.

KEY TERMS AND CONCEPTS

Price Level	Inflation	Employment Rate	Natural Unemployment
Price Index	Real Income	Labor Force Participation Rate	Full Employment
Consumer Price Index (CPI)	Nominal Income	Frictional Unemployment	Cyclical Unemployment Rate
Base Year	Unemployment Rate	Structural Unemployment	

QUESTIONS AND PROBLEMS

1. If the unemployment rate is 4 percent, it does not follow that the employment rate is 96 percent. Explain why.
2. Explain how the CPI is computed.
3. What criteria must be met for a person to be characterized as unemployed?
4. What is the relationship between your nominal income and the inflation rate if you are more than keeping up with inflation?
5. What is the difference between a job leaver and a reentrant?
6. If the price of, say, oranges has risen, does it follow that the price level has risen too? Explain your answer.
7. How is a discouraged worker different from an unemployed worker?

8. How does structural unemployment differ from frictional unemployment?
9. What is the difference between the employment rate and the labor force participation rate?
10. What does it mean if the expenditure weights of the market basket used to compute the CPI are changed?
11. What is "natural" about natural unemployment?
12. Show that if the percentage rise in prices is equal to the percentage rise in nominal income, then one's real income does not change.
13. What does it mean to say that the country is operating at full employment?
14. What does the CPI in the base year equal? Explain your answer.

WORKING WITH NUMBERS AND GRAPHS

1. Suppose 60 million people are employed, 10 million unemployed, and 30 million not in the labor force. What does the civilian noninstitutional population equal?

2. Suppose 100 million people are in the civilian labor force and 90 million people are employed. How many people are unemployed? What is the unemployment rate?

3. Change the current-year prices in Exhibit 1 to $1 for pens, $28 for shirts, and $32 for a pair of shoes. What is the CPI for the current year based on these prices?

4. Jim earned an annual salary of $15,000 in 1965. What is this equivalent to in 2005 dollars? (Use Exhibit 2 to find the CPI in the years mentioned.)

5. A house cost $10,000 in 1976. What is this equivalent to in 2001 dollars? (Use Exhibit 2 to find the CPI in the years mentioned.)

6. Using the following data, compute (a) the unemployment rate, (b) the employment rate, and (c) the labor force participation rate.

Civilian noninstitutional population	200 million
Number of employed persons	126 million
Number of unemployed persons	8 million

7. Based on the following data, compute (a) the unemployment rate, (b) the structural unemployment rate, and (c) the cyclical unemployment rate.

Frictional unemployment rate	2 percent
Natural unemployment rate	5 percent
Civilian labor force	100 million
Number of employed persons	82 million

8. Using Exhibit 2, compute the percentage change in prices between (a) 1966 and 1969, (b) 1976 and 1986, and (c) 1990 and 1999.

9. Assume the market basket contains 10X, 20Y, and 45Z. The current-year prices for goods X, Y, and Z are $1, $4, and $6, respectively. The base-year prices are $1, $3, and $5, respectively. What is the CPI in the current year?

10. If the CPI is 150 and nominal income is $100,000, what does real income equal?.

CHAPTER 7

MACROECONOMIC MEASUREMENTS, PART II: GDP AND REAL GDP

Introduction Each day in the United States, many thousands of goods and services are produced. How do we measure all this economic activity? One of the principal ways is to compute GDP, or gross domestic product. GDP is one of the most important economic measurements used by economists. In this chapter we explain what GDP is and discuss how to compute it. We then turn to a discussion of Real GDP and how to compute it.

GROSS DOMESTIC PRODUCT

In any given year, people in the United States produce goods and services—television sets, books, pencil sharpeners, DVD players, attorney services, haircuts, and much more. Have you ever wondered what the total dollar value is for all those goods and services? In 2009, it was $14.26 trillion. In other words, in 2009, people living and working in the United States produced $14.26 trillion worth of goods and services. That dollar amount—$14.26 trillion—is what economists call the gross domestic product. Simply put, gross domestic product (GDP) is the *total market value of all final goods and services produced annually within a country's borders.*

Gross Domestic Product (GDP)
The total market value of all final goods and services produced annually within a country's borders.

Calculating GDP

To show how GDP is computed, suppose the following data represent the prices and quantities of three goods produced in a tiny economy this year.

Goods	Quantities Produced of Each Good	Price of Each Good
A	10	$2
B	20	$3
C	30	$5

What is the GDP in this tiny economy? GDP is the total market value of all final goods and services produced annually within a country's borders. GDP, then, is the sum (Σ) of the prices (P) of all goods times the quantities (Q) of those goods produced.

$$GDP = \Sigma PQ$$

In our case:

$$GDP = (\$2 \times 10 \text{ units}) + (\$3 \times 20 \text{ units}) + (\$5 \times 30 \text{ units}) = \$230$$

Final Goods and Intermediate Goods

In our definition of GDP, reference was made to "final goods and services." If GDP is the total market value of these final goods and services, why do we need to specify them as *final*? There is a difference between a final good and an intermediate good. A final good (or service) is a good in the hands of the final user, the ultimate consumer. It is the orange juice that the consumer buys in the store.

So, then, what are the oranges that go to make the orange juice? The oranges are an *intermediate good.* An intermediate good is an input to the production of a final good. In other words, the oranges were used to produce orange juice (the final good).

Only expenditures on final goods are counted when computing GDP to avoid the *double counting* that would occur if we counted expenditures on both final and intermediate goods. Double counting refers to counting a good more than once when computing GDP. To illustrate, if we count the oranges and the orange juice, then we count the oranges twice because they are in the orange juice.

Final Good
A good in the hands of its final user.

Intermediate Good
A good that is an input to the production of a final good.

Double Counting
Counting a good more than once when computing GDP.

(f)inding ECONOMICS

In a Factory, Restaurant, and Law Office James works in a car factory in Detroit. Where is the economics? Obviously, cars are being produced in the car factory in Detroit. The production of these cars will add to the GDP for the current year.

Marion works as a cook in a coffee house. Bill has just ordered an egg salad sandwich on rye (toasted) with cole slaw and a root beer. Where is the economics? Marion will make the sandwich and cole slaw. These two items plus the root beer are part of the GDP for the current year.

Oliver is in his attorney's office talking about his upcoming court case. Where is the economics? The service the attorney is providing to Oliver is part of the GDP for the current year. ▲ ▲ ▲

What GDP Omits

Some exchanges that take place in an economy are not included in GDP. These trades range from sales of used cars to illegal drug deals.

CERTAIN NONMARKET GOODS AND SERVICES If a family hires a person through the classified section of the newspaper to cook and clean, the service is counted in GDP. If family members perform the same tasks, however, their services are not counted in GDP. In the first case, a service is bought and sold for a price in a market setting. In the second case, it is not; no transaction takes place.

Some nonmarket goods are included in GDP. For example, the market value of food produced on a farm and consumed by the farm family is estimated, and this imputed value is part of GDP.

UNDERGROUND ACTIVITIES, BOTH LEGAL AND ILLEGAL The underground economy consists of unreported exchanges that take place outside the normal recorded markets. Some underground activities involve illegal goods (e.g., cocaine), and others involve legal goods and tax evasion. Illegal goods and services are not counted in

Gross Family Product

One of the ways to understand GDP is to think of what it would be comparable to in a family. Instead of talking about what a country produces in a year, let's talk about what a family produces. Let's call the total market value of what the family produces gross family product (GFP).

Just as not every country has the same GDP, not every family has the same GFP. One family can have a higher or lower GFP than another. The difference in GFP might be because more people are producing in one family than in another. For example, family A is composed of five individuals, and family B is composed of eight. More family members (more resources) can produce more output.

The same holds for countries. China might have a higher GDP than, say, France because China has a larger population. The national Chinese "family" is larger than the French "family."

Of course, one family might have a higher GFP than another for other reasons. For example, even with the same number of persons in two families, one family might have a higher GFP. Perhaps the members of,

say, family A work more hours than those of family B. All other things equal, more work can result in more output.

The same holds for countries. The GDP of one country might be higher than the GDP of another because the workers in one country work more hours a week than those in the other country.

Finally, consider that even when the size of two families is the same and when the number of hours worked each week by the two families is the same, one family could still have a higher GFP than another. To understand why, keep in mind that GFP measures the total market value of the family output. Note the phrase "total market value," computed by multiplying the price of each unit of output by the number of units produced. If a family is producing chairs, then its GFP will be equal to the price of each chair multiplied by the number of chairs produced. One hundred dollars ($100) per chair multiplied by, say, 100 chairs equals a GFP of $10,000. If another family produces, say, 100 shirts at a price of $25, its GPF will be lower. Thus one family's GFP might be higher than another's GFP because the per-unit price of what it produces is higher.

GDP because no record exists of the related transactions. There are no written records of illegal drug sales, illegal gambling, and illegal prostitution. Nor are there written records of some legal activities that individuals want to keep from government notice. For example, a gardener might agree to do gardening work only on the condition that he is paid in cash. Obviously, a person may legally buy or sell gardening services, but the transaction might not be recorded if one or both parties do not want it to be. Why might the gardener want to be paid in cash? Perhaps he doesn't want to pay taxes on the income received—an objective more easily accomplished if no written record of the income is generated.

SALES OF USED GOODS GDP measures *current production* (i.e., production occurring during the current year). A used car sale, for example, does not enter into the current-year statistics because the car was counted when it was originally produced.

FINANCIAL TRANSACTIONS The trading of stocks and bonds is not counted in GDP because it does not represent the production of new assets. It is simply the trading of existing assets (the exchange of stocks or bonds for money).

Transfer Payment
A payment to a person that is not made in return for goods and services currently supplied.

GOVERNMENT TRANSFER PAYMENTS A transfer payment is a payment to a person that is not made in return for goods and services currently supplied. Government transfer payments, such as Social Security benefits and veterans' benefits, are not counted in GDP because they are not payments to individuals for *current production*.

Happiness and the Economist

In one survey, students at Harvard University were asked whether they would prefer (a) $50,000 a year while others got $25,000 a year or (b) $100,000 a year while others got $200,000 a year. A majority of the students chose (a). In other words, they chose a lower absolute income but a higher relative income. They chose to be poorer in absolute terms, as long as they could be richer in relative terms.

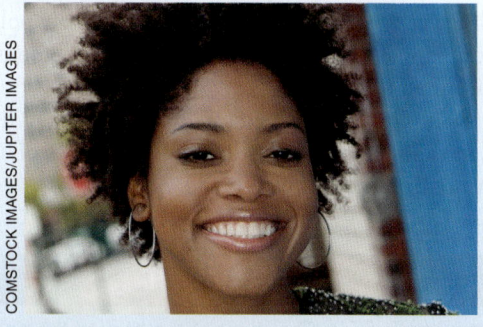

COMSTOCK IMAGES/JUPITER IMAGES

Sometimes, researchers conclude from such a survey that an increase in absolute standard of living (say, as measured by per-capita GDP) does not matter as much to happiness as a rise in one's relative standard of living (say, as measured by moving up from being poor to being middle income or from being middle income to being "rich"). In short, what matters is not so much how we are doing but how we are doing relative to everyone else.

Now the real question is whether survey results—such as the Harvard University student survey—are meaningful. For example, what would we observe if people cared more about their relative standing than their absolute standing? Some economists have suggested that more affluent people would move into poorer neighborhoods so that they could experience higher relative incomes. The economists go on to say that because we don't see this very often, then individuals do not care about their relative income as much as the survey results suggest. Another question is what would we *not* see if people cared about their relative incomes? Poor immigrants would not come to a rich country; after all, when poor immigrants come to a rich country, they know they will be near the bottom of the income scale. Yet they come, perhaps because they enjoy a higher absolute income in the rich country than they would in the country they leave.

What can we learn about economists? A key lesson is that economists don't always trust survey results—or what people say when answering certain questions. For economists, if we want to know something about people's preferences, we should observe how they act instead of noting what they say.

LEISURE The length of the workweek has fallen in the United States since the beginning of the twentieth century, and the leisure time individuals have to consume has increased. Leisure is a good in much the same way that cars, houses, and shoes are goods. But leisure is not counted in GDP because it is too difficult to quantify.

GDP Is Not Adjusted for Bads Generated in the Production of Goods

Economic growth often comes with certain bads (anything from which individuals receive disutility or dissatisfaction). For example, producing cars, furniture, and steel often generates air and water pollution, which most people consider as bads. GDP counts the goods and services, but it does not deduct the air and water pollution. Thus, some economists argue that GDP overstates our overall economic welfare.

Per Capita GDP

If we divide a country's GDP by the population in the country, we get *per-capita GDP*. For example, if a country has a GDP of $5 trillion and its population is 200 million, per-capita GDP is $25,000 ($5 trillion ÷ 200 million people). In 2009, the per-capita GDP in the United States was $46,400.

Is Either GDP or Per-Capita GDP a Measure of Happiness or Well-Being?

Are the people in a country with a higher GDP or higher per-capita GDP better off or happier than the people in a country with a lower GDP or lower per-capita GDP? We cannot answer that question because well-being and happiness are subjective. A person with more goods may be happier than a person with fewer goods, but possibly not. The person with fewer goods but a lot of leisure, little air pollution, and a relaxed way of life may be much happier than the person with many goods, little leisure, and a polluted, stressful environment.

So it is possible to read too much into GDP figures. GDP figures are useful for obtaining an estimate of the productive capabilities of an economy, but they do not necessarily measure happiness or well-being.

SELF-TEST

(Answers to Self-Test questions are in Answers to Self-Test Questions at the back of the book.)

1. Why aren't stock purchases and sales counted in GDP?

2. Suppose the GDP for a country is $0. Does this mean that there was no productive activity in the country? Explain your answer.

THE EXPENDITURE APPROACH TO COMPUTING GDP FOR A REAL-WORLD ECONOMY

In a tiny economy, we can compute GDP by simply multiplying the quantity of each good produced by the quantity of the good produced:

$$GDP = \Sigma PQ$$

The U.S. economy is anything but tiny. Economists cannot simply multiply the price of each good produced by the quantity of it. In a large economy, GDP can be measured in a number of different ways. A principal way is called the *expenditure approach* to measuring GDP. In this approach, economists sum the spending (on final goods and services) in usually four sectors of the economy: (1) household, (2) business, (3) government, and (4) foreign.

In each of these four sectors, economic actors buy goods and services; in other words, they spend. By sector, the expenditures are called, respectively, (1) *consumption;* (2) gross private domestic investment, or simply *investment;* (3) government consumption expenditures and gross investment, or simply *government purchases;* and (4) *net exports.*

Sectors of the Economy	Spending Called . . .
Household	Consumption
Business	Investment
Government	Government purchases
Foreign	Net Exports

Before we see how economists add up the expenditures of these sectors, let's discuss each of the expenditure components.

CONSUMPTION Consumption (*C*) includes spending on:

- *Durable goods.* Durable goods are goods that are expected to last for more than three years, such as refrigerators, ovens, or cars.
- *Nondurable goods.* Nondurable goods are goods that are not expected to last for more than three years, such as food.
- *Services.* Services are intangible items such as lawn care, car repair, and entertainment.

Consumption expenditures in the United States usually account for 70 percent of GDP. In short, consumption is the largest spending component of GDP.

INVESTMENT Investment (*I*) is the sum of:

- Purchases of newly produced capital goods.
- Changes in business inventories, sometimes referred to as inventory investment.
- Purchases of new residential housing.[1]

The sum of the purchases of newly produced capital goods and the purchases of new residential housing is often referred to as fixed investment. In other words:

Investment = Fixed investment + Inventory investment.

Fixed investment is the larger of the two components.

GOVERNMENT PURCHASES Government purchases (*G*) include federal, state, and local government purchases of goods and services and gross investment in highways, bridges, and so on. Not included in government purchases are government transfer payments, which are payments to persons that are not made in return for currently supplied goods and services. Social Security benefits and welfare payments are two examples of transfer payments; neither is a payment for current productive efforts.

NET EXPORTS People, firms, and governments in the United States sometimes purchase foreign-produced goods. These purchases are referred to as imports (*IM*). Foreign residents, firms, and governments sometimes purchase U.S.-produced goods. These purchases are referred to as exports (*EX*). If imports are subtracted from exports, we are left with net exports (*NX*).

$$NX = EX - IM$$

Obviously, net exports (*NX*) can be positive or negative. If exports are greater than imports, then *NX* is positive; if imports are greater than exports, then *NX* is negative.

Computing GDP Using the Expenditure Approach

So the expenditure approach to measuring or computing GDP calls for the totaling of the purchases of final goods and services made in the four sectors of the economy (see Exhibit 1). This may give you reason to pause because our earlier definition of GDP did not mention *purchases* of final goods and services. Rather, we defined GDP as the total market value of all final goods and services *produced* annually within a nation's borders.

Consumption
The sum of spending on durable goods, nondurable goods, and services.

Investment
The sum of all purchases of newly produced capital goods, changes in business inventories, and purchases of new residential housing.

Inventory Investment
Changes in the stock of unsold goods.

Fixed Investment
Business purchases of capital goods, such as machinery and factories, and purchases of new residential housing.

Government Purchases
Federal, state, and local government purchases of goods and services and gross investment in highways, bridges, and so on.

Government Transfer Payments
Payments to persons that are not made in return for currently supplied goods and services.

Imports
Total domestic (U.S.) spending on foreign goods.

Exports
Total foreign spending on domestic (U.S.) goods.

Net Exports
Exports minus imports.

---

1. For purposes of computing GDP, the purchases of new residential housing (although undertaken by members of the household sector) are considered investment.

EXHIBIT 1

The Expenditure Approach to Computing GDP

The expenditure components of GDP are consumption, investment, government purchases, and net exports. The exhibit shows what is included in each of these components.

The discrepancy is cleared up quickly when we note that national income accountants (persons who compute GDP for the government) assume that anything produced but not sold to consumers is "bought" by the firm that produced it. In other words, if a car is produced but not sold, it goes into business inventory and is consider "purchased" by the automaker firm that produced it. Thus, we can compute GDP by summing the purchases made by the four sectors of the economy. GDP equals consumption (C) plus investment (I) plus government purchases (G) plus net exports ($EX - IM$).

$$GDP = C + I + G + (EX - IM)$$

EXHIBIT 2

Components of GDP (Expenditure Approach)

The expenditure approach to computing GDP sums the purchases made by final users of goods and services. The expenditure components include consumption, investment, government purchases, and net exports. The data are for 2009.

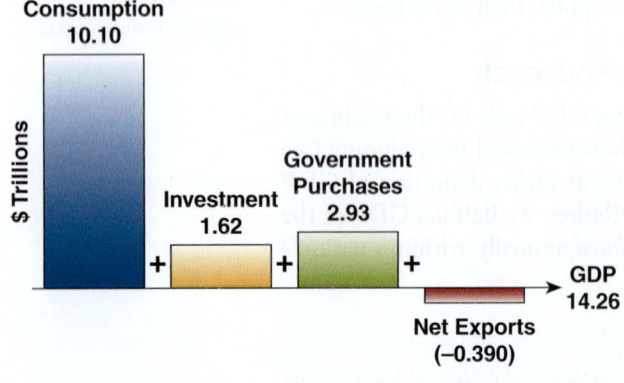

Exhibit 2 shows the dollar amounts of the four components of GDP for the United States in 2009.

Common Misconceptions about Increases in GDP

Are all increases in GDP good for the economy? To answer this question, consider that if investment rises and no other component of GDP declines, GDP will rise. Recall that investment can rise for one of three reasons: (1) Firms may purchase more newly produced capital goods (firms buy more factories and machinery); (2) individuals may purchase new residential housing (someone buys a new home); or (3) firms' inventory investment rises. Further, firms' inventory investment can rise in two ways:

- *Planned inventory investment.* Firms may deliberately produce more units of a good and add them to inventory.

- *Unplanned inventory investment.* Consumers don't buy as many units of output as firms have produced, and unsold units are added to inventory.

Now compare two settings:

- *Setting 1.* Firms purchase more newly produced capital goods (more factories and machinery). As a result, investment rises and so does GDP, all other things remaining constant.

- *Setting 2.* Buyers don't buy as many units of output as firms have produced. The unsold units find their way into (unplanned) inventory investment. As a result, investment rises and so GDP rises too, all other things remaining constant.

Is the higher GDP in settings 1 and 2 equivalent? We think not. As far as the health and strength of the economy are concerned, the increase in GDP in setting 1 is superior to the increase in GDP in setting 2.

SELF-TEST

1. Describe the expenditure approach to computing GDP in a real-world economy.

2. Will GDP be smaller than the sum of consumption, investment, and government purchases if net exports are negative? Explain your answer.

3. If GDP is $400 billion and the country's population is 100 million, does it follow that each individual in the country has $40,000 worth of goods and services?

THE INCOME APPROACH TO COMPUTING GDP FOR A REAL-WORLD ECONOMY

A second way to compute GDP, the income approach, and the expenditure approach should give us the same dollar amount of GDP. Let's look at an example. In a given economy, 10 units of good A are produced, and 20 units of good B are produced. Further, the price of good A is $1, and the price of good B is $2. If buyers purchase all the units of each of the two goods, then they will have spent $50 on these two goods: ($1 × 10 units) + ($2 × 20 units) = $50. In other words, the expenditure approach to measuring GDP gives us $50 of GDP in this little economy.

However, money spent by one person is money earned by another. The person who sells 10 units of good A at $1 per unit receives an income of $10. The $10 spent by the buyer is $10 earned by the seller.

Exhibit 3 shows a circular flow diagram of the economy. This diagram illustrates that, in a simple economy, GDP computed by summing the purchases of the four sectors of the economy is equal to GDP computed by summing the income earned by the different resources. In other words, dollar purchases (or dollar expenditures) equal dollar income. More specifically, money spent to buy goods and services ends up flowing to the resources that produce them. (Again, think in terms of a tiny economy in which one person buys 10 oranges for $1 each. His expenditures equal $10. But the $10 also represents income for the person who sold the buyer the oranges. An expenditure for one person is income for another.)

Two steps are involved in computing GDP using the income approach. First, compute national income. Second, adjust national income for certain things. The end result is GDP.

EXHIBIT 3

The Circular Flow: Total Purchases (Expenditures) Equal Total Income in a Simple Economy

The exhibit shows an economy with four sectors: Households, Business Firms, Government, and Foreign Economies. Each sector purchases goods and services. The sum of these purchases is GDP [GDP = C + I + G + (EX − IM)].

The purchases (expenditures) made in product markets flow to business firms. Business firms then use these monies to buy resources in resource markets. In other words, these monies flow to the owners (suppliers) of land, labor, capital, and entrepreneurship. The sum of these resource payments is total income, which flows to households. In this simple economy, where some things have been ignored, total purchases (expenditures) equal total income. Because total purchases (expenditures) equal GDP and total purchases equal total income, it follows that GDP equals total income.

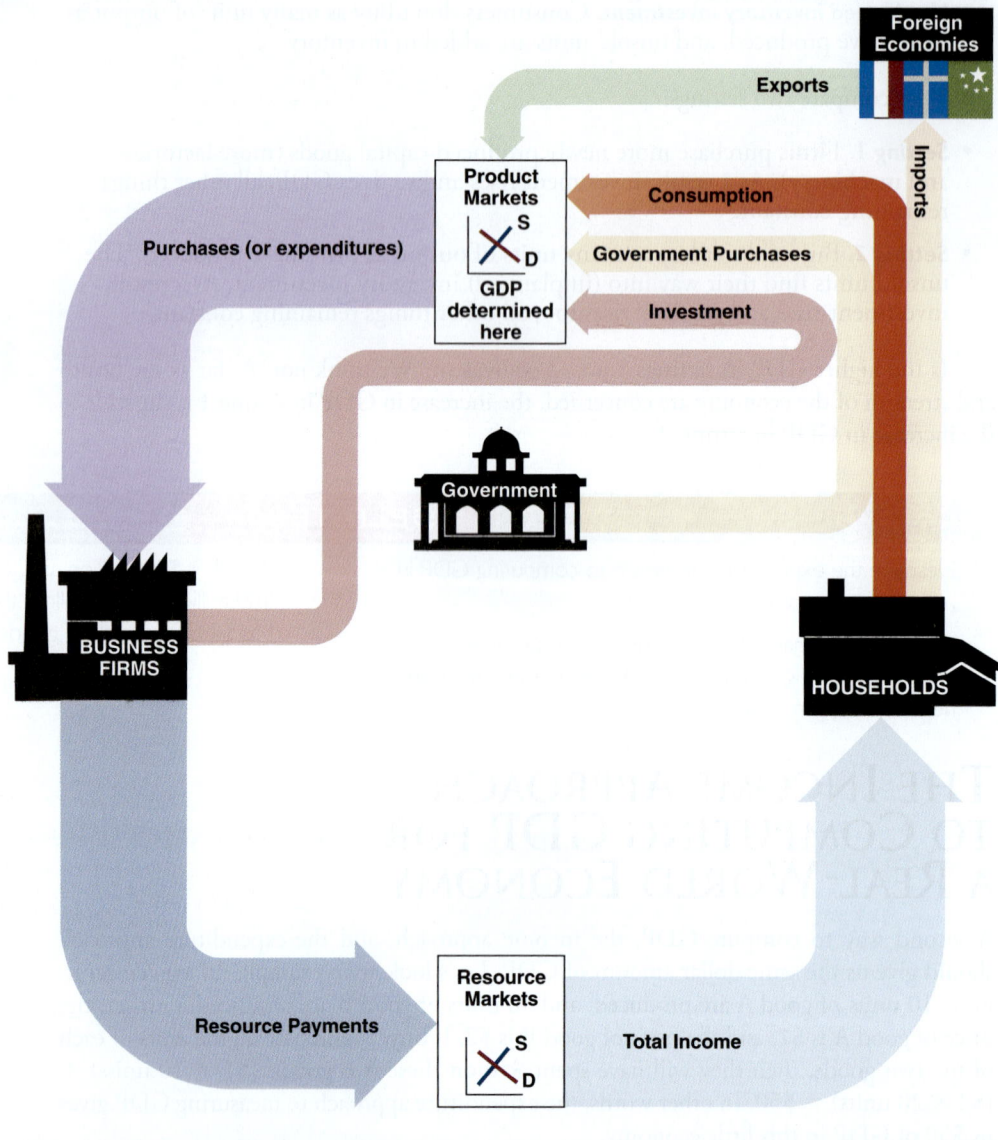

National Income

Total income earned by U.S. citizens and businesses, no matter where they reside or are located. National income is the sum of the payments to resources (land, labor, capital, and entrepreneurship): National income = Compensation of employees + Proprietors' income + Corporate profits + Rental income of persons + Net interest.

Computing National Income

National income is the sum of five components: (1) compensation of employees, (2) proprietors' income, (3) corporate profits, (4) rental income of persons, and (5) net interest.

COMPENSATION OF EMPLOYEES The compensation of employees is equal to the total of (1) wages and salaries paid to employees, (2) employers' contributions to Social Security and employee benefit plans, and (3) the monetary value of fringe benefits, tips, and paid vacations. The compensation of employees is the largest component of national income. In 2009, in the United States it was $7.84 trillion.

PROPRIETORS' INCOME Proprietors' income includes all forms of income earned by self-employed individuals and the owners of unincorporated businesses, including

1820

Most people are interested in knowing what the per-capita GDP is today in different countries. Also interesting is the per-capita GDP in different countries over the years. For example, what country had the highest per-capita GDP in, say, 1820? The answer is the Netherlands. In 1900, New Zealand was the high country. The following three tables identify the top 10 countries in various years in terms of per-capita GDP.

EXHIBIT 4

	1820			1900			1950	
Rank	Country	Per-Capita GDP	Rank	Country	Per-Capita GDP	Rank	Country	Per-Capita GDP
1	Netherlands	$1,561	1	New Zealand	$4,320	1	United States	$9,573
2	Australia	$1,528	2	Australia	$4,299	2	Switzerland	$8,939
3	Austria	$1,295	3	United States	$4,096	3	New Zealand	$8,495
4	Belgium	$1,291	4	Belgium	$3,652	4	Venezuela	$7,424
5	United States	$1,287	5	Netherlands	$3,533	5	Australia	$7,218
6	Denmark	$1,225	6	Switzerland	$3,531	6	Canada	$7,047
7	France	$1,218	7	Germany	$3,134	7	Sweden	$6,738
8	Sweden	$1,198	8	Denmark	$2,902	8	Denmark	$6,683
9	Germany	$1,112	9	Austria	$2,901	9	Netherlands	$5,850
10	Italy	$1,092	10	France	$2,849	10	Belgium	$5,346

unincorporated farmers. Included in farm income is an estimate of the value of the food grown and consumed on farms.

CORPORATE PROFITS Corporate profits include all the income earned by the stockholders of corporations. Some of the profits are paid to stockholders in the form of dividends, some are kept within the firm to finance investments (these are called *undistributed profits* or *retained earnings*), and some are used to pay corporate profits taxes. (The portion of corporate profits used to pay corporate profits taxes is counted as income "earned" by households even though households do not receive the income.)

RENTAL INCOME (OF PERSONS) Rental income is the income received by individuals for the use of their nonmonetary assets (land, houses, offices). It also includes returns to individuals who hold copyrights and patents. Finally, it includes an imputed value to owner-occupied houses. For example, someone may own the house she lives in and therefore not pay any rent, but for purposes of national income accounting, a rental value is imputed. In short, home ownership is viewed as a business that produces a service that is sold to the owner of the business.

NET INTEREST Net interest is the interest income received by U.S. households and government minus the interest they paid out.

NATIONAL INCOME We can summarize national income and its components as follows:

$$
\begin{aligned}
\text{National income} = \;&\text{Compensation of employees} \\
&+ \text{Proprietors' income} \\
&+ \text{Corporate profits} \\
&+ \text{Rental income} \\
&+ \text{Net interest}
\end{aligned}
$$

From National Income to GDP: Making Some Adjustments

After computing national income, we might think that there is nothing else to do—that national income should equal GDP. We naturally think that every dollar spent is someone's income. But when we check the actual figures for national income and GDP, we find that they are not equal. In other words, not every dollar spent is someone else's income. For example, if Jones spends $10 to buy a book, $9.50 of the $10 might end up in the seller's pocket as income, but remaining 50¢ might go for taxes.

With this in mind, the income approach to computing GDP requires us to add certain things to national income and to subtract certain things from it. The following equation and Exhibit 5 show what must be added to and subtracted from national income to compute GDP. Keep the equation and exhibit in mind as you continue to read.

$$
\begin{aligned}
\text{GDP} = \;&\text{National income} \\
&- \text{Income earned from the rest of the world} \\
&+ \text{Income earned by the rest of the world} \\
&+ \text{Indirect business taxes} \\
&+ \text{Capital consumption allowance} \\
&+ \text{Statistical discrepancy}
\end{aligned}
$$

INCOME EARNED FROM THE REST OF THE WORLD, INCOME EARNED BY THE REST OF THE WORLD In computing national income, we include the income earned by U.S. citizens who work and live in other countries, but we do not include the income earned by foreigners who work and live in the United States. If we want to compute GDP, we have to adjust for both these incomes. We do so by (1) subtracting from

---

EXHIBIT 5

The Income Approach to Computing GDP

The exhibit identifies the components of national income and the adjustments necessary to compute GDP using the income approach.

GDP: Proceed with Caution

Making incorrect comparisons between countries based on GDP figures is easy to do. For example, a person might notice that Austria's GDP ($374 billion) is smaller than Germany's GDP ($2,810 billion) and conclude that Austrians are not as well off as Germans.

First, however, we would expect a country with a smaller population to have a smaller GDP than a country with a larger population. With fewer people, usually less output is produced. Austria has a population of 8.2 million, whereas Germany has a population of 82 million. In other words, Germany has over 10 times the population of Austria; so we would expect it to have a higher GDP.

Also, GDP doesn't matter as much as per-capita GDP. For example, currently Austria has a higher per-capita GDP ($39,400) than Germany ($34,200).

But even per-capita GDP can be deceiving. When an economist states that the per-capita GDP of, say, Austria, is $39,400, this is the dollar amount each person in Austria would have *if* the GDP of the country

© IMAGE COPYRIGHT FEVERPITCH, 2009. USED UNDER LICENSE FROM SHUTTERSTOCK.COM

were divided equally among the entire population—in other words, if everyone in the country had an equal slice of GDP.

In actuality, not everyone in the country gets an equal slice. Some people have a much smaller slice than others. Whereas one person may have a slice equal to $400,000, another person might have a slice equal to $7,000.

Finally, keep in mind that we can witness an increase in GDP in two ways. GDP will rise if the inhabitants of a country actually produce more goods and services and if output remains constant while only prices rise. A rise in GDP due to only rising prices does not mean the same thing as a rise in GDP due to rising output while prices remain constant. Obviously, the overall standard of living of the people in the country is better served when GDP rises because output is higher than when it rises due to increasing prices.

The bottom line is that GDP is a useful economic variable that is readily measured and reported on. But we need to be careful to use it incorrectly when making comparisons, discussing well-being, and drawing conclusions.

national income the income earned from the rest of the world (this is income that U.S. citizens living abroad earned by producing and selling goods) and (2) adding to national income the income earned by the rest of the world (this is income that non-U.S. citizens earned by producing and selling goods in the United States).

INDIRECT BUSINESS TAXES Indirect business taxes are made up mainly of excise taxes, sales taxes, and property taxes. These taxes are not part of national income because they are not considered a payment to any resource (land, labor, etc.). Think of them as monies collected by government, not payments to land, labor, capital, or entrepreneurship.

Indirect taxes are included in the purchases of goods and services (you pay a sales tax when you buy most goods) and so are included when the expenditure approach is used to compute GDP. Therefore, we must add indirect business taxes to national income.

CAPITAL CONSUMPTION ALLOWANCE Some capital goods are used up in the production process through natural wear, obsolescence, or accidental destruction (e.g., the

Capital Consumption Allowance (Depreciation)
The estimated amount of capital goods used up in production through natural wear, obsolescence, and accidental destruction.

machinery that breaks down and cannot be repaired). The cost to replace these capital goods is called the capital consumption allowance, or depreciation. It is added to national income because we want a measure of all the income earned in the economy. National income, by itself, doesn't include the income payments implicit in the capital consumption allowance.

STATISTICAL DISCREPANCY GDP and national income are computed using different sets of data. Hence, statistical discrepancies or pure computational errors often occur and must be accounted for in the national income accounts.

Other National Income Accounting Measurements

Besides gross domestic product (GDP) and national income, three other national income accounting measurements are important: net domestic product, personal income, and disposable income. All five measurements—gross domestic product, national income, net domestic product, personal income, and disposable income—are often used interchangeably to measure the output produced and income earned in an economy.

Net Domestic Product

Net Domestic Product (NDP)
GDP minus the capital consumption allowance.

If we use the expenditure approach to compute GDP, we add consumption, investment, government purchases, and net exports. Investment (or more specifically, gross private domestic investment) includes fixed investment and inventory investment. Some of the fixed investment, however, is used to replace worn-out or obsolete capital goods, not to produce new goods. In short, gross private domestic investment contains the capital consumption allowance. If we subtract the capital consumption allowance from GDP, we are left with net domestic product (NDP). NDP measures the total value of new goods available in the economy in a given year after worn-out capital goods have been replaced.

$$\text{Net domestic product (NDP)} = \text{GDP} - \text{Capital consumption allowance}$$

Personal Income

Not all income earned is received, and not all income received is earned. An example of income earned but not received is undistributed profits, which stockholders earn but do not receive. Instead, the corporation usually reinvests the undistributed profits. An example of income received but not earned is Social Security benefits.

Personal Income
The amount of income that individuals actually receive. It is equal to national income minus undistributed corporate profits, social insurance taxes, and corporate profits taxes, plus transfer payments.

    Personal income is the amount of income that individuals actually receive. It is equal to national income minus such major earned-but-not-received items as undistributed corporate profits, social insurance taxes (Social Security contributions), and corporate profits taxes, plus transfer payments (which are received but not earned).

$$\begin{aligned}
\text{Personal income} = {} & \text{National income} \\
& - \text{Undistributed corporate profits} \\
& - \text{Social insurance taxes} \\
& - \text{Corporate profits taxes} \\
& + \text{Transfer payments}
\end{aligned}$$

Disposable Income

Disposable Income
The portion of personal income that can be used for consumption or saving. It is equal to personal income minus personal taxes (especially income taxes).

The portion of personal income that can be used for consumption or saving is referred to as disposable personal income, or simply disposable income. It is equal to personal income minus personal taxes (especially income taxes). Sometimes disposable income is referred to as spendable income, take-home pay, or after-tax income.

$$\text{Disposable income} = \text{Personal income} - \text{Personal taxes}$$

REAL GDP

This section defines Real GDP, shows how to compute it, and then explains how it is used to measure economic growth.

Why We Need Real GDP

In 2006, the U.S. GDP was about $13.39 trillion. One year later, in 2007, GDP was about $14.07 trillion. Although you know GDP was higher in 2007 than in 2006, do you know *why*?

As you think about your answer, look at GDP in a one-good economy. Suppose 10 units of this good X are produced and each unit is sold for $10; the GDP in the economy is $100.

$$\text{GDP} = \$10 \times 10 \text{ units} = \$100$$

The GDP rises from $100 to $250. Why? It could rise because price increased from $10 to $25:

$$\text{GDP} = \$25 \times 10 \text{ units} = \$250$$

Or it could rise because the quantity of output produced increased from 10 units to 25 units:

$$\text{GDP} = \$10 \times 25 \text{ units} = \$250$$

Or it could rise because price increased to $12.50 and the quantity increased to 20 units:

$$\text{GDP} = \$12.50 \times 20 \text{ units} = \$250$$

To gauge the health of the economy, economists want to know why the GDP increased. If GDP increased simply because price increased, then the economy is not growing. For an economy to grow, more output must be produced.

Because an increase in GDP can be due in part simply to an increase in price, a more meaningful measure is Real GDP. Real GDP is GDP adjusted for price changes.

Real GDP
The value of the entire output produced annually within a country's borders, adjusted for price changes.

Computing Real GDP

One way to compute Real GDP is to find the value of the output for the different years in terms of the same prices, that is, the base-year prices. Consider the following data for our one-good economy:

Year	Price of Good X	Quantity Produced of Good X (units)	GDP
1	$10	100	$10 × 100 = **$1,000**
2	$12	120	$12 × 120 = **$1,440**
3	$14	140	$14 × 140 = **$1,960**

The data show why GDP is higher in years 2 and 3: Both price and quantity have increased. However, we want to separate the part of GDP that is higher due to an increase in quantity from the part that is higher due to an increase in price. We want the Real GDP, the part of GDP that is higher because the quantity of output is higher.

To compute Real GDP for any year, multiply the quantity of the good produced in a given year by the price in the base year. If year 1 is the base year, we multiply the quantity of the good produced in year 2 by the price of the good in year 1. To find Real GDP in year 3, we multiply the quantity of the good produced in year 3 by the price of the good in year 1.

Year	Price of Good X	Quantity Produced of Good X (units)	GDP	Real GDP
1 (Base Year)	$10	100	$10 × 100 = **$1,000**	$10 × 100 = **$1,000**
2	$12	120	$12 × 120 = **$1,440**	$10 × 120 = **$1,200**
3	$14	140	$14 × 140 = **$1,960**	$10 × 140 = **$1,400**

The General Equation for Real GDP

The real world has more than one good and more than one price. The general equation used to compute Real GDP is:

$$\text{Real GDP} = \sum(\text{Base-year prices} \times \text{Current-year quantities})$$

$\sum$, the Greek capital letter sigma, stands for summation. Thus, Real GDP is the sum of all the current-year quantities times their base-year prices. In 2009, Real GDP in the United States was $12.98 trillion.

What Does It Mean If Real GDP Is Higher in One Year Than in Another?

If GDP is, say, $9 trillion in year 1 and $9.5 trillion in year 2, we cannot be sure why it has increased from one year to the next. (1) Did prices rise while output remained constant? (2) Did output rise while prices remained constant? (3) Or did prices and output both rise?

However, if Real GDP is, say, $8 trillion in year 1 and $8.3 trillion in year 2, we know why it has increased. Real GDP rises only if output rises. In other words, Real GDP rises only if more goods and services are produced.

Real GDP, Economic Growth, and Business Cycles

Suppose you have to choose between two countries. In country A, Real GDP grows by 3 percent each year. In country B, Real GDP is the same each year; if Real GDP was $500 billion last year, it is $500 billion in the current year, and it will be $500 billion next year. In which of the two countries would you prefer to live, *ceteris paribus*?

Or make a choice between countries C and D. In country C, Real GDP takes a roller coaster ride, alternating between rising and falling. It rises for some months, then falls, then rises again, then falls, and so on. In country D, Real GDP simply rises year after year. In which of the two countries would you prefer to live, *ceteris paribus*?

If you chose one country over the other in each of these two cases, then you are implicitly saying that Real GDP matters to you. One of the reasons economists study Real GDP is that it matters to you and others. In other words, because Real GDP is important to you, it is important to economists.

Economists study two major macroeconomic topics that have to do with Real GDP: *economic growth* and *business cycles*.

ECONOMIC GROWTH Annual economic growth has occurred if Real GDP in one year is higher than Real GDP in the previous year. For example, if Real GDP is $8.1 trillion in one year and $8.3 trillion in the next, the economy has undergone economic growth. The growth rate is equal to the (positive) percentage change in Real GDP and is computed as follows:

Economic Growth

Increases in Real GDP.

$$\text{Percentage change in Real GDP} = \left(\frac{\text{Real GDP}_{\text{later year}} - \text{Real GDP}_{\text{earlier year}}}{\text{Real GDP}_{\text{earlier year}}} \right) \times 100$$

THE UPS AND DOWNS IN THE ECONOMY: THE BUSINESS CYCLE If Real GDP is on a roller coaster—rising and falling and rising and falling—the economy is said to be going through a business cycle. Economists usually talk about four or five phases of the business cycle. We identify five in the following list and in Exhibit 6.

Business Cycle

Recurrent swings (up and down) in Real GDP.

1. **Peak.** At the *peak* of the business cycle, Real GDP is at a temporary high. In Exhibit 6, Real GDP is at a temporary high at Q_1.

2. **Contraction.** The *contraction* phase represents a decline in Real GDP. According to the standard definition of *recession,* two consecutive quarter declines in Real GDP constitute a recession.

3. **Trough.** The low point in Real GDP, just before it begins to turn up, is called the *trough* of the business cycle.

4. **Recovery.** The *recovery* is the period when Real GDP is rising. It begins at the trough and ends at the initial peak. The recovery in Exhibit 6 extends from the trough until Real GDP is again at Q_1.

5. **Expansion.** The *expansion* phase refers to increases in Real GDP beyond the recovery. In Exhibit 6, it refers to increases in Real GDP above Q_1.

EXHIBIT 6

The Phases of the Business Cycle

The phases of a business cycle include the peak, contraction, trough, recovery, and expansion. A business cycle is measured from peak to peak.

An entire business cycle is measured from peak to peak. The typical business cycle is approximately four to five years, although a few have been shorter and some have been longer.

ⓕinding ECONOMICS

After Graduating from College Yoram has just graduated from college. He has been searching for a job in his chosen field of accounting, but so far he hasn't been offered a job he would like. Where is the economics?

The state (or health) of the economy is closely tied to whether business firms are hiring or firing. When the economy is growing, firms are usually hiring employees; when the economy is in a slump (a recession), firms are often firing employees. As far as one's job prospects go, graduating when the economy is strong and growing is better than when it is weak and declining. ▲ ▲ ▲

NATIONAL BUREAU OF ECONOMIC RESEARCH (NBER) AND RECESSIONS The standard definition of a recession is two consecutive quarter declines in Real GDP, but this is not the only definition of a recession. The National Bureau of Economic Research has this to say about a recession.

> *A recession is a period between a peak and a trough . . . During a recession, a significant decline in economic activity spreads across the economy and can last from a few months to more than a year.*

The NBER definition is therefore different from the standard definition of a recession. According to the NBER, "a recession is a significant decline in activity [that] spreads across the economy."

OFFICE HOURS

"Why Do We Use the *Expenditure* Approach to Measure Production?"

STUDENT:

When GDP was first defined, emphasis was placed on goods and services being *produced*. The definition of GDP was "the total market value of all final goods and services *produced* annually with a country's borders."

INSTRUCTOR:

Yes, that is correct.

STUDENT:

But when we computed GDP, we simply summed the *expenditures* made by each of the four sectors of the economy. In other words, we added consumption, investment, government purchases, and net exports.

Now here is my problem. When we define GDP, we speak about production— final goods and services *produced*. But when we compute GDP, production doesn't seem to come up. Instead we sum *expenditures* made by the four sectors of the economy.

My point is simple: A good can be produced that is not purchased. So if we add up only expenditures (or purchases), aren't we underestimating production?

INSTRUCTOR:

I see your point. What you are saying is perhaps 100 chairs, say, are produced in the year, but only 75 of them are purchased. In that case, counting only purchases (or expenditures) underestimates production. And production is what we really want to get at because GDP is defined as the total market value of all final goods and services produced.

STUDENT:

Yes, that's right. That's what I am getting at.

INSTRUCTOR:

Well, remember one important category of expenditures: investment. Investment consists of the expenditures of the business sector. We know that investment is the sum of fixed investment and inventory investment, but let's focus on inventory investment for a minute. Think of how goods might get into inventory. One way is for the firm to deliberately produce goods and put some into inventory. In other words, a company produces 1,000 chairs, sends 900 of them to different retailers, and then puts 100 into inventory in case there is an unexpected increase in demand for chairs. We'll call these 100 chairs planned inventory.

SELF-TEST

1. Suppose GDP is $6 trillion in year 1 and $6.2 trillion in year 2. What has caused the rise in GDP?

2. Suppose Real GDP is $5.2 trillion in year 1 and $5.3 trillion in year 2. What has caused the rise in Real GDP?

3. Can an economy be faced with endless business cycles and still see its Real GDP grow over time? Explain your answer.

Now think of another way that chairs can be added to inventory. Suppose that when the firm sends those 900 chairs to different retailers, not all of the chairs sell. Only 700 of them sell. What will retailers do with the remaining 200 chairs? One thing they might do is return them to the producer. So what does the firm do with those 200 returned chairs. For now, they put them into inventory. We'll call these 200 chairs unplanned inventory.

Here is the important point: The 300 chairs in inventory (100 chairs in planned inventory and 200 chairs in unplanned inventory) are part of overall investment. In other words, if investment for the year equals $2.1 trillion (for the economy), the market value of the 300 chairs in inventory are part of that $2.1 trillion.

When computing GDP, we count those 300 chairs the same way we count the 700 that were produced and purchased. In short, everything produced in the economy is purchased by someone. In our example, the 300 chairs were "purchased" by the firm that produced them.

STUDENT:

Let me see if I have this right. If a firm produces a good and it is bought by, say, a consumer, that good is counted in GDP. But if the good is not bought by a consumer, then it is considered to be purchased by the firm that produced it. In other words, the chair company produces 1,000 chairs, sells 700 to consumers, and "sells" 300 to itself. It "buys" 300 of its own chairs. Is that right?

INSTRUCTOR:

That's right.

STUDENT:

But isn't that cheating somehow? After all, the 300 chairs weren't actually sold to anyone? They certainly weren't sold in the way we usually think of something being sold.

INSTRUCTOR:

That's true. But remember what we are trying to get at with GDP: the total market value of all final goods and services produced. Those 300 chairs were certainly produced. Looking at the 300 chairs as being purchased by the firm that produced them is simply a way of counting them. And counting those 300 chairs is what we want to do when we are trying to measure GDP.

STUDENT:

Yes, I see that now.

POINTS TO REMEMBER

1. GDP is the total market value of all final goods and services *produced* annually within a country's borders.

2. We can use the expenditure approach to measure production as long as all goods and services produced but not sold to end consumers are considered to be "purchased" by the firm that produced them.

GROSS DOMESTIC PRODUCT

- Gross domestic product (GDP) is the total market value of all final goods and services produced annually within a country's borders.
- Either the expenditure approach or the income approach can be used to compute GDP.
- To avoid the problem of double counting, only final goods and services are included in GDP.
- GDP omits certain nonmarket goods and services, both legal and illegal underground activities, the sale of used goods, financial transactions, transfer payments, and leisure (even though leisure is a good). Finally, GDP is not adjusted for the bads (e.g., pollution) that sometimes accompany production.

EXPENDITURES

- The expenditures on U.S. goods and services include consumption, gross private domestic investment (investment), government consumption expenditures and gross investment (government purchases), and net exports (exports–imports).
- Consumption includes spending on durable goods, nondurable goods, and services.
- Investment includes purchases of newly produced capital goods (fixed investment), changes in business inventories (inventory investment), and the purchases of new residential housing (also fixed investment).
- Government purchases include federal, state, and local government purchases of goods and services and gross investment in highways, bridges, and so on. Government purchases do not include transfer payments.
- Net exports equal the total foreign spending on domestic goods (exports) minus the total domestic spending on foreign goods (imports).

COMPUTING GDP

- Using the expenditure approach, GDP $= C + I + G + (EX - IM)$. In other words, GDP equals consumption plus investment plus government purchases plus net exports.

MEASUREMENTS OTHER THAN GDP

- Net domestic product (NDP) equals gross domestic product (GDP) minus the capital consumption allowance.

$$\text{NDP} = \text{GDP} - \text{Capital consumption allowance}$$

- National income equals the sum of resource, or factor, payments.

$$
\begin{aligned}
\text{National income} = \ & \text{Compensation of employees} \\
& + \text{Proprietors' income} \\
& + \text{Corporate profits} \\
& + \text{Rental income} \\
& + \text{Net interest}
\end{aligned}
$$

- Personal income equals national income minus undistributed corporate profits, social insurance taxes, and corporate profits taxes, plus transfer payments.

$$
\begin{aligned}
\text{Personal Income} = \ & \text{National income} \\
& - \text{Undistributed corporate profits} \\
& - \text{Social insurance taxes} \\
& - \text{Corporate profits taxes} \\
& + \text{Transfer payments}
\end{aligned}
$$

- Disposable Income = Personal income − Personal taxes

REAL GDP

- Real GDP is GDP adjusted for price changes. It is GDP in base-year dollars.

ECONOMIC GROWTH AND BUSINESS CYCLES

- Annual economic growth has occurred if Real GDP in one year is higher than Real GDP in the previous year.
- The business cycle has five phases: peak, contraction, trough, recovery, and expansion. A complete business cycle is measured from peak to peak.

Gross Domestic Product (GDP)	Investment	Imports	Net Domestic Product (NDP)
Final Good	Inventory Investment	Exports	Personal Income
Intermediate Good	Fixed Investment	Net Exports	Disposable Income
Double Counting	Government Purchases	National Income	Real GDP
Transfer Payment	Government Transfer	Capital Consumption	Economic Growth
Consumption	Payments	Allowance (Depreciation)	

QUESTIONS AND PROBLEMS

1. A business firm produces a good this year that it doesn't sell. As a result, the good is added to the firm's inventory. How does this inventory good find its way into GDP?

2. In the first quarter of the year, Real GDP was $400 billion; in the second quarter, it was $398 billion; in the third quarter, it was $399 billion; and in the fourth quarter, it was $395 billion. Has there been a recession? Explain your answer.

3. Why does GDP omit the sales of used goods? Of financial transactions? Of government transfer payments?

4. Does the expenditure approach to computing GDP measure U.S. spending on all goods, U.S. spending on only U.S. goods, or U.S. and foreign spending on only U.S. goods? Explain your answer.

5. The manuscript for this book was keyed by the author. Had he hired someone to do the keying, GDP would have been higher than it was. What other activities would increase GDP if they were done differently? What activities would decrease GDP if they were done differently?

6. What is the difference between a recovery and an expansion?

7. Discuss the problems you see in comparing the GDPs of two countries, say, the United States and the People's Republic of China.

8. Define each of the following terms:
   a. Contraction
   b. Business cycle
   c. Trough
   d. Disposable income
   e. Net domestic product

9. Which of the following are included in the calculation of this year's GDP? (a) 12-year-old Johnny mowing his family's lawn; (b) Dave Malone buying a used car; (c) Barbara Wilson buying a bond issued by General Motors; (d) Ed Ferguson's receipt of a Social Security payment; (e) the illegal drug transaction at the corner of Elm and Fifth.

10. Economists prefer to compare Real GDP figures for different years instead of comparing GDP figures. Why?

11. "I just heard on the news that GDP is higher this year than it was last year. This means that we're better off this year than last year." Comment.

WORKING WITH NUMBERS AND GRAPHS

1. Net exports are –$114 billion and exports are $857 billion. What are imports?

2. Consumption spending is $3.708 trillion, spending on nondurable goods is $1.215 trillion, and spending on services is $2.041 trillion. What does spending on durable goods equal?

3. Inventory investment is $62 billion and total investment is $1.122 trillion. What does fixed investment equal?

4. In year 1, the prices of goods X, Y, and Z are $2, $4, and $6 per unit, respectively. In year 2, the prices of goods X, Y, and Z are $3, $4, and $7, respectively. In year 2, twice as many units of each good are produced as in year 1. In year 1, 20 units of X, 40 units of Y, and 60 units of Z are produced. If year 1 is the base year, what does Real GDP equal in year 2?

5. Nondurable goods spending = $400 million, durable goods spending = $300 million, new residential housing spending = $200 million, and spending on services = $500 million. What does consumption equal?

6. According to the circular flow diagram in Exhibit 3, consumption spending flows into U.S. product markets, but import spending does not. But U.S. households buy imported goods in U.S. markets, don't they? Explain.

7. If Real GDP is $487 billion in year 1 and $498 billion in year 2, what is the economic growth rate equal to?

8. The following figure shows a business cycle. Identify each of the following as a phase of the business cycle:
   a. Point A
   b. Between points A and B
   c. Point B
   d. Between points B and C
   e. Point D

CHAPTER 8

© VASILY SMIRNOV/FOTOLIA.COM

AGGREGATE DEMAND AND AGGREGATE SUPPLY

Introduction Businesses make decisions based on what is happening in the economy today and on what they expect will happen in the economy in the future. For example, their profitability is based in part on the wages they must pay their employees, the prices of their nonlabor inputs, the productivity of their workers, and business taxes. If businesses want to expand in the future, they must consider all these things and try to predict their future sales. If they trade overseas, they must worry about exchange rates and foreign real national income. We discuss all such things and more in this chapter.

A WAY TO VIEW THE ECONOMY

This chapter begins our theoretical discussion of an economy. We can think of an economy as consisting of two major activities: buying and producing. See Exhibit 1. Specifically, goods and services are produced, and goods and services are bought. When economists speak about aggregate demand (*AD*), they are speaking about the buying side of the economy. When economists speak about aggregate supply, they are speaking about the producing side of the economy.

Buying side of the economy = Aggregate demand

Producing side of the economy = Aggregate supply

With respect to production, two time periods are relevant: production in the short run and production in the long run. When referring to short-run aggregate supply (*SRAS*), economists are speaking about production in the short run. When referring to long-run aggregate supply (*LRAS*), they are speaking about production in the long run.

Production in the short run = Short-run aggregate supply

Production in the long run = Long-run aggregate supply

EXHIBIT 1

An Economy

There are two sides to an economy: a buying side and a producing side. There are two time periods that relate to the producing side: production in the short run and production in the long run. Buying side = Aggregate demand (AD); Production in the short run = Short-run aggregate supply (SRAS); Production in the long run = Long-run aggregate supply (LRAS).

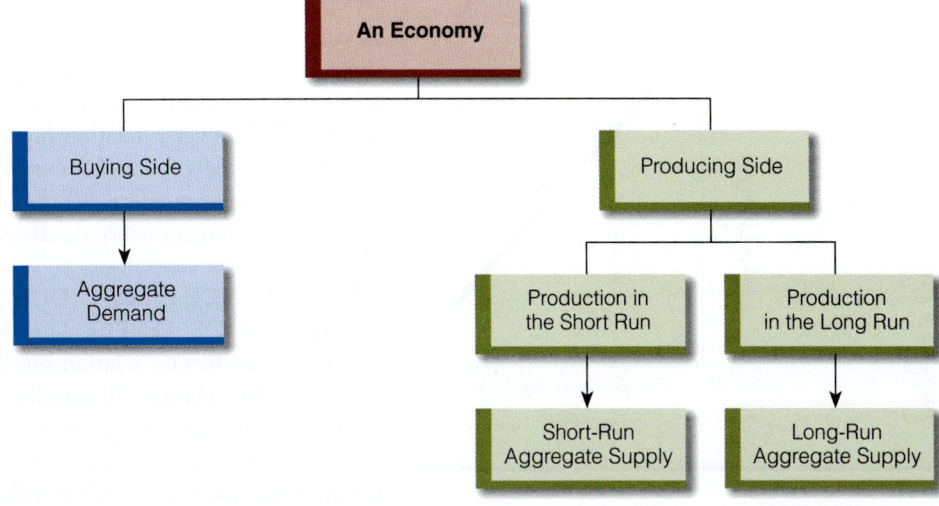

The framework of analysis we use is called aggregate demand–aggregate supply (*AD−AS*). That framework of analysis has three parts:

1. Aggregate demand (*AD*)

2. Short-run aggregate supply (*SRAS*)

3. Long-run aggregate supply (*LRAS*)

AGGREGATE DEMAND

Recall from the last chapter that people, firms, and governments buy U.S. goods and services. Aggregate demand is the quantity demanded of these U.S. goods and services, or the quantity demanded of U.S. Real GDP, at various price levels, *ceteris paribus*. For example, the following whole set of data represents aggregate demand:

Aggregate Demand

The quantity demanded of all goods and services (Real GDP) at different price levels, *ceteris paribus*.

Aggregate Demand

Price Index	Quantity Demanded of Goods and Services (Quantity Demanded of Real GDP)
100	$1,200 billion worth of goods and services
110	$1,000 billion worth of goods and services
120	$800 billion worth of goods and services

An aggregate demand (AD) curve is the graphical representation of aggregate demand. An *AD* curve is shown in Exhibit 2. Notice that it is downward sloping, indicating an inverse relationship between the price level (*P*) and the quantity demanded of Real GDP (*Q*):

Aggregate Demand (AD) Curve

A curve that shows the quantity demanded of all goods and services (Real GDP) at different price levels, *ceteris paribus*.

EXHIBIT 2

The Aggregate Demand Curve

The aggregate demand curve is downward sloping, specifying an inverse relationship between the price level and the quantity demanded of Real GDP.

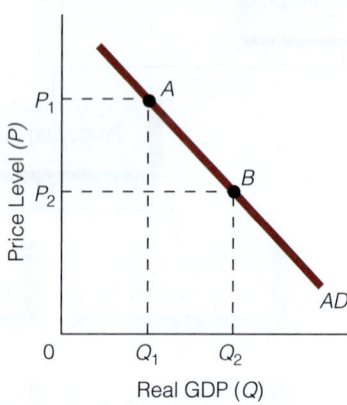

Aggregate Demand Curve
The price level and quantity demanded of Real GDP are inversely related.

As the price level rises, the quantity demanded of Real GDP falls; as the price level falls, the quantity demanded of Real GDP rises, *ceteris paribus*.

Why Does the Aggregate Demand Curve Slope Downward?

Asking why the *AD* curve slopes downward is the same as asking why the relationship between the price level and the quantity demanded of Real GDP is inverse. This inverse relationship and the resulting downward slope of the *AD* curve are explained by (1) the real balance effect, (2) the interest rate effect, and (3) the international trade effect.

REAL BALANCE EFFECT (DUE TO A CHANGE IN THE PRICE LEVEL) The real balance effect states that the inverse relationship between the price level and the quantity demanded of Real GDP is established through changes in the value of monetary wealth, or the value of a person's monetary assets. Changes in monetary wealth usually take the form of increased or decreased purchasing power, that is, the quantity of goods and services that can be purchased with a unit of money.

Real Balance Effect
The change in the purchasing power of dollar-denominated assets that results from a change in the price level.

Monetary Wealth
The value of a person's monetary assets. Wealth, as distinguished from monetary wealth, refers to the value of all assets owned, both monetary and nonmonetary. In short, a person's wealth equals his or her monetary wealth (e.g., $1,000 cash) plus nonmonetary wealth (e.g., a car or a house).

Purchasing Power
The quantity of goods and services that can be purchased with a unit of money. Purchasing power and the price level are inversely related: As the price level goes up (down), purchasing power goes down (up).

Interest Rate Effect
The changes in household and business buying as the interest rate changes (in turn, a reflection of a change in the demand for or supply of credit brought on by price level changes).

To illustrate, consider a person who has $50,000 in cash. Suppose the price level falls. As this happens, the purchasing power of the person's $50,000 rises. The $50,000, which once could buy 100 television sets at $500 each, can now buy 125 sets at $400 each. An increase in the purchasing power of the person's $50,000 is identical to saying that his monetary wealth has increased. (Isn't the $50,000 more valuable when it can buy more than when it can buy less?) And, as he becomes wealthier, he buys more goods.

So a fall in the price level causes purchasing power to rise, which increases a person's monetary wealth. As people become wealthier, the quantity demanded of Real GDP rises.

Suppose the price level rises. In this event, the purchasing power of the $50,000 falls. The $50,000, which once could buy 100 television sets at $500 each, can now buy 80 sets at $625 each. A decrease in the purchasing power of the person's $50,000 is identical to saying that his monetary wealth has decreased. And as he becomes less wealthy, he buys fewer goods.

In summary, a rise in the price level causes purchasing power to fall, which decreases a person's monetary wealth. As people become less wealthy, the quantity demanded of Real GDP falls.

INTEREST RATE EFFECT (DUE TO CHANGE IN THE PRICE LEVEL) The interest rate effect states that the inverse relationship between the price level and the quantity demanded of Real GDP is established through changes in the part of household and business spending that is sensitive to changes in interest rates.

A person buys a fixed bundle of goods (food, clothing, and shelter) each week. Suppose the price level falls, increasing the purchasing power of the person's money. With more purchasing power (per dollar), she can purchase her fixed bundle of goods with less money. What does she do with part of this increase in her monetary wealth? She saves it. In terms of simple supply-and-demand analysis, the supply of credit increases. Subsequently, the price of credit (the interest rate) drops. As the interest rate drops, households and businesses borrow more; so they end up buying more goods. Thus, the quantity demanded of Real GDP rises.

Now suppose the price level rises, decreasing the purchasing power of the person's money. With less purchasing power (per dollar), she cannot purchase her fixed bundle of goods with the same amount of money. If she wants to continue to buy the goods, she needs to acquire more money. To do that, she goes to a bank and requests a loan. In terms of simple supply-and-demand analysis, the demand for credit increases. Consequently, the interest rate rises. As the interest rate rises, households borrow less to finance, say, automobile purchases, and firms borrow less to finance new capital goods spending. Thus, the quantity demanded of Real GDP falls.

INTERNATIONAL TRADE EFFECT (DUE TO A CHANGE IN THE PRICE LEVEL) The international trade effect is the change in foreign sector spending as the price level changes. The inverse relationship between the price level and the quantity demanded of Real GDP is established through foreign sector spending, which includes U.S. spending on foreign goods (imports) and foreign spending on U.S. goods (exports).

Suppose the price level in the United States falls. As this happens, U.S. goods become relatively cheaper than foreign goods. As a result, both Americans and foreigners buy more U.S. goods. The quantity demanded of U.S. Real GDP rises.

Suppose the price level in the United States rises. In that event, U.S. goods become relatively more expensive than foreign goods. As a result, both Americans and foreigners buy fewer U.S. goods. The quantity demanded of U.S. Real GDP falls.

For a review of the three effects—real balance, interest rate, and international trade—see Exhibit 3.

> **International Trade Effect**
> The change in foreign sector spending as the price level changes.

ⓕinding ECONOMICS

In a Store Buying a Watch Jim is in a store buying a watch imported from Switzerland. What does this purchase have to do with a downward-sloping aggregate demand curve? When we ask Jim why he's buying a Swiss watch, he tells us that the Swiss watch is cheaper than the American watch. The reason could very well be that the U.S. price level has recently risen relative to the Swiss price level. In other words, when Jim buys the Swiss watch instead of the American watch, we could be seeing the international trade effect in action. ▲ ▲ ▲

An Important Word on the Three Effects

As explained, the aggregate demand curve is downward sloping because of the real balance, interest rate, and international trade effects. However, keep in mind that what caused these three effects is a change in the price level. In other words, when discussing, say, the interest rate effect, we are talking about the interest rate effect of *a change in the price level.*

Price level changes → Interest rate effect

Why is this point important? The interest rate can change due to things *other than the price level changing*, and not everything that changes the interest rate leads to a movement from one point to another point on the *AD* curve. Other things that change the interest rate can lead to a shift in the *AD* curve instead. We will have more to say about this later. For now, though, simply keep in mind the cause of each of the three effects: a change in the price level—the variable on the vertical axis in Exhibit 2.

A Change in Quantity Demanded of Real GDP Versus a Change in Aggregate Demand

A change in the price level brings about a change in the quantity demanded of Real GDP. As the price level falls, the quantity demanded of Real GDP rises, *ceteris paribus.* In Exhibit 4(a), a change in the quantity demanded of Real GDP is represented as a *movement* from one point (*A*) on AD_1 to another point (*B*) on AD_1.

EXHIBIT 3

Why the Aggregate Demand Curve Is Downward Sloping

This exhibit outlines the three effects that explain why the *AD* curve is downward sloping. Each effect relates to a change in the price level (*P*) leading to a change in the quantity demanded of Real GDP (*Q*).

Type of Effect	How It Works	Graphical Representation of What Happens
Real Balance Effect (due to a change in the price level)	*Price level falls* → purchasing power rises → monetary wealth rises → **buy more goods.**	
	Price level rises → purchasing power falls → monetary wealth falls → **buy fewer goods.**	
Interest Rate Effect (due to a change in the price level)	*Price level falls* → purchasing power rises → less money needed to buy fixed bundle of goods → save more → supply of credit rises → interest rate falls → businesses and households borrow more at lower interest rate → **buy more goods.**	
	Price level rises → purchasing power falls → borrow money in order to continue to buy fixed bundle of goods → demand for credit rises → interest rate rises → businesses and households borrow less at higher interest rate → **buy fewer goods.**	
International Trade Effect (due to a change in the price level)	*Price level in U.S. falls* relative to foreign price levels → U.S. goods relatively less expensive than foreign goods → both Americans and foreigners **buy more U.S. goods.**	
	Price level in U.S. rises relative to foreign price levels → U.S. goods relatively more expensive than foreign goods → both Americans and foreigners **buy fewer U.S. goods.**	

EXHIBIT 4

A Change in the Quantity Demanded of Real GDP Versus a Change in Aggregate Demand

(a) A change in the quantity demanded of Real GDP is graphically represented as a *movement* from one point, A, on AD_1 to another point, B, on AD_1. A change in the quantity demanded of Real GDP is the result of a change in the price level. (b) A change in aggregate demand is graphically represented as a *shift* in the aggregate demand curve from AD_1 to AD_2.

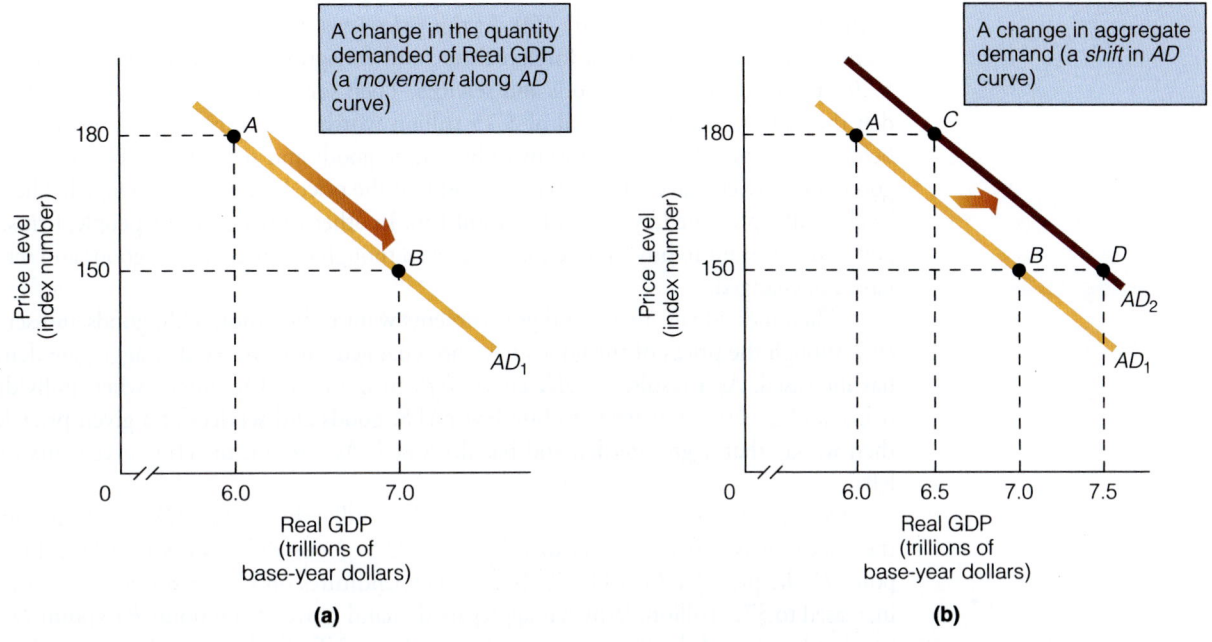

(a)

(b)

A change in aggregate demand is represented in Exhibit 4(b) as a *shift* in the aggregate demand curve from AD_1 to AD_2. When the aggregate demand curve shifts, the quantity demanded of Real GDP changes even though the price level remains constant. For example, at a price level (index number) of 180, the quantity demanded of Real GDP on AD_1 in Exhibit 4(b) is $6.0 trillion. But at the same price level (180), the quantity demanded of Real GDP on AD_2 is $6.5 trillion.

thinking like AN ECONOMIST

Shift Factors Versus Movement Factors, Once Again To the economist, not all factors are alike. For some factors, the change is from one point to another on the same curve. These are *movement factors*. The price level is a movement factor. Raise it, and we move up on the AD curve; lower it, and we move down.

Other factors, if they change, shift curves. These are *shift factors*. We turn now to discuss shift factors with respect to the AD curve. ●●●

Changes in Aggregate Demand: Shifts in the *AD* Curve

What can change aggregate demand? What can cause aggregate demand to rise, and what can cause it to fall?

The simple answer is that aggregate demand changes when spending on U.S. goods and services changes. If spending increases at a given price level, aggregate demand rises; if spending decreases at a given price level, aggregate demand falls.

Spending increases at a given price level → AD rises

Spending decreases at a given price level → AD falls

Suppose the price level in the economy is represented by the consumer price index (CPI) and the index is currently 150. At this price level, U.S. residents, firms, and governments, along with foreigners, foreign firms, and foreign governments, want to buy, say, $7.0 trillion worth of U.S. goods and services. Then something changes, and all of a sudden they all want to buy a total of $7.5 trillion worth of U.S. goods and services. Now, before you conclude that they want to buy more goods and services because the prices of goods and services have fallen, keep in mind that the price level has not changed. The price level—still represented by the CPI—is still 150. In other words, all these people, firms, and governments want to buy more U.S. goods even though the prices of the goods and services have not changed.

When individuals, firms, and governments want to buy more U.S. goods and services even though the prices of the goods have not changed, then we say that aggregate demand has increased. As a result, the *AD* curve *shifts* to the right. Of course, when individuals, firms, and governments want to buy fewer U.S. goods and services at a given price level, then we say that aggregate demand has decreased. As a result, the *AD* curve shifts to the left.

Exhibit 4(b) shows a change in aggregate demand (a shift in the *AD* curve). At point *B,* the price level is 150, and total expenditures on U.S. goods and services are $7.0 trillion. At point *D,* the price level is still 150, but total expenditures on U.S. goods and services have increased to $7.5 trillion. Why has aggregate demand moved from point *B* to point *D*; that is, what has caused the increase in total expenditures? To find out, we have to look at the components of total expenditures.

How Spending Components Affect Aggregate Demand

The last chapter identified four major spending components: consumption (*C*), investment (*I*), government purchases (*G*), and net exports (*NX*). Let's keep the numbers simple: *C* = $100, *I* = $100, *G* = $100, *EX* = $50, and *IM* = $15. If *EX* = $50 and *IM* = $15, then net exports = $35.

Using these dollar figures, we calculate that $335 is spent on U.S. goods and services. We get this dollar amount by finding the sum of consumption, investment, government purchases, and net exports.

Total expenditures on U.S. goods and services = C + I + G + NX

Obviously, this dollar amount will go up if (1) *C* rises, (2) *I* rises, (3) *G* rises, and/or (4) *NX* rises. In other words, a rise in consumption, investment, government purchases, or net exports will raise spending on U.S. goods and services:

C↑, I↑, G↑, NX↑ → Total expenditures on U.S. goods and services↑

Now, what will cause spending on U.S. goods to go down? Obviously, it will decline if (1) *C* falls, (2) *I* falls, (3) *G* falls, and/or (4) *NX* falls.

C↓, I↓, G↓, NX↓ → Total expenditures on U.S. goods or services↓

Because we now know what causes total expenditures on U.S. goods and services to change, we can relate the components of spending to (U.S.) aggregate demand. If, *at a given price level*:

- Consumption, investment, government purchases, or net exports *rise*, aggregate demand will rise and the *AD* curve will shift to the right.

- If consumption, investment, government purchases, or net exports *fall*, aggregate demand will fall and the *AD* curve will shift to the left.

We can write these relationships as:

If, at a given price level, $C\uparrow$, $I\uparrow$, $G\uparrow$ $NX\uparrow$, then $AD\uparrow$

If, at a given price level, $C\downarrow$, $I\downarrow$, $G\downarrow$, $NX\downarrow$, then $AD\downarrow$

The flow charts in Exhibit 5 show how changes in spending components affect aggregate demand.

Why Is There More Total Spending?

Here is a question that an economics professors might place on an exam:

True or false? The price level falls and total spending rises. As a result of total spending rising, aggregate demand in the economy rises and the AD curve shifts rightward.

You may think the answer is true—perhaps because you are accustomed to thinking that if total spending rises, aggregate demand rises. But aggregate demand rises only if total spending rises at *a given price level.*

To illustrate the difference between (1) total spending rising at a falling price level and (2) total spending rising at a given price level, consider the following two examples.

- *Example 1.* The price level falls, and goods and services become cheaper. As a result of lower prices, individuals start to buy more goods and services. As a result, total spending rises.

EXHIBIT 5

Changes in Aggregate Demand

The flow charts show how aggregate demand changes given changes in various spending components.
C = consumption, I = investment, G = government purchases, NX = net exports, EX = exports, IM = imports. Keep in mind that $NX = EX - IM$.

(a)   (b)

- *Example 2.* The price level does not change. Still, something in the economy changes so that people start buying more goods and services. As a result of their buying more goods and services, total spending in the economy rises.

In both cases, total spending rises. But in example 1, total spending rises because prices have fallen. This leads to a *movement* down a given *AD* curve. In example 2, total spending rises even when prices remain unchanged. This leads to a *shift* rightward in the *AD* curve.

Lesson learned: Total spending can rise for one of two reasons. The first deals with a decline in prices and leads to a *movement* along a given *AD* curve. The second deals with a change in some factor other than prices and leads to a *shift* in the *AD* curve.

Factors That Can Change C, I, G, and NX (EX – IM) and Therefore Can Change AD (Shift the AD Curve)

What can change aggregate demand in the economy? The answer is a change in consumption, investment, government purchases, and/or net exports (exports minus imports). So, for example, if someone asks you why *AD* increased, you might say because consumption increased.

But suppose the person then asks, "What caused consumption to increase?" Your answer to one question simply leads to another. If a change in consumption changes aggregate demand, what changes consumption? The same question can be asked about changes in investment, government purchases, and net exports (i.e., exports and imports). For example, if aggregate demand increased because investment increased, then what caused investment to increase?

This section looks at some of the many factors that can change consumption, investment, and net exports. A later chapter considers the factors that can change government purchases.

CONSUMPTION Four factors can affect consumption: wealth, expectations about future prices and income, the interest rate, and income taxes.

Wealth
The value of all assets owned, both monetary and nonmonetary.

1. *Wealth.* Individuals consume not only on the basis of their present income but also on the basis of their wealth. Each of two individuals has an income of $80,000 a year. One has $75,000 in the bank, and the other has no assets at all. We would expect the person with $75,000 in the bank to spend more of her income on consumption goods this year. Greater wealth makes individuals feel financially more secure and thus more willing to spend.

- Increases in wealth lead to increases in consumption. If consumption increases, aggregate demand rises and the *AD* curve shifts to the right.

- Decreases in wealth lead to a fall in consumption, which leads to a fall in aggregate demand. Consequently, the *AD* curve shifts to the left.

$$\text{Wealth}\uparrow \rightarrow C\uparrow \rightarrow AD\uparrow$$

$$\text{Wealth}\downarrow \rightarrow C\downarrow \rightarrow AD\downarrow$$

2. *Expectations About Future Prices and Income.* Individuals' expectations of future prices can increase or decrease aggregate demand:

- If individuals expect *higher* prices in the future, they increase their current consumption expenditures to buy goods at the lower current prices. The increase in consumption leads to an increase in aggregate demand.

- If individuals expect *lower* prices in the future, they decrease current consumption expenditures. The reduction in consumption leads to a decrease in aggregate demand.

$$\text{Expect higher future prices} \rightarrow C\uparrow \rightarrow AD\uparrow$$

$$\text{Expect lower future prices} \rightarrow C\downarrow \rightarrow AD\downarrow$$

Similarly, expectations regarding income can affect aggregate demand:

- Expectations of a *higher* future income increase consumption, leading to an increase in aggregate demand.
- Expectations of a *lower* future income decrease consumption, leading to a decrease in aggregate demand.

$$\text{Expect higher future income} \rightarrow C\uparrow \rightarrow AD\uparrow$$

$$\text{Expect lower future income} \rightarrow C\downarrow \rightarrow AD\downarrow$$

3. *Interest Rate.* Current empirical work shows that spending on consumer durables is sensitive to the interest rate.

   - Buyers often pay for these items by borrowing; so an *increase* in the interest rate increases the monthly payment amounts linked to the purchase of durables and thereby reduces their consumption. The reduction in consumption leads to a decline in aggregate demand.
   - Alternatively, a *decrease* in the interest rate reduces monthly payment amounts and thereby increases the consumption of durables. The increase in consumption leads to an increase in aggregate demand.

$$\text{Interest rate} \uparrow \rightarrow C\downarrow \rightarrow AD\downarrow$$

$$\text{Interest rate} \downarrow \rightarrow C\uparrow \rightarrow AD\uparrow$$

4. *Income Taxes.* Let's consider personal income taxes, that is, the taxes a person pays on earned income.

   - As income taxes *rise*, disposable income decreases. When people have less take-home pay to spend, consumption falls. Consequently, aggregate demand decreases.
   - A *decrease* in income taxes has the opposite effect; it raises disposable income. When people have more take-home pay to spend, consumption rises and aggregate demand increases.

$$\text{Income taxes} \uparrow \rightarrow C\downarrow \rightarrow AD\downarrow$$

$$\text{Income taxes} \downarrow \rightarrow C\uparrow \rightarrow AD\uparrow$$

⨍inding ECONOMICS

In a Housing Downturn A newspaper article reads as follows: "Housing prices have fallen over the past six months, and economists are concerned that this might lead to less overall demand in the economy." Can you find the economics here? Do housing prices have anything to do with aggregate demand? Let's work backward. First, a decline in aggregate demand can be caused by a decline in consumption. Second, a decline in consumption can be caused by a change in any of four factors: wealth, expectations about future prices and income, the interest rate, and income taxes.

(continued)

finding ECONOMICS (continued)

Let's focus on wealth. If housing prices fall, people who own houses will find themselves with less overall wealth. (Think of a person whose house is worth $500,000 one month and $450,000 six months later. She has suffered a decline in wealth.) As a result, these people reduce their consumption, and aggregate demand falls. ▲ ▲ ▲

INVESTMENT Three factors can change investment: the interest rate, expectations about future sales, and business taxes.

1. *Interest Rate.* Changes in interest rates affect business decisions.

   • As the interest rate *rises*, the cost of an investment project rises and businesses invest less. As investment decreases, aggregate demand decreases.

   • As the interest rate *falls*, the cost of an investment project falls and businesses invest more. Consequently, aggregate demand increases.

$$\text{Interest rate} \uparrow \rightarrow I\downarrow \rightarrow AD\downarrow$$

$$\text{Interest rate} \downarrow \rightarrow I\uparrow \rightarrow AD\uparrow$$

2. *Expectations About Future Sales.* Businesses invest because they expect to sell the goods they produce.

   • If businesses become *optimistic* about future sales, investment spending grows and aggregate demand increases.

   • If businesses become *pessimistic* about future sales, investment spending contracts and aggregate demand decreases.

$$\text{Businesses become optimistic about future sales} \rightarrow I\uparrow \rightarrow AD\uparrow$$

$$\text{Businesses become pessimistic about future sales} \rightarrow I\downarrow \rightarrow AD\downarrow$$

3. *Business Taxes.* Businesses naturally consider expected after-tax profits when making their investment decisions.

   • An *increase* in business taxes lowers expected profitability. With less profit expected, businesses invest less. As investment spending declines, so does aggregate demand.

   • A *decrease* in business taxes, on the other hand, raises expected profitability and investment spending. This increases aggregate demand.

$$\text{Business taxes} \uparrow \rightarrow I\downarrow \rightarrow AD\downarrow$$

$$\text{Business taxes} \downarrow \rightarrow I\uparrow \rightarrow AD\uparrow$$

NET EXPORTS Two factors can change net exports: foreign real national income and the exchange rate.

1. *Foreign Real National Income.* Just as Americans earn a national income, so do people in other countries. That is the foreign national income. By adjusting this foreign national income for price changes, we obtain foreign real national income.

   • As foreign real national income *rises*, foreigners buy more U.S. goods and services. Thus, U.S. exports (*EX*) rise. As exports rise, net exports rise, *ceteris paribus*. As net exports rise, aggregate demand increases.

- This process works in reverse. As foreign real national income *falls*, foreigners buy fewer U.S. goods and exports fall. This lowers net exports, reducing aggregate demand.

Foreign real national income ↑ → U.S. exports ↑ → U.S. net exports ↑ → AD↑

Foreign real national income ↓ → U.S. exports ↓ → U.S. net exports ↓ → AD↓

2. *Exchange Rate.* The exchange rate is the price of one currency in terms of another currency; for example, $1.25 may be exchanged for €1. A currency has appreciated in value if more of a foreign currency is needed to buy it. A currency has depreciated in value if more of it is needed to buy a foreign currency. For example, a change in the exchange rate from $1.25 = €1 to $1.50 = €1 means that more dollars are needed to buy 1 euro; the euro has appreciated. And because more dollars are needed to buy €1, the dollar has depreciated.

- *Depreciation* in a nation's currency makes foreign goods more expensive. Consider an Irish coat that is priced at €200 when the exchange rate is $1.25 = €1. To buy the Irish coat for €200, an American has to pay $250 ($1.25 for each of €200 for a total of $250). Now suppose the dollar depreciates to $1.50 = €1. The American now has to pay $300 for the coat.

- This process is symmetrical. An *appreciation* in a nation's currency makes foreign goods cheaper. For example, if the exchange rate goes from $1.25 = €1 to $1 = €1, the Irish coat will cost the American only $200.

The depreciation and appreciation of the U.S. dollar affect net exports.

- As the dollar *depreciates*, foreign goods become more expensive, Americans cut back on imported goods, and foreigners (whose currency has appreciated) increase their purchases of U.S. exported goods. If exports rise and imports fall, net exports increase and aggregate demand increases.

- As the dollar *appreciates*, foreign goods become cheaper, Americans increase their purchases of imported goods, and foreigners (whose currency has depreciated) cut back on their purchases of U.S. exported goods. If exports fall and imports rise, net exports decrease, thus lowering aggregate demand.

Dollar depreciates → U.S. exports ↑ and U.S. imports ↓ → U.S. net exports ↑ → AD↑

Dollar appreciates → U.S. exports ↓ and U.S. imports ↑ → U.S. net exports ↓ → AD↓

See Exhibit 6 for a summary of the factors that change aggregate demand.

Exchange Rate
The price of one currency in terms of another currency.

Appreciation
An increase in the value of one currency relative to other currencies.

Depreciation
A decrease in the value of one currency relative to other currencies.

ⓣhinking like AN ECONOMIST

The W-X-Y-Z Explanation In the last discussion, we said, for example, that if the dollar depreciates, U.S. exports will rise and U.S. imports will fall, in turn causing U.S. net exports to rise, in turn causing aggregate demand to rise. A summarization of this type of argument might go like this: A change in W leads to a change in X, which leads to a change in Y, which leads to change in Z. Let's call this kind of explanation the W-X-Y-Z explanation.

Economists often think in terms of one thing changing something else, which in turn changes still something else, and so on. Some people find this kind of thinking curious. They ask, "Why not simply say that W leads to Z instead of saying that W leads to X, which leads to Y, which leads to Z?"

Saying that W leads to Z might make things easier (there would be less to remember), but what the shortcut gains in ease, it loses in completeness. It is best to explain just how one thing eventually leads to something else happening. ●●●

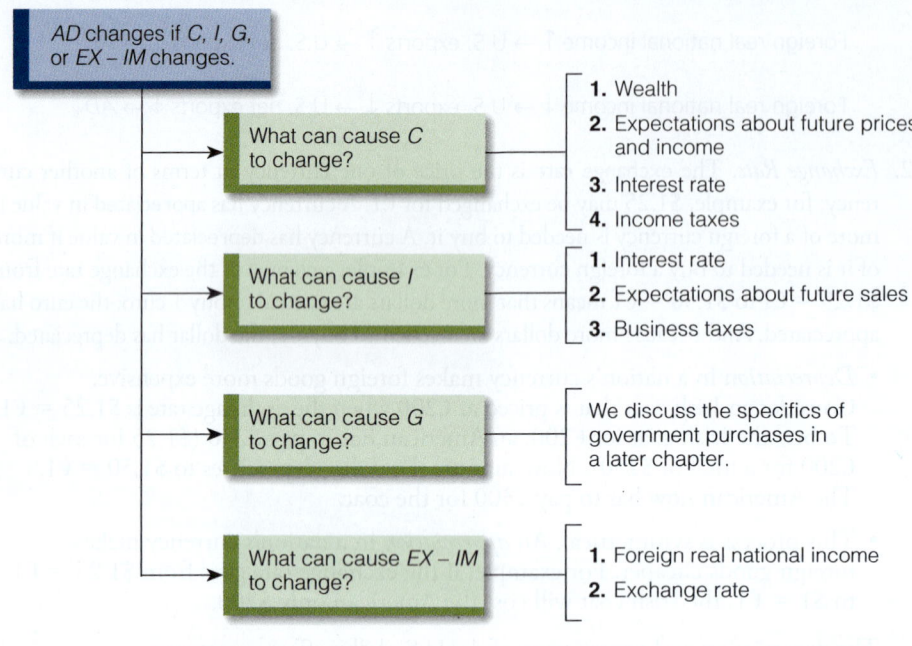

EXHIBIT 6

Factors That Change Aggregate Demand

Aggregate demand (AD) changes whenever consumption (C), investment (I), government purchases (G), or net exports (EX − IM) change. The factors that can affect C, I, and EX − IM, thereby indirectly affecting aggregate demand, are listed.

AD changes if C, I, G, or EX − IM changes.

What can cause C to change?
1. Wealth
2. Expectations about future prices and income
3. Interest rate
4. Income taxes

What can cause I to change?
1. Interest rate
2. Expectations about future sales
3. Business taxes

What can cause G to change?
We discuss the specifics of government purchases in a later chapter.

What can cause EX − IM to change?
1. Foreign real national income
2. Exchange rate

Can a Change in the Money Supply Change Aggregate Demand?

Changes in such factors as interest rates, business taxes, exchange rates, and the like can change aggregate demand (indirectly) by directly changing consumption, investment, and net exports. What about the money supply? Can a change in the money supply lead to a change in aggregate demand?

Let's see. Suppose the money supply rises from, say, $1,400 billion to $1,500 billion. Will this change in the money supply result in an increase in aggregate demand? Most economists would say that it does, but they differ on how. One way to explain the effect (in the context of our discussion) is as follows: (1) A change in the money supply affects interest rates, (2) a change in interest rates changes consumption and investment, and (3) a change in consumption and investment affects aggregate demand. Therefore a change in the money supply is a catalyst in a process that ends with a change in aggregate demand. (We will have much more to say about the money supply and interest rates in later chapters.)

If Consumption Rises, Does Some Other Spending Component Have to Decline?

Suppose C = $100, I = $100, G = $100, and NX = $100. Total expenditures equal $400. Now suppose C rises by $50 to $150. Must one or more other spending components decline by $50? In other words, if one spending component rises, does another spending component have to decline? To answer that question, we need to talk about two factors: the money supply and velocity.

Let's say that the money supply in the economy is $1 and that $1 is currently in the hands of Joe. Joe takes the $1 and buys good X from Jackie. Later, Jackie takes the $1 (she earlier received from Joe) and buys good Y from John. Still later, John takes the $1 (he earlier received from Jackie) and buys good Z from Jill.

When Would You Want to Be Paid in a Currency Other Than U.S. Dollars?

Most people who work in the United States are paid in dollars, but when would you not want to be paid in dollars? In thinking about the question, consider the exchange rate between the dollar and the euro. Suppose the exchange rate is $1 = €1 and this exchange rate is expected to stay constant. Your employer owes you $10,000. Does it matter if the employer pays you in dollars or euros? At the current exchange rate, $10,000 is the same as €10,000; so whether you are paid in euros or dollars does not matter.

Now suppose that you expect the exchange rate to change to $2 = €1 and that you expect the dollar to depreciate and the euro to appreciate. Does the currency in which you are paid matter? Yes, it does. Being paid in euros is preferable because the euro is expected to appreciate in value.

To see why, ask yourself what happens if you are paid $10,000 in contrast to €10,000. If the exchange rate changes to $2 = €1 after you are paid $10,000, then the $10,000 dollars is all you have. But if you are paid €10,000, you would have $20,000 because €10,000 can be exchanged for $20,000 dollars at the new rate.

So let's refine the original question: If you are usually paid in dollars, when would you prefer not to be paid in dollars? The answer is when you think the value of the dollar is going to fall relative to other currencies.

Here's the problem, though. Most of us who work for U.S. employers don't have the option of getting paid in the currency of our choice. Most of us cannot go to our employer and say, "This month, could you please pay me in euros instead of dollars?"

However, you can always convert the currency in which we are paid into another currency. Suppose that you are always paid in dollars but think the value of the dollar is going to decline relative to the euro. Your employer pays you $10,000 when the exchange rate is $1 dollar = €1 and you think the dollar is going to depreciate in value relative to the euro. You immediately take the $10,000 your employer paid you and exchange the dollars for €10,000. Then you wait. If the exchange rate actually does change to, say, $2 for €1, you then exchange your €10,000 for $20,000.

So, although we may not be able to get our employers to pay us in the currency of our choice, we can always do something to pay ourselves in the currency of our choice. We can always take the currency in which we are paid (e.g., dollars) and immediately exchange them for a different currency. In short, if you want to be paid in euros or yen or pesos, your employer may not comply with your wishes, but you have the option of acting on your own wishes.

Here is what we know: We started with a money supply of just $1, and that dollar changed hands three times. The number of times a dollar changes hands (or is spent) to buy final goods and services is what economists call velocity. (If we were dealing with a money supply of more than just $1, we would define velocity not as "the number" but as the *average number* of times a dollar is spent to buy final goods and services in a year.) In our simple example, velocity is 3.

The product of our money supply ($1) and velocity (3) is $3, which represents the total amount of spending in the economy. From our example, two things are obvious: First, total spending in the economy can be a greater dollar amount than the money supply. Proof: In our example, the money supply was $1, but total spending equaled $3. Second, total spending depends on the money supply and velocity. Proof: Total spending in our example was the product of the money supply *times* velocity.

Let's return to the original question: If consumption rises, must some other spending component decline? The answer is yes if neither the money supply nor velocity changes. But the answer is no if either the money supply or velocity rises.

To illustrate how the answer can be yes, suppose again that the money supply is $1 and velocity is 3 and that total spending is therefore $3. Let's break up our total of $3 spending this way: $1 goes for consumption, $1 goes for investment, and $1 goes for government

Velocity

The average number of times a dollar is spent to buy final goods and services in a year.

purchases. Consumption rises to $2, and the money supply and velocity remain at $1 and 3, respectively. So total spending is still $3, and therefore a $1 increase in consumption necessitates a decline in some other spending component by $1. After all, total spending is locked in at $3; if one spending component rises by a certain amount, another spending component(s) must decline by the same amount.

But total spending isn't locked in if either the money supply or velocity change. Again, suppose that consumption rises from $1 to $2 but that velocity or the money supply increases. Then no other spending component needs to change. To see why, suppose the money supply has risen to $1.40 and velocity is still 3. Total spending now is $4.20 instead of $3; so consumption could have risen to $2 without any decline in investment or government purchases. In other words, *C* can equal $2 and *I* can still equal $1, and *G* can still equal $1 (or even more at $1.20).

The same is true if the money supply remains constant at $1 and velocity increases from 3 to 4. At velocity of 4, total spending is $4. Again, consumption can rise to $2 without requiring any decline in another spending component.

We recap:

- If both the money supply and velocity are constant, a rise in one spending component (such as consumption) necessitates a decline in one or more other spending components.

- If either the money supply or velocity rises, one spending component can rise without requiring other spending components to decline.

SELF-TEST

(Answers to Self-Test questions are in Answers to Self-Test Questions at the back of the book.)

1. Explain the real balance effect.

2. Explain what happens to the *AD* curve if the dollar appreciates relative to other currencies.

3. The money supply has risen, but total spending has declined. Is this possible? Explain your answer.

SHORT-RUN AGGREGATE SUPPLY

Aggregate Supply
The quantity supplied of all goods and services (Real GDP) at different price levels, *ceteris paribus.*

Aggregate demand is one side of the economy; aggregate supply is the other. **Aggregate supply** is the quantity supplied of all goods and services (Real GDP) at various price levels, *ceteris paribus.* Aggregate supply includes both short-run aggregate supply (*SRAS*) and long-run aggregate supply (*LRAS*). Short-run aggregate supply is discussed in this section.

Short-Run Aggregate Supply Curve: What It Is and Why It Is Upward Sloping

Short-Run Aggregate Supply (SRAS) Curve
A curve that shows the quantity supplied of all goods and services (Real GDP) at different price levels, *ceteris paribus.*

A short-run aggregate supply (*SRAS*) curve (see Exhibit 7) shows the quantity supplied of all goods and services (Real GDP or output) at different price levels, *ceteris paribus.* Notice that the *SRAS* curve is upward sloping: As the price level rises, firms increase the quantity supplied of goods and services; as the price level drops, firms decrease the quantity supplied of goods and services. Why is the *SRAS* curve upward sloping? Economists have put forth a few explanations; we discuss two of them.

STICKY WAGES   Some economists believe that wages are sticky, or inflexible. This may be because wages are locked in for a few years due to labor contracts that workers and management enter into. For example, management and labor may agree to lock in wages for the next one to three years. Both labor and management may see this as in their best interest.

Management has some idea of what its labor costs will be during the time of the contract, and workers may have a sense of security knowing that their wages can't be lowered. Wages may also be sticky because of certain social conventions or perceived notions of fairness. Whatever the specific reason for sticky wages, let's see how they provide an explanation of an upward-sloping *SRAS* curve.

Firms pay *nominal wages* (e.g., $30 an hour), but they often decide how many workers to hire based on real wages. *Real wages* are nominal wages divided by the price level.

$$\text{Real wage} = \frac{\text{Nominal wage}}{\text{Price level}}$$

For example, suppose that the nominal wage is $30 an hour and that the price level, as measured by a price index, is 1.50.[1] The real wage is therefore $20.

- The quantity supplied of labor is *directly related* to the real wage: As the real wage rises, the quantity supplied of labor rises; as the real wage falls, the quantity supplied of labor falls. In short, more individuals are willing to work and current workers are willing to work more at higher real wages than at lower real wages.

Real wage ↑ → Quantity supplied of labor ↑

Real wage ↓ → Quantity supplied of labor ↓

- The quantity demanded of labor is *inversely related* to the real wage: As the real wage rises, the quantity demanded of labor falls; as the real wage falls, the quantity demanded of labor rises. Firms will employ more workers the cheaper it is to hire them.

Real wage ↑ → Quantity demanded of labor ↓

Real wage ↓ → Quantity demanded of labor ↑

So, suppose that a firm has agreed to pay its workers $30 an hour for the next three years and that it has hired 1,000 workers. When it agreed to this nominal wage, it thought that the price index would remain at 1.50 and that the real wage would stay at $20.

Now suppose the price index *falls* to 1.25. In that event, the real wage rises to $24 ($30 ÷ 1.25), which is higher than the firm expected when it agreed to lock in nominal wages at $30 an hour. If the firm had known that the real wage would turn out to be $24 (and not remain at $20), it would never have hired 1,000 workers. It would have hired, say, 800 workers instead.

So what does the firm do? As we stated, there is an inverse relationship between the real wage and the quantity demanded of labor (the number of workers that firms want to hire). Now that the real wage has risen (from $20 to $24), the firm cuts back on its labor (say, from 1,000 to 800 workers). With fewer workers working, less output is produced.

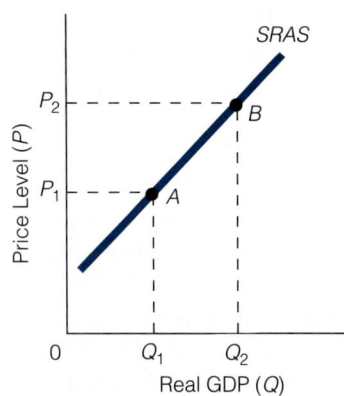

Short-Run Aggregate Supply Curve
The price level and quantity supplied of Real GDP are directly related.

EXHIBIT 7

The Short-Run Aggregate Supply Curve

The short-run aggregate supply curve is upward sloping, specifying a direct relationship between the price level and the quantity supplied of Real GDP.

1. Alternatively, you can view the price index as 1.50 times 100, or 150. In this case, the formula for the real wage would change to Real wage = (Nominal wage ÷ Price level) × 100.

So, if wages are sticky, a decrease in the price level (which pushes real wages up) will result in a decrease in output. This is what an upward-sloping *SRAS* curve represents: As the price level falls, the quantity supplied of goods and services declines.

Decline in price level and constant nominal wage → Real wage ↑ → Firms hire fewer workers → *Decline in quantity supplied of Real GDP*

WORKER MISPERCEPTIONS Another explanation for the upward-sloping *SRAS* curve holds that workers may misperceive real wage changes. To illustrate, if the nominal wage is $30 an hour and the price level, as measured by a price index, is 1.50, then the real wage is $20. Now suppose the nominal wage falls to $25 and the price level falls to 1.25. The real wage is still $20 ($25 ÷ 1.25 = $20), *but workers may not know this.* They know their nominal wage has fallen (i.e., they are earning $25 an hour instead of $30). They also may know that the price level is lower, but they may not know initially *how much* lower the price level is. For example, suppose they mistakenly believe the price level has fallen from 1.50 to 1.39. They will then think that their real wage has actually fallen from $20 ($30 ÷ 1.50) to $17.98 ($25 ÷ 1.39). In response to the misperceived falling real wage, workers may reduce the quantity of labor they are willing to supply. With fewer workers (resources), firms produce less.

So, if workers misperceive real wage changes, then a fall in the price level will bring about a decline in output, which is illustrative of an upward-sloping *SRAS* curve.

Nominal wages and *price level decline* by equal percentage → Real wage remains constant → But workers mistakenly think real wage has fallen → Workers reduce quantity supplied of labor → *Less output is produced*

What Puts the "Short Run" in the *SRAS* Curve?

According to most macroeconomists, the *SRAS* curve slopes upward because of sticky wages or worker misperceptions. No matter what the explanation, things are likely to change over time. Wages will not be sticky forever (labor contracts will expire), and workers will figure out that they misperceived real wage changes. Only for a period of time—identified as the short run—are these issues likely to be relevant.

Changes in Short-Run Aggregate Supply: Shifts in the *SRAS* Curve

A change in the quantity supplied of Real GDP is brought about by a change in the price level and is shown as a *movement* along the *SRAS* curve. But what can change short-run aggregate supply? What can *shift* the *SRAS* curve? The factors that can shift the *SRAS* curve are wage rates, prices of nonlabor inputs, productivity, and supply shocks.

WAGE RATES Changes in wage rates have a major impact on the position of the *SRAS* curve because wage costs are usually a firm's major cost item. The impact of a rise or fall in equilibrium wage rates can be understood in terms of the following equation:

Profit per unit = Price per unit − Cost per unit

Higher wage rates mean higher costs and, at constant prices, translate into lower profits and a reduction in the number of units (of a given good) that firms will want to produce. Lower wage rates mean lower costs and, at constant prices, translate into higher profits and an increase in the number of units (of a given good) firms will decide to produce.

The impact of higher and lower equilibrium wages is shown in Exhibit 8. At the given price level, P_1 on $SRAS_1$, the quantity supplied of Real GDP is Q_1. When wage rates become higher, a firm's profits at a given price level decrease. Consequently, the firm reduces production. In the diagram, this change corresponds to moving from Q_1 to Q_2, which at the given price level is point *B* on a new aggregate supply curve ($SRAS_2$). Thus, a rise in equilibrium wage rates leads to a leftward shift in the aggregate supply curve. For a fall in equilibrium wage rates, the steps are simply reversed.

PRICES OF NONLABOR INPUTS There are other inputs to the production process besides labor. Changes in the prices of nonlabor inputs affect the *SRAS* curve in the same way as changes in wage rates do. An increase in the price of a nonlabor input (e.g., oil) shifts the *SRAS* curve leftward; a decrease in their price shifts the *SRAS* curve rightward.

PRODUCTIVITY *Productivity* is the output produced per unit of input employed over some period of time. Although various inputs can become more productive, let's consider the labor input. An increase in labor productivity means businesses will produce more output with the same amount of labor, causing the *SRAS* curve to shift rightward. A decrease in labor productivity means businesses will produce less output with the same amount of labor, causing the *SRAS* curve to shift leftward. A host of factors lead to increased labor productivity, including a more educated labor force, a larger stock of capital goods, and technological advancements.

SUPPLY SHOCKS Major natural or institutional changes that affect aggregate supply are referred to as *supply shocks*. Supply shocks are of two varieties. *Adverse supply shocks* shift the *SRAS* curve leftward. Bad weather that wipes out a large part of the Midwestern wheat crop would be a supply shock. So would a major cutback in the supply of oil coming to the United States from the Middle East. *Beneficial supply shocks* shift the *SRAS* curve rightward; for example, a major oil discovery or unusually good weather leading to increased production of a food staple. These supply shocks are reflected in resource or input prices.

Exhibit 9 summarizes the factors that affect short-run aggregate supply.

EXHIBIT 8

Wage Rates and a Shift in the Short-Run Aggregate Supply Curve

A rise in wage rates shifts the short-run aggregate supply curve leftward. A fall in wage rates shifts the short-run aggregate supply curve rightward.

EXHIBIT 9

Changes in Short-Run Aggregate Supply The flow charts show how short-run aggregate supply changes given changes in several factors.

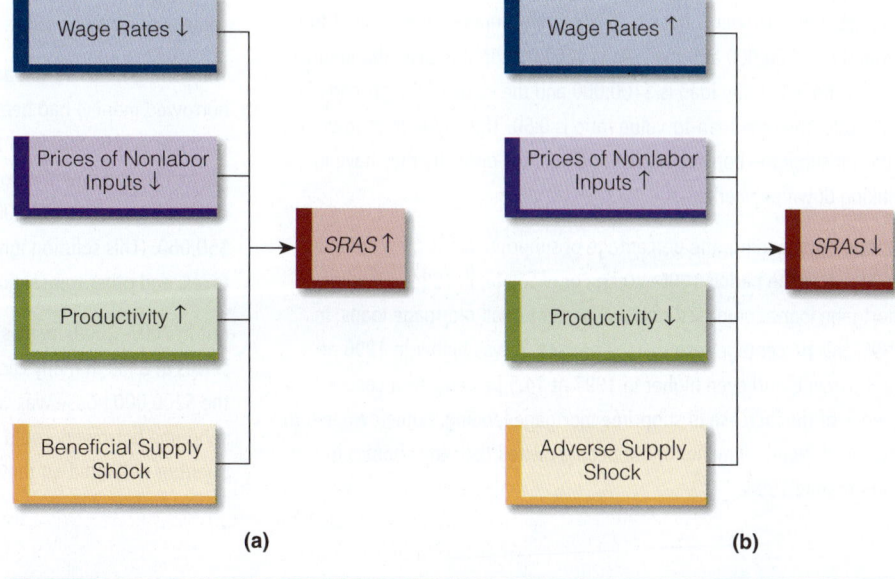

(a)   (b)

Subprime Lending, House Price Declines, and Loan Defaults

In 2008–2009, we heard much about subprime lending, especially as it relates to the mortgage loan market. What is a subprime loan, and what is controversial about it? First, a subprime loan is simply a loan made at an elevated credit risk. In contrast, prime loans are made to persons who have a strong credit history and a record of paying back loans. Subprime loans are usually made to persons who usually do not have a good credit history and may have been delinquent on paying back loans in the past.

A lender can research a person's credit risk by checking his or her FICO (Fair Isaac Corporation) credit score. These scores usually run between 300 and 850. A score below 620 usually denotes high risk and places a person in the subprime pool of borrowers.

One difference between a prime and a subprime loan is that the latter has a higher loan-to-value ratio. In other words, the subprime loan amount is a greater-than-usual percentage of the value of, say, the property the borrower is buying. To illustrate, suppose the value of the property is $200,000 and the loan is $200,000. In this case, the loan-to-value ratio is 1. If the loan is $100,000 and the value of the property is $200,000, then the loan-to-value ratio is 0.50. The higher loan-to-value ratio for subprime borrowers partly reflects the difficulty they have in making down payments.

In mortgage lending, the percentage of subprime loans grew substantially during the period 1995–2003. For example, in 1994, subprime mortgage loans comprised only 4.5 percent of all mortgage loans. In 1995, this percentage rose to 10.2 percent. It was higher in 1996 at 12.3 percent, and even higher in 1997 at 14.5 percent. As a consequence of the increase in subprime mortgage lending, home ownership increased. Nearly 9 million more people owned their own homes in 2003 than in 1994.

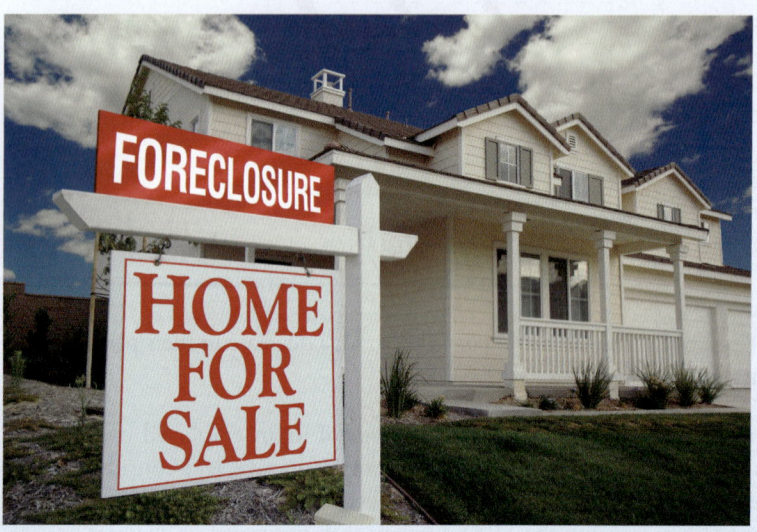

© ANDY DEAN/FOTOLIA.COM

In 2007–2009, subprime lending came under discussion and review, largely because many subprime borrowers were unable to pay off their loans. They were unable to pay off their loans to a large degree because the subprime loans were made at low interest rates that could change if interest rates in general were to rise. To illustrate, you are a subprime borrower paying an initial rate of 5 percent on a $200,000 loan. Your monthly payment is $1,073. Your subprime loan agreement states that your interest rate will rise by the same percentage as some specified interest rate in the economy (such as the Treasury bill rate or some other rate). At some point, this interest rate goes up by 300 basis points (3 percent). Now you pay a new interest rate of 8 percent instead of 5 percent, and your monthly payment is $1,467—$394 more than you were previously paying. You would have been all right if interest rates hadn't risen; you were able to pay $1,073 a month. Now, however, you are having a hard time making your increased monthly mortgage payment. In such a situation, some subprime borrowers defaulted on their loans.

Things might not be so bad if the house (that you bought with the borrowed money) had been rising in value. For example, suppose you took out a $200,000 loan to buy the house priced at $200,000 (no down payment), and now the house is worth $250,000. You could, of course, sell the house for $250,000, pay off the $200,000 loan, and pocket the $50,000. (This solution ignores such things as real estate commissions, taxes, and other transaction costs.)

But in 2007–2009, many subprime mortgage borrowers found themselves in a fix. In many cases, the value of the houses had fallen. Now the $200,000 house was worth, say, $145,000. In this situation, many subprime borrowers could not sell the property and either were delinquent or defaulted on their loans.

Something More to Come: Peoples' Expectations

So far, in this chapter we have said that several factors are capable of shifting the *SRAS* curve: wage rates, prices of nonlabor inputs, productivity, and supply shocks. In a later chapter (Chapter 16), we will begin to discuss how peoples' expectations (of certain key economic variables) can affect the price level and Real GDP. At that point, we will add another factor that can shift the *SRAS* curve: the *expected price level*.

1. If wage rates decline, explain what happens to the short-run aggregate supply (*SRAS*) curve?

2. Give an example of an increase in labor productivity.

3. Discuss the details of the worker misperceptions explanation for the upward-sloping *SRAS* curve.

PUTTING *AD* AND *SRAS* TOGETHER: SHORT-RUN EQUILIBRIUM

In this section, we put aggregate demand and short-run aggregate supply together to achieve short-run equilibrium in the economy. Aggregate demand and short-run aggregate supply determine the price level, Real GDP, and the unemployment rate in the short run.

How Short-Run Equilibrium in the Economy Is Achieved

Exhibit 10 shows an aggregate demand (*AD*) curve and a short-run aggregate supply (*SRAS*) curve. The quantity demanded of Real GDP and the quantity supplied of Real GDP are illustrated at three different price levels: P_1, P_2, and P_E.

At P_1, the quantity supplied of Real GDP (Q_2) is greater than the quantity demanded (Q_1). There is a surplus of goods. As a result, the price level drops, firms decrease output, and consumers increase consumption. Why do consumers increase consumption as the price level drops? (*Hint:* Think of the real balance, interest rate, and international trade effects.)

At P_2, the quantity supplied of Real GDP (Q_1) is less than the quantity demanded (Q_2). There is a shortage of goods. As a result, the price level rises, firms increase output, and consumers decrease consumption.

In instances of both surplus and shortage, economic forces are moving the economy toward *E*, where the quantity demanded of Real GDP equals the (short-run) quantity supplied of Real GDP. This is the point of short-run equilibrium. P_E is the short-run equilibrium price level; Q_E is the short-run equilibrium Real GDP.

A change in aggregate demand, in short-run aggregate supply, or in both will obviously affect the price level and/or Real GDP. For example, an increase in aggregate demand

EXHIBIT 10

Short-Run Equilibrium

At P_1, the quantity supplied of Real GDP is greater than the quantity demanded. As a result, the price level falls and firms decrease output. At P_2, the quantity demanded of Real GDP is greater than the quantity supplied. As a result, the price level rises and firms increase output. Short-run equilibrium occurs at point *E*, where the quantity demanded of Real GDP. equals the (short-run) quantity supplied. This is at the intersection of the aggregate demand (*AD*) curve and the short-run aggregate supply (*SRAS*) curve. (Note: Although real-world *AD* and *SRAS* curves can, and likely do, have some curvature to them, we have drawn both as straight lines, This does not affect the analysis. Whenever the analysis is not disturbed, we follow suit throughout this text.)

Short-Run Equilibrium
The condition in the economy when the quantity demanded of Real GDP equals the (short-run) quantity supplied of Real GDP. This condition is met where the aggregate demand curve intersects the short-run aggregate supply curve.

raises the equilibrium price level and, in the short run, Real GDP [Exhibit 11(a)]. An increase in short-run aggregate supply lowers the equilibrium price level and raises Real GDP [Exhibit 11(b)]. A decrease in short-run aggregate supply raises the equilibrium price level and lowers Real GDP [Exhibit 11(c)].

Thinking in Terms of Short-Run Equilibrium Changes in the Economy

We know that certain factors can lead to a change in aggregate demand or in short-run aggregate supply. We also know that if either aggregate demand or short-run aggregate supply changes, the price level and Real GDP will also change in the short run.

Exhibit 12 shows us how changes in *AD* or *SRAS* can impact the economy and change *P* and *Q*. (Refer to Exhibit 12 as we continue our discussion.) For example, when a factor changes, we ask ourselves a series of questions:

- Does the factor affect the *AD* curve or the *SRAS* curve? If the answer is neither, then there will be no change in either curve.

- If the answer is the *AD* curve, then does it shift to the right or to the left?

- If the answer is the *SRAS* curve, does it shift to the right or to the left?

After the shift in one or more curves, we identify the new equilibrium and what has happened to both the price level and Real GDP in the short run.

To illustrate, suppose there is an adverse supply shock in the economy:

- The shock shifts the *SRAS* curve leftward.

- Nothing has changed on the demand side of the economy, so the *AD* curve remains stable.

- A leftward shift in the *SRAS* curve in the face of an unchanged *AD* curve increases the price level and decreases Real GDP.

EXHIBIT 11

Changes in Short-Run Equilibrium in the Economy

(a) An increase in aggregate demand increases the price level and Real GDP. (b) An increase in short-run aggregate supply decreases the price level and increases Real GDP. (c) A decrease in short-run aggregate supply increases the price level and decreases Real GDP.

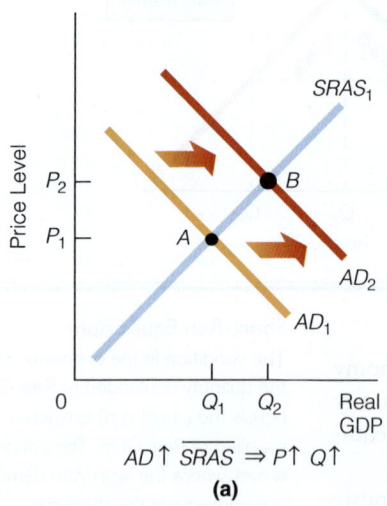

$AD\uparrow \overline{SRAS} \Rightarrow P\uparrow Q\uparrow$

(a)

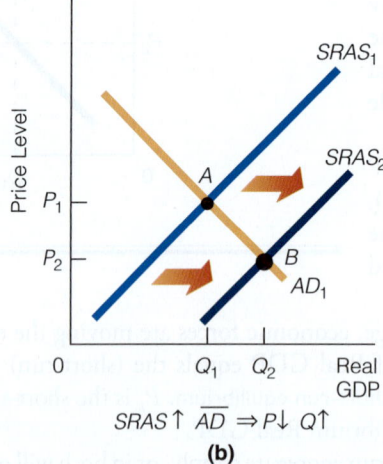

$SRAS\uparrow \overline{AD} \Rightarrow P\downarrow Q\uparrow$

(b)

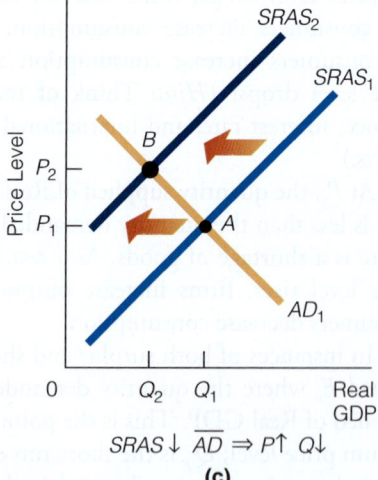

$SRAS\downarrow \overline{AD} \Rightarrow P\uparrow Q\downarrow$

(c)

EXHIBIT 12

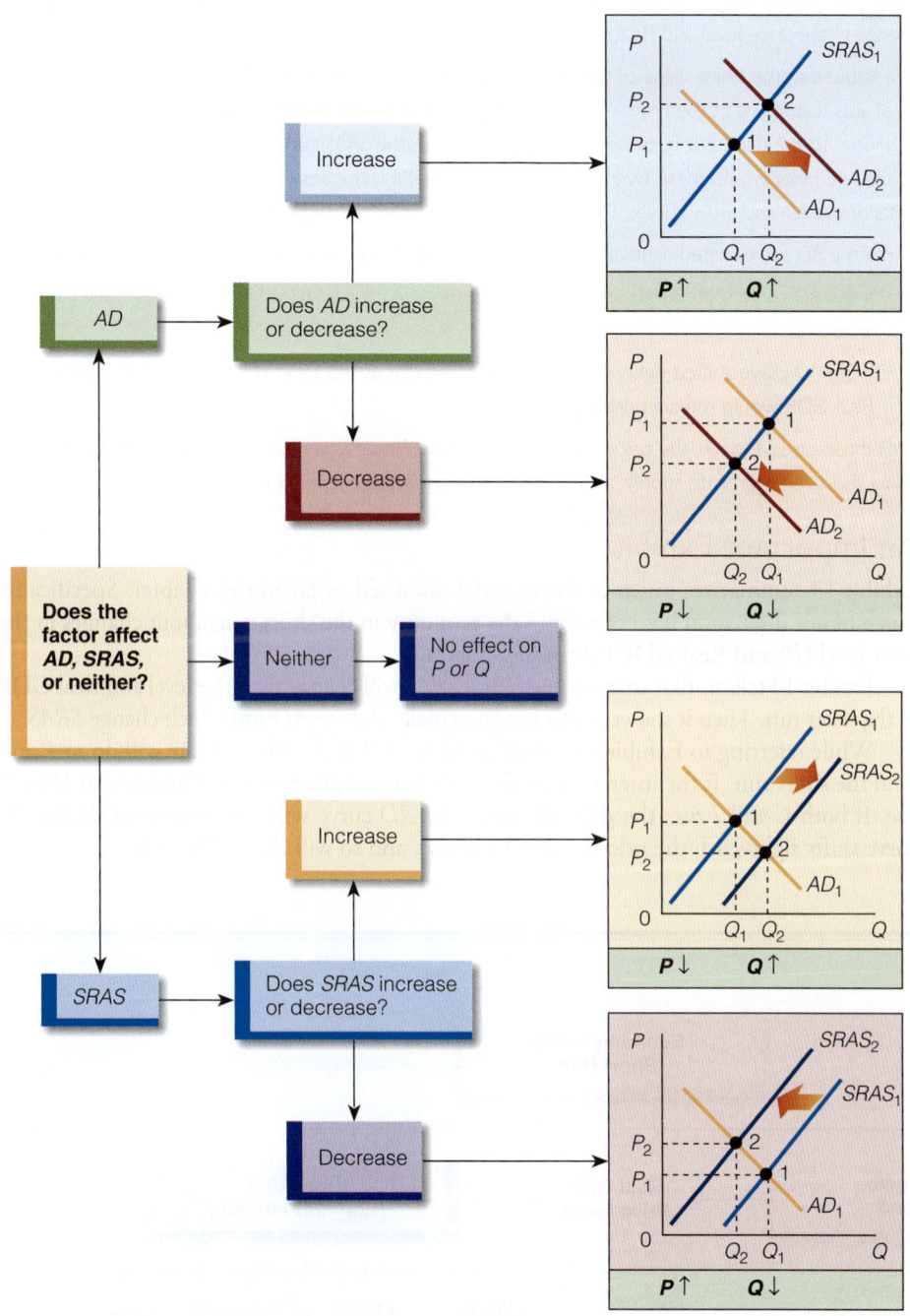

How a Factor Affects the Price Level and Real GDP in the Short Run

In the exhibit, P = price level and Q = Real GDP.

(f)inding ECONOMICS

In Dollars and in Oil In November 2007 the barrel price of oil was rising. On November 1, 2007, it had risen to $96 a barrel, and in the same month the value of the dollar was falling in foreign exchange markets. In fact, the value of the dollar had been falling for some time. Although the value of $1 was €0.83 in January 2006, it had fallen to €0.69 by November 1, 2007. In other words, the

(continued)

dollar had depreciated over that time period. Now what does all this have to do with the predicted change in the price level and Real GDP?

We know that the falling value of the dollar would lead to greater U.S. exports, and this is exactly what was happening at the time. As a result, U.S. net exports were rising, pushing the *AD* curve in the economy to the right. But because oil prices were rising, the *SRAS* curve in the economy was shifting to the left. How would these two changes affect Real GDP? The answer depends on the relative shifts of the *AD* and *SRAS* curves. Picture, in your mind's eye, the three possibilities:

- If the *AD* curve shifted rightward more than the *SRAS* curve shifted leftward, then Real GDP will rise.
- If the *AD* curve shifted rightward by less than the *SRAS* curve shifted leftward, then Real GDP would fall.
- If the *AD* curve shifted rightward by the same amount as the *SRAS* curve shifted leftward, then Real GDP would remain unchanged.

In all three cases, though, the price level would increase. Rising aggregate demand, combined with falling short-run aggregate supply, always results in a rising price level. ▲ ▲ ▲

An Important Exhibit

Exhibit 13 summarizes much of the material discussed so far in this chapter. Specifically, much of our discussion has been about the economy in the short run, about changes in the price level (*P*) and Real GDP (*Q*) in the short run.

Exhibit 13 tells us that changes in *AD* and *SRAS* will change the price level and Real GDP in the short run. Then it shows which factors actually change *AD* and which change *SRAS*.

While referring to Exhibit 13, consider what a fall in the interest rate will do to *P* and *Q* in the short run. If the interest rate falls, both consumption (*C*) and investment (*I*) will rise. If both *C* and *I* rise, the *AD* will rise or the *AD* curve will shift rightward. If the *AD* curve shifts rightward, the price level (*P*) will rise, and so will Real GDP (*Q*).

EXHIBIT 13

A Summary Exhibit of *AD* and *SRAS*

economics 24/7

Your First Job After College May Depend on the *AD* and *SRAS* Curves

There are some things that exist that you can see with your physical eyes. For example, a car exists, and you can see a car with your physical eyes.

There are some things that exist that you can only see with your mind's eye. For example, there actually is an *AD* curve in an economy, but no one has ever seen a real *AD* curve with his physical eyes. No one has walked into his backyard, looked up into the sky, and seen the country's *AD* curve. We can only see *AD* curves with our mind's eye. We then draw those *AD* curves on paper or a board.

Now although we cannot see the real *AD* curve in the economy, we know it exists and we also know that where it is positioned (when transferred to a two-dimensional diagram) affects your job prospects after college. Put it this way: You might have thought that learning what the *AD* curve looks like, and what makes it shift right or left, has nothing to do with you. But that's incorrect. To see why, suppose that you will be graduating from college in, say, two years. In two years, there will be an *AD* curve in the economy just as there is an *AD* curve in the economy right now.

But where will that *AD* curve in two years be positioned relative to the *AD* curve that exists right now? Let's suppose between now and then, something happens in the economy to shift the *AD* curve to the left. Will that matter to you? Well, think of what lower *AD* means in the economy, all other things remaining constant. It means that less Real GDP will be produced. Fewer houses will be built, fewer cars will be produced, fewer attorney services will be demanded. Now again ask: Will that matter to you? It certainly will matter to you if, two years from now when you graduate from college, you are looking for a job. Lower aggregate demand, which translates into less Real GDP, will translate into fewer employers visiting colleges to hire college graduates. It will translate into fewer employers reading your résumé and getting back to you for a job interview.

Our point is a simple one: In a textbook, or on a classroom board, the *AD* curve may look like something that is unrelated to you and your everyday life. But that isn't true at all. That *AD* curve may have much to do with how hard or easy it is for you to get your first job after college.

LONG-RUN AGGREGATE SUPPLY

In this section, we discuss long-run aggregate supply and draw a long-run aggregate supply (*LRAS*) curve. We also discuss long-run equilibrium and explain how it differs from short-run equilibrium.

Going from the Short Run to the Long Run

Graphically, short-run equilibrium is at the intersection of the *AD* curve and the (upward-sloping) *SRAS* curve. As explained earlier, economists give different reasons for an upward-sloping *SRAS* curve, which have to do either with sticky wages or with worker misperceptions. So, when either of these two conditions holds, short-run equilibrium

EXHIBIT 14

Long-Run Aggregate Supply (*LRAS*) Curve

The *LRAS* curve is a vertical line at the level of Natural Real GDP. It represents the output the economy produces when all economywide adjustments have taken place and workers do not have any relevant misperceptions.

Natural Real GDP

The Real GDP that is produced at the natural unemployment rate. The Real GDP that is produced when the economy is in long-run equilibrium.

Long-Run Aggregate Supply (*LRAS*) Curve

The *LRAS* curve is a vertical line at the level of Natural Real GDP. It represents the output the economy produces when wages and prices have adjusted to their final equilibrium levels and when workers do not have any relevant misperceptions.

identifies the Real GDP that the economy produces. In time, though, wages become unstuck, and misperceptions turn into accurate perceptions. In that event, the economy is said to be in the *long run*. In other words, these two conditions do not hold in the long run.

An important macroeconomic question is, "*Will the level of Real GDP that the economy produces in the long run be the same as in the short run?*" Most economists say that it will not. They argue that, in the long run, the economy produces the full-employment Real GDP, or the Natural Real GDP (Q_N). The aggregate supply curve that identifies the output the economy produces in the long run, the long-run aggregate supply (*LRAS*) curve, is portrayed as the vertical line in Exhibit 14.

Long-run equilibrium identifies the level of Real GDP the economy produces when wages and prices have adjusted to their final equilibrium levels and when workers have no relevant misperceptions. Graphically, this occurs at the intersection of the *AD* and *LRAS* curves. Further, the level of Real GDP that the economy produces in long-run equilibrium is the Natural Real GDP (Q_N).

Short-Run Equilibrium, Long-Run Equilibrium, and Disequilibrium

The two equilibrium states in an economy—short-run and long-run—are graphically shown in Exhibit 15. In Exhibit 15(a), the economy is at point 1, producing Q_1 amount of Real GDP. At point 1, the quantity supplied of Real GDP (in the short run) is equal to the quantity demanded of Real GDP, and both are Q_1. The economy is in short-run equilibrium. In Exhibit 15(b), the economy is at point 1, producing Q_N. In other words, it is producing Natural Real GDP. The economy is in long-run equilibrium when it produces Q_N.

In both short-run and long-run equilibrium, the quantity supplied of Real GDP equals the quantity demanded. So what is the difference between short-run equilibrium and long-run equilibrium? In long-run equilibrium, the quantities supplied and demanded of Real

EXHIBIT 15

Equilibrium States of the Economy

There are two equilibrium states in the economy: short-run equilibrium, shown in part (a), and long-run equilibrium, shown in part (b). During the time an economy moves from one equilibrium to another, it is said to be in disequilibrium.

Reality Can Be Messy, and Correct Predictions Can Be Difficult to Make

In a textbook, we can change one factor and then trace its effects through the economy, ultimately to the price level and Real GDP. For instance, a decline in business taxes will lead to a rise in investment, which in turn will lead to a rise in aggregate demand. Now, assuming that SRAS has not changed, a rise in AD will lead to a rise in the price level and a rise in Real GDP. Here are the links:

$$\text{Business taxes} \downarrow \rightarrow C\uparrow \rightarrow AD\uparrow \rightarrow P\uparrow\ Q\uparrow$$

where C = consumption, AD = aggregate demand, P = price level, and Q = Real GDP.

In reality, though, more than one thing can change at a time. Or at a minimum, two or more things could change within a few days or weeks of each other. To illustrate, suppose a factor on the demand side of the economy changes at about the same time as a factor on the supply side. Specifically, wealth rises at the same time as the price of nonlabor inputs rises. What ultimately happens to the price level and Real GDP? Let's break the problem down into small parts and find out.

1. A rise in wealth will raise AD. The AD curve shifts rightward.

2. A rise in nonlabor input prices will lower SRAS. The SRAS curve will shift leftward.

3. Because both the AD and SRAS curves are changing at the same time or at about the same time, the overall change in the price level and Real GDP will depend on the relative shifts of the AD and SRAS curves.

4. If the AD curve shifts rightward by more than the SRAS curve shifts leftward. the price level and Real GDP will rise. (You may want to draw this.)

5. If, however, the AD curve shifts rightward by less than the SRAS curve shifts leftward, then the price level will rise and Real GDP will fall.

6. Finally, if the AD curve shifts rightward to the same degree that the SRAS curve shifts leftward, Real GDP will not change and the price level will rise.

All this has something to say about economists' predictions. Making correct predictions in economics is easy when only one thing changes and everything else remains constant. Making correct predictions is much harder when more than one thing changes at a time and when the changes pull the economy in opposite directions. We have seen a little of this type of complexity in our example. Specifically, although the increase in AD tends to raise Real GDP, the decrease in SRAS tends to lower it. What will be the final effect on Real GDP? As we have seen, it depends on the relative shifts in AD and SRAS.

The lesson: Reality in economics can be messy.

GDP equal Natural Real GDP [Exhibit 15(b)]. But in short-run equilibrium, the quantities supplied and demanded of Real GDP are either more or less than Natural Real GDP.

Let's illustrate that difference with numbers. Suppose Q_N = $9.0 trillion. In long-run equilibrium, the quantity supplied of Real GDP equals the quantity demanded: $9.0 trillion. In short-run equilibrium, the quantity supplied of Real GDP equals the quantity demanded, but neither equals $9.0 trillion. For example, the quantity supplied of Real GDP could equal the quantity demanded of Real GDP at $8.5 trillion.

When the economy is in neither short-run nor long-run equilibrium, it is said to be in *disequilibrium.* Essentially, disequilibrium is the state of the economy as it moves from one short-run equilibrium to another or from short-run equilibrium to long-run equilibrium. In disequilibrium, the quantity supplied and the quantity demanded of Real GDP are not equal.

Long-Run Equilibrium
The condition that exists in the economy when wages and prices have adjusted to their (final) equilibrium levels and when workers do not have any relevant misperceptions. Graphically, long-run equilibrium occurs at the intersection of the AD and LRAS curves.

SELF-TEST

1. What is the difference between short-run equilibrium and long-run equilibrium?

2. Diagrammatically represent an economy that is in neither short-run nor long-run equilibrium.

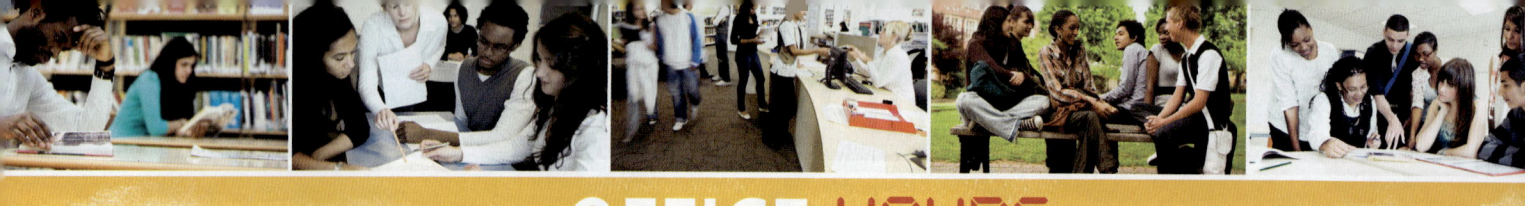

OFFICE HOURS

"What Purpose Does the *AD–AS* Framework Serve?"

> **STUDENT:**
>
> What purpose does the *AD–AS* framework serve?

> **INSTRUCTOR:**
>
> One purpose is to link some variables to other variables.

> **STUDENT:**
>
> How so?

> **INSTRUCTOR:**
>
> Well, consider a rise in income taxes. We learned in this chapter that a rise in income taxes will lead to a decline in consumption. And we know that a decline in consumption will lead to a decline in aggregate demand. Finally, we know that a decline in aggregate demand will lead to a decline in both the price level and Real GDP. In other words, the *AD–AS* framework helps us to link a rise in *income taxes* to a decline in both the *price level* and *Real GDP*.

> **STUDENT:**
>
> Oh, I see. It's sort of like the *AD–AS* framework is a road. We start at one point on the road (where income taxes are being raised), and then we follow the road until we come to the end (where the price level and Real GDP have declined).

> **INSTRUCTOR:**
>
> That's a good way of putting it. Let's now start at another point along the road. Let's start with a decline in wage rates.

> **STUDENT:**
>
> If wage rates decline, short-run aggregate supply increases (the *SRAS* curve shifts to the right). As a result, the price level declines and Real GDP rises.

CHAPTER SUMMARY

AGGREGATE DEMAND

- Aggregate demand refers to the quantity demanded of all goods and services (Real GDP) at different price levels, *ceteris paribus.*
- The aggregate demand (*AD*) curve slopes downward, indicating an inverse relationship between the price level and the quantity demanded of Real GDP.
- The *AD* curve slopes downward because of the real balance, interest rate, and international trade effects.
- The real balance effect states that the inverse relationship between the price level and the quantity demanded of Real GDP is established through changes in the value of a person's monetary wealth, or money holdings. Specifically, a fall in the price level causes purchasing power to rise, increasing a person's monetary wealth. As people become wealthier, they buy more goods. A rise in the price level causes purchasing power to fall, reducing a person's monetary wealth. As people become less wealthy, they buy fewer goods.
- The interest rate effect states that the inverse relationship between the price level and the quantity demanded of Real GDP is established through changes in household and business spending that is sensitive to changes in interest rates. If the price level rises, a person needs more money to buy a fixed bundle of goods. In an effort to acquire more money, the demand for credit rises, as does the interest rate. As the interest rate rises, businesses and households borrow less and buy fewer goods. Thus, the quantity demanded of Real GDP falls. If the price level falls, a person needs less money to buy a fixed bundle of goods. Part of the increase in a person's monetary wealth is saved; so the supply of credit rises, and the interest rate falls. As the interest rate falls, businesses and households borrow more and buy more goods. Thus, the quantity demanded of Real GDP rises.
- The international trade effect states that the inverse relationship between the price level and the quantity demanded of Real GDP is established through foreign sector spending. Specifically, as the price level in the United States rises, U.S. goods become relatively more expensive than foreign goods, and both Americans and foreigners buy fewer U.S. goods. The quantity demanded of U.S. Real GDP falls. As the price level in the United States falls, U.S. goods become relatively less expensive than foreign goods, and both Americans and foreigners buy more U.S. goods. The quantity demanded of U.S. Real GDP rises.
- At a given price level, a rise in consumption, investment, government purchases, or net exports will increase aggregate demand

POINTS TO REMEMBER

1. The *AD–AS* framework serves to link some variables to others. For example, a change in income taxes can ultimately be linked to a change in the price level and Real GDP.

2. The *AD–AS* framework helps us to understand changes in both the price level and Real GDP.

and shift the *AD* curve to the right. At a given price level, a fall in consumption, investment, government purchases, or net exports will decrease aggregate demand and shift the *AD* curve to the left.

FACTORS THAT CAN CHANGE C, I, AND NX (EX − IM) AND THEREFORE CHANGE AD

- The following factors can change consumption: wealth, expectations about future prices and income, the interest rate, and income taxes. The following factors can change investment: the interest rate, expectations about future sales, and business taxes. The following factors can change net exports (exports less imports): foreign real national income and the exchange rate. A change in the money supply can affect one or more spending components (e.g., consumption) and therefore affect aggregate demand.

MONEY SUPPLY AND VELOCITY

- Velocity is the average number of times a dollar is spent to buy final goods and services in a year.
- If money supply and velocity are constant, a rise in one spending component (such as consumption) necessitates a decline in one or more other components. If either the money supply or velocity rises, a rise in one component does not necessitate a decline in the others.

SHORT-RUN AGGREGATE SUPPLY

- Aggregate supply is to the quantity supplied of all goods and services (Real GDP) at different price levels, *ceteris paribus.*
- The short-run aggregate supply (*SRAS*) curve is upward sloping, indicating a direct relationship between the price level and the quantity supplied of Real GDP.
- A decrease in wage rates, a decrease in the price of nonlabor inputs, an increase in productivity, and beneficial supply shocks all shift the *SRAS* curve to the right. An increase in wage rates, an increase in the price of nonlabor inputs, a decrease in productivity, and adverse supply shocks all shift the *SRAS* curve to the left.

SHORT-RUN EQUILIBRIUM

- Graphically, short-run equilibrium exists at the intersection of the *AD* and *SRAS* curves. A shift in either or both of these curves can change the price level and Real GDP. For example, an increase in aggregate demand increases the price level and Real GDP, *ceteris paribus.*

LONG-RUN AGGREGATE SUPPLY AND LONG-RUN EQUILIBRIUM

- The long-run aggregate supply (*LRAS*) curve is vertical at the Natural Real GDP level.

- Graphically, long-run equilibrium exists at the intersection of the *AD* and *LRAS* curves. It is the condition that exists in the economy when all economywide adjustments have taken place and workers do not hold any (relevant) misperceptions. In long-run equilibrium, the quantity demanded of Real GDP equals the quantity supplied of Real GDP, which equals Natural Real GDP.

THREE STATES OF AN ECONOMY

- An economy can be in short-run equilibrium, long-run equilibrium, or disequilibrium.

KEY TERMS AND CONCEPTS

Aggregate Demand
Aggregate Demand (*AD*) Curve
Real Balance Effect
Monetary Wealth
Purchasing Power

Interest Rate Effect
International Trade Effect
Wealth
Exchange Rate
Appreciation

Depreciation
Velocity
Aggregate Supply
Short-Run Aggregate Supply
 (*SRAS*) Curve

Short-Run Equilibrium
Natural Real GDP
Long-Run Aggregate Supply
 (*LRAS*) Curve
Long-Run Equilibrium

QUESTIONS AND PROBLEMS

1. How will an increase in the money supply affect aggregate demand?

2. An economist is sitting in the Oval Office of the White House, across the desk from the president of the United States. The president asks, "How does the unemployment rate look for the next quarter?" The economist answers, "It's not good. I don't think Real GDP is going to be as high as we initially thought. The problem seems to be foreign income; it's just not growing at the rate we thought it was going to grow." How can foreign income affect U.S. unemployment?

3. Explain how expectations about future sales will affect investment.

4. What is the difference between short-run equilibrium and long-run equilibrium?

5. Explain how expectations about future prices and income will affect consumption.

6. Identify the details of each of the following explanations for an upward-sloping *SRAS* curve:
   a. Sticky-wage explanation
   b. Worker-misperception explanation

7. Explain what is likely to happen to U.S. export and import spending as a result of the dollar depreciating in value.

8. In the short run, what is the impact on the price level and Real GDP of each of the following?
   a. An increase in consumption brought about by a decrease in interest rates
   b. A decrease in exports brought about by an appreciation of the dollar
   c. A rise in wage rates
   d. A beneficial supply shock
   e. An adverse supply shock
   f. A decline in productivity

9. Explain what happens to aggregate demand in each of the following cases:
   a. The interest rate rises
   b. Wealth falls
   c. The dollar depreciates relative to foreign currencies
   d. Households expect lower prices in the future
   e. Business taxes rise

10. A change in the price level affects which of the following?
   a. The quantity demanded of Real GDP
   b. Aggregate demand
   c. Short-run aggregate supply
   d. The quantity supplied of Real GDP

11. The amount of Real GDP (real output) that households are willing and able to buy may change if there is a change in either (a) the price level or (b) some nonprice factor, such as wealth, interest rates, and the like. Do you agree or disagree? Explain your answer.

12. Explain how each of the following will affect short-run aggregate supply:
   a. An increase in wage rates
   b. A beneficial supply shock
   c. An increase in the productivity of labor
   d. A decrease in the price of a nonlabor resource (e.g., oil)

13. There is a difference between a change in the interest rate that is brought about by a change in the price level and a change in the interest rate that is brought about by a change in some factor other than the price level. The first will change the quantity demanded of Real GDP, and the second will change the *AD* curve. Do you agree or disagree with this statement? Explain your answer.

14. What is the difference between a change in the quantity supplied of Real GDP and a change in short-run aggregate supply?

15. Graphically portray each of the following: (a) a change in the quantity demanded of Real GDP and (b) a change in aggregate demand.

16. Will a direct increase in the price of U.S. goods relative to foreign goods lead to a change in the quantity demanded of Real GDP or to a change in aggregate demand? Will a change in the exchange rate that subsequently increases the price of U.S. goods relative to foreign goods lead to a change in the quantity demanded of Real GDP or to a change in aggregate demand? Explain your answers.

17. Explain each of the following: (a) real balance effect, (b) interest rate effect, and (c) international trade effect.

18. Can total spending be a greater dollar amount than the money supply? Explain your answer.

19. Is aggregate demand a specific dollar amount? For example, is it correct to say that aggregate demand is $9 trillion this year?

20. Under what conditions can consumption rise without some other spending component declining?

WORKING WITH NUMBERS AND GRAPHS

1. Suppose that at a price index of 154, the quantity demanded of U.S. Real GDP is $10.0 trillion worth of goods. Do these data represent aggregate demand or a point on an aggregate demand curve? Explain your answer.

2. Diagrammatically represent the effect on the price level and Real GDP in the short run of each of the following:

   a. An increase in wealth

   b. An increase in wage rates

   c. An increase in labor productivity

3. Diagrammatically represent the following, and identify the effect on Real GDP and the price level in the short run:

   a. An increase in *SRAS* that is greater than the increase in *AD*

   b. A decrease in *AD* that is greater than the increase in *SRAS*

   c. An increase in *SRAS* that is less than the increase in *AD*

4. In the following figure, which part is representative of each of the following?

   a. A decrease in wage rates

   b. An increase in the price level

   c. A beneficial supply shock

   d. An increase in the price of nonlabor inputs

(b)

(c)

(a)

CHAPTER 9

CLASSICAL MACROECONOMICS AND THE SELF-REGULATING ECONOMY

Introduction For hundreds of years, scientists have tried to understand humankind and their surroundings. Biologists have observed and conducted experiments to understand human and animal behavior. Ecologists have developed models to try to understand the relationships between the plants and animals in forests and oceans. Astronomers have constructed increasingly powerful telescopes to try to understand phenomena in space. And economists have built and tested theories to try to understand the economy. This chapter presents one view about how the economy works.

THE CLASSICAL VIEW

The term *classical economics* is often used to refer to an era in the history of economic thought that stretched from about 1750 to the early 1900s. Although classical economists lived and wrote many years ago, their ideas are often employed by some modern-day economists.

Classical Economists and Say's Law

You know from your study of supply and demand that markets can experience temporary shortages and surpluses, such as a surplus in the apple market. But can the economy have a general surplus, that is, a general glut of goods and services? The classical economists thought not, largely because they believed in Say's law (named after J. B. Say). In its simplest version, Say's law states that supply creates its own demand.

This law is most easily understood in terms of a barter economy. Consider a person baking bread in a barter economy; the baker is a supplier of bread. According to Say, the baker works at his trade because he plans to demand other goods. As he is baking bread, the baker is thinking of the goods and services he will obtain in exchange for it. Thus, his act of supplying bread is linked to his demand for other goods. Supply creates its own demand.

If supplying some goods leads to a simultaneous demand for other goods, then Say's law implies that there cannot be either (1) a general overproduction of goods (where supply in the economy is greater than demand) or (2) a general underproduction of goods (where demand in the economy is greater than supply).

Say's Law
Supply creates its own demand. Production creates enough demand to purchase all the goods and services produced.

182

On the other hand, if the baker is baking bread in a money economy, does Say's law hold? Over a period of time, the baker earns an income as a result of supplying bread, but what does he do with the income? One use of the money is to buy goods and services. However, his demand for goods and services does not necessarily match the income that he generates by supplying bread. The baker may spend less than his full income because he saves. So we might think that Say's law does not hold in a money economy because the act of supplying goods and services—thus earning income—need not create an equal amount of demand.

But the classical economists disagreed. They argued that even in a money economy, where individuals sometimes spend less than their full incomes, Say's law still holds. Their argument was partly based on the assumption of interest rate flexibility.

Classical Economists and Interest Rate Flexibility

For Say's law to hold in a money economy, the funds saved must give rise to an equal amount of funds invested; that is, what leaves the spending stream through one door must enter it through another door. If not, then some of the income earned from supplying goods may not be used to demand goods (good-bye Say's law). As a result, goods will be overproduced.

The classical economists argued that saving is matched by an equal amount of investment because of interest rate flexibility in the credit market. In Exhibit 1, I represents investment and S represents saving. I_1 is downward sloping, indicating an inverse relationship between the amount of funds firms invest and the interest rate (i). The reason for the downward slope is straightforward. The interest rate is the cost of borrowing funds. The higher the interest rate is, the fewer funds firms borrow and invest; the lower the interest rate, the more funds firms borrow and invest.

S_1 is upward sloping, indicating a direct relationship between the amount of funds that households save and the interest rate. The reason is that the higher the interest rate is, the higher the reward is for saving (or the higher the opportunity cost of consuming). So fewer funds are consumed and more funds are saved. Market-equilibrating forces move the credit market to interest rate i_1 and the equilibrium point E_1. At E_1, the number of dollars households save ($100,000) equals the number of dollars firms invest ($100,000).

Suppose now that saving increases at each interest rate level. In Exhibit 1, the saving increase is represented by a rightward shift in the saving curve from S_1 to S_2. The classical economists believed that an increase in saving puts downward pressure on the interest rate, moving it to i_2, thereby increasing the number of dollars firms invest. Ultimately, the number of dollars households save ($120,000) once again equals the number of dollars firms invest ($120,000). Interest rate

EXHIBIT 1

The Classical View of the Credit Market

In classical theory, the interest rate is flexible and adjusts so that saving equals investment. Thus, if saving increases and the saving curve shifts rightward from S_1 to S_2 (arrow 1), the increase in saving eventually puts pressure on the interest rate and moves it downward from i_1 to i_2 (arrow 2). A new equilibrium is established at E_2 (arrow 3), where once again the amount households save equals the amount firms invest.

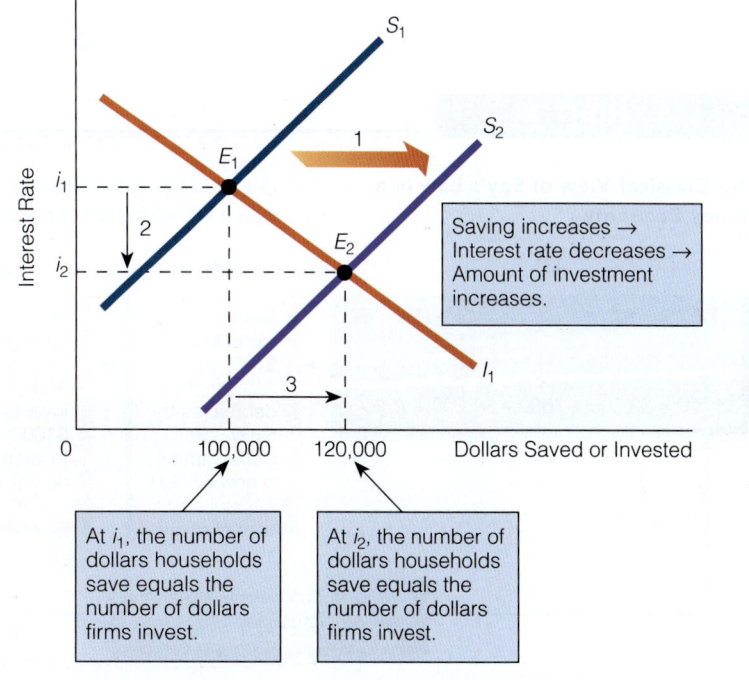

Saving increases → Interest rate decreases → Amount of investment increases.

At i_1, the number of dollars households save equals the number of dollars firms invest.

At i_2, the number of dollars households save equals the number of dollars firms invest.

flexibility ensures that saving equals investment. (What goes out one door comes in the other.) In short, changes in the interest rate uphold Say's law in a money economy where there is saving.

Let's use a few numbers to illustrate what classical economists were saying. At a given price level, total expenditures (*TE*) in a very tiny economy are $5,000. Total expenditures (total spending on domestic goods and services) equal the sum of consumption (*C*), investment (*I*), government purchases (*G*), and net exports (*EX − IM*). If *C* = $3,000, *I* = $600, *G* = $1,200, and *EX − IM* = $200, then

$$TE = C + I + G + (EX − IM)$$

$$\$5,000 = \$3,000 + \$600 + \$1,200 + \$200$$

The $5,000 worth of goods and services that the four sectors of the economy want to purchase also happens to be the exact dollar amount of goods and services that suppliers want to sell.

What happens when saving is increased in the economy? Saving (*S*) is equal to the amount of a person's disposable income (*Y_d*) minus consumption (*C*). For example, if Harriet earns a disposable income of $40,000 a year and spends $38,000, she saves $2,000.

$$\text{Saving } (S) = \text{Disposable income } (Y_d) − \text{Consumption } (C)$$

For saving to increase, consumption must decrease. See Exhibit 2. If saving increases by $100, then consumption must fall from $3,000 to $2,900. At first glance, this seems to imply that total expenditures will fall to $4,900. But classical economists disagreed. They said that investment will increase by $100, going from $600 to $700. Total expenditures will remain constant at $5,000 and will be equal to the dollar amount of the goods and services that suppliers want to sell.

$$TE = C + I + G + (EX − IM)$$

$$\$5,000 = \$2,900 + \$700 + \$1,200 + \$200$$

EXHIBIT 2

The Classical View of Say's Law in a Money Economy

According to classical economists, a decrease in consumption and subsequent increase in saving will be matched by an equal increase in investment. Thus, there is no change in total expenditures.

(1)

$$TE = C + I + G + (EX − IM)$$

$$\$5,000 = \$3,000 + \$600 + \$1,200 + \$200$$

(2)

Saving increases by $100; so consumption decreases by $100. Consumption is now $2,900.

(3)

The additional saving lowers the interest rate and increases investment by $100. Investment is now $700.

(4)

$$TE = C + I + G + (EX − IM)$$

$$\$5,000 = \$2,900 + \$700 + \$1,200 + \$200$$

TE is $5,000 before and after saving increased.

According to the classical view of the economy, then, Say's law holds both in a barter economy and in a money economy. In a money economy, according to classical economists, interest rates will adjust to equate saving and investment. Therefore, any fall in consumption (and consequent rise in saving) will be matched by an equal rise in investment. In essence, at a given price level, total expenditures will not decrease as a result of an increase in saving.

What does an increase in saving imply for aggregate demand (*AD*)? An earlier chapter explains that aggregate demand changes only if total spending in the economy changes at a given price level. Therefore, because total spending does not change as a result of an increase in saving, aggregate demand does not change.

Classical Economists on Prices and Wages: Both Are Flexible

Classical economists believed that most, if not all, markets are competitive; that is, supply and demand operate in all markets. If, for example, the labor market has a surplus, the surplus will be temporary. Soon the wage rate will decline, and the quantity supplied of labor will equal the quantity demanded of it. Similarly, given a shortage in the labor market, the wage rate will rise, and the quantity supplied will equal the quantity demanded.

What holds for wages in the labor market holds for prices in the goods and services market. Prices will adjust quickly to any surpluses or shortages, and equilibrium will be quickly reestablished. In short, the classical view is that prices and wages are flexible: They rise and decline in response to shortages and surpluses.

SELF-TEST

(Answers to Self-Test questions are in Answers to Self-Test Questions at the back of the book.)

1. Explain Say's law in terms of a barter economy.

2. According to classical economists, if saving rises and consumption spending falls, will total spending in the economy decrease? Explain your answer.

3. What is the classical position on prices and wages?

THREE STATES OF THE ECONOMY

The background information in this section will enable you to understand the views of economists who believe that the economy is self-regulating. Specifically, we discuss three states of the economy, the correspondence between the labor market and the three states of the economy, and more.

Real GDP and Natural Real GDP: Three Possibilities

In the last chapter, Natural Real GDP was defined as the Real GDP produced at the natural unemployment rate. The Real GDP is produced when the economy is in long-run equilibrium.

Economists often refer to three possible states of an economy when considering the relationship between Real GDP and Natural Real GDP:

- Real GDP is less than Natural Real GDP.
- Real GDP is greater than Natural Real GDP.
- Real GDP is equal to Natural Real GDP.

Let's now graphically portray each of these three possible states of the economy.

REAL GDP IS LESS THAN NATURAL REAL GDP (RECESSIONARY GAP) Exhibit 3(a) shows an *AD* curve, an *SRAS* curve, and the *LRAS* curve. It also shows that Natural Real GDP (Q_N) is produced in the long run.

Short-run equilibrium is at the intersection of the *AD* and *SRAS* curves; so, in Exhibit 3(a), short-run equilibrium is at point 1. The Real GDP level that the economy is producing at point 1 is designated by Q_1.

Compare Q_1 with Q_N. Obviously, Q_1 is less than Q_N. In other words, the economy is currently producing a level of Real GDP in the short run that is less than its Natural Real GDP level. When the Real GDP that the economy is producing is less than its Natural Real GDP, the economy is said to be in a **recessionary gap**.

Recessionary Gap
The condition in which the Real GDP that the economy is producing is less than the Natural Real GDP and the unemployment rate is greater than the natural unemployment rate.

REAL GDP IS GREATER THAN NATURAL REAL GDP (INFLATIONARY GAP) In Exhibit 3(b), the *AD* and *SRAS* curves intersect at point 1; so short-run equilibrium is at point 1. The Real GDP level that the economy is producing at point 1 is designated by Q_1. Compare Q_1 with Q_N. Obviously, Q_1 is greater than Q_N. In other words, the economy is currently producing a level of Real GDP in the short run that is greater than its Natural Real GDP level or potential output. When the Real GDP that the economy is producing is greater than its Natural Real GDP, the economy is said to be in an inflationary gap.

Inflationary Gap
The condition in which the Real GDP that the economy is producing is greater than the Natural Real GDP and the unemployment rate is less than the natural unemployment rate.

REAL GDP IS EQUAL TO NATURAL REAL GDP (LONG-RUN EQUILIBRIUM) In Exhibit 3(c), the *AD* and *SRAS* curves indicate that short-run equilibrium is at point 1. The Real GDP level that the economy is producing at point 1 is designated by Q_1.

Again compare Q_1 and Q_N. This time, Q_1 is equal to Q_N. In other words, the economy is currently producing a level of Real GDP that is equal to its Natural Real GDP or potential output. When the Real GDP that the economy is producing is equal to its Natural Real GDP, the economy is in *long-run equilibrium.*

EXHIBIT 3

Real GDP and Natural Real GDP: Three Possibilities

In (a), the economy is currently in short-run equilibrium at a Real GDP level of Q_1. Q_N is Natural Real GDP or the potential output of the economy. Notice that $Q_1 < Q_N$. When this condition ($Q_1 < Q_N$) exists, the economy is said to be in a recessionary gap.

In (b), the economy is currently in short-run equilibrium at a Real GDP level of Q_1. Q_N is Natural Real GDP or the potential output of the economy. Notice that $Q_1 > Q_N$. When this condition ($Q_1 > Q_N$) exists, the economy is said to be in an inflationary gap.

In (c), the economy is currently operating at a Real GDP level of Q_1, which is equal to Q_N.

In other words, the economy is producing its Natural Real GDP or potential output. When this condition ($Q_1 = Q_N$) exists, the economy is said to be in long-run equilibrium.

(a)

(b)

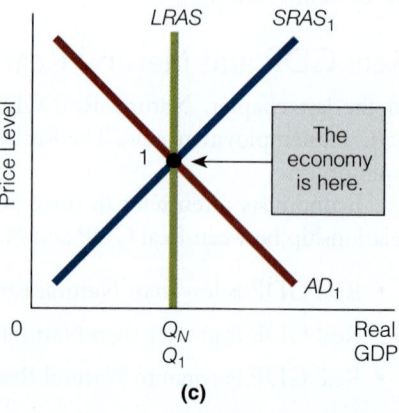

(c)

thinking like AN ECONOMIST

Thinking in Threes The economist often thinks in threes. For the economist, a market has either (1) a shortage, (2) a surplus, or (3) equilibrium. Similarly, for the economist, an economy is in:

- Either a recessionary gap, producing a level of Real GDP lower than Natural Real GDP.

- Or an inflationary gap, producing a level of Real GDP higher than Natural Real GDP.

- Or long-run equilibrium, producing a level of Real GDP equal to Natural Real GDP. ●●●

The Labor Market and the Three States of the Economy

If the economy can be in three possible states, so can the labor market. We identify the three possible states of the labor market and then tie each to a possible state of the economy.

We know that the labor market consists of the demand for and the supply of labor. Like a goods market, the labor market can manifest (1) equilibrium, (2) a shortage, or (3) a surplus. So the three possible states of the labor market are:

- *Equilibrium.* When the labor market is in equilibrium, the same number of jobs are available as the number of people who want to work. The quantity demanded of labor is equal to the quantity supplied.

- *Shortage.* When the labor market has a shortage, more jobs are available than are people who want to work. The quantity demanded of labor is greater than the quantity supplied.

- *Surplus.* When the labor market has a surplus, more people want to work than there are jobs available; the quantity supplied of labor is greater than the quantity demanded.

RECESSIONARY GAP AND THE LABOR MARKET The unemployment rate that exists when the economy produces Natural Real GDP is, of course, the natural unemployment rate. So if the economy is in a recessionary gap, is the labor market in equilibrium, shortage, or surplus?

In way of an answer, suppose the economy is in a recessionary gap, producing a Real GDP level of $9 trillion (worth of goods and services) when Natural Real GDP, or potential output, is $10 trillion. Is the existing unemployment rate producing $9 trillion worth of goods and services greater or less than the natural unemployment rate that exists when the economy is producing $10 trillion worth of goods and services? In fact, the unemployment rate is greater than the natural unemployment rate because fewer workers are needed to produce a Real GDP of $9 trillion than are needed to produce a Real GDP of $10 trillion. *Ceteris paribus,* the unemployment rate will be higher at a Real GDP level of $9 trillion than it is at a level of $10 trillion.

So, when the economy is in a recessionary gap, the unemployment rate is *higher* than the natural unemployment rate. This conclusion implies a surplus in the labor market: The quantity supplied of labor is greater than the quantity demanded; that is, more people want to work than there are jobs available.

If the economy is in a recessionary gap, the unemployment rate is higher than the natural unemployment rate, and a surplus exists in the labor market.

INFLATIONARY GAP AND THE LABOR MARKET Now suppose the economy is in an inflationary gap, producing a Real GDP level of $11 trillion (worth of goods and services) when Natural Real GDP, or potential output, is $10 trillion.

Again, the unemployment rate that exists when the economy produces Natural Real GDP is the natural unemployment rate. Is the unemployment rate that exists when the economy is producing $11 trillion worth of goods and services greater or less than the natural unemployment rate when the economy is producing $10 trillion worth? The unemployment rate is less than the natural unemployment rate because more workers are needed to produce a Real GDP of $11 trillion than are needed to produce a Real GDP of $10 trillion. *Ceteris paribus,* the unemployment rate will be lower at a Real GDP level of $11 trillion than it is at $10 trillion.

So, when the economy is in an inflationary gap, the unemployment rate is *lower* than the natural unemployment rate. This conclusion implies a shortage in the labor market: The quantity demanded of labor is greater than the quantity supplied; that is, more jobs are available than there are people who want to work.

> *If the economy is in an inflationary gap, the unemployment rate is less than the natural unemployment rate, and a shortage exists in the labor market.*

LONG-RUN EQUILIBRIUM AND THE LABOR MARKET Finally, suppose the economy is in long-run equilibrium. It is producing a Real GDP level equal to Natural Real GDP. In this state, the unemployment rate in the economy is the same as the natural unemployment rate. This conclusion implies that the labor market has neither a shortage nor a surplus but is in equilibrium.

> *If the economy is in long-run equilibrium, the unemployment rate equals the natural unemployment rate, and the labor market is in equilibrium.*

The following table summarizes three possible states of the economy and the related states of the labor market.

State of the Economy	What Do We Call It?	Relationship Between Unemployment Rate and Natural Unemployment Rate	State of the Labor Market
Real GDP < Natural Real GDP	Recessionary gap	Unemployment rate > Natural Unemployment rate	Surplus exists
Real GDP > Natural Real GDP	Inflationary gap	Unemployment rate < Natural Unemployment rate	Shortage exists
Real GDP = Natural Real GDP	Long-run equilibrium	Unemployment rate = Natural Unemployment rate	Equilibrium exists

Common Misconceptions About the Unemployment Rate and the Natural Unemployment Rate

Some people mistakenly think that the economy's unemployment rate *cannot* be lower than the natural unemployment rate (as it is in an inflationary gap). In other words, if the natural unemployment rate is 5 percent, then the unemployment rate can never be 4 percent. But that assumption is a myth.

To explain why, we need to look at two production possibilities frontiers. In Exhibit 4, the two production possibilities frontiers are the physical PPF (purple curve) and the institutional PPF (blue curve). The physical PPF illustrates different combinations of goods that the economy can produce given the physical constraints of (1) finite resources and (2) the current state of technology. The institutional PPF illustrates different combinations of goods that the economy can produce given the two physical constraints of (1) finite resources and (2) the current state of technology, plus (3) any institutional constraints. Broadly defined, an institutional constraint is anything that prevents economic agents from producing the maximum Real GDP that is physically possible.

For example, the minimum wage law, which is an institutional constraint, specifies that workers must be paid at least the legislated minimum wage. One effect of this law is that unskilled persons whose value to employers falls below the legislated minimum wage will not be hired. Having fewer workers means less output, *ceteris paribus.* (This is why the institutional PPF lies closer to the origin than the physical PPF.)

EXHIBIT 4

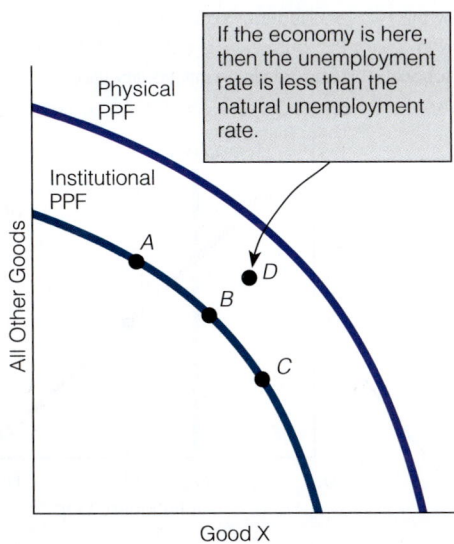

If the economy is here, then the unemployment rate is less than the natural unemployment rate.

The Physical and Institutional PPFs

A society has both a physical PPF and an institutional PPF. The physical PPF illustrates different combinations of goods the economy can produce given the physical constraints of (1) finite resources and (2) the current state of technology. The institutional PPF illustrates different combinations of goods the economy can produce given the physical constraints of (1) finite resources, (2) the current state of technology, and (3) any institutional constraints. The economy is at the natural unemployment rate if it is located on its institutional PPF, such as at points A, B, or C. An economy can never operate beyond its physical PPF, but it is possible for it to operate beyond its institutional PPF because institutional constraints are not always equally effective. If the economy does operate beyond its institutional PPF, such as at point D, then the unemployment rate in the economy is lower than the natural unemployment rate.

Within the confines of society's physical and institutional constraints is a natural unemployment rate. This situation is represented by any point on the institutional PPF. In the exhibit, points *A, B,* and *C* are all such points.

An economy can never operate beyond its physical PPF, but it can operate beyond its institutional PPF. For example, suppose inflation reduces the purchasing power of the minimum wage, thus reducing or eliminating the constraining influence of the minimum wage law on the unskilled labor market.[1] This change would make one of society's institutional constraints ineffective, allowing the economy to temporarily move beyond the institutional constraint. This is shown as point *D* in Exhibit 4. At point *D,* the unemployment rate that exists in the economy is less than the natural unemployment rate.

THREE STATES OF THE ECONOMY AND TWO PPF CURVES So an economy can operate beyond its institutional PPF but below its physical PPF. Now, let's tie the three states of an economy to the institutional and physical PPF curves.

Exhibit 5 shows the institutional PPF and the physical PPF, along with three points: *A, B,* and *C.* Point *A,* below the institutional PPF, represents an economy in a recessionary gap, where the economy is producing less than Natural Real GDP, Q_N. Point *B,* on the institutional PPF, represents an economy in long-run equilibrium, producing Natural Real GDP. Finally, point *C,* beyond the institutional PPF but below the physical PPF, represents an economy in an inflationary gap, where the economy is producing more than Natural Real GDP. Thus, each of the three states of the economy—recessionary gap, inflationary gap, and long-run equilibrium—can be identified as a point in relation to both the institutional PPF and physical PPF.

---

1. Inflation reduces the real (inflation-adjusted) minimum wage. If the minimum wage rate is $6 and the price level is 1.00, the real minimum wage is $6 ($6 ÷ the price level, 1.00). If the price level rises to 2.00, then the real minimum wage rate falls to $3. The lower the real minimum wage is, the greater the number of unskilled workers whom employers will hire, because the demand curve for unskilled workers is downward sloping.

EXHIBIT 5

Three States of the Economy and Two PPFs

In this exhibit, we show three states of the economy in terms of the institutional PPF

and physical PPF. Point A, which is below the institutional PPF, represents an economy in a recessionary gap. Point B, on the institutional PPF, represents an economy in long-run

equilibrium. Point C, beyond the institutional PPF but below the physical PPF, represents an economy in an inflationary gap.

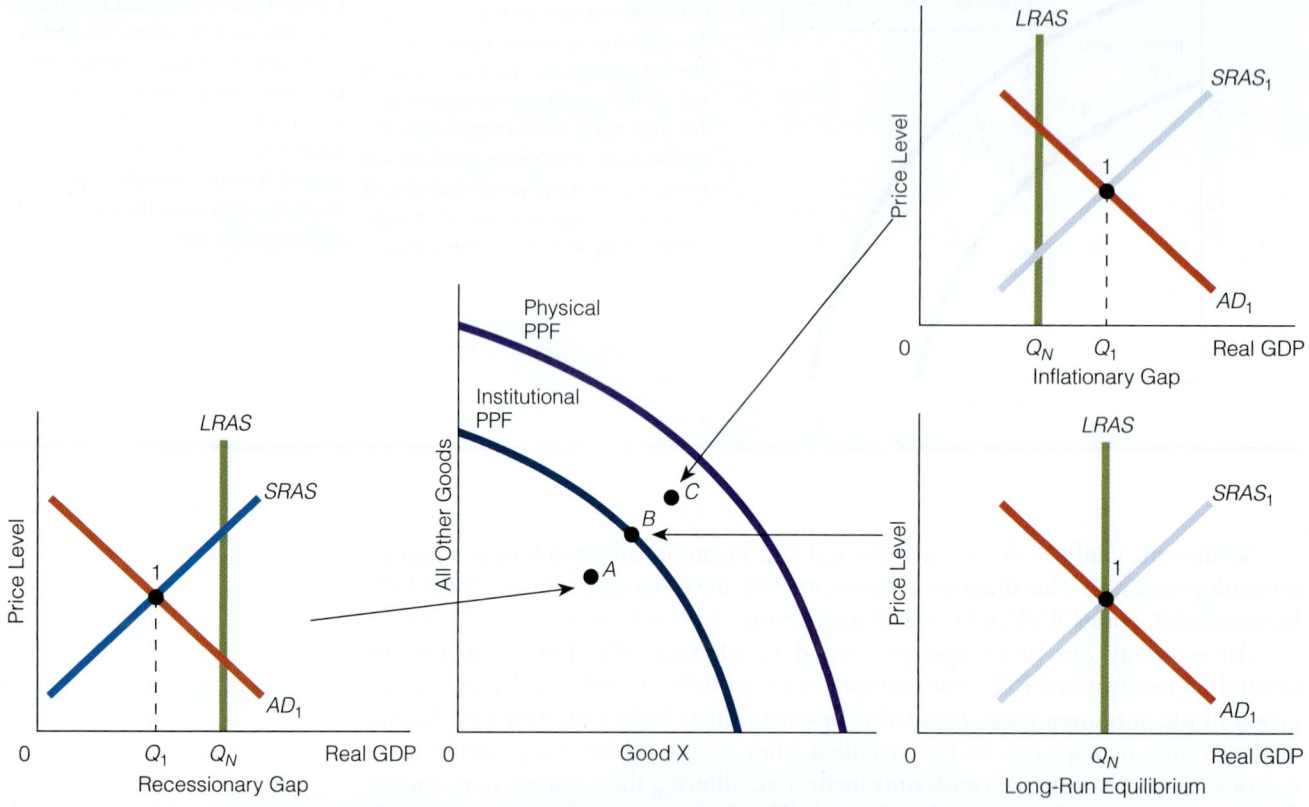

finding ECONOMICS

In a Country's Institutional PPF Assume that in year 1 country A's unemployment rate is equal to its natural unemployment rate at 4.7 percent. In year 2, its unemployment rate is still equal to its natural unemployment rate at 5.4 percent. What was going on in the country over the two years? Where is the economics?

We know that if a country's unemployment rate is equal to its natural unemployment rate, then the country is operating on its institutional PPF. (It is also operating at long-run equilibrium.) Because country A's unemployment rate is equal to its natural unemployment rate in years 1 and 2, the country must be operating on its institutional PPF in both years. But why are both the unemployment and natural unemployment rates higher (each at 5.4 percent) in year 2 than in year 1? What does this difference mean? Obviously the country's institutional PPF has shifted inward between the two years (assuming no change in the country's physical PPF). In other words, some institutional changes came about between years 1 and 2—perhaps changes in the regulatory climate—that made it more difficult to produce goods and services. ▲▲▲

SELF-TEST

1. What is a recessionary gap? An inflationary gap?

2. What is the state of the labor market when the economy is in a recessionary gap? In an inflationary gap?

3. If the economy is in an inflationary gap, locate its position in relation to the two PPFs discussed in this section.

THE SELF-REGULATING ECONOMY

Some economists believe that the economy is self-regulating. In other words, if the economy is not at the natural unemployment rate (or full employment)—that is, it is not producing Natural Real GDP—then it can move on its own to this position. The notion of a self-regulating economy is very classical, but it is also a view held by some modern-day economists. This section describes how a self-regulating economy works.

What Happens If a Self-Regulating Economy Is in a Recessionary Gap?

If the economy is in a recessionary gap,

1. it is producing a Real GDP level that is less than Natural Real GDP,

2. the unemployment rate is greater than the natural unemployment rate, and

3. a surplus exists in the labor market.

Exhibit 6(a) illustrates this case for a Real GDP of $9 trillion and a Natural Real GDP of $10 trillion. What, if anything, happens in the economy? According to economists who believe the economy is self-regulating, the surplus in the labor market begins to exert downward pressure on wages.[2] In other words, as old wage contracts expire, business firms negotiate contracts that pay workers lower wage rates.

As wage rates fall, the *SRAS* curve begins to shift to the right, ultimately moving from $SRAS_1$ to $SRAS_2$, as in Exhibit 6(b). As a result of the increase in short-run aggregate supply, the price level falls. As the price level falls, the quantity demanded of Real GDP rises due to the real balance, interest rate, and international trade effects (all discussed in the last

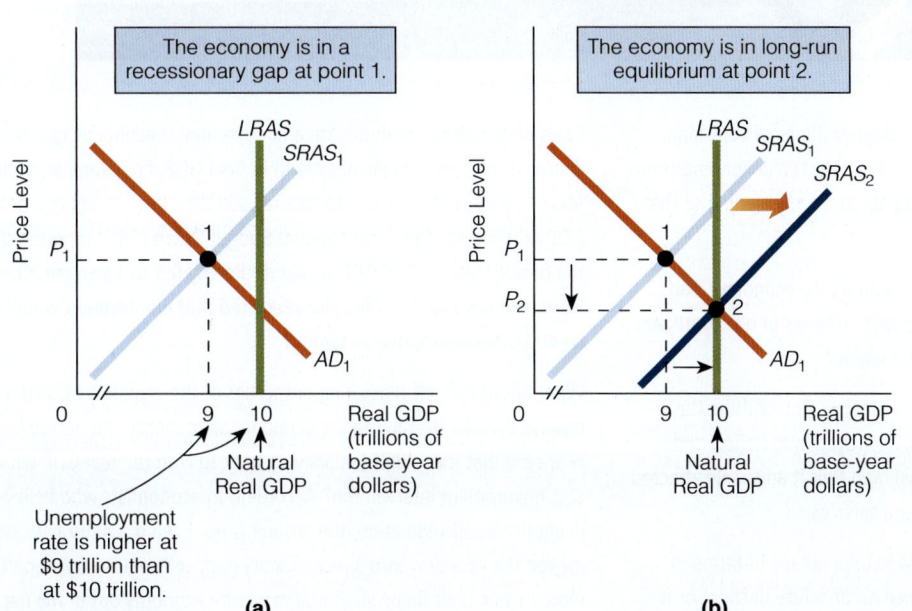

(a)   **(b)**

EXHIBIT 6

The Self-Regulating Economy: Removing a Recessionary Gap

(a) The economy is at P_1 and Real GDP of $9 trillion. Because Real GDP is less than Natural Real GDP ($10 trillion), the economy is in a recessionary gap and the unemployment rate is higher than the natural unemployment rate. (b) Wage rates fall, and the short-run aggregate supply curve shifts from $SRAS_1$ to $SRAS_2$. As the price level falls, the real balance, interest rate, and international trade effects increase the quantity demanded of Real GDP. Ultimately, the economy moves into long-run equilibrium at point 2.

---

2. In this discussion of how the self-regulating economy eliminates a recessionary gap, we have emphasized wages (in the labor market) adjusting downward. Resource prices other than wages may fall as well.

Natural Disasters and the Economy

Do natural disasters (such as hurricanes, tornadoes, earthquakes, and some fires) affect the economy? Katrina was a major hurricane that hit the central Gulf Coast on the morning of August 29, 2005. The

AP PHOTO/RIC FELD

storm caused catastrophic damage along the coastlines of Louisiana, Mississippi, and Alabama. The levees that separated Lake Pontchartrain from the city of New Orleans were damaged, ultimately leading to the flooding of about 80 percent of the city.

How does something like Hurricane Katrina affect the economy? Can Katrina (or any natural disaster) be interpreted in terms of our aggregate demand–aggregate supply framework of analysis?

Katrina is an adverse supply shock to the economy, thus shifting the *SRAS* curve to the left. Katrina essentially destroyed lives (labor) and capital (production facilities, oil platforms), and thus it adversely affected the economy's ability to produce goods and services.

Think of what a shift leftward in the *SRAS* curve means in terms of Real GDP. Either Real GDP will experience an absolute decline, or it will not grow as much as it would have had Katrina not hit. (With respect to the latter possibility, think of Katrina as shifting the *SRAS* curve leftward at the same time that other forces in the economy are shifting it rightward. Even if the forces shifting the *SRAS* curve

rightward are stronger than the leftward forces, like Katrina, the left-shifting forces still have an effect on the final position of the *SRAS* curve.)

Soon after Katrina, both private and government economic groups changed their predictions of growth in Real GDP. For example, both Merrill Lynch and Bank of America revised their growth figures for Real GDP downward. The Congressional Budget Office (CBO) reported that the growth rate in Real GDP would decline by 0.5 to 1 percent due to Hurricane Katrina. The CBO also predicted that employment would fall by 400,000 persons due to Katrina.

What about the self-regulating properties of the economy? Could a natural disaster destabilize the economy permanently, so destabilizing an economy that it couldn't find its way back to Natural Real GDP without, say, government intervention? According to economists who believe the economy is self-regulating, the answer is no. Even if a natural disaster moved the economy into a recessionary gap, self-regulating properties would soon exert themselves and move the economy out of the gap. In other words, if a natural disaster happened to move Real GDP below its natural level, in time wages would fall, the *SRAS* curve would shift rightward, and the economy would self-regulate itself toward its Natural Real GDP level.

chapter). As the price level falls, the economy moves from one point on the *AD* curve to a point farther down on the same curve. In Exhibit 6(b), this is a move from point 1 to point 2.

As long as the economy's Real GDP is less than its Natural Real GDP, the price level continues to fall. Ultimately, the economy moves to long-run equilibrium at point 2, corresponding to P_2 and a Natural Real GDP of $10 trillion.

> Recessionary gap →
> Unemployment rate > Natural unemployment rate →
> Surplus in labor market → Wages fall → *SRAS* curve shifts to the right →
> Economy moves into long-run equilibrium

What Happens If the Economy Is in an Inflationary Gap?

If the economy is in an inflationary gap,

1. it is producing a Real GDP level that is greater than Natural Real GDP,

2. the unemployment rate is less than the natural unemployment rate, and

3. a shortage exists in the labor market.

Exhibit 7(a) illustrates this case for a Real GDP of $11 trillion and a Natural Real GDP of $10 trillion. What happens in the economy in this situation? According to economists who believe the economy is self-regulating, the shortage in the labor market begins to exert upward pressure on wages. In other words, as old wage contracts expire, business firms negotiate contracts that pay workers higher wage rates.

EXHIBIT 7

The Self-Regulating Economy: Removing an Inflationary Gap

(a) The economy is at P_1 and Real GDP of $11 trillion. Because Real GDP is greater than Natural Real GDP ($10 trillion), the economy is in an inflationary gap and the unemployment rate is lower than the natural unemployment rate. (b) Wage rates rise, and the short-run aggregate supply curve shifts from $SRAS_1$ to $SRAS_2$. As the price level rises, the real balance, interest rate, and international trade effects decrease the quantity demanded of Real GDP. Ultimately, the economy moves into long-run equilibrium at point 2.

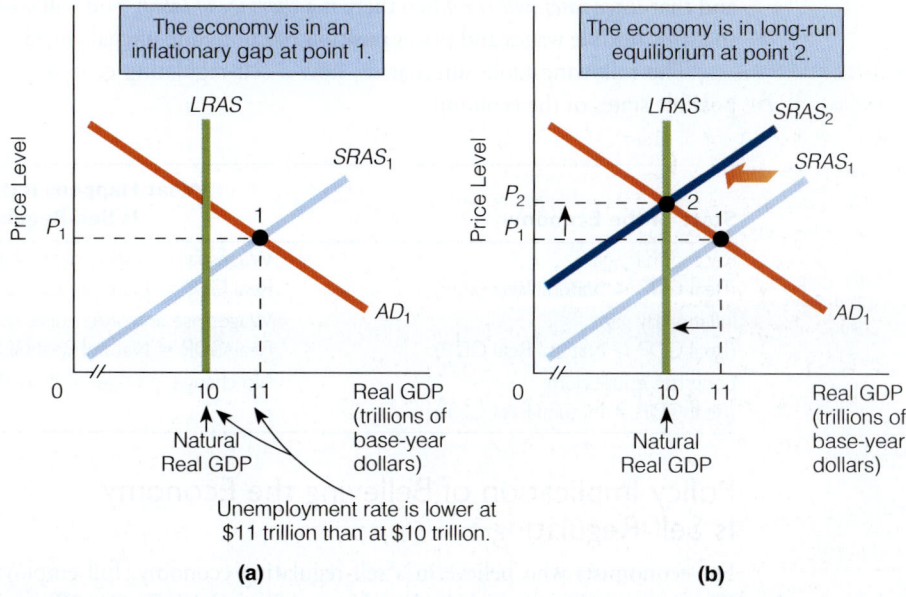

(a)

(b)

As wage rates rise, the *SRAS* curve begins to shift to the left, ultimately moving from *SRAS*₁ to *SRAS*₂ in Exhibit 7(b). As a result of the decrease in short-run aggregate supply, the price level rises. As the price level rises, the quantity demanded of Real GDP falls due to the real balance, interest rate, and international trade effects. The economy moves from one point on the *AD* curve to a point farther up on the same curve. In Exhibit 7(b), this is a move from point 1 to point 2.

As long as the economy's Real GDP is greater than its Natural Real GDP, the price level will continue to rise. Ultimately, the economy moves to long-run equilibrium at point 2, corresponding to *P*₂, and a Natural Real GDP of $10 trillion.

> Inflationary gap →
> Unemployment rate < Natural unemployment rate →
> Shortage in labor market → Wages rise → *SRAS* curve shifts to the left →
> Economy moves into long-run equilibrium

The Self-Regulating Economy: A Recap

We have seen that if the economy is in a recessionary gap, wage rates fall (along with other resource prices), and the *SRAS* curve shifts to the right, the price level falls, and the economy moves down the *AD* curve. The economy moves in the direction of long-run equilibrium, ultimately achieving the Natural Real GDP level.

If the economy is in an inflationary gap, wage rates rise (along with other resource prices), and the *SRAS* curve shifts to the left. At the same time, the price level rises and the economy moves up the *AD* curve. The economy moves in the direction of long-run equilibrium, ultimately achieving the Natural Real GDP level.

Flexible wage rates (and other resource prices) play a critical role in the self-regulating economy. For example, suppose wage rates are not flexible and do not fall in a recessionary gap. Then the *SRAS* curve does not shift to the right, the price level does not fall, and the economy doesn't move down the *AD* curve toward long-run equilibrium. Similarly, if wage rates are not flexible and do not rise in an inflationary gap, then the economy won't move up the *AD* curve toward long-run equilibrium.

The economists who say the economy is self-regulating believe that wage rates and other resource prices are *flexible* and that they move up and down in response to market conditions. These economists believe that *wage rates will fall* when there is a *surplus of labor* and that *wage rates will rise* when there is a *shortage of labor.* You will see in the next chapter that this flexible wages and prices position has not gone unchallenged.

The following table summarizes how a self-regulating economy works for the three possible states of the economy.

State of the Economy	What Happens If the Economy Is Self-Regulating?
Recessionary gap (Real GDP < Natural Real GDP)	Wages fall and *SRAS* curve shifts to the right until Real GDP = Natural Real GDP.
Inflationary gap (Real GDP > Natural Real GDP)	Wages rise and *SRAS* curve shifts to the left until Real GDP = Natural Real GDP.
Long-run equilibrium (Real GDP = Natural Real GDP)	No change in wages and no change in *SRAS*.

Policy Implication of Believing the Economy Is Self-Regulating

For economists who believe in a self-regulating economy, full employment is the norm: *The economy always moves back to Natural Real GDP.* Stated differently, if the economy contracts an "illness"—in the form of a recessionary or an inflationary gap—it is capable of healing itself through changes in wages and prices. This position on how the economy works has led these economists to advocate a macroeconomic policy of laissez-faire, or noninterference. In these economists' view, government does not have an economic management role to play.

laissez-faire
A public policy of not interfering with market activities in the economy.

Changes in a Self-Regulating Economy: Short Run and Long Run

If the economy is self-regulating, how does a change in aggregate demand affect the economy in the short run and the long run? In Exhibit 8(a), the economy is initially in long-run equilibrium at point 1. An increase in aggregate demand is brought about by, say, an increase in government purchases (a possibility discussed in the last chapter). The AD curve shifts right from AD_1 to AD_2, and in the short run the economy moves to point 2, with both Real GDP and the price level higher than at point 1. Now at point 2, the economy is in an inflationary gap. If the economy is self-regulating, wages will soon rise, and the $SRAS$ curve will shift to the left—ultimately from $SRAS_1$ to $SRAS_2$. The economy will end up at point 3 in long-run equilibrium.

Let's examine the changes in the short run and the long run. As a result of an increase in aggregate demand, Real GDP rises, and the price level rises in the short run. In addition, because Real GDP rises, the unemployment rate falls. In the long run, when the economy is at point 3, it is producing exactly the same level of Real GDP that it was producing originally (Q_N), but at a higher price level.

Conclusion: If the economy is self-regulating, an increase in aggregate demand can raise the price level and Real GDP in the short run, but in the long run the only effect is a

---

EXHIBIT 8

Changes in a Self-Regulating Economy: Short Run and Long Run

In (a) the economy is initially at point 1 in long-run equilibrium. Aggregate demand rises and the AD curve shifts right from AD_1 to AD_2. The economy is at point 2 in the short run, with a higher Real GDP and a higher price level than at point 1. The economy is also in an inflationary gap at point 2. If the economy is self-regulating, wages will soon rise, the $SRAS$

curve will shift left from $SRAS_1$ to $SRAS_2$, and the economy will be in long-run equilibrium at point 3. At point 3, the economy is producing the same Real GDP as it did at point 1. In other words, in the long run, an increase in aggregate demand only raises the price level. In (b) the economy is initially at point 1 in long-run equilibrium. Aggregate demand falls and the AD curve shifts left from AD_1 to AD_2. The economy is at point 2 in the short run, with a

lower Real GDP and a lower price level than at point 1. The economy is also in a recessionary gap. If the economy is self-regulating, wages will soon fall, the $SRAS$ curve will shift right from $SRAS_1$ to $SRAS_2$, and the economy will be in long-run equilibrium at point 3. At point 3, the economy is producing the same Real GDP as it did at point 1. In other words, in the long run, a decrease in aggregate demand only lowers the price level.

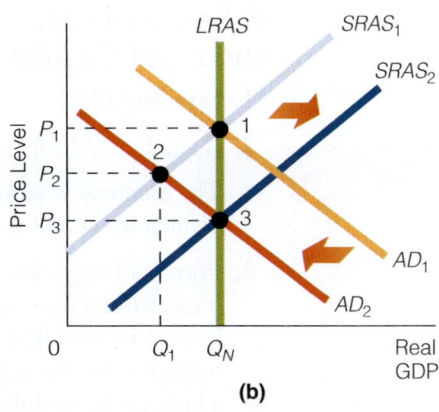

(a)   (b)

rise in the price level. In other words, in the long run, we have only higher prices to show for an increase in aggregate demand.

Now let's consider what happens if aggregate demand falls. In Exhibit 8(b), the economy is initially in long-run equilibrium at point 1 when aggregate demand decreases. The AD curve shifts left from AD_1 to AD_2, and in the short run the economy moves to point 2, with both Real GDP and the price level lower than at point 1.

Now at point 2, the economy is in a recessionary gap. If the economy is self-regulating, wages will soon fall and the $SRAS$ curve will shift to the right—ultimately from $SRAS_1$ to $SRAS_2$. The economy winds up at point 3 in long-run equilibrium.

Again, let's examine the changes in the short run and the long run. As a result of a decrease in aggregate demand, Real GDP falls in the short run, as does the price level. In addition, because Real GDP falls, the unemployment rate rises. In the long run, when the economy is at point 3, it is producing exactly the same level of Real GDP that it was producing originally (Q_N), but at a lower price level.

Conclusion: If the economy is self-regulating, a decrease in aggregate demand can lower the price level and Real GDP in the short run, but in the long run the only effect is a lower price level.

Change in AD	In the Short Run	In the Long Run
$AD \uparrow$	$P \uparrow, Q \uparrow$	$P \uparrow$, Q does not change
$AD \downarrow$	$P \downarrow, Q \downarrow$	$P \downarrow$, Q does not change

Let's return to Exhibit 8(a) to clarify a point about long-run equilibrium. In the exhibit, the economy starts at point 1 in long-run equilibrium and then moves to point 2. At point 2, both the price level and Real GDP are higher than they were at point 1. In other words, if AD rises, both the price level and Real GDP rise in the short run. If the economy is self-regulating, it does not remain at point 2 but rather moves to point 3, where it is again in long-run equilibrium. At point 3, the price level is higher than it was at point 2, but Real GDP is lower. Why, then, don't we say that Real GDP is lower in the long run than it is in the short run, instead of saying that Real GDP does not change in the long run? The answer is that the long run is measured from one long-run equilibrium point to another long-run equilibrium point. In terms of Exhibit 8(a), we look at the long run by comparing points 1 and 3. When we make this comparison, we notice two things: The price level is higher at point 3 than at point 1, and Real GDP is the same.

A Recap of Classical Macroeconomics and a Self-Regulating Economy

1. Say's law holds.

2. Interest rates change such that savings equals investment.

3. The economy is self-regulating, making full employment and an economy producing Natural Real GDP the norm.

4. Prices and wages are flexible. In other words, if the economy is in a recessionary gap, wages fall and the economy soon moves itself toward producing Natural Real GDP (at a lower price level than in the recessionary gap). If the economy is in an inflationary gap, wages rise and the economy soon moves itself toward producing Natural Real GDP (at a higher price level than in the inflationary gap).

5. Because the economy is self-regulating, laissez-faire is the policy prescription.

Business-Cycle Macroeconomics and Economic-Growth Macroeconomics

In Chapter 8, we introduced the *AD—AS* model, involving the aggregate demand (*AD*) curve, the short-run aggregate supply (*SRAS*) curve, and the long-run aggregate supply (*LRAS*) curve. In this chapter, working mainly with two of those three curves (the *AD* and *SRAS* curves), we did two things: First, we showed what would happen if a self-regulating economy were in either a recessionary or an inflationary gap (see Exhibits 6 and 7). In both cases, the short-run aggregate supply curve would shift so that the economy moved into long-run equilibrium. Second, we started from a point of long-run equilibrium and introduced a change in aggregate demand (see Exhibit 8). We explained what happens in the economy (specifically to the price level and Real GDP) in both the short run and the long run.

You have enough background now to understand the difference between business-cycle macroeconomics and economic-growth macroeconomics. Both can be explained with respect to Real GDP and a few curves. In some upcoming chapters, we will deal with business-cycle macroeconomics, that is, with changes in the *AD* and *SRAS* curves around a *fixed LRAS* curve. But in other chapters, we will be dealing with economic-growth macroeconomics, that is, with *rightward-shifting* changes in the *LRAS* curve. Business-cycle and economic-growth macroeconomics essentially make up two categories of macroeconomics. Keep these two categories in mind as you continue your study of macroeconomics.

BUSINESS-CYCLE MACROECONOMICS In this chapter, we have been looking at the *business cycle*, that is, the recurrent ups and downs in Real GDP. To understand the business cycle, refer to Exhibit 8 (a). The economy starts off in long-run equilibrium at point 1. Next, the aggregate demand shifts to the right. In the short run, Real GDP rises from Q_N to Q_1. Eventually, though, the *SRAS* curve shifts to the left, the economy is back in long-run equilibrium at point 3, and Real GDP returns to its natural level at Q_N.

We could describe what happened this way: Real GDP initially rose and then fell with respect to a *fixed LRAS* curve. This is what business-cycle macroeconomics deals with: changes in Real GDP (up and down) around a *fixed LRAS* curve.

In many upcoming chapters, we will delve into business-cycle macroeconomics: What shifts the *AD* curve? Why might Real GDP initially rise and then fall? Macroeconomists often have to ask and then try to answer such questions relating to business-cycle macroeconomics.

ECONOMIC-GROWTH MACROECONOMICS If business-cycle macroeconomics can be described as changes in Real GDP with respect to a *fixed LRAS* curve, then economic-growth macroeconomics can be described as increases in Real GDP due to a *rightward-shifting LRAS* curve. In Exhibit 9, we start with AD_1

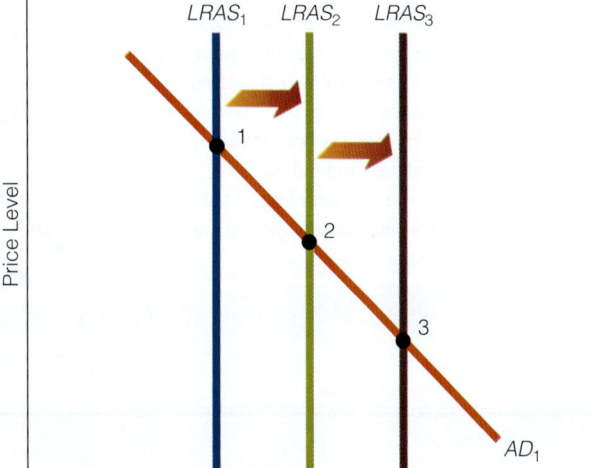

EXHIBIT 9

Economic-Growth Macroeconomics

Economic-growth macroeconomics deals with rightward shifts in the long-run aggregate supply curve (*LRAS*).

If the Economy Is Removing Itself from a Recessionary Gap, Where Is the Declining Price Level?

Suppose, in year 1, that the economy is in a recessionary gap, that it is self-regulating, and that it is beginning to remove itself from the recessionary gap. In other words, wages are beginning to fall, and the SRAS curve is beginning to shift rightward. As a result, the price level is beginning to decline.

Recessionary gap → Wages begin to fall → SRAS begins to shift rightward → Price level begins to decline

In year 2, the economy is no longer in a recessionary gap. It is in long-run equilibrium, producing the Natural Real GDP (Q_N). But here is the problem: The price level hasn't declined. This development is odd because if the economy were in a recessionary gap and the economy is self-regulating, we would expect the price level to be lower once the economy removes itself from a recessionary gap. For example, look at Exhibit 6(b) to see that the price level is lower at point 2 (once the economy has removed itself from a recessionary gap) than at point 1 (when it was in a recessionary gap).

Does a constant price level mean that the economy is not self-regulating? Not at all. While the economy was self-regulating (and the SRAS curve was shifting to the right), aggregate demand in the economy might have risen. Moreover, the rise in aggregate demand could be totally unrelated to the change occurring on the supply side of the economy (as evidenced by the SRAS curve's shift to the right).

Think of it this way: The SRAS is the right hand, and it is moving. The AD curve is the left hand; it is moving too, and its movement is unrelated to what the right hand (SRAS) is doing. In the end, both hands (both the SRAS and the AD curves) determine what happens to the price level.

In Exhibit 10, the economy is initially at point 1, in a recessionary gap. The self-regulating properties of the economy are in force, wages are falling, and the SRAS curve is shifting rightward from $SRAS_1$ to $SRAS_2$. At the same time, something has occurred to increase aggregate demand. For example, government purchases or the money supply might have increased, and the AD curve shifts rightward from AD_1 to AD_2. In the end, the two new curves—$SRAS_2$ and AD_2—intersect at point 2 in the exhibit. The economy is no longer in a recessionary gap, and the price level has remained constant.

Here's what we should take away from this discussion: Two (or more) things can happen at the same time in an economy, and unless we understand this, we may assume something is false when it is true. If the economy is removing itself from a recessionary gap, we expect the price level to decline, but it doesn't. So is the economy not self-regulating? No. Something else could have been happening at the same time the economy was removing itself from a recessionary gap, and this "something else" (in our example, a rise in aggregate demand) could offset the falling price level.

EXHIBIT 10

A Self-Regulating Economy with Aggregate Demand Increasing

The economy is initially in a recessionary gap at point 1. As the economy is self-regulating and the SRAS curve shifts to the right, something unrelated to the self-regulating properties of the economy occurs. Specifically, aggregate demand rises and the AD curve shifts rightward. The economy ends up at point 2, out of the recessionary gap but with no change in the price level.

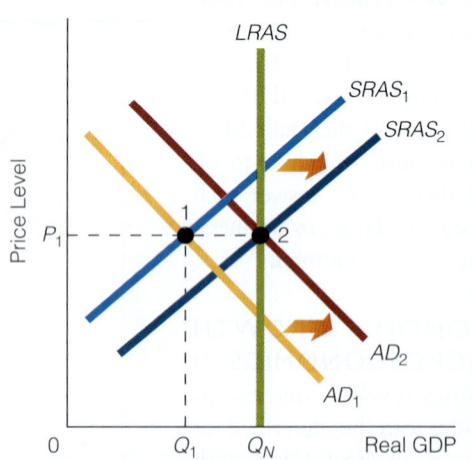

and $LRAS_1$. Long-run equilibrium is at point 1, and Natural Real GDP is Q_{N1}. Now suppose the $LRAS$ curve shifts rightward, first to $LRAS_2$ and then to $LRAS_3$. At the same time, Real GDP rises, first to Q_{N2} and then to Q_{N3}. These rightward shifts in the long-run aggregate supply ($LRAS$) curve illustrate economic growth. Our study of economic-growth macroeconomics deals with the factors that can lead to a rightward shift in $LRAS$.

SELF-TEST

1. If the economy is self-regulating, what happens if it is in a recessionary gap?

2. If the economy is self-regulating, what happens if it is in an inflationary gap?

3. If the economy is self-regulating, how do changes in aggregate demand affect the economy in the long run?

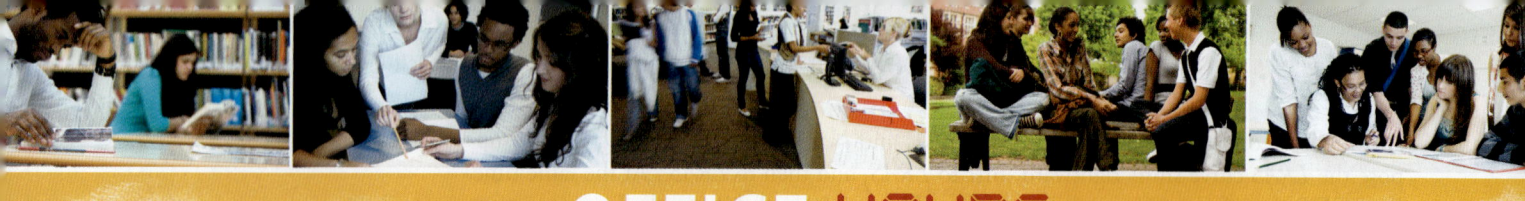

OFFICE HOURS

"Do Economists Really Know What the Natural Unemployment Rate Equals?"

STUDENT:

Do economists know what the natural unemployment rate equals at any given moment?

INSTRUCTOR:

They estimate it but can't be absolutely sure that their estimate of the natural unemployment rate is the same as the actual rate. After all, not all economists get the same estimate for the natural unemployment rate. One economist might estimate it at 4.3 percent, whereas another estimates it at 4.6 percent.

STUDENT:

Well, if that's true, then not every economist would agree that the economy is in, say, a recessionary gap if the unemployment rate is, say, 4.5 percent. Am I correct?

INSTRUCTOR:

You are correct. For example, the economist who thinks the natural unemployment rate is 4.3 percent will think the economy is in a recessionary gap if the actual unemployment rate is 4.5 percent, but the economist who thinks the natural unemployment rate is 4.6 percent will not. Here's an analogy: Smith thinks that Brown's normal body temperature is 98.9 degrees, and Jones thinks it is only 98.6 degrees. If Brown's body temperature today is 98.9 degrees, Jones will think Brown is running a low-grade fever, but Smith will not.

STUDENT:

Does getting a too-high or too-low estimate of the natural unemployment rate matter to the economy? In other words, do the incorrect estimates (that economists sometimes make) matter?

INSTRUCTOR:

Actually, the answer is yes and no. The answer is no if the economy is self-regulating and government doesn't plan to try to move the economy out of either a recessionary or inflationary gap by implementing economic policies. As in the example of misestimating Brown's normal body temperature, if no one plans to give Brown any medicine, then misestimating his body temperature probably doesn't matter.

CHAPTER SUMMARY

SAY'S LAW

- Say's law states that supply creates its own demand. All economists believe that Say's law holds in a barter economy, where there can be no general overproduction or underproduction of goods. Classical economists believed that Say's law also holds in a money economy. In their view, even if consumption drops and saving rises, economic forces are at work producing an equal increase in investment. According to classical economists, interest rates are flexible, and they move to a level where the amount of saving and the amount of investment in an economy are equal.

CLASSICAL ECONOMISTS ON MARKETS, WAGES, AND PRICES

- Classical economists believed that most, if not all, markets are competitive and that wages and prices are flexible.

THREE STATES OF THE ECONOMY

- Natural Real GDP is the level of Real GDP produced when the economy is operating at the natural unemployment rate.

But in later chapters you are going to read about the government implementing economic policies to try to remove the economy from either a recessionary or inflationary gap. Then misestimating the natural unemployment rate does matter.

To illustrate, suppose the natural unemployment rate has fallen from 5.0 percent to 4.7 percent, but economists and government economic policy makers have not figured this out yet. In other words, they still believe that the natural unemployment rate is 5.0 percent. Now if the actual unemployment rate is 4.7 percent, then the economy is in long-run equilibrium. Economists and government economic policy makers, however, mistakenly believe that the economy is in an inflationary gap (with the actual unemployment rate of 4.7 percent lower than their too-high estimate of 5.0 percent). Thinking the economy is in an inflationary gap, economists expect prices to rise in the future. To offset the higher prices in the future, they propose a reduction in the growth rate of the money supply in the hopes of reducing aggregate demand (shifting the *AD* curve to the left). The Federal Reserve [the monetary authority] follows suit and reduces the growth rate of the money supply, and the *AD* curve shifts leftward. But notice the effect of this in terms of our *AD–AS* model. A reduction in aggregate demand throws the economy into a recessionary gap. (Remember, the economy was actually in long-run equilibrium when the monetary policy action was carried out.)

Our conclusion is simple: A misestimate of the natural unemployment rate, if acted on, can move an economy from long-run equilibrium into a recessionary gap.

Back to the original question: Does getting a too-high or too-low estimate of the natural unemployment rate matter to the economy? The answer is yes, it certainly can matter to the economy.

- The economy can be producing a Real GDP level that (1) is equal to Natural Real GDP, (2) is greater than Natural Real GDP, or (3) is less than Natural Real GDP. In other words, the economy can be in (1) long-run equilibrium, (2) an inflationary gap, or (3) a recessionary gap, respectively.
- In long-run equilibrium, the Real GDP that the economy is producing is equal to the Natural Real GDP. The unemployment rate in the economy is equal to the natural unemployment rate, and the labor market is in equilibrium.
- In a recessionary gap, the Real GDP that the economy is producing is less than the Natural Real GDP. The unemployment rate in the economy is greater than the natural unemployment rate, and a surplus exists in the labor market.

- In an inflationary gap, the Real GDP that the economy is producing is greater than the Natural Real GDP. The unemployment rate in the economy is less than the natural unemployment rate, and a shortage exists in the labor market.

THE INSTITUTIONAL AND PHYSICAL PRODUCTION POSSIBILITIES FRONTIERS

- The physical PPF illustrates different combinations of goods that the economy can produce given the physical constraints of (1) finite resources and (2) the current state of technology. The institutional PPF illustrates different combinations of goods that the economy can produce given the two physical constraints of (1) finite resources and (2) the current state of technology, plus (3) any institutional constraints.

- If an economy is operating on its institutional PPF, it is operating at the natural unemployment rate. If it is operating at a point beyond the institutional PPF but below the physical PPF, it is operating at an unemployment rate less than the natural unemployment rate.

THE SELF-REGULATING ECONOMY

- Some economists contend that the economy can eliminate both recessionary and inflationary gaps smoothly and quickly by itself.
- If the economy is self-regulating and in a recessionary gap, then the unemployment rate in the economy is greater than the natural unemployment rate, and a surplus exists in the labor market. As wage contracts expire, wage rates fall. As a result, the SRAS curve shifts to the right, and the price level falls. As the price level falls, the quantity demanded of Real GDP rises.

Ultimately, the economy moves into long-run equilibrium, where it produces Natural Real GDP.

- If the economy is self-regulating and in an inflationary gap, then the unemployment rate in the economy is less than the natural unemployment rate, and a shortage exists in the labor market. As wage contracts expire, wage rates rise. As a result, the SRAS curve shifts to the left, and the price level rises. As the price level rises, the quantity demanded of Real GDP falls. Ultimately, the economy moves into long-run equilibrium, where it produces Natural Real GDP.

BUSINESS-CYCLE MACROECONOMICS AND ECONOMIC-GROWTH MACROECONOMICS

- This text presents both business-cycle and economic-growth macroeconomics. Business-cycle macroeconomics deals with changes in Real GDP around a fixed LRAS curve. Economic-growth macroeconomics deals with increases in Real GDP due to a rightward-shifting LRAS curve.

KEY TERMS AND CONCEPTS

| Say's Law | Recessionary Gap | Inflationary Gap | Laissez-faire |

QUESTIONS AND PROBLEMS

1. What does it mean to say that the economy is in a recessionary gap? In an inflationary gap? In long-run equilibrium?

2. According to economists who believe in a self-regulating economy, what happens—step by step—when the economy is in a recessionary gap? What happens when the economy is in an inflationary gap?

3. According to classical economists, does an increase in saving shift the AD curve to the left? Explain your answer.

4. Explain how an economy can operate beyond its institutional PPF but not beyond its physical PPF.

5. Explain why saving rises as the interest rate rises.

6. Describe the relationship of the (actual) unemployment rate to the natural unemployment rate in each of the following economic states: (a) a recessionary gap, (b) an inflationary gap, and (c) long-run equilibrium.

7. How do you explain why investment falls as the interest rate rises?

8. Diagrammatically represent an economy in (a) an inflationary gap, (b) a recessionary gap, and (c) long-run equilibrium.

9. According to classical economists, does Say's law hold in a money economy? Explain your answer.

10. What is the state of the labor market in (a) a recessionary gap, (b) an inflationary gap, (c) long-run equilibrium?

11. What is the classical economics position on (a) wages, (b) prices, and (c) interest rates?

12. Suppose that the economy is self-regulating, that the price level is 132, that the quantity demanded of Real GDP is $4 trillion, that the quantity supplied of Real GDP in the short run is $3.9 trillion, and that the quantity supplied of Real GDP in the long run is $4.3 trillion. Is the economy in short-run equilibrium? Will the price level in long-run equilibrium be greater than, less than, or equal to 132? Explain your answers.

13. Beginning in long-run equilibrium, explain what happens to the price level and Real GDP in the short run and in the long run as a result of (a) a decline in AD, (b) a rise in AD, (c) a decline in SRAS, and (d) a rise in SRAS.

14. Suppose that the economy is self-regulating, that the price level is 110, that the quantity demanded of Real GDP is $4 trillion, that the quantity supplied of Real GDP in the short run is $4.9 trillion, and that the quantity supplied of Real GDP in the long run is $4.1 trillion. Is the economy in short-run equilibrium? Will the price level in long-run equilibrium be greater than, less than, or equal to 110? Explain your answers.

15. Jim says, "I think it's a little like when you have a cold or the flu. You don't need to see a doctor. In time, your body heals itself. That's sort of the way the economy works too. We don't really need government coming to our rescue every time the economy gets a cold." According to Jim, how does the economy work?

16. Explain the importance of the real balance, interest rate, and international trade effects to long-run (equilibrium) adjustment in the economy.

17. Yvonne is telling her friend Wendy that wages are rising but that so is the unemployment rate. She tells Wendy that she may be the next person to be fired at her company and that she may have to move back in with her parents. What does the economy have to do with Yvonne's possibly of having to move back in with her parents?

18. If wage rates are not flexible, can the economy be self-regulating? Explain your answer.

WORKING WITH NUMBERS AND GRAPHS

1. In the following figure, which point is representative of:
   a. The economy on its *LRAS* curve
   b. The economy in a recessionary gap
   c. The economy in an inflationary gap

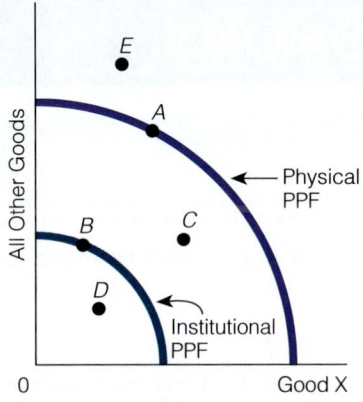

2. In the following figure, which of parts (a)–(c) is consistent with or representative of:
   a. The economy operating at the natural unemployment rate
   b. A surplus in the labor market
   c. A recessionary gap
   d. A cyclical unemployment rate of zero

3. Diagrammatically represent the following:
   a. An economy in which *AD* increases as it is self-regulating out of a recessionary gap
   b. An economy in which *AD* decreases as it is self-regulating out of an inflationary gap

4. Economist Jones believes there is always sufficient (aggregate) demand in the economy to buy all the goods and services supplied at full employment. Diagrammatically represent what the economy looks like for Jones.

5. Diagrammatically show what happens when the institutional constraints in the economy become less effective.

CHAPTER 10

KEYNESIAN MACROECONOMICS AND ECONOMIC INSTABILITY: A CRITIQUE OF THE SELF-REGULATING ECONOMY

Introduction In the last chapter we discussed the economy as a self-regulating mechanism. For example, we learned that an economy can remove itself from a recessionary gap. In this chapter we challenge that assertion and discuss the views of economists who believe that the economy may not be able to self-regulate at Natural Real GDP. In other words, the economy may not be able to move itself out of a recessionary gap. The ideas in this chapter are mostly those of one man, John Maynard Keynes, who taught economics at Cambridge University in England.

QUESTIONING THE CLASSICAL POSITION AND THE SELF-REGULATING ECONOMY

John Maynard Keynes, an English economist, changed how many economists viewed the economy. Keynes's major work, *The General Theory of Employment, Interest and Money*, was published in 1936. Just prior to its publication, the Great Depression had plagued many countries of the world. Looking around at the world during that time, one had to wonder whether the classical view of the economy could be right. Unemployment was sky-high in many countries, and many economies had been contracting. Where was Say's law, with its promise that there would be no general gluts? When was the self-regulating economy going to heal itself of its depression illness? Where was full employment? And, given the depressed state of the economy, could anyone any longer believe that laissez-faire was the right policy? With the Great Depression as recent history, Keynes and the Keynesians thought that although their theory might not be right in every detail, they certainly had enough evidence to say that the classical view of the economy was wrong.

Keynes challenged all four of the following classical position beliefs: (1) Say's law holds, so that insufficient demand in the economy is unlikely. (2) Wages, prices, and interest rates are flexible. (3) The economy is self-regulating. (4) Laissez-faire is the right and sensible economic policy.

Keynes's Criticism of Say's Law in a Money Economy

According to classical economists and Say's law, if consumption spending falls because saving increases, then total spending will not fall, because the added saving will simply bring about more investment spending. This will happen through changes in the interest rate. The added saving will put downward pressure on the interest rate, and at a lower interest rate businesses will borrow and invest more. Through changes in the interest rate, the amount of saving will always equal the amount invested.

Keynes disagreed. He didn't think that added saving will necessarily stimulate an equal amount of added investment spending. Exhibit 1 illustrates Keynes's point of view. Let consumption equal $3,000, investment equal $600, government purchases equal $1,200, and net exports equal $200. Then saving increases by $100, lowering consumption to $2,900. According to the classical economists, investment will rise by $100 at the same time, going from $600 to $700. Keynes asked, what is the guarantee that an increase in investment will equally match an increase in saving? What if saving rises by $100 (and consumption goes down by $100), but investment rises by, say, only $40 (instead of $100)? Then the original equation $TE = C + I + G + (EX - IM)$ changes from

$$TE = \$3{,}000 + \$600 + \$1{,}200 + \$200$$
$$= \$5{,}000$$

to

$$TE = \$2{,}900 + \$640 + \$1{,}200 + \$200$$
$$= \$4{,}940$$

not to

$$TE = \$2{,}900 + \$700 + \$1{,}200 + \$200$$
$$= \$5{,}000$$

EXHIBIT 1

Keynes's View of Say's Law in a Money Economy

According to Keynes, a decrease in consumption and subsequent increase in saving may not be matched by an equal increase in investment. Thus, a decrease in total expenditures may occur.

$TE = C + I + G + (EX - IM)$

$\$5{,}000 = \$3{,}000 + \$600 + \$1{,}200 + \$200$

Saving increases by $100, so consumption decreases by $100. Consumption is now $2,900.

According to Keynes, the additional $100 savings may not lead to a $100 increase in investment. Suppose investment rises by only $40, so total investment is now $640.

$TE = C + I + G + (EX - IM)$

$\$4{,}940 = \$2{,}900 + \$640 + \$1{,}200 + \$200$

Notice that TE is $5,000 before saving increased and $4,940 after it increased.

Thus, total expenditures decrease from $5,000 to $4,940. And if, at a given price level, total spending falls, so will aggregate demand. In other words, according to Keynes, aggregate demand could fall if saving increases.

Of course, a classical economist would retort that, as a result of a $100 increase in saving, interest rates will fall enough to guarantee that investment will increase by $100. Keynes countered by saying that individuals save and invest for a host of reasons and that no single factor, such as the interest rate, links these activities.

Furthermore, whereas the classical economists believed that saving and investment depend on the interest rate, Keynes believed that both saving and investment depend on a number of factors that may be far more influential than the interest rate. Keynes held that saving is more responsive to changes in income than to changes in the interest rate and that investment is more responsive to technological changes, business expectations, and innovations than to changes in the interest rate.

Consider the difference between Keynes and the classical economists on saving.

- The classical economists held that saving is directly related to the interest rate: As the interest rate goes up, saving rises; as the interest rate goes down, saving falls, *ceteris paribus*.

- Keynes thought this assumption might not always be true. Suppose individuals are saving for a certain goal—say, a retirement fund of $100,000. They might save less per period at an interest rate of 10 percent than at an interest rate of 5 percent because a higher interest rate means that they can save less per period and still meet their goal by retirement. For example, if the interest rate is 5 percent, they need $50,000 in savings to earn $2,500 in interest income per year. If the interest rate is 10 percent, they need only $25,000 in savings to earn $2,500 in interest.

As for investment, Keynes believed that the interest rate is important in determining the level of investment, but not as important as other variables, such as the expected rate of profit on investment. Keynes argued that if business expectations are pessimistic, then much investment is unlikely, regardless of how low the interest rate is.

Keynes on Wage Rates

As explained in the last chapter, if the unemployment rate in the economy is greater than the natural unemployment rate, a surplus exists in the labor market: The number of job seekers is high relative to the number of jobs available. Consequently, according to classical economists, wage rates will fall.

Keynes didn't see the adjustment as so simple. Instead, he asserted, employees will naturally resist an employer's efforts to cut wages, and labor unions may resist wage cuts. In short, wage rates may be inflexible in a downward direction.

If Keynes is correct and wage rates will not fall, is the economy then unable to get itself out of a recessionary gap? The unequivocal answer is yes. If employee and labor union resistance prevents wage rates from falling, then the *SRAS* curve will not shift to the right. If it does not shift to the right, the price level won't come down. If the price level does not come down, buyers will not purchase more goods and services and move the economy out of a recessionary gap. In terms of Exhibit 2, the economy is stuck at point 1. It cannot get to point 2.

Keynes believed that the economy is inherently unstable and that it may not automatically cure itself of a recessionary gap. *It may not be self-regulating.*

Different Markets, Different Rates of Adjustment

Keynes's notion that wages may not fall to their equilibrium level brings up the issue of various markets and the adjustment path in each. Let's first look at a market in which prices equilibrate very quickly: the stock market. Consider the market for stock A. There is a demand for this stock and a supply of it. If the demand rises, the price of the stock will rise. If the demand falls, the price of the stock will fall. Stock prices are flexible (upward and downward), and they move quickly to their equilibrium value. For example, the demand for stock A might rise at 10 o'clock in the morning, and one minute later, at 10:01, the new higher equilibrium price of stock A is reached.

Now not all markets adjust to their equilibrium values as quickly as the stock market. Many economists argue that the labor market might be very different from the

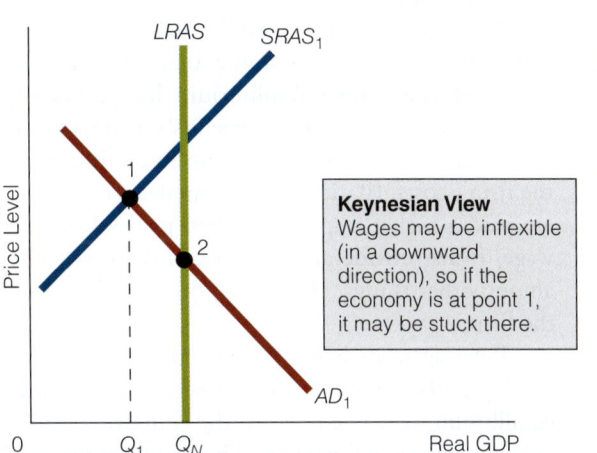

EXHIBIT 2

The Economy Gets Stuck in a Recessionary Gap

If the economy is in a recessionary gap at point 1, Keynes held that wage rates may not fall. The economy may be stuck in the recessionary gap.

stock market. Many economists argue that, in the labor market, wages may adjust very slowly to their new equilibrium values. For some period of time, wages may not adjust at all, especially when there is a surplus of labor and we would expect wages to decline.

Exhibit 3 shows the demand for and supply of labor. Currently, the labor market is in equilibrium at W_1. At this wage, the quantity demanded of labor equals the quantity supplied of labor, and both are 100 workers. Now let's suppose the demand for goods and services declines in the economy; that is, the aggregate demand (AD) curve shifts leftward. As a result of lower AD in the economy, firms are producing and selling fewer goods and services. Therefore, their demand for labor decreases; in Exhibit 3, the demand for labor curve shifts leftward from D_1 to D_2. If the labor market were like the stock market and equilibrated quickly to its new equilibrium wage rate (W_2), the labor market would move to point 2. Fewer people would be working at point 2 than at point 1, and the people who were working would be earning less (W_2 instead of W_1). Also, 25 people would have been fired.

Keynesian economists often argue that the labor market does not adjust the same way or as quickly as the stock market. In other words, wage rates aren't likely to fall simply because the demand for labor has declined (from D_1 to D_2). The wage rate W_1 is likely to be inflexible downward; that is, it isn't likely to *decline*—at least for some time.

Why is the wage rate inflexible downward? One explanation has to do with long-term labor contracts. To illustrate, suppose management and workers enter into a three-year contract that specifies a wage rate of $20 an hour for the duration of the contract. Management might want to enter into such a contract for two reasons: fewer labor negotiations and fewer worker strikes, both of which effectively diminish or disappear while the contract is in force. Workers want to

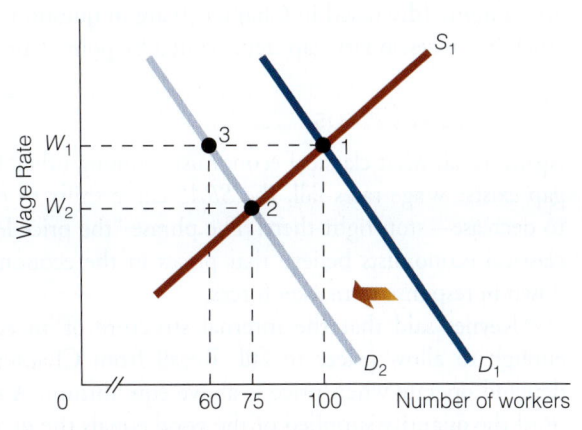

EXHIBIT 3

The Labor Market and Inflexible Wages Downward

We start with D_1 and S_1 and the labor market in equilibrium at point 1. The equilibrium wage rate is W_1. The demand for labor declines, and the new equilibrium wage rate is W_2. Will employers end up paying W_2? "Not necessarily," say economists who believe the wage rate (in the labor market) is inflexible downward. The reasons they offer include long-term labor contracts, fear of declining productivity resulting from lower wages, and avoiding having disgruntled workers in the workplace.

enter into such a contract also for two reasons: wage security and fewer strikes (strikes are costly for workers too).

There may also be solid microeconomic reasons for inflexible wages downward. Some economists argue that firms at times find it in their best interest to pay wage rates above equilibrium levels. For example, according to efficiency wage models, labor productivity depends on the wage rate that the firm pays its employees. Specifically, a cut in wages can cause a decline in labor productivity, which, in turn, raises the firm's costs. (Basically, these models say that workers are more productive when they are paid a higher wage than when paid a lower one.) By paying an above-equilibrium wage, firms provide an incentive to workers to be productive and to do less shirking, among other things. If shirking declines, so do the monitoring (management) costs of the firm.

Refer again to Exhibit 3, and think of how things look from the perspective of the employer, the person hiring workers. The demand for labor has declined, and the new equilibrium wage rate is W_2. If the employer decides to go with the new equilibrium wage rate, two things will happen: The employer has to (1) fire 25 workers and (2) pay the 75 remaining workers a lower wage rate than they were previously receiving. This means the employer is likely to have to face 75 disgruntled workers every day. Now, disgruntled workers (who may not understand *why* the employer has decided to pay them less) are not likely to be the same as when they were paid more. They may be less productive, shirk more, perhaps even steal from the employer.

Will things be much different if the employer continues to pay W_1 and keeps 60 workers instead of 75 workers (in other words, fire 40 workers instead of 25)? Some economists argue that paying W_1 might be better for the employer than paying the lower wage of W_2. At W_2, the employer has 75 workers who are angry because they are being paid a lower wage—and the employer has to work with these 75 disgruntled workers every day. But if the employer pays W_1 instead of W_2 and fires 40 workers, they will all be disgruntled, but they won't be disgruntled *at work*. They are disgruntled *at home*, away from the employer. The remaining 60 workers are not disgruntled because they haven't had their wage rate lowered and they haven't been fired. In fact, they may appreciate their employer all the more for not cutting their wage rates and for not firing them.

To recap, Keynesian economists often argue that the labor market is not the same as the stock market. The stock market equilibrates quickly to changes in demand and supply. The labor market may adjust slowly. In particular, a lowered demand for labor may not be met with a declining wage rate. Wage rates might be inflexible downward (at least for some time). If wage rates are inflexible downward, then the self-regulating properties of an economy (discussed in Chapter 9) are in question. Specifically, an economy might get stuck in a recessionary gap, represented by point 1 in Exhibit 2.

Keynes on Prices

Again, recall what classical economists (among others) believe occurs when a recessionary gap exists: Wage rates fall, the *SRAS* curve shifts to the right, and the price level begins to decrease—stop right there! The phrase "the price level begins to decrease" tells us that classical economists believe that prices in the economy are flexible: They move up and down in response to market forces.

Keynes said that the internal structure of an economy is not always competitive enough to allow prices to fall. Recall from Chapter 3 how the forces of supply and demand operate when price is above equilibrium. A surplus is generated, and price falls until the quantity supplied of the good equals the quantity demanded. Keynes suggested that anticompetitive or monopolistic elements in the economy sometimes prevent price from falling.

Efficiency Wage Models
These models hold that it is sometimes in the best interest of business firms to pay their employees higher-than-equilibrium wage rates.

The Financial and Economic Crisis of 2007–2009: Can a Housing Bust Lead to an Imploding Economy?

In the last chapter we discussed a self-regulating economy: When the economy is in a recessionary gap, it regulates itself back to long-run equilibrium. In this chapter, we state that an economy could get stuck in a recessionary gap if wages are inflexible downward. Some economists use the model in this chapter to explain the events of the latest financial and economic crisis.

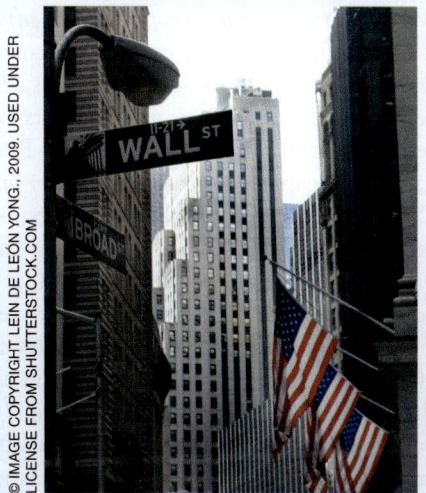

© IMAGE COPYRIGHT LEIN DE LEÓN YONG., 2009. USED UNDER LICENSE FROM SHUTTERSTOCK.COM

Suppose an economy in long-run equilibrium undergoes a shock, such as the bursting of the housing bubble, with the prices of houses dropping. In the United States, housing prices started declining in mid-2006. Because the value of a house is a part of a person's overall wealth, a decline in it leads to a decline in a person's wealth. As a result of a decline in wealth, the person is poorer (or less rich) and consequently cuts back on consumption. A decline in consumption leads to a decline in aggregate demand, and so the aggregate demand curve shifts leftward, as in Exhibit 4(a), and the economy is now in a recessionary gap.

If the economy were self-regulating, it could get itself out of the recessionary gap. But if wages are inflexible downward, the economy is stuck in the recessionary gap.

Look at the labor market in Exhibit 4(b). The labor market is initially in equilibrium at point 1. As a result of aggregate demand falling in the economy [see Exhibit 4(a)], firms are selling less output. So they do not need as much labor, and the demand for labor shifts leftward in Exhibit 4(b). Because the wage rate is flexible downward, the number of workers hired in the labor market falls from 10 million to 8 million. Two million workers are fired. As workers are fired, their incomes fall; as a result of lower incomes, individuals cut back on consumption. So aggregate demand shifts leftward again and into a deeper recessionary gap. See Exhibit 4(c).

What does this exposition tell us? A housing bust (declining house prices) can be the catalyst for an economy that falls into a recessionary gap. Further, if the economy is not self-regulating, a cascade of events can cause the economy to "implode" upon itself. A decline in aggregate demand leads to a recessionary gap that, if wages are inflexible downward, leads to some workers being fired, leading in turn to lower incomes and another decline in aggregate demand. Thus the recessionary gap deepens. Graphically, in Exhibit 4, instead of being between Q_1 and Q_2, the recessionary gap is between Q_1 and Q_3.

EXHIBIT 4

(a) — Price Level vs Real GDP: LRAS, SRAS$_1$, points 2 and 1, AD_1, AD_2; Q_1 Q_N on Real GDP axis.

(b) — Wage Rate vs Number of workers (millions): S_1, points 2 and 1 at W_1, D_1, D_2; 8 and 10 on axis.

(c) — Price Level vs Real GDP: LRAS, SRAS$_1$, points 2, 1, and 3, AD_1, AD_2, AD_3; Q_3 Q_2 Q_1 on Real GDP axis.

Is It a Question of the Time It Takes for Wages and Prices to Adjust?

Classical economists believed that both wages and prices are flexible and adjust downward in a recessionary gap. Keynes, however, suggested that wages and prices are not flexible in a downward direction and may not adjust downward in a recessionary gap.

Many economists today take a position somewhere between Keynes's and that of the classical economists. For them, the question is not whether wages and prices are flexible downward, but *how long it takes for them to adjust downward.*

In Exhibit 5, suppose the economy is currently in a recessionary gap at point 1. The relevant short-run aggregate supply curve is $SRAS_1$, where the wage rate is $10 per hour and the price level is P_1. Classical economists expect the wage rate and price level will fall, whereas Keynes said this may not happen. But did Keynes mean that if the economy is in a recessionary gap, *the wage rate will never fall and the price level will never adjust downward?* Most economists think not. The question is *how long* the wage rate and price level will take to fall. Will they fall in a few weeks? In a few months? In five years? The question is relevant because the answer determines how long an economy will be in a recessionary gap and thus how long the economy takes to self-regulate.

Look at the question this way: If it takes only a few weeks or months for wage rates to fall (say, to $8 an hour), for the short-run aggregate supply curve to shift from $SRAS_1$ to $SRAS_2$, and for the price level to fall from P_1 to P_2, then, for all practical purposes, the economy is almost instantaneously self-regulating. But if all this takes years to happen, the economy can hardly be considered self-regulating over any reasonable amount of time.

The classical position is that the time required for wages and prices to adjust downward is short enough to call the economy self-regulating. The Keynesian position is that the time is long enough to say that the economy is not self-regulating. Instead, the Keynesians believe that the economy is inherently unstable and that it can exist in a recessionary gap for a long time.

ⓣhinking like AN ECONOMIST

Different Assumptions, Different Conclusions The economist knows that assumptions affect conclusions. For example, classical economists assumed that wages are flexible, but Keynes assumed that wages might be inflexible at times. This difference in assumptions affects policy conclusions. For example, classical economists, assuming wages are flexible, will reach different policy conclusions than will Keynes, who is assuming wages are inflexible. ▪▪▪

EXHIBIT 5

A Question of How Long It Takes for Wage Rates and Prices to Fall

Suppose the economy is in a recessionary gap at point 1. Wage rates are $10 per hour, and the price level is P_1. The issue may not be whether wage rates and the price level fall, but how long they take to reach long-run levels. If they take a short time, then classical economists are right: The economy is self-regulating. If they take a long time—perhaps years—then Keynes is right: The economy is not self-regulating over any reasonable period of time.

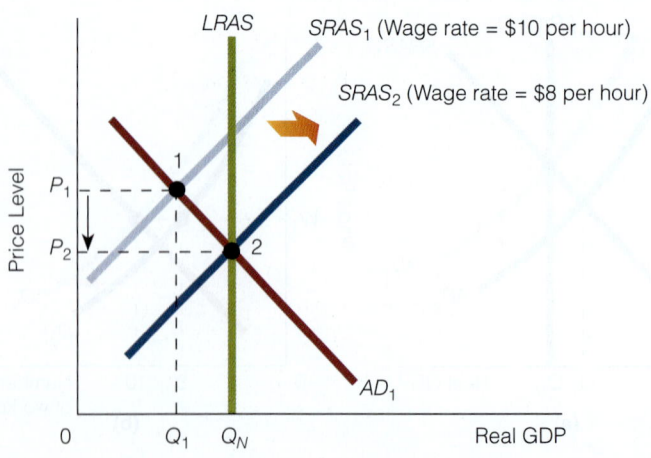

Was Keynes a Revolutionary in Economics?

John Maynard Keynes was born in Cambridge, England, on June 5, 1883, and died at Tilton (in Sussex) on April 21, 1946. His father was John Neville Keynes, an eminent economist and author of *The Scope and Method of Political Economy*. Keynes's mother was one of the first female students to attend Cambridge University and for a time presided as mayor of the city of Cambridge.

Keynes was educated at Eton and at King's College, Cambridge, where he received a degree in mathematics in 1905. At Cambridge, he studied under the well-known and widely respected economist Alfred Marshall. In 1925, Keynes married Russian ballerina Lydia Lopokova. He was prominent in British social and intellectual circles and enjoyed art, theater, opera, debate, and collecting rare books.

Many economists rank Keynes's *The General Theory of Employment, Interest and Money* (published on February 4, 1936) alongside Adam Smith's *Wealth of Nations* and Karl Marx's *Das Kapital* as the most influential economic treatises ever written.

Before the publication of *The General Theory*, Keynes presented the ideas contained in the work in a series of university lectures that he gave between October 10, 1932, and December 2, 1935. Ten days after his last lecture, he sent off to the publisher the manuscript for what was to become *The General Theory*.

Keynes's lectures were said to be both shocking (he was pointing out the errors of the classical school) and exciting (he was proposing something new). One of the students at these lectures was Lorie Tarshis, who later wrote the first Keynesian introductory textbook, *The Elements of Economics*. In another venue, Tarshis wrote about

the Keynes lectures and specifically about why Keynes's ideas were revolutionary.

TIM GIDAL/PICTURE POST/GETTY IMAGES

I attended that first lecture, naturally awed but bothered. As the weeks passed, only a stone would not have responded to the growing excitement these lectures generated. So I missed only two over the four years—two out of the thirty lectures. And like others, I would feel the urgency of the task. No wonder! These were the years when everything came loose; when sober dons and excitable students seriously discussed such issues as: Was capitalism not doomed? Should Britain not take the path of Russia or Germany to create jobs? Keynes obviously believed his analysis led to a third means to prosperity far less threatening to the values he prized, but until he had developed the theory and offered it in print, he knew that he could not sway government. So he saw his task as supremely urgent. I was also a bit surprised by his concern over too low a level of output. I had been assured by all I had read that the economy would bob to the surface, like a cork held under water—and output would rise, of its own accord, to an acceptable level. But Keynes proposed something far more shocking: that the economy could reach an equilibrium position with output far below capacity. That was an exciting challenge, sharply at variance with the views of Pigou and Marshall who represented "The Classical [Orthodox] School" in Cambridge, and elsewhere.[1]

1. L. Tarshis, "Keynesian Revolution," in *The New Palgrave: A Dictionary of Economics*, vol. 3 (London: Macmillan Press, 1987), p. 48.

The following chart is a quick review of some of the differences in the views of the classical economists and Keynes.

	Classical Economists	**Keynes**
Say's Law	Holds in a money economy. In other words, all output produced will be demanded.	May not hold in a money economy. In other words, more output may be produced than will be demanded.
Savings	Amount saved and interest rate are directly related. Savers save more at higher interest rates and save less at lower interest rates.	Savers may not save more at higher interest rates or save less at lower interest rates. If savers have a savings goal in mind, then a higher interest rate means savers can save less and still reach their goal.
Investment	Amount invested is inversely related to interest rate. Businesses invest more at lower interest rates and invest less at higher interest rates.	If expectations are pessimistic, a lower interest rate may not stimulate additional investment.
Prices	Flexible	May be inflexible downward.
Wages	Flexible	May be inflexible downward.

SELF-TEST

(Answers to Self-Test Questions are in Answers to Self-Test Questions at the back of the book.)

1. What do Keynesians mean when they say the economy is inherently unstable?

2. "What matters is not whether the economy is self-regulating, but whether prices and wages are flexible and adjust quickly." Comment.

3. According to Keynes, why might aggregate demand be too low?

THE SIMPLE KEYNESIAN MODEL

Economists build models and theories to better understand the economic world. Of the many such models, we have already discussed a few: the theory of supply and demand and the classical theory of interest rates. In this section, we identify and discuss a few of the key components and themes of another prominent macroeconomics model: *the simple Keynesian model*.

Assumptions

In the simple Keynesian model, certain simplifying assumptions hold.

- First, the price level is assumed to be constant until the economy reaches its full-employment or Natural Real GDP level.

- Second, there is no foreign sector: the model represents a *closed economy*, not an *open economy*. So total spending in the economy is the sum of consumption, investment, and government purchases.

- Third, the monetary side of the economy is excluded.

The Consumption Function

Although Keynes was interested in the level of total spending in general, he was particularly concerned about consumption. Consumption (C) was a major concern because it is by far the largest slice of the total spending pie.

Keynes made three basic points about consumption:

1. Consumption depends on disposable income (income minus taxes).

2. Consumption and disposable income move in the same direction.

3. When disposable income changes, consumption changes by less.

These three points make a specific statement about the relationship between consumption and disposable income: the consumption function, which can written as:

$$C = C_0 + (MPC)(Y_d)$$

You know that C is consumption, and we use Y_d to specify disposable income. Let's look at MPC and C_0. Think of consumption (as specified by the consumption function) as made up of two parts:

- *Autonomous consumption* (C_0) is independent of disposable income.
- *Induced consumption* [$MPC(Y_d)$] depends on disposable income.

MPC stands for marginal propensity to consume, which is the ratio of the change in consumption to the change in disposable income:

$$\text{Marginal propensity to consume} = \frac{\text{Change in consumption}}{\text{Change in disposable income}}$$

$$MPC = \frac{\Delta C}{\Delta Y_d}$$

The Greek symbol delta (Δ) stands for "change in." Thus, the MPC is equal to the change in consumption divided by the change in disposable income. To illustrate, suppose consumption rises from $800 to $900 as disposable income rises from $1,000 to $1,200. If we divide the change in consumption ($100) by the change in disposable income ($200), we see that the MPC equals 0.50. (Notice that the MPC is always a positive number between 0 and 1 because of Keynes's points 2 and 3.)

C_0 is autonomous consumption, which changes *not* as disposable income changes, but rather due to other factors.

The difference between autonomous and induced consumption can be illustrated with an example. Suppose your taxes are lowered and your disposable income consequently rises. With more disposable income, you buy more goods and services (e.g., entertainment, books, DVDs). The increase in disposable income has *induced* you to consume more; hence the name *induced consumption*. Next, suppose that, even though your disposable income has not changed, for some reason you are consuming more. You might be consuming more medication because you have recently become ill, or you might be consuming more car maintenance services because your car just broke down. Whatever the reason, you are consuming more of various goods and services even though your disposable income has not changed at all. This type of consumption is autonomous (i.e., independent) of disposable income; hence the name *autonomous consumption*.

Look again at the consumption function:

$$\text{Consumption} = \text{Autonomous consumption}$$
$$+ (\text{Marginal propensity to consume} \times \text{Disposable income})$$
$$C = C_0 + (MPC \times Y_d)$$

Consumption Function
The relationship between consumption and disposable income. In the consumption function used in this text, consumption is directly related to disposable income and is positive even at zero disposable income: $C = C_0 + (MPC)(Y_d)$.

Marginal Propensity to Consume (MPC)
The ratio of the change in consumption to the change in disposable income: $MPC = \Delta C/\Delta Y_d$.

Autonomous Consumption
The part of consumption that is independent of disposable income.

Suppose C_0 is $800, the *MPC* is 0.80, and Y_d is $1,500, and we insert these numbers into the consumption function:

$$C = \$800 + (0.80 \times \$1,500) = \$800 + \$1,200 = \$2,000$$

So what will cause an increase in consumption? Consumption, *C*, will increase if any of the variables (C_0, *MPC*, or Y_d) increases. Thus, *C* can be increased in three ways:

1. *Raise autonomous consumption.* Suppose in our example that autonomous consumption, C_0, goes from $800 to $1,000. This change will raise consumption to $2,200: $C = \$1,000 + (0.80 \times \$1,500) = \$2,200$.

2. *Raise disposable income.* Suppose disposable income, Y_d, goes from $1,500 to $1,800. This change will raise consumption to $2,240: $C = \$800 + (0.80 \times \$1,800) = \$2,240$. The increase in consumption from $2,000 to $2,240 is due to an increase of $240 in induced consumption, which the increase in disposable income induced.

3. *Raise the MPC.* Suppose the *MPC* rises to 0.90. This change will raise consumption to $2,150: $C = \$800 + (0.90 \times \$1,500) = \$2,150$.

In Exhibit 6, C_0 is equal to $200 billion and the *MPC* is equal to 0.80; thus, $C = \$200$ billion $+ (0.8)(Y_d)$. We then calculated different levels of consumption (column 3) for different levels of disposable income (column 1).

Consumption and Saving

In Exhibit 6, we also calculated the saving levels (column 5) at the different disposable income levels. How did we calculate these levels? We know that $C = C_0 + (MPC)(Y_d)$ and that households can only consume or save. So it follows that saving, *S*, is the difference between disposable income and consumption:

$$\text{Saving} = \text{Disposable income} - \text{Consumption}$$
$$= \text{Disposable income} - [\text{Autonomous consumption}$$
$$+ (\text{Marginal propensity to consume} \times \text{Disposable income})]$$
$$S = Y_d - [C_0 - (MPC \times Y_d)]$$

EXHIBIT 6

Consumption and Saving at Different Levels of Disposable Income (in billions)

Our consumption function is $C = C_0 + (MPC)$ (Y_d), where C_0 has been set at $200 billion and $MPC = 0.80$. Saving is the difference between Y_d and C: $S = Y_d - [C_0 + (MPC)$ $(Y_d)]$. All dollar amounts are in billions.

(1) Disposable Income Y_d	(2) Change in Disposable Income ΔY_d	(3) Consumption $C = C_0 + (MPC)(Y_d)$	(4) Change in Consumption	(5) Saving $S = Y_d - [C_0 + (MPC)(Y_d)]$	(6) Change in Saving
$ 800	$__	$ 840	$__	−$40	$__
1,000	200	1,000	160	0	40
1,200	200	1,160	160	40	40
1,400	200	1,320	160	80	40
1,600	200	1,480	160	120	40
1,800	200	1,640	160	160	40

The marginal propensity to save (MPS) is the ratio of the change in saving to the change in disposable income:

Marginal Propensity to Save (MPS)
The ratio of the change in saving to the change in disposable income: $MPS = \Delta S / \Delta Y_d$.

$$\text{Marginal propensity to save} = \frac{\text{Change in saving}}{\text{Change in disposable income}}$$

$$MPS = \frac{\Delta S}{\Delta Y_d}$$

Disposable income can be used only for consumption or saving; that is, $C + S = Y_d$. So any change to disposable income can change only consumption or saving. Therefore, the marginal propensity to consume (MPC) plus the marginal propensity to save (MPS) must equal 1.

$$\text{Marginal propensity to consume} + \text{Marginal propensity to save} = 1$$

$$MPC + MPS = 1$$

In Exhibit 6, the MPC is 0.80; so the MPS is 0.20.

The Multiplier

We know from the consumption function that a rise in autonomous consumption (C_0) will raise consumption (C) and, in turn, raise total spending. But *how much* will total spending rise? If C_0 rises by $40 billion, will total spending rise by $40 billion? According to Keynes, total spending would not rise by only $40 billion. The rise in C_0 will act as a catalyst to additional spending, and total spending will rise, in this case, by *more than* $40 billion.

For example, suppose an economy consists of 10 people, represented by the letters $A-J$. Person A increases his autonomous consumption by buying $40 more additional goods from person B. Now person B has witnessed an increase in her income of $40. According to Keynes, person B will spend some fraction of this additional income, and how much she spends depends on her marginal propensity to consume (MPC). If her MPC is 0.80, then she will spend 80 percent of $40, or $32. If she spends this additional $32 on purchasing goods from person C, then person C's income rises by $32 and now he will spend some percentage of that additional income. Again, how much he will spend depends on his MPC. If we again assume that the MPC is 0.80, then person C spends $25.60.

Person A increases his *autonomous consumption* by $40 →

This generates $40 *additional income* for person B →

Person B increases her *consumption* by $32 →

This generates $32 *additional income* for person C →

Person C increases his *consumption* by $25.60 →

And so on and so on.

This is the *multiplier process*: An initial rise in autonomous consumption leads to a rise in consumption for one person, generating additional income for another person, and leading to additional consumption spending by that person, and so on and so on.

Suppose we sum the initial rise in autonomous spending ($40) and all the additional spending it generates through the multiplier process. How much additional spending will have been generated? In other words, by how much will total expenditures rise?

Multiplier
The number that is multiplied by the change in autonomous spending to obtain the overall change in total spending. The multiplier (m) is equal to $1 \div (1 - MPC)$. If the economy is operating below Natural Real GDP, then the multiplier is the number that is multiplied by the change in autonomous spending to obtain the change in Real GDP.

The answer depends on the value of the multiplier. The multiplier (m) is equal to 1 divided by $1 - MPC$.

$$\text{Multiplier } (m) = \frac{1}{1 - MPC}$$

For example, if the $MPC = 0.80$ (in each round of spending), then the multiplier equals 5:

$$
\begin{aligned}
\text{Multiplier } (m) &= \frac{1}{1 - MPC} \\
&= \frac{1}{1 - 0.80} \\
&= \frac{1}{0.20} \\
&= 5
\end{aligned}
$$

Our original increase in autonomous consumption ($40), multiplied by the multiplier (5), equals $200. So in our example, a $40 increase in autonomous consumption would increase total spending by $200.

Just as consumption has an autonomous spending component, so do investment and government purchases. The multiplier process holds for these sectors too.

The process also holds for a decrease in autonomous spending by one of these sectors of total spending. So, in general,

Change in total spending = Multiplier × Change in autonomous spending

To illustrate, suppose business owners become optimistic about the future of the economy. They believe that members of the household and government sectors will soon start buying more goods and services. In the expectation of better times, businesses buy more factories and capital goods, and so investment spending rises. In this case, investment spending has risen, even without any change in income or Real GDP; hence, the rise is in autonomous investment spending. According to the multiplier analysis, this additional autonomous investment spending will change total spending by some multiple. For example, if the multiplier is 5, then a $1 increase in autonomous investment will raise total spending by $5.

The Multiplier and Reality

So, in simple terms, a change in autonomous spending leads to a *greater change* in total spending. Also, in the simple Keynesian model, the change in total spending is *equal to* the change in Real GDP (assuming that the economy is operating below Natural Real GDP). The reason is that, in the model, prices are assumed to be constant until Natural GDP is reached; so any change in nominal total spending is equal to the change in *real* total spending.

However, two reality checks are necessary. First, the multiplier takes time to have an effect. In a textbook, going from an initial increase in autonomous spending to a multiple increase in either total spending or Real GDP takes only seconds. In the real world, this process takes many months.

Second, for the multiplier to increase Real GDP, *idle resources must exist at each spending round*. After all, if Real GDP is increasing (output is increasing) at each spending round, *idle resources must be available to be brought into production*. If they are not available, then increased spending will simply result in higher prices without an increase in Real GDP. Simply put, GDP will increase but not Real GDP.

The Multiplier on Spring Break

During the weeklong spring break, many college students put away their books; pack their shorts, swimsuits, and tanning oil; jump into their cars; and head for the beaches. As they are driving to Fort Lauderdale, Galveston, Myrtle Beach, Daytona Beach, San Diego, and other coastal cities, the multiplier is getting ready to go to work.

Look at it this way. When college students from around the country head for, say, Daytona Beach, they have dollars in their pockets. They will spend many of these dollars in Daytona Beach on food and drink, motel rooms, dance clubs, and so on. As far as Daytona Beach is concerned, the dollars represent autonomous spending. More important, the dollars can raise the total income of Daytona Beach by some multiple. College students buy pizzas, beer, and sodas. The people who sell these items find their incomes rising. They, in turn, spend some fraction of their increase in income, generating additional income for

AP PHOTO/DAYTONA BEACH NEWS-JOURNAL, JIM TILLER

still others, who spend some fraction of their increase in income, and so on and so on.

For example, suppose college students spend $7 million in Daytona Beach during spring break. If the MPC is, say, 0.60 in Daytona Beach and if all the added income generated is spent in Daytona Beach, then college students will increase nominal income in that town by $17.5 million:

$$\frac{1}{1 - MPC} \times \$7 \text{ million}$$
$$= \frac{1}{0.40} \times \$7 \text{ million}$$
$$= 2.5 \times \$7 \text{ million}$$
$$= \$17.5 \text{ million}$$

Do the people who live in Daytona Beach want college students to visit their city during spring break? Many of them do because it means extra dollars in their pockets. College students from out of town, together with the multiplier, often make for robust economic times!

SELF-TEST

1. How is autonomous consumption different from consumption?

2. If the MPC is 0.70, what does the multiplier equal?

3. What happens to the multiplier as the MPC falls?

THE SIMPLE KEYNESIAN MODEL IN THE *AD–AS* FRAMEWORK

The first section of this chapter presented a few of Keynes's criticisms of the self-regulating economy, or classical position. The second section identified and discussed some of the key components of the simple Keynesian model, particularly the consumption function and the multiplier. In this section, we analyze the simple Keynesian model in terms of the aggregate demand and aggregate supply (*AD–AS*) framework. In the next section, we discuss the simple Keynesian model in terms of the total expenditures and total production (*TE–TP*) framework.[2]

---

2. Some instructors may choose to assign only one of these two sections. It is clear at the end of the chapter which questions and problems go with which sections.

Shifts in the Aggregate Demand Curve

Because there is no foreign sector in the simple Keynesian model, total spending consists of consumption (C), investment (I), and government purchases (G). Because the economy has no monetary side, changes in any of these variables (C, I, G) can shift the AD curve. For example, a rise in consumption will shift the AD curve to the right; a decrease in investment will shift it to the left.

Let's consider aggregate demand in terms of what we know about the consumption function and the multiplier. A rise in autonomous consumption (C_0) will raise consumption (C) and therefore shift the AD curve to the right. How much the AD curve will shift depends on the multiplier. In our earlier example, autonomous consumption C_0 increases by $40, and the multiplier ($m$) is 5.

$$\text{Change in total spending} = \text{Multiplier} \times \text{Change in autonomous spending}$$
$$= m \times \Delta C_0$$
$$= 5 \times \$40$$
$$= \$200$$

Exhibit 7 illustrates how the AD curve shifts in this situation. The original aggregate demand curve is AD_1. Autonomous consumption (C_0) rises by $40, shifting the curve to AD_2, but the AD curve does not stay here. Because of the multiplier, the initial autonomous consumption spending generates more spending, eventually pushing the AD curve to AD_3. In other words, at the end of the process, the AD curve has shifted from AD_1 to AD_3. Part of this shift ($40) is due to the initial rise in autonomous consumption, and part ($160) is due to the multiplier.

The Keynesian Aggregate Supply Curve

As noted, in the simple Keynesian model, the price level is assumed to be constant until it reaches its full-employment or Natural Real GDP level. What does this assumption say about the Keynesian aggregate supply curve?

Think back to the discussions of aggregate demand and aggregate supply in the last two chapters and in the first section of this chapter. The AD curve is downward sloping, and the $SRAS$ curve is upward sloping. Therefore, any shift in the AD curve (rightward or leftward) will automatically change (raise or lower) the price level. If the price level is assumed to be constant, then the Keynesian aggregate supply curve must have a horizontal section.

As shown in Exhibit 8, the Keynesian aggregate supply (AS) curve has both a horizontal section and a vertical section. The AS curve is horizontal until Q_N, or Natural Real GDP, because the simple Keynesian model assumes that the price level is constant until Q_N is reached. Given this AS curve, what happens in the economy when the AD curve shifts? An increase in aggregate demand from AD_1 to AD_2 raises Real GDP from Q_1 to Q_2 but does not change the price level. (The price level remains at P_1.) On the other hand, once the economy has reached Q_N, any increases in aggregate demand change the price level. For example, an increase in aggregate demand from

The Multiplier and Aggregate Demand

An initial increase in autonomous consumption raises total spending and shifts the aggregate demand curve from AD_1 to AD_2. The AD curve does not end here, however. Because of the multiplier, the increase in autonomous spending generates additional income and additional spending, shifting the aggregate demand curve to AD_3.

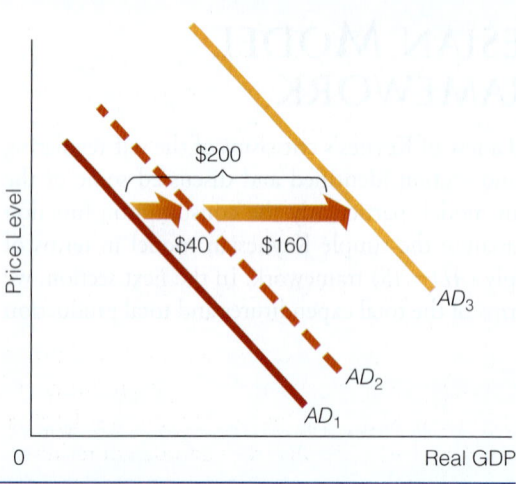

AD_3 to AD_4 raises the price level from P_2 to P_3.

According to Keynes, a change in autonomous spending (e.g., a change in autonomous consumption) will stimulate additional spending in the economy. In our example, a rise in autonomous consumption of $40 generated an additional $160 worth of spending so that total spending increased by $200. (The multiplier was 5 because we assumed the MPC was 0.80.)

Consider this question: Under what condition will a $200 *increase in total spending* lead to a $200 *increase in Real GDP?* That happens when the

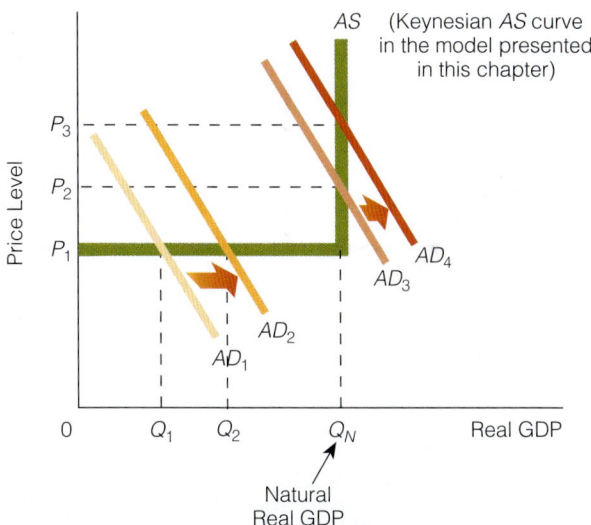

EXHIBIT 8

The *AS* Curve in the Simple Keynesian Model

The *AS* curve in the simple Keynesian model is horizontal until Q_N (Natural Real GDP) and vertical at Q_N. It follows that any changes in aggregate demand in the horizontal section do not change the price level, but any changes in aggregate demand in the vertical section do change the price level.

aggregate supply curve is horizontal, that is (in the simple Keynesian model), when the economy is currently producing less than Natural Real GDP. In other words, the AD curve in the economy must be shifting rightward (due to the increased spending) but must be within the *horizontal section* of the Keynesian AS curve.

finding ECONOMICS

In Unchanging Prices Suppose you read in the newspaper that the three sectors of a closed economy (household, business, and government) are all spending more but that, so far, there has been little to no change in the price level. Where is the economics?

The picture that should come to mind is the Keynesian aggregate supply curve—in particular, the horizontal section of the curve. Increases in aggregate demand in the horizontal section of the aggregate supply curve do not raise the price level. ▲ ▲ ▲

The Economy in a Recessionary Gap

If, according to classical economists, the economy is self-regulating, then a recessionary gap or an inflationary gap is only temporary. In time, the economy moves into long-run equilibrium and produces Natural Real GDP (Q_N).

Keynes did not accept that the economy always works this way, believing rather that the economy could get stuck in a recessionary gap. As shown in Exhibit 9, the economy could therefore be stuck at Q_1 (its equilibrium position) and unable to get to Q_N on its own. In other words, the economy is at point A, and it is not able to get to point B. Keynes believed that the private sector—consisting of the household and business sectors—may not be able to move the economy from point A to point B. Stated differently, neither consumption nor investment will rise enough to shift the aggregate demand curve from its current position (AD_1).

But suppose the interest rate in the economy falls. Won't this be enough to get businesses to invest more, and thus won't the AD curve begin to shift rightward, headed for point B? Not necessarily, said Keynes, who didn't believe that investment spending was always responsive to changes in interest rates. For example, suppose businesses are pessimistic about future sales, and the interest rate drops. Are businesses going to invest more just because interest rates have dropped, or might they feel so pessimistic that they choose not to invest, despite the lower interest rate? Keynes believed that the latter scenario could be the case.

EXHIBIT 9

Can the Private Sector Remove the Economy from a Recessionary Gap?

The economy is at point A producing Q_1. Q_1 is less than Q_N, so the economy is in a recessionary gap. The question is whether the private sector (consisting of consumption and investment spending) can remove the economy from the recessionary gap by increasing spending enough to shift the aggregate demand curve rightward to go through point B. Keynes believed that sometimes it could not. No matter how low interest rates fell, investment spending would not rise because of pessimistic business expectations with respect to future sales.

Economy is here in a recessionary gap and in equilibrium too.

Government's Role in the Economy

In the self-regulating economy of the classical economists, government does not have a management role to play. The private sector (households and businesses) is capable of self-regulating the economy at its Natural Real GDP level. On the other hand, Keynes believed that the economy is not self-regulating and that economic instability is a possibility. In other words, the economy could get stuck in a recessionary gap.

Economic instability opens the door to government's playing a role in the economy. According to Keynes and to many Keynesians, if the private sector cannot self-regulate the economy at its Natural Real GDP level, then maybe the government must help. In terms of Exhibit 9, maybe the government has a role to play in shifting the AD curve rightward so that it goes through point B. We discuss the role government might play in the economy in the next chapter.

ⓣhinking like AN ECONOMIST

From How the Economy Works to One's Policy Positions An economist's view of the economy (how the economy works) and policy suggestions are often linked. For example, classical economists and their modern-day counterparts, who view the economy as inherently stable, believe in a laissez-faire policy: Government should keep its hands off the economy. Keynesians, however, who view the economy as inherently unstable, suggest that government has an economic role to play. In short, policy suggestions are sometimes a consequence of how one views the internal, or inherent, workings of an economy. ●●●

The Theme of the Simple Keynesian Model

In terms of AD and AS, the essence of the simple Keynesian model can be summarized in five statements:

1. The price level is constant until Natural Real GDP is reached.

2. The AD curve shifts if there are changes in C, I, or G.

3. According to Keynes, the economy could be in equilibrium and in a recessionary gap too. In other words, the economy can be at point A in Exhibit 9.

4. The private sector may not be able to get the economy out of a recessionary gap. In other words, the private sector (households and businesses) may not be able to increase C or I enough to get the AD curve in Exhibit 9 to intersect the AS curve at point B.

5. The government may have a management role to play in the economy. According to Keynes, government may have to raise aggregate demand enough to stimulate the economy to move it out of the recessionary gap and to its Natural Real GDP level.

6. We show the simple Keynesian model in the AD–AS framework in Exhibit 10 in both flowchart form (a) and in diagrammatic form (b).

EXHIBIT 10

The Simple Keynesian Model in the AD–AS Framework

The purpose of the simple Keynesian model is to explain changes in Real GDP. In (a) the model is presented as a flowchart. Real GDP is determined by aggregate demand and aggregate supply. Aggregate demand depends on C, consumption; I, investment; and G, government purchases. In (b) we show a diagrammatic exposition of the model in the AD–AS framework.

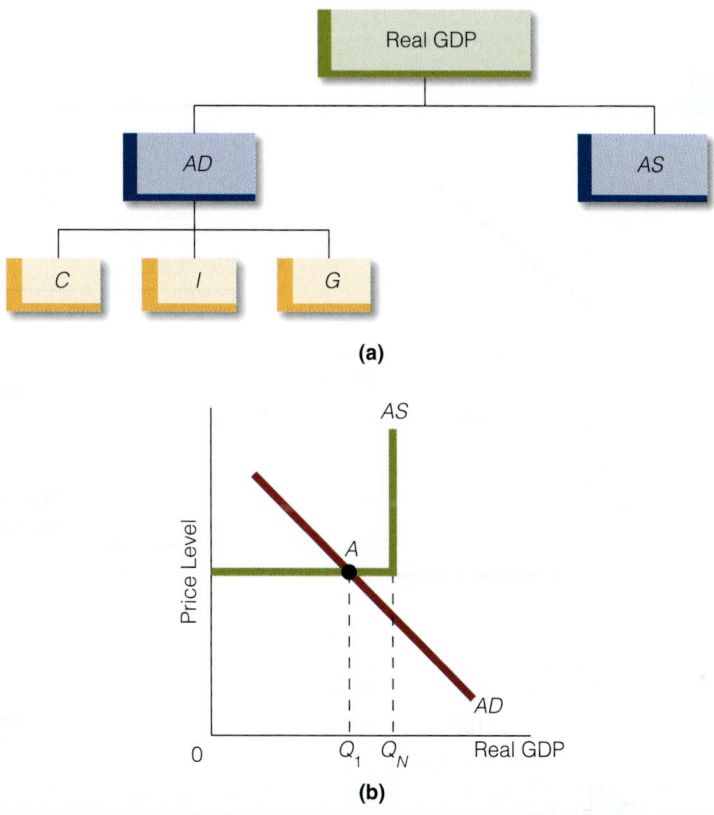

(a)

(b)

---

1. What was Keynes's position on the self-regulating properties of an economy?

2. What will happen to Real GDP if autonomous spending rises and the economy is operating in the horizontal section of the Keynesian AS curve? Explain your answer.

3. An economist who believes the economy is self-regulating is more likely to advocate laissez-faire than one who believes the economy is inherently unstable. Do you agree or disagree? Explain your answer.

THE SIMPLE KEYNESIAN MODEL IN THE *TE–TP* FRAMEWORK

Just as a story can be told into different languages, an economic model can be presented in various frameworks. The last section presented the simple Keynesian model in terms of the familiar (diagrammatic) *AD–AS* framework of analysis. But the simple Keynesian model was first presented not in terms of *AD–AS*, but in terms of the *TE–TP* framework. This framework has been known by different names, three of which are the Keynesian cross, income expenditure, and total expenditure–total production. In our discussion, we will refer to it as total expenditure–total production, or simply the *TE–TP* framework.

Deriving a Total Expenditures (TE) Curve

Just as we derived *AD* and *AS* curves in the *AD–AS* framework, we want to derive a total expenditures (*TE*) curve in the *TE–TP* framework. Total expenditures are the sum of its parts: consumption, investment, and government purchases. To derive a *TE* curve, first derive a diagrammatic representation of consumption, investment, and government purchases, as shown in Exhibit 11.

EXHIBIT 11

The Derivation of the Total Expenditures (TE) Curve

At different levels of Real GDP, we sum consumption (a), investment (b), and government purchases (c) to derive *TE* curve (d).

(a)

Consumption ($ Trillions)	
At Q_1	7.0
At Q_2	7.5

+

(b)

Investment ($ Trillions)	
At Q_1	1.0
At Q_2	1.0

+

(c)

Government Purchases ($ Trillions)	
At Q_1	1.5
At Q_2	1.5

=

(d)

Total Expenditures ($ Trillions)	
At Q_1	9.5
At Q_2	10.0

1. *Consumption.* As disposable income rises, so does consumption, as shown arithmetically in columns (1) and (3) of Exhibit 6. Because the *MPC* is less than 1, consumption rises by less than disposable income rises. Consumption also rises as Real GDP rises, but again by a smaller percentage. For example, if Real GDP rises by $100, consumption may rise by $80. Exhibit 11(a) shows consumption as an upward-sloping curve. Notice that as Real GDP rises from Q_1 to Q_2, consumption rises from $7 trillion to $7.5 trillion.

2. *Investment.* To simplify things in deriving *TE*, the investment curve in Exhibit 11(b) is constant at $1 trillion, whether Real GDP is Q_1 or Q_2.

3. *Government purchases.* We simplify the government spending curve too. In Exhibit 11(c), government purchases are constant at $1.5 trillion, regardless of the amount of Real GDP.

Exhibit 11(d) shows a *TE* curve. We simply added the components of total expenditures at the two Real GDP levels (Q_1 and Q_2), plotted the relevant points, and then drew a line through the points. At Q_1, total expenditures are $9.5 trillion, and at Q_2, they are $10.0 trillion. The *TE* curve is upward-sloping.

What Will Shift the *TE* Curve?

The *TE* curve in the *TE*−*TP* framework plays the same role as the *AD* curve in the *AD*−*AS* framework. Both the *AD* curve and the *TE* curve shift with a change in *C*, *I*, or *G*. For example, a rise in *C* will shift the *TE* curve upward; a decline in *I* will shift the *TE* curve downward.

Comparing Total Expenditures (*TE*) and Total Production (*TP*)

Businesses produce the goods and services that are bought in the three sectors of the economy (household, business, and government). Sometimes, though, businesses produce too much or too little in comparison to what the three sectors buy. For example, suppose businesses produce $10 trillion worth of goods and services, but the three sectors buy only $9.5 trillion worth. In this case, businesses have produced too much relative to what the three sectors of the economy buy.

Alternatively, businesses might produce $10 trillion worth of goods and services, but the three sectors of the economy buy $10.5 trillion worth. In this case, businesses have produced too little relative to what the three sectors of the economy buy. (If you are wondering how the three sectors of the economy can possibly buy more than businesses produce, the answer has to do with the goods that businesses hold in inventory. We will soon explain the process.)

Finally, businesses could produce $10 trillion worth of goods and services, and the three sectors of the economy could buy exactly $10 trillion worth. In this case, businesses have produced exactly the right amount of goods and services.

Thus, the economy may be in one of three possible states in the *TE*−*TP* framework: The total expenditures (*TE*) of the three sectors of the economy can be less than, greater than, or equal to the dollar value of total production (*TP*). In other words:

$$TE < TP$$
$$TE > TP$$
$$TE = TP$$

According to many economists, if the economy is currently operating where $TE < TP$ or $TE > TP$ (both states are described as disequilibrium), it will eventually move to where $TE = TP$ (where the economy is in equilibrium). The next section explains how this happens.

ⓣhinking like AN ECONOMIST

Thinking in Threes The concept of threes first came up when we discussed a single market (in Chapter 3), specifically when we said that a market could be in equilibrium, shortage, or surplus. In other words, a market had three possible states. In Chapter 9, we said the economy could be producing a Real GDP level either greater than, less than, or equal to Natural Real GDP; that is, an economy may have three possible states. Now we are saying that total expenditures (*TE*) can be either less than, greater than, or equal to total production—once again, three possible states. ▪▪▪

Moving from Disequilibrium to Equilibrium

Business firms hold an inventory of their goods to guard against unexpected changes in the demand for their product. For example, General Motors may hold an inventory of a certain type of car in case the demand for it unexpectedly and suddenly increases.

Although we know why business firms hold an inventory of their goods, we don't know *how much* inventory they will hold. For example, we do not know whether General Motors will hold an inventory of 1,000 cars, 2,000 cars, or 10,000 cars. (Inventories are usually held in terms of, say, a 45- or 60-day supply, but we have simplified things.) We do know that General Motors and all other business firms have some *optimum inventory*, which is "just the right amount" of inventory—not too much and not too little. With this in mind, consider two cases that illustrate how business inventory levels play an important role in the economy's adjustment from disequilibrium to equilibrium in the *TE−TP* framework.

CASE 1: *TE < TP*   Assume that business firms hold an optimum inventory level of $300 billion worth of goods, that the firms produce $11 trillion worth of goods and services, and that the three sectors of the economy buy $10.8 trillion worth of goods and services. In this case, producers produce more than individuals buy (*TE < TP*). The difference is added to inventories, and inventory levels rise unexpectedly to $500 billion, which is $200 billion more than the $300 billion that firms see as optimal.

This unexpected rise in inventories signals to firms that they have *overproduced*. Consequently, they cut back on the quantity of goods they are producing. The cutback in production causes Real GDP to fall, bringing Real GDP closer to the (lower) output level that the three sectors of the economy are willing and able to buy. Ultimately, *TP* will equal *TE*.

CASE 2: *TE > TP*   Assume that business firms hold their optimum inventory level ($300 billion worth of goods), that they produce $10.4 trillion worth of goods, and that members of the three sectors buy $10.6 trillion worth of goods. How can individuals buy more than businesses produce? Firms make up the difference out of inventory. In our example, inventory levels fall from $300 billion to $100 billion because individuals purchase $200 billion more of goods than firms produced (to be sold). This is why firms maintain inventories in the first place: to be able to meet an unexpected increase in sales.

The unexpected fall in inventories signals to firms that they have *underproduced*. Consequently, they increase the quantity of goods they produce. The rise in production causes Real GDP to rise, in the process bringing Real GDP closer to the (higher) real output that the three sectors are willing and able to buy. Ultimately, *TP* will equal *TE*.

THE GRAPHICAL REPRESENTATION OF THE THREE STATES OF THE ECONOMY IN THE *TE–TP* FRAMEWORK   The three states of the economy are represented in Exhibit 12. The exhibit shows a *TE* curve, which we derived earlier, and a *TP* curve, which is simply a 45-degree line (45 degrees because it bisects the 90-degree angle at the origin). Notice that, at any point on the *TP* curve, total production is equal to Real

EXHIBIT 12

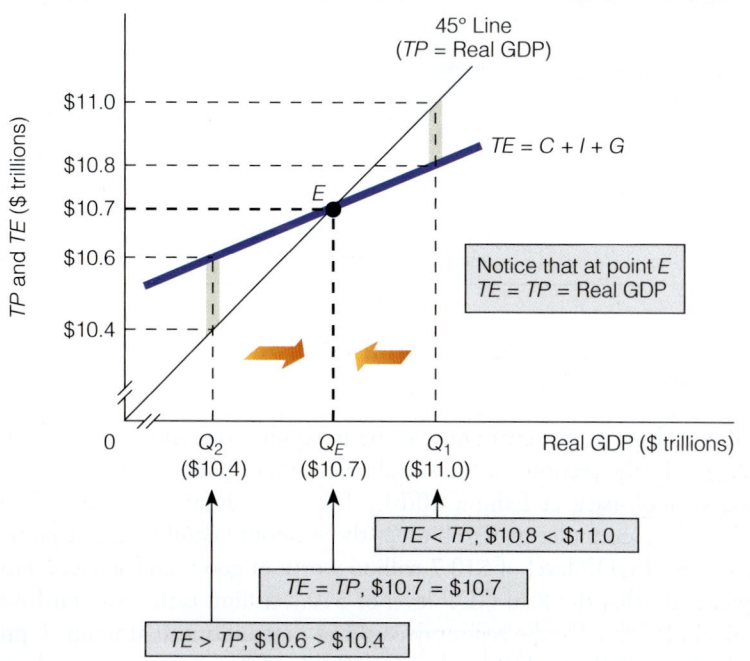

The Three States of the Economy in the *TE* − *TP* Framework

At Q_E, $TE = TP$ and the economy is in equilibrium. At Q_1, $TE < TP$. This results in an unexpected increase in inventories, which signals firms that they have overproduced, which leads firms to cut back production. The cutback in production reduces Real GDP. The economy tends to move from Q_1 to Q_E. At Q_2, $TE > TP$. This results in an unexpected decrease in inventories, which signals firms that they have underproduced, which leads firms to raise production. The increased production raises Real GDP. The economy tends to move from Q_2 to Q_E.

GDP (TP = Real GDP).[3] This is because TP and Real GDP are different names for the same thing. Real GDP, remember, is simply the total market value of all final goods and services produced annually within a country's borders, adjusted for price changes.

Look at the three Real GDP levels in the exhibit. At Q_1, Real GDP is $11 trillion. At this Real GDP level, TE is $10.8 trillion and TP is $11 trillion. This illustrates Case 1, in which producers produce more than individuals buy ($TE < TP$), with the difference added to inventories. This unexpected rise in inventories signals to firms that they have overproduced, and consequently they cut back on the quantity of goods they produce. The cutback in production causes Real GDP to fall, ultimately bringing Real GDP down to Q_E ($10.7 trillion in the exhibit).

Now look at Q_2, where Real GDP is $10.4 trillion. At this Real GDP level, TE equals $10.6 trillion and TP equals $10.4 trillion. This illustrates Case 2, in which the three sectors of the economy buy more goods and services than business firms have produced ($TE > TP$). Business firms draw from inventories to make up the difference between what they have produced and what the three sectors of the economy buy. Inventories then fall below optimum levels, and consequently businesses increase the quantity of goods they produce. The rise in production causes Real GDP to rise, ultimately moving Real GDP up to Q_E (again, $10.7 trillion).

When the economy is producing Q_E, or $10.7 trillion worth of goods and services, it is in equilibrium. At this Real GDP level, TP and TE are the same at $10.7 trillion. The following table summarizes some key points about the state of the economy in the $TE − TP$ framework.

---

3. Earlier, we said that the *TE* curve plays the role in the *TE*−*TP* framework that the *AD* curve plays in the *AD*−*AS* framework. In other words, roughly speaking, the *AD* curve is the *TE* curve. Similarly, the *TP* curve plays the role in the *TE*−*TP* framework that the *AS* curve plays in the *AD*−*AS* framework. In other words, roughly speaking, the *TP* curve is the *AS* curve. In the *AD*−*AS* framework, equilibrium is at the intersection of the *AD* and *AS* curves. As you will soon learn, in the *TE*−*TP* framework, equilibrium is at the intersection of the *TE* and *TP* curves.

State of the Economy	What Happens to Inventories?	What Do Firms Do?
TE < TP Individuals are buying less output than firms produce.	Inventories rise above optimum levels.	Firms cut back production to reduce inventories to their optimum levels.
TE > TP Individuals are buying more output than firms produce.	Inventories fall below optimum levels.	Firms increase production to raise inventories to their optimum levels.
TE = TP	Inventories are at their optimum levels.	Firms neither increase nor decrease production.

The Economy in a Recessionary Gap and the Role of Government

According to Keynes, the economy can be in equilibrium and in a recessionary gap too, as explained in the section on the simple Keynesian model in the $AD-AS$ framework. [To review, look back at Exhibit 10(b).] The same situation can exist in the $TE-TP$ framework. For example, in Exhibit 12, the economy equilibrates at point E and thus produces a Real GDP level of $10.7 trillion worth of goods and services. However, there is no guarantee that the Real GDP level of $10.7 trillion is the Natural Real GDP level. As shown in Exhibit 13, the economy could be in equilibrium at point A, producing Q_E, when the Natural Real GDP level is Q_N. Because the economy is producing at a Real GDP level that is less than Natural Real GDP, it is in a recessionary gap.

How does the economy get out of the recessionary gap? Will the private sector (households and businesses) be capable of pushing the TE curve in Exhibit 13 upward so that it goes through point B so that Q_N is produced? According to Keynes, the economy is not necessarily going to do so. Keynes believed that government may be necessary to get the economy out of a recessionary gap. For example, government may have to raise its purchases (raise G) so that the TE curve shifts upward and goes through point B.

Equilibrium in the Economy

Of the many debates in macroeconomics, one concerns equilibrium in the economy: where the economy naturally ends up after all adjustments have been made. As explained in the last chapter, some economists believe that the economy is self-regulating and that an economy naturally ends up in the long run producing Natural Real GDP. In this chapter, we have talked about economists who believe that the economy can be inherently unstable and that it can naturally end up producing a level of Real GDP less than Natural Real GDP. To the first group of economists, equilibrium is a desirable state of affairs; to the second group, equilibrium may not be if Real GDP is less than Natural Real GDP.

EXHIBIT 13

The Economy: In Equilibrium, and in a Recessionary Gap Too

Using the $TE-TP$ framework, the economy is currently in equilibrium at point A, producing Q_E. Natural Real GDP, however, is greater than Q_E, so the economy is in a recessionary gap as well as being in equilibrium.

The Theme of the Simple Keynesian Model

In terms of *TE* and *TP*, the essence of the simple Keynesian model can be summed up in five statements:

1. The price level is constant until Natural Real GDP is reached.

2. The *TE* curve shifts if there are changes in *C, I,* or *G*.

3. According to Keynes, the economy could be in equilibrium and in a recessionary gap too. In other words, the economy can be at point *A* in Exhibit 13.

4. The private sector may not be able to get the economy out of a recessionary gap. In other words, the private sector (households and businesses) may not be able to increase *C* or *I* enough to get the *TE* curve in Exhibit 13 to rise and pass through point *B*.

5. The government may have a management role to play in the economy. According to Keynes, government may have to raise *TE* enough to stimulate the economy to move it out of the recessionary gap and to its Natural Real GDP level.

We show the simple Keynesian model in the *TE−TP* framework in Exhibit 14 in both flowchart form (a) and in diagrammatic form (b).

SELF-TEST

1. What happens in the economy if total production (*TP*) is greater than total expenditures (*TE*)?

2. What happens in the economy if total expenditures (*TE*) are greater than total production (*TP*)?

EXHIBIT 14

Real GDP

TE

45° line
TP

C   I   G

(a)

The Simple Keynesian Model in the *TE−TP* Framework

The purpose of the simple Keynesian model is to explain changes in Real GDP. In (a) the model is presented as a flowchart. Real GDP is determined by total expenditures (*TE*) and total product (*TP*). Total expenditures (*TE*) depend on *C,* consumption; *I*, investment; and *G*, government purchases. In (b) is a diagrammatic exposition of the model in the *TE−TP* framework.

45° line (*TP* = Real GDP)

TP and *TE*

A

TE = *C* + *I* + *G*

Q_1 Real GDP

(b)

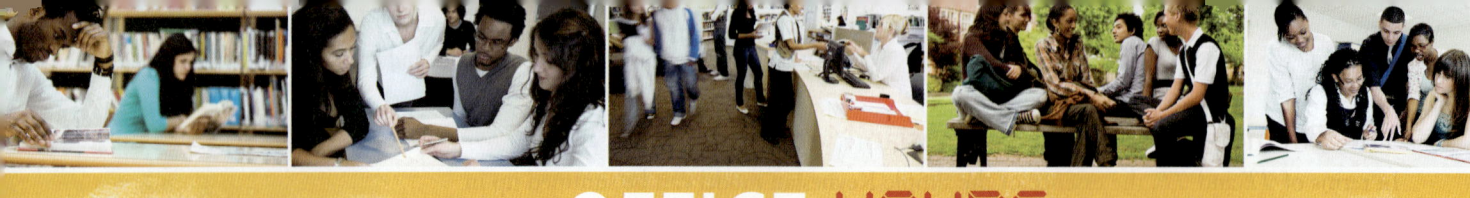

OFFICE HOURS

"Does a Lot Depend on Whether Wages are Flexible or Inflexible?"

STUDENT:

Can what we learned in this chapter be seen as a criticism of what we learned in the last chapter?

INSTRUCTOR:

Much of it can be viewed as a criticism. Specifically, in the last chapter you learned the views of economists who believe that the economy *is* self-regulating. In this chapter you learned the views of economists who believe that the economy *is not always* self-regulating.

STUDENT:

What is at the heart of the disagreement between these two groups of economists?

INSTRUCTOR:

That's a good question. One thing at the heart of the disagreement is whether wages are flexible or inflexible. To illustrate, look back at Exhibit 2. There you see an economy in a recessionary gap. Now if wages are flexible (as stated in the last chapter), then they will soon fall, and the *SRAS* curve in Exhibit 2 will shift to the right. In time, the economy will remove itself from a recessionary gap, to point 2 in the exhibit. However, if wages are inflexible downward (as stated in this chapter), then wages will not fall, the *SRAS* will not shift to the right, and the economy will remain stuck—at point 1 in the exhibit—in a recessionary gap.

STUDENT:

Suppose the economists who say the economy can get stuck in a recessionary gap are right. What then? Does the economy just stay stuck forever?

INSTRUCTOR:

What these economists usually propose is a government response. Specifically, they advocate fiscal or monetary policy to get the economy unstuck. We haven't discussed either fiscal or monetary policy yet, but we plan to in the next chapter.

STUDENT:

It seems to me that a lot depends on whether wages are flexible or inflexible. If wages are flexible, the economy self-regulates, removes itself from a recessionary gap, and thus requires no government

response. On the other hand, if wages are inflexible (downward), the economy can get stuck in a recessionary gap, and a government response may be needed.

INSTRUCTOR:

That's right. And because much depends on whether wages are flexible or inflexible, economists research such things as wages in various industries. For example, trying to find out whether wages in industries X and Y are flexible or inflexible may seem abstruse and esoteric to many people—who cares?—but, as you have just pointed out, a lot can depend on having the right answers.

POINTS TO REMEMBER

1. Not all economists agree on how the economy works. In the last chapter, you learned the views of economists who believe that the economy is self-regulating. In this chapter, you learned the views of economists who believe that the economy is not always self-regulating.

2. Often, much depends on what may appear to be a small issue. An economist tells you she is researching the degree of flexibility of wages in industry X. You may think, "What a small issue to research. Who cares about the degree of flexibility of wages? After all, they are what they are." However, as we have shown, sometimes these so-called small issues can make a big difference, such as whether government becomes involved in the economy.

CHAPTER SUMMARY

KEYNES ON WAGE RATES AND PRICES

- Keynes believed that wage rates and prices may be inflexible downward. He said that employees and labor unions will resist employer's wage cuts and that, because of anticompetitive or monopolistic elements in the economy, prices will not fall.

KEYNES ON SAY'S LAW

- Keynes did not agree that Say's law would necessarily hold in a money economy. He thought it was possible for consumption to fall (for saving to increase) by more than investment increased. Consequently, a decrease in consumption (or increase in saving) could lower total expenditures and aggregate demand in the economy.

CONSUMPTION FUNCTION

- Keynes made three points about consumption and disposable income: (1) Consumption depends on disposable income. (2) Consumption and disposable income move in the same direction. (3) As disposable income changes, consumption changes by less. These three ideas are incorporated into the consumption function, $C = C_0 + (MPC \times Y_d)$, where C_0 is autonomous consumption, MPC is the marginal propensity to consume, and Y_d is disposable income.

THE MULTIPLIER

- A change in autonomous spending will bring about a multiple change in total spending. The overall change in spending is equal to the multiplier $[1/(1 - MPC)]$ times the change in autonomous spending.

THE SIMPLE KEYNESIAN MODEL IN THE AD–AS FRAMEWORK

- Changes in consumption, investment, and government purchases will change aggregate demand.

- A rise in C, I, or G will shift the AD curve to the right.
- A decrease in C, I, or G will shift the AD curve to the left.
- The aggregate supply curve in the simple Keynesian model has both a horizontal section and a vertical section. The kink between the two sections is at the Natural Real GDP level. If aggregate demand changes in the horizontal section of the curve (when the economy is operating below Natural Real GDP), Real GDP changes, but not the price level. If aggregate demand changes in the vertical section of the curve (when the economy is operating at Natural Real GDP), the price level changes but not Real GDP.

THE SIMPLE KEYNESIAN MODEL IN THE TE–TP FRAMEWORK

- Changes in consumption, investment, and government purchases will change total expenditures.
- A rise in C, I, or G will shift the TE curve upward.
- A decrease in C, I, or G will shift the TE curve downward.
- If total expenditures (TE) equal total production (TP), the economy is in equilibrium. If $TE < TP$, the economy is in disequilibrium and inventories will unexpectedly rise, signaling firms to cut back production. If $TE > TP$, the economy is in disequilibrium and inventories will unexpectedly fall, signaling firms to increase production.
- Equilibrium occurs where $TE = TP$. The equilibrium level of Real GDP may be less than the Natural Real GDP level, and the economy may be stuck at this lower level of Real GDP.

A KEYNESIAN THEME

- Keynes proposed that the economy could reach its equilibrium position with Real GDP below Natural Real GDP; that is, the economy could be in equilibrium and in a recessionary gap too. Furthermore, he argued that the economy may not be able to get out of a recessionary gap by itself. Government may need to play a management role in the economy.

KEY TERMS AND CONCEPTS

Efficiency Wage Models	Marginal Propensity to	Autonomous Consumption	Multiplier
Consumption Function	Consume (*MPC*)	Marginal Propensity to Save (*MPS*)	

QUESTIONS AND PROBLEMS

Questions 1–5 are based on the first section of the chapter, questions 6–12 are based on the second section, questions 13–20 are based on the third section, and questions 21–25 are based on the fourth section.

1. According to some economists, why might business firms pay wage rates above market-clearing levels?
2. How is Keynes's position different from the classical position with respect to wages, prices, and Say's law?

3. How was Keynes's position different from the classical position with respect to saving and investment?

4. Classical economists assumed that wage rates, prices, and interest rates are flexible and will adjust quickly. Consider an extreme case: Suppose classical economists believed that wage rates, prices, and interest rates will adjust instantaneously. What would the classical aggregate supply (AS) curve look like? Explain your answer.

5. Give two reasons explaining the possibility that wage rates may not fall.

6. Explain the multiplier process.

7. What is the relationship between the MPC and the multiplier?

8. Look at the Keynesian consumption function: $C = C_0 + (MPC \times Y_d)$. What part of it relates to autonomous consumption? What part of it relates to induced consumption? Define autonomous consumption and induced consumption.

9. Explain how a rise in autonomous spending can increase total spending by some multiple.

10. Using the Keynesian consumption function, prove numerically that, as the MPC rises, saving declines.

11. In which factors will a change lead to a change in consumption?

12. Given the Keynesian consumption function, how would a cut in income tax rates affect consumption? Explain your answer.

13. Suppose consumption rises while investment and government purchases remain constant. How will the AD curve shift in the simple Keynesian model? Under what condition will the rise in Real GDP be equal to the rise in total spending?

14. Can a person believe that wages are inflexible downward for, say, one year and also believe in a self-regulating economy? Explain your answer.

15. "In the simple Keynesian model, increases in AD that occur below Natural Real GDP will have no effect on the price level." Do you agree or disagree with this statement? Explain your answer.

16. According to Keynes, an increase in saving and a decrease in consumption may lower total spending in the economy. But how could this happen if the increased saving lowers interest rates (as shown in the last chapter)? Wouldn't a decrease in interest rates increase investment spending, thus counteracting the decrease in consumption spending?

17. What does the aggregate supply curve look like in the simple Keynesian model?

18. What factors will shift the AD curve in the simple Keynesian model?

19. According to Keynes, can the private sector always remove the economy from a recessionary gap? Explain your answer.

20. According to Keynes, can an increase in saving shift the AD curve to the left? Explain your answer.

21. Identify the three states of the economy in terms of TE and TP.

22. If Real GDP is $10.4 trillion in Exhibit 12, what is the state of business inventories?

23. What role do inventories play in the equilibrating process in the simple Keynesian model (as described in the TE–TP framework)?

24. How will a rise in government purchases change the TE curve in Exhibit 12?

25. Explain how to derive a total expenditures (TE) curve.

WORKING WITH NUMBERS AND GRAPHS

Questions 1–2 are based on the second section of the chapter, questions 3–4 are based on the third section, and questions 5–8 are based on the fourth section.

1. Compute the multiplier in each of the following cases:
   a. MPC = 0.60
   b. MPC = 0.80
   c. MPC = 0.50

2. Write an investment function (equation) that specifies two components:
   a. Autonomous *investment spending*
   b. *Induced inve*stment spending

3. Economist Smith believes that changes in aggregate demand affect only the price level, and economist Jones believes that changes in aggregate demand affect only Real GDP. What do the AD and AS curves look like for each economist?

4. Explain the two statements (that appear at the the top of the next page) using the following figure:

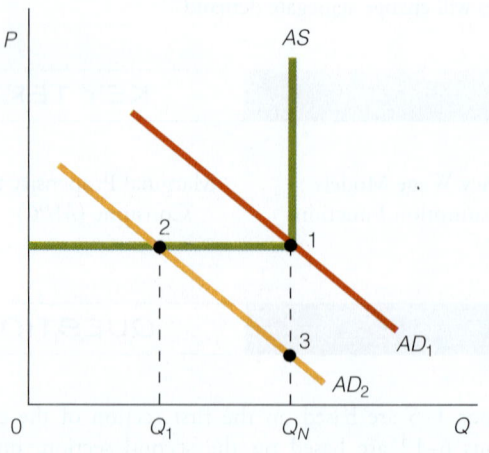

a. According to Keynes, aggregate demand may be insufficient to bring about the full-employment output level (or Natural Real GDP).

b. A decrease in consumption (due to increased saving) is not matched by an increase in investment spending.

5. The *TE* curve in Exhibit 11(d) is upward sloping because the consumption function is upward sloping. Explain.

6. In Exhibit 11(d), what does the vertical distance between the origin and the point at which the *TE* curve cuts the vertical axis represent?

7. In the figure at the right, explain what happens if:

a. The economy is at Q_1

b. The economy is at Q_2

8. In the figure at the right, if Natural Real GDP is Q_2, in what state is the economy at point *A*?

CHAPTER 11

FISCAL POLICY AND THE FEDERAL BUDGET

Introduction This chapter deals with fiscal policy and the federal budget. Fiscal policy consists of changes in government expenditures and/or taxes to achieve economic goals, such as low unemployment, stable prices, and economic growth. In the United States, the Congress and the president, together, fashion fiscal policy. We begin our discussion with some facts and figures about government expenditures and taxation, and we then go on to discuss the effect of fiscal policy on the economy.

THE FEDERAL BUDGET

The federal budget has two, not necessarily equal, parts: government expenditures and tax revenues. You are familiar with the term *government purchases* from earlier chapters. Government expenditures—sometimes simply called government spending—are not the same as government purchases. Government expenditures are the sum of government purchases and government transfer payments.[1]

Government Expenditures

In 2009, the federal government spent $3.518 trillion, which was 24.7 percent of GDP for that year. The following table shows government spending as a percentage of GDP in other years:

---

1 Remember from an earlier chapter that government purchases are the purchases of goods and services by government at all levels. Transfer payments are payments to persons, such as Social Security payments, that are not made in return for goods and services currently supplied. In this chapter, the terms *government expenditures, government spending, government purchases,* and *transfer payments* all refer to the *federal* government.

Year	Government Spending as a Percentage of GDP
2000	18.2
2001	18.2
2002	19.1
2003	19.7
2004	19.6
2005	19.9
2006	20.1
2007	19.6
2008	20.7
2009	24.7

The bulk of the $3.518 trillion in government spending in 2009 was spent on four programs: national defense, Social Security, Medicare, and Medicaid. These four programs together accounted for 60 percent of all government spending that year.

Government Tax Revenues

The federal government imposes taxes and fees that generate revenue. In 2009, government revenues totaled $2.104 trillion. This was 14.8 percent of GDP for the year. The following table shows government tax revenues as a percentage of GDP in other years:

Year	Government Tax Revenues as a Percentage of GDP
2000	20.6
2001	19.5
2002	17.6
2003	16.2
2004	16.1
2005	17.3
2006	18.2
2007	18.5
2008	17.5
2009	14.8

The bulk of government tax revenues comes from three taxes: the individual income tax, the corporate income tax, and Social Security taxes. In 2009, these three taxes accounted for 92.35 percent of total government tax revenues; the income tax by itself accounted for 43.46 percent of total government revenues.

Budget Projections

Here are the projections for government spending and tax revenues in various years:

Year	Government Spending ($ trillions)	Government Tax Revenues ($ trillions)
2011	$3.650	$2.670
2012	3.613	2.964
2013	3.756	3.214
2014	3.940	3.465
2015	4.105	3.625

EXHIBIT 1

Three Income Tax Structures

The three income tax structures outlined are the progressive, proportional, and regressive.

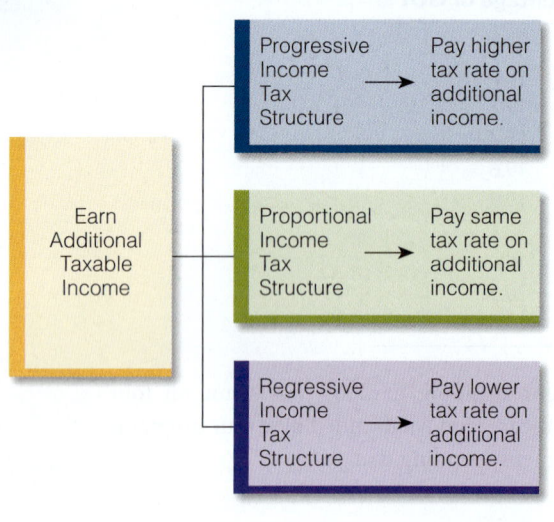

INCOME TAX STRUCTURES An income tax structure can be progressive, proportional, or regressive. Under a progressive income tax, the tax rate increases as a person's taxable income level rises. To illustrate, suppose Davidson pays taxes at the rate of 15 percent on a taxable income of $20,000. When his (taxable) income rises to, say, $30,000, he pays at a rate of 28 percent. And when his income rises to, say, $55,000, he pays at a rate of 31 percent. A progressive income tax is usually capped. Currently, the U.S. income tax structure is progressive, with six (marginal) tax rates, ranging (in 2009) from a low of 10 percent to a high of 35 percent.

Under a proportional income tax, the same tax rate is used for all income levels. A proportional income tax is sometimes referred to as a *flat tax*. For example, Kuan's pays taxes at a rate of 10% whether her taxable income is $10,000 or $100,000.

Under a regressive income tax, the tax rate decreases as a person's taxable income level rises. For example, Lowenstein's tax rate is 10 percent when her taxable income is $10,000 and 8 percent when her taxable income rises to $20,000.

See Exhibit 1 for a review of the three income tax structures.

Progressive Income Tax
An income tax system in which one's tax rate rises as taxable income rises (up to some point).

Proportional Income Tax
An income tax system in which a person's tax rate is the same regardless of taxable income.

Regressive Income Tax
An income tax system in which a person's tax rate declines as his or her taxable income rises.

🄵inding ECONOMICS

In How a Presidential Candidate Speaks A presidential candidate is speaking before a large group in Des Moines, Iowa, and he has just called the current income tax structure unfair. Someone from the crowd asks him what he means by "unfair." The candidate responds that individuals shouldn't pay a higher tax rate just because they earn a higher income. We should all pay the same tax rate, he argues. Where is the economics?

Obviously the candidate favors a proportional income tax (i.e., a flat tax). Under both a progressive and a regressive income tax structure, individuals pay different tax rates at different taxable income levels. Only with a proportional income tax do individuals pay the same tax rate no matter what their taxable income is. ▲ ▲ ▲

WHO PAYS THE INCOME TAX? Economists often look at the tax situations of different income groups. For example, in 2007, the top 1 percent of income earners in the United States earned 22.83 percent of the total income earned that year and paid 40.42 percent of the total federal income taxes collected. The following data show the income and taxes for various income groups in 2007. The column labeled "Income Split Point" identifies the dollar amount you would have had to earn in 2007 to be in the income group in that row. For example, to be in the top 1 percent of income earners in 2007, you would have had to earn more than $410,096.

Income Group	Group's Share of Total Income	Group's Share of Federal Income Taxes	Income Split Point
Top 1%	22.83	40.42	Greater than $410,096
Top 5%	37.44	60.63	Greater than $160,041
Top 10%	48.05	71.22	Greater than $113,018
Top 25%	68.71	85.59	Greater than $66,532
Top 50%	87.44	97.11	Greater than $32,879
Bottom 50%	12.26	2.89	Less than $32,879

Two Plumbers, New Year's Eve, and Progressive Taxation

Many people believe that if two people do the same job, they should be paid the same dollar amount. The question of equal pay for equal work often arises in discussions about the jobs performed by men and women. In other words, if a man and a woman do the same job, many people say that they should be paid the same dollar amount.

Sometimes the question of equal pay for equal work is extended to equal after-tax pay for equal work. That is, if two people do the same job, then they should earn the same after-tax income. However, a progressive income tax structure sometimes makes this impossible.

To illustrate, suppose under a progressive income tax structure, a person who earns between $50,000 and $60,000 pays income tax at a tax rate of 20 percent. For every dollar earned over $60,000 but under $70,000, a person pays at a tax rate of 30 percent.

Consider two plumbers, Smith and Jones. By December 30, Jones has earned $58,000 for the year, and Smith has earned $60,000. Each is asked to do the same kind of plumbing job on December 31, New Year's Eve. Each plumber

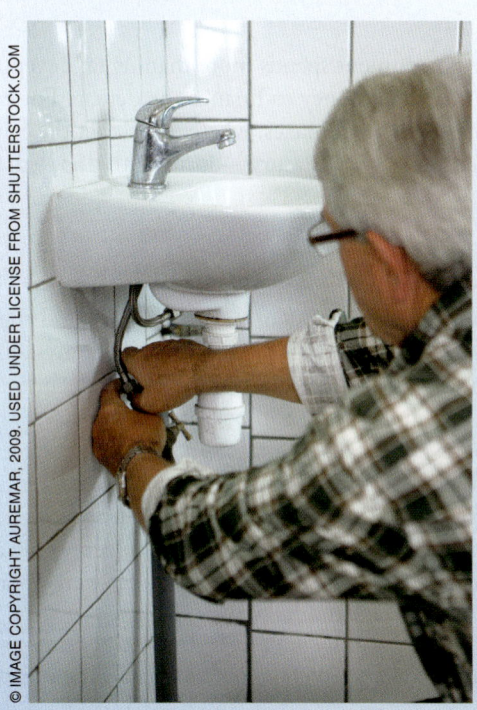

© IMAGE COPYRIGHT AUREMAR, 2009, USED UNDER LICENSE FROM SHUTTERSTOCK.COM

charges $1,000 for the job. So Jones and Smith receive equal pay for equal work.

The after-tax income that each receives for the job makes for a different story. On the additional $1,000 that Jones earns, she pays at a tax rate of 20 percent. So she pays $200 in taxes and gets to keep $800 in after-tax income. Smith, on the other hand, now has an annual income of $61,000 and thus falls into a higher marginal tax bracket. He pays at a tax rate of 30 percent on the additional $1,000. So Smith pays $300 in taxes and has $700 in after-tax income. Smith does the same job as Jones but earns only $700 in after-tax pay, whereas Jones earns $800 after taxes.

Our conclusion: The progressive income tax structure can turn equal pay for equal work into unequal after-tax pay for equal work. Stated differently, a person can be in favor of either progressive income taxes or equal after-tax pay for equal work, but not both. Sometimes, you have to decide between one or the other.

Budget Deficit, Surplus, or Balance

The government budget can be in one of three states:

- If government expenditures are greater than tax revenues, the federal government runs a budget deficit.
- If tax revenues are greater than government expenditures, the federal government runs a budget surplus.
- If government expenditures equal tax revenues, the federal government runs a balanced budget.

In 2009, the budget deficit was $1,414 billion, and budget deficits are projected for ensuing years. Here are the projected deficits in absolute dollars and as percentages of GDP for the years following 2009:

Budget Deficit
Government expenditures greater than tax revenues.

Budget Surplus
Tax revenues greater than government expenditures.

Balanced Budget
Government expenditures equal to tax revenues.

Year	Deficit ($ billions)	Deficit as a Percentage of GDP (%)
2010	$1,349	9.2
2011	980	6.5
2012	650	4.1
2013	539	3.2
2014	475	2.7
2015	480	2.6
2016	521	2.7

If the government spends more than its tax revenue and thus runs a budget deficit, where does it get the money to finance the deficit? For example, if the government spends $100 and has $70 only in taxes, where does it get the $30 difference? The federal government—actually the U.S. Treasury—borrows the $30; that is, it finances the budget deficit with borrowed funds.

Structural and Cyclical Deficits

Suppose the budget is currently balanced, and then Real GDP in the economy drops. As Real GDP drops, the tax base of the economy falls, and, if tax rates are held constant, tax revenues will fall. Another result of the decline in Real GDP is that transfer payments (e.g., unemployment compensation) will rise. Thus, government expenditures will rise as tax revenues fall. As a result, a balanced budget turns into a budget deficit—a result of the downturn in economic activity, not from current spending and taxing decisions by the government. Economists use the term cyclical deficit to describe the part of the budget deficit that is a result of a downturn in economic activity. The remainder of the deficit—the part that would exist if the economy were operating at full employment—is called the structural deficit. In other words,

Cyclical Deficit
The part of the budget deficit that is a result of a downturn in economic activity.

Structural Deficit
The part of the budget deficit that would exist even if the economy were operating at full employment.

Total budget deficit = Structural deficit + Cyclical deficit

To illustrate, suppose the economy is in a recessionary gap, government expenditures are currently $2.3 trillion, and tax revenues are $2.0 trillion. Thus, the (total) budget deficit is $300 billion. Economists estimate what government expenditures and tax revenues would be if the economy were operating at full employment. Assume they estimate that government expenditures would be only $2.2 trillion and that tax revenues would be $2.1 trillion. The structural deficit—the deficit that would exist at full employment—is therefore $100 billion. The cyclical deficit—the part of the budget deficit that is a result of economic downturn—is $200 billion.

The Public Debt

A budget deficit occurs when government expenditures are greater than tax revenues for a *single year*. The public debt, sometimes called the "federal" or "national debt," is the *total* amount the federal government owes its creditors. Some of this debt is held by agencies of the United States government; that is, one entity in the government owes it to another. The remainder of the debt is held by the public and is referred to either as *public debt held by the public* or as *net public debt*. On July 8, 2010, the public debt was $13.19 trillion, and the public debt held by the public was $8.63 trillion. (You can find the current public debt on the Bureau of the Public Debt website at http://www.publicdebt .treas.gov/.) The public debt was at its lowest on January 1, 1835, totaling $33,733.05 on that day. In 2009, the public debt held by the public was 53 percent of GDP. This

Public Debt
The total amount that the federal government owes its creditors.

percentage is expected to rising in upcoming years, reaching 60.3 percent in 2010, 65.3 percent in 2011, 66.6 percent in 2012, and 66.3 percent in 2013.

Valued-Added Tax

Some persons have proposed higher taxes or new taxes to deal with the enlarged budget deficits and growing public debt. One tax that has been suggested is the value-added tax (VAT). Some have proposed VAT as a supplementary revenue source; others, as a substitute for current taxes.

There are two things to understand about a value-added tax: the value-added part and the tax part.

THE VALUE-ADDED PART *Value added* is the difference between what a producer sells a (final) good for and what it pays for an (intermediate) good. For example, suppose a farmer finds a seed and plants it. In time, wheat appears. The farmer harvests the wheat and sells it to a baker for $1. The value added is $1.00.

- The farmer sells the wheat to the baker for $1.00.
- The farmer doesn't buy any intermediate goods (so intermediate goods "purchased" = $0.00).
- Value added = $1.00 − $0.00 = $1.00.
- Dollar amount kept by farmer = $1.00.

The baker, who has purchased wheat, turns it into a loaf of bread, which he sells to a (final) consumer for $1.40. The value added is $0.40.

- The baker sells the loaf of bread to a consumer for $1.40.
- The baker bought the wheat (the intermediate good) from the farmer for $1.00.
- Value added = $1.40 − $1.00 = $0.40.
- Dollar amount kept by baker = $0.40.

Notice two things:

- The sum of the values added ($1.00 + $0.40) is equal to the price paid by the final consumer for the loaf of bread ($1.40).

  Sum of values added ($1.00 + $0.40) = Price of the loaf of bread purchased by consumer ($1.40)

- The value added at each stage of production is equal to the dollar amount kept by the farmer and baker. For instance, the valued added by the farmer was $1.00 and this is the amount he kept.

THE TAX PART VAT is a *tax* applied to the *value added* at *each stage of production.* Suppose the VAT rate is 10 percent. A VAT rate of 10 percent applied to the $1.00 value added by the farmer is $0.10. A VAT tax rate of 10 percent applied to the $0.40 value added by the baker is $0.04. The total VAT ends up being $0.14.

Value added by farmer	$1.00
VAT rate of 10% applied to value added by farmer	$0.10
Value added by baker	$0.40
VAT rate of 10% applied to valued added by baker	$0.04
Total VAT = $0.10 + $0.04	$0.14

To see how the $0.14 ends up with government, we need to revisit our farmer-baker example, but this time with a VAT applied. Initially, the farmer charges the baker $1.00 for wheat. This time, with a VAT tax rate of 10 percent, he charges the baker 10 percent more or $1.10 for the wheat. Here is how things now look for the farmer:

- The farmer sells the wheat to the baker for $1.10.
- The farmer turns over 10¢ to the government (this is the VAT at the farmer's stage of production).
- The farmer keeps $1.00, which is the amount he kept when there was no VAT.

Whereas the baker sold a loaf of bread to the consumer for $1.40, this time, with a VAT rate of 10 percent, he charges 10 percent more, or $1.54 for a loaf of bread. Here is how things now look for baker:

- The baker sells the loaf of bread to the consumer for $1.54.
- The baker paid $1.10 for the wheat.
- The baker turns over $0.04 to government (this is the VAT at the baker's stage of production).
- The baker keeps $1.54 *minus* $1.10 (what he paid to the farmer) *minus* $0.04 (what he turned over to government) or $0.40, which is what he kept when there was no VAT.

Finally, here are how things look for the consumer and government:

- Without VAT, the customer paid $1.40 a loaf of broad. With VAT, she pays $1.54
- Without VAT, government collected no VAT revenues. With VAT, government collects $0.14 in VAT revenue.

So, the VAT (1) generates tax revenue and (2) raises prices.

VAT COMPARED TO A SALES TAX The VAT is nothing more than a less visible sales tax. To illustrate, in the example of the farmer and baker, this time we impose, instead of VAT, a sales tax of 10 percent at the point of final purchase. In other words, our consumer buys a loaf of bread for a price of $1.40 plus a 10 percent sales tax of $0.14: Price + Tax = $1.54.

Notice two things: (1) The consumer pays $1.54 for the bread when a VAT is applied and when a sales tax is applied. (2) The sales tax of $0.14 is exactly equal to the VAT.

In other words, government has two ways to generate $0.14 in tax revenue: impose VAT or a sales tax. Either way, the customer ends up paying $1.54 for a loaf of bread, and government generates $0.14 in tax revenue.

Finally, in comparing VAT with a sales tax, critics often stress the point that a VAT is less visible than a sales tax. If a sales tax is raised from, say, 5 percent to 6 percent, almost everyone who buys something is aware of the tax increase. The sales receipt plainly identifies the new, higher sales tax. But if the VAT rate is raised by the same amount, not everyone will know that the VAT has been raised. People may simply think that sellers are charging higher prices because the VAT is not itemized separately from what sellers charge other sellers. In the farmer-baker example, with VAT, the farmer simply charged the baker $1.10 for wheat instead of $1.00, and the baker simply charged the consumer $1.54 instead of $1.40 for a loaf of bread. With VAT, consumers find it hard to distinguish between the seller's charging a higher price because the VAT rate has been raised and the seller's charging a higher price even without the VAT rate being raised. The VAT critics add: When a sales tax is raised, people look to government and say, "*Government* raised my taxes." When VAT is raised, people say, "*Sellers* raised the prices I pay."

1. Explain the differences among progressive, proportional, and regressive income tax structures.

2. What percentage of all income taxes was paid by the top 5 percent of income earners in 2007? What percentage of total income did this income group receive in 2007?

3. What three taxes account for the bulk of federal tax revenues?

4. What is the cyclical budget deficit?

FISCAL POLICY

As explained in the last chapter, some economists believe that the economy is inherently unstable. They argue that government should play a role in managing the economy because the economy can get stuck in a recessionary gap. They believe government should try to move the economy out of the recessionary gap and toward Natural Real GDP.

A major way government can influence the economy is through its *fiscal policy*. Fiscal policy consists of changes in government expenditures and/or taxes to achieve economic goals, such as low unemployment, price stability, and economic growth.

Some Relevant Fiscal Policy Terms

Expansionary fiscal policy consists of increases in government expenditures and/or decreases in taxes to achieve macroeconomic goals. Contractionary fiscal policy is implemented through decreases in government expenditures and/or increases in taxes to achieve these goals.

- *Expansionary fiscal policy.* Government expenditures are up and/or taxes are down.
- *Contractionary fiscal policy.* Government expenditures are down and/or taxes are up.

When deliberate government actions bring about changes in its expenditures and taxes, fiscal policy is said to be *discretionary*. For example, a decision by Congress to increase government spending by, say, $10 billion in an attempt to lower the unemployment rate is an act of discretionary fiscal policy. In contrast, a change in either government expenditures or in taxes that occurs automatically in response to economic events is referred to as automatic fiscal policy. To illustrate, suppose Real GDP in the economy turns down, causing more people to become unemployed and, as a result, automatically receive unemployment benefits. These added unemployment benefits automatically boost government spending.

Two Important Notes

In your study of this chapter, keep in mind the following two important points:

1. In this chapter, we deal only with *discretionary fiscal policy*, that is, deliberate actions on the part of policy makers to affect the economy through changes in government spending and/or taxes.

2. We assume that any change in government spending is due to a change in government purchases, not to a change in transfer payments. In other words, we assume that transfer payments are constant so that changes in government spending are a reflection only of changes in government purchases.

Fiscal Policy
Changes in government expenditures and/or taxes to achieve economic goals, such as low unemployment, stable prices, and economic growth.

Expansionary Fiscal Policy
Increases in government expenditures and/or decreases in taxes to achieve particular economic goals.

Contractionary Fiscal Policy
Decreases in government expenditures and/or increases in taxes to achieve economic goals.

Discretionary Fiscal Policy
Deliberate changes of government expenditures and/or taxes to achieve economic goals.

Automatic Fiscal Policy
Changes in government expenditures and/or taxes that occur automatically without (additional) congressional action.

DEMAND-SIDE FISCAL POLICY

This section focuses on how government spending and taxes—fiscal policy—can affect the demand side of the economy, that is, aggregate demand.

Shifting the Aggregate Demand Curve

How do changes in government purchases (G) and taxes (T) affect aggregate demand? Recall that a change in consumption, investment, government purchases, or net exports can change aggregate demand and therefore shift the AD curve. For example, an increase in government purchases (G) increases aggregate demand and shifts the AD curve to the right. A decrease in G decreases aggregate demand and shifts the AD curve to the left.[2]

A change in taxes (T) can affect consumption, investment, or both, and they therefore can affect aggregate demand. For example, a decrease in income taxes increases disposable (after-tax) income, permitting individuals to increase their consumption. As consumption rises, the AD curve shifts to the right. An increase in taxes decreases disposable income, lowers consumption, and shifts the AD curve to the left.

Fiscal Policy: Keynesian Perspective (Economy Is Not Self-Regulating)

The model of the economy in Exhibit 2(a) shows a downward-sloping AD curve and an upward-sloping $SRAS$ curve. As you can see, the economy is initially in a recessionary gap at point 1. Aggregate demand is too low to move the economy to equilibrium at the

---

EXHIBIT 2

Fiscal Policy in Keynesian Theory: Ridding the Economy of Recessionary and Inflationary Gaps

(a) In Keynesian theory, expansionary fiscal policy eliminates a recessionary gap. Increased government purchases, decreased taxes, or both lead to a rightward shift in the aggregate demand curve from AD_1 to AD_2, restoring the economy to the natural level of Real GDP, Q_N. (b) Contractionary fiscal policy is used to eliminate an inflationary gap. Decreased government purchases, increased taxes, or both lead to a leftward shift in the aggregate demand curve from AD_1 to AD_2, restoring the economy to the natural level of Real GDP, Q_N.

In Keynesian theory, expansionary fiscal policy moves the economy here.

(a)
Expansionary Fiscal Policy for a Recessionary Gap

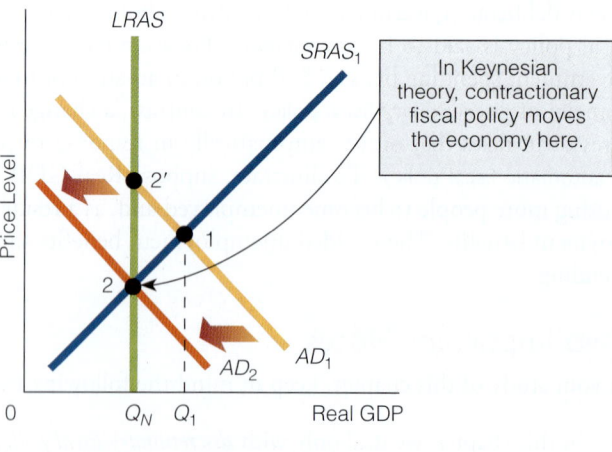

In Keynesian theory, contractionary fiscal policy moves the economy here.

(b)
Contractionary Fiscal Policy for an Inflationary Gap

---

2. Later in this chapter, when we discuss crowding out, we question the effect of an increase in government purchases on aggregate demand.

Natural Real GDP level. The Keynesian *perspective* of the economy is that the economy is not self-regulating. So the Keynesian *prescription* is to enact expansionary fiscal policy measures (an increase in government purchases or a decrease in taxes) to shift the aggregate demand curve rightward from AD_1 to AD_2 and to move the economy to the Natural Real GDP level at point 2.

Why not simply wait for the short-run aggregate supply curve to shift rightward and intersect the aggregate demand curve at point 2′? Again, the Keynesians usually respond that the economy is not self-regulating, making one of two arguments. (1) The economy is stuck at point 1 and won't move naturally to point 2′, perhaps because wage rates won't fall. (2) The short-run aggregate supply curve takes too long to shift rightward, and in the interim we must deal with the high cost of unemployment and a lower level of Real GDP. In Exhibit 2(b), the economy is initially in an inflationary gap at point 1. In this situation, Keynesians are likely to propose a contractionary fiscal measure (a decrease in government purchases or an increase in taxes) to shift the aggregate demand curve leftward from AD_1 to AD_2 and move the economy to point 2.

In Exhibit 2, fiscal policy has worked as intended. In panel (a), the economy was in a recessionary gap, and expansionary fiscal policy eliminated the gap. In panel (b), the economy was in an inflationary gap, and contractionary fiscal policy eliminated it. In (a) and (b), fiscal policy is at its best and working as intended.

Crowding Out: Questioning Expansionary Fiscal Policy

Not all economists believe that fiscal policy works as just described. Some economists bring up the subject of *crowding out.* Crowding out is a decrease in private expenditures (consumption, investment, etc.) as a consequence of increased government spending or the financing needs of a budget deficit.

Crowding out can be direct or indirect, as described in these two examples:

1. *Direct effect.* The government spends more on public libraries, and individuals buy fewer books at bookstores.[3]

2. *Indirect effect.* The government spends more on social programs and defense without increasing taxes; as a result, the size of the budget deficit increases. Consequently, the government must borrow more funds to finance the larger deficit. The increase in borrowing causes the demand for credit (i.e., the demand for loanable funds) to rise, which in turn causes the interest rate to rise. As a result, investment drops. More government spending indirectly leads to less investment spending.

TYPES OF CROWDING OUT In the first example, the government spends more on public libraries. Let's say that the government spends $2 billion more on public libraries and that consumers choose to spend not $1 less on books at bookstores. Obviously, there is no crowding out, or *zero crowding out*.

Now suppose that, after the government has spent $2 billion more on public libraries, consumers choose to spend $2 billion less at bookstores. Obviously, crowding out exists, and the degree of crowding out is dollar for dollar. When $1 of government spending offsets $1 of private spending, complete crowding out is said to exist.

Finally, suppose that, after the government has spent $2 billion more on public libraries, consumers spend $1.2 billion less on books at bookstores. Again, crowding out occurs, but it is not dollar for dollar, not complete crowding out. Incomplete crowding out occurs when the decrease in one or more components of private spending only partially offsets the increase in government spending.

Crowding Out
The decrease in private expenditures that occurs as a consequence of increased government spending or the financing needs of a budget deficit.

Complete Crowding Out
A decrease in one or more components of private spending that completely offsets the increase in government spending.

Incomplete Crowding Out
The decrease in one or more components of private spending that only partially offsets the increase in government spending.

---

3 We are not saying that, for example, if the government spends more on public libraries, individuals will necessarily buy fewer books at bookstores; rather, if they do, this would be an example of crowding out. The same holds for example 2.

The following table summarizes the different types of crowding out:

Type of Crowding Out	Example
Zero crowding out (sometimes called "no crowding out")	Government spends $2 billion more, and private sector spending stays constant.
Complete crowding out	Government spends $2 billion more, and private sector spends $2 billion less.
Incomplete crowding out	Government spends $2 billion more, and private sector spends $1.2 billion less.

GRAPHICAL REPRESENTATION OF CROWDING OUT In the event of *complete* or *incomplete crowding out* occurs, expansionary fiscal policy will have less impact on aggregate demand and Real GDP than Keynesian theory predicts. Let's look at the graphical representation of crowding out. Exhibit 3 illustrates the consequences of complete and incomplete crowding out and, for comparison, includes zero crowding. As shown Exhibit 3, here are the three possibilities for crowding out:

- *Zero crowding out (no crowding out).* In Exhibit 3, the economy is initially at point 1, with Real GDP at Q_1. Expansionary fiscal policy shifts the aggregate demand curve to AD_2 and moves the economy to point 2. Among other things, the implicit assumption is that there is zero (no) crowding out. Real GDP has increased from Q_1 to Q_N. Therefore, the unemployment rate will fall from its level at Q_1 to a lower level at Q_N. So, if there is no crowding out, expansionary fiscal policy increases Real GDP and lowers the unemployment rate.

- *Incomplete crowding out.* The aggregate demand curve shifts (on net) only to AD_2' because a fall in private expenditures *partially offsets* the initial stimulus in aggregate demand due to increased government spending. The economy moves to point 2', and Real GDP increases from Q_1 to Q_2'. Therefore, the unemployment rate will fall from what it was at Q_1 to what it is at Q_2'. Also, the changes in both Real GDP and the unemployment rate are smaller with incomplete crowding out than with zero crowding out. So, given incomplete crowding out, expansionary fiscal policy increases Real GDP and lowers the unemployment rate, but not as much as with zero crowding out.

- *Complete crowding out.* A fall in private expenditures *completely offsets* the initial stimulus in aggregate demand due to increased government spending, and the aggregate demand curve does not move (on net) at all. Real GDP does not change, and neither does the unemployment rate. So, with

---

EXHIBIT 3

Zero (No), Incomplete, and Complete Crowding Out

The exhibit shows the effects of zero, incomplete, and complete crowding out in the AD–AS framework. Starting at point 1, expansionary fiscal policy shifts the aggregate demand curve to AD_2 and moves the economy to point 2 and Q_N. The Keynesian theory that predicts this outcome assumes zero, or no, crowding out; an increase in, say, government spending does not reduce private expenditures. With incomplete crowding out, an increase in government spending causes private expenditures to decrease by less than the increase in government spending. The net result is a shift in the aggregate demand curve to AD_2'. The economy moves to point 2' and Q_2'. With complete crowding out, an increase in government spending is completely offset by a decrease in private expenditures, and the net result is that aggregate demand does not increase at all. The economy remains at point 1 and Q_1.

The increase (if any) in Real GDP due to expansionary fiscal policy depends on the degree of crowding out.

complete crowding out, expansionary fiscal policy has no effect on the economy. The economy remains at point 1.

See Exhibit 4 for a summary flowchart of the different types of crowding out.

ⓣhinking like AN ECONOMIST

Policy Is Not Necessarily Effective An ill person goes to the doctor and asks for medicine; the doctor prescribes the medicine, and the person goes home. After a few days, the medicine has not made the person well. The same can be sometimes said about economic policy. Keep in mind what we are and what we are not saying. We are not saying that economic policy is never effective; we are simply saying it is not *necessarily* effective. So far in our discussion, crowding out is only one reason fiscal policy may not be effective. Lags, which we discuss next, are another. ● ● ●

Lags and Fiscal Policy

Even if we prove beyond a shadow of a doubt that there is no (zero) crowding out, should fiscal policy then be used to solve the problems of inflationary and recessionary gaps? Many economists would answer not necessarily, because of *lags*. There are five types of lags:

1. *The data lag.* Policy makers are not aware of changes in the economy as soon as they happen. For example, if the economy turns down in January, the decline may not be apparent for two to three months.

2. *The wait-and-see lag.* After policy makers are aware of a downturn in economic activity, they rarely enact counteractive measures immediately. Instead, they usually adopt a relatively cautious wait-and-see attitude to be sure that the observed events are not just short-run phenomena.

EXHIBIT 4

Expansionary Fiscal Policy (Government Spending Increases), Crowding Out, and Changes in Real GDP and the Unemployment Rate

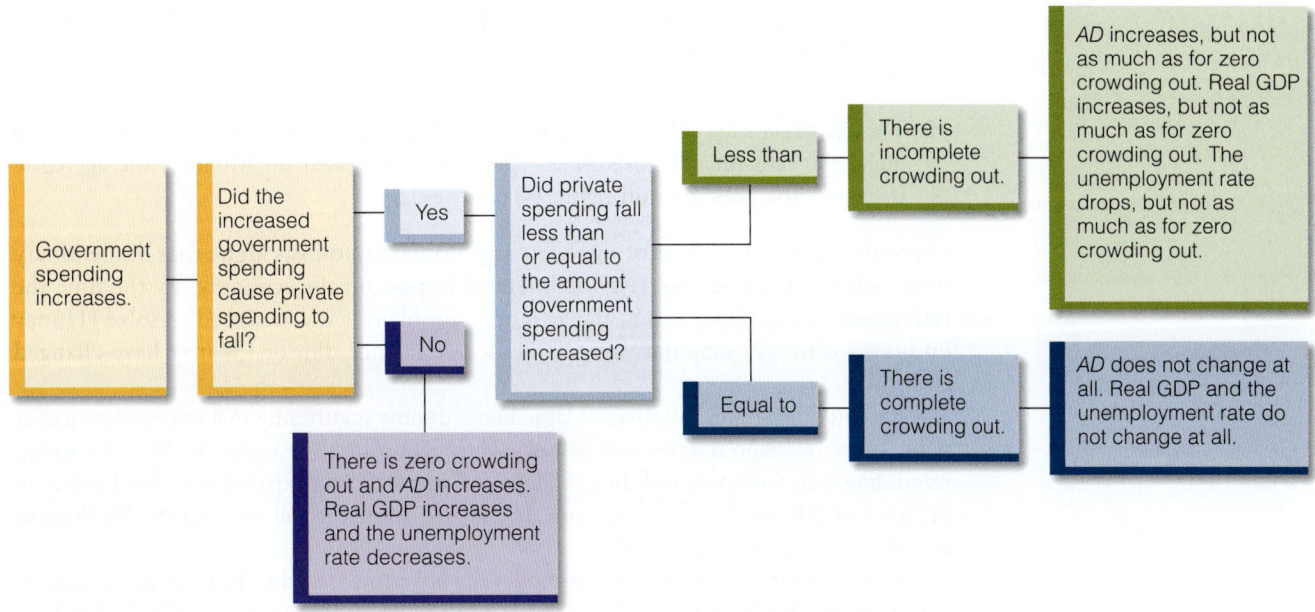

The Recession and the Stimulus Bill

The U.S. economy moved into a recession at the end of 2007. In terms of the *AD–AS* diagram [Exhibit 2(a)], the economy was in a recessionary gap, producing less than Natural Real GDP, or Q_N. From a Keynesian perspective, expansionary fiscal policy is recommended. The objective is to increase spending in the economy so that the *AD* curve shifts rightward, leading to a rise in Real GDP.

On February 17, 2009, President Barack Obama signed the American Recovery and Reinvestment Act of 2009 into law. This act was popularly known as "the stimulus bill." It was an expansionary fiscal policy measure that was made up of some tax cuts and a rise in government purchases. The total dollar amount of stimulus was $787 billion.

The stimulus bill had its proponents and opponents among economists. Some economists argued

AP PHOTO/DAVID ZALUBOWSKI

that the stimulus bill was definitely needed to move the economy out of the recession. They argued that the stimulus bill would work, that is, stimulate spending in the economy, shift the *AD* curve to the right, and remove the economy from the recession. Moreover, they argued that the multiplier (in the economy) was high enough to remove the economy from the recessionary gap given the dollar amount of stimulus. [In the last chapter, we discussed the simple Keynesian multiplier : $1 \div (1 - MPC)$, so that, if $MPC = 0.80$, the multiplier is 5.]

Not all economists agreed, arguing that crowding out would be a problem. In fact, some economists argued that every dollar of government stimulus would lead to one less dollar of private sector spending. In other words, crowding out would be complete.

3. *The legislative lag.* After policy makers decide that some type of fiscal policy measure is required, Congress or the president has to propose the measure, build political support for it, and get it passed. The legislative lag can take many months.

4. *The transmission lag.* Once enacted, a fiscal policy measure takes time to go into effect. For example, a discretionary expansionary fiscal policy measure mandating increased spending for public works projects requires construction companies to submit bids for the work, prepare designs, negotiate contracts, and so on.

5. *The effectiveness lag.* After being actually implemented, a policy measure takes time to affect the economy. If government spending is increased on Monday, the aggregate demand curve does not shift rightward on Tuesday.

Given the cumulative effect of these five lags, some economists argue that discretionary fiscal policy is not likely to have the intended impact on the economy. By the time the full impact of the policy is felt, the economic problem it was designed to solve (1) may no longer exist, (2) may not exist to the degree it once did, or (3) may have changed altogether.

Exhibit 5 illustrates the effect of lags. The economy is currently in a recessionary gap at point 1. The recession is under way before government officials recognize it. After it is recognized, however, Congress and the president consider enacting expansionary fiscal policy in the hope of shifting the *AD* curve from AD_1 to AD_2 so that it will intersect the *SRAS* curve at point 1′, at Natural Real GDP.

In the interim, unknown to everybody, the economy is said to be healing, or regulating, itself: the *SRAS* curve is already shifting to the right. Government officials don't see this change because collecting and analyzing data about the economy takes time.

Thinking that the economy is not healing itself or not healing itself quickly enough, the government enacts expansionary fiscal policy. In time, the *AD* curve shifts rightward. But by the time the increased demand is felt in the goods and services market, the *AD* curve intersects the *SRAS* curve at point 2. In effect, the government has moved the economy from point 1 to point 2, not, as it had intended, from point 1 to point 1′. The government has moved the economy into an inflationary gap. Instead of stabilizing and moderating the ups and downs in economic activity (the business cycle), the government has intensified the fluctuations.

EXHIBIT 5

Fiscal Policy May Destabilize the Economy

In this scenario, the *SRAS* curve is shifting rightward (healing the economy of its recessionary gap), but this information is unknown to policy makers. Policy makers implement expansionary fiscal policy, and the *AD* curve ends up intersecting *SRAS*₂ at point 2 instead of intersecting *SRAS*₁ at point 1′. Policy makers thereby move the economy into an inflationary gap, thus destabilizing the economy.

Crowding Out, Lags, and the Effectiveness of Fiscal Policy

Economists who believe that the crowding out is zero and that lags are insignificant conclude that fiscal policy is effective at moving the economy out of a recessionary gap. Economists who believe that crowding out is complete and/or that lags are significant conclude that fiscal policy is ineffective in this respect.

SELF-TEST

1. How does crowding out create questions about the effectiveness of expansionary demand-side fiscal policy? Give an example.

2. How might lags reduce the effectiveness of fiscal policy?

3. Give an example of the indirect effect of crowding out.

SUPPLY-SIDE FISCAL POLICY

Fiscal policy effects may be felt on the supply side as well as on the demand side of the economy. For example, a reduction in tax rates may alter an individual's incentive to work and produce, thus altering aggregate supply.

Marginal Tax Rates and Aggregate Supply

When fiscal policy measures affect tax rates, they may affect both aggregate supply and aggregate demand. Consider a reduction in an individual's marginal tax rate. The marginal (income) tax rate is equal to the change in a person's tax payment divided by the change in the person's taxable income.

$$\text{Marginal tax rate} = \frac{\Delta \text{ Tax payment}}{\Delta \text{ Taxable income}}$$

For example, if Serena's taxable income increases by $1 and her tax payment increases by $0.28, her marginal tax rate is 28 percent. If her taxable income increases by $1 and her tax payment increases by $0.35, then her marginal tax rate is 35 percent.

Marginal (Income) Tax Rate

The change in a person's tax payment divided by the change in taxable income: ΔTax payment $\div$ ΔTaxable income.

EXHIBIT 6

The Predicted Effect of a Permanent Marginal Tax Rate Cut on Aggregate Supply

A cut in marginal tax rates increases the attractiveness of productive activity relative to leisure and tax-avoidance activities and shifts resources from the latter to the former, thus shifting rightward both the short-run and the long-run aggregate supply curves.

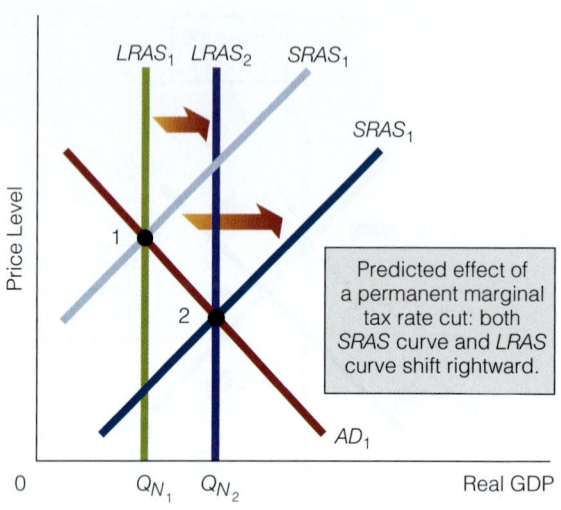

All other things held constant, lower marginal tax rates increase the incentive to engage in productive activities (work) relative to leisure and tax-avoidance activities.[4] As resources shift from leisure to work, short-run aggregate supply increases. When the lower marginal tax rates are permanent (not a one-shot phenomenon), most economists predict that not only the short-run aggregate supply curve but also the long-run aggregate supply curve will shift rightward. Exhibit 6 illustrates the predicted effect of a permanent marginal tax rate cut on aggregate supply.

The Laffer Curve: Tax Rates and Tax Revenues

Laffer Curve
The curve, named after Arthur Laffer, that shows the relationship between tax rates and tax revenues. According to the Laffer curve, as tax rates rise from zero, tax revenues rise, reach a maximum at some point, and then fall with further increases in tax rates.

High tax rates are followed by attempts of ingenious men to beat them as surely as snow is followed by little boys on sleds.

—Arthur Okun, economist (1928–1980)

If (marginal) income tax rates are reduced, will income tax revenues increase or decrease? Most people think the answer is obvious: lower tax rates mean lower tax revenues. Economist Arthur Laffer explained why this may not be the case. As the story is told, Laffer, while dining with a journalist at a restaurant in Washington, D.C., drew the curve in Exhibit 7 on a napkin. The curve came to be known as the Laffer curve. Laffer's objective was to explain the possible relationships between tax rates and tax revenues. In the exhibit, tax revenues are on the vertical axis, and tax rates are on the horizontal axis. Laffer made three major points about the curve:

EXHIBIT 7

The Laffer Curve

When the tax rate is either 0 or 100 percent, tax revenues are zero. Starting from a zero tax rate, increases in tax rates first increase (region A to B) and then decrease (region B to C) tax revenues. Starting from a 100 percent tax rate, decreases in tax rates first increase tax revenues (region C to B) and then decrease tax revenues (region B to A). This suggests there is some tax rate that maximizes tax revenues.

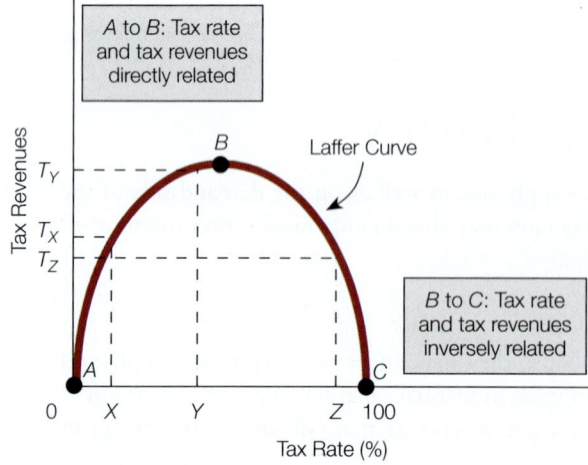

1. Zero tax revenues will be collected at two (marginal) tax rates: 0 percent and 100 percent. Obviously, no tax revenues will be raised if the tax rate is zero, and if the tax rate is 100 percent, no one will work and earn income because the entire amount would be taxed away.

---

4. When marginal tax rates are lowered, two things happen: (1) individuals will have more disposable income, and (2) the amount of money that individuals can earn (and keep) by working increases. As a result of the first effect, individuals will choose to work less. As a result of the second effect, individuals will choose to work more. Whether an individual works less or more on net depends on whether effect 1 is stronger than or weaker than effect 2. We have assumed that effect 2 is stronger than effect 1; so, as marginal tax rates decline, the net effect is that individuals work more.

2. An increase in tax rates could cause tax revenues to increase. For example, an increase in tax rates from X percent to Y percent will increase tax revenues from T_X to T_Y.

3. A decrease in tax rates could cause tax revenues to increase. For example, a decrease in tax rates from Z percent to Y percent will increase tax revenues from T_Z to T_Y. This point brought public attention to the Laffer curve.

Both an *increase* and a *decrease* in tax rates at different times can increase tax revenues due to the interrelationships among tax rates, the tax base, and tax revenues. Tax revenues equal the tax base times the (average) tax rate:[5]

$$\text{Tax revenues} = \text{Tax base} \times \text{(average) Tax rate}$$

Tax Base

In terms of income taxes, the total amount of taxable income. Tax revenue = Tax base × (average) Tax rate.

For example, a tax rate of 20 percent multiplied by a tax base of $100 billion generates $20 billion of tax revenues.

Obviously, tax revenues are a function of two variables: (1) the tax rate and (2) the tax base. Whether tax revenues increase or decrease when the average tax rate is lowered depends on whether the tax base expands by a greater or lesser percentage than the percentage reduction in the tax rate. Exhibit 8 illustrates the point. The tax rate starts at 20 percent, with a tax base of $100 billion and tax revenues of $20 billion. As the tax rate is reduced, the tax base expands: The rationale is that individuals work more, invest more, enter into more trades, and shelter less income from taxes at lower tax rates.

However, the real question is *how much* does the tax base expand following the tax rate reduction? Suppose the tax rate in Exhibit 8 is reduced to 15 percent. In Case 1, the reduction increases the tax base to $120 billion: A 25 percent decrease in the tax rate (from 20 to 15 percent) causes a 20 percent increase in the tax base (from $100 billion to $120 billion). Tax revenues drop to $18 billion. In Case 2, the tax base expands by 50 percent to $150 billion. Because the tax base increases by a greater percentage than the percentage decrease in the tax rate, tax revenues increase (to $22.5 billion).

Of course, either case is possible. In the Laffer curve, tax revenues increase if a tax rate reduction is made on the downward sloping portion of the curve (between points B and C in Exhibit 7); tax revenues decrease following a tax rate reduction on the upward sloping portion of the curve (between points A and B).

EXHIBIT 8

Tax Rates, the Tax Base, and Tax Revenues

Tax revenues equal the tax base times the (average) tax rate. If the percentage reduction in the tax rate is greater than the percentage increase in the tax base, tax revenues decrease (Case 1). If the percentage reduction in the tax rate is less than the percentage increase in the tax base, tax revenues increase (Case 2). All dollar amounts are in billions of dollars.

	(1) Tax Rate	(2) Tax Base	(3) Tax Revenues (1) × (2)	Summary
Start with:	20%	$100	$20	—
Case 1:	15	120	18	↓ Tax rate ↓ Tax revenues
Case 2:	15	150	22.5	↓ Tax rate ↑ Tax revenues

5. First, the average tax rate is equal to an individual's tax payment divided by taxable income (tax payment ÷ taxable income). Second, a lower average tax rate requires a lower marginal tax rate. This follows from the average-marginal rule, which states that if the marginal magnitude is below the average magnitude, then the average is pulled down; if the marginal is above the average, the average is pulled up. Simply put, if an individual pays less tax on an additional taxable dollar (which is evidence of a marginal tax rate reduction), then his or her average tax naturally falls.

ⓣhinking Like AN ECONOMIST

Incentives Matter Contrast how an economist thinks about a tax cut with how the layperson thinks about it. The layperson probably believes that a reduction in tax rates will reduce tax revenues, focusing just on the arithmetic. An economist, however, focuses on the economic incentives, asking a number of questions. What does a lower tax rate imply in terms of a person's incentive to engage in productive activity? How does a lower tax rate affect one's trade-off between work and leisure? The layperson likely sees only the arithmetic effect of a tax cut; the economist sees the incentive effect. ●●●

Fiscal Policy and Expectations

Even if, when tax rates are lowered, people do not work more and produce more, it cannot necessarily be said that lower tax rates do not stimulate work and production. Consider two different settings. In setting 1, income tax rates are lowered in year 1 with no further cuts expected in future years. In setting 2, income tax rates are lowered in year 1 with further cuts expected in future years. In setting 1, suppose tax cuts are implemented, and individuals don't respond by working more and producing more. Then we could confidently say, all other things being equal, that lower tax rates do not seem to stimulate work and production. But in setting 2, suppose tax cuts are implemented, and individuals don't

OFFICE HOURS

"Is There a Looming Fiscal Crisis?"

STUDENT:

I've been reading what some economists have been saying about the future state of the federal budget. They say there is a looming fiscal crisis ahead. What do they mean by "a looming fiscal crisis"?

INSTRUCTOR:

They are looking at the changing demographics in the United States, combined with rising health costs. As baby boomers retire and become eligible for Social Security and Medicare (and to a lesser extent, Medicaid), we can expect that Social Security, Medicare, and Medicaid spending will rise.

STUDENT:

Will it rise by much? Is this a big spending problem headed our way?

INSTRUCTOR:

Well, if our current federal tax burden were to remain constant over the years, it has been estimated that we will be able to pay for only three federal programs and nothing else by the year 2050: Social Security, Medicare, and Medicaid. In short, the so-called looming fiscal crisis is due to the expected growth in Social Security, Medicare, and Medicaid spending in the future. In 2005, spending on these three programs comprised 8.4 percent of GDP. This is projected to be 11 percent in 2020 and 18.1 percent in 2050.

STUDENT:

That will mean the public debt will grow, won't it?

INSTRUCTOR:

Not only will it grow in absolute terms, but it will grow as a percentage of GDP too.

respond immediately by working more and producing more. We should not conclude that lower tax rates don't stimulate work and production because the tax rates in year 1 are relatively higher than the tax rates expected in future years (such as years 2, 3, and so on). In other words, although the tax cut in year 1 reduced tax rates, the tax rate is still higher in year 1 than it will be in years 2, 3, and 4. People may simply be waiting for tax rates to go down more before they start working more and producing more (and thus earning more income on which to pay taxes).

Now look at the opposite condition: raising tax rates. Raising tax rates should lead to individuals' cutting back on work and production, but this effect isn't necessarily predicted if tax rates are expected to rise more in future years. In fact, raising the tax rate in year 1, with an expected tax rate hike to follow in year 2, could actually get people to work and produce more in year 1. In relative terms, the tax rate is lower in year 1 than it will be in year 2.

SELF-TEST

1. Give an arithmetic example to illustrate the difference between the marginal and average tax rates.

2. If income tax rates rise, will income tax revenues rise too?

STUDENT:

Let me see if I have this correct. You're saying (1) that Social Security, Medicare, and Medicaid spending are likely to grow in the future and that these three programs will comprise a larger share of the federal budget than they do today; (2) that if current spending and tax policies continue, both the budget deficit and the public debt will grow as a percentage of GDP. Is this the looming fiscal crisis we hear so much about?

INSTRUCTOR:

Yes, that's correct.

STUDENT:

So what does this mean for our future? Are taxes going to have to be raised? Is spending going to have to be cut? Or are we just going to continue on course and end up having to deal with large budget deficits and debt (as a percentage of GDP)?

INSTRUCTOR:

We're not sure what will happen. What we do know is that some stark fiscal realities are awaiting us. One way of identifying the problem (or the stark reality ahead) is to measure the *fiscal gap*. This is the amount of spending reductions or tax revenue increases needed (say, over the next four decades) if we want to keep our debt-to-GDP ratio at what it is today. It has been estimated (at the low end of estimates) that the fiscal gap requires annual tax revenue increases or spending cuts totaling 5–7 percent of projected GDP for the next four decades. Here's what that means. The Congressional Budget Office forecasts the 2011 GDP at about $15 trillion. If we take 5 percent of this, we get $750 billion. The federal government would need to either (1) cut spending

by this amount in 2011, or (2) raise tax revenues by this amount in 2011, or (3) raise tax revenues by, say, $400 billion and cut spending benefits by $350 billion (for a total of $750 billion), and so on.

POINTS TO REMEMBER

1. It is likely that in future years the combined spending on Social Security, Medicare, and Medicaid will grow as a percentage of the federal budget.

2. If the nation's current spending and tax policies continue, both the budget deficit and the public debt in the hands of the public will grow as a percentage of GDP.

CHAPTER SUMMARY

GOVERNMENT SPENDING

- In 2009, the federal government spent $3.518 trillion. This was 24.7 percent of the country's GDP. About 60 percent of the money went for Social Security, Medicare, Medicaid, and national defense.
- With a proportional income tax, everyone pays taxes at the same rate, regardless of income level. With a progressive income tax, a person pays taxes at a higher rate (up to some top rate) as the income level rises. With a regressive income tax, a person pays taxes at a lower rate as the income level rises.
- The federal income tax is a progressive income tax.

TAXES

- In 2009, the federal government took in $2.104 trillion in tax revenues. Most of this came from three taxes: the individual income tax, the corporate income tax, and Social Security taxes.

DEFICITS, SURPLUSES, AND THE PUBLIC DEBT

- If government expenditures are greater than tax revenues, a budget deficit results; if government expenditures are less than tax revenues, a budget surplus results. If government expenditures equal tax revenues, the budget is balanced. Budget deficits are predicted for the near future.
- A cyclical deficit is the part of the budget deficit that is a result of a downturn in economic activity.
- A structural deficit is the part of the deficit that would exist if the economy were operating at full employment.
- Total budget deficit = Structural deficit + Cyclical deficit.
- The public debt is the total amount that the federal government owes its creditors.

FISCAL POLICY: GENERAL REMARKS

- Fiscal policy consists of changes in government expenditures and/or taxes to achieve economic goals. Expansionary fiscal policy is composed of increases in government expenditures and/or decreases in taxes. Contractionary fiscal policy entails decreases in government expenditures and/or increases in taxes.

DEMAND-SIDE FISCAL POLICY: A KEYNESIAN PERSPECTIVE

- In Keynesian theory, demand-side fiscal policy can be used to rid the economy of a recessionary gap or an inflationary gap. A recessionary gap calls for expansionary fiscal policy, and an inflationary gap calls for contractionary fiscal policy. Ideally, fiscal policy changes aggregate demand by enough to rid the economy of either a recessionary gap or an inflationary gap.

CROWDING OUT

- Crowding out is the decrease in private expenditures that occurs as a consequence of increased government spending and/or the greater financing needs of a budget deficit. The crowding-out effect suggests that expansionary fiscal policy does not work to the degree that Keynesian theory predicts.
- Complete (incomplete) crowding out occurs when the decrease in one or more components of private spending completely (partially) offsets the increase in government spending.

WHY DEMAND-SIDE FISCAL POLICY MAY BE INEFFECTIVE

- Demand-side fiscal policy may be ineffective at achieving certain macroeconomic goals because of (1) crowding out and (2) lags.

SUPPLY-SIDE FISCAL POLICY

- When fiscal policy measures affect tax rates, they may affect both aggregate supply and aggregate demand. It is generally accepted that a marginal tax rate reduction increases the attractiveness of work relative to leisure and tax-avoidance activities and thus leads to an increase in aggregate supply.
- Tax revenues equal the tax base multiplied by the (average) tax rate. Whether tax revenues decrease or increase as a result of a tax rate reduction depends on whether the percentage increase in the tax base is greater or less than the percentage reduction in the tax rate. If the percentage increase in the tax base is greater than the percentage reduction in the tax rate, then tax revenues will increase. If the percentage increase in the tax base is less than the percentage reduction in the tax rate, then tax revenues will decrease.

KEY TERMS AND CONCEPTS

Progressive Income Tax
Proportional Income Tax
Regressive Income Tax
Budget Deficit
Budget Surplus

Balanced Budget
Cyclical Deficit
Structural Deficit
Public Debt
Fiscal Policy

Expansionary Fiscal Policy
Contractionary Fiscal Policy
Discretionary Fiscal Policy
Automatic Fiscal Policy
Crowding Out

Complete Crowding Out
Incomplete Crowding Out
Marginal (Income) Tax Rate
Laffer Curve
Tax Base

QUESTIONS AND PROBLEMS

1. Some economists argue for the use of fiscal policy to solve economic problems; others argue against it. What are some of the arguments on both sides?

2. Georgia Dickens is sitting with a friend at a coffee shop, and they are talking about the new tax bill. Georgia thinks that cutting tax rates at this time would be wrong: "Lower tax rates," she says, "will lead to a larger budget deficit, and the budget deficit is already plenty big." Do lower tax rates mean a larger deficit? Why or why not?

3. Why is crowding out an important issue in the debate over the use of fiscal policy?

4. Will tax revenue necessarily rise if tax rates are lowered? Explain your answer.

5. Explain two ways crowding out may occur.

6. What is the difference between a marginal tax rate and an average tax rate?

7. What is the difference between discretionary fiscal policy and automatic fiscal policy?

8. Will tax cuts that the public perceives to be temporary affect the *SRAS* and *LRAS* curves differently than tax cuts that are perceived to be permanent? Explain your answer.

9. What is the difference between a structural deficit and a cyclical deficit?

10. The economy is in a recessionary gap, and both Smith and Jones advocate expansionary fiscal policy. Does it follow that both Smith and Jones favor so-called big government?

11. Jim favors progressive taxation and equal after-tax pay for equal work. Comment.

12. Identify and explain the five lags associated with fiscal policy.

13. A progressive income tax always raises more revenue than a proportional income tax. Do you agree or disagree? Explain your answer.

14. Tax cuts will likely affect aggregate demand and aggregate supply. Does it matter which is affected more? Explain in terms of the *AD–AS* framework.

15. Is it true that, under a proportional income tax structure, a person who earns a high income will pay more in taxes than a person who earns a low income? Explain your answer.

16. Explain how expansionary fiscal policy can, under certain conditions, destabilize the economy.

17. What percentage of total income did the top 5 percent of income earners earn in 2007? What percentage of federal income taxes did this group pay in 2007?

18. Is crowding out equally likely under all economic conditions? Explain your answer.

19. The bulk of federal government expenditures go for four programs. What are they?

20. The debate over using government spending and taxing powers to stabilize the economy involves more than technical economic issues. Do you agree or disagree? Explain your answer.

21. How much were government expenditures in 2009? How much were government tax revenues in 2009?

22. Give a numerical example to illustrate the difference between complete crowding out and incomplete crowding out.

23. What is the difference between government expenditures and government purchases?

WORKING WITH NUMBERS AND GRAPHS

Use the following table to answer questions 1–4:

Taxable	Income Taxes
$1,000–$5,000	10% of taxable income
$5,001–$10,000	$500 + 12% of everything over $5,000
$10,001–$15,000	$1,100 + 15% of everything over $10,000

1. If a person's income is $6,000, how much does he pay in taxes?

2. If a person's income is $14,000, how much does she pay in taxes?

3. What is the marginal tax rate on the 10,001st dollar? What is the marginal tax rate on the 10,000th dollar?

4. What is the average tax rate of someone with a taxable income of $13,766?

5. A hypothetical society has three income earners, and all three must pay income taxes. The taxable income of Smith is $40,000, the taxable income of Jones is $100,000, and the taxable income of Brown is $200,000.

a. How much tax revenue is raised under a proportional income tax when the tax rate is 10 percent? How much is raised if the tax rate is 15 percent?

b. A progressive tax system is installed with a rate of 5 percent on an income of $0–$40,000, a rate of 8 percent on income over $40,000 and under $100,000, and a rate of 15 percent on all income over $100,000. Will this system raise more or less tax revenue than a proportional tax rate of 10 percent? Explain your answer.

6. Graphically show how fiscal policy works in the ideal case.

7. Graphically illustrate how government can use supply-side fiscal policy to get an economy out of a recessionary gap.

8. Graphically illustrate the following:

a. Fiscal policy destabilizes the economy

b. Fiscal policy eliminates an inflationary gap

c. Fiscal policy only partly eliminates a recessionary gap

CHAPTER 12

SUSAN VAN ETTEN

MONEY, BANKING, AND THE FINANCIAL SYSTEM

Introduction This chapter is about money: how it emerged out of a barter economy and the functions it serves. It is also about banking: how it came to exist and how it looks today. Finally, it is about the financial system in the United States; specifically, about what it is and what it does.

MONEY: WHAT IS IT AND HOW DID IT COME TO BE?

The story of money starts with a definition and a history lesson. This section discusses what money is and isn't (the definition) and how money came to be (the history lesson).

Money: A Definition

To the layperson, the words "income," "credit," and "wealth" are synonyms for "money." In each of the next three sentences, the word "money" is used incorrectly; the word in parentheses is the word an economist would use.

1. How much money (income) did you earn last year?

2. Most of her money (wealth) is tied up in real estate.

3. It sure is difficult to get money (credit) in today's tight mortgage market.

In economics, the words "money," "income," "credit," and "wealth" are not synonyms. The most general definition of money is any good that is widely accepted for purposes of exchange (payment for goods and services) and the repayment of debt.

Three Functions of Money

Money has three major functions; it is a:

1. medium of exchange.

Money
Any good that is widely accepted for purposes of exchange and the repayment of debt.

2. unit of account.

3. store of value.

MONEY AS A MEDIUM OF EXCHANGE If money did not exist, goods would have to be exchanged by barter, that is, exchanging goods and services for other goods and services without the use of money. If you wanted a shirt, you would have to trade some good in your possession, say, a jackknife, for it. But first you would have to locate a person who has a shirt and who wants to trade it for a knife. In a money economy, searching for a seller is not necessary. You can either (1) exchange money for a shirt or (2) exchange the knife for money and then the money for the shirt. The buyer of the knife and the seller of the shirt do not have to be the same person. Money is the medium through which the exchange occurs; it acts as a medium of exchange. As such, money reduces the *transaction costs* of exchanges. Exchange is easier and less time-consuming in a money economy than in a barter economy.

Barter
Exchanging goods and services for other goods and services without the use of money.

MONEY AS A UNIT OF ACCOUNT A unit of account is a common measure in which values are expressed. In a barter economy, the value of every good is expressed in terms of all other goods; there is no common unit of measure. For example, 1 horse might equal 100 bushels of wheat, or 200 bushels of apples, or 20 pairs of shoes, or 10 suits, or 55 loaves of bread, and so on. In a money economy, a person doesn't have to know the price of an apple in terms of oranges, pizzas, chickens, or potato chips, as in a barter economy. A person needs only to know the price in terms of money. And because all goods are denominated in money, determining relative prices is easy and quick. For example, if 1 apple is $1 and 1 orange is 50¢, then 1 apple is worth 2 oranges.

Medium of Exchange
Anything that is generally acceptable in exchange for goods and services; a function of money.

Unit of Account
A common measure in which relative values are expressed; a function of money.

MONEY AS A STORE OF VALUE The store of value function is related to a good's ability to maintain its value over time. This is the least exclusive function of money because other goods—for example, paintings, houses, and stamps—can store value too. At times, money has not maintained its value well, such as during high-inflationary periods. For the most part, though, money has served as a satisfactory store of value. This function allows us to accept payment in money for our productive efforts and to keep that money until we decide how we want to spend it.

Store of Value
The ability of an item to hold value over time; a function of money.

From a Barter to a Money Economy: The Origins of Money

The thing that differentiates man and animals is money.

—*Gertrude Stein*

At one time, there was trade but no money. Instead, people bartered. They traded 1 apple for 2 eggs, a banana for a peach.

Today we live in a money economy, but how did we move from a barter to a money economy? Did a king or queen issue an edict: "Let there be money"? Actually, money evolved in a much more natural, market-oriented manner.

Making exchanges takes longer (on average) in a barter economy than in a money economy because the *transaction costs* are higher in a barter economy. In other words, the time and effort incurred to consummate an exchange are greater in a barter economy than in a money economy.

In a barter economy, suppose Smith wants to trade apples for oranges. He locates Jones, who has oranges. Smith offers to trade apples for oranges, but Jones tells Smith that she does not like apples and would rather have peaches. Smith must either (1) find someone who has oranges and who wants to trade oranges for apples or (2) find someone who has peaches and who wants to trade peaches for apples, after which he must return to Jones and trade peaches for oranges. Suppose Smith continues to search and finds Brown, who

Double Coincidence of Wants
In a barter economy, a requirement, which must be met before a trade can be made. It specifies that a trader must find another trader who at the same time is willing to trade what the first trader wants and wants what the first trader has.

has oranges and wants to trade oranges for (Smith's) apples. In economics terminology, Smith and Brown are said to have a double coincidence of wants. Two people have a double coincidence of wants if what the first person wants is what the second person has and what the second person wants is what the first person has. A double coincidence of wants is a necessary condition for a trade to take place.

In a barter economy, some goods are more readily accepted than others in exchange. This characteristic may originally be the result of chance, but when traders notice the difference in marketability, their behavior tends to reinforce the effect. Suppose that, of 10 goods A–J, good G is the most marketable (the most acceptable) of the 10. On average, good G is accepted 5 of every 10 times it is offered in an exchange, whereas the remaining goods are accepted, on average, only 2 of every 10 times. Given this difference, some individuals accept good G simply because of its relatively greater acceptability, even though they have no plans to consume it. They accept good G because they know they can easily trade it for most other goods at a later time (unlike the item originally in their possession). Thus the marketability of good G snowballs. The more people accept good G for its relatively greater acceptability, the greater its relative acceptability becomes, in turn causing more people to accept it.

This is how money evolved. When good G's acceptance evolves to the point that it is widely accepted for purposes of exchange, good G is money. Historically, goods that have evolved into money include gold, silver, copper, cattle, salt, cocoa beans, and shells.

thinking Like AN ECONOMIST

The Effects of Self-Interest The statement that people in a barter economy "accept good G because they know they can easily trade it for most other goods at a later time (unlike the item originally in their possession)" brings up the role of self-interest. At some point in time, people in a barter economy simply wanted to make life easier on themselves; they wanted to cut down on the time and energy required to obtain their preferred bundle of goods. In other words, they began to accept the most marketable or acceptable of all goods out of self-interest—a process that eventually led to the creation of money. ▲ ▲ ▲

finding ECONOMICS

In a POW Camp You wouldn't think you could find money in a prisoner of war (POW) camp, but you can. During World War II, an American, R. A. Radford, was captured and imprisoned in a POW camp. While in the camp, he made some observations about economic developments, which he later described in the journal *Economica*. He noted that the Red Cross would periodically distribute packages to the prisoners that contained such goods as cigarettes, toiletries, chocolate, cheese, jam, margarine, and tinned beef. Not all the prisoners had the same preferences for the goods. For example, some liked chocolate more than others; some smoked cigarettes, and others did not. Because of their preferences, the prisoners began to trade, say, a chocolate bar for cheese, and a barter system emerged. After a short while, money appeared in the camp, but not U.S. dollars or any other government currency. The good that emerged as money—the good that was widely accepted for purposes of exchange—was cigarettes. As Radford noted, "The cigarette became the standard of value. In the permanent camp people started by wandering through the bungalows calling their offers—'cheese for seven [cigarettes] . . . .'" ▲ ▲ ▲

Money, Leisure, and Output

Exchanges take less time in a money economy than in a barter economy because a double coincidence of wants is unnecessary: everyone is willing to trade for money. The movement from a barter to a money economy therefore frees up some of the transaction time, which people can use in other ways.

economics 24/7

English and Money

In the world of barter, some goods are more widely accepted than others.

In the world of languages, some languages may be more widely used than others. Today, the most widely used language appears to be English.

English is spoken not only by native English speakers but by many other people around the world. English is the language of computers and the Internet. You can see English on posters everywhere in the world. You can hear it in pop songs sung in Tokyo. English is the working language of the Asian trade group ASEAN (Association of Southeast Asian Nations). It is the language of 98 percent of German research physicists and of 83 percent of German research chemists. It is the official language of the European Central Bank, even though the bank is in Frankfurt,

© IMAGE COPYRIGHT BRUCE AMOS, 2011. USED UNDER LICENSE FROM SHUTTERSTOCK.COM

Germany. It is found in official documents in Phnom Penh, Cambodia. Singers all over the world sing in English. Alcatel, a French telecommunications company, uses English as its internal language. By 2050, half the world's population is expected to be proficient in English.

In a barter economy, if more people accept a good in exchange, then more people will want to accept it. Might the same be true of a language? If more people speak English, then will more non-English-speaking people want to learn English? Just as money lowers the transaction costs of making exchanges, English might lower the transaction costs of communicating.

Is the world evolving toward one universal language, and is that language English?

To illustrate, suppose making trades takes 10 hours a week in a barter economy, but only 1 hour in a money economy. In a money economy, then, each week has 9 hours that don't have to be spent making exchanges and that people can use for other purposes. Some will use them to work, others will use them for leisure, and still others will divide the 9 hours between work and leisure. Thus, a money economy is likely to have both more output (because of the increased production) and more leisure time than a barter economy. In other words, a money economy is likely to be richer in both goods and leisure than a barter economy.

A person's standard of living depends, to a degree, on the number and quality of goods consumed and on the amount of leisure consumed. We would expect the average person's standard of living to be higher in a money economy than in a barter economy.

ﬁnding ECONOMICS

With William Shakespeare in London (1595) It is 1595, and William Shakespeare is sitting at a desk writing the Prologue to *Romeo and Juliet.* Where is the economics?

More specifically, what is the connection between Shakespeare's writing a play and the emergence of money out of a barter economy? In a money economy, individuals usually specialize in the production of one good or service because they can do so. In a barter economy, specializing is extremely costly. For Shakespeare, living in a barter economy would mean writing plays all day and then going out and trying to trade what he had written that day for apples, oranges, chickens, and bread. Would the baker trade two loaves of bread for two pages of Romeo and Juliet? Had Shakespeare lived in a barter economy, he would have soon learned that he did not have a double

(continued)

finding ECONOMICS *(continued)*

coincidence of wants with many people and that if he were going to eat and be housed, he would need to spend time baking bread, raising chickens, and building a shelter instead of thinking about Romeo and Juliet.

In a barter economy, trade is difficult; so people produce for themselves. In a money economy, trade is easy, and so individuals produce one thing, sell it for money, and then buy what they want with the money. A William Shakespeare who lived in a barter economy no doubt spent his days very differently from the William Shakespeare who lived in England in the sixteenth century. Put bluntly: without money, the world might never have enjoyed *Romeo and Juliet*. ▲ ▲ ▲

DEFINING THE MONEY SUPPLY

If money is any good that is widely accepted for purposes of exchange, is a $10 bill money? Is a dime money? Is a checking account or a savings account money? What constitutes money? In other words, what is included in the money supply? Two frequently used definitions of the money supply are M1 and M2.

M1

M1 is sometimes referred to as the *narrow definition of the money supply* or as *transactions money*. It is money that can be directly used for everyday transactions—to buy gas for the car, groceries to eat, and clothes to wear. M1 consists of currency held outside banks (by members of the public for use in everyday transactions), checkable deposits, and traveler's checks.

M1
Currency held outside banks plus checkable deposits plus traveler's checks.

$$M1 = \text{Currency held outside banks}$$
$$+ \text{ Checkable deposits}$$
$$+ \text{ Traveler's checks}$$

A couple of the components of M1 have specific definitions:

Currency
Coins and paper money.

Federal Reserve Notes
Paper money issued by the Federal Reserve.

Checkable Deposits
Deposits on which checks can be written.

- Currency includes coins minted by the U.S. Treasury and paper money. About 99 percent of the paper money in circulation is in the form of Federal Reserve notes issued by the Federal Reserve District Banks (the Fed).

- Checkable deposits are deposits on which checks can be written. Demand deposits, which are checking accounts that pay no interest, are one kind of checkable deposit. Two others are NOW (negotiated order of withdrawal) and ATS (automatic transfer from savings) accounts, which do pay interest on their balances.

In March 2010 checkable deposits equaled $835 billion, currency held outside banks equaled $871 billion, and traveler's checks were $6 billion. M1, the sum of these figures, was $1,712 billion.

Money Is More Than Currency

Most laypersons hear the word "money" and think of currency—paper money (dollar bills) and coins. For example, if a thief stops you on a dark street at night and demands, "Your money or your life," you can be sure he wants your currency. People often equate money and currency. To an economist, though, money is more than just currency. According to the M1 definition, money is currency, checkable deposits, and traveler's checks. (However, if robbed by a thief, an economist would be unlikely to hand over her currency and then write a check too.)

eBay and Match.com

One of the benefits of money's emerging out of a barter economy is that it lowers the transaction costs of making exchanges. In a barter economy, transaction costs are relatively high because no one can be sure that the person who has what you want wants what you have. With the emergence of money, the transaction costs of making exchanges drop because everyone is willing to trade for money.

Just as money has lowered the transaction costs of making exchanges, so has the Internet. Through the Internet, people can find other people they might want to exchange with faster and more easily.

Consider life before the Internet and before both eBay and Match.com. Suppose a person in London has an old Rolling Stones album for sale. He is not sure how to find someone who might want to buy it. Today, the seller simply goes online to eBay and posts the album for sale. In perhaps a matter of hours, people who want to buy the album are bidding

match.com®

COURTESY OF MATCH.COM

on it. eBay and the Internet lower the transaction costs of bringing buyer and seller together.

Or consider Match.com, an online dating service. When people date each other, an exchange of sorts is going on. Each person is effectively saying to the other, "I demand some of your time, which I hope you will supply to me."

One of the transaction costs of dating is actually finding a person to date. Match.com and the Internet, however, lower the transaction costs. The dating service is a little like eBay, in that you are offering to "sell" yourself. Instead of describing a Rolling Stones album, you describe yourself. Then, in a sense, people bid on you by getting in touch—and you bid on others.

What do money, eBay, and Match.com tell us about life? People want to trade with each other, and part of being able to trade is lowering the transaction costs. Money, eBay, and Match.com fill the bill.

M2

M2 is commonly referred to as the *broad definition of the money supply.* M2 is made up of M1 plus savings deposits (including money market deposit accounts), small-denomination time deposits, and money market mutual funds (retail).

$$
\begin{aligned}
M2 = M1 \\
&+ \text{Savings deposits (including money market deposit accounts)} \\
&+ \text{Small-denomination time deposits} \\
&+ \text{Money market mutual funds (retail)}
\end{aligned}
$$

Again, several components of M2 need to be defined:

- A savings deposit, sometimes called a *regular savings deposit,* is an interest-earning account at a commercial bank or thrift institution. (Thrift institutions include savings and loan associations, mutual savings banks, and credit unions.) Normally, checks cannot be written on savings deposits, and the funds in savings deposits can be withdrawn at any time without a penalty payment.

- A time deposit is an interest-earning deposit with a *specified maturity date.* Time deposits are subject to penalties for early withdrawal, that is, withdrawal before the maturity date. Small-denomination time deposits are less than $100,000.

- A money market deposit account (MMDA) is an interest-earning account at a bank or thrift institution, and usually a minimum balance is required. Most MMDAs offer limited check-writing privileges. For example, the owner of an MMDA might be

M2
M1 plus savings deposits (including money market deposit accounts) plus small-denomination time deposits plus money market mutual funds (retail).

Savings Deposit
An interest-earning account at a commercial bank or thrift institution. Normally, checks cannot be written on savings deposits, and the funds in a savings deposit can be withdrawn at any time without a penalty payment.

Time Deposit
An interest-earning deposit with a specified maturity date. Time deposits are subject to penalties for early withdrawal, that is, withdrawal before the maturity date. Small-denomination time deposits are less than $100,000.

Money Market Deposit Account (MMDA)
An interest-earning account at a bank or thrift institution, for which a minimum balance is usually required and most of which offer limited check-writing privileges.

Money Market Mutual Fund (MMMF)

An interest-earning account at a mutual fund company, for which a minimum balance is usually required and most of which offer limited check-writing privileges. Only retail MMMFs are part of M2.

able to write only a certain number of checks each month, and/or each check may have to be above a certain dollar amount (e.g., $500).

- A money market mutual fund (MMMF) is an interest-earning account at a *mutual fund company*. Usually, a minimum balance is required for an MMMF account, and most offer limited check-writing privileges. MMMFs held by large institutions are referred to as institutional MMMFs. MMMFs held by all others (e.g., by individuals) are referred to as retail MMMFs. *Only retail MMMFs are part of M2.*

In March 2010, M2 was $8,512 billion.

Where Do Credit Cards Fit In?

A credit card is commonly referred to as plastic money, but it is not money. A credit card is an instrument or a document that makes it easier for the holder to obtain a loan. When Tina Ridges hands the department store clerk her MasterCard or Visa, she is, in effect, spending someone else's money (which already existed). The department store submits the claim to the bank, the bank pays the department store, and then the bank bills the holder of its credit card. By using her credit card, Tina spends someone else's money, and she ultimately must repay her credit card debt with money. These transactions shift around the existing quantity of money among individuals and firms, but they do not change the total.

SELF-TEST

(Answers to Self-Test questions are in Answers to Self-Test Questions at the back of the book.)

1. Why (not how) did money evolve out of a barter economy?

2. If individuals remove funds from their checkable deposits and transfer them to their money market accounts, will M1 fall and M2 rise? Explain your answer.

3. How does money reduce the transaction costs of making trades?

HOW BANKING DEVELOPED

Just as money evolved, so did banking. This section discusses the origins of banking and sheds some light on and aids in understanding modern banking.

The Early Bankers

Our money today is easy to carry and transport, but it was not always so portable. For example, when money consisted principally of gold coins, carrying it about was neither easy nor safe. First, gold is heavy. Second, gold was not only inconvenient for customers to carry, but it was also inconvenient for merchants to accept; gold was heavy and unsafe to carry around. Third, a person transporting thousands of gold coins can easily draw the attention of thieves. Yet storing gold at home can also be risky. Most individuals therefore turned to their local goldsmiths for help because they had safe storage facilities. Goldsmiths were thus the first bankers. They took in other people's gold and stored it for them. To acknowledge that they held deposited gold, goldsmiths issued receipts, called *warehouse receipts*, to their customers.

Once people's confidence in the receipts was established, they used the receipts to make payments instead of using the gold itself. In time, the paper warehouse receipts circulated as money. For instance, if Franklin wanted to buy something from Mason that was priced at 10 gold pieces, he could simply give his warehouse receipt to Mason instead of going to the goldsmith, obtaining the gold, and then delivering it to Mason. For both Franklin and Mason, using the receipts was easier than exchanging the actual gold.

At this stage of banking, warehouse receipts were fully backed by gold; they simply represented gold in storage. Goldsmiths later began to recognize that, on an average day, few people redeemed their receipts for gold. Many individuals traded the receipts for goods

Economics on the Yellow Brick Road

I'll get you, my pretty.

—**Wicked Witch of the West in**
The Wizard of Oz

In 1893, the United States fell into economic depression. The stock market crashed, banks failed, workers were laid off, and many farmers lost their farms. Some people blamed the depression on the gold standard. They proposed that, instead of having only gold backing U.S. currency, the monetary standard should be bimetallic; that is, both gold and silver should back the currency. This change, they said, would lead to an increase in the money supply. Many people thought that, with more money in circulation, economic hard times would soon be a thing of the past.

One of the champions of silver was William Jennings Bryan, the Democratic candidate for the U.S. presidency in 1896. Bryan had established himself as a friend to the many Americans who had been hurt by the economic depression, especially farmers and industrial workers. Bryan's views were shared by L. Frank Baum, the author of *The Wonderful Wizard of Oz*, the book that was the basis for the 1939 movie, *The Wizard of Oz*.

Baum blamed the gold standard for the hardships faced by farmers and workers during the depression. Baum saw the farmer and the worker as the so-called common man, and he saw William Jennings Bryan as the best possible hope for the common man in this country.

Many people believe that Baum's most famous work, *The Wonderful Wizard of Oz*, is an allegory for the presidential election of 1896.[1] Some say that Dorothy, in the book and the movie, represents Bryan. Both Dorothy and Bryan were young (Bryan was a 36-year-old presidential candidate). Like the cyclone in the movie that transported Dorothy to

MGM/THE KOBAL COLLECTION

the Land of Oz, the delegates at the 1896 Democratic convention lifted Bryan into a new political world, the world of presidential politics.

As Dorothy begins her travels to the Emerald City (Washington, D.C.) with Toto (the Democratic party) to meet the Wizard of Oz, she travels down a yellow brick road (the gold standard). On her way, she meets the scarecrow (the farmer), the tin man (the industrial worker), and the cowardly lion, who some believe represents the Populist party of the time. (The Populist party was sometimes depicted as a lion in the political cartoons of the time. It was a cowardly lion in that, as some say, it did not have the courage to fight an independent campaign for the presidency in 1896.) The message is clear: Bryan, with the help of the Democratic and Populist parties and with the votes of the farmers and the industrial workers, will travel to Washington.

But then, when Dorothy and the others reach the Emerald City, they are denied their wishes, just as Bryan is denied the presidency. He loses the election to William McKinley.

But the story is not over. There is still the battle with the Wicked Witch of the West, who wears a golden cap (the gold standard). When the Wicked Witch sees Dorothy's silver shoes—they were changed to ruby in the movie—she desperately wants them for their magical quality. But she is not to get her way. Dorothy kills the Wicked Witch of the West. She then clicks her silver shoes together, and they take her back home, where all is right with the world.

---

1. This interpretation is based on "William Jennings Bryan on the Yellow Brick Road," by John Geer and Thomas Rochon, *Journal of American Culture* (Winter 1993) and "The Wizard of Oz: Parable on Populism," by Henry Littlefield, *American Quarterly* (1964).

and seldom requested the gold itself. In short, the receipts had become money, widely accepted for purposes of exchange.

Sensing opportunity, goldsmiths began to lend some of the stored gold, realizing that they could earn interest on the loans without defaulting on their pledge to redeem the warehouse receipts when presented. In most cases, however, the gold borrowers also preferred warehouse receipts to the actual gold. Thus the warehouse receipts came to represent a greater amount of gold than was actually on deposit. Consequently, the money supply increased, now measured in terms of gold and the paper warehouse receipts issued by the goldsmith-bankers.

Fractional Reserve Banking
A banking arrangement that allows banks to hold reserves equal to only a fraction of their deposit liabilities.

Federal Reserve System (the Fed)
The central bank of the United States.

Reserves
The sum of bank deposits at the Fed and vault cash.

Thus fractional reserve banking had begun. In a fractional reserve system, banks create money by holding on reserve only a fraction of the money deposited with them and lending the remainder. Our modern-day banking operates within such a system.

The Bank's Reserves and More

Many banks have an account with the Federal Reserve System (the Fed), the central bank of the United States. These accounts are very similar to the checking accounts that individuals have with a commercial bank. Economists refer to this account with the Fed as either a *reserve account* or *bank deposits at the Fed*. Banks also have currency or cash in their vaults—called vault cash—on the bank premises. The sum of (1) bank deposits at the Fed and (2) the bank's vault cash is known as reserves.

$$\text{Reserves} = \text{Bank deposits at the Fed} + \text{Vault cash}$$

For example, if a bank currently has $4 million in deposits at the Fed and $1 million in vault cash, it has $5 million in reserves.

THE REQUIRED RESERVE RATIO AND REQUIRED RESERVES The Fed mandates that member commercial banks must hold a certain fraction of their checkable deposits in *reserve form*. In other words, that fraction of checkable deposits must be in the form of bank deposits at the Fed and/or vault cash because the sum of these two accounts equals reserves.

Required Reserve Ratio (r)
A percentage of each dollar deposited that must be held in reserve form (specifically, as bank deposits at the Fed or vault cash).

Required Reserves
The minimum dollar amount of reserves a bank must hold against its checkable deposits, as mandated by the Fed.

Reserve Requirement
The Fed rule that specifies the amount of reserves a bank must hold to back up deposits.

Excess Reserves
Any reserves held beyond the required amount; the difference between (total) reserves and required reserves.

The fraction of checkable deposits that banks must hold in reserve form is called the required reserve ratio (r). The dollar amount of those deposits is called required reserves, and the rule specifying the amount of reserves that a bank must hold to back up deposits is the reserve requirement. To find the required reserves for a given bank, multiply the required reserve ratio by checkable deposits (in the bank):

$$\text{Required reserves} = r \times \text{Checkable deposits}$$

For example, assume that customers have deposited $40 million in a neighborhood bank and that the Fed has set the required reserve ratio at 1/10 or 10 percent. Required reserves for the bank equal $4 million (0.10 × $40 million = $4 million).

EXCESS RESERVES The difference between a bank's (total) reserves and its required reserves is its excess reserves:

$$\text{Excess reserves} = \text{Reserves} - \text{Required reserves}$$

For example, if the bank's (total) reserves are $5 million and its required reserves are $4 million, then it holds excess reserves of $1 million.

Note: Banks can use excess reserves to make loans. Before late 2008, the Fed did not pay interest on any reserves (required or excess); so banks had a monetary incentive to create loans with their excess reserves. That incentive was lessened when the Fed began paying interest on reserves in late 2008.

SELF-TEST

1. A bank reduces its deposits at the Fed by $5 million and increases its vault cash by $5 million. What happens to the bank's reserves?

2. If a bank has $87 million in checkable deposits, and it is required to hold $6 million in reserves (required reserves = $6 million), what is the required reserve ratio equal to?

3. If excess reserves are $4 million and (total) reserves are $6 million, what do required reserves and checkable deposits equal? Assume the required reserve ratio is 8 percent.

THE FINANCIAL SYSTEM

A financial system is essentially a means of getting people with surplus funds together with people who have a shortage of funds. Stated differently, it is a means of getting savers and borrowers together.

Why is getting lenders and borrowers together important? The short answer is getting them together is a way to put good ideas into action. Suppose you have saved funds that you want to lend. Elsewhere, someone has a shortage of funds but an idea for a new business venture. That person doesn't have the necessary funds to launch his new business venture. He needs to find people like you—people with funds to lend—who wouldn't mind trading him your funds now in return for his making interest payments to you later.

Thus an economy that can get saved funds to borrowers can not only benefit the lenders but the borrowers too. And it can also benefit others. If the borrower really does have a good idea for a new business venture, future customers will benefit when the business is up and running. Maybe the firm will produce something that many thousands of others want to buy.

Direct and Indirect Finance

Lenders can get together with borrowers directly or indirectly; that is, there are two types of finance: direct and indirect. In direct finance, the lenders and borrowers come together in a market setting, such as the bond market. In the bond market, people who want to borrow funds issue bonds. For example, company A might issue a bond that promises to pay an interest rate of 10 percent annually for the next 10 years. A person with funds to lend might then buy that bond for a particular price. The buying and selling in a bond market are simply lending and borrowing. The buyer of the bond is the lender, and the seller of the bond is the borrower.

In indirect finance, lenders and borrowers go through a financial intermediary, which takes in funds from people who want to save and then lends the funds to people who want to borrow. For example, a commercial bank is a financial intermediary, doing business with both savers and borrowers. Through one door the savers come in, looking for a place to deposit their funds and earn regular interest payments. Through another door come the borrowers, seeking loans on which they will pay interest. The bank, or the financial intermediary, ends up channeling the saved funds to borrowers.

Direct Finance
Borrowers and lenders come together in a market setting, such as in the bond market.

Indirect Finance
Funds are loaned and borrowed through a financial intermediary.

Financial Intermediary
A financial intermediary transfers funds from those who want to lend funds to those who want to borrow them.

Adverse Selection and Moral Hazard Problems

When it comes to lending and borrowing, both adverse selection and moral hazards can arise. Both are the result of asymmetric information. Asymmetric information relates to one side of a transaction having information that the other side does not have. Suppose Ursula is going to sell her house. As the seller of the house, she has more information about the house than potential buyers. Ursula knows whether the house has plumbing problems, cracks in the foundation, and so on. Potential buyers do not.

The effect of asymmetric information can be either an adverse selection problem or a moral hazard problem. The adverse selection problem occurs *before* the loan is made, and the moral hazard problem occurs *afterward*.

Asymmetric Information
Relates to an economic agent on one side of a transaction having information that an economic agent on the other side of the transaction does not have.

BEFORE THE LOAN IS MADE An adverse selection problem occurs when the parties on one side of the market, having information not known to others, self-select in a way that adversely affects the parties on the other side of the market. Think of it this way: Two people want a loan. One person is a good credit risk, and the other is a bad credit risk. The person who is the bad credit risk is the person more likely to ask for the loan.

Suppose two people, Steven and Olivia, want to borrow $10,000, and Jason has $10,000 to lend. Olivia wants to borrow the $10,000 to buy a piece of equipment for her small business. She plans to pay back the loan, and she takes her loan commitments very seriously. Steven wants to borrow the $10,000 so that he can go to Las Vegas and play roulette.

Adverse Selection
A phenomenon that occurs when the parties on one side of the market, who have information not known to others, self-select in a way that adversely affects the parties on the other side of the market.

He will pay back the loan only if he scores big in Las Vegas. He is not the type of person who takes his loan commitments seriously. Who is more likely to ask Jason for the loan, Steven or Olivia? Steven is because he knows that he will pay back the loan only if he wins big in Las Vegas; he sees a loan as essentially "free money." Heads, Steven wins; tails, Jason loses.

Now if Jason gives a little thought to his lending activities, he may realize that there are borrowers like Steven in the world. Ideally, Jason wants to lend only to the Olivias of the world, but Jason can't always tell who is an Olivia and who is a Steven. Olivia will tell Jason the truth about what she wants to do with the loan, and she is likely to pay back the loan. Steven, on the other hand, may lie to Jason about what he plans to do with the loan, and he is not as likely to pay back the loan as Olivia.

If Jason can't tell the Olivias from the Stevens, what can he do? He might just decide not to give a loan to anyone. In other words, his inability to solve the adverse selection problem (that is, to tell the good risks from the bad risks) may be enough for him to decide not to lend to anyone.

At this point, a financial intermediary can help. A financial intermediary, such as a bank, does not require Jason to worry about who will and who will not pay back a loan. Jason needs simply to turn over his saved funds to the bank, in return for the bank's promise to pay him a 5 percent interest rate per year. Then, the bank takes on the responsibility of trying to separate the Olivias from the Stevens. The bank will run a credit check on everyone (the Olivias and Stevens alike); the bank will collect information on who has a job and who doesn't; the bank will ask the borrower to put up some collateral on the loan; and so on. In other words, the bank's job is to solve the adverse selection problem.

Moral Hazard

A condition that exists when one party to a transaction changes his or her behavior in a way that is hidden from and costly to the other party.

AFTER THE LOAN IS MADE The moral hazard problem exists when one party to a transaction changes his or her behavior in a way that is hidden from and costly to the other party. Suppose you want to lend some saved funds. You give Tracy a $5,000 loan because she promised you that she was going to use the funds to help her get through college. Instead, once Tracy receives the $5,000, she decides to use the funds to buy some clothes and take a vacation to St. Thomas in the Caribbean.

Because of such potential moral hazard problems, you might decide to cut back on granting loans. You want to protect yourself from borrowers who do things that are costly to you. Again, a financial intermediary has a role to play. A financial intermediary, such as a bank, might try to solve the moral hazard problem by specifying that a loan can only be used for a particular purpose (e.g., paying for college). It might require the borrower to provide regular information on and evidence of how the borrowed funds are being used, giving out the loan in installments ($1,000 this month, $1,000 next month), and so on.

A Thought Experiment: No Financial Intermediaries

If financial intermediaries did not exist, how would life be different? Would there be as much lending and borrowing activity in a world? Because adverse selection and moral hazard problems reduce the amount of lending (and therefore borrowing), and because financial intermediaries help to solve these two problems, then there would be more lending and borrowing in a world with financial intermediaries than in one without them.

The next question is whether having more lending and borrowing is preferable to having less. To answer this question, recall that lending and borrowing is a process of channeling funds to those who can use those funds to start businesses, to come up with new products, to establish new and better production techniques, and to do other beneficial things. So lending and borrowing are not only beneficial to the lender and the borrower, but to others too. Your current material standard of living would probably not be as high as it is had you not lived in a country with substantial borrowing and lending.

The FDIC and Intended and Unintended Effects

In Chapter 1, we talked about the unintended consequences of actions. For example, a policy maker might undertake policy A because she wants effect X. She gets X, but she also gets the unintended effect Y, which she doesn't want.

As an example, in 1934, the federal government, through the Federal Deposit Insurance Corporation (FDIC), started insuring deposits in banks. Today, the FDIC insures bank depositors up to $250,00. If you have any dollar amount in a bank between $1 and $250,00 and that bank fails (goes out of business), you are guaranteed to get your money back. You will not suffer a loss.

The intended effect of instituting the FDIC and guaranteeing depositors up to $250,000 is to reduce the probability of a run on a bank and a bank panic. A run on a bank is exactly what it sounds like: individuals "run" to the bank to withdraw their funds because they think the bank might fail. A bank panic occurs when a run on one bank leads to runs on other banks. However, if you know you will get your money back, you have less reason to run to the bank and withdraw your funds. In turn, the bank isn't pushed into a position where it can't pay back its depositors' money.

The unintended effect of the FDIC guarantee is that depositors have less incentive to monitor the bank's activities and the bank has an increased incentive to take on riskier loans than it would if the FDIC did not exist.

Second, lending and borrowing allow people to consume earlier in life than they would otherwise be able to. To illustrate, Maria is 26 years old and wants to buy a condominium. Condos in her area sell for about $300,000, but Maria does not have $300,000; she has only $20,000. Without lending and borrowing, Maria would have to do without the condo until she can save $300,000. But with borrowing and lending, Maria can make a $20,000 down payment on the condo and borrow the remaining $280,000. She can begin living in the condo many years earlier than would otherwise be possible.

In conclusion, lending and borrowing not only provide the financing for new businesses and the production of new products, production techniques, and so on, but they also permit individuals to enjoy the benefits of certain goods and services for a greater number of years than would be possible without lending and borrowing. Because someone will lend her $280,000, Maria gets to enjoy the benefits of her condo for many additional years.

The Bank's Balance Sheet

We can learn a lot about banks by looking at a bank's balance sheet, which lists the bank's assets and liabilities. An asset is anything of value that the bank owns or has claim to. A liability is anything that the bank owes to someone else. A few examples of a bank's assets are the *reserves* the bank holds, any loans the bank has made to borrowers, and any securities the bank might own. A few examples of a bank's liabilities are the checkable deposits it holds for its customers, any nontransaction deposits (such as small-denomination time deposits), and any loans the bank has taken out (for example, a loan the bank might have received from the Fed). Exhibit 1 shows a simplified but typical balance sheet for a bank.

A Bank's Business: Turning Liabilities into Assets

A bank's business is to turn its liabilities into assets. Suppose you open up a checkable deposit account with bank A and deposit $10,000 into the account. Your checkable deposit is a liability for the bank. The balance in the checkable deposit account is what the bank *owes* you. The bank then turns the bulk of the funds in your checkable deposit account into an asset. Specifically, the bank might use the bulk of those funds to grant a

Balance Sheet
A record of the assets and liabilities of a bank.

Asset
Anything of value that is owned or that one has claim to.

Liability
Anything that is owed to someone else.

The Financial Crisis, Risky Loans, and Bank Insolvency

At the end of 2008 and throughout 2009, many banks found themselves holding unpaid loans, many of them mortgage loans to home buyers. To understand what was happening at this time, compare two settings.

In setting 1, a person wants to buy a house that is priced at $500,000. The person is asked to make a 20 percent down payment ($100,000) to take out a mortgage loan for the balance ($400,000). Time passes, and the person who took out the loan can't make the monthly payments. What course of action does he have? As long as the house's price hasn't fallen below $400,000, he can sell the property and repay the balance of the loan. In other words, suppose the price of the house has fallen to $425,000. Our house owner and mortgage loan borrower can sell the house for $425,000 and repay the $400,000 loan, leaving him with $25,000. Obviously, the mortgage borrower has ended up losing some of his $100,000 down payment.

In setting 2, a person wants to buy a house that is priced at $500,000. This time, though, the person is not asked for a down payment. The bank gives the buyer a mortgage loan for the entire price of the house: a $500,000 loan. Again, suppose that the person who took out the loan has a hard time making her monthly payments. What now? Can she sell the house and repay the loan? Yes, as long as the price of the house is still $500,000 (ignoring real estate fees and closing costs). But what if

the price of the house has fallen to $425,000. The person who bought the house and took out the $500,000 loan may simply walk away from the house and the loan. The house reverts to the bank, but the bank can't sell the house for a high enough price to recover its loan amount. It sells the house for $425,000 and takes a $75,000 loss on the mortgage loan of $500,000.

Setting 1 describes the state of the mortgage loan business in the 1970s, 1980s, and early 1990s. Setting 2 describes the state of the mortgage loan business in the late 1990s and the early-to-mid 2000s. Why banks moved from one setting to the other is a long story that we will speak about in a later chapter. For now, we are interested in how setting 2 changes things for the bank, especially with respect to the prospects of insolvency.

The peak of the housing boom (rising home prices) in the United States came in mid-2006. Since then, house prices have fallen. The decline in house prices, combined with the percentage of homeowners who can't make their monthly house payments, has the effect of loans going bad for banks. Some of the loans (which, in hindsight, turned out to be risky) were not paid off in full for one reason or another. As a result, the assets of the banks declined, and consequently so did the bank's capital (its net worth). Banks found themselves either falling over, or close to the edge, of the insolvency cliff.

Exhibit 1

A Bank's Balance Sheet

Here we show a bank's balance sheet. On the left-hand side are assets (what others owe to the bank): reserves (equal to bank deposits at the Fed plus vault cash), any loans it has made to others (e.g., a car loan the bank gave to someone), and any securities it owns. On the right-hand side are liabilities (what the bank owes to others): checkable deposits (held for its customers), nontransaction deposits (e.g., small-denomination time deposits), and borrowings of the banks (i.e., any loans the banks may have taken out). Also, it is customary to show bank capital (or net worth) -- which is the difference between assets and liabilities -- on the right-hand side of the balance sheet. In this balance sheet, assets are $110 million and liabilities are $100 million; so bank capital (or net worth) is $10 million.

Assets ($ millions)		Liabilities ($ millions)	
Reserves	10	Checkable deposits	50
Loans	90	Nontransaction deposits (e.g., small-denomination time deposits)	50
Securities	10	Borrowings	0
		Bank Capital (net worth)	10

loan to someone. So, therefore, a bank wants liabilities because liabilities are its sources of funds—the seeds, if you will—for growing its assets.

The difference between a bank's assets and liabilities constitutes the bank's capital, or its net worth:

$$\text{Bank capital (or net worth)} = \text{Assets} - \text{Liabilities}$$

For example, if a bank has $120 million in assets and $112 million in liabilities, its net worth (or the bank's capital) is equal to $8 million. Typically, a bank's capital is recorded on the right-hand side of its balance sheet, as shown in Exhibit 1.

The bank's capital can be viewed as a cushion against insolvency, which exists when a bank's liabilities are greater than its assets. An insolvent bank has failed and can be shut down.

$$\text{Insolvency} \rightarrow \text{Liabilities} > \text{Assets}$$

The larger the bank's capital, the bigger the cushion against bank failure or insolvency; the smaller the bank's capital, the smaller the cushion against bank failure or insolvency.

Insolvency
A condition in which one's liabilities are greater than one's assets.

SELF-TEST

1. Jack promises Samantha that he will pay for any expenses she has on her trip beyond $1,000. Does this create an adverse selection or moral hazard problem? Explain your answer.

2. Bank A finds that many of the loans it extended to individuals are not being paid back. How do the defaults affect bank A's capital or net worth?

3. What do financial intermediaries do?

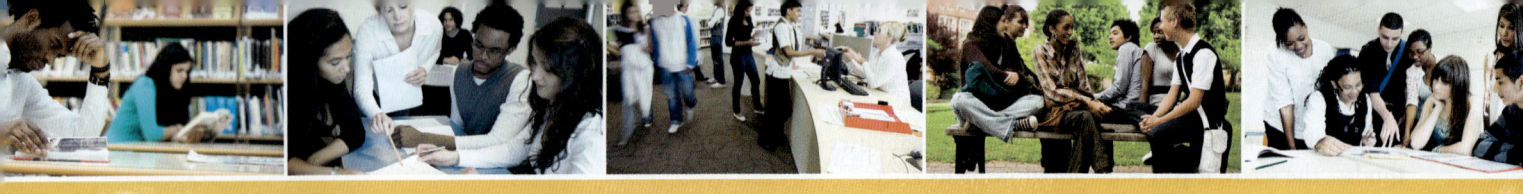

OFFICE HOURS

"I Thought Money Had to Be Backed by Gold to Have Value"

STUDENT:

We know that M1 is equal to currency held outside banks plus checkable deposits plus traveler's checks. None of these components of the money supply are backed by gold. But don't they have to be backed by gold before they can have any value?

INSTRUCTOR:

Your question essentially tries to identify that "thing" that gives money value. So let's suppose that paper money were backed by gold. In other words, if you take $100 in paper money, and turn it in to the federal government, it would give you in return $100 worth of gold. At first glance, you might say that paper money has value because it is backed by gold. But then the question becomes what gives gold value? What is gold backed by?

STUDENT:

Nothing backs up gold. For example, gold isn't backed by copper or anything else.

INSTRUCTOR:

Our point is a simple one: it is a myth that paper money has to be backed by a commodity—such as gold—before it can have value. Our paper money has value because of its *general acceptability*. Specifically, you accept a dollar bill in payment for your goods and services because you know others will accept the dollar bill in payment. To illustrate, suppose our paper money were not generally accepted. Suppose one day that the supermarket clerk would not accept the paper dollars you offered as payment for groceries. Suppose the plumber and the gas station attendant would not take your paper

dollars for fixing your kitchen drain and for servicing your car. In such a case, would you be as likely to accept paper dollars in exchange for what you sell? Probably not. You accept paper dollars because you know that other people will accept them when you spend them. Money has value to people because it is widely accepted in exchange for other valuable goods.

POINTS TO REMEMBER

1. It is a myth that paper money has to be backed by a commodity (such as gold) before it can have value.
2. General acceptability gives money value.

CHAPTER SUMMARY

WHAT MONEY IS

- Money is any good that is widely accepted for purposes of exchange and in the repayment of debts.
- Money serves as a medium of exchange, a unit of account, and a store of value.
- Money evolved out of a barter economy as traders attempted to make exchange easier. A few goods that have been used as money are gold, silver, copper, cattle, rocks, and shells.
- Our money today has value because of its general acceptability.

THE MONEY SUPPLY

- M1 includes currency held outside banks, checkable deposits, and traveler's checks.
- M2 includes M1, savings deposits (including money market deposit accounts), small-denomination time deposits, and money market mutual funds (retail).
- Credit cards are not money. When a credit card is used to make a purchase, a liability is incurred. This is not the case when money is used to make a purchase.

RESERVES, REQUIRED AND EXCESS

- Reserves equal bank deposits at the Fed plus vault cash. The dollar amount of reserves a bank must hold is equal to the required reserve ratio times its checkable deposits: Required reserves = $r \times$ Checkable deposits, where r = required reserve ratio. Excess

reserves is the difference between total reserves and required reserves: Excess reserves = Reserves − Required reserves.

THE FINANCIAL SYSTEM

- A financial system is a means of getting people with surplus funds (with funds to lend) together with people who have a shortage of funds (who want to borrow funds).
- Asymmetric information relates to one side of a transaction having information that the other side of the transaction does not. The two types of asymmetric information problems are adverse selection and moral hazard.
- Adverse selection is a phenomenon that occurs when the parties on one side of the market, who have information not known to others, self-select in a way that adversely affects the parties on the other side of the market.
- Moral hazard is the condition that exists when one party to a transaction changes his or her behavior in a way that is hidden from and costly to the other party.

A BANK'S BALANCE SHEET

- A bank's balance sheet records its assets and liabilities.
- A bank's business is to turn its liabilities into assets.
- Bank capital, or net worth, is the difference between a bank's assets and its liabilities. Bank capital (net worth) = Assets − Liabilities.
- A bank is insolvent if its liabilities are greater than its assets.

KEY TERMS AND CONCEPTS

Money	Checkable Deposits	Federal Reserve System	Financial Intermediary
Barter	M2	(the Fed)	Asymmetric Information
Medium of Exchange	Savings Deposit	Reserves	Adverse Selection
Unit of Account	Time Deposit	Required Reserve Ratio (r)	Moral Hazard
Store of Value	Money Market Deposit	Required Reserves	Balance Sheet
Double Coincidence of Wants	Account (MMDA)	Reserve Requirement	Asset
M1	Money Market Mutual	Excess Reserves	Liability
Currency	Fund (MMMF)	Direct Finance	Insolvency
Federal Reserve Notes	Fractional Reserve Banking	Indirect Finance	

QUESTIONS AND PROBLEMS

1. Explain the difference between a bank's loans and its borrowings.
2. Define the following:
   a. Time deposit

   b. Money market mutual fund
   c. Money market deposit account
   d. Fractional reserve banking
   e. Reserves

3. Explain how financial intermediaries help to solve adverse selection and moral hazard problems when it comes to lending and borrowing.

4. Why isn't a credit card money?

5. Identify each of the following as either an adverse selection or a moral hazard problem:

   a. Poor drivers apply for car insurance more than good drivers.

   b. The federal government promises to help banks that get into financial problems.

   c. The federal government insures checkable deposits (promises to repay the holder of the checkable deposit if the bank fails).

6. What is a financial system, and why would a country with a well-developed and fully functionally financial system be better off than a country without it?

7. Explain the process by which goldsmiths could increase the money supply.

8. If you were on an island with 10 other people and there were no money, do you think money would emerge on the scene? Why or why not?

9. "Money is a means of lowering the transaction costs of making exchanges." Do you agree or disagree? Explain your answer.

10. "People in a barter economy came up with the idea of money because they wanted to do something to make society better off." Do you agree or disagree with this statement? Explain your answer.

11. Explain why gold backing is not necessary to give paper money value.

12. Does inflation, which is an increase in the price level, affect the three functions of money? If so, how?

13. Money makes trade easier. Would having a money supply twice as large as it is currently make trade twice as easy? Would having a money supply half its current size make trade half as easy?

14. Suppose the value of the dollar declines relative to other currencies. How does the decline affect the three functions of money?

15. "A barter economy would have very few comedians." Do you agree or disagree with this statement? Explain your answer.

16. "How much money did you make last year?" What is wrong with that statement?

17. Can M1 fall as M2 rises? Can M1 rise without M2 rising too? Explain your answers.

WORKING WITH NUMBERS AND GRAPHS

1. Checkable deposits are $50 million, and required reserves are $4 million. What is the required reserve ratio?

2. The required reserve ratio is 9 percent, required reserves are $10 million, and (total) reserves are $50 million. What do excess reserves equal? What do checkable deposits equal?

3. A bank's assets are $90 million, and its liabilities are $71 million. Its assets increase by 10 percent, and its liabilities increase by 6 percent. What is the *percentage change* in the bank's capital, or net worth?

4. A bank currently has $100 million checkable deposits, $4 million in reserves, and $8 million in securities. If the required reserve ratio is 10 percent, is the bank meeting its legal reserve requirements? Explain.

CHAPTER 13

THE FEDERAL RESERVE SYSTEM

©LEE SNIDER/PHOTOIMAGES/CORBIS

Introduction Tourists in Washington, D.C., usually visit the White House, the Capitol building, and the Supreme Court building, in which major decisions are made that affect peoples' lives. Such decisions affecting peoples' lives are also made in another building in Washington, D.C., but tourists rarely visit it: the Federal Reserve building. In this building, the Board of Governors of the Federal Reserve System and the members of the Federal Open Market Committee determine U.S. monetary policy. We provide you with many of the details of the Federal Reserve System in this chapter.

THE STRUCTURE AND FUNCTIONS OF THE FEDERAL RESERVE SYSTEM (THE FED)

The Federal Reserve System is the central bank of the United States. Other nations have central banks, such as the Bank of Sweden, the Bank of England, the Banque de France, the Bank of Japan, the Deutsche Bundesbank, and the like.

The Structure of the Fed

The Federal Reserve System came into existence with the Federal Reserve Act of 1913 and began operations in November 1914. The act divided the country into Federal Reserve Districts. As Exhibit 1 shows, there are 12 districts, each with a Federal Reserve Bank and its own president.

Within the Fed, a seven-member Board of Governors coordinates and controls the activities of the Federal Reserve System. The board members serve 14-year terms and are appointed by the president with U.S. Senate approval. To limit political influence on Fed policy, the terms of the governors are staggered—with one new appointment every other year—so that a president cannot "pack" the board. The president also designates one member as chairman of the board for a four-year term.

The major policy-making group in the Fed is the Federal Open Market Committee (FOMC). Authority to conduct open market operations—the buying and selling of government securities—rests with the FOMC (more on open market operations later in the

Board of Governors
The governing body of the Federal Reserve System.

Federal Open Market Committee (FOMC)
The 12-member policy-making group in the Fed. The committee has the authority to conduct open market operations.

Open Market Operations
The buying and selling of government securities by the Fed.

EXHIBIT 1

Federal Reserve Districts and Federal Reserve Bank Locations

The boundaries of the Federal Reserve Districts, the cities in which a Federal Reserve Bank is located, and the location of the Board of Governors (Washington, D.C.) are all noted on the map.

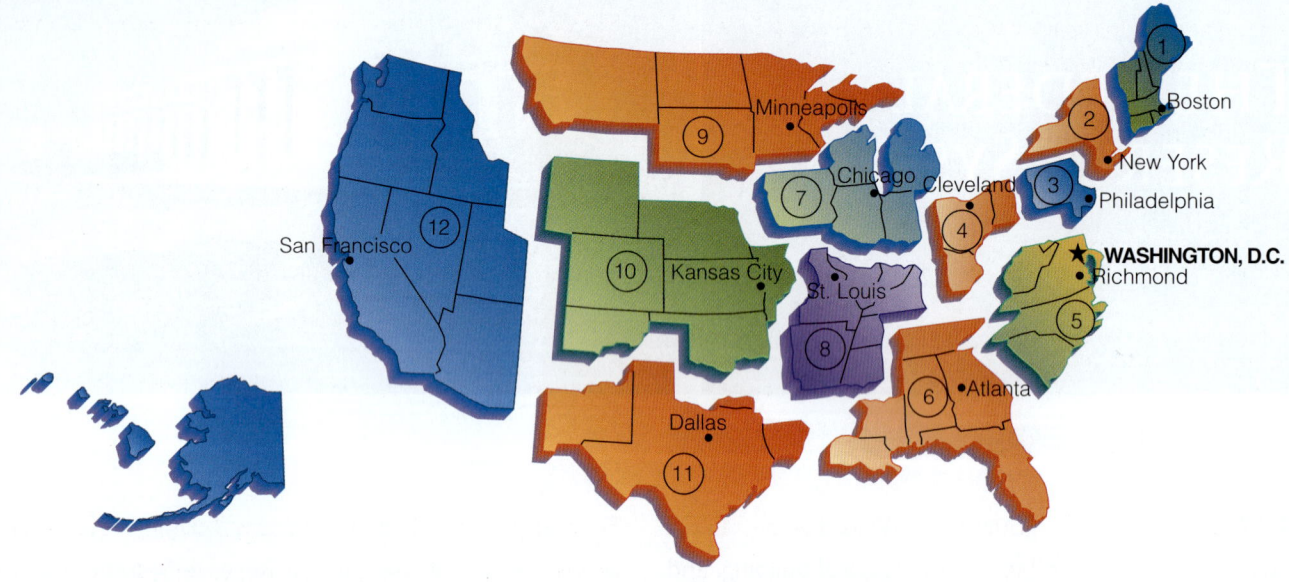

chapter). The FOMC has 12 members: the seven-member Board of Governors and five Federal Reserve District Bank presidents. The president of the Federal Reserve Bank of New York holds a permanent seat on the FOMC because a large amount of financial activity takes place in New York City and because the New York Fed is responsible for executing open market operations. The other four positions are rotated among the Federal Reserve District Bank presidents.

The most important responsibility of the Fed is to conduct monetary policy, or control the money supply. Monetary policy consists of changes in the money supply that are intended to achieve stated macroeconomic goals. More specifically, *expansionary monetary policy* aims to increase the money supply, and *contractionary monetary policy* aims to decrease it. The Fed has tools at its disposal to both increase and decrease the money supply. In a later chapter, we will discuss monetary policy in detail and show how, under certain conditions, it can remove an economy from both recessionary and inflationary gaps.

Monetary Policy

Changes in the money supply or in the rate of change of the money supply, intended to achieve stated macroeconomic goals.

Functions of the Fed

The Fed has eight major responsibilities or functions:

1. *Controlling the money supply.* A full explanation of how the Fed plays this role comes later in the chapter.

2. *Supplying the economy with paper money (Federal Reserve notes).* The Federal Reserve Banks have Federal Reserve notes on hand to meet the demands of the banks and the public. During the Christmas season, for example, more people withdraw larger-than-usual amounts of $1, $5, $20, $50, and $100 notes from banks. Needing to replenish their vault cash, banks turn to their Federal Reserve Banks, which meet cash needs by

economics 24/7

Inside an FOMC Meeting

The major policy-making group in the Federal Reserve System is the Federal Open Market Committee (FOMC), which, to a large degree, makes decisions about monetary policy. The FOMC meets eight times a year, each time on a Tuesday. The meeting is held in the board room of the Federal Reserve Building. The following events occur at a typical FOMC meeting.

8:00 a.m.

The board room is swept for electronic bugs.

8:45–9:00 a.m.

People begin to arrive for the meeting. In addition to the 12 members of the FOMC, about 37 other people will be present.

8:59 a.m.

The chairman of the Board of Governors of the Federal Reserve System walks through the door that connects his office to the board room and takes his place at the table.

9:00 a.m.

The FOMC meeting commences. The first agenda item is a presentation by the manager of the System Open Market Account at the Federal Reserve Bank of New York. He discusses the financial and foreign exchange markets and provides certain details about open market operations.

A Little Later …

The director of research and statistics at the Federal Reserve Board presents the forecast of the U.S. economy. The forecast has previously been circulated to the FOMC members. The latest economic data are reviewed and discussed.

A Little Later …

The 12 members of the FOMC present their views of local and national economic conditions.

A Little Later …

The director of monetary affairs presents policy options. These policy options have been previously circulated. The chairman of the Board of Governors gives his opinion of the economy and of the policy options.

A Little Later …

A general discussion among all the members of the FOMC takes place. At issue is the state of the U.S. economy and current policy options. After the discussion, the chairman summarizes his sense of the policy options. Then the members vote on the options. The chair votes first, the vice chair votes second, and the remaining FOMC members vote in alphabetical order.

A Little Later …

The FOMC discusses the wording of the announcement it will make regarding its decision.

Between 11:30 a.m. and 1:30 p.m.

The meeting usually adjourns.

2:15 p.m.

The decision of the FOMC is released to the public.

©JAY MARTIN/BLOOMBERG NEWS/LANDOV

---

issuing more paper money (acting as passive suppliers of paper money). The money is actually printed at the Bureau of Engraving and Printing in Washington, D.C., but it is issued to commercial banks by the 12 Federal Reserve Banks.

3. *Providing check-clearing services.* When someone in San Diego writes a check to a person in Los Angeles, what happens to the check? The process by which funds change hands when checks are written is called the *check-clearing process.* That process is summarized in Exhibit 2.

   a. Harry Saito writes a $1,000 check on his San Diego bank account and sends it to Ursula Pevins in Los Angeles.

EXHIBIT 2

The Check-Clearing Process

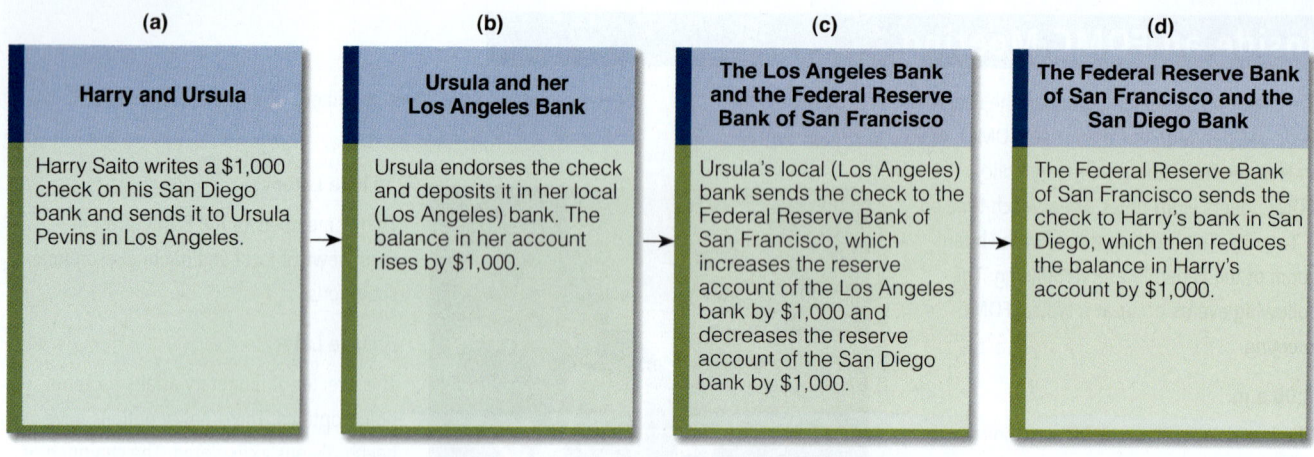

(a)	(b)	(c)	(d)
Harry and Ursula	**Ursula and her Los Angeles Bank**	**The Los Angeles Bank and the Federal Reserve Bank of San Francisco**	**The Federal Reserve Bank of San Francisco and the San Diego Bank**
Harry Saito writes a $1,000 check on his San Diego bank and sends it to Ursula Pevins in Los Angeles.	Ursula endorses the check and deposits it in her local (Los Angeles) bank. The balance in her account rises by $1,000.	Ursula's local (Los Angeles) bank sends the check to the Federal Reserve Bank of San Francisco, which increases the reserve account of the Los Angeles bank by $1,000 and decreases the reserve account of the San Diego bank by $1,000.	The Federal Reserve Bank of San Francisco sends the check to Harry's bank in San Diego, which then reduces the balance in Harry's account by $1,000.

b. Ursula takes the check to her local bank, endorses it, and deposits it in her checking account. The balance in her account rises by $1,000.

c. Ursula's Los Angeles bank sends the check to its Federal Reserve District Bank, located in San Francisco. The Federal Reserve Bank of San Francisco increases the reserve account of the Los Angeles bank by $1,000 and decreases the reserve account of the San Diego bank by $1,000.

d. The Federal Reserve Bank of San Francisco sends the check to Harry's bank in San Diego, which then reduces the balance in Harry's checking account by $1,000. Harry's bank in San Diego either keeps the check on record or sends it to Harry with his monthly bank statement.

4. *Holding depository institutions' reserves.* As explained in the last chapter, banks are required to keep reserves against customer deposits either in their vaults or in reserve accounts at the Fed. These accounts are maintained by the 12 Federal Reserve Banks for member banks in their respective districts.

5. *Supervising member banks.* Without warning, the Fed can examine the books of member commercial banks to assess the nature of the loans the banks have made, monitor compliance with bank regulations, check the accuracy of bank records, and so on. If the Fed finds that a bank has not been maintaining established banking standards, it can pressure the institution to do so.

6. *Serving as the government's banker.* The federal government collects and spends large sums of money. As a result, it needs a checking account for many of the same reasons an individual does. Its primary checking account is with the Fed, which is the government's banker.

7. *Serving as the lender of last resort.* A traditional function of a central bank is to serve as the lender of last resort for banks suffering cash management, or liquidity, problems.

U.S. Treasury Securities
Bonds and bond-like securities issued by the U.S. Treasury when it borrows.

8. *Handling the sale of U.S. Treasury securities (auctions).* U.S. Treasury securities (bills, notes, and bonds) are sold to raise funds to pay the government's bills. The Federal Reserve District Banks receive the bids for these securities and process them in time for weekly auctions.

Some History of the Fed

Slightly before the passage of the Federal Reserve Act in 1913, there was disagreement about how many districts and banks there should be. Many people thought there should be as few banks as possible—6 to 8—because concentrating activities in only a few cities would enhance efficiency and ease of operation. The Secretary of State at the time, William Jennings Bryan, wanted 50 district banks. He called for a "branch at every major crossroad." It was to be neither 6 nor 50; instead, there was a compromise. Section 2 of the Federal Reserve Act states that "not less than eight nor more than twelve cities" would be designated as Federal Reserve cities.

After the number of cities was determined to be 8 to 12, a commission was set up to identify both the boundaries of the Federal Reserve Districts and the locations of the district banks. The commission was composed of the Comptroller of the Currency, the Secretary of the Treasury, and the Secretary of Agriculture. They had to choose from among the 37 cities that had applied to be locations of a district bank. The commission settled on a 12-bank, 12-city plan. It decided the boundaries of the districts on the basis of trade. In other words, the commission decided the boundaries should include cities or towns that traded the most with each other. If the residents of cities X and Y traded a lot with each other but the residents of city Z did not trade much with the residents of cities X and Y, then cities X and Y should be included in the same district but Z should not. Instead, city Z should be part of the district that included cities with which it traded.

Some commercial banks protested both the number of district banks and the boundaries decided on by the committee. These banks filed petitions for review of the plan with the Federal Reserve Board, thought to be the only group that could alter the plan.[1]

The petitions for review are said to have rekindled the debate about the actual number of district cities. Three members of the Federal Reserve Board wanted to reduce the number of district banks because they thought that one-half of the banks were stronger than the other half were, and they wanted all banks to be of equal strength. Three other members of the Board wanted to stay with the original plan of 12 district banks. This left one member of the Board to break the tie. It looked as though that person's vote was going to be cast for a reduction in the number of district banks. At that point, one of the supporters of the original 12-bank plan went to the Attorney General of the United States and asked for an opinion stating that the Board did not have the authority to alter the original plan. The Attorney General gave that opinion. The Board, afraid of attracting any negative publicity by disagreeing and challenging the opinion, accepted it.

---

1. Before there was a Board of Governors of the Federal Reserve System, there was the Federal Reserve Board. The Banking Act of 1935, approved on August 23, 1935, changed the name of the Federal Reserve Board to the Board of Governors of the Federal Reserve System.

Common Misconceptions About the U.S. Treasury and the Fed

Some persons confuse the U.S. Treasury with the Fed. They mistakenly believe that the U.S. Treasury does some of the things that the Fed does. However, there are major differences between the Treasury and the Fed.

- The U.S. Treasury is a budgetary agency; the Fed is a monetary agency.

- When the federal government spends funds, the Treasury collects the taxes and borrows the funds needed to pay suppliers and others. In short, the Treasury has an obligation to manage the financial affairs of the federal government. Except for coins, the Treasury does not issue money. It cannot create money out of thin air as the Fed can. (We will soon explain exactly how the Fed does this.)

- The Fed is principally concerned with the availability of money and credit for the entire economy. It does not issue Treasury securities. It does not have an obligation to meet the financial needs of the federal government. Its responsibility is to provide a stable monetary framework for the economy.

(Answers to Self-Test questions are in Answers to Self-Test Questions at the back of the book.)

1. The president of which Federal Reserve District Bank holds a permanent seat on the Federal Open Market Committee (FOMC)?

2. What is the most important responsibility of the Fed?

3. "The Fed acts as lender of last resort." What does that statement mean?

THE MONEY SUPPLY EXPANSION PROCESS

This section describes the important money supply process, specifically, how the Fed can increase and decrease the money supply. Before we begin, we offer a quick review of reserves, required reserves, and excess reserves.

A Quick Review of Reserves, Required Reserves, and Excess Reserves

In the last chapter, we made the following points:

1. A bank's reserves equal its bank deposits at the Fed (the balance in its reserve account at the Fed) plus its vault cash.

$$\text{Reserves} = \text{Bank deposits at the Fed} + \text{Vault cash}$$

2. A bank's required reserves are equal to the required reserve ratio (r) times its checkable deposits.

$$\text{Required reserves} = r \times \text{Checkable deposits}$$

3. A bank's excess reserves equal its reserves minus its required reserves.

$$\text{Excess reserves} = \text{Reserves} - \text{Required reserves}$$

4. A bank can use its excess reserves to create new loans.

The Money Supply Expansion Process

We start with the definition of the M1 money supply:

$$\begin{aligned} \text{M1} = \;&\text{Currency held outside banks} \\ &+ \text{Checkable deposits} \\ &+ \text{Traveler's checks} \end{aligned}$$

Let's suppose that checkable deposits are $10,000 and that the other two components of the money supply equal $0. It follows that the money supply is $10,000.

$$\text{Money supply} = \$10,000$$

For now we are going to assume that the entire $10,000 in checkable deposits is held in one bank: bank A. We will also assume that the required reserve ratio is 10 percent and that bank A is currently holding $1,000 in required reserves and no excess reserves. Here is the relevant part of the balance sheet for bank A:

Bank A			
Assets		**Liabilities**	
Reserves	$1,000	Checkable Deposits	$10,000
Loans	$9,000		

THE FED CONDUCTS AN OPEN MARKET PURCHASE The Fed conducts an open market purchase, which is a type of open market operation; specifically, it buys government securities from a bank. In this example it buys $500 worth of government securities from bank A. (Although government securities are assets for banks, we have not shown these assets on Bank A's balance sheet in order that we may focus only on reserves, loans, and checkable deposits.) Bank A turns over the government securities to the Fed, and, in return, the Fed must pay bank A $500.

Where does the Fed get the $500 to pay bank A? The answer is *out of thin air*. Bank A currently has a reserve account (bank deposits at the Fed) of $1,000. The Fed simply changes the balance in that account (with a stroke of a computer key) from $1,000 to $1,500. Here is what the balance sheet now looks like for bank A:

Open Market Purchase
The buying of government securities by the Fed.

Bank A			
Assets		**Liabilities**	
Reserves	$1,500	Checkable Deposits	$10,000
Loans	$9,000		

THE SITUATION FOR BANK A The balance sheet for bank A shows $1,500 in reserves and $10,000 in checkable deposits. If the required reserve ratio is 10 percent, bank A is required to hold only $1,000 in reserves. So bank A has $500 in *excess reserves*.

Suppose bank A takes the entire $500 in excess reserves and creates a loan for Jill. Specifically, it grants Jill a $500 loan in the form of a new checkable deposit with a balance of $500. In other words, instead of giving Jill $500 in currency, bank A simply tells Jill that she now has a checkable deposit (a checking account) with the bank and that the balance in the account is $500.

WHAT IS THE MONEY SUPPLY NOW? Checkable deposits started off at $10,000 in bank A but are now $10,500. The extra $500 checkable deposit is the *new deposit* that the bank created for Jill. The money supply is now $10,500.

Money Supply = $10,500

Here is what happened to increase the money supply:

Open market purchase → More reserves for bank A
→ Bank A created more loans in the form of
new checkable deposits
→ Money supply increased

THE PROCESS CONTINUES Jill now takes the $500 loan from bank A (in the form of a new checkable deposit) and spends it. Specifically, she writes a check for $500 to Joe for the materials she buys from him. Joe then takes the $500 (he received from Jill) and deposits the full amount into his checking account at bank B. The situation for bank B looks like this:

Bank B			
Assets		**Liabilities**	
Reserves	$500	Checkable Deposits	$500
		(Joe's account)	

Where did $500 in reserves in bank B come from? When the check that Jill wrote to Joe clears, bank A has to turn over $500 to bank B. To make this happen, bank A instructs the Fed to move $500 out of its reserve account and deposit the amount into bank B's reserve account.

Bank B's balance sheet shows $500 in reserves and $500 in checkable deposits. But if the required reserve ratio is 10 percent, bank B is required to hold only $50 in reserves. Bank B has $450 in excess reserves.

Bank B uses the entire $450 in excess reserves to create a loan of $450 for Jamal in the form of a checkable deposit. In other words, bank B creates a new checkable deposit of $450.

WHAT IS THE MONEY SUPPLY NOW? The money supply of $10,000 went up to $10,500 because bank A extended a loan (created a new checkable deposit) for Jill. Bank B then extended a loan (created a new checkable deposit) of $450; so the money supply is now $10,950.

Money supply = $10,950

Some people might think that because Jill's checkable deposit balance went from $500 to $0 when her check cleared, the money supply should now be $10,450, not $10,950. But this point ignores the fact that when Jill pays off her $500 loan to bank A, the bank can lend the $500 to someone else. Thus, bank A can create a new checkable deposit of $500 to take the place of Jill's old one of $500.

THE EFFECTS OF NO CASH LEAKAGE AND ZERO EXCESS RESERVES HELD BY BANKS Up to this point, we have assumed two things.

First, we assumed that both banks A and B always used *all their excess reserves* to create loans (new checkable deposits); that is, the two banks did not hold any excess reserves. If they had held some positive amount of excess reserves, the money supply would have been affected. Specifically, suppose that when bank A had $500 in excess reserves, it created only a $200 loan (instead of a $500 loan) and held $300 in excess reserves. In that case, the money supply would have increased from $10,000, but only to $10,200, not $10,500. In other words, the more excess reserves banks hold, the smaller the increase will be in the money supply.

Second, when Jill paid $500 to Joe, Joe deposited the entire $500 into bank B, but, of course, Joe didn't have to do that. Instead, he could have deposited only $200 of the $500 into bank B and asked for $300 in currency. In this case, there would have been a cash leakage of $300. Bank B's reserves would have increased by only $200, not $500, and the bank could not have created a new loan (a new checkable deposit) of $450.

Given no cash leakage and zero excess reserves held by banks, how much does the money supply increase? The money supply story is ongoing. As we move from bank B to bank C to bank D and so on, each new bank creates some new loans (new checkable deposits), but each time the amount created is smaller than the amount that the previous bank created. Whereas bank A created $500 and bank B created $450, bank C might create $405, and so on. See Exhibit 3. In total, all the banks (together) create $5,000 in new checkable deposits. Here is the equation we use to calculate this amount:

$$\Delta \text{Checkable deposits (or money supply)} = \frac{1}{r} \times \Delta R$$

where r = the required reserve ratio and ΔR = the change in reserves resulting from the initial injection of funds. In our example, r = 10 percent and ΔR = $500. In the equation, the reciprocal of the required reserve ratio ($1/r$) is known as the simple deposit multiplier. The arithmetic for the example is:

Cash Leakage
Occurs when funds are held as currency instead of deposited into a checking account.

Simple Deposit Multiplier
The reciprocal of the required reserve ratio, $1/r$.

EXHIBIT 3

The Fed, Banks, and an Increase in Checkable Deposits or the Money Supply

We assume that $r = 10$ percent, there is no cash leakage, banks hold zero excess reserves, and the Fed ends up increasing the reserves in bank A's reserve account by $500 due to an open market purchase. As a result of the Fed's open market purchase, bank A finds itself with $500 in excess reserves that it uses to create a new loan or new checkable deposit. This starts a process that ends with all relevant banks together creating $5,000 in new checkable deposits (or money).

Creation of New Checkable Deposits, given:

(i) $r = 10\%$
(ii) No cash leakage
(iii) Banks hold zero excess reserves
(iv) $500 increase in reserves for bank A as a result of Fed's open market purchase

Bank	Increase in Checkable Deposits	New Required Reserves	New Checkable Deposits Created by Extending New Loans
A	$ 0	$ 0	$ 500
B	500	50	450
C	450	45	405
D	405	40.50	364.50
⋮	⋮	⋮	⋮
Total			$ 5,000

$$\Delta\text{Checkable deposits (or money supply)} = \frac{1}{0.10} \times \$500$$
$$= 10 \times \$500$$
$$= \$5,000\text{[3]}$$

The change in checkable deposits (or the money supply) is $5000; thus, the Fed's open market purchase resulted in the money supply *rising* from $10,000 to $15,000.

The Money Supply Contraction Process

Let's again start with bank A and its balance sheet:

Bank A			
Assets		**Liabilities**	
Reserves	$1,000	Checkable Deposits	$10,000
Loans	$9,000		

We will also assume that the initial money supply is $10,000:

Money supply = $10,000

This time the Fed undertakes an open market sale, that is, it sells government securities. Let's say the Fed sells $400 worth of government securities to bank A. The Fed turns the securities over to bank A and then subtracts $400 from bank A's reserve account. Just as

Open Market Sale
The selling of government securities by the Fed.

---

3. In the equation, we are looking at the change in checkable deposits or the money supply. Because checkable deposits are the only component of the money supply that is changing (currency and traveler's checks aren't changing), any change in the checkable deposits is equal to the change in the money supply.

the Fed can create money *out of thin* air, it can make it disappear *into thin air*. Here is what bank A's balance sheet (as before, we do not show the securities on the balance sheet so that we can focus on reserves, loans, and checkable deposits) now looks like:

Bank A			
Assets		**Liabilities**	
Reserves	$600	Checkable Deposits	$10,000
Loans	$9,000		

Reserve Deficient
The situation that exists when a bank holds fewer reserves than specified by the required reserve ratio.

Reserves for bank A have gone from $1,000 to $600. Given that checkable deposits are $10,000, bank A is reserve deficient. If the required reserve ratio is 10 percent, bank A is required to hold $1,000 in reserves ($10,000 × 0.10) . But after the open market sale, bank A is holding only $600 in reserves, and so it is reserve deficient by $400.

When a bank is reserve deficient, it can do a number of things: It can (1) try to get a loan from another bank; (2) try to get a loan from the Fed; or (3) apply some of its loan repayments to the reserve deficiency position. In our example, it chooses option 3. On the day bank A becomes reserve deficient, Harry walks into the bank and pays back the $400 loan he took out months ago.

If bank A weren't reserve deficient, it would probably create a $400 loan (new checkable deposit) for someone else with the $400 it received from Harry. In that case, although Harry's checkable deposit balance would go to zero, someone else's checkable deposit balance would rise by $400. The creation of the loan by the bank would keep the money supply constant.

But because the bank is reserve deficient, it keeps the $400 as reserves. As a result, checkable deposits *decline* by $400; so the money supply declines by $400 to $9,600.

$$\text{Money supply} = \$9,600$$

The contraction of the money supply does not stop with bank A. It moves on to banks B, C, D, and others. To illustrate, suppose the loan repayment that Harry made to bank A was written on a check issued by bank B. When the check clears, the reserves of bank B decline, and it finds itself reserve deficient. Bank B, then, applies loan repayments to its reserve deficiency position. The effect continues with banks C, D, and so on.

To find out how much checkable deposits (the money supply) will decline, apply the equation used earlier:

$$\Delta\text{Checkable deposits (or money supply)} = \frac{1}{r} \times \Delta R$$

where r = the required reserve ratio and ΔR = the change in reserves resulting from the initial removal of funds. In our example, r = 10 percent and $\Delta R = -\$400$
The arithmetic is:

$$\Delta\text{Checkable deposits (or money supply)} = \frac{1}{0.10} \times -\$400$$
$$= 10 \times -\$400$$
$$= -\$4,000$$

The change in checkable deposits (or the money supply) is $-\$4,000$; thus, the Fed's open market sale resulted in the money supply *falling* from $10,000 to $6,000.

OTHER FED TOOLS AND RECENT FED ACTIONS

The Fed has other tools to change the money supply. In the last section, we saw how the Fed can use open market operations to change the money supply. In this section, we discuss a few other tools.

The Required Reserve Ratio

Look again at the equation for computing the change in the money supply:

$$\Delta\text{Checkable deposits (or money supply)} = \frac{1}{r} \times \Delta R$$

Notice the role that the required reserve ratio plays in the equation. If $r = 10$ percent, then the simple deposit multiplier $(1 \div r)$ is 10. For a \$1 change in reserves, the change in checkable deposits (money supply) is \$10. If the Fed lowers the required reserve ratio to, say, 5 percent, then the simple deposit multiplier is 20 $(1 \div 0.05 = 20)$. Now a \$1 rise in reserves will lead to a \$20 increase in the money supply. If instead the required reserve ratio is raised to 20 percent, the simple deposit multiplier $(1 \div r)$ is 5 $(1 \div 0.20 = 5)$. So a \$1 rise in reserves will lead to a \$5 increase in the money supply.

In summary:

- Lowering the required reserve ratio will increase the money supply.
- Raising the required reserve ratio will decrease the money supply.

$$r \downarrow \rightarrow \frac{1}{r} \uparrow \rightarrow \text{Money supply} \uparrow$$
$$r \uparrow \rightarrow \frac{1}{r} \downarrow \rightarrow \text{Money supply} \downarrow$$

The Discount Window and the Federal Funds Market

If bank A wants a \$1 million loan, it can go to the Fed or to another bank (say, bank B) for it. The loan the bank gets from the Fed is called a discount loan, and the interest rate a bank pays for a discount loan is called the discount rate. The discount rate is set by the Fed.

The loan that bank A might get from another bank is usually called an *overnight loan* (because it is typically a loan of short duration, such as overnight). The market in which banks lend reserves to one another, usually for short periods, is called the *market for reserves* or the federal funds market. The interest rate that bank A pays for an overnight loan is called the federal funds rate, which is determined in the federal funds market. Specifically, the demand for and the supply of reserves determine the federal funds rate, in much the same way that the demand for and supply of apples determines the price of apples.

The discount rate is another tool the Fed can use to regulate the money supply. If the Fed wants to increase the money supply, it can drop the discount rate below the federal funds rate. To illustrate, suppose the federal funds rate is 5 percent. All the Fed has to do is set the discount rate at, say, 3 percent. Now bank A has an incentive to go to the Fed instead of to another bank for the \$1 million. The Fed gives the bank the \$1 million discount loan by increasing the balance in the bank's reserve account by \$1 million. With more reserves, the bank can create more loans (more checkable deposits), and, as a result, the money supply rises.

In summary:

Fed sets discount rate below federal funds rate → Banks borrow from Fed →
Banks have more reserves → Banks may make more loans and
checkable deposits → Money supply rises

Alternatively, if the Fed wants to contract the money supply, it can set the discount rate above the federal funds rate. Now banks will not go to the Fed for loans, and as the banks repay discount loans taken out in the past, reserves in the banking system decline. (When a bank repays a discount loan, the Fed *subtracts* the repayment from the bank's reserve account.)

Discount Loan
A loan the Fed makes to a commerical bank.

Discount Rate
The interest rate the Fed charges depository institutions that borrow reserves from it; the interest rate charged on a discount loan.

Federal Funds Rate
The interest rate in the federal funds market; the interest rate banks charge one another to borrow reserves.

Federal Funds Market
A market where banks lend reserves to one another, usually for short periods.

In summary:

Fed sets discount rate above federal funds rate → Banks do not borrow from the
Fed, and as banks repay past discount loans → Banks have fewer reserves →
Money supply declines

The Fed and the Federal Funds Rate Target

Federal Funds Rate Target
The interest rate that the Fed wants
the federal funds market rate to be.

So far, we have identified three tools the Fed has at its disposal to change the money
supply: conducting open market operations, changing the required reserve ratio, and
changing the discount rate relative to the federal funds rate. Normally, however, if the Fed
wants to change the money supply, it takes two measures: (1) It sets a federal funds rate
target and then (2) uses open market operations to change the federal funds rate so as to
"hit" the target.

Suppose the current federal funds rate is 4 percent, and the Fed sets a federal funds rate
target of 3 percent. The Fed then conducts an open market purchase, which, as we know,
has the effect of injecting reserves into the banking system. As a result of the open market
purchase, the supply of reserves in the market for reserves rises. As the supply of reserves
rises, the price of those reserves—the federal funds rate—falls. The Fed continues these
transactions until the federal funds rate falls from 4 percent to 3 percent, the federal funds
rate target.

Dealing with a Financial Crisis

The actions the Fed takes might differ depending on whether it is simply trying to
change the money supply to meet a macroeconomic objective, such as price stability,
or dealing with a financial crisis. (You will read about the financial crisis of 2007–2009
in Chapter 18.) In way of analogy, your pace is very different if you are taking a
leisurely walk than if you are running a race. The same type of difference exists for
the Fed when it is managing everyday monetary policy compared to dealing with a
financial crisis.

The Fed did three things to deal with the 2007–2009 financial crisis:

- Created the term auction facility (TAF) program
- Extended the lender-of-last-resort function beyond banks
- Bought securities from institutions other than banks

**Term Auction Facility (TAF)
Program**
A program under which the Fed
auctions funds to depository institutions. Each TAF auction is for a
fixed amount, with the TAF rate
determined by the auction process
(subject to a minimum bid rate).

TERM AUCTION FACILITY (TAF) PROGRAM In addition to issuing discount loans
to banks, in late 2007 the Fed created another way banks could get loans from it. Specifically, it created the term auction facility (TAF) program. In this program, instead of banks
asking for a specific dollar loan (as in a discount loan), the Fed first identifies the total
amount of credit it wants to extend (for example, $20 billion). Then it allows banks to bid
on the funds. The bidding process determines the TAF rate (interest rate) for the loans.

If the Fed already offers discount loans to banks, why set up the TAF program? In a
sense, if a bank can already get a loan by knocking on door 1 at the Fed, why add door 2
(TAF)?

One reason is that discount loans often come with a stigma attached. Specifically, if a
bank is in sound financial condition, it customarily borrows from institutions in the private
sector (such as another bank). A discount loan is intended for banks that cannot get loans
elsewhere; thus a bank that requests a discount loan is often viewed as admitting it is in
poor financial health. The bank might not want to make such an admission to either the
Fed or the market.

The Fed dealt with the stigma issue by stating that, as far as it was concerned, no
stigma was attached to borrowing from the term auction facility. It dealt with the issue of

economics 24/7

Flying in with the Money[2]

A banker at a commercial bank located about 200 miles from the Federal Reserve Bank of Minneapolis was frantic. A large crowd was outside his bank, and the people wanted their money now. The banker got on the phone and called the Federal Reserve Bank in Minneapolis. He told the people at the Minneapolis Fed that there was a "mad run" on his bank. If the Fed did not come to his rescue soon, he would be out of currency and unable to give the customers of his bank their money.

Where was their money? Why didn't he have it to give to them? As this chapter explained, banks need to have on hand only a fraction of their customers' deposits.

The Federal Reserve System responded to the call for currency. The Federal Reserve Bank of Minneapolis chartered a small plane, and two Fed officials took it, along with a half million dollars in small-denomination bills, to the nearby town.

Upon approaching the town, the pilot flew the plane over Main Street to dramatize its arrival in the town: the Federal Reserve was flying in to the rescue. The plane landed at a nearby field. From the field, the Fed officials were escorted into town by the police, and the money was stacked in the bank's windows. The sight of all the money calmed the bank's customers, who were now assured they could get their money if they wanted. A banking panic was averted in a very dramatic way.

---

2. This feature is based on "Born of a Panic: Forming the Federal Reserve System," *The Region* (August 1998).

---

confidentiality in the market by stating that it would not release any information on the participants in the TAF program, except as required by law.

Finally, by determining the TAF rate through a competitive bidding process, banks found that borrowing through the term auction facility was cheaper than with discount loans.

EXTENDING THE LENDER-OF-LAST-RESORT FUNCTION BEYOND BANKS

As the lender of last resort for banks, the Fed ensures that banks can obtain the funds they need. If a bank has financial problems, it can seek funds from the Fed. During the financial crisis, the Fed extended its lender-of-last-resort function to institutions other than banks.

BUYING SECURITIES FROM INSTITUTIONS OTHER THAN BANKS During normal economic times, the Fed buys Treasury securities from banks if it wants to increase reserves in the banking system to raise the money supply. During the financial crisis, the Fed not only bought securities from nonbank institutions, but often bought securities that were not Treasury issues. Often they were mortgage-backed securities that institutions owned that were declining in value.

SELF-TEST

1. How does the money supply change as a result of (a) an increase in the discount rate, (b) an open market purchase, (c) an increase in the required reserve ratio?

2. What is the difference between the federal funds rate and the discount rate?

3. If bank A borrows $10 million from bank B, what happens to the reserves in bank A? What happens in the banking system?

4. If bank A borrows $10 million from the Fed, what happens to the reserves in bank A? What happens in the banking system?

OFFICE HOURS

"Can Something I Do End Up Changing the Money Supply?"

STUDENT:

Let me see if I have this right: if I put $100 in my checking account at a bank, the bank then takes that $100 and adds it to vault cash, so that $100 becomes part of the bank's reserves, right?

INSTRUCTOR:

Yes, that's right.

STUDENT:

And then the bank holds a percentage of that $100 in reserve form and lends out the rest. So it might hold $10 of the $100 in its vault and lend out the remaining $90.

INSTRUCTOR:

That's correct.

STUDENT:

Now here's the part I am unsure of. When a bank gives out a loan of $90, does it actually lend out the $90 of currency (let's say nine $10 bills) or simply create a new checkable deposit of $90 for someone?

INSTRUCTOR:

It creates a new checkable deposit of $90.

STUDENT:

But then that means the full $100 currency is still in the bank's vault, right? When does $90 of the $100 leave the vault?

INSTRUCTOR:

Suppose the person who received the $90 loan (or new checkable deposit) writes a check to Marie. Marie then deposits the $90 check in another bank. When the check clears, the $90 is transferred from the first bank (in which you deposited your money) to Marie's bank. And then Marie's bank takes a fraction of that $90 and creates a loan with it, and the process continues.

STUDENT:

So, in the end, some portion of that $100 that I deposited into the bank ends up creating loans for a lot of people. Is that correct?

INSTRUCTOR:

That is correct.

STUDENT:

But this makes it sound like I can change the money supply by simply deciding to put $100 currency into a bank instead of keeping that $100 in my wallet. Is this true?

INSTRUCTOR:

Let's put it this way: by putting $100 currency into a bank, you change the composition of the money supply. Specifically, $100 less in currency is held outside banks and $100 more in checkable deposits. Then the banking system can take the $100 and create a multiple of it in terms of new checkable deposits, thereby raising the money supply.

POINTS TO REMEMBER

1. An individual (any member of the public) can change the composition of the money supply.
2. A change in the composition of the money supply can lead to a dollar change in the money supply

CHAPTER SUMMARY

THE FEDERAL RESERVE SYSTEM

- There are 12 Federal Reserve Districts. The Board of Governors controls and coordinates the activities of the Federal Reserve System. The Board is made up of seven members, each appointed to a 14-year term. The major policy-making group in the Fed is the Federal Open Market Committee (FOMC). It is a 12-member group made up of the seven members of the Board of Governors and five Federal Reserve District Bank presidents.
- The major responsibilities of the Fed are to (1) control the money supply, (2) supply the economy with paper money (Federal Reserve notes), (3) provide check-clearing services, (4) hold depository institutions' reserves, (5) supervise member banks, (6) serve as the government's banker, (7) serve as the lender of last resort, and (8) serve as a fiscal agent for the Treasury.

CONTROLLING THE MONEY SUPPLY

- The following Fed actions increase the money supply: lowering the required reserve ratio, purchasing government securities on the open market, and lowering the discount rate relative to the federal funds rate.
- The following Fed actions decrease the money supply: raising the required reserve ratio, selling government securities on the open market, and raising the discount rate relative to the federal funds rate.

OPEN MARKET OPERATIONS

- An open market purchase by the Fed increases the money supply.
- An open market sale by the Fed decreases the money supply.

THE REQUIRED RESERVE RATIO

- An increase in the required reserve ratio leads to a decrease in the money supply.
- A decrease in the required reserve ratio leads to an increase in the money supply.

DISCOUNT LOANS AND OVERNIGHT LOANS

- A bank obtains discount loans from the Fed and overnight loans from other banks. The interest rate it pays for a discount loan is called the discount rate. The interest rate a bank pays another bank for a loan is called the federal funds rate.
- The discount rate is set by the Fed. The federal funds rate is determined by market forces in the market for reserves (federal funds market).
- If the Fed sets the discount rate below the federal funds rate, banks will borrow from the Fed, and the banks will end up with more reserves. These reserves can be used to create more loans and checkable deposits, thus increasing the money supply.
- If the Fed sets the discount above the federal funds rate, banks will choose not to borrow from the Fed. As the banks repay past discount loans, they have fewer reserves, thus decreasing the money supply.

THE FEDERAL FUNDS RATE TARGET

- The Fed sets a federal funds rate target. Then it uses open market operations to change the federal funds rate so as to hit the target. For example, if the current federal funds rate is 4 percent, and the target is 3 percent, the Fed can conduct an open market purchase, which results in reserves being injected into the banking system. As the supply of reserves rises, the federal funds rate declines.

KEY TERMS AND CONCEPTS

Board of Governors
Federal Open Market Committee (FOMC)
Open Market Operations
Monetary Policy

U.S. Treasury Securities
Open Market Purchase
Cash Leakage
Simple Deposit Multiplier
Open Market Sale

Reserve Deficient
Reserve Requirement
Discount Loan
Discount Rate
Federal Funds Rate

Federal Funds Market
Federal Funds Target Rate
Term Auction Facility (TAF) Program

QUESTIONS AND PROBLEMS

1. Explain how an open market sale decreases the money supply.
2. Explain how an open market purchase increases the money supply.
3. What are the differences between the Fed and the U.S. Treasury?
4. Identify the major responsibilities of the Federal Reserve System.

5. Explain how a check is cleared through the Federal Reserve System.

6. The Fed can change the discount rate directly and the federal funds rate indirectly. Explain.

7. What does it mean to say the Fed serves as the lender of last resort?

8. The Fed has announced a new, lower target for the federal funds rate; it wants to lower the federal funds rate from its present level. What does setting a lower target for the federal funds rate have to do with open market operations?

9. Suppose you read in the newspaper that all last week the Fed conducted open market purchases and that on Tuesday of last week it lowered the discount rate. What would you say the Fed is trying to do?

10. Explain how a decrease in the required reserve ratio increases the money supply.

11. Suppose bank A borrows reserves from bank B. Now that bank A has more reserves than previously, will the money supply increase? Explain your answer.

12. Suppose the Fed raises the required reserve ratio, a move that is normally thought to reduce the money supply. However, banks find themselves with a reserve deficiency after the required reserve ratio is increased and are likely to react by requesting a loan from the Fed. Does this action prevent the money supply from contracting as predicted? Explain your answer.

WORKING WITH NUMBERS AND GRAPHS

1. If reserves increase by $2 million and the required reserve ratio is 8 percent, what is the maximum change in checkable deposits?

2. If reserves increase by $2 million and the required reserves ratio is 10 percent, what is the maximum change in checkable deposits?

3. If the federal funds rate is 6 percent and the discount rate is 5.1 percent, to whom will a bank be more likely to go for a loan: another bank or the Fed? Explain your answer.

4. Complete the following table:

Federal Reserve Action	Effect on the Money Supply (up or down?)
Lower the discount rate	A
Conduct open market purchase	B
Lower required reserve ratio	C
Raise the discount rate	D
Conduct open market sale	E
Raise the required reserve ratio	F

THE MARKET FOR RESERVES (OR THE FEDERAL FUNDS MARKET)

Monetary policy can be conducted in various ways. One is to target a specific money supply, such as M1 or M2. Suppose the M1 money supply is currently $1 trillion and the Fed wants to raise it to $1.1 trillion. The $1.1 trillion is the Fed's specific monetary target. The Fed then undertakes to increase the money supply until it hits its monetary target. For example, it might undertake an open market purchase or lower the required reserve ratio, either of which would lead to an increase in the money supply. If, by chance, the Fed overshot its monetary target and the money supply increased to some dollar figure over $1.1 trillion, the Fed then could reverse course. It could undertake an open market sale to bring the money supply back down to $1.1 trillion.

Today, the Fed does not usually have a specific money supply target in its execution of monetary policy. Instead, it tries to target a set federal funds rate. Suppose the federal funds rate is currently 4 percent and the Fed wants to lower it to 3 percent. Three percent is its federal funds rate target. Because the federal funds rate is determined in the market for reserves (or the federal funds market), we need to explain how that market works before we can explain what the Fed can do to reach its federal funds rate target.

THE DEMAND FOR RESERVES

The demand for reserves originates with banks. A bank may have a demand for reserves for a few reasons. A bank may demand reserves because it has to hold a certain amount of reserves against its checkable deposits. For example, if the required reserve ratio is, say, 10 percent, then for every $1 in checkable deposits a bank holds, it must hold 10¢ in reserves. So if the required reserve ratio is raised (by the Fed), a bank needs to hold more reserves for every $1 of checkable deposits. In Exhibit 1, the demand for reserves is downward-sloping. On the vertical axis is the federal funds rate, and on the horizontal axis is the quantity of reserves. When the bank needs more reserves, the demand curve for reserves (*D*) shifts to the right; if the required reserve ratio is lowered, a bank needs to hold fewer reserves for every $1 of checkable deposits, and therefore the demand curve for reserves shifts to the left.

Banks demand reserves also because they believe they may face large checkable deposit withdrawals. Suppose a bank believes that its depositors may soon withdraw large amounts of their

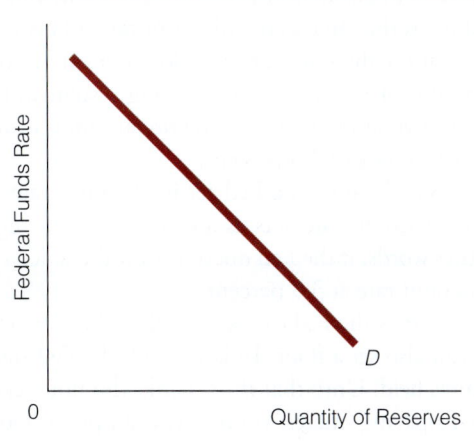

The Demand for Reserves

The demand for reserves curve (in the market for reserves or the federal funds market) is downward sloping: the federal funds rate and the quantity demanded of reserves are inversely related. As the federal funds rate moves down, holding reserves becomes cheaper, and therefore banks will buy more "insurance" to guard against checkable deposit withdrawals. As the federal funds rate moves up, holding reserves becomes more expensive, and banks will buy less "insurance" to guard against checkable deposit withdrawals. A change in expected deposit outflows and the required reserve ratio can lead to a shift in the demand for reserves.

money from their checkable deposits. To have the funds to meet the anticipated withdrawals, banks may decide to hold more reserves than they are required to by the required reserve ratio. For example, instead of holding 10¢ in reserves against every $1 in checkable deposits, they might increase that reserve holding to 20¢ or 30¢ or more.

The demand curve for reserves is downward sloping because, as the federal funds rate moves down, it becomes cheaper to hold reserves, and therefore banks will buy more "insurance" to guard against checkable deposit withdrawals. As the federal funds rate moves up, it becomes more expensive to hold reserves, and banks will buy less "insurance" to guard against checkable deposit withdrawals.

THE SUPPLY OF RESERVES

The supply of reserves comes from essentially two sources. The first source is the Fed. For example, when the Fed undertakes open market operations, it changes the supply of reserves. An open market purchase increases the supply of reserves (in the banking system); an open market sale decreases the supply of reserves.

The second source of reserves comes from banks taking out discount loans from the Fed. If a bank borrows from the Fed, the supply of reserves increases in the banking system. If a bank pays back a discount loan to the Fed, the supply of reserves decreases.

TWO DIFFERENT SUPPLY CURVES FOR RESERVES

Exhibit 2(a)–(b) shows two supply curves. In (a), we assume that the federal funds rate target [designated by an asterisk (*)] is currently ffr_1^* or 3.0 percent at the intersection of the D_1 and S_1 curves. We also assume that the Fed has set the discount rate ($dr_1 = 3.5$ percent) slightly above the federal funds rate target. In recent years, the Fed has customarily set the discount rate slightly above its federal funds rate target. To see why, let's suppose the demand curve in (a) shifts to the right from D_1 to D_2. Will the federal funds rate rise to ffr_2' (3.7 percent)? Under most conditions, the answer is no. Banks would prefer to borrow from the Fed at the discount rate of 3.5 percent instead of borrowing from other banks at the federal funds rate of 3.7 percent. In other words, equilibrium in the market for reserves is likely to occur at point 2 in the exhibit, where the new federal funds rate is 3.5 percent, which is the same as the discount rate. (This is why the supply of reserves curve has a kink in it at the discount rate and does not extend vertically above this point.) The equilibrium amount of reserves in the banking system will rise from R_1 to R_2, the difference between these two amounts being the dollar amount of discount loans that banks take out at the discount rate of 3.5 percent.

So why does the Fed set its discount rate slightly above the target federal funds rate? The discount rate acts as a ceiling on how high the federal funds rate is likely to go. In other words, if the Fed doesn't want the federal funds rate to go over 3.5 percent, it sets the discount rate at 3.5 percent.

Just as the Fed can set a ceiling above which the federal funds rate is not likely to rise, it can also set a floor. In late 2008, the Fed started to pay an interest rate on reserves that banks held. Until that time, banks did not receive any interest on reserves. To see how the Fed's paying interest on reserves can put a floor on the federal funds rate, look at Exhibit 2(b). The reserves market is initially in equilibrium at point 1. The federal funds rate target is the equilibrium federal funds rate of 3.0 percent, and the equilibrium amount of reserves is R_1. Now suppose that the Fed is willing to pay an interest rate on reserves of ir_1 ($ir_1 = 2.5$ percent) and that the demand for reserves curve shifts leftward from D_1 to D_2. Will the

EXHIBIT 2

The Supply of Reserves

Two supply of reserves curves. (a) A kink in the curve at the discount rate. To understand the kink, start with a federal funds rate of 3.0 percent. Next, the demand for reserves curve shifts from D_1 to D_2. Whether the federal funds rate will rise to 3.7 percent is possible but not likely if banks decide to borrow from the Fed at the lower discount rate of 3.5 percent. In other words, the federal funds rate rises to only 3.5 percent. The discount rate acts as a ceiling on the federal funds rate.

(b) A supply of reserves with two kinks. The uppermost kink, as explained, occurs at the discount rate. The lower one occurs at the interest rate the Fed pays (to banks) on reserves. To understand the lower kink, start with a federal funds rate of 3.0 percent. Next, the demand for reserves curve shifts from D_1 to D_2. The federal funds rate might fall to 2.3 percent, but it is not likely because banks would rather receive an interest rate of 2.5 percent from the Fed than lend to other banks and receive an interest rate of 2.3 percent. The interest rate the Fed pays on reserves acts as a floor on the federal funds rate.

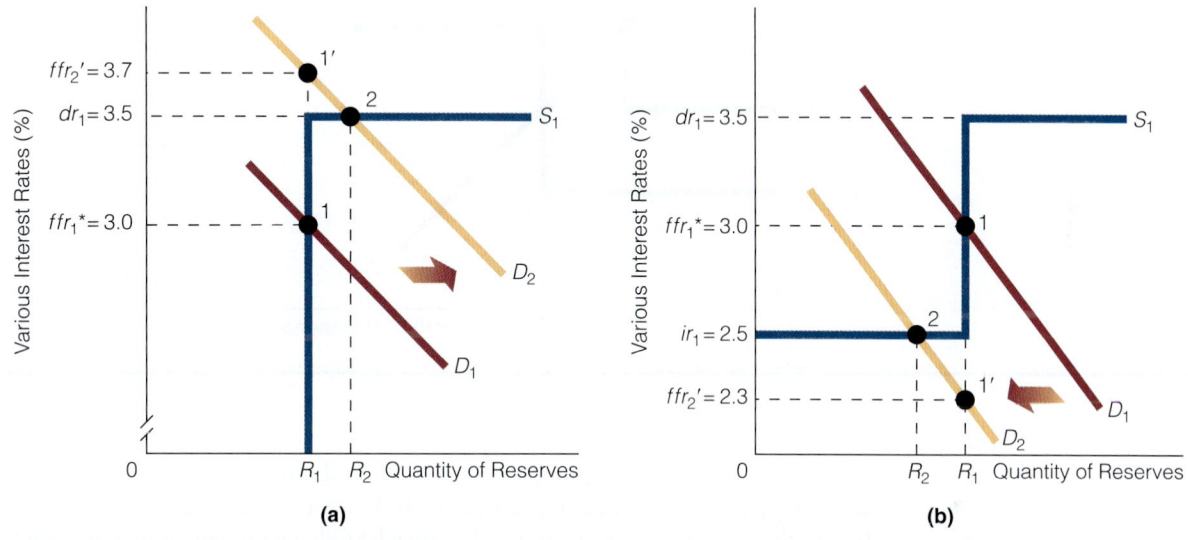

(a) (b)

federal funds rate fall to ffr_2, (2.3 percent)? Not likely, because no bank will prefer to lend reserves to another bank at a federal funds rate of 2.3 percent when it can simply keep the reserves and gain an interest rate on reserves of 2.5 percent. (The difference between R_1 and R_2 can be seen as a "negative discount loan," in that it is the amount that banks are "lending" to the Fed, for which the Fed pays them interest.) So the federal funds rate is not likely to fall to 2.3 percent. Instead, it is likely to only fall to 2.5 percent. In other words, the interest rate that the Fed pays on reserves acts as a floor below which the federal funds rate will not fall.

THE CORRIDOR AND CHANGING THE FEDERAL FUNDS RATE

In Exhibit 2(b), the supply curve (of reserves) has two kinks in it: one at the interest rate that the Fed pays on reserves and another at the discount rate. The vertical section between the kinks—or, simply, the vertical section of the supply curve—is called the *corridor*. The federal funds rate moves within this corridor. In other words, the federal funds rate can rise or fall within the corridor, but nowhere else. If the corridor were between a discount rate of 7 percent and an interest rate paid on reserves of 3 percent, the federal funds rate would be somewhere between a high of 7 percent and a low of 3 percent. If the Fed increases the length of the corridor by, say, increasing the discount rate from 7 percent to 8 percent, then the federal funds rate will be somewhere between a high of 8 percent and a low of 3 percent.

EXHIBIT 3

Changing the Federal Funds Rate

The equilibrium federal funds rate is 3.0 percent. The Fed then decides to lower the federal funds rate to 2.5 percent. To do this, the Fed undertakes an open market purchase, increasing reserves from R_1 to R_2. At the same time, it lowers the discount rate from 3.5 percent to 3.0 percent and lowers the interest rate it pays on reserves from 2.5 percent to 2.0 percent. The new supply of reserves curve is S_2, and the new equilibrium federal funds rate is 2.5 percent.

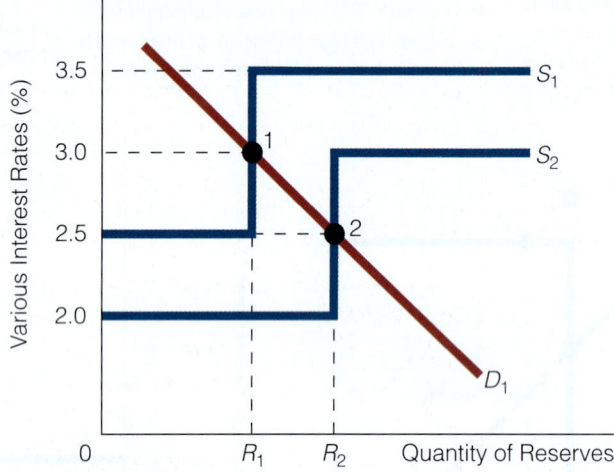

Now look at Exhibit 3. Suppose the federal fund rate is currently at 3.0, the discount rate is 3.5 percent, and the interest rate the Fed pays on reserves is 2.5 percent. The Fed decides that it wants to try to bring the federal funds rate down to its target rate of 2.5 percent. What can it do to achieve its objective of lowering the federal funds rate? It can undertake an open market purchase, thus increasing reserves from R_1 to R_2. At the same time as it increases reserves, it might then lower its discount rate from 3.5 percent to, say, 3.0 percent, and the interest it pays on reserves from 2.5 percent to, say, 2.0 percent, so that the new supply curve is S_2. The demand curve for reserves intersects the supply curve of reserves at point 2 in the exhibit. The equilibrium federal funds rate is now 2.5 percent.

MONEY AND THE ECONOMY

Introduction Does the money supply matter to the economy? Does a rise or fall in the money supply make a difference? In this chapter we talk about the money supply and its effects on the economy. We discuss changes in the money supply and in the price level, changes in the money supply and in Real GDP, and changes in the money supply and interest rates.

MONEY AND THE PRICE LEVEL

Classical economists believed that changes in the money supply affect the price level in the economy. Their position was based on the equation of exchange and on the simple quantity theory of money.

The Equation of Exchange

The equation of exchange is an identity stating that the money supply (M) multiplied by velocity (V) must be equal to the price level (P) times Real GDP (Q).

$$MV \equiv PQ$$

where $\equiv$ means "must be equal to." This is an identity, and an identity is valid for all values of the variables.

As we learned in an earlier chapter, *velocity* is the average number of times a dollar is spent to buy final goods and services in a year. For example, assume an economy has only five $1 bills. In January, the first of the $1 bills moves from Smith's hands to Jones's hands to buy good X. Then in June, it goes from Jones's hands to Brown's hands to buy good Y. And in December, it goes from Brown's hands to Peterson's hands to buy good Z. Over the course of the year, this dollar bill has changed hands three times.

The other dollar bills also change hands during the year. The second dollar bill changes hands five times; the third, six times; the fourth, two times; and the fifth, seven times. Given this information, we can calculate the average number of times a dollar changes hands in purchases. In this case, the number is 4.6, which is velocity.

Equation of Exchange
An identity stating that the money supply (M) times velocity (V) must be equal to the price level (P) times Real GDP (Q): $MV \equiv PQ$.

Velocity
The average number of times a dollar is spent to buy final goods and services in a year.

289

In a large economy such as ours, counting how many times each dollar changes hands is impossible; so calculating velocity as we did in our example is impossible. For a large economy, we use a different method.

- First, we calculate GDP.
- Next, we calculate the average money supply (M).
- Finally, we divide GDP by the average money supply to obtain velocity (V).

$$V \equiv \frac{GDP}{M}$$

For example, if $4,800 billion worth of transactions occur in a year (GDP) and the average money supply during the year is $800 billion ($M$), then a dollar must have been used an average of 6 times during the year to purchase goods and services:

$$V \equiv \frac{\$4,800 \text{ billion}}{\$800 \text{ billion}}$$

Because GDP is equal to $P \times Q$, this identity can be written

$$V \equiv \frac{P \times Q}{M}$$

Multiplying both sides by M, we get

$$MV \equiv PQ$$

which is the equation of exchange. Thus, the equation of exchange is derived from the definition of velocity.

The equation of exchange can be interpreted in different ways:

1. The money supply multiplied by velocity must equal the price level times Real GDP: $M \times V \equiv P \times Q$.

2. The money supply multiplied by velocity must equal GDP: $M \times V \equiv$ GDP (because $P \times Q \equiv$ GDP).

3. Total spending or expenditures (measured by MV) must equal the total sales revenues of business firms (measured by PQ): $MV \equiv PQ$.

The third way of interpreting the equation of exchange is perhaps the most intuitively easy to understand: The total expenditures (of buyers) must equal the total sales (of sellers). Consider a simple economy with only one buyer and one seller. If the buyer buys a book for $20, then the seller receives $20. Stated differently, the money supply in the example ($20) times velocity (1) is equal to the price of the book ($20) times the quantity of the book (1).

From the Equation of Exchange to the Simple Quantity Theory of Money

The equation of exchange is an identity, not an economic theory. To turn it into a theory, we make some assumptions about the variables in the equation. Many eighteenth-century classical economists, as well as American economist Irving Fisher (1867–1947) and English economist Alfred Marshall (1842–1924), made the following assumptions:

1. Changes in velocity are so small that for all practical purposes velocity can be assumed to be constant (especially over short periods of time).

2. Real GDP, or Q, is fixed in the short run.

Hence, they turned the equation of exchange, which is simply true by definition, into a theory by assuming that both V and Q are fixed, or constant. With these two assumptions, we have the simple quantity theory of money: If V and Q are constant, then changes in M will bring about *strictly proportional* changes in P. In other words, the simple quantity theory of money predicts that changes in the money supply will bring about strictly proportional changes in the price level.

Exhibit 1 shows the assumptions and predictions of the simple quantity theory. On the left side of the exhibit, the key assumptions of the simple quantity theory are noted: V and Q are constant. Also, $M \times \overline{V} = P \times \overline{Q}$ is noted. We use the equals sign ($=$) instead of the identity sign ($\equiv$) because we are speaking about the simple quantity theory, not the equation of exchange. (The equals sign can be read as "is predicted to be equal"; that is, given our assumptions, $M \times V$, or MV, is predicted to be equal to $P \times Q$, or PQ.)

Starting with the first row, the money supply is $500, velocity is 4, the price level, or price index, is $2, and Real GDP ($Q$) is 1,000 units.[1] Therefore, GDP equals $2,000. In the second row, the money supply increases by 100 percent, from $500 to $1,000, and both V and Q are constant, at 4 and 1,000, respectively. The price level moves from $2 to $4. On the right side of the exhibit, we see that a 100 percent increase in M predicts a 100 percent increase in P. Changes in P are predicted to be strictly proportional to changes in M. In the third row, M increases by 50 percent, and P is predicted to increase by 50 percent. In the fourth row, M decreases by 20 percent, and P is predicted to decrease by 20 percent.

So the simple quantity theory assumes that both V and Q are constant in the short run and therefore predicts that changes in M lead to strictly proportional changes in P.

How well does the simple quantity theory of money predict? Do changes in the money supply actually lead to *strictly proportional* changes in the price level? For example, if the money supply goes up by 7 percent, does the price level go up by 7 percent? If the money supply goes down by 4 percent, does the price level go down by 4 percent? The answer is that the strict proportionality between changes in the money supply and changes in the price level does not show up in the data (at least not very often).

Generally, though, the evidence supports the spirit (or essence) of the simple quantity theory of money: the higher the growth rate in the money supply, the greater the growth

Simple Quantity Theory of Money
The theory assuming that velocity (V) and Real GDP (Q) are constant and predicting that changes in the money supply (M) lead to strictly proportional changes in the price level (P).

EXHIBIT 1

Assumptions of Simple Quantity Theory					Predictions of Simple Quantity Theory	
M	×	**$\overline{V}$** =	**P**	×	**$\overline{Q}$**	**% Change in M**	**% Change in P**
$500	4		$2		1,000		
1,000	4		4		1,000	+ 100%	+ 100%
1,500	4		6		1,000	+ 50	+ 50
1,200	4		4.80		1,000	− 20	− 20

Assumptions and Predictions of the Simple Quantity Theory of Money

The simple quantity theory of money assumes that both V and Q are constant. (A bar over each indicates this in the exhibit.) The prediction is that changes in M lead to strictly proportional changes in P. (Note: For purposes of this example, think of Q as "so many units of goods" and of P as the "average price paid per unit of these goods.")

---

1. You are used to seeing Real GDP expressed as a dollar figure and a price index as a number without a dollar sign in front of it. We have switched things for purposes of this example because it is easier to think of Q as "so many units of goods" and P as "the average price paid per unit of those goods."

The California Gold Rush, or Really Expensive Apples

Soon there was too much money in California and too little of everything else.
—J. S. Holiday, *The World Rushed In*

The only peacetime rise [in prices] comparable in total magnitude [to the 40 to 50 percent rise in prices from 1897 to 1914] followed the California gold discoveries in the early 1850s. . . .
—Milton Friedman and Anna Schwartz, *A Monetary History of the United States, 1867–1960*

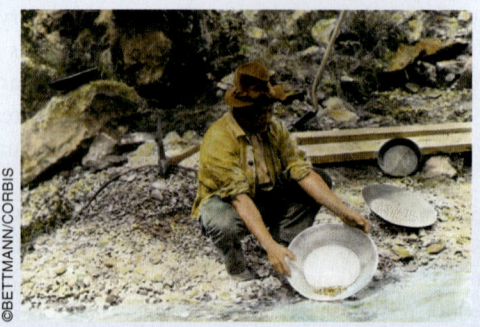
©BETTMANN/CORBIS

John Sutter was a Swiss immigrant who arrived in California in 1839. On the chilly morning of January 24, 1848, James Marshall, a carpenter, was busy at work building a sawmill for Sutter. Then something glistening caught his eye, and he reached down and picked it up. Marshall said to the workers he had hired, "Boys, by God I believe I have found a gold mine." Marshall later wrote, "I reached my hand down and picked it up; it made my heart thump, for I was certain it was gold. The piece was about half the size and shape of a pea. Then I saw another."

In time, Marshall and his workers came across more gold, and before long people from all across the United States and from many other countries headed to California. The California gold rush had begun.

The California gold rush resulted in an increase in the amount of money in circulation and illustrates how such a fairly dramatic increase

can affect prices. As more gold was mined and the supply of money went up, prices began to rise. Although prices rose generally across the country, the earliest and most dramatic price rises occurred in and near the areas where gold was discovered. Near the gold mines, the prices of food and clothing shot up. For example, whereas a loaf of bread sold for 4¢ in New York (equivalent to 84¢ today), near the mines the price was 75¢ (the equivalent of $15.67 today). Eggs sold for about $2 each ($41 today), apples for $4 ($83.59), a butcher's knife for $30 ($626), and boots went for $100 a pair ($2,089).

In San Francisco, land prices soared dramatically because of the city's relative closeness to the mines. In 18 months, real estate that cost $16 (the equivalent of $334 today) before gold was discovered jumped to $45,000 ($940,000 today).

The sharp rise in prices created by the California gold discoveries followed other gold discoveries too. For example, the gold stock of the world is estimated to have doubled from 1890 to 1914, due both to discoveries (in South Africa, Alaska, and Colorado) and to improved methods of mining and refining gold. During this period, world prices increased too.

rate in the price level. To illustrate, we would expect that a growth rate in the money supply of, say, 40 percent would generate a greater increase in the price level than, say, a growth rate in the money supply of 4 percent. Generally, this effect is what we see. For example, countries with more rapid increases in their money supplies often witness more rapid increases in their price levels than do countries that witness less rapid increases in their money supplies.

The Simple Quantity Theory of Money in an *AD–AS* Framework

In this section, we analyze the simple quantity theory of money in the *AD–AS* framework.

THE *AD* CURVE IN THE SIMPLE QUANTITY THEORY OF MONEY The simple quantity theory of money builds on the equation of exchange. Recall that one way of interpreting the equation of exchange is that the total expenditures of buyers (MV) must equal the total sales of sellers (PQ). Thus, MV is the total expenditures of buyers, and PQ is the total sales of sellers. Let's take the total expenditures of buyers a few steps further:

$$MV = \text{Total expenditures}$$

However, total expenditures (TE) is defined as the sum of the expenditures made by the four sectors of the economy (consumption, investment, government purchases, and net exports):

$$TE = C + I + G + (EX - IM)$$

Because $MV = TE$,

$$MV = C + I + G + (EX - IM)$$

At a given price level, anything that changes C, I, G, EX, or IM changes aggregate demand and thus shifts the aggregate demand (AD) curve. If MV equals $C + I + G + (EX - IM)$, then *a change in the money supply (M) or a change in velocity (V) will change aggregate demand and therefore lead to a shift in the AD curve.* In other words, aggregate demand depends on *both* the money supply and velocity. Specifically:

- An increase in the money supply will increase aggregate demand and shift the AD curve to the right.
- A decrease in the money supply will decrease aggregate demand and shift the AD curve to the left.
- An increase in velocity will increase aggregate demand and shift the AD curve to the right.
- A decrease in velocity will decrease aggregate demand and shift the AD curve to the left.

But *in the simple quantity theory of money, velocity is assumed to be constant.* Thus, only changes in the money supply can shift the AD curve.

The AD curve for the simple quantity theory of money is shown in Exhibit 2(a). The (M, V) next to the curve is a reminder of which factors can shift the AD curve. The bar over V (for velocity) indicates that velocity is assumed to be constant.

THE AS CURVE IN THE SIMPLE QUANTITY THEORY OF MONEY In the simple quantity theory of money, the level of Real GDP is assumed to be constant in the short run. Exhibit 2(b) shows Real GDP fixed at Q_1. The AS curve is vertical at this level of Real GDP.

AD AND AS IN THE SIMPLE QUANTITY THEORY OF MONEY Exhibit 2(c) shows both the AD and AS curves in the simple quantity theory of money. Suppose AD_1 is initially operational. In the exhibit, AD_1 is based on a money supply of $800 billion and a velocity of 2. The price level is P_1.

Now suppose we increase the money supply to $820 billion, and velocity remains constant at 2. According to the simple quantity theory of money, the price level will increase, and it does. The increase in the money supply shifts the AD curve from AD_1 to AD_2 and pushes up the price level from P_1 to P_2.

Suppose that instead of increasing the money supply, we decrease it to $780 billion, again with velocity remaining constant at 2. According to the simple quantity theory of money, the price level will decrease, and it does. The decrease in the money supply shifts the AD curve from AD_1 to AD_3 and pushes the price level down from P_1 to P_3.

EXHIBIT 2

The Simple Quantity Theory of Money in the AD–AS Framework

(a) In the simple quantity theory of money, the AD curve is downward sloping. Velocity is assumed to be constant, so changes in the money supply will change aggregate demand. (b) In the simple quantity theory of money, Real GDP is fixed in the short run. Thus, the AS curve is vertical. (c) In the simple quantity theory of money, an increase in the money supply will shift the AD curve rightward and increase the price level. A decrease in the money supply will shift the AD curve leftward and decrease the price level.

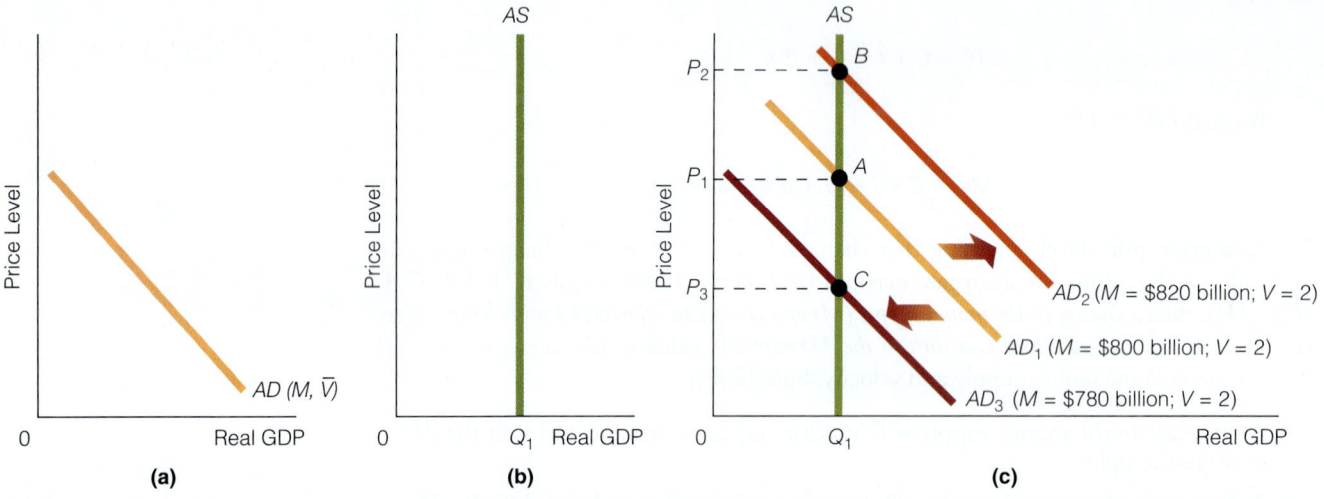

(a)   (b)   (c)

Dropping the Assumptions that V and Q Are Constant

If we drop the assumptions that velocity (V) and Real GDP (Q) are constant, we have a more general theory of the factors that cause changes in the price level. In this theory, changes in the price level depend on three variables:

1. Money supply

2. Velocity

3. Real GDP

Let's again start with the equation of exchange.

$$M \times V \equiv P \times Q \tag{1}$$

If the equation of exchange holds, then

$$P \equiv \frac{M \times V}{Q} \tag{2}$$

Equation 2 shows that the money supply, velocity, and Real GDP determine the price level. In other words, the price level depends on the money supply, velocity, and Real GDP.

What kinds of changes in M, V, and Q will bring about inflation (an increase in the price level), *ceteris paribus*? Obviously, an increase in M or V or a decrease in Q will cause the price level to rise. For example, if velocity rises, the price level will rise; that is, an increase in velocity is inflationary.

Inflationary tendencies: $M\uparrow$, $V\uparrow$, $Q\downarrow$

What will bring about deflation (a decrease in the price level), *ceteris paribus*? Obviously, a decrease in M or V or an increase in Q will cause the price level to fall. For example, if the money supply declines, the price level will drop; that is, a decrease in the money supply is deflationary.

Deflationary tendencies: $M\downarrow$, $V\downarrow$, $Q\uparrow$

(Answers to Self-Test questions are in Answers to Self-Test Questions at the back of the book.)

1. If $M \times V$ increases, why does $P \times Q$ have to rise?

2. What is the difference between the equation of exchange and the simple quantity theory of money?

3. Predict what will happen to the AD curve as a result of each of the following:

   a. The money supply rises.

   b. Velocity falls.

   c. The money supply rises by a greater percentage than velocity falls.

   d. The money supply falls.

MONETARISM

Economists who call themselves *monetarists* have not been content to rely on the simple quantity theory of money. They do *not* hold that velocity is constant, nor do they hold that output is constant. Monetarist views on the money supply, velocity, aggregate demand, and aggregate supply are discussed in this section.

The Four Monetarist Positions

We begin with a brief explanation of the four positions held by monetarists. Then we discuss how, based on these positions, monetarists view the economy.

VELOCITY CHANGES IN A PREDICTABLE WAY In the simple quantity theory of money, velocity is assumed to be constant; therefore, only changes in the money supply bring about changes in aggregate demand. Monetarists do not assume that velocity is constant, but rather that it can and does change. However, they believe that velocity changes in a predictable way, that is, not randomly, but in a way that can be understood and predicted. Monetarists hold that velocity is a function of certain variables—the interest rate, the expected inflation rate, the frequency with which employees receive paychecks, and more—and that changes in it can be predicted.

AGGREGATE DEMAND DEPENDS ON THE MONEY SUPPLY AND ON VELOCITY Earlier, we showed that total expenditures in the economy (*TE*) equal *MV*. To better understand the economy, some economists—such as Keynesians—focus on the spending components of *TE* (*C, I, G, EX,* and *IM*). Other economists—such as monetarists—focus on the money supply (*M*) and velocity (*V*). For example, Keynesians often argue that changes in *C, I, G, EX,* or *IM* can change aggregate demand, whereas monetarists often argue that *M* and *V* can change aggregate demand.

THE *SRAS* CURVE IS UPWARD-SLOPING In the simple quantity theory of money, the level of Real GDP (*Q*) is assumed to be constant in the short run. So the aggregate supply curve is vertical, as shown in Exhibit 3. According to monetarists, Real GDP may change in the short run, and therefore the *SRAS* curve is upward sloping.

THE ECONOMY IS SELF-REGULATING (PRICES AND WAGES ARE FLEXIBLE)

Monetarists believe that prices and wages are flexible. Monetarists therefore believe that the economy is self-regulating; it can move itself out of a recessionary or inflationary gap and into long-run equilibrium, producing Natural Real GDP.

Monetarism and *AD–AS*

If monetarists tend to stress velocity and the money supply when discussing how the economy works, what effect does this view have in the *AD–AS* framework? Exhibit 3 helps to explain some of the highlights of monetarism. Each of the four parts (a)–(d) is considered separately.

PART (a) The economy is initially in long-run equilibrium, producing Natural Real GDP (Q_N) at price level P_1. Monetarists believe that changes in the money supply will change aggregate demand. For example, suppose the money supply rises from $800 billion to $820 billion. If velocity is constant, the *AD* curve shifts to the right, from AD_1 to AD_2 in the exhibit. As a result, Real GDP rises to Q_1, and the price level rises to P_2. And, of course, if Real GDP rises, the unemployment rate falls, *ceteris paribus*.

According to monetarists, the economy is in an inflationary gap at Q_1. However, given the monetarist belief in a self-regulating economy, soon wages will be bid up because the unemployment rate in an inflationary gap is less than the natural unemployment rate. The increase in wages will cause the *SRAS* curve to shift leftward from $SRAS_1$ to $SRAS_2$. The economy will return to long-run equilibrium, producing the same level of Real GDP as it did originally (Q_N), but at a higher price level.

What monetarists predict will happen to the economy in the short run due to an increase in the money supply is slightly different from what they predict will happen in the long run. In the short run, Real GDP will rise and the unemployment rate will fall. In the long run, Real GDP will return to its natural level, as will the unemployment rate, and the price level will be higher.

PART (b) The economy is initially in long-run equilibrium, producing Natural Real GDP (Q_N) at price level P_1. A decrease in the money supply, holding velocity constant, will shift the *AD* curve to the left from AD_1 to AD_2. This will reduce Real GDP to Q_1 and reduce the price level to P_2. Because Real GDP has fallen, the unemployment rate will rise.

According to monetarists, the economy in part (b) is in a recessionary gap. Monetarists hold that the economy can get itself out of a recessionary gap because the economy is self-regulating. In time, wages will fall, the *SRAS* curve will shift to the right, and the economy will be back in long-run equilibrium producing Q_N, albeit at a lower price level.

Again, the short- and long-run effects of a decrease in the money supply differ, according to monetarists. In the short run, Real GDP will fall and the unemployment rate will rise. In the long run, Real GDP will return to its natural level, as will the unemployment rate, and the price level will be lower.

PART (c) Again, we start with the economy in long-run equilibrium. Instead of the money supply, velocity changes. An increase in velocity causes the *AD* curve to shift to the right from AD_1 to AD_2. As a result, Real GDP rises, as does the price level. The unemployment rate falls as Real GDP rises.

EXHIBIT 3

Monetarism in an *AD–AS* Framework

According to monetarists, changes in the money supply and velocity can change aggregate demand. In (a), an increase in the money supply shifts the *AD* curve to the right and raises Real GDP and the price level. Monetarists believe the economy is self-regulating; in time it moves back to its Natural Real GDP level at a higher price level. The same self-regulating properties are present in (b)–(d).

According to monetarists, the economy is in an inflationary gap, but in time it will move back to long-run equilibrium. So in the short run, an increase in velocity raises Real GDP and lowers the unemployment rate. In the long run, Real GDP returns to its natural level, as does the unemployment rate, and the price level is higher.

PART (d) The economy is in long-run equilibrium. A decrease in velocity causes the *AD* curve to shift to the left from AD_1 to AD_2. As a result, Real GDP falls, as does the price level. The unemployment rate rises as Real GDP falls.

According to monetarists, the economy is in a recessionary gap, but in time it will move back to long-run equilibrium. So in the short run, a decrease in velocity lowers Real GDP and increases the unemployment rate. In the long run, Real GDP returns to its natural level, as does the unemployment rate, and the price level is lower.

The Monetarist View of the Economy

The diagrammatic exposition of monetarism in Exhibit 3 reveals that monetarists believe that:

- The economy is self-regulating.
- Changes in velocity and the money supply can change aggregate demand.
- Changes in velocity and the money supply will change the price level and Real GDP in the short run but only the price level in the long run.

We need to make one other important point with respect to monetarists. Consider this question: Can a change in velocity offset a change in the money supply? Suppose velocity falls and the money supply rises. By itself, a decrease in velocity will shift the *AD* curve to the left. And, by itself, an increase in the money supply will shift the *AD* curve to the right. The decline in velocity could shift the *AD* curve to the left by the same amount as the increase in the money supply shifts the *AD* curve to the right. If so, then a change in the money supply would have no effect on Real GDP, on the short-run price level, and on the long-run price level. In other words, changes in monetary policy may be ineffective at changing Real GDP and the price level.

Monetarists think that this condition—a change in velocity completely offsetting a change in the money supply—does not occur often. They believe (1) that velocity does not change very much from one period to the next (i.e., it is relatively stable) and (2) that changes in velocity are predictable (as mentioned earlier). In other words, monetarists believe velocity is relatively stable and predictable.

So in the monetarist view of the economy, changes in velocity are not likely to offset changes in the money supply. Therefore, *changes in the money supply will largely determine changes in aggregate demand and thus changes in Real GDP and the price level.* For all practical purposes, an increase in the money supply will raise aggregate demand, increase both Real GDP and the price level in the short run, and increase only the price level in the long run. A decrease in the money supply will lower aggregate demand, decrease both Real GDP and the price level in the short run, and decrease only the price level in the long run.

SELF-TEST

1. What do monetarists predict will happen in the short run and in the long run as a result of each of the following? (In each case, assume the economy is currently in long-run equilibrium.)

   a. Velocity rises.

   b. Velocity falls.

   c. The money supply rises.

   d. The money supply falls.

2. Can a change in velocity offset a change in the money supply (on aggregate demand)? Explain your answer.

INFLATION

In everyday usage, the word "inflation" refers to any increase in the price level. Economists, though, like to differentiate between two types of increases in the price level: a one-shot increase and a continued increase.

One-Shot Inflation

One-shot inflation is exactly what it sounds like: a one-shot, or one-time, increase in the price level. Suppose the CPI for years 1 to 5 is as follows:

Year	CPI
1	100
2	110
3	110
4	110
5	110

Notice that the price level is higher in year 2 than in year 1, but after year 2 it does not change. In other words, it takes a one-shot jump in year 2 and then stabilizes. This is an example of one-shot inflation, which can originate on either the demand side or the supply side of the economy.

ONE-SHOT INFLATION: DEMAND-SIDE INDUCED In Exhibit 4(a), the economy is initially in long-run equilibrium at point 1. Suppose the aggregate demand curve shifts rightward from AD_1 to AD_2. As this happens, the economy moves to point 2, where the price level is P_2. At point 2 in Exhibit 4(b), the Real GDP the economy is producing (Q_2) is greater than Natural Real GDP; so the unemployment rate in the economy is lower than the natural unemployment rate. Consequently, as old wage contracts expire, workers are paid higher wage rates because unemployment is relatively low. As wage rates rise, the SRAS curve shifts leftward from $SRAS_1$ to $SRAS_2$. The long-run equilibrium position is at point 3. The price level and Real GDP at each of the three points are as follows:

Point	Price Level	Real GDP
1 (start)	P_1	$Q_1 = Q_N$
2	P_2	Q_2
3 (end)	P_3	$Q_1 = Q_N$

EXHIBIT 4

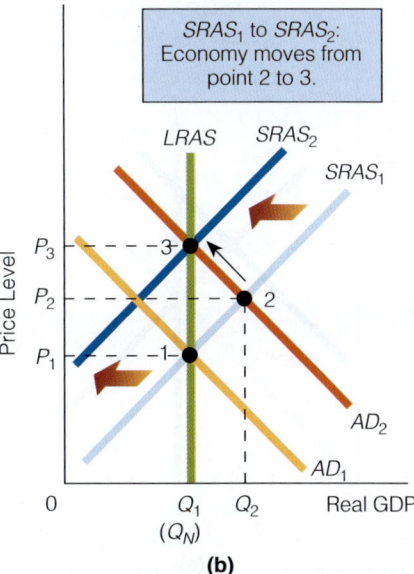

One-Shot Inflation: Demand-side Induced

(a) The aggregate demand curve shifts rightward from AD_1 to AD_2. As a result, the price level increases from P_1 to P_2; the economy moves from point 1 to point 2. (b) Because the Real GDP the economy produces (Q_2) is greater than Natural Real GDP, the unemployment rate that exists is less than the natural unemployment rate. Wage rates rise, and the short-run aggregate supply curve shifts leftward from $SRAS_1$ to $SRAS_2$. Long-run equilibrium is at point 3.

Notice that at point 3 the economy is at a higher price level than at point 1, but at the same Real GDP level.

Price levels that go from P_1 to P_2 to P_3 may seem like more than a one-shot increase. But because the price level stabilizes (at P_3), we cannot characterize it as continually rising. So the change in the price level is representative of one-shot inflation.

ONE-SHOT INFLATION: SUPPLY-SIDE INDUCED In Exhibit 5(a), the economy is initially in long-run equilibrium at point 1. Suppose the short-run aggregate supply curve shifts leftward from $SRAS_1$ to $SRAS_2$ because, say, oil prices increase. As the curve shifts, the economy moves to point 2, where the price level is P_2.

At point 2 in Exhibit 5(b), the Real GDP that the economy is producing (Q_2) is less than Natural Real GDP; so the unemployment rate in the economy is greater than the natural unemployment rate. Consequently, as old wage contracts expire, workers are paid lower wage rates because unemployment is relatively high. As wage rates fall, the short-run aggregate supply curve shifts rightward from $SRAS_2$ to $SRAS_1$. The long-run equilibrium position is at point 1 again. (If wage rates are somewhat inflexible, moving from point 2 back to point 1 may take some time.) The price level and Real GDP at each of the three points are as follows:

Point	Price Level	Real GDP
1 (start)	P_1	$Q_1 = Q_N$
2	P_2	Q_2
3 (end)	P_1	$Q_1 = Q_N$

Because the price level initially increased from P_1 to P_2, this case is descriptive of one-shot inflation.

CONFUSING DEMAND-INDUCED AND SUPPLY-INDUCED ONE-SHOT INFLATION Demand-induced and supply-induced types of one-shot inflation are easy

---

EXHIBIT 5

One-Shot Inflation: Supply-Side Induced

(a) The short-run aggregate supply curve shifts leftward from $SRAS_1$ to $SRAS_2$. As a result, the price level increases from P_1 to P_2; the economy moves from point 1 to point 2.
(b) Because the Real GDP the economy produces (Q_2) is less than Natural Real GDP, the unemployment rate that exists is greater than the natural unemployment rate. Some economists argue that when this happens, wage rates will fall and the short-run aggregate supply curve will shift rightward from $SRAS_2$ (back to $SRAS_1$). Long-run equilibrium is at point 1.

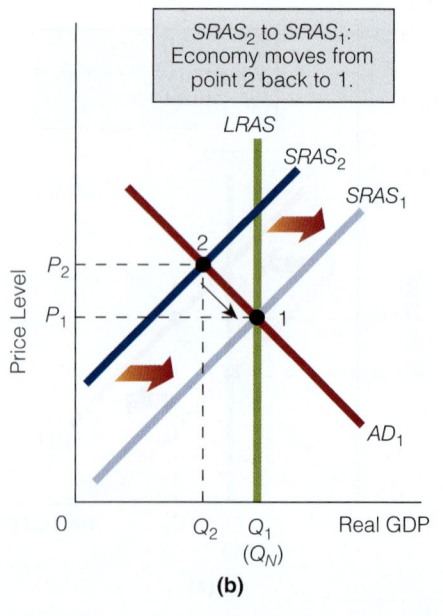

to confuse.[2] To illustrate, suppose the Federal Reserve System increases the money supply. With more money in the economy, there can be greater total spending at any given price level. Consequently, the *AD* curve shifts rightward.

Next, prices begin to rise, and, soon afterward, wage rates begin to rise (because the economy is in an inflationary gap). Many employers, perhaps unaware that the money supply has increased, certainly are aware that they are paying their employees higher wages. Thus, employers may think the higher price level is due to higher wage rates, not to the increased money supply that preceded the higher wage rates. But they would be wrong. What may look like a supply-induced rise in the price level is really demand-induced.

We can tell this same story in terms of the diagrams in Exhibit 4. In (a), the *AD* curve shifts rightward because, as explained, the money supply increases. Employers, however, are unaware of what has happened in part (a). What they see is part (b). They end up paying higher wage rates to their employees, and the *SRAS* curve shifts leftward. Unaware that the *AD* curve shifted rightward in (a) but aware that the *SRAS* curve shifted leftward in (b), employers mistakenly conclude that the rise in the price level originated with a supply-side factor (higher wage rates), not with a demand-side factor (an increase in the money supply).

ⓣhinking Like AN ECONOMIST

Your Eyes Can Deceive You People tend to believe that what they see with their own eyes or what they experience directly in their daily lives causes the effects they notice. In our last example, employers mistakenly believed that the stimulus for the rise in the price level was a rise in wage rates (which they had experienced firsthand), not an increase in the money supply (which they probably did not know had occurred). But the economist knows that the cause of a phenomenon may be far removed from our personal orbit. This awareness is part of the economic way of thinking. ▲ ▲ ▲

ⓕinding ECONOMICS

In a Remodeling Job Jan is getting her house remodeled. Today her contractor told her that the price he pays for many of his supplies has increased and that the remodeling is going to cost "a little more." That night, Jan says to her husband, Mike, "I guess that's the way life is sometimes. Costs go up; so prices go up." Where is the economics? Could Jan somehow be the real reason that her contractor's costs went up?

What Jan may not see is that she and others who want their houses remodeled are increasing the demand for remodeling. As a result, the demand rises for things such as tile, wood, nails, cement, and related materials. The higher prices for tile, nails, and wood are the higher costs the remodeler is talking about; so when he tells Jan his costs have risen, he is telling the truth. Jan then blames the higher costs for her having to pay more for her remodeling job. Actually, the higher demand stemming from her and others starts the process that ends in higher costs for the remodeler and in higher prices for her. ▲ ▲ ▲

Continued Inflation

Suppose the CPI for years 1 to 5 is as follows:

Year	CPI
1	100
2	110
3	120
4	130
5	140

---

2. Sometimes the terms "demand-side inflation" and "supply-side inflation" are used.

Grade Inflation: It's All Relative

Inflation can sometimes be deceptive. Suppose Jones produces and sells motorcycles. The average price for one of his motorcycles is $10,000. Unknown to Jones, the Fed increases the money supply. Months pass, and then one day Jones notices that the demand for his motorcycles has increased. Jones raises the prices of his motorcycles and earns a higher dollar income.

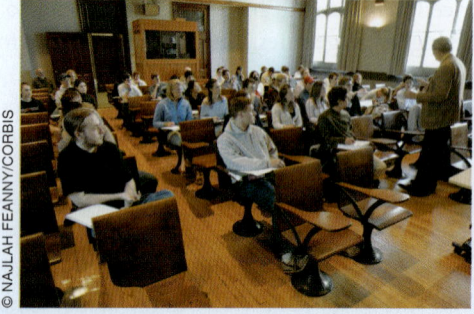

© NAJLAH FEANNY/CORBIS

Jones is excited about earning more income, but soon he realizes that the prices of many of the things he buys have increased too. Food, clothing, and housing prices have all gone up. Jones is earning a higher dollar income, but he is also paying higher prices. In relative terms, Jones's financial position may be the same as it was before the price of motorcycles increased.

Now let's consider grade inflation. Beginning in the 1960s, the average GPA at most colleges and universities across the country began to rise. Whereas professors once gave out the full range of grades—A, B, C, D, and F—today many professors give only As and Bs and a few Cs. The so-called Gentleman's C, once a mainstay on many college campuses, is said to have been replaced by the Gentleperson's B.

Grade inflation can deceive you, just as general price inflation deceived Jones. To illustrate, suppose you get higher grades (without studying more or working harder). Your average grade goes from, say, C+ to B,

and you believe you have an advantage over other college and university students. You reason that with higher grades, you will have a better chance of getting a good job or of getting into graduate school.

But you do only if your grades go up *and no one else's do*. In other words, your relative position must improve. Grade inflation at thousands of colleges and universities across the country prevents you from gaining that advantage. You get higher grades, but so does everyone else. Your GPA increases from, say, 2.90 to 3.60, but other students' GPAs increase similarly.

So, as long as other students are getting higher grades too, better grades for you do not necessarily make it easier for you to compete with others for a job or for admission to graduate school. In essence, grade inflation, like general price inflation, is deceptive. With price inflation, you may initially think your financial position has improved because you are earning more for what you sell, but then you realize that you have to pay more for the things you buy. With grade inflation, you may initially think you have an advantage over other students because you are receiving higher grades, but then you learn that everyone else is getting higher grades too. Your relative position may be the same as it was before grade inflation boosted your GPA.

Continued Inflation
A continued increase in the price level.

Notice that the CPI goes from 100 to 110, then from 110 to 120, and so on. Each year the CPI is higher than the year before. This continued increase in the price level is an example of continued inflation.

FROM ONE-SHOT INFLATION TO CONTINUED INFLATION Continued increases in aggregate demand can turn one-shot inflation into continued inflation. (Later in this chapter we describe what leads to continued increases in aggregate demand.) The process is illustrated in Exhibit 6. (The diagram looks scary, but not when you take it one step at a time.)

Beginning at point 1 in Exhibit 6(a), the aggregate demand curve shifts rightward from AD_1 to AD_2. The economy moves from point 1 to point 2. At point 2, the unemployment rate in the economy is less than the natural unemployment rate. As a result, wage rates rise and cause the short-run aggregate supply curve to shift leftward from $SRAS_1$ to $SRAS_2$. The economy moves from point 2 to point 3. At point 3, the economy is in long-run equilibrium.

Suppose that at point 3 the economy experiences *another* rightward shift in the aggregate demand curve (to AD_3). The process keeps repeating itself, and the economy moves from point 3 to point 4 to point 5. Still *another* rightward shift in the aggregate demand

EXHIBIT 6

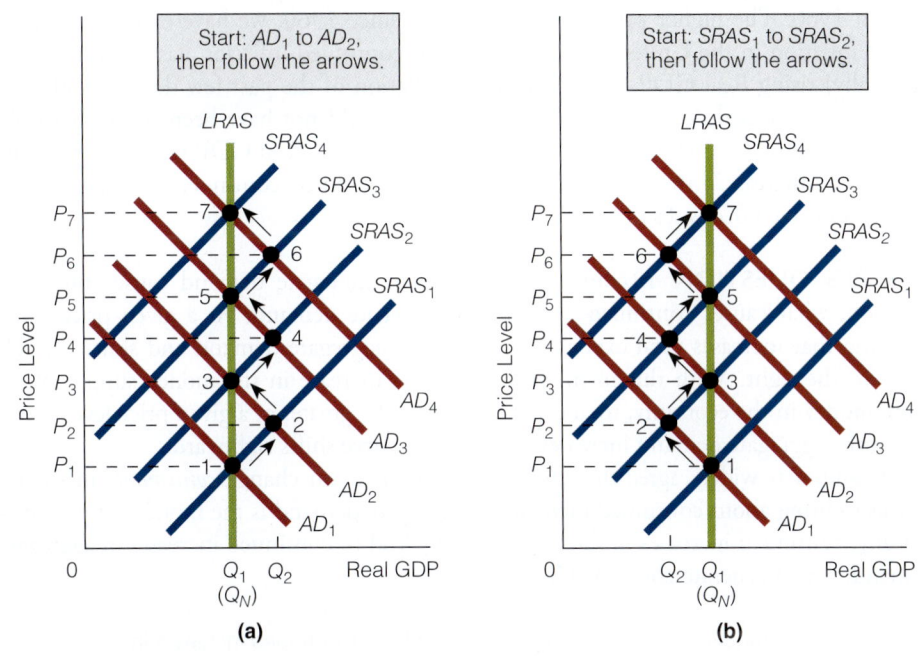

Changing One-Shot Inflation into Continued Inflation

(a) The aggregate demand curve shifts rightward from AD_1 to AD_2. The economy initially moves from point 1 to point 2 and finally to point 3. Continued increases in the price level are brought about through continued increases in aggregate demand. (b) The short-run aggregate supply curve shifts leftward from $SRAS_1$ to $SRAS_2$. The economy initially moves from point 1 to point 2. The economy will return to point 1 unless there is an increase in aggregate demand. We see here, as in (a), that continued increases in the price level are brought about through continued increases in aggregate demand.

curve moves the economy from point 5 to point 6 to point 7. The exhibit stops at point 7, but it could have continued. The result of this process is a *continually rising price level*—from P_1 to P_7 and beyond. Continued increases in aggregate demand cause continued inflation.

Continued inflation from the supply side of the economy is illustrated in Exhibit 6(b). Beginning at point 1, the short-run aggregate supply curve shifts leftward from $SRAS_1$ to $SRAS_2$. The economy moves from point 1 to point 2. At point 2, the unemployment rate in the economy is greater than the natural unemployment rate. According to some economists, the natural tendency is for wage rates to fall and for the $SRAS$ curve to shift rightward, moving the economy back to point 1.

This natural tendency of the economy to return to point 1 will be offset, however, if the aggregate demand curve shifts rightward. Then, instead of moving from point 2 back to point 1, the economy moves from point 2 to point 3. At point 3, the economy is in long-run equilibrium, and the price level is higher than at point 2.

Suppose the economy experiences another leftward shift in the aggregate supply curve (to $SRAS_3$). The economy moves from point 3 to point 4 and would naturally return to point 3 unless the aggregate demand curve shifts rightward. If it does, the economy moves to point 5. The same process moves the economy from point 5 to point 6 to point 7, where the exhibit stops. This process results in a continually rising price level—from P_1 to P_7 and beyond. Again, *continued increases in aggregate demand cause continued inflation.*

THE EFFECT OF CONTINUED DECLINES IN SRAS Can continued declines in $SRAS$ cause continued inflation? For example, suppose a labor union continually asks for and receives higher wages. As wages continually increase, the $SRAS$ curve will continually shift leftward, leading to a continually rising price level. This could happen but isn't likely. Every time workers ask for and receive higher wages—shifting the $SRAS$ curve leftward—Real GDP declines. Because not as many workers are needed to produce a lower Real GDP as are needed to produce a higher Real GDP, some of the workers will lose their jobs. Labor unions are not likely to adopt a policy that would put more and more of their members out of work.

There is another argument against declines in *SRAS* causing continued inflation. The CPI and the Real GDP level for, say, 1960 indicate that today both are higher than they were in 1960. The higher price level means that, since 1960, we have experienced continued inflation in the United States but that this continued inflation has accompanied a (generally) rising Real GDP. If the continued inflation of the past few decades had been caused by continued declines in *SRAS,* Real GDP would not have been rising. It would have been falling (as *SRAS* declines, the price level rises and Real GDP falls). In short, the continued inflation in the United States had to be caused by continued increases in *AD,* not by continued decreases in *SRAS.*

THE BIG QUESTION If continued increases in aggregate demand cause continued inflation, what causes continued increases in aggregate demand? At a given price level, anything that increases total expenditures increases aggregate demand and shifts the *AD* curve to the right. With this in mind, consider an increase in the money supply. With more money in the economy, total expenditures can be greater at a given price level. Consequently, aggregate demand increases, and the *AD* curve shifts rightward.

Economists widely agree that the only factor that can change *continually* in such a way as to bring about continued increases in aggregate demand is the money supply. Specifically, continued increases in the money supply lead to continued increases in aggregate demand, which generate continued inflation.

Continued increases in the money supply → Continued increases in
aggregate demand → Continued inflation

The money supply is the *only* factor that can continually increase without causing a reduction in one of the four components of total expenditures (consumption, investment, government purchases, or net exports). This point is important because someone might ask, "Can't government purchases continually increase and so cause continued inflation?" This is unlikely for two reasons:

- Government purchases cannot go beyond both real and political limits. The real upper limit is 100 percent of GDP. No one knows what the political upper limit is, but it is likely to be less than 100 percent of GDP. In either case, once government purchases reach their limit, they can no longer increase.

- Some economists argue that government purchases that are not financed with new money may crowd out one of the other expenditure components (see Chapter 11.) Thus, increases in government purchases are not guaranteed to raise total expenditures because if government purchases rise, consumption may fall to the degree that government purchases have increased. For example, for every additional dollar government spends on public education, households may spend $1 less on private education.

The emphasis on the money supply as the only factor that can continue to increase and thus cause continued inflation has led most economists to agree with Nobel Laureate Milton Friedman that "inflation is always and everywhere a monetary phenomenon."

SELF-TEST

1. The prices of houses, cars, and television sets have increased. Has there been inflation?

2. Is continued inflation likely to be supply side induced? Explain your answer.

3. What type of inflation is Milton Friedman referring to when he says that "inflation is always and everywhere a monetary phenomenon"?

MONEY AND INTEREST RATES

Let's review how changes in the money supply affect different economic variables.

What Economic Variables Does a Change in the Money Supply Affect?

Money supply can affect interest rates, but to understand how, we need to review how the money supply affects different economic variables. Specifically:

1. *Money and the supply of loans.* The last chapter explained the actions of the Fed that change the money supply. For example, when the Fed undertakes an open market purchase, the money supply increases, as do reserves in the banking system. With greater reserves, banks can extend more loans. In other words, as a result of the Fed's conducting an open market purchase, the supply of loans rises. Similarly, when the Fed conducts an open market sale, the supply of loans decreases.

2. *Money and Real GDP.* This chapter shows how a change in the money supply can change aggregate demand and thereby change the price level and Real GDP in the short run. For example, look back at Exhibit 3(a). The economy starts at point 1, producing Q_N. An increase in the money supply shifts the AD curve rightward, from AD_1 to AD_2. In the short run, the economy moves to point 2 and produces a higher level of Real GDP (Q_1). Similarly, in the short run, a decrease in the money supply produces a lower level of Real GDP [see Exhibit 3(b)].

3. *Money and the price level.* This chapter also shows how a change in the money supply can change the price level. Again, look back at Exhibit 3(a). Initially, at point 1, the price level is P_1. An increase in the money supply shifts the AD curve rightward from AD_1 to AD_2. In the short run, the price level in the economy moves from P_1 to P_2. In the long run, the economy is at point 3 and the price level is P_3. Exhibit 3(b) shows how a decrease in the money supply affects the price level.

So changes in the money supply affect (1) the supply of loans, (2) Real GDP, and (3) the price level.

Can the money supply affect anything else? Many economists say that because the money supply affects the price level, it also affects the *expected inflation rate*, which is the inflation rate that you expect. For example, your expected inflation rate—the inflation rate you expect will be realized over the next year—may be 5 percent, 6 percent, or some other rate. Changes in the money supply affect the expected inflation rate, either directly or indirectly. The equation of exchange indicates that the greater the increase in the money supply is, the greater the rise in the price level will be. And we would expect that the greater the rise in the price level is, the higher the expected inflation rate will be, *ceteris paribus*. For example, we would predict that a money supply growth rate of, say, 10 percent a year generates a greater actual inflation rate and a larger expected inflation rate than a money supply growth rate of 2 percent a year.

So, changes in the money supply (or changes in the rate of growth of the money supply) can affect:

1. the supply of loans.

2. Real GDP.

3. the price level.

4. the expected inflation rate.

The Money Supply, the Loanable Funds Market, and Interest Rates

Exhibit 7(a) shows the loanable funds market. The demand for loanable funds (D_{LF}) is downward sloping, indicating that borrowers will borrow more funds as the interest rate declines. The supply of loanable funds (S_{LF}) is upward sloping, indicating that lenders will lend more funds as the interest rate rises. The equilibrium interest rate (i_1 percent) is determined through the forces of supply and demand. If there is a surplus of loanable funds, the interest rate falls; if there is a shortage of loanable funds, the interest rate rises.

Anything that affects either the supply of or the demand for loanable funds will obviously affect the interest rate. All four of the factors that are affected by changes in the money supply—the supply of loans, Real GDP, the price level, and the expected inflation rate—affect either the supply of or demand for loanable funds.

THE SUPPLY OF LOANS A Fed open market purchase increases reserves in the banking system and therefore increases the supply of loanable funds. As a result, the interest rate declines [see Exhibit 7(b)]. This change in the interest rate due to a change in the supply of loanable funds is called the liquidity effect.

REAL GDP A change in Real GDP affects both the supply of and the demand for loanable funds.

First, how does Real GDP affect the supply of loanable funds? When Real GDP rises, people's wealth is greater. (Real GDP consists of goods, and goods are a component of wealth.) When people became wealthier, they often demand more bonds (in much the same way that they may demand more houses, cars, and jewelry). Demanding more bonds (buying more bonds), however, is nothing more than lending more money to others. When you buy a bond issued by company A, you are essentially giving the company a loan. The company says. "Do you want to buy this bond for $10,000?" You say yes. When you buy the bond from the company for $10,000, you essentially give the company a $10,000 loan, which it is obligated to repay with interest. When the company pays off the bond to you, it returns the $10,000 plus interest. So, as Real GDP rises, individuals become wealthier, and they tend to buy more bonds, that is, extend more loans. The supply of loanable funds increases.

Second, how does Real GDP affect the demand for loanable funds? When Real GDP rises, profitable business opportunities usually abound, and businesses issue or supply more bonds to take advantage of those opportunities. But, supplying more bonds is nothing more than demanding more loanable funds. So, when Real GDP rises, corporations issue or supply more bonds, thereby demanding more loanable funds.

In summary, when Real GDP increases, both the supply of and the demand for loanable funds increase. The overall effect on the interest rate is that, usually, the demand for loanable funds increases by more than the supply so that the interest rate rises. The change in the interest rate due to a change in Real GDP is called the income effect. See Exhibit 7(c).

THE PRICE LEVEL A downward-sloping *AD* curve is explained by (1) the real balance effect, (2) the interest rate effect, and (3) the international trade effect (see Chapter 8). With respect to the interest rate effect, when the price level rises, the purchasing power of money falls. People may therefore increase their demand for credit or loanable funds to borrow the funds necessary to buy a fixed bundle of goods. This change in the interest rate due to a change in the price level is called the price-level effect. See Exhibit 7(d).

THE EXPECTED INFLATION RATE A change in the expected inflation rate affects both the supply of and demand for loanable funds. Suppose the expected inflation rate is zero and that when the expected inflation rate is zero, the equilibrium interest rate is 6

Liquidity Effect
The change in the interest rate due to a change in the supply of loanable funds.

Income Effect
The change in the interest rate due to a change in Real GDP.

Price-Level Effect
The change in the interest rate due to a change in the price level.

EXHIBIT 7

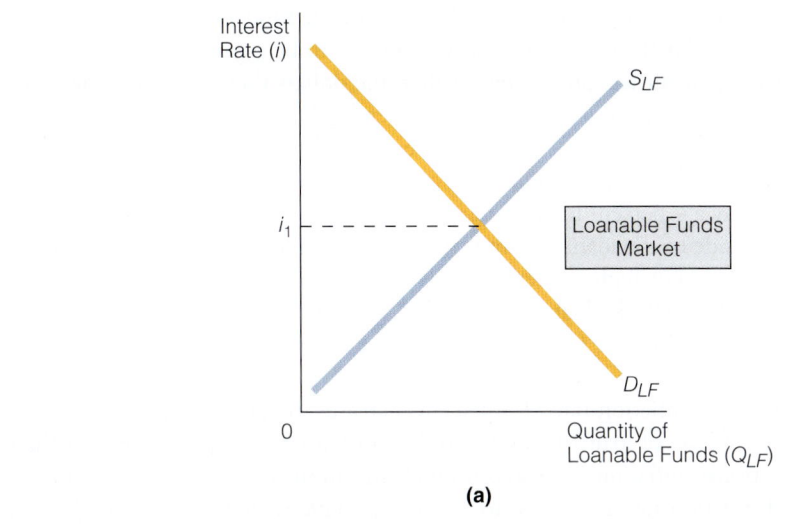

(a)

The Interest Rate and the Loanable Funds Market

The loanable funds market is shown in part (a). The demand for loanable funds is downward sloping; the supply of loanable funds is upward sloping. Part (b) shows the liquidity effect, part (c) shows the income effect, part (d) shows the price-level effect, and part (e) shows the expectations effect.

(b)

(c)

(d)

(e)

percent, as in Exhibit 7(e). Now suppose the expected inflation rate rises from 0 percent to 4 percent. What will this rise in the expected inflation rate do to the demand for and supply of loanable funds? Borrowers (demanders of loanable funds) will be willing to pay 4 percent more interest for their loans because they expect to be paying back the loans with dollars that have 4 percent less buying power than the dollars they are borrowing. If they wait to buy goods they want, the prices will have risen by 4 percent. To beat the price rise, consumers are willing to pay up to 4 percent more to borrow money to purchase the goods now. In effect, the demand for loanable funds curve shifts rightward so that at Q_1 borrowers are willing to pay a 4 percent higher interest rate.

On the other side of the loanable funds market, the lenders (the suppliers of loanable funds) require a 4 percent higher interest rate to compensate them for the 4 percent less valuable dollars with which the loan will be repaid. In effect, the supply of loanable funds curve shifts leftward, so that at Q_1 lenders will receive an interest rate of 10 percent. See Exhibit 7(e).

Thus an expected inflation rate of 4 percent increases the demand for loanable funds and decreases the supply of loanable funds. So the interest rate is 4 percent higher than it was when the expected inflation rate was zero. A change in the interest rate due to a change in the expected inflation rate is referred to as the **expectations effect** (or *Fisher effect*, after economist Irving Fisher).

Exhibit 8 summarizes how a change in the money supply directly and indirectly affects the interest rate.

Expectations Effect
The change in the interest rate due to a change in the expected inflation rate.

EXHIBIT 8

How the Fed Affects the Interest Rate

This exhibit summarizes the way the Fed (through its monetary policy) affects the interest rate. For example, an open market operation (OMO) directly affects the supply of loanable funds and affects the interest rate. An OMO also affects Real GDP, the price level, and the expected inflation rate, and therefore indirectly affects either the supply of or demand for loanable funds, which in turn affects the interest rate.

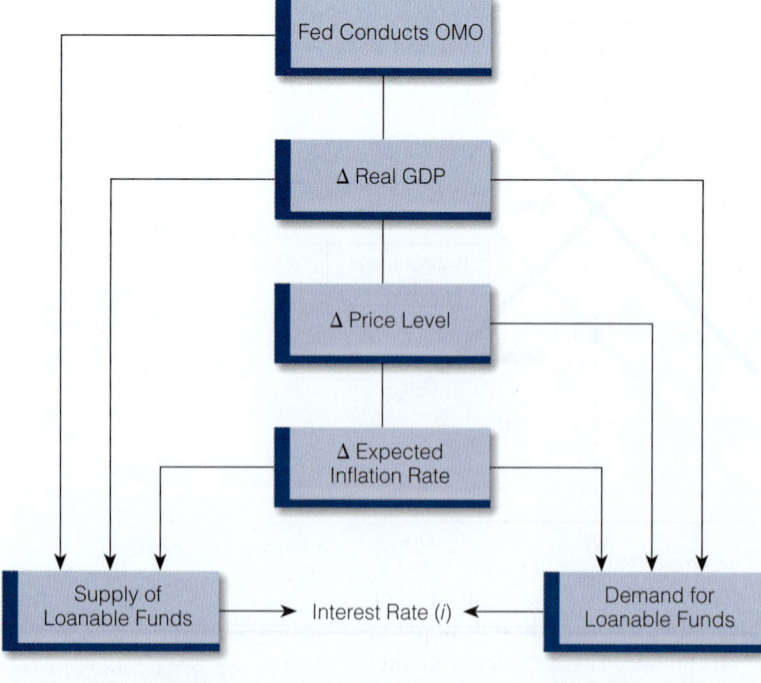

THE DIFFERENCE BETWEEN THE PRICE-LEVEL EFFECT AND THE EXPECTATIONS EFFECT To many people, the price-level effect sounds the same as the expectations effect. After all, both have something to do with the price level.

But they are different. Consider a one-shot change in the money supply that ultimately moves the price level from a price index of 120 to a price index of 135. The price-level effect refers to the change in the interest rate that is related to the actual rise in price level. The demand for loanable funds creeps up steadily as the price index rises from 120 to 121, to 122, to 123, and so on to 135. Once the price index hits 135, though, there is no further reason for the demand for loanable funds to rise because the price level isn't rising anymore.

As the price level is rising, people's expected inflation rate is rising. They may feel they know where the price level is headed (from 120 to 135) and adjust accordingly. Once the price level hits 135 (and given that the change in the money supply is one-shot), the expected inflation rate falls to zero. Any change in the interest rate due to a rise in the expected inflation rate is now over, and therefore the expected inflation rate no longer has an effect on the interest rate. But certainly the price level still has an effect because the price level is higher than it was originally. In the end, the effect on the interest rate due to a rise in the price level remains, and the effect on the interest rate due to a rise in the expected inflation rate disappears.

What Happens to the Interest Rate as the Money Supply Changes?

Suppose the Fed takes action to raise the rate of growth of the money supply from, say, 3 percent to 5 percent a year. What effect does this action have on the interest rate? Some people will quickly say that it will lower the interest rate, thinking perhaps that only the liquidity effect comes into play. In other words, as the Fed increases the rate of growth of the money supply, more reserves enter the banking system, more loans are extended, and the interest rate falls [Exhibit 7(b)].

That would be the right answer if all an increase in the money supply growth rate did was to affect the supply of loanable funds, but, as explained, this isn't the only effect. Real GDP changes, the price level changes, and the expected inflation rate changes, and all these changes affect the loanable funds market, just as the Fed action did. Figuring out what happens to the interest rate is a matter of trying to figure out when each effect (liquidity, income, price-level, and expectations) occurs and how strong each is.

To illustrate, suppose on December 31 everyone expects the Fed to continue to increase the money supply at a growth rate of 2 percent a year. Then, on January 1, the Fed announces that it will increase the rate of growth in the money supply to 4 percent and will begin open market purchases to effect this outcome immediately. One second after the announcement, people's expected inflation rate may rise. The expectations effect begins to affect interest rates immediately. On January 2, the interest rate is therefore higher than it was one day earlier.

- *Point 1 in time:* Fed says it will increase the growth rate of the money supply.
- *Point 2 in time:* If the expectations effect kicks in immediately, then . . .
- *Point 3 in time:* Interest rates rise.

At point 3 in time, a natural conclusion is that an increase in the rate of growth in the money supply *raises* the interest rate. The problem with this conclusion, though, is that *not all the effects (liquidity, income, etc.) have occurred yet.* In time, the liquidity effect puts downward pressure on the interest rate. Suppose the liquidity effect goes to work on January 15, and the interest rate begins to fall from what it was on January 2. Then, someone on January 15 could say, "Obviously, an increase in the rate of growth of the money supply *lowers* interest rates."

- *Point 4 in time:* Liquidity effect kicks in.
- *Point 5 in time:* As a result of what happened at point 4, the interest rate drops. The interest rate is now lower than it was at point 3.

The point is that a change in the money supply affects the economy in many ways: changing the supply of loanable funds directly, changing Real GDP and therefore changing the demand for and supply of loanable funds, changing the expected inflation rate, and so on. The *timing* and *magnitude* of these effects determine the changes in the interest rate.

The Nominal and Real Interest Rates

If you were to call a bank and ask what it charges for, say, a car loan, the bank would quote an interest rate. The quoted interest rate is the rate we have been discussing, the interest rate that comes about through the interaction of the demand for and supply of loanable funds. Sometimes, this interest rate is called the nominal interest rate, or market interest rate.

Nominal Interest Rate
The interest rate actually charged (or paid) in the market; the market interest rate: Nominal interest rate = Real interest rate + Expected inflation rate.

The nominal interest rate may not be the true cost of borrowing because part of the nominal interest rate is a reflection of the expected inflation rate. Suppose the nominal interest rate is 9 percent, and the expected inflation rate is 2 percent. If you take out a loan for $10,000 at 9 percent, you will have to pay back the loan amount ($10,000) plus $900 in interest at the end of the year. In other words, for a $10,000 loan, you have to repay $10,900.

Now suppose the expected inflation rate turns out to be the actual inflation rate. As an example, people expect the inflation rate to be 2 percent, and it turns out to be 2 percent. In this case, the dollars you pay back will be worth less—by 2 percent—than the dollars you borrowed. In other words, you borrowed dollars that were worth 2 percent more in purchasing power than the dollars you repaid.

This fact should be taken into account in determining your real cost of borrowing. Economists would say that the real cost of borrowing was not 9 percent, but 7 percent. The real cost of borrowing is sometimes called the **real interest rate**, which is equal to the nominal interest rate minus the expected inflation rate.[3]

Real Interest Rate
The nominal interest rate minus the expected inflation rate. When the expected inflation rate is zero, the real interest rate equals the nominal interest rate.

$$\text{Real interest rate} = \text{Nominal interest rate} - \text{Expected inflation rate}$$

Given this equation, the nominal interest rate is therefore equal to the real interest rate plus the expected inflation rate.

$$\text{Nominal interest rate} = \text{Real interest rate} + \text{Expected inflation rate}$$

SELF-TEST

1. If the expected inflation rate is 4 percent and the nominal interest rate is 7 percent, what is the real interest rate?

2. Is it possible for the nominal interest rate to rise immediately following an increase in the money supply? Explain your answer.

3. The Fed affects only the interest rate via the liquidity effect. Do you agree or disagree? Explain your answer.

---

3. A broader definition is Real interest rate = Nominal interest rate − Expected rate of change in the price level. This definition is useful because we will not always be dealing with an expected inflation rate; we could be dealing with an expected deflation rate.

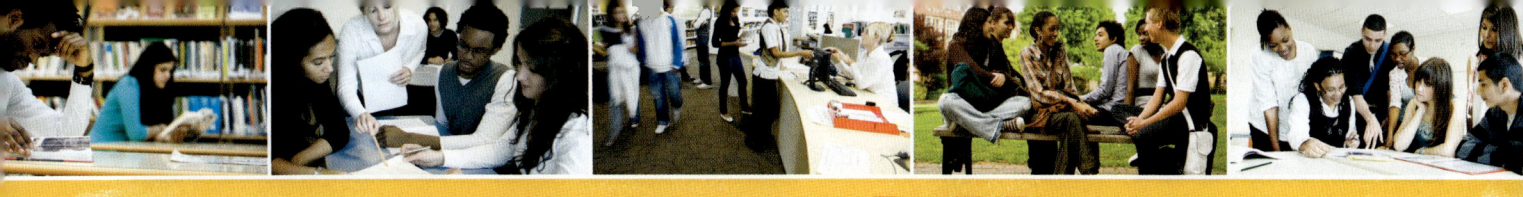

"What Is the Current Expected Inflation Rate?"

STUDENT:

Is there some way to figure out the expected inflation rate at any given time?

INSTRUCTOR:

One way to find out the expected inflation rate is to look at the spread—the difference—between the yield on conventional bonds and the yield on indexed bonds with the same maturity.

STUDENT:

What's a a conventional bond? What's an inflation-indexed bond?

INSTRUCTOR:

An inflation-indexed bond guarantees the purchaser a certain real rate of return, but a conventional, or nonindexed, bond does not. For example, suppose you purchase an *inflation-indexed*, 10-year, $1,000 bond that pays 4 percent interest. If there is no inflation, the annual interest payment is $40. But if the inflation rate is 3 percent, the bond issuer marks up the value of your security by 3 percent—from $1,000 to $1,030. Your annual interest payment is then 4 percent of this new higher amount, that is, 4 percent of $1,030, or $41.20.

Now investors are willing to accept a lower yield on inflation-indexed bonds because they get something that they don't get with conventional bonds: protection against inflation. So while a conventional bond may yield, say, 6 percent, an inflation-indexed bond may yield 4 percent. The spread is the difference between the two rates.

STUDENT:

And how does the spread or difference relate to the expected inflation rate?

INSTRUCTOR:

Well, the spread is a measure of the inflation rate that investors expect will exist over the life of the bond. To illustrate with real numbers, let's say that we go to www.bloomberg.com/ and learn that an *inflation-indexed* 10-year Treasury bond has an interest rate of 1.72 percent and that a conventional 10-year Treasury bond has an interest rate

of of 4.02. The difference, or spread, is therefore 2.3 percent. In other words, on this day, investors (or the so-called market) expect that the inflation rate is going to be 2.3 percent.

So, by checking the spread between interest rates on conventional and inflation-indexed bonds of the *same maturity* (that is, both mature in the same number of months or years), you can see what the market expects the inflation rate will be. As the spread widens, the market expects a higher inflation rate; as it narrows, the market expects a lower inflation rate.

POINTS TO REMEMBER

1. We discussed two types of bonds: inflation-indexed and convential. Each type of bonds pays an interest rate.

2. The spread, or difference, between the interest rates on a convential and an inflation-indexed bond is the market's expected inflation rate. The larger the spread is, the higher is the expected inflation rate (the inflation rate the market expects in the future). The smaller the spread, the lower the expected inflation rate (the lower the inflation rate the market expects in the future).

CHAPTER SUMMARY

THE EQUATION OF EXCHANGE

- The equation of exchange is an identity: $MV \equiv PQ$. The equation of exchange can be interpreted in different ways: (1) The money supply multiplied by velocity must equal the price level times Real GDP: $M \times V \equiv P \times Q$. (2) The money supply multiplied by velocity must equal GDP: $M \times V \equiv GDP$. (3) Total expenditures (measured by MV) must equal the total sales revenues of business firms (measured by PQ): $MV \equiv PQ$.

- The equation of exchange is not a theory of the economy. However, the equation of exchange can be turned into a theory by making assumptions about some of the variables. For example, if we assume that both V and Q are constant, then we have the simple quantity theory of money, which predicts that changes in the money supply cause *strictly proportional* changes in the price level.

- A change in the money supply or a change in velocity will change aggregate demand and therefore lead to a shift in the *AD* curve. Specifically, either an increase in the money supply or an increase in velocity will increase aggregate demand and therefore shift the *AD* curve to the right. A decrease in the money supply or a decrease in velocity will decrease aggregate demand and therefore shift the *AD* curve to the left.

- In the simple quantity theory of money, Real GDP is assumed to be constant in the short run. This means the *AS* curve is vertical. Also, velocity is assumed to be constant so that only a change in money supply can change aggregate demand. In the face of a vertical *AS* curve, any change in the money supply shifts the *AD* curve and changes only the price level, not Real GDP.

MONETARISM

- According to monetarists, if the economy is initially in long-run equilibrium, (1) an increase in the money supply will raise the price level and Real GDP in the short run and will raise only the price level in the long run; (2) a decrease in the money supply will lower the price level and Real GDP in the short run and will lower only the price level in the long run; (3) an increase in velocity will raise the price level and Real GDP in the short run and will raise only the price level in the long run; (4) a decrease in velocity will lower the price level and Real GDP in the short run and will lower only the price level in the long run.

ONE-SHOT INFLATION AND CONTINUED INFLATION

- One-shot inflation can result from an increase in aggregate demand or a decrease in short-run aggregate supply.

- For one-shot inflation to change to continued inflation, a continued increase in aggregate demand is necessary and sufficient. Continued increases in the money supply cause continued increases in aggregate demand and continued inflation.

THE MONEY SUPPLY AND INTEREST RATES

- Changes in the money supply can affect the interest rate by means of the liquidity, income, price-level, and expectations effects.

- The change in the interest rate due to a change in the supply of loanable funds is called the liquidity effect. The change in the interest rate due to a change in Real GDP is called the income effect. The change in the interest rate due to a change in the price level is called the price-level effect. The change in the interest rate due to a change in the expected inflation rate is called the expectations effect (or Fisher effect).

NOMINAL AND REAL INTEREST RATES

- Real interest rate = Nominal interest rate − Expected inflation rate.

- Nominal interest rate = Real interest rate + Expected inflation rate.

KEY TERMS AND CONCEPTS

Equation of Exchange	One-Shot Inflation	Income Effect	Nominal Interest Rate
Velocity	Continued Inflation	Price-Level Effect	Real Interest Rate
Simple Quantity Theory of Money	Liquidity Effect	Expectations Effect	

QUESTIONS AND PROBLEMS

1. Suppose the money supply increased 30 days ago. Whether the nominal interest rate is higher, lower, or the same today as it was 30 days ago depends on what? Explain your answer.

2. Suppose the objective of the Fed is to increase Real GDP. To this end, it increases the money supply. Can anything offset the increase in the money supply so that Real GDP does not rise? Explain your answer.

3. The money supply rises on Tuesday, and by Thursday the interest rate has risen. Is the rise more likely the result of the income effect or of the expectations effect? Explain your answer.

4. In monetarism, how will each of the following affect the price level in the short run?

   a. An increase in velocity

   b. A decrease in velocity

   c. An increase in the money supply

   d. A decrease in the money supply

5. To a potential borrower, which would be more important: the nominal interest rate or the real interest rate? Explain your answer.

6. According to monetarism, an increase in the money supply will lead to a rise in Real GDP in the long run. Do you agree or disagree with this statement? Explain your answer.

7. The money supply rises. Is the interest rate guaranteed to decline initially? Why or why not?

8. According to the simple quantity of money, what will happen to Real GDP and the price level as the money supply rises? Explain your answer.

9. With respect to the interest rate:

   a. What is the liquidity effect?

   b. What is the price-level effect?

   c. What is the expectations effect?

10. In the simple quantity theory of money, what will lead to an increase in aggregate demand? In monetarism, what will lead to an increase in aggregate demand?

11. In recent years, economists have argued about the true value of the real interest rate at any one time and over time. Given that the Nominal interest rate = Real interest rate + Expected inflation rate, then Real interest rate = Nominal interest rate − Expected inflation rate. Why do you think there is so much disagreement over the true value of the real interest rate?

12. In the simple quantity theory of money, the *AS* curve is vertical. Explain why.

13. Explain how demand-induced, one-shot inflation may seem like supply-induced, one-shot inflation.

14. Can the money supply support a GDP level greater than itself? Explain your answer.

15. "One-shot inflation may be a demand-side (of the economy) or a supply-side phenomenon, but continued inflation is likely to be a demand-side phenomenon." Do you agree or disagree with this statement? Explain your answer.

16. What are the assumptions and predictions of the simple quantity theory of money? Does the simple quantity theory of money predict well?

17. What is the difference in the long run between a one-shot increase in aggregate demand and a one-shot decrease in short-run aggregate supply?

WORKING WITH NUMBERS AND GRAPHS

1. How will things change in the *AD–AS* framework if a change in the money supply is completely offset by a change in velocity.

2. Graphically show each of the following:

   a. Continued inflation due to supply-side factors

   b. One-shot, demand-induced inflation

   c. One shot, supply-induced inflation

3. Use the figure to answer questions a and b.

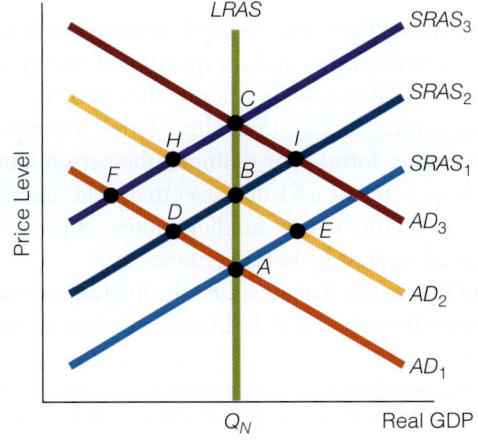

a. The economy is at point *A* when there is a one-shot, demand-induced inflation. Assuming no other changes in the economy, at what point will the economy settle (assuming the economy is self-regulating)?

b. The economy is at point *A* when it is faced with two adverse supply shocks. The Fed tries to counter these shocks by increasing aggregate demand. What path will the economy follow?

4. Starting at a position of long-run equilibrium, use the monetarist model to graphically portray what happens to the price level and Real GDP in the short run and in the long run, as a result of the following: (a) rise in the money supply, (b) decline in velocity.

5. What does the real interest rate equal given the following?

   a. Nominal interest rate = 8 percent; expected inflation rate = 2 percent

   b. Nominal interest rate = 4 percent; expected inflation rate = −4 percent

   c. Nominal interest rate = 4 percent; expected inflation rate = 1 percent?

6. What does the nominal interest rate equal, given the following?

   a. Real interest rate = 3 percent; expected inflation rate = 1 percent

   b. Real interest rate = 5 percent; expected inflation rate = −3 percent

MONETARY POLICY

Introduction When it comes to monetary policy, most economists agree that the goals of monetary policy are to stabilize the price level, to achieve low unemployment, and to promote economic growth, among other things. What they sometimes disagree about is the degree to which, and under what conditions, monetary policy achieves these goals. In this chapter we discuss monetary policy, beginning with the details of the money market. Then we discuss how changes in the money market—brought about by changes in the money supply—can affect the economy.

TRANSMISSION MECHANISMS

Transmission Mechanism
The routes, or channels, traveled by the ripple effects that the money market creates and that affect the goods and services market (represented by the aggregate demand and aggregate supply curves in the *AD–AS* framework).

Demand for Money (Balances)
The inverse relationship between the quantity demanded of money balances and the price of holding money balances.

Changes in one market can often ripple outward to affect other markets. The routes, or channels, that these ripple effects travel are known as the transmission mechanism. In this section we discuss two transmission mechanisms: the Keynesian and the monetarist.

The Money Market in the Keynesian Transmission Mechanism

Like all markets, the money market has two sides: a demand side and a supply side.[1]

THE DEMAND FOR MONEY In an illustration of the demand for money (balances), the price of holding money balances is on the vertical axis, and the quantity of money is on the horizontal axis. The price of holding money balances—specifically, the opportunity cost of holding money—is the interest rate. By holding money, individuals forfeit the opportunity to hold that portion of their wealth in other forms. For example, the person who holds $1,000 in cash gives up the opportunity to purchase a $1,000 asset that yields interest (e.g., a bond). Thus the interest rate is the opportunity cost of holding money. A person can be described as "paying the price" of forfeited interest by holding money.

Exhibit 1(a) illustrates the demand for money (balances). As the interest rate increases, the opportunity cost of holding money increases, and individuals choose to hold less

---

1. In everyday language, the term "money market" is often used to refer to the market for short-term securities, where there is a demand for and a supply of short-term securities. This is not the money market discussed here. In this money market, there is a demand for and a supply of *money*.

money. As the interest rate decreases, the opportunity cost of holding money decreases, and individuals choose to hold more money.

THE SUPPLY OF MONEY Exhibit 1(b) shows the supply of money as a vertical line at the quantity of money that is largely determined by the Fed. The money supply is largely but not exclusively determined by the Fed because both banks and the public are important players in the money supply process (as explained in earlier chapters). For example, when banks do not lend their entire excess reserves, the money supply is not as large as it is when they do.

EQUILIBRIUM IN THE MONEY MARKET The money market is in equilibrium when the quantity demanded of money equals the quantity supplied. In Exhibit 2, equilibrium exists at the interest rate i_1. At a higher interest rate, i_2, the quantity supplied of money is greater than the quantity demanded, and there is an excess supply of money ("too much" money). At a lower interest rate, i_3, the quantity demanded of money is greater than the quantity supplied, and there is an excess demand for money ("too little" money). Only at i_1 are the quantity demanded and the quantity supplied of money equal. At i_1, there are no shortages or surpluses of money and no excess demands or excess supplies. Individuals are holding the amounts of money they want to hold.

EXHIBIT 1

The Demand for and Supply of Money

(a) The demand curve for money is downward sloping. (b) The supply curve of money is a vertical line at the quantity of money that is largely but not exclusively determined by the Fed.

(a)

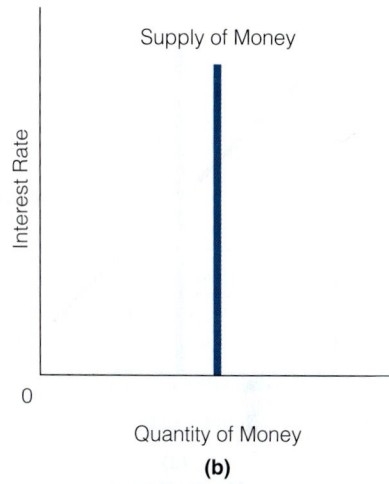

(b)

The Keynesian Transmission Mechanism: Indirect

The Keynesian route between the money market and the goods and services market is an indirect one. Exhibit 3 is a market-by-market depiction of the Keynesian transmission mechanism.

1. *The money market.* Suppose the money market is in equilibrium at interest rate i_1 in part (a). Then, the Fed increases the reserves of the banking system through an open market purchase, resulting in an increase in the money supply. The money supply curve shifts rightward from S_1 to S_2. The reserves of the banking system are increased, resulting in more loans being made. A greater supply of loans puts downward pressure on the interest rate, as reflected in the movement from i_1 to i_2.

2. *The investment goods market.* A fall in the interest rate stimulates investment. In the investment goods market in part (b), investment rises from I_1 to I_2.

EXHIBIT 2

Equilibrium in the Money Market

At an interest rate of i_1, the money market is in equilibrium: There is neither an excess supply of money nor an excess demand for money.

EXHIBIT 3

The Keynesian Transmission Mechanism

The exhibit shows how the Keynesian transmission mechanism operates given an increase in the money supply. (a) An increase in the money supply brings on a lower interest rate. (b) As a result, investment increases. (c) As investment increases, total expenditures rise and the aggregate demand curve shifts rightward. Real GDP rises from Q_1 to Q_2.

(a)
Money Market

(b)
Investment Goods Market

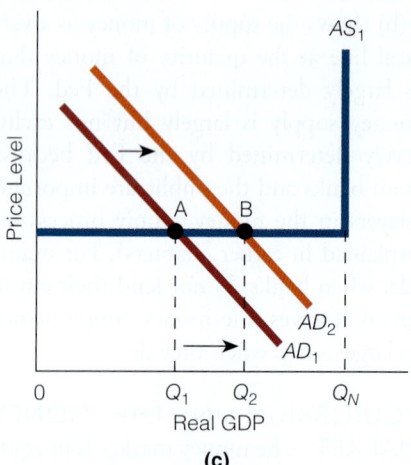

(c)
Goods and Services Market
(*AD–AS* framework)

3. *The goods and services market (AD–AS framework).* Recall that the Keynesian model has a horizontal aggregate supply curve in the goods and services market until full employment or Natural Real GDP is reached (see Chapter 10). The decline in the interest rate has brought about an increase in investment, as shown in part (b). Rising investment increases total spending in the economy and shifts the *AD* curve to the right [part (c)]. As a result, Real GDP rises from Q_1 to Q_2, and the price level does not change.

In summary, when the money supply increases, the Keynesian transmission mechanism works as follows: An increase in the money supply lowers the interest rate, which causes investment to rise and the *AD* curve to shift rightward. As a result, Real GDP increases. The process works in reverse for a decrease in the money supply.

$$\text{Money supply} \uparrow \rightarrow i \downarrow \rightarrow I \uparrow \rightarrow AD \uparrow \rightarrow Q \uparrow, \bar{P}$$
$$\text{Money supply} \downarrow \rightarrow i \uparrow \rightarrow I \downarrow \rightarrow AD \downarrow \rightarrow Q \downarrow, \bar{P}$$

The Keynesian Mechanism May Get Blocked

The Keynesian transmission mechanism is *indirect.* Changes in the money market *do not directly affect* the goods and services market (and thus Real GDP) because the investment goods market stands between the two markets. Possibly (although not likely), the link between the money market and the goods and services market could be broken in the investment goods market. Here's how.

INTEREST-INSENSITIVE INVESTMENT Some Keynesian economists believe that investment is not always responsive to interest rates. For example, when business firms are pessimistic about future economic activity, a decrease in interest rates will do little, if anything, to increase investment. When investment is completely insensitive to changes in interest rates, the investment demand curve is vertical, as in Exhibit 4(a).

EXHIBIT 4

(a)
Interest-Insensitive Investment

(b)
Liquidity Trap

Breaking the Link Between the Money Market and the Goods and Services Market: Interest-Insensitive Investment and the Liquidity Trap

The Keynesian transmission mechanism allows the link between the money market and the goods and services market to be broken in two places. (a) If investment is totally interest sensitive, a change in the interest rate will not change investment; therefore, aggregate demand and Real GDP will not change. (b) If the money market is in the liquidity trap, an increase in the money supply will not lower the interest rate. It follows that there will be no change in investment, aggregate demand, or Real GDP.

This condition has an affect on the Keynesian transmission mechanism described in Exhibit 3. If the investment demand curve is vertical (instead of downward sloping), a fall in interest rates will not increase investment; if investment does not increase, neither will aggregate demand or Real GDP. Thus, the Keynesian transmission mechanism would be short-circuited in the investment goods market, severing the link between the money market in part (a) of Exhibit 3 and the goods and services market in part (c).

$$\text{Money supply} \uparrow \rightarrow i\downarrow$$
$$\text{Investment insensitive to changes in } i \rightarrow \overline{I} \rightarrow \overline{AD} \rightarrow \overline{Q}, \overline{P}$$

THE LIQUIDITY TRAP Keynesians have sometimes argued that the demand curve for money could become horizontal at some low interest rate. In Exhibit 4(b), the demand curve for money becomes horizontal at i_1. This horizontal section is referred to as the liquidity trap.

If the money supply is increased (e.g., from S_1 to S_2) when the money market is in the liquidity trap, the money market moves from point 1 to point 2, and individuals are willing to hold all the additional money supply at the given interest rate. Once again, this condition breaks the Keynesian transmission mechanism illustrated in Exhibit 3. Obviously, if an increase in the money supply does not lower the interest rate, then neither investment, aggregate demand, nor Real GDP changes. The liquidity trap can thus break the link between the money market and the goods and services market.

$$\text{Money supply} \uparrow$$
$$\text{Liquidity trap} \rightarrow \overline{I} \rightarrow \overline{I} \rightarrow \overline{AD} \rightarrow \overline{Q}, \overline{P}$$

Because the Keynesian transmission mechanism is indirect, both *interest-insensitive investment demand* and the *liquidity trap* may occur. Therefore, Keynesians conclude that at times monetary policy will be unable to increase Real GDP and decrease unemployment. Viewing the money supply as a string, some economists have argued that you cannot push on a string. In other words, you cannot always force Real GDP up by increasing (pushing up) the money supply.

See Exhibit 5 for a review of the Keynesian transmission mechanism and how it may get blocked.

Liquidity Trap
The horizontal portion of the demand curve for money.

EXHIBIT 5

The Keynesian View of Monetary Policy

According to the Keynesian transmission mechanism, if the Fed increases reserves in the banking system and therefore raises the money supply, the interest rate will drop, stimulating investment and aggregate demand. Consequently, Real GDP will rise. However, things may not work out this way if there is a liquidity trap or if investment is insensitive to changes in the interest rate.

BOND PRICES, INTEREST RATES, AND THE LIQUIDITY TRAP The liquidity trap, or the horizontal section of the demand curve for money, seems to come out of the clear blue sky. Why might the demand curve for money become horizontal at some low interest rate? To understand the explanation, you must first understand the relationship between bond prices and interest rates.

Consider Jessica Howard, who buys good X for $100 today and sells it one year later for $110. Her actual rate of return is 10 percent; the difference between the selling price and buying price ($10) divided by the buying price ($100) is 10 percent. Now suppose good X is a bond. Jessica buys the bond for $100 and sells it one year later for $110. Her actual interest rate return is the same: 10 percent. If Jessica buys the bond for $90 instead of $100 but still sells it for $110, her interest rate return is 22 percent: $20 ÷ $90 = 22 percent. The point is simple: *As the price of a bond decreases, the actual interest rate return, or the interest rate, increases.*

So bond prices and interest rates are inversely related. For example, last year Rob bought a bond for $1,000 that promises to pay him $100 a year in interest. The annual interest rate return is 10 percent: $100 ÷ $1,000 = 10 percent. Suppose, however, the market, or nominal, interest rate is higher now than last year when Rob bought his bond. Now bond suppliers have to promise to pay $120 a year to someone who buys a $1,000 bond.

The change in rate has an effect on the price Rob can get in the market for the $1,000 bond he bought last year, assuming he wants to sell it. If a purchaser can buy a new $1,000 bond that pays $120 a year, why pay Rob $1,000 for an (old) bond that pays only $100? Rob has to lower the price of his bond below $1,000, but the question is by how much? The price has to be far enough below $1,000 so that the interest rate return on his old bond will be competitive with (i.e., equal to) the interest rate return on new bonds.

Rob's bond will sell for $833. At that price, a buyer of his bond will receive $100 a year and an interest rate of 12 percent—the same interest rate offered by a new $1,000 bond paying $120 a year. In other words, $100 is the same percentage of $833 as $120 is of $1,000: 12 percent. Therefore, *the market interest rate is inversely related to the price of old or existing bonds.*

This relationship can help you understand how a liquidity trap comes to be. At a low interest rate, the money supply increases but does not result in an excess supply of money. Interest rates are very low, and so bond prices are very high. Would-be buyers believe that bond prices are so high that they have no place to go but down. So individuals would rather hold all the additional money supply than use it to buy bonds, .

finding ECONOMICS

In Rising Demand for Bonds Kenneth reads in the newspaper that the demand for bonds is rising. Is there any information here that relates to the interest rate? Yes, if the demand for bonds is rising, then the price of bonds will rise too. Because the price of bonds and the interest rate are inversely related, the interest rate is about to decline. ▲ ▲ ▲

The Monetarist Transmission Mechanism: Direct

Monetarist theory proposes a direct link between the money market and the goods and services market. The monetarist transmission mechanism is short. Changes in the money market have a direct impact on aggregate demand, as illustrated in Exhibit 6. An increase in the money supply from S_1 to S_2 in part (a) leaves individuals with an excess supply of money. As a result, they increase their spending on a wide variety of goods. Households buy more refrigerators,

EXHIBIT 6

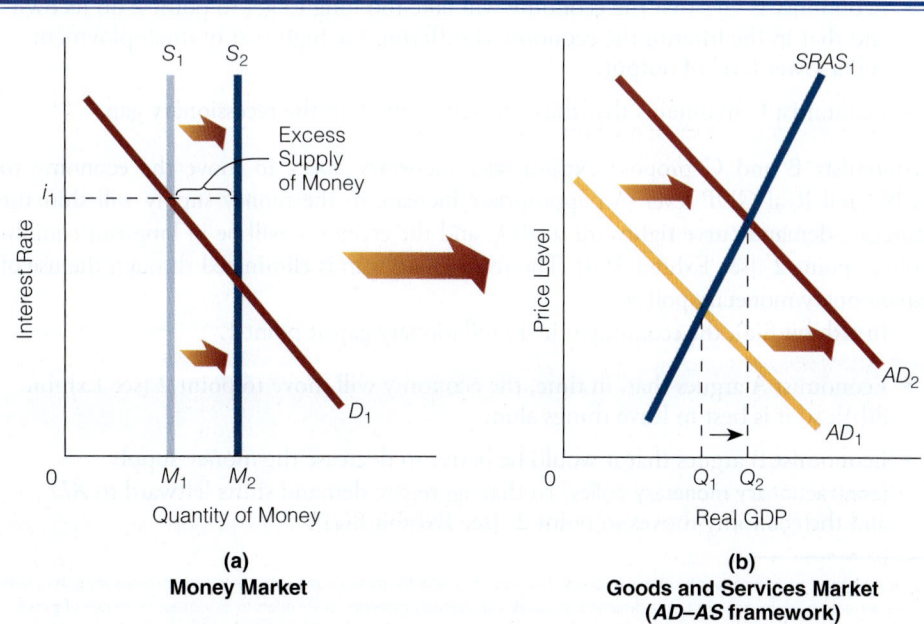

(a)
Money Market

(b)
Goods and Services Market
(***AD–AS* framework**)

The Monetarist Transmission Mechanism

The monetarist transmission mechanism is short and direct. Changes in the money market directly affect aggregate demand in the goods and services market. For example, an increase in the money supply leaves individuals with an excess supply of money that they spend on a wide variety of goods.

personal computers, television sets, clothes, and vacations. Businesses purchase additional machinery. The aggregate demand curve in part (b) is directly affected. In the short run, Real GDP rises from Q_1 to Q_2. The process works in reverse for a decrease in the money supply.

$$\text{Money supply} \uparrow \rightarrow AD\uparrow \rightarrow Q\uparrow, P\uparrow$$
$$\text{Money supply} \downarrow \rightarrow AD\downarrow \rightarrow Q\downarrow, P\downarrow$$

The Keynesian transmission mechanism from the money market to the goods and services market is indirect; the monetarist transmission mechanism is direct.

SELF-TEST

(Answers to Self-Test questions are in Answers to Self-Test Questions at the back of the book.)

1. Explain the inverse relationship between bond prices and interest rates.

2. "According to the Keynesian transmission mechanism, as the money supply rises, there is a direct impact on the goods and services market." Do you agree or disagree with this statement? Explain your answer.

3. Explain how the monetarist transmission mechanism works when the money supply rises.

MONETARY POLICY AND THE PROBLEM OF INFLATIONARY AND RECESSIONARY GAPS

In Chapter 11, we explained how expansionary and contractionary fiscal policies might be used to move the economy out of recessionary and inflationary gaps, respectively, and questioned the effectiveness of fiscal policy. In this section, we discuss how monetary policy might be used to eliminate both recessionary and inflationary gaps.

In Exhibit 7(a), the economy is in a recessionary gap at point 1; aggregate demand is too low to bring the economy into equilibrium at Natural Real GDP.

- Economist A argues that, in time, the short-run aggregate supply curve will shift rightward to point 2 [see Exhibit 7(b)]; so it is best to leave things alone.

- Economist B says that the economy will take too long to get to point 2 on its own and that in the interim the economy is suffering the high cost of unemployment and a lower level of output.

- Economist C maintains that the economy is stuck in the recessionary gap.

Expansionary Monetary Policy
The policy by which the Fed increases the money supply.

Economists B and C propose expansionary monetary policy to move the economy to its Natural Real GDP level. An appropriate increase in the money supply will shift the aggregate demand curve rightward to AD_2, and the economy will be in long-run equilibrium at point 2′ [see Exhibit 7(c)]. The recessionary gap is eliminated through the use of expansionary monetary policy.[2]

In Exhibit 8(a), the economy is in an inflationary gap at point 1.

- Economist A argues that, in time, the economy will move to point 2 [see Exhibit 8(b)]; so it is best to leave things alone.

Contractionary Monetary Policy
The policy by which the Fed decreases the money supply.

- Economist B argues that it would be better to decrease the money supply (contractionary monetary policy) so that aggregate demand shifts leftward to AD_2 and the economy moves to point 2′ [see Exhibit 8(c)].

---

2. In a static framework, expansionary monetary policy means an increase in the money supply, and contractionary monetary policy refers to a decrease in the money supply. In a dynamic framework, expansionary monetary policy refers to an increase in the rate of growth of the money supply, and contractionary monetary policy means a decrease in the growth rate of the money supply. In the real world, where things are constantly changing, the growth rate of the money supply is more indicative of the direction of monetary policy.

EXHIBIT 7

Monetary Policy and a Recessionary Gap

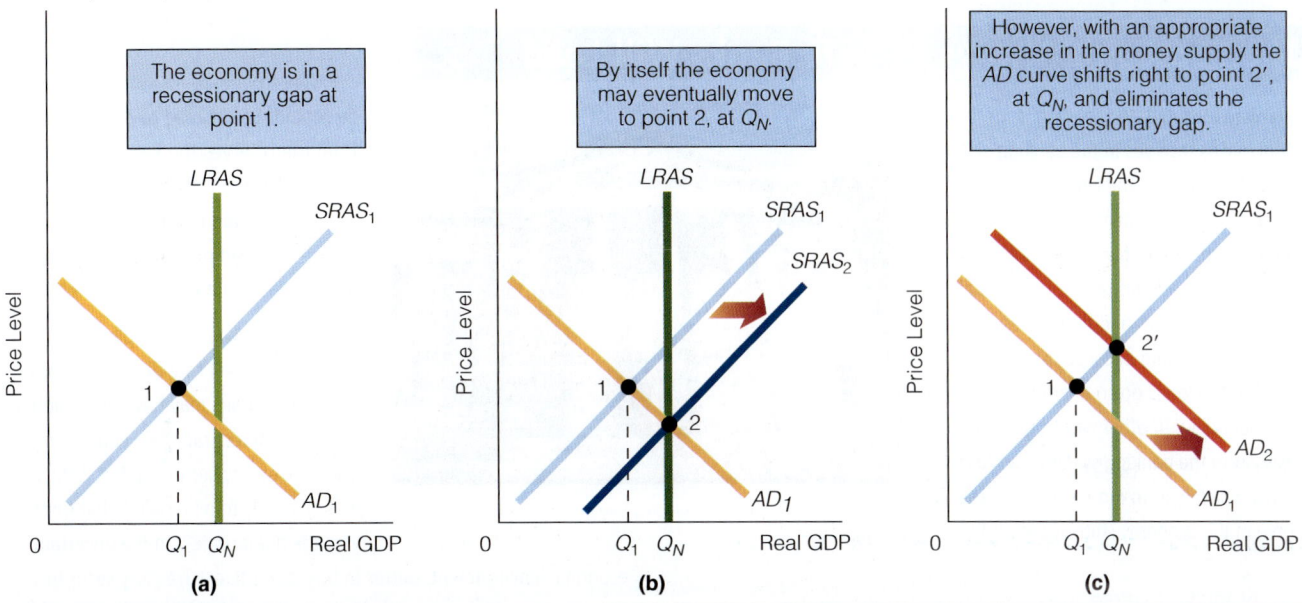

> The economy is in a recessionary gap at point 1.

> By itself the economy may eventually move to point 2, at Q_N.

> However, with an appropriate increase in the money supply the AD curve shifts right to point 2', at Q_N, and eliminates the recessionary gap.

(a)   (b)   (c)

- Economist C agrees with economist B and points out that the price level is lower at point 2' than at point 2, although Real GDP is the same at both points.

Most Keynesians believe that the natural forces of the market economy work much faster and more assuredly in eliminating an inflationary gap than in eliminating a recessionary gap. In terms of Exhibits 7 and 8, they argue that the short-run aggregate supply curve in Exhibit 8(b) is much more likely to shift leftward to point 2, eliminating the

EXHIBIT 8

Monetary Policy and an Inflationary Gap

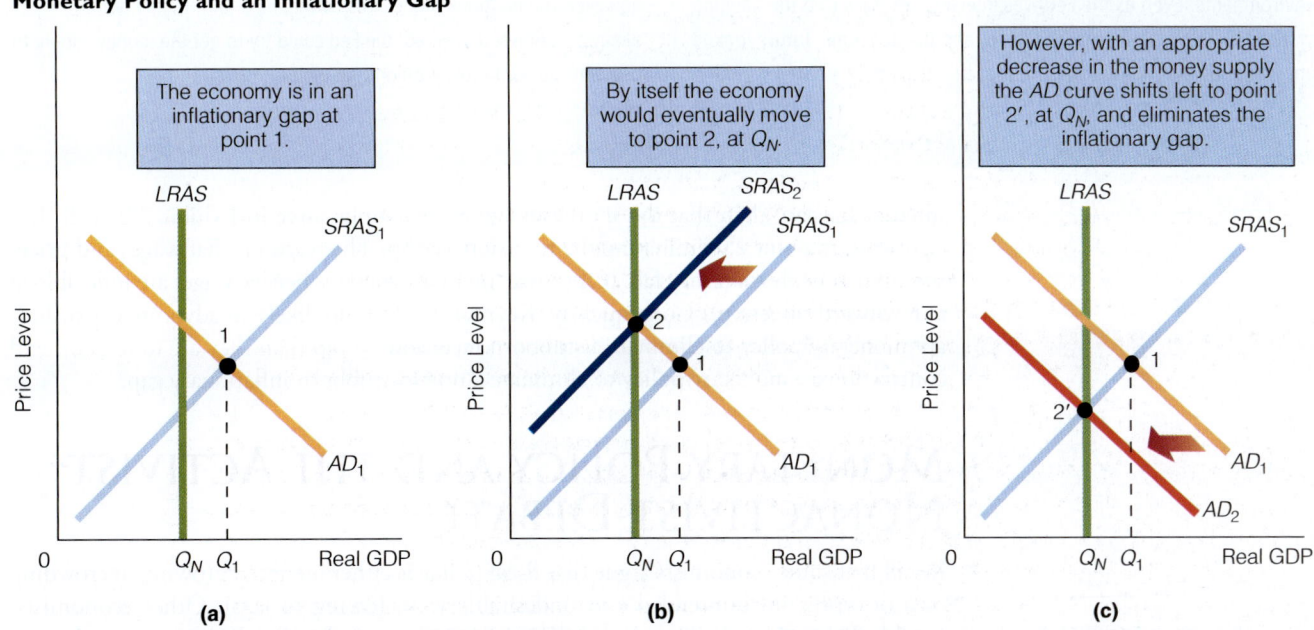

> The economy is in an inflationary gap at point 1.

> By itself the economy would eventually move to point 2, at Q_N.

> However, with an appropriate decrease in the money supply the AD curve shifts left to point 2', at Q_N, and eliminates the inflationary gap.

(a)   (b)   (c)

The Fed Can't Always be Sure Banks Will Lend

One way to stimulate spending is for the Fed to increases reserves in the banking system. Recall the process: The Fed injects reserves into the banking system (say, by undertaking an open market purchase), and then banks use the additional reserves to make loans to individuals and firms. These loans stimulate spending because the people who take out the loans do so in order to increase their spending. In other words, greater reserves in the banking system lead to more loans, which lead to more spending. The AD curve in the economy shifts rightward.

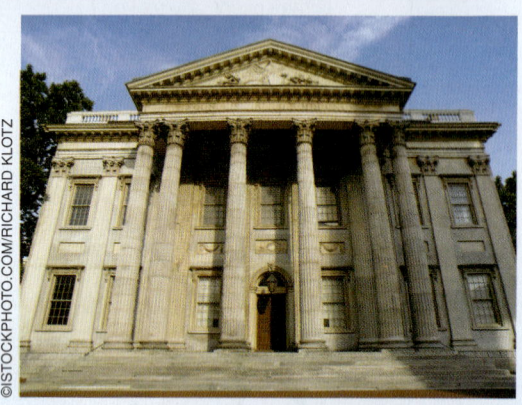

©ISTOCKPHOTO.COM/RICHARD KLOTZ

Reserves increase → More Loans → More Spending → AD curve shifts rightward

However, things do not always work out the way the Fed intends. Something the Fed cannot do is force banks to lend out reserves. At the end of 2008 and into much of 2009, banks were adding to their reserves, but they weren't turning them into loans, largely because of the financial shape they were in. At the time, many banks were either insolvent (their liabilities were greater than their assets) or close to being insolvent. When banks are close to being insolvent, they are particularly wary of making loans, especially in uncertain environments. Even as the Fed was injecting reserves into the banking system, some businesses were failing, and the economic future looked uncertain. Banks couldn't be sure that the loans they created would

be repaid. So, instead of creating loans from the reserves the Fed was injecting into the banking system, the banks took the reserves and bought safe Treasury securities or simply earned the interest rate the Fed paid on reserves.

The banks looked at their plight this way: the interest rate they could earn by creating loans may have been higher than the interest rate they could earn by buying Treasury securities, but if the loans weren't likely to be repaid, what good was the higher rate? In the uncertain economic environment, better to buy low-interest Treasury securities than to create higher-interest loans that wouldn't be repaid.

The ineffectiveness of the Fed at getting the banks to increase their lending caused some economists to wonder whether monetary policy didn't work anymore or, at minimum, didn't work when the economic future looked bleak or uncertain. The so-called textbook model of how monetary policy works (say, in a recessionary gap) is that the Fed undertakes open market purchases, reserves flow into the banking system, banks take the reserves and create loans and new checkable deposits, the money supply rises, and the AD curve shifts to the right. (This is how it works in this textbook.) In 2008 and much of 2009, however, the textbook model was correct most of the time but not always. At times, it seemed, the Fed could try to get the money supply to rise, but the banks just wouldn't go along.

inflationary gap, than that the short-run aggregate supply curve in Exhibit 7(b) will shift rightward to point 2, eliminating the recessionary gap. The reason is that wages and prices rise more quickly than they fall. (Of course, many Keynesians believe wages are inflexible in a downward direction.) Consequently, Keynesians are more likely to advocate expansionary monetary policy to eliminate a stubborn recessionary gap than they are to recommend contractionary monetary policy to eliminate a not-so-stubborn inflationary gap.

MONETARY POLICY AND THE ACTIVIST-NONACTIVIST DEBATE

Recall that some economists argue that fiscal policy is either ineffective (owing to crowding out) or works in unintended and undesirable ways (owing to lags). Other economists, notably Keynesians, believe that neither is the case and that fiscal policy not only can, but should, be used to smooth out the business cycle. This point of contention is part of the activist–nonactivist debate, which encompasses both fiscal and monetary policy. This section addresses the *monetary policy* component of the activist–nonactivist debate.

Activists argue that monetary policy should be deliberately used to smooth out the business cycle. They are in favor of economic fine-tuning, which is the (usually frequent) use of monetary policy to counteract even small undesirable movements in economic activity. Sometimes, the monetary policy they advocate is called either *activist* or *discretionary monetary policy*.

Nonactivists argue *against* the use of activist or discretionary monetary policy. Instead, they propose a rules-based monetary policy. Sometimes, the monetary policy they propose is called either *nonactivist* or *rules-based monetary policy*. An example of a rules-based monetary policy is one based on a predetermined steady growth rate in the money supply, such as allowing the money supply to grow 3 percent a year, no matter what is happening in the economy.

The Case for Activist (or Discretionary) Monetary Policy

The case for activist (or discretionary) monetary policy rests on three major claims:

1. *The economy does not always equilibrate quickly enough at Natural Real GDP.* Consider the economy at point 1 in Exhibit 7(a). Some economists maintain that, left on its own, the economy will eventually move to point 2 in part (b). Activists argue that the economy takes too long to move from point 1 to point 2 and that in the interim too much output is lost and too high an unemployment rate must be tolerated. They believe that an activist monetary policy speeds things along so that higher output and a lower unemployment rate can be achieved more quickly.

2. *Activist monetary policy works; it is effective at smoothing out the business cycle.* Activists are quick to point to the undesirable consequences of the constant monetary policy of the mid-1970s. In 1973, 1974, and 1975, the money supply growth rates were 5.5 percent, 4.3 percent, and 4.7 percent, respectively. These percentages represent a nearly constant growth rate in the money supply. The economy, however, went through a recession during this time; Real GDP fell between 1973 and 1974 and between 1974 and 1975. Activists argue that an activist and flexible monetary policy would have reduced the high cost the economy had to pay in terms of lost output and high unemployment.

3. *Activist monetary policy is flexible; nonactivist (rules-based) monetary policy is not.* Activists argue that flexibility is a desirable quality in monetary policy; inflexibility is not. Implicitly, activists maintain that the more closely monetary policy can be designed to meet the particulars of a given economic environment, the better. For example, at certain times the economy requires a sharp increase in the money supply and at other times, a sharp decrease; at still other times, only a slight increase or decrease is needed. Activists argue that activist (discretionary) monetary policy can change as the monetary needs of the economy change; nonactivist, rules-based, or "the-same-for-all-seasons" monetary policy cannot.

The Case for Nonactivist (or Rules-Based) Monetary Policy

The case for nonactivist (or rules-based) monetary policy also rests on three major claims:

1. *In modern economies, wages and prices are sufficiently flexible to allow the economy to equilibrate at reasonable speed at Natural Real GDP.* For example, nonactivists point to the sharp drop in union wages in 1982 in response to high unemployment. In addition, they argue that government policies largely determine the flexibility of wages and prices. For example, when government decides to cushion people's unemployment (e.g., through unemployment compensation), wages will not fall as quickly as when government does nothing. Nonactivists believe that a laissez-faire, hands-off approach by government promotes speedy wage and price adjustments and thus a quick return to Natural Real GDP.

Activists
Persons who argue that monetary and fiscal policies should be deliberately used to smooth out the business cycle.

Fine-tuning
The (usually frequent) use of monetary and fiscal policies to counteract even small undesirable movements in economic activity.

Nonactivists
Persons who argue against the deliberate use of discretionary fiscal and monetary policies. They believe in a permanent, stable, rule-oriented monetary and fiscal framework.

Monetary Policy and Blue Eyes

Two days before the beginning of the fall semester at a college in the Midwest, Suzanne, a student at the college, was waiting in line to register for classes. As she waited, she looked through the fall schedule. She had to take an economics principles course at 10 a.m., and two sections were listed for that time. Hernandez was the instructor for one section; Jones, for the other. Suzanne, not knowing which section to take, asked the person behind her in line if he had ever taken a course with either instructor. The person said that he had taken a course with Hernandez and that he was very good. That was enough for Suzanne; she signed up for Hernandez's class.

© PHOTODISC GREEN/GETTY IMAGES

While a student in Hernandez's class, Suzanne met the person whom she ended up marrying. His name is Bob. Suzanne often says to Bob, "You know, if that guy behind me in line that day had said that Hernandez wasn't a good teacher or hadn't said anything at all, I might never have taken Professor Hernandez's class. I might have taken Jones's class instead, and I would never have met you. I'd probably be married to someone else right now." This (untrue) story is representative of the many little things that happen every day. Little events can make big differences.

Consider another story (this one about monetary policy) that is also not true but that, if it hasn't happened, certainly can.

A few years ago, Real GDP was below its natural level, and the Fed decided to increase the money supply. As a result, the *AD* curve in the economy shifted to the right. One of the first places to feel the new demand in the economy was Denver, where economic activity increased.

Jake, who lived in Austin at the time, was out of work and looking for a job. He heard about the job prospects in Denver, and so one day he got into his car and headed for Denver. Luckily for him, a few days after arriving in Denver, he got a job and rented an apartment near his workplace. He became a friend of Nick, who lived in the apartment across the hall.

Nick, knowing that Jake was new in town, asked Jake if he wanted a date with his girlfriend's friend, Melanie, and Jake said yes. Jake and Melanie ended up dating for two years, and they've been married now for ten years. They have three children, all of whom have blue eyes.

One day, the youngest child asked her mother why she had blue eyes. Her mother told her it's because both she and her daddy have blue eyes. And that's not an incorrect explanation, as far as it goes. But we can't help wondering if the youngest child has blue eyes because of an event that took place years ago, an event that has to do with the Fed and the money supply. After all, if the Fed hadn't increased the money supply when it did, maybe Denver's job prospects wouldn't have been so attractive, and maybe Jake wouldn't have left Austin. And, if Jake had not left Austin, he wouldn't have married Melanie and had three children, each with blue eyes.

We're just speculating, of course.

2. *Activist monetary policies may not work.* Some economists argue that there are really two types of monetary policy: (1) monetary policy that is anticipated by the public and (2) monetary policy that is not. Anticipated monetary policy may not be effective at changing Real GDP or the unemployment rate. We discuss this subject in detail in the next chapter, but here is a brief explanation. Suppose the public correctly anticipates that the Fed will soon increase the money supply by 10 percent. Consequently, the public reasons that aggregate demand will increase from AD_1 to AD_2, as shown in Exhibit 9, and prices will rise.

Workers are particularly concerned about the expected higher price level because they know higher prices decrease the buying power of their wages. In an attempt to maintain their real wages, workers bargain for and receive higher money wage rates, thereby shifting the short-run aggregate supply curve from $SRAS_1$ to $SRAS_2$ in Exhibit 9.

Now, if the *SRAS* curve shifts leftward (owing to higher wage rates) to the same degree as the *AD* curve shifts rightward (owing to the increased money supply), Real

GDP does not change but stays constant at Q_1. Thus, *a correctly anticipated increase in the money supply will be ineffective at raising Real GDP.*

3. *Activist monetary policies are likely to be destabilizing rather than stabilizing; they are likely to make matters worse, not better.* Nonactivists point to *lags* as the main reason that activist (or discretionary) monetary policies are likely to be destabilizing. (The total lag consists of the data, wait-and-see, legislative, transmission, and effectiveness lags discussed in Chapter 11.) Nonactivists argue that a long lag (e.g., 12 to 20 months) makes it almost impossible to conduct effective activist monetary policy. By the time the Fed's monetary stimulus arrives on the scene, the economy may not need any stimulus, and thus the policy measures will likely destabilize the economy. In this instance, the stimulus makes things worse rather than better.

Exhibit 10 illustrates the last point. Suppose the economy is currently in a recessionary gap at point 1. The recession is under way before Fed officials recognize it. Once they become aware of the recession, however, the officials consider expanding the money supply in the hopes of shifting the AD curve from AD_1 to AD_2 so that it will intersect the $SRAS$ curve at point 1′, at Natural Real GDP.

In the interim, however, unknown to everybody, the economy is regulating itself: The $SRAS$ curve is shifting to the right. Fed officials don't realize that this shift is occurring because collecting and analyzing data about the economy take time. Thinking that the economy is not regulating itself, or not regulating itself quickly enough, Fed officials implement expansionary monetary policy, and the AD curve shifts rightward. By the time the increased money supply is felt in the goods and services market, the AD curve intersects the $SRAS$ curve at point 2. In short, the Fed has moved the economy from point 1 to point 2—not, as it had hoped, from point 1 to point 1′. The Fed has moved the economy into an inflationary gap. Instead of stabilizing and moderating the business cycle, the Fed has intensified it.

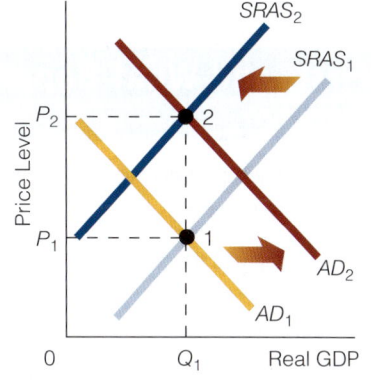

EXHIBIT 9

Expansionary Monetary Policy and No Change in Real GDP

If expansionary monetary policy is anticipated (thus, a higher price level is anticipated), workers may bargain for and receive higher wage rates. It is possible that the $SRAS$ curve will shift leftward to the same degree that expansionary monetary policy shifts the AD curve rightward. Result: No change in Real GDP.

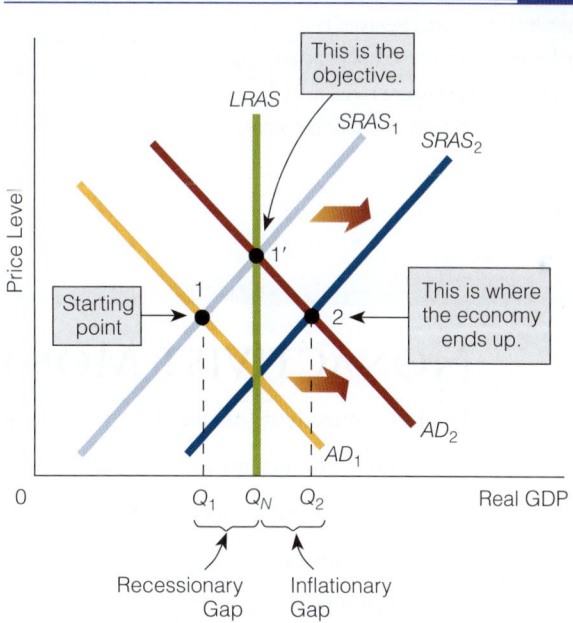

EXHIBIT 10

Monetary Policy May Destabilize the Economy

In this scenario, the $SRAS$ curve is shifting rightward (ridding the economy of its recessionary gap), but Fed officials do not realize this is happening. They implement expansionary monetary policy, and the AD curve ends up intersecting $SRAS_2$ at point 2 instead of intersecting $SRAS_1$ at point 1′. Fed officials end up moving the economy into an inflationary gap and thus destabilizing the economy.

SELF-TEST

1. Why are Keynesians more likely to advocate expansionary monetary policy to eliminate a recessionary gap than they are to advocate contractionary monetary policy to eliminate an inflationary gap?

2. How might monetary policy destabilize the economy?

3. Does an economy stuck in a recessionary gap make the case for activist (expansionary) monetary policy stronger or weaker? Explain your answer.

Who Gets the Money First, and What Happens to Relative Prices?

Besides expansionary and contractionary monetary policies and their effects on Real GDP and the price level, other effects have to be considered:

- The distribution of the increase in the money supply (in the case of expansionary monetary policy).
- How a change in the money supply might affect relative prices (as opposed to the price level).

Let's look at how these two effects interact. When the money supply expands (say, from $1.41 trillion to $1.42 trillion), not every member of the public gets some of the new money. To illustrate, suppose the Fed undertakes an open market purchase, which results in a rise in reserves in the banking system. Faced with greater (and excess) reserves, banks start to make more loans (new checkable deposits). The first economic actors to get the new money (as a result of the open market purchase) are the banks; the second economic actors are the individuals and firms who take out loans.

Now let's say that one of the second economic actors is Caroline, who spends the money from her new loan to buy good X from Richard. If Caroline would not have purchased good X without the loan, then the demand for good X presumably rises because of the loan (which the bank created as a result of the Fed's open market purchase). Therefore, if the demand for good X rises, so will its absolute (or money) price. If the absolute price of good X rises, so will its relative price, *ceteris paribus*. Conclusion: An increase in the money supply can change not only the price level, but relative prices too.

Of course, an increase in the money supply changes relative prices because not everyone gets the new money at the same time. Caroline gets the new money before the seller of good X (Richard) gets it, and so on. When the money supply is increased, some people get the new money before others, and so the goods and services these people buy rise in price relative to the prices of the goods and services they do not buy. If the Carolines of the world (who get the new money first) buy good X and not good Y, and the non-Carolines of the world (who get the new money later) buy good Y, we can expect that, initially, the price of good X will rise relative to good Y.

NONACTIVIST MONETARY PROPOSALS

The four nonactivist (or rules-based) monetary proposals are as follows:

1. Constant-money-growth-rate rule
2. Predetermined-money-growth-rate rule
3. The Taylor rule
4. Inflation targeting

Constant-Money-Growth-Rate Rule

Many nonactivists argue that the sole objective of monetary policy is to stabilize the price level. To this end, they propose a *constant-money-growth-rate rule.* One version of the rule is:

> *The annual money supply growth rate will be constant at the average annual growth rate of Real GDP.*

For example, if the average annual Real GDP growth rate is approximately 3.3 percent, the money supply should be put on automatic pilot and be permitted to grow at an annual rate of 3.3 percent. The money supply will grow at this rate regardless of the state of the economy.

Some economists predict that a constant-money-growth-rate rule will bring about a stable price level over time because of the equation of exchange ($MV \equiv PQ$). If the average annual growth rate in Real GDP (Q) is 3.3 percent and the money supply (M) grows at 3.3 percent, the price level should remain stable over time. Advocates of this rule argue that in some years the growth rate in Real GDP will be below its average rate, causing an increase in the price level, and that in other years the growth rate in Real GDP will be above its average rate, causing a fall in the price level, but over time, the price level will be stable.

Predetermined-Money-Growth-Rate Rule

Critics of the constant-money-growth-rate rule point out that it makes two assumptions: (1) Velocity is constant; (2) the money supply is defined correctly. Critics argue that velocity has not been constant in some periods. Also, not yet clear is which definition of the money supply is the proper one and therefore which money supply growth rate should be fixed: M1, M2, or some broader monetary measure.

Largely in response to the charge that velocity is not always constant, some nonactivists prefer the following rule:

> The annual growth rate in the money supply will be equal to the average annual growth rate in Real GDP minus the growth rate in velocity.

In other words,

$$\%\Delta M = \%\Delta Q - \%\Delta V$$

With this rule, the growth rate of the money supply is not fixed. It can vary from year to year, but it is predetermined in that it is dependent on the growth rates of Real GDP and velocity. For this reason, we call it the *predetermined-money-growth-rate rule*. To illustrate the workings of this rule, consider the following extended version of the equation of exchange:

$$\%\Delta M + \%\Delta V = \%\Delta P + \%\Delta Q$$

Suppose $\%\Delta Q$ is 3 percent and $\%\Delta V$ is 1 percent. The rule specifies that the growth rate in the money supply should be 2 percent. This growth rate would keep the price level stable; there would be a 0 percent change in P:

$$\%\Delta M + \%\Delta V = \%\Delta P + \%\Delta Q$$
$$2\% + 1\% = 0\% + 3\%$$

The Fed and the Taylor Rule

Economist John Taylor has argued for a middle ground, of sorts, between activist and nonactivist monetary policy. He has proposed that monetary authorities use a rule to guide them in making their discretionary decisions.

His rule has come to be known as the *Taylor rule*, which specifies how policy makers should set the federal funds rate target (recall from an earlier chapter that the federal funds rate is the interest rate banks charge one another for reserves). The economic thinking implicit behind the Taylor rule is that there is some federal funds rate target that is consistent with (1) stabilizing inflation around a rather low inflation rate and (2) stabilizing Real GDP around its full-employment level. The aim is to find this target and then to use the Fed's tools to hit it.

Here is how John Taylor, for whom the Taylor Rule is named, defines the particulars of the rule:

> The federal funds rate target "should be one-and-a-half times the inflation rate plus one-half times the GDP gap plus one."[3]

Algebraically, the Taylor Rule specifies:

Federal funds rate target = 1.5 (inflation rate) + 0.5 (GDP gap) + 1

---

3. See John Taylor, *Getting Office Track* (Hoover Institution Press, 2009), p. 67.

In this equation, the GDP gap measures the percentage deviation of Real GDP from its potential level. Let's use the rule to find the federal funds rate target that Taylor recommends to the Fed. Suppose the inflation rate is 5 percent and the GDP gap is 3 percent. Putting these percentages in our equation, we get:

$$\text{Federal funds rate target} = 1.5\ (5\ \text{percent}) + 0.5\ (3\ \text{percent}) + 1$$
$$= 7.5 + 1.5 + 1$$
$$= 10\ \text{percent}$$

Inflation Targeting

Inflation Targeting
Targeting that requires the Fed to keep the inflation rate near a predetermined level.

Many economists recommend inflation targeting, which requires that the Fed try to keep the inflation rate near a predetermined level. Three major issues surround inflation targeting. The first deals with whether the inflation rate target should be a specific percentage rate (e.g., 2.5 percent) or a narrow range (e.g., 1.0–2.5 percent). Second, whether it is a specific percentage rate or range, what should the rate or range be? For example, if it is specific percentage rate, should it be, say, 2.0 percent or 3.5 percent? The last issue deals with whether the inflation rate target should be announced or not. In other words, if the Fed adopts an inflation rate target of, say, 2.5 percent, should the target be disclosed to the public?

OFFICE HOURS

"Does Monetary Policy Always Have the Same Effects?"

STUDENT:

Does monetary policy always have the same effects?

INSTRUCTOR:

Instead of my giving you the answer, think back to the Keynesian transmission mechanism and try to answer your question.

STUDENT:

In the transmission mechanism, an increase in the money supply lowers the interest rate. The lower interest rate then increases investment. And the increased investment raises aggregate demand.

INSTRUCTOR:

Ask yourself whether the lower interest rate always raises investment.

STUDENT:

No, it doesn't always raise investment. If investment is interest insensitive, the lower interest rate will leave investment unchanged.

INSTRUCTOR:

There is something else too. Suppose investment is responsive to changes in the interest rate. In other words, if the interest rate falls, investment will rise. But the question is whether investment always rises by the same amount. For example, if in year 1 the interest rate falls from 6 percent to 5 percent and investment rises from $300 billion to $400 billion, does it follow that every time the interest rate falls from 6 percent to 5 percent, investment will rise by $100 billion?

STUDENT:

I see your point. You're saying that, although investment might always rise as the interest rate falls, it doesn't necessarily rise by the same

Numerous central banks in the world practice inflation targeting, and they announce their targets. For example, the Bank of Canada has set a target of 2 percent (inflation), and it has been announcing its inflation target since 1991. Other central banks that practice inflation targeting are the Bank of England, the Central Bank of Brazil, the Bank of Israel, and the Reserve Bank of New Zealand.

For an inflation rate target approach, the Fed would undertake monetary policy actions to keep the actual inflation rate near or at its target. For example, if its target rate is 2 percent and the actual inflation rate is, say, 5 percent, it would cut back the growth rate in the money supply (or the absolute money supply) to bring the actual inflation rate nearer to the target.

The proponents of inflation targeting argue that such a policy is more in line with the Fed's objective of maintaining near price stability. The critics of inflation targeting often argue that such a policy would constrain the Fed at times, such as when it might need to overlook the target to deal with a financial crisis.

SELF-TEST

1. Would a rules-based monetary policy produce price stability?

2. Suppose the inflation rate is 4 percent and the GDP gap is 5 percent. What is the Taylor rule recommendation for the federal funds rate target?

amount every time. If it doesn't rise by the same amount every time, then there is no guarantee that aggregate demand will rise by the same amount every time (because increases in investment lead to increases in aggregate demand).

INSTRUCTOR:

That's correct. We'd now have to conclude that expansionary monetary policy won't always increase aggregate demand by the same amount. In other words, a money supply expansion of $30 billion might raise aggregate demand more at one time than at some other time.

STUDENT:

So one answer to my question—whether monetary policy always has the same effects—is, no, monetary policy doesn't always change aggregate demand by the same amount.

INSTRUCTOR:

That's correct. This discussion also helps us to understand why economists—even those of the same school of thought—might disagree with each other. For example, suppose Smith and Jones both believe that monetary policy affects the economy through the Keynesian transmission mechanism. Just because both accept the Keynesian transmission mechanism, they don't both necessarily think that a given increase in the money supply is going to affect aggregate demand to the same degree. Although both might agree that an expansion in the money supply will increase aggregate demand, they might disagree as to how much aggregate demand will increase. Smith might think aggregate demand will rise only a little because investment will not rise much when the interest rate drops. Jones might think aggregate demand will rise a lot because investment will rise a lot when the interest rate drops.

POINTS TO REMEMBER

1. Monetary policy doesn't always have the same effects. With reference to the Keynesian transmission mechanism, expansionary monetary policy might lead to a large change in investment at some times (when investment is highly responsive to changes in the interest rate) and only a small change in investment at other times (when investment is somewhat insensitive to changes in the interest rate). Expansionary monetary policy therefore might not always change aggregate demand to the same degree.

2. Even economists of the same school of thought can disagree with each other at times. For example, although two economists might agree that a rise in the money supply will change investment (or aggregate demand), they might disagree as to how much investment (or aggregate demand) will change.

CHAPTER SUMMARY

THE KEYNESIAN TRANSMISSION MECHANISM

- The Keynesian route between the money market and the goods and services market is indirect. Changes in the money market must affect the investment goods market before the goods and services market is affected. Assuming that no liquidity trap exists and investment is not interest insensitive, the transmission mechanism works as follows for an increase in the money supply: an increase in the money supply lowers the interest rate and increases investment, thereby increasing aggregate demand and thus shifting the *AD* curve rightward. Consequently, Real GDP rises. Under the same assumptions, the transmission mechanism works as follows for a decrease in the money supply: a decrease in the money supply raises the interest rate and decreases investment, thereby decreasing aggregate demand and thus shifting the *AD* curve leftward. As a result, Real GDP falls.

- The Keynesian transmission mechanism may be short-circuited either by the liquidity trap or by interest-insensitive investment. Both are Keynesian notions. If either is present, Keynesians predict that expansionary monetary policy will be unable to change Real GDP.

THE MONETARIST TRANSMISSION MECHANISM

- The monetarist route between the money market and the goods and services market is direct. Changes in the money supply affect aggregate demand. An increase in the money supply causes individuals to increase their spending on a wide variety of goods.

BOND PRICES AND INTEREST RATES

- Interest rates and the prices of old or existing bonds are inversely related.

THE ACTIVIST–NONACTIVIST DEBATE

- Activists argue that monetary policy should be deliberately used to smooth out the business cycle; they favor using activist, or discretionary, monetary policy to fine-tune the economy. Nonactivists argue against the use of discretionary monetary policy; they propose nonactivist, or rules-based, monetary policy.

- The case for discretionary monetary policy rests on three major claims: (1) The economy does not always equilibrate quickly enough at Natural Real GDP. (2) Activist monetary policy works. (3) Activist monetary policy is flexible, and flexibility is a desirable quality in monetary policy.

- The case for nonactivist monetary policy rests on three major claims: (1) There is sufficient flexibility in wages and prices in modern economies to allow them to equilibrate at reasonable speed at Natural Real GDP. (2) Activist monetary policies may not work. (3) Activist monetary policies are likely to make matters worse rather than better.

NONACTIVIST (OR RULES-BASED) MONETARY PROPOSALS

- The constant-money-growth-rate rule states that the annual money supply growth rate will be constant at the average annual growth rate of Real GDP.

- The predetermined-money-growth-rate rule states that the annual growth rate in the money supply will be equal to the average annual growth rate in Real GDP minus the growth rate in velocity.

- The Taylor rule specifies: Federal funds rate target = 1.5 (inflation rate) + 0.5 (GDP gap) + 1.

- Inflation targeting requires the Fed to keep the inflation rate near a predetermined level.

KEY TERMS AND CONCEPTS

Transmission Mechanism	Liquidity Trap	Contractionary Monetary	Fine-tuning
Demand for Money	Expansionary Monetary	Policy	Nonactivists
(Balances)	Policy	Activists	Inflation Targeting

QUESTIONS AND PROBLEMS

1. It has been suggested that nonactivists are not concerned with the level of Real GDP and unemployment because most (if not all) nonactivist monetary proposals set as their immediate objective the stabilization of the price level. Discuss.

2. Monetary policy can affect relative prices. Do you agree or disagree with this statement? Explain your answer.

3. Explain how the Keynesian transmission mechanism works.

4. How does inflation targeting work?

5. Explain how the monetarist transmission mechanism works.

6. Argue the case for and against a monetary rule.

7. Explain how it is possible to have too much money.

8. Both activists and nonactivists make good points for their respective positions. Do you think activists could say anything to nonactivists to convince them to accept the activist position, and vice versa? If so, what is it? If not, why not?

9. Why is the demand curve for money downward sloping?

10. The discussion of supply and demand in Chapter 3 noted that if two goods are substitutes, the price of one and the demand for the other are directly related. For example, if Pepsi-Cola and Coca-Cola are substitutes, an increase in the price of Pepsi-Cola will increase the demand for Coca-Cola. Suppose that bonds and stocks are substitutes. We know that interest rates and bond prices are inversely related. What do you predict is the relationship between stock prices and interest rates? Explain your answer.

11. If bond prices fall, will individuals want to hold more or less money? Explain your answer.

12. Suppose it were proved that liquidity traps do not occur and that investment is not interest insensitive. Would this be enough to disprove the Keynesian claim that expansionary monetary policy is not always effective at changing Real GDP? Why or why not?

13. Consider the following: Two researchers, A and B, are trying to determine whether eating fatty foods leads to heart attacks. The researchers proceed differently. Researcher A builds a model in which fatty foods may first affect X in one's body, and if X is affected, then Y may be affected, and if Y is affected, then Z may be affected. Finally, if Z is affected, the heart is affected, and the individual has an increased probability of suffering a heart attack. Researcher B doesn't proceed in this step-by-step fashion. She conducts an experiment to see whether people who eat many fatty foods have more, fewer, or the same number of heart attacks as people who eat few fatty foods. Which researcher's methods have more in common with the research methodology implicit in the Keynesian transmission mechanism? Which researcher's methods have more in common with the research methodology implicit in the monetarist transmission mechanism? Explain your answer.

14. Suppose the combination of more accurate data and better forecasting techniques would make it easy for the Fed to predict a recession 10 to 16 months in advance. Would this strengthen the case for activism or nonactivism? Explain your answer.

WORKING WITH NUMBERS AND GRAPHS

1. Manuel bought a bond last year for $10,000 that promises to pay him $900 a year. This year, he can buy a bond for $10,000 that promises to pay $1,000 a year. If Manuel wants to sell his old bond, what is its price likely to be?

2. Charu bought a bond last year for $10,000 that promises to pay her $1,000 a year. This year, investors can buy a bond for $10,000 that promises to pay $800 a year. If Charu wants to sell her old bond, what is its price likely to be?

3. The annual average percentage change in Real GDP is 2.3 percent, and the annual average percentage change in velocity is 1.1 percent. Using the monetary rule discussed in the text, what percentage change in the money supply will keep prices stable (on average)?

4. Graphically show that the more interest insensitive the investment demand curve is, the less likely it is that monetary policy will be effective at changing Real GDP.

5. Which panel in the figure best describes the situation in each of parts (a)–(d)?

   a. Expansionary monetary policy that effectively removes the economy from a recessionary gap

   b. Expansionary monetary policy that is destabilizing

   c. Contractionary monetary policy that effectively removes the economy from an inflationary gap

   d. Monetary policy that is ineffective at changing Real GDP

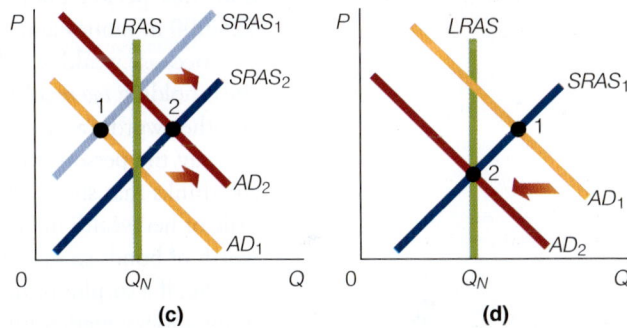
(c)   (d)

6. Graphically portray the Keynesian transmission mechanism under the following conditions:

   a. A decrease in the money supply

   b. No liquidity trap

   c. Downward-sloping investment demand

7. Graphically portray the monetarist transmission mechanism when the money supply declines.

8. According to the Taylor rule, if inflation is 8 percent and the GDP gap is 3 percent, what is the recommendation for the federal funds rate target?

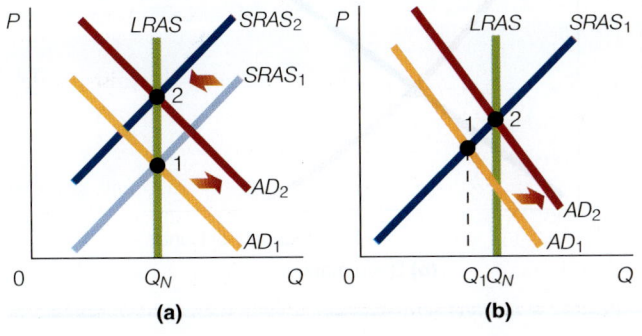
(a)   (b)

APPENDIX D

BOND PRICES AND THE INTEREST RATE

Bond prices and the interest rate are inversely related: as the price of bonds rises, the interest rate falls; as the price of bonds falls, the interest rate rises. In this appendix, we explain this relationship by looking closely at the money market and the bond market.

The money market is shown in equilibrium in Exhibit 1(a). The equilibrium interest rate is 5 percent. The bond market is shown in equilibrium in Exhibit 1(b). The equilibrium bond price is P_{B1}.

Suppose people have only two ways to hold their wealth: in money or in bonds. In other words, a person must always decide, "How much of my wealth do I hold in money and how much do I hold in bonds?" If someone's wealth is currently equal to $100,000, does this person hold $50,000 (of that wealth) in money and $50,000 in bonds, or $25,000 in money and $75,000 in bonds, and so on?

Because wealth can be held only in the form of money and bonds, if someone thinks she is holding *too much* money, she also must be thinking that she is holding too few bonds. In other words, a surplus of money necessarily implies a shortage of bonds. To illustrate, let's say the person is currently holding $25,000 in money and $75,000 in bonds. Then she thinks that she is holding too much money; so she must also think she is holding too little of her wealth in bonds. She might want to take $5,000 of her money and buy $5,000 worth of bonds so that she has $20,000 in money and $80,000 in bonds.

So, if a surplus of money signifies a shortage of bonds, then, in market terms, a surplus in the money market implies a shortage in the bond market.

Suppose our person believes that she is holding *too little* money. Instead of holding $25,000 in money, she would prefer to hold $30,000 in money. But, of course, holding

---

EXHIBIT 1

The Money Market and the Bond Market

(a) The money market in equilibrium at an interest rate of 5 percent. (b) The bond market is in equilibrium at a bond price of P_{B1}. When one of these markets is in equilibrium, the other is too.

(a) Money market

(b) Bond market

too little money necessarily implies that our person is holding too much of her wealth in bonds. In other words, a shortage of money implies a surplus of bonds.

So, a shortage in the money market implies a surplus in the bond market. Let's recap:

Holding too much of one's wealth in money → Holding too little of one's wealth in bonds

or

Surplus in the money market → Shortage in the bond market

and

Holding too little of one's wealth in money → holding too much of one's wealth in bonds

or

Shortage in the money market → Surplus in the bond market

Now let's look at Exhibit 2. At point 1 in each market, both the money market and the bond market are in equilibrium. People are holding just the right amount of money and just the right amount of bonds. Suppose the Fed undertakes an action that increases the money supply. The money supply curve in Exhibit 2(a) shifts rightward from S_1 to S_2. At the initial interest rate of 5 percent, the money market now has a surplus of money.

EXHIBIT 2

Changes in the Money Market Affect the Bond Market

(a) The money market is initially in equilibrium at point 1; the equilibrium interest rate is 5 percent. (b) The bond market is initially in equilibrium at point 1; the equilibrium bond price is P_{B1}. The Fed increases the money supply. In the money market [shown in (a)], the supply of money curve shifts rightward from S_1 to S_2. At the interest rate of 5 percent, there is now a surplus of money. With their surplus of money, individuals start to buy more bonds, so the demand for bonds curve in panel (b) shifts rightward from D_1 to D_2. The result is a shortage of bonds in the bond market at the price of P_{B1}. Both markets are now in disequilibrium. The equilibrating process in the bond market pushes bond prices up. As bond prices rise, the interest rate falls, and that happens in the money market [shown in (a)]. Eventually, both markets are back in equilibrium. The equilibrium interest rate is now 4 percent, and the price of bonds is now P_{B2}.

(a) Money market

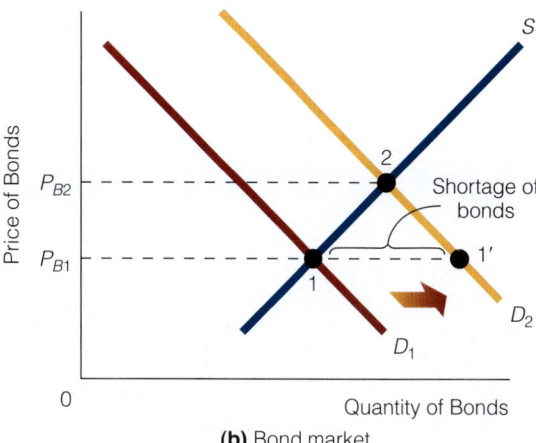

(b) Bond market

But, as we recall, a surplus of money in the money market must mean a shortage of bonds in the bond market.

How does this shortage manifest itself? As a result of the surplus in the money market, individuals take their "surplus money" and start to buy bonds. The demand for bonds in the bond market shifts rightward from D_1 to D_2. So now there is a surplus of money in the money market at 5 percent and a shortage of bonds in the bond market at P_{B1}. Both markets are in disequilibrium at the specified interest rate and bond price.

The markets will begin to equilibrate. In the bond market, the price of bonds will begin to rise toward P_{B2}. As the price of bonds rises, the interest rate in the money market starts to fall, moving toward its equilibrium level of 4 percent. Finally, both markets are in equilibrium: the money market is at 4 percent and the bond market at P_{B2}.

APPENDIX SUMMARY

• Suppose that an individual can hold his wealth only in terms of money and bonds. So if a person believes he is holding too much of his wealth in money, he also believes that he is holding too little of it in bonds. Similarly, if he believes he is holding too little of his wealth in money, he also believes that he is holding too much of it in bonds.

• A surplus in the money market implies a shortage in the bond market. A shortage in the money market implies a surplus in the bond market.

QUESTIONS AND PROBLEMS

1. Draw both the money market and bond market in equilibrium. Next, explain and diagrammatically show what happens to the interest rate and the price of bonds as a result of the Fed's increasing the money supply.

2. Draw both the money market and bond market in equilibrium. Next, explain and diagrammatically show what happens to the interest rate and the price of bonds as a result of the Fed's decreasing the money supply.

3. Identify the state of the bond market (equilibrium, shortage, surplus), given each of the following:

   a. Shortage in the money market

   b. Surplus in the money market

   c. Equilibrium in the money market

4. Fed actions affect the money market but not the bond market. Do you agree or disagree with this statement? Explain your answer.

CHAPTER 16

EXPECTATIONS THEORY AND THE ECONOMY

© AP PHOTO/PETAR PETROV

Introduction In this chapter, we discuss two expectations theories: adaptive and rational. We begin our discussion of expectations theory and the economy with a debate that raged within the economic profession years ago over the shape of the Phillips curve.

PHILLIPS CURVE ANALYSIS

The Phillips curve is used to analyze the relationship between inflation and unemployment. We begin the discussion of the Phillips curve by focusing on the work of three economists: A. W. Phillips, Paul Samuelson, and Robert Solow.

The Phillips Curve

In 1958, A. W. Phillips of the London School of Economics published a paper in the economics journal, *Economica*: "The Relation Between Unemployment and the Rate of Change of Money Wages in the United Kingdom, 1861–1957." As the title suggests, Phillips collected data about the rate of change in money wages, sometimes referred to as *wage inflation*, and about *unemployment rates* in the United Kingdom over almost a century. He then plotted the rate of change in money wages against the unemployment rate for each year. Finally, he fit a curve to the data points (Exhibit 1).

AN INVERSE RELATIONSHIP The curve, which came to be known as the Phillips curve, is downward sloping, suggesting that the rate of change of money wage rates (wage inflation) and unemployment rates are *inversely related*.[1] This inverse relationship, in turn, suggests a trade-off between wage inflation and unemployment. Higher wage inflation means lower unemployment; lower wage inflation means higher unemployment.

Phillips Curve

A curve that originally showed the relationship between wage inflation and unemployment and that now more often shows the relationship between price inflation and unemployment.

---

1. Early explanations *for the* inverse relationship between wage inflation and unemployment focused on the state of the labor market, given changes in aggregate demand. When aggregate demand is increasing, businesses expand production and hire more employees. As the unemployment rate falls, the labor market becomes tighter, and employers find it increasingly difficult to hire workers at old wages. Businesses must offer higher wages to obtain additional workers. Unemployment and money wage rates move in opposite directions.

EXHIBIT 1

The Original Phillips Curve

This curve was constructed by A. W. Phillips, using data for the United Kingdom from 1861 to 1913. (The relationship here is also representative of the experience of the United Kingdom through 1957.) The original Phillips curve suggests an inverse relationship between wage inflation and unemployment; it represents a wage inflation–unemployment trade-off. (Note: Each dot represents a single year.)

Policy makers concluded from the Phillips curve that lowering both wage inflation and unemployment was impossible; they could do only one or the other. So the combination of low wage inflation and low unemployment was unlikely. This was the bad news.

The good news was that rising unemployment and rising wage inflation did not go together either. Thus, the combination of high unemployment and high wage inflation was unlikely.

Samuelson and Solow: The Americanization of the Phillips Curve

In 1960, two American economists, Paul Samuelson and Robert Solow, published an article in the *American Economic Review* in which they fit a Phillips curve to the U.S. economy from 1935 to 1959. In addition to using American data instead of British data, they measured *price inflation rates* (instead of wage inflation rates) against unemployment rates. They found an inverse relationship between (price) inflation and unemployment (see Exhibit 2).[2]

Stagflation
The simultaneous occurrence of high rates of inflation and unemployment.

Economists concluded from the Phillips curve that stagflation, or high inflation together with high unemployment, was extremely unlikely. The economy could register (1) high unemployment and low inflation or (2) low unemployment and high inflation. Also, economists noticed that the Phillips curve presented policy makers with a *menu of choices*. For example, policy makers could choose to move the economy to any of the points on the Phillips curve in Exhibit 2. If they decided that, say, point *A*, with high unemployment and low inflation, was preferable to point *D*, with low unemployment and high inflation, then so be it. Getting the economy to the desired point was simply a matter of reaching the right level of aggregate demand. To Keynesian economists, who were gaining a reputation for advocating fine-tuning the economy (i.e., using small-scale measures to counterbalance undesirable economic trends), this conclusion seemed consistent with their theories and policy proposals.

EXHIBIT 2

The Phillips Curve and a Menu of Choices

Samuelson and Solow's early work using American data showed that the Phillips curve was downward sloping. Economists reasoned that stagflation was extremely unlikely and that the Phillips curve presented policy makers with a menu of choices—point *A*, *B*, *C*, or *D*.

THE CONTROVERSY BEGINS: ARE THERE REALLY TWO PHILLIPS CURVES?

This section discusses the work of Milton Friedman and the hypothesis that there are two, not one, Phillips curves.

Things Aren't Always as We Think

In the 1970s and early 1980s, economists began to question many of the conclusions about the Phillips curve—questions

---

2. Today, when economists speak of the Phillips curve, they are usually referring to the relationship between price inflation rates and unemployment rates instead of the relationship between wage inflation rates and unemployment rates.

largely prompted by events after 1969. Exhibit 3 shows U.S. inflation and unemployment rates for the years 1961–2003. The 1961–1969 period, which is shaded, depicts the original Phillips curve trade-off between inflation and unemployment. The remaining period, 1970–2003, as a whole does not, although some subperiods, such as 1976–1979, do.

In the period 1970–2003, note that stagflation—high unemployment and high inflation—is possible. For example, 1975, 1981, and 1982 are definitely years of stagflation. The existence of stagflation implies that a trade-off between inflation and unemployment may not always exist.

Friedman and the Natural Rate Theory

Milton Friedman, in his presidential address to the American Economic Association in 1967 (published in the *American Economic Review*), attacked the idea of a *permanent* downward-sloping Phillips curve. Friedman's key point was that there are two Phillips curves, not one: a short-run Phillips curve and a long-run Phillips curve. Friedman said, "There is always a temporary tradeoff between inflation and unemployment; there is no permanent tradeoff." Specifically, *there is a trade-off in the short run but not in the long run.*

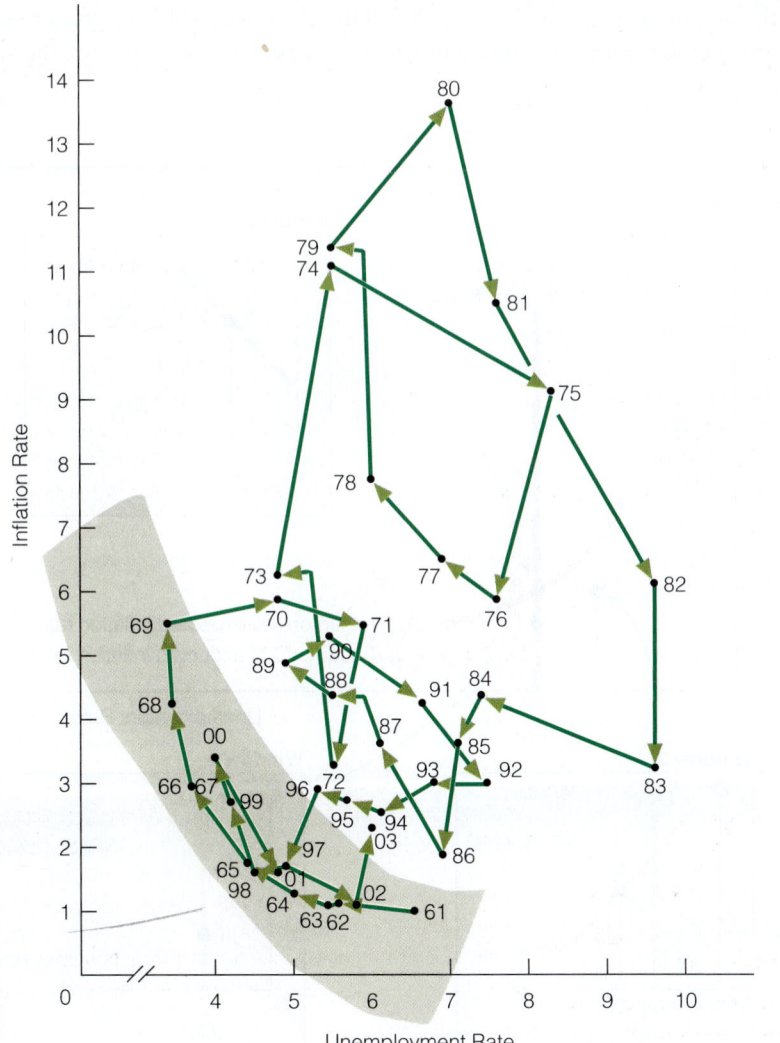

EXHIBIT 3

The Diagram That Raises Questions: Inflation and Unemployment, 1961–2003

The period 1961–1969 clearly depicts the original Phillips curve trade-off between inflation and unemployment. The later period, 1970–2003, as a whole, does not. However, some subperiods do, such as 1976–1979. The diagram presents empirical evidence that stagflation may exist; an inflation–unemployment trade-off may not always hold.

Friedman's discussion not only introduced two types of Phillips curves but also opened the macroeconomics door wide, once and for all, to expectations theory: the idea that people's expectations about economic events affect economic outcomes.

Exhibit 4 illustrates both the short- and long-run Phillips curves. In window 1, the economy is in long-run equilibrium, operating at Q_1, which is equal to Q_N. In the main diagram, the economy is at point 1 at the natural rate of unemployment, U_N. Further and most important, *we assume that the expected inflation rate and the actual inflation rate are the same* at 2 percent.

Now suppose government *unexpectedly* increases aggregate demand from AD_1 to AD_2, as shown in window 2. As a result, the *actual* inflation rate increases (say, to 4 percent), but in the short run (immediately after the increase in aggregate demand), individual decision makers do not know this. Consequently, the *expected* inflation rate remains at 2 percent. In short, aggregate demand increases at the same time that people's expected inflation rate remains constant.

Because of this combination of events, certain consequences unfold. The higher aggregate demand causes temporary shortages and higher prices. Businesses then respond to higher prices and higher profits by increasing output. Higher output requires more employees, and so businesses start hiring more workers. As hiring increases, many currently unemployed individuals find work. Furthermore, many of the newly employed persons accept the prevailing wage rate because they think the wages will have greater purchasing power (because they expect the inflation rate to be 2 percent) than, in fact, the wages will turn out to have.

EXHIBIT 4

Short-Run and Long-Run Phillips Curves

Starting at point 1 in the main diagram, and assuming that the expected inflation rate stays constant as aggregate demand increases, the economy moves to point 2. As the expected inflation rate changes and comes to equal the actual inflation rate, the economy moves to point 3. Points 1 and 2 lie on a short-run Phillips curve. Points 1 and 3 lie on a long-run Phillips curve. (Note: The percentages in parentheses following the *SRAS* curves in the windows refer to the expected inflation rates.)

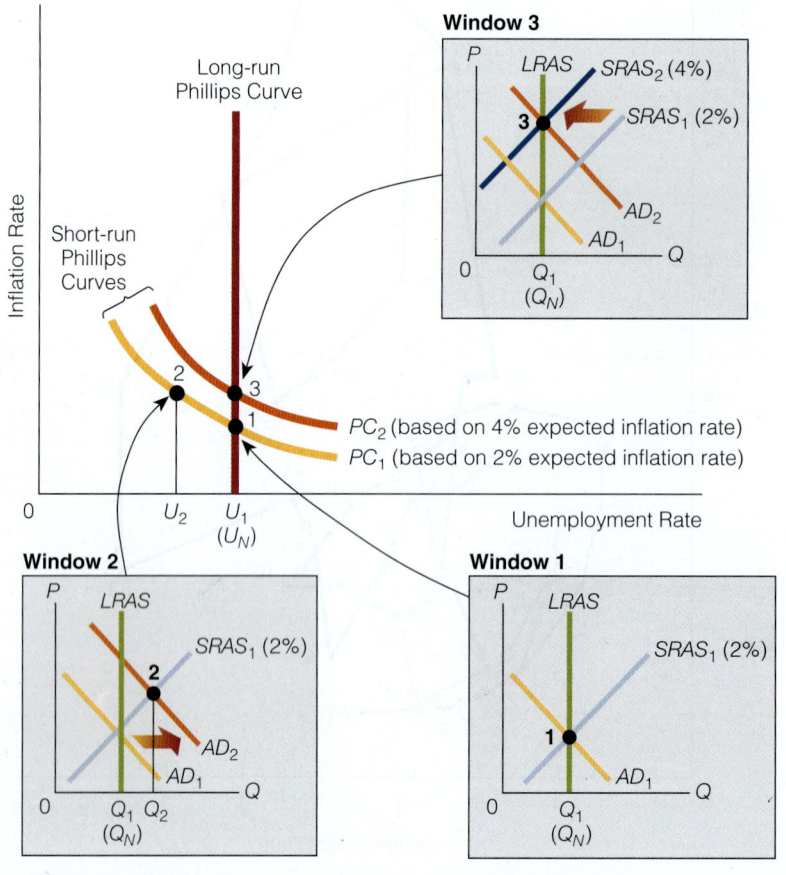

So far, the results of an increase in aggregate demand with no change in the expected inflation rate are (1) an increase in Real GDP from Q_1 to Q_2 (see window 2) and (2) a corresponding decrease in the unemployment rate from U_1 to U_2 (see the main diagram). Thus, the economy has moved from point 1 to point 2 in the main diagram.

The question is whether point 2 is a stable equilibrium. Friedman answered that it is not. He argued that, *as long as the expected inflation rate is not equal to the actual inflation rate, the economy is not in long-run equilibrium.*

For Friedman, as for most economists today, the movement from point 1 to point 2 on PC_1 is a short-run movement. Economists refer to PC_1, along which short-run movements occur, as a *short-run Phillips curve.*

In time, inflation expectations begin to change. As prices continue to climb, wage earners realize that their real (i.e., inflation-adjusted) wages are lower than they thought. In hindsight, they realize that they accepted nominal (money) wages based on an expected inflation rate (2 percent) that was too low. So they revise their inflation expectations upward.

At the same time, some wage earners quit their jobs because they choose not to continue working at such low *real wages.* Eventually, the combination of some workers quitting their jobs and most (if not all) workers revising their inflation expectations upward causes wage rates to move upward.

Higher wage rates shift the short-run aggregate supply curve from $SRAS_1$ to $SRAS_2$ (see window 3), ultimately moving the economy back to Natural Real GDP and to the natural rate of unemployment at point 3 (see the main diagram). The curve that connects point 1, where the economy started, and point 3, where it ended, is called the *long-run Phillips curve.*

Thus, the short-run Phillips curve exhibits a trade-off between inflation and unemployment, whereas the long-run Phillips curve does not. This idea is implicit in what has come to be called the Friedman natural rate theory (or the *Friedman fooling theory*). According to this theory (Exhibit 5), in the long run, the economy returns to its natural rate of unemployment, and it moved away from the natural unemployment rate in the first place only because workers were fooled (in the short run) into thinking the inflation rate was lower than it was.

Friedman Natural Rate Theory
Within the Phillips curve framework, the idea that, in the long run, unemployment is at its natural rate and that there is a long-run Phillips curve, which is vertical at the natural rate of unemployment.

EXHIBIT 5

Mechanics of the Friedman Natural Rate Theory

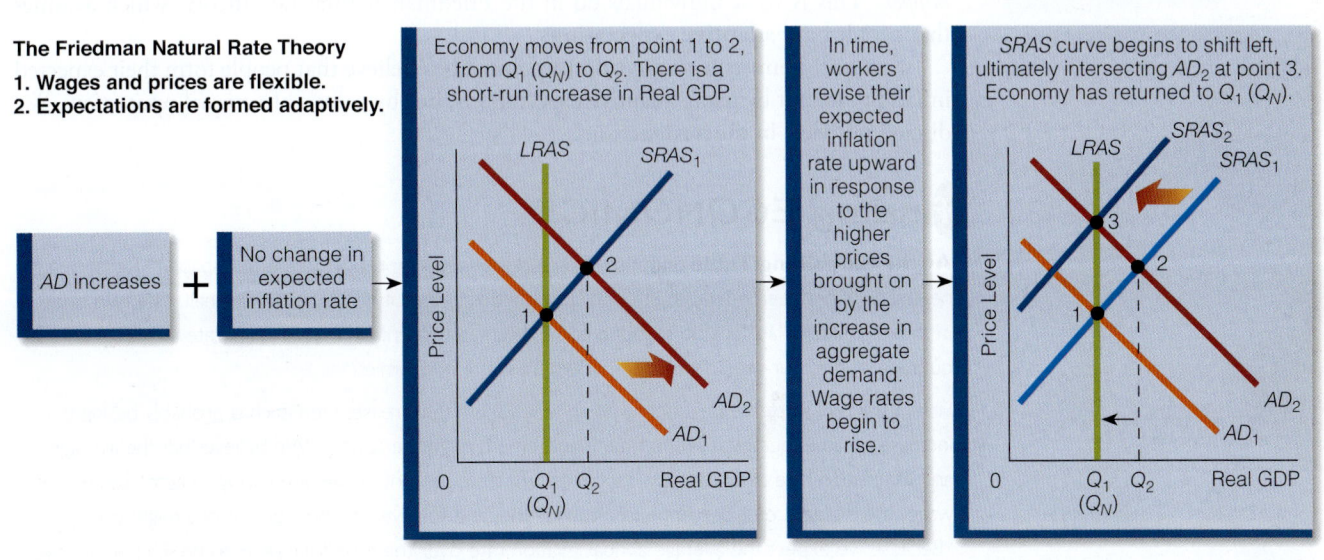

The Friedman Natural Rate Theory
1. **Wages and prices are flexible.**
2. **Expectations are formed adaptively.**

AD increases + No change in expected inflation rate

Economy moves from point 1 to 2, from Q_1 (Q_N) to Q_2. There is a short-run increase in Real GDP.

In time, workers revise their expected inflation rate upward in response to the higher prices brought on by the increase in aggregate demand. Wage rates begin to rise.

SRAS curve begins to shift left, ultimately intersecting AD_2 at point 3. Economy has returned to Q_1 (Q_N).

How, specifically, do people's expectations relate to the discussion of the short- and long-run Phillips curves? In Exhibit 4, the economy starts out at point 1 in the main diagram, and then something happens: Aggregate demand increases. This increase raises the inflation rate, *but workers don't become aware of the change in the inflation rate for a while.* In the interim, their expected inflation rate is too low, and, as a result, they are willing to work at jobs (and produce output) that they wouldn't work at if they perceived the inflation rate realistically.

In time, workers perceive the inflation rate realistically. Their expected inflation rate is no longer too low; it has risen to equal the actual inflation rate. The response, as predicted, is that the unemployment rate rises and output falls.

So, because workers' expectations (of inflation) are, in the short run, inconsistent with reality, workers produce more output than they would produce if their expectations were consistent with reality. This is how people's expectations can affect such real economic variables as Real GDP and the unemployment rate.

ⓣhinking Like AN ECONOMIST

Perceptions of Reality Matter People say they base their actions on reality. When it rains, the pull out an umbrella; when they have a hard time seeing, they get their eyes checked. People also base their actions on their *perceptions* of reality, as workers do in the Friedman natural rate theory. Although the inflation rate has actually increased, workers don't perceive the change. Thus, in the short run (during the time period in which they misperceive reality), workers base their actions not on reality, but on their perception of it. ▪▪▪

How Do People Form Their Expectations?

Implicit in the Friedman natural rate theory is an assumption about how individuals form their expectations. Essentially, the theory holds that individuals form their expected inflation rate by looking at *past inflation rates*. Suppose someone were to ask you your expected inflation rate for the upcoming year. Would your response be closer to 50 percent or to 2 percent? If you arrive at your expected inflation rate using adaptive expectations, the answer is closer to 2 percent than to 50 percent because you haven't seen recent past inflation rates of 50 percent. But you have seen recent past inflation rates near 2 percent.

Notice that, with adaptive expectations, individuals look to the past—they look over their shoulders to see what *has happened*—in formulating their best guess as to what *will happen*. This is what individuals do in the Friedman natural rate theory, which assumes that people have **adaptive expectations**.

Some economists have argued this point. They believe that people form their expected inflation rate not by using adaptive expectations, but by means of *rational expectations*. We discuss this view in the next section.

Adaptive Expectations
Expectations that individuals form from past experience and modify slowly as the present and the future become the past (i.e., as time passes).

ⓕinding ECONOMICS

At the Bargaining Table Suppose you read the following report in the newspaper: "Recent wage negotiations between management and labor unions in the city have come to a halt. The two sides in the negotiations are unable so far to come to an agreement on annual wage rate increases for the duration of the four-year contract . . . ." Where is the economics?

First, if the two sides are negotiating an annual wage rate increase, then each is probably basing the increase on an expected inflation rate. Management might be saying, "We believe that the average annual inflation rate over the next four years will be 2 percent; so we are willing to agree to an annual wage rate increase of 2 percent each year for the next four years. The labor unions might be saying, "Because we expect the average annual inflation rate over the next four years to be 3.5 percent, we believe that 3.5 percent is the right annual wage rate increase for us." ▪▪▪

SELF-TEST

(Answers to Self-Test questions are in Answers to Self-Test Questions at the back of the book.)

1. What condition must exist for the Phillips curve to present policy makers with a permanent menu of choices (between inflation and unemployment)?

2. Is there a trade-off between inflation and unemployment? Explain your answer.

3. The Friedman natural rate theory is sometimes called the fooling theory. Who is being fooled, and what are they being fooled about?

RATIONAL EXPECTATIONS AND NEW CLASSICAL THEORY

Rational expectations have played a major role in the Phillips curve controversy. We discuss rational expectations and new classical theory next.

Rational Expectations

In the early 1970s, a few economists, including Robert Lucas of the University of Chicago (winner of the 1995 Nobel Prize in Economics), began to question the short-run trade-off between inflation and unemployment. Essentially, Lucas combined the natural rate theory with rational expectations.[3]

Rational expectations holds that individuals form the expected inflation rate not only on the basis of their past experience with inflation (looking over their shoulders), but also on their predictions about the effects of present and future policy actions and events (looking around and ahead). In short, the expected inflation rate is formed by looking at the past, present, and future. To illustrate, suppose the inflation rate has been 2 percent for the past seven years. Then, the chairman of the Fed's Board of Governors speaks about "sharply stimulating the economy." Rational expectationists argue that the expected inflation rate might immediately jump upward based on the current announcement by the chairman.

A major difference between adaptive and rational expectations is the *speed* at which the expected inflation rate changes. If the expected inflation rate is formed adaptively, then it is slow to change. Because it is based only on the past, individuals wait until the present becomes the past before changing their expectations. If the expected inflation rate is formed rationally, it changes quickly because it is based on the past, present, and future.

Rational Expectations
Expectations that individuals form based on past experience and on their predictions about the effects of present and future policy actions and events.

Do People Really Anticipate Policy?

One assumption of rational expectations is that people anticipate policy. Suppose you chose people at random on the street and asked them, "What do you think the Fed will do in the next few months?" Do you think you would be more likely to receive an intelligent answer or the response, "What's the Fed?" Most readers of this text would probably expect the second answer. In fact, the general feeling is that the person on the street knows little about economics or economic institutions. So, no, people don't really anticipate policy. But suppose you chose people at random in the Wall Street area of Manhattan and asked

---

3. Rational expectations appeared on the economic scene in 1961, when John Muth published "Rational Expectations and the Theory of Price Movements" in *Econometrica*. For about 10 years, the article received little attention from the economics profession. Then, in the early 1970s, with the work of Robert Lucas, Thomas Sargent, Neil Wallace, Robert Barro, and others, the article began to be noticed.

the same question. In this case, the answer is likely to be well thought out; at least *these* people anticipate policy.

However, not all persons need to anticipate policy. *As long as some do*, the consequences may be the same *as if* all persons do. For example, Juanita Estevez is anticipating policy if she decides to buy 100 shares of SKA because her best friend, Tammy Higgins, heard from her friend Kenny Urich that his broker, Roberta Gunter, told him that SKA's stock is expected to go up. Juanita is anticipating policy because it is likely that Roberta Gunter obtained her information from a researcher in the brokerage firm who makes it his business to watch the Fed and to anticipate its next move.

Of course, anticipating policy is not done just for the purpose of buying and selling securities. Labor unions hire professional forecasters (Fed watchers) to predict future inflation rates, which is important information to have during wage contract negotiations. Banks hire forecasters to predict inflation rates, which they incorporate into the interest rates they charge. Export businesses hire forecasters to predict the future exchange-rate value of the dollar. The average investor may subscribe to a business or investment newsletter for information in order to predict interest rates, the price of gold, or next year's inflation rate more accurately. The person thinking of refinancing a mortgage watches one of the many financial news shows on television to find out about the government's most recent move and how it will affect interest rates in, say, the next three months.

finding ECONOMICS

While Playing a Game of Chess Where is the economics in a game of chess? Chess players often anticipate each others' moves. Player 1 might be thinking that if she moves from e4 to e5, player 2 will move from b5 to c6. But then the first player asks herself, "What comes next? Will my opponent then be likely to move from c3 to d6?"

What people do in a game of chess and what they do when predicting government policy actions might not be all that different. In a game of chess you are playing to win, and whether you win depends on how well you can anticipate your opponent's moves. Anticipating policy actions is not much different, as you will shortly see. How well you do in the economy also has a lot to do with how well you anticipate government policy actions. ▲ ▲ ▲

Price Level Expectations and the *SRAS Curve*

We know that various factors can shift the *SRAS* curve—wage rates, the price of nonlabor inputs, supply shocks, and so on. In this chapter, we want to show how a change in expectations can lead to a shift in the *SRAS* curve.

REAL WAGE The real (inflation-adjusted) wage is equal to the nominal wage divided by the price level.

$$\text{Real wage} = \frac{\text{Nominal Wage}}{\text{Price Level}} \times 100$$

Suppose that the nominal wage is $40 and that the price level, as represented by a price index, is 110. The real wage is therefore $36.36: $40 ÷ 110. Obviously, a person's real wage will rise if either the nominal wage rises or the price level declines, or if both occur. For example, suppose the price level falls from 110 to 95. The real wage rises to $42.10. And, under certain conditions, as one's real wage rises, one chooses to work more. Conversely, as one's real wage falls, one chooses to work less.

Price level falls → Real wage rises → Work more

Price level rises → Real wage falls → Work less

WORKING MORE OR LESS AND SHIFTS IN THE *SRAS* CURVE Labor is an input into the production process; so more labor (either in terms of individuals or labor hours) means more output. When people work more, more output is produced; so the *SRAS* curve shifts rightward. When people work less, less output is produced; so the *SRAS* curve shifts leftward.

Now we can connect the expected price level to the *SRAS* curve.

- *Example 1.* Suppose individuals expect the price level to decline. Thus they expect their real wages to rise and will work more. Working more produces more output; so the *SRAS* curve shifts rightward.

  Expect price level to fall → Expect real wage to rise → Work more → Produce more
  output → *SRAS* curve shifts rightward

- *Example 2.* Suppose individuals expect the price level to rise. Thus they expect their real wage to decline and will work less. Working less produces less output; so the *SRAS* curve shifts leftward.

  Expect price level to rise → Expect real wage to fall → Work less → Produce less
  output → *SRAS* curve shifts leftward

Exhibit 6 shows three *SRAS* curves. After each curve is the expected price level in parentheses. The higher the expected price level is, the closer the *SRAS* curve lies to the vertical axis, or the origin. The lower the expected price level is, the farther away from the vertical axis, or origin, the *SRAS* lies. Therefore, a rise in the expected price level will shift the *SRAS* curve to the left; a fall in the expected price level will shift the *SRAS* curve to the right.

Expected and Actual Price Levels

The difference between an actual price level and an expected price level is fairly clear.

- The *actual price level* is exactly what it sounds like: the price level that actually exists. For example, someone might say that the price level today is 140. This, then, is the actual price level. We will use P_A to represent the actual price level.

Price Level (vertical axis)

SRAS₃ (expected price level = 170)
SRAS₁ (expected price level = 150)
SRAS₂ (expected price level = 120)

0   Real GDP

EXHIBIT 6

The Expected Price Level and the *SRAS* Curve

Every *SRAS* curve is based on some expected price level. For example, *SRAS*₁ in the exhibit is based on an *expected price level* of 150. As the expected price level rises, the *SRAS* curve shifts leftward; as the expected price level falls, the *SRAS* curve shifts rightward.

- The *expected price level* is what you expect the price level will be sometime in the future. For example, you might expect that the price level in, say, one year will be 150. This is your expected price level. We will use P_{EX} to represent the expected price level.

Obviously, individuals' expectations (P_{EX}) can have one of three relationships with the actual price level (P_A):

$$P_{EX} = P_A$$
$$P_{EX} > P_A$$
$$P_{EX} < P_A$$

To illustrate, the Fed increases the money supply, and the *AD* curve shifts rightward. If the *SRAS* curve is upward sloping, then there will be a short-run and a long-run effect on the price level. Suppose that when the economy is back in long-run equilibrium, the actual price level *(P_A)* will be 155. But when the Fed increases the money supply, you expect that the price level in the future will be 165. In other words, your expected price level is greater than the actual price level: $P_{EX} > P_A$. Obviously you made a mistake; specifically, you overestimated what the price level would be. You "guessed" too high. In the new classical theoretical framework using rational expectations, "guessing" too high, too low, or just right can have an effect on the economy. We show how next.

New Classical Economics and Four Different Cases

New classical theory holds that individuals have rational expectations and that prices and wages are flexible. With these two points in mind, we apply new classical theory to four different cases (or settings):

- Case 1: Policy Correctly Anticipated
- Case 2: Policy Incorrectly Anticipated (Bias Upward)
- Case 3: Policy Incorrectly Anticipated (Bias Downward)
- Case 4: Policy Unanticipated

Each setting relates to a different perspective individuals have with respect to economic policy. We discuss monetary policy, but everything we say with respect to monetary policy in the upcoming discussion also holds for demand-side fiscal policy.

CASE 1: POLICY CORRECTLY ANTICIPATED An economy is in long-run equilibrium, as shown at point 1 in Exhibit 7. The actual price level is 100, and $SRAS_1$ is based on the expected price level of 100. In other words, in long-run equilibrium the actual price level (P_A) and the expected price level (P_{EX}) are the same.

Starting point: $P_A = P_{EX}$

The Fed increases the money supply, and this Fed policy action is *correctly anticipated* by the public. What "correctly anticipated" means here is that individuals know not only that the Fed is increasing the money supply, but also know how much the money supply is increasing and what the actual price level will be when the economy reaches its new long-run equilibrium position. The exhibit shows that the actual price level *will be* 110 when the economy reaches its new long-run equilibrium at point 2.

Now how does the fact that individuals are correctly anticipating policy (and the consequences of that policy) affect the *expected price level*? If individuals know where the actual price level is headed (i.e., to 110), they will immediately change their expected price

EXHIBIT 7

Policy Correctly Anticipated

We assume that rational expectations hold, that wages and prices are flexible, that any policy action is anticipated correctly, and that the economy is in long-run equilibrium. The actual price level is 100, and the expected price level (which the $SRAS_1$ curve is based on) is also 100. The Fed increases the money supply, and the AD curve shifts rightward. Because policy is anticipated correctly, individuals know that the new long-run equilibrium price level will be 110. Knowing this, they change their expected price level to 110. As a result, the $SRAS$ curve shifts leftward from $SRAS_1$ to $SRAS_2$. Keep in mind that the AD and $SRAS$ change at the same time. In other words, the AD curve shifts rightward at the same time the $SRAS$ curve shifts leftward. The result is that the Fed action leads to a higher price level but does not change Real GDP. The Fed action is ineffective at changing Real GDP; thus we have the policy ineffectiveness proposition (PIP) holding.

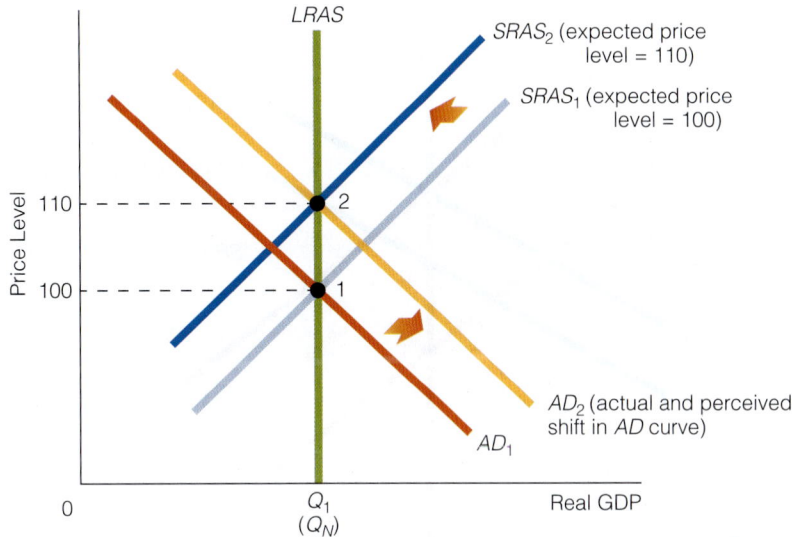

level to 110. Look at it this way: reality is changing in the economy; the price level is going to rise from 100 to 110 because of the Fed action. Correctly anticipating the new price level is like having a crystal ball and knowing exactly what is going to happen. So individuals immediately change their expectations of the future based on their correctly viewed perception of what is really going to happen.

Now if the expected price level changes to 110, the $SRAS$ curve in the exhibit will shift leftward from $SRAS_1$ to $SRAS_2$. However, the $SRAS$ curve shifts leftward at essentially the same time that the AD curve shifts rightward. The economy therefore moves from point 1 (its starting point) to point 2 (or ending point).

Exhibit 7 shows that even though the Fed increases the money supply (and the AD curve shifts rightward), Real GDP does not change. We started at Q_1 (or Q_N) and ended up at Q_1 (or Q_N). Therefore, if policy is correctly anticipated and if rational expectations hold, the only thing an increase in the money supply does in the economy is raise the price level. It does not change Real GDP. In other words, the Fed policy action was ineffective at changing Real GDP. This is called the policy ineffectiveness proposition (PIP).

CASE 2: POLICY INCORRECTLY ANTICIPATED (BIAS UPWARD) Again, an economy starts at long-run equilibrium, shown as point 1 in Exhibit 8. The two operational curves are AD_1 and $SRAS_1$. $SRAS_1$ is based on an expected price level (P_{EX}) of 100, which is the same as the actual price level (P_A).

Starting point: $P_A = P_{EX}$

Policy Ineffectiveness Proposition (PIP)

If (1) a policy change is correctly anticipated, (2) individuals form their expectations rationally, and (3) wages and prices are flexible, then neither fiscal policy nor monetary policy is effective at meeting macroeconomic goals.

EXHIBIT 8

Policy Incorrectly Anticipated—Bias Upward

(1) The economy starts in long-run equilibrium at point 1 and $P_A = P_{EX}$. (2) The Fed increases the money supply, and the AD curve actually shifts rightward from AD_1 to AD_2. (3) Individuals have incorrectly anticipated the Fed action. They believe the Fed has increased the money supply more than it actually has, and so they believe the AD curve has shifted from AD_1 to AD_3. This is a mistake. (4) Mistakenly assuming that the AD curve has shifted rightward from AD_1 to AD_3, individuals think the new actual price level will end up being 118, where the AD_3 curve intersects the LRAS curve. Accordingly, they change their expected price level to 118, and the SRAS curve shifts leftward from $SRAS_1$ to $SRAS_2$. (5) The short-run equilibrium for the economy turns out to be at point 2. (6) Eventually, individuals figure out that they made a mistake—that the real AD curve is AD_2, not AD_3. So the new long-run equilibrium will be 110, not 118 (as earlier believed). As a result, individuals now readjust their expected price level down from 118 to 110. Accordingly, the SRAS curve shifts rightward from $SRAS_2$ to $SRAS_3$. The economy is now in long-run equilibrium at point 3, and the expected price level is equal to the actual price level.

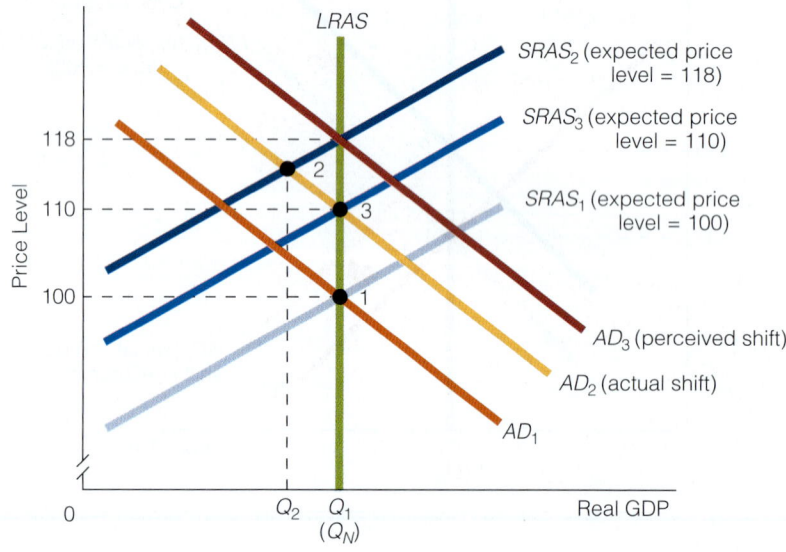

The Fed increases the money supply, and the AD curve shifts rightward from AD_1 to AD_2. This time, individuals mistakenly believe that the AD curve has shifted to the rightward by more than it has. In other words, they mistakenly think that the AD curve has shifted from AD_1 to AD_3. Individuals have thus *incorrectly anticipated policy with an upward bias*. In other words, they think that the AD curve has shifted more than it really has.

Obviously individuals have made a mistake, and this mistake is going to have consequences. Specifically, because individuals mistakenly believe the AD curve in the economy is AD_3 now, they think the new long-run equilibrium price level (where AD_3 intersects LRAS) will be 118; that is, their expected price level is 118. But the actual price level is never going to be 118. The actual price level in the future is going to 110, where the AD_2 intersects LRAS. So the expected price level is higher than what the actual price will be.

$$P_{EX} > P_A$$

Now as a result of individuals changing their expected price level from 100 to 118, the SRAS curve shifts leftward from $SRAS_1$ to $SRAS_2$. So far, then, the AD curve has actually shifted from AD_1 to AD_2, and the SRAS curve has shifted from $SRAS_1$ to $SRAS_2$. So, in the short run, the economy ends up at the intersection of AD_2 and $SRAS_2$, at point 2 in the exhibit. This is an odd result because we are accustomed to believing that an increase in the money supply leads to higher, not lower, Real GDP in the short run, but that is not what we see in Exhibit 8. Instead, Real GDP has fallen from Q_1 to Q_2. In other words, expansionary monetary policy has actually led to a decline in Real GDP. But why? It happened because of the mistake people made; specifically, they anticipated the Fed action incorrectly—with a bias upward.

The time will come when individuals realize that they made a mistake. In time, they will realize that the price level never actually increased to 118 and that AD_3 in the exhibit never really existed. They only perceived all that. In time, they will realize that the operational AD curve in the economy *is* AD_2 and that the long-run equilibrium price level consistent with this aggregate demand curve is 110. Accordingly, they will adjust their expected price level downward from 118 to 110. As they do, the $SRAS$ curve shifts rightward from $SRAS_2$ to $SRAS_3$, and the economy moves into long-run equilibrium at point 3. The long-run equilibrium condition of $P_A = P_{EX}$ holds at point 3.

Let's recap: (1) The economy starts in long-run equilibrium at point 1, and $P_A = P_{EX}$. (2) The Fed increases the money supply, and the AD curve actually shifts rightward from AD_1 to AD_2. (3) Individuals have incorrectly anticipated the Fed action. They believe the Fed has increased the money supply more than it actually did, and so they believe the AD curve has shifted from AD_1 to AD_3. This is a mistake. (4) Mistakenly assuming that the AD curve has shifted rightward from AD_1 to AD_3, individuals think the new actual price level will end up being 118, which is where the AD_3 curve intersects the $LRAS$ curve. Accordingly, they change their expected price level to 118, and the $SRAS$ curve shifts leftward from $SRAS_1$ to $SRAS_2$. (5) The short-run equilibrium for the economy turns out to be at point 2. Interestingly, because individuals have incorrectly anticipated policy with a bias upward, an increase in the money supply actually leads to a decline in Real GDP in the short run. (6) Eventually, individuals figure out that they made a mistake—that the real AD curve is AD_2, not AD_3. So the new long-run equilibrium will be 110, not 118 (as earlier believed). As a result, individuals now adjust their expected price level down from 118 to 110. Accordingly, the $SRAS$ curve shifts rightward from $SRAS_2$ to $SRAS_3$. The economy is now in long-run equilibrium at point 3, and the expected price level is equal to the actual price level.

CASE 3: POLICY INCORRECTLY ANTICIPATED (BIAS DOWNWARD) Just as individuals can incorrectly anticipate policy with a bias upward, they can also incorrectly anticipate policy with a bias downward. In Exhibit 9, an economy starts in long-run equilibrium at point 1. The Fed increases the money supply, and the AD curve shifts from AD_1 to AD_2. Individuals mistakenly think the AD curve has shifted from AD_1 to AD_3. In other words, they believe the Fed has increased the money supply by less than it actually has. They have incorrectly anticipated policy with a bias downward.

Because individuals have incorrectly anticipated policy with a bias downward, they mistakenly believe that the new actual long-run equilibrium price level will be 110. So they change their expected price level from 100 to 110, and the $SRAS$ curve shifts leftward from $SRAS_1$ to $SRAS_2$. Short-run equilibrium for the economy comes at the intersection of AD_2 and $SRAS_2$, at point 2. In the short run, an increase in the money supply has increased Real GDP from Q_1 to Q_2.

Eventually, individuals realize they have made a mistake. Eventually, they realize that AD_3 does not exist and that AD_2 is the only operational AD curve in the economy. So the new long-run equilibrium price level will be 115. Realizing that the long-run equilibrium level will be 115, individuals revise their expected price level from 110 to 115, and the $SRAS$ curve shifts from $SRAS_2$ to $SRAS_3$. The economy is now in long-run equilibrium at point 3, and the expected price level equals the actual price level.

CASE 4: POLICY UNANTICIPATED Besides correctly anticipating the new price level, and incorrectly anticipating it with bias upward or downward, the only possibility left is not anticipating it at all.

In Exhibit 10, an economy starts in long-run equilibrium at point 1. Here the actual price level equals the expected price level. The Fed increases the money supply so that the

EXHIBIT 9

Policy Incorrectly Anticipated—Bias Downward

An economy starts in long-run equilibrium at point 1. The expected price level is equal to the actual price level. The Fed increases the money supply, and the AD curve shifts rightward from AD_1 to AD_2. However, individuals mistakenly believe the AD curve has shifted rightward by less, from AD_1 to AD_3. As a result of this mistake, individuals mistakenly believe that the new long-run equilibrium price level will be 110. They then change their expected price level to 110, and the SRAS curve shifts leftward from $SRAS_1$ to $SRAS_2$. The short-run equilibrium in the economy comes at point 2. Eventually, individuals realize their mistake. They come to understand that AD_2 is the only operational AD curve in the economy and that the long-run equilibrium price level consistent with AD_2 is 115. They revise their expected price level from 110 to 115, and the SRAS curve shifts leftward from $SRAS_2$ to $SRAS_3$. The economy moves into long-run equilibrium at point 3.

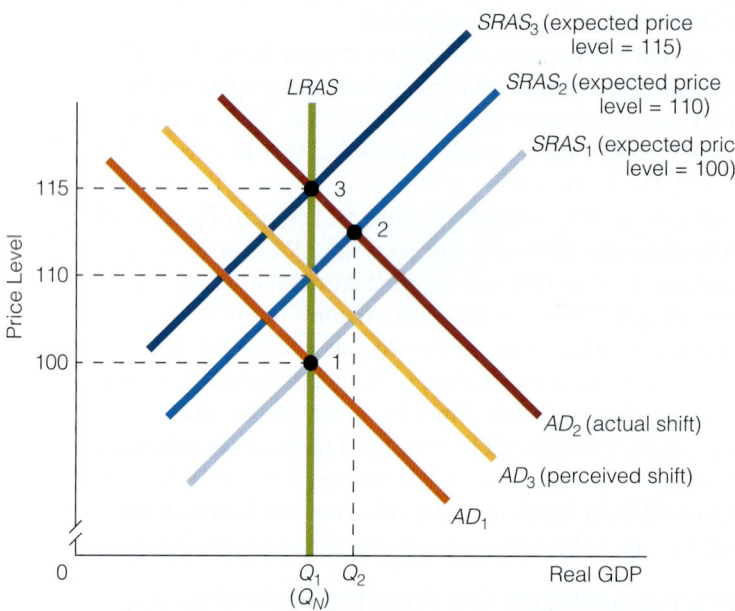

EXHIBIT 10

Policy Unanticipated

An economy starts in long-run equilibrium at point 1. The Fed increases the money supply, and the AD curve shifts rightward from AD_1 to AD_2. The policy action by the Fed is unanticipated; so individuals mistakenly believe that the AD curve in the economy has not shifted. Thus there is no reason for them to believe that the price level will soon change and therefore no reason for them to revise their expected price level. As a result, the SRAS curve does not shift and in the short run, the economy moves to point 2. In time, individuals revise their expected price level upward, and the SRAS curve shifts leftward. The economy moves back into long-run equilibrium at point 3.

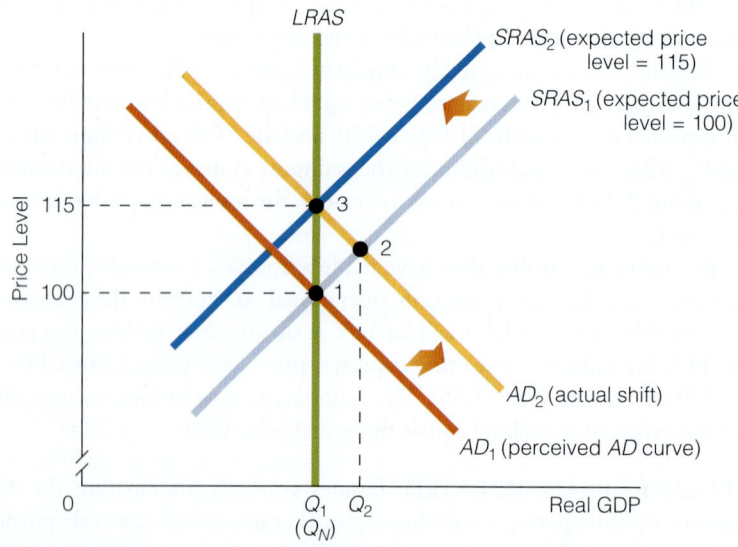

Deficits, Money, Expectations, and Unintended Effects

Suppose Congress continually takes actions that result in large budget deficits, and every time the deficit increases, the Fed says that it will *not monetize the deficit*. To *monetize the deficits* means to turn the Treasury securities (that have been issued to finance the deficit) into money. Here is an example of moneting the deficit. On Monday the Congress increases government purchases; as a result, the deficit rises by $100 billion. To finance the $100 billion addition to the deficit, the Treasury has to borrow the funds. It does so by issuing (selling) Treasury securites (Treasury debt). Commerical banks buy these newly issued Treasury securities and hold them as assets. Later, the Fed steps in and conducts an open market purchase; specifically, it buys the Treasury securities from the banks. As a result of the purchase, reserves in the banking system rise, and banks can create new loans (checkable deposits). Assuming that the banks choose to do so, the money supply rises. The effect: what started off as an increase in the deficit has ended with an increase in the money supply. The deficit has been monetized.

Suppose that every time the Fed promises not to monetize the deficit, it breaks its promise. In other words, the deficit rises, the Fed promises not to monetize the deficit (the promise), but it ends up monetizing the deficit anyway (the action). The promise is different from the action.

It isn't likely that promises that are not consistent with actions will be believed. More likely, individuals will soon learn to translate promises into expected actions. In other words, the Fed says it will not monetize the deficit, and individuals translate the Fed statement into, "We [the Fed] will probably end up monetizing at least *some* of the deficit."

What does all this mean in terms of expectations and unintended effects on the economy? To answer the question, suppose the economy is in long-run equilibrium, producing Natural Real GDP. Suddenly, members of Congress undertake policy actions that increase the size of the deficit. Soon after, the Fed states that it will not monetize the deficit, but—and here is the point—the Fed has made that statement before and then taken different actions. So this time indviduals *expect* the Fed to end up monetizing some of the deficit. As a result, they expect the *AD* curve in the economy to shift rightward and the price level to rise. Based on what they perceive as a soon-to-be rising price level, they revise their expected price level upward, and then the *SRAS* curve shifts leftward.

Now suppose this time the Fed actually holds to its promise and does not monetize the deficit. All of a sudden the Fed's actions match its promise. What happens now? The *SRAS* curve has shifted leftward, but the *AD* curve remains unchanged. The result is a short-run decline in Real GDP below Natural Real GDP. The economy is now in a recessionary gap.

The economy ended up in a recessionary gap because:

- The Fed had previously made promises that it didn't keep.
- Individuals learned to translate Fed promises into likely actions, even if the actions were inconsistent with the promises.
- Individuals based their behavior on what they thought the Fed would do given its past performance.
- This time, the Fed kept to its promise, and as a result the economy moved into a recessionary gap.

The lesson: If the Fed says one thing and continually does another, then unintended effects may follow when it does what it says it will do. The unintended effect in our example was the economy falling into a recessionary gap.

AD curve shifts rightward from AD_1 to AD_2. In this case, individuals do not anticipate this policy action by the Fed; it is unanticipated. What this means is that individuals do not notice that the *AD* curve in the economy has shifted. They mistakenly believe AD_1 (not AD_2) is the operational (i.e., the true) *AD* curve in the economy. Because they do not know the *AD* curve has shifted, they do not expect any change in the price level. They expect it to remain at 100. Individuals therefore have no reason to revise their expected price level, and it stays at 100.

In the short run, the economy moves to point 2. So a rising money supply leads to a rise in Real GDP in the short run. In time, individuals will realize that things have changed and that the Fed's action has shifted the *AD* curve in the economy rightward. In short, they will come to realize that the operational *AD* curve in the economy is AD_2, not AD_1. Individuals will then realize the long-run equilibrium price level consistent with

economics 24/7

Rational Expectations in the College Classroom

If people hold rational expectations, the outcome of a policy will be different if the policy is unanticipated than if it is anticipated. Specifically, unanticipated policy changes can move the economy away from the natural unemployment rate, but correctly anticipated policy changes cannot. Does something similar happen in a college classroom?

Suppose Ana's history class starts at 9:00 a.m., and she "naturally" arrives 1 minute before class starts. In other words, her so-called natural waiting time is 1 minute.

The first day of class, Ana arrives at 8:59, her instructor arrives at 8:59:30, and she starts class promptly at 9:00 a.m.

The second day of class, Ana arrives at 8:59, her instructor arrives at 9:01:30, and she starts class at 9:02 a.m. On this day, Ana has waited 3 minutes, which is more than her natural waiting time of 1 minute.

The timing of the start of class on the third, fourth, and fifth days is the same as on the second. So for the second through fifth days, Ana is operating at more than her natural waiting time.

Rational expectations hold that people will not continue to make the same mistake. In this case, Ana will take her professor's recent arrival time into account and adjust her timing accordingly. On the sixth day

©BANANA STOCK/JUPITER IMAGES

of class, instead of arriving at 8:59, Ana arrives at 9:01. This day, the instructor again arrives at 9:01:30 and begins class at 9:02 a.m., and Ana has moved back to her natural waiting time of 1 minute.

So far, Ana's natural waiting time was met on the first day of class. On the second through fifth days of class, the professor obviously changed her policy as to her arrival time. Ana didn't anticipate this change of policy; so she was fooled into waiting more than her natural waiting time. But Ana did not continue to make the same mistake. She adjusted to her professor's policy change and went back to her 1-minute natural waiting time.

Now let's change the scenario. At the end of the first day of class, the professor announces, "I know I arrived at class at 8:59:30 today, but I won't do this again. From now on, I will arrive at 9:01:30."

In this situation, the professor has announced her policy change. Ana hears the announcement and correctly anticipates the professor's arrival time from now on. With this information, she adjusts her behavior. Instead of arriving at class at 8:59, she arrives at 9:01. Thus, she has correctly anticipated her professor's policy change, and she will remain at her natural waiting time (she will not move from it, even temporarily).

AD_2 is 115. Accordingly, they will revise their expected price level upward to 115, and the $SRAS$ curve will shift leftward from $SRAS_1$ to $SRAS_2$. The economy will move into long-run equilibrium at point 3, and the expected price level will be equal to the actual price level.

Comparing Exhibits 9 and 10

The short-run equilibrium positions in Exhibits 9 and 10 led to the same conclusion: that an increase in the money supply could increase Real GDP in the short run. In Exhibit 10, the policy was unanticipated; in Exhibit 9, we assumed that the policy was incorrectly anticipated—bias downward. So how could two very different assumptions lead to the same short-run outcome? The answer is that Q_2 in Exhibit 10 represents a higher Real GDP level than Q_2 in Exhibit 9. For example, if Q_2 in Exhibit 10 is \$12 trillion, then Q_2 in Exhibit 9 is less—say, \$11 trillion. If we assumed that the policy was unanticipated in Exhibit 9, the short-run equilibrium point would not be at point 2, but at the intersection of the AD_2 and $SRAS_1$ curves. This point is not identified in Exhibit 9, but it is to the southeast of point 2. If we viewed the Real GDP level that corresponds to this point, it would be greater than Q_2 in the exhibit.

ⓣhinking Like AN ECONOMIST

What People Think Can Matter to Outcomes Think of how economics might differ from chemistry. In chemistry, if you add two molecules of hydrogen to one molecule of oxygen, you always get water. What is often frustrating to economists is that sometimes the layperson thinks that economics works like chemistry: X plus Y should always give us Z. Sadly, that is not how economics works. If you add expansionary monetary policy to an economy, you don't always get a rise in short-run Real GDP. Sometimes you get a rise (when policy is unanticipated), sometimes no change (when policy is correctly anticipated), and other times a decline (when policy is incorrectly anticipated, bias upward).

The factor affecting economics that is not at work in chemistry is the human factor. What new classical economists teach us about human beings is that their perceptions of things (vis-à-vis reality) have a large part to play in determining outcomes. ●●●

SELF-TEST

1. Does the policy ineffectiveness proposition (PIP) always hold?

2. When policy is unanticipated, what difference is there between the natural rate theory built on adaptive expectations and the natural rate theory built on rational expectations?

3. Identify the changes in the price level and Real GDP in both the short run and the long run as a result of the Fed's increasing the money supply. Assume that the Fed action is incorrectly anticipated (bias upward), wages and prices are flexible, and individuals hold rational expectations.

NEW KEYNESIANS AND RATIONAL EXPECTATIONS

The new classical theory assumes that wages and prices are flexible. In this theory, an increase in the expected price level results in an immediate and equal rise in wages and prices, and the aggregate supply curve immediately shifts to the long-run equilibrium position.

In response to the new classical assumption of flexible wages and prices, a few economists developed what has come to be known as the *new Keynesian rational expectations theory.* This theory assumes that rational expectations are a reasonable characterization of how expectations are formed, but it drops the new classical assumption of complete wage and price flexibility. According to this theory, long-term labor contracts often prevent wages and prices from fully adjusting to changes in the expected price level. (In other words, prices and wages are somewhat sticky, rigid, or inflexible.)

Consider the possible situation at the end of the first year of a three-year wage contract. Workers realize that the actual price level is higher than they expected when they negotiated the contract, but they are unable to do much about it because their wages are locked in for the next two years. Price rigidity might also come into play because firms often engage in fixed-price contracts with their suppliers. As discussed in Chapter 10, Keynesian economists today assert that, for microeconomic-based reasons, long-term labor contracts and above-market wages are sometimes in the best interest of both employers and employees (the efficiency wage theory).

To see what the theory predicts, look at Exhibit 11. The economy is initially in long-run equilibrium at point 1. The public correctly anticipates an increase in aggregate demand from AD_1 to AD_2, and, as a result, the expected price level changes. Because of some wage and price rigidities, however, the short-run aggregate supply curve does not shift all the way from $SRAS_1$ to $SRAS_2$, and the economy does not move from point 1 to point 2 (as in new classical theory). The short-run aggregate supply curve shifts instead to $SRAS'_2$ because rigidities prevent complete wage and price adjustments. In the short run,

The Short-Run Response to Aggregate Demand–Increasing Policy (in the New Keynesian Theory)

Starting at point 1, an increase in aggregate demand is correctly anticipated. As a result, the short-run aggregate supply curve shifts leftward, but not all the way to $SRAS_2$ (as would be the case in the new classical theory). Instead it shifts only to $SRAS'_2$ because of some wage and price rigidities; the economy moves to point 2′ (in the short run), and Real GDP increases from Q_N to Q_A. If the policy had been unanticipated, Real GDP would have increased from Q_N to Q_{UA}.

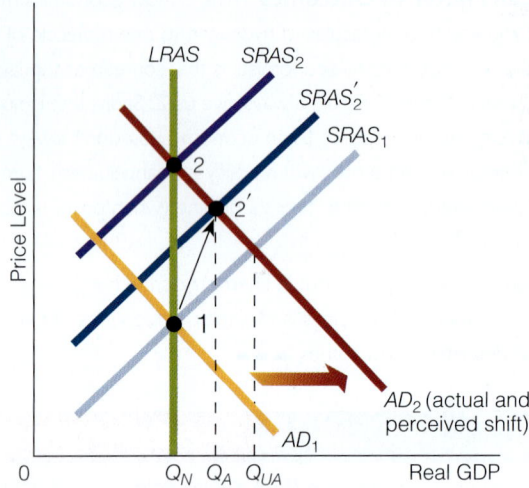

the economy moves from point 1 to point 2′, from Q_N to Q_A. Had the policy been unanticipated, Real GDP would have increased from Q_N to Q_{UA} in the short run.

LOOKING AT THINGS FROM THE SUPPLY SIDE: REAL BUSINESS CYCLE THEORISTS

Throughout this chapter, changes in Real GDP have originated on the demand side of the economy. When discussing the Friedman natural rate theory, the new classical theory, and the new Keynesian theory, we began our analysis by shifting the *AD* curve to the right. Then we explained what happens in the economy as a result. The presentation so far in this chapter seems to assume that all changes in Real GDP originate on the demand side of the economy. In fact, some economists believe this to be true.

Other economists do not. One group of such economists, called *real business cycle theorists*, believe that changes on the supply side of the economy can lead to changes in Real GDP and unemployment. Real business cycle theorists argue that a decrease in Real GDP (which refers to the recessionary or contractionary part of a business cycle) can be brought about by a major supply-side change that reduces the capacity of the economy to produce. Moreover, they argue that what looks like a contraction in Real GDP originating on the demand side of the economy can be, in essence, the effect of what has happened on the supply side.

In Exhibit 12, an adverse supply shock reduces the capacity of the economy to produce. This effect is represented by a shift inward in the economy's production possibilities frontier or a leftward shift in the long-run aggregate supply curve from $LRAS_1$ to $LRAS_2$. This moves the economy from point *A* to point *B*. As shown in the exhibit, a leftward shift in the long-run aggregate supply curve means that Natural Real GDP has fallen.

As a result of the leftward shift in the *LRAS* curve and the decline in Real GDP, firms reduce their demand for labor and scale back employment. Due to the lower demand for labor (which puts downward pressure on money wages) and the higher price level, real

EXHIBIT 12

Real business cycle:
LRAS curve shifts before
AD curve shifts

Real Business Cycle Theory

We start with a supply-side change capable of reducing the capacity of the economy to produce. This is manifested by a leftward shift of the long-run aggregate supply curve from $LRAS_1$ to $LRAS_2$ and a fall in the Natural Real GDP level from Q_{N1} to Q_{N2}. A reduction in the productive capacity of the economy filters to the demand side of the economy and, in our example, reduces consumption, investment, and the money supply. The aggregate demand curve shifts leftward from AD_1 to AD_2.

wages fall. As real wages fall, workers choose to work less, and unemployed persons choose to extend the length of their unemployment. Due to less work and lower real wages, workers have less income. Lower incomes soon lead workers to reduce consumption.

Either because consumption has fallen or because businesses have become pessimistic (prompted by the decline in the productive potential of the economy), or because of both reasons, businesses have less reason to invest. As a result, firms borrow less from banks, the volume of outstanding loans falls, and thus the money supply falls. A decrease in the money supply causes the aggregate demand curve to shift leftward, from AD_1 to AD_2 in Exhibit 12, and the economy moves to point C.

Real business cycle theorists sometimes point out how easily a demand-induced decline in Real GDP can be confused with a supply-induced decline. In our example, both the aggregate supply side and the aggregate demand side of the economy change, but the aggregate supply side changes first. If the change in aggregate supply is overlooked, and only the changes in aggregate demand are observed (or specifically, a change in one of the variables that can change aggregate demand, such as the money supply), then the contraction in Real GDP will appear to be demand induced. In terms of Exhibit 12, the leftward shift in the *LRAS* curve would be overlooked, but the leftward shift in the *AD* curve would be observed, giving the impression that the contraction is demand induced.

If real business cycle theorists are correct, the cause–effect analysis of a contraction in Real GDP would be turned upside down. As just one example, changes in the money supply may be an *effect* of a contraction in Real GDP (which originates on the supply side of the economy), not its *cause*.

SELF-TEST

1. *The Wall Street Journal* reports that the money supply has recently declined. Is the decline consistent with a demand-induced business cycle, with a supply-induced business cycle, or with both? Explain your answer.

2. How are new Keynesians who believe people hold rational expectations different from new classical economists who believe people hold rational expectations?

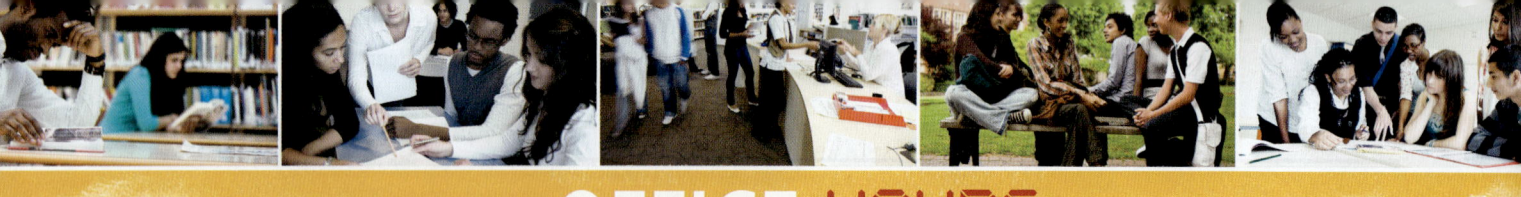

OFFICE HOURS

"Does New Classical Theory Call the Effects of Fiscal and Monetary Policy into Question?"

STUDENT:

When I started this course in macroeconomics, I was hoping to learn the unequivocal answers to some simple questions, such as what effect does fiscal policy have on the economy? What effect does monetary policy have on the economy? I don't think I am learning this. For example, fiscal and monetary policy seems to have different effects on Real GDP in the short run depending on whether policy is unanticipated, incorrectly anticipated, or correctly anticipated. Am I right about this?

INSTRUCTOR:

You're right. A given policy action (such as expansionary monetary policy) can have different effects on Real GDP (in the short run) depending on whether the policy is unanticipated, correctly anticipated, and so on.

STUDENT:

What am I supposed to learn from this?

INSTRUCTOR:

The obvious point, which you've identified, is that policy actions have different effects depending on the degree to which individuals correctly anticipate the policy. The not so obvious point is that it might not be wise to use government policy actions to stabilize the economy.

STUDENT:

How do you come to that point? What are the details?

INSTRUCTOR:

Let's say that the economy is currently in a recessionary gap and Real GDP is $11 trillion. Policy makers want to raise the GDP level to Natural Real GDP at, say, $11.2 trillion. To achieve this goal, either expansionary fiscal or monetary policy is implemented. Are we guaranteed to raise Real GDP from $11 trillion to $11.2 trillion?

STUDENT:

No.

CHAPTER SUMMARY

THE PHILLIPS CURVE

- A. W. Phillips plotted a curve to a set of data points that exhibited an inverse relationship between wage inflation and unemployment. This curve came to be known as the Phillips curve. From the Phillips curve relationship, economists concluded that neither the combination of low inflation and low unemployment nor the combination of high inflation and high unemployment was likely.

- Economists Paul Samuelson and Robert Solow fit a Phillips curve to the U.S. economy. Instead of measuring wage inflation against unemployment rates (as Phillips did), they measured price inflation against unemployment rates. They found an inverse relationship between inflation and unemployment rates.

- Based on the findings of Phillips and Samuelson and Solow, economists concluded the following: (1) Stagflation, or high inflation and high unemployment, is extremely unlikely. (2)

The Phillips curve presents policy makers with a menu of different combinations of inflation and unemployment rates.

FRIEDMAN NATURAL RATE THEORY

- Milton Friedman pointed out that there are two types of Phillips curves: a short-run and a long-run Phillips curve. The short-run Phillips curve exhibits the inflation–unemployment trade-off; the long-run Phillips curve does not. Consideration of both short- and long-run Phillips curves opened macroeconomics to expectations theory.

- The Friedman natural rate theory holds that, in the short run, a decrease (increase) in inflation is linked to an increase (decrease) in unemployment, but in the long run, the economy returns to its natural rate of unemployment. In other words, there is a trade-off between inflation and unemployment in the short run, but not in the long run.

Why is that?

Well, according to new classical economists, it's because individuals may incorrectly anticipate the policy in such as way as to reduce Real GDP instead of raising it.

That's right. Suppose, for example, the Fed plans to raise the money supply by $10 billion, but the public mistakenly believes the Fed will raise the money supply by, say, $18 billion. In the short run, the *AD* curve will shift to the right and the *SRAS* curve will to shift to the left, but the *SRAS* curve will be shifting left *by more than* the *AD* curve will be shifting to the right. (This happened in Exhibit 8.) And the result will be a decline, not an increase, in Real GDP—at least in the short run.

So the monetary policy action can end up doing the very opposite of what it was intended to do. It was intended to raise Real GDP, but it lowered it instead.

That's correct. What the new classical economists are really pointing out is that we can't always be sure of a discretionary policy action's effect on Real GDP. In turn, this should make economists less sure, or

a little more humble, when it comes to advocating certain economic policy actions for government to implement.

POINTS TO REMEMBER

1. According to new classical economists, economic policy actions may not always have the intended effect on Real GDP in the short run.
2. Economic policy actions may accomplish the opposite of what they were intended to accomplish.

- The Friedman natural rate theory was expressed in terms of adaptive expectations. Individuals formed their inflation expectations by considering past inflation rates. Later, some economists expressed the theory in terms of rational expectations. Rational expectations theory holds that individuals form their expected inflation rate by considering present and past inflation rates, as well as all other available and relevant information—in particular, the effects of present and future policy actions.

NEW CLASSICAL THEORY

- Implicit in the new classical theory are two assumptions: (1) Individuals form their expectations rationally. (2) Wages and prices are completely flexible.
- In the new classical theory, policy has different effects (1) when it is unanticipated, (2) when it is incorrectly anticipated—bias upward, (3) when it is incorrectly anticipated—bias downward, and (4) when it is correctly anticipated. To illustrate, consider two cases: (A) when policy is incorrectly anticipated—bias upward and (B) when policy is correctly anticipated. Assume

that in both cases a demand-side policy increases aggregate demand in the economy. In case A, the *AD* curve will shift rightward by less than the *SRAS* initially shifts leftward, bringing about a decline in Real GDP in the short run. In case B, the *AD* curve will shift rightward to the same degree, and at the same time, but in the opposite direction of the *SRAS* curve. In this case, Real GDP does not change.

NEW KEYNESIAN THEORY

- Implicit in the New Keynesian theory are two assumptions: (1) Individuals form their expectations rationally. (2) Wages and prices are not completely flexible in the short run.
- If policy is correctly anticipated, the economic effects predicted by the new classical theory and the new Keynesian theory are not the same in the short run. Because the new Keynesian theory assumes that wages and prices are not completely flexible in the short run, given an anticipated change in aggregate demand, the short-run aggregate supply curve cannot immediately shift to its long-run equilibrium position. The new Keynesian theory

predicts a short-run trade-off between inflation and unemployment (in the Phillips curve framework).

REAL BUSINESS CYCLE THEORY

- Real business cycle contractions (in Real GDP) originate on the supply side of the economy. A contraction in Real GDP might follow this pattern: (1) An adverse supply shock reduces the economy's ability to produce. (2) The *LRAS* curve shifts leftward. (3) As a result, Real GDP declines and the price level rises. (4) The number of persons employed falls, as do real wages, owing to a decrease in the demand for labor (which lowers money wages) and a higher price level. (5) Incomes decline. (6) Consumption and investment decline. (7) The volume of outstanding loans declines. (8) The money supply falls. (9) The *AD* curve shifts leftward.

KEY TERMS AND CONCEPTS

Phillips Curve
Stagflation

Friedman Natural Rate
Theory

Adaptive Expectations
Rational Expectations

Policy Ineffectiveness
Proposition (PIP)

QUESTIONS AND PROBLEMS

1. New Keynesian theory holds that wages are not completely flexible because of such things as long-term labor contracts. New classical economists often respond that experience teaches labor leaders to develop and bargain for contracts that allow for wage adjustments. Do you think the new classical economists have a good point? Why or why not?

2. "The policy ineffectiveness proposition (connected with new classical theory) does not eliminate policy makers' ability to reduce unemployment through aggregate demand–increasing policies because they can always increase aggregate demand by more than the public expects." What might be the weak point in this argument?

3. Assume a current short-run trade-off between inflation and unemployment, as well as a change in technology that permits the wider dispersion of economic policy news. How would the change affect the trade-off? Explain your answer.

4. What is a major difference between adaptive and rational expectations? Give an example of each.

5. Suppose a permanent downward-sloping Phillips curve existed and offered a menu of choices of different combinations of inflation and unemployment rates to policy makers. How do you think society would go about deciding which point on the Phillips curve it wanted to occupy?

6. According to Friedman, how do we know when the economy is in long-run equilibrium?

7. Why is the new classical theory associated with the word "classical"? Why has it been said that classical theory failed where new classical theory succeeds, because the former could not explain the business cycle (the ups and downs of the economy), but the latter can?

8. What does it mean to say that the Phillips curve presents policy makers with a menu of choices?

9. Explain both the short- and long-run movements of the Friedman natural rate theory, assuming expectations are formed adaptively.

10. The expected inflation rate is 5 percent, and the actual inflation rate is 7 percent. According to Friedman, is the economy in long-run equilibrium? Explain your answer.

11. Explain both the short- and long-run movements of the new classical theory, assuming expectations are formed rationally and policy is unanticipated.

12. In the real business cycle theory, why can't the change in the money supply prompted by a series of events catalyzed by an adverse supply shock be considered the cause of the business cycle?

13. Suppose the government undertakes an expansionary fiscal policy measure that raises aggregate demand, but individuals incorrectly anticipate the policy measure (bias upward). What will the short- and long-run changes be in the price level and Real GDP?

14. "Even if some people do not form their expectations rationally, the new classical theory is not necessarily of no value." Discuss this statement.

15. What evidence can you point to that suggests individuals form their expectations adaptively? What evidence can you point to that suggests individuals form their expectations rationally?

WORKING WITH NUMBERS AND GRAPHS

1. Illustrate graphically what would happen in the short run and in the long run if individuals hold rational expectations, prices and wages are flexible, and individuals underestimate the decrease in aggregate demand.

2. In each of the following figures, the starting point is 1. Which part illustrates each of the following?

   a. Friedman natural rate theory (short run)

WORKING WITH NUMBERS AND GRAPHS

b. New classical theory (unanticipated policy, short run)

c. Real business cycle theory

d. New classical theory (incorrectly anticipated policy, over-estimating increase in aggregate demand, short run)

e. Policy ineffectiveness proposition (PIP)

(a)

(b)

(c)

(d)

3. Illustrate graphically what would happen in the short run and in the long run if individuals hold adaptive expectations, if prices and wages are flexible, and if aggregate demand decreases.

CHAPTER 17

© IMAGE COPYRIGHT ANDRESR, 2009. USED UNDER LICENSE FROM SHUTTERSTOCK.COM

ECONOMIC GROWTH: RESOURCES, TECHNOLOGY, IDEAS, AND INSTITUTIONS

Introduction Rarely do we think of how we came to have the standard of living we enjoy. Most of us live in comfortable houses, drive nice cars, work on fast computers, enjoy exciting sporting events, attend lively jazz concerts, visit relaxing vacation spots, go to the movies and restaurants, and have many other things to be grateful for. To a large degree, our lives are so enriched because we were born in a country that has experienced a relatively high rate of economic growth. How might your life be different if the U.S. economy had had a lower growth rate over, say, the last century? To answer this question, you need to know the causes of economic growth.

A FEW BASICS ABOUT ECONOMIC GROWTH

Absolute Real Economic Growth
An increase in Real GDP from one period to the next.

The term "economic growth" refers either to absolute real economic growth or to per-capita real economic growth. Absolute real economic growth is an increase in Real GDP from one period to the next. Exhibit 1 shows absolute real economic growth (or the percentage change in Real GDP) for the United States for the period 1998–2009.

Per-Capita Real Economic Growth
An increase from one period to the next in per-capita Real GDP, which is Real GDP divided by population.

Per-capita real economic growth is an increase from one period to the next in per-capita Real GDP, which is Real GDP divided by population.

$$\text{Per-capita Real GDP} = \frac{\text{Real GDP}}{\text{Population}}$$

Do Economic Growth Rates Matter?

Suppose the (absolute) real economic growth rate is 4 percent in one country and 3 percent in another. The difference in growth rates may not seem very significant. But if the growth rates are sustained over a long period of time, the people who live in each country will see a real difference in their standard of living. For example, if a country's economic growth rate

EXHIBIT 1

Absolute Real Economic Growth Rates for the United States, 1998–2009

This exhibit shows the absolute real economic growth rates (or percentage change in Real GDP) in the United States for the period 1998–2006.

Source: *Economic Report of the President*, 2010.

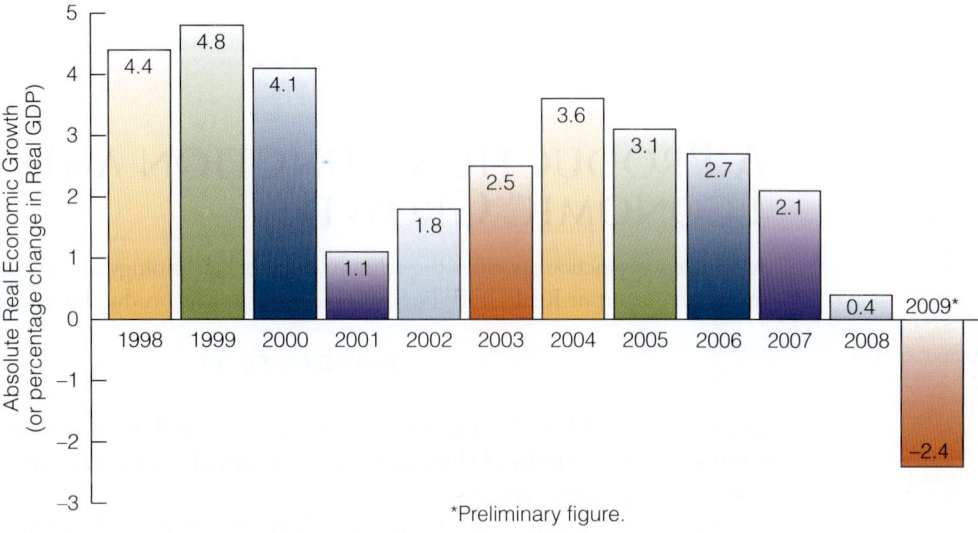

*Preliminary figure.

is 5 percent each year, its Real GDP will double in 14 years. If a country has a 2 percent annual growth rate, its Real GDP will double in 35 years. In other words, a country with a 5 percent growth rate can double its Real GDP in 21 fewer years than a country with a 2 percent growth rate. (To calculate the time required for any variable to double, simply divide its percentage growth rate into 70. This is called the *rule of 70*.)

finding ECONOMICS

In a Night Out It is 6 p.m. and Xavier is driving his new $45,000 car to a restaurant. He and a friend have dinner at the restaurant. The bill comes to $86.75. After dinner, Xavier and his friend attend a play. Later that night, they return to Xavier's 3,500-square-foot house. They sit out by the swimming pool and talk about everything and nothing. Where is the economics? Is economic growth relevant to the evening?

Economic growth is the silent actor of the evening. Because Xavier and his friend live in a country that has experienced economic growth over the years, their night can be as comfortable and satisfying for them as it is.

Or look at it this way. People like Xavier and his friend are all over the world. Not all of them *can* have the same evening. Individuals living in countries that experienced much less economic growth over the years are not as likely to experience the same kind of evening as did Xavier and his friend.

Here is a startling fact: About 24,000 people die every day from hunger or hunger-related causes. Three-fourths of the deaths are children under the age of 5. The vast majority of people who die of hunger live in countries of the world that have experienced relatively little economic growth. ▲▲▲

⊕hinking Like AN ECONOMIST

Economic Growth Matters Economic growth has been a major topic of discussion for economists for over two centuries. Adam Smith, the founder of modern economics, wrote a book on the subject that was published in 1776: *An Inquiry into the Nature and Causes of the Wealth of Nations*. In the book, Smith set out to answer the question of why some countries are rich and others are poor. Today, we'd ask, "Why do some countries have a high per-capita Real GDP and others have a low per-capita Real GDP? For economists, getting the right answer to this question is of major importance to the lives of millions—if not billions—of people. ▲▲▲

A PRODUCTION FUNCTION AND ECONOMIC GROWTH

Production Function

A function that specifies the relation between technology and the quantity of factor inputs to output or Real GDP.

A production function specifies the relation between technology and the quantity of factor inputs to output or Real GDP. For example, look at this production function:

$$\text{Real GDP} = T(L, K)$$

The L stands for labor; the K stands for capital; the T stands for the technology coefficient. Suppose we have 4 units of labor and 2 units of capital. In all, we have 6 units of our two resources, labor and capital.

In an earlier chapter, an advance in technology was defined as being able to produce more output (more Real GDP) with a given level of resources, such as labor and capital. The T, or technology coefficient, in our production function captures this idea. Suppose we set our T equal to 0.40. Given that L equals 4 and K equals 2, our production function now reads:

$$\text{Real GDP} = 0.4\,(4 + 2)$$
$$\text{Real GDP} = 0.4\,(6)$$
$$\text{Real GDP} = 2.4 \text{ units of output}$$

In other words, we have taken so much labor and capital, added it together at a certain level of technology—evidenced in a technology coefficient of 0.4—and ended up with 2.4 units of output or Real GDP.

Obviously, given our production function, which focuses on the three factors of T, L, and K, an increase in any one of these factors will lead to a rise in Real GDP. For example, if we increase labor from 4 to 8 units, Real GDP will rise to 4 units of output. Alternatively, if we raise T from 0.4 to 0.5, holding labor at 4 units and capital at 2 units, Real GDP will rise from 2.4 units to 3.0 units.

The Graphical Representation of the Production Function

Exhibit 2(a) represents the production function graphically. Real GDP (Q) is on the vertical axis, and labor (L) is on the horizontal axis. The curve in the two-dimensional space is the graphical representation of the production function. At a given level of labor, L_1, we get Q_1 amount of Real GDP. A change in labor, say from L_1 to L_2, will give us more Real GDP, as shown in Exhibit 2(b).

Now a change in either K or T will shift the production function up or down. For example, Exhibit 2(c) shows what happens to the production function if K rises. Initially $K = 1$, and this, combined with L_1 and a given technology coefficient, produces Q_1 Real GDP.

If K rises to 2, and this higher K is combined with the same amount of labor and the same technology coefficient, Real GDP rises to Q_2.

Exhibit 2(d) shows what happens if the technology coefficient rises. Initially, $T = 0.4$. Combining this with a given amount of labor and capital produces a Real GDP level of Q_1. If T rises to 0.5 and nothing else changes, then Real GDP rises to Q_2.

EXHIBIT 2

The Production Function

(a) The production function is based on labor (L), capital (K), and technology (technology coefficient, T). (b) Changes in L lead to changes in Real GDP (Q). (c) A rise in capital leads to a shift upward in the production function and to more Real GDP (for a given level of L and a given technology coefficient). (d) A rise in the technology coefficient leads to a shift upward in the production function and to more Real GDP (for a given level of L and K).

(a)

(b)

(c)

(d)

So our production function specifies that output or Real GDP depends on labor, capital, and the technology coefficient (which captures the essence of advances in technology). Specifically, a rise in labor will move us from one point to another on the same production function, ending with more Real GDP. A rise in capital or a rise in the technology coefficient will lead to a shift upward in the production function, ending with more Real GDP.

From the Production Function to the *LRAS* Curve

The changes in and the movements along the production function can be linked to shifts in the *LRAS* curve. In Exhibit 3(a), we start with L_1, which gives us Real GDP of Q_1. We then take Q_1 from panel (a) and move it to panel (b). This is the Real GDP that the economy is producing when it is at the natural unemployment rate; this is Natural Real GDP. This level of Real GDP is consistent with $LRAS_1$ in the exhibit.

Suppose, in panel (a), we raise labor to L_2. This change in labor moves us along our production function, from point 1 to point 2 at a higher Real GDP level, Q_2. In panel (b), this new, higher Real GDP is consistent with $LRAS_2$.

Therefore, a rise in labor moves us along the given production function and shifts the *LRAS* curve to the right. If you superimpose an *AD* curve on panel (b), you see that a shift rightward in the *LRAS* curve brings about a lower price level and a higher Real GDP level. With a heightened Real GDP level, we have economic growth.

In panel (c), again we start with L_1, which gives us Q_1 Real GDP. If the technology coefficient rises from 0.4 to 0.5, the production function shifts upward. At a given level of labor and capital, we have more Real GDP, Q_2. Carrying over the changes in Real GDP from panel (c) to panel (d), we see that a rise in the technology coefficient shifts the *LRAS* curve to the right. Again, we have economic growth.

Emphasis on Labor

Exhibit 3 showed that a rise in labor would lead to a rightward shift in the *LRAS* curve. In other words, a rise in labor would result in economic growth. Then what might lead to a rise in labor? In other words, if *X* and *Y* lead to a rise in labor, then *X* and *Y* are factors that promote economic growth.

One such factor that is often mentioned is taxes. Specifically, some economists propose promoting economic growth by cutting taxes on such activities as working. The idea is that, if the marginal income tax rate is cut, workers will work more, and, as they work more, output will rise. Think of this in terms of the labor market. Exhibit 4(a) shows a labor market that is in equilibrium at point 1. The equilibrium quantity of labor in this market is L_1. If L_1 is put into our production function, as shown in panel (b), it gives us Q_1 amount of Real GDP. Finally, if Q_1 from panel (b) is placed in panel (c), Q_1 is consistent with the $LRAS_1$ curve.

Now suppose we lower taxes on income. As a result, the labor supply curve in panel (a) shifts rightward. In other words, as the overall return on working increases due to a drop in income taxes, more people decide to go to work, and many of those already working decide to work more. The new equilibrium quantity of labor, L_2, is shown in panel (a). If we carry over the greater quantity of labor to panel (b), showing our production function, more labor produces the higher level of Real GDP, Q_2. Then, in panel (c), the new higher level of Real GDP corresponds to a new *LRAS* curve, $LRAS_2$.

Therefore, lower income taxes shift the labor supply to the right, raising the equilibrium quantity of labor, which produces more Real GDP or shifts the *LRAS* curve to the right. Again, we have witnessed economic growth.

EXHIBIT 3

The Production Function and the LRAS Curve

(a) More labor (L) leads to more Real GDP (shown in terms of the production function). (b) More L shifts the LRAS curve to the right.

(c) A higher technology coefficient shifts the production function up and brings about more Real GDP, Q. (d) A heightened technology coefficient leads to a rightward shift in the LRAS curve. (Although not shown in this exhibit, a rise

in K would do the same thing as a rise in the technology coefficient in terms of shifting up the production function and shifting the LRAS curve to the right.)

(a)

(b)

(c)

(d)

Growth and Morality[1]

There is more to life, liberty, and the pursuit of happiness than a faster car and an iPod nano.

—The Economist (November 10, 2005)

Almost everyone agrees that economic growth, especially sustained economic growth, can produce more, better, and newer goods and services. But what else can it do, if anything? According to economist Benjamin Friedman, it can make people happier, more tolerant, more willing to settle disputes in a peaceful manner, and more inclined to favor an open and democratic society. It can also make people more willing to work toward improving the environment and reducing poverty.

© IMAGE COPYRIGHT PETRENKO ANDRIY, 2009. USED UNDER LICENSE FROM SHUTTERSTOCK.COM

The thought that economic growth can do more than give us more goods and services goes back to Adam Smith. According to Smith, when a nation is acquiring more—when it is getting richer—most of the people are happy and comfortable. When a nation is just maintaining its wealth or declining, its people are not as happy or as comfortable.

What Friedman essentially argues is that economists have looked at the benefits of economic growth too narrowly. They have stressed the rising material standard of living that comes with economic growth. But this perspective, says Friedman, ignores the political, social, and moral aspects of economic growth. In his book, *The Moral Consequences of Economic Growth*, he says that "a rising standard of living lies not just in the concrete improvements it brings to how individuals live but in how it shapes the social, political, and ultimately the moral character of a people."

If Friedman is correct that economic growth affects people not only economically but politically, socially, and morally too, then we need to ask why. Friedman says it has such influence because people's sense of how well off they are is made relative to their (own) past. People feel happiest (and the most tolerant of others) when they believe their standard of living is rising—in other words, if they are better off this year than last year. When they have this sense, people care less about where they stand relative to others. But if they are not witnessing an increase in their standard of living relative to their past, they begin to care more about how they are doing relative to others. This comparison with others usually results in frustration and possibly social friction.

Friedman does not argue that there are absolutely no costs to growth. Instead, he simply makes the point that the benefits emanating from growth may be greater and more far-reaching than we initially thought.

1. This feature is based on "Why the Rich Must Get Richer," *The Economist*, November 10, 2005.

Emphasis on Capital

So more labor can lead to economic growth, but so can more capital. How much capital is available depends on such things as the tax treatment of capital returns and interest rates. Consider two settings. In the first, taxes on the returns to capital are high; in the second, taxes on the returns to capital are low. Which setting offers a stronger incentive to employ capital in the production process? When taxes on the returns to capital are low, we predict the following: as taxes decline on the returns from capital, more capital is utilized in the production process, thus shifting upward the production function and thereby shifting the *LRAS* curve to the right.

The interest rate can also affect the amount of capital employed, because firms often borrow the funds to buy the capital goods used in production. In short, the process can

EXHIBIT 4

The Labor Market, the Production Function, and the *LRAS* Curve

(a) Lower taxes on income shifts the labor supply curve rightward from S_{LF1} to S_{LF2}. As a result of the lower taxes and the shift rightward in the labor supply curve, the equilibrium amount of

labor rises from L_1 to L_2. (b) More labor leads to more Real GDP in terms of the production function. (c) More Real GDP corresponds to a rightward shift in the *LRAS* curve.

(a)

(b)

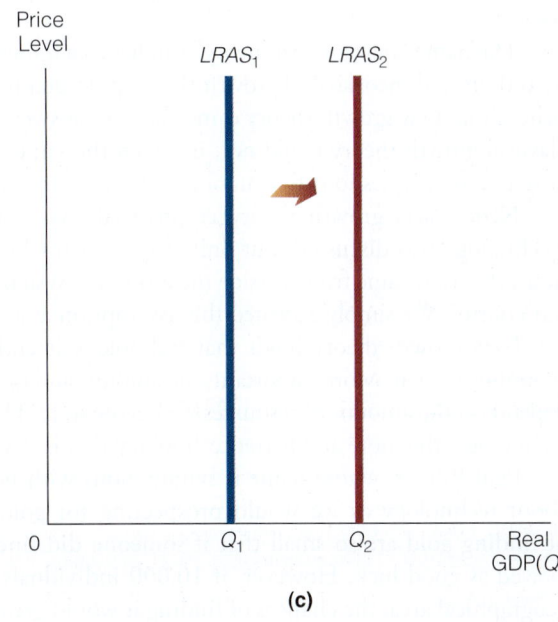

(c)

work like this: A decline in interest rates prompts firms to borrow more. The firms use the borrowed funds to purchase capital goods. As they purchase and utilize more capital (in the production process), the production function shifts upward and the *LRAS* curve shifts rightward.

Emphasis on Other Resources: Natural Resources and Human Capital

Our production function so far has included only two resources—labor and capital—and technology. When building economic growth models, economists often specify a production function of this sort.

However, for reasons of completeness, a more fully specified production function would also include natural resources (*NR*) and human capital (*H*). For example, producing goods—such as wood to produce chairs, desks, and paper—often takes natural resources. In fact, economists often speak in terms of four resources (Chapter 1): land, labor, capital, and entrepreneurship. The resource of land is simply another name for natural resources.

Producing many goods also takes human capital, which is different from the kind of capital we represented as *K*. The capital referred to earlier is *physical capital*—such things as machines, computers, and factories. Human capital is what you acquire by attending college and the skills and knowledge you pick up through education, training, and experience. You enroll in a number of courses, learn certain material, and acquire certain thinking skills; these are all components of human capital.

Human Capital
The knowledge and skills a person acquires through education, training, and experience.

Adding human capital and natural resources to our production function leads us to specify that function this way:

$$\text{Real GDP} = T(L, K, NR, H)$$

Emphasis on the Technology Coefficient and Ideas

Beginning in the 1980s, economists began discussing economic growth differently than they did in previous decades. They placed more attention on technology, ideas, institutions, and education. The discussion often took place under the rubric of *new growth theory*.

The name "new growth theory" implies that a theory of economic growth came before it, and, indeed, neoclassical growth theory preceded new growth theory. Some economists believe that new growth theory came about to answer some of the questions that new neoclassical growth theory could not, in much the same way that a new medical theory may arise to answer questions that an old medical theory cannot answer.

Neoclassical growth theory emphasized two resources: labor and physical capital. Technology was discussed, but only very tangentially. Technology was said to be exogenous; that is, it came from outside the economic system. It fell out of the sky; it was outside our control. We simply accepted this assumption as a given.

New growth theory holds that technology is endogenous; it is a central part of the economic system. More important, the amount and quality of technology that is developed depend on the amount of resources we devote to it: The more resources that go to develop technology, the more and better technology that is developed.

Paul Romer, whose name is synonymous with new growth theory, asks us to think about technology as we would prospecting for gold. For one individual, the chances of finding gold are so small that if someone did find gold, the strike would simply be viewed as good luck. However, if 10,000 individuals are looking for gold across a wide geographical area, the chances of finding it would greatly improve. As with gold prospecting, so it is with technological advances. If one person is trying to advance technology, his or her chances of success are much smaller than if hundreds or thousands of persons are trying.

New growth theory also emphasizes the process of discovering and formulating ideas as they relate to technological advances. The emphasis is on ideas rather than on objects, which are material, tangible things, such as natural resources and capital goods. Some countries are poor because they lack objects (natural resources and capital goods). Yet some countries have had very few objects and have been able to grow economically. For example, in the 1950s, Japan had few natural resources and capital goods, but still it grew economically. Some economists believe that Japan grew because it had access to ideas or knowledge.

Discovery and Ideas

If discovering ideas is important to technological advances and therefore to economic growth, then we need to figure out ways to promote the discovery process. One way is for business firms not to get locked into doing things one way and one way only. They must let their employees—from the inventor in the lab to the worker on the assembly line—try new ways of getting the job done. Some might carry this further: businesses need to create an environment that is receptive to new ideas. They need to encourage their employees to try new ways of doing things.

Employee flexibility, which is a part of the discovery process, is becoming a larger part of the U.S. economy. To some degree, this process is seen in the amount of time and effort firms devote to discovery in contrast to the amount of time they devote to actually manufacturing goods. Consider the computer software business. Millions of dollars and hundreds of thousands of work hours are devoted to coming up with new and useful software, whereas only a tiny fraction of the work effort and hours go into making, copying, and shipping the disks or CDs that contain the software.

Expanding Our Horizons

Romer has said that "economic growth occurs whenever people take resources and rearrange them in ways that are more valuable." Let's focus on the word "rearrange." We can think of rearranging as in rearranging the pieces of a puzzle, as in changing the ingredients in a recipe, or as in rearranging the way workers go about their daily work. When we rearrange anything, we do that "thing" differently. Sometimes, differently is better, and sometimes it is worse.

Think of how you study for a test. Perhaps you read the book first, go back and underline, study the book, and then finally study your lecture notes. Would it be better to study differently? You won't know until you try.

As with studying for a test, so it is with producing a car, computer software, or a shopping mall. We do not find better ways of doing things unless we experiment. And with repeated experiments, we often discover new and better ideas, ideas that ultimately lead to economic growth. The research and development of new medicines makes for a good example. Sometimes, what makes a mildly effective medicine into a very effective one is a change in one or two molecules of a certain chemical. A small change—a change perhaps no one would ever think would matter—can make a large difference.

A policy prescription follows from this mind-set: we should think of ways to make the process of discovering ideas, experimenting with different ways of doing things, and developing new technology more likely. Without this kind of effort, we are likely to diminish our growth potential. If we believe ideas are important to economic growth, then we need to have ideas about how to generate more ideas. Paul Romer calls these *meta-ideas*: ideas about how to support the production and transmission of other ideas.

Some ways have been proposed. Perhaps we need to invest more funds in education or research and development. Or perhaps we need to find ways to better protect people's ideas (few people will invest the time, money, and effort to discover better ideas if the ideas can easily be stolen).

In the twenty-first century, countries with the most natural resources and capital goods aren't likely to be the ones that grow the fastest. If new growth theory is correct, the successful ones will be those that have discovered how to encourage and develop the most and best ideas.

Institutions Matter

Crops don't grow equally well in all soils. Some soils are more conducive to the growing than others. Similarly, many economists argue that some environments are more conducive to economic growth than others.

One of the ways economists differentiate one environment from another is in terms of its institutions. But what are institutions in this context? Douglass North, a well respected economist in this area of research, defines an institution as "the rules of the game in a society or, more formally, the humanly devised constraints that shape human interaction." Specifically, institutions consist of a country's rules and regulations, laws, customs, and business practices. Consider two countries, A and B, each with different institutions. In country A, the rule of law operates (no one is above the law), contracts are enforced, private property rights are protected, and free international trade is permitted. In country B, the rule of law does not hold, contracts are not always enforced, private property is not protected (and is often seized), and high tariffs and quotas are placed on imported goods. In North's terminology, the "rules of the game" are different in these two countries.

Here are a few of the institutions that most economists agree are conducive to economic growth:

- Property rights structure
- The legal system
- Growth-promoting policies versus transfer-promoting policies
- Other institutions

PROPERTY RIGHTS STRUCTURE Think of two property rights structures, X and Y. Under X, a person is allowed to own property (a piece of land, a business, a store, an invention, etc.); that is, private property is permitted. Under Y, a person is not allowed to own property; private property is not permitted. The incentive to produce goods and services is hardly the same in each of the two property rights structures. Undoubtedly, the incentive to produce is greater under property rights structure X than Y. Why produce anything under Y if what you produce does not belong to you? In short, different property rights structures come with different incentives to produce. All other things equal, the property rights structures that permit individuals to own property will be more conducive to production and economic growth than those that do not.

Now consider two other property rights structures, A and B. Under both, individuals are allowed to own property. But in A, a person's private property rights are not as well protected as in B. For example, in A, the government sometimes confiscates a person's private property; in B, this never happens. Again, the incentive to produce is not the same under A and B. The more secure the private property rights are, the greater the incentive is to produce. Why produce if what you produce might be taken away from you?

Therefore, not only do private property rights matter to production and economic growth; so does the security of those private property rights.

THE LEGAL SYSTEM In country A, the legal system is dependable, honest, and dedicated to enforcing legitimate contracts and to protecting private property. In country B, the legal system is the polar opposite. In which country, A or B, are individuals more likely to have a greater incentive to start businesses, lend and borrow funds, invest, produce goods, and innovate—all important to the process of economic growth? Most economists would say in country A, where the legal system is dependable, honest, and sound. That conclusion becomes quickly obvious once you think of what is involved with starting a business, lending and borrowing, investing, innovating, and producing: dealing with other people. If you start a business, you will often need to deal with other people to finance the business,

---

Institution
The rules of the game in a society or, more formally, the humanly devised constraints that shape human interaction; the rules and regulations, laws, customs, and business practices of a country.

Economic Freedom and Growth Rates

Does economic freedom matter to a country's economic growth rate? There is some evidence that it does. Consider the time in which there were two Germanys: an East Germany and a West Germany. The two Germanys were much the same in terms of culture, people, climate, language, and so on, except West Germans enjoyed more economic freedom than East Germans. Did this major difference between the two Germanys matter to economic growth? Most economists answer yes. Between 1950 and 1991, the average annual growth rate in East Germany was 1.3 percent; in West Germany it was 4.4 percent.

© BLICKWINKEL / ALAMY

The same sort of difference holds between North Korea and South Korea. South Korea permits much more economic freedom than North Korea. Does this difference affect economic growth rates? During the second half of the twentieth century, the average annual growth rate in South Korea was more than three times higher than in North Korea.

The evidence from the two Koreas and two Germanys tells us that economic freedom does matter to economic growth, especially when other factors (that matter to growth) are much the same between the countries.

But when the other factors are not the same, problems arise. Suppose country A has less economic freedom than country B. Will country A grow less than country B during the next 5 or 10 years? Not necessarily. The economic growth rate in a country could depend on the economic base from which the growth emanates. Suppose that country A has a Real GDP of $10 billion, that country B has a Real GDP of $100 billion, and that Real GDP grows by $2 billion in both countries. The economic growth rate in country A (the country with less economic freedom) is 20 percent, but the economic growth rate in country B (the country with more economic freedom) is only 2 percent. Does it follow that economic freedom is a hindrance to economic growth? Not at all. It may simply look that way because something different between the two countries—namely, the economic base from which growth emanates—isn't being considered.

to hire workers, to buy from suppliers, and so on. In your dealings with other people, you need to be assured that your agreements (or contracts) with them are upheld and enforced and that others cannot steal from you and get away with it. This is why the legal system is important to economic growth. A legal system that is dependable, honest, and dedicated to enforcing legitimate contracts, and protecting private property reduces the transaction costs of dealing with others, thus providing individuals with a greater incentive to engage in activities conducive to economic growth.

GROWTH-PROMOTING POLICIES VERSUS TRANSFER-PROMOTING POLICIES

Consider two types of economic policies: growth-promoting policies and transfer-promoting policies. A growth-promoting policy increases Real GDP; it enlarges the size of the economic pie. A transfer-promoting policy leaves the size of the economic pie unchanged, but it increases the size of the slice that one group gets relative to another.

Religious Beliefs and Economic Growth

For given religious beliefs, increases in church attendance tend to reduce economic growth. In contrast, for given church attendance, increases in some religious beliefs—notably heaven, hell, and an afterlife—tend to increase economic growth.

—Robert Barro and Rachel McCleary[2]

Economists have been studying economic growth for more than 200 years. Some of the questions they have asked and tried to answer are:

- Why are some nations rich and others poor?
- What causes economic growth?
- Why do some nations grow faster than others?

Of the causes of economic growth discussed in this chapter, we do not include cultural determinants. Yet some economic researchers argue that explanations for economic growth should be broadened to include cultural determinants. Culture may influence personal traits, they argue, which may in turn affect economic growth. For example, personal traits such as honesty, thriftiness, the willingness to work hard, and openness to strangers may be related to economic growth.

Two Harvard economists, Robert Barro and Rachel McCleary, have analyzed one such cultural determinant: the role of religion in economic growth. Their work was based partly on the World Values Survey, which looked at a representative sample of people in 66 countries on all six inhabited continents between 1981 and 1997. The survey asked at least 1,000 people in each country about their basic values and beliefs: What is their religious affiliation? How often do they attend a religious service? Were they raised religiously or not?

Barro and McCleary found that economic growth corresponds negatively with church attendance (nations with a high rate of attendance at religious services grow more slowly than those with lower rates of attendance) but positively with religious beliefs in heaven, hell, and an afterlife. Specifically, in countries where the belief in heaven, hell, and an afterlife is strong, the growth of gross domestic product runs about 0.5 percent higher than average. (This result takes into account other factors that influence growth rates, such as education.) Perhaps more telling, the belief in hell matters more to economic growth than the belief in heaven. Barro and McCleary suggest that religious beliefs stimulate growth because they help to sustain aspects of individual behavior that enhance productivity.

2. Robert Barro and Rachel McCleary, "Religion and Economic Growth (NBER Working paper No. 9682).

For example, suppose group A, a special interest group, currently gets 1/1,000 of the economic pie, and the economic pie is $1,000. The group gets a $1 slice. Group A wants to get more than a $1 slice, and it can do so in one of two ways. The first is to lobby for a policy that increases the size of its slice of the economic pie. In other words, group A gets a larger slice (say, a $2 slice) at the expense of someone else's getting a smaller slice. Alternatively, group A can lobby for a policy that increases the size of the pie—say, from $1,000 to $1,500. In this case, group A gets not the full increase of $500, but 1/1,000 of the increase, or 50¢. So group A has to decide whether it is better to lobby for a growth-promoting policy (where it gets 1/1,000 of any increase in Real GDP) or for a transfer-promoting policy (where it gets 100 percent of any transfer).

According to Mancur Olson, in *The Rise and Decline of Nations*, special interest groups are more likely to argue for transfer-promoting policies than growth-promoting policies, and the cost–benefit calculation of each policy is the reason.[3] This behavior affects economic growth in that the more special interest groups there are in a country, the more likely it is that transfer-promoting policies will be lobbied for instead of growth-promoting policies. Individuals will try to get a larger slice of a constant-sized economic pie rather than trying to increase the size of the pie. In short, numerous and politically strong special interest groups are detrimental to economic growth.

3. Mancur Olson, *The Rise and Decline of Nations* (New Haven, CT, and London: Yale University Press, 1982).

OTHER INSTITUTIONS Other institutions are often mentioned as conducive to economic growth: open and competitive markets, free (international) trade, policies that promote economic freedom, a stable monetary system, unburdensome taxes and regulations, and a strong and effective educational system.

1. Explain how a decline in taxes that affects the labor market can end up shifting the *LRAS* curve to the right.

2. What is the difference between physical and human capital?

3. What is the difference between neoclassical growth theory and new growth theory with respect to technology?

4. In the production function specified in Exhibit 2(a), what variable(s) are movement factors (will move us along the production function)? What variable(s) are shift factors (will shift the production function)?

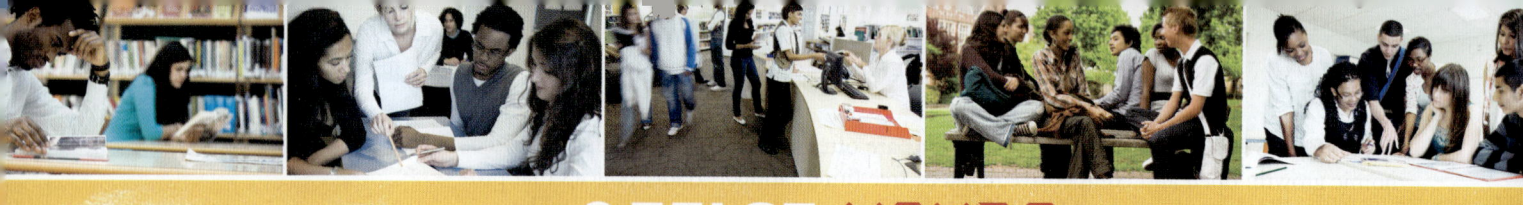

OFFICE HOURS

"What Is the Difference Between Business Cycle Macroeconomics and Economic Growth Macroeconomics?"

STUDENT:

I am searching for a way to put the macroeconomics in this chapter in perspective with the macroeconomics in the other chapters. Can you help?

INSTRUCTOR:

In most of the previous chapters, the *LRAS* curve did not move. It was fixed at some Natural Real GDP level. In this chapter, we discussed the factors that can shift the *LRAS* curve; we discussed how the economy can move from one Real GDP level to a higher Real GDP level. This was obvious in all the exhibits.

Let me add some economic terminology to the discussion. In previous chapers we mainly discussed business cycle macroeconomics. In this chapter we discussed economic growth macroeconomics.

STUDENT:

Specifically, what does business cycle macroeconomics deal with?

INSTRUCTOR:

It deals with two things: (1) differences between Real GDP and Natural Real GDP and (2) ways of moving the economy to its Natural Real GDP level. Suppose Natural Real GDP is $11 trillion and the current Real GDP in the economy is $10 trillion. Obviously, since Real GDP is less than Natural Real GDP, the economy is in a recessionary gap. If the economy is self-regulating, it will eventually move to its Natural Real GDP level. If it is not self-regulating, then perhaps monetary or fiscal policy can be used to move the economy to its Natural Real GDP level.

STUDENT:

How does business cycle macroeconomics differ from what was discussed in this chapter?

INSTRUCTOR:

In this chapter, we mainly discussed economic growth. This topic deals with the economy moving from one Natural Real GDP level to a higher one—specifically, how the economy might move from a Natural Real GDP level of, say, $11 trillion to a higher Natural Real GDP level of, say, $11.7 trillion.

STUDENT:

Does it follow that when we're discussing how the economy moves from one Natural Real GDP level to a higher one, we are simultaneously discussing rightward shifts in the *LRAS* curve?

INSTRUCTOR:

Yes, that's correct. In fact, let's define business cycle macroeconomics and economic growth macroeconomics with respect to the *LRAS* curve. Business cycle macroeconomics deals with economic activity occurring around a single *LRAS* curve. Economic growth macroeconomics (starting from an efficient level of production) deals with rightward shifts in the *LRAS* curve.

POINTS TO REMEMBER

1. Business cycle macroeconomics deals with economic activity occurring around a single *LRAS* curve (or around a specific Natural Real GDP level).
2. Economic growth macroeconomics (starting from an efficient level of production) deals with rightward shifts in the *LRAS* curve (or moving from a lower to a higher level of Natural Real GDP).

CHAPTER SUMMARY

ECONOMIC GROWTH

- Absolute real economic growth refers to an increase in Real GDP from one period to the next.
- Per-capita real economic growth refers to an increase from one period to the next in per-capita Real GDP, which is Real GDP divided by population.

THE PRODUCTION FUNCTION

- A production function specifies the relation between technology and the quantity of factor inputs to output or Real GDP.
- Real GDP $= T(L, K)$. This production function specifies that Real GDP or output is a function of technology—as evidenced in the technology coefficient, T—labor (L), and (physical) capital (K). Another production function is Real GDP $= T(L, K, NR, H)$. This production function specifies that Real GDP or output is a function of technology—as evidenced in the technology coefficient, T—labor (L), (physical) capital (K), natural resources (NR), and human capital (H).

THE PRODUCTION FUNCTION AND ECONOMIC GROWTH

- Using the production function Real GDP $= T(L, K)$, we know that increases in T, L, and K will raise Real GDP and that decreases in T, L, and K decrease Real GDP. Also, changes in Real GDP, as a result of changes in T, L, and K, will lead to shifts in the $LRAS$ curve. For example, a rise in K will raise Real GDP, leading to a rightward shift in the $LRAS$ curve.

- A change in taxes affects the supply of labor of supply curve, thus leading to a change in the amount of labor employed in the labor market. In turn, this change in the amount of labor employed leads to a change in Real GDP and to a shift in the $LRAS$ curve. See Exhibit 4.
- How much capital is employed in the production process depends on such things as the tax treatment of capital's returns and interest rates.

NEW GROWTH THEORY

- New growth theory holds that technology is endogenous; neoclassical growth theory holds that technology is exogenous. When something is endogenous, it is part of the economic system, under our control or influence. When something is exogenous, it is not part of the system; it is assumed to be given to us, often mysteriously through a process that we do not understand.
- According to Paul Romer, discovering and implementing new ideas are what causes economic growth.
- Certain institutions can promote the discovery of new ideas and therefore promote economic growth.

ECONOMIC GROWTH AND SPECIAL INTEREST GROUPS

- According to Mancur Olson, the more special interest groups a country has, the more likely it is that transfer-promoting policies will be lobbied for instead of growth-promoting policies. Individuals will try to get a larger slice of a constant-size economic pie rather than trying to increase the size of the pie.

KEY TERMS AND CONCEPTS

| Absolute Real Economic Growth | Per-Capita Real Economic Growth | Production Function Human Capital | Institution |

QUESTIONS AND PROBLEMS

1. What is *new* about new growth theory?
2. Why might special interest groups favor transfer-promoting policies over growth-promoting policies?
3. What do interest rates and the tax treatment of the returns to capital have to do with economic growth?
4. Some property rights structures provide more and stronger incentives to produce goods and services than other such structures do. Do you agree or disagree with this statement? Explain your answer.
5. What does it mean to say that "a change in labor moves us along a given production function"?
6. What is an institution? Why might institutions matter to how much economic growth a country experiences?
7. Identify how changes in L, K, and T can lead to changes in output or Real GDP.
8. What is the difference between business cycle macroeconomics and economic growth macroeconomics?
9. Why might per-capita real economic growth be a more useful measurement than absolute real economic growth?
10. How does discovering and implementing new ideas cause economic growth?

WORKING WITH NUMBERS AND GRAPHS

1. The economy of country X is currently growing at 2 percent a year. How many years will it take to double the Real GDP of country X?

2. Explain numerically how an advance in technology can lead to more output or Real GDP.

3. A rise in physical capital can raise Real GDP and lead to a rightward shift in the *LRAS* curve. Show this diagrammatically.

4. A change in the labor market can change the equilibrium amount of labor employed, thus leading to a change in Real GDP and to a shift in the *LRAS* curve. Show this diagrammatically.

CHAPTER 18

THE FINANCIAL CRISIS OF 2007–2009

AP PHOTO/SUSAN WALSH, FILE

Introduction Every now and then, a major economic event takes center stage in the news. The most recent such event occurred in September and October of 2008, when people throughout the United States first learned of a financial crisis. For weeks, the talk in the country was of banks and other financial institutions, mortgage-backed securities and collateralized debt obligations, leverage, subprime loans, and who did what when. This chapter is about the events leading up to September and October of 2008 and beyond.

RECENT ECONOMIC EVENTS

To understand recent economic events, first consider an economy as consisting of two sectors: the financial sector and the real sector. The financial sector consists of financial institutions: commercial banks, investment banks, hedge funds, brokerage firms, and others. The real sector consists of firms that produce goods and services, individuals who buy goods and services, and individuals who work for firms, among others.

To a large extent, the financial sector deals with borrowing and lending activities. It takes money that is saved and lends it out. Within the financial sector are financial intermediaries, which are firms that bring borrowers and lenders together. If company X is a financial intermediary, people go to X and deposit their savings. Then X lends out the savings to others. In other words, it grants loans to people using the money other people have saved.

During the period 2007–2009, a financial crisis hit the United States. A financial crisis occurs when financial firms and financial markets undergo a major disruption, making it difficult for persons to obtain loans from banks and other financial institutions. Problems contributing to the financial crisis included people not paying back the loans they took out from the banks, depositors becoming afraid that their deposits were not safe at the banks and en masse trying to withdraw them, banks having a hard time getting loans from other banks, and banks finding themselves with declining asset values, moving them toward insolvency (when their liabilities are greater than their assets).

Problems in the financial sector can bleed over into the real sector, producing problems, such as decreased borrowing and lending, decreased economic activity, a decline in

Financial Intermediary
A firm that transfers funds from those who want to lend funds to those who want to borrow funds.

Insolvency
The condition when liabilities are greater than assets.

sales, a rise in unemployment, and much more. In other words, if the financial sector gets sick, that sickness can do harm to the real sector. That is what happened in the United States in the crisis of 2007–2009. A crisis in the financial sector adversely affected the real sector of the U.S. economy.

The problems in both the financial and real sectors of the economy have called forth certain government programs. Some have been designed to affect the financial sector, such as the *Troubled Asset Relief Program* (TARP), popularly referred to as part of the financial bailout. Some programs have been designed to affect the real sector, such as the $787 billion fiscal stimulus bill (expansionary fiscal policy). In addition, the Federal Reserve recently played a role in trying to deal with the problems in both the financial and real sectors.

Thus, the financial crisis in this country has affected the real sector of the economy, evoking a response from Congress and the Fed, directed at addressing the problems in both the financial and real sectors of the economy.

The rest of this chapter is about the financial crisis, the real sector crisis, and the actions of the Congress and the Federal Reserve. In short, it is about the 2007–2009 economic events and government actions directed at the economy. Within that general discussion, we will discuss the causes and effects of the financial crisis.

THE FINANCIAL CRISIS AS A BALANCE SHEET PROBLEM

Balance Sheet
A record of the assets and liabilities of a bank.

Asset
Anything owned or that one has claim to that has value.

Liability
Anything that is owed to someone else.

Net Worth (or Capital)
The difference between assets and liabilities. For example, if assets are $100 and liabilities are $80, net worth, or capital, is $20.

Financial institutions have balance sheets consisting of assets, liabilities, and net worth (or capital). For a financial institution, an asset is anything that has value and that generates a flow of income. For example, suppose a commercial bank makes a loan to you for $40,000. You agree to pay $1,200 a month on the loan for so many months. Your loan is an *asset* as far as the bank is concerned. That loan has value to the bank and generates a flow of income for the bank, specifically, $1,200 a month.

A liability (for the bank) is something that it owes. For example, suppose you go to your local bank and open up a checking account. You deposit $5,000 into the account. Your deposit is the bank's *liability*. The bank owes you the $5,000. Another way of looking at that deposit is to say that you are lending the money to the bank. With that $5,000, the bank will make a loan to someone else. It will pay you 3 percent on your deposit, and then lend it to someone else for, say, 4.5 percent.

Let's say the bank has $100 in assets and $80 in liabilities. The difference between its assets and its liabilities is its net worth, or capital: $20. One way to view capital is as a buffer against insolvency. Suppose that the bank initially has assets of $100 and liabilities of $80. Then the value of its assets falls to $85. This might happen if people to whom the bank lent money do not pay it back. The bank can survive this $15 loss in the value of its assets because the capital of $20 cushioned the blow. The value of the bank's assets would have to fall enough to wipe out the entire capital amount before the bank is deemed insolvent. In other words, a $15 decline in asset value wouldn't do it, but a $21 decline would.

The financial crisis can be viewed as a *balance sheet problem*. Many financial firms had assets on their balance sheets that declined in value. As these assets lost value, some financial institutions found themselves insolvent; other financial institutions found themselves coming perilously close to insolvency.

When a financial institution is either insolvent or close to insolvency, the real sector in the economy is affected. If the institution is insolvent, it can go out of the lending business, reducing the amount of lending in the economy. With less lending (and consequently less borrowing), there is less economic activity, which can show up as less buying and less producing. Less buying and producing can, in turn, result in firms going out of business, people getting fired from their jobs, and so on. Even if a bank isn't insolvent but is simply close, it could simply pull back on its lending activities, thereby reducing economic activity in the real sector of the economy.

There are other consequences. As a bank becomes insolvent or close to insolvent, it may find that one of two things happen. First, people may not want to deposit funds in the bank. After all, if a bank is having a problem paying off its liabilities, why put your money there. If you put your money in that bank today, it might not be able to pay you back tomorrow. Also, knowing that a bank is likely to become insolvent, depositors in that bank might make a *run* on it. They might think that if the bank is having a hard time paying off its liabilities, isn't it better for me to be one of the first people the bank pays off? There might not be enough money to pay everyone off.

Part of the run-on-the-bank problem these days is mitigated by the Federal Deposit Insurance Corporation (FDIC). The FDIC insures deposits in banks up to $250,000 per depositor. This insurance cuts down on people running to banks to get their money out if they think the bank is having problems. But it does so at the cost of pushing banks into taking a little more risk than they might take on if deposits weren't insured by the FDIC. To illustrate, if depositors' money is insured by the federal government, the bank knows that it isn't as likely to see a lot of people asking for their money all at once. This environment makes it less likely that the bank will worry about having to pay off all its depositors at once. Consequently, the banks may make riskier loans (riskier loans come with higher expected returns) than it would if its liabilities (specifically, its depositors' deposits) were not insured. But, of course, making riskier loans may raise the probability that the bank will become insolvent. After all, riskier loans do not get paid back as often as less risky loans.

ⓣhinking Like **AN ECONOMIST**

Unintended Effects Economists know that actions can have both intended and unintended effects. The intended effect of insuring bank deposits is to reduce bank runs. The unintended effect is to push banks into taking on more risk than they would have if bank deposits were not insured. ▪▪▪

Which Assets Were Risky?

The assets on the banks' balance sheets that lost value because they turned out to be risky were the *subprime mortgage loans*, other nontraditional mortgage loans, *mortgage-backed securities* (MBS), and *collateralized debt obligations* (CDOs).

Subprime mortgage loans and other nontraditional mortgage loans fall into the same category. They are mortgage loans granted to persons who might have low credit ratings or some other factors that suggest they could default on the debt repayment. Anyone who is not paying for a house with cash has to take out a mortgage loan. Mortgage loans often come with certain restrictions. They might specify that a borrower must make a down payment equal to the a specified percentage (say, 10 percent) of the purchase price of the house, that he needs a certain dollar income, that he has a good credit history, and so on. Generally speaking, mortgage lending practices were stricter in the 1970s and 1980s than they were in the late 1990s and early 2000s. In other words, lending practices loosened up in the latter years. A drastic loosening is reflected in subprime and other nontraditional mortgage loans. With subprime loans, loans were being given out to persons who could not have qualified for traditional loans (with larger down payments, better documentation of income, and so on).

Mortgage-backed securities (MBS) are a type of asset-backed security that is secured by a mortgage or collection of mortgages. Here is how an MBS is created. Bank A has made 5,000 mortgage loans, some of which are subprime and other nontraditional loans. It bundles all 5,000 loans into a package, which consists of the expected future payments that

Subprime Mortgage Loan

A nontraditional mortgage loan granted to persons who might have low credit ratings or some other factors that suggest they could default on the debt repayment.

Mortgage-Backed Securities (MBS)

A type of asset-backed security that is secured by a mortgage or collection of mortgages.

will be made on the 5,000 loans. For example, one of the 5,000 loans was made to Smith, who pays $2,400 a month on her mortgage loan. The bank cuts up the package of 5,000 loans into slices and sells them; these slices are the mortgage-backed securities themselves. Thus, they are called mortgage-backed securities because they are backed by (or composed of) mortgage loans. For example, if you buy a slice that represents 1/1,000 of the pool of mortgages, then what you will receive is 1/1,000 of the payments made on the 5,000 loans in the pool.

Collateralized debt obligations (CDOs) are like mortgage-backed securities, except that the slices are not equal. Some people who hold certain slices get paid before other people with other slices. These are called *tranches*, which are simply slices with different risk.

What is important is that the value of an MBS and a CDO depends on the people who are paying off their mortgage loans. If a lot of people do not pay off their loans, then the MBSs and CDOs lose their value. Look at it this way. You buy a slice of an MBS for $10,000, which entitles you to a payment of $500 a month for x number of years. What happens to your payments of $500 a month if the borrowers do not pay off their mortgage loans? All of a sudden, you do not receive the payments you thought you were going to receive, and your MBS is worthless.

In 2006, some people with subprime and other nontraditional loans were not able to make their monthly payments on their mortgage loans. (We explain why later.) As a result, banks and other financial institutions experienced a decline in the value of their assets: the subprime loans, other nontraditional loans, MBSs, and CDOs listed as assets on their balance sheets. As the value declined, some banks and financial institutions slid into insolvency, and others were coming ever closer to insolvency.

Three Questions

At this point, the story of the financial crisis goes in different directions, which are related to three questions:

- Why were many of the people who had taken out subprime and other nontraditional loans unable to make their monthly payments?

- Why did traditional lending give way to subprime and other nontraditional lending?

- Why didn't the banks and other financial institutions have a bigger capital buffer (against insolvency) when they found themselves with loans that were not being paid off and MBSs and CDOs that were losing their value?

The answer to the first question has to do with the housing market. Related to the housing market is a discussion of the Fed and its monetary policy and a global savings glut.

The answer to the second question relates to Congress, two presidents, Fannie Mae and Freddie Mac, and securitization.

The answer to the third question relates to leverage and regulatory capital arbitrage.

SELF-TEST

(Answers to Self-Test questions are in Answers to Self-Test Questions at the back of the book.)

1. Explain how the net worth, or capital, of a bank can act as a buffer against insolvency.

2. Explain how a decline in a bank's assets values could lead to less lending activity.

3. What is a financial crisis?

THE FED, INTEREST RATES, AND HOUSING PRICES

We know that the Fed sets a target for the federal funds rate, which is the interest rate banks charge each other for loans. For example, if bank A wants to borrow $4 million from bank B, it would pay bank B the federal funds rate for the loan.

Now the Fed does not set the federal funds rate by edict. Instead it undertakes certain monetary actions so that the market federal funds rate equals its federal funds rate target. To illustrate, if the current market federal funds rate is 5 percent and the Fed's target federal funds rate is 3 percent, the Fed will inject reserves into the banking system so that the federal funds rate falls to 3 percent.

Exhibit 1 shows the federal funds rate for the period from a little before 2001 to 2007. In January of 2001, the federal funds rate was 6 percent, but it was much lower at 1.75 percent in December 2001. During the period 2002–2005, it is in the 1–2 percent range. Then, in June 2006, the federal funds rate rises to 5.25 percent. What is behind the decline in the federal funds rate, some argue, is that, beginning in 2001, the Fed dramatically lowered its federal funds rate target. That target is especially low during the period 2002–2005.

The Fed pursued such a low federal funds rate target because it believed that if the federal funds rate decreased, so would other interest rates in the economy (especially short-term rates). And the Fed wanted to lower interest rates in the economy for a number of reasons. It was trying to stimulate economic activity. It was afraid that if it didn't nudge interest rates down, the economy might fall into a recession. And it seemed to be worried about deflation.

The specific reason for the low interest rate policy is not as important as the fact that a low interest rate policy had certain effects. One major effect is that the Fed's low federal fund targets led to a decline in mortgage interest rates. Here is the process. When the Fed lowers its federal funds rate target, it ends up injecting reserves into the banking system to bring the actual federal funds rate down to its new lower target level. As a byproduct of more reserves in the banking system, banks can make more loans—such as mortgage loans. Thus, mortgage rates decline. When mortgage rates decline, more people take out mortgage loans to buy houses; it is cheaper to buy a house when mortgage rates are low than when they are high. Another effect is that people take out bigger loans than they would have taken out at higher interest rates.

So the Fed's low federal funds rate target policy made it possible for more people to take out mortgage loans. But more people with loans—and some people with bigger loans—added demand to the housing market. As demand in the housing market rose, so did housing prices.

The Global Savings Glut and Low Interest Rates

At this point in our story, some economists mention the "global savings glut" as an alternative explanation for lower interest rates. A *global savings glut* describes an excess of savings over investment. Emerging countries in the world began to save more, and much

EXHIBIT 1

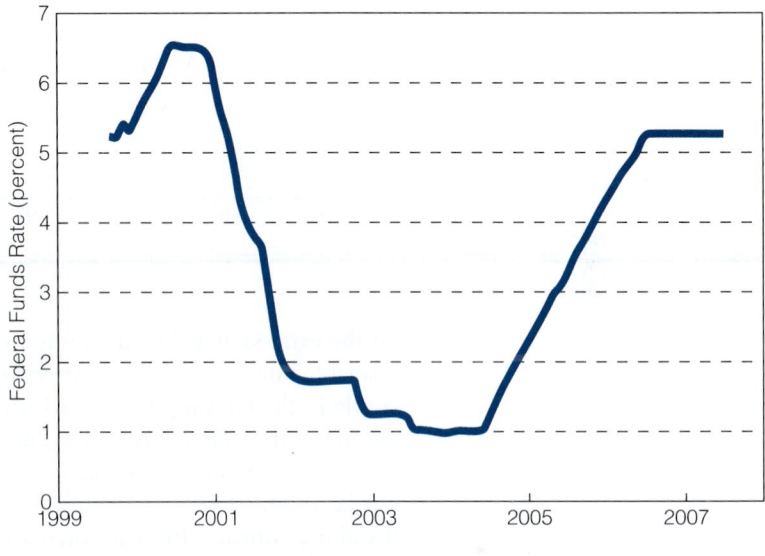

The Federal Funds Rate for Various Years

The federal funds rate starts out relatively high in early 2001 and then starts to decline. The federal funds rate is in the 1–2 percent category in 2002–2005.

EXHIBIT 2

Global Savings and Investment as a Percentage of World GDP

Global savings is a smaller percentage of World GDP in the period 2002–2004 than it was in the 1970s and 1980s. John Taylor has argued that the data here are more nearly representative of a savings shortage during the period 2002–2004 than a savings glut.

of the extra savings found its way to the United States, where it increased the supply of loanable funds and lowered interest rates. The increased supply of loanable funds played a role in the housing story, in which low mortgage interest rates were already leading to greater borrowing to buy houses and rising house prices.

Some economists have questioned whether there was a global savings glut. One in particular is John Taylor of Stanford University. Taylor makes a major point with the help of Exhibit 2, which is from an International Monetary Fund study that shows global savings and global investment as a share of World GDP for different years. For example, global investment is approximately 22 percent of World GDP in 2004, and savings is slightly over 21 percent of World GDP in the same year. The point that Taylor makes is that global savings as a percentage of World GDP was lower in the period 2002–2004 than it was in 1970s and 1980s. Yet interest rates in the United States were low in the period 2002–2004. In other words, low interest rates in the United States correspond to the time when savings as a percentage of World GDP is low. But one would have thought that low interest rates would have corresponded to a time when savings as percentage of World GDP was high, not low.

If emerging and developing countries supposedly sent their excess savings to the United States, in the process lowering interest rates, what did their savings and investment look like as percentages of GDP? Exhibit 3(a) shows that the savings rate as a percentage of emerging countries' GDP rose during the period from 2002 to 2008. According to the global savings glut story, we would expect that the rising savings rate in emerging countries would lower interest rates in the United States. Yet look at the mortgage rates in the United States [Exhibit 3(b)] on a 30-year mortgage during the period 1998–2009. Specifically, during the period 2000–2008—the period in which savings rates in emerging countries were rising—mortgage rates fell from 2000 to 2003. They stayed low during the period 2003 to 2005, and then they began to rise. In other words, the rising savings rate in emerging countries is consistent with both *falling* and *rising* mortgage interest rates, not simply with lowering interest rates.

Our Story So Far

So far, we know that the banks had balance sheet problems. When the assets on their balance sheets began to decline in value (especially the subprime loans, MBSs, and CDOs), some banks became insolvent and other banks came critically close to insolvency. As a

EXHIBIT 3

Savings and Investment Rates and 30-Year Conventional Mortgage Rates, Various Years

(a) Savings and investment in emerging and developing countries as a percentage of the GDP in these countries. (b) The

30-year conventional mortgage rate for various years.

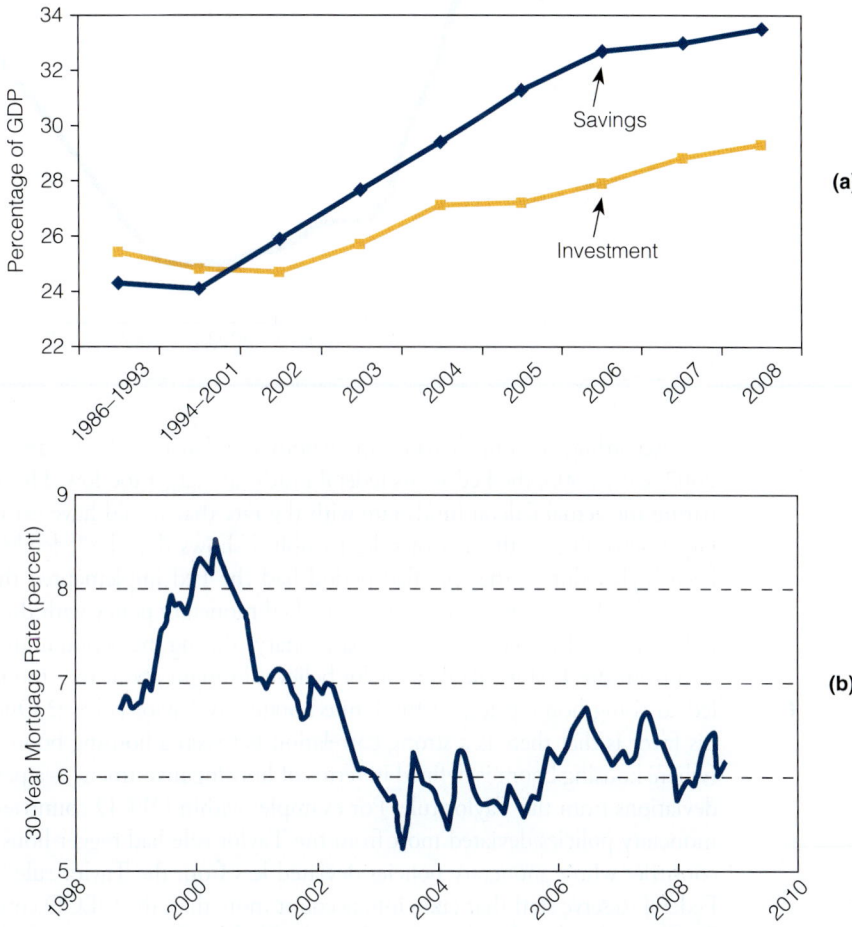

(a)

(b)

result, banks pulled back their lending, and the reduction in lending adversely affected the real sector of the economy. What we do not yet know is *why* the people who had taken out subprime and other nontraditional loans could not pay back their loans, thus adversely affecting the values of MBSs and CDOs. To explain that part of the story, we need to know more about low interest rates and the housing price boom. This takes us to a discussion of the Taylor rule.

THE TAYLOR RULE AND INTEREST RATES

As mentioned in earlier chapters, the Taylor rule is a monetary rule of sorts; it is a recommendation of how the Fed should set its federal funds rate target. Essentially, it says that the Fed should raise the federal funds interest rate when inflation increases and lower it when GDP declines. It specifies how much the federal funds rate should change in different circumstances.

EXHIBIT 4

Federal Funds Rate, Actual and Consistent with the Taylor Rule, Various Years

The actual federal funds rate and the federal funds rate consistent with the Taylor rule for various years.

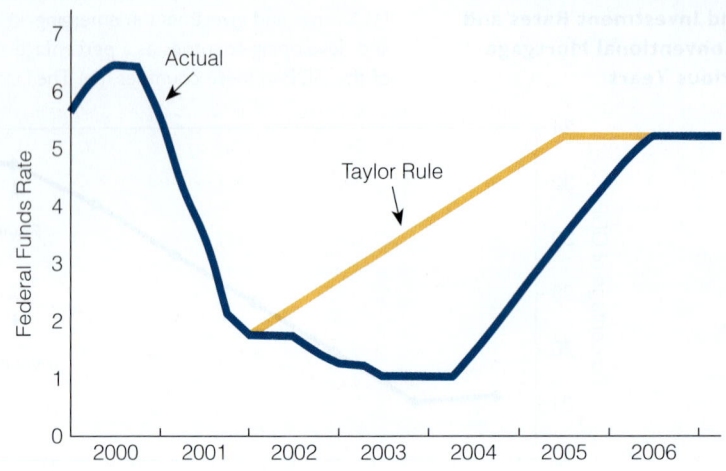

According to John Taylor (for whom the Taylor rule is named), during the period 2002–early 2006, the Fed set its federal funds rate target too low. He concludes this by comparing the actual federal funds rate with the rate that would have existed had the Fed set its target according to the Taylor rule. Exhibit 4 shows that the federal funds rate would have been higher during the specified period had the Fed implemented the Taylor rule. Taylor concludes that, when we compare actual Fed monetary policy with the Taylor rule monetary policy, the Fed's policy was "too expansionary" during the period in question. It is this deviation from the Taylor rule that Taylor believes brought about the "too low" interest rates that led to rising house prices in the United States. Is Taylor correct? One piece of evidence in his favor is that there is a strong correlation between a housing boom in different countries (where housing boom is defined in terms of housing investment as a percentage of GDP) and deviations from the Taylor rule. For example, within OECD countries, the countries whose monetary policies deviated most from the Taylor rule had bigger housing booms than those countries whose monetary policies deviated less from the Taylor rule.[1] However, a study by Federal Reserve staff that takes into account more than the OECD countries contradicts that finding, indicating that deviations from the Taylor rule are not correlated with housing prices.

Alan Greenspan Responds

Alan Greenspan was chair of the Federal Reserve from 1987 to 2006. He has argued in favor of the global savings glut explanation for the decline in interest rates and against the position held by John Taylor. Greenspan argues that the Taylor rule is not really a fail-safe monetary rule for the Fed to follow because it cannot be applied to asset prices (such as house prices). Greenspan's argument is essentially: (1) John Taylor uses the Taylor rule to argue that the Fed held interest rates too low during the early 2000s. In other words, if the Fed had set monetary policy using the Taylor rule during that period, interest rates wouldn't have been too low, and there wouldn't have been a housing boom. (2) But, says Greenspan, the Taylor rule is structured in such a way as to indicate a proper federal funds rate target necessary to balance the trade-off between inflation and unemployment. And the type of inflation that the Taylor rule addresses is *product-price inflation,* not *asset-price*

---

1. OECD stands for Organization for Economic Co-operation and Development, with 30 member countries: Australia, Austria, Belgium, Canada, Czech Republic, Denmark, Finland, France, Germany, Greece, Hungary, Iceland, Ireland, Italy, Japan, Korea, Luxembourg, Mexico, the Netherlands, New Zealand, Norway, Poland, Portugal, Slovak Republic, Spain, Sweden, Switzerland, Turkey, United Kingdom, and the United States.

inflation (such as house price inflation). (3) So, unless there is a strong correlation between the consumer price index (CPI) and house prices—and Greenspan says there isn't—then the Taylor rule is *inappropriate* to use when trying to figure out the causes of sharp increases in house prices.

Greenspan has also argued that the boom in housing was caused by low long-term interest rates (such as the 30-year fixed mortgage rate), not short-term interest rates. Moreover, he argues that the Fed has much more control over short-term interest rates (such as the federal funds rate) than over long-term interest rates. Greenspan notes:

> In the United States, the house price bubble was driven by the low level of the 30 year fixed rate mortgage that decline from its mid-2000 peak, six months prior to the FOMC (Federal Open Market Committee) easing of the federal funds rate in January, 2001.[2]

Rising House Prices, Delinquency Rates, and Foreclosures

During the period 2003–2005, housing prices were rising. But during the same period, delinquency rates (on adjustable rate mortgages, whose interest rate is adjusted periodically depending on various factors) and foreclosure rates were falling. In other words, as house prices were rising, more people were paying off their mortgages loans and fewer people were being foreclosed upon. There is perhaps a good reason for the inverse relationship between housing prices and delinquency and foreclosure rates. When house prices are rising, home owners are gaining equity in their homes. Equity is the difference between the price the house can be sold for and what one owes on the house. To illustrate, if you owe $500,000 on a house and the price of the house is $600,000, you have $100,000 in equity. If the price of the house rises to $650,000, your equity rises to $150,000. When housing prices decline, the benefits of holding on to a house decline. In particular, if the price of the house falls below the value of the mortgage loan (if, for instance, the house can be sold for no more than, say, $480,000 and the mortgage loan is $500,000), some people will not pay off their loans.

Looking at delinquency and foreclosure rates only during a period of rising prices can give a false picture of the risks inherent in giving out mortgage loans. To illustrate, suppose that, during years 1–10, house prices are falling, while delinquency and foreclosure rates are up. During years 11–20, house prices are rising, while delinquency and foreclosure rates are down. Suppose a lender who is considering giving out mortgage loans in year 21 looks only at years 11–20 to get some idea of how risky mortgage loans are. The lender might come away thinking they are not risky at all (because delinquency and foreclosure rates are relatively low). But the picture is very different for years 1–10 and even more different for the period of years 1–20. The point is that, if lenders during the early 2000s were looking only at recent past behavior in delinquency and foreclosure rates when deciding how risky mortgage loans are, then they *underestimated* the risk of mortgage loans. The mortgage loans they were giving out were riskier than they thought they were.

So, if the low interest rate policy of the Fed pushed up home prices, it also led to lower delinquency and foreclosure rates. Lenders, who perhaps were viewing less than the complete time span of delinquency and foreclosure rates, then mistakenly thought that granting mortgage loans was a less risky business than it was. With the benefit of hindsight, we now know that too many risky mortgage loans ended up being made. Hence the subprime loans, the MBSs, and the CDOs, and eventually the declining asset values on banks' balance sheets.

Adjustable Rate Mortgage
A mortgage loan where the interest rate on the loan is adjusted periodically depending on various factors.

Equity (in a House)
The difference between the price the house can be sold for and what one owes on the house.

SELF-TEST

1. What is the global-savings-glut explanation of rising housing prices? What is the Fed-low-interest-rate explanation of rising housing prices?

2. According to John Taylor, who or what caused the boom in housing prices in the United States in the early 2000s?

---

2. *The Crisis*, by Alan Greenspan, Second Draft: March 9, 2010.

THE POLITICS OF HOUSING

Mortgage lending standards in the United States declined in the 1990s and early 2000s. To understand why, we need to compare traditional and nontraditional lending practices. In traditional lending, borrowers must provide proof of income, employment, and assets. In nontraditional lending, borrowers may not be asked to provide proof of income, employment, and assets. Also, in traditional lending, down payments are a larger percentage of the house being purchased than in nontraditional lending. For example, a typical down payment in traditional mortgage lending is 20 percent. In nontraditional mortgage lending it could be 2–5 percent.

In the 1990s and early 2000s, the mortgage market saw a change in the composition of mortgage lending—away from more traditional lending and toward more nontraditional lending. For example, many lenders waived requirements that borrowers document their incomes, assets, and employment information and required down payments of only 2 or 3 percent or, in some cases, 0 percent.

Why lending practices declined makes for an interesting story that tells what was going on in both the private sector and in government. In this section, we talk about what was going on in government, especially as it relates to the politics of housing.

The Community Reinvestment Act

The Community Reinvestment Act (CRA) was passed in 1977. Its purpose was to encourage financial institutions to meet the needs of borrowers in all segments of their communities, including low- and moderate-income borrowers. In 1995, Congress revised the CRA to give banks a stronger incentive to increase the percentage of mortgage loans (among other loans) going to low- and moderate-income borrowers. Some have argued that Congress was essentially imposing quotas on banks to apply "innovative or flexible" standards to meet the borrowing needs of these borrowers. Some have argued that essentially the CRA forced banks to relax lending standards so that they could make loans that they otherwise would not have made. Some take a different position, arguing that banks did not have to give out loans they didn't want to. However, banks that were not in compliance with CRA could find their applications for new branches, mergers, or acquisitions denied. According to economist Thomas Sowell:

> . . . when legislation was pending in 1999 to permit banks to diversify into selling investment securities, the White House urged "that banks given unsatisfactory ratings under the 1977 Community Reinvestment Act be prohibited from enjoying the new diversification privileges" of this legislation. Accordingly, when Congress passed legislation removing existing prohibitions against banks affiliating with securities or insurance firms, this new scope of banking operations was in fact reserved for those banks that had a "satisfactory record of meeting community credit needs or better, at the most recent examination of each such institution"—that is, banks that met government-imposed quotas.[3]

FANNIE MAE AND FREDDIE MAC

Fannie Mae (Federal National Mortgage Association, FNMA) came into existence in 1938 to add demand to the housing market. Specifically, Fannie Mae would buy mortgage loans from banks that had originated the loans. For example, bank A might make a mortgage loan to a borrower and then sell the mortgage loan to Fannie Mae, in the process receiving funds from Fannie Mae with which to create more mortgages. In 1970, Freddie Mac (Federal Home Loan Mortgage Corporation, FHLMC) was established to do much the same things as Fannie Mae.

---

3. Thomas Sowell, *The Housing Boom and Bust* (New York: Basic Books, 2010), p. 39.

Fannie Mae and Freddie Mac got the money they used to buy the mortgage loans from banks in a number of ways. One way was to borrow it. Another way was by creating mortgage-backed securities and then selling them. (They also insured them.) Suppose an MBS issued by Fannie Mae includes the loan repayments of 10,000 mortgage loans, and 100 of them are not repaid. Fannie Mae steps in and pays off those loans, but to do so, Fannie Mae has to have enough capital (net worth). In the recent financial crisis, Fannie Mae did not have enough capital to pay off all the loans that were not being repaid. Although Fannie Mae did not have explicit and formal backing from the U.S. government, many of the investors who bought the MBSs that Fannie issued thought the U.S. government would come to Fannie Mae's rescue should she need it. They were proved right. In

September 2008, the U.S. government committed $200 billion (as needed on a quarterly basis) to Fannie Mae to correct any deficiencies in its net worth.

Beginning in the early 1990s, government pressure was placed on both Fannie Mae and Freddie Mac to increase their purchases of mortgages made to low- to moderate-income families. In 1996, the Department of Housing and Urban Development (HUD) stipulated that 42 percent of all mortgages purchased by Fannie Mae and Freddie Mac were to be given to individuals with incomes below the median incomes in their areas. In 1999, the quota was raised to 50 percent. In short, HUD placed pressure on Fannie and Freddie to buy nontraditional loans, and that pressure came not only from HUD, but also from key members of Congress. In 2000, Fannie bought $1.2 billion worth of subprime mortgages; in 2001, the amount rose to $9.2 billion; and in 2003, to $15 billion. In 2004, both Fannie and Freddie had spent $175 billion on subprime loans.

The buying of subprime loans by Fannie and Freddie and the emergence of MBSs backed by subprime loans created a market in subprime lending. Specifically, the large-scale expansion of Fannie and Freddie into the subprime loan business made it profitable for other financial institutions to grant subprime loans in order to sell them to Fannie and Freddie.

THE ROLE OF LEVERAGE AND REGULATORY CAPITAL ARBITRAGE

In this section we discuss the role of leverage and regulatory capital arbitrage in the financial crisis.

Leverage

Leverage is the use of borrowed funds to increase the returns that can be earned with a given amount of capital. Suppose a bank has $100 in assets (which are primarily outstanding loans), $92 in liabilities, and $8 in capital, or net worth. Its leverage ratio—the ratio of its assets to capital—is 100 to 8, or 12½ to 1.[4] Now suppose the bank's assets increase in value by 10 percent. The bank's assets are now $110, and its liabilities are still $92. The bank now has $18 worth of capital. In other words, the 10 percent increase in the value of the bank's assets has more than doubled the bank's capital (from $8 to $18). This is an increase of 125 percent.

Leverage
The use of borrowed funds to increase the returns that can be earned with a given amount of capital.

---

4. One can use different leverage ratios to get an idea of a firm's ability to meet its financial obligations. We have used one particular leverage ratio in our discussion here.

Now change the example. Suppose the bank borrows $5 so that its liabilities rise to $97. Now the bank has only $3 in capital. Its leverage ratio rises from 100 to 8 (12½ to 1) to 100 to 3 (33⅓ to 1). The bank is said to be much more highly leveraged now than it was before. If the assets of the bank rise by 10 percent to $110, the capital rises from $3 to $13, for an increase of 333 percent. The lesson is that borrowing to increase the leverage ratio raises the percentage rise in capital, given a rise in the value of assets. In other words, if the value of assets is rising, a high leverage ratio increases the percentage rise in capital.

There is a downside to a high leverage ratio. A decline in asset values magnifies losses. Suppose that when the bank had a leverage ratio of 12½ to 1, its assets declined in value by 4 percent. The value of its assets fall in value from $100 to $96 as its liabilities remain constant at $92. The bank's capital falls from $8 to $4, for a decline of 50 percent. Of course, the bank is still solvent because its assets are still greater than its liabilities.

However, if the bank has a leverage ratio of 33⅓ to 1 when its assets decline in value by 4 percent to $96, it is now insolvent. Its liabilities are $97. The bank has negative capital (–$1).

So, if a bank is highly leveraged (i.e., has a high leverage ratio), even a small decline in the value of its assets can push it into insolvency. Part of the explanation of the financial crisis of 2007–2009 is that many banks (and other financial institutions) were highly leveraged. So, when the value of their assets (some of which were subprime loans and MBSs backed by subprime loans) declined, they were thrown into insolvency or came very close to insolvency.

When financial institutions are highly leveraged, the availability of credit in the economy can suffer if asset values decline. Suppose a bank, in order to meet its legal capital requirements, must have 5 percent of capital to back every $1 of a loan (an asset) that it grants. If the bank has $100 billion in loans outstanding, it must have $5 billion in capital. If the bank's capital falls to $4 billion as a result of the value of its loans declining, the bank now has to do something to be in compliance with the 5 percent requirement? The owners either to have add more capital to the bank, or the bank has to cut back its loans to $80 billion ($4 billion is 5 percent of $80 billion). So a fall in capital of $1 billion can lead to a $20 billion reduction in bank loans.

A reduction in loans occurring at a number of banks at the same time can dramatically affect the amount of lending and borrowing in the economy. And, as we know, a decline in credit can affect the real sector of the economy, reducing economic activity, leading to a decline in purchases and sales, and raising unemployment.

Regulatory Capital Arbitrage

Regulatory capital is the amount of capital that a financial institution must hold because of regulatory requirements. For example, a bank may have to have 5 percent capital for every $1 of a loan it creates. Regulatory capital requirements exist for the sake of bank safety. Supposedly, if a bank is meeting its regulatory capital requirements, it is a safe and sound bank that is unlikely to suffer insolvency due to any losses it may incur.

The important question, though, is *how much* capital is required to keep a bank safe and sound? Is a capital requirement of 10 percent too high or a capital requirement of 2 percent too low? After all, a high capital requirement might make a bank safe and sound (and less likely to become insolvent), but it can also lower a bank's returns. That is the lesson of leverage: A higher leverage ratio increases gains when assets values rise. So there is a *return-safety trade-off* that speaks to how much capital a bank should hold. More capital means more safety, but it also means lower returns when asset values are rising.

Some economists have argued that regulatory capital arbitrage explains why banks (and other financial institutions) were as highly leveraged as they were and why. When asset values began to decline, a cascading effect set in that ended with credit being less available in the economy.

The question of how much capital regulators should require banks to hold is based on the concept of *risk-weighted assets*. The idea is that not all assets are alike; some are

Too Big to Fail

At one time, the phrase "too big to fail" meant that a company was so large and so diversified in its businesses (conducting business in numerous different areas in different countries) that a downturn in one business area or in one country wouldn't really hurt it; it would still be successful in many other areas. It had its eggs in a lot of different baskets, all over the world; so a broken egg in one or two places didn't mean failure. It was, in a sense, "too big to fail."

Today the term "too big to fail" means something different. It refers to a company or institution that is so big that, if the government were to allow it to fail, there would be negative repercussions for other companies and for the economy as a whole. A more accurate descriptive phrase might be "too big to *let* fail," but still the phrase "too big to fail" is used instead.

Think of the too-big-to-fail (TBTF) company or institution today as occupying the center of a circle, with its many appendages (much like an octopus) extended outward. If the TBTF institution fails, then the repercussions flow outward to adversely affect others. So, to prevent others from being hurt by its failure, government must step in and prevent it from failing, even if it has to use taxpayer funds to do so. In fact, some argue that taxpayer funds are wisely used for such purposes. Better to use $500 billion of taxpayer funds to save the economy than to let the economy contract, resulting in rising unemployment, bankruptcies, and dwindling tax revenues.

In the financial crisis of 2007–2009, both Fannie Mae and Freddie Mac were considered too big to fail, as was General Motors, some investment and commercial banks, and some financial services and insurance companies (such as American International Group, AIG).

Businesses that are TBTF and that are therefore bailed out when they are in trouble have competitive market advantages vis-à-vis

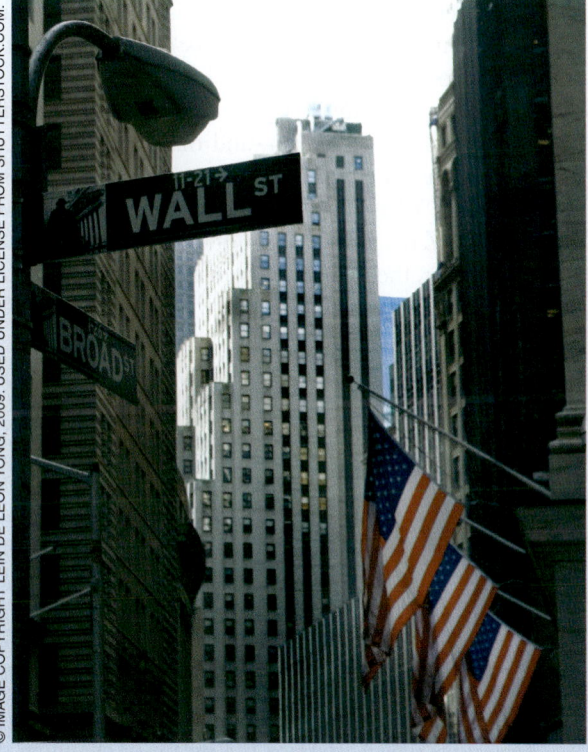

© IMAGE COPYRIGHT LEIN DE LEÓN YONG, 2009. USED UNDER LICENSE FROM SHUTTERSTOCK.COM.

companies that are small enough to let fail. Suppose bank A is considered TBTF but that banks B–Z are not. Many depositors will want to put their money in bank A instead of banks B–Z because they feel safer putting their money there. After all, if their bank—Bank A—has any problems, the government will bail it out.

So banks (and other institutions) that are TBTF are often shielded from risk because they know they will be bailed out if they run into problems. So why not take on the risk in search of the high returns? After all, if the returns materialize, they win; but if they don't, and it looks like failure is around the corner, they will be bailed out. Heads, we win; tails, the taxpayer loses. In other words, being TBTF creates a *moral hazard problem*; a party that is insulated from risk behaves differently than it would behave it if weren't shielded from risk. (Think of how fast you might drive if you knew it were impossible for you to be hurt in a car accident.)

In 2007–2010, with respect to the TBTF issue, some individuals argued that some institutions were truly too big to fail because, if they did fail, not only they, but many others, would feel the consequences. Better to save them today than to let many others suffer tomorrow. Other individuals argued that by not allowing these institutions to fail, the government simply increased the probability that other financial crises would follow. In other words, when government protects institutions from failure, it simply increases the probability that those institutions will fail in the future. Finally, some argued that the least worst course of action was to bail out some TBTF institutions—this time—but then to pass regulatory measures that break up TBTF institutions into a smaller sizes so that TBTF institutions no longer exist. In other words, being "too big to fail" is too big.

riskier than others. To illustrate, if bank A holds assets X and Y, and asset X is very risky and asset Y is not so risky, then the bank should hold more capital for asset X than for asset Y.

Under the 1988 Basel Accord (Basel I), international standards for risk-based capital requirments were introduced. Specifically, banks have to hold capital equivalent to 8 percent of their risk-weighted assets. To understand this, think of a bank with two assets: Treasury bonds and uncollateralized commercial loans. The Treasury bonds are not risky assets. The bank can be sure that the U.S. Treasury is going to redeem those bonds. In comparison, the uncollateralized commercial loans are risky. The bank cannot be sure that all its commercial loans will be paid off. Because Treasury bonds are less risky than uncollateralized commercial loans, the bank would be expected to hold more capital against its commercial loans than its Treasury bonds.

As a concrete example of *regulatory capital arbitrage*, suppose that a bank has three kinds of assets—X, Y, and Z—and that they differ in their degrees of riskiness. In other words, each class of asset has a different *risk weight*. Asset X has zero risk; so zero capital is required. Asset Y has a risk weight of 50 percent; so 50¢ of capital is needed for every $1 of Y asset. Asset Z has a risk weight of 80 percent; so 80¢ of capital is needed for every $1 of Z asset. Further, the total amount of each asset is $100 for a total of $300 in assets. To find the amount of risk-weighted assets, we multiply the amount of each asset by its risk weight and then sum the results:

$$\text{Risk-weighted assets} = (\$100X \times 0 \text{ percent}) + (\$100Y \times 50 \text{ percent}) \\ + (\$100Z \times 80 \text{ percent}) = \$130$$

Now if the requirement is that financial institutions must hold 8 percent capital against their risk-weighted assets, the financial institution with $130 of risk-weighted assets has to hold capital equal to 8 percent of $130, or $10.40:

$$\text{Amount of capital a bank must hold} = \$130 \times 8 \text{ percent} \\ = \$10.40$$

Regulatory Capital Arbitrage

A means of changing the composition of assets in such a way as to lower the overall amount of capital a financial institution holds for a given level of assets.

Securitization

The process by which financial institutions aggregate debt (such as loans) in a pool and then issue securities backed by the pool.

Special-Purpose Vehicle (SPV)

A legal entity created to fulfill narrow, specific, or temporary objectives.

Regulatory capital arbitrage is a means of changing the composition of assets in such a way as to lower the overall amount of capital a financial institution holds for a given level of assets. A financial institution might want to practice regulatory capital arbitrage because of what was explained earlier about leverage: hold either less capital for a given amount of assets or more assets for a given amount of capital. In other words, a higher leverage ratio means higher returns as long as asset values are rising. One way of increasing returns, then, is to reduce the amount of capital one needs to hold given the overall capital requirements. Regulatory capital arbitrage offers a means.

Securitization—the process by which financial institutions aggregate debt (such as loans) in a pool and then issue securities backed by the pool—is one way to accomplish regulatory capital arbitrage. To illustrate, suppose a bank has $100 in mortgages for which it needs to hold $4 in capital. If the bank can create a collateralized debt obligation (CDO) out of these mortgages, it may be able to reduce its capital to *less* than $4. Here's how. The CDO that the bank creates is sold to a **special-purpose vehicle (SPV)** that issues bonds based on the money that is expected to be forthcoming from the monthly mortgage payments. The bonds are divided up into tranches with different priorities. For example, senior tranches take priority over junior tranches; that is, when the money comes in from the mortgage loans, the people who hold the senior tranches are paid first, then the people who hold the junior tranches are paid. In other words, the people holding the senior tranches are shielded from losses relative to the people holding the junior tranches.

So, if most of the mortgage loans are high-quality loans, then most of the risk can be placed in the bottom few tranches, and the higher tranches are safe. The senior tranches get a higher credit rating than the junior tranches. What does all this have to do with the amount of capital a bank holds? By getting high credit ratings for the senior tranches, a bank can lower the risk weight on those assets and, as a result, lower the amount of capital it has to hold for them. Even though the junior tranches require *more* capital, the lower capital requirements on the senior tranches can be organized so that they *outweigh* the requirements on the junior tranches so that overall requirements decline. In other words, securitization is the means by which regulatory capital arbitrage lowers capital requirements.

Where We Are So Far

The Fed implemented a low interest rate policy in the early 2000s. Low mortgage rates led to increased mortgage borrowing and added demand to the housing market. As a result, house prices increased. At the same time:

- Banks were lowering lending standards to comply with the CRA.

- Fannie and Freddie came under political pressure to buy nontraditional loans (such as subprime loans) and to create a strong secondary market for mortgage-backed securities backed by nontraditional loans.

- Fannie and Freddie securitization and private securitization was going on, the latter of which was the means of achieving regulatory capital arbitrage, a process that increased leverage ratios in financial institutions.

House Prices Decline

As long as house prices were rising, the dance continued. It took only a small decline in house prices, though, to start things unraveling. And house prices did begin to decline, as shown in Exhibit 5. As house prices came down, some recent home buyers saw the prices they could sell their houses for fall below their loan amounts. (For many new homeowners, even a small price decline brought the value of their homes below the loan amount because they had put down very low—or no—down payments. In other words, their loan amounts were nearly equal to the purchase price of the house.)

Also, some of the mortgage loans that the borrowers had taken out had been adjustable rate mortgages, with a low interest payment in the early years, followed by a reset of the interest rate in later years. What these people found is that their low interest rates

EXHIBIT 5

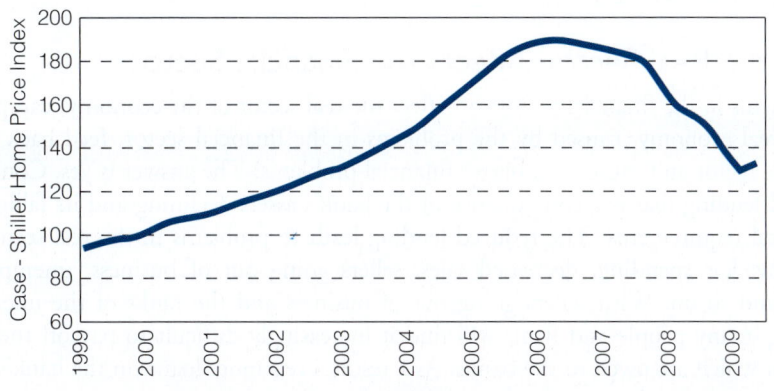

The Case-Shiller Home Price Index

House prices begin to decline in mid-2006.

were being reset at higher levels because mortgage rates had risen since they had taken out their loans.

As house prices declined, delinquency rates and foreclosure rates rose for two reasons: (1) Some individuals found their loan amounts greater than the price they could sell their houses for. (2) Other individuals found their mortgage rates resetting at higher rates, making for monthly payments that they could not afford. The banks holding assets in the form of subprime loans and MBSs then started to feel the consequences of the higher delinquency and foreclosure rates. Because of their high leverage ratios, they could not absorb much of a decline in asset values before they were insolvent or nearly so.

Domino Effects

When one bank finds that it cannot meet its capital requirements, how it responds can adversely affect other banks. For example, if bank A has to hold 5 percent of the value of its loans outstanding in capital, and it has $100 billion in loans outstanding, it must then hold $5 billion in capital. If the bank capital falls to $4 billion because the value of its loans is declining, it must reduce its assets to, say, $80 billion to be in compliance with the 5 percent capital requirement. The reduction in loans outstanding leads to less lending in the economy, which, as we know, can reduce economic activity.

Instead of reducing its outstanding loans to meet its capital requirement, suppose bank A sells some of its assets, including some mortgage-backed securities. Because bank A is in trouble and has to sell some of its MBSs, it might sell the securities at a lower price than it would have liked. Thereafter, bank B, now holding MBSs as assets on its balance sheet, finds the value of its assets declining, thus lowering its capital. As a result, bank B has less than enough capital to meets its capital requirements, and so it sells some of its MBSs to bank C, just as bank A did before. Soon bank C finds itself in the same position as bank B did earlier. And so on.

Thus the banks fall one after another, like dominos. The more dominos that fall, the more likely we are to see a big cutback in lending activity on the part of banks in order to meet their capital requirements. And the bigger the cutback in lending activity is, the more pronounced the effect will be in the real sector of the economy.

At the time, another problem could compound the problems of the banks. As word got out that a bank was near insolvency, the bank might find it harder to borrow money. Suppose bank A's assets have declined and it is approaching insolvency, and bank B hears that bank A is having problems. If bank A happens to ask bank B for a loan, bank B declines because it is afraid that bank A, faced with declining asset values, might not be able to repay the loan. (Banks ultimately must pay off their liabilities out of their assets. If the bank has assets of $100 and liabilities of $80, it could sell off its assets for $100 and pay off all $80 of its liabilities. But if its assets fall in value to, say, $70, then even if it sells off all its assets, it still couldn't pay off all its liabilities.)

How the Real Sector Affects the Financial Sector

If problems in the financial sector can affect the real sector of the economy, can problems in the real economy, caused by the problems in the financial sector, feed back into the financial sector and cause even bigger financial problems? The answer is yes. Consider the reduced lending that is a consequence of the bank's assets declining and its falling below its capital requirements. The reduced lending leads to problems in the real sector of the economy: less spending, decreased sales, sellers going out of business, unemployment rising, and so on. With sellers going out of business and the ranks of the unemployed swelling, many people and firms will find it increasingly difficult to pay off their debts, many of which are owed to the banks. As a result, even more loans on the bank's balance sheet lose value, pushing the bank ever closer to insolvency.

The Government Response

The federal government responded to the financial crisis and to the problems in the real sector of the economy in a number of ways. The responses can be categorized as *bailouts*, *fiscal stimulus*, and *easy money*.

- *Bailouts.* The $700 billion Troubled Asset Relief Program (TARP) took several forms: the U.S. Treasury's buying some of the bad assets on the banks' balance sheets, such as MBSs, and the government investing directly in some of the largest banks in the country, thus increasing the capital in banks. Also considered a bailout were the federal loans to General Motors and Chrysler in December 2008 to prevent the bankruptcy of these companies.

- *Fiscal Stimulus.* The Congress passed and President Obama signed a $787 billion fiscal stimulus bill in February 2009 in the hopes of injecting demand into the economy.

- *Easy Money.* In November 2008, the Federal Reserve announced that it would buy $800 billion of private debt. This was its attempt to increase lending and borrowing in the economy.

SELF-TEST

1. Explain how a high leverage ratio can lead to insolvency if assets decline in value.

2. What happens in the financial sector can affect the real sector, and what happens in the real sector can affect the financial sector. Do you agree or disagree? Explain your answer.

3. What is regulatory capital arbitrage?

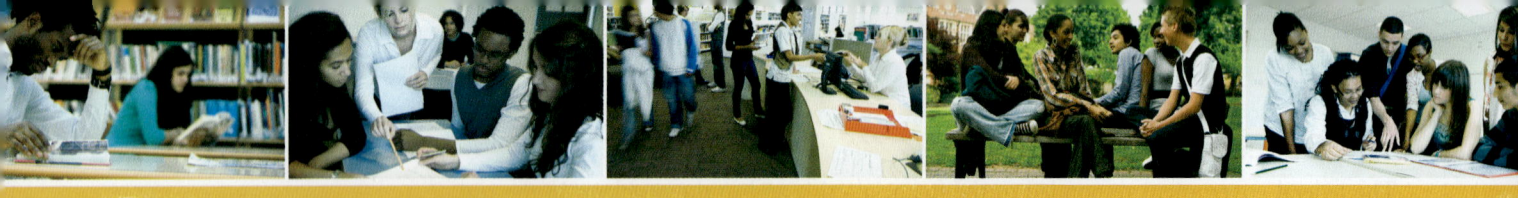

"Do Economists and the Public Always Understand the Causes of Financial Crises?"

STUDENT:

Are all economists agreed on the causes of the financial crisis? If the answer is no, why?

INSTRUCTOR:

First, all economists are not agreed on the cause of the financial crisis. In this chapter, principal players in causing the crisis were the Fed's low federal funds rate target policy, the politics of housing, and regulatory capital arbitrage. Most economists would agree that these factors all played a role in the financial crisis, but not all economists agree that each factor was of equal weight. For example, some economists might weight regulatory capital arbitrage as much more important to explaining the financial crisis than, say, the politics of housing (as described in the chapter). Also, not all economists agree that the Fed's low federal funds rate target policy mattered. Instead, it was the global savings glut.

STUDENT:

Is it a little like the Great Depression? Not all economists agree as to the cause of the Great Depression?

INSTRUCTOR:

Yes, it's somewhat like that. You're right that not all economists agree as to the cause(s) of the Great Depression, and among those economists who "sort of" agree on the main factors that caused the Great Depression, not all of them place equal weight on the various factors.

STUDENT:

Another issue that bothers me a little is the fact that when something big happens on the economic scene—like a financial crisis—the lay public seems to be all over the map commenting on what they think caused the crisis. For example, some people seem to think the latest

---

CHAPTER SUMMARY

A VIEW OF THE ECONOMY

- One way to view the economy is as consisting of two sectors: a financial sector and a real sector. The financial sector consists of financial institutions—commercial banks, investment banks, hedge funds, brokerage firms, and more. The real sector consists of firms that produce goods and services, individuals that buy goods and services, individuals that work for firms, and more.

A FINANCIAL CRISIS

- A financial crisis occurs when financial firms and financial markets undergo a major disruption. In turn, these problems make it difficult for persons to obtain loans from banks and other financial institutions.
- Problems in the financial sector can affect the real sector.

- One way to view a financial crisis is as a balance sheet problem. Specifically, the assets of financial institutions are declining in value, which reduces the net worth (or capital) of the institutions and moves them closer to insolvency. As these institutions approach or reach insolvency, they pull back on lending activities. Pulling back on their lending activities can, in turn, adversely affect the real sector of the economy.

RISKY ASSETS

- Describing the financial crisis as a balance sheet problem requires us to identify the assets that declined in the mid-2000s, causing asset values for financial institutions to decline and moving them closer to insolvency. These assets include subprime loans, other nontraditional loans, mortgage-backed securities, and collateralized debt obligations.

financial crisis was caused by government, specifically, the Fed and Congress and Fannie and Freddie. Others seem to blame the banks and other financial institutions for taking excessive risks. With respect to the latter, you sometimes hear that the financial community was just out to make a lot of money as fast as possible and so they pushed off these subprime loans to a lot of people. It seems to me that what we think about the cause of the crisis has a lot to do with what we then think is the right preventive medicine for the next crisis.

> **INSTRUCTOR:**

In other words, if the cause of the crisis is that financial institutions weren't regulated enough, then the solution is to regulate banks more. Or if the cause of the crisis was a too lenient Fed combined with a lot of politics in the housing market, then the solution is some sort of monetary rule for the Fed and the depoliticization of the housing market.

> **STUDENT:**

Yes, that is what I am taking about. If you think X caused the crisis, then you want to do something about X. But if you think Y caused the crisis, then, of course, you want to do something about Y.

> **INSTRUCTOR:**

I can only agree with you on that. Whatever one believes about the causes of the financial crisis does seem to influence his or her opinion of what should be done to prevent another such crisis.

POINTS TO REMEMBER

1. Not all economists are agreed on the cause(s) of the financial crisis. Not all members of the public are agreed on the cause(s) of the financial crisis.

2. What one identifies as the cause(s) of the financial crisis does influence his opinion of what should be done to prevent another financial crisis.

THE FED, THE FEDERAL FUNDS RATE TARGET, AND THE GLOBAL SAVINGS GLUT

- Some economists argue that the Fed set its target federal funds rate "too low" in the early 2000s, especially during the period 2002–2005. This had consequences, one of which was that mortgage rates declined, giving individuals an incentive to borrow to buy a house. As a result, the low mortgage interest rates fueled buying in the housing market, driving up house prices.

- Some economists argue that the cause of the low interest rates was the global savings glut. Specifically, emerging countries in the world began to save more, and these extra savings found their way to the United States, where they increased the supply of loanable funds and lowered interest rates (one interest rate in particular was the mortgage interest rate). The low mortgage interest rates fueled buying in the housing market, driving up house prices.

THE TAYLOR RULES AND INTEREST RATES

- According to economist John Taylor, the Fed set its federal funds rate target "too low" during the early 2000s, as measured by what it would be if it were set by the Taylor rule. Accordingly, the low interest rates that followed fueled borrowing and the sharp rise in housing prices. One piece of evidence Taylor cited as evidence in favor of his argument is that there is a strong correlation between a housing boom in different countries and deviations from the Taylor Rule.

- Alan Greenspan has argued that low long-term interest rates, not short-term interest rates, were the causing of the housing boom. Moreover, the Fed, he argues, has more control over short-term rates (such as the federal funds rate) than over long-term rates (such as the 30-year fixed mortgage rate).

THE POLITICS OF HOUSING

- Mortgage lending standards decline in the 1990s and early 2000s in the United States. There was a move away from traditional lending practices to nontraditional lending practices.

- The Community Reinvestment Act (CRA) was passed in 1977 to encourage financial institutions to meet the needs of borrowers in all segments of their communities. In 1995, Congress revised the CRA to give banks a stronger incentive to increase the percentage of mortgage loans (among other loans) going to low- and moderate-income borrowers.

- Beginning in the early 1990s, government pressure was placed on both Fannie Mae and Freddie Mac to increase their purchases of mortgages made to low- to moderate-income families.

- The entrance of Fannie Mae and Freddie Mac into the market of buying subprime loans and creating mortgage-backed securities created a market in subprime lending. Specifically, the large-scale expansion of Fannie and Freddie into the subprime loan business made it profitable for other financial institutions to grant subprime loans in order to sell them to Fannie and Freddie.

THE ROLE OF LEVERAGE

- Leverage is the use of borrowed funds to increase the returns that can be earned with a given amount of capital.

- Consider a bank with $100 in assets, $92 in liabilities, and $8 net worth or capital. Its leverage ratio—the ratio of its assets to its capital—is 100 to 8, or 12½ to 1.

- A bank with a higher leverage ratio has a higher percentage rise in capital when asset values are rising. Bank A has $100 in assets, $92 in liabilities, and $8 net worth, or capital. Its leverage ratio is 12½ to 1. If asset values rise to $110, its capital is now $18. Going from capital of $8 to $18 is a 125 percent rise in capital. Bank B has $100 in assets, $97 in liabilities, and capital of $3. If assets values rise to $110, its capital is now $13. Going from $3 to $13 capital is a 333 percent rise in capital. Therefore, if asset values are expected to rise, highly leveraged banks will witness a higher percentage rise in their capital than low-leveraged banks will witness. Alternatively, when asset values are expected to decline, highly leveraged banks will witness a higher percentage of decline in their capital than low-leveraged banks will. Finally, a bank with a high leverage ratio is more likely to fall into insolvency when assets decline in value than is a bank with a low leverage ratio.

REGULATORY CAPITAL, RISK-WEIGHTED ASSETS, AND REGULATORY CAPITAL ARBITRAGE

- Regulatory capital is the amount of capital that a financial institution must hold because of regulatory requirements.

- Regulatory capital arbitrage is a means of changing the composition of assets in such a way as to lower the overall amount of capital a financial institution holds for a given level of assets.

- Financial institutions can increase returns (during a time of rising asset values) by engaging in regulatory capital arbitrage. One way to do this is through securitization. Regulatory capital arbitrage is part of the reason banks and other financial institutions had high leverage ratios when asset values were increasing.

THINGS BEGIN TO UNRAVEL

- The decline in house prices and the rise in interest rates caused delinquency rates and foreclosure rates to rise, for two reasons: (1) Some individuals found their loan amounts greater than the price they could sell their houses for. (2) Other individuals found their mortgage rates resetting at higher rates.

- Banks that held assets in the form of subprime loans and mortgage-backed securities began to feel the effects of heightened delinquency and foreclosure rates. As a result, asset values for banks began to decline. Because of the high leverage ratios, it didn't take much of a decline in asset values before banks were either insolvent or nearly so.

- As banks became insolvent or approached insolvency, they pulled back on their lending, reducing economic activity in the real sector of the economy.

- Problems in the real sector began to feed back into the financial sector.

KEY TERMS AND CONCEPTS

Financial Intermediary	Net Worth (or Capital)	Equity (in a Home)	Special-Purpose Vehicle
Insolvency	Subprime Mortgage Loans	Leverage	(SPV)
Balance Sheet	Mortgage-Backed Securities	Regulatory Capital	
Asset	(MBS)	Regulatory Capital Arbitrage	
Liability	Adjustable Rate Mortgage	Securitization	

QUESTIONS AND PROBLEMS

1. Explain how FDIC insurance can cause banks to take on riskier loans than they would if FDIC didn't exist.

2. What are some differences between a subprime loan and a traditional loan? What is the difference between a mortgage-backed security and a collateralized debt obligation?

3. What is an asset? A liability? Net worth, or capital?

4. Explain how a low federal funds rate target can influence mortgage interest rates.

5. What does it mean to say that the financial crisis can be viewed as a balance sheet problem?

6. The financial sector can affect the real sector, and the real sector can affect the financial sector. Do you agree or disagree? Explain your answer.

7. What role, if any, did Congress, Fannie Mae, and Freddie Mac play in creating a market for subprime lending?

8. It has been said that the decline in house prices precipitated the financial crisis. How so?

9. What role, if any, did the CRA play in relaxing lending standards?

10. What role does securitization play in regulatory capital arbitrage?

11. Is there any connection between rising housing prices and delinquency and foreclosure rates? Explain your answer.

12. Explain the process of regulatory capital arbitrage.

13. What role does Alan Greenspan say that short-term interest rates (such as the federal funds rate) played in the housing boom? What role did long-term interest rates play?

14. Illustrate with a numerical example how a high leverage ratio produces a different percentage rise in capital than a lower leverage ratio when asset values are rising.

15. Some argue that the global savings glut acted as a catalyst for the boom in housing prices in the early 2000s. What is their argument?

16. What does it mean to say a bank has a leverage ratio of 10 to 1?

17. Some argue that the Fed acted as a catalyst for the boom in housing prices in the early 2000s. What is their argument?

WORKING WITH NUMBERS AND GRAPHS

1. A bank has $1 million in assets and $700,000 in liabilities. What is its net worth? What is its leverage ratio?

2. The bank identified in the previous question finds that its assets increase in value by 15 percent. By what percentage does its capital increase?

3. A bank has $1 million in assets and $920,000 in liabilities. What is its net worth? What is its leverage ratio?

4. The bank identified in the previous question finds that its assets decline in value by 4 percent. By what percentage does its capital decrease?

5. A bank has $400 in asset X, $500 in asset Y, and $300 in asset Z. Each asset has a different risk weight. Asset X has a risk weight of 10 percent, Y has a risk weight of 40 percent, and Z has a risk weight of 70 percent. What dollar amount do risk-weighted assets equal? Assuming that the bank has to hold capital equal to 7 percent of its risk-weighted assets, how much capital does the bank have to hold?

CHAPTER 19

DEBATES IN MACROECONOMICS OVER THE ROLE AND EFFECTS OF GOVERNMENT

Introduction Most of this book has been about economics, with mention of government here and there. This chapter discusses some of the things that economists have to say about government, especially with respect to the role and effects of government in the economy.

MACROECONOMICS AND GOVERNMENT: THE DEBATE

Macroeconomists are agreed on some things. For example, if you ask 10 economists to identify the tools the Fed has at its disposal to change the money supply, you are likely to get the same answer from all 10 economists. If you ask 10 economists to identify the assumptions in the simple quantity theory of money, again you are likely to get the same answer from all 10.

However, macroeconomists are not agreed on some things. If you ask 10 economists how sensitive investment is likely to be to a change in the interest rate in the current environment, not all 10 are likely to give you the same answer. Some might say that investment is likely to change a lot in response to a change in the interest rate. In other words, the elasticity of investment (the percentage change in investment given a percentage change in the interest rate) is likely to be high. Other economists might disagree and argue that investment will not change much (or at all) if the interest rate changes.

This type of issue—*how much* will investment fall if the interest rate rises—is an *empirical issue*. Although all economists might agree that investment will fall if the interest rate rises, they will not all agree as to *how much* it will fall. Other empirical issues that economists might not agree on are *how much* will aggregate demand rise if government increases its spending or *how flexible or inflexible* wages are in the current economic environment.

Besides disagreements that focus on empirical issues, economists often express disagreement over the role government *should* play in the economy given their understanding of how the economy works. Suppose three economists agree that Real GDP is headed down, that prices are headed up, and that the prospects for economic growth look bleak for the near future. Even though all three economists have the same diagnosis, they will

Elasticity of Investment
A measure of the responsiveness of investment to changes in the interest rate.

not necessarily recommend the same government policies. The first economist might argue that government should do nothing (no government medicine), the second might argue that medicine X is needed, and the third might recommend medicine Z. The first economist has government doing nothing, the second economist has the government doing X, and the third economist has government doing Z.

Ask most students of macroeconomics (especially those who taking their first course in macroeconomics) what they would like to take away from the course, and they say something like this: "We would like to get explanations for the various macroeconomic phenomena (recessions, inflation, high unemployment) and what is the right approach to deal with a particular macroeconomic phenomenon." Their thinking is like a doctor's: "What is wrong with the patient, and what is the best medicine for the patient to take to get well?" In economic terms, the questions would be, "What is wrong with the economy, and what is the best policy to enact to get the economy well?" But the answers in economics are not so clear-cut. President Harry S. Truman once said, "Give me a one-handed economist. All my economists say 'On the one hand, and then on the other hand.'" No doubt students of macroeconomics experience some of Truman's frustration with economists.

Because this is probably your first college course in macroeconomics, you would probably be content with a "one-handed" answer. But you wouldn't be getting an accurate picture of economics theory and its effects on policy. To present an accurate picture, you need to hear some of the debates in macroeconomics, especially as they relate to the role of government in the economy. Some of what we will discuss here has been discussed in earlier chapters, sometimes with a different emphasis. The outline in this chapter is fairly straightforward. We identify a number of macroeconomic topics. Next, we explain how government comes up in the discussions of various economists with respect to that topic.

TAX CUTS, TAX REVENUE, AND BUDGET DEFICITS

Suppose the federal government is running a budget deficit; government spending is greater than tax revenues. To reduce the size of the deficit, some economists propose income tax cuts. Other economists argue that income tax cuts will not lead to a smaller deficit. The source of the disagreement between the two sets of economists is the issue of whether tax cuts will or will not raise tax revenue.

One group of economists argues this way: (1) If income tax rates are cut, individuals will choose to work and produce more. (2) As a result, they will generate more income and the tax base will rise. (3) If the tax base rises by more than tax rates are cut, then tax revenue will rise. (4) More tax revenue will end up reducing the size of the budget deficit.

Another group of economists challenges assumption 3. They argue that that the tax base is not likely to rise by more than tax rates are cut, so that result 4 will be less tax revenue and therefore a bigger budget deficit.

The discussion goes back to this equation, first identified in Chapter 11:

$$\text{Tax revenues} = \text{Tax base} \times \text{(average) Tax rate}$$

Almost all economists will agree that if the tax rate is cut, the tax base will rise, but not all economists agree as to *how much* the tax base will rise. In other words, if the tax rate is cut 10 percent, will the tax base rise by more than, less than, or as much as the cut in the tax rate?

What separates economists here is an empirical issue. Specifically, economists sometimes disagree on what is likely to happen given a certain action. In other words, if tax rates are cut, then what? Do tax revenues rise, decline, or remain constant?

To recap in terms of these differing economic perspectives:

- *Economist A:* Tax cuts will raise tax revenue, and increased tax revenue will decrease the size of the budget deficit.

- *Economist B:* Tax cuts will lower tax revenue, and decreased tax revenue will increase the size of the budget deficit.

THE ECONOMY: SELF-REGULATING OR NOT?

One major debate in macroeconomics focuses on whether the economy is self regulating. Specifically, if an economy is in a recessionary gap, can it move itself into long-run equilibrium? To a degree, the answer depends on whether wages are flexible or inflexible downward. If wages are flexible, then an economy can remove itself from a recessionary gap. Hence, government need not get involved in managing the economy. But if wages are inflexible downward, then an economy cannot remove itself from a recessionary gap; an economy can get stuck in a recessionary gap. The economy can get unstuck only by means of economic policy enacted by either the Congress or the president (in terms of fiscal policy) or by the Fed (in terms of monetary policy).

To recap in terms of these differing economic perspectives:

- *Economist A:* Wages are flexible, so that if the economy is in a recessionary gap, it will soon remove itself from the gap. Government doesn't have to do anything.

- *Economist B:* Wages are inflexible downward, so that if the economy is in a recessionary gap, it may be stuck there. The best course of action is for the federal government to implement expansionary fiscal policy or for the Fed to implement expansionary monetary policy to remove the economy from the recessionary gap.

MORE GOVERNMENT SPENDING OR A CUT IN TAXES: WHICH GIVES A BIGGER BANG FOR THE BUCK?

The economy is in a recessionary gap, and economists call for a demand-side expansionary fiscal policy measure. As we know, expansionary fiscal policy consists of (1) an increase in government purchases or (2) a cut in taxes or (3) both. Not all economists are likely to agree on the best way to proceed. One economist will argue that a rise in government purchases will give the economy the "biggest bang for the buck." A $1 rise in government purchases will (by changing aggregate demand) raise Real GDP by more than a $1 cut in taxes. In other words, the government spending multiplier [the number that, when multiplied by the change in government spending, gives us the change in total spending (and, if prices are constant, the change in Real GDP)] is larger than the tax multiplier [the number that, when multiplied by the change in taxes, gives us the change in total spending (and if prices are constant, the change in Real GDP]. Another economist argues just the opposite: the tax multiplier is larger than the government spending multiplier, so a $1 cut in taxes will raise Real GDP by more than a $1 rise in government purchases.

Suppose that the government spending multiplier is 1.4 and the tax multiplier is 3. This means that a $1 rise in government spending will increase Real GDP by $1.40, and a $1 tax cut will increase Real GDP by $3. Now the debate and disagreement among economists can focus on the value of the two multipliers.

In the standard textbook Keynesian analysis, there is reason to believe that the government spending multiplier is larger than the tax multiplier. Here is the reasoning: when

Government Spending Multiplier
The number that, when multiplied by the change in government spending, gives us the change in total spending (and, if prices are constant, the change in Real GDP).

Tax Multiplier
The number that, when multiplied by the change in taxes, gives us the change in total spending (and if prices are constant, the change in Real GDP).

government spends $1, the entire $1 enters the spending stream. However, when government cuts taxes by $1, individuals spend some of the dollar they now get to keep and save some of it. In other words, they might spend 60¢ of the dollar and save 40¢. What separates economists, though, is that not all economists hold to the standard textbook analysis. Some economists argue that the standard textbook analysis does not take into account all the ways that tax cuts can be stimulative.

To recap in terms of these differing economic perspectives:

- *Economist A:* The economy needs expansionary fiscal policy to remove it from a recessionary gap. Government should either raise its spending or cut taxes. I believe the government spending multiplier is larger than the tax multiplier; so I suggest government increase its spending.

- *Economist B:* The economy needs expansionary fiscal policy to remove it from a recessionary gap. Government should either raise its spending or cut taxes. I believe the tax multiplier is larger than the government spending multiplier, so I suggest government cut taxes.

MORE GOVERNMENT SPENDING OR A CUT IN TAXES: THE SIZE AND SCOPE OF GOVERNMENT

The *size* of government relates to the resources over which government has command. Suppose the economy has 100 units of labor, with 30 of the units allocated through government and 70 units through the private sector. Government grows in size, relative to the private sector, if it begins to allocate more than 30 units of labor and the private sector begins to allocate less than 70 units of labor.

The *scope* of government relates to what government does. Suppose government can provide for the national defense, build roads and bridges, provide schools, institute and operate Social Security. The scope of government relates to how many things government actually does. If it only provides for the national defense and builds roads and bridges, then its scope is more limited than if it provides for the national defense, builds roads and bridges, and implements and operates Social Security.

Both a rise in government purchases and a cut in taxes are expansionary fiscal policy measures, but both don't have the same impact on the size and scope of government. To illustrate, suppose economist A calls specifically for more government spending to get the economy out of a recessionary gap. The argument is standard fare: a rise in government purchases increases aggregate demand and removes the economy from the recessionary gap.

But couldn't a tax cut, instead of greater government spending, do the same thing? For instance, an income tax cut will raise after-tax (or disposable) income. With greater after-tax income, individuals will buy more goods and services, thus increasing consumption in the economy. And a rise in consumption will raise aggregate demand, perhaps by enough to remove the economy out of a recessionary gap.

The decision between government spending and tax cuts depends partly on the effect that each has on the size and scope of government. Economist A favors bigger government (government making more decisions); when it comes to advocating increased government purchases or tax cuts, he argues for increased government purchases. He sees increased government purchases as increasing the size and possibly the scope of government. Economist B favors smaller government (government making fewer decisions); when it comes to advocating increased government purchases or tax cuts, she argues for tax cuts. She sees cutting taxes as decreasing the size and possibly the scope of government.

To recap in terms of these differing economic perspectives:

- *Economist A:* Expansionary fiscal policy is needed to raise aggregate demand and remove the economy from a recessionary gap. The choice of fiscal policy measures is between more government spending or a cut in taxes. Since I am in favor of bigger government, I choose more government spending.

- *Economist B:* Expansionary fiscal policy is needed to raise aggregate demand and remove the economy from a recessionary gap. The choice of fiscal policy measures is between more government spending or a cut in taxes. Since I am in favor of smaller government, I choose a cut in taxes.

THE DEGREE OF CROWDING OUT

Suppose 10 out of 10 economists agree that the economy is in a recessionary gap. Seven of them argue that an expansionary fiscal policy measure in the form of greater government spending will remove the economy from the recessionary gap. Their argument is that if government purchases increase, aggregate demand in the economy will rise, and the economy will move out of the recessionary gap. Also, any increase in government purchases will not crowd out any private sector spending (i.e., spending by households and businesses).

The other three economists see things a little differently. They argue that a lot of crowding out is likely, thus weakening the impact of the expansionary fiscal policy measure. Their argument is that if government purchases increase, aggregate demand probably will not rise enough to remove the economy from the recessionary gap because for every dollar the government spends, it has to borrow a dollar. In short, to get an additional dollar to spend, government must first borrow it. If the borrowed dollars come from the private sector, then the private sector will have fewer dollars to spend on various goods and services; so more government spending means less private sector spending. The rise in aggregate demand due to more government spending is largely offset by a reduction in aggregate demand because of less private sector spending. In the end, aggregate demand will change little, if at all, so that government will have been ineffective in its attempt to remove the economy from the recessionary gap. In terms of jobs, jobs created or saved because of increased government spending are offset by jobs destroyed by a decline in private sector spending.

To recap in terms of these differing economic perspectives:

- *Economist A:* A rise in government purchases will increase aggregate demand and remove the economy from the recessionary gap because little or no crowding out will occur. A rise in government purchases will end up increasing the number of jobs in the economy.

- *Economist B:* A rise in government purchases will not increase aggregate demand and remove the economy from the recessionary gap because of complete (or nearly complete) crowding out.

THE POLITICS OF GOVERNMENT SPENDING

Consider two settings. In setting 1, fiscal policy emerges in a political vacuum. In setting 2, it umdergoes a political process. The fiscal policy created in a political vacuum is probably not going to be the same as the fiscal policy that arises from a political process. For example, government spends $100 on good X in setting 1. Will it spend $100 on good X in setting 2? Probably not. In setting 2, it might spend more or less on good X. In fact, in setting 2, it might not spend any money on good X.

As an example, in 2008–2009, the U.S. economy was on a downward slide—Real GDP was declining, the unemployment rate was rising, and some companies were cutting employment, while others were closing down. Many economists argued that an expansionary policy measure was needed to strengthen the economy (specifically, to turn the decline in Real GDP around, to reduce the unemployment rate, etc.). Some economists called for more government spending. However, the government-needs-to-spend-more group contained factions. Some argued that the important objective for the economy is that government spends more; of lesser importance was what government spent the money on. In other words, whether government spent money having people dig ditches and then filling them up or building bridges and roads, a dollar spent is a dollar spent as far as the economy goes.

Other economists disagreed, arguing that how the money was spent would make a difference in the effect on the economy. Money spent on having people dig ditches and then filling them up is not as beneficial to the economy as spending money to build bridges and roads. More importantly, these same economists argued that much of the additional money spent by government would end up motivated by politics instead of economics. In other words, members of Congress might find a large spending bill just the cover they needed to reward their political allies. Of course, from an economic perspective, if a dollar spent here is the same as a dollar spent there, rewarding one's political allies does not come with an economywide cost. But if spending a dollar in some ways is more productive for the economy than spending it in other ways, them how the dollar is spent matters a lot.

To recap in terms of these differing economic perspectives:

- *Economist A:* An expansionary fiscal policy measure is needed to increase Real GDP, lower the unemployment rate, and so on. I propose $100 billion more in government spending. It doesn't really matter what the $100 billion is spent on; the important thing is that the money is spent.

- *Economist B:* An expansionary fiscal policy measure is needed to increase Real GDP, lower the unemployment rate, and so on. Ideally, the economy needs $100 billion more in government spending. But how the money is spent will be determined by Congress, and Congress is likely to be motivated by political interests. Furthermore, not all spending is the same. Some spending is better for the economy than other spending. I think much of the spending that we will get from Congress will be motivated by politics instead of by economics, and sometimes the spending motivated by politics will be of little help in turning the economy around. In the end, I have my doubts as to how effective an increase in government spending will be in aiding the economy.

MONETARY POLICY: RULES VERSUS DISCRETION

With regard to the creation of monetary policy, some economists argue in favor of a rule-based system, whether it is the Taylor rule or setting the growth of the money supply equal to some fixed percentage rate (such as 3 percent). Other economists argue in favor of discretion for the Fed, saying that the Fed needs to have the flexibility to create the best monetary policy possible given the circumstances.

The debate between these economists centers around two major points. The first has to do with the effects of different types of monetary policy: rule-based versus discretionary. Those who advocate rule-based monetary policy often say that it is more likely than discretionary monetary policy to produce nearly stable prices, low unemployment, low and stable interest rates, and the right overall conditions for sustained economic growth. Economists who advocate discretionary monetary policy argue that it is more likely to achieve the

economics 24/7

What Does a Stimulus Bill Look Like?

In February 2009, the U.S. Congress passed a $787 billion stimulus bill (an expansionary fiscal policy measure). At the time the bill passed, various economists had different things to say about it. Some argued that it was the right thing to do to stimulate the economy. Some argued that it wouldn't stimulate the economy. Some argued that the bill was filled with "political pork," which wasn't always consistent with the kind of spending and tax cuts needed to jump-start the economy. On February 17, 2009, the *Wall Street Journal* published the details of the stimulus bill in terms of (1) classification—such as spending or tax provisions, (2) keyword, (3) description, and (4) cost. The full details of the stimulus can be found at http://online.wsj.com/public/resources/documents/STIMULUS_FINAL_0217.html. Here we show you only a small sample of a few provisions in the stimulus bill.

© IMAGE COPYRIGHT TRAVEL BUG, 2009. USED UNDER LICENSE FROM SHUTTERSTOCK.COM

Classification	Keyword	Description	Cost ($ millions)
Spending	Farming	Loans to rural homeowners	$ 200
Aid	Food	Adult and child day care meals and snacks	100
Spending	Commerce	Extra money for Census	1,000
Spending	Science	NASA climate research	400
Spending	Energy	Training of electric grid workers	100
Spending	Government	Oversight of Small Business Administration spending	10
Spending	Arts	Grants to fund art projects in nonprofit sector	50
Aid	Education	Increase in Pell grants	17,114
Spending	Military	Army child development centers	80
Spending	State	Passport and training funding for State Department	90
Spending	Transportation	Grants for highway improvements	29,000
Aid	Aid to States	Aid to states to balance education budgets prevent cutbacks and modernize schools	40,600
Tax provisions	Business tax cuts	Tax cuts for low-income housing investors	143
Aid	Other tax cuts	U.S. lumber, steel and other companies can keep money they were given from Canadian and Mexican import duties	90
Aid	Individual Aid	Extension of jobless benefits up to 33 weeks	29,960
Tax provision	Individual tax cut	Tax credit up to $2,500 for tuition and college expenses	13,907
Aid	Healthcare	Federal aid to states for Medicare spending	90,044
Spending	Transportation	Grants to Amtrak	1,300
Spending	Housing	Repairs and modernization of public housing projects	1,000
Tax provisions	Energy tax cuts	Tax credit for plug-in electric vehicle conversion	2,002
Spending	Outdoors	Priority road, bridge, and trail repairs	180

desired economic results because the monetary authority has the flexibility to shape the best monetary policy to the existing circumstances.

The second major point is that rules-based monetary policy advocates often assert that discretionary monetary policy, all too often, is motivated by political instead of economic interests. A rules-based monetary policy removes monetary policy from politics, they argue, in the end, making for better monetary policy. The money supply is too important an economic variable, with too many far-reaching effects, to have politicians pushing it one way or another to serve their short-run, the-next-election-is-around-the-corner interests.

To recap in terms of these differing economic perspectives:

- *Economist A:* A monetary rule is preferred to a discretionary Fed. The former is more likely to bring about stable prices, low unemployment, and so on. In addition, a monetary rule removes monetary policy from politics.

- *Economist B:* A discretionary Fed is preferred to a monetary rule. The Fed needs the flexibility to tailor monetary policy to the existing circumstances.

BAILOUTS

Not all economists are agreed as to whether government should bail out companies in financial problems. Suppose a large company employs thousands of workers, pays millions of dollars in taxes to the state in which it is located, buys hundreds of parts from its suppliers in assembling its product, and has thousands of bondholders and stockholders. Then the company finds itself in dire financial straits—so dire that the company finds it difficult to repay its debt or to obtain loans. Without some financial assistance, the company will probably go out of business. If it does, its home state will lose millions of dollars in tax revenue, employees will lose their jobs, its suppliers lose sales revenues (perhaps causing them to go out of business), fire workers, and so on, and thousands of investors will see their personal wealth diminished. Does the government have a role to play in bailing out this company?

One way to answer that question is to ask another: "Who loses if the company goes out of business?" Certainly the owners of the business lose, but then there might be others, such as the employees who lose their jobs, the suppliers of the company who lose business, the state that loses the tax revenue, and the investors who lose personal wealth. If the total dollar amount of loss is $50 billion and the federal government bailout of the company comes to $30 billion in taxpayer funds, then, for $30 billion, a $50 billion loss could be averted. Some would argue that bailing out the company (and, one step removed, those who would be adversely affected by the company's failure) would be economically advantageous. In fact, this was the argument when the federal government bailed out several financial institutions and both General Motors and Chrysler during the financial and economic crisis in the mid-to-late 2000s. A little bailing out here and there may be better than letting large businesses fail and in the process drag down others with them.

AP PHOTO/MARK LENNIHAN, FILE

However, another viewpoint goes like this: (1) The people ultimately doing the bailing out—the taxpayers—incur the cost of the bailout, while others receive the benefits (such as the company owners, the employees, and others). Why should the taxpayers pay the costs while others receive the benefits, especially when many of the taxpayers have less income than the persons who are bailed out? (2) If firms know they will be bailed out, they will take more risks than if they know they won't be. The possibility of a bailout creates an environment in which more and more firms will need bailouts. The owners and managers of firms will want to take ever more risk because if high returns follow, then they are the winners, but if failure comes, the federal government, with taxpayer funds in hand, will bail them out. "Heads, we win; tails, others lose." That will bring on many more business failures than "heads, we win; tails, we lose."

To recap in terms of these differing economic perspectives:

- *Economist A:* Ideally, bailing out companies is not a good idea. But Company X is a large company, and if it goes out of business, that will adversely affect hundreds of thousands of persons. Bailing out the company is better than letting it fail; we lose more by letting the company fail than by saving it. Some companies are simply too big to be allowed to fail. Their failure is like an earthquake, adversely affecting all the people around them. To save the innocent, you sometimes have to save the not-so-innocent.

- *Economist B:* Who is "we" when you say, "We lose more by letting the company fail than by saving it?" Some persons gain by having the company bailed out, and others lose. Furthermore, if we continue to tell companies that the federal government will be there if they fail, we simply create an environment in which we privatize gains (the companies keep the gains if there are any) and socialize the costs (spread the costs among millions of taxpayers if the companies end up in financial problems). In the end, this will lead to more companies that "need" to be bailed out.

Demand-Side and Supply-Side Views of the Economy and Government Tools to Change Real GDP

Much of our discussion of macroeconomics has been in terms of aggregate demand and aggregate supply. Whereas the *AD* curve was always represented as downward sloping, the *AS* curve was shown in different ways according to the macroeconomic model. For example, in the simple quantity theory of money, the *AS* curve is vertical. In many other models we represented, it is upward sloping. Exhibit 1(a)–(b) shows two aggregate supply curves.

Each of these two aggregate supply curves has its own meaning in terms of changes in aggregate demand. If the aggregate supply curve is vertical and aggregate demand rises—the *AD* curve shifts rightward—the price level will rise, but Real GDP will not change. See Exhibit 1(c). But if the aggregate supply curve is upward sloping, a rise in aggregate demand will raise both the price level and Real GDP. See Exhibit 1(d).

Depending on your view of whether the real aggregate supply curve is vertical or upward sloping, how would you respond to this question? "Assuming that the objective is to raise Real GDP, would it be preferable for government to try to increase aggregate demand or aggregate supply?"

The economists who view the *AS* curve as vertical will say that government cannot do anything to raise Real GDP from the demand side of the economy, because changes in *AD* don't change Real GDP if the *AS* curve is vertical. Forget an increase in government purchases, a demand-side tax cut, or expansionary monetary policy. These actions may change *AD*, but a change in *AD*—in the face of a vertical AS curve—will lead only to a change in prices, not in Real GDP. The only way for Real GDP to rise is for the *AS* curve to shift rightward.

Of course, economists who view the *AS* curve as upward sloping will disagree. For them, both a change in *AD* and a change in *AS* will affect Real GDP. Changes in Real GDP may be realized by changes that originate on either the demand side or the supply side of the economy. If the aggregate supply curve is upward sloping, an increase in

EXHIBIT 1

The Aggregate Supply Curve and What Government Can and Cannot Do

Two aggregate supply curves: (a) The curve is vertical; (b) it is upward sloping. In this text, we have often spoken of each of these two differently shaped curves. (c) Changes in aggregate demand will not change Real GDP if the aggregate supply curve is vertical.

(d) Changes in aggregate demand will change Real GDP if the aggregate supply curve is upward sloping. For the vertical-AS economist, changes in Real GDP originate only on the supply-side economy; so government policy that aims to affect the demand side of the economy will change only prices, not Real GDP. For the upward-sloping-AS economist, changes in Real GDP can originate on either

the demand side or the supply side of the economy; so government policy that aims to affect either side of the economy will not only change prices, but Real GDP too. For the vertical-AS economist, government has fewer tools (demand-side fiscal policy and monetary policy won't work) to change Real GDP than the upward-sloping AS economist would say government has.

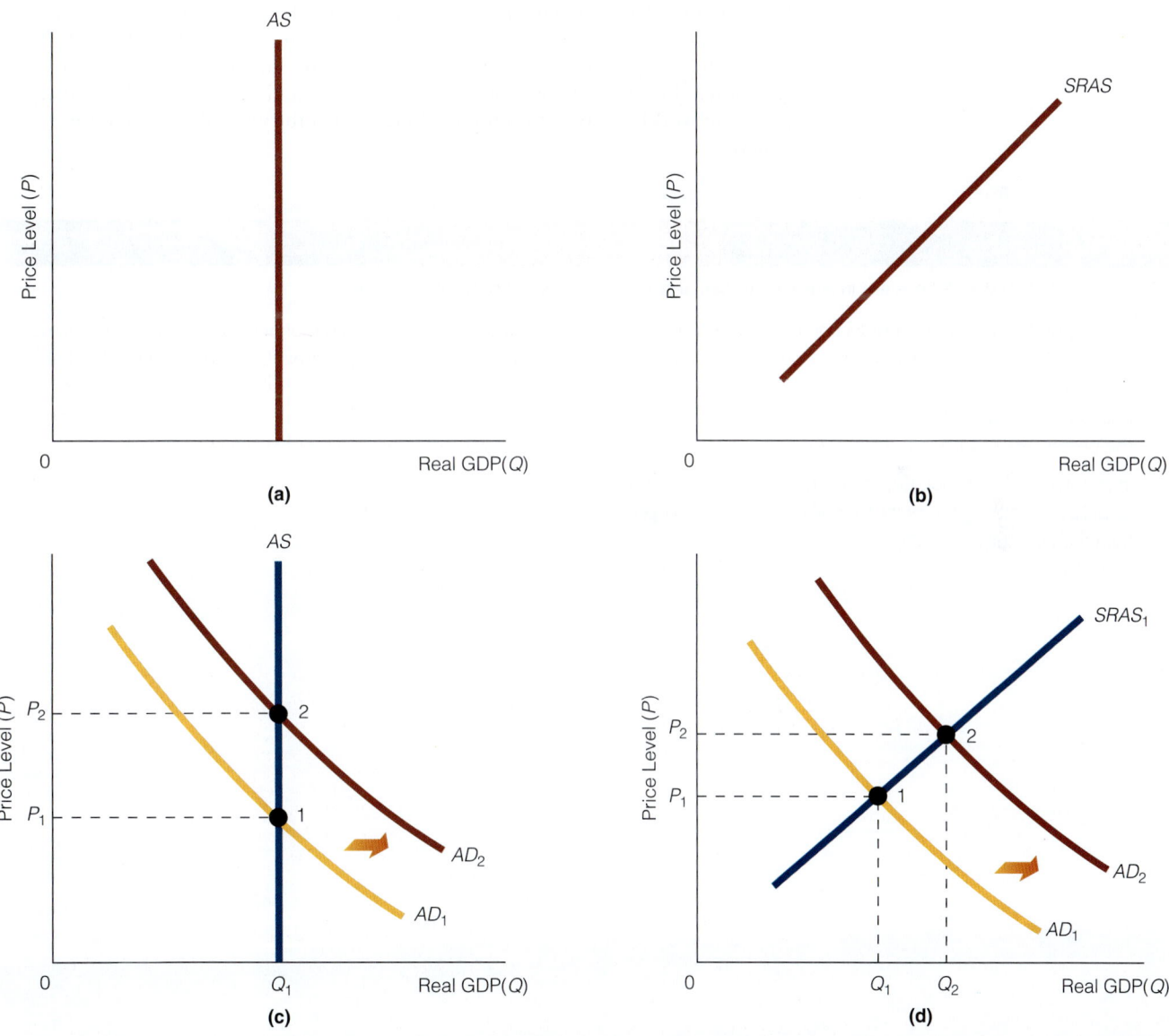

aggregate demand will lead to a rise in Real GDP (at least in the short run), as will an increase in aggregate supply. Viewing things from the demand side of the economy, these economists would argue that a rise in government purchases, a demand-side tax cut, and monetary policy will all be effective at changing Real GDP.

Comparing our two camps of economists, the vertical-*AS* group sees fewer government tools (demand-side fiscal policy and monetary policy won't work) capable of raising Real GDP than do the upward-sloping *AS* economists.

To recap in terms of these differing economic perspectives:

- *Economist A:* The aggregate supply curve is vertical. Therefore, government actions designed to change aggregate demand in the economy will not lead to changes in Real GDP. Changes in Real GDP come from the supply side of the economy, not the demand side. Government has fewer tools (demand-side fiscal policy and monetary policy won't work) capable of raising Real GDP than the upward-sloping *AS* economist believes.

- *Economist B:* The aggregate supply curve is upward sloping (in the short run). Government actions designed to change aggregate demand in the economy will lead to changes in Real GDP (at least in the short run). Changes in Real GDP (in the short run) can come from either the demand side or the supply side of the economy. Government has more tools (demand-side fiscal policy and monetary policy do work) capable of raising Real GDP than the vertical-*AS* economist believes.

SELF-TEST

(Answers to Self-Test questions are in Answers to Self-Test Questions at the back of the book.)

1. Economist A believes that a reduction in tax rates will lead to increased tax revenue, and economist B believes the opposite. What does each believe with respect to the relationship between the percentage change in tax rates and the percentage change in the tax base?

2. In the standard textbook Keynesian analysis, there is reason to believe that the government spending multiplier is larger than the tax multiplier. Why?

3. Not all economists agree on what constitutes the optimal size and scope of government. Therefore, they won't all agree as to the preferred fiscal policy measure to stimulate the economy—increased government purchases or tax cuts. Do you agree or disagree? Explain your answer.

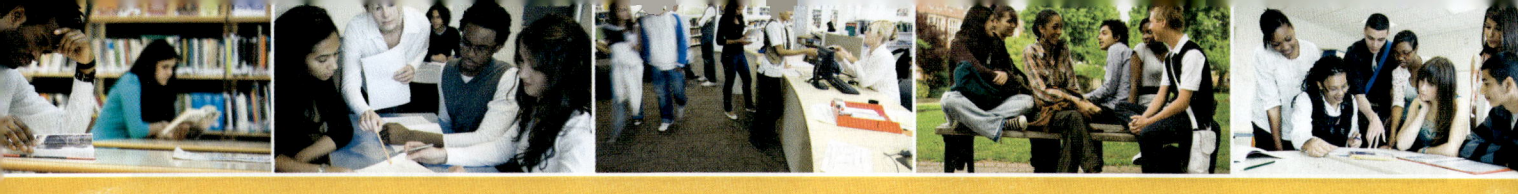

OFFICE HOURS

"What Kinds of Debates Do Macroeconomists Have?"

STUDENT:

I'd like some way to categorize the kinds of debates that macroeconomists have. Can you help here?

INSTRUCTOR:

Four words: theory, policy, empirics, and government. Here is what we mean by each. Economists sometimes debate theory. For example, think of the economist who builds a theory that assumes wages are inflexible downward and the one who builds a theory that assumes flexible wages.

Economists often debate the kind of policy that will best solve the economic problem at hand. To illustrate, economist A might argue that a supply-side tax cut is better able to solve the problem of lagging economic growth than a demand-side rise in government spending. Economist B might argue the opposite, especially if the increased government spending is directed toward research and development.

Economists often debate empirical results. To illustrate, economist A could say that during period X, the data show that expansionary fiscal policy did raise aggregate demand and did increase Real GDP. Economist B might argue that during period X, many things occurred, only one of which was the implementation of expansionary fiscal policy. Monetary policy was also expansionary during the period, and it, more than expansionary fiscal policy, is the reason why aggregate demand increased and Real GDP increased.

Economists also debate the role government should play in the economy. Often how they argue here is related to their views of how the economy works. For example, as we have stated in this chapter and others, consider an economist who believes that the evidence is consistent with a self-regulating economy—one that regulates itself quickly. He is less likely to advocate government macroeconomic interventions in the economy than an economist who believes that the evidence is consistent with either an unstable economy or with an economy that is unacceptably slow in self-regulating.

STUDENT:

One other question about debates in macroeconomics: I've heard about freshwater and saltwater economists. What do these two terms mean, and what is the essential difference between them when it comes to government's role in the economy?

INSTRUCTOR:

Sometimes these macroeconomic differences between economists find a home in two words: freshwater and saltwater, specifically, freshwater economists and saltwater economists. At universities such as Chicago, Minneapolis, and Rochester, which are all located near the Great Lakes, so-called freshwater economists can be found. At universities such as Harvard, MIT, and UC Berkeley—all near oceans—saltwater economists can be found.

Of course, the proximity to freshwater or saltwater isn't what fundamentally separates economists. It is differences in theory, policy, and the role of government. With respect to the latter, freshwater economists see a smaller role for government than do saltwater economists.

POINTS TO REMEMBER

1. The debates in macroeconomics often focus on theory, policy, empirics, and government.
2. It is not uncommon for an economist's view of how the economy works to influence his or her view on the role government should play in the economy.

CHAPTER SUMMARY

In this chapter, the summary is presented in terms of the opposing views of economists on macroeconomic issues.

TAX CUTS, TAX REVENUE, AND BUDGET DEFICITS

- *Economist A:* Tax cuts will raise tax revenue, and increased tax revenue will decrease the size of the budget deficit.
- *Economist B:* Tax cuts will lower tax revenue, and decreased tax revenue will increase the size of the budget deficit.

THE ECONOMY: SELF-REGULATING OR NOT?

- *Economist A:* Wages are flexible, so if the economy is in a recessionary gap, it will soon remove itself from the gap. Government need not do anything.
- *Economist B:* Wages are inflexible downward, so if the economy is in a recessionary gap, it may be stuck there. The best course of action is for the federal government to implement expansionary fiscal policy or for the Fed to implement expansionary monetary policy to remove the economy from the recessionary gap.

MORE GOVERNMENT SPENDING OR A CUT IN TAXES: WHICH GIVES A BIGGER BANG FOR THE BUCK?

- *Economist A:* The economy needs expansionary fiscal policy to remove it from a recessionary gap. Government should either raise its spending or cut taxes. I believe the government spending multiplier is larger than the tax multiplier; so I suggest government increase its spending.
- *Economist B:* The economy needs expansionary fiscal policy to remove it from a recessionary gap. Government should either raise its spending or cut taxes. I believe the tax multiplier is larger than the government spending multiplier; so I suggest government cut taxes.

MORE GOVERNMENT SPENDING OR A CUT IN TAXES: THE SIZE AND SCOPE OF GOVERNMENT

- *Economist A:* Expansionary fiscal policy is needed to raise aggregate demand and to remove the economy from a recessionary gap. The choice of fiscal policy measures is between either more government spending or a cut in taxes. Since I am in favor of bigger government, I choose more government spending.
- *Economist B:* Expansionary fiscal policy is needed to raise aggregate demand and to remove the economy from a recessionary gap. The choice of fiscal policy measures is between more government spending or a cut in taxes. Since I am in favor of smaller government, I choose a cut in taxes.

THE DEGREE OF CROWDING OUT

- *Economist A:* A rise in government purchases will increase aggregate demand and remove the economy from the recessionary gap because little or no crowding out will occur. A rise in government purchases will increase the number of jobs in the economy.
- *Economist B:* A rise in government purchases will not increase aggregate demand and remove the economy from the recessionary gap because of complete (or nearly complete) crowding out.

THE POLITICS OF GOVERNMENT SPENDING

- *Economist A:* An expansionary fiscal policy measure is needed to increase Real GDP, lower the unemployment rate, and so on. I propose $100 billion more in government spending. What the $100 billion is spent on does not matter; the important thing is that the money is spent.
- *Economist B:* An expansionary fiscal policy measure is needed to increase Real GDP, lower the unemployment rate, and so on. Ideally, the economy needs $100 billion more in government spending. But how the money will be spent will be determined by Congress, which is likely to be motivated by political interests when it determines how the money is spent. Furthermore, not all spending is the same. Some spending is better for the economy than other spending. I think much of the spending will be motivated by politics instead of economics, and sometimes the spending motivated by politics will be of little help in turning the economy around. In the end, I have my doubts as to how effective an increase in government spending will be in aiding the economy.

MONETARY POLICY: RULES OR DISCRETION?

- *Economist A:* A monetary rule is preferred to a discretionary Fed. The former is more likely to bring about stable prices, low unemployment and so on. In addition, a monetary rule removes monetary policy from politics.
- *Economist B:* A discretionary Fed is preferred to a monetary rule. The Fed needs the flexibility to tailor monetary policy to existing circumstances.

BAILOUTS

- *Economist A:* Ideally, bailing out companies is not a good idea. But Company X is a large company that, if it goes out of business, will adversely affect hundreds of thousands of persons. Bailing out the company is better than letting it fail. We lose more by letting the company fail than by saving it. Some companies are simply too big to be allowed to fail. Their failure is like an earthquake, adversely affecting all the people. To save the innocent, you sometimes have to save the not-so-innocent.
- *Economist B:* Who is "we" when you say, "We lose more by letting the company fail than by saving it?" Some persons gain by having the company bailed out, and others lose. Furthermore, if we continue to tell companies that the federal government will be there if they fail, we simply create an environment in which we privatize gains (the companies keep the gains if there are any) and socialize the costs (spread the costs among millions of taxpayers if

the companies end up in financial problems). In the end, this will lead to more companies that "need" to be bailed out.

DEMAND-SIDE VERSUS SUPPLY-SIDE VIEW OF THE ECONOMY AND GOVERNMENT TOOLS TO CHANGE REAL GDP

- *Economist A:* The aggregate supply curve is vertical. Therefore, government actions designed to change aggregate demand in the economy will not lead to changes in Real GDP. Changes in Real GDP come from the supply side of the economy, not the demand side. Government has fewer tools (demand-side fiscal policy and monetary policy won't work) capable of raising Real GDP than the upward-sloping *AS* economist believes.

- *Economist B:* The aggregate supply curve is upward sloping (in the short run). Government actions designed to change aggregate demand in the economy will lead to changes in Real GDP (at least in the short run). Changes in Real GDP (in the short run) can come from either the demand side or the supply side of the economy. Government has more tools (demand-side fiscal policy and monetary policy do work) capable of raising Real GDP than the vertical-*AS* economist believes.

KEY TERMS AND CONCEPTS

Elasticity of Investment

Government Spending Multiplier

Tax Multiplier

QUESTIONS AND PROBLEMS

1. There is little doubt that if income tax rates are cut, the size of the budget deficit will increase. Do you agree or disagree? Explain your answer.

2. Something is referred to as a "double-edged sword" if it can have both favorable and unfavorable consequences. In what way might government bailouts of failing companies or financial institutions be a double-edged sword? Explain your answer.

3. What do the values of the government spending and tax multipliers have to do with "getting the biggest bang for the buck"?

4. Outline the details of the debate between economists who favor a rules-based monetary policy and those who favor a discretionary monetary policy.

5. The shape of the aggregate supply curve matters to one's view of the ability of government to change Real GDP by way of demand-side fiscal policy and monetary policy. Do you agree or disagree? Explain your answer.

6. Whether an economist argues in favor of a rise in government spending (as an expansionary fiscal policy measure) could have something to do with the degree of crowding out he expects as a result of the measure. Do you agree or disagree? Explain your answer.

7. Whether an economist argues in favor of a rise in government spending or a cut in taxes (as an expansionary fiscal policy measure) could have something to do with whether she views the government spending multiplier as greater or less than the tax multiplier. Do you agree or disagree? Explain your answer.

8. Some economists argue that if the economy currently needs to be stimulated to remove it from a recessionary gap, *how* government spends more money (on X or Y) matters less than the fact that it spends more money. Do all economists agree? If not, what do they say in response?

9. How an economist thinks the economy works—is it self-regulating or not?—influences his opinion of the role government should play in trying to stabilize the economy. Do you agree or disagree? Explain your answer.

10. Whether an economist argues in favor of a rise in government spending or a cut in taxes (as an expansionary fiscal policy measure) could have something to do with how he views the current size and scope of government in relationship to his optimal size and scope of government. Do you agree or disagree? Explain your answer.

11. Can tax revenue rise and the budget deficit decline as a result of an income tax rate cut? Explain your answer.

WORKING WITH NUMBERS AND GRAPHS

1. A $40 reduction in taxes increases Real GDP by $100, and a $50 increase in government spending increases Real GDP by $120. What does the tax multiplier equal? What does the government spending multiplier equal?

2. A rise in aggregate demand raises Real GDP and the price level. Draw the aggregate supply curve consistent with these results. Next, a rise in aggregate demand raises the price level but leaves Real GDP unchanged. Draw the aggregate supply curve consistent with these results.

CHAPTER 20

ELASTICITY

Introduction In New York City, a Broadway play is performed in a theater with 1,500 seats. Will the play take in more revenue if the average ticket price for a performance is $70 or if it is $120? If you said $120, consider some other questions: Will the play take in more revenue if the average price is $120 or $180?

Will it take in more revenue if the average price is $180 or $250? Are you beginning to get suspicious? Perhaps the highest ticket price won't generate the greatest amount of revenue, but which ticket price will? The answer may surprise you.

ELASTICITY: PART 1

The law of demand states that price and quantity demanded are inversely related, *ceteris paribus.* But it doesn't tell us by what percentage the quantity demanded changes as price changes. Suppose price rises by 10 percent. As a result, quantity demanded falls, but by what percentage does it fall? The notion of price elasticity of demand can help answer this question. The general concept of elasticity provides a technique for estimating the response of one variable to changes in another. It has numerous applications in economics.

Price Elasticity of Demand

The law of demand states that there is a *directional relationship* between price and quantity demanded: price and quantity demanded are inversely related. The law of demand does not tell us how much quantity demanded declines as price rises. The *magnitudinal relationship* between price and quantity demanded brings us to a discussion of price elasticity of demand, which is a measure of the responsiveness of quantity demanded to changes in price. More specifically, it addresses the percentage change in quantity demanded for a given percentage change in price. (Keep in mind "percentage change," not just "change.")

Let's say that a seller of a good—a computer—raises the price by 10 percent, and as a result the quantity demanded for the computer falls by 20 percent. The percentage change

Price Elasticity of Demand
A measure of the responsiveness of quantity demanded to changes in price.

in quantity demanded (Q_d)—20 percent—divided by the percentage change in price (P)—10 percent—is called the *coefficient of price elasticity of demand* (E_d).

$$E_d = \frac{\text{Percentage change in quantity demanded}}{\text{Perentage change in price}} = \frac{\%\Delta Q_d}{\%\Delta P}$$

In the formula, E_d = coefficient of price elasticity of demand, or simply elasticity coefficient, % = percentage, and Δ stands for "change in."

If we apply the calculation to our simple example—where quantity demanded changes by 20 percent and price changes by 10 percent—we get 2. An economist would say either, "The coefficient of price elasticity of demand is 2" or, more simply, "Price elasticity of demand is 2." Either expression means that the percentage change in quantity demanded will be 2 times any percentage change in price.[1] If price changes 5 percent, the quantity demanded will change 10 percent; if price changes 10 percent, the quantity demanded will change 20 percent.

WHERE IS THE MISSING MINUS SIGN? Price and quantity demanded move in opposite directions: When price rises, quantity demanded falls; when price falls, quantity demanded rises. In our example, when price rises by 10 percent, the quantity demanded falls by 20 percent. When you divide a *minus 20 percent* by a *positive 10 percent*, you don't get 2; you get −2. Instead of saying that the price elasticity of demand is 2, you might think the price elasticity of demand is −2. However, by convention, economists usually simplify things by using the absolute value of the price elasticity of demand; thus they drop the minus sign.

FORMULA FOR CALCULATING PRICE ELASTICITY OF DEMAND Using percentage changes to calculate price elasticity of demand can lead to conflicting results depending on whether price rises or falls. Therefore, economists use the following formula to calculate price elasticity of demand:[2]

$$E_d = \frac{\dfrac{\Delta Q_d}{Q_{d\,\text{average}}}}{\dfrac{\Delta P}{P_{\text{average}}}}$$

In the formula, ΔQ_d stands for the absolute change in Q_d. For example, if Q_d changes from 50 units to 100 units, then ΔQ_d is 50 units. ΔP stands for the absolute change in price. For example, if price changes from \$12 to \$10, then ΔP is \$2. $Q_{d\,\text{average}}$ stands for the average of the two quantities demanded, and P_{average} stands for the average of the two prices.

For the price and quantity demanded data in Exhibit 1, the calculation is:

$$E_d = \frac{\dfrac{50}{75}}{\dfrac{2}{11}} = 3.67$$

Because we use the average price and average quantity demanded in the price elasticity of demand equation, 3.67 may be considered the price elasticity of demand at a point *midway between the two points identified on the demand curve.* For example, in Exhibit 1, 3.67 is the price elasticity of demand between points A and B on the demand curve.

---

1. This assumes we are changing price from its current level.
2. This formula is sometimes called the midpoint formula for calculating price elasticity of demand.

EXHIBIT 1

Calculating Price Elasticity of Demand

We identify two points on a demand curve. At point A, price is $12 and quantity demanded is 50 units. At point B, price is $10 and quantity demanded is 100 units. When calculating price elasticity of demand, we use the *average* of the two prices and the *average* of the two quantities demanded. The formula for price elasticity of demand is:

$$E_d = \frac{\dfrac{\Delta Q_d}{Q_{d\,average}}}{\dfrac{\Delta P}{P_{average}}}$$

For example, the calculation is:

$$E_d = \frac{\dfrac{50}{75}}{\dfrac{2}{11}} = 3.67$$

Elasticity Is Not Slope

Some tend to think that slope and price elasticity of demand are the same, but they are not. Suppose we identify a third point on the demand curve in Exhibit 1. The following table shows the price and quantity demanded for our three points.

Point	Price	Quantity Demanded
A	$12	50
B	10	100
C	8	150

To calculate the *price elasticity of demand* between points A and B, we divide the percentage change in quantity demanded (between the two points) by the percentage change in price (between the two points). Using the price elasticity of demand formula, we get 3.67.

The *slope of the demand curve* between points A and B is the ratio of the change in the variable on the vertical axis to the change in the variable on the horizontal axis. The slope of the demand curve reflects the change, not a percentage change.

$$\text{Slope} = \frac{\Delta \text{Variable on vertical axis}}{\Delta \text{Variable on horizontal axis}} = \frac{-2}{50} = -0.04$$

Now let's calculate the price elasticity of demand and the slope between points B and C. The price elasticity of demand is 1.80; the slope is still −0.04.

From Perfectly Elastic to Perfectly Inelastic Demand

Look back at the equation for the elasticity coefficient and think of it as

$$E_d = \frac{\text{Percentage change in quantity demanded}}{\text{Percentage change in price}} = \frac{\text{Numerator}}{\text{Denominator}}$$

Focusing on the numerator and denominator, we realize that the numerator can be (1) greater than, (2) less than, or (3) equal to the denominator. These three cases, along with two peripherally related cases, are discussed in the following paragraphs. Exhibits 2 and 3 provide summaries of the discussion.

Price Elasticity of Demand

Demand may be elastic, inelastic, unit elastic, perfectly elastic, or perfectly inelastic.

Elasticity Coefficient	Responsiveness of Quantity Demanded to a Change in Price	Terminology
$E_d > 1$	Quantity demanded changes proportionately more than price changes: $\%\Delta Q_d > \%\Delta P$.	Elastic
$E_d < 1$	Quantity demanded changes proportionately less than price changes: $\%\Delta Q_d < \%\Delta P$.	Inelastic
$E_d = 1$	Quantity demanded changes proportionately to price change: $\%\Delta Q_d = \%\Delta P$.	Unit elastic
$E_d = \infty$	Quantity demanded is extremely responsive to even very small changes in price.	Perfectly elastic
$E_d = 0$	Quantity demanded does not change as price changes.	Perfectly inelastic

Graphical Representation of Price Elasticity of Demand

(a) The percentage change in quantity demanded is greater than the percentage change in price: $E_d > 1$ and demand is elastic.

(b) The percentage change in quantity demanded is less than the percentage change in price: $E_d < 1$ and demand is inelastic. (c) The percentage change in quantity demand is equal to percentage change in price: $E_d = 1$ and

demand is unit elastic. (d) A small change in price reduces quantity demanded to zero: $E_d = \infty$ and demand is perfectly elastic. (e) A change in price does not change quantity demanded: $E_d = 0$ and demand is perfectly inelastic.

ELASTIC DEMAND ($E_d > 1$) See Exhibit 3(a). If the numerator (percentage change in quantity demanded) is greater than the denominator (percentage change in price), the elasticity coefficient is greater than 1, and demand is elastic. This is elastic demand; that is, the quantity demanded changes proportionately more than price changes. A 10 percent increase in price causes, say, a 20 percent reduction in quantity demanded ($E_d = 2$).

Percentage change in quantity demanded > Percentage change in price →

$E_d > 1 \rightarrow$ Demand is elastic

INELASTIC DEMAND ($E_d < 1$) See Exhibit 3(b). If the numerator (percentage change in quantity demanded) is less than the denominator (percentage change in price), the elasticity coefficient is less than 1, and demand is inelastic. This is inelastic demand; that is, the quantity demanded changes proportionately less than price changes. A 10 percent increase in price causes, say, a 4 percent reduction in the quantity demanded ($E_d = 0.4$).

Percentage change in quantity demanded < Percentage change in price →

$E_d < 1 \rightarrow$ Demand is inelastic

UNIT ELASTIC DEMAND ($E_d = 1$) See Exhibit 3(c). If the numerator (percentage change in quantity demanded) equals the denominator (percentage change in price), the elasticity coefficient is 1. This is unit elastic demand; that is, the quantity demanded changes proportionately to price changes. For example, a 10 percent increase in price causes a 10 percent decrease in quantity demanded ($E_d = 1$). In this case, demand exhibits unitary elasticity, or is unit elastic.

Percentage change in quantity demanded = Percentage change in price →

$E_d = 1 \rightarrow$ Demand is unit elastic

PERFECTLY ELASTIC DEMAND ($E_d = \infty$) See Exhibit 3(d). If quantity demanded is extremely responsive to changes in price, the result is perfectly elastic demand. For example, buyers are willing to buy all units of a seller's good at $5 per unit but nothing at $5.10. A small percentage change in price causes an extremely large percentage change in quantity demanded (from buying all to buying nothing). The percentage is so large, in fact, that economists say it is infinitely large.

PERFECTLY INELASTIC DEMAND ($E_d = 0$) See Exhibit 3(e). If quantity demanded is completely unresponsive to changes in price, the result is perfectly inelastic demand. A change in price causes no change in quantity demanded. For example, suppose the price of *Dogs Love It* dog food rises 10 percent (from $2 to $2.20), and Jeremy doesn't buy any less of it per week for his dog. Jeremy's demand for *Dogs Love It* dog food is thus perfectly inelastic between a price of $2 and $2.20.

PERFECTLY ELASTIC AND PERFECTLY INELASTIC DEMAND CURVES Even though you are used to seeing a downward sloping demand curve, Exhibit 3 shows two demand curves that are not downward sloping. But aren't all demand curves supposed to be downward sloping because, according to the law of demand, an inverse relationship exists between price and quantity demanded? In the real world, no demand curves are perfectly elastic (horizontal) or perfectly inelastic (vertical) at all prices. Thus, the perfectly elastic and perfectly inelastic demand curves in Exhibit 3 should be viewed as representations of the extreme limits between which all real-world demand curves fall.

However, a few real-world demand curves do *approximate* the perfectly elastic and inelastic demand curves in Exhibit 3(d) and (e); that is, they come very close. For example, the demand for a particular farmer's wheat approximates the perfectly elastic demand curve in panel (d). A later chapter discusses the perfectly elastic demand curve for firms in perfectly competitive markets.

finding ECONOMICS

At the Local Coffee Bar You buy 7 coffees at the local coffee bar each week when the price of a cup of coffee is $2, and you buy 5 coffees a week when the price is $2.50. Where is the economics?

Actually, economics appears in two places. First, the law of demand is visible because you buyer *fewer* cups of coffee at the higher price. Second, calculating your price elasticity of coffee between the lower and higher prices is easy. It is 1.5, which means your demand for coffee is *elastic*. ▲ ▲ ▲

Price Elasticity of Demand and Total Revenue (Total Expenditure)

Total revenue (*TR*) of a seller equals the price of a good times the quantity of the good sold.[3] For example, if the hamburger stand down the street sells 100 hamburgers today at $1.50 each, its total revenue is $150.

Total Revenue (*TR*)
Price times quantity sold.

Suppose the hamburger vendor raises the price of a hamburger to $2. What do you predict will happen to total revenue? Most people say it will increase in the widespread belief that higher prices bring higher total revenue. However, total revenue may increase, decrease, or remain constant. Suppose price rises to $2, but because of the higher price, the quantity of hamburgers sold falls to 50. Total revenue is now $100 (whereas it was $150). Whether total revenue rises, falls, or remains constant after a price change depends on whether the percentage change in the quantity demanded is less than, greater than, or equal to the percentage change in price. Thus, price elasticity of demand influences total revenue.

Elastic Demand and Total Revenue

If demand is elastic, the percentage change in quantity demanded is greater than the percentage change in price. Given a price rise of, say, 5 percent, the quantity demanded falls by more than 5 percent—say, 8 percent—having an effect on total revenue. Because quantity demanded falls, or sales fall off, by a greater percentage than the percentage rise in price, total revenue decreases. In short, if demand is elastic, a price rise decreases total revenue.

$$\text{Demand is elastic: } P\uparrow \rightarrow TR\downarrow$$

If demand is elastic and price falls, the quantity demanded rises (price and quantity demanded are inversely related) by a greater percentage than the percentage fall in price, causing total revenue to increase. In short, if demand is elastic, a price fall increases total revenue.

$$\text{Demand is elastic: } P\downarrow \rightarrow TR\uparrow$$

---

3. In this discussion, "total revenue" and "total expenditure" are equivalent terms. *Total revenue* equals price times the quantity sold. *Total expenditure* equals price times the quantity purchased. If something is sold, it must be purchased, making total revenue equal to total expenditure. The term "total revenue" is used when looking at things from the point of view of the sellers in a market. The term "total expenditure" is used when looking at things from the point of view of the buyers in a market. Buyers make expenditures; sellers receive revenues.

EXHIBIT 4

Price Elasticity of Demand and Total Revenue

In (a) demand is elastic between points A and B. A fall in price, from P_1 to P_2, will increase the size of the total revenue rectangle from $0P_1AQ_1$ to $0P_2BQ_2$. A rise in price, from P_2 to P_1, will decrease the size of the total revenue rectangle from $0P_2BQ_2$ to $0P_1AQ_1$. In other words, when demand is elastic, price and total revenue are inversely related. In (b) demand is inelastic between points A and B. A fall in price, from P_1 to P_2, will decrease the size of the total revenue rectangle from $0P_1AQ_1$ to $0P_2BQ_2$. A rise in price, from P_2 to P_1, will increase the size of the total revenue rectangle from $0P_2BQ_2$ to $0P_1AQ_1$. In other words, when demand is inelastic, price and total revenue are directly related.

(a)   **(b)**

Exhibit 4(a) shows the relationship between a change in price and total revenue if demand is elastic. Between points A and B on the demand curve, demand is elastic. At point A, price is P_1 and the quantity demanded is Q_1. Total revenue is equal to the rectangle $0P_1AQ_1$. Now suppose we lower price to P_2. After the price decline, total revenue is now the rectangle $0P_2BQ_2$, which, as you can see, is larger than rectangle $0P_1AQ_1$. In other words, if demand is elastic and price declines, total revenue will rise.

Of course, when price moves in the opposite direction, rising from P_2 to P_1, then the total revenue rectangle becomes smaller. In other words, if demand is elastic and price rises, total revenue will fall.

INELASTIC DEMAND AND TOTAL REVENUE If demand is inelastic, the percentage change in quantity demanded is less than the percentage change in price. If price rises, quantity demanded falls but by a smaller percentage than the percentage rise in price. As a result, total revenue increases. So if demand is inelastic, a price rise increases total revenue. However, if price falls, the quantity demanded rises by a smaller percentage than the percentage fall in price, and total revenue decreases. If demand is inelastic, a price fall decreases total revenue; price and total revenue are directly related.

Demand is inelastic: $P\uparrow \rightarrow TR\uparrow$

Demand is inelastic: $P\downarrow \rightarrow TR\downarrow$

You can see the relationship between inelastic demand and total revenue in Exhibit 4(b), where demand is inelastic between points A and B on the demand curve. If we start at P_1 and lower price to P_2, the total revenue rectangle goes from $0P_1AQ_1$ to the smaller total revenue rectangle $0P_2BQ_2$. In other words, if demand is inelastic and price falls, total revenue will fall.

Drug Busts and Crime

Most people agree that the sale or possession of drugs such as cocaine and heroin should be illegal, but sometimes laws may have unintended effects. Do drug laws have unintended effects? Let's analyze the enforcement of drug laws in terms of supply, demand, and price elasticity of demand.

AP PHOTO/CP, NATHAN DENETTE

Suppose for every $100 of illegal drug sales, 60 percent of the $100 paid is obtained by illegal means. That is, buyers of $100 worth of illegal drugs obtain $60 of the purchase price from criminal activities such as burglaries, muggings, and similar illegal acts.

In Exhibit 5, the demand for and supply of cocaine in a particular city are represented by D_1 and S_1. The equilibrium price of $50 an ounce and the equilibrium quantity of 1,000 ounces give cocaine dealers a total revenue of $50,000. If 60 percent of this total revenue is obtained by the criminal activities of cocaine buyers, then $30,000 worth of crime

has been committed to purchase the $50,000 worth of cocaine.

A drug bust in the city reduces the supply of cocaine. The supply curve shifts leftward from S_1 to S_2, the equilibrium price rises to $120 an ounce, and the equilibrium quantity falls to 600 ounces. The demand for cocaine is inelastic between the two prices, at 0.607. When demand is inelastic, an increase in price will raise total revenue. The total revenue received by cocaine dealers is now $72,000. If, again, we assume that 60 percent of the total revenue paid comes from criminal activity, then $43,200 worth of crime has been committed to purchase the $72,000 worth of cocaine.

Therefore, if the demand for cocaine is inelastic and people commit crimes to buy drugs, then a drug bust can actually increase the amount of drug-related crime. Obviously, this is an unintended effect of the enforcement of drug laws.

EXHIBIT 5

Drug Busts and Drug-Related Crime

In the exhibit, P = price of cocaine, Q = quantity of cocaine, and TR = total revenue from selling cocaine. At a price of $50 for an ounce of cocaine, equilibrium quantity is 1,000 ounces and total revenue is $50,000. If $60 of every $100 cocaine purchase is obtained through

crime, then $30,000 worth of crime is committed to purchase $50,000 worth of cocaine. As a result of a drug bust, the supply of cocaine shifts leftward; the price rises and the quantity falls. Because we have assumed the demand for cocaine is inelastic, total revenue rises to $72,000. Sixty percent of this comes from criminal activities, or $43,200.

	P	Q	TR	Dollar Amount of TR Obtained Through Crime
Before Drug Bust	$50	1,000	$50,000	$30,000
After Drug Bust	120	600	72,000	43,200

EXHIBIT 6

Elasticities, Price Changes, and Total Revenue

If demand is elastic, a price rise leads to a decrease in total revenue (*TR*), and a price fall leads to an increase in total revenue. If demand is inelastic, a price rise leads to an increase in total revenue and a price fall leads to a decrease in total revenue. If demand is unit elastic, a rise or fall in price does not change total revenue.

Moving from the lower price, P_2, to the higher price, P_1, does just the opposite. If demand is inelastic and price rises, the total revenue rectangle becomes larger; that is, total revenue rises.

UNIT ELASTIC DEMAND AND TOTAL REVENUE If demand is unit elastic, the percentage change in quantity demanded equals the percentage change in price. If price rises, the quantity demanded falls by the same percentage as the percentage rise in price. Total revenue does not change. If price falls, the quantity demanded rises by the same percentage as the percentage fall in price. Again, total revenue does not change. If demand is unit elastic, a rise or fall in price leaves total revenue unchanged.

For a review of the relationship between price elasticity of demand and total revenue, see Exhibit 6.

ⓣhinking Like AN ECONOMIST

Price and Total Revenue Ask some people what will happen if a seller raises the selling price of a product, and they will tell you that total revenue is bound to rise: "Sellers want higher prices because they take in more money at higher prices than at lower prices." As you have just learned, this is not always true. If demand is inelastic and price rises, then total revenue rises too. But if demand is elastic and price rises, then total revenue falls. Finally, if demand is unit elastic and price rises, then total revenue remains unchanged. Simply put, saying that total revenue always rises as sellers raise prices is a myth. ▪▪▪

ⓕinding ECONOMICS

In an Earthquake Suppose an earthquake in Los Angeles destroys 10 percent of the apartment stock. Where is the economics?

As a result of the earthquake, we can expect the average rent for an apartment in the city to rise. Some people go further and argue that because of the earthquake, landlords will take in more total revenue than they did before the earthquake, but this is not necessarily true. Suppose the rent before the earthquake is $2,000 and 100,000 apartments are rented. The monthly total revenue is $200 million. Now suppose the earthquake reduces the number of apartments to 90,000. As a result of a lower supply of apartments, the average rent rises to, say, $2,100 a month. At this higher rent per month, the monthly total revenue from apartments is $189 million. Total revenue is lower because the demand for apartments between the lower rent and the higher rent is elastic. If demand is elastic and price rises, then total revenue falls. ▲▲▲

SELF-TEST

(Answers to Self-Test questions are in Answers to Self-Test Questions at the back of the book.)

1. On Tuesday, the price and quantity demanded are $7 and 120 units, respectively. Ten days later, the price and quantity demanded are $6 and 150 units, respectively. What is the price elasticity of demand between the $7 and $6 prices?

2. What does a price elasticity of demand of 0.39 mean?

3. Identify what happens to total revenue as a result of each of the following:

   a. Price rises and demand is elastic.

   b. Price falls and demand is inelastic.

   c. Price rises and demand is unit elastic.

   d. Price rises and demand is inelastic.

   e. Price falls and demand is elastic.

4. Alexi says, "When a seller raises his price, his total revenue rises." What is Alexi implicitly assuming?

ELASTICITY: PART 2

This section discusses the elasticity ranges of a straight-line downward-sloping demand curve and the determinants of price elasticity of demand.

Price Elasticity of Demand Along a Straight-Line Demand Curve

The price elasticity of demand for a straight-line downward-sloping demand curve varies from highly elastic to highly inelastic. Consider the price elasticity of demand at the upper range of the demand curve in Exhibit 7(a). Whether the price falls from $9 to $8 or rises from $8 to $9, using the price elasticity of demand formula, we calculate the price elasticity of demand as 5.66.[4]

Now consider the price elasticity of demand at the lower range of the demand curve in Exhibit 7(a). Whether the price falls from $3 to $2 or rises from $2 to $3, we calculate the price elasticity of demand as 0.33.

In other words, along the range of the demand curve identified, price elasticity goes from being greater than 1 (5.66) to being less than 1 (0.33). Obviously, on its way from being greater than 1 to being less than 1, price elasticity of demand must be equal to 1. In Exhibit 7(a), we have identified the price elasticity of demand as equal to 1 at the *midpoint* of the demand curve.[5]

The elastic and inelastic ranges along the straight-line downward-sloping demand curve can be related to a total revenue curve [Exhibit 7(b)]. If we start in the elastic range of the demand curve in Exhibit 7(a) and lower price, total revenue rises, as shown in Exhibit 7(b). That is, as price is coming down within the elastic range of the demand curve in part (a), total revenue is rising in part (b).

When price has fallen enough that we move into the inelastic range of the demand curve in part (a), further price declines simply lower total revenue, as shown in part (b). Therefore, total revenue is at its highest— its peak—when price elasticity of demand equals 1.

EXHIBIT 7

Price Elasticity of Demand Along a Straight-Line Demand Curve

In (a), the price elasticity of demand varies along the straight-line downward-sloping demand curve. There is an elastic range to the curve (where $E_d > 1$) and an inelastic range (where $E_d < 1$). At the midpoint of any straight-line downward-sloping demand curve, price elasticity of demand is equal to 1 ($E_d = 1$). Part (b) shows that in the elastic range of the demand curve, total revenue rises as price is lowered. In the inelastic range of the demand curve, further price declines result in declining total revenue. Total revenue reaches its peak when price elasticity of demand equals 1.

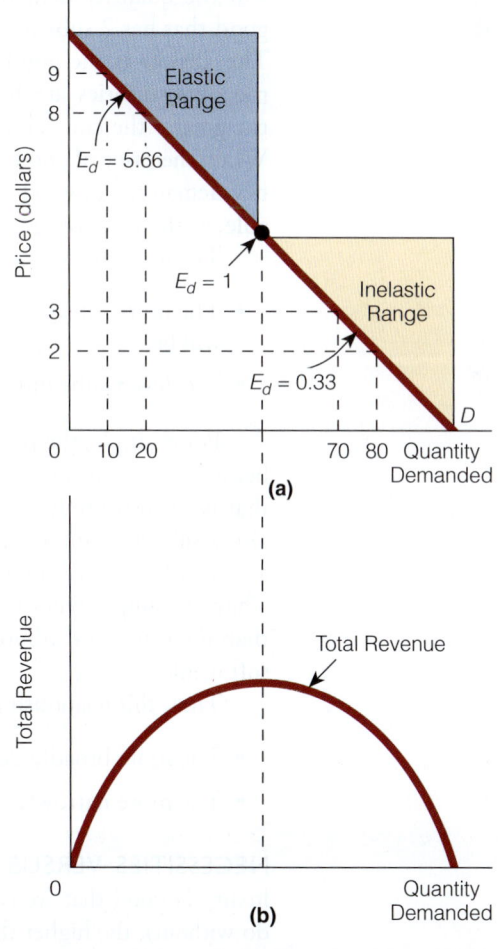

---

4. Keep in mind that our formula uses the average of the two prices and the average of the two quantities demanded. You may want to look back at the formula to refresh your memory.
5. For any straight-line downward-sloping demand curve, price elasticity of demand equals 1 at the midpoint of the curve.

Determinants of Price Elasticity of Demand

Four factors are relevant to the determination of price elasticity of demand:

1. Number of substitutes

2. Necessities versus luxuries

3. Percentage of one's budget spent on the good

4. Time

Because all four factors interact, we hold all other things constant as we discuss each.

NUMBER OF SUBSTITUTES Suppose good A has 2 substitutes and good B has 15 substitutes. Assume that each of the 2 substitutes for good A is as good a substitute (or a good enough substitute) for that good as each of the 15 substitutes is for good B.

Let the price of each good rise by 10 percent. The quantity demanded of each good decreases. Will the percentage change in the quantity demanded of good A be greater or less than the percentage change in quantity demanded of good B? In other words, will the quantity demanded be more responsive to the 10 percent price rise for the good that has 2 substitutes (good A) or for the good that has 15 substitutes (good B)? The answer is the good with 15 substitutes, good B. The reason is that the greater the opportunities are for substitution (good B has more substitutes than good A), the greater the cutback in the quantity of the good purchased will be as its price rises. When the price of good A rises 10 percent, people can turn to 2 substitutes. The quantity demanded of good A falls, but not by as much as if 15 substitutes had been available, as there are for good B.

The relationship between the availability of substitutes and price elasticity is clear:

- The more substitutes a good has, the higher the price elasticity of demand will be.

- The fewer substitutes a good has, the lower the price elasticity of demand.

For example, the price elasticity of demand for Chevrolets is higher than for all cars because there are more substitutes for Chevrolets than there are for cars. Everything that is a substitute for a car (taking a bus, getting on a train, walking, bicycling, etc.) is also a substitute for a specific type of car, such as a Chevrolet, but some substitutes for a Chevrolet (Ford, Toyota, Chrysler, Mercedes-Benz, etc.) are not substitutes for a car. They are simply types of cars. There are more substitutes for this economics textbook than there are for textbooks. There are more substitutes for Coca-Cola than there are for soft drinks.

Thus, this relationship can be restated as:

- The more broadly defined the good is, the fewer the substitutes it will have.

- The more narrowly defined the good, the more the substitutes.

NECESSITIES VERSUS LUXURIES Generally, the more that a good is considered a luxury (a good that we can do without) rather than a necessity (a good that we cannot do without), the higher the price elasticity of demand will be. For example, consider two goods: jewelry and a medicine for controlling high blood pressure. If the price of jewelry rises, cutting back on purchases is easy; no one really needs jewelry to live. However, if the price of the medicine for controlling one's high blood pressure rises, cutting back is not so easy. We expect the price elasticity of demand for jewelry to be higher than for high blood pressure medicine.

PERCENTAGE OF ONE'S BUDGET SPENT ON THE GOOD Claire Rossi has a monthly budget of $3,000. Of this monthly budget, she spends $3 per month on pens and $400 per month on dinners at restaurants. In terms of percentages, she spends 0.1 percent of her monthly budget on pens and 13 percent of her monthly budget on dinners at restaurants. Suppose both the price of pens and the price of dinners at restaurants double. Claire is likely to be more responsive to the change in the price of restaurant dinners than to the change in the price of pens. Claire feels the pinch of a doubling in the price of a good on which she spends 0.1 percent of her budget a lot less than a doubling in price of a good on which she spends 13 percent. Claire is more likely to ignore the increased price of pens than she is to ignore the heightened price of restaurant dinners. Buyers are (and thus the quantity demanded is) more responsive to price as the percentage of their budget that goes for the purchase of the good increases.

- The greater the percentage of one's budget that goes to purchase a good, the higher the price elasticity of demand will be.
- The smaller the percentage of one's budget that goes to purchase a good, the lower the price elasticity of demand will be.

TIME As time passes, buyers have greater opportunities to be responsive to a price change. If the price of electricity went up today and you knew about it, you probably would not change your consumption of electricity today as much as you would three months from today. As time passes, you have more chances to change your consumption by finding substitutes (natural gas), changing your lifestyle (buying more blankets and turning down the thermostat at night), and so on.

- The more time that passes (since the price change), the higher the price elasticity of demand for the good will be.
- The less time that passes, the lower the price elasticity of demand for the good will be.

In other words, the price elasticity of demand for a good is higher in the long run than in the short run.

finding ECONOMICS

In Apples and Pens Parker buys a lot more apples when their price falls, but he doesn't buy many more pens when the price of pens falls. Where is the economics?

Obviously, Parker's price elasticity of demand is different for apples than for pens. Even without percentage changes, from the little information given, Parker's price elasticity of demand for apples seems to be greater than his price elasticity of demand for pens. ▲ ▲ ▲

SELF-TEST

1. If good X has 7 substitutes and demand is inelastic, then if there are 9 substitutes for good X, will demand be elastic? Explain your answer.

2. Price elasticity of demand is predicted to be higher for which good of the following combinations of goods? Explain your answers.

a. Dell computers or computers
b. Heinz ketchup or ketchup
c. Perrier water or water

Mad Men and Price Elasticity of Demand

The AMC television show *Mad Men* is about people who work in a Madison Avenue advertising agency in the early 1960s. The creative talent behind the success of the agency is Don Draper. If you watch Don Draper at work, you soon learn that one of his talents is his ability to make the consumer feel some connection to the product he is advertising. In other words, the product he is advertising—whether it is potato chips, a camera, or a cigarette brand—is unique in that it "makes" the consumer feel some special connection to it. For example, here is what Don Draper says in a meeting about the Kodak slide projector:

© AMC/COURTESY EVERETT COLLECTION

> Well, technology is a glittering lure. But there is the rare occasion when the public can be engaged on a level beyond flash, if they have a *sentimental bond* with the product.
>
> [In] my first job, I was in-house at a fur company, with this old-pro copywriter, a Greek named Teddy. Teddy told me the most important idea in advertising is new. Creates an itch. You simply put your product in there as a kind of calamine lotion.
>
> But he also talked about a deeper bond with the product. Nostalgia. It's delicate, but potent. *(lights switch off) (changes slide on the slide projector)*
>
> Teddy told me that in Greek, "nostalgia" literally means "the pain from an old wound." *(changes slide)*
>
> It's a twinge in your heart far more powerful than memory alone. *(changes slide)*
>
> This device [Kodak slide projector] isn't a spaceship, it's a time machine. *(changes slide)*
>
> It goes backwards, forwards, *(changes slide)* takes us to a place where we ache to go again. *(changes slide)*
>
> It's not called the wheel. It's called the carousel. *(changes slide)*
>
> It lets us travel the way a child travels. *(changes slide)*
>
> Round and around, and back home again. *(changes slide)*
>
> To a place where we know we are loved. *(changes slide)*

What is the economic logic behind designing an ad campaign that makes the consumer feel some connection to the product being advertised?

If the campaign is successful, it can change the price elasticity of demand of the product. Suppose 10 products (A–J) are close substitutes for one other. Don Draper is hired to think up an ad campaign for product A. If Draper can come up with a campaign that gets consumers feeling some special connection to product A, he can differentiate product A from its substitutes. In other words, consumers may come to think that product B or C aren't really good substitutes for product A, because they don't have the same connection to B and C as they do to A.

At that point, we know that the fewer substitutes a product has (even if only in the minds of buyers), the lower its price elasticity of demand will be. If Draper can effectively eliminate the substitutes for product A, he effectively lowers the price elasticity of demand for product A.

Now if he can lower it enough to bring it below 1, then the demand for the good is *inelastic*. And if demand is inelastic, you can raise the price of the product and have greater total revenue too.

But will profit rise? At a higher price for the product, fewer units will be sold, and if fewer units are sold, then fewer need to be produced; so total costs will decline.

In the end, the story goes like this: (1) Don Draper advertises the product so that consumers feel some connection to the product. (2) Because consumers feel a connection to the product, they don't see as many substitutes for the product as they once did. (3) Because consumers see fewer substitutes for the product, the price elasticity of demand for the product declines. (4) If it declines enough to make the demand for the product inelastic, then the seller of the product can raise the price and increase total revenue. (5) Fewer units of the product will be sold at the higher price, which means fewer units have to be produced; so total costs decline; (6) If total revenue rises and total costs decline, profit rises.

OTHER ELASTICITY CONCEPTS

This section looks at three other elasticities:

- Cross elasticity of demand
- Income elasticity of demand
- Price elasticity of supply

Cross Elasticity of Demand

Cross elasticity of demand measures the responsiveness in the quantity demanded of one good to changes in the price of another good. It is calculated by dividing the percentage change in the quantity demanded of one good by the percentage change in the price of another.

$$E_c = \frac{\text{Percentage change in quantity demanded of one good}}{\text{Percentage change in price of another good}}$$

where E_c stands for the coefficient of cross elasticity of demand, or elasticity coefficient.

This concept is often used to determine whether two goods are substitutes or complements and the degree to which one good is a substitute for or a complement to the other. Consider Skippy peanut butter and Jif peanut butter. Suppose that when the price of Jif increases by 10 percent, the quantity demanded of Skippy increases by 45 percent. The cross elasticity of demand for Skippy with respect to the price of Jif is:

$$E_c = \frac{\text{Percentage change in quantity demanded of Skippy}}{\text{Percentage change in price of Jif}}$$

$$E_c = \frac{45}{10} = 4.5$$

In this case, the cross elasticity of demand is a positive 4.5. When the cross elasticity of demand is positive, the percentage change in the quantity demanded of one good (in the numerator) moves in the same direction as the percentage change in the price of the other good (in the denominator). This is a characteristic of goods that are substitutes. As the price of Jif rises, the demand curve for Skippy shifts rightward, causing the quantity demanded of Skippy to increase at every price. So if $E_c > 0$, the two goods are substitutes.

$$E_c > 0 \rightarrow \text{Goods are substitutes}$$

If the elasticity coefficient is negative, $E_c < 0$, then the two goods are complements.

$$E_c < 0 \rightarrow \text{Goods are complements}$$

A negative cross elasticity of demand occurs when the percentage change in the quantity demanded of one good (numerator) and the percentage change in the price of another good (denominator) move in opposite directions. For example, suppose the price of cars increases by 5 percent, and the quantity demanded of car tires decreases by 10 percent. Calculating the cross elasticity of demand, we have -10 percent $\div$ 5 percent $= -2$. Cars and car tires are complements.

The concept of cross elasticity of demand can be very useful. A company that sells cheese might ask what goods are substitutes for cheese. The answer would help the company identify its competitors. The company could identify substitutes for

Cross Elasticity of Demand
A measure of the responsiveness in quantity demanded of one good to changes in the price of another good.

cheese by calculating the cross elasticity of demand between cheese and other goods. A positive cross elasticity of demand would indicate that the two goods were substitutes, and the higher the cross elasticity of demand is, the greater the degree of substitution will be.

Income Elasticity of Demand

Income Elasticity of Demand
A measure of the responsiveness of quantity demanded to changes in income.

Income elasticity of demand measures the responsiveness of quantity demanded to changes in income. It is calculated by dividing the percentage change in quantity demanded of a good by the percentage change in income.

$$E_y = \frac{\text{Percentage change in quantity demanded}}{\text{Percentage change in income}}$$

where E_y = coefficient of income elasticity of demand, or elasticity coefficient.

Income elasticity of demand is positive, $E_y > 0$, for a *normal good*. Recall that a normal good is one whose demand and thus whose quantity demanded increase, given an increase in income. Thus, for a normal good, the variables in the numerator and denominator in the income elasticity of demand formula move in the same direction.

$$E_y > 0 \rightarrow \text{Normal good}$$

In contrast to a normal good, the demand for an *inferior good* decreases as income increases. Income elasticity of demand for an inferior good is negative, $E_y < 0$.

$$E_y < 0 \rightarrow \text{Inferior good}$$

We calculate the income elasticity of demand for a good using the same approach we used to calculate price elasticity of demand.

$$E_y = \frac{\dfrac{\Delta Q_d}{Q_{d\,\text{average}}}}{\dfrac{\Delta Y}{Y_{\text{average}}}}$$

where $Q_{d\,\text{average}}$ is the average quantity demanded, and Y_{average} is the average income.

Suppose income increases from \$500 to \$600 per month, and as a result quantity demanded of good X increases from 20 units to 30 units per month. We have

Income Elastic
The condition when the percentage change in quantity demanded of a good is greater than the percentage change in income.

Income Inelastic
The condition when the percentage change in quantity demanded of a good is less than the percentage change in income.

Income Unit Elastic
The condition when the percentage change in quantity demanded of a good is equal to the percentage change in income.

$$E_y = \frac{\dfrac{10}{25}}{\dfrac{100}{550}} = 2.2$$

E_y is a positive number; so good X is a normal good. Also:

- Because $E_y > 1$, demand for good X is said to be **income elastic**. In other words, the percentage change in quantity demanded of the good is greater than the percentage change in income.

- If $E_y < 1$, the demand for the good is said to be **income inelastic**.

- If $E_y = 1$, then the demand for the good is **income unit elastic**.

Greenhouse Gases and Gas-Efficient Cars

Here is an often heard argument:
(1) Greenhouse gases generated by human activity, such as driving cars, are causing global warming. (2) If the car industry were forced to produce more gas-efficient cars, we would burn less gas. (3) Therefore, fewer greenhouses gases would be emitted.

To this argument an economist might respond, "It's not guaranteed to turn out that way." Suppose that the price of a gallon of gasoline is $3.80, that one car gets 16 miles to a gallon, and that another car gets 32 miles a gallon. Lyle, who owns the car that gets 16 miles to a gallon, travels an average of 160 miles a week; so he needs to buy 10 gallons of gasoline each week for a total cost of $38. His price for driving each mile is 24¢ (10 gallons × $3.80 = $38 and $38 ÷ 160 miles = 24¢ per mile).

Lyle trades in his car for one that gets 32 miles a gallon. If he continues to travel an average of 160 miles a week, he now needs to buy only 5 gallons of gasoline each week. With less gas purchased, less gas is used (to drive his car), and fewer greenhouse gases are emitted. Things work out just as intended.

But one thing is being overlooked. The cost of driving a mile is lower for Lyle when he drives the 32-mile-per-gallon car than when he drives the 16-mile-per-gallon car. When he drives the 16-mile-per-gallon car,

© PAUL THOMPSON IMAGES / ALAMY

he pays 24¢ to drive a mile. When he drives the 32-mile-per-gallon car, he pays only 12¢ to drive a mile (5 gallons × $3.80 = $19 and $19 ÷ 160 miles = 12¢ per mile). Lyle must still drive 160 miles to and from work each week, but he doesn't necessarily continue to drive *only* 160 miles each week when the price of driving a mile drops to 12¢. If Lyle's demand curve for driving is downward sloping, we can expect him to drive more miles at the lower price per mile.

Suppose Lyle's demand for driving is elastic. In other words, the percentage change in the miles Lyle drives is greater than the percentage change in the price of driving. Let's say that as the price of driving falls from 24¢ to 12¢ a mile, Lyle increases his driving from 160 miles a week to 370 miles a week. At 24¢ a mile and 160 miles a week, Lyle used to purchase and use 10 gallons of gas. At 12¢ a mile and 370 miles a week, Lyle purchases and uses 11.56 gallons of gas (370 miles ÷ 32 miles per gallon = 11.56 gallons). Because more greenhouse gases are emitted using 11.56 gallons of gas a week than when using 10 gallons of gas a week, we can see that Lyle's gas-efficient car doesn't really lower greenhouse gas emissions. In fact, if everyone is like Lyle, gas-efficient cars will actually increase greenhouse gases in the atmosphere. (Obviously, things don't have to turn out this way. Lyle's demand for driving could be inelastic.)

Price Elasticity of Supply

Price elasticity of supply measures the responsiveness of quantity supplied to changes in price. It is calculated by dividing the percentage change in quantity supplied of a good by the percentage change in the price of the good.

> **Price Elasticity of Supply**
> A measure of the responsiveness of quantity supplied to changes in price.

$$E_s = \frac{\text{Percentage change in quantity supplied}}{\text{Percentage change in price}}$$

where E_s stands for the coefficient of price elasticity of supply, or elasticity coefficient. We use the same approach to calculate the price elasticity of supply that we used to calculate the price elasticity of demand.

In addition, supply can be classified as elastic, inelastic, unit elastic, perfectly elastic, or perfectly inelastic (Exhibit 8).

- Elastic supply ($E_s > 1$) refers to a percentage change in quantity supplied that is greater than the percentage change in price.

Percentage change in quantity supplied > Percentage change in price →

$E_s > 1$ → Elastic supply

- Inelastic supply ($E_s < 1$) refers to a percentage change in quantity supplied that is less than the percentage change in price.

Percentage change in quantity supplied < Percentage change in price →

$E_s < 1$ → Inelastic supply

EXHIBIT 8

Price Elasticity of Supply

(a) The percentage change in quantity supplied is greater than the percentage change in price: $E_s > 1$ and supply is elastic. (b) The percentage change in quantity supplied is less than the percentage change in price: $E_s < 1$ and supply is inelastic. (c) The percentage change in quantity supplied is equal to the percentage change in price: $E_s = 1$ and supply is unit elastic. (d) A small change in price changes quantity supplied by an infinite amount: $E_s = \infty$ and supply is perfectly elastic. (e) A change in price does not change quantity supplied: $E_s = 0$ and supply is perfectly inelastic.

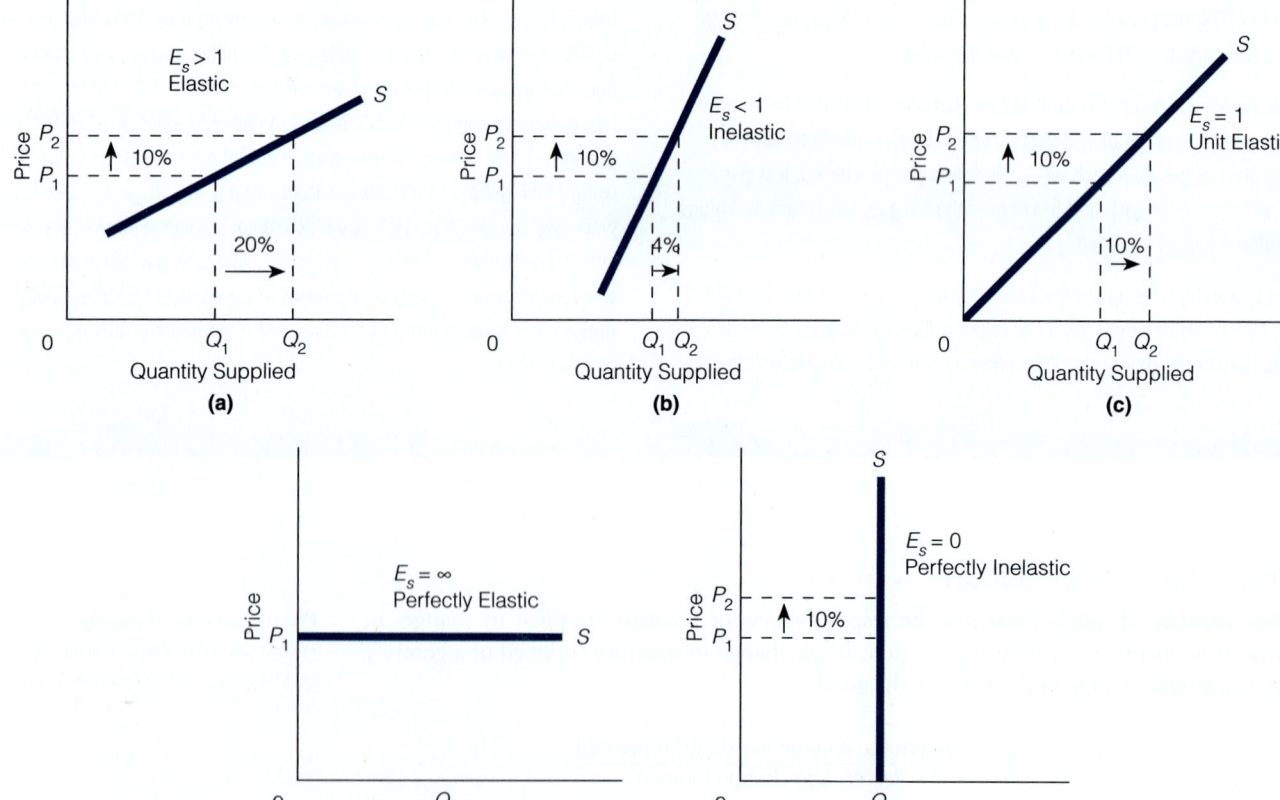

- Unit elastic supply ($E_s = 1$) refers to a percentage change in quantity supplied that is equal to the percentage change in price.

  Percentage change in quantity supplied = Percentage change in price →

  $E_s = 1$ → Unit elastic supply

- In the case of perfectly elastic supply ($E_s = \infty$), a small change in price changes the quantity supplied by an infinitely large amount (and thus the supply curve, or a portion of the overall supply curve, is horizontal).

- In the case of perfectly inelastic supply ($E_s = 0$), a change in price brings no change in quantity supplied (and thus the supply curve, or a portion of the overall supply curve, is vertical).

See Exhibit 9 for a summary of the elasticity concepts.

Price Elasticity of Supply and Time

The longer the period of adjustment is to a change in price, the higher the price elasticity of supply will be. (We are referring to goods whose quantity supplied can increase with time, a characteristic of most goods. It does not, however, cover, say, original Picasso paintings.) The obvious reason is that additional production takes time or may be impossible.

For example, suppose that the demand for new housing increases in your city and that the increase occurs all at once on Tuesday, placing upward pressure on the price of housing. The number of houses supplied will not be much different on Saturday than it was on Tuesday. It will take time for suppliers to determine whether the increase in demand is permanent. If they decide it is temporary, not much will change. If contractors decide it

EXHIBIT 9

Summary of the Four Elasticity Concepts

Type	Calculation	Possibilities	Terminology
Price elasticity of demand	$\dfrac{\text{Percentage change in quantity demanded}}{\text{Percentage change in price}}$	$E_d > 1$	Elastic
		$E_d < 1$	Inelastic
		$E_d = 1$	Unit elastic
		$E_d = \infty$	Perfectly elastic
		$E_d = 0$	Perfectly inelastic
Cross elasticity of demand	$\dfrac{\text{Percentage change in quantity demanded of one good}}{\text{Percentage change in price of another good}}$	$E_c < 0$	Complements
		$E_c > 0$	Substitutes
Income elasticity of demand	$\dfrac{\text{Percentage change in quantity demanded}}{\text{Percentage change in income}}$	$E_y > 0$	Normal good
		$E_y < 0$	Inferior good
		$E_y > 1$	Income elastic
		$E_y < 1$	Income inelastic
		$E_y = 1$	Income unit elastic
Price elasticity of supply	$\dfrac{\text{Percentage change in quantity supplied}}{\text{Percentage change in price}}$	$E_s > 1$	Elastic
		$E_s < 1$	Inelastic
		$E_s = 1$	Unit elastic
		$E_s = \infty$	Perfectly elastic
		$E_s = 0$	Perfectly inelastic

House Prices and the Elasticity of Supply

House prices increased in the United States during the years 1998 through mid-2006. House prices did not rise by the same percentage in all cities and states, however. For example, house prices increased more in Los Angeles than in Houston, Texas. House prices increased more in Florida than in Idaho. Why didn't house prices rise by the same percentage in every location? Why did they rise more in some places than in others?

One reason could be that demand didn't increase by the same amount in all locations. The demand for houses in, say, San Francisco could have risen by more than the demand for houses in Topeka, Kansas. No doubt this is part of the explanation.

But another part of the explanation has to do with supply. As the price of a good rises, we expect the quantity supplied (of the good) to rise too. In other words, the supply curve of the good is upward sloping. But, although the supply curve of housing is upward sloping, not all supply curves have the same elasticity of supply.

For example, Exhibit 10 shows two supply curves, S_1 and S_2. S_1 has lower elasticity of supply than S_2. Now suppose that S_1 represents the supply curve of housing in city 1 and that S_2 represents the supply curve of housing in city 2. Suppose the demand for housing in each city rises from D_1 to D_2, as in Exhibit 10. As a result, the price of houses rises in both cities, but it rises by more in city 1 than in city 2. In other words, the lower the elasticity of supply is, the greater the increase in price will be.

But why would the elasticity of supply be lower for housing in city 1 than in city 2? The answer could have to do with land use regulations. Suppose that each city has 1,000 vacant areas and that house developers are able to put houses up on only 10 percent of vacant land in city 1, whereas in city 2 house developers are able to put houses up on 70 percent of it. For a given rise in price, the developers in city 2 can put up more houses (of a given size and plot size) than developers in city 1 can put up. As a result, if the demand for houses rises by the same amount in city 1 and city 2, more houses will be built in city 2 than in 1, and so the price of houses will rise by less in city 2 than in city 1.

EXHIBIT 10

House Prices and Elasticity of Supply

S_1 represents the supply of housing in city 1, and S_2 represents the supply of housing in city 2. S_1 has lower elasticity of supply than S_2. Suppose the demand for housing in each city rises from D_1 to D_2 As a result, the price of houses rises in both cities, but it rises by more in city 1 than city 2. In other words, the lower the elasticity of supply, the greater the increase in price.

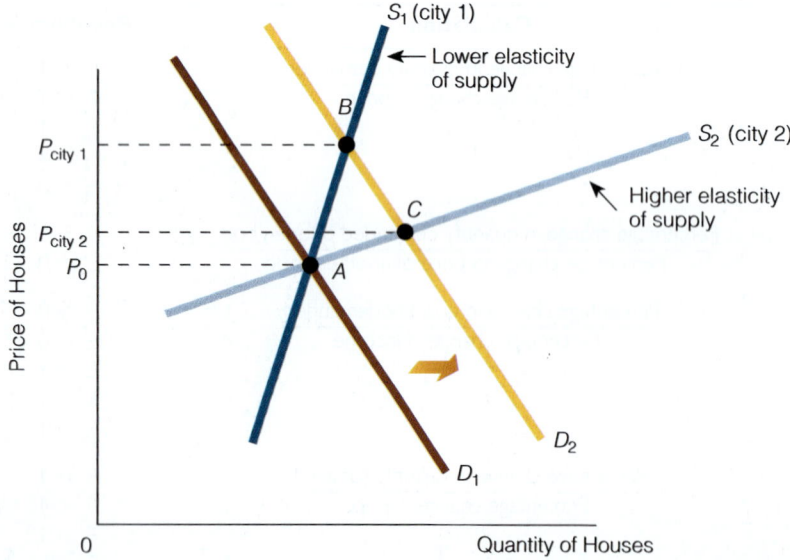

is permanent, they need time to move resources from the production of other things into the production of new housing. Simply put, the change in quantity supplied of housing is likely to be different in the long run than in the short run, given a change in price. This effect translates into a higher price elasticity of supply in the long run than in the short run.

ⓣhinking Like AN ECONOMIST

Think Ratios In a way, this chapter is about ratios. A ratio describes how one thing changes (the numerator) relative to a change in something else (the denominator). For example, when we discuss price elasticity of demand, we investigate how quantity demanded changes as price changes; when we discuss income elasticity of demand, we explore how quantity demanded changes as income changes. Economists often think in terms of ratios because they are often comparing the change in one variable to the change in another. ●●●

THE RELATIONSHIP BETWEEN TAXES AND ELASTICITY

Before explaining how elasticity affects taxes and tax revenues, we explore how supply and demand determine who pays a tax.

Who Pays the Tax?

Many people think that if government places a tax on the seller of a good, the seller actually pays the tax. However, the *placement* of a tax is not the same as its *payment*, and placement does not guarantee payment.

Suppose the government imposes a tax on sellers of music DVDs. Sellers are taxed $1 for every DVD they sell: sell a DVD, send $1 to the government. The government action changes the equilibrium in the DVD market. In Exhibit 11, before the tax is imposed, the equilibrium price and the quantity of tapes are $15 and Q_1, respectively. The tax per DVD shifts the supply curve leftward from S_1 to S_2. The vertical distance between the two supply curves represents the $1-per-DVD tax, because what matters to sellers is how much they keep for each DVD sold, not how much buyers pay. For example, if sellers are keeping $15 per DVD for Q_1 DVDs before the tax is imposed, then they want to keep as much after the tax is imposed. But if the tax is $1, the only way they can keep $15 per DVD for Q_1 DVDs is to receive $16 per DVD. They receive $16 per DVD from buyers, turn over $1 to the government, and keep $15. In other words, each quantity on the new supply curve, S_2, corresponds to a $1 higher price than it did on the old supply curve, S_1.

However, the new equilibrium price will not necessarily be $1 higher than the old equilibrium price. In this case, the new equilibrium happens

EXHIBIT 11

Who Pays the Tax?

A tax placed on the sellers of DVDs shifts the supply curve from S_1 to S_2 and raises the equilibrium price from $15.00 to $15.50. Part of the tax is paid by buyers through a higher price paid ($15.50 instead of $15.00), and part of the tax is paid by sellers through a lower price kept ($14.50 instead of $15.00).

to be at a price of $15.50 and a quantity of Q_2. Buyers pay $15.50 per DVD after the tax is imposed, as opposed to $15.00 before the tax was imposed. The difference between the new and old prices is the amount of the $1.00 tax that buyers pay per DVD. In this example, buyers pay 50¢, or one-half of the $1.00 tax per DVD.

> Before the tax, buyers pay $15.00.
>
> After the tax, buyers pay $15.50.

The sellers receive $15.50 per DVD from buyers after the tax is imposed, as opposed to $15.00 per DVD before the tax was imposed, but they do not get to keep $15.50 per DVD. One dollar has to be turned over to the government, leaving the sellers with $14.50. Before the tax was imposed, however, sellers received and kept $15.00 per DVD. In this example, the difference between $15.00 and $14.50—50¢—is the amount of the tax per DVD that sellers pay.

> Before the tax, sellers receive $15.00 and keep $15.00.
>
> After the tax, sellers receive $15.50 and keep $14.50.

So, although the full tax was *placed* on the sellers, they *paid* only one-half of it; although none of the tax was placed on buyers, they paid one-half of it too. The lesson is that government can place a tax on whomever it wants, but the laws of supply and demand determine who actually ends up paying it.

ⓣhinking Like AN ECONOMIST

Placement Can Be Different from Payment According to a layperson, if the government places a tax on entity A, then entity A pays the tax. The economist knows that the placement and the payment of a tax are two different things. Government may determine the placement of a tax, but supply and demand determine who pays. ● ● ●

Elasticity and the Tax

In our tax example, buyers paid half of the $1 tax and sellers paid half, but this is not the outcome in every situation. The buyer can pay more than half the tax. In fact, the buyer can pay the full tax if demand for the good is perfectly inelastic, as in Exhibit 12(a). The tax shifts the supply curve from S_1 to S_2, and the equilibrium price rises from $15.00 to $16.00. In other words, if demand is perfectly inelastic and a tax is placed on the sellers of a good, buyers pay the full tax as part of a higher price.

Parts (b)–(d) of Exhibit 12 show other cases. In part (b), demand is perfectly elastic. The tax shifts the supply curve from S_1 to S_2, but the equilibrium price does not change. Sellers must therefore pay the full tax if demand is perfectly elastic. In part (c), supply is perfectly elastic, and buyers pay the full tax. In part (d), a change in price causes no change in quantity supplied. If sellers try to charge a higher price than $15 for their good (and thus try to get buyers to pay some of the tax), a surplus will result, driving the price back down to $15. In this case, sellers pay the full tax. Although the exhibit does not show this possibility, sellers would receive $15, turn over $1 to the government, and keep $14 for each unit sold.

Degree of Elasticity and Tax Revenue

Of two sellers, seller A faces a perfectly inelastic demand for her product and is currently selling 10,000 units a month. Seller B faces an elastic demand for his product and is

EXHIBIT 12

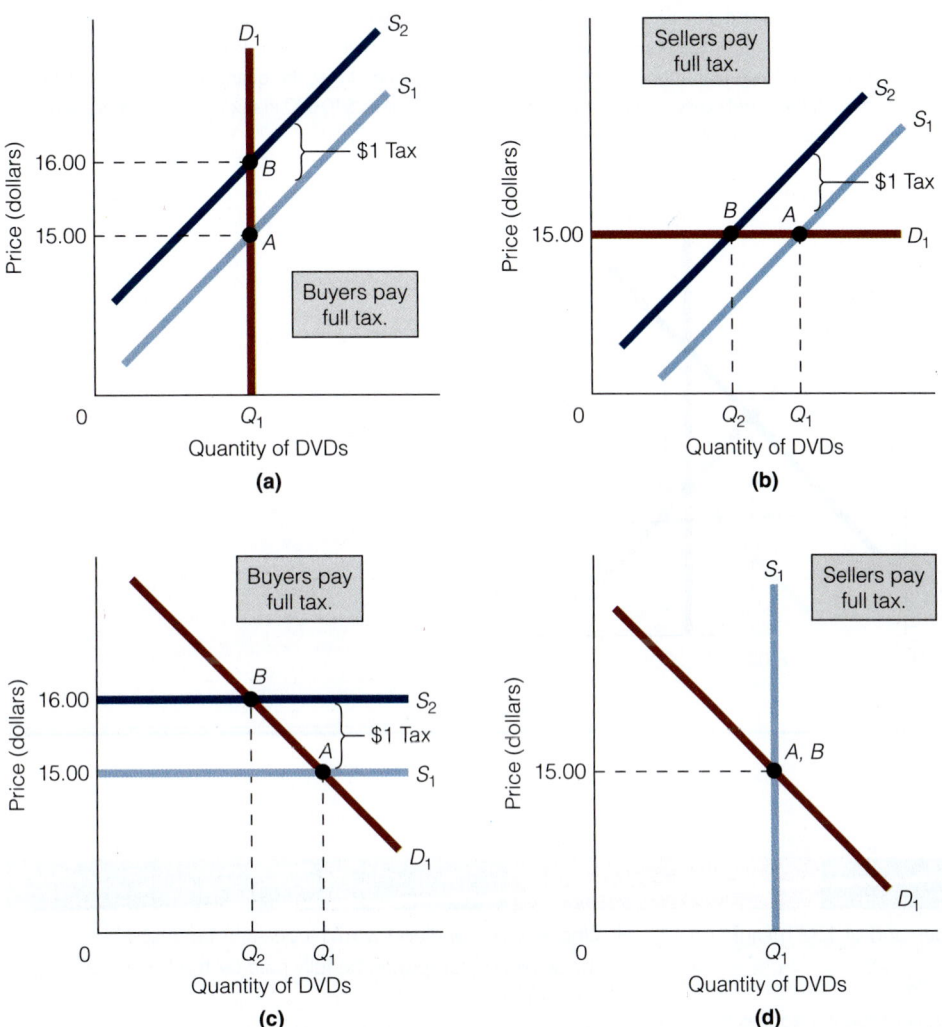

(a)

(b)

(c)

(d)

Different Elasticities and Who Pays the Tax

Four extreme cases are illustrated here. If demand is perfectly inelastic (a) or if supply is perfectly elastic (c), buyers pay the full tax even though the tax may be placed entirely on sellers. If demand is perfectly elastic (b) or if supply is perfectly inelastic (d), the full tax is paid by the sellers.

currently selling 10,000 units a month. Government is thinking about placing a $1 tax per unit of product sold on one of the two sellers. If government's objective is to maximize tax revenues, it should tax seller A, because that seller is facing the inelastic demand curve.

In Exhibit 13, the demand curve facing seller A is D_1; the demand curve facing seller B is D_2. S_1 represents the supply curve for both firms. Currently, both firms are at equilibrium at point A, selling 10,000 units. If government places a $1 tax per unit sold on seller A, the supply curve shifts to S_2, and the equilibrium is now at point C. Because demand is perfectly inelastic, A still sells 10,000 units. Tax revenue equals the tax ($1) times 10,000 units, or $10,000. If government places the $1 tax per unit sold on seller B, tax revenue will be only $8,000. When the tax shifts the supply curve to S_2, the equilibrium moves to point B, where only 8,000 units are sold.

The lesson is that given the $1 tax per unit sold, tax revenues are maximized by placing the tax on the seller who faces the more inelastic (less elastic) demand curve.

EXHIBIT 13

Maximizing Tax Revenues

Two sellers, A and B, are each currently selling 10,000 units of their good. A faces the demand curve D_1 and B faces D_2. If the objective is to maximize tax revenues with a $1 tax per unit of product sold and only one seller can be taxed, taxing A will maximize tax revenues and taxing B will not. Note that after the tax has been placed, the supply curve shifts from S_1 to S_2. A is in equilibrium at point C, selling 10,000 units, and B is in equilibrium at point B, selling 8,000 units. Because tax revenues equal the tax per unit times the quantity of output sold, taxing A raises $10,000 in tax revenues whereas taxing B raises $8,000.

SELF-TEST

1. What does an income elasticity of demand of 1.33 mean?

2. What does perfectly inelastic supply signify?

3. Why will government raise more tax revenue if it applies a tax to a good with inelastic demand than if it applies the tax to a good with elastic demand?

4. Under what condition would a per-unit tax placed on the sellers of computers be fully paid by the buyers of computers?

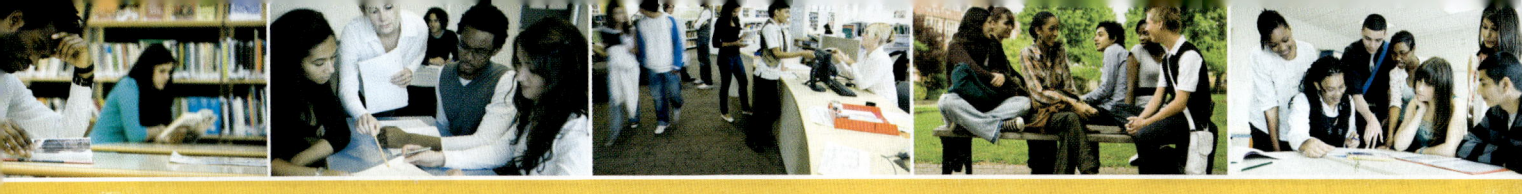

OFFICE HOURS

"What Is the Relationship Between Different Price Elasticities of Demand and Total Revenue?"

STUDENT:

I'm still not sure I understand the relationship between price elasticity of demand and total revenue.

INSTRUCTOR:

Let's use some numbers to illustrate the relationship. Here we have identified two points on a demand curve:

Price	Quantity Demanded
$10	110
$12	100

The price elasticity of demand between these two points is 0.52; so demand is inelastic. Now let's find the total revenue at each price. If we assume we are in equilibrium (at which quantity demanded is equal to quantity supplied), then total revenue at $10 is $1,100. (We get this amount by multiplying $10 times 110.) When price is $12, total revenue is $1,200. We conclude that if price elasticity of demand is less than 1 (demand is inelastic), a price rise will raise total revenue. Therefore, if we lower price (from $12 to $10), total revenue will decline.

Now let's change one of the numbers in the table—100 to 80. We now have this:

Price	Quantity Demanded
$10	110
$12	80

If we compute the new price elasticity of demand, we get 1.73, meaning that demand is elastic. Now let's compute total revenue at each price. At $10, that's $1,100. At the higher price of $12, total revenue is $960. So, if price elasticity is greater than 1 (demand is elastic) and if price rises, total revenue falls. And, of course, if price falls (from $12 to $10), total revenue will rise.

STUDENT:

So in the first example, when demand was inelastic, we raised price, and total revenue increased. But in the second example, when demand was elastic and we raised price, total revenue decreased.

INSTRUCTOR:

Yes, that's correct. When demand is inelastic, the directional change in price brings about the same directional change in total revenue: When price rises, total revenue rises; when price falls, total revenue falls. But when demand is elastic, the directional change in price brings about an opposite directional change in total revenue: When price rises, total revenue falls; when price falls, total revenue rises.

POINTS TO REMEMBER

1. When demand is inelastic, price and total revenue move in the same direction.
2. When demand is elastic, price and total revenue move in opposite directions.

CHAPTER SUMMARY

PRICE ELASTICITY OF DEMAND

- Price elasticity of demand is a measure of the responsiveness of quantity demanded to changes in price.
- If the percentage change in quantity demanded is greater than the percentage change in price, demand is elastic.
- If the percentage change in quantity demanded is less than the percentage change in price, demand is inelastic.
- If the percentage change in quantity demanded is equal to the percentage change in price, demand is unit elastic.
- If a small change in price causes an infinitely large change in quantity demanded, demand is perfectly elastic.
- If a change in price causes no change in quantity demanded, demand is perfectly inelastic.
- The coefficient of price elasticity of demand (E_d) is negative, signifying the inverse relationship between price and quantity demanded. For convenience, however, the absolute value of the elasticity coefficient is used.

TOTAL REVENUE AND PRICE ELASTICITY OF DEMAND

- Total revenue equals price times quantity sold. Total expenditure equals price times quantity purchased. Total revenue equals total expenditure.
- If demand is elastic, price and total revenue are inversely related: as price rises (falls), total revenue falls (rises).
- If demand is inelastic, price and total revenue are directly related: as price rises (falls), total revenue rises (falls).
- If demand is unit elastic, total revenue is independent of price: as price rises (falls), total revenue remains constant.

DETERMINANTS OF PRICE ELASTICITY OF DEMAND

- The more substitutes a good has, the higher the price elasticity of demand; the fewer substitutes a good has, the lower the price elasticity of demand.
- The more that a good is considered a luxury instead of a necessity, the higher the price elasticity of demand will be.
- The greater the percentage of one's budget that goes to purchase a good, the higher the price elasticity of demand will be; the smaller the percentage of one's budget that goes to purchase a good, the lower the price elasticity of demand.
- The more time that passes (since a price change), the higher the price elasticity of demand will be; the less time that passes, the lower the price elasticity of demand.

CROSS ELASTICITY OF DEMAND

- Cross elasticity of demand measures the responsiveness in the quantity demanded of one good to changes in the price of another good.

- If $E_c > 0$, two goods are substitutes. If $E_c < 0$, two goods are complements.

INCOME ELASTICITY OF DEMAND

- Income elasticity of demand measures the responsiveness of quantity demanded to changes in income.
- If $E_y > 0$, the good is a normal good. If $E_y < 0$, the good is an inferior good.
- If $E_y > 1$, demand is income elastic. If $E_y < 1$, demand is income inelastic. If $E_y = 1$, demand is income unit elastic.

PRICE ELASTICITY OF SUPPLY

- Price elasticity of supply measures the responsiveness of quantity supplied to changes in price.
- If the percentage change in quantity supplied is greater than the percentage change in price, supply is elastic.
- If the percentage change in quantity supplied is less than the percentage change in price, supply is inelastic.
- If the percentage change in quantity supplied is equal to the percentage change in price, supply is unit elastic.
- Price elasticity of supply is higher in the long run than in the short run.

TAXES AND ELASTICITY

- The placement of a tax is different from its payment. For example, a tax may be placed on the seller of a good, and both the seller and buyer end up paying the tax.
- In this chapter, we discuss a per-unit tax that was placed on the seller of a specific good (DVDs). This tax shifted the supply curve of DVDs leftward. The vertical distance between the old supply curve (before the tax) and the new supply curve (after the tax) was equal to the per-unit tax.
- If a per-unit tax is placed on the seller of a good, both the buyer and the seller will pay part of the tax if the demand curve is downward sloping and the supply curve is upward sloping.
- The more inelastic the demand is, the larger the percentage of the tax is that the buyer will pay.
- The more elastic the demand, the smaller the percentage of the tax is that the buyer will pay.
- When demand is perfectly inelastic or supply is perfectly elastic, buyers pay the full tax.
- When demand is elastic or supply is perfectly inelastic, sellers pay the full tax.

KEY TERMS AND CONCEPTS

Price Elasticity of Demand
Elastic Demand
Inelastic Demand
Unit Elastic Demand

Perfectly Elastic Demand
Perfectly Inelastic Demand
Total Revenue (*TR*)

Cross Elasticity of Demand
Income Elasticity of Demand
Income Elastic

Income Inelastic
Income Unit Elastic
Price Elasticity of Supply

QUESTIONS AND PROBLEMS

1. Suppose Austin, Texas, is hit by a tornado that destroys 25 percent of the housing in the area. Would you expect the total expenditure on housing after the tornado to be greater than, less than, or equal to what it was before the tornado? Explain your answer.

2. A tax is placed on the sellers of a good. What happens to the percentage of this tax that buyers pay as the price elasticity of demand for the good decreases? Explain your answer.

3. Identify whether total revenue rises, falls, or remains constant for each of the following:

   a. Demand is inelastic, and price falls.

   b. Demand is elastic, and price rises.

   c. Demand is unit elastic, and price rises.

   d. Demand is inelastic, and price rises.

   e. Demand is elastic, and price falls.

4. "If government wishes to tax certain goods, it should tax goods that have inelastic rather than elastic demand." What is the rationale for this statement?

5. Suppose a straight-line downward-sloping demand curve shifts rightward. Is the price elasticity of demand higher, lower, or the same between any two prices on the new (higher) demand curve than on the old (lower) demand curve?

6. In 1947, the U.S. Department of Justice brought a suit against the DuPont Company (which at the time sold 75 percent of all the cellophane in the United States) for monopolizing the production and sale of cellophane. In court, the DuPont Company tried to show that cellophane was only one of several goods in the market in which it was sold. It argued that its market was not the cellophane market but the flexible packaging materials market, which included (besides cellophane) waxed paper, aluminum foil, and other such products. DuPont pointed out that it had only 20 percent of all sales in this more broadly defined market. Using this information, discuss how the concept of cross elasticity of demand would help establish whether DuPont should have been viewed as a firm in the cellophane market or as a firm in the flexible packaging materials market.

7. Suppose the current price of gasoline at the pump is $1 per gallon and that 1 million gallons are sold per month. A politician proposes to add a 10¢ tax to the price of a gallon of gasoline. She says the tax will generate $100,000 tax revenues per month (1 million gallons × $0.10 = $100,000). What assumption is she making?

8. Assume the demand for product A is perfectly inelastic. Further, assume that the buyers of A get the funds to pay for it by stealing.

   a. If the supply of A decreases, what happens to its price?

   b. What happens to the amount of crime committed by the buyers of A?

9. Prove that price elasticity of demand is not the same as the slope of a demand curve

10. Suppose you learned that the price elasticity of demand for wheat is 0.7 between the current price for wheat and a price $2 higher per bushel. Do you think farmers collectively would try to reduce the supply of wheat and drive the price up $2 higher per bushel? Explain your answer. Assuming that they would try to reduce supply, what problems might they have in actually doing so?

11. For each of the following, identify where demand is elastic, inelastic, perfectly elastic, perfectly inelastic, or unit elastic:

    a. Price rises by 10 percent, and the quantity demanded falls by 2 percent.

    b. Price falls by 5 percent, and the quantity demanded rises by 4 percent.

    c. Price falls by 6 percent, and the quantity demanded does not change.

    d. Price rises by 2 percent, and the quantity demanded falls by 1 percent.

12. How might you determine whether toothpaste and mouthwash manufacturers are competitors?

13. Explain how a seller can determine whether the demand for his or her good is inelastic, elastic, or unit elastic between two prices.

14. In each of the following pairs of goods, which has the higher price elasticity of demand?

    a. Airline travel in the short run or airline travel in the long run

    b. Television sets or Sony television sets

    c. Cars or Fords

    d. Telephones or AT&T telephones

    e. Popcorn or Orville Redenbacher's popcorn

WORKING WITH NUMBERS AND GRAPHS

1. A college raises its annual tuition from $23,000 to $24,000, and its student enrollment falls from 4,877 to 4,705. Compute the price elasticity of demand. Is demand elastic or inelastic?

2. As the price of good X rises from $10 to $12, the quantity demanded of good Y rises from 100 units to 114 units. Are X and Y substitutes or complements? What is the cross elasticity of demand?

3. The quantity demanded of good X rises from 130 to 145 units as income rises from $2,000 to $2,500 a month. What is the income elasticity of demand?

4. The quantity supplied of a good rises from 120 to 140 as price rises from $4 to $5.50. What is the price elasticity of supply?

5. In the following figure, what is the price elasticity of demand between the two prices on D_1? On D_2?

CHAPTER 21

CONSUMER CHOICE: MAXIMIZING UTILITY AND BEHAVIORAL ECONOMICS

© 2010 JUPITERIMAGES

Introduction Just before purchasing a computer, a book, or an iPod, what do you think about? Do you say, "Do I want this or not?" Many people would give this answer. Economists have put this response under a microscope and rephrase it: "The marginal utility of this item divided by its price is greater than the marginal utility of other items divided by their prices; so I am going to make this purchase because it will increase my overall utility." You may not believe now that you—or anyone else—would think this way, but you may believe it after reading this chapter.

UTILITY THEORY

Water is cheap, and diamonds are expensive. But water is necessary to life and diamonds are not. Isn't it odd—even paradoxical—that what is necessary to life is cheap, and what is not necessary is expensive? Eighteenth-century economist Adam Smith wondered about this question. He observed that often things with the greatest value in use (or that are the most useful) have a relatively low price, and things with little or no value in use have a high price. Smith's observation came to be known as the diamond-water paradox, or the paradox of value. The paradox challenged economists, and they sought a solution to it. This section begins to develop parts of the solution they found.

Utility: Total and Marginal

Saying that a good gives you utility is the same as saying that it has the power to satisfy your wants or that it gives you satisfaction. For example, suppose you buy your first unit of good X, and you get a certain amount of utility, say, 10 utils from it. (Utils are an artificial construct used to measure utility; we realize you have never seen a util—no one has.) You buy a second unit of good X, and, once again, you get a certain amount of utility from this second unit, say, 8 utils. You purchase a third unit and receive 7 utils. The sum of the amount of utility you obtain from each of the 3 units is the total utility you receive from purchasing good X: 25 utils. Total utility is the total satisfaction one receives from consuming a particular quantity of a good (in this example, 3 units of good X).

Diamond-Water Paradox
The observation that things with the greatest value in use sometimes have little value in exchange and things with little value in use sometimes have the greatest value in exchange.

Utility
A measure of the satisfaction, happiness, or benefit that results from the consumption of a good.

Util
An artificial construct used to measure utility.

Total Utility
The total satisfaction a person receives from consuming a particular quantity of a good.

Marginal Utility
The additional utility a person receives from consuming an additional unit of a good.

Total utility is different from marginal utility. Marginal utility is the *additional* utility gained from consuming an additional unit of good *X*. Marginal utility (*MU*) is the change in total utility (ΔTU) divided by the change in the quantity (ΔQ) consumed of a good:

$$MU = \frac{\Delta TU}{\Delta Q}$$

where the change in the quantity consumed of a good is usually equal to 1 unit.

To illustrate, suppose you receive 10 utils of total utility from consuming 1 apple and 19 utils of total utility from consuming 2 apples. The marginal utility of the second apple (the additional utility of consuming an additional apple) is 9 utils. As a person consumes more apples, total utility rises, but marginal utility (additional utility received from the additional apple) falls. In other words, total utility rises as marginal utility falls.

ⓣhinking Like AN ECONOMIST

Total Utility and Marginal Utility Can Move in Opposite Directions The economist knows that marginal utility and total utility can move in opposite directions. So a rise in total utility doesn't mean that marginal utility is rising too. To illustrate, look at the table:

(1) Number of Apples Consumed	(2) Total Utility (utils)	(3) Marginal Utility (utils)
1	10	10
2	19	9
3	27	8

Moving from one to two to three apples, total utility rises, but marginal utility falls. ●●●

Law of Diminishing Marginal Utility

Do you think the marginal utility of the second unit is greater than, less than, or equal to the marginal utility of the first unit? Consider the difference in marginal utility between the third unit and the second unit or between the fifth unit and the fourth unit (had we extended the number of units consumed). In general, the question is whether the marginal utility of the following unit is greater than, less than, or equal to that of the preceding unit.

Law of Diminishing Marginal Utility
The marginal utility gained by consuming equal successive units of a good will decline as the amount consumed increases.

Economists have generally answered "less than." The law of diminishing marginal utility states that, for a given time period, the marginal utility gained by consuming equal successive units of a good declines as the amount consumed increases. In other words, the number of utils gained by consuming the first unit of a good is greater than the number of utils gained by consuming the second unit (which is greater than the number gained by the third, which is greater than the number gained by the fourth, and so on).

The law of diminishing marginal utility is illustrated in Exhibit 1. The table in part (a) shows both the total utility of consuming a certain number of units of a good and the marginal utility of consuming additional units. The graph in part (b) shows the total utility curve for the data in part (a), and the graph in part (c) shows the marginal utility curve for the data in part (a). The graphs in parts (b) and (c) show that total utility can increase as marginal utility decreases. This relationship between total utility and marginal utility is important in unraveling the diamond-water paradox.

The law of diminishing marginal utility is based on the idea that if a good has a variety of uses but only 1 unit of the good is available, then the consumer will use the first unit to satisfy his or her most urgent want. If 2 units are available, the consumer will use the second unit to satisfy a less urgent want. Suppose that good X can be used to satisfy wants

EXHIBIT 1

(1) Units of Good X	(2) Total Utility (utils)	(3) Marginal Utility (utils)
0	0	—
1	10	10
2	19	9
3	27	8
4	34	7
5	40	6

(a)

Total Utility, Marginal Utility, and the Law of Diminishing Marginal Utility

TU = total utility and MU = marginal utility. (a) Both total utility and marginal utility are expressed in utils. Marginal utility is the change in total utility divided by the change in the quantity consumed of the good, $MU = \Delta TU/\Delta Q$. (b) Total utility curve. (c) Marginal utility curve. Together, (b) and (c) demonstrate that total utility can increase (b) as marginal utility decreases (c).

This is a marginal utility curve. It is derived by plotting the data in columns 1 and 3 in part (a) and then connecting the points.

This is a total utility curve. It is derived by plotting the data in columns 1 and 2 in part (a) and then connecting the points.

(b)   **(c)**

A through E, with A being the most urgent and E being the least. Also, B is more urgent than C, C is more urgent than D, and D is more urgent than E. We can chart the wants as follows:

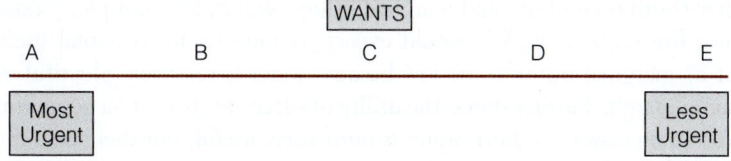

Suppose the first unit of good X can satisfy any one—but only one—of wants A through E. An individual will choose to satisfy the most urgent want, A, instead of B, C, D, or E, because people ordinarily satisfy their most urgent want before all others. If you were dying of thirst in a desert (having gone without water for 3 days) and came across a quart of water, you would drink, not wash your hands; that is, you would satisfy your most urgent want first. Washing your hands in the water would give you less utility than drinking it.

THE MILLIONAIRE AND THE PAUPER: WHAT THE LAW SAYS AND DOESN'T SAY Who gets more utility from one more dollar, a poor man or a millionaire?

Most people would say that a poor man gets more utility from one more dollar because the poor man has far fewer dollars than the millionaire. To a millionaire, one more dollar is nothing. A millionaire has so many dollars, one more doesn't mean a thing.

Some people think the law of diminishing marginal utility substantiates the claim that a millionaire gets less utility from one more dollar than a poor man does. Unfortunately, though, this interpretation is a misreading of the law. The law says that, for the millionaire or the poor man, an additional dollar is worth less than the dollar that preceded it. Let's say the millionaire has $2 million and the poor man has $1,000. We now give each of them one more dollar. The law of diminishing marginal utility says that (1) the additional dollar is worth less to the millionaire than her two-millionth dollar and (2) the additional dollar is worth less to the poor man than his one-thousandth dollar. That is all the law says. We do not and cannot know whether the additional dollar is worth more or less to the millionaire than it is to the poor man. In summary, the law says something about the millionaire and about the poor man (both persons value the last dollar less than the next-to-last dollar), but it does not say anything about the millionaire's utility compared to the poor man's utility.

Interpersonal Utility Comparison
Comparing the utility one person receives from a good, service, or activity with the utility another person receives from the same good, service, or activity.

To compare the utility the millionaire gets from the additional dollar with the utility the poor man gets from it is to fall into the trap of making an interpersonal utility comparison. The utility that one person gets cannot be scientifically or objectively compared with the utility that another person gets from the same thing because utility is subjective. Who knows for certain how much satisfaction (utility) the millionaire gets from the additional dollar, compared with that of the poor man? The poor man may care little for money; he may shun it, consider the love of it the root of all evil, and prefer to consume the things in life that do not require money. On the other hand, the millionaire may be interested only in amassing more money. We must not guess at the utility that someone obtains from consuming a certain item, compare it to our guess of the utility that another person obtains from consuming the same item, and then call our guesses scientific facts.

thinking Like AN ECONOMIST

Seeming Reasonable Is Not Enough The economist knows that what looks true or seems true may not be true. Although assuming that the millionaire receives less utility from an additional dollar than a pauper may seem perfectly reasonable, the assumption does not make it so. At one time, believing that the world was flat seemed perfectly reasonable, but we know that the world is not flat. ●●●

The Solution to the Diamond-Water Paradox

Goods have both total utility and marginal utility. Water, for example, is extremely useful; we cannot live without it. We would expect its total utility (its total usefulness) to be high but its marginal utility to be low because water is relatively plentiful. As the law of diminishing marginal utility states, the utility of successive units of a good diminishes as its consumption increases. In short, water is immensely useful, but there is so much of it that individuals place relatively little value on another unit of it.

In contrast, diamonds are not as useful as water. We would expect the total utility of diamonds to be lower than that of water, but their marginal utility to be high. Because there are relatively few diamonds in the world, their consumption (in contrast to water consumption) takes place at relatively high marginal utility. Diamonds, which are rare, are used only for their few valuable uses. Water, which is plentiful, gets used for its many valuable uses and for its not so valuable uses (e.g., spraying the car with the hose for 2 more minutes even though you are 99 percent sure that the soap is fully rinsed off).

So the total utility of water is high because water is extremely useful. The total utility of diamonds is comparatively low because diamonds are not as useful as water. The marginal utility of water is low because water is so plentiful that people consume it at low

Why Did I Buy the Gym Membership?

Many people buy a gym membership but do not regularly use it. This is usually how things go. A person visits a gym. He sees people working out; he sees all the different exercise machines. A gym employee tells him that a membership is a great deal, only $1 a day. He signs up for a membership. He visits the gym every other day for the first week of his membership. Then weeks go by without his visiting. He begins to feel guilty about not using his membership; so he drags himself to the gym. A few more weeks pass, and then he drags himself to the gym one more time. Finally, three months pass without his going at all. One day he gets on the phone and cancels his gym membership. He doesn't even want to add up how much he has spent for a gym membership he rarely used. He sits down, has a bowl of ice cream, and watches television.

LOURENS SMAK/ALAMY

What has happened is that our gym member has underestimated the law of diminishing marginal utility applied to exercising at a gym. When he first visits the gym and looks at all the people working out, he might feel that here is a place where utility can be gained. But that utility might simply be the utility he expects to receive on his *first visit* to the gym times the number of visits. In other words, he expects to receive, say,

100 utils on his first visit, and he plans to visit the gym 90 days a year. That is a total of 9,000 utils.

What our gym member overlooks is that the utility on his second visit might be less than the utility on his first visit. In other words, the law of diminishing marginal utility might apply to exercising at the gym. For all we know, there could be a dramatic drop-off in marginal utility with, say, the third or fourth visit. His marginal utility per visit might go something like this: first visit, 100 utils; second visit, 80 utils; third visit, 20 utils; fourth visit, 5 utils.

In short, our gym member's decision to join the gym might have been made based on his thinking that he wouldn't experience diminishing marginal utility, when in fact that is exactly what he does experience.

Now let's return to the gym employee who told our prospective gym member that the gym membership was a great deal: only $1 a day. That $1 a day might have been a great deal for the first day (the first visit to the gym), because our gym member received more than one dollar's worth of utility on the first visit. But then diminishing marginal utility kicked in, and by the time he got to the fifth visit, he no longer was receiving more than one dollar's worth of utility.

marginal utility. The marginal utility of diamonds is high because diamonds are so scarce that people consume them at high marginal utility.

Prices therefore reflect marginal utility, not total utility.

CONSUMER EQUILIBRIUM AND DEMAND

This section identifies the condition necessary for consumer equilibrium and then discusses the relationship between equilibrium and the law of demand. The analysis is based on the assumption that individuals seek to maximize utility.

Equating Marginal Utilities per Dollar

Suppose there are only two goods in the world: apples and oranges. At present, a consumer is spending his entire income consuming 10 apples and 10 oranges a week. For a particular week, the marginal utility (MU) and price (P) of each are as follows:[1]

$$MU_{oranges} = 30 \text{ utils}$$
$$MU_{apples} = 20 \text{ utils}$$
$$P_{oranges} = \$1$$
$$P_{apples} = \$1$$

So the consumer's marginal (last) dollar spent on apples returns 20 utils per dollar, and his marginal (last) dollar spent on oranges returns 30 utils per dollar. The ratio MU_O/P_O (O = oranges) is greater than the ratio MU_A/P_A (A = apples):

$$\frac{MU_O}{P_O} > \frac{MU_A}{P_A}$$

If the consumer recognizes this fact one week, he might redirect his purchases of apples and oranges the next week: "If I buy an orange, I receive more utility [30 utils] than if I buy an apple [20 utils]. It's better to buy 1 more orange with $1 and 1 less apple. I gain 30 utils from buying the orange, which is 10 utils more than if I buy the apple."

As the consumer buys 1 more orange and 1 less apple, however, the marginal utility of oranges falls (recall what the law of diminishing marginal utility says about consuming additional units of a good), and the marginal utility of apples rises (the consumer is consuming fewer apples). Because the consumer has bought 1 more orange and 1 less apple, he now has 11 oranges and 9 apples. At this new combination of goods,

$$MU_O = 25 \text{ utils}$$
$$MU_A = 25 \text{ utils}$$
$$P_O = \$1$$
$$P_A = \$1$$

Now, the ratio MU_O/P_O equals the ratio MU_A/P_A. The consumer is getting exactly the same amount of utility (25 utils) per dollar from each of the two goods. There is no way for the consumer to redirect his purchases (i.e., buy more of one good and less of another good) and have more utility. Thus the consumer is in equilibrium; that is, he or she derives the same marginal utility per dollar for all goods. The condition for **consumer equilibrium** is

$$\frac{MU_A}{P_A} = \frac{MU_B}{P_B} = \frac{MU_C}{P_C} = \cdots = \frac{MU_Z}{P_Z}$$

where the letters A–Z represent all the goods a person buys.[2]

Consumer Equilibrium
The equilibrium that occurs when the consumer has spent all income and the marginal utilities per dollar spent on each good purchased are equal: $MU_A/P_A = MU_B/P_B = \ldots = MU_Z/P_Z$, where the letters A–Z represent all the goods a person buys.

---

1. You may wonder where we get these marginal utility figures. They are points on hypothetical marginal utility curves, such as the one in Exhibit 1. What is important is that one number is greater than the other. We could easily have picked other numbers, such as 300 and 200.
2. We are assuming that the consumer exhausts his or her income and that saving is treated as a good.

A person in consumer equilibrium has *maximized total utility.* By spending his or her dollars on goods that give the greatest marginal utility and in the process bringing about the consumer equilibrium condition, the consumer is adding as much to total utility as possible.

finding ECONOMICS

In Everyday Choices You are standing in a store trying to decide whether to buy another pair of shoes or one more sweater. What is the economics?

You might be seeking consumer equilibrium. Consumer equilibrium exists when the marginal utility–price (*MU/P*) ratios for all goods are the same, in this case, when the *MU/P* ratio for shoes is the same as the *MU/P* ratio for the sweater. As you are standing there trying to decide which to buy more of and which not to buy more of, you are deciding on how best you can spend that next dollar. If you feel that you will get more utility (or satisfaction) per dollar by buying one more pair of shoes instead of one more sweater, then you will buy another pair of shoes. If you feel that you will get more utility per dollar by buying one more sweater instead of one more pair of shoes, then you will buy another sweater. Maybe you have thought, "I never try to achieve consumer equilibrium." But that is exactly what you do if you have purchased one more unit of one good instead of one more unit of another good because you thought it was "worth it." ▲▲▲

Maximizing Utility and the Law of Demand

Suppose a consumer of oranges and apples is currently in equilibrium; that is,

$$\frac{MU_O}{P_O} = \frac{MU_A}{P_A}$$

When in equilibrium, the consumer is maximizing utility. Now suppose the price of oranges falls. The situation now becomes:

$$\frac{MU_O}{P_O} > \frac{MU_A}{P_A}$$

The consumer will attempt to restore equilibrium by buying more oranges. This behavior —buying more oranges when their price falls—is consistent with the law of demand.

Therefore, the consumer's attempt to reach equilibrium—which is another way of saying that the consumer is seeking to maximize utility—is consistent with the law of demand. Utility maximization is consistent with the law of demand. The next time someone says that she doesn't maximize utility, ask her if she buys more units of a good when the price is lowered, that is, whether her behavior is consistent with the law of demand. If she says yes, then you can be sure she maximizes utility because utility maximization is consistent with the law of demand.

Should the Government Provide the Necessities of Life for Free?

Some people argue that because food and water are necessities of life and no one can live without them, charging for them is wrong. The government should provide them to everyone for free. Similarly, others argue that medical care is a necessity for those who are sick. Without proper care, sick people will either die or experience an extremely low quality of life. Making people pay for medical care is wrong. The government should provide it for free to those who need it. Each argument labels something as a necessity of life (food, water, medical care) and then makes the policy proposal that government should provide the necessity for free.

How You Pay for Good Weather

Suppose two cities are alike in every way except one: the weather. One is called Good-Weather City (*GWC*) and the other Bad-Weather City (*BWC*). In *GWC*, temperatures are moderate all year (70 degrees) and the sky is always blue. In *BWC*, the winter brings snow and freezing rain, and the summer brings high humidity and high temperatures. *BWC* has all the forms of weather that people dislike. We assume that people get more utility from living in good weather than from living in bad weather and that the median price (*P*) of a home in the two cities is the same: $200,000. In terms of marginal utility and housing prices,

©BRAND X PICTURES/JUPITER IMAGES

$$\frac{MU_{GWC}}{P_{H,GWC}} > \frac{MU_{BWC}}{P_{H,BWC}}$$

That is, the marginal utility of living in *GWC* (*MU*$_{GWC}$) divided by the price of a house in *GWC* (*P*$_{H,GWC}$) is greater than the marginal utility of living in *BWC* (*MU*$_{BWC}$) divided by the price of a house in *BWC* (*P*$_{H,BWC}$). *GWC* offers greater utility per dollar than does *BWC*.

At least some people will move from *BWC* to *GWC*. The people in *BWC* who want to move will put their houses up for sale, increasing the supply of houses for sale and lowering the price. As these people move to *GWC*, they increase the demand for houses there, and house prices in *GWC* begin to rise.

This process will continue until the price of a house in *GWC* has risen high enough, and the price of a house in *BWC* has fallen low enough, so that the *MU/P* ratios in the two cities are the same. In other words, the process continues until:

$$\frac{MU_{GWC}}{P_{H,GWC}} = \frac{MU_{BWC}}{P_{H,BWC}}$$

At this point, a consumer receives the same utility per dollar in the two cities; the two cities are the same.

Consider a young couple who have to choose which city to live in. They will not necessarily choose *GWC* because it has a better climate. *GWC* has a better climate than *BWC*, but *BWC* has lower housing prices. One partner says, "Let's live in *GWC*. Think of all that great weather we'll enjoy. We can go outside every day." The other partner says, "But if we live in *BWC*, we can have either a much bigger and better house for the money or more money to spend on things other than housing. Think of the better cars and clothes we'll be able to buy or the vacations we'll be able to take because we won't have to spend as much money to buy a house."

What has happened is that the initial greater satisfaction of living in *GWC* (the higher utility per dollar) has been eroded by people moving there, thereby raising housing prices. GWC doesn't look as good as it once did. On the other hand, *BWC* doesn't look as bad as it once did. It still doesn't have the good climate that *GWC* has, but it now has lower housing prices. The utility per dollar of living in *BWC* has risen as a consequence of lowered housing prices.

As long as one city is better (in some way) than another, people will move to it. In the process, they will change things just enough so that it is no longer relatively better. In the end, you have to pay for paradise.

Suppose government did give food, water, and medical care to everyone for free—at zero price (although not at zero taxes). At zero price, people would want to consume these goods up to the point of zero marginal utility for each good. If the marginal utility of the good (expressed in dollars) is greater than its price, people can derive more utility from purchasing the good than they lose in parting with the dollar price of the good. For example, if the price of a good is $5, an individual will continue consuming the good as long as the marginal utility derived from it is greater than $5. If the price is $0, the person will continue to consume the good as long as the marginal utility derived from it is greater than $0.

Resources must be used to produce every unit of a good consumed. If the government uses scarce resources to provide goods with low marginal utility (which food, water, and medical care would have at zero price), then fewer resources are available to produce other

Do Rats Maximize Utility?

Certainly, rats do not understand marginal utility. They cannot define it, compute it, or do anything else with it. But do they act *as if* they equate *MU/P* ratios? Do they observe the law of demand? Consider an experiment conducted by economists at Texas A&M University, who undertook to study the "buying" behavior of two white rats. Each rat was put in a laboratory cage with two levers. By pushing one lever, a rat obtained root beer; by pushing the other lever, it obtained a nonalcoholic collins mix. Every day, each rat was given a so-called fixed income of 300 pushes. (When the combined total of pushes on the two levers reached 300, the levers could not be pushed down until the next day.) The prices of root beer and collins mix were both 20 pushes per milliliter. Given this income and these prices, one rat settled in to consuming 11 milliliters of root beer and 4 milliliters of collins mix. The other rat settled in to consuming almost all root beer.

Then the prices of the two beverages were changed. The price of collins mix was halved while the price of root beer was doubled.[3]

Using economic theory, we would predict that with these new prices, the consumption of collins mix would increase and the consumption of root beer would decrease. This is exactly what happened. Both rats began to consume more collins mix and less root beer. Both rats had downward-sloping demand curves for collins mix and root beer.

Therefore, if the behavior of rats is consistent with the law of demand and if the law of demand is consistent with equating *MU/P* ratios, then the rat's behavior is consistent with maximizing utility. Obviously the research on rats says that you can be maximizing utility without knowing it.

---

3. The researchers raised the price of root beer by reducing the quantity of root beer dispensed per push. This is the same as increasing the number of pushes necessary to obtain the original quantity.

---

goods. The resources could then be redirected to producing goods with a higher marginal utility, thereby raising total utility.

The people who argue that certain goods should be provided free implicitly assume that the not so valuable uses of food, water, and medical care are valuable enough to warrant a system of taxes to pay for the complete provision of them at zero price. It is questionable, however, whether the least valuable uses of food, water, and health care are worth the sacrifices of other goods that would necessarily be forfeited if more of these goods were produced.

Think about the question this way: Currently, water is relatively cheap, and people use it for its valuable purposes and its not so valuable purposes. But if water were cheaper than it is—if its price were zero—would it be used to satisfy its more valuable uses, its not so valuable uses, and its absolutely least valuable use? If food had a zero price, would it be used to satisfy its more valuable uses, its not so valuable uses, and its absolutely least valuable use (food fights perhaps)?

thinking Like AN ECONOMIST

Yes, There Can Be Too Much of a Good Thing As odd as it may sound to say so, there is such a thing as too much health care. The right amount of health care is the amount at which the marginal benefit or marginal utility (of an additional unit of health care) equals the marginal cost. Let's say that the marginal cost of health care is $40 but that, under the free-health-care-for-everyone system, no one directly pays even one cent for personal health care. All health-care bills are paid by the federal government with tax monies. In such a case, an individual is likely to continue consuming health care until his marginal utility equals zero. In other words, a person will consume, say, the one-hundredth unit of health care even though the one-hundredth unit comes with only $0.0000001 worth of benefits to him and a cost of $40 to society at large. If individuals are getting not even a penny's worth of benefits from care that cost $40 to provide, economist say that this is too much health care. ●●●

1. Alesandro purchases two goods, X and Y, and the utility gained for the last unit purchased of each is 16 utils and 23 utils, respectively. The prices of X and Y are $1 and $1.75, respectively. Is Alesandro in consumer equilibrium? Explain your answer.

2. In a two-good world (goods A and B), what does it mean to be in consumer disequilibrium?

BEHAVIORAL ECONOMICS

Economists are interested in how people behave with respect to marginal utility. Economic theory predicts that when the MU/P ratio for one good is greater than it is for another, individuals will buy more of the good with the higher MU/P ratio and less of the good with the lower MU/P ratio. Individuals, seeking to maximize their utility, will buy more of one good and less of another until the MU/P ratios for all goods are the same.

In traditional economic theories and models, individuals are assumed to be rational, self-interested, and consistent. For about the last 30 years, however, behavioral economists have challenged the traditional economic models. Behavioral economists argue that some human behavior does not fit neatly—at a minimum, easily—into the traditional economic framework. In this section, we describe some of the findings of behavioral economists.

Are People Willing to Reduce Others' Incomes?

Two economists, Daniel Zizzo and Andrew Oswald, set up a series of experiments with four groups, each with four people. Each person was given the same amount of money and asked to gamble with it. At the end of each act of gambling, two of the four persons in each group had won money and two had lost some. Then each of the four people in each group was given the opportunity to pay (or forfeit) some amount of money (to a bank) to reduce the take of the others in the group. To illustrate, in the group consisting of Smith, Matsui, Brown, and Riverra, Smith and Riverra had more money after gambling, and Matsui and Brown had less. All four were given the opportunity to reduce the amount of money held by the others in the group. For example, Brown could pay to reduce Smith's money, Matsui could pay to reduce Riverra's, and so on.

A reasonable expectation is that no one will spend money to hurt someone else if doing so means leaving himself poorer. However, Zizzo and Oswald found that 62 percent of the participants did just that: they made themselves worse off to make someone else worse off.

People behave this way possibly because they are more concerned with relative rank and status than with absolute well-being. Thus, the poorer of the two individuals doesn't mind paying, say, 25¢ if he can reduce the richer person's take by, say, $1. After the poorer person pays 25¢, the gap between him and the richer person is smaller.

Some economists argue that such behavior is irrational and inconsistent with utility maximization. Other economists say it is no such thing. They argue that if people get utility from relative rank, then, in effect, they are buying a move up the relative rank ladder by reducing the size of the gap between themselves and others.

Is $1 Always $1?

Do people treat money differently depending on where it comes from? Traditional economics argues that they should not; after all, a dollar is a dollar is a dollar. Specifically, $1 that someone gives you as a gift is no different from $1 you earn or $1 you find on the street. When people treat some dollars differently from other dollars, they are *compartmentalizing*. They are saying that dollars in some compartments (of their minds) are valued differently from dollars in other compartments.

economics 24/7

Which Is Better: A Tax Rebate or a Tax Bonus?[4]

Suppose the economy is heading into a recession and both the president and Congress feel that the best way to stimulate the economy (and head off a recession or dampen it) is to get people to spend more money. Congress and the president agree on tax rebates; in effect, the federal government would write out checks and send them to people. Then the people would spend the money on various goods and services, stimulating the economy in the process.

But if the objective is to get people to spend money, wouldn't a tax bonus be better than a tax rebate? According to Nicholas Epley, at the University of Chicago Graduate School of Business, it could be. Here is Epley in his own words:

> Changing the way that identical income is described can significantly affect how people spend it. In an experiment I conducted at Harvard with my colleagues Dennis Mak and Lorraine Chen Idson, participants were given a $50 check. They were told that this money came from a faculty member's research budget, financed indirectly through tuition dollars. Roughly half

of the participants had this money described as a "rebate," whereas the others had it described as a "bonus." When unexpectedly contacted one week later, participants who got a "rebate" reported spending less than half of what those who got a "bonus" reported spending ($9.55 versus $22.04, respectively).[5]

According to Epley, a rebate to most people is different from a bonus. A rebate is equated with *returned income*, whereas a bonus is equated with *extra income*. And his results show that people spend a greater percentage of extra income than they spend of returned income. He concludes that if the objective of the president and Congress is to get people to spend money (and to stimulate the economy), then they should speak of tax bonuses and not tax rebates.

---

4. This feature is based on "Rebate Psychology" by Nicholas Epley in *The New York Times*, January 31, 2008.
5. Ibid.

Suppose you plan to see a Broadway play, the ticket for which costs $100. You buy the $100 ticket on Monday to see the play on Friday night. When Friday night arrives, you realize you have lost the ticket. Do you spend another $100 to buy another ticket (assuming another ticket can be purchased)?[6]

Now let's change the circumstances slightly. Instead of buying the ticket on Monday, you plan to buy the ticket at the ticket window on Friday night. At the ticket window on Friday night, you realize you have lost $100 somewhere between home and the theater. Assuming you still have enough money to buy a $100 ticket to the play, do you buy it?

Regardless of how you answer each question, some economists argue that your answers should be consistent. If you say no to the first question, you should say no to the second. If you say yes to the first, you should say yes to the second. The two questions, based on two slightly different settings, present you with essentially the same choice.

However, many people, when asked the two questions, say that they will not pay an additional $100 to buy a second ticket (having lost the first one) but will spend an additional $100 to buy a first ticket (having lost $100 in cash between home and the theater). Some people argue that spending an additional $100 on an additional ticket is the same as paying $200 to see the play—and that is just too much to pay. However, they don't see themselves as spending $200 to see the play when they lose $100 and pay $100 for a ticket. In either case, though, $200 is gone. Behavioral economists argue that people who answer the two questions differently (yes to one and no to the other) are

---

6. This example comes from Gary Belsky and Thomas Gilovich, *Why Smart People Make Big Money Mistakes and How to Correct Them* (New York: Simon & Schuster, 1999).

compartmentalizing. They are treating two $100 amounts in two different ways, as if they come from two different compartments. For example, if a person will not buy a second $100 ticket (having lost the first $100 ticket) but will buy a first ticket (having lost $100 cash), her behavior is effectively indicating that $100 lost on a ticket is different from $100 lost in cash.

Consider another situation. You earn $1,000 by working hard at a job and also win $1,000 at the roulette table in Las Vegas. Would you feel freer to spend the $1,000 you won than to spend the $1,000 you earned? If the answer is yes, then you are treating money differently depending on where it came from and on what you had to do to get it. Nothing is necessarily wrong or immoral about that, but it is interesting because $1,000 is $1,000 is $1,000—no matter where it came from and no matter what you had to do to get it.

Finally, consider an experiment conducted by two marketing professors. Drazen Prelec and Duncan Simester once organized a sealed-bid auction for tickets to a Boston Celtics basketball game. Half the participants in the auction were told that if they had the winning bid, they had to pay in cash. The other half of the participants were told that if they had the winning bid, they had to pay with a credit card.

Assuming that the two groups were divided randomly and that neither group showed a stronger or weaker preference for seeing the Celtics game, the average bid from the people who had to pay cash should have been the same as the average bid from the people who had to pay with a credit card. But this didn't happen. The average bid of the people who had to pay with a credit card was higher than the average bid of the people who had to pay with cash. Using a credit card somehow caused people to bid higher dollar amounts than they would have bid if they had to pay cash. Money from the credit card compartment seemed to be more quickly or easily spent than money from the cash compartment.

Coffee Mugs and the Endowment Effect

In an economic experiment, coffee mugs were allocated randomly to half the people in a group. Each person with a mug was asked to state a price at which he would be willing to sell his mug. Each person without a mug was asked to state a price at which he would be willing to buy a mug.

Even though the mugs were allocated randomly (in other words, the people who received mugs did not necessarily value them more than those who did not receive them), the lowest price at which the owner would sell the mug was, on average, higher than the highest price at which a buyer would pay to buy a mug. For example, the sellers wouldn't sell the mugs for less than $15, and buyers wouldn't pay more than $10.

This outcome—called the *endowment effect*—is odd. Even though we have no reason to believe that the people who received the mugs valued them more than the people who didn't receive them, people seem to place a high value on something (like a mug) simply because they own it. In other words, they seem to show an inclination to hold on to what they have.

If this tendency applies to you, think of what it means. When you go into a store to buy a sweater, you might determine that a sweater is worth no more to you than, say, $40 and that you are not willing to pay more than $40 for it. But if someone gave you the sweater as a gift and you were asked to sell it, you wouldn't be willing to sell it for less than, say, $50. Owning the sweater makes it more valuable to you.

Economist David Friedman says that such behavior is not limited to humans.[7] He points out that some species of animals exhibit territorial behavior; that is, they are more

---

7 See his "Economics and Evolutionary Psychology" at his website, http://www.daviddfriedman.com/Academic/econ_and_evol_psych/economics_and_evol_psych.html.

likely to fight to keep what they have than to fight to get what they do not have. As Friedman notes, "It is a familiar observation that a dog will fight harder to keep his own bone than to take another dog's bone."

Friedman argues that this type of behavior in humans makes perfect sense in a hunter-gatherer society. Here is what Friedman has to say:

Now consider the same logic [found in the fact that a dog will fight harder to keep the bone he has than to take a bone from another dog] in a hunter-gatherer society—in which there are no external institutions to enforce property rights. Imagine that each individual considers every object in sight, decides how much each is worth to him, and then tries to appropriate it, with the outcome of the resulting Hobbesian struggle determined by some combination of how much each wants things and how strong each individual is. It does not look like a formula for a successful society, even on the scale of a hunter-gatherer band.

There is an alternative solution, assuming that humans are at least as smart as dogs, robins, and fish. Some method, possibly as simple as physical possession, is used to define what "belongs to" whom. Each individual then commits himself to fight very hard to protect his "property"—much harder than he would be willing to fight in order to appropriate a similar object from someone else's possession—with the commitment made via some psychological mechanism presumably hardwired into humans. The result is both a considerably lower level of (risky) violence and a considerably more prosperous society.

The fact that the result is attractive does not, of course, guarantee that it will occur—evolution selects for the reproductive interest of the individual, not the group. But in this case they are the same. To see that, imagine a population in which some individuals have adopted the commitment strategy [outlined above—that is, fighting for what you physically possess], and some have adopted different commitment strategies—for example, a strategy of fighting to the death for whatever they see as valuable. It should be fairly easy to see that individuals in the first group will, on average, do better for themselves—hence have (among other things) greater reproductive success—than those in the second group.

How do I commit myself to fight very hard for something? One obvious way is some psychological quirk that makes that something appear very valuable to me. Hence the same behavior pattern that shows up as territorial behavior in fish and ferocious defense of bones in dogs shows up in Cornell students [who were given the coffee mugs] as an endowment effect. Just as in the earlier cases, behavior that was functional in the environment in which we evolved continues to be observed, even in an environment in which its function has largely disappeared.[8]

We value X more highly if we have it than if we do not have it because such behavior at one point in our evolution made possible a system of property rights in a world where the alternative was the Hobbesian jungle.

Does the Endowment Effect Hold Only for New Traders?

The endowment effect has not gone untested. John List, an economist at the University of Maryland, wanted to know whether new traders were more likely than experienced traders to experience the endowment effect. He went to a sports card exchange where people trade regularly. In one experiment, he took aside a group of card fans and gave them such things as sports autographs and sports badges. He then gave them the opportunity to trade. He observed that the more experience traders had (at trading such items), the less prone they were to the endowment effect.

One criticism of this experiment was that new traders were less likely to trade than experienced traders because novices were not sure of the value of the sports autographs. To meet this criticism, List conducted another experiment with chocolate and coffee mugs, where he was sure everyone did know the values of the items. Once again, he observed

---

8. Ibid., p. 10.

$40 and Two People[9]

The ultimatum game involves two people and one pot of money. One person divides the money between himself and the other person. The other person can either accept his portion of the money or reject it. If he rejects it, then neither person gets any money. To illustrate, suppose Jack is going to divide $40 between himself and Bill. Jack gives himself $35, and he gives Bill $5. At this point, Bill can either accept or reject the $5 that Jack has apportioned to him. If he accepts it, then he gets the $5 and Jack gets the $35. But if he rejects it, neither he nor Jack gets any money.

In Bill's position, would you accept the $5 or reject it? Often, your strategy may depend on whether this is a one-time deal or there are other rounds of play. If there are other rounds of play, you might reject the initial offer of $5, so that you send a message to Jack: Either divide the money more nearly equal (closer to $20 each), or I will make sure you get nothing. Over several rounds of play, this strategy may give you the most money overall.

But if it is a one-round game, does rejecting the deal make sense, no matter how Jack divides the money? If Jack gives himself $35 and you $5 and if you reject the deal, you do not get the $5. If you accept the deal, you get at least the $5. When economists have experimented with the ultimatum game, they find that many participants reject the money offer if it is not close to half the money. In other words, they are likely to reject an offer of $35–$5 (where they receive the $5) or an offer of $30–$10. They are likely to accept, though, an offer of $20–$20.

Some economists reason that this tendency to reject uneven splits of the money shows people are more concerned with their relative income position than with their absolute income position. In other words, how much income one has does not seem to matter as much as how much income one has relative to others.

In one experiment, performed by economist Terence Burnham of Harvard University, the results showed that men with higher testosterone levels were more likely to reject unequal offers of money than those with lower testosterone levels. Five of seven men with the highest testosterone levels in the group rejected an unequal offer, whereas only one of 19 men with lower testosterone rejected the same offer. Since high testosterone is highly correlated with social dominance (in many societies), one conclusion might be that the higher a man's testosterone level is, the more relative position (as opposed to absolute position) seems to matter.

Another way of looking at the results of the ultimatum game is to say that sometimes people are irrational. In other words, turning down, say, a $35–$5 offer is irrational because having $5 is better than not having $5. Of course, another perspective is that rejecting such an offer is not irrational at all for someone who is trying to maximize his or her relative position in society, not the number of dollars. In such a case, rejecting offers that lower one's relative position is rational.

---

9. This feature is based on "Money Isn't Everything" in *The Economist*, July 5, 2007.

---

some endowment effect, but it was not as evident as in the sports memorabilia case, and—more important—only newer traders demonstrated the effect. In other words, experience as a trader seems to make one less prone to the endowment effect.

SELF-TEST

1. Brandon's grandmother is very cautious about spending money. Yesterday, she gave Brandon a gift of $100 for his birthday. Brandon also received a gift of $100 from his father, who isn't nearly as cautious about spending money as Brandon's grandmother. Brandon believes that buying frivolous things with his grandmother's gift would be wrong, but not with his father's gift. Is Brandon compartmentalizing? Explain your answer.

2. Summarize David Friedman's explanation of the endowment effect.

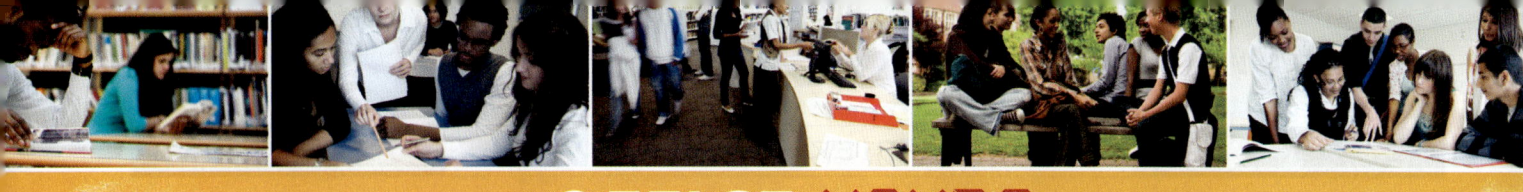

OFFICE HOURS

"Is There an Indirect Way of Proving the Law of Diminishing Marginal Utility?"

STUDENT:

In class, you proved that the law of demand is consistent with utility maximization. This was an important proof for me because I had always accepted the law of demand as true, but I never really felt easy with the idea that indivduals seek to maximize utility. Your proof that the law of demand is consistent with utility maximization helps put this earlier uneasiness of mine to rest.

Having said that, is there any similar proof of the law of diminishing marginal utility? The law of diminishing marginal utility sounds true, but can it be proven so?

INSTRUCTOR:

Yes, there is. To illustrate, let's start with something that we know is true because it is so obvious: people trade. Now it's not likely that they would trade if the law of diminishing marginal utility did not hold.

STUDENT:

In other words, you're saying that the law of diminishing marginal utility is consistent with the fact that people trade.

INSTRUCTOR:

Yes. Consider two people, Smith and Jones. Smith has 100 apples and Jones has 100 oranges. As Smith consumes her apples, marginal utility declines. Her tenth apple doesn't give her as much utility as her ninth and so on. The same is true for Jones with respect to oranges. In other words, as Smith and Jones consume successive units of what they have, marginal utility falls.

At some point, Smith's marginal utility of consuming another apple is likely less than her marginal utility of consuming something different—such as an orange. And at some point, Jones's marginal utility of consuming another orange is likely less than his marginal utility of consuming something different—say, an apple. When this point comes, Smith and Jones will trade. For Smith, the marginal utility of an apple will be less than the marginal utility of an orange, and she will gladly trade an apple for an orange. For Jones, the marginal utility of an orange will be less than the marginal utility of an apple, and he will gladly trade an orange for an apple.

Now suppose the law of diminishing marginal utility did not exist. Smith would have the same marginal utility when she consumed her first and her one-hundredth apple, and this marginal utility would always be greater than her marginal utility for an orange. The same would be true for Jones with respect to oranges. In this case, Smith and Jones would not trade with each other. The law of diminishing marginal utility, at work on both apples and oranges, gets Smith and Jones eventually to trade.

POINTS TO REMEMBER

1. The law of demand is consistent with utility maximization.
2. The law of diminishing marginal utility is consistent with the fact that individuals trade.

CHAPTER SUMMARY

THE LAW OF DIMINISHING MARGINAL UTILITY

- The law of diminishing marginal utility holds that as the amount of a good consumed increases, the marginal utility of the good decreases.

- The law of diminishing marginal utility should not be used to make interpersonal utility comparisons. For example, the law does not say that a millionaire receives less (or more) utility from an additional dollar than a poor man does. All it says is that, for both the millionaire and the poor man, the last dollar has less value than the next-to-last dollar has.

THE DIAMOND-WATER PARADOX

- The diamond-water paradox states that what has great value in use sometimes has little value in exchange and that what has little value in use sometimes has great value in exchange. A knowledge of the difference between total utility and marginal utility is necessary to unravel the diamond-water paradox.

- A good can have high total utility and low marginal utility. For example, water's total utility is high, but because water is so plentiful, its marginal utility is low. In short, water is immensely useful, but it is so plentiful that individuals place relatively low value on another unit of it. In contrast, diamonds are not as useful as water, but because there are few diamonds in the world, the marginal utility of diamonds is high. In summary, a good can be extremely useful and have a low price if the good is in plentiful supply (high value in use, low value in exchange). On the other hand, a good can be of little use and have a high price if the good is in short supply (low value in use, high value in exchange).

CONSUMER EQUILIBRIUM

- Individuals seek to equate marginal utilities per dollar. For example, if a person receives more utility per dollar spent on good A than on good B, she will reorder her purchases and buy more A and less B. The tendency is to move away from the condition $MU_A/P_A > MU_B/P_B$ to the condition $MU_A/P_A = MU_B/P_B$. The latter condition represents consumer equilibrium (in a two-good world).

MARGINAL UTILITY ANALYSIS AND THE LAW OF DEMAND

- Marginal utility analysis can be used to illustrate the law of demand, which states that price and quantity demanded are inversely related, *ceteris paribus*. Starting from consumer equilibrium in a world containing only two goods, A and B, a fall in the price of A will cause MU_A/P_A to be greater than MU_B/P_B. As a result, the consumer will purchase more of good A to restore herself to equilibrium.

BEHAVIORAL ECONOMICS

- Behavioral economists argue that some human behavior does not fit neatly—at a minimum, easily—into the traditional economic framework.

- Behavioral economists believe they have identified human behaviors that are inconsistent with the model of men and women as rational, self-interested, and consistent: (1) Individuals are willing to spend some money to lower the incomes of others even if doing so lowers their own incomes. (2) Individuals don't always treat $1 as $1; some dollars seem to be treated differently than others. (3) Individuals sometimes value X more if it is theirs than if it isn't theirs and they are seeking to acquire it.

KEY TERMS AND CONCEPTS

Diamond-Water Paradox
Utility
Util

Total Utility
Marginal Utility
Law of Diminishing Marginal Utility

Interpersonal Utility Comparison
Consumer Equilibrium

QUESTIONS AND PROBLEMS

1. Is it possible to get so much of a good that it turns into a bad? If so, give an example.

2. "If we take $1 away from a rich person and give it to a poor person, the rich person loses less utility than the poor person gains." Comment.

3. The law of diminishing marginal utility is consistent with the fact that people trade. Do you agree or disagree. Explain your answer.

4. Give a numerical example that illustrates total utility rising as marginal utility declines.

5. List five sets of two goods (each set is composed of two goods; for example, diamonds and water are one set) where the good with the greater value in use has a lower value in exchange than does the good with the lower value in use.

6. Of two similar houses on a street, one faces the ocean and the other does not. How might we determine the price of an ocean view? Explain your answer.

7. Is there a logical link between the law of demand and the assumption that individuals seek to maximize utility? (*Hint:* Think of how the condition for consumer equilibrium can be used to express the inverse relationship between price and quantity demanded.)

8. How is buying a house in a good school district like sending children to a private school?

9. Describe five everyday examples of you or someone else making an interpersonal utility comparison.

10. What is the endowment effect?

11. Individuals who buy second homes usually spend less for them than they do for their first homes. Why is this the case?

12. After each toss of the coin, one person has more money and one person has less. If the person with less money cares about relative rank and status, will he be willing to pay, say, $1 to reduce the other person's winnings by, say, 50¢? Will he be willing to pay 25¢ to reduce the other person's winnings by $1? Explain your answers.

13. The marginal utility of good A is 4 utils, and its price is $2, and the marginal utility of good B is 6 utils, and its price is $1. Is the individual consumer maximizing (total) utility if she spends a total of $3 by buying one unit of each good? If not, how can more utility be obtained?

14. Do you think people with high IQs are in consumer equilibrium (equating marginal utilities per dollar) more often than people with low IQs? Why or why not?

15. If a person consumes fewer units of a good, will marginal utility of the good increase as total utility decreases? Why or why not?

WORKING WITH NUMBERS AND GRAPHS

1. The marginal utility for the third unit of X is 60 utils, and the marginal utility for the fourth unit of X is 45 utils. If the law of diminishing marginal utility holds, what is the minimum total utility?

2. Fill in blanks A–D in the following table.

Units of Good Consumed	Total Utility (utils)	Marginal Utility (utils)
1	10	10
2	19	A
3	B	8
4	33	C
5	35	D

3. The total utilities of the first 5 units of good X are 10, 19, 26, 33, and 40 utils, respectively. In other words, the total utility of 1 unit is 10 utils, the total utility of 2 units is 19 utils, and so on. What is the marginal utility of the third unit?

Use the following table to answer questions 4 and 5.

Units of Good X	TU of Good X (utils)	Units of Good Y	TU of Good Y (utils)
1	20	1	19
2	35	2	32
3	48	3	40
4	58	4	45
5	66	5	49

4. If George spends $5 (total) a week on good X and good Y, and if the price of each good is $1 per unit, then how many units of each good does he purchase to maximize utility?

5. Given the number of units of each good that George purchases in question 4, what is his total utility?

6. Draw the marginal utility curve for a good that has constant marginal utility.

7. The marginal utility curve for units 3–5 of good X is below the horizontal axis. Draw the corresponding part of the total utility curve for good X.

APPENDIX E

BUDGET CONSTRAINT AND INDIFFERENCE CURVE ANALYSIS

This chapter uses marginal utility theory to discuss consumer choice. Sometimes budget constraint and indifference curve analysis are used instead, especially in upper-division economics courses. We examine this important topic in this appendix.

THE BUDGET CONSTRAINT

Budget Constraint

All the combinations, or bundles, of two goods a person can purchase, given a certain money income and prices for the two goods.

Societies have production possibilities frontiers, and individuals have **budget constraints**. A budget constraint is built on three components: two prices and the individual's income. To illustrate, O'Brien has a monthly income of $1,200. In a world of two goods, X and Y, O'Brien can spend his total income on X, he can spend his total income on Y, or he can spend part of his income on X and part on Y. The price of X is $100 and the price of Y is $80. If O'Brien spends his total income on X, he can purchase a maximum of 12 units; if he spends his total income on Y, he can purchase a maximum of 15 units. Locating these two points on a two-dimensional diagram and then drawing a line between them, as shown in Exhibit 1, gives us O'Brien's budget constraint. Any point on the budget constraint, as well as any point below it, represents a possible combination (or bundle) of the two goods available to O'Brien.

Slope of the Budget Constraint

The slope of the budget constraint has special significance. The absolute value of the slope represents the relative prices of the two goods, X and Y. In Exhibit 1, the slope, or P_X/P_Y, is equal to 1.25, indicating that the relative price of 1 unit of X is 1.25 units of Y.

What Will Change the Budget Constraint?

If any of the three variables changes—two prices and the individual's income—the budget constraint changes. Not all changes are alike, however. Consider a fall in the price of good X from $100 to $60. With this change, the maximum number of units of good X purchasable with an income of $1,200 rises from 12 to 20. The budget constraint revolves away from the origin, as shown in Exhibit 2(a). The number of O'Brien's possible combinations of the two goods increases; more bundles of the two goods are available after the price decrease than before.

Consider what happens to the budget constraint if the price of good X rises. If it goes from $100 to, say,

$$\frac{\text{Income}}{\text{Price of good Y}} = \frac{\$1,200}{\$80} = 15$$

$$\frac{\text{Income}}{\text{Price of Good X}} = \frac{\$1,200}{\$100} = 12$$

EXHIBIT 2

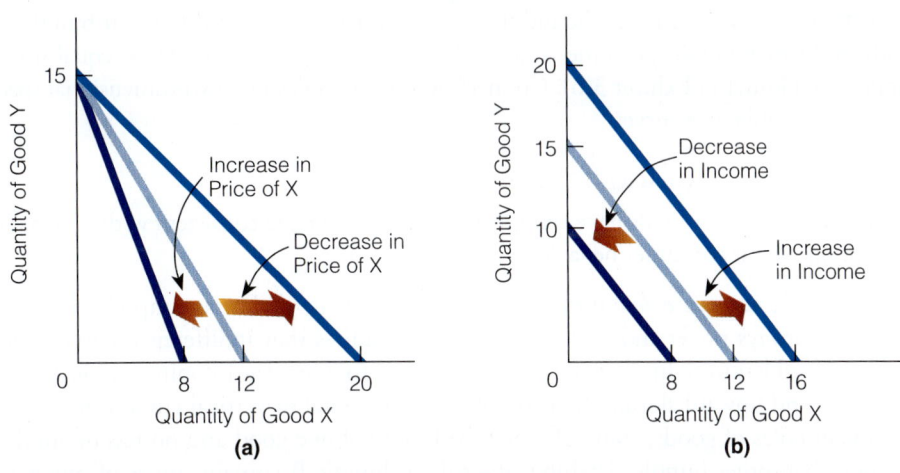

Changes in the Budget Constraint

(a) A change in the price of good X or good Y will change the slope of the budget constraint. (b) A change in income will change the position of the budget constraint while the slope remains constant. Whenever a budget constraint changes, the number of combinations (bundles) of the two goods available to the individual changes too.

$150, the maximum number of units of good X falls from 12 to 8. The budget constraint revolves toward the origin. As a consequence, the number of bundles available to O'Brien decreases. Therefore, a change in the price of either good changes the slope of the budget constraint, with the result that relative prices and the number of bundles available to the individual also change.

We turn now to a change in income. If O'Brien's income rises to $1,600, the maximum number of purchasable units of X rises to 16, and the maximum number of units of Y rises to 20. The budget constraint shifts rightward (away from the origin) and is parallel to the old budget constraint. As a consequence, the number of bundles available to O'Brien increases [Exhibit 2(b)]. If O'Brien's income falls from $1,200 to $800, the extreme end points on the budget constraint become 8 and 10 for X and Y, respectively. The budget constraint shifts leftward (toward the origin) and is parallel to the old budget constraint. As a consequence, the number of bundles available to O'Brien falls.

INDIFFERENCE CURVES

An individual can, of course, choose any bundle of the two goods on or below the budget constraint. If she spends her total income and therefore chooses a point on the budget constraint, this action raises two important questions: (1) Which bundle of the many bundles of the two goods does the individual choose? (2) How does the individual's chosen combination of goods change, given a change in prices or income? Both questions can be answered by combining the budget constraint with the graphical expression of the individual's preferences: indifference curves.

CONSTRUCTING AN INDIFFERENCE CURVE

A person can be indifferent between two bundles of goods. Suppose that bundle A consists of 2 pairs of shoes and 6 shirts and that bundle B consists of 3 pairs of shoes and 4 shirts. A person who is indifferent between these two bundles is implicitly saying that one is as good as the other. She is likely to say this, though, only if she receives equal total utility from the two bundles. If not, she would prefer one bundle to the other.

Indifference Set

A group of bundles of two goods that give an individual equal total utility.

Indifference Curve

The curve that represents an indifference set and that shows all the bundles of two goods giving an individual equal total utility.

If we tabulate all the different bundles from which the individual receives equal utility, we have an indifference set. We can then plot the data in the indifference set and draw an indifference curve. Consider the indifference set in Exhibit 3(a). Of the four bundles of goods, A–D, each bundle gives the same total utility as every other one. These equal-utility bundles are plotted in Exhibit 3(b). Connecting these bundles in a two-dimensional space gives us an indifference curve.

Characteristics of Indifference Curves

Indifference curves for goods have certain characteristics that are consistent with reasonable assumptions about consumer behavior.

1. *Indifference curves are downward sloping (from left to right).* The assumption that consumers always prefer more of a good to less requires that indifference curves slope downward left to right. Consider the alternatives to downward sloping: vertical, horizontal, and upward sloping (left to right). A horizontal or vertical curve would combine bundles of goods, some of which had more of one good and no less of another good than other bundles [Exhibit 4(a–b)]. (If bundle B contains more of one good and no less of another good than bundle A, an individual would not be indifferent between them. Individuals prefer more to less.) An upward-sloping curve would combine bundles of goods, some of which had more of both goods than other bundles [Exhibit 4(c)]. More simply, indifference curves are downward sloping because a person has to get more of one good in order to maintain a level of satisfaction (utility) when giving up some of another good.

2. *Indifference curves are convex to the origin.* As we move down and to the right along the indifference curve, it becomes flatter. For example, at 8 units of milk [point *A* in Exhibit 3(b)], the individual is willing to give up 3 units of milk to get an additional unit of orange juice (and thus move to point *B*). At point *B*, where she has 5 units of milk, she is willing to give up only 2 units of milk to get an additional unit of orange juice (and thus move to point *C*). Finally, at point *C*, with 3 units of milk, she is now willing to give up only 1 unit of milk to get an additional unit of orange juice. Therefore, the more of one good that an individual has, the more units he will give up to get an additional unit of another good; the less of one good that an individual has, the fewer units he will give up to get an additional unit of another good.

EXHIBIT 3

An Indifference Set and an Indifference Curve

An indifference set is a number of bundles of two goods in which each bundle yields the same total utility. An indifference curve represents an indifference set. In this exhibit, data from the indifference set (a) are used to derive an indifference curve (b).

An Indifference Set

Bundle	Milk (units)	Orange Juice (units)
A	8	3
B	5	4
C	3	5
D	2	6

(a)

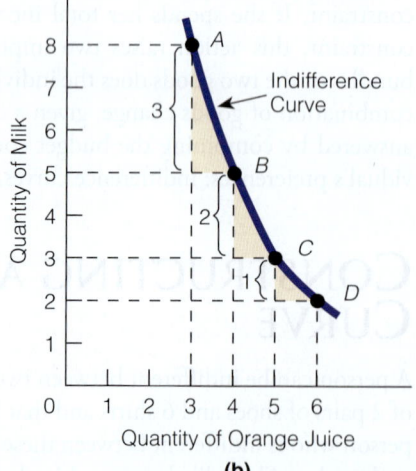

(b)

EXHIBIT 4

Indifference Curves for Goods Do Not Look Like This

(a) Bundle B has more milk and no less orange juice than bundle A, so an individual would prefer B to A and not be indifferent between them. (b) Bundle B has more orange juice and no less milk than bundle A, so an individual would prefer B to A and not be indifferent between them. (c) Bundle B has more milk and more orange juice than bundle A, so an individual would prefer B to A and not be indifferent between them.

(a)

(b)

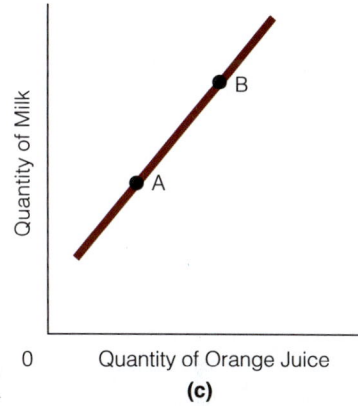

(c)

This is reasonable: our observation is a reflection of diminishing marginal utility at work. As the quantity of a good consumed increases, the marginal utility of that good decreases; therefore, the more of one good an individual has, the more units he can (and will) sacrifice to get an additional unit of another good and still maintain total utility. Stated differently, if the law of diminishing marginal utility did not exist, saying that indifference curves of goods are convex to the origin would not make sense.

An important peripheral point about marginal utilities is that *the absolute value of the slope of the indifference curve*—the marginal rate of substitution—*represents the ratio of the marginal utility of the good on the horizontal axis to the marginal utility of the good on the vertical axis:*

$$\frac{MU_{\text{good on horizontal axis}}}{MU_{\text{good on vertical axis}}}$$

Marginal Rate of Substitution The amount of one good an individual is willing to give up to obtain an additional unit of another good and maintain equal total utility.

Let's look carefully at this assertion. First, the absolute value of the slope of the indifference curve is the marginal rate of substitution (*MRS*). The *MRS* is the amount of one good an individual is willing to give up to obtain an additional unit of another good and maintain equal total utility. For example, in Exhibit 3(b), we see that moving from point *A* to point *B*, the individual is willing to give up 3 units of milk to get an additional unit of orange juice, with total utility remaining constant (between points *A* and *B*). The marginal rate of substitution is therefore 3 units of milk for 1 unit of orange juice in the area between points *A* and *B*. Further, the absolute value of the slope of the indifference curve (the *MRS*) is equal to the ratio of the *MU* of the good on the horizontal axis to the *MU* of the good on the vertical axis. How can this be? If an individual giving up 3 units of milk and receiving 1 unit of orange juice maintains her total utility, then (in the area under consideration) the marginal utility of orange juice is approximately three times the marginal utility of milk. In general terms

Absolute value of the slope of the indifference curve = Marginal rate of substitution

$$= \frac{MU_{\text{good on horizontal axis}}}{MU_{\text{good on vertical axis}}}$$

EXHIBIT 5

An Indifference Map

A few of the many possible indifference curves are shown. Any point in the two-dimensional space is on an indifference curve. Indifference curves farther away from the origin represent greater total utility than those closer to the origin.

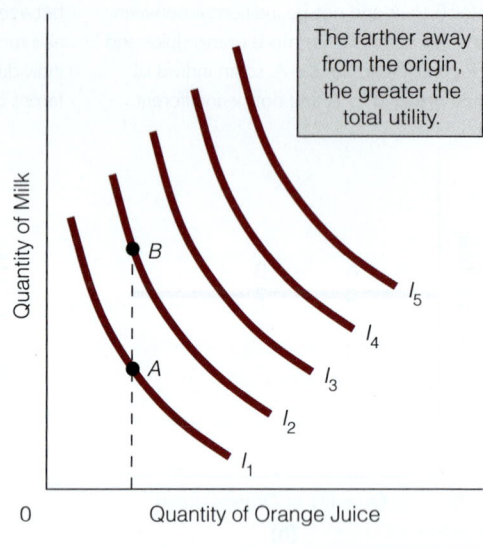

The farther away from the origin, the greater the total utility.

3. *Indifference curves that are farther from the origin are preferable because they represent larger bundles of goods.* Exhibit 3(b) shows only one indifference curve. However, different bundles of the two goods exist and have indifference curves passing through them. These bundles have less of both goods or more of both goods than those in Exhibit 3(b). Illustrating a number of indifference curves on the same diagram gives us an **indifference curve map,** which represents a number of indifference curves for a given individual with reference to two goods.

See Exhibit 5. Although only five indifference curves have been drawn, many more could have been added. For example, many indifference curves lie between I_1 and I_2. Also, the farther away from the origin an indifference curve lies, the higher the total utility is that it represents. Compare point A on I_1 and point B on I_2. At point B, there is the same amount of orange juice as at point A but more milk. Point B is therefore preferable to point A, and, because B is on I_2 and A is on I_1, I_2 is preferable to I_1. The reason is simple: An individual receives more utility at any point on I_2 (because more goods are available) than at any point on I_1.

Indifference Curve Map

A map that represents a number of indifference curves for a given individual with reference to two goods.

Transitivity

The principle whereby if A is preferred to B, and B is preferred to C, then A is preferred to C.

4. *Indifference curves do not cross (intersect).* Indifference curves do not cross because individuals' preferences exhibit **transitivity,** the principle whereby if A is preferred to B, and B is preferred to C, then A is preferred to C. For example, if Kristin prefers Coca-Cola to Pepsi-Cola and she also prefers Pepsi-Cola to root beer, then she must prefer Coca-Cola to root beer. If she said she preferred root beer to Coca-Cola, she would be contradicting her earlier preferences. To say that an individual has transitive preferences means that she maintains a logical order of preferences over a given time period.

Consider what intersecting indifference curves would represent. In Exhibit 6, indifference curves I_1 and I_2 intersect at point A, which lies on both I_1 and I_2. An individual must be indifferent between A and B because they lie on the same indifference curve. The same holds for A and C. But if the individual is indifferent between A and B and between A and C, then she must be indifferent between B and C. But C has more of both goods than B, and thus the individual will not be indifferent between B and C; she will prefer C to B. We cannot have transitive preferences and make sense of crossing indifference curves. We can, however, have transitive preferences and make sense of noncrossing indifference curves. We go with the latter.

EXHIBIT 6

Crossing Indifference Curves Are Inconsistent with Transitive Preferences

Point A lies on both indifference curves I_1 and I_2. This means that the individual is indifferent between A and B and between A and C, which results in her (supposedly) being indifferent between B and C. But individuals prefer more to less (when it comes to goods) and, thus, would prefer C to B. We cannot have transitive preferences and make sense of crossing indifference curves.

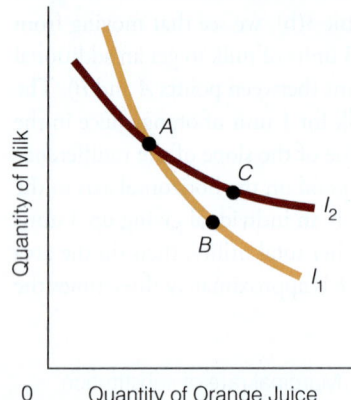

THE INDIFFERENCE MAP AND THE BUDGET CONSTRAINT COME TOGETHER

Together, the indifference map and the budget constraint illustrate consumer equilibrium. We have the following facts:

- The individual has a budget constraint.
- The absolute value of the slope of the budget constraint is the relative prices of the two goods under consideration, say, P_X/P_Y.
- The individual has an indifference map.
- The absolute value of the slope of the indifference curve at any point is the marginal rate of substitution, which is equal to the marginal utility of one good divided by the marginal utility of another good, MU_X/MU_Y.

The necessary condition for consumer equilibrium is obviously that the individual will try to reach a point on the highest indifference curve possible. This point is where the slope of the budget constraint is equal to the slope of an indifference curve (or where the budget constraint is tangent to an indifference curve). At this point, consumer equilibrium is established and the following condition holds:

$$\frac{P_X}{P_Y} = \frac{MU_X}{MU_Y}$$

In Exhibit 7, this condition is met at point E. Note that this condition looks similar to the condition for consumer equilibrium described in this chapter. By rearranging the terms in the condition, we get[1]

$$\frac{MU_X}{P_X} = \frac{MU_Y}{P_Y}$$

EXHIBIT 7

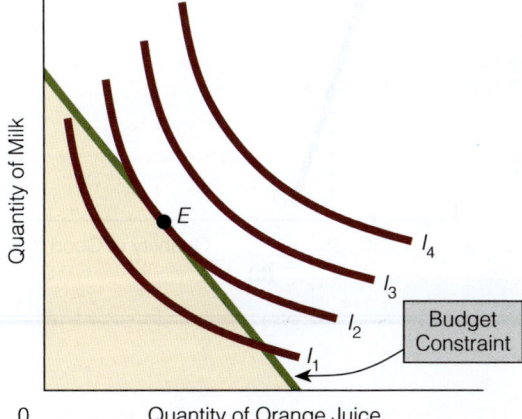

Consumer Equilibrium

Consumer equilibrium exists at the point where the slope of the budget constraint is equal to the slope of an indifference curve, or where the budget constraint is tangent to an indifference curve. In the exhibit, this point is E. Here $P_X/P_Y = MU_X/MU_Y$; or, rearranging, $MU_X/P_X = MU_Y/P_Y$.

---

1. Start with $P_X/P_Y = MU_X/MU_Y$ and cross-multiply. This gives $P_X MU_Y = P_Y MU_X$. Next divide both sides by P_X. This gives $MU_Y = P_Y MU_X/P_X$. Finally, divide both sides by P_Y. This gives $MU_Y/P_Y = MU_X/P_X$.

FROM INDIFFERENCE CURVES TO A DEMAND CURVE

We can now derive a demand curve within a budget constraint–indifference curve framework. Exhibit 8(a) shows two budget constraints, one reflecting a $10 price for good X and the other reflecting a $5 price for good X. As the price of X falls, the consumer moves from point A to point B. At B, 35 units of X are consumed; at A, 30 units of X. So, a lower price for X results in greater consumption of X. By plotting the relevant price and quantity data, we derive a demand curve for good X in Exhibit 8(b).

EXHIBIT 8

From Indifference Curves to a Demand Curve

(a) At a price of $10 for good X, consumer equilibrium is at point A with the individual consuming 30 units of X. As the price falls to $5, the budget constraint moves outward (away from the origin), and the consumer moves to point B and consumes 35 units of X. Plotting the price-quantity data for X gives a demand curve for X in (b).

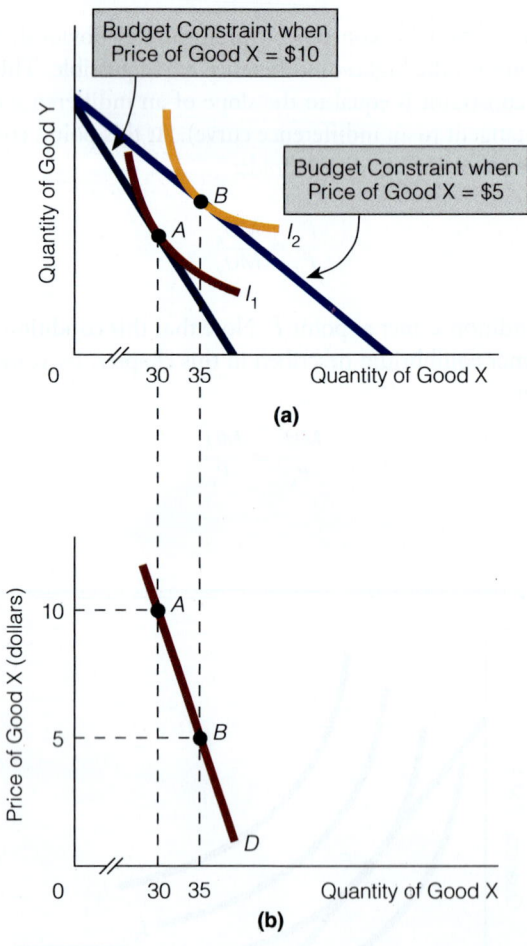

APPENDIX SUMMARY

- A budget constraint represents all combinations of bundles of two goods that a person can purchase, given a certain money income and prices for the two goods.
- An indifference curve shows all the combinations or bundles of two goods that give an individual equal total utility.
- Indifference curves are downward sloping, they are convex to the origin, and they do not cross. The farther away from the origin an indifference curve is, the greater total utility it represents for the individual.
- Consumer equilibrium is at the point where the slope of the budget constraint equals the slope of the indifference curve.
- A demand curve can be derived within a budget constraint–indifference curve framework.

KEY TERMS AND CONCEPTS

Budget Constraint
Indifference Set

Indifference Curve
Marginal Rate of Substitution

Indifference Curve Map

Transitivity

QUESTIONS AND PROBLEMS

1. Diagram the following budget constraints:
   a. Income = $4,000; P_X = $50; P_Y = $100
   b. Income = $3,000; P_X = $25; P_Y = $200
   c. Income = $2,000; P_X = $40; P_Y = $150
2. Explain why indifference curves:
   a. are downward sloping
   b. are convex to the origin
   c. do not cross
3. Explain why consumer equilibrium is equivalent whether using marginal utility analysis or indifference curve analysis.
4. Derive a demand curve using indifference curve analysis.

CHAPTER 22

© DIGITAL VISION/GETTY IMAGES

PRODUCTION AND COSTS

Introduction Everyone deals with business firms on a daily basis. People buy goods from firms: cars, clothes, food, books, entertainment, and other products. And people work for firms as accountants, truck drivers, secretaries, vice presidents, and editors. Our lives are constantly intermingled with business firms, as buyers of goods and as sellers of our labor services. Even though we deal with business firms daily, most of us probably know little about them. Why do they exist? What do they try to maximize? How do they go about producing the goods they produce? What concepts must firms concern themselves with? In this chapter we answer many of these questions.

WHY FIRMS EXIST

Business Firm
An entity that employs factors of production (resources) to produce goods and services to be sold to consumers, other firms, or the government.

A business firm is an entity that employs resources, or factors of production, to produce goods and services to be sold to consumers, other firms, or the government. To understand why firms exist, we must explain worker behavior, markets, and the questions a firm must answer.

The Market and the Firm: Invisible Hand Versus Visible Hand

Through the forces of supply and demand, the market guides and coordinates individuals' actions, and it does so in an impersonal manner. No one orders buyers to reduce quantity demanded when price increases; they just do it. No one orders sellers to increase quantity supplied when price increases; they just do it. No one orders more resources to be moved into the production of personal computers when the demand and price for personal computers increase. The market guides individuals from the production of one good into the production of another. It coordinates individuals' actions so that suppliers and demanders find mutual satisfaction at equilibrium. As economist Adam Smith observed, individuals in a market setting are "led by an invisible hand to promote an end which was no part of their intention."

Contrast the invisible hand of the market with the visible hand of a manager in a firm. The manager tells the employee on the assembly line to make more computer chips. The manager tells the employee to design a new engine, to paint the lamps green, to put steak and lobster on the menu. Thus, both the invisible hand of the market and the visible hand of the firm's manager guide and coordinate individuals' actions. There is, in other words, both market coordination and managerial coordination.

If the market is capable of guiding and coordinating individuals' actions, why did firms (and managers) arise in the first place? Why do firms exist?

The Alchian and Demsetz Answer

Economists Armen Alchian and Harold Demsetz suggest that firms are formed when benefits can be obtained from individuals working as a team.[1] Sometimes, the sum of what individuals can produce as a team is greater than the sum of what they can produce alone:

Sum of team production > Sum of individual production

Consider 11 individuals, all making shoe boxes. Each working alone produces 10 shoe boxes per day, for a total daily output of 110 shoe boxes. If they work as a team, however, the same 11 individuals can produce 140 shoe boxes. The added output (30 shoe boxes) may be reason enough for them to work together as a team and to create a firm.

Shirking in a Team

Although forming a firm can increase output, team production can have problems that do not occur in individual production. One problem of team production is shirking, which occurs when workers put forth less than the agreed-to effort. The amount of shirking increases in teams because the costs of shirking to individual team members are lower than when they work alone.

Consider five individuals, Alice, Bob, Carl, Denise, and Elizabeth, who form a team to produce light bulbs because they realize that the sum of their team production will be more than the sum of their individual production. They agree to team-produce light bulbs, sell them, and split the proceeds five equal ways. On an average day, they produce 140 light bulbs and sell each one for $2. Total revenue per day is $280, with each of the five team members receiving $56. Then Carl begins to shirk. Owing to his shirking, production falls to 135 light bulbs per day, and total revenue falls to $270 per day. Each person now receives $54. Notice that while Carl did all the shirking, Carl's reduction in pay was only $2, one-fifth of the $10 drop in total revenue.

In situations (such as team production) where one person receives all the benefits from shirking and pays only a part of the costs, economists predict there will be more shirking than when the person who shirks bears the full cost of shirking.

THE MONITOR (MANAGER): TAKING CARE OF SHIRKING The monitor (or manager) plays an important role in the firm. The monitor reduces the amount of shirking by firing shirkers and rewarding the productive members of the firm. In doing this, the monitor can preserve the benefits that often come with team production (increased output) and reduce, if not eliminate, the costs associated with team production (increased shirking). But then the question is who or what monitors the monitor? How can the monitor be kept from shirking?

One possibility is to give the monitor an incentive not to shirk by making him or her a residual claimant of the firm. A residual claimant receives the excess of revenues over costs (profits) as income. If the monitor shirks, then profits are likely to be lower (or even zero or negative), and therefore the monitor will receive less income.

Market Coordination
The process in which individuals perform tasks, such as producing certain quantities of goods, based on changes in market forces, such as supply, demand, and price.

Managerial Coordination
The process in which managers direct employees to perform certain tasks.

Shirking
The behavior of a worker who is putting forth less than the agreed-to effort.

Monitor
A person in a business firm who coordinates team production and reduces shirking.

Residual Claimants
Persons who share in the profits of a business firm.

1. Armen Alchian and Harold Demsetz, "Production, Information Costs, and Economic Organization," *American Economic Review* 62 (December 1972): 777–795.

🄕inding ECONOMICS

In a Classroom Project Terry's sociology professor has broken her sociology class into teams of five persons each. Each team has to research a particular topic, write a 10-page paper, and then present the paper to the class. The grade that the paper and presentation receive will be the same grade that each member of the team receives for the assignment. Terry has been complaining recently that two of the members in particular don't make the team meetings regularly and are not doing their share of the assignment. Where is the economics here?

It sounds as though at least two team members are shirking. Shirking often happens in team environments where no one monitors the team or where there is no residual claimant. When the cost of shirking is spread over the entire team, instead of being incurred only by the person who shirks, there will be more shirking than when the shirker feels the full cost of his or her shirking. ▲ ▲ ▲

Ronald Coase on Why Firms Exist

Ronald Coase, winner of the 1991 Nobel Prize in Economics, argued that "the main reason why it is profitable to establish a firm would seem to be that there is a cost of using the price mechanism."[2] Stated differently, firms exist either to economize on buying and selling everything or to reduce transaction costs.

For example, suppose it takes 20 different operations to produce good X. One way to produce good X, then, is to enter into a separate contract with everyone necessary to complete the 20 different operations. If we assume that one person completes one and only one operation, then we have 20 different contracts. Obviously, costs are associated with preparing and monitoring all these contracts. A firm is a recipe for reducing these costs, effectively replacing many contracts with one.

Here is what Coase had to say:

The costs of negotiating and concluding a separate contract for each exchange transaction which takes place on a market must also be taken into account. . . . It is true that contracts are not eliminated when there is a firm, but they are greatly reduced. A factor of production (or the owner thereof) does not have to make a series of contracts as would be necessary, of course, if this co-operation were a direct result of the working of the price mechanism. For this series of contracts is substituted one. At this state, it is important to note the character of the contract into which a factor enters that is employed within a firm. The contract is one whereby the factor [the employee], for a certain remuneration (which may be fixed or fluctuating), agrees to obey the directions of an entrepreneur within certain limits.[3]

Markets: Outside and Inside the Firm

When we put the firm under the microeconomic microscope, basically we see a market of sorts at work. Economics is largely about trades or exchanges; it is about market transactions. In supply-and-demand analysis, the exchanges are between the buyers of goods and services and the sellers of goods and services. In the theory of the firm, the exchanges take place at two levels: (1) at the level of individuals coming together to form a team and (2) at the level of workers choosing a monitor.

Let's look at the theory of the firm in the context of exchange. Individuals initially come together because they realize that the sum of what they can produce as a team is greater than the sum of what they can produce as individuals. In essence, each individual trades working alone for working in a team. Later, after the team has been formed, the team members learn that shirking reduces the amount of the added output they came together to capture in the first place. Now the team members enter into another trade or market transaction. They trade some control over their daily behavior—specifically, they

---

2. Ronald Coase, "The Nature of the Firm," *Economica*, November 1937.
3. Ibid.

trade an environment in which the cost of shirking is low for an environment in which the cost of shirking is high—to receive a larger absolute amount of the potential benefits that drew them together. In this trade the monitor appears: some individuals buy the monitoring services that other individuals sell.

As you continue your study of microeconomics, look for the markets that appear at different levels of analysis.

Two Sides to Every Business Firm

There are two sides to every market—a buying side (demand) and a selling side (supply). Similarly, there are two sides to every business firm—a revenue side and a cost side. We can see both sides of a firm by focusing in on profit. The firm's objective is to maximize profit, where profit is the difference between total revenue and total cost.

$$\text{Profit} = \text{Total revenue} - \text{Total cost}$$

Looking at this profit equation, it is easy to understand what any firm would like; specifically, it would like its total revenue to be as high as possible and its total cost to be as low as possible. That way, its profit is as high as possible.

Total revenue is equal to the price of a good multiplied by the quantity of the good sold. For example, if a business firm sells 100 units of X at $10 per unit, its total revenue is $1,000. In the next chapter we will begin our discussion of the firm's total revenue. In this chapter we discuss the side of the firm that deals with total cost. Of course, the total cost that a firm incurs does not simply fall out of the sky. It is related to the production of the firm. Produce nothing, no costs; producing something, costs. So, this chapter is focused on production and costs.

More on Total Cost

A disagreement sometimes arises as to what total cost should include. To illustrate, suppose Jill currently works as an attorney earning $80,000 a year. One day, dissatisfied with her career, Jill quits her job as an attorney and opens a pizzeria. After one year of operating the pizzeria, Jill sits down to compute her profit. She sold 20,000 pizzas at a price of $10 per pizza; so her total revenue (for the year) is $200,000. Jill computes her total costs by adding the dollar amounts she spent for everything she bought or rented to run the pizzeria. She spent $2,000 on plates, $3,000 on cheese, $4,000 on soda, $20,000 for rent in the mall where the pizzeria is located, $2,000 for electricity, and so on. The dollar payments Jill made for everything she bought or rented are called her *explicit costs*. An explicit cost is a cost that is incurred when an actual (monetary) payment is made. So Jill sums her explicit costs, which turn out to be $90,000. Then she computes her profit by subtracting $90,000 from $200,000, giving her a profit of $110,000.

A few days pass before Jill tells her friend Marian that she earned a $110,000 profit her first year of running the pizzeria. Marian asks, "Are you sure your profit is $110,000?" Jill assures her that it is. "Did you count the salary you earned as an attorney as a cost?" Marian asks. Jill tells Marian that she did not count the $80,000 salary as a cost of running the pizzeria because the $80,000 is not something she paid out to run the pizzeria. "I wrote a check to my suppliers for the pizza ingredients, soda, dishes, and so on," Jill says, "but I didn't write a check to anyone for the $80,000."

Marian says that, although Jill did not pay out $80,000 in salary to run the pizzeria, still she forfeited $80,000 to run it. "What you could have earned but didn't is a cost to you of running the pizzeria," says Marian.

Jill's $80,000 salary is what economists call an *implicit cost*. An implicit cost is a cost that represents the value of resources used in production for which no actual (monetary)

Profit
The difference between total revenue and total cost.

Explicit Cost
A cost incurred when an actual (monetary) payment is made.

Implicit Cost
A cost that represents the value of resources used in production for which no actual (monetary) payment is made.

payment is made. It is a cost incurred as a result of a firm's using resources that it owns or that the owners of the firm contribute to it.

If total cost is computed as explicit costs plus implicit costs, then Jill's total cost of running the pizzeria is $90,000 plus $80,000, or $170,000. Subtracting $170,000 from a total revenue of $200,000 leaves a profit of $30,000.

ⓣhinking like AN ECONOMIST

What Does the Person "Give Up"? The economist wants to know what a person gives up when she goes into business for herself. What she gives up isn't only the money she pays for resources (to run the business), but also the job she would have had (and the income she would have earned) had she not gone into business for herself. ●●●

Accounting Profit Versus Economic Profit

Accounting Profit
The difference between total revenue and explicit costs.

Economists refer to the first profit that Jill calculated ($110,000) as *accounting profit*. Accounting profit is the difference between total revenue and total cost, where total cost equals explicit costs [see Exhibit 1(a)].

Accounting profit = Total revenue − Total cost (Explicit costs)

Economic Profit
The difference between total revenue and total cost, including both explicit and implicit costs.

Economists refer to the second profit calculated ($30,000) as *economic profit*. Economic profit is the difference between total revenue and total cost, where total cost equals the sum of explicit and implicit costs [see Exhibit 1(b)].

Economic profit = Total revenue − Total cost (Explicit costs + Implicit costs)

To illustrate the difference between explicit and implicit costs, suppose a person has $100,000 in the bank, earning an interest rate of 5 percent a year. This amounts to $5,000 in interest a year. Now suppose the person takes the $100,000 out of the bank to start a business. The $5,000 in *lost interest* is included in the implicit costs of owning and operating the firm. To see why, let's change the example somewhat. Assume the person does not use her $100,000 in the bank to start a business but leaves it in the bank and instead takes out a $100,000 loan at an interest rate of 5 percent. The interest she has to pay on the loan—$5,000 a year—certainly would be an explicit cost and would take away from overall profit. It just makes sense, then, to count the $5,000 interest that the owner doesn't earn if she uses her own $100,000 to start the business (instead of taking out a loan) as a cost, albeit implicit.

Zero Economic Profit Is Not as Bad as It Sounds

Economic profit is usually lower (never higher) than accounting profit. Whereas economic profit is the difference between total revenue and total cost (where total cost is the sum of explicit and implicit costs), accounting profit is the difference between total revenue and only explicit costs. Thus, a firm could earn both a positive accounting profit and a zero

---

EXHIBIT 1

Accounting and Economic Profit

Accounting profit equals total revenue minus explicit costs. Economic profit equals total revenue minus both explicit and implicit costs.

(a)

(b)

economic profit. In economics, a firm that makes a zero economic profit is said to be earning a normal profit.

Normal profit = Zero economic profit

However, the owner of a firm should not be worried about making zero economic profit for the year just ending. A zero economic profit—as bad as it may sound—means the owner has generated total revenue sufficient to cover total cost—that is, *both explicit and implicit costs*. If, for example, the owner's implicit cost is a (forfeited) $100,000 salary working for someone else, then earning a zero economic profit means he has done as well as he could have done in his next best (alternative) line of employment.

When we realize that zero economic profit (or normal profit) means doing as well as could have been done, we understand that it isn't bad to make zero economic profit. Zero accounting profit, however, is altogether different; it implies that some part of total cost has not been covered by total revenue.

Normal Profit
Zero economic profit. A firm that earns normal profit is earning revenue equal to its total costs (explicit plus implicit costs). This is the level of profit necessary to keep resources employed in the firm.

finding ECONOMICS

In a Sports Bar Frank is sitting at the bar, watching the game on the nearby television set. The bartender asks him whether he wants another drink, and he says yes. The bartender and Frank start talking, and Frank learns that the bartender owns the bar. In fact, he opened up the bar 10 years ago. Is it more likely that before the bartender opened up the bar, he was working at a high-paying job or at a medium-paying job? Is there any economics here?

Think implicit costs. There are benefits to the bartender of owning and operating a sports bar, but there are costs too. Some costs are explicit (rent for the bar, pretzels, TV sets, beer, etc.), and some are implicit (specifically, the salary he earned in the job he had before he was the owner and bartender). The higher those implicit costs are, the less likely it is that the bartender would have quit the job to open a sports bar. ▲ ▲ ▲

SELF-TEST

(Answers to Self-Test questions are in Answers to Self-Test Questions at the back of the book.)

1. Will individuals form teams or firms in all settings?

2. Suppose everything about two people is the same except that currently one person earns a high salary and the other person earns a low salary. Which is more likely to start his or her own business and why?

3. Is accounting profit or economic profit larger? Why?

4. When can a business owner be earning a profit but not covering costs?

PRODUCTION

Production is a transformation of resources or inputs into goods and services. You may think of production as you might think of making a cake. It takes certain ingredients to make a cake—sugar, flour, and so on. Similarly, it takes certain resources, or inputs, to produce a computer, a haircut, a piece of furniture, or a house.

Economists often talk about two types of inputs in the production process: fixed and variable. A fixed input is an input whose quantity cannot be changed as output changes. To illustrate, suppose the McMahon and McGee Bookshelf Company has rented a factory under a six-month lease: McMahon and McGee, the owners of the company, have contracted to pay the $2,500 monthly rent for six months—no matter what. Whether McMahon and McGee produce one bookshelf or 7,000, the $2,500 rent for the factory must be paid. The factory is a fixed input in the production process of bookshelves.

Fixed Input
An input whose quantity cannot be changed as output changes.

Variable Input
An input whose quantity can be changed as output changes.

A **variable input** is an input whose quantity can be changed as output changes. Examples of variable inputs for the McMahon and McGee Bookshelf Company include wood, paint, nails, and so on. These inputs can (and most likely will) change as the production of bookshelves changes. As they produce more bookshelves, McMahon and McGee purchase more of these inputs; as they produce fewer bookshelves, they purchase fewer of these inputs. Labor might also be a variable input for McMahon and McGee. As they produce more bookshelves, they might hire more employees; as they produce fewer bookshelves, they might lay off some.

If any of the inputs of a firm are fixed inputs, then it is said to be producing in the *short run*. In other words, the **short run** is a period of time in which some inputs are fixed.

Short Run
A period of time in which some inputs in the production process are fixed.

If none of the inputs of a firm is a fixed input—if all inputs are variable—then the firm is said to be producing in the *long run*. In other words, the **long run** is a period of time in which all inputs can be varied (no inputs are fixed).

Long Run
A period of time in which all inputs in the production process can be varied (no inputs are fixed).

When firms produce goods and services and then sell them, they necessarily incur costs. In this section we discuss the production activities of the firm in the short run, leading to the law of diminishing marginal returns and marginal costs. In the next section we tie the production of the firm to all the costs of production in the short run. We then turn to an analysis of production in the long run.

Common Misconception About the Short Run and Long Run

Individuals naturally think that the long run is a longer period of time than the short run. For example, if the short run is 6 months, then the long run is, say, 10 months. But this is not the right way to differentiate the short run from the long run. Think of each as a period of time during which some condition exists. The short run is the period of time during which at least one input is fixed, and it could be a period of 6 months, 2 years, and so on. The long run is not necessarily longer in months and years than the short run. It is simply the period of time during which all inputs are variable (i.e., no input is fixed). In terms of days, weeks, and months, the short run could be a longer period of time than the long run.

Production in the Short Run

Suppose two inputs (or resources), labor (L) and capital (C), are used to produce some good. Furthermore, suppose one of those inputs—capital—is fixed. Obviously, because an input is fixed, the firm is producing in the short run.

In Exhibit 2, column 1 shows the units of the fixed input, capital (fixed at 1 unit). Column 2 shows different units of the variable input, labor. Notice that we go from 0 (no workers) through 10 units (10 workers). Column 3 shows the quantities of output produced with 1 unit of capital and different amounts of labor. (The quantity of output is sometimes referred to as the *total physical product*, or *TPP*.) For example, 1 unit of capital and 0 units of labor produce 0 output; 1 unit of capital and 1 unit of labor produce 18 units of output; 1 unit of capital and 2 units of labor produce 37 units of output; 1 unit of capital and 3 units of labor produce 57 units of output; and so on.

Marginal Physical Product (MPP)
The change in output that results from changing the variable input by one unit, holding all other inputs fixed.

Column 4 shows the marginal physical product of the variable input. The **marginal physical product (MPP)** of a variable input is equal to the change in output that results from changing the variable input by one unit, *holding all other inputs fixed*. Because in our example the variable input is labor, we are talking about the *MPP* of labor. Specifically, the *MPP* of labor is equal to the change in output, *Q*, that results from changing labor, *L*, by one unit, *holding all other inputs fixed*.

$$MPP \text{ of labor} = \Delta Q / \Delta L$$

EXHIBIT 2

(1) Capital (C), fixed input (units)	(2) Labor (L), variable input (number of workers)	(3) Quantity of Output, Q (units)	(4) Marginal Physical Product (MPP) of labor, MPP of labor = ΔQ/ΔL, Δ(3)/Δ(2) (units)
1	0	0	
1	1	18	18
1	2	37	19
1	3	57	20
1	4	76	19
1	5	94	18
1	6	111	17
1	7	127	16
1	8	137	10
1	9	133	–4
1	10	125	–8

Production in the Short Run and the Law of Diminishing Marginal Returns

In the short run, as additional units of a variable input are added to a fixed input, the marginal physical product of the variable input may increase at first. Eventually, the marginal physical product of the variable input decreases. The point at which marginal physical product decreases is the point at which diminishing marginal returns have set in.

Notice that the marginal physical product of labor first rises (from 18 to 19 to 20), then falls (from 20 to 19 to 18 to 17 to 16 to 10), and then becomes negative (–4 and –8). When the *MPP* is rising, we say there is increasing *MPP*; when it is falling, there is diminishing *MPP*; and when it is negative, there is negative *MPP*.

Focus on the point at which the *MPP* first begins to decline—with the addition of the fourth worker. The point at which the marginal physical product of labor first declines is the point at which diminishing marginal returns are said to have set in. Diminishing marginal returns are common in production—so common, in fact, that economists refer to the law of diminishing marginal returns (or the law of diminishing marginal product). The law of diminishing marginal returns states that *as ever larger amounts of a variable input are combined with fixed inputs, eventually the marginal physical product of the variable input will decline.*

The question is why the *MPP* of the variable input eventually declines. To answer this question, think of adding agricultural workers (variable input) to 10 acres of land (fixed input). The workers must clear the land, plant the crop, and then harvest the crop. In the early stages of adding labor to the land, perhaps the *MPP* rises or remains constant. But eventually, as we continue to add more workers to the land, it becomes overcrowded with workers. Workers are stepping around each other, stepping on the crops, and so on. Because of these problems, output growth begins to slow.

It may seem strange that the firm in Exhibit 2 would ever hire beyond the third worker. After all, the *MPP* of labor is at its highest (20) with the third worker. Why hire the fourth worker if the *MPP* of labor is going to fall to 19? The firm may hire the fourth worker because the worker adds output. It would be one thing if the quantity of output were 57 units with three workers and fell to 55 units with the addition of the fourth worker, but this isn't the case. With the addition of the fourth worker, output rises from 57 units to 76 units. The firm has to ask and answer two questions: (1) What can the additional 19 units of output be sold for? (2) What does it cost to hire the fourth worker? Suppose the additional 19 units can be sold for $100, and it costs the firm $70 to hire the fourth worker. In that case, hiring the fourth worker makes sense.

Law of Diminishing Marginal Returns

As ever larger amounts of a variable input are combined with fixed inputs, eventually the marginal physical product of the variable input will decline.

Whose Marginal Productivity Are We Talking About?

Look back at Exhibit 2, and note the data that follows the fourth worker. When the fourth worker is added, the quantity of output rises from 57 units to 76 units. Also, marginal productivity is 19 units. It is easy to fall into the trap of believing that 19 units is the marginal productivity of the fourth worker, but this is a misreading of the data. It's not as though the fourth worker walks through the door, and we attach the number "19" to him. Instead, 19 is the marginal productivity of labor when there are four workers working with the one (fixed) unit of capital. The number can be as easily attached to the first, second, or third worker as it can be to the fourth worker.

thinking like AN ECONOMIST

Comparing One Thing to Another In economics, when making decisions, you usually compare one thing to something else. To illustrate, suppose you need to decide how much time to devote to studying. Would you consider just the additional benefits of spending more time studying, or would you consider the additional costs of spending more time studying too? You would want to consider both.

Similarly, when a firm has to decide how many workers to hire, it wouldn't consider only the additional benefits of hiring more workers (as measured by their additional output times the price the additional output could be sold for). Instead, it would consider the additional benefits against the additional costs of hiring more workers. ●●●

Marginal Physical Product and Marginal Cost

A firm's costs are tied to its production. Specifically, the *marginal cost* (*MC*) of producing a good is a reflection of the marginal physical product (*MPP*) of the variable input. Our objective in this section is to prove that this statement is true. Before doing so, we need to define and discuss some economic cost concepts.

SOME ECONOMIC COST CONCEPTS Certainly, a cost is incurred whenever a fixed input or variable input is employed in the production process. The costs associated with fixed inputs are called fixed costs. The costs associated with variable inputs are called variable costs.

Because the quantity of a fixed input does not change as output changes, neither do fixed costs. Payments for such things as fire insurance (the same amount every month), liability insurance, and the rental of a factory and machinery are usually considered fixed costs. Whether the business produces 1, 10, 100, or 1,000 units of output, the rent for its factory is not likely to change. The rent is whatever amount was agreed to with the owner of the factory for the duration of the rental agreement.

Because the quantity of a variable input changes with output, so do variable costs. For example, it takes labor, wood, and glue to produce wooden bookshelves. The quantity of all these inputs (labor, wood, and glue) changes as the number of wooden bookshelves produced changes.

The sum of fixed costs and variable costs is total cost (*TC*). If total fixed costs (*TFC*) are $100 and total variable costs (*TVC*) are $300, then total cost (*TC*) is $400.

$$TC = TFC + TVC$$

Given total cost, we can formally define marginal cost. Marginal cost (*MC*) is the change in total cost, *TC*, that results from a change in output, *Q*.

$$MC = \frac{\Delta TC}{\Delta Q}$$

THE LINK BETWEEN *MPP* AND *MC* In Exhibit 3, we establish the link between the marginal physical product of a variable input and marginal cost. The first four columns

Fixed Costs
Costs that do not vary with output; the costs associated with fixed inputs.

Variable Costs
Costs that vary with output; the costs associated with variable inputs.

Total Cost (*TC*)
The sum of fixed costs and variable costs.

Marginal Cost (*MC*)
The change in total cost that results from a change in output: $MC = \Delta TC/\Delta Q$.

present much of the same data first presented in Exhibit 2. Essentially, column 3 shows the different quantities of output produced by 1 unit of capital (fixed input) and various amounts of labor (variable input), and column 4 shows the *MPP* of labor. Exhibit 3(a) shows the *MPP* curve, which is based on the data in column 4. Notice that the *MPP* curve first rises and then falls.

In column 5, we have identified the total fixed cost (*TFC*) of production as $40. (Recall that fixed costs do not change as output changes.) For column 6, we have assumed that each worker is hired for $20; so when there is only 1 worker, total variable cost (*TVC*) is $20; when there are 2 workers, total variable cost is $40; and so on. Column 7 shows total cost at various output levels; the total cost figures in this column are simply the sum of the fixed costs in column 5 and the variable costs in column 6. Finally, in column 8, we compute marginal cost. Exhibit 3(b) shows the *MC* curve, which is based on the data in column 8.

Columns 4 and 8 show the *MPP* and *MC,* respectively. Notice that when the *MPP* is rising (from 18 to 19 to 20), marginal cost is decreasing (from $1.11 to $1.05 to $1.00),

EXHIBIT 3

Marginal Physical Product and Marginal Cost

(a) The marginal physical product of labor curve. The curve is derived by plotting the data from columns 2 and 4 in the exhibit. (b) The marginal cost curve. The curve is derived by plotting the data from columns 3 and 8 in the exhibit. Notice that as the *MPP* curve rises, the *MC* curve falls; and as the *MPP* curve falls, the *MC* curve rises.

(1) Capital (C), fixed input (units)	(2) Labor (L), variable input (workers)	(3) Quantity of Output, Q (units)	(4) Marginal Physical Product (MPP) of labor, MPP of labor = $\Delta Q/\Delta L$ = $\Delta(3)/\Delta(2)$ (units)	(5) Total Fixed Cost (TFC)	(6) Total Variable Cost (TVC)	(7) Total Cost (TC), (5) + (6)	(8) Marginal Cost (MC), $\Delta TC/\Delta Q$, $\Delta(7)/\Delta(3)$
1	0	0		$40	$ 0	$40	
			18				$1.11
1	1	18		40	20	60	
			19				$1.05
1	2	37		40	40	80	
			20				$1.00
1	3	57		40	60	100	
			19				$1.05
1	4	76		40	80	120	
			18				$1.11
1	5	94		40	100	140	
			17				$1.17
1	6	111		40	120	160	
			16				$1.25
1	7	127		40	140	180	

(a)

(b)

and when the *MPP* is falling (from 20 to 19, etc.), marginal cost is increasing (from $1.00 to $1.05, etc.). In other words, the *MPP* and *MC* move in opposite directions. You can also see this by comparing the *MPP* curve with the *MC* curve. When the *MPP* curve is going up, the *MC* curve is moving down, and when the *MPP* curve is going down, the *MC* curve is going up. Of course, all this is common sense: As marginal physical product rises—or, to put it differently, as the productivity of the variable input rises—we would expect costs to decline. And as the productivity of the variable input declines, we would expect costs to rise.

In conclusion, then, what the *MC* curve looks like depends on what the *MPP* curve looks like. Recall that the *MPP* curve must have a declining portion because of the law of diminishing marginal returns. So if the *MPP* curve first rises and then (when diminishing marginal returns set in) falls, the *MC* curve must first fall and then rise.

ANOTHER WAY TO LOOK AT THE RELATIONSHIP BETWEEN *MPP* AND *MC* An easy way to see that marginal physical product and marginal cost move in opposite directions is to reexamine the definition of marginal cost (the change in total cost divided by the change in output). The change in total cost is the additional cost of an additional unit of the variable input (see Exhibit 3). The change in output is the marginal physical product of the variable input. Thus, marginal cost is equal to the additional cost of an additional unit of the variable input divided by the input's marginal physical product. In Exhibit 3, the variable input is labor; so $MC = W/MPP$, where MC = marginal cost, W = wage, and MPP = marginal physical product of labor. The following table reproduces column 4 from Exhibit 3, notes the wage, and computes *MC* using the equation $MC = W/MPP$.

MPP	Variable Cost (W)	W/MPP = MC
18 units	$20	$20/18 = $1.11
19	20	20/19 = 1.05
20	20	20/20 = 1.00
19	20	20/19 = 1.05
18	20	20/18 = 1.11
17	20	20/17 = 1.17
16	20	20/16 = 1.25

Now compare the marginal cost figures in the last column in the table with the marginal cost figures in column 8 of Exhibit 3. Whether marginal cost is defined as equal to $\Delta TC/\Delta Q$ or as equal to W/MPP, the result is the same. The latter way of defining marginal cost, however, explicitly shows that as *MPP* rises, *MC* falls and that as *MPP* falls, *MC* rises.

$$\frac{W}{MPP \uparrow} = MC \downarrow$$

$$\frac{W}{MPP \downarrow} = MC \uparrow$$

Average Productivity

When the press or laypersons use the word *productivity*, they are usually referring to *average physical product* instead of *marginal physical product*. To illustrate the difference, suppose 1 worker can produce 10 units of output a day and 2 workers can produce 18 units of output a day. Marginal physical product is 8 units (MPP of labor $= \Delta Q/\Delta L$). Average physical product, which is output divided by the quantity of labor, is equal to 9 units.

$$AP \text{ of labor} = \frac{Q}{L}$$

High School Students, Staying Out Late, and More

Can marginal cost affect a person's behavior? Let's analyze two different situations in which it might.

High School Students and Staying Out Late

A 16-year-old high school student asks her parents if she can have the car tonight. She says she plans to go with some friends to a concert. Her parents ask what time she will get home. She says that she plans to be back by midnight.

The girl's parents tell her that she can have the car and that they expect her home by midnight. If she's late, she will lose her driving privileges for a week.

Later that night, it is midnight and the 16-year-old is 15 minutes away from home. When she realizes she can't get home until 12:15 a.m., will she continue on home? She may not. The marginal cost of staying out later is now zero. In short, whether she arrives home at 12:15, 1:15, or 2:25, the punishment is the same: she will lose her driving privileges for a week. There is no additional cost for staying out an additional minute or an additional hour. There may, however, be additional benefits. Her punishment places a zero marginal cost on staying out after midnight. Once midnight has come and gone, the additional cost of staying out later is zero.

No doubt her parents would prefer her to get home at, say, 12:01 rather than at 1:01 or even later. If this is the case, then they should not have made the marginal cost of staying out after midnight zero. They should have increased the marginal cost of staying out late for every minute (or 15-minute period) that the 16-year-old was late. In other words, one of the parents might have said, "For the first 15 minutes you're late, you'll lose 1 hour of driving privileges, for the second 15 minutes you're late, you'll lose 2 hours of driving privileges, and so on." This would have presented our teen with a rising marginal cost of staying out late. With a rising marginal cost, it is more likely she will get home close to midnight.

Crime

Suppose that the sentence for murder in the first degree is life imprisonment, that the sentence for burglary is 10 years, and that the burglary rate has skyrocketed in the past few months. Many of the city residents have become alarmed, calling on the police and other local and state officials to do something about the rising burglary rate.

Someone proposes that the way to lower the burglary rate is to increase the punishment for it. Instead of only 10 years in prison, make the punishment stiffer. In his zeal to reduce the burglary rate, a state legislator proposes that burglary carry the same punishment as first-degree murder: life in prison. That will certainly get the burglary rate down, he argues. After all, who will take the chance of committing a burglary knowing that if he gets caught and convicted, he will spend the rest of his days in prison?

Unfortunately, by making the punishment for burglary and murder the same, the marginal cost of murdering someone while burglarizing a home falls to zero. To illustrate, suppose Smith is burglarizing a home and the residents walk in on him. Realizing the residents can identify him as the burglar, Smith shoots and kills them. If he gets apprehended for burglary, the penalty is the same as it is for murder. Raising the cost of burglary from 10 years to life imprisonment may reduce the number of burglaries, but it may have the unintended effect of also raising the murder rate.

Usually, when the term *labor productivity* is used in the newspaper and in government documents, it refers to the average (physical) productivity of labor on an hourly basis. By computing the average productivity of labor for different countries and noting the annual percentage changes, we can compare labor productivity between and within countries. Government statisticians have chosen 1992 as a benchmark year (a year against which we measure other years). They have also set a productivity index, (a measure of productivity) for 1992 equal to 100. By computing a productivity index for other years and noting whether each index is above, below, or equal to 100, they know whether productivity is rising, falling, or remaining constant, respectively. Finally, by computing the percentage change in productivity indexes from one year to the next, they know the rate at which productivity is changing.

Suppose the productivity index for the United States is 120 in year 1 and 125 in year 2. Because the productivity index is higher in year 2 than in year 1, labor productivity increased over the year; that is, output produced increased per hour of labor expended.

SELF-TEST

1. If the short run is 6 months, does it follow that the long run is longer than 6 months? Explain your answer.

2. "As we add more capital to more labor, eventually the law of diminishing marginal returns will set in." What is wrong with this statement?

3. Suppose a marginal cost (MC) curve falls when output is in the range of 1 unit to 10 units. Then it flattens out and

remains constant over an output range of 10 units to 20 units, and then rises over a range of 20 units to 30 units. What does this have to say about the marginal physical product (MPP) of the variable input?

EXHIBIT 4

Total, Average, and Marginal Costs

TFC equals $100 (column 2) and TVC is as noted in column 4. From the data, we

calculate AFC, AVC, TC, ATC, and MC. The curves associated with TFC, AFC, TVC, AVC, TC, ATC, and MC are shown in diagrams at the

bottom of the corresponding columns. (Note: Scale is not the same for all diagrams.)

(1) Quantity of Output, Q (units)	(2) Total Fixed Cost (TFC)	(3) Average Fixed Cost (AFC) $AFC = TFC/Q$ $= (2)/(1)$	(4) Total Variable Cost (TVC)	(5) Average Variable Cost (AVC) $AVC = TVC/Q$ $= (4)/(1)$
0	$100	—	$ 0	—
1	100	$100.00	50	$50.00
2	100	50.00	80	40.00
3	100	33.33	100	33.33
4	100	25.00	110	27.50
5	100	20.00	130	26.00
6	100	16.67	160	26.67
7	100	14.28	200	28.57
8	100	12.50	250	31.25
9	100	11.11	310	34.44
10	100	10.00	380	38.00

COSTS OF PRODUCTION: TOTAL, AVERAGE, MARGINAL

Continuing our discussion of the costs of production, the easiest way to see the relationships among the various costs is with the example in Exhibit 4.

Column 1 of Exhibit 4 shows the various quantities of output, ranging from 0 units to 10 units.

Column 2 shows the total fixed costs of production with *TFC* set at $100. Recall that fixed costs do not change as output changes. Therefore, *TFC* is $100 when output is 0 units, 1 unit, or 2 units, and so on. Because *TFC* does not change as *Q* changes, the *TFC* curve in the exhibit is a horizontal line at $100.

In column 3, we have computed average fixed cost (AFC), which is total fixed cost divided by quantity of output.

$$AFC = \frac{TFC}{Q}$$

Average Fixed Cost (AFC)
Total fixed cost divided by quantity of output: $AFC = TFC/Q$.

EXHIBIT 4

Continued

(6) Total Cost (TC) $TC = TFC + TVC$ $= (2) + (4)$	(7) Average Total Cost (ATC) $ATC = TC/Q$ $= (6)/(1)$	(8) Marginal Cost (MC) $MC = \Delta TC/\Delta Q$ $= \Delta(6)/\Delta(1)$
$100.00	—	—
150.00	$150.00	$50.00
180.00	90.00	30.00
200.00	66.67	20.00
210.00	52.50	10.00
230.00	46.00	20.00
260.00	43.33	30.00
300.00	42.86	40.00
350.00	43.75	50.00
410.00	45.56	60.00
480.00	48.00	70.00

For example, look at the fourth entry in column 3. To get a dollar amount of $33. 33, we simply took *TFC* at 3 units of output, which is $100, and divided by 3. Notice that the *AFC* curve in the exhibit continually declines.

In column 4, we have simply entered some hypothetical data for total variable cost (*TVC*). The *TVC* curve in the exhibit rises because variable costs are likely to increase as output increases.

In column 5, we have computed average variable cost (*AVC*), which is total variable cost divided by quantity of output.

$$AVC = \frac{TVC}{Q}$$

For example, look at the third entry in column 5. To get a dollar amount of $40.00, we simply took *TVC* at 2 units of output, which is $80, and divided by 2. Notice that the *AVC* curve declines and then rises.

Column 6 shows total cost (*TC*). Total cost is the sum of total variable cost and total fixed cost. Notice that the *TC* curve does not start at zero because, even when output is zero, there are some fixed costs. In this example, total fixed cost (*TFC*) at zero output is $100. The total cost (*TC*) curve must start at $100 instead of at $0.

Column 7 shows average total cost (*ATC*), which is total cost divided by quantity of output. Average total cost is sometimes called *unit cost.*

$$ATC = \frac{TC}{Q}$$

Alternatively, we can say that *ATC* equals the sum of *AFC* and *AVC*.

$$ATC = AFC + AVC$$

To understand why this makes sense, remember that *TC* = *TFC* + *TVC*. Thus, if we divide all total magnitudes by quantity of output (*Q*), we necessarily get *ATC* = *AFC* + *AVC*. Notice that the *ATC* curve falls and then rises.

Column 8 shows marginal cost (*MC*), which is the change in total cost divided by the change in output.

$$MC = \frac{\Delta TC}{\Delta Q}$$

The *MC* curve has a declining portion and a rising portion. When *MC* is declining, the *MPP* is rising. When *MC* is rising, the *MPP* of the variable input is falling. Obviously, the low point on the *MC* curve is when diminishing marginal returns set in.

Exhibit 5 brings together much of the material we have discussed relating to production and costs in the short run.

ⓣhinking like AN ECONOMIST

Deducing Things from What Is Known Economists often deduce things from what they know, as we just did when discussing *MPP* and *MC.* Here is what we know: *MPP* and *MC* are inversely related; as *MPP* rises, *MC* falls, and as *MPP* falls, *MC* rises. When diminishing marginal returns kick in, *MPP* begins to decline. We deduce, then, that when diminishing marginal returns kick in, *MC* begins to rise. ● ● ●

The AVC and ATC Curves in Relation to the MC Curve

What do the average total and average variable cost curves look like in relation to the marginal cost curve? To explain, we need to discuss the average-marginal rule, which is best defined with an example.

Average Variable Cost (AVC)
Total variable cost divided by quantity of output: AVC = TVC/Q.

Average Total Cost (ATC), or Unit Cost
Total cost divided by quantity of output: ATC = TC/Q.

Average-Marginal Rule
When the marginal magnitude is above the average magnitude, the average magnitude rises; when the marginal magnitude is below the average magnitude, the average magnitude falls.

EXHIBIT 5

A Review of Production and Costs in the Short Run

Concept	Explanation	Example	Other information (if relevant)
Production in the short run	Firm is producing with at least one input that is fixed.	Firm produces with capital and labor and capital is the fixed input and labor is the variable input.	
Marginal Physical Product (MPP)	$MPP = \Delta Q/\Delta \text{Variable Input}$	If $\Delta Q = 40$ units, and ΔVariable Input $= 1$, then $MPP = 40$ units.	
Law of Diminishing Marginal Returns	The law of diminishing marginal returns states that as ever larger amounts of a variable input are combined with a fixed input, eventually the MPP of the variable input declines.	See Exhibit 2. Diminishing marginal returns "kick in" with the addition of the fourth worker.	The law of diminishing marginal returns holds only in the short run, when at least one input is fixed.
Total Cost (TC)	$TC = TFC + TVC$	Let $TFC = \$10$, and $TVC = \$40$; it follows that $TC = \$50$.	
Total Fixed Cost (TFC)	$TFC = AFC \times Q$	Let $AFC = \$4$ and $Q = 40$ units; it follows that $TFC = \$160$.	TFC is constant over quantity of output. For example, TFC is, say, \$100 when quantity of output is 10 units and also when quantity of output is 20 units
Total Variable Cost (TVC)	$TVC = AVC \times Q$	Let $AVC = \$6$ and $Q = 40$ units; it follows that $TVC = \$240$.	TVC changes as quantity of output changes.
Average Fixed Cost (AFC)	$AFC = TFC/Q$	Let $TFC = \$50$ and $Q = 10$; it follows that $AFC = \$5$.	AFC declines as quantity of output rises.
Average Variable Cost (AVC)	$AVC = TVC/Q$	Let $TVC = \$120$ and $Q = 20$; it follows that $AVC = \$10$.	
Average Total Cost (ATC)	(1) $ATC = TC/Q$ (2) $ATC = AFC + AVC$	(1) Let $TC = \$50$ and $Q = \$5$; it follows that $ATC = \$5$. (2) Let $AFC = \$4$ and $AVC = \$1$; it follows that $ATC = \$5$.	ATC is the same as *unit cost*. Also, notice that ATC can be computed two ways, as we show at the left in the second column.
Marginal Cost (MC)	$MC = \Delta TC/\Delta Q$	Suppose that TC increases from \$40 to \$45 as quantity of output rises from 101 to 101 units. It follows that MC, which is the change in total cost divided by the change in quantity of output, is \$5.	There is a second way of computing MC. Here it is: $MC = W/MPP$, where $W = $ wage rate, and $MPP = $ marginal physical product.

Suppose that 20 persons are in a room and that each person weighs 170 pounds. Your task is to calculate the average weight. This is accomplished by adding the individual weights and dividing by 20. Obviously, this average weight will be 170 pounds. Now an additional person enters the room. We will refer to this additional person as the marginal (additional) person, and we will call the additional weight he brings into the room the marginal weight.

Let's suppose the weight of the marginal person is 275 pounds. The average weight based on the 21 persons now in the room is 175 pounds. The new average weight is greater than the old average weight. The average weight was pulled up by the weight of the additional person. In short, *when the marginal magnitude is above the average magnitude, the average magnitude rises.* This is one part of the average-marginal rule.

Suppose the weight of the marginal person is less than the average weight of 170 pounds, such as 65 pounds. Then the new average is 165 pounds. In this case, the average weight was pulled down by the weight of the additional person. Thus, *when the marginal magnitude is below the average magnitude, the average magnitude falls.* This is the other part of the average-marginal rule.

$$\text{Marginal} < \text{Average} \rightarrow \text{Average} \downarrow$$
$$\text{Marginal} > \text{Average} \rightarrow \text{Average} \uparrow$$

We can apply the average-marginal rule to find out what the average total and average variable cost curves look like in relation to the marginal cost curve. The following analysis holds for both the average total cost curve and the average variable cost curve.

We reason that

1. if marginal cost is below (less than) average variable cost, average variable cost is falling; and

2. if marginal cost is above (greater than) average variable cost, average variable cost is rising.

This reasoning implies that the relationship between the average variable cost curve and the marginal cost curve must look like that in Exhibit 6(a). In region 1 of (a), marginal cost is below average variable cost, and, consistent with the average-marginal rule, average variable cost is falling. In region 2 of (a), marginal cost is above average variable cost, and average variable cost is rising. In summary, the relationship between the average variable cost curve and the marginal cost curve in Exhibit 6(a) is consistent with the average-marginal rule.

In addition, because average variable cost is pulled down when marginal cost is below it and pulled up when marginal cost is above it, the marginal cost curve must intersect the average variable cost curve at the latter's lowest point. This lowest point is point L in Exhibit 6(a).

The same relationship that exists between the *MC* and *AVC* curves also exists between the *MC* and *ATC* curves, as shown in Exhibit 6(b). In region 1 of (b), marginal cost is below average total cost, and, consistent with the average-marginal rule, average total cost is falling. In region 2 of (b), marginal cost is above average total cost, and average total cost is rising. The marginal cost curve must therefore intersect the average total cost curve at the latter's lowest point.

There is no relationship between the average fixed cost curve and the marginal cost curve. We can indirectly see why by recalling that average fixed cost is simply total fixed cost (which is constant over output) divided by output ($AFC = TFC/Q$). As output (Q) increases and total fixed cost (TFC) remains constant, average fixed cost (TFC/Q) must decrease continuously [see Exhibit 6(c)].

EXHIBIT 6

Average and Marginal Cost Curves

(a) The relationship between *AVC* and *MC*.
(b) The relationship between *ATC* and *MC*.
The *MC* curve intersects both the *AVC* and *ATC*

curves at their respective low points (*L*). This is consistent with the average-marginal rule.
(c) The *AFC* curve declines continuously.

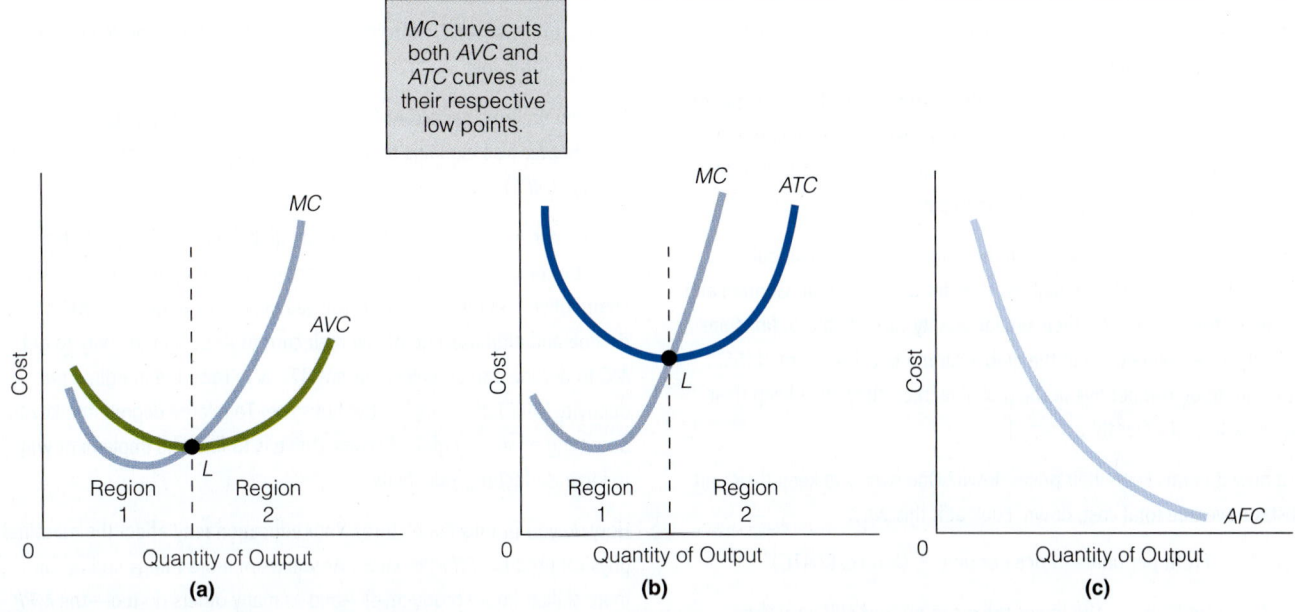

MC curve cuts both *AVC* and *ATC* curves at their respective low points.

finding ECONOMICS

Why Doesn't Oliver Cheat? Oliver is sitting in class taking a test, and his teacher is out of the class. He could easily look over at his neighbor's paper (which is uncovered) to see what the answer to question 25 is, but he doesn't. Why doesn't he cheat? Does it have anything to do with the average-marginal rule?

There may be a guilt cost to Oliver cheating, but let's ignore that reason for a moment. Even without a guilt cost and without the chance of being caught, Oliver may still not cheat for a reason that could have something to do with the average-marginal rule. People usually cheat by copying the work of someone they believe is smarter than they are. Suppose Oliver believes that his grade on the test will be 65 and that Ian (who is sitting next to him) will receive a grade of 60. Oliver's grade of 65 can be viewed as the average grade and Ian's as the marginal grade. Because the marginal grade is less than the average grade, the marginal will pull down the average. There's no need to cheat if copying someone else's work only lowers Oliver's grade. Oliver is more likely to cheat if he thinks cheating will raise his grade, but this can only occur if he cheats off a person whose grade is likely to be higher than his (when he doesn't cheat). ▲ ▲ ▲

Tying Short-Run Production to Costs

To see how costs are tied to production, let's summarize some of our earlier discussions (see Exhibit 7). We assume production takes place in the short run; so there is at least one fixed input. Suppose we initially add units of a variable input to the fixed input, and the marginal physical product of the variable input (e. g., labor) rises. As a result of *MPP* rising, marginal cost (*MC*) falls. When *MC* has fallen enough to be below average variable cost (*AVC*), we know from the average-marginal rule that *AVC* will begin to decline. Also, when *MC* has fallen enough to be below average total cost (*ATC*), *ATC* will begin to decline.

What Matters to Global Competitiveness?

What does a country need to do to be competitive in the global marketplace? The usual answer is that it needs to produce goods that people in other countries want to buy at prices they want to pay. For example, for the United States to be competitive in the global car and computer markets, U.S. firms must produce cars and computers at prices that people all over the world are willing and able to pay.

Price is a major factor in the race to be competitive in the global market. If U.S. firms charge higher prices for their cars than German and Japanese firms charge for their similar-quality cars, then U.S. firms are unlikely to be competitive in the global car market. Therefore, if U.S. firms are to be competitive in the global market, they must keep their prices down, all other things equal.

But how do firms keep their prices down? One way is to keep their unit cost, or average total cost, down. Look at it this way:

$$\text{Profit per unit} = \text{Price per unit} - \text{Unit cost } (ATC)$$

The lower unit cost is, the lower price can go and still earn the producer/seller an acceptable profit per unit. That is, to be competitive on price, firms must be competitive on unit cost; they need to find ways to lower unit cost. This chapter shows how unit cost declines when marginal cost (MC) is below unit cost (ATC). In other words, to lower ATC, marginal cost must fall and go below (current) average total cost.

But how do firms get MC to fall and eventually go below current ATC? This chapter also explains that before MC can decline, marginal physical product (MPP) must rise.

To summarize, to be competitive in the global marketplace, U.S. firms must be competitive on price. To be competitive on price, firms must be competitive on unit cost (ATC). This requires firms to get their MC to decline and ultimately go below their current ATC. And the way to get MC to decline and go below current ATC is to raise the marginal productivity (MPP) of the inputs the firms use. To a large degree, the key to becoming or staying globally competitive is to find and implement ways to increase factor productivity.

How do you fit into the picture? Your education may affect the marginal physical product (MPP) of labor. As you learn more things and become more skilled (more productive)—and as many others do too—the MPP of labor in the United States rises. The rise in the MPP of labor, in turn, lowers firms' marginal cost, which ideally will decline enough to pull both average variable and average total costs down. As this happens, U.S. firms can become more competitive on price and still earn a profit.

EXHIBIT 7

Tying Production to Costs

What happens in terms of production (MPP rising or falling) affects MC, which in turn eventually affects AVC and ATC.

Eventually, though, the law of diminishing marginal returns will set in. When this happens, the *MPP* of the variable input declines. As a result, *MC* rises. When *MC* has risen enough to be above *AVC*, *AVC* will rise. Also, when *MC* has risen enough to be above *ATC*, *ATC* will rise.

So what happens in terms of production (rising or falling *MPP*) affects *MC*, which in turn eventually affects *AVC* and *ATC*. In short, the cost of a good is tied to its production.

✆hinking like AN ECONOMIST

Seeing How Things Came to Be In economics, learning what comes before an event is important. To illustrate, suppose *ATC* is rising. Can you see the process that brought this event (*ATC* rising) at this particular moment?

Let's take one step back at a time. *ATC* is rising because (one step back) *MC* rose to a level above *ATC*. But why did *MC* rise to a level above *ATC* or why is *MC* rising at all? *MC* is rising because *MPP* (one step back) is declining. But why is *MPP* declining? *MPP* is declining because (one step back) the law of diminishing marginal returns set in.

Looking at a tree, you see its branches and leaves. If you look back, though, you can see the seed that was planted and that grew into the tree. You can do the same in economics. When looking at rising *ATC*, most of us simply see rising *ATC*. But if you look far enough back, you can see the law of diminishing marginal returns growing into rising *ATC*. ▪▪▪

One More Cost Concept: Sunk Cost

Sunk cost is a cost incurred in the past that cannot be changed by current decisions and therefore cannot be recovered. For example, suppose that a firm must purchase a $10,000 government license before it can legally produce and sell lamp poles and that the government will not buy back the license or allow it to be resold. The $10,000 the firm spends to purchase the license is a sunk cost. It is a cost that, after it has been incurred (the $10,000 was spent), cannot be changed by a current decision (the firm cannot go back into the past and undo what was done) and cannot be recovered (the government will neither buy back the license nor allow it to be resold).

Let's consider another example of a sunk cost. Suppose Jeremy buys a movie ticket, walks into the theater, and settles down to watch the movie. Thirty minutes into the movie, he realizes that he hates it. The money he paid for the ticket is a sunk cost. The cost was incurred in the past, it cannot be changed, and it cannot be recovered. (We are assuming that movie theaters do not give your money back if you dislike the movie.)

ECONOMISTS' ADVICE: IGNORE SUNK COSTS Economists advise individuals to ignore sunk costs. To illustrate, for Jeremy, who bought the movie ticket but dislikes the movie, the movie ticket is a sunk cost. Now suppose Jeremy says the following to himself as he is watching the movie:

> *I paid to watch this movie, but I really hate it. Should I get up and walk out or should I stay and watch the movie? I think I'll stay and watch the movie because if I leave, I'll lose the money I paid for the ticket.*

The error that Jeremy is making is believing that if he walks out of the theater, he will lose the money he paid for the ticket. But he has already lost the money for the ticket. Whether he stays and watches the movie or leaves, the money is gone forever. It is a sunk cost.

An economist would advise Jeremy to ignore what has happened in the past and what can't be undone. In other words, ignore sunk costs. The question is not what have I already lost? Nothing can be done about what has been lost. Instead, Jeremy should ask and answer these questions: What do I gain (what are my benefits) if I stay and

Sunk Cost
A cost incurred in the past that cannot be changed by current decisions and therefore cannot be recovered.

Producing a Grade in a College Course

One way to think of your taking a college course is as a consumer. To illustrate, you might think of an economics lecture the same way you would a movie. You sit in the classroom and watch the lecturer lecture. You sit in a theater and watch the movie on the screen.

Another (and perhaps "more nearly accurate") way to think of your taking a college course is as a producer. But if, by taking a course, you are a producer, what is it exactly that you are producing? The immediate answer is a grade. You work at producing an A, or a B, or a C, and so on.

If we dig below the surface of the grade, though, what you really are producing is knowledge for yourself. The grade is simply a reflection of the knowledge, in the sense that a higher grade reflects more knowledge produced by you for you, and a lower grade reflects less knowledge produced by you for you.

Now one of the ways to understand what production and costs are about is to think through your actions as a producer. With this in mind, let's consider your producing a grade in a college course.

In your production of a grade, there are both fixed and variable costs. Your paper and pen (that you use to take notes) are largely fixed inputs. The cost of these items constitutes your fixed cost. No matter what grade you produce, or how much knowledge you acquire, your paper and pen cost is not going to change. It is the same whether you end up producing an A, B, or C in the course.

Your variable costs relate to how carefully you listen, how carefully you take notes, and how many course assignments you complete. We would expect that the variable costs will rise as you listen more carefully, take more careful notes, and work on and turn in more assignments.

If we add your pen and paper costs (fixed costs) to your listening and note-taking costs (variable costs), we have the total cost of producing the grade.

Now consider marginal cost. Marginal cost is the change in total cost given a change in quantity of output. The "quantity of output" term here can be misleading, because rarely does a student sitting in class think of

his or her producing so many units of a good, the way a computer firm produces computers or a furniture firm produces furniture. Still, the student produces something, and that something can be roughly described as "units of knowledge." The more units of knowledge produced (by you for you), the higher the grade. So, is there a positive marginal cost of producing a higher grade?

We expect that there would be, and you probably would agree if you have ever made a mental note of the "extra work" it takes you to move your current course grade up from an 89 (B+) to a 92 (A−). In other words, the marginal cost (to you) of producing a higher grade in the course, or acquiring more knowledge from the course, is positive and not zero. [As an aside, it could very well be the case that different students incur a different marginal cost of moving their grade up from an 89 to a 92. In other words, it might be less costly (or easier) for some students to raise their grade 5 points than it is for other students.]

Let's compare the marginal cost of raising *your grade* in two courses, A and B. The marginal cost of raising your grade by 5 points is $100 of extra effort in course A and $300 of extra effort in course B. Many students may express the difference here by saying, "Course B is a tougher course than course A." ("Econ 302 is a lot tougher than Sociology 270.") Will the difference in marginal cost in the two courses affect your behavior? Will it be the deciding factor in which of the two courses you decide to enroll in (assuming you don't have to take both courses)? It could be, assuming the benefits of taking the two courses are the same. All other things being equal, you will probably prefer to take course A than course B.

Finally, do sunk costs exist in a college course? Suppose you took a midterm last week and received a low grade. Are the costs associated with taking the midterm a sunk cost? Well, a cost is sunk if it was (1) incurred in the past, (2) cannot be changed by current decisions, and therefore (3) cannot be recovered. The costs associated with taking the midterm were (1) incurred last week, (2) cannot be changed by a current decision because we assume your professor will not let you retake the midterm, and therefore (3) cannot be recovered. Hence, the costs associated with taking the midterm are sunk.

watch the movie? What do I lose (what are my costs) if I stay and watch the movie? If what Jeremy expects to gain by staying and watching the movie is greater than what he expects to lose, he should stay and watch the movie. However, if what he expects to lose by staying and watching the movie is greater than what he expects to gain, he should leave.

To see this point more clearly, let's say that Jeremy has decided to stay and watch the movie because he doesn't want to lose the price of the movie ticket. Two minutes after he makes this decision, you walk up to him and offer him $200 to leave the theater. Do you think Jeremy will say, "I can't leave the movie theater because if I do, I will lose the price of the movie ticket"? Or do you think he is more likely to take the money and leave? Most people will say that Jeremy will take the $200 and leave the movie theater simply because if he doesn't leave, he loses the opportunity to receive $200.

However, wouldn't he have forfeited something—albeit not $200—if no one offered him $200 to leave? He might have given up at least $1 in benefits doing something else. In short, he must have had some opportunity cost of staying at the movie theater before the $200 was offered. The problem is that somehow, by letting sunk cost influence his decision, Jeremy was willing to ignore this opportunity cost of staying at the theater. The $200 offer only made this opportunity cost of staying at the movie theater obvious.

Consider another situation. Alicia purchases a pair of shoes on sale (no refunds), wears them for a few days, and then realizes they are uncomfortable. An economist would recommend that Alicia simply not wear the shoes. To an economist, the cost of the shoes is a sunk cost because it (1) was incurred in the past, (2) cannot be changed by a current decision, and (3) cannot be recovered. An economist would advise Alicia not to base her current decision as to whether to wear the shoes on what has happened and what cannot be changed. If Alicia lets what she has done and can't undo influence her present decision, she runs the risk of compounding her mistake.

To illustrate, if Alicia decides to wear the uncomfortable shoes because she thinks it is a waste of money not to, she may end up with an even bigger loss: certainly less comfort and possibly a trip to the podiatrist. The relevant question she must ask herself is not, "What did I give up by buying the shoes?" The right question is, "What will I give up by wearing the uncomfortable shoes?"

The message is that a present decision can affect only the future, never the past. Bygones are bygones; sunk costs are sunk costs.

BEHAVIORAL ECONOMICS AND SUNK COST In a real-life experiment, two researchers randomly distributed discounts to buyers of subscriptions to Ohio University's 1982–1983 theater season.[4] One group of ticket buyers paid the normal ticket price of $15 per ticket, a second group received $2 off per ticket, and a third group received $7 off per ticket. In short, some buyers paid lower ticket prices than others.

The researchers found that people who paid more for their tickets attended the theater performances more often than those who paid less. Some people argue that this is because people who paid more for their tickets somehow wanted to attend the theater more than those who paid less. But this isn't likely because the discounts to buyers were distributed randomly. Instead, it seems to be that the more someone paid for the ticket (everyone paid for the ticket before the night of the performance), the greater the sunk cost. And the greater the sunk cost, the more likely individuals were to attend the theater performance. In other words, at least some people were not ignoring sunk cost.

ⓣhinking like AN ECONOMIST

Viewing Sunk Cost as a Constraint Microeconomics emphasizes that all economic actors deal with objectives, constraints, and choices. Let's focus briefly on constraints. All economic actors would prefer to have fewer rather than more constraints and to have constraints that offer more rather than less latitude. For example, a firm would probably prefer to be constrained in having to buy its resources from five suppliers rather than from only one supplier. A consumer would rather have a budget constraint of $4,000 a month instead of $2,000 a month.

(continued)

---

4. Hal Arkes and Catherine Blumer, "The Psychology of Sunk Cost," *Organizational Behavior and Human Decision Processes* 124 (1985).

Adding One More Person to a Caribbean Cruise

We know that marginal cost is the change in total cost divided by the change in quantity of output (produced). For example, if total cost is $100 when 10 units of output are produced, and it rises to $120 when 11 units are produced, then marginal cost is $20. Specifically, marginal cost is the additional cost of the additional unit of output.

© IMAGE COPYRIGHT OCULO, 2009. USED UNDER LICENSE FROM SHUTTERSTOCK.COM

When it comes to producing goods, it is perhaps natural to think of marginal cost as some positive dollar amount. But sometimes marginal cost can be zero. To illustrate, consider a cruise line company that is offering Caribbean cruises. Currently, the cruise liner that will leave for the Caribbean 5 days from today has a 99 percent occupancy rate and a 1 percent vacancy rate. In other words, there are still a few of the ship's cabins that have not been "sold" yet. Now ask yourself what the marginal cost is for the cruise line if one more person (an additional person) joins the cruise. Does the addition of one more person increase the fuel costs of the cruise line company? Probably not. The amount of gasoline needed to move the ship from point X to point Y is independent of how many persons are on the cruise liner. Does the addition of one more person increase the labor costs of the cruise line? Specifically, will the cruise line company have to hire more staff because one more person joins the cruise? Probably not. Probably the only additional cost that the additional person produces for the cruise line company is the cost of extra food (for the person) and a few other minor incidentals. In short, the marginal cost for the extra person is probably very low. So low, in fact, that it is probably close to zero. So, without straying too far from the truth, we can say that the marginal cost of adding one more person to the cruise is zero.

Here are the facts so far: (1) We started with an occupancy rate of 99 percent; (2) We then asked what the marginal cost of adding one more person to the cruise would be. Our answer, for all practical purposes, was zero. Now we ask: Will the fact that the marginal cost is zero for the additional person influence the cruise line company if it tries to increase the occupancy rate from 99 to 100 percent, beginning 5 days before the cruise? Will the cruise line executives think that *the ship is headed to the Caribbean anyway, and adding one more person really doesn't increase the company costs by much, if any, so why not lower the price of the Caribbean to bring in additional customers? Better to sail with more paying customers than fewer paying customers—especially when the last few customers don't raise our costs.* Fact is, cruise line executives often reason this way, and that is why you will often find "last-minute cruise line deals" advertised.

ⓣhinking like AN ECONOMIST (continued)

Person A considers sunk cost when she makes a decision, and person B ignores it when he makes a decision. Does one person face fewer constraints, *ceteris paribus?* The person who ignores sunk cost, person B, faces fewer constraints. Person A acts as if a constraint is there—the constraint of sunk cost, the constraint of having to rectify a past decision—when it really exists only in person A's mind.

In this sense, the fabricated constraint of sunk cost is very different from the real constraint of, say, scarcity. Whether a person believes it or not, scarcity exists. People are constrained by scarcity, just as they are by the force of gravity, whether they know it or not. But people are not constrained by sunk cost if they choose not to be. If you let bygones be bygones, if you realize that sunk cost is a cost that has been incurred and can't be changed, then it cannot constrain you when making a current decision.

Economists look at things this way: there are enough constraints in the world. You are not made better off by behaving as if there is one more than there actually is. ● ● ●

SELF-TEST

1. Identify two ways to compute average total cost (*ATC*).

2. Would a business ever sell its product for less than cost? Explain your answer.

3. What happens to unit costs as marginal costs rise? Explain your answer.

4. Do changes in marginal physical product influence unit costs? Explain your answer.

PRODUCTION AND COSTS IN THE LONG RUN

This section discusses production and long-run costs. As noted, in the long run, there are no fixed inputs and no fixed costs. Consequently, the firm has *greater flexibility* in the long run than in the short run. (Because we discuss both short-run and long-run average total cost curves, we distinguish between them with prefixes: *SR* for short run and *LR* for long run.)

Long-Run Average Total Cost Curve

In the short run, because there are fixed costs and variable costs, total cost is the sum of the two. But in the long run, there are no fixed costs; so variable costs *are* total costs. This section focuses on (1) the long-run average total cost (*LRATC*) curve and (2) what it looks like.

Consider the manager of a firm that produces bedroom furniture. When all inputs are variable, the manager must decide what the situation of the firm should be in the upcoming short-run period. For example, he might need to determine the size of the plant—small, medium, or large. Once this decision is made, the firm is locked into a specific plant size for the short run. Associated with each of the three different plant sizes is a short-run average total cost (*SRATC*) curve, as illustrated in Exhibit 8 (a).

EXHIBIT 8

Long-Run Average Total Cost Curve (*LRATC*)

(a) There are three short-run average total cost curves for three different plant sizes. If these are the only plant sizes, the long-run average total cost curve is the heavily shaded, blue scalloped curve. (b) The long-run average total cost curve is the heavily shaded, blue smooth curve. The *LRATC* curve in (b) is not scalloped because it is assumed that there are so many plant sizes that the *LRATC* curve touches each *SRATC* curve at only one point.

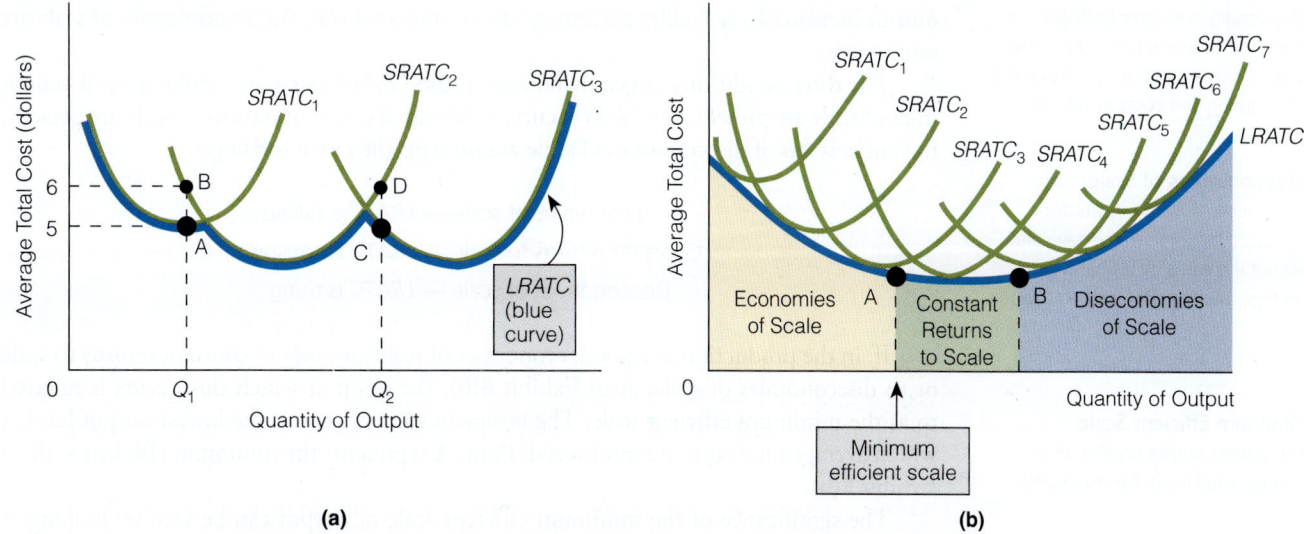

(a)

(b)

Suppose the manager of the firm wants to produce output level Q_1. Obviously, he will choose the plant size represented by $SRATC_1$. This gives a lower unit cost of producing Q_1 than the plant size represented by $SRATC_2$, which has a higher unit cost of producing Q_1 ($6 as opposed to $5).

However, if the manager chooses to produce Q_2, he will choose the plant size represented by $SRATC_3$ because the unit cost of producing Q_2 is lower with that plant size than it is with the plant size represented by $SRATC_2$.

Long-Run Average Total Cost (*LRATC*) Curve

A curve that shows the lowest (unit) cost at which the firm can produce any given level of output.

If we were to ask the same question for every (possible) output level, we would derive the long-run average total cost (*LRATC*) curve. The *LRATC* curve shows the lowest unit cost at which the firm can produce any given level of output. In Exhibit 8(a), the *LRATC* consists of the portions of the three *SRATC* curves that are tangential to the blue curve; it is the scalloped blue curve.

Exhibit 8(b) shows a host of *SRATC* curves and one *LRATC* curve. In this case, the *LRATC* curve is not scalloped, as in part (a). The *LRATC* curve is smooth in part (b) because we assume there are many plant sizes in addition to the three represented in (a). In other words, although they have not been drawn, short-run average total cost curves representing different plant sizes exist in (b) between $SRATC_1$ and $SRATC_2$, between $SRATC_2$ and $SRATC_3$, and so on. In this case, the *LRATC* curve is smooth and touches each *SRATC* curve at one point.

Economies of Scale, Diseconomies of Scale, and Constant Returns to Scale

Economies of Scale

Economies that exist when inputs are increased by some percentage and output increases by a greater percentage, causing unit costs to fall.

Suppose two inputs, labor and capital, are used together to produce a good. If inputs are increased by some percentage (say, 100 percent) and if output increases by a greater percentage (more than 100 percent), then unit costs fall and economies of scale are said to exist.

For example, suppose good X is made with two inputs, Y and Z, and it takes 20 Y and 10 Z to produce 5 units of X. The cost of each unit of input Y is $1, and the cost of each unit of input Z is $1. Thus, a total cost of $30 is required to produce 5 units of X. The unit cost (average total cost) of good X is $6 ($ATC = TC/Q$). Now consider a doubling of inputs Y and Z to 40 Y and 20 Z and a more than doubling in output, say, to 15 units of X. This means a total cost of $60 is required to produce 15 units of X, and the unit cost (average total cost) of good X is $4.

Constant Returns to Scale

The condition when inputs are increased by some percentage and output increases by an equal percentage, causing unit costs to remain constant.

An increase in inputs can have two other results. If inputs are increased by some percentage and output increases by an equal percentage, then unit costs remain constant, and constant returns to scale are said to exist. If inputs are increased by some percentage and output increases by a smaller percentage, then unit costs rise, and diseconomies of scale are said to exist.

Diseconomies of Scale

The condition when inputs are increased by some percentage and output increases by a smaller percentage, causing unit costs to rise.

The three conditions can easily be seen in the *LRATC* curve in Exhibit 8(b): if economies of scale are present, the *LRATC* curve is falling; if constant returns to scale are present, the curve is flat; if diseconomies of scale are present, the curve is rising.

Economies of scale → *LRATC* is falling
Constant returns to scale → *LRATC* is constant
Diseconomies of scale → *LRATC* is rising

Minimum Efficient Scale

The lowest output level at which average total costs are minimized.

If, in the production of a good, economies of scale give way to constant returns to scale or to diseconomies of scale, as in Exhibit 8(b), the point at which this occurs is referred to as the minimum efficient scale. The minimum efficient scale is the lowest output level at which average total costs are minimized. Point A represents the minimum efficient scale in Exhibit 8(b).

The significance of the minimum efficient scale of output can be seen by looking at the long-run average total cost curve between points A and B in Exhibit 8(b). Between these points, there are constant returns to scale; the average total cost is the same over the various output levels between the two points. This means that larger firms (firms producing greater output levels) within this range do not have a cost advantage over smaller firms that operate at the minimum efficient scale.

Keep in mind that economies of scale, diseconomies of scale, and constant returns to scale are relevant only in the long run. Implicit in the definition of the terms and explicit in our examples, all inputs necessary to the production of a good are changeable (not fixed). Because no input is fixed, economies of scale, diseconomies of scale, and constant returns to scale are relevant only in the long run.

Exhibit 9 reviews some of the material we have discussed about production and costs in the long run.

Why Economies of Scale?

Up to a certain point, long-run unit costs of production fall as a firm grows, for two main reasons: (1) Growing firms offer greater opportunities for employees to specialize. Individual workers can become highly proficient at narrowly defined tasks, often producing more output at lower unit costs. (2) Growing firms (especially large, growing firms) can take advantage of highly efficient mass production techniques and equipment that ordinarily require large setup costs and thus are economical only if they can be spread over a large number of units. For example, assembly line techniques are usually relatively cheap when millions of units of a good are produced but are expensive when only a few thousand units are produced.

Why Diseconomies of Scale?

Diseconomies of scale usually arise at the point where a firm's size causes coordination, communication, and monitoring problems. In very large firms, managers often find it difficult to coordinate work activities, communicate their directives to the right persons

EXHIBIT 9

A Review of Production and Costs in the Long Run

Concept	Explanation	Example	Other information (if relevant)
Production in the long run	There are no fixed inputs in the production process. All inputs are variable.	Firms use two inputs, capital (C) and labor (L) and both are variable.	
Economics of scale	Percentage increase in output is greater than percentage increase in inputs.	Inputs increase by, say, 5 percent, and quantity of output increases by, say, 9 percent.	When the firm experiences economics of scale, its LRATC (long-run average total cost) curve declines.
Diseconomies of scale	Percentage increase in output is less than percentage increase in inputs.	Inputs increase by, say, 5 percent, and quantity of output increases by, say, 2 percent.	When the firm experiences diseconomics of scale, its LRATC (long-run average total cost) curve rises.
Constant returns to scale	Percentage increase in output is equal to percentage increase in inputs.	Inputs increase by, say, 5 percent, and quantity of output increases by 5 percent.	When the firm experiences constant returns to scale, its LRATC curve is constant.

in a timely way, and monitor personnel effectively. The business operation simply gets too big. There is, of course, a monetary incentive not to pass the point of operation where diseconomies of scale exist, and firms usually find ways to avoid them. They will reorganize, divide operations, hire new managers, and so on.

Minimum Efficient Scale and Number of Firms in an Industry

Some industries are composed of a smaller number of firms than other industries. Or we can say there is a different degree of concentration in different industries.

The minimum efficient scale (*MES*) as a percentage of U.S. consumption or total sales is not the same for all industries. For example, in industry X, *MES* as a percentage of total sales might be 6.6, and in industry Y, it might be 2.3. In other words, firms in industry X reach the minimum efficient scale of plant and thus exhaust economies of scale at an output level of 6.6 percent of total industry sales, whereas firms in industry Y experience economies of scale only up to an output level of 2.3 percent of total industry sales.

Clearly, we would expect to find fewer firms in industry X. By dividing the *MES* as a percentage of total sales into 100, we can estimate the number of efficient firms it takes to satisfy total consumption for a particular product. For the product produced by industry X, it takes 15 firms (100/6.6 = 15). For the product produced by industry Y, it takes 43 firms.

SHIFTS IN COST CURVES

In discussing the shape of short- and long-run cost curves, we assumed that certain factors remained constant. We discuss a few of these factors now and describe how changes in them can shift cost curves.

Taxes

Consider a tax on each unit of a good produced. Suppose company X has to pay a tax of $3 for each unit of X it produces. What effects will this have on the firm's cost curves? The tax won't affect the firm's fixed costs because the tax is paid only when output is produced, and fixed costs are present even if output is zero. (If the tax is a lump-sum tax—that is, the company pays a lump sum no matter how many units of X it produces—then the tax will affect fixed costs.) We conclude that the tax does not affect fixed costs and therefore cannot affect average fixed cost.

The tax will affect variable costs. As a consequence of the tax, the firm has to pay more for each unit of X it produces. Because variable costs rise, so does total cost. This means that average variable cost and average total cost rise and that the representative cost curves shift upward. Finally, because marginal cost is the change in total cost divided by the change in output, marginal cost rises and the marginal cost curve shifts upward.

Input Prices

A rise or fall in variable input prices causes a corresponding change in the firm's average total, average variable, and marginal cost curves. For example, if the price of steel rises, the variable costs of building skyscrapers rise, and so must average variable cost, average total cost, and marginal cost. The cost curves shift upward. If the price of steel falls, the opposite effects occur.

Technology

Technological changes often bring either (1) the capability of using fewer inputs to produce a good (e.g., the introduction of the personal computer reduced the hours necessary to key and edit a manuscript) or (2) lower input prices (e.g., technological improvements in transistors led to price reductions in the transistor components of calculators). In either case, technological changes of this variety lower variable costs and consequently lower average variable cost, average total cost, and marginal cost. The cost curves shift downward.

1. Give an arithmetical example to illustrate economies of scale.

2. What would the *LRATC* curve look like if there were always constant returns to scale? Explain your answer.

3. Firm A charged $4 per unit when it produced 100 units of good X, and it charged $3 per unit when it produced 200 units. Furthermore, the firm earned the same profit per unit in both cases. How can this happen?

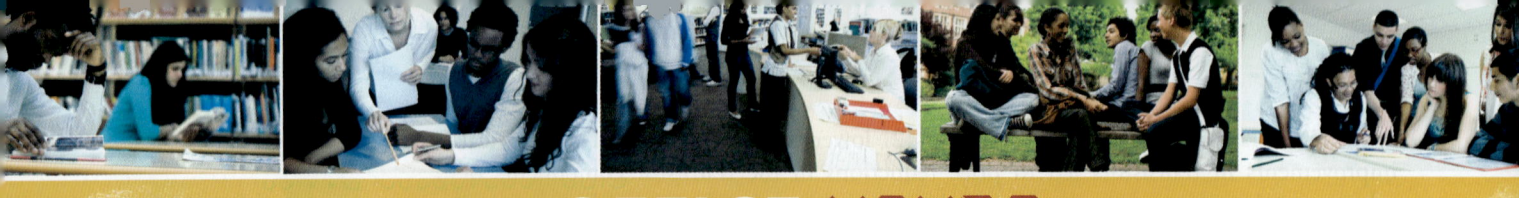

OFFICE HOURS

"What Is the Difference Between the Law of Diminishing Marginal Returns and Diseconomies of Scale?"

STUDENT:

I'm not sure I understand the difference between the law of diminishing marginal returns and diseconomies of scale. They sound similar to me.

INSTRUCTOR:

The law of diminishing marginal returns holds in the short run when at least one input is fixed. In our example in class, we held capital constant (at one unit) and changed the units of labor. Diseconomies of scale are relevant to the long run, which is a period when all inputs are variable. In other words, no input is fixed.

STUDENT:

But don't both the law of diminishing marginal returns and diseconomies of scale have something to do with less output per unit of input?

INSTRUCTOR:

Let's define each and see. The law of diminishing marginal returns says that as we add additional units of a variable input (such as labor) to a fixed input (such as capital), we get to a point where the marginal physical product of the variable input (the marginal physical product of labor) declines.

This has to do with less output per unit of input. Specifically, as we add additional units of the variable input to the fixed input, our output might rise, but it rises at a decreasing rate. To illustrate, adding the fourth worker to the production process might raise output from 100 units to 120 units (an addition of 20 units), but adding the fifth worker increases output from 120 units to 135 units (which is an addition of 15 units).

STUDENT:

Okay, then, how is the law of diseconomies of scale different?

INSTRUCTOR:

Here is an example of diseconomies of scale. The firm increases each of its inputs by, say, 10 percent, but its output rises by only 3 percent. In other words, its output rises less than the increase in its inputs.

Also, notice that we don't hold any input fixed. We have assumed that there are two inputs the firm uses, labor and capital, and that it increases its usage of each input by 10 percent.

STUDENT:

Are we getting less output per unit of input, as we did with respect to the law of diminishing marginal returns?

INSTRUCTOR:

Yes and no. We are getting less output per unit of input if we compare diseconomies of scale with, say, economies of scale. To illustrate, with economies of scale, we might increase each input by 10 percent and end up with 20 percent more output. With diseconomies of scale, we increase each input by 10 percent and end up with, say, only 3 percent more output. Obviously, when diseconomies of scale exist we get less output for each percentage increase in inputs than we do when economies of scale exist.

POINTS TO REMEMBER

1. The law of diminishing marginal returns holds in the short run when at least one input is fixed.
2. Diseconomies of scale are relevant to the long run, which is a period when all inputs are variable.

490

CHAPTER SUMMARY

THE FIRM

- Armen Alchian and Harold Demsetz argue that firms are formed when individuals derive benefits from working as a team—specifically, when the sum of what individuals can produce as a team is greater than the sum of what individuals can produce alone: Sum of team production > Sum of individual production.

- Team production has its advantages and disadvantages. The chief advantage (in many cases) is the positive difference between the output produced by the team and the sum of the output produced by individuals working alone. The chief disadvantage is the increased shirking in teams. The role of the monitor (manager) in the firm is to preserve the increased output and to reduce or eliminate the increased shirking. The monitors have a monetary incentive not to shirk their monitoring duties when they are residual claimants.

- Ronald Coase argued that firms exist to reduce the "costs of negotiating and concluding a separate contract for each exchange transaction which takes place on a market." In short, firms exist to reduce transaction costs.

EXPLICIT COST AND IMPLICIT COST

- An explicit cost is incurred when an actual (monetary) payment is made. An implicit cost represents the value of resources used in production for which no actual (monetary) payment is made.

ECONOMIC PROFIT AND ACCOUNTING PROFIT

- Economic profit is the difference between total revenue and total cost, including both explicit and implicit costs. Accounting profit is the difference between total revenue and explicit costs. Economic profit is usually lower (never higher) than accounting profit. Economic profit (not accounting profit) motivates economic behavior.

PRODUCTION AND COSTS IN THE SHORT RUN

- The short run is a period in which some inputs are fixed. The long run is a period in which all inputs can be varied. The costs associated with fixed and variable inputs are referred to as fixed costs and variable costs, respectively.

- Marginal cost is the change in total cost that results from a change in output.

- The law of diminishing marginal returns states that as ever larger amounts of a variable input are combined with fixed inputs, eventually the marginal physical product of the variable input will decline. As this happens, marginal cost rises.

- The average-marginal rule states that if the marginal magnitude is above (below) the average magnitude, the average magnitude rises (falls).

- The marginal cost curve intersects the average variable cost curve at its lowest point. The marginal cost curve intersects the average total cost curve at its lowest point. There is no relationship between marginal cost and average fixed cost.

PRODUCTION AND COSTS IN THE LONG RUN

- In the long run, because there are no fixed costs, variable costs equal total costs.

- The long-run average total cost curve is the envelope of the short-run average total cost curves. It shows the lowest unit cost at which the firm can produce a given level of output.

- If inputs are increased by some percentage and output increases by a greater percentage, then unit costs fall and economies of scale exist. If inputs are increased by some percentage and output increases by an equal percentage, then unit costs remain constant and constant returns to scale exist. If inputs are increased by some percentage and output increases by a smaller percentage, then unit costs rise and diseconomies of scale exist.

- The minimum efficient scale is the lowest output level at which average total costs are minimized.

SUNK COST

- Sunk cost is a cost incurred in the past that cannot be changed by current decisions and therefore cannot be recovered. A person or firm that wants to minimize losses will hold sunk costs to be irrelevant to present decisions.

SHIFTS IN COST CURVES

- A firm's cost curves will shift if there is a change in taxes, input prices, or technology.

KEY TERMS AND CONCEPTS

Business Firm	Profit	Fixed Input	Law of Diminishing Marginal
Market Coordination	Explicit Cost	Variable Input	Returns
Managerial Coordination	Implicit Cost	Short Run	Fixed Costs
Shirking	Accounting Profit	Long Run	Variable Costs
Monitor	Economic Profit	Marginal Physical Product	Total Cost (*TC*)
Residual Claimant	Normal Profit	(*MPP*)	Marginal Cost (*MC*)

Average Fixed Cost (*AFC*)
Average Variable Cost (*AVC*)
Average Total Cost (*ATC*),
   or Unit Cost

Average-Marginal Rule
Sunk Cost
Long-Run Average Total Cost
   (*LRATC*) Curve

Economies of Scale
Constant Returns to
   Scale

Diseconomies of Scale
Minimum Efficient
   Scale

QUESTIONS AND PROBLEMS

1. Some individuals decry the decline of the small family farm and its replacement with the huge corporate megafarm. Discuss the possibility that this is a consequence of economies of scale.

2. The average variable cost curve and the average total cost curve get closer to each other as output increases. What explains this?

3. Explain the difference between managerial coordination and market coordination.

4. Explain why earning zero economic profit is not as bad as it sounds.

5. Is the managerial coordination that goes on within a business firm independent of market forces? Explain your answer.

6. Why does the *AFC* curve continually decline (and get closer and closer to the quantity axis)?

7. Explain why even conscientious workers will shirk more when the cost of shirking falls.

8. What is the difference between diseconomies of scale and the law of diminishing marginal returns?

9. Illustrate the average-marginal rule in a noncost setting.

10. When would total costs equal fixed costs?

11. "A firm that earns only normal profit is not covering all its costs." Do you agree or disagree? Explain your answer.

12. Is studying for an economics exam subject to the law of diminishing marginal returns? If so, what is the fixed input? What is the variable input?

13. Explain why a firm might want to produce its good even after diminishing marginal returns have set in and marginal cost is rising.

14. Under what condition would Bill Gates be the richest person in the United States and earn zero economic profit?

15. People often believe that large firms in an industry have cost advantages over small firms in the same industry. For example, they might think a big oil company has a cost advantage over a small oil company. For this to be true, what condition must exist? Explain your answer.

16. We know there is a link between productivity and costs. For example, recall the link between the marginal physical product of the variable input and marginal cost. With this in mind, what link might there be between productivity and prices?

17. Some people's everyday behavior suggests that they do not hold sunk costs irrelevant to present decisions. Give some examples different from those presented in this chapter.

18. The government says that firm X must pay $1,000 in taxes simply because it is in the business of producing a good. What cost curves, if any, does this tax affect?

19. Based on your answer to question 18, does *MC* change if *TC* changes?

WORKING WITH NUMBERS AND GRAPHS

1. Determine the appropriate dollar amount for each lettered space.

(1) Quantity of Output, Q (units)	(2) Total Fixed Cost (dollars)	(3) Average Fixed Cost (AFC)	(4) Total Variable Cost (TVC)	(5) Average Variable Cost (AVC)	(6) Total Cost (TC)	(7) Average Total Cost (ATC)	(8) Marginal cost (MC)
0	$200	A	$0		V		
1	200	B	30	L	W	GG	QQ
2	200	C	50	M	X	HH	RR
3	200	D	60	N	Y	II	SS
4	200	E	65	O	Z	JJ	TT
5	200	F	75	P	AA	KK	UU
6	200	G	95	Q	BB	LL	VV
7	200	H	125	R	CC	MM	WW
8	200	I	165	S	DD	NN	XX
9	200	J	215	T	EE	OO	YY
10	200	K	275	U	FF	PP	ZZ

2. Give a numerical example to show that as marginal physical product (*MPP*) rises, marginal cost (*MC*) falls.

3. Price = $20, quantity = 400 units, unit cost = $15, implicit costs = $4,000. What does economic profit equal?

4. If economic profit equals accounting profit, what do implicit costs equal?

5. If accounting profit is $400,000 greater than economic profit, what do implicit costs equal?

6. If marginal physical product is continually declining, what does marginal cost look like? Explain your answer.

7. If the *ATC* curve is continually declining, what does this imply about the *MC* curve? Explain your answer.

PERFECT COMPETITION

Introduction Every firm shares two things with all other firms. First, every firm has to answer certain questions: (1) What price should the firm charge for the good it produces and sells? (2) How many units of the good should the firm produce? (3) How much of the resources that the firm needs to produce its good should it buy? Regardless of whether a firm sells shirts or cars, whether it is large or small, whether it is located in Georgia or Maine, it must answer all three of these questions. Period.

Second, every firm finds itself operating in a certain market structure. A market structure is a firm's environment or setting, whose characteristics influence the firm's pricing and output decisions. This chapter focuses on a particular market structure: perfect competition.

Market Structure
The environment of a firm, whose characteristics influence the firm's pricing and output decisions.

Perfect Competition
A theory of market structure based on four assumptions: (1) There are many sellers and buyers; (2) sellers sell a homogeneous good; (3) buyers and sellers have all relevant information; (4) entry into or exit from the market is easy.

THE THEORY OF PERFECT COMPETITION

The theory of perfect competition is built on four assumptions:

1. *There are many sellers and many buyers, none of which is large in relation to total sales or purchases.* This assumption speaks to both demand (the number of buyers) and supply (the number of sellers). Given many buyers and sellers, each buyer and each seller may act independently of other buyers and sellers, respectively, and each is such a small a part of the market as to have no influence on price.

2. *Each firm produces and sells a homogeneous product.* Each firm sells a product that is indistinguishable from all other firms' products in a given industry. (For example, a buyer of wheat cannot distinguish between Farmer Stone's wheat and Farmer Gray's wheat.) As a consequence, buyers are indifferent to the sellers.

3. *Buyers and sellers have all relevant information about prices, product quality, sources of supply, and so forth.* Buyers and sellers know who is selling what, at what prices, at what quality, and on what terms. In short, they know everything that relates to buying, producing, and selling the product.

4. *Firms have easy entry and exit.* New firms can enter the market easily, and existing firms can exit the market easily. There are no barriers to entry or exit.

Before discussing the perfectly competitive firm in the short and long run, we discuss some of the characteristics of the perfectly competitive firm that result from these four assumptions.

A Perfectly Competitive Firm Is a Price Taker

A perfectly competitive firm is a price taker, which is a seller that does not have the ability to control the price of its product; it "takes" the price determined in the market. For example, if Farmer Stone is a price taker, he can increase or decrease his output without significantly affecting the price of his product.

Why is a perfectly competitive firm a price taker? A firm is restrained from being anything but a price taker if it finds itself one among many firms where its supply is small relative to the total market supply (assumption 1 in the theory of perfect competition), and it sells a homogeneous product (assumption 2) in an environment where buyers and sellers have all relevant information (assumption 3).

Some people might suggest that the assumptions of the theory of perfect competition give economists what they want. In other words, economists want the perfectly competitive firm to be a price taker, and so they choose the assumptions that make it so. But this isn't the case. Economists start out with certain assumptions and then logically conclude that the firm for which these assumptions hold, or that behaves as if these assumptions hold, is a price taker; that is, it has no control over price. Afterward, economists test the theory by observing whether it accurately predicts and explains the real-world behavior of some firms.

The Demand Curve for a Perfectly Competitive Firm Is Horizontal

The perfectly competitive setting has many sellers and many buyers. Together, all buyers make up the market demand curve; together, all sellers make up the market supply curve. An equilibrium price is established at the intersection of the market demand and market supply curves [Exhibit 1(a)].

When the equilibrium price has been established, a single perfectly competitive firm faces a horizontal (flat, perfectly elastic) demand curve at the equilibrium price [Exhibit 1(b)]. In short, the firm takes the equilibrium price as given—hence the firm is a price taker—and sells all quantities of output at this price.[1]

WHY DOES A PERFECTLY COMPETITIVE FIRM SELL AT EQUILIBRIUM PRICE? If a perfectly competitive firm tries to charge a price higher than the market-established equilibrium price, it won't sell any of its product. The reasons are that the firm sells a homogeneous product, its supply is small relative to the total market supply, and all buyers are informed about where they can obtain the product at the lower price.

If the firm wants to maximize profits, it does not offer to sell its good at a lower price than the equilibrium price. Why should it? It can sell all it wants at the market-established equilibrium price. The equilibrium price is the only relevant price for the perfectly competitive firm.

Price Taker

A seller that does not have the ability to control the price of the product it sells; the seller "takes" the price determined in the market.

---

1. The horizontal demand curve means *not* that the firm can sell an infinite amount at the equilibrium price, but that price will be virtually unaffected by the variations in output that the firm may find it practicable to make.

EXHIBIT 1

Market Demand Curve and Firm Demand Curve in Perfect Competition

(a) The market, composed of all buyers and sellers, establishes the equilibrium price. (b) A single perfectly competitive firm then faces a horizontal (flat, perfectly elastic) demand curve. We conclude that the firm is a price taker; it takes the equilibrium price established by the market and sells any and all quantities of output at this price. (The capital *D* represents the market demand curve; the lowercase *d* represents the single firm's demand curve.)

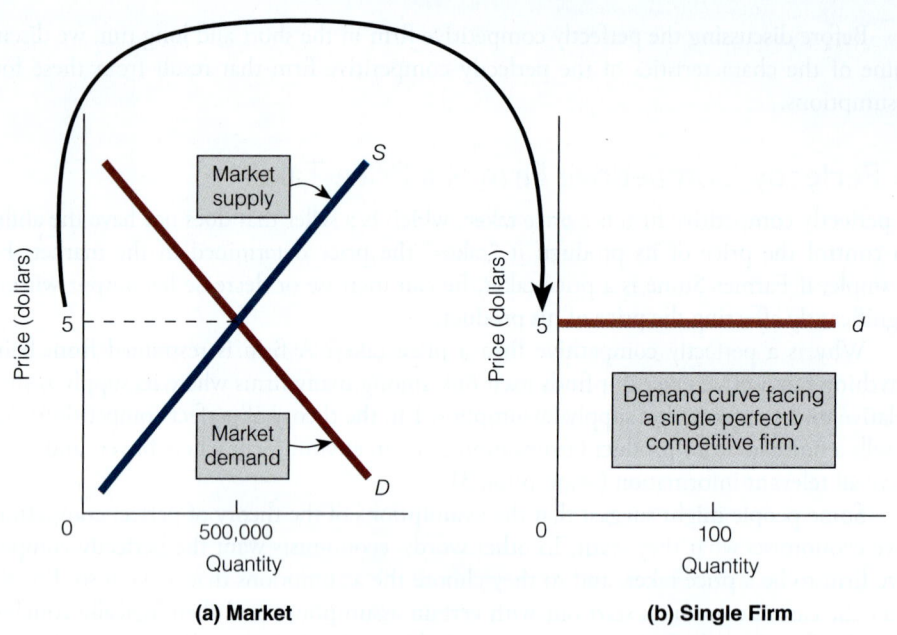

(a) Market

(b) Single Firm

𝕗inding ECONOMICS

When Selling Shares of Stock Roberta wakes up in the morning and turns on her computer. She checks the prices of the stocks she owns. The price of stock X is selling at $35 per share. She had bought 200 shares of the stock when the price was only $11, and now she decides to sell. She places a sell order with her online broker and in a matter of minutes she has sold her 200 shares of stock. Where is the economics? Does Roberta's sale of stock have anything to do with operating in a perfectly competitive market?

If Roberta wants to sell her shares of stock X, she must sell at the current market price. Roberta, as a seller of stock, is a price taker. She cannot sell her shares of stock at $2 over the current price, and she will not sell below the market price. Why should she sell her shares of stock at $9 when she can sell them at the current market price of $11? ▲▲▲

Common Misconceptions About Demand Curves

The law of demand posits an inverse relationship between price and quantity demanded. So it follows that if a demand curve is to represent the law of demand graphically, it must be downward sloping. A common misconception, though, is to think that *all* demand curves have to be downward sloping. Why this is not true can be explained by distinguishing the market demand curve from the demand curve faced by a single firm.

In Exhibit 1(a), the market demand curve is downward sloping, positing an inverse relationship between price and quantity demanded, *ceteris paribus*. The *single* perfectly competitive firm's demand curve does not contradict this relationship; it simply represents the pricing situation in which the *single* perfectly competitive firm finds itself. Recall from an earlier chapter that the more substitutes a good has, the higher the price elasticity of demand will be. In the perfectly competitive market setting, there are many substitutes for the firm's product—so many, in fact, that the firm's demand curve is perfectly elastic.

Intuitively, a single perfectly competitive firm's supply is such a *small percentage* of the total market supply that the firm cannot perceptibly influence price by changing its quantity of output. To put it differently, the firm's supply is so small, compared with the total market supply, that the inverse relationship between price and quantity demanded, although present, cannot be observed on the firm's level, although it is observable on the market level.

The Marginal Revenue Curve of a Perfectly Competitive Firm Is the Same as Its Demand Curve

Total revenue is the price of a good multiplied by the quantity sold. If the equilibrium price is $5, as in Exhibit 2(a), and the perfectly competitive firm sells 3 units of its good, its total revenue is $15. If the firm sells an additional unit, bringing the total number of units sold to 4, its total revenue is $20.

A firm's marginal revenue (MR) is the change in total revenue (TR) that results from selling one additional unit of output (Q):

$$MR = \frac{\Delta TR}{\Delta Q}$$

Marginal Revenue (MR)
The change in total revenue (TR) that results from selling one additional unit of output (Q).

Column 4 in Exhibit 2(a) shows that the firm's marginal revenue ($5) at any output level is always equal to the equilibrium price ($5). For a perfectly competitive firm, therefore, price (P) is equal to marginal revenue.

For a Perfectly Competitive Firm, P = MR

If price is equal to marginal revenue, then *the marginal revenue curve for the perfectly competitive firm is the same as its demand curve.*

A demand curve plots price against quantity, whereas a marginal revenue curve plots marginal revenue against quantity. If price equals marginal revenue, then the demand curve and marginal revenue curve are the same [Exhibit 2(b)].

For a Perfectly Competitive Firm, demand curve = Marginal revenue curve

EXHIBIT 2

The Demand Curve and the Marginal Revenue Curve for a Perfectively Competitive Firm

(a) By computing marginal revenue, we find that it is equal to price. (b) By plotting columns 1 and 2, we obtain the firm's demand curve; by plotting columns 2 and 4, we obtain the firm's marginal revenue curve. The two curves are the same.

(1) Price	(2) Quantity	(3) Total Revenue = (1) × (2)	(4) Marginal Revenue = $\Delta TR/\Delta Q$ = $\Delta(3)/\Delta(2)$
$5	1	$ 5	$5
5	2	10	5
5	3	15	5
5	4	20	5

(a)

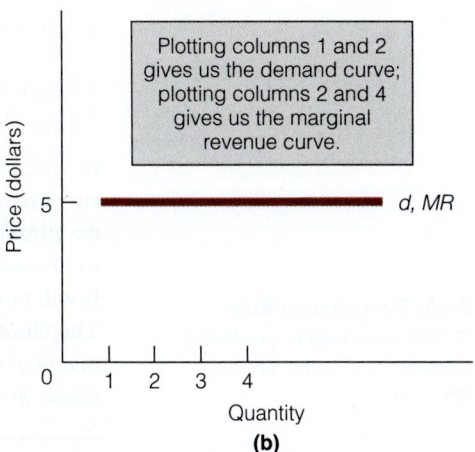

Plotting columns 1 and 2 gives us the demand curve; plotting columns 2 and 4 gives us the marginal revenue curve.

(b)

Theory and Real-World Markets

The theory of perfect competition describes how firms act in a market structure where (1) there are many buyers and sellers, none of whom is large in relation to total sales or purchases; (2) sellers sell a homogeneous product; (3) buyers and sellers have all relevant information; and (4) market entry and exit are easy. These assumptions are closely met in some real-world markets, such as some agricultural markets and a small subset of the retail trade. The stock market, with its hundreds of thousands of buyers and sellers of stock, is also sometimes cited as an example of perfect competition.

The four assumptions of the theory of perfect competition are also *approximated* in some real-world markets. In such markets, the number of sellers may not be large enough for every firm to be a price taker, but the firm's control over price may be negligible. The amount of control may be so negligible, in fact, that the firm acts *as if* it were a perfectly competitive firm.

Similarly, buyers may not have all relevant information concerning price and quality. However, they may still have a great deal of information, and the information they do not have may not matter. The products that the firms in the industry sell may not be homogeneous, but the differences may be inconsequential.

In short, a market that does not *exactly* meet the assumptions of perfect competition may nonetheless *approximate* the assumptions to a degree that it behaves *as if* it were a perfectly competitive market. If so, the theory of perfect competition can be used to predict the market's behavior.

SELF-TEST

(Answers to Self-Test questions are in Answers to Self-Test Questions at the back of the book.)

1. "If a firm is a price taker, it does not have the ability to control the price of the product it sells." What does this statement mean?

2. Why is a perfectly competitive firm a price taker?

3. The horizontal demand curve for the perfectly competitive firm signifies that it cannot sell any of its product for a price higher than the market equilibrium price. Why not?

4. Suppose the firms in a real-world market do not sell a homogeneous product. Does it necessarily follow that the market is not perfectly competitive?

PERFECT COMPETITION IN THE SHORT RUN

For the perfectly competitive firm, a price taker, price is equal to marginal revenue, $P = MR$, and therefore the firm's demand curve is the same as its marginal revenue curve. This section discusses the amount of output the firm will produce in the short run.

What Level of Output Does the Profit-Maximizing Firm Produce?

In Exhibit 3, the perfectly competitive firm's demand curve (d) and marginal revenue curve (MR, which is the same as d) are drawn at the equilibrium price of $5. The firm's marginal cost curve (MC) is also shown. On the basis of these curves, the firm will continue to increase its quantity of output as long as marginal revenue is greater than marginal cost. It will not produce units of output for which marginal revenue is less than marginal cost. Therefore, the firm will stop increasing its quantity of output when marginal revenue and marginal cost are equal. The profit maximization rule for a firm says *produce the quantity of output at which MR = MC.*[2] In Exhibit 3, $MR = MC$ at 125 units of output.

Profit Maximization Rule
Profit is maximized by producing the quantity of output at which $MR = MC$.

---

2. The profit maximization rule is the same as the loss-minimization rule because maximizing profits is impossible without minimizing losses. The profit-maximization rule holds for *all firms*, not just for perfectly competitive firms.

For the perfectly competitive firm, the profit maximization rule can be written as $P = MC$ because for the perfectly competitive firm, $P = MR$. In perfect competition, profit is maximized when

$$P = MR = MC$$

The Perfectly Competitive Firm and Resource Allocative Efficiency

Resources (or inputs) are used to produce goods and services; for example, wood may be used to produce a chair. To the buyers of the goods, the resources used in the production of goods have an exchange value that is approximated by the price that people pay for the good. For example, when buying a chair for $100, Smith values the resources used to produce the chair by at least $100. Wood that is used to produce chairs cannot be used to produce desks. Hence, the opportunity cost of producing chairs is best measured by its marginal cost.

Now suppose that 100 chairs are produced and that, at this quantity, the price is greater than marginal cost; for example, the price is $100 and the marginal cost is $75. Obviously, buyers place a higher value on wood when it is used to produce chairs than when it is used to produce an alternative good.

Producing a good—any good—until price equals marginal cost ensures that all units of the good are produced that are of greater value to buyers than the alternative goods that might have been produced. In other words, a firm that produces the quantity of output at which price equals marginal cost ($P = MC$) is said to exhibit **resource allocative efficiency**.

Does the perfectly competitive firm exhibit resource allocative efficiency? We know two things about this type of firm: First, the perfectly competitive firm produces the quantity of output at which $MR = MC$. Second, for this firm $P = MR$. If the perfectly competitive firm produces the output at which $MR = MC$ and if for this firm $P = MR$, then the firm produces the output at which $P = MC$. In short, the perfectly competitive firm *is* resource allocative efficient.

Also, for a perfectly competitive firm, profit maximization and resource allocative efficiency are not at odds. (Whether they might be for other market structures is discussed in the next two chapters.) The perfectly competitive firm seeks to maximize profit by producing the quantity of output at which $MR = MC$. Because for the firm $P = MR$, it automatically accomplishes resource allocative efficiency ($P = MC$) when it maximizes profit ($MR = MC$).

The Quantity of Output the Perfectly Competitive Firm Will Produce

The firm's demand curve is horizontal at the equilibrium price. Its demand curve is its marginal revenue curve. The firm produces that quantity of output at which $MR = MC$.

Resource Allocative Efficiency
The situation when firms produce the quantity of output at which price equals marginal cost: $P = MC$.

ⓣhinking Like AN ECONOMIST

Profit Maximization Can Be Consistent with Consumer Welfare With good X, as with all goods, there is a right and a wrong quantity to produce. From the perspective of consumers, the right quantity is the efficient quantity. The consumer says to the manufacturers of X: "Keep producing X as long as its price is greater than its marginal cost. Stop when $P = MC$." Let's say that $P = MC$ when the quantity of X is 10,000 a month.

The question now is whether the manufacturers of X want to produce 10,000 units of X a month. For manufacturers, the right quantity of X is the quantity at which $MR = MC$. In other words, manufacturers will continue making units of X as long as MR is greater than MC, and they will stop when $MR = MC$.

(continued)

thinking Like AN ECONOMIST (continued)

For a perfectly competitive firm, we know that $P = MR$; so what consumers want (produce until $P = MC$) is really the same thing that manufacturers want (produce until $MR = MC$). Simply put, when manufacturers do what is in their best interest—produce until $MR = MC$—*they are automatically producing the efficient amount of the good, which is what consumers want. Who would have thought it?* ●●●

To Produce or Not to Produce: That Is the Question

The following cases illustrate three applications of the profit maximization (loss minimization) rule by a perfectly competitive firm.

CASE 1: PRICE IS ABOVE AVERAGE TOTAL COST Exhibit 4(a) illustrates the perfectly competitive firm's demand and marginal revenue curves. If the firm follows the profit maximization rule and produces the quantity of output at which marginal revenue equals marginal cost, it will produce 100 units of output—the profit-maximizing quantity of output. At this quantity of output, price is above average total cost. Using the information in the exhibit, we can make the following calculations:

EXHIBIT 4

Profit Maximization and Loss Minimization for the Perfectly Competitive Firm: Three Cases

(a) In case 1, $TR > TC$ and the firm earns profits. It continues to produce in the short run. (b)

In case 2, $TR < TC$ and the firm takes a loss. It shuts down in the short run because it minimizes its losses by doing so; it is better to lose $400 in fixed costs than to take a loss of $450. (c) In case 3, $TR < TC$ and the firm takes a loss.

It continues to produce in the short run because it minimizes its losses by doing so; it is better to lose $80 by producing than to lose $400 in fixed costs.

$P > ATC\ (> AVC)$

$TR = \$1{,}500$
$TC = \$1{,}100$
$TVC = \$700$
$TFC = \$400$
Profits = \$400
Continue to produce in the short run.

$P < AVC\ (< ATC)$

$TR = \$200$
$TC = \$650$
$TVC = \$250$
$TFC = \$400$
Losses = \$450
Shut down in the short run.

$ATC > P > AVC$

$TR = \$720$
$TC = \$800$
$TVC = \$400$
$TFC = \$400$
Losses = \$80
Continue to produce in the short run.

(a) Case 1

(b) Case 2

(c) Case 3

Case 1		
Equilibrium price (P)	=	$15
Quantity of output produced (Q)	=	100 units
Total revenue (P × Q = $15 × 100)	=	$1,500
Total cost (ATC × Q = $11 × 100)	=	$1,100
Total variable cost (AVC × Q = $7 × 100)	=	$700
Total fixed cost (TC − TVC = $1,100 − $700)	=	$400
Profits (TR − TC = $1,500 − $1,100)	=	$400

Therefore, for the perfectly competitive firm, if price is above the average total cost, the firm maximizes profits by producing the quantity of output at which $MR = MC$.

CASE 2: PRICE IS BELOW AVERAGE VARIABLE COST Exhibit 4(b) illustrates the case in which price is below the average variable cost. The equilibrium price at which the perfectly competitive firm sells its good is $4. At this price, total revenue is less than both total cost and total variable cost, as the following calculations indicate. To minimize its loss, the firm should shut down.

Case 2		
Equilibrium price (P)	=	$4
Quantity of output produced (Q)	=	50 units
Total revenue (P × Q = $4 × 50)	=	$200
Total cost (ATC × Q = $13 × 50)	=	$650
Total variable cost (AVC × Q = $5 × 50)	=	$250
Total fixed cost (TC − TVC = $650 − $250)	=	$400
Profits (TR − TC = $200 − $650)	=	−$450

If the firm produces in the short run, it will take a loss of $450. If it shuts down, its loss will be less, losing its fixed costs, which amount to the difference between total cost and variable cost ($TFC + TVC = TC$, so $TC − TVC = TFC$). This is $400 ($650−$250). So between the two options of producing in the short run or shutting down, the firm minimizes its losses by choosing to shut down ($Q = 0$). It will lose $400 by shutting down, whereas it will lose $450 by producing in the short run.

Therefore, if price is below the average variable cost, the perfectly competitive firm minimizes losses by choosing to shut down—that is, by not producing.

CASE 3: PRICE IS BELOW AVERAGE TOTAL COST BUT ABOVE AVERAGE VARIABLE COST Exhibit 4(c) illustrates the case in which price is below average total cost but above average variable cost. The equilibrium price at which the perfectly competitive firm sells its good is $9. If the firm follows the profit maximization rule, it will produce 80 units of output. At this price and quantity of output, total revenue is less than total cost (hence, the firm will incur a loss), but total revenue is greater than total variable cost. The calculations are as follows:

Case 3		
Equilibrium price (P)	=	$9
Quantity of output produced (Q)	=	80 units
Total revenue (P × Q = $9 × 80)	=	$720
Total cost (ATC × Q = $10 × 80)	=	$800
Total variable cost (AVC × Q = $5 × 80)	=	$400
Total fixed cost (TC − TVC = $800 − $400)	=	$400
Profits (TR − TC = $720 − $800)	=	−$80

If the firm decides to produce in the short run, it will take a loss of $80. If it shuts down, it will lose its fixed costs, which, in this case, are $400 ($TC - TVC = \$800 - \$400$). Continuing to produce in the short run is better than to shutting down. Losses are minimized by producing.

Therefore, if price is below average total cost but above average variable cost, the perfectly competitive firm minimizes its losses by continuing to produce in the short run instead of shutting down.

Common Misconceptions over the Shutdown Decision

Asked when a business firm should shut down (stop producing), the layperson is likely to say when the firm is no longer earning a profit. In economics, that is when price is lower than average total cost ($P < ATC$). But that could be the wrong way to go, as we have just shown. Even if price is below average total cost and a loss is being incurred, a firm should not necessarily shut down. The shutdown decision depends, in the short run, on whether the firm loses more by shutting down than by not shutting down. Even though price is below average total cost, it could still be above average variable cost, and, if it is, the firm minimizes its losses (in the short run) by continuing to produce than by shutting down.

SUMMARY OF CASES 1–3 *A perfectly competitive firm produces in the short run as long as price is above average variable cost (cases 1 and 3).*

$$P > AVC \rightarrow \text{Firm produces}$$

A perfectly competitive firm shuts down in the short run if price is less than average variable cost (case 2).

$$P < AVC \rightarrow \text{Firm shuts down}$$

We can summarize the same information in terms of total revenue and total variable costs. *A perfectly competitive firm produces in the short run as long as total revenue is greater than total variable costs (cases 1 and 3).*

$$TR > TVC \rightarrow \text{Firm produces}$$

A perfectly competitive firm shuts down in the short run if total revenue is less than total variable costs (case 2).

$$TR < TVC \rightarrow \text{Firm shuts down}$$

Exhibit 5 reviews some of the material discussed in this last section. Exhibit 6 reviews, in a question and answer format, some of the material discussed in the last few sections.

EXHIBIT 5

What Should a Perfectly Competitive Firm Do in the Short Run?

The firm should produce in the short run as long as price (P) is above average variable cost (AVC). It should shut down in the short run if price is below average variable cost.

EXHIBIT 6

Q&A About Perfect Competition

Question	Answer
What four assumptions is the theory of perfect competition built on?	1. There are many buyers and many sellers. 2. Each firm produces and sells a homogeneous good. 3. Buyers and sellers have all relevant information about prices, product quality, sources of supply, and so forth. 4. Firms have easy entry into the market and easy exit out of the market.
What does it mean to say the perfectly competitive firm is a price taker?	The perfectly competitive firm *takes* the market-determined equilibrium price as the price at which it sells its product. The firm has no ability to control the price of the product it sells.
At what price does the perfectly competitive firm sell its product?	It sells at the price determined by the market. In other words, market demand and market supply determine the price of the good—say, $10—and then the firm takes this price as the price at which it will sell its product.
What quantity does the single perfectly competitive firm produce?	The quantity at which $MR = MC$.
How do we know if the perfectly competitive firm is earning profit or incurring a loss?	If $P > ATC$ for the firm, then it is earning profit. If $P < ATC$ for the firm, then it is incurring a loss.
What is resource allocative efficiency, and is the perfectly competitive firm resource allocate efficient?	Resource allocative efficiency exists if firms produce the quantity of output at which $P = MC$. The perfectly competitive firm is resource allocative efficient. Proof: (1) The firm produces the quantity of output at which $MR = MC$. (2) In perfect competition, $P = MR$. (3) Since $P = MR$, and the firm produces the quantity at which $MR = MC$, then $P = MC$. Hence, the firm is resource allocative efficient.

The Perfectly Competitive Firm's Short-Run Supply Curve

The perfectly competitive firm produces (supplies output) in the short run if price is above average variable cost. It shuts down (does not supply output) if price is below average variable cost. Therefore, the **short-run (firm) supply curve** of the firm is the portion of its marginal cost curve that lies above the average variable cost curve. Only a price above average variable cost will induce the firm to supply output. The short-run supply curve of the perfectly competitive firm is illustrated in Exhibit 7.

Short-Run (Firm) Supply Curve
The portion of the firm's marginal cost curve that lies above the average variable cost curve.

From Firm to Market (Industry) Supply Curve

If the perfectly competitive firm's short-run supply curve is the part of its marginal cost curve above its average variable cost curve, deriving the **short-run market (industry) supply curve** is a simple matter.[3] We horizontally add the short-run supply curves for all firms in the perfectly competitive market or industry.

Short-Run Market (Industry) Supply Curve
The horizontal addition of all existing firms' short-run supply curves.

3. In discussing market structures, the words "industry" and "market" are often used interchangeably when a single-product industry is under consideration, which is the case here.

EXHIBIT 7

The Perfectly Competitive Firm's Short-Run Supply Curve

The short-run supply curve is that portion of the firm's marginal cost curve that lies above the average variable cost curve.

Consider, for simplicity, an industry made up of three firms: A, B, and C [see Exhibit 8(a)]. At a price of P_1, firm A supplies 10 units, firm B supplies 8 units, and firm C supplies 18 units. One point on the market supply curve thus corresponds to P_1 on the price axis and 36 units $(10 + 8 + 18 = 36)$ on the quantity axis.[4] If we follow this procedure for all prices, we have the short-run market supply curve. This market supply curve, shown in the market setting in part (b) of the exhibit, is used along with the market demand curve (derived in Chapter 3) to determine equilibrium price and quantity.

Why Is the Market Supply Curve Upward Sloping?

When the demand and supply curves were introduced in Chapter 3, the supply curve was drawn upward-sloping. To understand why, consider the following questions and answers.

- *Question 1:* Why do we draw market supply curves upward-sloping?

EXHIBIT 8

Deriving the Market (Industry) Supply Curve for a Perfectly Competitive Market

In (a) we add (horizontally) the quantity supplied by each firm to derive the market supply curve. The market supply curve and the market demand curve are shown in (b). Together, they determine equilibrium price and quantity.

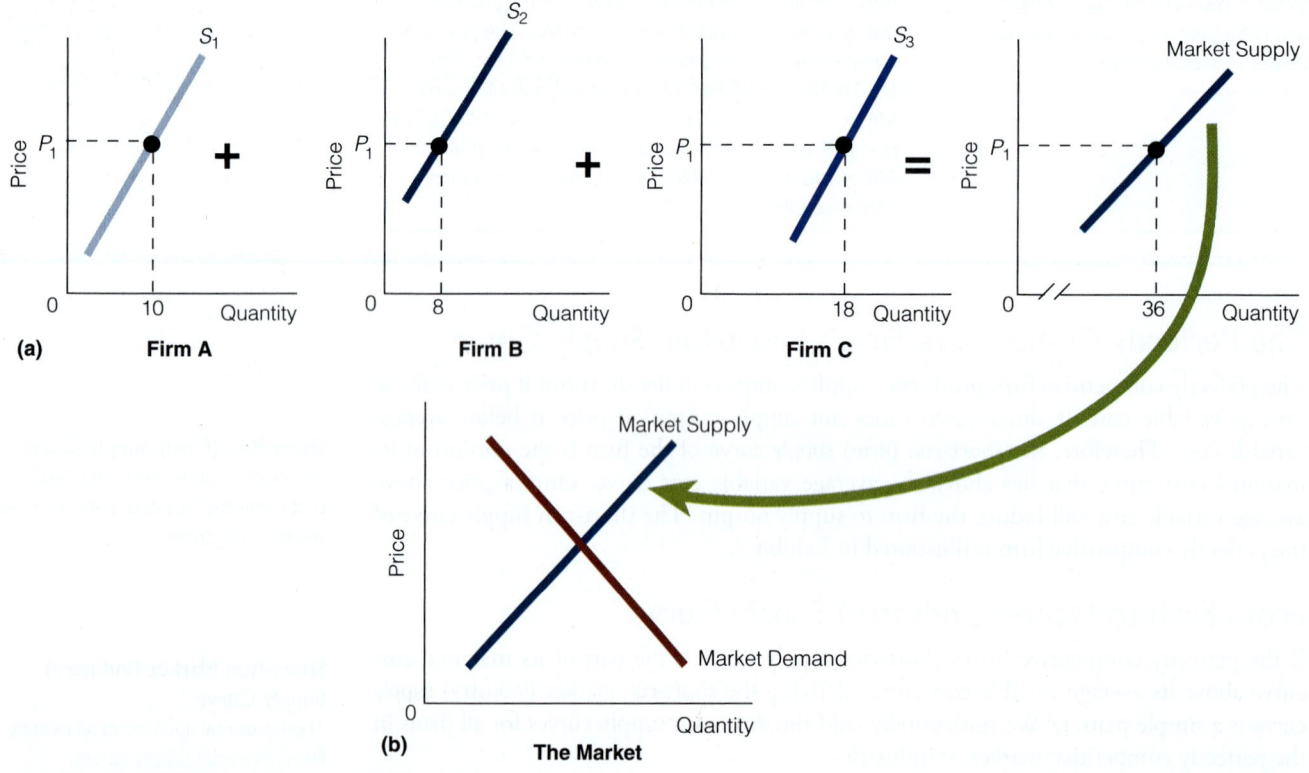

---

4. We add one qualification: Each firm's supply curve is drawn on the assumption that the prices of the variable inputs are constant.

economics 24/7

The Gary Cooper, Bob Hope, or the Purple Heart Medal Stamp

Every year, the U.S. Postal Service issues commemorative stamps to honor or to commemorate a place, event, or person. In the past, commemorative stamps have been issued of Frank Sinatra, Sugar Ray Robinson, Hattie McDaniel, Benjamin Franklin, the settlement of Jamestown, Bob Hope, Gary Cooper, the Purple Heart medal, flags of the nation, and so on.

Why does the U.S. Postal Service issue these special commemorative stamps? To find out, let's analyze why people buy stamps.

Most people buy stamps to send letters or other items through the mail. When a stamp is placed on a letter, the Postal Service is required to deliver the letter to the address on the envelope. Suppose the average variable cost (AVC) of producing a stamp is 7¢, regardless of the likeness on the front, and the unit variable cost of delivering a stamped letter is 19¢. The sum of the unit variable costs of producing the stamp and delivering the letter is 26¢.

AVC stamp = AVC producing the stamp + AVC delivering the letter

AP PHOTO/USPS

For simplicity, we assume $AFC = 0$; so $AVC = ATC$. In other words, the per-unit cost of the stamp is 26¢. So, if the price of a stamp is 44¢, the U.S. Postal Service earns a per-unit profit of 18¢ per stamp issued and used.

If the U.S. Postal Service wants to increase its per-unit profit, one way to do so is to issue stamps that people won't put on items to be mailed, that is, to issue stamps that people want to collect.

Hence the commemorative stamps that the U.S. Postal Service issues and sells. Many people buy these stamps not to mail letters, but to collect them. When the stamp is not used, the U.S. Postal Service doesn't incur the unit variable cost of delivering mail. Thus the average total cost of the commemorative stamp falls by the amount of the AVC of delivering the letter, which in turn means the ATC of the stamp falls to 7¢ (the AVC of producing the stamp). Consequently, the profit per unit for issuing collectors' stamps rises to 37¢ for a 44¢ stamp.

- *Answer:* Because market supply curves are the horizontal addition of firms' supply curves, and firms' supply curves are upward sloping.
- *Question 2:* But why are firms' supply curves upward sloping?
- *Answer:* Because the supply curve for each firm is the portion of its marginal cost (MC) curve that is *above* its average variable cost (AVC) curve—and this portion of the MC curve is upward sloping.
- *Question 3:* But why do MC curves have an upward-sloping portion?
- *Answer:* According to the law of diminishing marginal returns, the marginal physical product (MPP) of a variable input eventually declines. When this happens, the MC curve begins to rise.

Conclusion: Because of the law of diminishing marginal returns, MC curves are upward sloping, and because MC curves are upward sloping, so are market supply curves.

finding ECONOMICS

In the Production of Air Conditioners Peter is willing to produce more air conditioners if the price of a unit is $800 than if it is $600. Where is the economics?

We can detect the law of supply in Peter's behavior—he produces more at a higher price than at a lower price—and we know that his supply curve is upward sloping. But is there more? As already explained, supply curves are upward sloping because a producer's supply curve is the portion of its MC curve above the AVC curve, and that portion of the MC curve is upward sloping. Finally, at least a portion of an MC curve is upward sloping because of the law of diminishing marginal returns. ▲▲▲

SELF-TEST

1. If a firm produces the quantity of output at which $MR = MC$, does it necessarily earn profits?

2. In the short run, if a firm finds that its price (P) is less than its average total cost (ATC), should it shut down its operation?

3. The layperson says that a firm maximizes profits when total revenue (TR) minus total cost (TC) is as large as possible and positive. The economist says that a firm maximizes profits when it produces the level of output at which $MR = MC$. Explain how the two ways of looking at profit maximization are consistent.

4. Why are market supply curves upward sloping?

PERFECT COMPETITION IN THE LONG RUN

The number of firms in a perfectly competitive market may not be the same in the short run as in the long run. For example, if the typical firm is making economic profits in the short run, new firms will be attracted to the industry, and the number of firms will increase. If the typical firm is sustaining losses, some existing firms will exit the industry, and the number of firms will decrease. This process is explained in greater detail later in this section. For now, we begin by outlining the conditions of long-run competitive equilibrium.

The Conditions of Long-Run Competitive Equilibrium

Long-Run Competitive Equilibrium
The condition where $P = MC = SRATC = LRATC$. Economic profit is zero, firms are producing the quantity of output at which price is equal to marginal cost, and no firm has an incentive to change its plant size.

The following conditions characterize long-run competitive equilibrium:

1. *Economic profit is zero: Price (P) is equal to short-run average total cost (SRATC).*

$$P = SRATC$$

The logic of this condition is clear when we analyze what will happen if price is above or below short-run average total cost. If it is above, positive economic profits will attract firms to the industry to obtain the profits. If price is below, losses will result, and some firms will want to exit the industry. Long-run competitive equilibrium cannot exist if firms have an incentive to enter or exit the industry in response to positive economic profits or losses. For long-run equilibrium to exist, there can be no incentive for firms to enter or exit. This condition is brought about by zero economic profit (normal profit), which is a consequence of the equilibrium price being equal to short-run average total cost.

2. *Firms are producing the quantity of output at which price (P) is equal to marginal cost (MC).*

$$P = MC$$

Perfectly competitive firms naturally move toward the output level at which marginal revenue (or price because, for a perfectly competitive firm, $MR = P$) equals marginal cost.

3. *No firm has an incentive to change its plant size to produce its current output; that is, at the quantity of output at which P = MC, the following condition holds:*

$$SRATC = LRATC$$

To understand this condition, suppose $SRATC > LRATC$ at the quantity of output established in condition 2. If this is the case, the firm has an incentive to change plant size in the long run because it wants to produce its product with the plant size that will give it the lowest average total cost (unit cost). It will have no incentive to change plant size when it is producing the quantity of output at which price equals marginal cost and $SRATC$ equals $LRATC$.

The three conditions necessary for long-run competitive equilibrium can be stated as shown in Exhibit 9: long-run competitive equilibrium exists when $P = MC = SRATC = LRATC$.

In conclusion, long-run competitive equilibrium exists when firms have no incentive to make any changes—that is, when there is no incentive for firms to:

1. enter or exit the industry.

2. produce more or less output.

3. change plant size.

EXHIBIT 9

(a) The Market

(b) The Firm

Long-Run Competitive Equilibrium

(a) Equilibrium in the market. (b) Equilibrium for the firm. In (b), $P = MC$ (the firm has no incentive to move away from the quantity of output at which this occurs, q_1); $P = SRATC$ (there is no incentive for firms to enter or exit the industry); and $SRATC = LRATC$ (there is no incentive for the firm to change its plant size).

⊕hinking Like AN ECONOMIST

Equilibrium Is Where Things Are Headed The concept of equilibrium is important in economics because equilibrium is where things are headed; in a way, it is the destination point. Suppose that firms in a perfectly competitive market are currently earning positive economic profit. At this point, say, 100 firms are in the market. But things are not likely to stay this way, and the number of firms is not likely to remain at 100. Firms are earning positive profits, and so firms not currently in the market will join the market, pushing the number of participants upward from 100. Only when all firms are earning normal profit (zero economic profit) will the number of firms remain where it is. Only then will the market be in equilibrium.[5]

(continued)

5. We are assuming that our other long-run equilibrium conditions hold, such as no firms want to change plant size and there is no incentive for any firm to produce any more or any less output.

When you get on a plane in, say, Los Angeles that is headed for New York City, you are fairly sure the trip is not over until you reach New York City. However, knowing when the trip is over in economics is not as easy. Theoretically, we know the trip is over when equilibrium has been reached. But what conditions indicate that equilibrium has been reached? ● ● ●

The Perfectly Competitive Firm and Productive Efficiency

Productive Efficiency
The situation when a firm produces its output at the lowest possible per-unit cost (lowest *ATC*).

A firm that produces its output at the lowest possible per-unit cost (lowest *ATC*) is said to exhibit productive efficiency. The perfectly competitive firm does this in long-run equilibrium, as shown in Exhibit 9. Productive efficiency is desirable from society's standpoint because perfectly competitive firms are economizing on society's scarce resources and therefore not wasting them.

To illustrate, suppose the lowest unit cost at which good X can be produced is $3, the minimum *ATC*. If a firm produces 1,000 units of good X at this unit cost, its total cost is $3,000. Now suppose the firm produces good X not at its lowest unit cost of $3, but at a slightly higher unit cost of $3.50. Total cost now equals $3,500. Resources worth $500 were employed producing good X that could have been used to produce other goods, had the firm exhibited productive efficiency. Society could have been richer in goods and services, but not now.

Industry Adjustment to an Increase in Demand

An increase in market demand for a product can throw an industry out of long-run competitive equilibrium. See Exhibit 10:

1. We start at long-run competitive equilibrium, where $P = MC = SRATC = LRATC$ (see part 1 in Exhibit 10).

2. Then market demand rises for the product produced by the firms in the industry, and the equilibrium price rises.

3. As a consequence, the demand curve faced by an individual firm (which is its marginal revenue curve) shifts upward.

4. Next, *existing firms* in the industry increase the quantity of output because marginal revenue now intersects marginal cost at a higher quantity of output.

5. In the long run, new firms begin to enter the industry because price is currently above average total cost, and there are positive economic profits.

6. As new firms enter the industry, the market (industry) supply curve shifts rightward.

7–8. As a consequence, equilibrium price falls until long-run competitive equilibrium is reestablished—that is, until once again economic profit is zero.

Look at the process again, from the initial increase in market demand to the reestablishment of long-run competitive equilibrium: price increased in the short run (owing to the increase in demand) and then decreased in the long run (owing to the increase in supply). Also, profits increased (owing to the increase in demand and consequent increase in price) and then decreased (owing to the increase in supply and consequent decrease in price). They went from zero to some positive amount and then back to zero.

The *up-and-down* movements in both price and profits in response to an increase in demand are important. Too often people see only the primary upward movements in both price and profits, and they ignore or forget the secondary downward movements. However, the secondary effects in price and profits are as important as the primary effects.

EXHIBIT 10

The Process of Moving from One Long-Run Competitive Equilibrium Position to Another

This exhibit describes what happens on both the market level and the firm level when

demand rises and throws an industry out of long-run competitive equilibrium.

(1)

The industry is in long-run competitive equilibrium. All firms earn zero economic profit.

(2)

For some reason, the market demand curve rises and price rises.

(3)

This raises the demand and marginal revenue curves for the firm, and it produces more output.

(4)

At a higher price and demand curve, firms in the industry are now earning positive economic profits.

(5)

Other firms (currently not in the industry) view the positive economic profits as an incentive to join the industry.

(6)

As new firms join the industry, the market supply curve shifts to the right and price declines.

(7)

This lowers the demand and marginal revenue curves for firms. Older firms, which made up the industry before market demand increased (back in box 2), cut back output.

(8)

Eventually, all firms earn zero economic profit and are in long-run competitive equilibrium.

The adjustment to an increase in demand brings up an important question: if price first rises owing to an increase in market demand and later falls owing to an increase in market supply, will the new equilibrium price be greater than, less than, or equal to the *original* equilibrium price? (In Exhibit 10, the new equilibrium is shown as equal to the original equilibrium price, but this need not be the case.)

For example, if the equilibrium price is $10 before the increase in market demand, will the new equilibrium price (after market and firm adjustments) be greater than, less than, or equal to $10? The answer depends on whether cost is remaining constant, increasing, or decreasing, respectively, in the industry.

CONSTANT-COST   In a constant-cost industry, average total costs (unit costs) do not change as output increases or decreases when firms enter or exit the market or industry. If market demand increases for a good produced by firms in a constant-cost industry, price will initially rise and then will finally fall to its original level, as shown in Exhibit 11(a). Point 1 represents long-run competitive equilibrium where economic profits are zero. Then demand increases, and price rises from P_1 to P_2. At P_2, there are positive economic profits, which cause the firms currently in the industry to increase output. We move up the supply curve, S_1, from point 1 to point 2. Next, new firms, drawn by the profits, enter the industry, causing the supply curve to shift rightward (S_2).

For a constant-cost industry, output is increased without a change in the price of inputs. Because of this, the firms' cost curves do not shift. But if costs do not rise to reduce the profits in the industry, then price must fall. (Profits can be reduced in two ways: through a rise in costs or a fall in price.) Price must fall to its original level (P_1) before profits can be zero, implying that the supply curve shifts rightward by the same amount that the demand curve shifts rightward. In the exhibit, this is a shift from S_1 to S_2. The two long-run equilibrium points (1 and 3), where economic profits are zero, define the long-run (industry) supply (*LRS*) curve. A constant-cost industry is thus characterized by a horizontal long-run supply curve.

INCREASING COST   In an increasing-cost industry, average total costs (unit costs) increase as output increases, and firms enter the industry; they decrease as output decreases, and firms exit the industry. If market demand increases for a good produced by firms in an increasing-cost industry, price will initially rise and then finally fall to a level above its original level.

Long-Run (Industry) Supply (*LRS*) Curve

Graphic representation of the quantities of output that the industry is prepared to supply at different prices after the entry and exit of firms are completed.

Constant-Cost Industry

An industry in which average total costs do not change as (industry) output increases or decreases when firms enter or exit the industry, respectively.

EXHIBIT 11

Long-Run Industry Supply Curves

LRS = Long-run industry supply. Each part illustrates the same scenario, but with different results depending on whether the industry has (a) constant costs, (b) increasing costs, or (c) decreasing costs. In each part, we start at long-run competitive equilibrium (point 1). Demand increases, price rises from P_1 to P_2, and there are positive economic profits. Consequently,

existing firms increase output and new firms are attracted to the industry. In (a), input costs remain constant as output increases, so the firms' cost curves do not shift. Profits fall to zero through a decline in price. This implies that in a constant-cost industry, the supply curve shifts rightward by the same amount as the demand curve shifts rightward. In (b), input costs increase as output increases. Profits

are squeezed by a combination of rising costs and falling prices. The new equilibrium price (P_3) for an increasing-cost industry is higher than the old equilibrium price (P_1). In (c), input costs decrease as output increases. The new equilibrium price (P_3) for a decreasing-cost industry is lower than the old equilibrium price (P_1).

(a) Constant-Cost Industry

(b) Increasing-Cost Industry

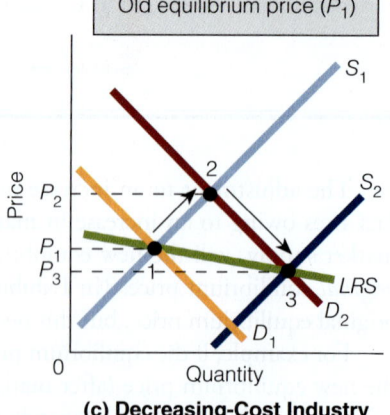

(c) Decreasing-Cost Industry

In Exhibit 11(b), as before, point 1 represents long-run competitive equilibrium. Demand increases, and price rises from P_1 to P_2. This shift brings about positive economic profits, which cause firms in the industry to increase output and new firms to enter the industry. So far, the process is the same as for a constant-cost industry. However, in an increasing-cost industry, as firms purchase more inputs to produce more output, some input prices rise and cost curves shift. In short, as industry output increases, profits are caught in a two-way squeeze: price is coming down, and costs are rising. If costs are rising as price is falling, then price will not have to fall to its original level before zero economic profits rule once again. In an increasing-cost industry, price will not have to fall as far to restore long-run competitive equilibrium as in a constant-cost industry. We would expect, then, that when an increasing-cost industry experiences an increase in demand, the new equilibrium price will be higher than the old equilibrium price. The supply curve shifts rightward by less than the demand curve shifts rightward. An increasing-cost industry is characterized by an upward-sloping long-run supply curve.

DECREASING-COST INDUSTRY In a decreasing-cost industry, average total costs (unit costs) decrease as output increases, and firms enter the industry; they increase as output decreases, and firms exit the industry. If market demand increases for a good produced by firms in a decreasing-cost industry, price will initially rise and then finally fall to a level below its original level. In Exhibit 11(c), price moves from P_1 to P_2 and then to P_3. In such an industry, average total costs decrease as new firms enter the industry; so price must fall below its original level to eliminate profits. A decreasing-cost industry is characterized by a downward-sloping long-run supply curve.

Increasing-Cost Industry
An industry in which average total costs increase as output increases and decrease as output decreases when firms enter and exit the industry, respectively.

Decreasing-Cost Industry
An industry in which average total costs decrease as output increases and increase as output decreases when firms enter and exit the industry, respectively.

ⓣhinking Like AN ECONOMIST

Common Misconceptions About Profits The layperson often views profits in much the same way as the English teacher views a period. Profits come at the end of a production process, and a period comes at the end of a sentence. In reality, profit is more like a comma, in that something comes after it. Profit is more like an ongoing process, as just explained: demand rises, causing price to rise, causing profits to rise. But things don't stop there. The higher profits call forth new firms into the market, causing the supply curve in the market to shift rightward, in turn causing price and profits to fall.

Think of how not knowing about the up-and-down movements in price and profits can lead to some unintended effects. The demand for a good rises, and with it both price and profits rise. Big profits are reported in the news, and politicians start talking about taxing those so-called high profits. However, might taxing those high profits stop the price-profits story from continuing? Without the profits, new firms don't enter the market. Without the new firms, supply doesn't increase. In other words, to tax the profits might have the unintended effect of reducing the supply of goods from what it would be if the profits weren't taxed. ●●●

Profit from Two Perspectives

From one perspective, profit serves as an *incentive* for individuals to produce. From another perspective, it serves as a *signal*.

Profit serves as an incentive by prompting or encouraging certain behavior. John produces furniture to sell because he hopes to earn profit; Jackie opens up a hair salon because she hopes to earn profit.

As a signal, profit acts a little like a neon sign, identifying where resources are most welcome. To illustrate, suppose company A produces good A and company B produces good B. Currently, company A is earning profits producing good A and company B is incurring a loss producing good B. To those viewing the profits and losses from the outside, it is as if the profits are signaling, "If you are thinking of producing either good A or B, choose A. That is where the profit can be found." Stated differently, it is as if profit tells others where resources are best allocated. Allocate them toward producing good A.

finding ECONOMICS

In the Computer Industry and Elsewhere Years ago, the prices of a personal computer, calculator, DVD recorder, and plasma television set were higher than they are today. Where is the economics? Do higher prices have anything to do with what we have just discussed—prices and profits?

The early introduction of these goods often came with (what in hindsight appears to be) high prices and high profits. The high profits called forth new firms into the market. The new firms ended up increasing supply and reducing prices and profits. (Other changes were occurring at the same time, such as changes in technology.) ▲ ▲ ▲

thinking Like AN ECONOMIST

Easy Entry into a Market Matters Once again demand rises, price rises, and profits go from zero to positive. Yet, as explained, this is not the end of the story as long as new firms can enter the market. But suppose they can't. If something prevents firms from entering the market, the end of the story will not be the same, with price moving down and profit returning to zero. The different ending points out how important easy entry into the market is to the story. Without easy entry, the story is a different story altogether: Prices are more likely to stay high, and profits are more likely to stay positive. ▲ ▲ ▲

Industry Adjustment to a Decrease in Demand

Demand can decrease as well as increase. Starting at long-run competitive equilibrium, market demand decreases. As a consequence, in the short run, the equilibrium price falls, effectively shifting the firm's demand curve (marginal revenue curve) downward. Some firms in the industry then decrease production because marginal revenue intersects marginal cost at a lower level of output, and some firms shut down.

In the long run, some firms will leave the industry because price is below the average total cost, and they are suffering ongoing losses. As firms leave the industry, the market supply curve shifts leftward. As a consequence, the equilibrium price rises and continues to rise until long-run competitive equilibrium is reestablished—that is, until there are, once again, zero economic profits (instead of negative economic profits). Whether the new equilibrium price is greater than, less than, or equal to the original equilibrium price depends on whether cost is decreasing, increasing, or remaining constant, respectively, in the industry.

Differences in Costs, Differences in Profits: Now You See It, Now You Don't

Two farmers, Hancock and Cordero, produce wheat. Farmer Cordero grows his wheat on fertile land; farmer Hancock grows her wheat in poor soil. Both farmers sell their wheat for the same price, but because of the difference in the quality of their land, Cordero has lower average total costs than Hancock, as shown in Exhibit 12. Given the initial situations of the two farmers (each farmer's ATC_1), we notice that Cordero is earning profits and Hancock is not. Cordero is earning profits because he pays lower average total costs than Hancock as a consequence of farming higher-quality land.

But Cordero is not likely to continue earning profits. Individuals will bid up the price of the fertile land that Cordero farms vis-à-vis the poor-quality land that Hancock

economics 24/7

Is it "Sellers Against Buyers" or "Sellers Against Sellers"?

Often, the noneconomist thinks that buyers and the sellers are at odds with each other. The sellers want to sell their goods at high prices, and the buyers want to buy the goods at low prices. This naturally puts buyers and sellers in a tug of war, each pulling in the opposite direction.

A tug of war between buyers and sellers is not always descriptive of what happens in the real world. To illustrate, suppose all firms in market X are earning positive economic profits. If entry into the market is easy—as it is in a perfectly competitive market—firms not currently in market X will *enter* the market to obtain some of those profits. The entry of the new firms into market X will shift the market supply curve to the right, lower price, and thus eliminate the positive economic profits. The positive economic profits will turn to zero economic profit.

Now ask yourself two questions:

1. Do the existing firms in the market oppose the entry of new firms into the market?

2. Whom do the new firms help and hurt?

Obviously, the existing firms will be unhappy if new firms enter the market because new firms erode their positive economic profits. In other words, the situation is not a case of seller against buyer; it is a case of seller against seller. More specifically, it is a case of existing sellers against new sellers. The existing sellers want to keep out the new ones.

Although the entry of new firms hurts existing firms, it benefits consumers. By entering the market, new firms increase supply and lower price. Lower prices benefit consumers.

In our story of two categories of sellers (existing and new) and consumers, here is how things stack up:

1. Existing sellers are opposed to new sellers.

2. If existing sellers try to keep new sellers out of the market, then existing sellers are at odds with consumers.

3. New sellers benefit consumers by entering the market and driving supply up and price down.

In other words, it is not a case of all sellers being against all buyers or of all buyers against all sellers. In our example, (1) some sellers are *against* other sellers (existing sellers against new sellers); (2) some sellers are *against* buyers (if existing sellers try to keep new sellers from raising supply and lowering prices); and (3) some sellers are *for* buyers" (if new sellers enter the market, raise supply, and lower prices for buyers).

EXHIBIT 12

(a) Farmer Hancock

(b) Farmer Cordero

Differences in Costs, Differences in Profits: Now You See It, Now It's Gone

At ATC_1 for both farmers, Cordero earns profits and Hancock does not. Cordero earns profits because the land he farms is of higher quality (more productive) than Hancock's land. Eventually, this fact is taken into account, by Cordero either paying higher rent for the land or incurring implicit costs for it. This moves Cordero's *ATC* curve upward to the same level as Hancock's, and Cordero earns zero economic profits. The profits have gone as payment (implicit or explicit) for the higher quality, more productive land.

How Is High-Quality Land like a Genius Software Engineer?

In the example of two farmers who produce wheat, Cordero was earning profits and Hancock was not because Cordero farmed higher-quality land. In time, though, Cordero's higher profits ended up going into higher rent for the higher-quality land. The profit therefore went as payment for the higher-quality, more productive resource responsible for the lower average total costs in the first place.

In the field of designing and developing computer software applications, suppose there are two companies, A and B. Software engineers work at both companies, but one of company A's software engineers is considered a genius within the software industry. Currently, the genius earns the same salary as other software engineers in the software industry.

Because the genius works for company A, company A comes up with better software applications than other companies. As a result, company A not only sells more software applications, but it can also charge higher prices for the software it sells. Thus, largely as a result of having hired

PAWEL KOPCZYNSKI/REUTERS /LANDOV

the genius software engineer, company A currently earns higher profits than company B.

If company A's higher profits are attributable to the genius software engineer, then other software companies will soon compete to hire him. He will soon find his salary being bid up. To keep the software genius, company A will have to turn over some of its profits to him in the form of salary. Profits on Wednesday turn in to the genius's salary on Thursday.

High-quality land is like a genius software engineer in that both are the source of profits and eventually those profits get transformed into something else. In the farming example, high profits get turned into higher rent for the higher-quality land. In the software engineer example, high profits (for company A) get turned into a higher salary for our genius software engineer. Stated differently, the higher-quality land in our first example "is" the genius software engineer in the second.

farms. In other words, if Cordero is renting his farmland, the rent he pays will increase to reflect the superior quality of the land. The rent will increase by an amount equal to the profits per time period—that is, an amount equal to the shaded portion in Exhibit 12(b). If Cordero owns the land, the superior quality of the land will have a higher implicit cost (Cordero can rent it for more than Hancock can rent her land, assuming Hancock owns her land). This process is reflected in the average total cost curve.

In Exhibit 12(b), ATC_2 reflects either the higher rent Cordero must pay for the superior land or the full implicit cost he incurs by farming the land he owns. In either case, when the average total cost curve reflects all costs, Cordero will be in the same situation as Hancock; he, too, will be earning zero economic profits.

The profit has gone as payment for the higher-quality, more productive resource responsible for the lower average total costs in the first place. Consequently, average total costs are no longer relatively lower for the person or firm that employs the higher-quality, more productive resource or input.

Profit and Discrimination

A firm's discriminatory behavior can affect its profits in the context of the model of perfect competition. Under the conditions of long-run competitive equilibrium, where firms are earning zero economic profits, the owner of a firm chooses not to hire an excellent worker (i.e., above average, let's say) simply because of that worker's race, religion, or gender. What happens to the owner of the firm who discriminates in any way? If he chooses not to employ high-quality employees because of their race, religion, or gender, then his costs will rise above those of competitors who hire the best employees irrespective of race, religion, or gender. Because he is initially earning zero profit, where $TR = TC$, the act of discrimination will raise TC and push the firm into taking economic losses. If the owner in the example is a manager, he may lose his job because the firm's owners may decide to replace managers earning subnormal profits. Thus, profit maximization by shareholders works to reduce discrimination.

Our conclusion is that if a firm is in a perfectly competitive market structure, it will pay penalties if it chooses to discriminate. Discrimination will not necessarily disappear, but it comes with a price tag. And according to economic theory, the more something costs, the less of it there will be, *ceteris paribus.*

TOPICS FOR ANALYSIS IN THE THEORY OF PERFECT COMPETITION

This section briefly analyzes three topics in the theory of perfect competition: higher costs and higher prices, advertising, and setting prices.

Do Higher Costs Mean Higher Prices?

Suppose that 600 firms are in an industry and that each firm sells the same product at the same price. Then one of these firms experiences a rise in its marginal costs of production. Someone immediately comments, "Higher costs for the firm today, higher prices for the consumer tomorrow," the assumption being that firms experiencing a rise in costs simply pass the higher costs on to consumers in the form of higher prices.

Passing along costs, however, cannot occur in a perfectly competitive market. Each firm in the industry is a price taker; furthermore, only one firm has experienced a rise in marginal costs. Because this firm supplies only a tiny percentage of the total market supply, the market supply curve is unlikely to undergo more than a negligible change. And if the market supply curve does not change, neither will equilibrium price. In short, a rise in costs incurred by one of many firms does not mean consumers will pay higher prices. Of course, if many of the firms in the industry experience a rise in costs, the market supply curve will be affected, along with price.

ⓣhinking Like AN ECONOMIST

A Reasonable-Sounding Argument Is Not Enough Sometimes, two or more explanations may seem equally reasonable. For example, if all firms in an industry sell their products for the same price, two explanations seem equally plausible: the firms collude on price or the firms are price takers. But for the economist, a reasonable explanation is not sufficient; she wants the correct explanation. The economist is skeptical of any explanation that simply sounds reasonable. She needs evidence (often in the form of data) to support the explanation. ▲ ▲ ▲

Will the Perfectly Competitive Firm Advertise?

Individual farmers don't advertise. You've never seen an advertisement for, say, farmer Johnson's milk for a couple of reasons. First, farmer Johnson sells a homogeneous product; so advertising his milk is the same as advertising every dairy farmer's milk. Second, farmer Johnson is in a perfectly competitive market; so he can sell all the milk he wants at the going price. Why should he advertise? From his viewpoint, advertising has all cost and no benefits.

However, a perfectly competitive industry might advertise. For example, if farmer Johnson won't advertise his milk, the milk industry might advertise milk in general in the

OFFICE HOURS

"Do You Have to Know the *MR* = *MC* Condition to Be Successful in Business?"

STUDENT:

Something seems odd to me. Some people are successful in business without knowing any of the material in this chapter. Isn't it possible for a person to be successful in business without knowing the *MR* = *MC* condition or the shutdown decision (shut down when *P* is less than *AVC*), and so on?

INSTRUCTOR:

Yes, but keep in mind that someone doesn't have to know the *MR* = *MC* condition to try to put it into operation. Most people don't know the physics behind the operation of a car, but they drive a car as if they do know the physics.

STUDENT:

Are you saying that we can know and not know something at the same time? That sounds odd to me.

INSTRUCTOR:

That's not exactly what I am saying. You can do something you don't know you're doing. Let me give you an example. Jack owns and operates his own business producing shoe boxes. He has never taken an economics course in his life, and he doesn't know the first thing about marginal revenue, marginal cost, average total cost, and so on. Not knowing these things doesn't mean he doesn't have to figure out how many shoe boxes to produce. So how does he do it without a knowledge of marginal revenue and marginal cost? All Jack has to know is that it is a good idea to keep producing shoe boxes when more money is coming in the front door (in additional revenue) than is going out the back door (in additional costs). That's it. That basic, very elemental idea is behind the *MR* = *MC* condition.

STUDENT:

Does the same hold for things like knowing when to continue producing a good and knowing when to shut down?

hope of shifting the market demand curve for milk to the right. This is actually what the milk industry hopes to do with its commercial message, "Got milk?"

Supplier-Set Price Versus Market-Determined Price: Collusion or Competition?

Suppose the only thing you know about an industry is that all the firms in it sell their products at the same price. To explain this, some people argue that the firms are colluding—that is, they come together, pick a price, and stick to it. This, of course, is one way for all firms to arrive at the same price for their products, but it is not the only way. Another way, as described in this chapter, is that all firms are price takers; that is, the firms are in a perfectly competitive market structure. In this case, there is no collusion.

1. In a perfectly competitive market, do higher costs mean higher prices?

2. If you see a product advertised on television, does it follow that the product cannot be produced in a perfectly competitive market?

INSTRUCTOR:

Yes. The economist advises to shut down when $P < AVC$, but this is just a slightly more sophisticated way of expressing the idea that a firm should shut down when it would lose more from not shutting down. Consider Yvonne who, like Jack, owns her own business. She is currently wondering whether she should stop producing a good. She may not know the first thing about the relationship between price and average variable cost, but certainly she can put some numbers down on paper and figure out how much money she loses if she shuts down and how much money she loses if she doesn't shut down.

STUDENT:

I think I see what you are getting at. The economist seems only to be formalizing what people do if they are trying to maximize their profits or minimize their losses. The average Joe or Jane in business simply continues producing additional units of a good as long as more money comes into the firm by selling the additional unit than is going out by producing it. Then the economist simply says, "Produce as long as MR is greater than MC." Am I right?

INSTRUCTOR:

Yes, you're right.

STUDENT:

Looking at things this way makes the material in this chapter seem a little easier and a little more grounded in reality.

INSTRUCTOR:

That's good to hear.

POINTS TO REMEMBER

1. Not knowing the $MR = MC$ condition doesn't mean that a real-world businessperson doesn't abide by it.

2. Many of the rules or conditions in this chapter (produce until $MR = MC$, shut down when $P < AVC$) are simply formalized ways of expressing what individuals in business settings do when they seek to maximize profits or minimize losses.

CHAPTER SUMMARY

THE THEORY OF PERFECT COMPETITION

- The theory of perfect competition is built on four assumptions: (1) There are many sellers and many buyers, none of whom is large in relation to total sales or purchases. (2) Each firm produces and sells a homogeneous product. (3) Buyers and sellers have all relevant information with respect to prices, product quality, sources of supply, and so on. (4) Entry into or exit from the industry is easy.

- The theory of perfect competition predicts the following: (1) Economic profits will be squeezed out of the industry in the long run by the entry of new firms; that is, zero economic profit exists in the long run. (2) In equilibrium, firms produce the quantity of output at which price equals marginal cost. (3) In the short run, firms will stay in business as long as price covers average variable costs. (4) In the long run, firms will stay in business as long as price covers average total costs. (5) In the short run, an increase in demand will lead to a rise in price; whether the price in the long run will be higher than, lower than, or equal to its original level depends on whether the firm is in an increasing-, decreasing-, or constant-cost industry.

THE PERFECTLY COMPETITIVE FIRM

- A perfectly competitive firm is a price taker. It sells its product only at the market-established equilibrium price.

- The perfectly competitive firm faces a horizontal (flat, perfectly elastic) demand curve. Its demand curve and its marginal revenue curve are the same.

- The perfectly competitive firm (as well as all other firms) maximizes profits (or minimizes losses) by producing the quantity of output at which $MR = MC$.

- For the perfectly competitive firm, price equals marginal revenue.

- A perfectly competitive firm is resource allocative efficient because it produces the quantity of output at which $P = MC$.

PRODUCTION IN THE SHORT RUN

- If $P > ATC$ ($> AVC$), the firm earns economic profits and will continue to operate in the short run.

- If $P < AVC$ ($< ATC$), the firm takes losses. It will shut down because the alternative (continuing to produce) increases the losses.

- If $ATC > P > AVC$, the firm takes losses. Nevertheless, it will continue to operate in the short run because the alternative (shutting down) increases the losses.

- The firm produces in the short run only when price is greater than the average variable cost. Therefore, the portion of its marginal cost curve that lies above the average variable cost curve is the firm's short-run supply curve.

CONDITIONS OF LONG-RUN COMPETITIVE EQUILIBRIUM

- Long-run competitive equilibrium exists when there is no incentive for firms (1) to enter or exit the industry, (2) to produce more or less output, and (3) to change plant size. We formalize these conditions as follows: (1) Economic profits are zero (that is, firms have no incentive to enter or exit the industry). (2) Firms are producing the quantity of output at which price is equal to marginal cost. (Firms have no incentive to produce more or less output. After all, when $P = MC$, it follows that $MR = MC$ for the perfectly competitive firm, and thus the firm is maximizing profits.) (3) $SRATC = LRATC$ at the quantity of output at which $P = MC$. (Firms do not have an incentive to change plant size.)

- A perfectly competitive firm exhibits productive efficiency because it produces its output in the long run at the lowest possible per-unit cost (lowest ATC).

INDUSTRY ADJUSTMENT TO A CHANGE IN DEMAND

- In a constant-cost industry, an increase in demand will result in a new equilibrium price equal to the original equilibrium price (before demand increased). In an increasing-cost industry, an increase in demand will result in a new equilibrium price higher than the original one. In a decreasing-cost industry, an increase in demand will result in a new equilibrium price lower than the original one.

- The long-run supply curve for a constant-cost industry is horizontal (flat, perfectly elastic). The long-run supply curve for an increasing-cost industry is upward sloping. The long-run supply curve for a decreasing-cost industry is downward sloping.

KEY TERMS AND CONCEPTS

Market Structure
Perfect Competition
Price Taker
Marginal Revenue (*MR*)
Profit Maximization Rule

Resource Allocative Efficiency
Short-Run (Firm) Supply
   Curve
Short-Run Market (Industry)
   Supply Curve

Long-Run Competitive
   Equilibrium
Productive Efficiency
Constant-Cost Industry

Long-Run (Industry) Supply
   (*LRS*) Curve
Increasing-Cost Industry
Decreasing-Cost Industry

QUESTIONS AND PROBLEMS

1. Profit serves as both an incentive and signal. Explain.

2. In your own words, explain resource allocative efficiency.

3. Do firms in a perfectly competitive market exhibit productive efficiency? Why or why not?

4. You read in a business magazine that computer firms are reaping high profits. With the theory of perfect competition in mind, what do you expect to happen over time to the following?

   a. Computer prices

   b. The profits of computer firms

   c. The number of computers on the market

   d. The number of computer firms

5. Many plumbers charge the same price for coming to your house to fix a kitchen sink. Is this because plumbers are colluding?

6. The perfectly competitive firm does not increase its quantity of output without limit even though it can sell all it wants at the going price. Why not?

7. Why is the marginal revenue curve for a perfectly competitive firm the same as its demand curve?

8. For a perfectly competitive firm, profit maximization does not conflict with resource allocative efficiency. Do you agree? Explain your answer.

9. Suppose the government imposes a production tax on one perfectly competitive firm in an industry. For each unit the firm produces, it must pay $1 to the government. Will consumers in this market end up paying higher prices because of the tax? Why or why not?

10. Explain why one firm sometimes appears to be earning higher profits than another but in reality is not.

11. In long-run competitive equilibrium, $P = MC = SRATC = LRATC$. Because $P = MR$, we can write the condition as $P = $

$MR = MC = SRATC = LRATC$. The condition thus consists of four parts: (a) $P = MR$, (b) $MR = MC$, (c) $P = SRATC$, and (d) $SRATC = LRATC$. Part (b)—$MR = MC$—exists because the perfectly competitive firm attempts to maximize profits, and this is how it does it. What are the explanations for parts (a), (c), and (d)?

12. Suppose all firms in a perfectly competitive market structure are in long-run equilibrium. Then demand for the firms' product increases. Initially, price and economic profits rise. Soon afterward, the government decides to tax most (but not all) of the economic profits, arguing that the firms in the industry did not earn the profits. They were simply the result of an increase in demand. What effect, if any, will the tax have on market adjustment?

13. Explain why a perfectly competitive firm will shut down in the short run if price is lower than the average variable cost but will continue to produce if price is below the average total cost but above the average variable cost.

14. "Firm A, one firm in a competitive industry, faces higher costs of production. As a result, consumers end up paying higher prices." Discuss.

15. Why study the theory of perfect competition if no real-world market completely satisfies all of the theory's assumptions?

16. "In a perfectly competitive market, firms always operate at the lowest per-unit cost." Is the statement true or false? Explain your answer.

17. The term "price taker" can apply to buyers as well as to sellers. A price-taking buyer is one who cannot influence price by changing the amount she buys. What goods do you buy for which you are a price taker? What goods do you buy for which you are not a price taker?

18. "The firm's entire marginal cost curve is its short-run supply curve." Is the statement true or false? Explain your answer.

WORKING WITH NUMBERS AND GRAPHS

1. Given the following information, state whether the perfectly competitive firm should shut down or continue to operate in the short run.

   a. $Q = 100$; $P = \$10$; $AFC = \$3$; $AVC = \$4$.

   b. $Q = 70$; $P = \$5$; $AFC = \$2$; $AVC = \$7$.

   c. $Q = 150$; $P = \$7$; $AFC = \$5$; $AVC = \$6$.

2. If total revenue increases at a constant rate, what does this condition imply about marginal revenue?

3. Using the table given here, what quantity of output should the firm produce? Explain your answer.

Q	TR	TC
0	$0	$0
1	100	50
2	200	110
3	300	180
4	400	260
5	500	360
6	600	480

4. Is the firm in question 3 a perfectly competitive firm? Explain your answer.

5. Explain how a market supply curve is derived.

6. Draw the following:

   a. A perfectly competitive firm that earns profits

   b. A perfectly competitive firm that incurs losses but that will continue operating in the short run

   c. A perfectly competitive firm that incurs losses and that will shut down in the short run

7. Why is the perfectly competitive firm's supply curve the portion of its marginal cost curve that is above its average variable cost curve?

8. In the following figure, what area(s) represent(s) the following at Q_1?

   a. Total cost

   b. Total variable cost

   c. Total revenue

   d. Loss (negative profit)

9. Why does the *MC* curve cut the *ATC* curve at the latter's lowest point?

10. Suppose all firms in a perfectly competitive market are in long-run equilibrium. Illustrate what a perfectly competitive firm will do if market demand rises.

MONOPOLY

Introduction Monopoly is at the opposite end of the market structure spectrum from perfect competition. We begin our discussion of monopoly by outlining the assumptions on which the theory of monopoly is built. We move on to talk about the quantity of output the monopolist wants to produce and the price (per unit) at which it sells that output. Much of this chapter focuses on the differences between the perfectly competitive firm and the monopoly firm.

THE THEORY OF MONOPOLY

The theory of monopoly is built on three assumptions:

1. *There is one seller.* In effect, the firm is the industry. Contrast this situation with perfect competition, where many firms make up the industry.

2. *The single seller sells a product that has no close substitutes.* Because there are no close substitutes for its product, the single seller—the monopolist or monopoly firm—faces little, if any, competition.

3. *The barriers to entry are extremely high.* In the theory of perfect competition, a firm can enter the industry easily. In the theory of monopoly, entering the industry is very hard (if not impossible) Extremely high barriers keep out new firms.

Examples of monopoly include many public utilities (local public utilities such as electricity, water, and gas companies) and the U.S. Postal Service (in the delivery of first-class mail).

Barriers to Entry: A Key to Understanding Monopoly

If a firm is a single seller of a product, why don't other firms enter the market and produce the same product? Legal barriers, economies of scale, or one firm's exclusive ownership of a scarce resource may make it difficult or impossible for new firms to enter the market.

Monopoly
A theory of market structure based on three assumptions: There is one seller, it sells a product that has no close substitutes exist, and the barriers to entry are extremely high.

Public Franchise
A right granted to a firm by government that permits the firm to provide a particular good or service and that excludes all others from doing so.

LEGAL BARRIERS Legal barriers include public franchises, patents, and government licenses. A public franchise is a right that government grants to a firm and that permits the firm to provide a particular good or service and excludes all others from doing so (thus eliminating potential competition by law). For example, the U.S. Postal Service has been granted the exclusive franchise to deliver first-class mail. Many public utilities operate under state and local franchises, as do food and gas suppliers along many state turnpikes.

In the United States, patents are granted to inventors of a product or process for a period of 20 years. During this time, the patent holder is shielded from competitors; no one else can legally produce and sell the patented product or process. The rationale behind patents is that they encourage innovation in an economy. Few people will waste their time and money trying to invent a new product if their competitors can immediately copy and sell it.

Entry into some industries and occupations requires a government-granted license. For example, radio and television stations cannot operate without a license from the Federal Communications Commission (FCC). In most states, a person needs to be licensed to join the ranks of physicians, dentists, architects, nurses, embalmers, barbers, veterinarians, and lawyers, among others.

Some cities also use licensing as a form of legal barrier. For example, the Taxi & Limousine Commission in New York City requires a person to have a taxi license, called a *taxi medallion,* to own and operate a taxi. The medallion is similar to a business license; a person needs it to lawfully operate a taxicab business.

The number of taxi medallions (licenses) has been fixed at about 12,000 for many years. The price of a medallion changes according to changes in the demand for them. In 1976, a medallion was about $45,000; in 1988, it was $125,000; and in January 2008, it was $429,000. Obviously, many people find $429,000 a barrier to entering the taxi business. Consequently, many economists believe that taxi medallions in New York City are a form of legal barrier.

ECONOMIES OF SCALE In some industries, low average total costs (low unit costs) are obtained only through large-scale production. Thus, if new entrants are to compete in the industry, they must enter it on a large scale. But having to produce on this scale is risky and costly, and it therefore acts as a barrier to entry. If economies of scale are so pronounced that only one firm can survive in the industry, the firm is called a natural monopoly. Often cited examples of natural monopoly include public utilities that provide gas, water, and electricity. A later chapter discusses government regulation of a natural monopoly.

Natural Monopoly
The condition where economies of scale are so pronounced that only one firm can survive.

EXCLUSIVE OWNERSHIP OF A NECESSARY RESOURCE Existing firms may be protected from the entry of new firms by the exclusive or nearly exclusive ownership of a resource needed to enter the industry. The classic example is the Aluminum Company of America (Alcoa), which for a time controlled almost all the sources of bauxite in the United States. Alcoa was the sole producer of aluminum in the country from the late nineteenth century until the 1940s. Many people today view the De Beers Company of South Africa as a monopoly because it controls such a large percentage of diamond production and sales. Strictly speaking, De Beers is more of a marketing cartel than a monopoly, although, as discussed in the next chapter, a successful cartel acts much like a monopolist.

finding ECONOMICS

At JFK Airport in New York City Nathan has just picked up his luggage in the baggage terminal of JFK Airport. He is heading out of the terminal to find a taxi. His destination is the Sheraton Manhattan hotel in midtown Manhattan. As he walks out the doors of the baggage terminal, a man says to him, "Looking for a taxi?" Nathan says yes. The man says, "Walk with me. I'm over here." When Nathan gets to the man's car, he realizes he is not a yellow taxi driver. The man is someone

(continued)

Monopoly and the Boston Tea Party

The original meaning of the word "monopoly" was an exclusive right to sell something. At one time, kings and queens granted monopolies to people whom they favored. The monopoly entitled the person to be the sole producer or seller of a particular good. If anyone dared to compete, the crown could have the offender fined or imprisoned.

The issue of monopoly came up in the early history of the America. In 1767, the British Parliament passed the Townsend Acts, which imposed taxes (or duties) on various products imported into the American colonies. The taxes were so hated in the colonies that they prompted protest and noncompliance, and the taxes were repealed in 1770, except for one: the tax on tea. Some historians state that the British Parliament left the tax on tea to show the colonists

© BETTMANN/CORBIS

that it had the right to raise tax revenue without seeking colonial approval. To get around the tax, the colonists started to buy tea from Dutch traders.

Then, in 1773, the British East India Company was in financial trouble. To help solve its financial problems, it sought a special privilege—a monopoly—from the British Parliament. In response, Parliament passed the Tea Act, which granted the company the sole right to export tea to the colonies—a monopoly. The combination of the tax and the monopoly right given to the British East India Company angered the colonists and is said to have led to the Boston Tea Party on December 16, 1773. The colonists who took part in the Boston Tea Party threw overboard 342 chests of tea owned by the monopoly-wielding British East India Company.

finding ECONOMICS (continued)

who does not have license to operate a taxi in New York City but who is offering transportation services. Nathan mentions this fact to the man, who says he is still willing to drive Nathan to his destination for the same price a taxi service would charge. Nathan ends up not going with him. Where is the economics?

What we *may* be witnessing is one of the effects of a legal barrier to entry. (We say "may" because we cannot be sure that the man who met Nathan really had Nathan's transportation interests in mind.) As explained earlier, a taxi medallion is needed to operate a taxi service in New York City. The limited number and expense of the medallions make for a high barrier for individuals who want to enter the taxi business and who might have all the abilities necessary to operate a successful business. The man whom Nathan encountered was trying to bypass this legal barrier. ▲ ▲ ▲

What Is the Difference Between a Government Monopoly and a Market Monopoly?

Sometimes high barriers to entry exist because competition is legally prohibited, and sometimes barriers exist independently. When high barriers take the form of public franchises, patents, or government licenses, competition is *legally* prohibited. When high barriers take the form of economies of scale or exclusive ownership of a resource, competition is not legally prohibited. In the latter cases, nothing legally prohibits rival firms from entering the market and competing, even though they may choose not to do so; there is no sign on the industry entrance that reads, "No competition allowed."

Some economists use the term "government monopoly" to refer to a monopoly that is legally protected from competition and the term "market monopoly" to refer to one that is not legally protected from competition. But these terms do not imply that one type is better or worse than the other.

(Answers to Self-Test questions are in Answers to Self-Test Questions at the back of the book.)

1. "There are always some close substitutes for the product any firm sells; therefore, the theory of monopoly (which assumes no close substitutes) cannot be useful." Comment.

2. How do economies of scale act as a barrier to entry?

3. How is a movie superstar like a monopolist?

MONOPOLY PRICING AND OUTPUT DECISIONS

Price Searcher

A seller that has the ability to control to some degree the price of the product it sells.

A monopolist is a **price searcher**, that is, a seller with the ability to control to some degree the price of the product it sells. In contrast to a price taker, a price searcher can raise its price and still sell its product—although it will not sell as many units as at the lower price. The pricing and output decisions of the price-searching monopolist are discussed in this section.

The Monopolist's Demand and Marginal Revenue

In the theory of monopoly, the monopoly firm is the industry, and the industry is the monopoly firm; they are one and the same. Thus the demand curve for the monopoly firm *is* the market demand curve, which is downward sloping. Because a downward-sloping demand curve posits an inverse relationship between price and quantity demanded, more is sold at lower prices than at higher prices, *ceteris paribus*. Unlike the perfectly competitive firm, the monopolist can raise its price and still sell its product (though not as much).

Because it faces a downward-sloping demand curve, to sell an additional unit of its product, the monopolist must necessarily lower price. For example, the monopoly seller originally planned to sell 2 units of X a day at $10 each and now wishes to sell 3 units a day. To sell more units, it must lower the price to, say, $9.75, and it sells the 3 units at $9.75 each.[1]

So to sell an additional unit, a monopoly firm must lower price on all previous units. Note that the terms "previous" and "additional" do not refer to an actual sequence of events. A firm doesn't sell 100 units of a good and then decide to sell one more unit. The firm is in an either–or situation. Either the firm sells 100 units over some period of time, or it sells 101 units over the same period of time. If the firm wants to sell 101 units, the price per unit must be lower than if it wants to sell 100 units.

A monopoly seller both gains and loses by lowering price. As Exhibit 1 shows, the monopolist in our example gains $9.75, the price of the additional unit sold, because price was lowered. It loses 50¢: 25¢ on the first unit it used to sell at $10, plus 25¢ on the second unit it used to sell at $10.

Gains are greater than losses; the monopolist's net gain from selling the additional unit of output is $9.25 ($9.75 − $0.50 = $9.25). This is the monopolist's *marginal revenue*, the change in total revenue that results from selling one additional unit of output. (Total revenue is $20 when 2 units are sold at $10 each and $29.25 when 3 units are sold at $9.75 each. The change in total revenue that results from selling one additional unit of output is $9.25.)

Notice that the price of the good ($9.75) is greater than the marginal revenue ($9.25): $P > MR$. This is the case for a monopoly seller or any price searcher. (Recall that for the firm in perfect competition, $P = MR$.)

For a monopolist, $P > MR$

---

1. This discussion of the behavior of a single-price monopolist, which is a monopolist that sells all units of its product for the same price. Later, we discuss a price-discriminating monopolist.

EXHIBIT 1

(1) P	(2) Q	(3) TR	(4) MR
$10.00	2	$20.00	—— $9.25
9.75	3	29.25	

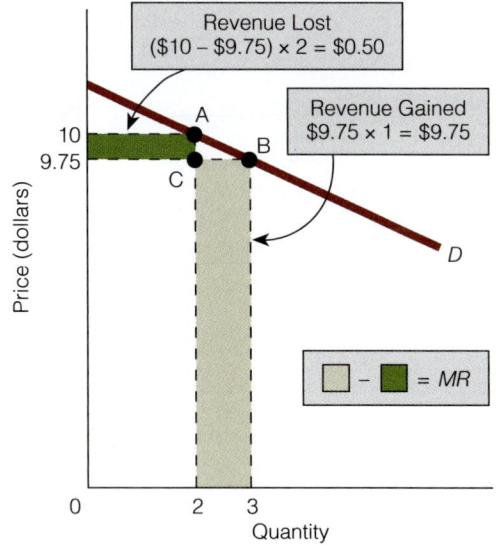

The Dual Effects of a Price Reduction on Total Revenue

To sell an additional unit of its good, a monopolist needs to lower price. This price reduction both gains revenue and loses revenue for the monopolist. In the exhibit, the revenue gained and revenue lost are shaded and labeled. Marginal revenue is equal to the larger shaded area minus the smaller shaded area.

The Monopolist's Demand and Marginal Revenue Curves Are Not the Same

In perfect competition, the firm's demand curve *is* the same as its marginal revenue curve. In monopoly, the firm's demand curve is not the same as its marginal revenue curve but rather lies *above* its marginal revenue curve.

The relationship between a monopolist's demand and marginal revenue curves is illustrated in Exhibit 2. The demand curve plots price and quantity (P and Q); the marginal revenue curve plots marginal revenue and quantity (MR and Q). Because price is greater than marginal revenue for a monopolist, its demand curve necessarily lies *above* its marginal revenue curve. (Note that price and marginal revenue are the same for the first unit of output; so the demand curve and the marginal revenue curve will share one point in common.)

Price and Output for a Profit-Maximizing Monopolist

The monopolist that seeks to maximize profit produces the quantity of output at which $MR = MC$ (as did the profit-maximizing perfectly competitive firm) and *charges the highest price per unit at which this quantity of output can be sold.*

In Exhibit 3, the highest price at which Q_1, the quantity at which $MR = MC$, can be sold is P_1. At Q_1, the monopolist charges a price that is greater than marginal cost, $P > MC$. Therefore, the monopolist is *not* resource allocative efficient.

Whether profits are earned depends on whether P_1 is greater or less than average total cost at Q_1. In short, the profit-maximizing price may be the loss-minimizing price. Monopoly profits and monopoly losses are illustrated in Exhibit 4.

EXHIBIT 2

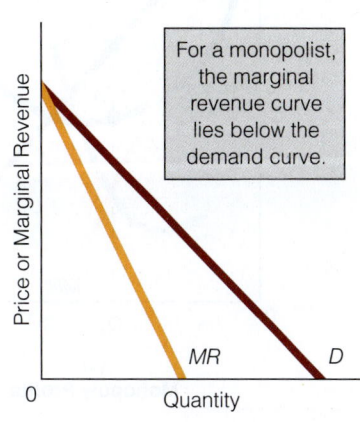

Demand and Marginal Revenue Curves

The demand curve plots price and quantity. The marginal revenue curve plots marginal revenue and quantity. For a monopolist, $P > MR$, so the marginal revenue curve must lie below the demand curve. (Note that when a demand curve is a straight line, the marginal revenue curve bisects the horizontal axis halfway between the origin and the point where the demand curve intersects the horizontal axis.)

EXHIBIT 3

The Monopolist's Profit-Maximizing Price and Quantity of Output

The monopolist produces the quantity of output (Q_1) at which $MR = MC$, and charges the highest price per unit at which this quantity of output can be sold (P_1). Notice that at the profit-maximizing quantity of output, price is greater than marginal cost, $P > MC$.

Some people argue that suggesting that a monopolist can take a loss is unrealistic. If the monopolist is the only seller in the industry, they maintain, it is guaranteed a profit. But even when a firm is the only seller of a product, it may not earn a profit. A monopolist cannot charge any price it wants for its good, but rather the highest price that the demand curve allows it to charge. In some instances, the highest price may be lower than the firm's average total costs (unit costs). If so, the monopolist incurs a loss, as shown in Exhibit 4(b).

EXHIBIT 4

Monopoly Profits and Losses

A monopoly seller is not guaranteed any profits. In (a), price is above average total cost at Q_1, the quantity of output at which $MR = MC$. Therefore, TR (the area $0P_1BQ_1$) is greater than TC (the area $0CAQ_1$), and profits equal the area CP_1BA. In (b), price is below average total cost at Q_1. Therefore, TR (the area $0P_1AQ_1$) is less than TC (the area $0CBQ_1$), and losses equal the area P_1CBA.

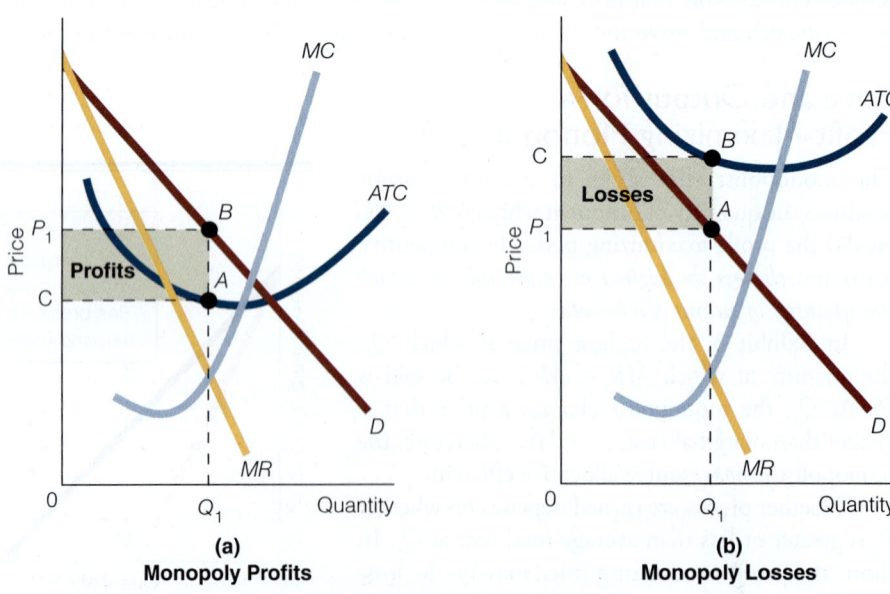

(a)
Monopoly Profits

(b)
Monopoly Losses

Comparing the Demand Curve in Perfect Competition with the Demand Curve in Monopoly

The perfectly competitive firm is a *price taker*; it has no control over the price of the product it sells. The monopoly firm is a *price searcher*; it has some control over the price of the product it sells. Essentially, what determines whether a firm is a price taker or a price searcher is the demand curve that it faces. The perfectly competitive firm faces a horizontal demand curve. The monopoly firm faces a downward-sloping demand curve. If a firm faces a horizontal (or flat) demand curve, then it is a price taker. If a firm faces a downward-sloping demand curve, then it is a price searcher. Let's remind ourselves what each demand curve implies about the firm's ability to control price. A horizontal (or flat) demand curve implies that the firm can sell its good at only *one price*: the price determined by the market. In other words, if the market-determined price is $10, then the perfectly competitive firm's demand curve is a horizontal line at $10. In contrast, a downward-sloping demand curve implies that the firm can sell its good at *different prices*. For example, it might sell 100 units at $12 per unit and 150 units at $11 per unit. In short, it "searches" for the best price among the many possible prices.

If a Firm Maximizes Revenue, Does It Automatically Maximize Profit Too?

Profit is the difference between total revenue (*TR*) and total cost (*TC*).

$$\text{Profit} = TR - TC$$

Since *TC* is the sum of total fixed costs (*TFC*) and total variable costs (*TVC*), we can rewrite our profit equation as:

$$\text{Profit} = TR - (TFC + TVC)$$

Maximizing profit is the same as maximizing total revenue under one condition: when *TVC* = 0. When *TVC* = 0, then *TVC* falls out of our profit equation and we are left with:

$$\text{Profit} = TR - TFC$$

Since *TFC* is constant as output increases, then a rise in *TR* will automatically increase profit by the same amount. To illustrate, if *TR* = $100 and *TFC* = $40, then profit is $60. If *TR* rises by $10 to $110, and *TFC* remains constant at $40, then profit rises to $70. The rise in *TR* is equal to the rise in profit: $10. Therefore, to maximize total revenue is to maximize profit.

Now change things a bit. Suppose *TVC* is not zero. We return to our profit equation of:

$$\text{Profit} = TR - (TFC + TVC)$$

Again, let *TR* = $100 and *TFC* = $40. But this time *TVC* = $20. It follows that profit is $40. Now if *TR* rises to $110, will profit again rise by $10, as it did in the previous example? Perhaps not, because what happens to profit depends on what happens not only to *TR*, but to *TVC* too. Suppose *TVC* rises to $37 as *TR* rises by $110. Now profit is $33. In other words, total revenue increased (from $100 to $110), but profit decreased (from $40 to $33).

Therefore, profit maximization is the same as revenue maximization only when there are no variable costs (i.e., when *TVC* = $0).

finding ECONOMICS

In the Price of Songs A musical artist is currently arguing with a few music company executives at BT Productions over the price of her next CD. She wants the CD priced lower than the music executives want to price it. Where is the economics?

The musical artist receives a royalty rate on total revenue: the bigger the total revenue is, the more income she earns. (A royalty rate of 10 percent applied to a total revenue of, say, $10 million is better than the same royalty rate applied to a total revenue of only $4 million.) In this setting, her objective is to choose a price that will maximize total revenue.

The situation is different for the music company. The company is interested in maximizing profit, not revenue. Maximizing revenue and maximizing profit are not the same thing as long as variable costs exist.

Exhibit 5 shows a demand curve and a marginal revenue curve for the CD. There are two marginal cost curves. The one for the music company (BT Productions) is positive and (we have assumed) constant. The other marginal cost curve is for the musical artist and is zero at all levels of output because the artist does not incur any costs of actually producing and selling the CD (this is the music company's job). Because the musical artist receives a royalty rate based on total revenue, she wants to maximize total revenue, which happens when $MR = 0$. Think about this for a moment: if MR is positive, then total revenue is rising because MR is *additional* revenue. When $MR = 0$, there is no additional revenue.

EXHIBIT 5

The Music Company and the Musical Artist Opt for Different Prices

The artist faces zero costs of producing and selling the CD; BT Productions, the music company, faces positive (and we assume) constant marginal costs. Both the artist and the music company may want to equate marginal revenue and marginal cost, but they do not have the same marginal cost. The artist wants Q_A CDs produced and sold at a price of P_A; the music company wants Q_{BT} CDs produced and sold at a price of P_{BT}.

Marginal revenue equals zero in Exhibit 5 at Q_A, which is also the point at which $MR = MC$ for the musical artist. The highest price (per unit) that this quantity can sell for is P_A. In other words, the musical artist wants the CD to have a price of P_A, the price that is best for her.

But the music company is better off producing Q_{BT}, where its MR equals its MC. The highest price (per unit) consistent with this quantity is P_{BT}. In other words, the best price for the music company is higher than the best price for the musical artist. ▲▲▲

PERFECT COMPETITION AND MONOPOLY

Because perfect competition and monopoly are at opposite ends of the (market structure) spectrum, there are major differences between them. In this section, we discuss those differences.

Price, Marginal Revenue, and Marginal Cost

Here are two key differences between perfect competition and monopoly:

1. For the perfectly competitive firm, $P = MR$; for the monopolist, $P > MR$. The perfectly competitive firm's demand curve *is* its marginal revenue curve; the monopolist's demand curve lies *above* its marginal revenue curve.

2. The perfectly competitive firm charges a price equal to marginal cost; the monopolist charges a price greater than marginal cost.

$$\text{Perfect competition: } P = MR \text{ and } P = MC$$
$$\text{Monopoly: } P > MR \text{ and } P > MC$$

Monopoly, Perfect Competition, and Consumers' Surplus

A monopoly firm differs from a perfectly competitive firm in terms of how much consumers' surplus buyers receive. To illustrate, Exhibit 6 shows a downward-sloping market demand curve, a downward-sloping marginal revenue curve, and a horizontal marginal cost (MC) curve. Although you are used to seeing upward-sloping marginal cost curves, nothing prevents marginal cost from being constant over some range of output. A horizontal MC curve simply means that marginal cost is constant. If the market in Exhibit 6 is perfectly competitive, the demand curve *is* the marginal revenue curve. Therefore, the

EXHIBIT 6

Monopoly, Perfect Competition, and Consumers' Surplus

If the market in the exhibit is perfectly competitive, the demand curve is the marginal revenue curve. The profit-maximizing output is Q_{PC} and price is P_{PC}. Consumers' surplus is the area $P_{PC}AB$. If the market is a monopoly market, the profit-maximizing output is Q_M and price is P_M. In this case, consumers' surplus is the area P_MAC. Consumers' surplus is greater in perfect competition than in monopoly; it is greater by the area $P_{PC}P_MCB$.

profit-maximizing output is Q_{PC} and the buyer will pay P_{PC} per unit of the good. Recall that consumers' surplus is the area under the demand curve and above the price. For the perfectly competitive firm, consumers' surplus is the area $P_{PC}AB$.[2]

In a monopoly market, the demand curve and the marginal revenue curve are different. The profit-maximizing output is where the MR curve intersects the MC curve; thus, the profit-maximizing output is Q_M, and the price the buyer pays is P_M. In the case of monopoly, consumers' surplus is P_MAC.

Obviously, consumers' surplus is greater in the perfectly competitive case than in the monopoly case by the area $P_{PC}P_MCB$. This is the loss in consumers' surplus due to monopolization.

Monopoly or Nothing?

Suppose you could push one of two buttons to determine the conditions under which a particular good is produced. If you push the first button, the good is produced under the conditions of perfect competition. If you push the second button, the good is produced under the conditions of monopoly. Which button would you push?

From a consumer's perspective, perfect competition would seem to be the better choice because it provides more output and a lower price than monopoly. In short, there is more consumers' surplus. Perfect competition would therefore seem to be superior to monopoly. But life doesn't always present a choice between perfect competition and monopoly. Sometimes it presents a choice between monopoly and nothing.

Exhibit 7 shows the demand curve (D) for a good, along with the relevant marginal revenue curve (MR) and two sets of MC and ATC curves. Assume that MC_1 and ATC_1 are the relevant cost curves. Because the MC_1 curve is so far above the MR curve, the two do not intersect. In other words, there is no profit-maximizing quantity of output for a firm to produce. Although there is demand for the particular good, the costs of producing it are so high that no firm will produce it. Consumers therefore receive no consumers' surplus from the purchase and consumption of the good.

But suppose a firm—a single firm—is able to lower costs to MC_2 and ATC_2. Now marginal cost is low enough for the firm to produce the good. The firm produces Q_M and charges a price of P_M. The area P_MAB is equal to consumers' surplus.

No doubt the firm producing this good and charging a price of P_M is a monopoly firm. However, consumers are better off having a monopoly firm produce the good than having no firm produce it. If no firm produces the good because costs are too high, consumers' surplus is zero. But when the monopoly firm produces the good, consumers' surplus is positive.

EXHIBIT 7

Monopoly or Nothing?

We start with the demand and marginal revenue curves and with $MC_1 = ATC_1$. Because cost is "so high," no firm produces the good. Later, a single firm figures out how to lower cost to $MC_2 = ATC_2$. This firm produces Q_M and charges the monopoly price of P_M per unit. Is monopoly preferable to no firm producing the good? From a consumer's perspective, the answer is yes. Consumers' surplus is zero when no firm produces the good, and consumers' surplus is area P_MAB when the monopoly firm produces the good.

---

2. The demand curve is downward sloping because we are looking at the market demand curve, not the firm's demand curve. All market demand curves are downward sloping.

So under certain conditions, a monopoly may be created in a market because a firm figures out a way to lower the cost of producing a good enough to make producing it worthwhile. Of course, once the monopoly firm exists, consumers would prefer that the good be produced under perfect competition than under monopoly conditions. But that is not always the relevant choice. Sometimes, the choice is between monopoly and nothing, and, when this is the choice, the consumers' surplus is greater with monopoly than it is with nothing.

THE CASE AGAINST MONOPOLY

Monopoly is often said to be inefficient in comparison with perfect competition. This section examines some of the shortcomings of monopoly.

The Deadweight Loss of Monopoly

Exhibit 8 shows demand, marginal revenue, marginal cost, and average total cost curves. For simplicity's sake, assume that the product is produced under constant cost conditions, so that marginal cost equals long-run average total cost. If the product is produced under perfect competition, output Q_{PC} is produced and is sold at a price of P_{PC}. At the competitive equilibrium output level, $P = MC$. If the product is produced under monopoly, output Q_M is produced and is sold at a price of P_M. At the monopoly equilibrium, $P > MC$.

Greater output is produced under perfect competition than under monopoly. The net value of the difference in these two output levels is said to be the **deadweight loss of monopoly**. In Exhibit 8, the value to buyers of increasing output from Q_M to Q_{PC} is equal to the maximum amount they would pay for this increase in output, designated by the area $Q_M CBQ_{PC}$. The costs that would have to be incurred to produce this additional output are designated by the area $Q_M DBQ_{PC}$. The difference between the two is the triangle *DCB, the amount buyers value the additional output over and above the costs of producing the additional output.* It is the loss attached to not producing the competitive quantity of output. The triangle *DCB* is referred to as the *deadweight loss triangle.*

Therefore, monopoly produces a quantity of output that is too small in comparison to the quantity of output produced in perfect competition. This difference in output results in a welfare loss to society.

Deadweight Loss of Monopoly
The net value (value to buyers over and above costs to suppliers) of the difference between the competitive quantity of output (where P = MC) and the monopoly quantity of output (where P > MC); the loss of not producing the competitive quantity of output.

Deadweight Loss and Rent Seeking as Costs of Monopoly

The monopolist produces Q_M, and the perfectly competitive firm produces the higher output level Q_{PC}. The deadweight loss of monopoly is the triangle (*DCB*) between these two levels of output. Rent-seeking activity is directed to obtaining the monopoly profits, represented by the area $P_{PC}P_M CD$. Rent seeking is a socially wasteful activity because resources are expended to transfer income rather than to produce goods and services.

Arnold Harberger was the first economist who tried to determine the actual size of the deadweight loss cost of monopoly in the manufacturing sector of the U.S. economy. He estimated the loss to be a small percentage of the economy's total output. Additional empirical work by other economists puts the figure at approximately 1 percent of total output.

Rent Seeking

Sometimes, individuals and groups try to influence public policy in the hope of redistributing (transferring) income from others to themselves. In Exhibit 8, the market produces Q_{PC} output and charges a price of P_{PC}. Suppose, however, that one of the, say, 100 firms currently producing some of Q_{PC} asks the government to grant it a monopoly; that is, firm A asks the government to prevent the 99 other firms from competing with it. Consider the benefit for firm A of becoming a monopolist (a single seller). Currently, it is earning zero economic profit because it is selling at a price that equals ATC. If it becomes a monopolist, though, it will earn profits equal to the area $P_{PC}P_MCD$ in Exhibit 8.

These profits are the result of a *transfer* from buyers to the monopolist. To see this, consider what happens to consumers' surplus. If the market in Exhibit 8 is perfectly competitive, consumers' surplus is equal to the area $P_{PC}AB$; if the market is monopolized, consumers' surplus is equal to the area P_MAC. The difference is the area $P_{PC}P_MCB$, the area that represents the loss in consumers' surplus if the market is monopolized. Part of this area—$P_{PC}P_MCD$—is transferred to the monopolist in terms of profits. *In other words, if the market is monopolized, part of the consumers' surplus that is lost to buyers becomes profits for the monopolist.* (The other part is the deadweight loss of monopoly, identified by the deadweight loss triangle.)

If firm A tries to get the government to transfer income in the form of consumers' surplus from buyers to itself, it is undertaking a *transfer-seeking activity.* In economics, such activities are usually called **rent seeking**. In other words, firm A is rent seeking.[3]

Economist Gordon Tullock has made the point that rent-seeking behavior is individually rational but socially wasteful. To see why, suppose the profits in Exhibit 8 (the area $P_{PC}P_MCD$) are equal to $10 million. Firm A wants the $10 million in profits; so it asks the government for a monopoly because it wants the government to prevent the 99 other firms from competing with it.

Firm A will not get its monopoly privilege simply by asking for it. The firm will have to spend money and time to convince government officials that it should give the firm this monopoly privilege. It will have to hire lobbyists, take politicians and other government officials to dinner, and perhaps make donations to some of them. Firm A will have to spend resources to get what it wants, and all the resources firm A uses to try to bring about a transfer from buyers to itself, says Tullock, are wasted. Those resources cannot be used to produce shoes, computers, television sets, and many other things that people would like to buy. The resources are instead used to try to transfer income from one party to another, not to produce more goods and services.

Society would be very different if no one produced anything but only invested time and money in rent seeking. For example, Jones would try to get what is Matsui's, Matsui would try to get what is Kahn's, and Kahn would try to get what is Patel's. No one would produce anything; everyone would simply spend time and money trying to get what currently belongs to someone else. In this world, no one would produce the food, the computers, and the cars.

Tullock makes the point that the resource cost of rent seeking should be added to the deadweight loss of monopoly. This addition, according to Tullock, makes the overall cost of monopoly to society higher than anyone initially thought.

Rent Seeking
Actions of individuals and groups who spend resources to influence public policy in the hope of redistributing (transferring) income to themselves from others.

---

3. The word "rent" (used in this context) often confuses people. In everyday life, "rent" refers to the payment for an apartment. In economics, rent, or more formally, economic rent, is a payment in excess of opportunity cost. The term "rent seeking" was introduced by economist Anne Krueger in her article "The Political Economy of the Rent-Seeking Society," *American Economic Review* 64 (June 1974): 291–303.

ⓣhinking Like AN ECONOMIST

No $10 Bills Here is a joke that tells us something about how economists think. Two economists are walking down the street. One sees a $10 bill lying on the sidewalk and asks the other, "Isn't that a $10 bill?" "Obviously not," says the other. "If it were, someone would have already picked it up." Specifically, economists believe that an opportunity for gain won't last long because someone will grab it—quickly. By the time you come along, it's gone.

Apply this thinking to what Gordon Tullock says about monopoly. As a seller, being a monopolist is better than being a competitive firm. Like a $10 bill lying on the sidewalk, a monopoly position is worth something. Just as people will pick up a $10 bill on the sidewalk, they will try to become monopolists. In terms of rent seeking, to which Tullock first called our attention, just as people will bend down to pick up the $10 bill, so will they invest resources to capture the monopoly rents. No opportunity for gain is likely to be ignored. ●●●

X-Inefficiency

Economist Harvey Leibenstein maintains that the monopolist is not under pressure to produce its good at the lowest possible cost; it can produce its good above the lowest possible unit cost and still survive. Certainly, the monopolist benefits if it can and does lower its costs, but it doesn't have to in order to survive (with the proviso that average total costs cannot be higher than price). When the monopolist operates at a cost that is higher than the lowest possible, Leibenstein refers to the organizational slack that is directly tied to this as X-inefficiency.

Obtaining accurate estimates of X-inefficiency is difficult, but, whatever its magnitude, forces are at work to mitigate it. For example, if a market monopoly is being run inefficiently, other people, realizing this, may attempt to buy the monopoly and to lower costs in order to make higher profits.

> **X-Inefficiency**
> The increase in costs due to the organizational slack in a monopoly resulting from the lack of competitive pressure to push costs down to their lowest possible level.

PRICE DISCRIMINATION

The monopoly seller may sell all units of its product for the same price, that is, be a single-price monopolist. However, under certain conditions, a monopolist could practice price discrimination, which occurs when the seller charges different prices for the product it sells and the price differences do not reflect cost differences.

Types of Price Discrimination

There are three types of price discrimination:

- *Perfect price discrimination:* Suppose a monopolist produces and sells 1,000 units of good X. It sells each unit separately, charging the highest price that each consumer would be willing to pay for the product rather than go without it. This practice is perfect price discrimination, sometimes called *discrimination among units.*

- *Second-degree price discrimination:* If a firm charges a uniform price per unit for one specific quantity, a lower price for an additional quantity, and so on, the monopolist practices second-degree price discrimination, sometimes called *discrimination among quantities.* For example, the monopolist might sell the first 10 units for $10 each, the next 20 units for $9 each, and so on.

- *Third-degree price discrimination:* If it charges different prices in various markets or charges different prices to various segments of the buying population, the monopolist practices third-degree price discrimination, sometimes called *discrimination among buyers.* For example, if your local pharmacy charges senior citizens lower prices for medicine than it charges nonsenior citizens, it practices third-degree price discrimination.

> **Price Discrimination**
> A price structure in which the seller charges different prices for the product it sells and the price differences do not reflect cost differences.
>
> **Perfect Price Discrimination**
> A price structure in which the seller charges the highest price that each consumer is willing to pay for the product rather than go without it.
>
> **Second-Degree Price Discrimination**
> A price structure in which the seller charges a uniform price per unit for one specific quantity, a lower price for an additional quantity, and so on.
>
> **Third-Degree Price Discrimination**
> A price structure in which the seller charges different prices in different markets or charges different prices to various segments of the buying population.

Why a Monopolist Wants to Price Discriminate

Suppose the following units of a product can be sold at varying maximum prices: first unit, $10; second unit, $9; third unit, $8; fourth unit, $7. If the monopolist wants to sell 4 units, and it charges the same price for each unit (it is a single-price monopolist), its total revenue is $28 ($7 × 4). If the monopolist practices perfect price discrimination, it charges $10 for the first unit, $9 for the second unit, $8 for the third unit, and $7 for the fourth unit. Its total revenue is $34 ($10 + $9 + $8 + $7). A comparison of total revenues with and without price discrimination explains why the monopolist would want to price discriminate. A perfectly price-discriminating monopolist receives the maximum price for each unit of the good it sells; a single-price monopolist does not.

For the monopolist who practices perfect price discrimination, price equals marginal revenue, $P = MR$. To illustrate, when the monopolist sells its second unit for $9 (having sold the first unit for $10), its total revenue is $19—or its marginal revenue is $9, which is equal to price.

Conditions of Price Discrimination

Why the monopolist would want to price discriminate is obvious. However, to price discriminate, the following conditions must hold:

1. *The seller must exercise some control over price; that is, it must be a price searcher.* If the seller is not a price searcher (if it is a price taker), it has no control over price and therefore cannot sell a good at different prices to different buyers.

2. *The seller must be able to distinguish among buyers who are willing to pay different prices.* Unless the seller can distinguish among buyers who would pay different prices, it cannot price discriminate. After all, how would it know whom to charge the higher or lower prices?

3. *Reselling the good to other buyers must be impossible or too costly.* Arbitrage, or buying low and selling high, must not be possible. If a buyer can resell the good, price discrimination is not possible because buyers of the good at a lower price will simply resell it to other buyers for a price lower than the original seller's higher price. In time, no one will pay the higher price.

Arbitrage
Buying a good at a low price and selling it for a higher price.

About Price Discrimination: Does Your Lower Price Mean My Higher Price?

Some people argue that if a firm charges one person $40 for its product and charges another person only $33, the first person is paying a higher price so that the second person can pay a lower price. This is not the case. Suppose the maximum price O'Neill will pay for good X is $40, and the maximum price Stevens will pay is $33. If a monopolist can and does perfectly price discriminate, it charges O'Neill $40 and charges Stevens $33.

O'Neill is not, however, somehow paying the higher price so that Stevens can pay the lower price. Consider whether the monopolist would have charged O'Neill a price under $40 if Stevens's maximum price had been $39 instead of $33. It probably would not have. Why should it when it could have received O'Neill's maximum price of $40?

The point is that the perfectly price-discriminating monopolist tries to get the highest price from each customer, irrespective of what other customers pay. In short, the price O'Neill is charged is independent of the price Stevens pays.

Moving to $P = MC$ Through Price Discrimination

We know that the perfectly competitive firm exhibits resource allocative efficiency; it produces the quantity of output at which $P = MC$. We also know that the single-price

Why Do District Attorneys Plea-Bargain?

© IMAGE COPYRIGHT JUNIAL ENTER-PRISES, 2010. USED UNDER LICENSE FROM SHUTTERSTOCK.COM

District attorneys sometimes offer the accused a chance to plead to a lesser charge in return for providing information about a crime or for agreeing to testify against someone. In short, the district attorneys will plea-bargain.

To some people, a district attorney who plea-bargains is similar to a seller who price discriminates. Suppose Smith and Jones have committed the same crime. The district attorney has the same type and amount of evidence against each person, and the chance of a successful prosecution is approximately the same in each case. A successful prosecution will end in a prison sentence of 25 years.

The district attorney offers Smith a plea bargain. In exchange for Smith's testimony against Brown, who is someone the DA's office has been after for a long time, Smith will be charged with a lesser crime and will serve only five years in prison. Thus, Smith can pay a smaller price for his crime than Jones must pay. In other words, each person commits the same crime, and each has an equal chance of being successfully prosecuted for that crime, but Smith (if he accepts the plea bargain) will serve five years in prison and Jones will serve 25 years.

Do district attorneys want to plea-bargain for a reason analogous to why sellers want to price discriminate?[4] A seller wants to price discriminate because it raises total revenue without affecting costs. For example, $10 is the highest price at which the first unit of a good can be sold, $9 for the second unit, $8 for the third unit, and $7 for the fourth unit. A single-price monopolist that wants to sell 4 units of the good charges a price of $7 per unit and earns total revenue of $28. But a perfectly price-discriminating monopolist charges the highest price per unit and gains total revenue of $34. In other words, price discrimination leads to higher total revenue.

District attorneys do not want to maximize total revenue, but they may want to maximize the number of successfully prosecuted crimes given certain budget constraints. Just as price discrimination leads to higher total revenue, plea bargaining may lead to more successfully prosecuted crimes. Smith and Jones committed the same crime, and, without a plea bargain, they both go to prison for 25 years. But if the DA offers Smith five years in return for help in sending Brown to prison, then, because of the plea bargain, three crimes are successfully prosecuted: the crimes committed by Smith, Jones, and Brown.

Finally, just as certain conditions have to be met before a seller can price discriminate, certain conditions have to be satisfied before district attorneys can plea-bargain successfully.

To price discriminate, a seller must exercise some control over the price of the product sold. To plea-bargain, a district attorney has to exercise some control over the sentence for the accused. In reality, district attorneys do exercise some control over sentences because they largely control the charges they bring. If they reduce the charges (say, from murder to manslaughter), they automatically affect the sentence.

A seller who price discriminates has to be able to distinguish among customers who are willing to pay different prices for the good sold. Similarly, a district attorney has to be able to distinguish among accused persons who do and do not have something to sell to the authorities. District attorneys seem to be able to do this. In many cases, the accused person who has something to sell will say so.

Finally, for price discrimination to exist, arbitrage has to be impossible or too costly. Obviously, reselling a plea bargain is not possible.

---

4. Be careful: We are not saying that a plea bargain is an act of price discrimination, broadly defined. We are saying that why sellers want to price discriminate and why district attorneys want to plea-bargain have certain similarities. Later in the feature, we explain that just as certain conditions need to be met to price discriminate, certain conditions need to be met for district attorneys to offer plea bargains and that there seems to be a rough similarity between the two sets of conditions.

monopolist produces the quantity of output at which $P > MC$, that is, it produces an inefficient level of output. But does the monopolist, which can and does practice perfect price discrimination, also produce an inefficient level of output?

The answer is no. For a perfectly price-discriminating monopolist, $P = MR$ (as is the case for the perfectly competitive firm). It follows that when the perfectly price-discriminating monopolist produces the quantity of output at which $MR = MC$, it automatically produces the quantity at which $P = MC$. In short, the perfectly price-discriminating monopolist and the perfectly competitive firm both exhibit resource allocative efficiency.

In part (a) of Exhibit 9, the perfectly competitive firm produces where $P = MC$. In part (b), the single-price monopolist produces where $P > MC$. In part (c), the perfectly price-discriminating monopolist produces where $P = MC$.

There is one important difference between the perfectly competitive firm and the perfectly price-discriminating monopolist. Although both produce where $P = MC$, the perfectly competitive firm charges the same price for each unit of the good it sells, and the perfectly price-discriminating monopolist charges a different price for each unit it sells.

Coupons and Price Discrimination

Third-degree price discrimination, or discrimination among buyers, is sometimes employed by means of cents-off coupons. (Third-degree price discrimination exists if a seller sells the same product at different prices to different segments of the population.)

One of the conditions of price discrimination is that the seller has to be able to distinguish among customers who are willing to pay different prices. For example, some sellers think that people who value their time highly are willing to pay a higher price for a product than people who do not. Sellers argue that people who place a high value on their time want to economize on the shopping time connected with the purchase. If sellers want to

---

EXHIBIT 9

Comparison of a Perfectly Competitive Firm, Single-Price Monopolist, and Perfectly Price-Discriminating Monopolist

For both the perfectly competitive firm and the perfectly price-discriminating monopolist,

$P = MR$ and the demand curve is the marginal revenue curve. Both produce where $P = MC$. The single-price monopolist, however, produces where $P > MC$ because for it, $P > MR$ and its demand curve lies above its marginal revenue curve. One difference

between the perfectly competitive firm and the perfectly price-discriminating monopolist is that the former charges the same price for each unit of the good it sells and the latter charges a different price for each unit of the good it sells.

(a)
Perfectly Competitive Firm

(b)
Single-Price Monopolist

(c)
Perfectly Price-Discriminating Monopolist

Do Colleges and Universities Price Discriminate?

Many colleges and universities practice price discrimination. For example, consider the university that gives out student or financial aid. The student aid is nothing more than a reduction in the tuition a student pays. As an example, University X states that it will give a low-income student, if admitted, $10,000 in student aid. So, if the tuition at the university is, say, $15,000, the student ends up paying only $5,000. The student with a high income does not get the student aid and therefore pays $15,000 upon admission. Even though the cost to the university to educate each student is the same, the students pay different tuition prices.

Another example is the university that offers a scholarship to an academic high achiever or to a star athlete (just coming out of high school). To either or both, the university offers a scholarship, which lowers the tuition the person pays.

If the universities price discriminate, they must meet all the conditions necessary for price discrimination:

- *The seller must be a price searcher*. First, universities are price searchers; they exercise some control over the tuition they charge.

In other words, universities can lower tuition and sell more or raise tuition and sell less.

- *The seller must be able to distinguish among buyers who would be willing to pay different prices*. Universities can distinguish among students (customers) who would be willing to pay different prices. For example, the student with few universities seeking him would probably be willing to pay more than the student with many options.

- *Reselling the good to other buyers must be impossible or too costly*. The service the university sells cannot be resold to someone else. For example, reselling an economics lecture is difficult. You cold, of course, tell someone what was covered in the lecture, perhaps for a small payment or a promise to do the same for you at a later date. But this is like telling someone about a movie. Reselling something that is consumed on the premises is often difficult or impossible.

Universities meet all three requirements.

---

price discriminate between these two types of customers—charging more to customers who value time more and charging less to customers who value time less—they must determine the category into which each of their customers falls.

If you were a seller, how would you go about this? Many real-world sellers place cents-off coupons in newspapers and magazines. They hypothesize that people who place a relatively low value on their time are willing to spend it clipping and sorting coupons. People who place a relatively high value on their time are not. In effect, price discrimination works much like the following in, say, a grocery store:

1. The posted price for all products is the same for all customers.

2. Both Linda and Josh put product X in their shopping carts.

3. When Linda gets to the checkout counter, the clerk asks, "Do you have any coupons today?" Linda says no. She is therefore charged the posted price for all products, including X.

4. When Josh gets to the checkout counter, the clerk asks, "Do you have any coupons today?" Josh says yes and gives the clerk a coupon for product X. Josh pays a lower price for it than Linda pays.

Thus, one of the uses of the cents-off coupon is to enable the seller to charge a higher price to one group of customers than to another group. (We say one of the uses because cents-off coupons are also used to induce customers to try a product.)

economics 24/7

If I Want ESPN, Why Am I Buying MSNBC Too?

Cable companies often bundle television and cable networks; that is, they include a number of television and cable networks in a package and offer them as a package. The basic cable package, for example, includes a number of networks—such as NBC, CBS, ABC, ESPN, MSNBC, Fox News, QVC, Bravo, Lifetime, and so on. Some people have asked, "Why do I have to pay for something I don't want? Why can't I buy only the channels I want to watch?"

That's a good question, and it doesn't come up in all contexts. For example, in the grocery store you don't find that milk, cereal, and raisins are packaged together (or bundled). So why is bundling used in some market settings but not in all of them?

One answer is that bundling is more likely when the marginal costs of delivering a good or service are low. Providing a new customer with a channel that many other customers already receive doesn't cost the cable company much in additional (marginal) cost. Once a customer has selected one cable channel to receive, it doesn't cost the cable company much to add other channels. Therefore, bundling is more common when the things being bundled have low marginal cost.

To understand why a company would want to bundle, suppose we have two cable customers, Hannah and Mia. Hannah places a value of $8 (a month) on having the ESPN channel and a value of $3 on having MSNBC. Mia places a value of $7 on having MSNBC and only $4 on ESPN. If the cable company sells each channel separately, and charges

the same price per channel per customer, it will likely charge $7 for ESPN (the highest price Mia is willing to pay) and $3 for MSNBC (the highest price Hannah is willing to pay). At these prices, both Hannah and Mia will buy both channels ($10 per person), and the cable company will receive a total revenue of $20 from the two customers.

Or the cable company can bundle the two channels and charge a price that makes it worthwhile for the two customers to buy the bundle. This price is $10.99 because $10.99 is less than the $11 value that each customer places on having the two channels. Now total revenue for the cable company is $21.98. In other words, bundling brings about a higher total revenue for the cable company (and not much more in total costs, if any at all). In the end, the cable company's profits rise.

One last point: Often the customer's intuition is that companies bundle in order to force customers to buy something they don't want to buy. Economist George Stigler questions that intuition. He argues that if a customer did not want one of the bundled goods, it would be cheaper for the company to leave out the unwanted good from the bundle. To illustrate, suppose a customer values good A at $10 and good B at $0. The highest price the company can get for bundled goods A and B is $10 because the customer won't pay more than $10 just because a worthless good was added to the bundle. Why, then, add good B to the bundle, especially if doing so incurs marginal cost to producing and delivering an additional unit of good B? It is better to simply charge $10 for good A.

finding ECONOMICS

At a Car Dealership Blake is shopping for a new car. At every dealership he has visited, the salesperson asked him what he does for a living. Where is the economics?

Think price discrimination. One of the conditions for price discrimination is that the seller must be able to distinguish among buyers who are willing to pay different prices. Willingness to pay is, of course, not the same as ability to pay, but the difference might not prevent the salesperson from thinking that the two are strongly correlated. The salespersons might be asking Blake what he does for a living in order to get some idea of what he can pay for the car. ▲▲▲

Buying a Computer and Getting a Printer for $100 Less Than the Retail Price

Some computer companies offer a rebate on a printer if you first buy a computer. In other words, buy the computer for $1,400 and then get $100 off the price of a printer that sells for $250. Instead of paying $1,650 for a computer and printer, you pay $1,550.

But at the time of purchase, you pay $1,650, not $1,550. Afterward, you can submit a rebate-request form online for the $100 rebate. So you pay $1,650, fill out the form, submit it, and get the $100 rebate.

Now the computer company could do things differently. It could certainly discount the computer plus printer at the time of purchase; that is, ask you to pay only $1,550 at the time of purchase. That way there would be no rebate form to fill out and to process, and no rebate check to send to the customer. But the company does not do things this way. Why not?

The answer has to do with price discrimination. The company will end up charging some customers $1,550 and other customers $1,650 for the computer and printer. It charges the lower price to the customers who submit the rebate form. It charges the higher price to the customers who do not submit the form.

By offering the $100 rebate, the company is effectively separating customers according to the value they place on their time. (See "Coupons and Price Discrimination.") Some sellers think that people who value their time more will pay a higher price for a product than those who value their time less. The company can separate those customers by offering a price reduction in the form of a rebate and then by waiting to see who requests the rebate. To those who request it, you give the rebate. They are the ones who aren't as willing to pay as much for the product as others.

SELF-TEST

1. What are some of the costs, or shortcomings, of monopoly?

2. What is the deadweight loss of monopoly?

3. Why must a seller be a price searcher (among other things) before he can price discriminate?

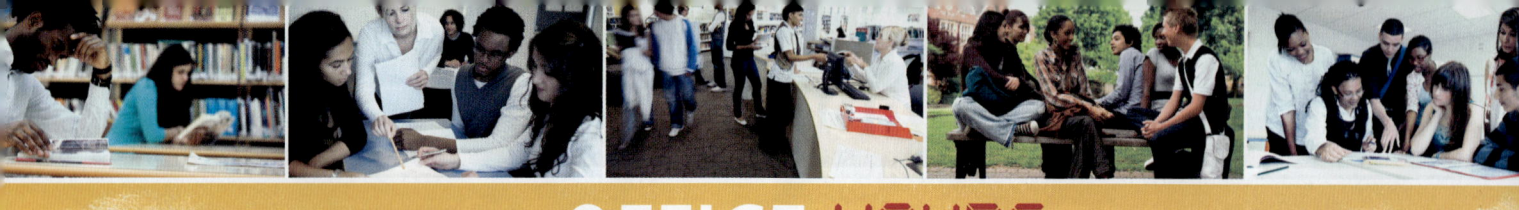

OFFICE HOURS

"Does the Single-Price Monopolist Lower Price Only on the Additional Unit?"

STUDENT:

You said that a single-price monopolist has to lower its price to sell an additional unit of the good it produces. Does this mean that it can sell the first unit of a good for, say, $20, but that if it wants to sell a second unit, it has to lower the price to, say, $19?

INSTRUCTOR:

I would say things a little differently. If the monopoly firm wants to sell one unit, it charges $20, but if it wants to sell two units, it must charge $19 for each of the two units.

STUDENT:

How is what you said different from what I said?

INSTRUCTOR:

I spoke of two units instead of the second unit.

STUDENT:

I don't see the critical difference.

INSTRUCTOR:

Your statement made it sound as though the monopolist earned $20 on the first unit and $19 on the second unit, but this is not how things work for a single-price monopolist. A single-price monopolist has to charge the same price for *every unit* of the good it sells. In other words, if it sells 100 units, it sells each of the 100 units for the same price. It doesn't sell the first unit for $20 and the second unit for $19 and so on.

STUDENT:

But I'm still confused. We know that a monopoly firm has to lower its price to sell an additional unit; so why can't we just say that it has to lower price to sell the *second* unit?

CHAPTER SUMMARY

THE THEORY OF MONOPOLY

- The theory of monopoly is built on three assumptions: (1) There is one seller. (2) The single seller sells a product for which there are no close substitutes. (3) The barriers to entry into the industry are extremely high.
- High barriers to entry may take the form of legal barriers (public franchise, patent, government license), economies of scale, or exclusive ownership of a scarce resource.

MONOPOLY PRICING AND OUTPUT

- The profit-maximizing monopolist produces the quantity of output at which $MR = MC$ and charges the highest price per unit at which this quantity of output can be sold.
- For the single-price monopolist, $P > MR$; therefore, its demand curve lies above its marginal revenue curve.

- The single-price monopolist sells its output at a price higher than its marginal cost, $P > MC$, and therefore is *not* resource allocative efficient.
- Consider a perfectly competitive market and a monopoly market, each with the same demand and marginal cost curves. Consumers' surplus is greater in the perfectly competitive market.

RENT SEEKING

- Activity directed at competing for and obtaining transfers is referred to as rent seeking. From society's perspective, rent seeking is a socially wasteful activity. People use resources to bring about a transfer of income from others to themselves instead of producing goods and services.

Because it has to lower price on the previous (the first) unit too if it wants to sell two units. To illustrate, suppose the price of a good is $20 and at this price the quantity demanded is 1 unit. At a price of $19, the quantity demanded rises to 2 units. What you said implied that the firm would sell the first unit for $20. Then, with that transaction done, it considers whether it wants to sell an additional unit (the second unit). If it does, it charges $19 for it.

That's not the way things happen. The firm—from the beginning, before any units of the good have been sold—has to decide whether it wants to sell 1 unit or 2. If it wants to sell only 1 unit, it charges $20. If it wants to sell 2 units, it sells each unit for $19.

STUDENT:

I think I understand now. That's what you must have meant in class when you said that the word "additional" doesn't refer to a sequence of events, as in sell the first unit, then sell the additional unit (the second unit), and so on. Instead, it is sell 1 unit at $4 *or* sell two units at $3 each, *or* sell three units at $2 each, and so on.

INSTRUCTOR:

Yes, that's correct.

POINTS TO REMEMBER

1. A single-price monopolist must lower its price to sell an additional unit of the good it produces.
2. The lower price (necessary to sell an additional unit) applies to the additional unit and *to all units that preceded it.*

PRICE DISCRIMINATION

- Price discrimination occurs when a seller charges different prices for its product and the price differences are not due to cost differences.
- Before a seller can price discriminate, certain conditions must hold: (1) The seller must be a price searcher. (2) The seller must be able to distinguish among customers who are willing to pay different prices. (3) Reselling the good to others must be impossible or too costly for a buyer.
- A seller that practices perfect price discrimination (charges the maximum price for each unit of product sold) sells the quantity of output at which $P = MC$. It exhibits resource allocative efficiency.
- The single-price monopolist is said to produce too little output because it produces less than would be produced under perfect competition. This is not the case for a perfectly price-discriminating monopolist.

KEY TERMS AND CONCEPTS

Monopoly
Public Franchise
Natural Monopoly
Price Searcher

Deadweight Loss of Monopoly
Rent Seeking
X-Inefficiency

Price Discrimination
Perfect Price Discrimination
Second-Degree Price Discrimination

Third-Degree Price Discrimination
Arbitrage

QUESTIONS AND PROBLEMS

1. Occasionally, students accuse their instructors, rightly or wrongly, of practicing grade discrimination. These students claim that the instructor "charges" some students a higher price for a given grade than he or she charges other students (by requiring some students to do more or better work). Unlike price discrimination, grade discrimination involves no money. Discuss the similarities and differences between the two types of discrimination. Which do you prefer less or perhaps dislike more? Why?

2. Is there a deadweight loss if a firm produces the quantity of output at which price equals marginal cost? Explain.

3. Rent seeking is individually rational but socially wasteful. Explain.

4. When a single-price monopolist maximizes profits, price is greater than marginal cost. In other words, buyers are willing to pay more for additional units of output than the units cost to produce. Given this, why doesn't the monopolist produce more?

5. A perfectly competitive firm will produce more output and charge a lower (per-unit) price than a single-price monopoly firm. Do you agree or disagree with this statement? Explain your answer.

6. Because the monopolist is a single seller of a product with no close substitutes, can it obtain any price for its good that it wants? Why or why not?

7. Under what condition will a monopoly firm incur losses?

8. The perfectly competitive firm exhibits resource allocative efficiency ($P = MC$), but the single-price monopolist does not. What is the reason for this difference?

9. Fast-food stores often charge higher prices for their products in high-crime areas than they charge in low-crime areas. Is this an act of price discrimination? Why or why not?

10. In general, coupons are more common on small-ticket items than they are on big-ticket items. Explain why.

11. A firm maximizes its total revenue. Does it automatically maximize its profit too? Why or why not?

12. For many years in California, car washes would advertise Ladies' Day. On one day during the week, a woman could have her car washed for a price lower than what a man would pay. Some people argued that this was a form of sexual discrimination. A California court accepted the argument and ruled that car washes could no longer have a Ladies' Day. Do you think this was a case of sexual discrimination or price discrimination? Explain your answer.

13. Make a list of market monopolies and a list of government monopolies. Which list is longer? Why do you think this is so?

14. Make a list of real-world price discrimination practices. Do they meet the conditions posited for price discrimination?

WORKING WITH NUMBERS AND GRAPHS

1. Draw a graph that shows a monopoly firm incurring losses.

2. A monopoly firm is currently earning positive economic profit, and the owner decides to sell it. He asks for a price that takes into account the economic profit. Explain and diagrammatically show what this does to the average total cost (ATC) curve of the firm.

3. Suppose a single-price monopolist sells its output (Q_1) at P_1. Then it raises its price to P_2, and its output falls to Q_2. In terms of Ps and Qs, what does marginal revenue equal?

Use the following figure to answer questions 4–6.

4. If the market is perfectly competitive, what does profit equal?

5. If the market is a monopoly market, what does profit equal?

6. Redraw the figure and label consumers' surplus when the market is perfectly competitive and when it is monopolized.

CHAPTER 25

MONOPOLISTIC COMPETITION, OLIGOPOLY, AND GAME THEORY

© ISTOCKPHOTO.COM/IIOFOTO

Introduction How do firms in a market act toward one other? Are they fiercely competitive, much as runners in a race to the finish line where only one can be the winner? Or do firms act like people strolling in a park on a warm spring day, without a care in the world and certainly without competition on their minds? As you read this chapter, keep these two images in mind. Also keep two words in mind: competition and collusion. This chapter is about both.

THE THEORY OF MONOPOLISTIC COMPETITION

The theory of monopolistic competition is built on three assumptions:

1. *There are many sellers and buyers.* This assumption holds for perfect competition too. For this reason, you might think the monopolistic competitor should be a price taker, but it is a price searcher, basically because of the next assumption.

2. *Each firm (in the industry) produces and sells a slightly differentiated product.* Differences among the products may be due to brand names, packaging, location, credit terms connected with the sale of the product, the friendliness of the salespeople, and so forth. Product differentiation may be real or imagined. For example, aspirin may be aspirin, but if some people view a name brand aspirin (such as Bayer) as better than a generic brand, product differentiation exists.

3. *Entry and exit are easy.* Monopolistic competition resembles perfect competition in this respect. There are no barriers to entry and exit, legal or otherwise. Examples of monopolistic competition include retail clothing, computer software, restaurants, and service stations.

Monopolistic Competition
A theory of market structure based on three assumptions: many sellers and buyers, firms producing and selling slightly differentiated products, and easy entry and exit.

The Monopolistic Competitor's Demand Curve

The perfectly competitive firm has many rivals, all producing the same good, and so the good it produces has an endless number of substitutes. The elasticity of demand for its product is extremely high—so high, in fact, that the demand curve it faces is horizontal (for all practical purposes).

The monopoly firm has practically no rivals, and it produces a good that has no substitutes. The elasticity of demand for its product is low, as reflected by its downward-sloping demand curve.

The monopolistic competitor, like the perfectly competitive firm, has many rivals. But unlike the perfectly competitive firm, its rivals do not sell exactly the same product as the monopolistic competitor sells. Because its product has substitutes, but not perfect ones, the elasticity of demand for its product is not as great as that of the perfectly competitive firm. Nor does its demand curve look like the one faced by the perfectly competitive firm. The monopolistic competitor's demand curve is not horizontal; it is downward sloping.

The Relationship Between Price and Marginal Revenue for a Monopolistic Competitor

Because a monopolistic competitor faces a downward-sloping demand curve, it has to lower price to sell an additional unit of the good it produces. (It is a price searcher.) For example, let's say that it can sell 3 units at $10 each but that it has to lower its price to $9 to sell 4 units. Its marginal revenue is therefore $6 (total revenue at 3 units is $30, and total revenue at 4 units is $36), which is below its price of $9. Thus, for the monopolistic competitor $P > MR$.

Output, Price, and Marginal Cost for the Monopolistic Competitor

The monopolistic competitive firm is the same as both the perfectly competitive firm and the monopoly firm in one regard: it produces the quantity of output at which $MR = MC$. In Exhibit 1, the firm produces q_1. For this quantity, the monopolistic competitor charges the highest price it can charge. This is P_1 in the exhibit.

For the monopolistic competitor, $P > MR$. Because the monopolistic competitor produces the quantity of output at which $MR = MC$, it must produce a level of output at which price is greater than marginal cost, $P > MC$. This is obvious in Exhibit 1.

The Monopolistic Competitive Firm's Output and Price

The monopolistic competitor produces that quantity of output for which $MR = MC$. This is q_1 in the exhibit. It charges the highest price consistent with this quantity, which is P_1.

Will There Be Profits in the Long Run?

If the firms in a monopolistic competitive market are currently earning profits, such as the firm in Exhibit 1, most likely they will not continue to earn profits in the long run. The assumption of easy entry and exit precludes this possibility. If firms in the industry are earning profits, new firms will enter the industry and reduce the demand that each firm faces. In other words, the demand curve for each firm may shift to the left. Eventually, competition will reduce economic profits to zero in the long run, as shown for the monopolistic competitive firm in Exhibit 2.

Note, however, that the answer to the question of whether firms will continue to earn profits in the long run was "most likely" they won't, instead of no. In monopolistic competition, new firms usually produce a *close substitute* for the product of existing firms rather than the *identical* one. In some instances, this difference may be enough to upset the zero economic profit condition in the long run. An existing firm may differentiate its product sufficiently in the minds of buyers such that it continues to earn profits, even though new firms enter the industry and compete with it.

Firms that try to differentiate their products from those of other sellers in ways other than price are said to be engaged in *nonprice competition.* This type of competition may take the form of advertising or of trying to establish a well-respected brand name, among other efforts. For example, soft drink companies' advertising often tries to stress the uniqueness of their product. In the past, Dr. Pepper has been advertised as "the unusual one," 7-Up as "the uncola," Wheaties as the "breakfast of champions," and Budweiser as the "king of beers." Apple has a well-respected name in personal computers, Bayer in aspirin, Marriott in hotels. Such well-respected names sometimes sufficiently differentiate products in the minds of buyers so that short-run profits are not easily, or completely, eliminated by the entry of new firms into the industry.

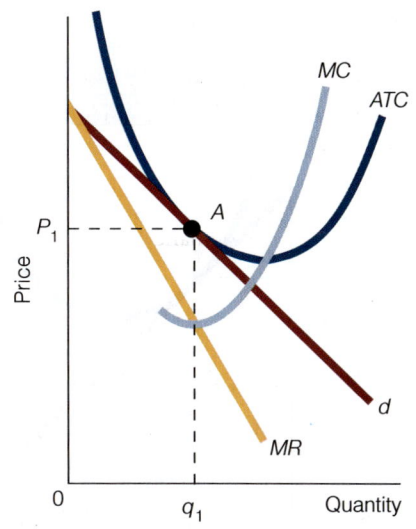

EXHIBIT 2

Monopolistic Competition in the Long Run

Because of easy entry into the industry, there are likely to be zero economic profits in the long run for a monopolistic competitor. In other words, $P = ATC$.

(f)inding ECONOMICS

On an Online Radio Service Abbie just found an online radio station that plays the songs and artists she wants to hear. She types in the title of the song or the name of the artist she would like to hear, and the online radio service creates a virtual radio station just for her. Where is the economics?

Firms can compete in terms of price or in areas other than price (price competition versus nonprice competition). With respect to free radio (radio you do not pay to hear), radio stations cannot compete on price, and so they must turn to nonprice competition. Customizing a radio station for a listener is a nonprice way of competing for listeners. ▲▲▲

Excess Capacity: What Is It, and Is It "Good" or "Bad"?

The theory of monopolistic competition makes a major prediction, which is generally referred to as the excess capacity theorem: a monopolistic competitor will produce an output smaller than the one that would minimize its unit costs of production.

At point *A* in Exhibit 3(a), the monopolistic competitor is in long-run equilibrium because profits are zero ($P = ATC$). Point *A* is *not* the lowest point on the average total cost curve; the lowest point is point *L*. Therefore, in long-run equilibrium, when the monopolistic competitor earns zero economic profits, it is not producing the quantity of output at which average total costs (unit costs) are minimized given the scale of plant. Exhibit 3 contrasts the perfectly competitive firm and the monopolistic competitor in long-run equilibrium. In part (b), the perfectly competitive firm is earning zero economic profits, and price (P_{Cl}) equals average total cost (ATC). Furthermore, the point at which price equals average total cost (point *L*) is the lowest point on the ATC curve. In long-run equilibrium, the perfectly competitive firm produces the quantity of output at which unit costs are minimized.

Look back at part (a). The monopolistic competitor is earning zero economic profits, and price (P_{MCl}) equals average total cost. If the monopolistic competitor produced the

Excess Capacity Theorem
A monopolistic competitor in equilibrium produces an output smaller than the one that would minimize its costs of production.

EXHIBIT 3

A Comparison of Perfect Competition and Monopolistic Competition: The Issue of Excess Capacity

The perfectly competitive firm produces a quantity of output consistent with lowest unit costs. The monopolistic competitor does not. If it did, it would produce q_{MC2} instead of q_{MC1}. The monopolistic competitor is said to underutilize its plant size or to have excess capacity.

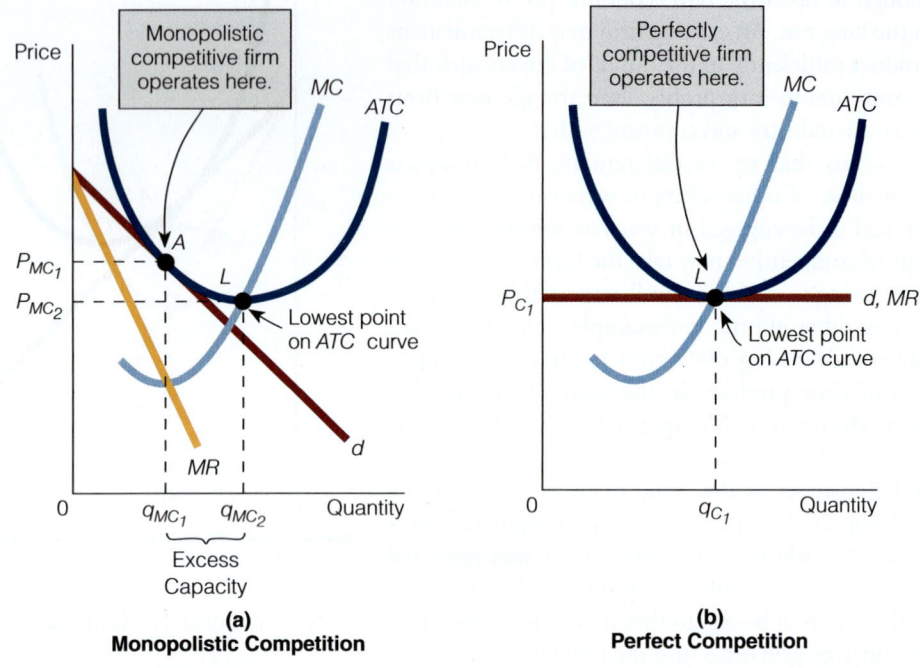

(a)
Monopolistic Competition

(b)
Perfect Competition

quantity of output at which unit costs are minimized, it would produce q_{MC2}. For this reason, it has been argued that the monopolistic competitor produces too little output (q_{MC1} instead of q_{MC2}) and charges too high a price (P_{MC1} instead of P_{MC2}). With respect to output, too little translates into the monopolistic competitor's underutilizing its present plant size; it is said to have *excess capacity*. In part (a), the excess capacity is equal to the difference between q_{MC2} and q_{MC1}.

Some have argued that the monopolistic competitor operates at excess capacity because it faces a downward-sloping demand curve. In Exhibit 3(a), the only way the firm would not operate at excess capacity is if its demand curve were tangent to the *ATC* curve at point *L*—the lowest point on the *ATC* curve. But for this to occur, the demand curve *would have to be horizontal*, which would require homogeneous products. A downward-sloping demand curve cannot be tangent to the *ATC* curve at point *L*.

In short, *the monopolistic competitor operates at excess capacity as a consequence of its downward-sloping demand curve,* and its downward-sloping demand curve is a consequence of differentiated products. A question that many economists ask but not all answer in the same way is this: *If excess capacity is the price we pay for differentiated products (more choice), is it too high a price?*

The Monopolistic Competitor and Two Types of Efficiency

We know that a firm is resource allocative efficient if it charges a price that is equal to marginal cost; that is, if $P = MC$. Because the monopolistic competitive firm charges a price that is greater than marginal cost ($P > MC$), it is not resource allocative efficient.

We also know that a firm is productive efficient if it charges a price that is equal to its lowest *ATC*. Because the monopolistic competitor operates at excess capacity, it is not productive efficient.

The People Wear Prada

Suppose you own a business that is considered a monopolistic competitive firm. Your business is one of many sellers, you sell a product slightly differentiated from the products of your competitors, and entry into and exit from the industry are easy. Would you rather your business were a monopoly firm? Wouldn't it be better for you to be the only seller of a product than to be one of many? Most business owners would answer yes. So we consider how monopolistic competitors may try to become monopolists.

One possibility is through a designer label. If a monopolistic competitor can, through the use of a designer label, persuade the buying public that her product is *more than just slightly differentiated* from those of her competitors, she stands a better chance of becoming a monopolist.

AP PHOTO/KEVORK DJANSEZIAN

(Remember that a monopolist produces a good that has no close substitutes.)

For example, many firms produce women's jeans, and, to many people, the jeans all look very much alike. To differentiate its product from the pack, a firm could add a designer label to the jeans to suggest uniqueness—that they are the only *Tag Jeans*, for example. For added impact, it could try to persuade the buying public through advertising that its jeans are "the" jeans worn by the most famous, best-looking people.

Think of a list of firms that have employed a designer label to try to outcompete their competitors: Gucci, Tommy Hilfiger, Perry Ellis, Liz Clairborne, Armani, Versace, Dolce & Gabbana, Prada, Valentino, Chanel, L.L. Bean, Da-Nang, Primp, and many others.

SELF-TEST

(Answers to Self-Test questions are in Answers to Self-Test Questions at the back of the book.)

1. How is a monopolistic competitor like a monopolist? How is it like a perfect competitor?

2. Why do monopolistic competitors operate at excess capacity?

OLIGOPOLY: ASSUMPTIONS AND REAL-WORLD BEHAVIOR

Unlike perfect competition, monopoly, and monopolistic competition, there is no one accepted theory of oligopoly. However, the different theories of oligopoly have the following common assumptions:

1. *There are few sellers and many buyers.* The assumption is usually that the few firms of an oligopoly are interdependent; each one is aware that its actions influence the others and that the actions of the other firms affect it. This interdependence among firms is a key characteristic of oligopoly.

2. *Firms produce and sell either homogeneous or differentiated products.* Aluminum is a homogeneous product produced in an oligopolistic market; cars are a differentiated product produced in an oligopolistic market.

3. *The barriers to entry are significant.* Economies of scale constitute perhaps the most significant barrier to entry in oligopoly theory, but patent rights, exclusive control of an essential resource, and legal barriers also act as barriers to entry.

Oligopoly

A theory of market structure based on three assumptions: few sellers and many buyers, firms producing either homogeneous or differentiated products, and significant barriers to entry.

The oligopolist is a price searcher. Like all other firms, it produces the quantity of output at which $MR = MC$.

The Concentration Ratio

Which industries today are dominated by a small number of firms, that is, are oligopolistic? Economists have developed the *concentration ratio* to help answer this question. The concentration ratio is the percentage of industry sales (or assets, output, labor force, or some other factor) accounted for by x number of firms in the industry. The x number in the definition is usually four or eight, but it can be any number (although it is usually small).

Concentration Ratio

The percentage of industry sales (or assets, output, labor force, or some other factor) accounted for by x number of firms in the industry.

> *Four-firm concentration ratio:* CR_4 = Percentage of industry sales accounted for by four largest firms
>
> *Eight-firm concentration ratio:* CR_8 = Percentage of industry sales accounted for by eight largest firms

A high concentration ratio implies that few sellers make up the industry; a low concentration ratio implies that more than a few sellers make up the industry.

As an example, let's calculate a four-firm concentration ratio for industry Z. Total industry sales for a given year are $5 million, and the four largest firms in the industry account for $4.5 million in sales. The four-firm concentration ratio is 0.90, or 90 percent ($5 million $\times$ 0.90 = $4.5 million). Industries with high four- and eight-firm concentration ratios in recent years are cigarettes, cars, tires, cereal breakfast foods, farm machinery, and soap and other detergents, to name a few.

Although concentration ratios are often used to determine the extent (or degree) of oligopoly, they are not perfect guides to industry concentration. Most important, they do not take into account foreign competition and competition from substitute domestic goods. For example, the U.S. automobile industry is concentrated, but it still faces stiff competition from abroad. A more relevant concentration ratio for this particular industry might be one computed on a worldwide basis.

PRICE AND OUTPUT UNDER THE CARTEL THEORY

In this section we discuss why oligopoly firms might want to form a cartel and some of the problems in doing so.

The Cartel Theory

Cartel Theory

A theory of oligopoly in which oligopolistic firms act as if there were only one firm in the industry.

Cartel

An organization of firms that reduces output and increases price in an effort to increase joint profits.

The key behavioral assumption of the cartel theory is that, within a given industry, oligopolists act as if there were only one firm. In short, they form a cartel to capture the benefits that would exist for a monopolist. A cartel is an organization of firms that reduces output and increases price in an effort to increase joint profits.

Forming and maintaining a cartel has its benefits. Exhibit 4 shows an industry in long-run competitive equilibrium. Price is P_1, and quantity of output is Q_1. The industry is producing the output at which price equals marginal cost and economic profits are zero. Now suppose the firms making up the industry form a cartel and reduce output to Q_C. The new price is P_C (cartel price), and profits are equal to the area CP_CAB, which can be shared among the members of the cartel. With no cartel, there are no profits; with a cartel, profits are earned. Thus, the firms have an incentive to form a cartel and to behave cooperatively rather than competitively.

However, firms may not be able to form a cartel, even though they have a profit incentive to do so. Also, even if they are able to form the cartel, the firms may not be able to maintain it. Firms that wish to form and maintain a cartel will encounter several problems, in addition to the fact that legislation prohibits certain types of cartels in the United States. Also, organizing and forming a cartel involves costs as well as benefits.[1]

THE PROBLEM OF FORMING THE CARTEL Even if it were legal, getting the sellers of an industry together to form a cartel can be costly, even when the number of sellers is small. Each potential cartel member may resist incurring the costs of forming the cartel because it stands to benefit more if other firms do the work. In other words, each potential member has an incentive to be a free rider—to stand by and take a free ride on the actions of others.

THE PROBLEM OF FORMULATING CARTEL POLICY Even if prospective firms form a cartel, next is the problem of formulating policy. For example, firm A might propose that each cartel member reduce output by 10 percent, and firm B advocates that all bigger cartel members reduce output by 15 percent and all smaller members reduce output by 5 percent. In fact, there may be as many policy proposals as there are cartel members, and reaching agreement may be difficult. Such disagreements become harder to resolve as the differences among cartel members in costs, size, and so forth, grow.

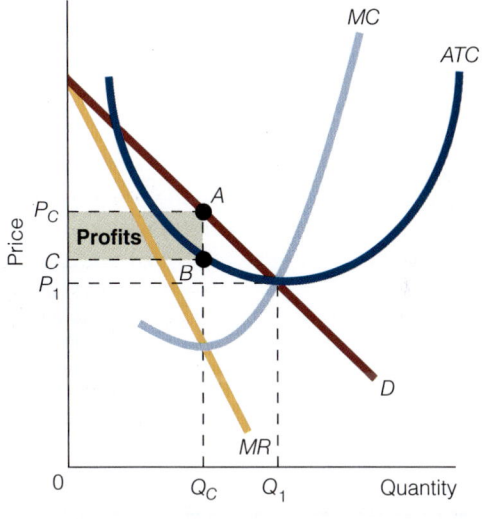

EXHIBIT 4

The Benefits of a Cartel (to Cartel Members)

We assume the industry is in long-run competitive equilibrium, producing Q_1 and charging P_1. There are no profits. A reduction in output to Q_C through the formation of a cartel raises prices to P_C and brings profits of $CP_C AB$.

(Note: In an earlier chapter, a horizontal demand curve faces the *firm*. Here a downward- sloping demand curve faces the *industry*. Don't be misled by this difference. No matter what type of demand curve we use, long-run competitive equilibrium is where $P = MC = SRATC = LRATC$.)

THE PROBLEM OF ENTRY INTO THE INDUSTRY
Even if the cartel members manage to agree on a policy that generates high profits, those high profits will provide an incentive for firms outside the industry to join the industry. If current cartel members cannot keep new suppliers from entering, the cartel is likely to break up.

THE PROBLEM OF CHEATING As paradoxical as it first appears, after the cartel agreement is made, members have an incentive to cheat on it. Exhibit 5 shows three situations for a *representative firm* of the cartel: (1) the situation before the cartel is formed; (2) the situation after the cartel is formed when all members adhere to the cartel price; and (3) the situation if the firm cheats on the cartel agreement, but the other cartel members do not.

Before the cartel is formed, the firm in the exhibit is in long-run competitive equilibrium; it produces output q_1, charges price P_1, and earns zero economic profits. Next, it reduces its output to q_C, as directed by the cartel (the cartel has set a quota for each member), and it charges the cartel price of P_C. Now the firm earns profits equal to the area $CP_C AB$.

What happens if the firm cheats on the cartel agreement and produces q_{CC} instead of the stipulated q_C? As long as other firms do not cheat, this firm views its demand curve as horizontal at the cartel price (P_C). The reason is simple: Because it is one of a number of firms, it cannot affect price by changing output. Therefore, it can produce and sell additional units of output without lowering price. So, if the firm cheats on the cartel agreement

---

1. Sometimes, economists discuss the benefits and costs of organizing a cartel without specifying the market structure. We have followed suit here by broadening our discussion of cartel theory to include market structures other than oligopoly. This will be noticeable in places. For example, even though there are few sellers in oligopoly, we discuss cartel theory in the context of both few and many sellers.

EXHIBIT 5

The Benefits of Cheating on the Cartel Agreement

The situation for a representative firm of a cartel: in long-run competitive equilibrium, it produces q_1 and charges P_1, earning zero economic profits. As a consequence of the cartel agreement, it reduces output to q_C and charges P_C. Its profits are the area CP_CAB. If it cheats on the cartel agreement and others do not, the firm will increase output to q_{CC} and reap profits of FP_CDE. Note, however, that if this firm can cheat on the cartel agreement, so can others. Given the monetary benefits gained by cheating, it is likely that the cartel will exist for only a short time.

| Quantity firm produces when it adheres to cartel agreement; profits = CP_CAB | Quantity firm produces when there is no cartel agreement; profits = 0 | Quantity firm produces when it cheats on the cartel agreement, but other firms do not; profits = FP_CDE |

and other firms do not, then the cheating firm can increase its profits from the smaller amount CP_CAB to the larger amount FP_CDE. Of course, if all the firms cheat, the cartel members are back where they started—with no cartel agreement and at price P_1.

This analysis illustrates a major theme of cartels: firms have an incentive to form a cartel, but, once it is formed, they have an incentive to cheat. As a result, some economists have concluded that even if cartels are formed successfully, they are not likely to be effective for long.

ⓣhinking like AN ECONOMIST

The Target Sometimes Moves In economics, there are moving targets. Consider the target of higher profits for the firms in an oligopolistic industry. After the firms form a cartel to capture the higher profits, the target of higher profits moves to where a cartel member must cheat on the cartel to hit it. But if all cartel members take aim at the target's new position, the target moves back to its original position—where cartel members must agree to stop cheating.

The layperson may think that an economic objective, or economic target, is stationary. All an economic actor has to do to hit it is to take careful aim. But the economist knows that sometimes the target moves, and a careful aim is not always enough. ▪▪▪

SELF-TEST

1. "Firms have an incentive to form a cartel, but, once it is formed, they have an incentive to cheat." What is the specific incentive to form the cartel? What is the incentive to cheat on the cartel?

2. Is an oligopolistic firm a price taker or price searcher? Explain your answer.

How Is a New Year's Resolution Like a Cartel Agreement?

In a cartel, one firm makes an agreement with another firm or other firms. In a New Year's resolution, you essentially make an agreement with yourself. So both cases—the cartel and the resolution—involve an agreement.

Both cases also raise the possibility of cheating on the agreement. Suppose your New Year's resolution is to exercise more, take better notes in class, and read one good book a month. You might set such objectives because you know you will be better off in the long run if you do these things. Then the short run enters into the picture. You have to decide between exercising today or plopping down in your favorite chair and watching television. You have to decide between starting to read *Moby Dick* or catching up on the latest entertainment news in *People* magazine. The part of you that wants to hold to the resolution is at odds with the part of you that wants to watch television or read *People*. Often, the television-watching, *People*-reading part wins out. Breaking a New Year's resolution—as you probably already know—is just too easy.

So is breaking a cartel agreement. For the firm that has entered into the agreement, the lure of higher profits is often too strong to resist. In addition, the firm is concerned that, if it doesn't break the

©SUPERSTOCK/JUPITER IMAGES

agreement (and cheat), some other firm might, and then it will have lost out completely.

In short, both resolutions and cartel agreements take a lot of willpower to hold them together. Willpower, it seems, is in particularly short supply, and something is needed to take its place. Both a resolution and a cartel agreement need something if they are to endure. Something or someone has to exact a penalty from the party who breaks the resolution or cartel agreement. Government sometimes plays this role for firms. Family members and friends occasionally play this role for individuals by reminding or reprimanding them if they fail to live up to their resolutions. (Usually, though, family members and friends are not successful.)

So we conclude:

- First, an agreement is at the heart of both a New Year's resolution and a cartel.
- Second, both the resolution and the cartel are subject to cheating behavior.
- Third, if the resolution and the cartel are to have a long life, they often need someone or something to prevent each party from breaking the agreement.

GAME THEORY, OLIGOPOLY, AND CONTESTABLE MARKETS

Of the four market structures (perfect competition, monopoly, monopolistic competition, and oligopoly), oligopoly is often described as the most difficult to analyze. Analysis is difficult because of the interdependence among firms in such a market. Economists often use game theory to get a workable understanding of the interdependence of oligopoly firms. Game theory is a mathematical technique used to analyze the behavior of decision makers who (1) try to reach an optimal position through game playing or the use of strategic behavior, (2) are fully aware of the interactive nature of the process at hand, and (3) anticipate the moves of other decision makers.

In this section, we describe a famous game and then use it to discuss oligopoly behavior. We also discuss the issue of contestable markets.

Game Theory
A mathematical technique used to analyze the behavior of decision makers who try to reach an optimal position for themselves through game playing or the use of strategic behavior, who are fully aware of the interactive nature of the process at hand and who anticipate the moves of other decision makers.

Prisoner's Dilemma

A well-known game in game theory, the prisoner's dilemma, illustrates a case in which individually rational behavior leads to a jointly inefficient outcome. The lesson of the game has been described this way: "You do what is best for you, I'll do what is best for me, and somehow we end up in a situation that is not best for either of us." Here is how the game is played.

THE FACTS   Two men, Bob and Nathan, are arrested and charged with jointly committing a crime. They are put into separate cells so that they cannot communicate with each other. The district attorney goes to each man separately and says the following:

- If you confess to the crime and agree to turn state's evidence and if your accomplice does not confess, I will let you off with a $500 fine.
- If your accomplice confesses to the crime and agrees to turn state's evidence and if you do not confess, I will fine you $5,000.
- If both you and your accomplice remain silent and refuse to confess to the crime, I will charge you with a lesser crime, which I can prove you committed, and both you and your accomplice will pay fines of $2,000.
- If both you and your accomplice confess, I will fine each of you $3,000.

THE OPTIONS AND CONSEQUENCES   Each man has two choices: confess or not confess, as shown in the grid in Exhibit 6. According to the possibilities laid out by the district attorney:

- *Box 1.* If both men do not confess, each pays a fine of $2,000.
- *Box 2.* If Nathan confesses and Bob does not, then Nathan gets off with the light fine of $500 and Bob pays the stiff penalty of $5,000.
- *Box 3.* If Nathan does not confess and Bob confesses, then Nathan pays the stiff penalty of $5,000 and Bob pays the light fine of $500.
- *Box 4.* Finally, if both men confess, each pays $3,000.

WHAT NATHAN THINKS   Nathan considers his choices and their possible outcomes. He reasons to himself, "I have two options, confess or not confess, and Bob has the same two options. Let me ask myself two questions:

- "*If Bob chooses not to confess, what is the best thing for me to do?* The answer is to confess because if I do not confess, I will end up in box 1 paying $2,000, but if

---

EXHIBIT 6

Prisoner's Dilemma

Nathan and Bob each have two choices: confess or not confess. No matter what Bob does, it is always better for Nathan to confess. No matter what Nathan does, it is always better for Bob to confess. Both Nathan and Bob confess and end up in box 4 where each pays a $3,000 fine. Both men would have been better off had they not confessed. That way they would have ended up in box 1 paying a $2,000 fine.

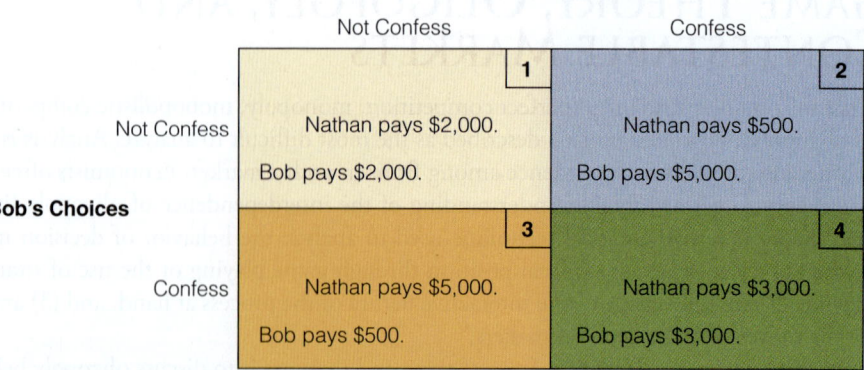

Nathan's Choices

	Not Confess	Confess
Not Confess	**1** Nathan pays $2,000. Bob pays $2,000.	**2** Nathan pays $500. Bob pays $5,000.
Confess	**3** Nathan pays $5,000. Bob pays $500.	**4** Nathan pays $3,000. Bob pays $3,000.

Bob's Choices

I confess I will end up in box 2, paying only $500. No doubt about it: If Bob chooses not to confess, I should confess."

- *"If Bob chooses to confess, what is the best thing for me to do?* The answer is to confess because, if I do not confess, I will end up in box 3 paying $5,000, but if I confess I will pay $3,000. No doubt about it, if Bob chooses to confess, I should confess."

NATHAN'S CONCLUSION Nathan concludes that no matter what Bob chooses to do—not confess or confess—he is always better off if he confesses. Nathan decides to confess to the crime.

THE SITUATION IS THE SAME FOR BOB Bob goes through the same mental process that Nathan does. Asking himself the same two questions Nathan asked himself, Bob gets the same answers and draws the same conclusion. Bob decides to confess to the crime.

THE OUTCOME The DA goes to each man and asks what he has decided. Both Nathan and Bob say, "I confess." The outcome is shown in box 4, with each man paying a fine of $3,000.

LOOK WHERE THEY COULD BE Another outcome, represented by one of the four boxes, is better for both Nathan and Bob than the one where each pays $3,000. In box 1, both Nathan and Bob pay $2,000. To get to box 1, all the two men had to do was keep silent and not confess.

CHANGING THE GAME What would happen if the DA gave Nathan and Bob another chance? Suppose she tells them that she will not accept their confessions. Instead, she wants them to talk it over together for 10 minutes, after which time she will come back, place each man in a separate room, and ask for his decision. The second time, she will accept each man's decision, no matter what.

Will a second chance change the outcome? Most people will say yes, arguing that Nathan and Bob will now see that their best choice is to remain silent so that each ends up with a $2,000 fine instead of a $3,000 fine. Let's assume this happens, and Nathan and Bob enter into an agreement to remain silent.

NATHAN'S THOUGHTS ON THE WAY TO HIS ROOM The DA returns and takes Nathan to a separate room. On the way, Nathan thinks to himself, "I'm not sure I can trust Bob. Suppose he goes back on our agreement and confesses. If I hold to the agreement and he doesn't, he'll end up with a $500 fine and I'll end up paying $5,000. Of course, if I break the agreement and confess and he holds to the agreement, then I'll reduce my fine to $500. Maybe the best thing for me to do is break the agreement and confess, hoping that he doesn't and I'll pay only $500. If I'm not so lucky, at least I'll protect myself from paying $5,000."

Once in the room, the DA asks Nathan what his decision is. He says, "I confess."

THE SITUATION IS THE SAME FOR BOB Bob sees the situation the same way Nathan does and again chooses to confess.

THE OUTCOME AGAIN Both men end up confessing a second time. Each pays $3,000, realizing that if they had been silent and kept to their agreement, their fine would be only $2,000 each.

ⓕinding ECONOMICS

In a Water Shortage During a water shortage, the water authority has asked people to conserve, but most people do not comply. Where is the economics?

The people are in a prisoner's dilemma setting. Specifically, each person might agree (with all others) that conserving water is a good thing to do, but then each person realizes that he is better off if everyone conserves except him. Everyone can think the same way, of course. In the end, we are likely to find few people conserving. ▲ ▲ ▲

Oligopoly Firms' Cartels and the Prisoner's Dilemma

When oligopoly firms enter into a cartel agreement, do they create a prisoner's dilemma? Most economists answer yes. To illustrate, two firms, A and B, produce and sell the same product and are in stiff competition with each other. The competition is so stiff that each earns only $10,000 profits. Soon the two firms decide to enter into a cartel agreement in which each agrees to raise prices and, after prices are raised, not to undercut the other. If they hold to the agreement, each firm will earn profits of $50,000. But if one firm holds to the cartel agreement and the other does not, the one that does not will earn profits of $100,000 and the one that does will earn $5,000 profits. Of course, if neither holds to the agreement, then both will be back where they started, earning $10,000 profits. The choices for the two firms and the possible outcomes are outlined in Exhibit 7.

Each firm is likely to behave as the two prisoners did in the prisoner's dilemma game. Each firm will see the chance to earn $100,000 by breaking the agreement (instead of $50,000 by holding to it); each will also realize that if it does not break the agreement and the other firm does, it will be in a worse situation than before entering into the cartel. Most economists predict that the two firms will end up in box 4 in Exhibit 7, earning the profits they did before they entered into the agreement. In summary, they will cheat on the cartel agreement and again be in competition—the very situation they wanted to escape.

The only way out of the prisoner's dilemma for the two firms is to have some entity enforce the cartel agreement so that the two firms do not cheat. As odd as it may sound, sometimes government has played this role. Normally we think of government as trying to break up cartel agreements because, after all, such agreements are illegal. Nevertheless, sometimes government acts as the enforcer, not the eliminator, of cartel agreements.

For example, the Civil Aeronautics Board (CAB) was created in the days of airline regulation to protect the airlines from so-called cutthroat competition. It had the power to set airfares, allocate air routes, and prevent the entry of new carriers into the airline industry.

EXHIBIT 7

Cartels and Prisoner's Dilemma

Many economists suggest that firms trying to form a cartel are in a prisoner's dilemma situation. Both firms A and B earn higher profits holding to a (cartel) agreement than not, but each will earn even higher profits it if breaks the agreement while the other firm holds to it. If cartel formation is a prisoner's dilemma situation, we predict that cartels will be short-lived.

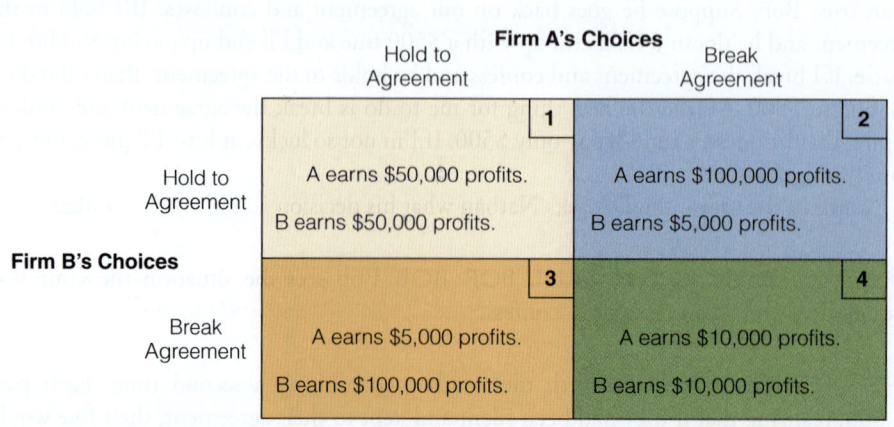

In the days before deregulation, the federal government's General Accounting Office estimated that airline fares would have been, on average, as much as 52 percent lower if the CAB had not been regulating them. Clearly, the CAB was doing for the airlines what an airline cartel would have done: prevent price competition, allocate routes, and prevent new entries into the industry.

In a similar vein, Judge Richard Posner has observed that "the railroads supported the enactment of the first Interstate Commerce Act, which was designed to prevent railroads from price discrimination, because discrimination was undermining the railroad's cartels."[2]

Are Markets Contestable?

Market structures, from perfect competition to oligopoly, have been traditionally defined in terms of the *number of sellers*. In perfect competition, there are many sellers; in monopoly, there is only one; in monopolistic competition, there are many; in oligopoly, there are few. The message is that the number of sellers in a market influences their behavior. For example, the monopoly seller is more likely to restrict output and charge higher prices than is the perfect competitor.

Some economists have shifted the emphasis from the number of sellers in a market to the issue of *entry into and exit from an industry*. This brings us to a discussion of contestable markets. A contestable market is one in which the following conditions are met:

1. *Entry into the market is easy, and exit from it is costless.*

2. *New firms entering the market can produce the product at the same cost as current firms.*

3. *Firms exiting the market can easily dispose of their fixed assets by selling them elsewhere.* Except for depreciation, fixed costs are not sunk but recoverable.

Suppose that eight firms are in an industry and that all of them are earning profits. Firms outside the industry notice this and decide to enter the industry (nothing prevents entry). They acquire the necessary equipment and produce the product at the same cost as current producers do. Time passes, and the firms that entered the industry decide to exit it. They can either switch their machinery into another line of production or sell their equipment for what they paid for it, less depreciation.

Perhaps the most important element of a contestable market is so-called hit-and-run entry and exit. New entrants can enter (hit), produce the product, take profits from current firms, and then exit costlessly (run).

The theory of contestable markets has been criticized because of its assumptions—in particular, the assumption that entry into the industry is free and exit is costless. However, even though this theory, like most theories, does not perfectly describe the real world, it has its usefulness.

At a minimum, the contestable markets theory has rattled orthodox market structure theory. Here are a few of its conclusions:

1. Even if an industry is composed of a small number of firms or even just one firm, the firms do not necessarily perform in a noncompetitive way. They might be extremely competitive if the market they are in is contestable.

2. Profits can be zero in an industry even if the number of sellers in the industry is small.

3. If a market is contestable, inefficient producers cannot survive. Cost inefficiencies invite lower-cost producers into the market, driving price down to minimum ATC and forcing inefficient firms to change their ways or exit the industry.

> **Contestable Market**
> A market in which entry is easy and exit is costless, new firms can produce the product at the same cost as current firms, and exiting firms can easily dispose of their fixed assets by selling them.

---

2. Richard A. Posner, "Theories of Regulation," *Bell Journal of Economics and Management Science* 5 (Autumn): 337.

4. If, as the previous conclusion suggests, a contestable market encourages firms to produce at their lowest possible average total cost and charge a price equal to average total cost, then they will also sell at a price equal to marginal cost. (The marginal cost curve intersects the average total cost curve at its minimum point.)

The theory of contestable markets has also led to a shift in policy perspectives. To some (but certainly not all) economists, the theory suggests a new way to encourage firms to act as perfect competitors. Rather than direct interference in the behavioral patterns of firms, efforts should perhaps be directed at lowering entry and exit costs.

A REVIEW OF MARKET STRUCTURES

Exhibit 8 reviews some of the characteristics and consequences of the four different market structures: perfect competition, monopoly, monopolistic competition, and oligopoly. The first four columns of the exhibit summarize the characteristics. The last column notes the long-run market tendencies of price and average total cost. The relationship between price and *ATC* indicates whether long-run profits are possible. In the exhibit, three of the four market structures (monopoly, monopolistic competition, and oligopoly) have superscript letters beside the possible profits. These letters refer to notes that describe alternative market tendencies given different conditions. For example, the market tendency in oligopoly is for $P > ATC$ and for profits to exist in the long run. Because oligopoly has significant barriers to entry, short-run profits cannot be reduced by competition from new firms entering the industry. However, the market tendency of price and average total cost may be different if the particular oligopolistic market is contestable.

APPLICATIONS OF GAME THEORY

Game theory, especially prisoner's dilemma, is applicable in a number of real-world situations. In this section, we discuss a few of these applications.

Grades and Partying

Your economics professor announces in class one day that on the next test, she will give the top 10 percent of the students in the class A's, the next 15 percent B's, and so on. Because studying to get, say, a 60 takes less time than a 90 on the test, you hope everyone studies

---

EXHIBIT 8

Characteristics and Consequences of Market Structures

Market Structure	Number of Sellers	Type of Product	Barriers to Entry	Long-Run Market Tendency of Price and *ATC*
Perfect competition	Many	Homogeneous	No	$P = ATC$ (zero economic profits)
Monopoly	One	Unique	Yes	$P > ATC$ (positive economic profits)[a, c]
Monopolistic competition	Many	Slightly differentiated	No	$P = ATC$ (zero economic profits)[b]
Oligopoly	Few	Homogeneous or differentiated	Yes	$P > ATC$ (positive economic profits)[a, c]

a. It is possible for positive profits to turn to zero profits through the capitalization of profits or rent-seeking activities.
b. It is possible for the firm to earn positive profits in the long run if it can differentiate its product sufficiently in the minds of the buying public.
c. It is possible for positive profits to turn to zero profits if the market is contestable.

only a little. If so, you can study only a little and earn a high letter grade. But, of course, everyone in the class is thinking the same thing.

Envision yourself entering into an agreement with your fellow students. You say the following to them one day:

> *There are 30 students in our class. Each of us can choose to study either two hours or four hours for the test. Our relative standing in the class will be the same whether we all study for two hours or all study for four hours. So why don't we all agree to study for only two hours. That way, we have two extra hours to do other things. I'd rather receive my B by studying for only two hours instead four.*

Everyone agrees with the logic of the argument and agrees to study only two hours. Of course, once all the students have agreed to this, they have an incentive to cheat on the agreement and study more. If everyone else in your class agrees to study two hours and you study four, you increase your relative standing in the class. You go from, say, a B to an A.

You and the other students in your class are in a prisoner's dilemma. Exhibit 9 shows the payoffs for you and for Jill, a representative other student. If both you and Jill study four hours, each receives an 85, which is a B (box 4). With your professor's new relative grading plan, if you study two hours and Jill studies two hours, the grade for each of you falls to 65, but now 65 is a B (box 1). In other words, in comparison with box 4, box 1 is better because you receive the same letter grade (B) in both cases but spend less time studying.

Of course, once you and Jill agree to lower your study time from four hours to two, each of you has an incentive to cheat on the agreement. If you study four hours and Jill studies two, then you raise your grade to an 85, which is now an A, whereas Jill's grade is 65, which now becomes a C (box 2). Of course, if Jill studies four hours and you study two, then Jill raises her grade to an 85, which is now an A, and your grade is 65, which is now a C (box 3).

EXHIBIT 9

Studying and Grades

Suppose your letter grade in class depends on how well you do relative to others. In this setting, you and the other students are in a prisoner's dilemma, which is shown here. If both you and Jill (a representative other student) each study 4 hours, each of you earns a point grade of 85, which is a B (box 4). If each of you studies 2 hours, each of you earns a point grade of 65, which is a B (box 1). Box 1 is preferred over box 4 because you get the same letter grade in each box, but you study less in box 1 than in box 4.

If you study 4 hours while Jill studies 2 hours, your point grade rises to 85 and Jill's point grade remains at 65. In this case, 85 is an A and 65 is a C (box 2). You are better off and Jill is worse off.

If you study 2 hours while Jill studies 4 hours, Jill's point grade rises to 85 and your point grade remains at 65. Jill earns a letter grade of A, and you earn a letter grade of C.

No matter what Jill decides to do—study 2 or 4 hours—it is always better for you to study 4 hours (assuming the costs of studying additional hours are less than the benefits of studying additional hours). The same holds for Jill. Our outcome, then, is box 4, where both you and Jill study 4 hours.

No matter what you think Jill is going to do, the best thing for you to do is study four hours.[3] The same holds for Jill with respect to whatever you choose to do. The outcome, then, is box 4, where both of you study four hours.

Ideally, what you and Jill need is a way to enforce your agreement not to study more than two hours. How might students do this? One way is to party. (That's right, party.) If you can get all the students in your class together and party, you can be fairly sure that no one is studying.

In general, students in the same class understand (1) that some professors set aside some percentage of A's for the top students in the class (no matter how low the top is) and (2) that they are in a prisoner's dilemma. They realize it would be better for them to cooperate and study less than to compete and study more. Instead of actually entering into an agreement to study less (sign on the dotted line), they think up ways to keep the studying time down. One way to keep the studying time down—one way to enforce the implicit and unspoken agreement not to study too much—is to do things with others that do not entail studying. One such institution that satisfies all requirements is partying: everyone is together, not studying.

The Arms Race

During much of the Cold War, the United States and the Soviet Union engaged in an arms race. Each country was producing armaments directed at the other. Occasionally, representatives of the two countries would meet and try to slow down the race. The United States would agree to cut armaments production if the Soviet Union did, and vice versa. Many arms analysts generally agreed that the arms agreements between the United States and the Soviet Union were unsuccessful. In other words, representatives of the two countries would meet and enter into an agreement not to compete so heavily on arms production, but then the countries would just keep competing.

The two countries were in a prisoner's dilemma. When both the United States and the Soviet Union were competing on arms production, they were in box 4 of Exhibit 10,

---

EXHIBIT 10

An Arms Race

In the days of the Cold War, the United States and the Soviet Union were said to be in an arms race. Actually, the arms race was a result of the two countries being in a prisoner's dilemma. Start with each country racing to produce more military goods than the other country; that is, each country is in box 4. In their attempt to move to box 1, they enter into an arms agreement (to reduce the rate at which they produce arms). But no matter what the Soviet Union does (hold to the arms agreement or break it), it is always better for the United States to break the agreement. The same holds for the Soviet Union with respect to the United States. The two countries end up in box 4. (Note: In the exhibit, the higher the number, the better the position for the country.)

| | **United States** | |
	Hold to Arms Agreement	Break Arms Agreement
Soviet Union Hold to Arms Agreement	**1** United States, 10 Soviet Union, 10	**2** United States, 15 Soviet Union, 5
Break Arms Agreement	**3** United States, 5 Soviet Union, 15	**4** United States, 7 Soviet Union, 7

---

3. We are assuming that the cost of studying two additional hours is lower than the benefits you receive by raising your grade one letter.

Grade Inflation at College

At Harvard in 1966, 22 percent of all grades were A's. By 2002, that percentage had risen to 46 percent.

Were the students at Harvard in 2002 a lot smarter than the students in 1966? Were the professors at Harvard in 2002 much better teachers than the professors in 1966? If neither smarter students nor better professors can explain the growing percentage of A's at Harvard overtime, then what does?

Many suggest it is grade inflation. Student performance on tests, exams, and papers that once received a grade of C today receives a grade of B; what once received a grade of B now receives a grade of A.

Harvard is not unusual when it comes to grade inflation. It exists on many other college campuses. College professors often acknowledge it

("Years ago this would be a C paper instead of a B paper"), and some complain about it. Some even go so far as wanting to change it—to end grade inflation. So, then, why don't they?

College professors might be in a prisoner's dilemma setting. To illustrate, suppose college professors (on a particular college campus) enter into an agreement with other college professors to stop inflating grades. Each professor now has the choice of holding to the agreement or breaking it (continuing to inflate grades). If a professor wants to raise the grades of his students relative to other students, he may chose to inflate grades—thinking that other professors are not inflating grades. The result? All (or almost all) professors will end up inflating grades.

each receiving a utility level of 7. Their collective objective was to move from box 4 to box 1, where each cooperated with the other and reduced its armaments production. In box 1, each country received a utility level of 10. The arms agreements that the United States and the Soviet Union entered into were attempts to get to box 1.

Of course, after the agreement was signed, each country had an incentive to cheat. Certainly, the United States would be better off if it increased its armaments production while the Soviet Union cut back its production. Then the United States could establish clear military superiority over the Soviet Union. The same held for the Soviet Union with respect to the United States.

The payoff matrix in Exhibit 10 makes it is easy to see that the best strategy for the United States or the Soviet Union was to compete. So the two countries ended up in box 4, racing to outproduce the other in arms.

Speed Limit Laws

Envision a world with no law against speeding. In this world, you and everyone else speeds. With everyone speeding, a good number of accidents occur each day, some of which may involve you. In time, everyone decides that something has to be done about the speeding. It is just too dangerous, everyone admits, to let it continue.

Someone offers a proposal: "Let's agree that we will post signs on the road that state the maximum speed. Furthermore, let's agree here and now that we will all obey the speed limits." The proposal sounds like a good one, and everyone agrees to it.

Of course, as we know by now, once the agreement not to speed is made, we have a prisoner's dilemma. Each person will be better off if he (and he alone) speeds while everyone else obeys the speed limit. In the beginning, everyone agrees to the speed limit; in the end, however, everyone breaks it.

What is missing, of course, is an effective enforcement mechanism. To move the speeders out of the classic prisoner's dilemma box (box 4 in our earlier examples) to box 1, someone or something has to punish people who do not cooperate. A law against speeding—backed up by the police and the court system—solves the prisoner's dilemma. The law, the police, and the court system change the payoff for cheating on the agreement.

The Fear of Guilt as an Enforcement Mechanism

Might there be a social purpose for feeling guilty? Consider the following scenario. John and Mary decide to get married. As part of their wedding vows, they promise to remain faithful to each other. In other words, each promises the other that he or she will not cheat. Of course, once two parties make such an agreement, often each party will be better off if one cheats and the other does not. In the case of John and Mary, John may think, "I can gain utility by cheating on Mary." Of course, Mary can think the same thing with respect to John. Their utility payoffs are shown in Exhibit 11.

Notice in part (a) that both Mary and John receive a utility level of 15 when one cheats but the other does not. Possibly, if each person felt some guilt over cheating, the utility level would be something lower than 15. In some sense, both Mary and John might prefer to feel guilty when cheating. After all, both would prefer to be in box 1, where neither is cheating, than in box 4, where both are cheating. In short, given that box 1 is better than box 4 for both Mary and John, we would expect that both would opt for some

---

EXHIBIT 11

Cheating and Guilt

Does guilt sometimes serve a useful social purpose? John and Mary are married and may be in a prisoner's dilemma. If Mary cheats on John, but John doesn't cheat on Mary, Mary may be better off and therefore moves from box 1 to box 2 in part (a). If John cheats on Mary, but Mary doesn't cheat on John, John may be better off and therefore moves from box 1 to box 3 in (a). Of course, if both cheat, they both end up in box 4, which is inferior for both to box 1. A sense of guilt for each person may change the payoffs in part (a). If each person feels guilty about cheating, then the payoff from cheating is lowered. Look at the new payoffs for each person in part (b). The payoff for cheating goes from 15 to 4 for both Mary and John. With the new, lower payoffs (resulting from a sense of guilt over cheating), both Mary and John remove themselves from a prisoner's dilemma and therefore are more likely to end up in box 1, a box that is better for both.

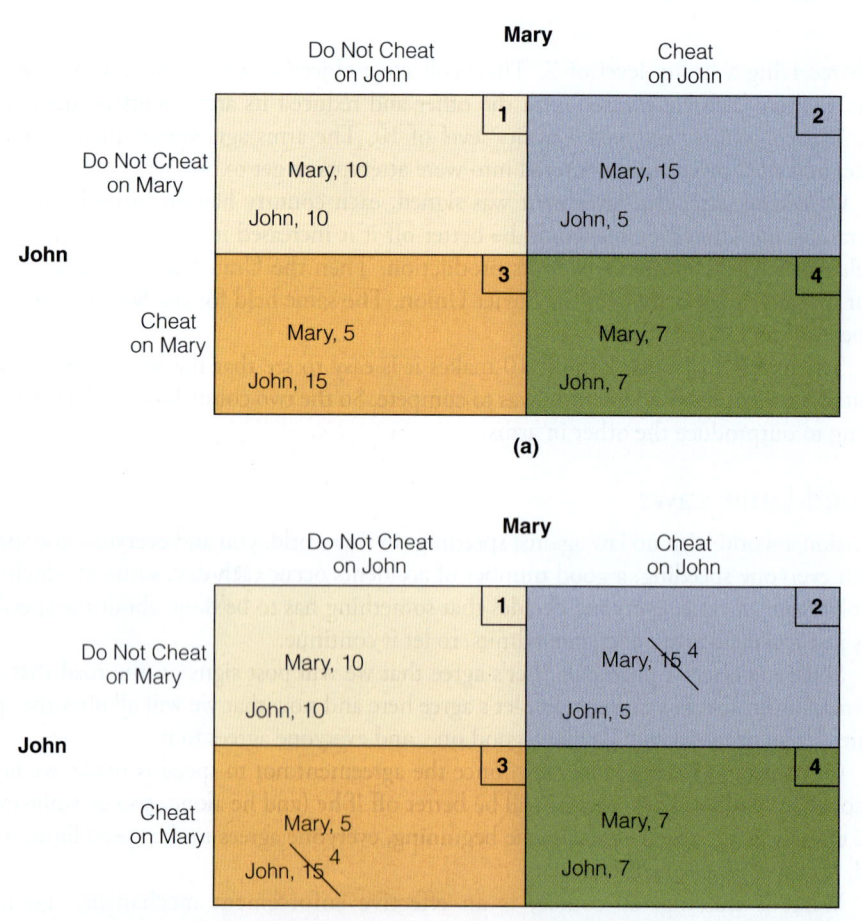

enforcement mechanism that prevented them from moving away from box 1. Didn't the speeders want a law against speeding, enforced by the police and courts?

Of course, John and Mary have no outside enforcement mechanism, but an internal sense of guilt over cheating might be a good substitute for such a mechanism. Instead of the police and the court system putting John and Mary in prison for cheating, each one's sense of guilt will put him or her in a personal jail. This idea is implied when someone says, "I can't do that; I would feel too guilty." In other words, many people want to prevent themselves from suffering the pangs of guilt in much the same way they don't want to suffer the pain of prison. Both guilt pangs and prison are *bads.* Both come with disutility.

Suppose that, as shown in Exhibit 11(b), a sense of guilt would change Mary's utility level in box 2 from 15 to 4 and would change John's utility level in box 3 from 15 to 4. Then neither Mary nor John would find it advantageous to cheat on the other if the spouse did not cheat.

In the end, the question is, when is guilt good? One answer is that guilt is good when the fear of it motivates two people to remove themselves from a setting they would prefer not to be in to a better setting. If the fear of guilt moves Mary and John from box 4 to box 1 (which is what they want), then the fear of guilt is good.

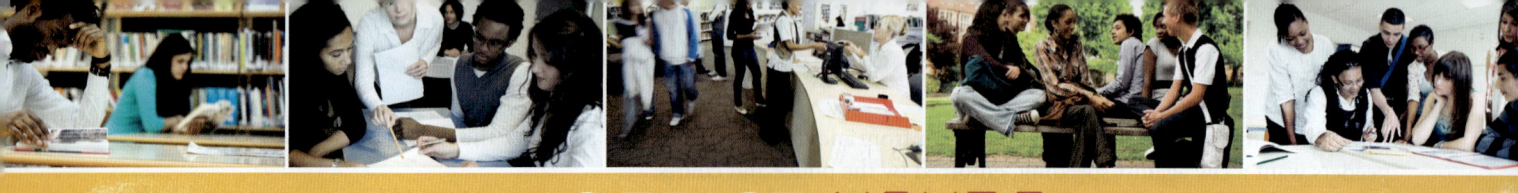

OFFICE HOURS

"Are Firms (as Sellers) Price Takers or Price Searchers?"

STUDENT:

Now that I have studied four different market structures, I want to see whether I have some things correct. First, am I correct that all firms—no matter the market structure—will seek to produce that quantity of output at which $MR = MC$?

INSTRUCTOR:

Yes, that's correct.

STUDENT:

And is it correct that a firm either faces a horizontal demand curve and is a price taker or faces a downward-sloping demand curve and is a price searcher? In other words, is it true that a firm is either one of two things: a price taker or a price searcher? To put it differently, (1) perfectly competitive firms are price takers and (2) monopoly, monopolostic competitive, and oligopolistic firms are price searchers.

INSTRUCTOR:

Yes, that's correct. To be more specific, if a firm is a price taker, it does not have to lower its price to sell additional units of a good. It can sell 100 units at $4 per unit, and it can sell 200 units at $4 a unit. But for a price searcher, the only way it can sell additional units of a good is by lowering price. In other words, it can sell 100 units at $4 per unit, but if it wants to sell 101 units, it has to charge less than $4 per unit.

STUDENT:

As to the issue of resource allocative efficiency ($P = MC$), am I right that a price taker is resource allocative efficient but a price searcher is not?

INSTRUCTOR:

Yes, that's correct.

POINTS TO REMEMBER

1. All firms seek to produce the quantity of output at which $MR = MC$.

2. A firm faces either a horizontal demand curve or a downward-sloping demand curve; that is, a firm is either a price taker or a price searcher, respectively.

3. Perfectly competitive firms are price takers, and monopoly, monopolistic competitive, and oligopolistic firms are price searchers.

4. A price taker is resource allocative efficient, and a price searcher is not.

CHAPTER SUMMARY

MONOPOLISTIC COMPETITION

- The theory of monopolistic competition is built on three assumptions: (1) There are many sellers and buyers. (2) Each firm in the industry produces and sells a slightly differentiated product. (3) Entry and exit are easy.
- The monopolistic competitor is a price searcher.
- For the monopolistic competitor, $P > MR$, and the marginal revenue curve lies below the demand curve.
- The monopolistic competitor produces the quantity of output at which $MR = MC$. It charges the highest price per unit for this output.
- Unlike the perfectly competitive firm, the monopolistic competitor does not exhibit resource allocative efficiency.
- The monopolistic competitive firm does not earn profits in the long run (because of easy entry into the industry) unless it can successfully differentiate its product (e.g., by brand name) in the minds of buyers.

EXCESS CAPACITY THEOREM

- The excess capacity theorem states that a monopolistic competitor will, in equilibrium, produce an output smaller than that at which average total costs (unit costs) are minimized. Thus, the monopolistic competitor is not productive efficient.

OLIGOPOLY ASSUMPTIONS

- All of the many different oligopoly theories are built on the following assumptions: (1) There are few sellers and many buyers. (2) Firms produce and sell either homogeneous or differentiated products. (3) The barriers to entry are significant.
- One of the key characteristics of oligopolistic firms is their interdependence.

CARTEL THEORY

- The cartel theory assumes that firms in an oligopolistic industry act in a manner consistent with there being only one firm in the industry.
- Four problems are associated with cartels: (1) the problem of forming the cartel, (2) the problem of formulating policy, (3) the problem of entry into the industry, and (4) the problem of cheating.
- Firms that enter into a cartel agreement are in a prisoner's dilemma situation, where individually rational behavior leads to a jointly inefficient outcome.

THE THEORY OF CONTESTABLE MARKETS

- The conditions for a contestable market are as follows: (1) Entry into the market is easy, and exit from it is costless. (2) New firms entering the market can produce the product at the same cost as current firms. (3) Firms exiting the market can easily dispose of their fixed assets by selling them elsewhere (less depreciation).
- Compared to orthodox market structure theories, the theory of contestable markets places more emphasis on the issue of entry into and exit from an industry and less emphasis on the number of sellers in an industry.

GAME THEORY

- Game theory is a mathematical technique used to analyze the behavior of decision makers (1) who try to reach an optimal position through game playing or the use of strategic behavior, (2) who are fully aware of the interactive nature of the process at hand, and (3) who anticipate the moves of other decision makers.
- The prisoner's dilemma game illustrates individually rational behavior leading to a jointly inefficient outcome.

KEY TERMS AND CONCEPTS

Monopolistic Competition	Oligopoly	Cartel Theory	Game Theory
Excess Capacity Theorem	Concentration Ratio	Cartel	Contestable Market

QUESTIONS AND PROBLEMS

1. Why does the interdependence of firms play a major role in oligopoly but not in perfect competition or monopolistic competition?

2. Concentration ratios have often been used to note the tightness of an oligopoly market. A high concentration ratio indicates a tight oligopoly market, and a low concentration ratio indicates a loose oligopoly market. Would you expect firms in tight markets to reap higher profits, on average, than firms in loose markets? Would it matter if the markets were contestable? Explain your answers.

3. There are 60 types or varieties of product X on the market. Is product X made in a monopolistic competitive market? Explain your answer.

4. Market theories are said to have the happy consequence of getting individuals to think in more focused and analytical ways. Is this true for you? Give examples to illustrate.

5. Does the theory of contestable markets shed any light on oligopoly pricing theories? Explain your answer.

6. Give an example of a prisoner's dilemma situation other than the ones mentioned in this chapter.

7. Would you expect cartel formation to be more likely in industries comprised of a few firms or in those that include many firms? Explain your answer.

8. How are oligopoly and monopolistic competition alike? How are they different?

9. Will there be profits in the long run in a monopolistic competitive market? Explain your answer.

10. Why might a producer use a designer label to differentiate her product from that of another producer?

11. "Excess capacity is the price we pay for production differentiation." Evaluate this statement in terms of monopolistic competition.

12. What, if anything, do all firms in all four market structures have in common?

WORKING WITH NUMBERS AND GRAPHS

1. Diagrammatically identify the quantity of output a monopolistic competitor produces and the price it charges.

2. Diagrammatically identify a monopolistic competitor that is incurring losses.

3. Total industry sales are $105 million. The top four firms account for sales of $10 million, $9 million, $8 million, and $5 million, respectively. What is the four-firm concentration ratio?

4. Refer to the following figure. Because of a cartel agreement, the firm has been assigned a production quota of q_2 units. The cartel price is P_2. What do the firm's profits equal if it adheres to the cartel agreement? What do the firm's profits equal if it breaks the cartel agreement and produces q_3?

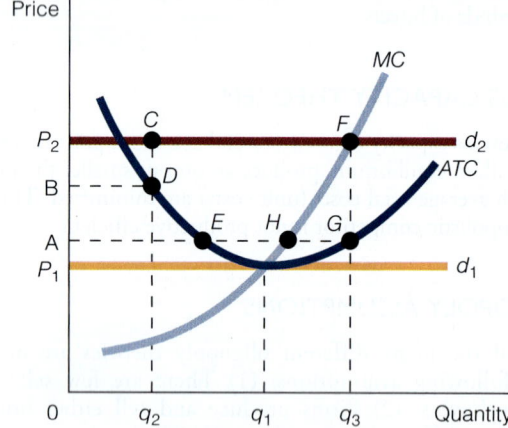

GOVERNMENT AND PRODUCT MARKETS: ANTITRUST AND REGULATION

© GLOW IMAGES/ALAMY

Introduction In Washington, D.C., you may see the building that houses the Department of Justice. One of the many duties of the Justice Department is the enforcement of the country's antitrust laws, whose stated purpose is to control monopoly and to preserve and promote competition. Does it matter to your life whether the Justice Department does a good, bad, or mediocre job of controlling monopoly and preserving and promoting competition? It matters in more ways than you can possibly imagine.

ANTITRUST

A monopoly (1) produces a smaller output than is produced by a perfectly competitive firm with the same revenue and cost considerations, (2) charges a higher price, and (3) causes a deadweight loss. Some economists argue that, based on these facts, government should place restrictions on monopolies. In addition, government should restrict the activities of cartels because the objective of a cartel is to behave as if it were a monopoly.

Other economists argue that monopolies do not have as much market power as some people think: witness the competition some monopolies face from broadly defined substitutes and imports. As for cartels, they usually contain the seeds of their own destruction; so it is only a matter of (a usually short) time before they fall apart naturally.

We are not concerned with the debate about whether to restrict monopoly power, but rather with how government deals with it, specifically antitrust laws and regulation. We examine antitrust law in this section and regulation in the next. Antitrust law is legislation passed for the stated purpose of controlling monopoly power and preserving and promoting competition. Let's look at the uses and effects of a few of the major antitrust acts.

Antitrust Law
Legislation passed for the stated purpose of controlling monopoly power and preserving and promoting competition.

Antitrust Acts

A few key acts that constitute U.S. antitrust policy are the

- Sherman Act (1890).
- Clayton Act (1914).

- Federal Trade Commission Act (1914).
- Robinson-Patman Act (1936).
- Wheeler-Lea Act (1938).
- Celler-Kefauver Antimerger Act (1950).

SHERMAN ACT (1890) The Sherman Act was passed when mergers of companies were common. (A *merger* occurs when two companies combine under single ownership of control.) At that time, the organization that companies formed by combining was called a trust; this, in turn, gave us the word *antitrust*.

The Sherman Act contains two major provisions:

Trust
A combination of firms that come together to act as a monopolist.

1. "Every contract, combination in the form of trust or otherwise, or conspiracy, in restraint of trade or commerce among the several states, or with foreign nations, is hereby declared to be illegal."

2. "Every person who shall monopolize, or attempt to monopolize, or combine or conspire with any other person or persons to monopolize any part of the trade or commerce . . . shall be guilty of a misdemeanor."

Some people have argued that the provisions of the Sherman Act are vague. For example, the act never explains which specific acts constitute a restraint of trade, although it declares such acts illegal.

CLAYTON ACT (1914) The Clayton Act makes the following business practices illegal when their effects "may be to substantially lessen competition or tend to create a monopoly":

1. *Price discrimination.* An example is charging different customers different prices for the same product when the price differences are not related to cost differences.

2. *Exclusive dealing.* This is selling to a retailer on the condition that the retailer not carry any rival products.

3. *Tying contracts.* Arrangements can be made whereby the sale of one product is dependent on the purchase of some other product or products.

4. *The acquisition of competing companies' stock if the acquisition reduces competition.* Some say a major loophole of the act is that it does not ban the acquisition of competing companies' physical assets and therefore does not prevent anticompetitive mergers from doing what they are intended to do.

5. *Interlocking directorates.* In this type of arrangement, the directors of one company sit on the board of another company in the same industry. These were made illegal, irrespective of their effects (i.e., interlocking directorates are illegal at all times, not just when their effects "may be to substantially lessen competition . . . .").

FEDERAL TRADE COMMISSION ACT (1914) The Federal Trade Commission Act contains the broadest and most general language of any antitrust act. It declares illegal "unfair methods of competition in commerce." In essence, it declares illegal acts that are judged to be "too aggressive" in competition. The problem is how to decide what is fair and what is unfair, what is aggressive but not too aggressive. This act also set up the Federal Trade Commission (FTC) to deal with "unfair methods of competition."

ROBINSON-PATMAN ACT (1936) The Robinson-Patman Act was passed in an attempt to decrease the failure rate of small businesses by protecting them from the

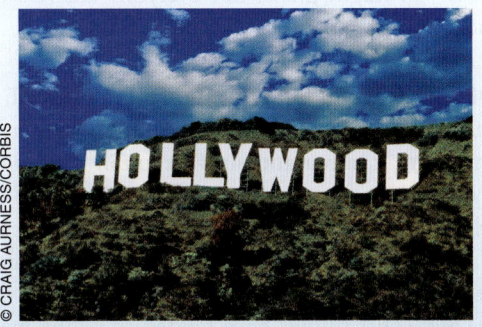

economics 24/7

Thomas Edison and Hollywood

Thomas Alva Edison was born in 1847 and died in 1931. In his 84 years of life, Edison was granted 1,093 patents. Almost everyone knows the role Edison played in the development of electric light and power, but not everyone knows the role he played in indirectly and unwittingly making Hollywood the film capital of the world.

© CRAIG AURNESS/CORBIS

Our story begins with an Edison invention—a machine called the kinetophonograph, which showed a moving picture that was synchronized with a phonograph record. Later, Edison invented the kinetoscope, a device that allowed users to deposit a coin and watch a short motion picture through a small hole.

After inventing the kinetophonograph and kinetoscope, Edison went on to construct the first building that was used solely to make movies. A hole in the ceiling of the building allowed the sun to shine through and illuminate the stage. The entire building was on a set of tracks so that it could be moved around to follow the sun. The first film that Edison produced was a 15-minute movie called *The Great Train Robbery*. Over the years, he produced more than 2,000 short films.

There is some evidence that Edison and a few other people tried to gain complete control over the movie industry in its early days. Edison played a critical role in putting together the Movie Trust, sometimes called the

Edison Trust, a group of ten film producers and distributors. The Movie Trust reportedly tried to eliminate its competition. First, the Movie Trust entered into a contract with Eastman Kodak Company, which manufactured film, to sell film only to it. Second, the Movie Trust refused to lease or sell equipment to certain filmmakers and theater owners. One of the independent movie producers whom the Movie Trust tried to run out of the industry was Carl Laemmie. Laemmie and some other movie producers decided to leave the East Coast, where the Movie Trust had the greatest control over the industry, and went to the West Coast, specifically to southern California. Others soon followed. The rush of independent filmmakers to southern California set the stage for the development of Hollywood as the film capital of the world. In 1917, the Movie Trust was dissolved by court order, but by then the movie industry had a new home. Laemmie, for example, founded Universal Studios in Hollywood in 1912.

Whether Hollywood would be the film capital of the world had it not been for the Movie Trust is doubtful. Without the exclusionary and anticompetitive tactics of the Movie Trust, the film capital of the world would probably be on the East Coast of the United States, very likely in or near New York City.

competition of large and growing chain stores. The large chain stores were receiving price discounts from suppliers and, in turn, passing the discounts on to their customers. As a result, small businesses had a difficult time competing, and many of them failed. The Robinson-Patman Act prohibits suppliers from offering special discounts to large chain stores unless they also offer the discounts to everyone else. Many economists believe that rather than preserving and strengthening competition, the Robinson-Patman Act limits it. The act seems to be more concerned about a certain group of competitors than about the process of competition and the buying public as a whole.

WHEELER-LEA ACT (1938) The Wheeler-Lea Act empowers the Federal Trade Commission to deal with false and deceptive acts or practices. Major moves in this area have been against advertising that the FTC has deemed false and deceptive.

CELLER-KEFAUVER ANTIMERGER ACT (1950) The Celler-Kefauver Act was designed to close the merger loophole in the Clayton Act (see point 4 of the Clayton Act). It bans anticompetitive mergers that occur as a result of one company's acquiring the physical assets of another company.

567

Unsettled Points in Antitrust Policy

Not always clear is where the lines should be drawn in implementing antitrust policy. Which firms should be allowed to enter into a merger and which prohibited? What constitutes restraint of trade? Which firms should be treated as monopolists and broken into smaller firms? Which firms should be left alone?

As you might guess, not everyone answers these questions the same way. In short, some points of antitrust policy are still unsettled.

DOES THE DEFINITION OF THE MARKET MATTER?

How a market is defined—broadly or narrowly—helps determine whether a firm is considered a monopoly. For example, in an important antitrust suit in 1945, a court ruled that Alcoa (Aluminum Company of America) was a monopoly because it had 90 percent of the virgin aluminum ingot market. If Alcoa's market had been broadened to include stainless steel, copper, tin, nickel, and zinc (some of the goods competing with aluminum), it is unlikely that Alcoa would have been ruled a monopoly.

Later court rulings have tended to define markets broadly rather than narrowly. For instance, in the DuPont case in 1956, the market relevant to DuPont was ruled to be the flexible wrapping materials market rather than the narrower cellophane market.

CONCENTRATION RATIOS

Concentration ratios have often been used to gauge the amount of competition in an industry, but their use presents two major problems. First, concentration ratios do not address the issue of foreign competition. For example, the four-firm concentration ratio may be very high, but the four firms that make up the concentration ratio may still face stiff competition from abroad. Second, a four-firm concentration ratio can remain stable over time despite competition among the four major firms in the industry.

In 1982, the Justice Department replaced the four- and eight-firm concentration ratios with the Herfindahl index, although it too is subject to some of the same criticisms as the concentration ratios. The Herfindahl index, which measures the degree of concentration in an industry, is equal to the sum of the squares of the market shares of each firm in the industry:

Herfindahl Index
An index that measures the degree of concentration in an industry, equal to the sum of the squares of the market shares of each firm in the industry.

$$\text{Herfindahl index} = (S_1)^2 + (S_2)^2 + \ldots + (S_n)^2$$

where S_1 through S_n are the market shares of firms 1 through n. For example, if 10 firms are in an industry and if each firm has a 10 percent market share, the Herfindahl index is 1,000 ($10^2 + 10^2 + 10^2 + 10^2 + 10^2 + 10^2 + 10^2 + 10^2 + 10^2 + 10^2 = 1,000$).

Exhibit 1 compares the Herfindahl index and the four-firm concentration ratio. When the four-firm concentration ratio is used, the top four firms (A–D) have a 48 percent market share, which generally is thought to describe a concentrated industry. A merger between any of the top four firms and any other firm (e.g., between firm B and firm G in Exhibit 1) would give the newly merged firm a greater market share than any existing firm and usually incur frowns at the Justice Department.

The Herfindahl index for the industry is 932, however, and the Justice Department generally considers any number less than 1,000 representative of an unconcentrated (or competitive) industry. An index between 1,000 and 1,800 is considered representative of a moderately concentrated industry, and an index greater than 1,800 is representative of a concentrated industry.

When is the Justice Department likely to take antitrust actions? According to the statement made at the website of the Antitrust Division of the Justice Department "transactions that increase the HHI [Herfindahl-Hirschman Index, a commonly accepted measure of market concentration] by more than 100 points in

EXHIBIT 1

Firms	Market Share
A	15%
B	12
C	11
D	10
E	8
F	7
G	7
H	6
I	6
J	6
K	6
L	6

Old Method: Four-Firm Concentration Ratio

15% + 12% + 11% + 10% = 48%

New Method: Herfindahl Index

Square the market share of each firm and then add:

$(15)^2 + (12)^2 + (11)^2 + (10)^2 + (8)^2 + (7)^2 + (7)^2 + (6)^2 + (6)^2$
$+ (6)^2 + (6)^2 + (6)^2 = 932$

A Comparison of the Four-Firm Concentration Ratio and the Herfindahl Index

Using the old method (in this case, the four-firm concentration ratio), the top four firms in the industry have a 48 percent market share. The Justice Department would likely frown on a proposed merger between any of the top four firms and any other firm. However, the Herfindahl index of 932 is representative of an unconcentrated industry.

concentrated markets [markets with an index greater than 1,800] presumptively raise antitrust concerns . . . ."[1]

To illustrate, suppose 8 firms are in an industry. Two of the firms, A and B, want to merge. The market share of firm A is 30 percent, and the market share of firm B is 22 percent. The market shares for the other six firms in the industry are 15 percent, 10 percent, 10 percent, 5 percent, 5 percent, and 3 percent. The Herfindahl index in this industry currently is 1,868 ($30^2 + 22^2 + 15^2 + 10^2 + 10^2 + 5^2 + 5^2 + 3^2$).

If the merger is approved, there will be 7, not 8, firms. Moreover, the market share of the merged firm (when A and B form one firm) will be 52 percent. The Herfindahl index after the merger will be 3,188. In other words, the increase will be 1,320 points if the firms merge. With this substantial increase in the index, the proposed merger is likely to be blocked.

INNOVATION AND CONCENTRATION RATIOS According to the 1999 *Economic Report of the President,* more than half of all productivity gains in the U.S. economy in the previous 50 years, as measured by output per labor hour, came from innovation and technical change. Because innovation and technical change are so important to our economic well-being, some economists argue that concentration ratios should not play so large a role in determining a merger's approval. The merger's effect on innovation should also be taken into account. There is some evidence that antitrust authorities are beginning to accept this line of thinking.

In the past, small firms in highly competitive markets with many rivals were thought to have a stronger incentive to innovate than firms in markets where only a few firms existed and where each firm had sizable market power. Increasingly, however, these small competitive firms seem often to face a greater risk of innovation than firms with substantial market power and therefore they tend to innovate less.

To illustrate, consider a market with 100 firms, each of which supplies one-hundredth of the market. Suppose one of these firms invests heavily in research and develops a new product or process. It has to worry about any of its 99 rivals soon developing a similar innovation and therefore reducing the value of its innovation. On the other hand, if a firm is one of four firms and has substantial market power, it doesn't face as much so-called innovative risk. It has only three, not 99, rivals to worry about. And, of course, the less likely it is that competitors can render one's own innovations less valuable, the higher the expected return from innovating will be.

1. See http://www.usdoj.gov/atr/public/testimony/hhi.htm.

Today, antitrust authorities say that they consider the benefits of both competition and innovation when ruling on proposed mergers. On the one hand, increased competition lowers prices for consumers. On the other hand, monopoly power may yield more innovation. If it does, then the lower prices brought about through increased competition have to be weighed against the increased innovation that may come about through greater market concentration and monopoly power.

ⓣhinking Like AN ECONOMIST

Different Roads to the Same Destination If a firm has a large share of the market, the economist will ask, "Is there only one possible explanation for this, or are there many?" If there are many, then the economist will try to find out which is the correct explanation. As an analogy, suppose someone gets the highest grade in three of three courses. There may well be more than one explanation: the person could be studying more than anyone else. Or the student could be innately smarter than anyone else. Or the individual could be cheating. The economist knows that usually different roads end up at the same destination. Trying to figure out which road was taken to the destination is part of the task economists set for themselves. ●●●

Antitrust and Mergers

There are three basic types of mergers.

Horizontal Merger
A merger between firms that are selling similar products in the same market.

Vertical Merger
A merger between companies in the same industry but at different stages of the production process.

Conglomerate Merger
A merger between companies in different industries.

1. A horizontal merger is a merger between firms that are selling similar products in the same market. For example, both companies A and B produce cars. If the two companies combine under single ownership of control, the merger is horizontal.

2. A vertical merger is a merger between companies in the same industry but at different stages of the production process. A vertical merger occurs between companies one of which buys (or sells) something from (or to) the other. For example, company C, which produces cars, buys tires from company D. If the two companies combine under single ownership of control, the merger is vertical.

3. A conglomerate merger is a merger between companies in different industries. For example, if company E, in the car industry, and company F, in the pharmaceutical industry, combine under single ownership of control, the result is a conglomerate.

Of the three types of mergers—vertical, horizontal, and conglomerate—the federal government looks most carefully at proposed horizontal mergers. These mergers are the most likely to change the degree of concentration, or competition, in an industry. For example, if General Motors (cars) and Ford Motor Company (cars) were to horizontally merge, competition in the car industry would be likely to decrease by more than if General Motors (cars) and BF Goodrich (tires) were to vertically merge. In the latter case, the competition among car companies and among tire companies is likely to be the same after the merger as it was before. (This is not necessarily the case. The government does not always approve vertical mergers; in some notable examples, it has not.)

Common Misconceptions About Antitrust Policy

Some people believe that all the big issues in antitrust policy have been settled. This belief is simply not true. For example, predatory pricing practices—such as selling a good for a low price to eliminate competitors—are deemed illegal. But difficult questions arise: How low must a price be before it is deemed predatory? How long must the low price persist before it is deemed predatory?

Also, in a monopoly case, the relevant market is not always obvious. For example, is the relevant market for soft drinks the soft drink market? Or is it the beverage market? Or is it the anything-to-drink market (which includes water, juices, coffee, tea, and so on)?

Finally, mergers and tying arrangements are deemed illegal if they "substantially reduce competition," but how much competition has to be reduced before it is "substantial"?

Network Monopolies

A network connects things. A telephone network connects telephones; the Internet (which is a network of networks) connects computers; and a bank network connects, among other things, automated teller machines (ATMs).

A **network good** is a good whose value increases as the expected number of units sold increases. A telephone is a network good; you buy a telephone to network with other people. It has little value to you if you expect only 100 people to buy telephones, but its value increases if you expect thousands or millions of people to buy telephones. Software is also a network good in the sense that if Smith and Jones both buy software X, they can then easily exchange documents. As new buyers buy a network good, the present owners of the good receive greater benefits because the network connects them to more people. For example, if Brown and Thompson also buy software X, Smith and Jones benefit more because they can exchange documents with two more people.

The production and sales of a network good can lead to monopoly. Suppose three companies (A, B, and C) make some version of network good X. Company A makes the most popular version; so its good is said to have the greatest network worthiness. Consequently, people who are thinking of buying good X buy it from company A. As more people purchase good X from company A, the network worthiness increases, prompting even more people to buy good X from company A rather than from the other two companies. Eventually, the customers of companies B and C may switch to company A, and at some point almost everyone buys good X from company A. Company A is a network monopoly.

ANTITRUST POLICY FOR NETWORK MONOPOLIES Currently, the antitrust authorities move against a network monopoly based on how it behaves, not because of what it is. For example, the authorities would not issue a complaint against company A in our example unless it undertook predatory or exclusionary practices to *maintain* its monopoly position.

INNOVATION IN NETWORK MONOPOLIES Recall that economists are undecided as to whether market share assists or detracts from innovation. For example, one firm among four firms may have less innovative risk than one firm among 100. Therefore, the firm with a larger market share would innovate more, *ceteris paribus*. Presumably, a network monopoly will have a large market share and therefore should be a major innovator.

Actually, the situation may be different for network monopolies because high switching costs sometimes accompany a network monopoly. To illustrate, suppose firm A produces network good A. Network good A begins to sell quite well, and, because it is a network good, its robust sales increase its value to potential customers. Potential customers turn into actual customers, and before long good A has set the market, or industry, standard.

Because network good A is now the industry standard and because network goods (especially those related to the high-tech industries) are sometimes difficult to learn, it may have a lock on the market. Specifically, a **lock-in effect** increases the costs of switching from good A to another good. Because of the relatively high switching costs, good A has some staying power in the market. Firm A, the producer of good A, thus has staying power too, possibly causing firm A to rest on its laurels. Instead of innovating—instead of trying to outcompete its existing and future rivals with better production processes or better products—it may do very little. Firm A will realize that the high switching costs keep customers from changing to a different network good. Some economists suggest that, in this environment, the network monopoly may have little reason to innovate.

Network Good
A good whose value increases as the expected number of units sold increases.

Lock-In Effect
The situation when a product or technology becomes the standard and is difficult or impossible to dislodge as the standard.

High-Priced Ink Cartridges and Expensive Minibars

Shopping for a printer for your computer, you see one priced at $69. "That's a good price," you think; so you buy it. Later, you learn that you have to pay $33 for an ink cartridge. The printer wasn't so well priced after all.

You spend the night at a hotel. Once in your room, you look in the minibar and decide to eat a small bag of almonds. You learn later, after looking at your bill, that the small bag of almonds came with a price tag of $6.

You sign up with a cell phone company, decide on a plan, and get a free cell phone. Later, you learn that for every minute you go over your allotted monthly number of minutes, you pay 33¢.

Because of such everyday occurrences, some economists today are talking about the hidden fee economy—an economy in which many main items for sale (a printer, a hotel room, cell phone service) come with high hidden fees that you did not expect when you purchased the main item.

According to two economists, David Laibson and Xavier Gabaix, firms reap certain benefits through hidden fees. (There are certain costs too, but sometimes the benefits are greater than the costs.) For example,[2] hotel X rents its rooms for $80 a night and has some hidden fees: $12 for parking, $6 for a small bag of almonds from the minibar, and $3 for a local call. Hotel Y rents its rooms for $95 a night, and it has no high hidden fees. It does not charge for parking or for a local call, and the small bag of almonds comes at the same price as at a grocery store. What are the major differences between the two hotels? On the basis of just the price of a room, hotel X is cheaper than hotel Y. Add in hidden and unexpectedly high fees, hotel X is a culprit and hotel Y is not.

The natural question is why doesn't hotel Y simply advertise the fact that its competitor, hotel X, is trying to dupe its customers by charging high hidden fees? (The ad might read, "Sure, hotel X has cheaper rooms, but what about all the hidden fees?") According to Laibon and Gabaix, that strategy could backfire because of one of the two types of customers

that frequent hotel X. One type of customer is unaware of the hidden fees and initially responds to the lower room rate of hotel X. With this customer, the strategy of pointing out the hidden fees of hotel X will be successful. Another type of customer is sophisticated when it comes to sellers' tactics. This customer realizes that if she doesn't park at hotel X, doesn't eat anything from the minibar, and makes calls on her cell phone instead of on the hotel telephone, she can then get a lower-priced room at hotel X. The ad by hotel Y simply notifies the sophisticated customer that she can get a good deal at the hotel with the hidden fees, as long as she doesn't purchase the goods or services that come with the high hidden fees.

So hotel Y gains and loses with its ad pointing out the high hidden fees of hotel X. It gains the clueless customers ("Thanks for telling me about those hidden fees!"), but it may lose some sophisticated customers ("Thanks for telling me about the lower-priced rooms your competitor is offering!"). If hotel Y thinks it will lose more sophisticated customers than it will gain clueless ones, it will not run the ad. Instead, it may simply join the ranks of hotels like hotel X and lower its room rate and increase the use of high hidden fees.

But consider something else. Barry Nalebuff, a professor of business strategy, has noted that a firm that charges hidden fees incurs a cost and that cost comes in the form of customers getting angry at the hidden fees. Angry customers, Nalebuff says, often turn their backs on sellers they are angry with. In other words, they seek out other (perhaps more up-front and straightforward) sellers to buy from.

In the end, it becomes a matter of a seller having to consider both the benefits and the costs of a hidden fees strategy. Perhaps initially the benefits outweigh the costs, but there is no guarantee that, in time, the costs won't rise above the benefits.

---

2. The source of the material in this feature (and the example) is Christopher Shea," The Hidden Economy," *The Boston Globe*, June 27, 2006.

SELF-TEST

(Answers to Self-Test questions are in Answers to Self-Test Questions at the back of the book.)

1. Why does it matter whether a market is defined broadly or narrowly for purposes of antitrust policy?

2. Suppose that 20 firms are in an industry and that each firm has a 5 percent market share. What is the four-firm concentration ratio for this industry? What is the Herfindahl index?

3. What is the advantage of the Herfindahl index over the four- and eight-firm concentration ratios? Explain your answer.

Macs, PCs, and People Who Are Different

Tracey currently works on a Windows-based PC but is thinking of switching to a Mac: "I have heard good things about a Mac, and part of me would like to switch to a Mac, but I have some problems. First, many more people use a PC than a Mac. Second, I'm not sure how long it will take me to get up to speed on a Mac. I don't think the learning curve is that steep, but it's something to consider."

© IMAGE COPYRIGHT DMITRY MELNIKOV, 2009. USED UNDER LICENSE FROM SHUTTERSTOCK.COM

What Tracey is noticing is that her Windows-based PC is a network good (a good whose value increases as the expected number of units sold increases). Tracey might stick with a PC partly because so many other people use PCs. This is not to say that a PC is not a good product. It's just that, despite how good a product it is, people either initially choose a PC instead of a Mac or stay with a PC instead of switching to a Mac partly because so many more millions of people use PCs than Macs.

Next, as Tracey has pointed out, she will have to learn how to do things differently if she switches from a PC to a Mac; that is, she incurs switching costs. The greater the switching costs are, the more likely Tracey will feel locked in to a PC. So thinking about switching from a PC to a Mac involves considering network goods and lock-in effects.

The concepts of a netwook good and the lock-in effect apply to other things. All of us were born into a certain world, where certain people were around us, speaking a certain language, listening to certain kinds of music, abiding by certain rules and customs, and so on. Might our immediate environment and the people, language, and customs we deal with in that environment be a network good of sorts? Specifically, consider the language we learned as children. We learn a language—any language—partly because other people speak it. There is no reason to learn Italian,

English, or Spanish if only a few people speak these languages.

Of course, when we learned a language as children, we didn't choose the language we would learn; we learned the language that the people around us spoke. What language would you have chosen to learn if you could have chosen one as an infant? It is very likely that you would have chosen the language that your parents and relatives were speaking.

Now, of course, that you have learned a language, learning another language comes with costs. This learning curve is analogous to the situation of a person who has learned how to operate a PC and is learning how to operate a Mac. In other words, switching costs are involved in learning a new language. To a degree, these costs might keep many people locked in to their native language.

Furthermore, just as learning a new language might be costly, learning how to deal with people who are different from you may be costly: people raised in a different culture, people who like different music than you, people who eat different foods, and so on. The PC–Mac issue might simply be presenting itself in a different guise. Speaking English, listening to rock 'n' roll, eating steak, and watching sports might be the network good in much the same way that the Windows-based PC is a network good. The switching costs of learning to speak Italian, listening to opera, eating different-tasting foods, and watching soccer might come with (what you deem to be) unusually high switching costs. To a degree, you might feel and be locked in to who you are and what you do (and perhaps even to what you think) because the switching costs are as high as they are.

REGULATION

This section examines the types of regulation, theories of regulation, the stated objectives of regulatory agencies, and the effects of regulation on natural and other monopolies.

The Case of Natural Monopoly

We know that if economies of scale are so pronounced or so large in an industry that only one firm can survive, that firm is a *natural monopoly*. Firms that supply local electricity, gas, and water service are usually considered natural monopolies.

EXHIBIT 2

The Natural Monopoly Situation

The only existing firm produces Q_1 at an average total cost of ATC_1. (Q_1 is the output at which $MR = MC$; to simplify the diagram, the MR curve is not shown.) Resource allocative efficiency exists at Q_2. There are two ways to obtain this output level: (1) The only existing firm can increase its production to Q_2, or (2) a new firm can enter the market and produce Q_3, which is the difference between Q_2 and Q_1. The first way minimizes total cost; the second way does not. This, then, is a natural monopoly situation: one firm can supply the entire output demanded at a lower cost than two or more firms can.

In Exhibit 2, the market consists of one firm, which produces Q_1 units of output at an average total cost of ATC_1. (Q_1 is the output at which $MR = MC$; to simplify the diagram, the MR curve is not shown.) At Q_1, the allocation of resources is inefficient. Resource allocative efficiency exists when the marginal benefit to demanders of the resources used in the goods they buy equals the marginal cost to suppliers of the resources used in the production of the goods they sell. In Exhibit 2, resource allocative efficiency exists at Q_2, corresponding to the point where the demand curve intersects the MC curve.

There are two ways to reach the higher, efficient quantity of output, Q_2: (1) The firm currently producing Q_1 could increase its output to Q_2. (2) Another firm could enter the market and produce Q_3—the difference between Q_2 and Q_1. Each way has its associated costs. If the firm currently in the market increases its production to Q_2, it incurs average total costs of ATC_2. If, instead, a new firm enters the market and produces Q_3, it incurs an average total cost of ATC_3. In this way, both firms together produce Q_2, but the new firm incurs average total costs of ATC_3, whereas the existing firm incurs average total costs of ATC_1.

As long as the objective is to increase output to the level of resource allocative efficiency, it is cheaper (total costs are lower) to have the firm currently in the market increase its output to Q_2 than to have two firms together produce Q_2. So the situation in Exhibit 2 describes a natural monopoly situation. *Natural monopoly* exists when one firm can supply the entire output demanded at lower cost than two or more firms can. A natural monopoly will evolve over time as the low-cost producer undercuts its competitors.

Some economists say that the natural monopolist will charge the monopoly price. In Exhibit 3, the natural monopoly firm produces Q_1, at which marginal revenue equals marginal cost, and charges price P_1, which is the highest price per unit consistent with the output it produces. Because it charges the monopoly price, some people argue that the natural monopoly firm should be regulated. The form that the regulation should take is a question addressed in the next section.

Regulating the Natural Monopoly

The natural monopoly may be regulated through price, profit, or output regulation.

1. *Price regulation.* Marginal cost pricing is one form of price regulation. The objective is to set a price for the natural monopoly firm that equals its marginal cost at the quantity of output at which demand intersects marginal cost. In Exhibit 4, this price is P_1. At this price, the natural monopoly takes a loss. At Q_1, average total cost is greater than price, thus total cost is greater than total revenue.[3] Obviously, the natural monopoly would rather go out of business than be subject to this type of regulation unless it receives a subsidy for its operation.

---

3. Remember that $TC = ATC \times Q$ and $TR = P \times Q$. Here $ATC > P$; so it follows that $TC > TR$.

2. *Profit regulation.* Government may want the natural monopoly to earn only zero economic profits. If so, government will require the natural monopoly to charge a price of P_2 (because $P_2 = ATC$) and to supply the quantity demanded at that price (Q_2). This form of regulation is often called *average cost pricing*. Theoretically, this may seem like a good way to proceed, but in practice it often turns out differently. The problem is that if the natural monopoly is always held to zero economic profits—and is not allowed to fall below or rise above this level—then it has an incentive to let costs rise. Higher costs—in the form of higher salaries or more luxurious offices—simply mean higher prices to cover the higher costs. In this case, average cost pricing is not likely to be an efficient way to proceed.

3. *Output regulation.* Government can mandate a quantity of output it wants the natural monopoly to produce. Suppose this is Q_3 in Exhibit 4, where there are positive economic profits because price is above average total cost. However, the natural monopoly could want even higher profits, and, at a fixed quantity of output, higher profits can be obtained by lowering costs. The natural monopolist might lower costs by reducing the quality of the good or service it sells, knowing that it faces no direct competition and that it is protected (by government) from competitors.

Government regulation of a natural monopoly does not always turn out the way it was intended. Regulation—whether it takes the form of price, profit, or output regulation—can distort the incentives of those who operate the natural monopoly. For example, if

EXHIBIT 3

The Profit-Maximizing Natural Monopoly

The natural monopoly that seeks to maximize profits will produce the quantity of output at which $MR = MC$ and charge the (monopoly) price, P_1.

Profit-maximizing natural monopoly will:

1. Produce Q_1 where $MR = MC$
2. Charge monopoly price, P_1

EXHIBIT 4

Regulating a Natural Monopoly

The government can regulate a natural monopoly through (1) price regulation, (2) profit regulation, or (3) output regulation. Price regulation usually means marginal cost pricing, and profit regulation usually means average cost pricing.

profit is regulated to the extent that zero economic profits are guaranteed, then the natural monopoly has little incentive to hold costs down. Furthermore, the owners of the natural monopoly have an incentive to try to influence the government officials or other persons who are regulating the firm.

In addition, each of the three types of regulation requires information. For example, if the government wishes to set price equal to marginal cost or average total cost for the natural monopoly, it must know the cost conditions of the firm.

Three problems arise in gathering information: (1) The cost information is not easy to determine, even for the natural monopoly itself. (2) The cost information can be rigged (to a degree) by the natural monopoly, and therefore the regulators will not get a true picture of the firm. (3) The regulators have little incentive to obtain accurate information because they are likely to keep their jobs and prestige even if they work with less than accurate information. (This raises another question: Who will ensure that the regulators do a good job?)

Regulatory Lag

The time period between when a natural monopoly's costs change and when the regulatory agency adjusts prices for it.

Finally, the issue of *regulatory lag* is indirectly related to information. Regulatory lag is the time period between when a natural monopoly's costs change and when the regulatory agency adjusts prices for it. For example, suppose the local gas company rates are regulated. The gas company's costs rise, and it seeks a rate hike through the local regulatory body. The rate hike is not likely to be approved quickly. The gas company will probably have to submit an application for a rate hike, document its case, have a date set for a hearing, argue its case at the hearing, and then wait for the regulatory agency to decide on the merits of the application. Many months may pass between the beginning of the process and the end. During that time, the regulated firm is operating in ways and under conditions that both the firm and the regulatory body might not have desired.

ⓣhinking Like **AN ECONOMIST**

Something Is Not Always Better Than Nothing The public is perhaps naturally inclined to think that a solution (e.g., regulation) to a problem (e.g., monopoly) is better than no solution at all—that something is better than nothing. The economist has learned, though, that a so-called solution can do one of three things: (1) solve a problem, (2) not solve a problem but do no damage, or (3) make the problem worse. Thinking through the entire range of possibilities is natural for an economist, who, after all, understands that solutions come with both costs and benefits. ●●●

Regulating Industries That Are Not Natural Monopolies

Some firms are regulated even though they are not natural monopolies. For instance, in the past, government has regulated both the airline and trucking industries. In the trucking industry, the Interstate Commerce Commission (ICC) fixed routes, set minimum freight rates, and erected barriers to entry. In the airline industry, the Civil Aeronautics Board (CAB) did much the same thing. Some economists view the regulation of competitive industries as unnecessary. They see it as evidence that the firms being regulated are, in turn, controlling the regulation to reduce their competition.

Theories of Regulation

Capture Theory of Regulation

A theory holding that no matter what the motive is for the initial regulation and the establishment of the regulatory agency, eventually the agency will be captured (controlled) by the special interests of the industry being regulated.

The capture theory of regulation holds that no matter what the motive is for the initial regulation and the establishment of the regulatory agency, eventually the agency will be captured (i.e., controlled) by the special interests of the industry being regulated. The following are a few of the interrelated points that have been put forth to support this theory:

1. In many cases, persons who have been in the industry are asked to regulate the industry because they know the most about it. Such regulators are likely to feel a bond with people in the industry, to see their side of the story more often than not, and thus to be inclined to cater to them.

2. At regulatory hearings, members of the industry attend in greater force than do taxpayers and consumers. The industry turns out in force because the regulatory hearing can affect it substantially and directly. In contrast, the effect on individual taxpayers and consumers is usually small and indirect (the effect is spread over millions of people). Thus, regulators are much more likely to hear and respond to the industry's side of the story.

3. Members of the regulated industry make a point of getting to know the members of the regulatory agency. They may talk frequently about business matters; perhaps they socialize. The bond between the two groups grows stronger over time, possibly having an impact on regulatory measures.

4. After they either retire or quit their jobs, regulators often go to work for the industries they once regulated.

The capture theory is markedly different from what has come to be called the public interest theory of regulation. This theory holds that regulators are seeking to do—and will do through regulation—what is in the best interest of the public or society at large.

An alternative to both theories is the public choice theory of regulation. This theory suggests that to understand the decisions of regulatory bodies, we must first understand how the decisions affect the regulators themselves. For example, a regulation that increases the power, size, and budget of the regulatory agency should not be viewed in the same way as a regulation that decreases the agency's power and size. The theory predicts that the outcomes of the regulatory process will tend to favor the regulators instead of either business interests or the public.

These are three interesting, different, and, at first sight, believable theories of regulation, and economists have directed much effort to testing them. There is no clear consensus yet, but in the area of business regulation, the adherents of the capture and public choice theories have been increasing.

The Costs and Benefits of Regulation

Suppose a business firm is polluting the air with smoke from its factories. The government passes an environmental regulation requiring such firms to purchase antipollution devices that reduce the smoke emitted into the air.

Among the benefits of this kind of regulation is the obvious one of cleaner air, but cleaner air can lead to other benefits. For example, people may have fewer medical problems in the future. In some parts of the country, pollution from cars and factories causes people to cough, feel tired, and experience eye discomfort. More important, some people have chronic medical problems from constantly breathing dirty air. Government regulation that reduces the amount of pollution in the air clearly helps these people.

However, regulation usually comes with costs as well as with benefits. For example, when a business firm incurs the cost of antipollution devices, its overall costs of production rise. Simply put, making its product is costlier for the firm after the regulation is imposed. As a result, the business firm may produce fewer units of its product, raising its product price and causing some workers to lose their jobs.

If you are a worker who loses your job, you may view the government's insistence on antipollution devices differently than if, say, you are someone suffering from chronic lung disease. If you have asthma, less pollution may be the difference between feeling well and feeling sick. If you are a worker for the business firm, less pollution may cost you your job. Ideally, you prefer a little less pollution in your neighborhood, but perhaps not at the cost of losing your job.

Economists are neither for nor against such government regulation. The job of the economist is to make the point that regulation involves both benefits and costs. To the person who sees only the costs, the economist asks, what about the benefits? To the person who sees only the benefits, the economist asks, what about the costs? Then, the economist goes on to outline the benefits and the costs as best as possible.

Public Interest Theory of Regulation

A theory holding that regulators are seeking to do—and will do through regulation—what is in the best interest of the public or society at large.

Public Choice Theory of Regulation

A theory holding that regulators are seeking to do—and will do through regulation—what is in their best interest (specifically to enhance their power and the size and budget of their regulatory agencies).

ⓕinding ECONOMICS

In an Irish Pub One person in an Irish pub says to a second person, "Remember the days when we could smoke in the pub?" The second person says, "I miss those days." Where is the economics?

What we see is regulation. At one time smoking was permissible in Irish pubs; today it is not. With regard to regulation, the question is often, who has the right to regulate? Critics of the Irish nonsmoking regulation argue that the pub owner should decide whether smoking will be allowed in the pub. Others argue differently, saying that people should not have to breathe in cigarette or cigar smoke if they don't want to. In other words, smoking is fine as long as others are not bothered by the smoke. ▲ ▲ ▲

Some Effects of Regulation Are Unintended

Besides outlining the benefits and costs of regulation, the economist tries to point out the possible unintended effects of regulation. To illustrate, suppose the government requires new cars to get an average of 40 miles per gallon of gasoline instead of, say, 30. Many people will say that this is a good requirement, reasoning that if car companies are made to produce cars that get better mileage, people will not need to buy and burn as much gasoline. Burning less gasoline means less air pollution.

This effect is not guaranteed, however. In fact, the effects could be quite different. If cars are more fuel efficient, people will buy less gasoline to drive from one place to another—say, from home to college. So the dollar cost per mile of driving will fall, and, as a result, people might drive more. Leisure driving on the weekend might become more common, people might begin to drive farther on vacations, and so on. If people begin to drive more, then the gasoline saving that resulted from the higher fuel economy standards might be offset or even outweighed. Higher gasoline consumption due to more driving will mean burning more gasoline and sending more pollutants into the air.

Thus a regulation requiring automakers to produce cars that get better fuel mileage may have an unintended effect. The net result might be that people purchase and burn more gasoline and thus produce more air pollution, not less as the government intended.

Deregulation

In the early 1970s, many economists, basing their arguments on the capture and public choice theories of regulation, argued that regulation was actually promoting and protecting market power instead of reducing it. They argued for deregulation. Since the late 1970s, many industries have been deregulated, including airlines, trucking, long-distance telephone service, and others.

Consider a few details relating to the deregulation of the airline industry. The Civil Aeronautics Act, which was passed in 1938, gave the Civil Aeronautics Authority (CAA) the authority to regulate airfares, the number of carriers on interstate routes, and the pattern of routes. The CAA's successor, the Civil Aeronautics Board (CAB), regulated fares in such a way that major air carriers could meet their average costs. An effect of this policy was that fares were raised so that high-cost, inefficient air carriers could survive. In addition, the CAB did not allow price competition among air carriers. As a result, air carriers usually competed in a nonprice dimension: they offered more scheduled flights, better meals, more popular in-flight movies, and so forth.

In 1978, under CAB Chairman Alfred Kahn, an economist, the airline industry was deregulated. With deregulation, airlines can compete on fares, initiate service along a new route, or discontinue a route. Empirical research after deregulation showed that passenger miles increased and fares decreased. For example, fares fell 20 percent in 1978 and approximately 14 percent between 1979 and 1984.

Deregulation has also led to a decline in costs in various industries. For example, a study by Clifford Winston of the Brookings Institution showed that since deregulation, costs in the airline industry have fallen 24 percent (per unit of output); in trucking, operating costs have fallen 30–35 percent per mile; in railroads, there has been a 50 percent decline in costs per ton-mile and a 141 percent increase in productivity; and in natural gas, there has been a 35 percent decline in operating and maintenance expenses.

SELF-TEST

1. What is a criticism of average cost pricing?
2. State the essence of the capture theory of regulation.
3. What is the difference between the capture theory and the public choice theory of regulation?
4. Are economists for or against regulation?

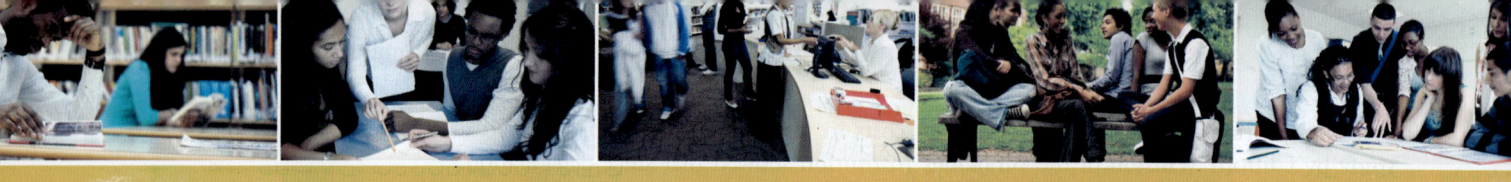

OFFICE HOURS

"What Is the Advantage of the Herfindahl Index?"

CHAPTER SUMMARY

DEALING WITH MONOPOLY POWER

- A monopoly produces less than a perfectly competitive firm produces (assuming the same revenue and cost conditions), charges a higher price, and causes a deadweight loss. This is the monopoly power problem, and solving it is usually put forth as a reason for antitrust laws and/or government regulatory actions. Some economists note, though, that government antitrust and regulatory actions do not always have the intended effect. In addition, such actions are sometimes implemented when there is no monopoly power problem to solve.

ANTITRUST LAWS

- Two major criticisms have been directed at the antitrust acts. First, some argue that the language in the laws is vague; for example, even though the words "restraint of trade" are used in the Sherman Act, the act does not clearly explain what actions constitute a restraint of trade. Second, it has been argued that some antitrust acts appear to hinder, rather than promote, competition; an example is the Robinson-Patman Act.

- Antitrust policy has a few unsettled points. One centers on the proper definition of a market, specifically whether it should be defined narrowly or broadly. How this question is answered has an impact on which firms are considered monopolies. In addition, the use of concentration ratios for identifying monopolies or deciding whether to allow two firms to enter into a merger has been called into question. Recently, concentration ratios have been largely replaced (for purposes of implementing antitrust policy) with the Herfindahl index, which is subject to some of the same criticisms as the concentration ratios. Antitrust authorities are also beginning to consider the benefits of innovation in ruling on proposed mergers.

REGULATION

- Even if we assume that the intent of regulation is to serve the public interest, we may not assume that it will do so. To work as

INSTRUCTOR:

Others have made that very point. In fact, both the four- and eight-firm concentration ratios, as well as the Herfindal index, have been criticized for implicitly arguing from firm size and industry concentration to market power. Both assume firms with large market shares have market power that they are likely to be abusing, but perhaps they're not. Size could be a function of efficiency, and a firm with a large market share could be serving the buying public well.

STUDENT:

Yes, that is what I was getting at. It seems to me that the process of how a firm got to be big matters.

INSTRUCTOR:

I should say that the terms "process" and "behavior" have come to mean more in recent years, particularly with economists and with the Antitrust Division of the U.S. Justice Department. With respect to behavior, more emphasis these days is placed on how the firm behaves—no matter its size and market power. To illustrate, two firms of equal size relative to other firms in their respective industries could behave differently. One firm reduces output and charges higher prices, and the other firm increases output and charges lower prices.

POINTS TO REMEMBER

1. In the two settings (four firms have 50 percent market share but the number of other firms in the industry is different), the four-firm concentration ratio is the same, but the Herfindahl index is not. The Herfindahl index supplies more information, specifically about the dispersion of firm size in an industry, than either the four- or eight-firm concentration ratio.

2. In recent years, process (how did the firm get to be big?) and behavior (how does the firm act?) have come to mean more when evaluating firms.

desired, (1) regulation must be based on complete information (e.g., the regulatory body must know the cost conditions of the regulated firm), and (2) it must not distort incentives (e.g., to keep costs down). Many economists are quick to point out that neither condition is likely to be fully met.

- Government uses three basic types of regulation to regulate natural monopolies: price, profit, or output regulation. Price regulation usually means marginal cost price regulation—that is, setting $P = MC$. Profit regulation usually means zero economic profits. Output regulation specifies a particular quantity of output that the natural monopoly must produce.

- The capture theory of regulation holds that no matter what the motive is for the initial regulation and the establishment of the regulatory agency, eventually, the agency will be captured (controlled) by the special interests of the industry being regulated. The public interest theory holds that regulators are seeking to do—and will do through regulation—what is in the best interest of the public or society at large. The public choice theory holds that regulators are seeking to do—and will do through regulation—what is in their best interest (specifically, enhance their own power, size, and budget).

KEY TERMS AND CONCEPTS

Antitrust Law
Trust
Herfindahl Index
Horizontal Merger

Vertical Merger
Conglomerate Merger
Network Good
Lock-In Effect

Regulatory Lag
Capture Theory of Regulation
Public Interest Theory of
 Regulation

Public Choice Theory of
 Regulation

QUESTIONS AND PROBLEMS

1. Why might profit regulation lead to rising costs for the regulated firm?

2. Explain how the lock-in effect might make it less likely for the firm (that benefits from the lock-in effect) to innovate.

3. What is the implication of saying that regulation is likely to affect incentives?

4. Discuss the advantages and disadvantages of regulation (as you see it).

5. Explain price regulation, profit regulation, and output regulation.

6. It is usually asserted that public utilities such as electric companies and gas companies are natural monopolies, but an assertion is not proof. How would you go about trying to prove (or disprove) that electric companies and the like are (or are not) natural monopolies? (*Hint:* Consider comparing the average total cost of a public utility that serves many customers with the average total cost of a public utility that serves relatively few customers.)

7. How does a vertical merger differ from a horizontal merger? Why would the government look more carefully at one than at the other?

8. The courts have ruled that it is a reasonable restraint of trade (and therefore permissible) for the owner of a business to sell his business and sign a contract with the new owner saying he will not compete with her within a vicinity of, say, 100 miles, for a period of, say, 5 years. If this is a reasonable restraint of trade, can you give an example of what you would consider an unreasonable restraint of trade? Explain how you decide what is a reasonable restraint of trade and what isn't.

9. What is one difference between the four-firm concentration ratio and the Herfindahl index?

10. In your opinion, what is the best way to deal with the monopoly power problem? Do you advocate antitrust laws, regulation, or something not discussed in the chapter? Give reasons for your answer.

11. Explain why defining a market narrowly or broadly can make a difference in how antitrust policy is implemented.

12. George Stigler and Claire Friedland studied both unregulated and regulated electric utilities and found no difference in the rates they charged. One could draw the conclusion that regulation is ineffective when it comes to utility rates. What ideas or hypotheses presented in this chapter might have predicted this result?

13. Why was the Robinson-Patman Act passed? The Wheeler-Lea Act? The Celler-Kefauver Antimerger Act?

14. What is the major difference between the capture theory of regulation and the public interest theory of regulation?

WORKING WITH NUMBERS AND GRAPHS

1. Calculate the Herfindahl index and the four-firm concentration ratio for the following industry:

Firms	Market Share (%)
A	17
B	15
C	14
D	14
E	12
F	10
G	9
H	9

Use the following figure to answer questions 2–4.

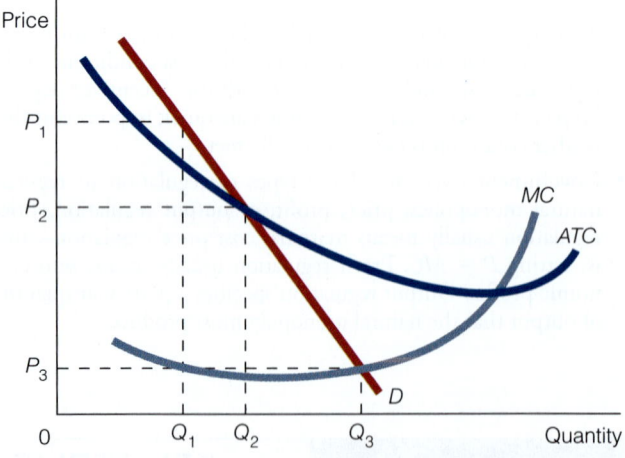

2. Is the firm in the figure a natural monopoly? Explain your answer.

3. Will the firm in the figure earn profits if it produces Q_3 and charges P_3? Explain your answer.

4. Which quantity in the figure is consistent with profit regulation? With price regulation? Explain your answers.

CHAPTER 27

FACTOR MARKETS: WITH EMPHASIS ON THE LABOR MARKET

Introduction Employees want to know why their salaries can't be higher; they would like to have more income for spending and saving. Employees might wonder, "Why am I not getting paid $10,000 more? Why not $20,000 more?" Of course, employers look at salaries differently; they would like to pay lower salaries. Employers may look at a salary and wonder, "Why couldn't I have paid $10,000 less? Why not $20,000 less?" Salaries are determined by economic forces. This chapter identifies the factors and the process affecting your pay. This chapter, without a doubt, is relevant to you.

FACTOR MARKETS

Just as there is a demand for and a supply of a product, there is a demand for and a supply of a factor, or resource, such as labor.

The Demand for a Factor

All firms purchase factors to make products to sell, whether they are perfectly competitive firms, oligopolistic firms, or whatever. For example, farmers buy tractors and fertilizer to produce crops to sell. General Motors buys steel to build cars to sell.

The demand for factors is a derived demand; that is, it is derived from and directly related to the demand for the product that the resources go to produce. If the demand for the product rises, so does the demand for the factors that go into the making of the product. If the demand for the product falls, so does the demand for the factors. For example, if the demand for a university education falls, so does the demand for university professors. If the demand for computers rises, so does the demand for skilled computer workers.

When the demand for a seller's product rises, the seller needs to decide how much more of a factor to buy. Marginal revenue product and marginal factor cost are relevant to this decision.

Derived Demand
Demand that is the result of some other demand. For example, factor demand is derived from the demand for the products that the factors go to produce.

finding ECONOMICS

In a Restaurant Frank is sitting in a restaurant giving his order to the server. Where is the economics?

It is to be found in the server. The demand for servers is a derived demand—derived from the demand for eating out at restaurants. If the demand for eating out falls, we can expect the demand for servers to fall; if the demand for eating out rises, we can expect the demand for servers to rise. ▲ ▲ ▲

Marginal Revenue Product: Two Ways to Calculate It

Marginal Revenue Product (MRP)
The additional revenue generated by employing an additional factor unit.

Marginal revenue product (*MRP*) is the additional revenue generated by employing an additional factor unit, such as one more unit of labor. For example, if a firm employs one more unit of a factor and its total revenue rises by $20, the *MRP* of the factor equals $20. Marginal revenue product can be calculated in two ways:

$$MRP = \frac{\Delta TR}{\Delta \text{Quantity of the factor}}$$

or

$$MRP = MR \times MPP$$

where *TR* = total revenue, *MR* = marginal revenue, and *MPP* = marginal physical product. Exhibit 1 presents data for a hypothetical firm to show the two methods for calculating *MRP*.

METHOD 1: *MRP* = Δ*TR*/Δ*QUANTITY OF THE FACTOR* Look at Exhibit 1(a).

- Column 1 shows the different quantities of factor X.
- Column 2 shows the quantity of output produced at the different quantities of factor X.
- Column 3 lists the price and the marginal revenue of the product that the factor goes to produce. We have assumed that the price of the product (*P*) equals the product's marginal revenue (*MR*). So the seller in Exhibit 1 is a perfectly competitive firm, for which *P* = *MR*.
- In column 4, we calculate the total revenue, or price multiplied by quantity.
- In column 5, we calculate the marginal revenue product (*MRP*) by dividing the change in total revenue (from column 4) by the change in the quantity of the factor.

METHOD 2: *MRP* = *MR* × *MPP* Now look at Exhibit 1(b). Columns 1 and 2 are the same as in Exhibit 1(a), and the other columns show the corresponding calculations.

The *MRP* Curve Is the Firm's Factor Demand Curve

Look again at column 5 in Exhibit 1, which shows the *MRP* for factor X. By plotting the data in column 5 against the quantity of the factor (in column 1), we derive the *MRP* curve for factor X. This curve is the same as the firm's demand curve for factor X (or simply the firm's factor demand curve) (see Exhibit 2).

MRP curve = Factor demand curve

EXHIBIT 1

Calculating Marginal Revenue Product (MRP)

There are two methods of calculating *MRP*. Part (a) shows one method (*MRP* = Δ*TR*/Δ*Quantity* of the factor), and (b) shows the other (*MRP* = *MR* × *MPP*).

(1) Quantity of Factor X	(2) Quantity of Output, Q	(3) Product Price, Marginal Revenue (P = MR)	(4) Total Revenue TR = P × Q = (3) × (2)	(5) Marginal Revenue Product of Factor X MRP = ΔTR/ΔQuantity of factor X = Δ(4)/Δ(1)
0	10*	$5	$ 50	—
1	19	5	95	$45
2	27	5	135	40
3	34	5	170	35
4	40	5	200	30
5	45	5	225	25

(a)

(1) Quantity of Factor X	(2) Quantity of Output, Q	(3) Marginal Physical Product MPP = Δ(2)/Δ(1)	(4) Product Price, Marginal Revenue (P = MR)	(5) Marginal Revenue Product of Factor X MRP = MR × MPP = (4) × (3)
0	10*	—	$5	—
1	19	9	5	$45
2	27	8	5	40
3	34	7	5	35
4	40	6	5	30
5	45	5	5	25

(b)

*Because the quantity of output is 10 at 0 units of factor X, other factors (not shown in the exhibit) must also be used to produce the good.

The *MRP* curve in Exhibit 2 is downward sloping. You can understand why when you recall that *MRP* can be calculated as *MRP* = *MR* × *MPP*. With regard to *MPP*, the marginal physical product of a factor, you know that, according to the law of diminishing marginal returns, eventually the *MPP* of a factor will diminish. Because *MRP* is equal to *MR* × *MPP* and because *MPP* will eventually decline, *MRP* will eventually decline too.

Value Marginal Product (VMP)
The price of the good multiplied by the marginal physical product of the factor: *VMP* = *P* × *MPP*.

Value Marginal Product

Value marginal product (*VMP*) is equal to the price of the product multiplied by the marginal physical product of the factor:

$$VMP = P \times MPP$$

For example, if *P* = $10 and *MPP* = 9 units, then *VMP* = $90. Think of *VMP* as a measure of the value that each factor unit adds to the firm's product or simply as *MPP* measured in dollars.

A firm wants to know the *VMP* of a factor because it helps in deciding how many units of the factor to

EXHIBIT 2

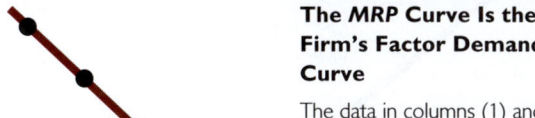

MRP Curve = Factor Demand Curve

Quantity of Factor X

The MRP Curve Is the Firm's Factor Demand Curve

The data in columns (1) and (5) in Exhibit 1 are plotted to derive the *MRP* curve. The *MRP* curve shows the various quantities of the factor the firm is willing to buy at different prices, which is what a demand curve shows. The *MRP* curve is the firm's factor demand curve.

hire. To illustrate, put yourself in the shoes of the owner of a firm that produces computers. One of the factors you need to produce computers is labor, and currently you are thinking of hiring an additional worker. Whether you actually hire the additional worker will depend on (1) how much better off you are—in dollars and cents—with the additional worker and (2) what you have to pay the new hire. Simply put, you want to know what the worker will do for you and what you will have to pay the worker. The *VMP* of a factor is a dollar measure of how much an additional unit of the factor will do for you.

An Important Question: Is *MRP* = *VMP*?

In the computations of *MRP* in Exhibit 1, price (*P*) was equal to marginal revenue (*MR*) because we assumed the firm was perfectly competitive. Because *P* = *MR* for a perfectly competitive firm, then for a perfectly competitive firm *MRP* = *VMP*. Given that

$$MRP = MR \times MPP$$

and

$$VMP = P \times MPP$$

then, because *P* = *MR* for a perfectly competitive firm,

$$MRP = VMP \text{ for a perfectly competitive firm}$$

See Exhibit 3(a).

Although *MRP* = *VMP* for perfectly competitive firms, this is not the case for firms that are price searchers (monopolist, monopolistic competitive, and oligopolistic firms). All

---

EXHIBIT 3

MRP and VMP Curves

$MRP = MR \times MPP$ and $VMP = P \times MPP$.
(a) The *MRP* (factor demand) curve and *VMP* curve. These are the same for a price taker, or

perfectly competitive firm, because *P* = *MR*.
(b) The *MRP* (factor demand) curve and *VMP* curve for a firm that is a price searcher (monopolist, monopolistic competitor, oligopolist). The

MRP curve lies below the *VMP* curve because for these firms, *P* > *MR*.

(a)

(b)

these firms face downward-sloping demand curves for their products. For all of these firms, $P > MR$, and so VMP (which is $P \times MPP$) is greater than MRP (which is $MR \times MPP$).[1] See Exhibit 3(b).

> $VMP > MRP$ for monopolists, monopolistic competitors, and oligopolists

Marginal Factor Cost: The Firm's Factor Supply Curve

Marginal factor cost (MFC) is the additional cost incurred by employing an additional factor unit. It is calculated as

$$MFC = \frac{\Delta TC}{\Delta \text{Quantity of the factor}}$$

where TC = total costs.

Let's suppose a firm is a factor price taker: it can buy all it wants of a factor at the equilibrium price. For example, suppose the equilibrium price for factor X is $5. If a firm is a factor price taker, it can buy any quantity of factor X at $5 per factor unit [see Exhibit 4(a)].

For this kind of firm, the marginal factor cost (MFC) curve (the firm's factor supply curve) would be horizontal (flat, or perfectly elastic), as shown in Exhibit 4(b).[2]

How Many Units of a Factor Should a Firm Buy?

Suppose you graduate with a BA in economics and go to work for a business firm. The first day on the job, you are involved in a discussion about factor X. Your employer asks you, "How many units of this factor should we buy?" What would you say?

Marginal Factor Cost (MFC)
The additional cost incurred by employing an additional factor unit.

Factor Price Taker
A firm that can buy all of a factor it wants at the equilibrium price. It faces a horizontal (flat, perfectly elastic) supply curve of factors.

EXHIBIT 4

Calculating MFC and Deriving the MFC Curve (the Firm's Factor Supply Curve)

In (a), MFC is calculated in column 4. Notice that the firm is a factor price taker because it can buy any quantity of factor X at a given price per factor unit ($5, as shown in column 2). In (b), the data from columns (1) and (4) are plotted to derive the MFC curve, which is the firm's factor supply curve.

(1) Quantity of Factor X	(2) Price of Factor X	(3) Total cost TC = (2) × (1)	(4) MFC = ΔTC/ΔQuantity of the factor = Δ(3)/Δ(1)
0	$5	$ 0	—
1	5	5	$5
2	5	10	5
3	5	15	5
4	5	20	5
5	5	25	5
6	5	30	5

(b)

---

1. An exception is the perfectly price-discriminating monopoly firm. For this firm, $P = MR$.
2. Although the MFC (factor supply curve) for the single factor price taker is horizontal, the market supply curve is upward sloping. This is similar to the situation for the perfectly competitive firm where the firm's demand curve is horizontal but the market (or industry) demand curve is downward sloping. In factor markets, we are simply talking about the supply side of the market instead of the demand side. The firm's supply curve is flat because it can buy additional factor units without driving up the price of the factor; it buys a relatively small portion of the factor. For the industry, however, higher factor prices must be offered to entice factors (e.g., workers) from other industries. The difference in the two supply curves—the firm's and the industry's—is basically a reflection of the different sizes of the firm and the industry.

Equating MRP and MFC

The firm continues to purchase a factor as long as the factor's *MRP* exceeds its *MFC*. In the exhibit, the firm purchases Q_1.

Your response is based on marginal analysis. "Continue buying additional units of the factor," you say, "until the additional revenue generated by employing an additional factor unit is equal to the additional cost incurred by employing an additional factor unit." Simply stated, keep buying additional units of the factor until *MRP* = *MFC*. In Exhibit 5, *MRP* equals *MFC* at a factor quantity of Q_1.

ⓣhinking Like AN ECONOMIST

Different Markets, Same Principles In the product market, a firm produces that quantity of output at which marginal revenue equals marginal cost, *MR* = *MC*. In the factor market, a firm buys the factor quantity at which marginal revenue product equals marginal factor cost, *MRP* = *MFC*. The economic principle of equating additional benefits with additional costs holds in both markets. ●●●

When There Is More Than One Factor, How Much of Each Factor Should the Firm Buy?

Until now, we have discussed the purchase of only one factor. Suppose a firm requires two factors, labor (*L*) and capital (*K*), to produce its product. How does it combine these two factors to minimize costs? Does it combine, say, 20 units of labor with 5 units of capital or perhaps 15 units of labor with 8 units of capital?

The firm purchases the two factors until the ratio of *MPP* to price for one factor equals the ratio of *MPP* to price for the other factor. In other words,

$$\frac{MPP_L}{P_L} = \frac{MPP_K}{P_K}$$

Least-Cost Rule

Rule that specifies the combination of factors that minimizes costs and so requires that the following condition be met: $MPP_1/P_1 = MPP_2/P_2 = \ldots = MPP_N/P_N$, where the numbers stand for the different factors.

This is the least-cost rule. To understand its logic, consider an example. Suppose for a firm that (1) the price of labor is $5, (2) the price of capital is $10, (3) an extra unit of labor results in an increase in output of 25 units, and (4) an extra unit of capital results in an increase in output of 25 units. Notice that MPP_L/P_L is greater than MPP_K/P_K: 25/$5 > 25/$10. Thus, for this firm, $1 spent on labor is more effective at raising output than $1 spent on capital. In fact, it is twice as effective.

Suppose the firm currently spends an extra $5 on labor and an extra $10 on capital. With this purchase of the two factors, the firm *is not* minimizing costs. It spends an additional $15 and produces 50 additional units of output. If, instead, it spent an additional

$10 on labor and $0 on capital, it could still have produced the 50 additional units of output and saved $5.

To minimize costs, the firm will rearrange its purchases of factors until the least-cost rule is met. To illustrate, if $MPP_L/P_L > MPP_K/P_K$, the firm buys more labor and less capital. As a result, the MPP of labor falls and the MPP of capital rises, bringing the two ratios closer in line. The firm continues to buy more of the factor whose MPP-to-price ratio is larger. It stops when the two ratios are equal.

thinking Like AN ECONOMIST

Two Different Settings, Same Principles We can compare a firm's least-cost rule with how buyers allocate their consumption dollars. A buyer of goods in the product market chooses combinations of goods so that the marginal utility of good A divided by the price of good A is equal to the marginal utility of good B divided by the price of good B; that is, $MU_A/P_A = MU_B/P_B$.

A firm buying factors in the factor market chooses combinations of factors so that the marginal physical product of, say, labor divided by the price of labor (the wage rate) is equal to the marginal physical product of capital divided by the price of capital; that is, $MPP_L/P_L = MPP_K/P_K$.

Thus consumers buy goods in the same way firms buy factors. This similarity points out something that you may have already sensed: although economic principles are few, they sometimes seem numerous because we find them in so many different settings.

The same economic principle lies behind equating the MU/P ratio for different goods in the product market and equating the MPP/P ratio for different resources in the resource market. In short, only one economic principle is at work in the two markets, not two different ones. That principle simply says that economic actors will, in their attempt to meet their objectives, arrange their purchases in such a way that they receive equal additional benefits per dollar of expenditure.

Seeing how a few economic principles operate in many different settings is part of the economic way of thinking. ● ● ●

SELF-TEST

(Answers to Self-Test questions are in Answers to Self-Test Questions at the back of the book.)

1. When a perfectly competitive firm employs one worker, it produces 20 units of output, and when it employs two workers, it produces 39 units of output. The firm sells its product for $10 per unit. What is the marginal revenue product connected with hiring the second worker?

2. What is the difference between marginal revenue product (*MRP*) and value marginal product (*VMP*)?

3. What is the distinguishing characteristic of a factor price taker?

4. How much labor should a firm purchase?

THE LABOR MARKET

Labor is a factor of special interest because, at one time or another, most people find themselves in the labor market. This section discusses first the demand for labor, then the supply of labor, and finally the two together. The section focuses on a firm that is a price taker in the product market (i.e., a perfectly competitive firm) and in the factor market.[3] In this setting, the demand for and supply of labor determine wage rates.

---

3. Keep in mind that, in the labor market here, neither buyers nor sellers have any control over wage rates. Consequently, supply and demand are our analytical tools. In the next chapter, we modify this analysis.

Shifts in a Firm's *MRP*, or Factor Demand, Curve

As explained, a firm's *MRP* curve is its factor demand curve, and marginal revenue product equals marginal revenue multiplied by marginal physical product:

$$MRP = MR \times MPP \tag{1}$$

For a perfectly competitive firm, where $P = MR$, we can write equation (1) as

$$MRP = P \times MPP \tag{2}$$

Now consider the demand for a specific factor input, labor. What will happen to the factor demand (*MRP*) curve for labor as the price of the product that the labor produces changes? In Exhibit 6, the initial product price is $10, and the initial factor demand curve is MRP_1. At the wage rate of W_1, the firm hires Q_1 labor. Suppose product price rises to $12. As we can see from equation (2), *MRP* rises. At each wage rate, the firm wants to hire more labor. For example, at W_1, it wants to hire Q_2 labor instead of Q_1. In short, a rise in product price shifts the firm's *MRP*, or factor demand, curve rightward. If product price falls from $10 to $8, *MRP* falls. At each wage rate, the firm wants to hire less labor. For example, at W_1, it wants to hire Q_3 labor instead of Q_1. In short, a fall in product price shifts the firm's *MRP*, or factor demand, curve leftward.

Changes in the *MPP* of the factor—reflected in a shift in the *MPP* curve—also change the firm's *MRP* curve. As we can see from equation (2), an increase in, say, the *MPP* of labor will increase *MRP* and shift the *MRP*, or factor demand, curve rightward. A decrease in *MPP* will decrease *MRP* and shift the *MRP*, or factor demand, curve leftward.[4]

EXHIBIT 6

Shifts in the Firm's *MRP*, or Factor Demand, Curve

It is always the case that $MRP = MR \times MPP$. For a perfectly competitive firm, where $P = MR$, it follows that $MRP = P \times MPP$. If *P* changes, *MRP* will change. For example, if product price rises, *MRP* rises, and the firm's *MRP* curve (factor demand curve) shifts rightward. If product price falls, *MRP* falls, and the firm's *MRP* curve (factor demand curve) shifts leftward. If *MPP* rises (reflected in a shift in the *MPP* curve), *MRP* rises and the firm's *MRP* curve shifts rightward. If *MPP* falls, *MRP* falls and the firm's *MRP* curve shifts leftward.

---

4. We are talking about a change in *MPP* that is reflected in a *shift* in the *MPP* curve, not a *movement* along a given *MPP* curve.

economics 24/7

Why Jobs Don't Always Move to a Low-Wage Country

Some people think that tariffs are needed to protect U.S. workers. They argue that without tariffs, U.S. companies will relocate to countries where wages are lower. They will produce their products there and then transport the products to the United States to sell them. Tariffs will make this scenario less likely because the gains the companies receive in lower wages will be offset by the tariffs imposed on their goods.

What this argument overlooks is that U.S. companies are interested not only in what they pay workers, but also in the marginal productivity of the workers. For example, suppose a U.S. worker earns $10 an hour and a Mexican worker earns $4 an hour. Say the marginal physical product (MPP) of the U.S. worker is 10 units of good X and the MPP of the Mexican worker is 2 units. Thus, we have lower wages in Mexico and higher productivity in the United States. Where will the company produce?

To answer this question, compare the output produced per $1 of cost in the two countries.

$$\text{Output produced per \$1 of cost} = \frac{MPP \text{ of the factor}}{\text{Cost of the factor}}$$

In the United States, at an MPP of 10 units of good X and a wage rate of $10, workers produce 1 unit of good X for every $1 they are paid:

$$\frac{MPP \text{ of U.S. labor}}{\text{Wage rate of U.S. labor}} = \frac{10 \text{ units of good X}}{\$10}$$
$$= 1 \text{ unit of good X per \$1}$$

In Mexico, at an MPP of 2 units and a wage rate of $4, workers produce half a unit of good X for every $1 they are paid:

$$\frac{MPP \text{ of Mexican labor}}{\text{Wage rate of Mexican labor}} = \frac{2 \text{ units of good X}}{\$4}$$
$$= 1/2 \text{ unit of good X per \$1}$$

Thus, the company gets more output per $1 of cost by using U.S. labor and will produce good X in the United States. It is cheaper to produce the good in the United States than it is in Mexico, even though wages are lower in Mexico.

In other words, U.S. companies look at the following ratios:

(1)
$$\frac{MPP \text{ of labor in U.S.}}{\text{Wage rate in U.S.}}$$

(2)
$$\frac{MPP \text{ of labor in country } X}{\text{Wage rate in country } X}$$

If ratio (1) is greater than ratio (2), U.S. companies will hire labor in the United States. As they do so, the MPP of labor in the United States will decline (according to the law of diminishing marginal returns). Companies will continue to hire labor in the United States until ratio (1) is equal to ratio (2).

© AP PHOTO/EDUARDO VERDUGO

Market Demand for Labor

We would expect the market demand curve for labor to be the horizontal addition of the firm's demand curves (MRP curves) for labor. However, this is not the case, as Exhibit 7 illustrates. Two firms, A and B, make up the buying side of the factor market, and the product price for both firms is P_1. Parts (a) and (b) in the exhibit show the MRP curves for the two firms based on this product price.

At a wage rate of W_1, firm A purchases 100 units of labor, the amount of labor at which its marginal revenue product equals marginal factor cost (or the wage). At this same wage rate, firm B purchases 150 units of labor. If we horizontally add the MRP curves of firms A and B, we get the MRP curve in part (c), where the two firms together purchase 250 units of labor at W_1.

Now assume the wage rate increases to W_2. In part (c), firms A and B move up the given MRP_{A+B} curve and purchase 180 units of labor. This may seem to be the end of the

EXHIBIT 7

The Derivation of the Market Demand Curve for Labor Units

Two firms, A and B, make up the buying side of the market for labor. At a wage rate of W_1, firm A purchases 100 units of labor and firm B purchases 150 units. Together, they purchase

250 units, as illustrated in (c). The wage rate rises to W_2, and the amount of labor purchased by both firms initially falls to 180 units, as shown in (c). Higher wage rates translate into higher costs, a fall in product supply, and a rise in product price from P_1 to P_2. Finally, an increased

price raises MRP and each firm has a new MRP curve. The horizontal "addition" of the new MRP curves shows they purchase 210 units of labor. Connecting the units of labor purchased by both firms at W_1 and W_2 gives the market demand curve.

(a) Firm A   (b) Firm B   (c) Firms A and B

process, but of course it is not because a higher wage rate increases each firm's costs and thus shifts its supply curve leftward. This, in turn, leads to an increase in product price to P_2.

Recall that the firm's marginal revenue product is equal to marginal revenue (or price, when the firm is perfectly competitive) times marginal physical product: $MRP = MR \times MPP = P \times MPP$. So if price rises (which it has), so does MRP, and therefore each firm faces a new MRP curve at the wage rate W_2. Parts (a) and (b) in Exhibit 7 illustrate these new MRP curves for firms A and B, and part (c) shows the horizontal addition of the *new MRP* curves. The firms together now purchase 210 units of labor at W_2.

After all adjustments have been made, connecting the units of labor purchased by both firms at W_1 and W_2 gives the market demand curve in part (c).

The Elasticity of Demand for Labor

Elasticity of Demand for Labor
The percentage change in the quantity demanded of labor divided by the percentage change in the wage rate.

If the wage rate rises, firms will cut back on the labor they hire. How much they cut back depends on the elasticity of demand for labor, which is the percentage change in the quantity demanded of labor divided by the percentage change in the price of labor (the wage rate).

$$E_L = \frac{\text{Percentage change in quantity demanded of labor}}{\text{Percentage change in wage rate}}$$

where E_L = coefficient of elasticity of demand for labor, or simply the elasticity coefficient.

For example, when the wage rate changes by 20 percent, the quantity demanded of a particular type of labor changes by 40 percent. The elasticity of demand for this type of labor is 2 (40 percent ÷ 20 percent), and the demand between the old wage rate and the new wage rate is elastic. There are three main determinants of elasticity of demand for labor:

• The elasticity of demand for the product that labor produces

• The ratio of labor costs to total costs

• The number of substitute factors

ELASTICITY OF DEMAND FOR THE PRODUCT THAT LABOR PRODUCES If the demand for the product that labor produces is highly elastic, a small percentage increase in price (e.g., owing to a wage increase that shifts the supply curve for the product leftward) will decrease the quantity demanded of the product by a relatively large percentage. In turn, this will greatly reduce the quantity of labor needed to produce the product, implying that the demand for labor is highly elastic too.

The relationship between the elasticity of demand for the product and the elasticity of demand for labor is as follows:

- The higher the elasticity of demand for the product, the higher the elasticity of demand for the labor that produces the product.
- The lower the elasticity of demand for the product, the lower the elasticity of demand for the labor that produces the product.

RATIO OF LABOR COSTS TO TOTAL COSTS Labor costs are a part of total costs. Consider two situations: in one, labor costs are 90 percent of total costs, and in the other, labor costs are only 5 percent of total costs. Then wages increase by $2 per hour. Total costs are affected more when labor costs are 90 percent of total costs (the $2-per-hour wage increase is being applied to 90 percent of all costs) than when labor costs are only 5 percent. Thus, price rises more when labor costs are a larger percentage of total costs. And, of course, the more price rises, the more the quantity demanded of the product falls. Therefore, labor, being a derived demand, is affected more. In short, for a $2-per-hour wage increase, the decline in the quantity demanded of labor is greater when labor costs are 90 percent of total costs than when labor costs are 5 percent of total costs.

The relationship between the ratio of labor cost to total cost and the elasticity of demand for labor is as follows:

- The higher the ratio of labor cost to total cost, the higher the elasticity of demand for labor (i.e., the greater the cutback in labor for any given wage increase).
- The lower the ratio of labor cost to total cost, the lower the elasticity of demand for labor (i.e., the less the cutback in labor for any given wage increase).

NUMBER OF SUBSTITUTE FACTORS The more substitutes labor has, the more sensitive buyers of labor will be to a change in its price. This principle was established in the discussion of price elasticity of demand. The more factors that can be substituted for labor, the more likely it is that firms will cut back on their use of labor if its price rises.

- The more substitutes there are for labor, the higher the elasticity of demand will be for it.
- The fewer substitutes for labor, the lower the elasticity of demand for labor.

Market Supply of Labor

As the wage rate rises, the quantity supplied of labor rises, *ceteris paribus*. The upward-sloping labor supply curve in Exhibit 8 illustrates this relationship. At a wage rate of W_1, individuals are willing to supply 100 labor units. At the higher wage rate of W_2, individuals are willing to supply 200 labor units. Some individuals who were not willing to work at a wage rate of W_1 are willing to work at a wage rate of W_2, and some individuals who were working at W_1 will be willing to

EXHIBIT 8

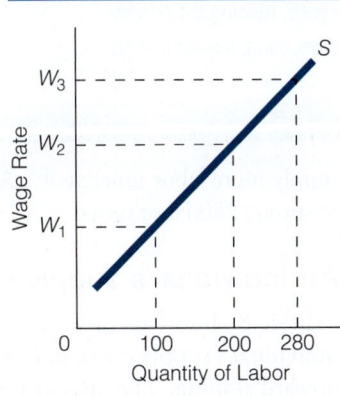

The Market Supply of Labor

A direct relationship exists between the wage rate and the quantity of labor supplied.

economics 24/7

How Crime, Outsourcing, and Multitasking Might Be Related

Consider three seemingly unrelated images of life in the United States in recent years:

1. *A lower crime rate.* For example, violent crime, property crime, and homicides were all down in the late 1990s and early 2000s.

2. *Increasingly more professional people outsourcing their routine tasks.* They are hiring people to run errands, buy groceries, plan parties, drop off dry cleaning, take pets to the vet, and do other chores.

3. *More people choosing to multitask—that is, to work on more than one task at a time.* If you drive a car at the same time as you talk to your office on your cell phone, you are multitasking.

Could all three images be the result of the same thing: higher real wages?[5] How might higher real wages affect crime, multitasking, and outsourcing?

Committing a crime has both costs and benefits. As long as the benefits are greater than the costs, crimes will be committed; increase the costs of crime relative to the benefits, and the crime rate will decline. Suppose part of the cost of crime is equal to the probability of being sentenced to jail multiplied by the real wage that would be earned if the person were not in jail.

Part of the cost of crime = Probability of jail sentence × Real wage

If this is the case, then, as the real wage rises, the overall cost of crime rises and fewer crimes will be committed.

Real wages also relate to individuals outsourcing their routine tasks. Suppose John and Mary are married and have two daughters. Mary works as a physician, and John works part-time as an accountant. Because John has chosen to work part-time, he takes care of many of the routine household tasks: buying the groceries, running the errands, and so on. If the real wage rises for accountants, John may rethink his part-time work. An increase in the real wage is the same as an increase in the reward from working, and so John may choose to work more. In fact, working full-time and paying someone else to run the errands, buy the groceries, and so on may be cheaper for him.

As for multitasking, as the real wage rises, one's time becomes more valuable. As time becomes more valuable, people want to economize on using it. One way to economize on time is to do several things simultaneously. Instead of spending 20 minutes driving to work and another 10 minutes talking on the phone, you kill two birds with one stone and talk on the phone while driving to work, saving 10 minutes. Of course, there is a downside (as economists are quick to point out). Talking on a hand-held cell phone while driving is not only illegal in some states, but it probably makes you and others around you less safe while driving.

If higher real wages can affect the crime rate, the amount of outsourcing, and how much people multitask, knowing what can cause real wages to rise becomes important. One way real wages can rise is through a technological advance that increases the quality of the capital goods used by labor. To illustrate, consider a technological advance that makes it possible for computers to complete more of their tasks in less time than before. As a result, the productivity of labor rises and the demand curve for labor shifts to the right. Higher demand for labor increases the nominal wage rate, and, as long as the price level doesn't rise by more than the nominal wage rate, the real wage rises too.

Can a technological advance indirectly lead to a lower crime rate, more outsourcing, and greater multitasking? We think so.

---

5. Nominal wages are dollar wages—such as $30 an hour. Real wages are nominal wages adjusted for price changes. Real wages measure what nominal wages can actually buy in terms of goods and services. So when real wages rise, people can buy more goods and services.

---

supply more labor units at W_2. At the even higher wage rate of W_3, individuals are willing to supply 280 labor units.

An Individual's Supply of Labor

Exhibit 8 shows an upward-sloping *market* supply curve of labor. Let's consider an individual's supply curve of labor—specifically, whether John's supply curve of labor is upward sloping. The answer depends on the relative strengths of the substitution and income effects.

John currently earns $10 an hour and works 40 hours a week. If John's wage rate rises to, say, $15 an hour, he will feel two effects, each pulling him in opposite directions.

1. *Substitution effect.* As his wage rate rises, John recognizes that the monetary reward from working has increased. As a result, John will want to work more—say, 45 hours a week instead of 40 hours (an additional 5 hours).

2. *Income effect.* As his wage rate rises, John knows that he can earn $600 a week (40 hours at $15 an hour) instead of $400 a week (40 hours at $10 an hour). If leisure is a normal good (the demand for which increases as income increases), then John will want to consume more leisure as his income rises. But the only way to consume more leisure is to work fewer hours. John might want to decrease his work hours per week from 40 to 37 hours (3 fewer hours).

The substitution effect pulls John in one direction (toward working 5 more hours), and the income effect pulls him in the opposite direction (toward working 3 fewer hours). Which effect is stronger? In our numerical example, the substitution effect is stronger; so, on net, John wants to work 2 more hours a week as his wage rate rises. This means that John's supply curve of labor is upward sloping between a wage rate of $10 and $15.

(f)inding ECONOMICS

In the Number of Hours a Person Works Larry works at a job where it is easy to get overtime. He has been earning $20 an hour for the last year, and most weeks he works 45 hours. He recently got a raise to $23 an hour. Since getting his $3-an-hour raise, he has been working about 40 hours a week. Where is the economics?

The economics can be found in the substitution and income effects. As a result of the higher wage, part of Larry wants to work more; this is the substitution effect at work. But part of Larry wants to work less; this is the income effect at work. In the end, Larry works fewer hours (40 instead of 45 hours), which means his income effect was stronger than his substitution effect. ▲ ▲ ▲

Shifts in the Labor Supply Curve

Changes in the wage rate change the quantity supplied of labor units; that is, they cause a *movement* along a given supply curve. Two factors of major importance, however, can *shift* the entire labor supply curve: wage rates in other labor markets and the nonmoney, or nonpecuniary, aspects of a job.

WAGE RATES IN OTHER LABOR MARKETS Deborah works as a technician in a television manufacturing plant, but she has skills suitable for a number of jobs. One day, she learns that the computer manufacturing plant on the other side of town is offering 33 percent more pay per hour. Deborah is also trained to work as a computer operator; so she decides to leave her current job and apply for work at the computer manufacturing plant. In short, the wage rate offered in other labor markets can bring about a shift of the supply curve in a particular labor market.

NONMONEY, OR NONPECUNIARY, ASPECTS OF A JOB Other things held constant, people prefer to avoid dirty, heavy, dangerous work in cold climates. An increase in the overall unpleasantness of a job (e.g., an increased probability of contracting lung cancer working in a coal mine) will cause a decrease in the supply of labor to that firm or industry and a leftward shift in its labor supply curve. An increase in the overall pleasantness of a job (e.g., employees are now entitled to a longer lunch break and use of the company gym) will cause an increase in the supply of labor to that firm or industry and a rightward shift in its labor supply curve.

EXHIBIT 9

Equilibrium in a Particular Labor Market

The forces of supply and demand bring about the equilibrium wage rate and quantity of labor. At the equilibrium wage rate, the quantity demanded of labor equals the quantity supplied. At any other wage rate, there is either a surplus or a shortage of labor.

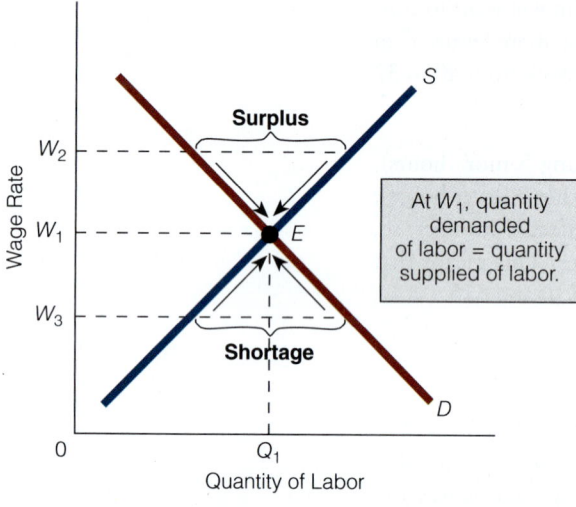

Putting Supply and Demand Together

Exhibit 9 illustrates a labor market. The equilibrium wage rate and quantity of labor are established by the forces of supply and demand. At a wage rate of W_2, there is a surplus of labor. Some people who want to work at this wage rate will not be able to find jobs, and a subset of this group will begin to offer their services for a lower wage rate. The wage rate will move down until it reaches W_1.

At a wage rate of W_3, there is a shortage of labor. Some demanders of labor will begin to bid up the wage rate until it reaches W_1. At the equilibrium wage rate, W_1, the quantity supplied of labor equals the quantity demanded of labor.

Why Do Wage Rates Differ?

To discover why wage rates differ, we must determine what conditions are necessary for everyone to receive the same pay. Assume the following conditions:

1. The demand for every type of labor is the same. (Throughout our analysis, any wage differentials caused by demand are short-run.)

2. The jobs have no special nonpecuniary aspects.

3. All labor is ultimately homogeneous and can costlessly be trained for different types of employment.

4. All labor is mobile at zero cost.

Given these conditions, there would be no difference in wage rates in the long run. Exhibit 10 shows two labor markets, A and B. Initially, the supply conditions are different, with a greater supply of workers in labor market B (S_B) than in labor market A (S_A). Because of the different supply conditions, more labor is employed in labor market B (Q_B) than in labor market A (Q_A), and the equilibrium wage rate in labor market B ($10) is lower than it is in labor market A ($30).

EXHIBIT 10

Wage Rate Equalization Across Labor Markets

Given the four necessary conditions (noted in the text), there will be no wage rate differences across labor markets. We start with a wage rate of $30 in labor market A and a wage rate of $10 in labor market B. Soon some individuals in B relocate to A. This increases the supply in one market (A), driving down the wage rate, and decreases the supply in the other market (B), driving up the wage rate. Equilibrium comes when the same wage rate is paid in both labor markets. This outcome critically depends on the necessary conditions holding.

(a) Labor Market A

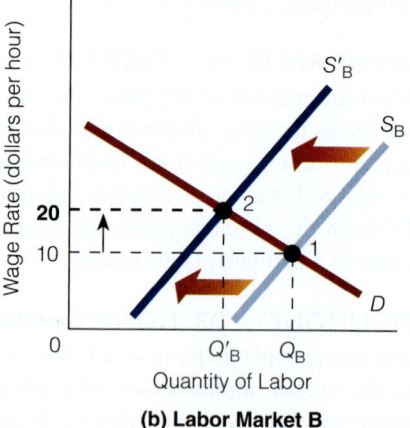

(b) Labor Market B

The differences in the wage rates between the two labor markets will not last. We have assumed (1) labor can move costlessly from one labor market to another (so labor moves from the lower-paying job to the higher-paying job); (2) the jobs have no special nonpecuniary aspects (no nonpecuniary reason for not moving); (3) labor is ultimately homogeneous (workers who work in labor market B can work in labor market A); and (4) if workers need training to move from one labor market to another, they not only are capable of being trained but also can acquire the training costlessly.

As a result, some workers in labor market B will relocate to labor market A, decreasing the supply of workers to S'_B in labor market B and increasing the supply to S'_A in market A. The relocation of workers ends when the equilibrium wage rate in both markets is the same at $20. Therefore, wage rates will not differ in the long run if our four conditions hold.

Given the conditions under which wage rates will not differ, we now know why wage rates do differ. Obviously, they differ because demand conditions are not the same in all labor markets (which explains only short-run wage differentials) and because supply conditions are not the same in all markets. Jobs *do have* nonpecuniary aspects, labor is *not* homogeneous, labor *cannot* be retrained without cost, and labor is *not* costlessly mobile.

Why Demand and Supply Differ Among Labor Markets

If wage rates differ because demand and supply conditions differ from one market to another, the next question is why. Let's consider the factors that affect the demand for and the supply of labor.

DEMAND FOR LABOR The market demand curve for labor is based on the *MRP* curves for labor of the individual firms in the market. So we need to look at what affects the components of *MRP*, namely, *MR* and *MPP*.

Marginal revenue, *MR*, is indirectly affected by product supply and demand conditions because these conditions determine price ($MR = \Delta TR/\Delta Q$ and $TR = P \times Q$). Thus, product demand and supply conditions affect factor demand. In short, because the supply and demand conditions in product markets are different, the demand for labor in labor markets will be different too.

The second factor, the marginal physical product of labor, is affected by individual workers' *own abilities and skills* (both innate and learned), the *degree of effort* they put forth on the job, and the *other factors of production* available to them. (American workers are more productive than workers in many other countries because they work with many more capital goods and much more technical know-how.) If all individuals had the same innate and learned skills and abilities, applied the same degree of effort on the job, and worked with the same amount and quality of other factors of production, wages would differ less than they currently do.

SUPPLY OF LABOR As noted, the supply conditions in labor markets are different. First, jobs have *different nonpecuniary qualities*. Working as a coal miner in West Virginia is not as attractive a job as working as a tour guide at a lush resort in Hawaii. We would expect this difference to be reflected in the supply of coal miners and tour guides.

Second, supply is also a reflection of the *number of persons who can actually do a job*. Williamson may want to be a nuclear physicist but may not have the ability in science and mathematics to become one. Johnson may want to be a basketball player but may not have the ability to become one.

Third, even if individuals have the ability to work at a certain job, they may perceive the *training costs as too high* (relative to the perceived benefits) to train for it. Tyler may have the ability to be a brain surgeon but views the years of schooling required to be too high a price to pay.

Fourth, sometimes the supply in different labor markets reflects a difference in the *cost of moving* across markets. Wage rates might be higher in Alaska than in Alabama for comparable labor because the workers in Alabama find the cost of relocating to Alaska too high relative to the benefits of receiving a higher wage.

In conclusion, because the wage rate is determined by supply-and-demand forces, the factors that affect these forces indirectly affect wage rates. Exhibit 11 summarizes these factors.

Why Did You Choose Your Major?

What happens in the labor market sometimes influences our lives. Consider a college student who is trying to decide whether to major in accounting or English. The student believes that English is more fun and interesting but that accounting, on average, will earn her enough additional income to compensate for the lack of fun in accounting. Specifically, at a $55,000 annual salary for accounting and a $39,000 annual salary for teaching English, the student is indifferent between accounting and English. But at a $56,000 annual salary for accounting and a $39,000 annual salary for teaching English, accounting moves ahead.

Of course, what accounting pays is determined by the demand for and supply of accountants. Given that fact, we see that other people influenced the student's decision to become an accountant. To illustrate, suppose Congress passes more intricate tax laws that require more accountants to figure them out. The change in the law increases the demand for accountants, which in turn raises the wage rate for them. And an increase in the wage rate for accountants increases the probability that more people—perhaps you—will major in accounting, not in English, philosophy, or history.

As you can see, economics—in which markets play a major role—helps explain why part of your life is the way it is.

EXHIBIT 11

The Wage Rate

A step-by-step framework that describes the factors that affect the wage rate.

The Wage Rate for a Street-Level Pusher in a Drug Gang

Gangs that deal drugs exist in almost every large city in the United States. It is not uncommon to see a 16- or 17-year-old gang member selling or delivering drugs in Los Angeles, New York, Chicago, Houston, or any other big city. In the public debate about drug dealing in these cities, one argument goes like this: "No wonder these kids sell drugs; it's the best job they can get. When your alternatives are working at McDonald's earning the minimum wage or selling drugs for big money, you sell drugs. If we want to get kids off the streets and out of gangs and if we want to stop them from selling drugs, we need to have something better for them than the minimum wage."

One question, however, is whether the young gang members who sell and deliver drugs really earn big money. Economics would predict that they don't. After all, the supply of people who can sell or deliver drugs is probably rather large. In fact, a recent study found that low-level foot soldiers in a drug gang actually earned very low wages.

Steven Levitt, an economist, and Sudhir Venkatesh, a sociologist, analyzed the data set of a drug-selling street gang.[6] They estimated that the average hourly wage rate in the gang was $6 at the time they started the study and $11 at the time they finished.[7] They also noted that the distribution of wages was extremely skewed. Actual street-level dealers (foot soldiers) appeared to earn less than the minimum wage. According to Levitt and Venkatesh,

> While these wages are almost too low to be believable, there are both theoretical arguments and corroborating empirical evidence in support of these numbers. From a theoretical perspective, it is hardly surprising that foot-soldier wages would be low given the minimal skill requirements for the job and the presence of a "reserve army" of potential replacements among the rank and file.

---

6. Steven Levitt and Sudhir Venkatesh, *An Economic Analysis of a Drug-Selling Gang's Finances*, NBER Working Paper No. W6592 (Cambridge, MA: National Bureau of Economic Research, 1998).
7. Wage rates are in 1995 dollars.

Marginal Productivity Theory

An analysis of some of the things we know from this chapter leads us to the following conclusions:

1. If a firm is a factor price taker, marginal factor cost is constant and equal to factor price, $MFC = P$. If the factor price taker hires labor, then, for the firm, $MFC = W$, where W is the wage rate.

2. Firms hire the factor quantity at which $MRP = MFC$.

3. Given points 1 and 2 together, a factor price taker pays labor a wage equal to its marginal revenue product: $W = MRP$. Because $MFC = W$ (point 1) and $MRP = MFC$ (point 2), then $W = MRP$.

4. If a firm is perfectly competitive, $MRP = VMP$.

5. If a firm is both perfectly competitive (a product price taker) and a factor price taker, it pays labor a wage equal to its value marginal product: $W = VMP$. Because $W = MRP$ (point 3) and $MRP = VMP$ (point 4), then $W = VMP$.

This is the marginal productivity theory, which states that if a firm sells its product and purchases its factors in competitive or perfect markets (i.e., it is a perfectly competitive firm and a factor price taker), it pays its factors their *MRP* or *VMP* (the two are equal for a product price taker).

The theory holds that, under the competitive conditions specified, if a factor unit is withdrawn from the productive process and the amount of all other factors remains the

Marginal Productivity Theory
Firms in competitive or perfect product and factor markets pay factors their marginal revenue products.

economics 24/7

It's a Party Every Night[8]

Workers who portray Disney characters at Disneyland and Disney World earn as little as $7.60 an hour. They can also suffer from certain injuries, many of which are the result of having to wear heavy costumes.

But even though the wages are low and the possibility of injury high, Disney doesn't seem to suffer from a lack of job applicants. More importantly, the people who work at the Disney parks (in all capacities) seem rather happy with their jobs. According to one employee, "It's a party every night."

Perhaps it's a party every night because many of the employees who play Disney characters are young (college student age), from various countries, and they live near each other in Disney-provided apartments. In other words, $7.60 an hour gets you work, plus certain social amenities, such as being able to get together with other people who are your age and single.

Another factor is in play. To keep the mood light and entertainment-based, Disney calls the people who work for the company not employees or workers, but cast members. And to become a cast member, one does not apply for a job; one auditions.

The other factor in play consists of the nonpecuniary aspects of a job with Disney. Other things held constant, we know that people prefer to avoid dirty, heavy, dangerous work in cold climates. An increase in a job's overall unpleasantness (e.g., an increased probability of

© AP PHOTO/NICK UT

contracting lung cancer working in a coal mine) will cause a decrease in the supply of labor to that firm or industry and a leftward shift in its labor supply curve. An increase in the overall pleasantness (e.g., a longer lunch break and use of the company gym) will cause an increase in the supply of labor to that firm or industry and a rightward shift in its labor supply curve.

Working as a Disney character seems to come with both the pleasant and the unpleasant. Wearing a heavy costume is unpleasant. Sustaining certain injuries from wearing a heavy costume is unpleasant. On the other hand, if you are young and single, socializing with other young and single persons is pleasant. Being called a cast member is pleasant. And some people might consider getting to party every night pretty pleasant.

On net, given that Disney doesn't have a difficult time finding cast members and that the wages for Disney characters are relatively low, the pleasantness of the job seems to outweigh its unpleasantness by a good amount. And it probably doesn't hurt that Disney advertises many of its jobs on a website called Yummy Jobs (yummyjobs.com).

---

8. This feature is adapted from "The Myth and Magic of Mickey Mouse," *Economist*, March 30, 2007.

---

same, then the decrease in the value of the product produced equals the factor payment received by the factor unit. To illustrate, suppose Wilson works for a perfectly competitive firm (firm X) producing good X. One day, he quits his job (but nothing else relevant to the firm changes). As a result, the total revenue of the firm falls by $100. If Wilson was paid $100, then he received his *MRP*. He was paid a wage equal to his contribution to the productive process.[9]

SELF-TEST

1. The demand for labor is a derived demand. What could cause the firm's demand curve for labor to shift rightward?

2. Suppose the coefficient of elasticity of demand for labor is 3. What does this mean?

3. Why are wage rates higher in one competitive labor market than in another? In short, why do wage rates differ?

4. Workers in labor market X do the same work as workers in labor market Y, but they earn $10 less per hour. Why?

---

9. Recall that *MRP* can be calculated in two ways: $MRP = \Delta TR/\Delta$Quantity of the factor, and $MRP = MR \times MPP$. In this example, we use the first method. When Wilson quits his job, the change in the denominator is 1 factor unit. If, as a result, *TR* falls by $100, then the change in the numerator must be $100.

Who Pays the Social Security Tax?

When Congress established the Social Security system, it instituted Social Security taxes and split the tax between the employer and the employee. By doing so, it intended to split the cost of the system. But economists know that taxes *placed* on one group of persons can be actually *paid* for by another group. To a large extent, this is so with the Social Security tax. Although half of the tax is placed on the employer and half is placed on the employee, the employee ends up paying almost all of the tax.

Exhibit 12 shows an approximation of this statement. We say "approximation" because most economists believe that the supply curve for labor *in the aggregate is extremely inelastic*. For simplicity, the supply curve is drawn as perfectly inelastic.

When no Social Security tax is placed on the employer, D_1 is the relevant demand curve for labor. The equilibrium wage rate is $19; that is, employers are willing to pay a maximum of $19 per hour (per worker) for Q_1 workers.

Now, instead of placing half the Social Security tax on the employer and half on the employee, let's take an extreme position and place the *entire tax on the employer*. Suppose employers calculate the Social Security tax on an hourly basis and find that they have to "pay" $1 per hour for every employee they hire. If $19 was the equilibrium wage rate *before the tax*, then employers are not willing to pay any more for the same number of workers *after the tax*. Employers are willing to pay labor only $19 per hour *minus* the hourly computed tax. In short, from the employer's perspective, the demand curve for labor falls by $1 for each alternative quantity of labor. In other words, the demand curve shifts leftward and down from D_1 to D_2. Given our vertical supply curve of labor, the new equilibrium wage rate is now $18 per worker for Q_1 workers.

So, if the supply curve is perfectly inelastic, and if the Social Security tax is *placed* wholly on employers, employees will end up *paying* the full tax in the form of lower wages.

CHRIS SCHMIDT/ISTOCKPHOTO

EXHIBIT 12

Who Pays the Social Security Tax?

With no Social Security tax, the equilibrium wage rate is $19 per hour; employers are willing to pay a maximum of $19 per hour (per worker) for Q_1 workers. With the Social Security tax fully placed on employer, and computed on an hourly basis, employers are willing to pay $19 per hour *minus* the hourly computed tax for Q_1 workers. Since we have assumed the hourly tax is $1 per employee, and that the supply curve for labor is perfectly inelastic in the aggregate, the new equilibrium wage rate is $18. Under the conditions stated, the employee ends up paying the full Social Security tax in the form of lower wages.

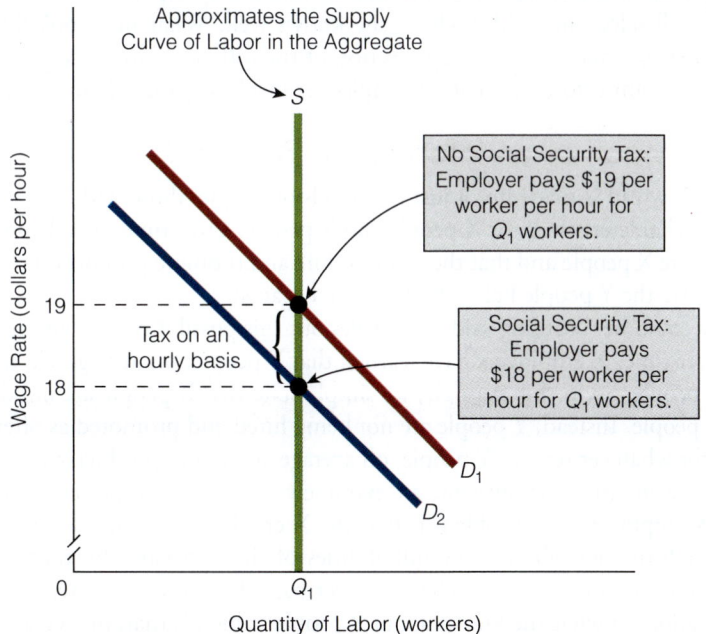

Approximates the Supply Curve of Labor in the Aggregate

S

No Social Security Tax: Employer pays $19 per worker per hour for Q_1 workers.

Social Security Tax: Employer pays $18 per worker per hour for Q_1 workers.

Tax on an hourly basis

19

18

D_1

D_2

Wage Rate (dollars per hour)

0   Q_1

Quantity of Labor (workers)

LABOR MARKETS AND INFORMATION

This section looks at job hiring, employment practices, and employment discrimination, as well as how information or the lack of it affects these processes.

Screening Potential Employees

Employers typically do not know exactly how productive a prospective employee will be. What the employer wants but lacks is complete information about the employee's future job performance. This need raises two questions:

1. *Why would an employer want complete information about a potential employee's future job performance?* The answer is obvious. Employers have a strong monetary incentive to hire good, stable, quick-learning, responsible, hardworking, punctual employees. One study found that corporate spending on training employees reached $40 billion annually. Obviously, corporations want to see the highest return possible for their training expenditures; so they try to hire employees who will make the training worthwhile.

2. *What does the employer do in the absence of such complete information?* This is where screening comes in.

Screening

The process employers use to increase the probability of choosing good employees based on certain criteria.

Screening is the process employers use to increase the probability of choosing good employees based on certain criteria. For example, as a step in the screening mechanism, an employer might ask a young college graduate searching for a job what his or her GPA was in college. The employer might know from past experience that persons with high GPAs turn out to be better employees, on average, than persons with low GPAs. Screening is one thing an employer does in the absence of complete information.

Promoting from Within

Sometimes employers promote from within the company because they have more information about present employees than about prospective employees.

Suppose the executive vice president in charge of sales is retiring from Trideck, Inc. The president of the company could hire an outsider to replace the vice president, but often she will select an insider whom she knows well. What may look like discrimination to outsiders, may simply be a reflection of the difference in costs to the employer of acquiring relevant information about employees inside and outside the company.

Discrimination or an Information Problem?

Suppose the world is made up of just two kinds of people: those with characteristic X and those with characteristic Y, or X people and Y people. Over time, it so happens that most employers are X people and that they tend to hire and promote proportionally more X than Y people. Are the Y people being discriminated against?

They could be. Nothing said so far rules out this possibility. But another explanation is that, over time, X employers have learned that Y people, on average, do not perform as well as X people. So in this example, we simply state that X people are not discriminating against Y people. Instead, Y people are not being hired and promoted as often as X people because, for whatever reason, Y people, on average, are not as productive.

Suppose in this environment, an extremely productive Y person applies for a job with an X employer. The problem is that the X employer does not know—that is, lacks complete information about—the full abilities of the Y person. Furthermore, acquiring complete information is costly. The employer bases her decision to reject the Y person's job application on what she knows about Y people, which is that, on average, they are not as productive as X people. She makes this decision not because she has something against

Y people but because acquiring complete information on every potential employee—X or Y—is simply too costly.

Legislation mandating equal employment opportunities requires employers to absorb some information costs to open the labor markets to all. All but the smallest of firms are required to search for qualified Y persons who can perform the job even if the employer believes that the average Y person cannot. Requiring employers to forgo the use of a screening mechanism typically increases firm costs and raises prices to consumers, but the premise of the legislation is that the social benefits of having more Y persons in the mainstream of society more than outweigh such costs.

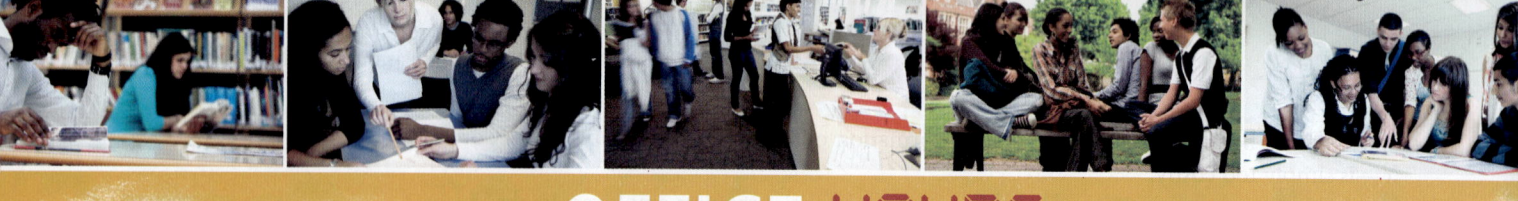
"Why Do Economists Think in Twos?"

STUDENT:

Before I read this chapter, I had thought that U.S. firms would rather pay low wages in other countries than to pay high wages in the United States. Now I realize that wages aren't the only thing that matters to a firm. The productivity of labor matters too.

INSTRUCTOR:

Does this ring a bell?

STUDENT:

What do you mean?

INSTRUCTOR:

Well, one of the things emphasized in the "Thinking Like an Economist" feature in various chapters is that economists often compare one thing to another when trying to determine what economic actors will do. To illustrate, when a firm decides where to hire labor, it compares wage rates to productivity in various countries. The firm compares marginal revenue to marginal cost when it decides how much of a good to produce. Marginal revenue product is compared to marginal factor cost when a firm decides how much of a factor to hire or buy. A consumer who decides to buy more or less of various goods compares marginal utility to price.

STUDENT:

What's the lesson? Why do economists seem to think in twos?

INSTRUCTOR:

The lesson goes back to something explained in Chapter 1: Usually, our activities have costs and benefits. Producing goods in the United States has a cost (paying high wages) and a benefit too (high

productivity). Producing an additional unit of a good (*MC*) has a cost but an additional benefit too (*MR*). Hiring an additional unit of labor comes with a cost (the wage rate) but with a benefit too (*VMP* or *MRP*). In the end, what matters is not the costs alone, nor the benefits alone, but the benefits relative to the costs.

POINTS TO REMEMBER

1. When firms are trying to decide where to hire workers (the United States or Mexico), wages are not the only factor that matters. Productivity matters too.
2. Economists often think in twos. They often compare the benefits and costs of doing X, where X can stand for various actions (e.g., hiring workers in various countries, producing an additional unit of a good, and so on).

CHAPTER SUMMARY

DERIVED DEMAND

- The demand for a factor is derived; hence, it is called a *derived demand.* Specifically, it is derived from and directly related to the demand for the product that the factor goes to produce; for example, the demand for auto workers is derived from the demand for autos.

MRP, MFC, VMP

- Marginal revenue product (*MRP*) is the additional revenue generated by employing an additional factor unit. Marginal factor cost (*MFC*) is the additional cost incurred by employing an additional factor unit. The profit-maximizing firm buys the factor quantity at which *MRP = MFC.*
- The *MRP* curve is the firm's factor demand curve; it shows how much of a factor the firm buys at different prices.
- Value marginal product (*VMP*) is a measure of the value that each factor unit adds to the firm's product. Whereas *MRP = MR × MPP, VMP = P × MPP.* For a perfectly competitive firm, *P = MR*; so *MRP = VMP.* For a monopolist, a monopolistic competitor, or an oligopolist, *P > MR*; so *VMP > MRP.*

THE LEAST-COST RULE

- A firm minimizes costs by buying factors in the combination at which the *MPP*-to-price ratio for each factor is the same. For example, for two factors, labor (*L*) and capital (*K*), the least-cost rule reads $MPP_L/P_L = MPP_K/P_K$.

LABOR AND WAGES

- A change in the price of the product that labor produces or a change in the marginal physical product of labor (reflected in a shift in the *MPP* curve) will shift the demand curve for labor.
- The higher (lower) the elasticity of demand is for the product that labor produces, the higher (lower) the elasticity of demand is for labor. The higher (lower) the ratio is of labor cost to total cost, the higher (lower) the elasticity of demand is for labor. The more (fewer) substitutes there are for labor, the higher (lower) the elasticity of demand is for labor.
- As the wage rate rises, the quantity supplied of labor rises, *ceteris paribus.*
- At the equilibrium wage rate, the quantity supplied of labor equals the quantity demanded of labor.

DEMAND FOR AND SUPPLY OF LABOR

- The demand for labor is affected by (1) marginal revenue and (2) marginal physical product. The supply of labor is affected by (1) wage rates in other labor markets, (2) the nonpecuniary aspects of the job, (3) the number of persons who can do the job, (4) training costs, and (5) moving costs.

MARGINAL PRODUCTIVITY THEORY

- Marginal productivity theory states that firms in competitive or perfect product and factor markets pay their factors their marginal revenue products.

KEY TERMS AND CONCEPTS

Derived Demand
Marginal Revenue Product
 (*MRP*)

Value Marginal Product (*VMP*)
Marginal Factor Cost
 (*MFC*)

Factor Price Taker
Least-Cost Rule
Elasticity of Demand for Labor

Marginal Productivity
 Theory
Screening

QUESTIONS AND PROBLEMS

1. The supply curve is horizontal for a factor price taker; however, the industry supply curve is upward sloping. Explain why this occurs.

2. Using the theory developed in this chapter, explain the following:
   a. Why a worker in Ethiopia is likely to earn much less than a worker in Japan
   b. Why the army expects recruitment to rise during economic recessions
   c. Why basketball stars earn relatively large incomes
   d. Why jobs that carry a health risk offer higher pay than jobs that do not, *ceteris paribus*

3. Compare the firm's least-cost rule to how buyers allocate their consumption dollars.

4. What might be one effect of government legislating wage rates?

5. "*VMP = MRP* for a price taker but not for a price searcher." Do you agree or disagree with this statement? Explain your answer.

6. What is the relationship between labor productivity and wage rates?

7. Why is the *MRP* curve a firm's factor demand curve?

8. What forces and factors determine the wage rate for a particular type of labor?

9. What does it mean to say that the demand for a factor is a derived demand?

10. Discuss the firm's objective, its constraints, and how it makes choices in its role as a buyer of resources.

11. How might you go about determining whether a person is worth the salary he or she is paid?

12. Prepare a list of questions that an interviewer is likely to ask an interviewee in a job interview. Try to identify which of the questions are part of the interviewer's screening process.

13. What do substitution and income effects have to do with the supply curve of labor?

14. Explain why the market demand curve for labor is not simply the horizontal addition of the firms' demand curves for labor.

15. Explain the relationship between each of the following pairs of concepts:

   a. The elasticity of demand for a product and the elasticity of demand for the labor that produces the product

   b. The ratio of labor cost to total cost and the elasticity of demand for labor

   c. The number of substitutes for labor and the elasticity of demand for labor

16. Discuss the factors that might prevent the equalization of wage rates for identical or comparable jobs across labor markets.

WORKING WITH NUMBERS AND GRAPHS

1. Determine the appropriate numbers for the lettered spaces.

(1) Units of Factor X	(2) Quantity of Output	(3) Marginal Physical Product of X (MPP_X)	(4) Product Price, Marginal Revenue $(P = MR)$	(5) Total Revenue	(6) Marginal Revenue Product of X (MRP_X)
0	15	0	$8	F	L
1	24	A	8	G	M
2	32	B	8	H	N
3	39	C	8	I	O
4	45	D	8	J	P
5	50	E	8	K	Q

2. Based on the table above, if the price of a factor is constant at $48, how many units of the factor will the firm buy?

3. In one diagram, draw the *VMP* curve and the *MRP* curve for an oligopolist. Explain why the curves look the way you drew them.

4. Explain why the factor supply curve is horizontal for a factor price taker.

5. Look at the two factor demand curves in the following figure. Is the price of the product that labor goes to produce higher for MRP_2 than for MRP_1? Explain your answer.

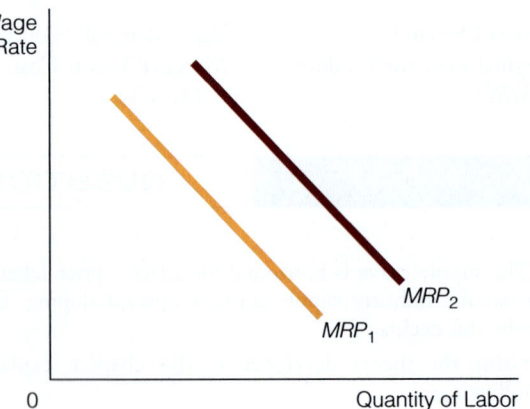

CHAPTER 28

WAGES, UNIONS, AND LABOR

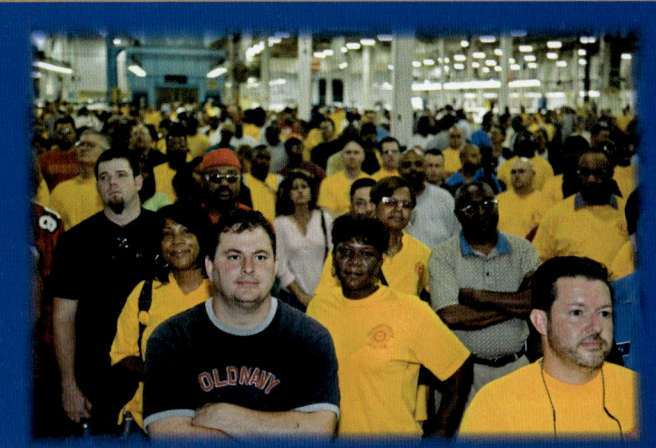

© JIM WEST/ALAMY

Introduction Certain organizations seem to engender controversy. Labor unions are such organizations. Some people are strongly prounion; others are strongly antiunion. And many millions of people between these extremes don't have a strong opinion on labor unions. In this chapter we discuss the objectives, practices, and effects of unions.

OBJECTIVES OF LABOR UNIONS

Labor unions usually seek one of three objectives:

- To employ all their members
- To maximize the total wage bill
- Or to maximize income for a limited number of union members

Employment for All Members

Suppose the demand curve in Exhibit 1 represents the demand for labor in a given union, and the total membership of the union is Q_1. If the objective of the union is to have its total membership employed, then the wage rate that must exist in the market is W_1. At W_1, firms want to hire the total union membership.

Maximizing the Total Wage Bill

The total wage bill paid to the membership of a union is equal to the wage rate multiplied by the number of labor hours worked. One objective of a labor union is to maximize this dollar amount, that is, to maximize the number of dollars coming *from* the employer *to* union members.

EXHIBIT 1

Labor Union Objectives

If total membership in the union is Q_1, and the union's objective is employment for all its members, it chooses W_1. If the objective is to maximize the total wage bill, it chooses W_2, where the elasticity of demand for labor equals 1. If the union's objective is to maximize the income of a limited number of union workers (represented by Q_3), it chooses W_3.

In Exhibit 1, the wage rate that maximizes the total wage bill is W_2. At W_2, the quantity of labor is Q_2, and the elasticity of demand for labor is equal to 1. Recall that total revenue (or total expenditure) is maximized when price elasticity of demand is equal to 1, or demand has unit elasticity. So the total wage bill is maximized at that point where the demand for labor is unit elastic. However, less union labor is working at W_2 than at W_1, indicating that there is a trade-off between higher wages and the employment of union members.

Maximizing Income for a Limited Number of Union Members

Some economists have suggested that a labor union might want neither total employment of its membership nor maximization of the total wage bill. Instead, it might prefer to maximize income for a *limited number* of union members, perhaps those with the most influence or seniority in the union. Suppose this group is represented by Q_3 in Exhibit 1. The highest wage at which this group can be employed is W_3; thus, the union might seek this wage rate instead of any lower rate.

Wage-Employment Trade-Off

Exhibit 1 suggests that a union can get higher wage rates, but some of the union members will lose their jobs in the process. Hence, the wage-employment trade-off depends on the *elasticity of demand for labor.*

To illustrate, consider the demand for labor in two unions, A and B, in Exhibit 2. Both unions bargain for a wage increase from W_1 to W_2. The quantity of labor drops much more in union B, where demand for labor is elastic between the two wage rates, than in union A, where the demand for labor is inelastic between the two wage rates. Union B is less likely than union A to push for higher wages, *ceteris paribus.* The reason is that the wage-employment trade-off is more pronounced for union B than for union A. Pushing for higher wages is simply costlier (in terms of union members' jobs) for union B than it is for union A.

EXHIBIT 2

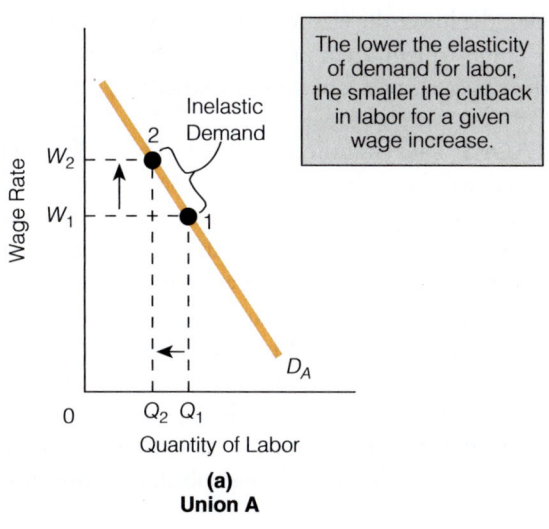

The lower the elasticity of demand for labor, the smaller the cutback in labor for a given wage increase.

(a)
Union A

(b)
Union B

The Wage-Employment Trade-Off: Two Cases

For union A, which has an inelastic demand for its labor between W_1 and W_2, a higher wage rate brings about a smaller cutback in the quantity of labor than for union B, which has an elastic demand for its labor between W_1 and W_2. We predict that union B will be less likely to push for higher wages than union A because its wage–employment trade-off is more pronounced.

𝒻inding ECONOMICS

In a Union Roundtable Discussion The leaders of a union are sitting around the table discussing what to do in the upcoming negotiations with management. One person argues for a 7 percent wage increase. Another person argues for a 10 percent wage increase, saying, "I don't think a 10 percent wage increase will lose us many jobs—if any." Where is the economics?

The economics is in the statement about the 10 percent wage increase. Believing that few jobs will be lost, if any, tells us she believes either that the wage–employment trade-off is small or that the demand for union labor is highly inelastic (maybe even perfectly inelastic if there will be *no loss* of jobs). ▲▲▲

PRACTICES OF LABOR UNIONS

This section explains how labor unions try to meet their objectives by influencing one or more of the following factors:

- The elasticity of demand for labor
- The demand for labor
- The supply of labor

We also discuss how unions can directly affect wages.

Affecting Elasticity of Demand for Union Labor

Exhibit 2 shows that the lower the elasticity of demand is for labor, the smaller the cutback in labor for any given wage increase will be. Obviously, the smaller the cutback in labor for a given wage increase, the better it is for the labor union. Given a choice between losing either 200 jobs or 50 jobs because of a wage rate increase of $2, the labor union prefers to lose the smaller number of jobs. Thus, a labor union looks for ways to lower the elasticity of demand for its labor, and it does so mainly by attempting to reduce the availability of substitutes.

AVAILABILITY OF SUBSTITUTE PRODUCTS Consider the autoworkers' union, whose members produce American automobiles. We know that the lower the elasticity of demand is for American automobiles, the lower the elasticity of demand will be for the labor that produces automobiles. So unions might attempt to reduce the availability of substitutes for the products they produce by such means as import restrictions.

AVAILABILITY OF SUBSTITUTE FACTORS The fewer the substitute factors are for union labor, the lower the elasticity of demand will be for union labor. Union labor has two general substitutes: nonunion labor and certain types of machines. For example, a musical synthesizer (which can sound like many different instruments) is a substitute for a group of musicians playing different instruments. Labor unions have often attempted to reduce the availability of substitute factors—both the nonunion and nonhuman. Thus, labor unions commonly oppose the relaxation of immigration laws; they usually favor the repatriation of illegal aliens; they generally are in favor of a high minimum wage (which increases the relative price of nonunion labor vis-à-vis union labor); and they usually oppose machines that can be substituted for their labor. Also, in the area of construction, unions usually specify that certain jobs are done by, say, electricians only (thus prohibiting substitute factors from being employed on certain jobs).

Affecting the Demand for Union Labor

Labor unions can try to meet their objectives by increasing the demand for union labor. All other things held constant, this leads to higher wage rates and more union labor employed. Labor unions can increase the demand for their labor in a number of ways.

INCREASING PRODUCT DEMAND Unions occasionally urge the buying public to buy the products produced by union labor. Union advertisements urge people to "look for the union label" or to look for the label that reads "Made in the U.S.A." As mentioned, unions sometimes also support legislation that either keeps out imports altogether or makes them more expensive.

INCREASING SUBSTITUTE FACTOR PRICES If union action leads to a rise in the relative price of factors that are substitutes for union labor, the demand for union labor rises. (If X and Y are substitutes and the price of X rises, so does the demand for Y.) For this reason, unions have often lobbied for an increase in the minimum wage—the wage received mostly by unskilled labor, which is a substitute for skilled union labor. The first minimum wage legislation was passed in 1938 when many companies were moving from the unionized North to the nonunionized South. The minimum wage made the nonunionized, relatively unskilled labor in the South more expensive and is said to have slowed the movement of companies to the South.

INCREASING MARGINAL PHYSICAL PRODUCT If unions can increase the productivity of their members, the demand for their labor will rise. With this in mind, unions prefer to add skilled labor to their ranks, and they sometimes undertake training programs for new entrants.

Affecting the Supply of Union Labor

Labor unions try to meet their objectives also by decreasing the supply of labor because a decreased supply translates into higher wage rates. One way to lower the supply below what it might be if the union did not exist is to control the supply of labor in a market.

Craft unions, in particular, have been moderately successful in getting employers to hire only union labor. In the past, they were successful at turning some businesses into closed shops. A closed shop is an organization in which an employee must belong to the

Closed Shop
An organization in which an employee must belong to the union before he or she can be hired.

union before being able to work. (In contrast, in an *open shop,* an employer may hire union or nonunion workers.) When unions can determine, or at least control in some way, the supply of labor in a given market, they can decrease it from what it would be otherwise. They can do this by restricting membership, by requiring long apprenticeships, or by rigid certification requirements. The closed shop was prohibited in 1947 by the Taft-Hartley Act.

The union shop, however, is legal in many states today. A union shop is an organization that does not require individuals to be union members to be hired but does require them to join the union within a certain period of time after becoming employed.

Today, unions typically argue for union shops, against open shops, and against the prohibition of closed shops. They also typically argue against state right-to-work laws (which some, but not all, states have), which make it illegal to require union membership for purposes of employment. (The Taft-Hartley Act allowed states to pass right-to-work laws and thus to override federal legislation that legalized union shops.) In short, the union shop is illegal in right-to-work states.

Affecting Wages Directly: Collective Bargaining

Besides increasing wage rates indirectly by influencing the demand for and supply of their labor, unions can directly affect wage rates through collective bargaining. Collective bargaining is the process whereby wage rates are determined by union's bargaining with management on behalf of all its members. In collective bargaining, union members act together as a single unit to increase their bargaining power with management. On the other side of the market, the employers of labor may also band together and act as one unit, with the same objective: to increase their bargaining power.

From the viewpoint of the labor union, collective bargaining is unlikely to be successful unless the union can strike. A strike occurs when unionized employees refuse to work at a certain wage or under certain conditions.

Exhibit 3 illustrates the effects of successful union collective bargaining. Suppose the initial wage rate that exists in the labor market is the competitive wage rate W_1. This is the wage rate that would exist if each employee were to bargain separately with management. The equilibrium quantity of labor is Q_1.

Management and the union (which represents all labor in this market) now sit down at a collective bargaining session. The union specifies that it wants a wage rate of W_2 and says that *none of its members will work at a lower wage rate.* Thus the union holds that the new supply curve is $S'S$—the heavy supply curve in Exhibit 3. In effect, the union is telling management that it cannot hire anyone for a wage rate lower than W_2.

Whether the union can bring about this higher wage rate (W_2) depends on whether it can prevent labor from

Union Shop
An organization in which a worker is not required to be a member of the union to be hired but must become a member within a certain period of time after being employed.

Collective Bargaining
The process whereby wage rates and other issues are determined by a union bargaining with management on behalf of all union members.

Strike
The union employees' refusal to work at a certain wage or under certain conditions.

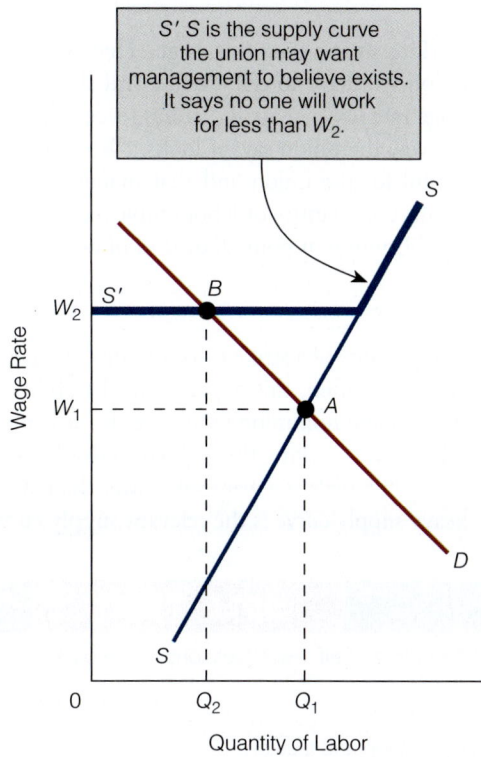

EXHIBIT 3

Successful Collective Bargaining by the Union

We start at a wage rate of W_1. The union's objective is to increase the wage rate to W_2. This means the union holds that the new supply curve of labor is $S'S$—the heavy supply curve. To convince management that the new supply curve looks as the union says it does, the union will have to either threaten a strike or call one. We assume that the union is successful at raising the wage rate to W_2. As a consequence, the quantity of labor employed is less than it would have been at W_1.

$S'S$ is the supply curve the union may want management to believe exists. It says no one will work for less than W_2.

Technology, the Price of Competing Factors, and Displaced Workers[1]

For most of the eighteenth century in England, spinners and weavers worked on hand-operated spinning wheels and looms. Then in the 1770s, a mechanical spinner was invented that required steam or water power, and so yarn-spinning factories were set up near water mills. The factory workers, working with mechanical spinners, could produce 100 times more yarn in a day than they could using hand-operated spinners.

Because of the increased supply of yarn, the price fell and the quantity demanded of yarn increased substantially. In turn, the heightened demand increased the demand for weavers who continued to use hand-operated looms. As a result, weavers' wages increased. In reaction to the higher wages for weavers, entrepreneurs and inventors began to experiment with different kinds of weaving machines. Their experiments began to pay off; in 1787, the power loom was invented, although it was not perfected until the 1820s. By the 1830s, two workers using a power loom could produce in one day 20 times what a weaver could produce on a hand-operated loom.

Soon, the weavers who used hand-operated looms found themselves without jobs, displaced by the the power loom. Some of the displaced workers showed their frustration and anger at their predicament by burning power looms and factories.

The story of spinners and weavers in eighteenth-century England helps us realize two important points about technology. First, as long as technology advances, some workers will be temporarily displaced. Second, an advance in technology often has an identifiable cause; it doesn't simply fall out of the sky. If it had not been for the higher weavers' wages, the power loom might not have been invented.

1. This feature is based on Elizabeth Hoffman, "How Can Displaced Workers Find Better Jobs?" in *Second Thoughts: Myths and Morals of U.S. Economic History*, ed. by Donald McCloskey (Oxford: Oxford University Press, 1993).

working at less than this wage. That is, if management does not initially agree to W_2, the union will have to call a strike and show management that it cannot hire any labor for a wage rate lower than W_2. It has to convince management that the new supply curve looks the way the union says it looks. (We assume that the strike threat, or actual strike, is successful for the union and that management agrees to the higher wage rate of W_2.) As a result, the quantity of labor employed, Q_2, is less than it would have been at W_1. The new equilibrium is at point B instead of point A.

Strikes

The purpose of a strike is to convince management that the supply curve is what the union says it is. Often, this depends on the ability of striking union employees to prevent non-striking and nonunion employees from working for management at a lower wage rate than the union is seeking through collective bargaining. For example, if management can easily hire individuals at a wage rate lower than W_2 in Exhibit 3, it will not be convinced that the heavy supply curve is the relevant supply curve.

SELF-TEST

(Answers to Self-Test questions are in Answers to Self-Test Questions at the back of the book.)

1. What will lower the demand for union labor?

2. What is the difference between a closed shop and a union shop?

3. What is the objective of a strike?

EFFECTS OF LABOR UNIONS

This section addresses two questions:

- What are the effects of labor unions on wage rates?
- Are the effects the same in all labor markets?

The Case of Monopsony

A single buyer in a factor market is known as a monopsony. Some economists refer to a monopsony as a buyer's monopoly; that is, whereas a monopoly is a single seller of a product, a monopsony is a single buyer.

For example, if a firm in a small town is the only buyer of labor because there are no other firms for miles around, the firm is a monopsony. Because it is a monopsony, it cannot buy additional units of a factor without increasing the price it pays for it (in much the same way that a monopolist in the product market cannot sell an additional unit of its good without lowering price.) The reason is that the supply of labor that the monopsonist faces is the market supply of labor.

Marginal factor cost increases as the monopsonist buys additional units of a factor, and the supply curve of the factor *is not the same* as the firm's marginal factor cost curve. [For a price taker in the factor market, marginal factor cost is constant, and the *MFC* curve is the same as the supply curve for the factor. A monopsonist is not a price taker in the factor market: marginal factor cost rises as it buys additional units of a factor, and its *MFC* curve and supply curve (for the factor) are not the same.]

As shown in Exhibit 4, marginal factor cost increases as additional units of the factor are purchased. Notice in part (a) that as workers are added, the wage rate rises. For example, for the monopsonist to employ two workers, the wage rate must rise from $6.00 per hour to $6.05. To employ three workers, the monopsonist must offer to pay $6.10. Comparing column 2 with column 4, we notice that the marginal factor cost for a monopsonist is greater than the wage rate (in the same way that for a monopolist in a product market, price is greater than marginal revenue). Plotting columns 1 and 2 gives the supply curve for the monopsonist [see Exhibit 4(b)]; plotting columns 1 and 4 gives the monopsonist's *MFC* curve. Because *MFC* is greater than the wage rate, the supply curve lies below the *MFC* curve.

Exhibit 4(b) shows that the monopsonist chooses to purchase Q_1 units of labor (where $MRP = MFC$) and that it pays a wage rate of W_1 (the wage rate necessary to get Q_1 workers to offer their services).

If the monopsonist were to pay workers what their services were worth to it (as represented by the *MRP* curve), it would pay a higher wage. Some persons contend that labor unions and collective bargaining are necessary when labor is paid less than its marginal revenue product. Furthermore, they argue that successful collective bargaining on the part of the labor union in this setting is not subject to the wage–employment trade-off it encounters in other settings, as illustrated in Exhibit 4(c).

In Exhibit 4(c), successful collective bargaining by the labor union moves the wage rate from W_1 to W_2. The labor union is essentially saying to the monopsonist that it cannot hire any labor below W_2. This changes the monopsonist's marginal factor cost curve from *MFC* to *MFC′*, which corresponds to the new supply curve the monopsonist faces, $S'S$. The monopsonist once again purchases the quantity of labor at which marginal revenue product equals the marginal factor cost. But now, because the marginal factor cost curve is *MFC′*, equality is at Q_2 workers and a wage rate of W_2. Therefore, over a range, there is no wage–employment trade-off for the labor union when it faces a monopsonist. It can raise both the wage rate and the number of workers employed.

Monopsony
A single buyer in a factor market.

EXHIBIT 4

The Labor Union and the Monopsonist

(a) For the monopsonist, *MFC* > wage rate. This implies that the supply curve the monopsonist faces lies below its *MFC* curve. (b) The monopsonist purchases Q_1 quantity of labor

and pays a wage rate of W_1, which is less than *MRP* (labor is being paid less than its *MRP*). (c) If the labor union succeeds in increasing the wage rate from W_1 to W_2 through collective bargaining, then the firm will also hire more

labor (Q_2 instead of Q_1). We conclude that in the case of monopsony, higher wage rates (over a range) do not imply fewer persons working.

(1) Workers	(2) Wage Rate	(3) Total Labor Cost (1) × (2)	(4) Marginal Factor Cost $\frac{\Delta(3)}{\Delta(1)}$
0	—	—	—
1	$6.00	$6.00	$6.00
2	6.05	12.10	6.10
3	6.10	18.30	6.20
4	6.15	24.60	6.30
5	6.20	31.00	6.40

(a)

(b)

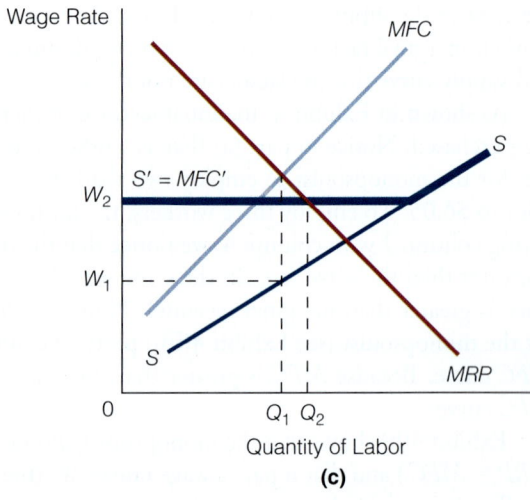

(c)

Unions' Effects on Wages

Most studies show that some unions have increased their members' wages substantially, whereas other unions have not done so at all. Work by H. Gregg Lewis concludes that during the period 1920–1979, the average wage of union members was 10 to 15 percent higher than that of comparable nonunion labor. (Keep in mind, though, that the union–nonunion wage differential can differ quite a bit in different years and among industries.) For data on this subject, see Exhibit 5.

THE UNION–NONUNION WAGE GAP Exhibit 6 illustrates the theoretical basis of the observation that higher union wages lead to lower nonunion wages or to a union–nonunion wage gap. Two sectors of the labor market are shown: the unionized sector in part (a) and the nonunionized sector in part (b). Assume that labor is homogeneous and that the wage rate is $15 an hour in both sectors.

EXHIBIT 5

Median Weekly Earnings in the Union and Nonunion Sectors, Selected Industries, 2008

In four of the five (selected) industries shown, union workers earned a higher weekly salary in 2008 than did nonunion workers. Overall in 2008, the median weekly salary was $829 for a union workers and $680 for a nonunion worker (not shown).

Source: Statistical Abstract of the United States, 2010

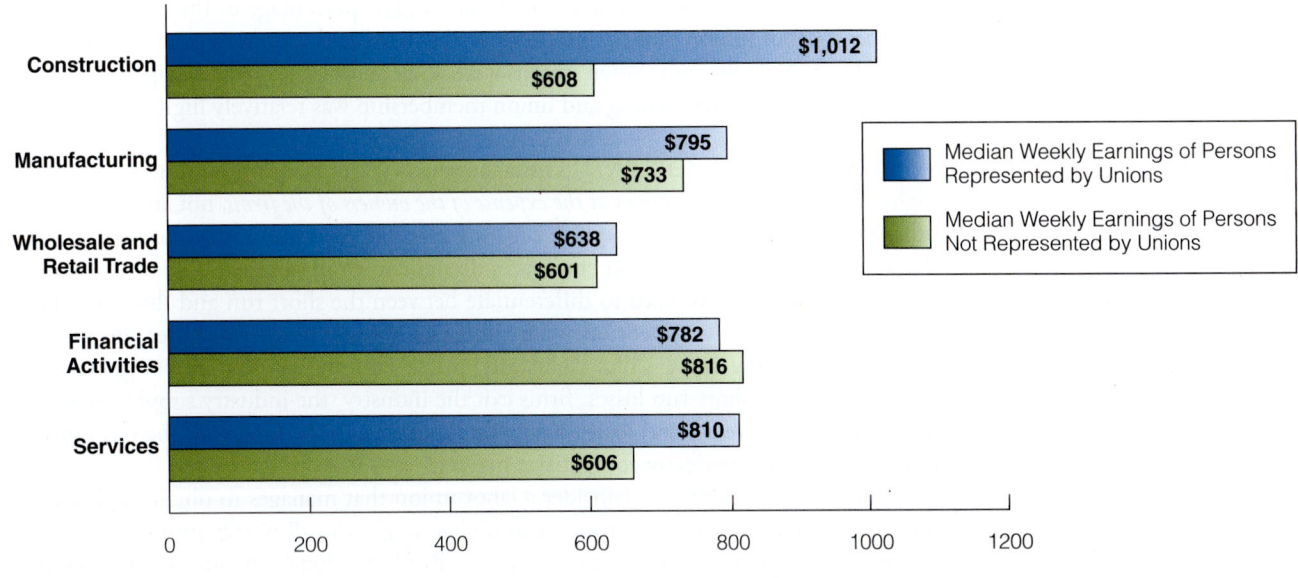

The labor union either collectively bargains to a higher wage rate of $18 an hour or manages to reduce supply so that the higher wage rate comes about (the exhibit shows a decrease in supply). As a consequence, less labor is employed in the unionized sector. If those now not working in the unionized sector can work in the nonunionized sector, then

EXHIBIT 6

The Effect of Labor Unions on Union and Nonunion Wages

We begin at a wage rate of $15 in both the unionized sector, (a), and the nonunionized sector, (b). Next, the union manages to increase its wage rate to $18 either through collective bargaining or by decreasing the supply of labor in the unionized sector (shown). Fewer persons now work in the unionized sector, and we assume that those persons who lose their jobs move to the nonunionized sector. The supply of labor in the nonunionized sector rises, and the wage rate falls.

Changes in supply conditions and wage rates in the unionized sector can cause changes in supply and wage rates in the nonunionized sector.

(a) Unionized Sector

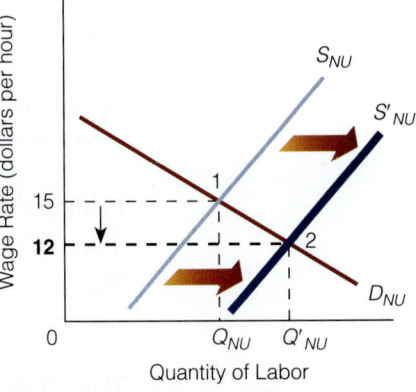

(b) Nonunionized Sector

the supply of labor in the nonunionized sector increases from S_{NU} to S'_{NU} and the wage rate in the nonunionized sector falls to $12 an hour. Therefore, there are theoretical and empirical reasons for believing that labor unions increase the wages of union employees and decrease the wages of nonunion employees.

However, the higher wages that union employees receive through unionization do not seem to outweigh the lower wages that nonunion employees receive in terms of the percentage of the national income that goes to labor. The percentage of the national income that goes to labor (union plus nonunion labor) has been fairly constant over time. In fact, it was approximately the same when unions were weak and union membership was relatively low as when unions were strong and union membership was relatively high.

WHY DON'T EMPLOYERS PAY? The layperson's view of labor unions is that they obtain higher wages for their members *at the expense of the owners of the firms,* not at the expense of other workers. The preceding section suggests that this perception may not be true—that the higher wages going to union employees do not come out of profits.

To explain why, we need to differentiate between the short run and the long run. In the theory of perfect competition, with short-run profits, new firms enter the industry, the industry supply curve shifts rightward, prices fall, and profits are competed away. Conversely, given short-run losses, firms exit the industry, the industry supply curve shifts leftward, prices increase, and losses finally disappear. So in the long run, there is zero economic profit in the perfectly competitive market.

In this market structure, consider a labor union that manages to obtain higher wages for its members. In the short run, these higher wages can diminish profits, as any cost increase would diminish profits, *ceteris paribus.* But in the long run, adjustments are made as firms exit the industry, supply curves shift, and prices change. In the long run, zero economic profit will exist. Therefore, in the short run, higher wages may come out of profits, but in the long run they probably do not.

ⓣhinking Like AN ECONOMIST

Primary and Secondary Effects Economists make the important distinction between primary and secondary effects, that is, between what happens in the short run and what happens in the long run. For example, higher wages for union workers may initially come at the expense of profits, but as time passes this may not continue to be the case. ●●●

Unions' Effects on Prices

One effect of labor unions is that union wages are relatively high and nonunion wages are relatively low. The higher union wages mean higher costs for the firms that employ union labor, and higher costs affect supply curves, which in turn affect product prices. Therefore, higher union wages will cause higher prices for the products that the union labor produces. Conversely, lower nonunion wages mean lower costs for the firms that employ nonunion labor and thus lower prices for the products produced by nonunion labor.

Unions' Effects on Productivity and Efficiency: Two Views

There are two major views of the effects that labor unions have on productivity and efficiency.

THE TRADITIONAL (OR ORTHODOX) VIEW The traditional view holds that labor unions have a negative impact on productivity and efficiency. Its proponents make the following arguments:

Are You Ready for Some Football?

Sometimes, firms that sell a similar good try to form a cartel so that they can act as a monopoly. Can firms that buy a factor do the same, that is, form a cartel so that they can act as a monopsony? Students know such a "firm." Many universities and colleges have banded together to buy the services of college-bound athletes. In other words, they have entered into a cartel agreement to reduce the monetary competition among themselves for college-bound athletes. The National Collegiate Athletic Association (NCAA) is the cartel or monopsony enforcer.

Here's how it works. The NCAA sets certain rules and regulations by which its member universities and colleges must abide or else face punishment and fines. For example, universities and colleges are prohibited from offering salaries to athletes to play on their teams. They are prohibited from making work for them at the university or paying them relatively high wage rates for a job that usually pays much less, such as, paying athletes $60 an hour to reshelve books in the university library. Universities and colleges are also prohibited from offering inducements to attract athletes, such as cars, clothes, and trips.

The stated objectives of these NCAA regulations are to maintain the amateur standing of college athletes, to prevent the rich schools from getting all the good players, and to enhance the competitiveness of college sports. Some economists suggest that some schools may have other objectives. They note that college athletics can be a revenue-raising activity for schools and that these institutions would rather pay college athletes less than their marginal revenue products (as a monopsony

© PAN AMERICA/JUPITER IMAGES

does) to play sports. Currently, universities and colleges openly compete for athletes by offering scholarships, free room and board, and school jobs. They also compete in terms of their academic reputations and the reputations of their sports programs (obviously, some find it easier to do this than others).

Although the practice is prohibited, some universities and colleges compete for athletes in ways not sanctioned by the NCAA; that is, they compete, as it is said, under the table. Such practices are evidence, some economists maintain, that certain schools are cheating on the cartel agreement. Such cheating usually benefits the college athletes, who receive a payment for their athletic abilities that is closer to their marginal revenue products. For example, some college athletes, many of whom come from families of modest means, drive flashy, expensive cars, which often come from community friends of the university or boosters of its sports program. The NCAA may prohibit such payments to college athletes, but, as we have seen, members of cartels (of the monopoly or monopsony variety) usually find ways of evading the rules.

Not all economists agree that the NCAA is a cartel. Some argue that paying college athletes would diminish the reputation of college athletics, thus decreasing the public demand for college sports programs. They conclude that the NCAA imposes its rules and regulations—one of which is that college athletes should not be paid to play sports—to keep college sports nonprofessional and in relatively high demand, not to suppress players' wages.

- Labor unions often have unnecessary staffing requirements and insist that only certain persons be allowed to do certain jobs. Because of this, the economy operates below its potential—that is, inefficiently.

- Strikes disrupt production and prevent the economy from realizing its productive potential.

- Labor unions drive an artificial wedge between the wages of comparable labor in the union and nonunion sectors of the labor market.

This last point warrants elaboration. In Exhibit 6, labor is homogeneous, and the wage rate is initially the same in both sectors of the labor market. Union efforts increase the wage rate in the union sector and decrease the wage rate in the nonunion sector. At this point, the marginal revenue product of persons who work in the union sector is higher than the marginal revenue product of individuals who work in the nonunion sector. [We are farther up the factor demand (*MRP*) curve in the union than in the nonunion sector.] If labor could move from the nonunionized sector to the unionized sector, it would be moving from where it is worth less to where it is worth more, but it cannot do so because of the supply-restraining efforts of the union. Economists call this a misallocation of labor; not all labor is employed where it is the most valuable.

A NEW VIEW: THE LABOR UNION AS A COLLECTIVE VOICE   There is evidence that, in some industries, union firms have a higher rate of productivity than nonunion firms. Some economists believe this effect is a result of the labor union's role as a collective voice mechanism for its members. Without a labor union, workers who are disgruntled with their jobs, who feel taken advantage of by their employers, or who feel unsafe in their work will leave their jobs and seek work elsewhere. Job exiting comes at a cost: it raises the turnover rate, results in lengthy job searches during which individuals are not producing goods and services, and raises training costs. Such costs can be reduced, it is argued, when a labor union acts as a collective voice for its members. Instead of individual employees having personally to discuss ticklish matters with their employer, the labor union does so for them. Overall, the labor union makes employees feel more confident, less intimidated, and more secure in their work. Such positive feelings usually mean happier, more productive employees. Some proponents of this view also hold that employees are less likely to quit their jobs. In fact, there is evidence that unionism does indeed reduce job quits.

Critics have contended, though, that the reduced job quits are less a function of the labor union's collective voice than of the labor union's institutional capability of increasing its members' wages. Also, the productivity-increasing aspects of the labor union, which are linked to its role as a collective voice mechanism, are independent of the productivity-decreasing aspects of the labor union in its role as a monopolizer of labor.

SELF-TEST

1. What is a major difference between a monopsonist and a factor price taker?

2. Under what conditions will the minimum wage increase the number of people working?

3. How could a collectively bargained higher wage rate in the unionized sector of the economy lead to a lower wage rate in the nonunionized sector of the economy?

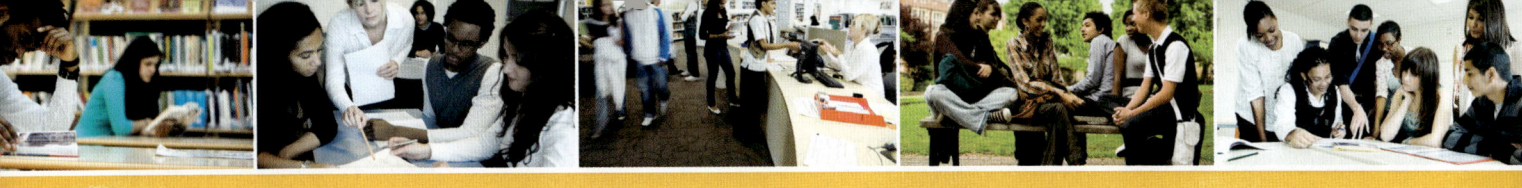

OFFICE HOURS

"Don't Higher Wages Reduce Profits?"

STUDENT:

I'm beginning to find that many things in economics are counterintuitive. Things I expect to be true turn out to be false, and things that I think are false turn out to be true.

INSTRUCTOR:

Are you thinking of something in particular?

STUDENT:

I had thought that labor unions obtained higher wages at the expense of the firm owners by reducing the owners' profits. Now I know that this is not necessarily true in the long run, especially in a perfectly competitive market.

INSTRUCTOR:

Any thoughts on why economics is full of the counterintuitive?

STUDENT:

I'm not sure.

INSTRUCTOR:

Well, part of the answer might have to do with how far we take the analysis. To illustrate, consider your example dealing with the labor union and profits. You had thought that the labor union obtained higher wages at the expense of the firm owners. That can be true in the short run. In other words, your intuition was correct for the short run. But when we extended the analysis beyond the immediate effects of higher wages, things began to turn out differently than you thought.

STUDENT:

So, is there a lesson here?

INSTRUCTOR:

Don't stop analyzing things too soon. The problem, though, is that we don't always know that we're stopping too soon.

STUDENT:

In other words, I saw the story this way: wages for members of labor unions rise, which causes profits to fall for owners of firms. But I should have seen it this way: wages for members of labor unions rise, profits fall for owners of firms, some firms leave the industry, the market supply curve shifts leftward, and price rises.

Of course, my problem, as you imply, was that I didn't know I should have gone beyond steps 1 and 2. I didn't know steps 3 through 5 were there. So I guess my question now is, how do you get to those steps if you don't know they exist?

INSTRUCTOR:

That's a good question. What you need is a device to use that can propel you onward. That device comes in the form of the question, is there anything else? To illustrate, go back to the way you initially saw the story: wages for members of labor unions rise, which causes profits to fall for owners of firms.

Now, instead of putting a period at the end of that, ask a question: If profits fall for the owners of firms, what, if anything, do falling profits lead to? This question—a form of the is-there-anything-else? question—propels you forward and reduces the probability that you will stop before you have tried to figure out the full story.

POINTS TO REMEMBER

1. Do higher wages lead to lower profits—end of story? Our answer depends on how far we take the analysis.
2. To propel our analysis forward, we often need to ask whether there is anything else.

CHAPTER SUMMARY

OBJECTIVES OF A UNION

- Objectives of a union include (1) employment for all its members, (2) maximization of the total wage bill, and (3) maximization of the income for a limited number of union members. A labor union faces a wage–employment trade-off; higher wage rates mean lower labor union employment. An exception is when a labor union faces a monopsonist; then the union can raise both wage rates and employment of its members (over a range). Exhibit 4(c) illustrates this possibility.

PRACTICES OF A LABOR UNION

- To soften the wage–employment trade-off, a labor union seeks to lower the elasticity of demand for its labor. Ways of doing this are (1) reducing the availability of substitute products and (2) reducing the availability of substitute factors for labor.

- Union wage rates can be increased indirectly by increasing the demand for union labor or by reducing the supply of union labor, or they can be increased directly by collective bargaining. To increase demand for its labor, a union might try to increase (1) the demand for the good it produces, (2) substitute factor prices, or (3) its marginal physical product. To decrease the supply of its labor, a union might argue for closed and union shops and against right-to-work laws.

- In a way, successful collective bargaining by a labor union changes the supply curve of labor that the employer faces. The labor union is successful if, through its collective bargaining efforts, it can prevent the employer from hiring labor at a wage rate below a union-determined level. In this case, the supply curve of labor becomes horizontal at this wage rate (see Exhibit 3).

MONOPSONY

- For a monopsonist, marginal factor cost rises as it buys additional units of a factor, and its supply curve lies below its marginal factor cost curve. The monopsonist buys the factor quantity at which $MRP = MFC$. The price of the factor is less than the monopsonist's marginal factor cost; so the monopsonist pays the factor less than its marginal revenue product.

EFFECTS OF UNIONS

- There is evidence that labor unions generally have the effect of increasing their members' wage rates (over what they would be without the union) and of lowering the wage rates of nonunion labor.

- The traditional view of labor unions holds that unions negatively affect productivity and efficiency by (1) arguing for and often obtaining unnecessary staffing requirements, (2) calling strikes that disrupt production, and (3) driving an artificial wedge between the wages of comparable labor in the union and nonunion sectors.

- The new view of labor unions holds that labor unions act as a collective voice mechanism for individual union employees and cause them to feel more confident in their jobs and less intimidated by their employers. This effort leads to more productive employees, who are less likely to quit.

KEY TERMS AND CONCEPTS

Craft (Trade) Union	Employee Association	Union Shop	Strike
Industrial Union	Closed Shop	Collective Bargaining	Monopsony
Public Employee Union			

QUESTIONS AND PROBLEMS

1. Organizing labor unions may be easier in some industries than in others. What industry characteristics make unionization easier?

2. Contrast the traditional (or orthodox) and new views of labor unions.

3. Most actions or practices of labor unions are attempts to affect one of three factors. What are they?

4. Unions can affect (a) a firm's profits, (b) the price consumers pay for a good, and (c) the wages received by nonunion workers. Do you agree or disagree? Explain your answer.

5. Explain why the monopsonist pays a wage rate less than labor's marginal revenue product.

6. What forces may lead to the breakup of an employer (monopsony) cartel?

7. What view is a labor union likely to hold on each of the following issues?
   a. Easing of the immigration laws
   b. A quota on imported products
   c. Free trade
   d. A decrease in the minimum wage

8. A discussion of labor unions usually evokes strong feelings. Some people argue vigorously against labor unions; others

argue with equal vigor for them. Some people see labor unions as the reason workers in this country enjoy as high a standard of living as they do; others see labor unions as the reason the country is not so well off economically as it might be. Speculate on why the topic of labor unions generates such strong feelings and emotions—often with such little analysis.

9. Identify one practice of labor unions consistent with the following:

a. Affecting the elasticity of demand for union labor

b. Increasing the demand for union labor

c. Decreasing the supply of labor union workers

10. Some persons argue that a monopsony firm exploits its workers if it pays them less than their marginal revenue products. Others disagree. They say that as long as the firm pays the workers their opportunity costs (which must be the case or

the workers would not stay with the firm), the workers are not being exploited. This view suggests that there are two definitions of exploitation:

a. Paying workers below their marginal revenue products (even if wages equal the workers' opportunity costs)

b. Paying workers below their opportunity costs

Keeping in mind that this may be a subjective judgment, which definition of exploitation do you think is more descriptive of the process and why?

11. What does the elasticity of demand for labor have to do with the wage–employment trade-off?

12. What is the effect of labor unions on nonunion wage rates?

13. Will a union behave differently if it wants to get all its members employed instead of maximizing the total wage bill? Explain your answer.

WORKING WITH NUMBERS AND GRAPHS

1. Determine the appropriate numbers for the lettered spaces.

(1) Workers	(2) Wage Rate	(3) Total Labor Cost	(4) Marginal Factor Cost
1	A	$12.00	$12.00
2	$12.10	24.20	E
3	12.20	C	F
4	B	D	12.60

2. Which demand curve for labor in the following figure exhibits the most pronounced wage–employment trade-off? Explain your answer.

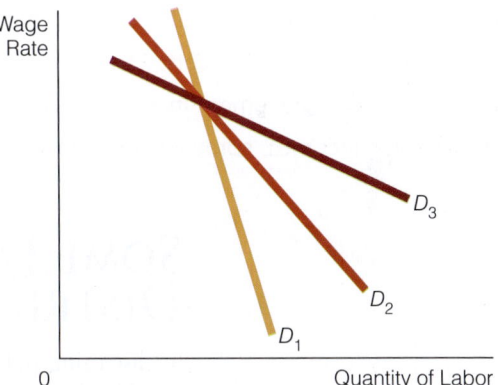

3. Diagrammatically explain how changes in supply conditions and wage rates in the unionized sector can cause changes in supply and wage rates in the nonunionized sector.

CHAPTER 29

© IMAGE COPYRIGHT DHOXAX, 2009. USED UNDER LICENSE FROM SHUTTERSTOCK.COM

THE DISTRIBUTION OF INCOME AND POVERTY

Introduction A random sample of people from the general population will have various incomes. Some people will be in the top 20 percent of income earners, some in the lowest 20 percent, and many others between these two extremes. In other words, some people earn high incomes, some earn low incomes, and many earn middle incomes. What factors influence the amount of income a person earns? Why are some people more likely than others to be poor? Why are some people more likely to be rich? You'll find the answers to these questions and many other questions about the distribution of income and poverty in this chapter.

SOME FACTS ABOUT INCOME DISTRIBUTION

In discussing public policy issues, people sometimes talk about a single fact when they should talk about a collection of facts. A single fact is usually not as informative as a collection of facts, in much the same way that a single snapshot does not tell as much of a story as a moving picture—a succession of snapshots. This section presents a collection of a few facts about the distribution of income.

Who Are the Rich and How Rich Are They?

By many interpretations, the lowest fifth (the lowest quintile) of households in the United States is considered poor, the top fifth is considered rich, and the middle three-fifths are considered middle income.[1]

In 2007, the lowest fifth (the poor) in the United States received 3.4 percent of the total money income, the second fifth received 8.7 percent, the third fifth received 14.8 percent, the fourth fifth received 23.4 percent, and the top fifth (the rich) received 49.7 percent (see Exhibit 1).[2]

---

1. A household consists of all people who occupy a housing unit. It includes the related family members and all unrelated people.
2. Percentages in this chapter do not always equal 100 due to rounding.

Has the income distribution become more or less equal over time? Exhibit 2 shows the income shares of households in 1967 and 2007. In 1967, the highest fifth (top) of households accounted for 43.8 percent of all income; in 2007, the percentage had risen to 49.7 percent.

At the other end of the income spectrum, in 1967, the lowest fifth received 4.0 percent of all income; in 2007, the percentage had fallen to 3.4 percent. The middle groups—the three-fifths of income recipients between the lowest fifth and the highest fifth—accounted for 52.3 percent of all income in 1967 and 46.9 percent in 2007.

Many people implicitly assume that the quintiles (the fifths) in income distributions contain equal shares of the population, but the official income quintiles of the Bureau of the Census do not contain equal shares of the population. The Census Bureau quintiles are unequal in size because they are based on a count of households rather than persons. In the United States, high-income households tend to be married couples with many members and earners. Low-income households tend to be single persons with little or no earnings. The average household in the top quintile contains 3.2 persons, and the average household in the bottom quintile contains 1.8 persons.

Some economists have argued that the unequal quintile populations skew the Census's measure of the income distribution. For example, in 2002, the top quintile contained 24.6 percent of the population, and the bottom quintile contained 14.3 percent of the population. In terms of head count, 69.4 million persons were in the highest fifth, and 40.3 million persons were in the lowest fifth.

If we adjust the income distribution so that each quintile actually contains 20 percent of the population, we get different results. In 2002, the income share of the lowest fifth rises from 3.5 percent to 9.4 percent, and the income share of the highest fifth falls from 49.7 percent to 39.6 percent.

Sometimes economists make further adjustments to income distribution. For example, the persons in each fifth do not all work the same number of hours. In 2002, individuals in the lowest fifth performed 4.3 percent of all the work in the U.S. economy, and those in the highest fifth performed 33.9 percent. To be fair, the low levels of paid employment in the lowest fifth reflect the low numbers of working-age population in this group. In 2002, the lowest fifth contained only 11.2 percent of all working-age adults, and the highest fifth contained 27.6 percent. However, when comparing working-age adults in the lowest fifth with working-age adults in the highest fifth, the average working-age adult in the lowest fifth worked about half as many hours a year as the working-age adult in the highest fifth.

The Effect of Age on the Income Distribution

In analyzing the income distribution, we have to distinguish between people who are poor for long periods of time (sometimes their entire lives) and people who are poor temporarily. Consider Sherri Holmer, who attends college and works part-time as a waitress at a nearby restaurant. Currently, her income is so low that she falls into the lowest quintile of income earners, but she isn't likely always to be in this quintile. After she graduates from college, Sherri's income will probably rise. If she is like most people, her income will rise during her twenties, thirties, and forties. In her late forties or early fifties, her income will take a slight downturn and then level off.

EXHIBIT 1

Distribution of Household Income Shares, 2007

The annual income shares for different quintiles of households is shown here.

Source: U.S. Bureau of the Census.

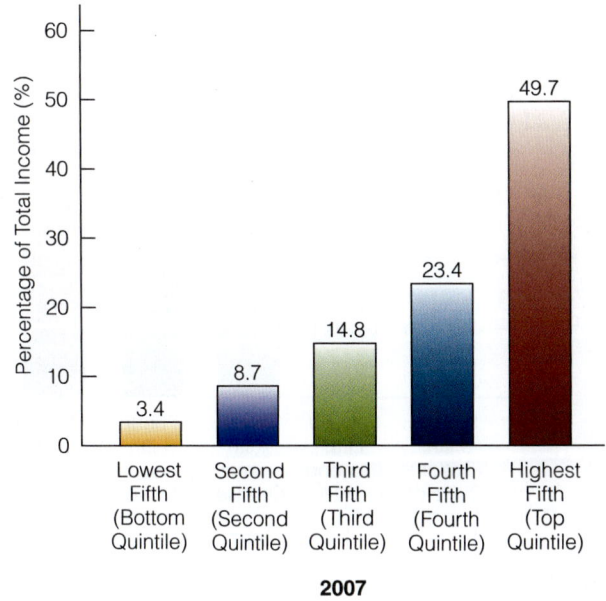

2007

EXHIBIT 2

Income Distribution, 1967 and 2007

Note that income shares have not been adjusted for such things as taxes and in-kind transfer payments, which are transfer payments made in terms of a specific good or service rather than in cash.

1967

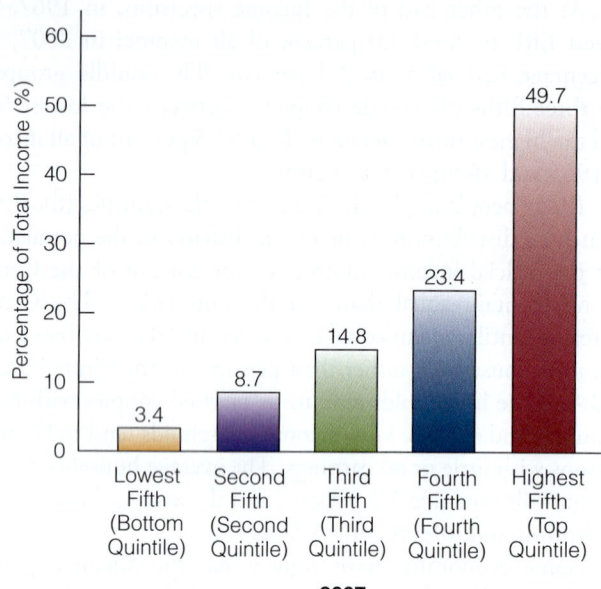

2007

Possibly—in fact, very likely—a person in her late twenties, thirties, or forties will have a higher income than a person in his early twenties or a person in her sixties, even though their total lifetime incomes will be identical. If we view each person over time, income equality is greater than if we view each person at a particular point in time (say, when one person is 58 years old and another is 68).

Exhibit 3 shows the incomes of John and Stephanie over a span of years. In 2000, John is 18 years old and earning $10,000 per year, and Stephanie is 28 years old and earning $30,000 a year. The income distribution between John and Stephanie is unequal in 2000.

EXHIBIT 3

Income Distribution at One Point in Time and Over Time

In each year, the income distribution between John and Stephanie is unequal, with Stephanie earning more than John in 2000, 2010, 2020, and 2030 and John earning more than Stephanie in 2040. In the five years specified, however, both John and Stephanie earned the same total income of $236,000, giving a perfectly equal income distribution over time.

Year	John's Age (years)	John's Income	Stephanie's Age (years)	Stephanie's Income
2000	18	$10,000	28	$30,000
2010	28	35,000	38	45,000
2020	38	52,000	48	60,000
2030	48	64,000	58	75,000
2040	58	75,000	68	26,000
Total		$236,000		$236,000

Ten years later, the income distribution is still unequal, with Stephanie earning $45,000 and John earning $35,000. In fact, the income distribution is unequal in every year shown in the exhibit. However, the total income earned by each person is $236,000, giving a perfectly equal income distribution over time.

In the United States, people seem to experience quite a bit of upward income mobility over time. The University of Michigan's Panel Survey on Dynamics tracked 50,000 Americans for 17 years. Of the people in the lowest fifth of the income distribution in 1975, only 5.1 percent were still there in 1991—and 29 percent of them were in the highest fifth.

t:hinking Like AN ECONOMIST

Why Poor? Many people believe that poor is poor, but not the economist, who wants to know why the person is poor. Is he poor because he is young and just starting out in life? Would he be poor if we were to consider the **in-kind transfer payments** or in-kind benefits he receives? Some people argue that when someone is poor, you do not ask questions; you simply try to help. But the economist knows that not everyone is in the same situation for the same reason and that the reason may determine whether you proceed with help and, if you do proceed, how to do so. Both the elderly person with a disability and the young, smart college student may earn the same low income, but you may feel more obliged to help the elderly person with a disability than the college student. ●●●

In-Kind Transfer Payments
Transfer payments, such as food stamps, medical assistance, and subsidized housing, that are made in a specific good or service rather than in cash.

A Simple Equation

The following simple equation combines four of the factors that determine a person's income:

$$\text{Individual income} = \text{Labor income} + \text{Asset income} + \text{Transfer payments} - \text{Taxes}$$

- *Labor income* is equal to the wage rate an individual receives multiplied by the number of hours worked.
- *Asset income* consists of such things as the return to saving, the return to capital investment, and the return to land.
- *Transfer payments* are payments to persons that are not made in return for goods and services currently supplied (e.g., Social Security payments and cash welfare assistance are government transfer payments).
- Finally, from the sum of labor income, asset income, and transfer payments, we subtract *taxes* to see what an individual is left with (i.e., individual income).

Transfer Payments
Payments to persons that are not made in return for goods and services currently supplied.

This equation provides a quick way of focusing on the direct and indirect factors affecting an individual's income and the degree of income inequality. The next section examines the conventional ways that income inequality is measured.

SELF-TEST

(Answers to Self-Test questions are in Answers to Self-Test Questions at the back of the book.)

1. How can government change the distribution of income?

2. "Income inequality at one point in time is sometimes consistent with income equality over time." Comment.

3. Smith and Jones have the same income this year: $40,000. Does it follow that their income came from the same sources? Explain your answer.

Statistics Can Mislead If You Don't Know How They Are Made

If you read that U.S. household income has not grown in the last 20 years, would you conclude that incomes in the United States are stagnant? Many people might think so, but it may not be true. A household consists of all the people who occupy a housing unit. Individual incomes can rise while household incomes remain unchanged if households become smaller over time.

To illustrate, suppose 10 households have four persons in each. Each person in each household earns $30,000 a year. So each household earns an income of $120,000 a year. Some years pass, each person's income in each household rises to $60,000, but two of every four persons in each household leave to set up a new household. In other words, we now have 20 households with two persons in each, and the total income of each of the 20 households is still $120,000. On an individual basis, certainly all 40 persons are better off earning $60,000 each than earning $30,000 each. But on the basis of household income, we get a very different picture.

Lesson: Individual income can rise while household income remains unchanged because households could be getting smaller as individual incomes rise.

Consider another assertion: "The middle class in this country is getting smaller and smaller." On the surface, this statement sounds fairly ominous. Where is the middle class going? Is it disappearing because it is becoming poorer or because it is becoming richer?

The problem is that if we have a fixed definition of the middle class—say, persons who earn between $40,000 and $50,000 a year—then a changing income distribution can cause the number of persons in that (middle-class) income range to fall. Suppose that of 10 people, the lowest-earning earns $10,000 a year, the next-lowest-earning person

earns $20,000 a year, and so on up to the highest-earning person, who earns $100,000 a year.

Incomes for various persons ($000)

10, 20, 30, 40, 50, 60, 70, 80, 90, 100

Let's say that the middle class consists of persons in the middle of the income distribution who earn between $40,000 and $70,000. In other words, the middle class consists of four persons. These four persons' incomes are enclosed in brackets.

10, 20, 30, [40, 50, 60, 70], 80, 90, 100

Years pass, and now everyone earns $50,000 more than before. So now the lowest-earning person earns $60,000 a year and the highest-earning person earns $150,000.

Incomes for various persons ($000)

60, 70, 80, 90, 100, 110, 120, 130, 140, 150

The income distribution has become skewed toward higher incomes. The middle class has been cut in half if we continue to define it as persons earning between $40,000 and $70,000 a year. Now only two persons fall within this category: the person who once earned $10,000 and now earns $60,000 and the person who once earned $20,000 and now earns $70,000.

Lesson: As individual incomes rise, the middle class can get smaller (and disappear altogether) if the definition of the middle class is a fixed income range. Contrary to what some people believe, a disappearing middle class does not necessarily connote a world of only the rich and the poor.

MEASURING INCOME EQUALITY

Two commonly used measures of income inequality are the Lorenz curve and the Gini coefficient.

Lorenz Curve
A graph of the income distribution that expresses the relationship between the cumulative percentage of households and the cumulative percentage of income.

The Lorenz Curve

The Lorenz curve represents the distribution of income; it expresses the relationship between cumulative percentage of households and *cumulative percentage of income.*

Exhibit 4 shows a hypothetical Lorenz curve. The data in part (a) are used to plot the Lorenz curve in part (b). According to (a), the lowest fifth of households has an income

EXHIBIT 4

A Hypothetical Lorenz Curve

The data in (a) were used to derive the Lorenz curve in (b). The Lorenz curve shows the cumulative percentage of income earned by the cumulative percentage of households. If all households received the same percentage of total income, the Lorenz curve would be the line of perfect income equality. The bowed Lorenz curve shows an unequal distribution of income. The more bowed the Lorenz curve is, the more unequal the distribution of income.

Quintile	Income Share (percent)	Cumulative Income Share (percent)
Lowest fifth	10%	10%
Second fifth	15	25
Third fifth	20	45
Fourth fifth	25	70
Highest fifth	30	100

(a)

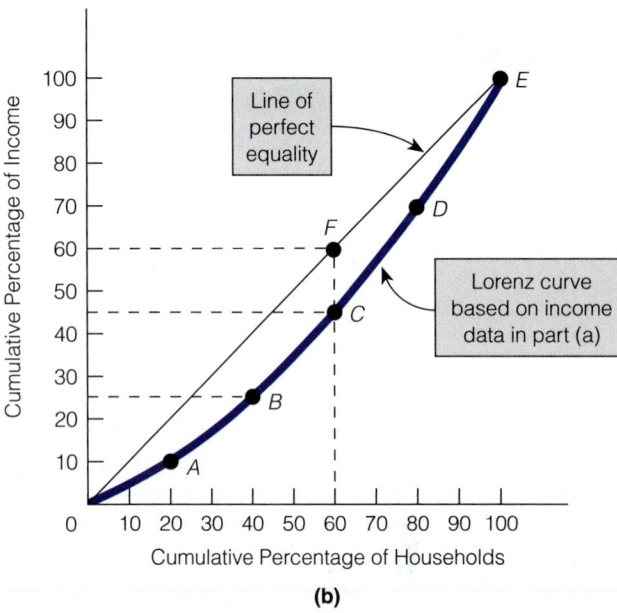

(b)

share of 10 percent, the second fifth has an income share of 15 percent, and so on. The Lorenz curve in (b) is derived by plotting five points.

- Point A represents the cumulative income share of the lowest fifth of households (10 percent of income goes to the lowest fifth of households).

- Point B represents the cumulative income share of the lowest fifth plus the second fifth (25 percent of income goes to two-fifths, or 40 percent, of the income recipients).

- Point C represents the cumulative income share of the lowest fifth plus the second fifth plus the third fifth (45 percent of income goes to three-fifths, or 60 percent, of the income recipients).

The same procedure is used for points D and E.

Connecting these points gives the Lorenz curve that represents the data in (a); the Lorenz curve is another way of depicting the income distribution in (a). Exhibit 5 illustrates the Lorenz curve for the United States based on the (money) income shares in Exhibit 1.

What would the Lorenz curve look like if there were perfect income equality among all households? In this case, every household would receive exactly the same percentage of total income, and the Lorenz curve would be the line of perfect income equality illustrated in Exhibit 4(b). At any point on this 45-degree line, the cumulative percentage of income (on the vertical axis) equals the cumulative percentage of households (on the horizontal axis). For example, at point F, 60 percent of the households receive 60 percent of the total income.

The Gini Coefficient

The Gini coefficient, a measure of the degree of inequality in the income distribution, is used in conjunction with the Lorenz curve. It is equal to the area between the line of perfect

Gini Coefficient
A measure of the degree of inequality in the income distribution.

EXHIBIT 5

Lorenz Curve for the United States, 2007

This Lorenz curve is based on the 2007 income shares for the United States.

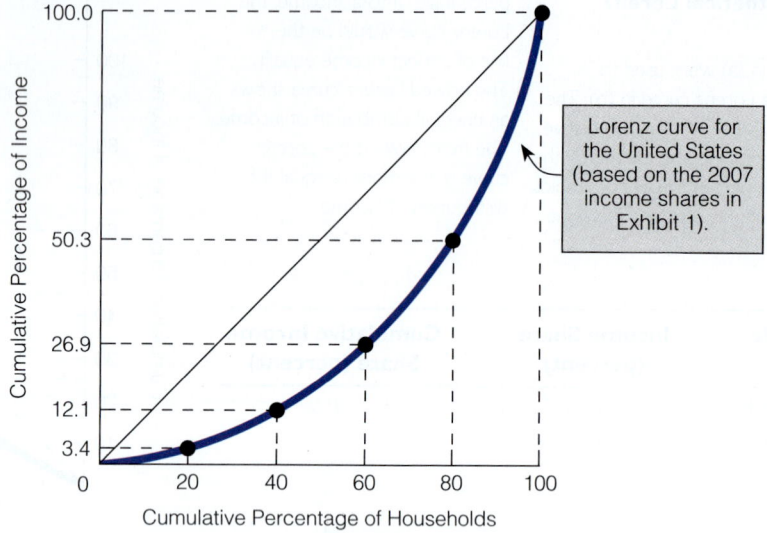

Lorenz curve for the United States (based on the 2007 income shares in Exhibit 1).

income equality (or 45-degree line) and the actual Lorenz curve, divided by the entire triangular area under the line of perfect income equality.

$$\text{Gini coefficient} = \frac{\text{Area between the life of perfect income equality and actual Lorenz curve}}{\text{Entire triangular area under the line of perfect income equality}}$$

Exhibit 6 illustrates both the line of perfect income equality and an actual Lorenz curve. The Gini coefficient is computed by dividing the shaded area (the area between the line of perfect income equality and the actual Lorenz curve) by the area $0AB$ (the entire triangular area under the line of perfect income equality).

The Gini coefficient is a number between 0 and 1. At one extreme, the Gini coefficient equals 0 if the numerator in the equation is 0, which means there is no area between the line of perfect income equality and the actual Lorenz curve, implying that they are the same. Thus a Gini coefficient of 0 means perfect income equality.

At the other extreme, the Gini coefficient equals 1 if the numerator in the equation is equal to the denominator. If this is the case, the actual Lorenz curve is as far away from the line of perfect income equality as is possible. Thus a Gini coefficient of 1 means complete income inequality. (In this situation, in terms of the actual Lorenz curve, one person would have all the total income, and no one else would have any. In Exhibit 4, a Lorenz curve representing complete income inequality would lie along the horizontal axis from 0 to A and then move from A to B.)

If a Gini coefficient of 0 represents perfect income equality and a Gini coefficient of 1 represents complete income inequality, then the larger the Gini coefficient is, the higher the degree of income inequality will be. Conversely, the smaller the Gini coefficient is, the lower the degree of income inequality. In 2007, the Gini coefficient in the United States was 0.450; in 1947, it was 0.376. In way of comparison, here are the Gini coefficients for some other countries: Russia, 0.423 (2008), Argentina, 0.49 (2007), Mexico 0.482 (2008), United Kingdom, 0.34 (2005), Spain, 0.32 (2005), Sweden, 0.23 (2005).

EXHIBIT 6

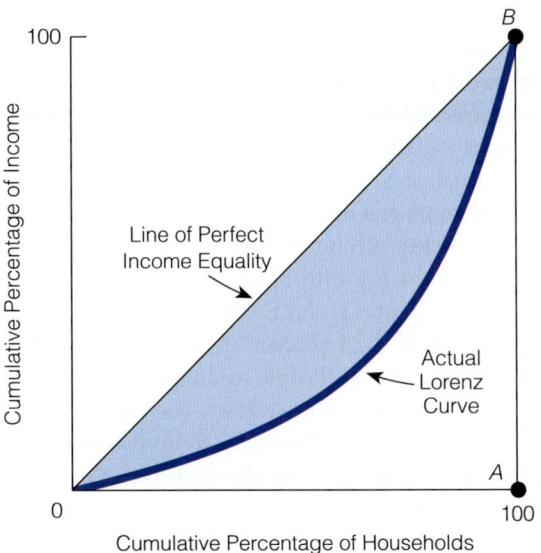

The Gini Coefficient

The Gini coefficient is a measure of the degree of income inequality. It is equal to the area between the line of perfect income equality and the actual Lorenz curve divided by the entire triangular area under the line of perfect income equality. In the diagram, this is equal to the shaded portion divided by the triangular area 0AB. A Gini coefficient of 0 means perfect income equality; a Gini coefficient of 1 means complete income inequality. The larger the Gini coefficient, the greater the income inequality; the smaller the Gini coefficient, the lower the income inequality

A Limitation of the Gini Coefficient

Although the Gini coefficient indicates a lot about the degree of inequality in income distribution, we have to be careful not to misinterpret it. For example, if the Gini coefficient is 0.33 in country 1 and 0.25 in country 2, we know that the income distribution is more equal in country 2 than in country 1. But in which country does the lowest fifth of households receive the larger percentage of income? The natural inclination is to answer, in the country with the more nearly equal income distribution: country 2.

However, this answer may not be true. Exhibit 7 shows two Lorenz curves. Overall, Lorenz curve 2 is closer to the line of perfect income equality than Lorenz curve 1; thus, the Gini coefficient is smaller for Lorenz curve 2 than for Lorenz curve 1. But the lowest 20 percent of households has a smaller percentage of total income with Lorenz curve 2 than with Lorenz curve 1.

Therefore, the Gini coefficient cannot tell us what is happening in different quintiles. If the Gini coefficient is lower in country 2 than in country 1, the lowest fifth of households do not necessarily have a greater percentage of total income in country 2 compared to country 1.

Common Misconceptions About Income Inequality

Some people suggest that in a country where income inequality is rising, individuals cannot become better off. Suppose a society is made up of five

EXHIBIT 7

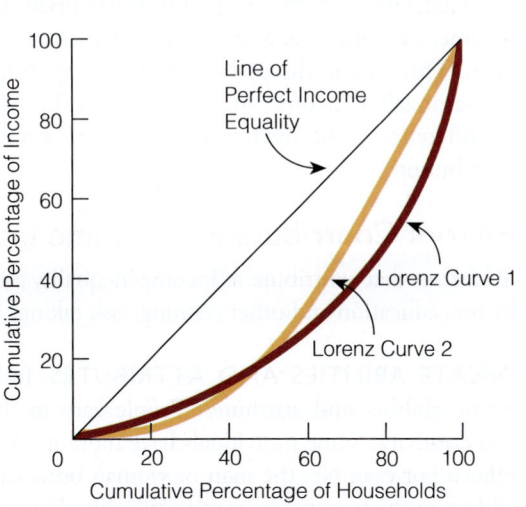

Limitation of the Gini Coefficient

By itself, the Gini coefficient cannot tell us anything about the income share of a particular quintile. Although there is a tendency to believe that the bottom quintile receives a larger percentage of total income the lower the Gini coefficient, this need not be the case. In the diagram, the Gini coefficient for Lorenz curve 2 is lower than the Gini coefficient for Lorenz curve 1. But, the bottom 20 percent of households obtains a smaller percentage of total income in the lower Gini coefficient case.

individuals, A–E. The yearly income for each individual is as follows: A earns $20,000, B earns $10,000, C earns $5,000, D earns $2,500, and E earns $1,250. The total yearly income in this society is $38,750, and the distribution of income is certainly unequal. A earns 51.61 percent of the income, B earns 25.81 percent, C earns 12.90 percent, D earns 6.45 percent, and E earns only 3.23 percent.

Now each person earns additional real income. A earns $10,000 more real income for a total of $30,000, B earns $3,000 more real income for a total of $13,000, C earns $2,000 more real income for a total of $7,000, D earns $1,000 more real income for a total of $3,500, and E earns $200 more real income for a total of $1,450. In terms of real income, each of the five persons is better off, but the income distribution has become even more unequal. For example, A (at the top fifth of income earners) now receives 54.60 percent of all income instead of 51.61 percent, and E (at the bottom fifth of income earners) now receives 2.64 percent instead of 3.23 percent. A newspaper headline might read, "The rich get richer as the poor get poorer." People reading this headline might naturally think that the poor in society are worse off. But we know they are not worse off in terms of the goods and services they can purchase. They have more real income than they had when the income distribution was less unequal. In short, everyone can be better off even if the income distribution becomes more unequal.

SELF-TEST

1. Starting with the top fifth of income earners and proceeding to the lowest fifth, suppose the income share of each group is 40 percent, 30 percent, 20 percent, 10 percent, and 5 percent. Can these percentages be right?

2. Country A has a Gini coefficient of 0.45. What does this mean?

WHY INCOME INEQUALITY EXISTS

The question of why income inequality exists can be answered by focusing on our simple equation:

Individual income = Labor income + Asset income + Transfer payments − Taxes

Generally, income inequality exists because people do not receive the same labor income, asset income, and transfer payments, and/or because they do not pay the same taxes. This section discusses some of the specific reasons that people don't receive, say, the same labor income and asset income by focusing on factors that often contribute to differences. The next section looks at some of the proposed standards of income distribution.

Factors Contributing to Income Inequality

Six factors that contribute to income inequality are innate abilities and attributes, work and leisure, education and other training, risk taking, luck, and wage discrimination.

INNATE ABILITIES AND ATTRIBUTES Individuals are not all born with the same innate abilities and attributes. People vary in their degrees of intelligence, appearance, and creativity. Some individuals have more marketable innate abilities and attributes than others. For example, the man or woman born with exceptionally good looks, the natural athlete, or the person who is musically gifted or mathematically adept is more likely to earn a higher income than someone with lesser abilities or attributes.

WORK AND LEISURE There is a trade-off between work and leisure: more work means less leisure, and less work means more leisure. Some individuals will choose to work more hours (or take a second job) and thus have less leisure, and this choice will be reflected in their labor income. They will earn a larger income than persons who choose not to work more, *ceteris paribus.*

EDUCATION AND OTHER TRAINING Economists usually refer to schooling and other types of training as an investment in human capital. To buy or to invest in a capital good, a person has to give up present consumption and does so in the hope that the capital good will increase future consumption.

Schooling can be looked on as capital. First, one must give up present consumption to obtain it. Second, by providing individuals with certain skills and knowledge, schooling can increase their future consumption over what it would be without schooling. Schooling, then, is human capital. In general, human capital includes education, the development of skills, and any other improvements that are particular to the individual and increase productivity.

Contrast a person who has obtained an education with a person who has not. The educated person is likely to have certain skills, abilities, and knowledge that the uneducated person lacks. Consequently, the educated person is likely to be worth more to an employer. Most college students know this; it is one of the reasons they attend college.

RISK TAKING Individuals have different attitudes toward risk. Some individuals are more willing to take on risk than others. Some of the individuals who are willing to take on risk will do well and rise to the top of the income distribution, and others will fall to the bottom. Individuals who prefer to play it safe aren't as likely to reach the top of the income distribution or to hit bottom.

LUCK When individuals can't explain why something has happened to them, they often say it was the result of good or bad luck. At times, the good or bad luck explanation makes sense; at other times, it is more of a rationalization than an explanation.

Good and bad luck may influence incomes. For example, the college student who studies biology only to find out in her senior year that the bottom has fallen out of the biology market has experienced bad luck. The farmer who hits oil while digging a well has experienced good luck. An automobile worker who is unemployed owing to a recession he had no part in causing is experiencing bad luck. A person who trains for a profession in which there is an unexpected increase in demand experiences good luck.

Although luck can and does influence incomes, it is not likely to have (on average) a great or long-run effect. The person who experiences good luck today and whose income reflects this fact isn't likely to experience luck-boosting income increases time after time. In the long run, such factors as innate ability and attributes, education, and personal decisions (e.g., how much work versus how much leisure) are more likely to have a greater, more sustained effect on income than luck.

WAGE DISCRIMINATION Wage discrimination exists when an employer pays different wages to individuals of equal ability and productivity, as measured by their marginal revenue products. For example, in the period since World War II, the median income of African Americans has been approximately 60 percent that of whites, and since the late 1950s, females working full-time have earned approximately 60–70 percent of the male median income. These differences between white and black incomes and between male and female incomes are not due wholly to discrimination. Most empirical studies show that approximately half the differences are due to variations in education, productivity, and job training (although one may ask whether discrimination has anything to do with the education, productivity, and job training differences). The remainder of the wage differential is due to other factors, one of which is hypothesized to be discrimination.

Human Capital
Education, development of skills, and anything else that is particular to the individual and that increases personal productivity.

Wage Discrimination
The situation in which individuals of equal ability and productivity (as measured by their contribution to output) are paid different wage rates.

Winner-Take-All Markets[3]

Two economists, Robert Frank and Philip Cook, published a book in 1995 titled *The Winner-Take-All Society*. A winner-take-all market is one in which the top producer or performer in the market earns appreciably more than others in the market. In fact, the top producers earn so much more than others that it is as if they "take it all." For example, in major moviemaking, the producer, director, and leading actor may earn much more than anyone else. In the sports market, the sports stars earn more than their fellow players. For example, the last year that Michael Jordan played basketball with the Chicago Bulls, he earned 121 times the salary of the lowest-paid player.

In their book, Frank and Cook argue that there are more winner-take-all markets today than in the past. They state that winner-take-all markets are nothing new in sports and entertainment. What is new, they argue, is that winner-take-all is becoming a common feature of other markets. Winner-take-all is becoming increasingly more descriptive in such fields as law, journalism, design, investment banking, and medicine.

© IMAGE COPYRIGHT CINEMAFESTIVAL, 2009. USED UNDER LICENSE FROM SHUTTERSTOCK.COM

The data seem to support what Frank and Cook are saying. Recent statistics show that so-called within-group income inequality has been rising. In other words, the winnings, as it were, have come to be concentrated in the hands of a smaller percentage of people in an industry. In 1980, for instance, major U.S. chief executive officers (CEOs) earned an average of 42 times the amount that an average American production worker earned; by 2003, this multiple had jumped to 301.[4] Other examples illustrate the same phenomenon, prompting Frank and Cook to comment that we are increasingly coming to live in a winner-take-all society.

To explain what has happened in recent years to bring about more winner-take-all markets and greater within-group income inequality, Frank and Cook identify two factors: (1) developments in communications, manufacturing technology, and transportation costs that let top performers serve broader markets (a global marketplace) and (2) implicit and explicit rules that have led to more competition for top performers.

Most people agree that discrimination exists, although they differ on how much they think it affects income. Also, discrimination is not always directed at employees by employers. For example, consumers may practice discrimination: Some white consumers may wish to deal only with white physicians and lawyers; some Asian Americans may wish to deal only with Asian American physicians and lawyers.

Income Differences: Some Are Voluntary, Some Are Not

Even in a world with no discrimination, differences in income would exist due to other factors. Some individuals would have more marketable skills than others, some individuals would decide to work harder and longer hours than others, some individuals would take on more risk than others, and some individuals would undertake more schooling and training than others. Thus, some degree of income inequality occurs because individuals are innately different and make different choices. However, some degree of income inequality is also due to factors unrelated to innate ability or choices—such as discrimination or luck.

In an ongoing and interesting debate on the topic of discrimination-based income inequality, the opposing sides weight various factors differently. Some people argue that wage discrimination would be reduced if markets were allowed to be more competitive, more open, and freer. They believe that in an open and competitive market with few barriers to entry and with no government protection of privileged groups, discrimination would

Developments in Communications, Manufacturing Technology, and Transportation Costs

In a winner-take-all market, the demand for goods and services is focused on a small number of suppliers—and not, as some may think, because government is limiting our choices. According to Frank and Cook, we are simply focusing on "the best" suppliers to a greater degree than before because of changes in technology, communications, and transportation costs. For example, consumers today do not have to settle for buying tires, cars, clothes, books, or much of anything else from regional or national producers of these items. They can buy these items from the best producers in the world. As Frank notes, whereas once a firm that produced a good tire in northern Ohio could be assured of selling tires in its regional market, today it cannot. Consumers buy tires from a handful of the best tire producers in the world.

Consider another example, in which technological development plays an important part. Before there were records, tapes, or CDs, a person had to go to a concert to hear music. After the technology was developed for producing records, tapes, and CDs, concertgoing was no longer necessary. The best singers and bands in the world could simply put their music on a record, tape, or CD, and anyone in the world could listen to it. A person living in a small town no longer had to go to a local concert to hear music performed by what may have been a very mediocre musician. Now, that person could listen to music performed by the best musicians in the world. Thus people's demand for music became focused on a smaller pool of musicians. As a consequence, these top musicians began to witness large increases in their earnings.

Within-Group Income Inequality

Frank and Cook argue that greater competition for top performers can be the result of a legal change. For example, the deregulation in airline, trucking, banking, brokerage, and other industries may have increased the salary competition for top performers, thus driving up their wages.

Deregulation can have such an effect because, in a deregulated environment, market competition comes to play a bigger role in determining outcomes—both good and bad. Specifically, in a deregulated environment, the potential for both profits and losses is greater than in a regulated (less competitive) environment. To capture the higher potential profits and to guard against the increased likelihood of losses, talented professionals become more valuable to a firm.

Also, perhaps as a result of a less regulated, more fiercely competitive product market, the once widely accepted practice of companies promoting from within is today falling by the wayside. Increasingly, companies search for the top talent in other firms and industries, not just the top talent in their company pool. Although at one time a top performer in a soft drink company could expect only soft-drink companies to compete for his or her services, that employee can now expect to receive offers from soft-drink companies, computer companies, insurance companies, and other types of firms.

---

3. This feature is based on Robert H. Frank, "Talent and the Winner-Take-All Society," *American Prospect* 17 (Spring 1994): 97–107.

4. The 2003 multiple is from *BusinessWeek's* 54th Annual Executive Compensation Survey, April 2004.

---

have a high price. Firms that didn't hire the best and the brightest—regardless of race, religion, or gender—would suffer. They would ultimately pay for their act of discrimination by having higher labor costs and lower profits. Individuals holding this view usually propose that government deregulate, reduce legal barriers to entry, and in general not hamper the workings of the free market mechanism.

Others contend that even if the government were to follow this script, much wage discrimination would still exist. They think government should play an active legislative role in reducing both wage discrimination and other types of discrimination that they believe ultimately result in wage discrimination, such as discrimination in education and in on-the-job training. Proponents of an active role for government usually believe that such policy programs as affirmative action, equal pay for equal work, and comparable worth (equal pay for comparable work) are beneficial in reducing both the amount of wage discrimination in the economy and the degree of income inequality.

SELF-TEST

1. Jack and Harry work for the same company, but Jack earns more than Harry. Is this evidence of wage discrimination? Explain your answer.

2. A person decides to assume a lot of risk in earning an income. How could this affect her income?

POVERTY

This section presents some facts about poverty and examines its causes.

What Is Poverty?

There are principally two views on poverty:

- *Poverty should be defined in absolute terms.* In absolute terms, poverty might be defined as follows: poverty exists when the income of a family of four is less than $10,000 per year.

- *Poverty should be defined in relative terms.* In relative terms, poverty might be defined as follows: poverty exists when the income of a family of four places it in the lowest 10 percent of income recipients.

Viewing poverty in relative terms means that poverty will always exist—unless, of course, income equality is absolute. Given any unequal income distribution, some individuals will always occupy the bottom rung of the income ladder; thus, there will always be poverty. This holds no matter how high the absolute standard of living is of the members of the society. For example, in a society of 10 persons where 9 earn $1 million per year and 1 earns $400,000 per year, the person earning $400,000 per year is in the bottom 10 percent of the income distribution. If poverty is defined in relative terms, this person is considered to be living in poverty.

The U.S. government defines poverty in absolute terms. The absolute poverty measure was developed in 1964 by the Social Security Administration based on findings of the Department of Agriculture. Called the poverty income threshold or poverty line, this measure refers to the income below which people are considered to be living in poverty. Individuals or families with incomes below the poverty income threshold, or poverty line, are considered poor.

The poverty threshold is updated yearly to reflect changes in the consumer price index. In 2007, the poverty income threshold was $21,203 for a family of four and $10,787 for an individual under 65 years old. For an individual 65 years and older, it was $9,444. Also in that year, 38.2 million people (in the United States), or 13 percent of the entire population, were living below the poverty line.

Poverty Income Threshold (Poverty Line)
The income level below which people are considered to be living in poverty.

Limitations of the Official Poverty Income Statistics

The official poverty income statistics have certain limitations and shortcomings.

- Poverty figures are based solely on money incomes. Many money-poor persons receive in-kind benefits. For example, a family of four with a money income of $21,203 in 2007 was defined as poor, although it might have received in-kind benefits worth, say, $4,000. If the poverty figures are adjusted for in-kind benefits, the percentage of persons living in poverty drops.

- Poverty figures are not adjusted for unreported income, leading to an overestimate of poverty.

- Poverty figures are not adjusted for regional differences in the cost of living, leading to both overestimates and underestimates of poverty.

- Government counters are unable to find some poor persons—such as some of the homeless—which leads to an underestimate of poverty.

Who Are the Poor?

Although the poor are persons of all religions, colors, genders, ages, and ethnic backgrounds, some groups are represented much more prominently in the poverty figures than others. For example, a greater percentage of African Americans and Hispanics than whites are poor. In 2007, 24.5 percent of African Americans, 21.5 percent of Hispanics, and 10.5 percent of whites lived below the poverty line.

A greater percentage of families headed by females than families headed by males are poor, and families with seven or more persons are much more likely to be poor than are families with fewer than seven. In addition, a greater percentage of young persons than other age groups are poor, and the uneducated and poorly educated are more likely to be poor than are the educated. Overall, a disproportionate percentage of the poor are African American or Hispanic, and they live in large families headed by a female who is young and has little education.

If we look at poverty in terms of absolute numbers instead of percentages, then more poor persons are white, largely because more whites are in the total population than other groups. In 2007, 25.1 million whites, 9.2 million African Americans, and 9.8 million Hispanics lived below the poverty line.

What Is the Justification for Government Redistributing Income?

Some individuals say there is no justification for government welfare assistance—that is, redistributing income. In their view, playing Robin Hood is not a proper role of government. Persons who make this argument say they are not against helping the poor (e.g., they are usually in favor of private charitable organizations), but they are against government using its powers to take from some to give to others.

Others who believe in government welfare assistance usually present the *public good–free rider* justification or the *social-insurance* justification. Proponents of the public good–free rider position make the following arguments: most individuals in society would feel better if there were little or no poverty. Witnessing the signs of poverty, such as slums, hungry and poorly clothed people, and the homeless, is distressing. Therefore, there is a demand for reducing or eliminating poverty.

The reduction or elimination of poverty is a *(nonexcludable) public good*—a good that if consumed by one person, can be consumed by other persons to the same degree and the consumption of which cannot be denied to anyone. That is, when poverty is reduced or eliminated, everyone will benefit from no longer viewing the ugly and upsetting sights of poverty, and no one can be excluded from such benefits.

If no one can be excluded from experiencing the benefits of poverty reduction, then individuals will not have any incentive to pay for what they can get for free. Thus, they will become free riders. Economist Milton Friedman sums up the force of the argument this way:

> I am distressed by the sight of poverty. I am benefited by its alleviation; but I am benefited equally whether I or someone else pays for its alleviation; the benefits of other people's charity therefore partly accrue to me. To put it differently, we might all of us be willing to contribute to the relief of poverty, provided everyone else did it. We might not be willing to contribute the same amount without such assurance.[5]

Accepting the public good–free rider argument means that government is justified in taxing all persons to pay for the welfare assistance of some.

The social-insurance justification is a different type of justification for government welfare assistance. It holds that individuals not currently receiving welfare think they might one day need it and thus are willing to take out a form of insurance for themselves by supporting welfare programs with their tax dollars and votes.

SELF-TEST

1. "Poor people will always exist." Comment.

2. What percentage of the U.S. population was living in poverty in 2007?

3. What is the general description of a disproportionate percentage of the poor?

5. Milton Friedman, *Capitalism and Freedom* (Chicago: University of Chicago Press, 1962), p. 191.

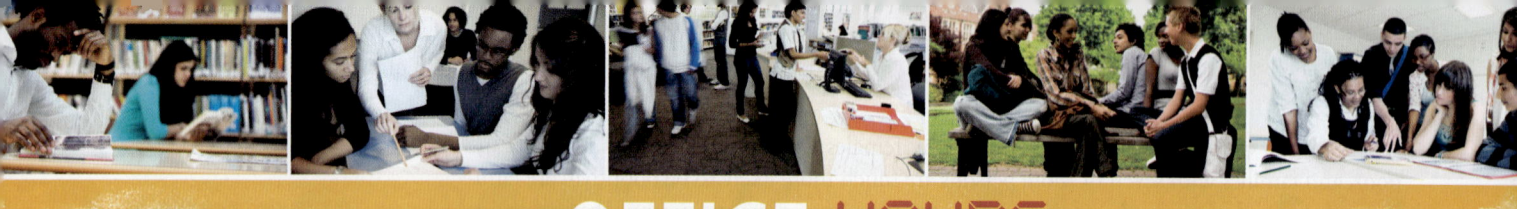

OFFICE HOURS

Are the Number of Persons in Each Fifth the Same?

STUDENT:

Earlier you said that in 2007, the lowest fifth of household income earners in the United States received 3.4 percent of the total money income, the second fifth received 8.7 percent, the third fifth received 14.8 percent, the fourth fifth received 23.4 percent, and the top fifth (the rich) received 49.7 percent. Am I right that each fifth contains the same number of individuals? In other words, if there are 100 individuals in the lowest fifth, it follows that there are 100 individuals in the top fifth too.

INSTRUCTOR:

No, you're not right. The quintiles (the fifths) are unequal in size because they are based on a count of households rather than persons, and not every household has the same number of persons in it. For example, one household can have 2 persons in it, and another has 4.

STUDENT:

Well, then, are more persons in the top fifth of income earners than in the lowest fifth of income earners?

INSTRUCTOR:

Yes. For example, in 2002, the top fifth contained 24.6 percent of the population, whereas the lowest fifth contained 14.3 percent of the population. Stated differently, the top fifth contained 69.4 million persons, and the lowest fifth contained 40.3 million persons.[6]

STUDENT:

What happens to the income distribution if we adjust each fifth so that it contains an equal number of persons? In other words, what happens if we adjust every fifth so that it contains 20 percent of the population?

INSTRUCTOR:

The income distribution becomes less unequal. To illustrate, if you look at the data for 2002 and deal with households instead of persons, you'd conclude that the lowest fifth received 3.5 percent of the total money income and the top fifth received 49.7 percent. Now if you adjust the fifths so that each has 20 percent of the population, the lowest fifth received 9.4 percent (instead of 3.5 percent) of the total money income and the top fifth received 39.6 percent (instead of 49.7 percent).

---

6. The adjusted income distributions in this feature come from Census Bureau data and a publication by Robert Rector and Rea Hederman, Jr., *Two Americas: One Rich, One Poor? Understanding Income Inequality in the United States* (August 24, 2004) at http://www.heritage.org/Research/Taxes/bg1791.cfm

CHAPTER SUMMARY

THE DISTRIBUTION OF INCOME

- In 2007, the lowest fifth of households received 3.4 percent of the total money income, the second fifth received 8.7 percent, the third fifth received 14.8 percent, the fourth fifth received 23.4 percent, the top fifth received 49.7 percent.

- The government can change the distribution of income through taxes and transfer payments. Individual income = Labor income + Asset income + Transfer payments − Taxes. Government directly affects transfer payments and taxes.

- The Lorenz curve represents the income distribution. The Gini coefficient is a measure of the degree of inequality in the distribution of income. A Gini coefficient of 0 means perfect income equality; a Gini coefficient of 1 means complete income inequality.

- Income inequality exists because individuals differ in their innate abilities and attributes, their choices regarding work and leisure, their education and other training, their attitudes about risk taking, the luck they experience, and the amount of wage discrimination directed against them. Some income inequality is the result of voluntary choices, and some is not.

STUDENT:

Can income distribution be adjusted for other things?

INSTRUCTOR:

Yes. For example, persons in each fifth do not all work the same number of hours. For example, in 2002, individuals in the lowest fifth performed 4.3 percent of all work in the U.S. economy, and those in the highest fifth performed 33.9 percent. To be fair, though, the low levels of paid employment in the lowest fifth reflect the low numbers of working-age population in this group. In 2002, the lowest fifth contained only 11.2 percent of all working-age adults, whereas the highest fifth contained 27.6 percent. However, when we compare working-age adults in the lowest fifth with working-age adults in the highest fifth, we learn that the average working-age adult in the lowest fifth worked about half as many hours a year as the working-age adult in the highest fifth.

Now if we adjust the income distribution to show us what it would be like if average working-age adult in the lowest fifth worked as many hours as the average working-age adult in the top fifth, the income distribution becomes less unequal. In 2002, the lowest fifth would receive 12.3 percent (instead of 3.5 percent) of the total money income, and the top fifth would receive 35.8 percent (instead of 49.7 percent).

STUDENT:

The income distribution seems as though it can be portrayed in different ways. We can adjust for taxes and transfer payments or choose not to; we can choose to adjust for number of persons or choose not to; we can adjust for number of hours worked or choose not to.

INSTRUCTOR:

You're right about that. And that is part of the reason for such heated debate over income distribution. Person A might think it's better to view the income distribution after having adjusted for something (such as taxes, transfer payments, the number of persons, and the like), and Person B might think it better to view the income distribution before adjusting.

POINTS TO REMEMBER

1. The bottom fifth of household income earners does not contain the same number of persons as the top fifth of household income earners. For example, in 2002, the top fifth contained 69.4 million persons, whereas the lowest fifth contained 40.3 million persons.
2. The income distribution (or distribution of income) can be adjusted for various factors. Such adjustments often change the degree of income equality/inequality of the income distribution.

POVERTY

- The income poverty threshold, or poverty line, is the income level below which a family or person is considered poor and living in poverty.
- Poverty income statistics have their limitations. The statistics are usually not adjusted for (1) in-kind benefits, (2) unreported and illegal income, and (3) regional differences in the cost of living. Furthermore, the statistics do not count the poor who exist but who are out of sight, such as some of the homeless.
- People who believe government should redistribute income from the rich to the poor usually base their argument on the public good–free rider justification or the social-insurance justification. The public good–free rider justification holds that many people are in favor of redistributing income from the rich to the poor and that the elimination of poverty is a public good. Unfortunately, individuals cannot create a public good because of the incentive everyone has to free-ride on the contributions of others. Consequently, government is justified in taxing all persons to pay for the welfare assistance of some. The social-insurance justification holds that individuals not currently receiving redistributed monies may one day find themselves in a position where they will need to; so they are willing to take out a form of insurance. In essence, they are willing to support redistribution programs today so that the programs exist if they should need them in the future.

In-Kind Transfer Payments
Transfer Payments

Lorenz Curve
Gini Coefficient

Human Capital
Wage Discrimination

Poverty Income Threshold
(Poverty Line)

QUESTIONS AND PROBLEMS

1. What role might each of the following play in contributing to income inequality?
   a. Risk taking
   b. Education
   c. Innate abilities and attributes

2. How would you determine whether the wage difference between two individuals is due to wage discrimination?

3. Compare the U.S. income distribution in 1967 with the income distribution in 2007. Has U.S. income inequality increased or decreased? What percentage of total money income did the top fifth of U.S. households receive in 2007?

4. Can more people live in poverty at the same time that a smaller percentage of people live in poverty? Explain your answer.

5. Would you expect greater income inequality in country A, where there is great disparity in age, or in country B, where there is little disparity in age? Explain your answer.

6. What is the effect of age on income distribution?

7. "The Gini coefficient for country A is 0.35, and for country B it is 0.22. Therefore, the bottom 10 percent of income recipients in country B have a greater percentage of the total income than the bottom 10 percent of the income recipients in country A." Do you agree or disagree? Why?

8. Welfare recipients would rather receive cash benefits than in-kind benefits, but much of the welfare system provides in-kind benefits. Is there any reason for not giving recipients their welfare benefits the way they want to receive them? Would it be better to move to a welfare system that provides benefits only in cash?

9. What percentage of total money income did the lowest fifth of households receive in 2007? The fourth fifth?

WORKING WITH NUMBERS AND GRAPHS

1. The lowest fifth of income earners have a 10 percent income share; the second fifth, a 17 percent income share; the third fifth, a 22 percent income share; the fourth fifth, a 24 percent income share; and the highest fifth, a 27 percent income share. Draw the Lorenz curve.

2. In Exhibit 7, using Lorenz curve 2, approximately what percentage of income goes to the second-highest 20 percent of households?

3. Is it possible for everyone's real income to rise even though the income distribution in a society has become more unequal? Prove your answer with a numerical example.

CHAPTER 30

INTEREST, RENT, AND PROFIT

CREATAS IMAGES/JUPITER IMAGES

Introduction The time between when individuals decide to start a business and the day they open their door for the first time can seem like forever. Starting up a business involves decisions and payments. Most likely, the entrepreneurs will need to obtain a loan, on which they will pay interest. They will need to find a suitable location and may need to pay rent on a piece of land. Finally, the grand opening day arrives, and the new owners can look forward to earning profit.

Interest, rent, and profit are the payments to capital, land, and entrepreneurship. A knowledge of these three payments is critical to understanding how markets operate and how economies function.

INTEREST

The word "interest" is used in two ways in economics. Sometimes, it refers to the price for credit or loanable funds. For example, Lars borrows $100 from Rebecca and a year later pays her back $110. The interest is $10.

Interest can also refer to the return that capital earns as an input in the production process. A person who buys a machine (a capital good) for $1,000 and earns $100 a year by using the productive services of the machine is said to earn $100 interest, or a 10 percent interest rate, on the capital.

Economists refer to both the price for loanable funds and the return on capital goods as interest because the two tend to become equal, as discussed later in this section.

Loanable Funds
Funds that someone borrows and another person lends, for which the borrower pays an interest rate to the lender.

Loanable Funds: Demand and Supply

The equilibrium interest rate, or the price for loanable funds (or credit), is determined by the demand for and supply of loanable funds (or credit). The demand for loanable funds is composed of the demand for consumption loans, the demand for investment loans, and government's demand for loanable funds [the U.S. Treasury may need to finance budget deficits by borrowing (demanding) loanable funds in the loanable funds market]. This chapter focuses on the demand for consumption loans and the demand for investment loans. The supply of loanable funds comes from people's saving and from newly created money. This chapter discusses only people's saving.

So, in this chapter, the demand for loanable funds is composed of the demand for (1) consumption loans and (2) investment loans. The supply of loanable funds is composed of people's saving.

THE SUPPLY OF LOANABLE FUNDS Savers are people who consume less than their current income. Without savers, there would be no supply of loanable funds. Savers receive an interest rate for the use of their funds, and the amount of funds saved and loaned is directly related to the interest rate.[1] Specifically, the supply curve of loanable funds is upward sloping: The higher the interest rate is, the greater the quantity supplied of loanable funds will be; the lower the interest rate, the less the quantity supplied of loanable funds.

THE DEMAND FOR LOANABLE FUNDS: CONSUMPTION LOANS Consumers demand loanable funds because they have a positive rate of time preference; that is, consumers prefer earlier availability of goods to later availability. For example, most people would prefer to have a car today than to have one five years from today.

There is nothing irrational about a positive rate of time preference; most, if not all, people have it. People differ, though, as to the *degree* of their preference for earlier availability. Some people have a high rate of time preference, signifying that they greatly prefer present to future consumption. ("I *must* have that new car today.") Other people have a low rate, signifying that they prefer present to future consumption only slightly. People with a high rate of time preference are less likely to postpone consumption than people with a low rate. People with a high rate of time preference feel they need to have things now.

Consumers' positive rate of time preference is the reason for a demand for consumption loans. Consumers borrow today to buy today; they will pay back the borrowed amount plus interest tomorrow. The interest payment is the price consumers borrowers to pay for the earlier availability of goods.

THE DEMAND FOR LOANABLE: INVESTMENT LOANS Investors (or firms) demand loanable funds (or credit) so that they can invest in capital goods and finance roundabout methods of production. A firm using a roundabout method of production first produces capital goods and then uses those goods to produce consumer goods.

Compare the direct method and the roundabout method for catching fish. In the direct method, a person uses his hands to catch fish. In the roundabout method, the person weaves a net (which is a capital good) and then uses the net to catch fish. Using the direct method, Charlie can catch 4 fish per day. Using the roundabout method, he can catch 10 fish per day. Suppose Charlie takes 10 days to weave a net. If Charlie does not weave a net and instead catches fish by hand, he can catch 1,460 fish per year (4 fish per day times 365 days). If, however, Charlie spends 10 days weaving a net (during which time he catches no fish), he can catch 3,550 fish the first year (10 fish per day times 355 days). Thus, the capital-intensive roundabout method of production is highly productive.

Because roundabout methods of production are so productive, investors are willing to borrow funds to finance them. For example, Charlie might reason, "I'm more productive if I use a fishing net, but I'll need to take 10 days off from catching fish and devote all my energies to weaving a net. What will I eat during the 10 days? Perhaps I can borrow some fish from my neighbor. I'll need to borrow 40 fish for the next 10 days. But I must make it worthwhile for my neighbor to enter into this arrangement, so I will promise to pay her back 50 fish at the end of the year. Thus, my neighbor will lend me 40 fish today

Positive Rate of Time Preference
A preference for earlier over later availability of goods.

Roundabout Method of Production
The production of capital goods that enhance productive capabilities.

---

[1]. Because a higher interest rate may have both a substitution effect and an income effect, many economists argue that a higher interest rate can lead to either more saving or less saving depending on which effect is stronger. We ignore these complications at this level of analysis and hold that the supply curve of loanable funds (from savers) is upward sloping.

in exchange for 50 fish at the end of the year. I realize I'm paying an interest rate of 25 percent [the interest payment of 10 fish is 25 percent of the number of fish borrowed, 40], but it will be worth it." The highly productive nature of the capital-intensive roundabout method of production is what makes the loan worthwhile.

The reasoning in the fish example is repeated whenever a firm makes a capital investment. Producing computers on an assembly line is a roundabout method of production compared with producing them one by one by hand. Making copies on a copying machine is a roundabout method of production compared with copying by hand. In both cases, firms are willing to borrow now, use the borrowed funds to invest in capital goods to finance roundabout methods of production, and pay back the loan with interest later. If roundabout methods of production were not productive, firms would not be willing to borrow.

THE LOANABLE FUNDS MARKET The sum of the demand for consumption loans and the demand for investment loans is the total demand for loanable funds. The demand curve for loanable funds is downward sloping: As interest rates rise, consumers' cost of earlier availability of goods rises, and they curtail their borrowing. Also, as interest rates rise, some investment projects that would be profitable at a lower interest rate will no longer be profitable. Therefore, the interest rate and the quantity demanded of loanable funds are inversely related.

Exhibit 1 illustrates the demand for and supply of loanable funds. The equilibrium interest rate occurs where the quantity demanded of loanable funds equals the quantity supplied of loanable funds.

The Price for Loanable Funds and the Return on Capital Goods Tend to Equality

As already explained, both the price for loanable funds and the return on capital are referred to as interest because they tend to equality. To illustrate, suppose the return on capital is 10 percent and the price for loanable funds is 8 percent. In this setting, firms will borrow in the loanable funds market and invest in capital goods. As they do so, the quantity of capital increases, and its return falls (capital is subject to diminishing marginal returns). In short, the return on capital and the price for loanable funds begin to approach each other.

Suppose, instead, that the percentages are reversed, and the price for loanable funds is 10 percent and the return on capital is 8 percent. In this situation, no one will borrow loanable funds at 10 percent to invest at 8 percent. Over time, the capital stock will decrease (capital depreciates over time; it doesn't last forever), its marginal physical product will rise, and the return on capital and the price for loanable funds will eventually equal each other.

Why Do Interest Rates Differ?

The supply-and-demand analysis in Exhibit 1 suggests that the economy has only one interest rate. In reality, it has many. For example, a major business is not likely to pay the same interest rate for an investment loan to purchase new machinery as the person next door pays for a consumption loan to buy a car. Some of the factors that affect interest rates are discussed next. In each case, the *ceteris paribus* condition holds.

RISK Any time a lender makes a loan, there is a possibility that the borrower will not repay it. Some borrowers are better credit risks than others. A major corporation with a long and established history is probably a better credit risk than a person who has been unemployed three

EXHIBIT 1

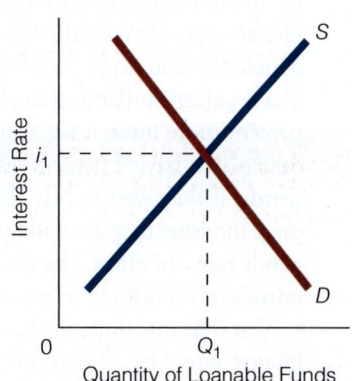

Loanable Funds Market

The demand curve shows the different quantities of loanable funds demanded at different interest rates. The supply curve shows the different quantities of loanable funds supplied at different interest rates. Through the forces of supply and demand, the equilibrium interest rate and the quantity of loanable funds at that rate are established as i_1 and Q_1.

times in the last seven years. The more risk associated with a loan, the higher the interest rate will be; the less risk associated with a loan, the lower the interest rate.

TERM OF THE LOAN In general, the longer the term of the loan is, the higher the interest rate will be; the shorter the term of the loan, the lower the interest rate. Borrowers are usually more willing to pay higher interest rates for long-term loans because the longer term gives them greater flexibility. Lenders require higher interest rates to part with their funds for extended periods.

COST OF MAKING THE LOAN A loan for $1,000 and a loan for $100,000 may require the same amount of record keeping, making the larger loan cheaper (per dollar) to process than the smaller loan. In addition, some loans require frequent payments (e.g., payments for a car loan), whereas others do not. This difference is likely to be reflected in higher administrative costs for loans with more frequent payments. Therefore, loans that cost more to process and administer will have higher interest rates than loans that cost less to process and administer.

ⓣhinking Like AN ECONOMIST

Tending to Equality In economics, factors typically converge. For example, in supply-and-demand analysis, the quantity demanded and the quantity supplied of a good tend to equality (through the equilibrating process). In consumer theory, the marginal utility–price ratios for different goods tend to equality. And, as just discussed, the price of loanable funds and the return on capital tend to equality.

In economics, many things tend to equality because equality is often representative of equilibrium. When quantity demanded equals quantity supplied, a market is said to be in equilibrium. When the marginal utility–price ratio for all goods is the same, the consumer is said to be in equilibrium. Inequality therefore often signifies disequilibrium. When the price of loanable funds is greater than the return on capital, there is disequilibrium.

The economist, knowing that equality often signifies equilibrium, looks for inequalities and then asks, "So what happens now?" ●●●

Nominal and Real Interest Rates

Nominal Interest Rate

The interest rate determined by the forces of supply and demand in the loanable funds market.

The nominal interest rate is the interest rate determined by the forces of supply and demand in the loanable funds market; it is the interest rate in current dollars. The nominal interest rate will change if the demand for or supply of loanable funds changes.

Individuals' expectations of inflation are one of the factors that can change both the demand for and supply of loanable funds. (Inflation occurs when the money prices of goods, on average, increase over time.) Exhibit 2 shows how inflation can affect the nominal interest rate. The current interest rate is 8 percent, and the actual and expected inflation rate are zero (actual inflation rate = expected inflation rate = 0 percent). Later, both the demanders and suppliers of loanable funds expect a 4 percent inflation rate. In anticipation of a 4 percent inflation rate, borrowers (demanders of loanable funds) are willing to pay 4 percent more interest for their loans because they expect to be paying back the loans with dollars that have 4 percent less buying power than the dollars they are being lent. In other words, if they wait to buy the goods, the prices will have risen by 4 percent. To beat the price increase, they are willing to pay up to 4 percent more to borrow funds to purchase the goods now. In effect, the demand for loanable funds curve shifts rightward, so that at Q_1 borrowers are willing to pay a 4 percent higher interest rate.

At the same time, the lenders (the suppliers of loanable funds) require a 4 percent higher interest rate (i.e., 12 percent) to compensate them for the 4 percent less valuable dollars in which the loan will be repaid. In effect, the supply of loanable funds curve shifts leftward, so that at Q_1 lenders will receive an interest rate of 12 percent.

Thus, an expected inflation rate of 4 percent increases the demand for loanable funds and decreases their supply, so that the interest rate is 4 percent higher than it was when the expected inflation rate was zero. In this example, 12 percent is the nominal interest rate. It is the interest rate in current dollars, and it includes the expected inflation rate.

If we adjust for the expected inflation rate, we have the real interest rate. The real interest rate is the nominal interest rate adjusted for the expected inflation rate; that is, it is the nominal interest rate minus the expected inflation rate (Real interest rate = Nominal interest rate – Expected inflation rate). In our example, the real interest rate is 8 percent (12 percent – 4 percent).

The real interest rate, not the nominal interest rate, matters to borrowers and lenders. Consider a lender who grants a $1,000 loan to a borrower at a 20 percent nominal interest rate at a time when the actual inflation rate is 15 percent. The amount repaid to the lender is $1,200, but $1,200 with a 15 percent inflation rate does not have the buying power that $1,200 with a zero inflation rate has. The 15 percent inflation rate wipes out much of the gain, and the lender's real return on the loan is not 20 percent, but rather only 5 percent. Thus, the rate lenders receive and borrowers pay (and therefore the rate they care about) is the real interest rate.

Expected Inflation and Interest Rates

We start at an 8 percent interest rate and an actual and expected inflation rate of 0 percent. Later, both borrowers and lenders expect an inflation rate of 4 percent. Borrowers are willing to pay a higher interest rate because they will be paying off their loans with cheaper dollars. Lenders require a higher interest rate because they will be paid back in cheaper dollars. The demand and supply curves shift such that at Q_1, borrowers are willing to pay and lenders require a 4 percent higher interest rate. The nominal interest rate is now 12 percent. The real interest rate is 8 percent (the Real interest rate = Nominal interest rate – Expected inflation rate).

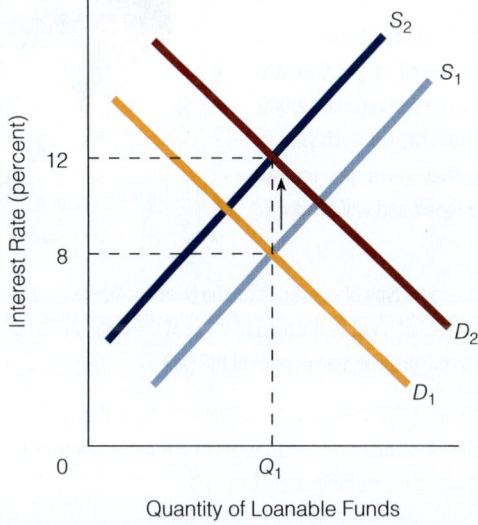

Present Value: What Is Something Tomorrow Worth Today?

Because of people's positive rate of time preference, $100 today is worth more than $100 a year from now. (Wouldn't you prefer to have $100 today to having $100 in a year?) Thus, $100 a year from now must be worth less than $100 today. The question is *how much* $100 a year from now is worth today. This question involves the concept of present value, which is the current worth of some future dollar amount (of receipts or income). In our example, present value refers to what $100 a year from now is worth today.

Present value (*PV*) is computed by using the following formula:

$$PV = \frac{A_n}{(1 + i)^n}$$

where A_n is the actual amount of income or receipts in some future year, i is the interest rate (expressed as a decimal), and n is the number of years in the future. The present value of $100 one year in the future at a 10 percent interest rate is $90.91:

$$PV = \frac{\$100}{(1 + 0.10)^1}$$
$$= \$90.91$$

Thus the right to receive $100 a year from now is worth $90.91 today. In other words, if $90.91 is put into a savings account paying a 10 percent interest rate, it would equal $100 in a year.

Real Interest Rate
The nominal interest rate adjusted for expected inflation, that is, the nominal interest rate minus the expected inflation rate.

Present Value
The current worth of some future dollar amount of income or receipts.

Is the Car Worth Buying?

Business firms often compute present values when trying to decide whether to buy capital goods. Should consumers do the same when they are thinking about buying a durable good (i.e., a good that will last for a few years), such as a car?

Suppose you're thinking about buying a car. The market price of the car is $15,500, and you anticipate that you will receive $2,000 worth of services from the car each year for the next 10 years, after which time the car will have to be scrapped and will have no salvage value.

Now ask yourself the same type of question that the business firm asks when it considers buying a capital good: Is the present value of the car more than, less than, or equal to the present market price of the car?

So you need to calculate the present value of the car. A car that yields $2,000 worth of benefits each year for 10 years at a 4 percent interest rate has a present value of approximately $16,223:

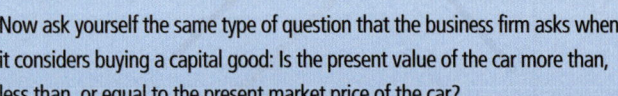

© IMAGE COPYRIGHT MONKEY BUSINESS IMAGES, 2009. USED UNDER LICENSE FROM SHUTTERSTOCK.COM

$$PV = \frac{\$2,000}{(1 + 0.04)^1} + \frac{\$2,000}{(1 + 0.04)^2} + \cdots + \frac{\$2,000}{(1 + 0.04)^{10}} = \$16,223$$
(approximately)

The market price of the car ($15,500) is less than its present value ($16,223); so purchasing the car is worthwhile.

You should also be attentive to the interest rate. All other things remaining constant, an increase in the interest rate will lower the present value of the car. For example, at a 7 percent interest rate, the present value of the car is approximately $15,377. Now the market price of the car ($15,500) is greater than the present value of the car ($15,377); the purchase is not worthwhile.

So we would expect fewer cars to be sold when the interest rate rises and more cars to be sold when the interest rate falls, because a change in the interest rate changes the present value of cars.

Suppose we wanted to know what a future income stream is worth today. Instead of what a future dollar amount is worth today, our objective is to find out what a series of future dollar amounts are worth today. The general formula is:

$$PV = \frac{\Sigma A_n}{(1 + i)^n}$$

where the Greek letter Σ stands for "sum of."

Suppose a firm buys a machine that will earn $100 a year for the next 3 years. What is this future income stream, at $100 per year for 3 years, worth today, that is, its present value? At a 10 percent interest rate, this income stream has a present value of $248.68:

$$PV = \frac{A_1}{(1 + 0.10)^1} + \frac{A_2}{(1 + 0.10)^2} + \frac{A_3}{(1 + 0.10)^3}$$
$$= \frac{\$100}{1.10} + \frac{\$100}{1.21} + \frac{\$100}{1.331}$$
$$= \$90.91 + \$82.64 + \$75.13 = \$248.68$$

finding ECONOMICS

In Living Longer Suppose that because of an advancement in medical science, people start living longer. Can living longer affect the price of antique cars, famous paintings, and fine jewelry? Where is the economics?

(continued)

Investment, Present Value, and Interest Rates

Firms will often increase their level of investment (e.g., purchase more capital goods) as interest rates fall. Suppose a firm is thinking of purchasing a capital good that costs $1,000. The firm expects that the capital good will add to its revenue in each of two years. In year 1, the capital good will add $600, and in year 2 it will add $500. Should the firm purchase the capital good?

One way to decide is to compare the cost of the capital good ($1,000) to the additional revenue the capital good will generate ($1,100). Since the additional revenue is greater than the cost of the capital good, the inclination to say the firm should buy the capital good is strong. But not all the additional revenue is generated in the first year of the life of the capital good. Some of that additional revenue—$500—comes in year 2.

So we need to compute the present value of a stream of revenue to be realized over two years. Here is the calculation:

$$PV = \frac{\$600}{(1 + i)^1} + \frac{\$500}{(1 + i)^2}$$

What the present value (PV) turns out to be depends, of course, on the interest rate. At the assumed interest rate of 10 percent, the present value is $958.67. Since the cost of the capital good ($1,000) is greater than the present value of the additional revenue generated by its use, the capital good is not worth purchasing.

But suppose the interest rate falls to 5 percent. Now the present value is $1,024.93. At the lower interest rate, the capital good is worth purchasing, because the present value of the additional revenue generated by the use of the capital good (or $1,024.93) is greater than its purchase price.

The point is simple: Lower interest rates raise present values, and higher present values that are connected with the purchase of capital goods lead firms to buy more capital goods (i.e., increase their investing).

finding ECONOMICS (continued)

It can be found in the concept of present value. Suppose that you are considering the purchase of a painting and that you would receive $2,000 worth of benefits a year from owning and viewing it. The dollar price you would be willing to pay for the painting is partly based on the present value of the benefits over the number of years you plan to enjoy the painting. The number of years could be higher because you expect to live longer. At a given interest rate, the longer you expect to live, the greater will be the present value of the benefits you receive from the painting, and the more you would be willing to pay for the painting. ▲▲▲

SELF-TEST

(Answers to Self-Test questions are in Answers to Self-Test Questions at the back of the book.)

1. Why does the price for loanable funds tend to equal the return on capital goods?

2. Why does the real interest rate, not the nominal interest rate, matter to borrowers and lenders?

3. What is the present value of $1,000 two years from today if the interest rate is 5 percent?

4. A business firm is thinking of buying a capital good, which will earn $2,000 a year for the next 4 years and cost $7,000. The interest rate is 8 percent. Should the firm buy the capital good? Explain your answer.

RENT

Economic Rent
Payment in excess of opportunity costs.

Pure Economic Rent
A category of economic rent where the payment is to a factor that is in fixed supply, implying that it has zero opportunity costs.

Mention the word "rent," and people naturally think of someone living in an apartment and making monthly payments to a landlord. This is not the type of rent discussed in this chapter. To an economist, rent means economic rent, that is, a payment in excess of opportunity costs (as discussed in an earlier chapter). A subset of economic rent, called pure economic rent, is a payment in excess of opportunity costs when opportunity costs are zero. Historically, the term "pure economic rent" was first used to describe the payment to the factor land, which is perfectly inelastic in supply.

In Exhibit 3, the total supply of land is fixed at Q_1 acres; there can be no more and no less than this amount of land. The payment for land (R_1) is determined by the forces of supply and demand. R_1 is more than sufficient to bring Q_1 acres into supply. In fact, by reason of the fixed supply of land (the supply curve is perfectly inelastic), the Q_1 acres would have been forthcoming at a payment of $0. In short, this land has zero opportunity costs. Therefore, the full payment—all of R_1—is referred to as pure economic rent.

David Ricardo, the Price of Grain, and Land Rent

In nineteenth-century England, people were concerned about the rising price of grains, which were a staple in many English diets. Some argued that grain prices were rising because land rents were going up rapidly. People began pointing fingers at the landowners, maintaining that the high rents the landowners received for their land made it more and more costly for farmers to raise grains. These higher costs, in turn, were passed on to consumers in the form of higher prices. According to this argument, the solution was to lower rents, which would lead to lower costs for farmers and eventually to lower prices for consumers.

English economist David Ricardo thought this reasoning was faulty. He contended that grain prices were high not because rents were high (as most individuals thought) but rather that rents were high because grain prices were high. In current economic terminology, his argument was as follows: land is a factor of production; therefore, the demand for it is derived. Land is also in fixed supply; therefore, the only thing that will change the payment made to land is a change in the demand for it. (The supply curve isn't going to shift, and thus the only thing that can change price is a shift in the demand curve.) Landowners have no control over the demand for land, which comes from other persons who want to use it.

In nineteenth-century England, the demand came from farmers who were raising grains and other foodstuffs. Landowners could not have pushed up land rents because they had no control over the demand for their land. Therefore, rents were high because the demand for land was high, and the demand for land was high because grain prices were high. Economists put it this way: *land rents are price determined, not price determining.*

EXHIBIT 3

Pure Economic Rent and the Total Supply of Land

The total supply of land is fixed at Q_1. The payment for the services of this land is determined by the forces of supply and demand. Because the payment is for a factor in fixed supply, it is referred to as pure economic rent.

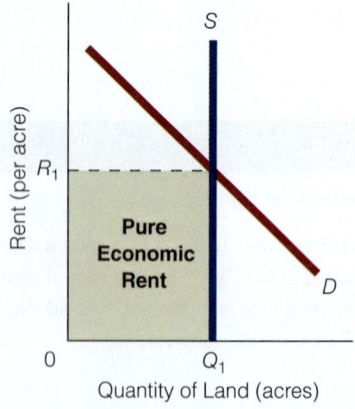

Grain Prices and Land Rent

David Ricardo argued that high grain prices cause high land rents. For example, suppose that there are three grades of land: excellent, good, and poor and that grain can be produced on each grade of land. The excellent land can produce 10 bushels of grain, the good land can produce 5 bushels of grain, and the poor land can produce 2 bushels of grain. Further, it costs $10 to farm each grade of land, and the price of grain is currently $1.50 a bushel.

Under these circumstances, not all three grades of land will be farmed. Only the excellent grade of land will be farmed because it can produce 10 bushels of grain, which can then be sold at $1.50 a bushel for a total revenue of $15. Because it costs $10 to farm this land, the farmer is then left with a $5 profit.

No one will farm the good or the poor land, though, because neither grade of land will earn the farmer any profit. The good land will cost $10 to farm but will generate only 5 bushels of grain for a total revenue of $7.50. The poor land will cost $10 to farm but will generate only 2 bushels of grain for a total revenue of $3.

So the excellent land is the only grade that will be farmed if the price of grain is $1.50 a bushel because it earns the farmer $5 in profit. But the $5 profit may not last. If the farmer leases the land, the profit of $5 will soon become $5 in land rent for the owner of the land. Farmers will compete among themselves to lease the land from its owner. With $5 profit, the first farmer says that he is willing to pay $1 in land rent for the land, but the second farmer says $2, and the third farmer

© IMAGE COPYRIGHT ORIENTALY, 2009. USED UNDER LICENSE FROM SHUTTERSTOCK.COM

says $3, and so on. The profit on the land will soon turn into land rent received by the owner of the land. The land rent will eventually go up to $5. In other words, the excellent land—given the price of grain at $1.50 a bushel—will fetch a rent of $5.

Now suppose the price of grain rises from $1.50 a bushel to $2.10 a bushel. Two things will happen at this higher price. First, the good land, which wasn't farmed when the price of grain was $1.50, will now be farmed. The good land generates 5 bushels of grain, which when sold at $2.10 a bushel will generate $10.50 in revenue. Since the cost of farming the land is $10, this leaves the farmer with a profit of 50¢. Farming the good land is now profitable.

Second, the land rent on the excellent land will rise from $5. At a grain price of $2.10 a bushel, the excellent land now generates $21 in revenue. Given a cost of farming the excellent land of $10, this amount of revenue generates $11 in profit, or only $6 in profit if we assume the farmer is paying the owner of the excellent land $5 in land rent. Either way, we can expect land rent to soon rise, as farmers compete for the land that is generating the additional profits. We expect the land rent ultimately to rise to $11.

So higher grain prices initially increase the profit on farming high-quality or excellent land. But higher profit ends up as higher land rent as farmers compete for the land. In short, high grain prices cause high land rents, and rising grain prices cause rising rents.

finding ECONOMICS

In a Sandwich and a Soft Drink in New York City During a visit to New York City, Rachel ordered a sandwich and soft drink for lunch in a restaurant. Her bill was $21. She complained to a friend later in the day, saying, "I don't know why everything is so expensive in New York. I paid $21 for a sandwich and drink today." Her friend replied, "Sandwich prices are high because the owner of the restaurant has to pay such high rent for his place." Where is the economics?

(continued)

finding ECONOMICS *(continued)*

Here is the same misperception about rents and prices that Ricardo found in the nineteenth century. Many people today complain that the prices in stores, hotels, and restaurants in New York City are high. When they notice the steep land rents, they reason that prices are high because land rents are high. But, as Ricardo pointed out, the reverse is true: land rents are high because prices are high. If the demand for living, visiting, and shopping in New York City were not as high as it is, the prices for goods would not be as high. In turn, the demand for land would not be as high, and therefore the payments to land would not be as high. ▲ ▲ ▲

The Supply Curve of Land Can Be Upward Sloping

Exhibit 3 depicts the supply of land as fixed—the case when the total supply of land is in question. For example, this country has only so many acres of land, and that amount is not likely to change.

Most subparcels of land, however, have competing uses. Consider 25 acres of land on the periphery of a major city. That parcel can be used for farmland, a shopping mall, or a road. If a parcel of land (as opposed to all land, or the total supply of land) has competing uses (the land can be used one way or another), then it has opportunity costs. Land that is used for farming could be used for a shopping mall. To reflect the opportunity cost of that land, the supply curve is upward sloping. The upward slope implies that if individuals want more land for a specific purpose—say, for a shopping mall—they must bid high enough to attract existing land away from other uses (e.g., farming). Exhibit 4 illustrates this phenomenon, where the equilibrium payment to land is R_1. The shaded area indicates the economic rent.

Economic Rent and Other Factors of Production

The concept of economic rent applies to economic factors besides land. For example, it applies to labor. Suppose Hanson works for company X and is paid $60,000 a year. Further suppose that in his next best alternative job, he would be earning $57,000. Hanson is

---

EXHIBIT 4

Economic Rent and the Supply of Land (Competing Uses)

A particular parcel of land, as opposed to the total supply of land, has competing uses, or positive opportunity costs. For example, to obtain land to build a shopping mall, the developers must bid high enough to attract existing land away from competing uses. The supply curve is upward sloping. At a payment of R_1, economic rent is identified as the payment in excess of (positive) opportunity costs.

receiving economic rent working for company X in that he is receiving a payment in excess of his opportunity costs—economic rent.

Or consider the local McDonald's that hires teenagers. It pays all its beginning employees the same wage, but not all beginning employees have the same opportunity cost. Suppose two teenagers, Tracy and Paul, sign on to work at McDonald's for $8.00 an hour. Tracy's next best alternative wage is $8.00 an hour working for her mother's business, and Paul's is $7.25 an hour, working in another store. Tracy receives no economic rent in her McDonald's job, but Paul receives 75¢ an hour economic rent in the same job.

Over time, teenagers and other beginning employees usually find that their opportunity costs rise (owing to continued schooling and job experience) and that the McDonald's wage no longer covers their opportunity costs. When this happens, they quit.

Economic Rent and Baseball Players: Perspective Matters

Economic rent differs depending on the perspective from which the factor is viewed. If a baseball star who earns $1 million a year playing baseball weren't playing the sport, he would be a coach at a high school. Therefore, the difference between what he is currently paid ($1 million a year) and what he would earn as a coach (say, $40,000 a year) is economic rent. This amounts to $960,000. Thus economic rent is determined by identifying the alternative to the baseball star's playing major league ball.

However, a different alternative would be identified by asking what is the alternative to the baseball star's playing baseball for his present team. The answer is that he probably can play for another team. For example, if he weren't playing for the Boston Red Sox, he might be playing for the Pittsburgh Pirates, earning $950,000 a year. His economic rent in this instance is only $50,000. So the player's economic rent as *a player for the Boston Red Sox* is $50,000 a year; his next best alternative is playing for the Pittsburgh Pirates earning $950,000 a year. But his economic rent as *a baseball player* is $960,000; his next best alternative is being a high school coach earning $40,000 a year.

Competing for Artificial and Real Rents

Individuals and firms compete for both *artificial rents* and *real rents*. An artificial rent is an economic rent that is artificially contrived by government; that is, it would not exist without government. Suppose government decides to award a monopoly right to one firm to produce good X. In so doing, it legally prohibits all other firms from producing good X. If the firm with the monopoly right receives a price for good X in excess of its opportunity costs, it receives a rent or monopoly profit because of government's supply restraint.

Firms that compete for the monopoly right to produce good X expend resources in a socially wasteful manner.[4] They use resources to lobby politicians in the hope of getting the monopoly, and those resources (from society's perspective) could be better used to produce goods and services.

Competing for real rents is different, however. If the rent is real (not artificially created) and if there are no barriers to competing for it, resources are used in a way that is socially productive. For example, suppose firm Z currently receives economic rent in the production of good Z. Government does not prohibit other firms from competing with firm Z; so some do. The other firms also produce good Z, thus increasing its supply and lowering its price. The lower price reduces the rent firm Z receives in its production of good Z. In the end, firm Z has less rent, and society has more of good Z and pays a lower price for it.

---

4. This may sound familiar. The process described where individuals expend resources lobbying government for a special privilege was described as rent seeking in Chapter 23.

Do People Overestimate Their Worth to Others, or Are They Simply Seeking Economic Rent?

Johnson is an accountant with seven years of experience and is currently earning $95,000 annually. One day, he walks into his employer's office and asks for a raise in salary to $105,000. His employer asks him why he thinks he deserves the $10,000 raise. Johnson says that he is sure he is worth that much. (If he is, he can leave his current company and receive an offer of $105,000 from another company. We don't know whether he can do so.)

His employer believes that Johnson is overestimating his worth to others. She thinks, "There's no way Johnson is worth $10,000 more a year. He is simply overestimating his worth."

However, Johnson is not necessarily overestimating his worth to others. He could believe his worth to others is $95,000—in other words, $95,000 is his opportunity cost. However, he could be attempting to receive economic rent ($10,000 more than his opportunity cost) by getting his employer to believe his opportunity cost is really $105,000. Thus, a person who may appear to others to be overestimating his worth may be merely attempting to obtain economic rent.

SELF-TEST

1. Give an example to illustrate that economic rent differs depending on the perspective from which the factor is viewed.

2. Nick's salary is pure economic rent. What does this imply about Nick's next best alternative salary?

3. What are the social consequences of firms competing for artificial rents, as opposed to competing for real rents (where there are no barriers to competing for real rents)?

PROFIT

The profits that appear in newspaper headlines are *accounting profits*, not economic profits. Economic profit is the difference between total revenue and total cost, and both explicit and implicit costs are included in total cost. Economists emphasize economic profit over accounting profit because economic profit determines entry into and exit from an industry. For the most part, this is how economic profit figured in the discussion of market structures in previous chapters.

In this section, we discuss profit as the payment to a resource. Recall the four resources, or factors of production: land, labor, capital, and entrepreneurship. Firms make payments to each of these resources: wages are the payment to labor, interest is the payment to capital, rent is the payment to land, and profit is the payment to entrepreneurship. Understanding the source of profits enables us to find out why economic profit exists.

Theories of Profit

Several different theories address the question of where profit comes from, that is, the source of profit. One theory holds that profit would not exist in a world of certainty; hence, uncertainty is the source of profit. Another theory is that profit is the return for alertness to broadly defined arbitrage opportunities. A third theory posits that profit is the return to the entrepreneur for innovation.

PROFIT AND UNCERTAINTY Uncertainty exists when a potential occurrence is so unpredictable that a probability cannot be estimated. (For example, what is the probability that the United States will enter a world war in 2020?) Risk, which many people mistake for uncertainty, exists when the probability of a given event can be estimated. (For example, a coin toss has a 50–50 chance of coming up heads.) Therefore, risks can be insured against, but uncertainties cannot.

Anything that can be insured against can be treated as just another cost of doing business, and thus insurance coverage is an input in the production process. Only uncertain events can cause a firm's revenues to diverge from costs (including insurance costs). The investor/decision maker who is adept at making business decisions under conditions of uncertainty earns a profit. For example, based on experience and some insights, an entrepreneur may believe that 75 percent of all college students will buy personal computers next year. This assessment, followed by investing in a chain of retail computer stores near college campuses, will ultimately prove to be right or wrong. The essential point is that the entrepreneur's judgment cannot be insured against. If correct, the entrepreneur will earn a profit; if incorrect, a loss.

PROFIT AND ARBITRAGE OPPORTUNITIES The way to make a profit, the advice goes, is to buy low and sell high (usually the same item). For example, someone might buy good X in New York for $10 and sell good X in London for $11. We might say that the person is alert to where she can buy low and sell high, thereby earning a profit. She is alert to what is called an arbitrage opportunity.

Sometimes, buying low and selling high does not refer to the same item. The opportunity can refer to buying factors in one set of markets at the lowest possible prices, combining the factors into a finished product, and then selling the product in another market for the highest possible price. An example of this is buying oranges and sugar (in the orange and sugar markets), combining the two, and selling an orange soft drink (in the soft drink market). If doing so results in profit, the person who undertook the act is considered alert to a (broadly defined) arbitrage opportunity. He saw that oranges and sugar together, in the form of an orange soft drink, would fetch more than the sum of oranges and sugar separately.

PROFIT AND INNOVATION In this theory, profit is the return to the entrepreneur as innovator—the person who creates new profit opportunities by devising a new product, production process, or marketing strategy. Viewed this way, profit is the return to innovative genius. People such as Thomas Edison, Henry Ford, and Richard Sears and Alvah Roebuck are said to have had innovative genius.

✿hinking Like AN ECONOMIST

About Interest, Land Rent, and Profits Throughout history, interest, land rent, and profits have often been attacked. For example, Henry George (1839–1897), who wrote the influential book *Progress and Poverty*, believed that all land rents were pure economic rents and should be heavily taxed. Landowners benefited simply because they had the good fortune to own land. In George's view, landowners did nothing productive. He maintained that the early owners of land in the American West reaped high land rents not because they had made their land more productive but because individuals from the East began to move West, driving up the price of land. In arguing for a heavy tax on land rents, George said there would be no supply response in land owing to the tax because land was in fixed supply.

Profits have also frequently come under attack. High profits are somehow thought to be evidence of corruption or manipulation. Those who earn profits are sometimes considered no better than thieves.

The economist thinks of interest, land rent, and profits differently from how many laypersons think of them. The economist understands that all are returns to resources, or factors of production. Most

(continued)

economics 24/7

Insuring Oneself Against Terrorism[5]

Meet Abbas Shaheed al-Taiee, an executive at the Iraq Insurance Company in Baghdad, Iraq. Mr. Shaheed is an innovator (entrepreneur) who came up with the idea of selling the Iraqi people something he thought they had a demand for: terrorism insurance.

Mr. Shaheed says terrorism insurance is his gift to the Iraqi people: "We have expanded the principles of life insurance to cover everything that happens in Iraq." The terrorism insurance policy looks much like an ordinary life insurance policy, except for a one-page rider that insures a person against (1) explosions caused by weapons of war and car bombs, (2) assassinations, and (3) terrorist attacks. According to Mr. Shaheed, it doesn't

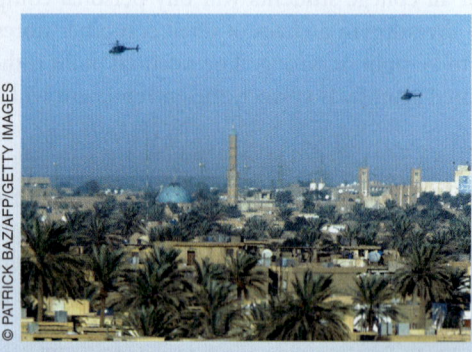

© PATRICK BAZ/AFP/GETTY IMAGES

matter who fires the shots or sets off the bombs. The policy pays off no matter who is at fault.

The cost of the policy depends on your occupation. If you have one of the safer occupations, the cost is $45 for about $3,500 worth of coverage (which is what an Iraqi police officer earns a year). If you have a relatively unsafe profession (e.g., a police officer or translator for a Western company), the cost is $90 for about $3,500 worth of coverage.

5. This feature is based on Robert F. Worth, "New Business Blooms in Iraq: Terror Insurance," *The New York Times*, March 21, 2006.

thinking Like AN ECONOMIST (continued)

people find it easy to understand that labor is a factor of production and that wages are the return to this factor. But understanding that land, capital, and entrepreneurship are also genuine factors of production, with returns that flow to them, seems more difficult.

Another overlooked point is that interest exists largely because individuals naturally have a positive rate of time preference. Those who dislike interest are in fact criticizing a natural characteristic of individuals. If the critics could change this natural trait and make individuals stop weighting present consumption higher than future consumption, interest would diminish.

A similar point can be made about profit. Some say profit is the consequence of living in a world of uncertainty. If those who do not like profit could make the world less uncertain, or bring certainty to it, then profit would disappear. ▲ ▲ ▲

What Is Entrepreneurship?

We have defined entrepreneurship as the talent of some people for organizing the resources of land, labor, and capital to produce goods, seek new business opportunities, and develop new ways of doing things. Taking the three profit theories together, we can define entrepreneurship more narrowly: *An entrepreneur bears uncertainty, is alert to arbitrage opportunities, and exhibits innovative behavior.* Most entrepreneurs probably exhibit different degrees of each. For example, Thomas Edison may have been more the innovator entrepreneur than the arbitrager entrepreneur.

Notice that entrepreneurship is not like the other factors of production (land, labor, capital) in that it cannot be measured. Entrepreneurship has no units of measurement, as do labor, capital, and land. Furthermore, an entrepreneur receives profit as a residual after the other factors of production have been paid. Thus, the actual dollar amount of profit depends on the payments to the other three factors of production.

What a Microwave Oven, an Oil Change, and an Errand Runner Have in Common

Many people today complain that they do not have enough time to do all they want to do. Where these people see a problem, the entrepreneur sees a business opportunity. If people do not have enough time to do what they want, the entrepreneur reasons, then perhaps they will be willing to pay for a product or service that economizes on their time and frees it for other uses.

A microwave oven, for example, reduces the time it takes to cook a meal, thus freeing time for other activities such as reading a book, working, sleeping, and so on.

Stanley Richards is another example. He recently started a business that economizes on people's time. Richards started a company called Stan's Mobile Car Service. For $29.95 plus tax, he drives to a customer's car, whether it is at home or at work, and changes the oil, lubricates the chassis, and checks the engine. He says that he expects to do 90 jobs a day after his three vans are in operation.

Or consider the professional errand runner, who will pick up the laundry, manage the house, feed the cat, pick up food for a party, and do other such things. In some large cities around the country, professional errand runners will do the things that two-earner families or working single men and women would rather pay someone to do than spend the time doing themselves.

Profit and Loss as Signals

Although profit and loss are often viewed in terms of the benefit or hurt they bring to persons, they also signal how a market may be changing. When a firm earns a profit, entrepreneurs in other industries view the profit as a signal that the firm is producing and selling a good that buyers value more than the factors that go into making the good. (The firm would not earn a profit unless its product had more value than the total of the payments to the other three factors of production.) The profit causes entrepreneurs to move resources into the production of the profit-linked good. In short, resources follow profit.

On the other hand, if a firm is taking a loss, the loss is a signal to the entrepreneur that the firm is producing and selling a good that buyers value less than the factors that go into making the good. The loss causes resources to move out of the production of the loss-linked good. Resources turn away from losses.

SELF-TEST

1. What is the difference between risk and uncertainty?

2. Why does profit exist?

3. "Profit is not simply a dollar amount; it is a signal." Comment.

OFFICE HOURS

"How Is Present Value Used in the Courtroom?"

STUDENT:

I've heard that present value is sometimes used in law cases. Is this true? And if so, how?

INSTRUCTOR:

Yes, it's true. It could be used in a divorce case. For example, suppose Jack and Carol are getting a divorce. Carol worked during the time Jack went to medical school. In the divorce, Carol and Jack agree to split the assets they own together: the house, the paintings, the jewelry, the cars, and so on. Carol claims that the Jack's medical degree is an asset that she should have part of. "After all," she says, "I helped pay for Jack's medical education."

STUDENT:

So is the objective now to find out what the medical degree is worth?

INSTRUCTOR:

Yes. And this is where present value comes in. Suppose Jack will earn $100,000 more each year for the next 25 years because he went to medical school. Carol's attorney needs to find the present value of this dollar amount, which turns out to be approximately $1.57 million. Now the court has to decide whether the medical degree is an asset whose proceeds should be divided between Carol and Jack.

STUDENT:

Does present value come up in any other cases?

INSTRUCTOR:

Yes. Present value is sometimes used in injury cases. For example, suppose Yvonne gets hit by a drunk driver and can't work any longer.

She might ask to be compensated for the injury plus the loss in her earning power. Her lawyer will need to find the present value of her lost earnings (over, say, the next 10 years).

POINTS TO REMEMBER

1. Present value can be used to determine today's worth of a medical education.
2. Present value can be used to determine today's worth of a loss in earning power.

CHAPTER SUMMARY

INTEREST

- Interest refers to (1) the price paid by borrowers for loanable funds and (2) the return on capital in the production process. These two definitions tend to become equal.

- The equilibrium interest rate (in terms of the price for loanable funds) is determined by the demand for and supply of loanable funds. The supply of loanable funds comes from savers, people who consume less than their current incomes. The demand for loanable funds comes from the demand for consumption and investment loans.

- Consumers demand loanable funds because they have a positive rate of time preference; they prefer earlier rather than later availability of goods. Investors (or firms) demand loanable funds so that they can finance roundabout methods of production.

- The nominal interest rate is the interest rate determined by the forces of supply and demand in the loanable funds market; it is the interest rate in current dollars. The real interest rate is the nominal interest rate adjusted for expected inflation. Specifically: Real interest rate = Nominal interest rate – Expected inflation rate (which means Nominal interest rate = Real interest rate + Expected inflation rate).

RENT

- Economic rent is a payment in excess of opportunity costs. A subset of this is pure economic rent, which is a payment in excess of opportunity costs when opportunity costs are zero. Historically, the term *pure economic rent* was used to describe the payment to the factor land because land (in total) was assumed to be fixed in supply (perfectly inelastic). Today, the terms "economic rent" and "pure economic rent" are also used when speaking about economic factors other than land.

- David Ricardo argued that high land rents were an effect of high grain prices, not a cause of them (in contrast to many of his contemporaries who thought high rents caused the high grain prices). Land rents are price determined, not price determining.

- The amount of economic rent a factor receives depends on the perspective from which the factor is viewed. For example, a university librarian earning $50,000 a year receives $2,000 economic rent if his next best alternative income at another university is $48,000. The economic rent is $10,000 if his next best alternative is in a nonuniversity (nonlibrarian) position that pays $40,000.

PROFIT

- Several theories address the question of the source of profit. One theory holds that profit would not exist in a world of certainty; hence, uncertainty is the source of profit. Another is that profit is the return for alertness to arbitrage opportunities. A third states that profit is the return to the entrepreneur for innovation.

- Taking the three profit theories together, we can say that profit is the return to entrepreneurship, which entails bearing uncertainty, being alert to arbitrage opportunities, and being innovative.

KEY TERMS AND CONCEPTS

Loanable Funds	Roundabout Method of	Real Interest Rate	Economic Rent
Positive Rate of Time	Production	Present Value	Pure Economic Rent
Preference	Nominal Interest Rate		

QUESTIONS AND PROBLEMS

1. "As the interest rate falls, firms are more inclined to buy capital goods. " Do you agree or disagree? Explain your answer.

2. In what ways are a baseball star who can do nothing but play baseball and a parcel of land similar?

3. Describe the effect of each of the following events on individuals' rate of time preference and thus on interest rates:

   a. A technological advance that increases longevity

   b. An increased threat of war

   c. Growing older

4. What type of person is most willing to pay high interest rates?

5. Make an attempt to calculate the present value of your future income.

6. Some people have argued that in a moneyless (or barter) economy, interest would not exist. Is this true? Explain your answer.

7. It has been said that a society with a high savings rate is a society with a high standard of living. What is the link (if any) between saving and a relatively high standard of living?

8. The real interest rate can remain unchanged as the nominal interest rate rises. Do you agree or disagree with this statement? Explain your answer.

9. "The more economic rent a person receives in his job, the less likely he is to leave the job and the more content he will be on the job." Do you agree or disagree? Explain your answer.

10. The interest rate on loan X is higher than the interest rate on loan Y. What might explain the difference in interest rates between the two loans?

11. What is the link between profit and uncertainty?

12. How would the interest rate change as a result of the following?

   a. A rise in the demand for consumption loans

   b. A decline in the supply of loanable funds

   c. A rise in the demand for investment loans

13. What is the overall economic function of profits?

14. What does having a positive rate of time preference have to do with positive interest rates?

15. What does it mean to say that land rent is price determined, not price determining?

16. What does it mean to say that an individual has a positive rate of time preference?

WORKING WITH NUMBERS AND GRAPHS

1. Compute the following:

   a. The present value of $25,000 each year for 4 years at a 7 percent interest rate

   b. The present value of $152,000 each year for 5 years at a 6 percent interest rate

   c. The present value of $60,000 each year for 10 years at a 6.5 percent interest rate

2. Bobby is a baseball player who earns $1 million a year playing for team X. If he weren't playing baseball for team X, he would be playing baseball for team Y and earning $800,000 a year. If he weren't playing baseball at all, he would be working as an accountant earning $120,000 a year. What is his economic rent as a baseball player playing for team X? What is his economic rent as a baseball player?

3. Diagrammatically represent pure economic rent.

CHAPTER 31

MARKET FAILURE: EXTERNALITIES, PUBLIC GOODS, AND ASYMMETRIC INFORMATION

ERIC O'CONNELL/CREATAS/JUPITER IMAGES

Introduction

Markets are a major topic in this book. We have analyzed how markets work, beginning with the simple supply-and-demand model, as well as various market structures: perfect competition, monopoly, and others. Goods and services are produced in markets. For example, cars are produced in car markets, houses are produced in housing markets, and computers are produced in computer markets. We now ask, do these markets produce the right amount (the optimal or ideal amount) of these various goods? What are the right amounts?

For example, what is the ideal or optimal amount of houses to produce, and does the housing market actually produce this amount?

When a market produces more or less than the ideal or optimal amount of a particular good, economists say there is market failure. Economists want to know under what conditions market failure may occur. This chapter presents three topics in which market failure is a prominent part of the discussion: externalities, public goods, and asymmetric information.

EXTERNALITIES

Sometimes, when goods are produced and consumed, side effects (spillover or third-party effects) are felt by people who are not directly involved in the market exchanges. In general, these side effects are called externalities because the costs or benefits are external to the persons who caused them. In this section, we discuss the various costs and benefits of activities and describe how and when activities cause externalities. We then explain graphically how externalities can result in market failure.

Costs and Benefits of Activities

Most activities in life have both costs and benefits. For example, when Jim sits down to read a book, reading has some benefits for Jim and some costs. These benefits and costs are private to him—they affect only him—hence, we call them *private benefits* and *private costs*.

Market Failure
A situation in which the market does not provide the ideal or optimal amount of a good.

Externality
A side effect of an action that affects the well-being of third parties.

Jim can also undertake an activity that has benefits and costs not only for him but also for others. Suppose he decides to smoke a cigarette in the general vicinity of Angelica. For Jim, smoking the cigarette has both benefits and costs—his private benefits and costs. But Jim's smoking might also affect Angelica in some way if, for example, she reacts to cigarette smoke by coughing. In this case, Jim's smoking might impose a cost on Angelica. Because the cost Jim imposes on her is external to him, we call it an *external cost*. Jim's activity imposes a *negative externality* on Angelica, for which she incurs an external cost. A negative externality exists when a person's or group's actions impose a cost (or adverse side effect) on others.

In a slightly different example, suppose Jim lives across the street from Yvonne and beautifies his front yard (which Yvonne can clearly see from her house) by planting trees, flowers, and a new lawn. Obviously, Jim receives some benefits and costs by beautifying his yard, but Yvonne enjoys some benefits too. Not only does she have a pretty yard to look at (in much the same way that someone might benefit by gazing at a beautiful painting), but Jim's beautification efforts may also raise the market value of Yvonne's property.

Because the benefit that Jim generates for Yvonne is external to him, it is an *external benefit*. Jim's activity generates a *positive externality* for Yvonne, for which she receives an external benefit. A positive externality exists when a person's or group's actions create a benefit (or beneficial side effect) for others.

ⓕinding ECONOMICS

In Students Talking in Class Blake sits near the back of the room in his biology class. Two students who sit near Blake often talk to each other while the class is in session. They usually whisper, but still their talking disturbs Blake. Where is the economics?

As far as Blake is concerned, the two talking students are doing something (talking during the class) that adversely affects him. For Blake, their talking is a negative externality. ▲ ▲ ▲

Marginal Costs and Benefits of Activities

When considering activities that have different degrees or amounts of costs and benefits (smoking one cigarette an hour or two, planting three trees or four), economists speak in terms of marginal benefits and costs. More specifically, for Jim, various activities have marginal private benefits (*MPB*) and marginal private costs (*MPC*). If Jim's activities generate external benefits or costs for others, then it makes sense to speak in terms of marginal external benefits (*MEB*) and marginal external costs (*MEC*).

To analyze the effects of an activity, we need to know the total marginal costs and benefits. So we sum them. The sum of marginal private costs (*MPC*) and marginal external costs (*MEC*) is referred to as marginal social costs (*MSC*).

$$MSC = MPC + MEC$$

In our example, Jim's smoking a cigarette imposed an external cost on Angelica. Suppose Jim's *MPC* of smoking a cigarette is $1, and Angelica's *MEC* of Jim's smoking a cigarette is $2. Therefore, the *MSC* of Jim smoking a cigarette (taking into account both Jim's private costs and Angelica's external costs) is $3.

The sum of marginal private benefits (*MPB*) and marginal external benefits (*MEB*) is called marginal social benefits (*MSB*).

$$MSB = MPB + MEB$$

Jim's beautifying his yard created an external benefit for Yvonne. Suppose Jim's *MPB* of beautifying his yard is $5, and Yvonne's *MEB* is $3. The *MSB* of Jim's beautifying his yard (at a given level of beautification) is therefore $8.

Negative Externality
The condition when a person's or group's actions impose a cost (an adverse side effect) on others.

Positive Externality
The condition that exists when a person's or group's actions create a benefit (beneficial side effect) for others.

Marginal Social Costs (MSC)
The sum of marginal private costs (*MPC*) and marginal external costs (*MEC*): *MSC* = *MPC* + *MEC*.

Marginal Social Benefits (MSB)
The sum of marginal private benefits (*MPB*) and marginal external benefits (*MEB*): *MSB* = *MPB* + *MEB*.

Social Optimality, or Efficiency, Conditions

For an economist, there is always a right amount of something. There is a right amount of time to study for a test, a right amount of exercise, and a right number of cars to be produced. The right amount, for an economist, is the socially optimal amount (output), or the efficient amount (output)—the amount at which $MSB = MSC$. In other words, the right amount of anything is the amount at which the MSB (of that thing) equals the MSC (of that thing). Later in this section, we illustrate this condition graphically.

Socially Optimal Amount (Output)
An amount that takes into account and adjusts for all benefits (external and private) and all costs (external and private); the amount at which $MSB = MSC$. Sometimes referred to as the efficient amount.

Three Categories of Activities

For the person who engages in an activity (whether producing a computer or studying for an exam), the activity almost always brings benefits and costs. It is hard to think of any activities in life in which private benefits and private costs do not exist.

Not so hard, however, is thinking of activities in life in which external benefits and external costs do not exist. For example, when reading a book, a person incurs benefits and costs, but probably no one else does. We can characterize this effect in the following way: $MPB > 0$, $MPC > 0$, $MEB = 0$, $MEC = 0$. Marginal private benefits and costs are both positive (greater than zero), but there are no marginal external benefits or costs. In other words, the activity has no positive or negative externalities.

Therefore, activities may be categorized according to whether negative or positive externalities exist, as shown in the following table:[1]

Category	Definition	Meaning in Terms of Marginal Benefits and Costs
1	No negative or positive externality	$MEC = 0$ and $MEB = 0$; it follows that $MSC = MPC$ and $MSB = MPB$
2	Negative externality but no positive externality	$MEC > 0$ and $MEB = 0$; it follows that $MSC > MPC$ and $MSB = MPB$
3	Positive externality but no negative externality	$MEB > 0$ and $MEC = 0$; it follows that $MSB > MPB$ and $MSC = MPC$

Externalities in Consumption and in Production

Externalities can arise because someone *consumes* something that has an external benefit or cost for others or because someone *produces* something that has an external benefit or cost for others. Consider two examples. Barbara plays the radio in her car loudly, adversely affecting drivers around her at the stoplight. In this situation, Barbara is consuming music and creating a negative externality for others. John produces cars in his factory. As a result of the production process, he emits pollution into the air that adversely affects some people who live downwind from the factory. In this situation, the negative externality is the result of John's producing a good.

Diagram of a Negative Externality

Exhibit 1 shows the downward-sloping demand curve, D, for some good. Because the demand curve represents the marginal private benefits received by the buyers of the good, it is the same as the MPB curve. Because there are no positive externalities in this case, $MPB = MSB$. So the demand curve is also the MSB curve. The supply curve, S, represents

---

1. Theoretically, there is a fourth category—where both a positive externality and a negative externality exist—but one would reasonably assume that this category has little, if any, practical relevance. For example, suppose Jim smokes a cigarette, and cigarette smoke is a negative externality for Angelica but a positive externality for Bobby. It is possible that what is a bad for Angelica is a good for Bobby, but little is added to the discussion (at this time) by reviewing such cases.

Switching Costs and Market Failure (Maybe)

Some economists believe that a series of events are occurring today. A company produces a good (say, software X), and it finds that its major costs of producing the software are up front at the research and development stage. After it has produced one copy of the software program, producing each additional copy is relatively cheap. The company sells software X at a price that is likely to generate a large number of sales. As some people buy the software program, additional people find it worth buying because the good is important in terms of networking with others. (For example, if many of the people you know use the spreadsheet Excel, you may choose Excel as your spreadsheet.) Because of its network externalities, software X becomes widely used in the industry. At some point, the good simply dominates the market with, say, 90 percent of market sales.

Some economists then ask whether software X is the best product or inferior to the substitutes that exist for it. For example, if software programs Y and Z are substitutes for X, is X superior to both Y and Z or is either Y or Z superior to X? A real-world example illustrates our point. Both Beta and VHS formats for VCRs came out at about the same time. VHS initially sold better than Beta, although Beta was a strong competitor. At some point, the higher percentage of VHS users in the market (relative to Beta users) seemed to matter to people who were considering buying a VCR. The VHS format seemed more common; so sharing videotapes with more people should be easier. At this point, the sales of VHS began to explode, and before long very few people were buying Beta. Some of the initial buyers of the Beta format even switched over to the VHS format. In the race between VHS and Beta, VHS won, not necessarily because it was superior to Beta, but simply because it had an early lead in the race. If network externalities are present, the early lead may be the only lead that is necessary to win the race for customers' dollars.

Some economists conclude that if only the early lead counts and not the quality of the product, then an inferior product that gets an early lead could outsell a superior product that comes to market later. So, if X outcompetes Y and Z not because it is superior but because it gets an early lead in the software market, then the market might have chosen the inferior product. Stated differently, market failure occurs in the sense that the market has failed to choose a superior product over an inferior one.

But not all economists agree. Some say that choosing an inferior product over a superior product does not constitute market failure. There must also be net benefits to switching (from the inferior to the superior product) that market participants are not acting on. To illustrate, suppose that the market has chosen software X, that it is inferior to software Y, and that the benefits of switching from X to Y are $30 and the costs of switching are $45. In this case, even if the market stays with software X, there is no market failure because switching to the superior product is not worthwhile. The market fails, argue these economists, only if the benefits of switching are, say, $30 and the costs are $10 (and therefore switching has net benefits), yet the market doesn't switch. In short, when the benefits and costs of switching are considered, what may initially look like a market failure may turn out not to be.

the marginal private costs (MPC) of the producers of the good. Equilibrium in this market setting is at E_1; Q_1 is the output—specifically, the market output.

Assume negative externalities arise as a result of the production of the good. For example, suppose the good happens to be cars whose production in a factory causes the emission of some air pollution. Due to the negative externalities, external costs associated with the production of the good are not taken into account at the market output. The marginal external costs linked to the negative externalities are taken into account by adding them (as best we can) to the marginal private costs. The result is the marginal social cost (MSC) curve shown in Exhibit 1. If all costs are taken into account (both external costs and private costs), equilibrium is at E_2, where $MSB = MSC$. The quantity produced at E_2 (Q_2) is the socially optimal output, or efficient output.

When negative externalities exist, the market output (Q_1) is greater than the socially optimal output (Q_2). The market is said to fail (hence market failure) because it *overproduces* the good connected with the negative externality. The shaded triangle in Exhibit 1 is the visible manifestation of the market failure. It represents the net social cost of producing the market output (Q_1) instead of the socially optimal output (Q_2), or of moving from the socially optimal output to the market output.

To understand exactly how the triangle in Exhibit 1 represents the net social cost of moving from the socially optimal output to the market output, look at Exhibit 2, where, as in Exhibit 1, Q_2 is the socially optimal output and Q_1 is the market output. If society moves from Q_2 to Q_1, who specifically benefits and how do we represent these benefits? Buyers benefit (they are a part of society) because they will be able to buy more output at prices they are willing to pay. Thus, the area under the demand curve between Q_2 and Q_1 represents the benefits to society of moving from Q_2 to Q_1 (see the shaded area in window 1 of Exhibit 2).

Next, if society moves from Q_2 to Q_1, both sellers and third parties incur costs. Sellers incur private costs, and third parties incur external costs. The area under S (the *MPC* curve) takes into account only part of society—sellers—and ignores third parties. The area under the *MSC* curve between Q_2 and Q_1 represents the full costs to society of moving from Q_2 to Q_1 (see the shaded area in window 2).

The shaded area in window 2 is larger than the one in window 1; so the costs to sellers and third parties of moving from Q_2 to Q_1 outweigh the benefits to buyers of moving from Q_2 to Q_1. The difference between the shaded areas is the triangle shown in the main diagram. Thus, the costs to society outweigh the benefits to society by the triangle. In short, the triangle in this example represents the net social cost of moving from Q_2 to Q_1, or of producing Q_1 instead of Q_2.

The Negative Externality Case

Because of a negative externality, marginal social costs (MSC) are greater than marginal private costs (MPC) and the market output is greater than the socially optimal output. The market is said to fail in that it overproduces the good.

Diagram of a Positive Externality

Exhibit 3 shows the downward-sloping demand curve, D, for some good. This curve represents the marginal private benefits received by the buyers of the good, and so it is the same as the *MPB* curve. The supply curve, S, represents the marginal private costs (*MPC*) of the producers of the good. The marginal social costs (*MSC*) are the same as the marginal private costs—$MPC = MSC$—because there are no negative externalities in this case. Equilibrium in this market setting is at E_1; Q_1 is the output—specifically, the market output.

Assume positive externalities arise as a result of the production of the good. For example, suppose Erica is a beekeeper who produces honey. The hives are near an apple orchard, and her bees occasionally fly over to the orchard and pollinate the blossoms, in the process making the orchard more productive. The orchard owner thus benefits from Erica's bees.

Because positive externalities exist, the production of the good has external benefits that are not taken into account at the market output. The marginal external benefits linked to the positive externalities are taken into account by adding them (as best we can) to the marginal private benefits. The result is the marginal social benefit (*MSB*) curve shown in Exhibit 3. If all benefits are taken into account (both external benefits and private benefits), equilibrium is at E_2, where $MSB = MSC$. The quantity produced at E_2 (Q_2)

EXHIBIT 2

The Triangle

Q_2 is the socially optimal output; Q_1 is the market output. If society moves from Q_2 to Q_1, buyers benefit by an amount represented by the shaded area in window 1, but sellers and third parties together incur greater costs, represented by the shaded area in window 2. The triangle (the difference between the two shaded areas) represents the net social cost to society of moving from Q_2 to Q_1, or of producing Q_1 instead of Q_2.

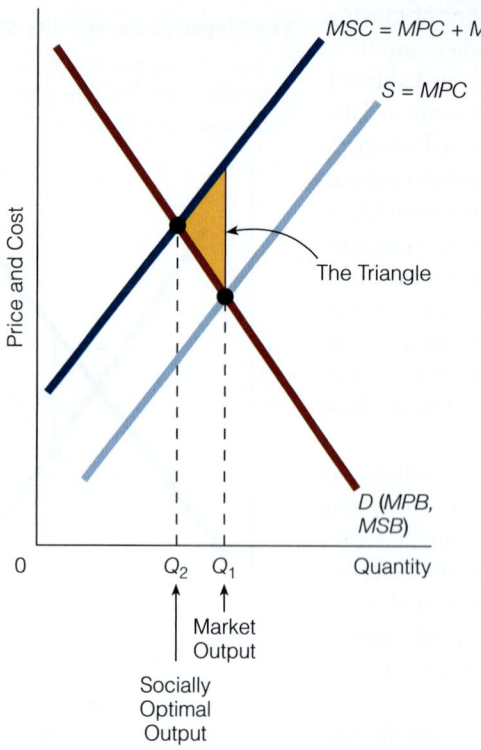

Window 1
Benefits of moving from Q_2 to Q_1

Window 2
Costs of moving from Q_2 to Q_1

EXHIBIT 3

The Positive Externality Case

Because of a positive externality, marginal social benefits (MSB) are greater than marginal private benefits (MPB) and the market output is less than the socially optimal output. The market is said to fail in that it underproduces the good.

is the socially optimal output, or efficient output.

The market output (Q_1) is less than the socially optimal output (Q_2) when positive externalities exist (just the opposite of when negative externalities exist). The market is said to fail (hence market failure) because it *under-produces* the good connected with the positive externality. The triangle in Exhibit 3 is the visible manifestation of the market failure. It represents the net social benefit *that is lost* by producing the market output (Q_1) instead of the socially optimal output (Q_2). Stated differently, at the socially optimal output (Q_2), society realizes greater benefits than at the market output (Q_1). So by being at Q_1, society loses out on some net benefits that it could obtain if it were at Q_2.

thinking Like AN ECONOMIST

The Benefits and the Costs of Making the Move An economist may seem to prefer the socially optimal output (where all benefits and costs are taken into account) to the market output (where only private benefits and costs are taken into account), but not necessarily. An economist prefers the socially optimal output to the market output (assuming they are different) only when the benefits of moving from the market output to the socially optimal output are greater than the costs. To illustrate, suppose $400 in benefits exists if we move from the market output to the socially optimal output, but the costs of making the move are $1,000. According to an economist, trying to make the adjustment would not be worthwhile. ● ● ●

SELF-TEST

(Answers to Self-Test questions are in Answers to Self-Test Questions at the back of the book.)

1. What is the major difference between the market output and the socially optimal output?

2. For an economist, is the socially optimal output preferred to the market output?

INTERNALIZING EXTERNALITIES

An externality is internalized if the persons or group generating the externality incorporate into their own private or *internal* cost-benefit calculations the external benefits (in the case of a positive externality) or the external costs (in the case of a negative externality). Simply put, internalizing externalities is the same as adjusting for externalities. An externality has been internalized, or adjusted for, *completely* if, as a result, the socially optimal output emerges. A few of the numerous ways to adjust for, or internalize, externalities are presented in this section.

Persuasion

Many negative externalities arise partly because persons or groups do not consider other individuals when they decide to undertake an action, like the person who plays his CD player loudly at 3 o'clock in the morning. Perhaps if he considered the external cost of his action to his neighbors, he either would not play the CD player at all or would tune it down.

Trying to persuade those who impose external costs on us to take these costs into account is one way to make the imposers adjust for—or internalize —externalities. In today's world, such slogans as "Don't Drink and Drive" and "Don't Litter" are attempts to persuade individuals to consider the effects of their actions on others. The golden rule of ethical conduct, "Do unto others as you would have them do unto you," makes the same point.

Taxes and Subsidies

Taxes and subsidies are sometimes used as corrective devices for a market failure. A tax adjusts for a negative externality; a subsidy adjusts for a positive externality.

Consider the negative externality case in Exhibit 1. The objective of a corrective tax would be to move the supply curve from S to the MSC curve (recall that a tax can shift a supply curve) and therefore move from the market-determined output, Q_1, to the socially optimal output, Q_2.

In the case of a positive externality, illustrated in Exhibit 3, the objective would be to subsidize the demand side of the market so that the demand curve moves from D to the MSB curve and output moves from Q_1 to the socially optimal output, Q_2.

However, taxes and subsidies also involve costs and consequences. For example, suppose, as illustrated in Exhibit 4, government misjudges the external costs when it imposes a tax on the supplier of a good. Instead of the supply curve moving from S_1 to S_2 (the MSC

Internalizing Externalities
An externality is internalized if the persons or group that generated the externality incorporate into their own private or internal cost-benefit calculations the external benefits (in the case of a positive externality) or the external costs (in the case of a negative externality).

A Corrective Tax Gone Wrong

Government may miscalculate external costs and impose a tax that moves the supply curve from S_1 to S_3 instead of from S_1 to S_2. As a result, the output level will be farther away from the socially optimal output than before the "corrective" tax was applied. Q_3 is farther away from Q_2 than Q_1 is from Q_2.

curve), it moves from S_1 to S_3. As a result, the output level will be farther away from the socially optimal output than it was before the corrective tax was applied.

Assigning Property Rights

Consider the idea that air pollution and ocean pollution—both of which are examples of negative externalities—are the result of the air and oceans being unowned. No one owns the air, no one owns the oceans. Because no one does, many individuals feel free to emit wastes into them. If private property, or ownership, rights in air and oceans could be established, the negative externalities would likely decrease. If someone owns a resource, then actions that damage it have a price; namely, the resource owner can sue for damages.

For example, in the early West, when grazing lands were open and unowned (common property), many cattle ranchers allowed their herds to overgraze. The reason was simple. No one owned the land, so no one could stop the overgrazing to preserve the value of the land. Even if one rancher decided not to allow his herd to graze, all he did was leave more grazing land for other ranchers. As a consequence of overgrazing, a future generation inherited barren, wasted land. From the point of view of future generations, the cattle ranchers who allowed their herds to overgraze were generating negative externalities.

If the Western lands had been privately owned, overgrazing would not have occurred because the monetary interests of the landowner would not have permitted it. The landowner would have charged ranchers a fee to graze their cattle, and more grazing would have entailed additional fees. There would have been less grazing at a positive fee than at a zero fee (the case when the lands were open and unowned). The externalities would have been internalized.

Voluntary Agreements

Externalities can sometimes be internalized through individual voluntary agreements. Suppose Pete and Sean live alone on a tiny island. They have agreed, between themselves, that Pete owns the northern part of the island and Sean owns the southern part. Pete occasionally plays his drums in the morning, and the sound awakens Sean, causing a negative externality problem. Pete wants to be free to play his drums in the morning, and Sean would like to sleep.

Suppose Sean values his sleep in the morning by a maximum of 6 oranges; that is, he would give up 6 oranges to be able to sleep without Pete playing his drums. On the other hand, Pete values drum playing in the morning by 3 oranges. He would give up a maximum of 3 oranges to be able to play his drums in the morning. Because Sean values his sleep by more than Pete values playing his drums, they have an opportunity to strike a deal. Sean can offer Pete some number of oranges greater than 3, but fewer than 6, to refrain from playing his drums in the morning. The deal will make both Pete and Sean better off.

In this example, the negative externality problem is successfully addressed through the individuals' voluntarily entering into an agreement. The condition for this output is that the *transaction costs*, or costs associated with making and reaching the agreement, must be low relative to the expected benefits of the agreement.

Combining Property Rights Assignments and Voluntary Agreements

The last two ways of internalizing externalities—property rights assignments and voluntary agreements—can be combined, as in the following example.[2] Suppose a rancher's cattle occasionally stray onto the adjacent farm and damage or eat some of the farmer's crops. The court assigns liability to the cattle rancher and orders him to prevent his cattle from straying; thus a property rights assignment solves the externality problem. As a result, the rancher puts up a strong fence to prevent his cattle from damaging his neighbor's crops.

But the court's property rights assignment may be undone by the farmer and the cattle rancher if they find that doing so is in their mutual interest. Suppose the rancher is willing to pay $100 a month to the farmer for permission to allow his cattle to stray onto the farmer's land, and the farmer is willing to give permission for $70 a month. Assuming trivial or zero transaction costs, the farmer and the rancher will undo the court's property rights assignment. For a payment of $70 or more a month, the farmer will allow the rancher's cattle to stray onto his land.

COASE THEOREM Suppose in our example that the court, instead of assigning liability to the cattle rancher, had given him the property right to allow his cattle to stray. What would the resource allocative outcome have been in this case? With the opposite property rights assignment, the cattle would have been allowed to stray (which was exactly the outcome of the previous property rights assignment after the cattle rancher and farmer voluntarily agreed to undo the decision). Therefore, *in the case of trivial or zero transaction costs, the property rights assignment does not matter to the resource allocative outcome.* In a nutshell, this is the Coase theorem.

The Coase theorem can be expressed in other ways, two of which are as follows: (1) In the case of trivial or zero transaction costs, a property rights assignment will be undone (exchanged) if it benefits the relevant parties to undo it. (2) In the case of trivial or zero transaction costs, the resource allocative outcome will be the same no matter who is assigned the property right.

The Coase theorem is significant for two reasons: (1) It shows that under certain conditions, the market can internalize externalities. (2) It provides a benchmark for analyzing externality problems; that is, it shows what will happen if transaction costs are trivial or zero.

PIGOU VERSUS COASE The first editor of the *Journal of Law and Economics* was Aaron Director. In 1959, Director published an article by Ronald Coase entitled "The Federal Communications Commission." In the article, Coase took issue with economist A. C. Pigou, a trailblazer in the area of externalities and market failure, who had argued that government should use taxes and subsidies to adjust for negative and positive externalities, respectively. Coase argued that in the case of negative externalities, whether the state should tax the person imposing the negative externality is not clear. First, Coase stressed the reciprocal nature of externalities, pointing out that it takes two to make a negative externality (who is harming whom is not always clear). Second, Coase proposed a market solution to externality problems that was not implicit in Pigou's work.

Aaron Director and others believed that Coase was wrong and Pigou was right. Coase, who was teaching at the University of Virginia at the time, was invited to discuss his thesis with Director and a handful of well-known economists. The group included Martin Bailey, Milton Friedman, Arnold Harberger, Reuben Kessel, Gregg Lewis, John McGee, Lloyd Mints, George Stigler, and, of course, Director.

The group met at Aaron Director's house one night. Before Coase began to outline his thesis, the group took a vote and found that everyone (with the exception of Coase) sided with Pigou. Then the sparks began to fly, with Friedman, it is reported, opening fire

Coase Theorem
In the case of trivial or zero transaction costs, the property rights assignment does not matter to the resource allocative outcome.

---

2. See Ronald Coase, "The Problem of Social Cost," *Journal of Law and Economics* 3 (October 1960): 1–44.

Telemarketers, Where Are You?

Effective October 1, 2003, the Federal Trade Commission (FTC) amended its Telemarketing Sales Rule (TSR), creating a National Do Not Call Registry. People could add their telephone numbers to the registry if they chose not to be called by telemarketers.

Essentially, the change in rules entails two property rights assignments:

- Before October 1, 2003, telemarketers had the right to call you on the phone.
- After October 1, 2003, they did not.

To determine whether the change in the property rights assignment was consistent with efficiency, think of what was happening before October 1, 2003. Surely, some people being called by telemarketers valued not being called more than the telemarketers valued calling them. For example, suppose that Smith valued not being called at $10 a month and that, collectively, the telemarketers valued calling him at $8 a month. If Smith were called, a net loss would arise. Perhaps the net loss is why so many individuals got angry over being called by telemarketers (especially around dinner time). However, some individuals likely placed a lower value on not being called than others. Therefore, calling these persons could have been efficient.

The Do Not Call Registry acts as a means for individuals to register how much they value not being called. Those who value not being called quite a bit will likely place their phone numbers on the registry. Those who do not place a high value on not being called will not. With the Do Not Call Registry, we are closer to achieving efficiency than we were without it. Telemarketers will call people who place a low value on not being called, and they will not call people who place a high value on not being called.

Some economists have proposed that an even better system to achieve efficiency exists. Instead of simply allowing individuals to register their phone numbers with the Do Not Call Registry, offer them the added advantage of stating the dollar price they value not being called. For example, Smith is willing to pay $1 not to be called by telemarketers. She registers her phone number with the Do Not Call Registry along with the $1 she is willing to pay not to be called by telemarketers. A telemarketer notices that Smith's phone number is registered and calls her only if he is willing to pay something more than $1 to Smith.

So telemarketers will call persons who value not being called less than the telemarketer values calling. They will not call persons who value not being called more than the telemarketer values calling.

on Coase. Coase answered the intellectual attacks of his colleagues, and, at the end of the debate, another vote was taken. Everyone sided with Coase against Pigou. It is reported that as the members of the group left Director's home that night, they said to one another that they had witnessed history in the making. The Coase theorem had taken hold in economics.

Beyond Internalizing: Setting Regulations

One way to deal with externalities, in particular with negative externalities, is for government to apply regulations directly to the activities that generate the externalities. For example, factories producing goods also produce smoke, which is often seen as a negative externality. Government may decide that the factory must install pollution-reducing equipment, that it can emit only a certain amount of smoke into the air per day, or that it must be moved to a less populated area.

Critics of this approach often note that regulations, once instituted, are difficult to remove even if conditions warrant removal. Also, regulations are often applied across the board when individual circumstances dictate otherwise. For example, factories in relatively pollution-free cities might be required to install the same pollution control equipment as factories in smoggy, pollution-ridden cities.

Finally, regulation entails costs. If government imposes regulations, it needs regulators (whose salaries must be paid), offices (to house the regulators), word processors (to produce the regulations), and more. As noted, dealing with externalities successfully may offer benefits, but the costs need to be considered as well.

DEALING WITH A NEGATIVE EXTERNALITY IN THE ENVIRONMENT

The environment has become a major economic, political, and social issue. Environmental problems are manifold and include acid rain, the greenhouse effect, deforestation (including the destruction of the rain forests), solid waste (garbage) disposal, water pollution, air pollution, and many more. This section discusses mainly air pollution.

Economists make three principal points about pollution. First, it is a negative externality. Second, and perhaps counterintuitively, no pollution is sometimes worse than some pollution. Third, the market can be used to deal with the problem of pollution. In this section, we discuss the last two points.

Is No Pollution Worse Than Some Pollution?

Certainly, if all other things are held constant, less pollution is preferred to more pollution, and therefore no pollution is preferred to some. However, some pollution might be preferred to no pollution when all other things are not held constant—in short, most of the time.

The world would be different with no pollution, and not only because it would have cleaner air, rivers, and oceans. Pollution is a by-product of the production of many goods and services. For example, steel probably could not be produced without some pollution as a by-product. Given the current state of pollution technology, less pollution from steel production means less steel and fewer products made from steel.

Pollution is also a by-product of many of the goods we use daily, including our cars. We could certainly end the pollution caused by cars tomorrow, but to do so we would have to give up driving cars. As long as driving cars has any benefits, we won't choose zero pollution. In short, zero pollution is not preferable to some positive amount of it when we realize that goods and services must be forfeited.

The same conclusion can be reached through Coasian-type analysis. Suppose there are two groups: polluters and nonpolluters. For certain units of pollution, the value of polluting to polluters might be greater than the value of a less polluted environment to nonpolluters. In the presence of trivial or zero transaction costs, a deal will be struck, and the outcome will be characterized by some positive amount of pollution.

Government Standards or Pollution Permits

Let's consider two methods of reducing pollution. In method 1, government sets pollution standards. In method 2, the government allocates pollution permits and allows them to be traded.

METHOD 1: GOVERNMENT SETS POLLUTION STANDARD Three firms, X, Y, and Z, are located in the same area. Currently, each firm is spewing 3 units of pollution into the area under consideration, for a total of 9 pollution units. The government wants to reduce the total pollution in the area to 3 units and, to accomplish this objective, sets pollution standards (or regulations) stating that each firm must reduce its pollution by 2 units.

Exhibit 5 shows the respective cost of eliminating each unit of pollution for the three firms. The costs are different because eliminating pollution is more difficult for some kinds

EXHIBIT 5

The Cost of Reducing Pollution for Three Firms

These are hypothetical data showing the cost of reducing pollution for three firms. The text shows that it is cheaper to reduce pollution through market environmentalism than through government standards or regulations.

	Firm X	Firm Y	Firm Z
Cost of Eliminating:			
First unit of pollution	$ 50	$ 70	$ 500
Second unit of pollution	75	85	1,000
Third unit of pollution	100	200	2,000

of firms than it is for others. For example, the air pollution that an automobile manufacturer produces might be more costly to eliminate than the air pollution from a clothing manufacturer. In other words, if the three firms eliminate pollution by installing antipollution devices in their factories, the cost of the antipollution devices may be much higher for an automobile manufacturer than for a clothing manufacturer.

The cost to firm X of eliminating its first 2 units is $125 ($50 + $75 = $125); the cost to firm Y of eliminating its first 2 units is $155; and the cost to firm Z of eliminating its first 2 units is $1,500. Thus, the total cost of eliminating 6 units of pollution is $1,780 ($125 + $155 + $1,500).

Total cost of eliminating 6 units of pollution through standards or regulations = $1,780

METHOD 2: MARKET ENVIRONMENTALISM AT WORK: GOVERNMENT ALLOCATES POLLUTION PERMITS AND THEN ALLOWS THEM TO BE BOUGHT AND SOLD The objective of government is still to reduce the pollution in the area of firms X, Y, and Z from 9 units to 3 units. This time, government issues one pollution permit (sometimes these permits are called allowances or credits) to each firm, telling each firm that it can emit 1 unit of pollution for each permit it has in its possession. Furthermore, the firms are allowed to buy and sell the permits.

Firm X has one pollution permit in its possession; so it can emit 1 unit of pollution and must eliminate the other 2. But firm X does not have to keep its pollution permit and emit 1 unit of pollution. Instead, it can sell its permit and take measures to emit no pollution. Might firm X be better off selling the permit and eliminating all 3 units of pollution?

Firm Y is in the same situation as firm X. This firm also has only one permit and must therefore eliminate 2 units of pollution. Firm Y also wonders whether it might be better off selling the permit and eliminating 3 units of pollution.

Firm Z is in a different situation. Exhibit 5 shows that this firm has to pay $500 to eliminate its first unit of pollution and $1,000 to eliminate its second unit. Firm Z wonders whether it might be better off buying the two other permits from firms X and Y and not eliminating any pollution at all.

So the owners of the three firms get together. The owner of firm Z says to the owners of the other firms, "I have to spend $500 to eliminate my first unit of pollution and $1,000 to eliminate my second unit. If either of you is willing to sell me your pollution permit for less than $500, I'm willing to buy it." The owners of the three firms agree on a price of $330 for a permit, and both firms X and Y sell their permits to firm Z. This exchange benefits all three parties. Firm X receives $330 for its permit and then spends $100 to eliminate its third unit of pollution. Firm Y receives $330 for its permit and then spends $200 to eliminate its third unit of pollution. Firm Z spends $660 for the two pollution permits instead of spending $1,500 to eliminate its first 2 units of pollution.

Under this scheme, firms X and Y eliminate all their pollution (neither firm has a pollution permit). Firm X spends $225 ($50 + $75 + $100) to eliminate all 3 units of its pollution, and firm Y spends $355 to do the same. The two firms together spend $580 ($225 + $355) to eliminate 6 units of pollution. The total cost of eliminating 6 units of pollution through market environmentalism is therefore only $580.

This cost is lower than the cost incurred by the three firms when government standards simply ordered each to eliminate 2 units of pollution (or 6 units for all three firms). The cost in that case was $1,780. In both cases, however, 6 pollution units were eliminated. So eliminating pollution is less costly when government allocates pollution permits that can be bought and sold than when it simply directs each firm to eliminate so many units of pollution.

Some argue that the dollar figure of $580 should be adjusted upward by $660 that firm Z paid to buy the two pollution permits, but that is not correct. Although the $660 is a real cost of doing business for firm Z, *it is not a cost to society of eliminating pollution.* The $660 was not actually used to eliminate pollution. It was simply a transfer from firm Z to firms X and Y. The distinction is between a resource cost, which signifies an expenditure of resources, and a transfer, which does not.

SELF-TEST

1. The layperson finds it odd that economists often prefer some pollution to no pollution. Explain how the economist reaches this conclusion.

2. Why does reducing pollution cost less by using market environmentalism than by setting standards?

3. Under market environmentalism, the dollar amount firm Z has to pay to buy the pollution permits from firms X and Y is not counted as a cost to society. Why not?

PUBLIC GOODS: EXCLUDABLE AND NONEXCLUDABLE

Many economists maintain that the market fails to produce nonexcludable public goods. In this section, we discuss public goods in general and nonexcludable public goods in particular.

Goods

Economists talk about two kinds of goods: private and public. A *private good* is a good whose consumption by one person reduces its consumption for another person. For example, a sweater, an apple, and a computer are all private goods. If one person is wearing a sweater, another person cannot wear (consume) it. If one person takes a bite of an apple, there is less apple for someone else to consume. If someone is using a computer, someone else can't use it. A private good is said to be **rivalrous in consumption**.

A **public good**, in contrast, is a good whose consumption by one person does not reduce its consumption by another. For example, a movie in a movie theater is a public good. If there are 200 seats in the theater, then 200 people can see the movie at the same time, and no one person's viewing of it detracts from another's. An economics lecture is also a public good. If there are 30 seats in the classroom, then 30 people can consume the economics lecture at the same time, and one person's consumption does not detract from any other's. The chief characteristic of a public good is that it is **nonrivalrous in consumption**, which means that its consumption by one person does not reduce its consumption by others.

All public goods are nonrivalrous in consumption, but they are not all the same. Some public goods are excludable and some are nonexcludable. A public good is **excludable** if it

Rivalrous in Consumption
A good whose consumption by one person reduces its consumption by others.

Public Good
A good whose consumption by one person does not reduce its consumption by another person—that is, it is nonrivalrous in consumption.

Nonrivalrous in Consumption
A good whose consumption does not reduce its consumption by others.

Excludable
A characteristic of a good whereby it is possible, or not prohibitively costly, to exclude someone from receiving its benefits after it has been produced.

is possible, or not prohibitively costly, to exclude someone from obtaining the benefits of it after it has been produced. For example, a movie in a movie theater is excludable in that persons who do not pay for admission can be excluded from seeing it. The same holds for an economics lecture. Someone who does not pay the tuition to attend the lecture can be excluded from consuming it. So both movies in movie theaters and economics lectures in classrooms are *excludable public goods.*

Nonexcludable

A characteristic of a good whereby it is impossible, or prohibitively costly, to exclude someone from receiving its benefits after it has been produced.

A public good is **nonexcludable** if it is impossible, or prohibitively costly, to exclude someone from obtaining the benefits of the good after it has been produced. National defense is a public good in that it is nonrivalrous in consumption. For example, if the U.S. national defense system is protecting people in New Jersey from incoming missiles, then it is automatically protecting people in New York as well. And just as important, protecting people in New Jersey does not reduce the degree of protection for the people in New York. Second, once national defense has been produced, excluding someone from consuming its services is impossible (or prohibitively costly). Thus, national defense is a *nonexcludable public good.* The same holds for flood control or large-scale pest control. After the dam has been built or the pest spray has been sprayed, excluding persons from benefiting from it is impossible.

The Free Rider

When a good is excludable (whether private or public), individuals can obtain the benefits of it only if they pay for it. For example, no one can consume an apple (a private good) or a movie in a movie theater (a public good) without first paying for it. This is not the case with a nonexcludable public good, though. Individuals can obtain the benefits of a nonexcludable public good without paying for it. Persons who do so are referred to as **free riders**. Because of the so-called *free-rider problem,* most economists hold that the market will fail to produce nonexcludable public goods or at least fail to produce them at a desired level.

Free Rider

Anyone who receives the benefits of a good without paying for it.

To illustrate, consider someone contemplating the production of nonexcludable public good X, which, because it is a public good, is also nonrivalrous in consumption. After good X has been produced and provided to one person, others have no incentive to pay for it (even if they demand it) because they can receive all of its benefits without paying. No one is likely to supply a good that people can consume without paying for it. The market, it is argued, will not produce nonexcludable public goods. The door then is opened to government involvement in the production of nonexcludable public goods. Many argue that if the market will not produce nonexcludable public goods, even though they are demanded, then the government must.

The free-rider argument is the basis for accepting government's (the public's or taxpayers') provision of nonexcludable public goods. However, a nonexcludable public good is not the same as a government-provided good. A nonexcludable public good is a good that is nonrivalrous in consumption and nonexcludable. A government-provided good is self-defined: a good that government provides. In some instances, a government-provided good is a nonexcludable public good, such as when the government furnishes national defense, but it need not be. The government furnishes mail delivery and education, two goods that are also provided privately and are excludable and thus not subject to free riding.

Nonexcludable Versus Nonrivalrous

The market fails to produce a demanded good only when the good is nonexcludable because the free-rider problem arises only if the good is nonexcludable. The rivalry-versus-nonrivalry issue is not relevant to the issue of market failure; that is, a good can be rivalrous or nonrivalrous in consumption and still be produced by the market. For example, a movie may be nonrivalrous in consumption but excludable too. And the market has no problem producing movies and movie theaters. The free-rider problem occurs only with goods that are nonexcludable.

economics 24/7

"They Paved Paradise and Put Up a Parking Lot"

Don't it always seem to go
That you don't know what you've got
'Til it's gone,
They paved paradise
And put up a parking lot

From *Big Yellow Taxi* by Joni Mitchell

Suppose Smith owns 5 acres of land in the middle of a large city. One day he is contacted by a man who wants to buy the land for $5 million. Smith asks the person what he plans to do with the land; the man says he represents a company that wants to "put up a parking lot." Smith is seriously thinking about selling the land to the man.

In time, the people who live and work in the area find out that Smith is contemplating selling the land to someone who wants to put up a parking lot. They urge Smith not to sell. They say that they like looking at Smith's land the way it is—natural and green. They tell Smith that his land is a green space in the city and that thousands of people enjoy passing by it every day. Smith tells the people that he is happy about that, but that he needs to pay his bills, and so he has to sell the land. Smith tells the people that they can buy the land themselves if they want to—assuming they are willing and able to pay $5 million for it.

So, of two groups of people, the first is represented by the man who wants to buy the land to put up a parking lot. This group includes the buyer, the company he represents, and all the people who would like to park their cars at the parking lot. Smith's land has a certain value to these people. Call these people "group P" (for parking lot).

The second group consists of the people who benefit from the land in its natural state. These might be the people who live or work by Smith's land or who pass by it regularly. They like seeing the land in its natural state, especially since so few places are left in the city where there is some green. We'll call this people "group G" (for green).

© IMAGE COPYRIGHT ANDREY KHROLENOK, 2009. USED UNDER LICENSE FROM SHUTTERSTOCK.COM

Which group, P or G, values the land more? There are three possibilities: (1) group P values the land more than group G, (2) group G values the land more than group P, and (3) each group values the land as much as the other.

So far, we know that group P values the land at (at least) $5 million because this is what they have agreed to pay for it. Suppose that group G values the land at $8 million. Group G, however, is probably not as able to express how much they value the land as group P. The members of group G face high transaction costs to find out how much each values the land and would be willing to pay to keep the land in its natural state. In contrast, the company that wants to put up a parking lot on the land can figure out relatively easily what persons are likely to pay for parking in the city. Other parking lots in the city are already charging *x* dollars per hour for parking.

Also, the land in its natural state is a nonexcludable public good. Everyone in the area around the land can see it, enjoy it, walk near it, and so on. If these people are asked to donate money to buy it so that it can stay in its natural state, many are likely to assume the role of free riders.

So the combination of high transaction costs and the likelihood of free riders are difficult problems to overcome. In other words, the $8 million value that group G places on the land might never be realized. And if isn't realized, then group G is not going to be able to bid for the land against group P.

Of course, things could be different. Maybe group P values the land much more than group G, but that isn't the point. *Even if* group G values the land more than group P, group G might find it harder to express their greater value for the land than group P. The "$8 million value of the land" is never heard, but the "$5 million value" is heard loud and clear in the form of a specific dollar offer to purchase. Not hearing the $8 million bid, then, leads Smith to believe that the high bid is $5 million. In this case, putting up a parking lot is really not the most valuable thing to do with the land.

economics 24/7

The Right Amount of National Defense

Because of free riders, the market is unlikely to produce nonexcludable public goods. This is the basis for accepting government's provision of such goods.

If the nonexcludable public good that government provides is national defense, a thorny issue immediately arises: What quantity and quality of national defense will government provide? Will it produce a large national defense with many technologically advanced weapons systems? Will it produce a small national defense with very few technologically advanced weapons systems but with a relatively large number of soldiers?

Providing a good is one thing; providing the precise number of units and the exact quality of the good that most people demand is quite another. Some Americans want a national defense that consists of U.S. armed forces present in many different countries around the world. They argue that the U.S. needs to have a presence in countries such as Saudi Arabia, Iraq, Germany, and other parts of the world because doing so is in the best interests of the safety and security of the United States. Other Americans vehemently disagree, demanding the type of national defense by which U.S. armed forces stay home until and unless the United States is provoked in some way—for example, by an attack on U.S. citizens residing in the United States. The point is simple: once government is expected to deliver a nonexcludable public good, people are likely to argue over its quantity and quality.

Things are noticeably different with private goods. People can choose the particular type of a private good they demand from the wide variety offered to them. For example, if one person wants brown shoes and another person wants black shoes, the person who wants brown shoes buys brown and the person who wants black buys black.

But there is usually only one nonexcludable public good for everyone to consume. There is, for example, only one U.S. national defense and national defense policy, and everyone in the United States, no matter what his or her individual preferences, consumes them as is. As a result, people often argue over, and try to change, the one nonexcludable public good that they all have to consume in a way that comes closer to matching their personal preferences.

The lighthouse makes for a good metaphor. For a long time, a lighthouse was thought to have the two characteristics of a nonexcludable public good: (1) It is nonrivalrous in consumption; any ship can use the light from the lighthouse, and one ship's use of it does not detract from another's. (2) It is nonexcludable; excluding any nonpaying ships from using the light is difficult. The lighthouse seemed to be a perfect good for government provision.

However, economist Ronald Coase found that in the eighteenth and early nineteenth centuries, many lighthouses were privately owned; the market had not failed to provide lighthouses. Economists were left to conclude either that the market could provide nonexcludable public goods or that the lighthouse was not a nonexcludable public good, as had been thought. Closer examination showed that although the lighthouse was nonrivalrous in consumption (it was a public good), the costs of excluding others from using it were fairly low (so it was an excludable public good). Lighthouse owners knew that usually only one ship was near the lighthouse at a time and that they could turn off the light if a ship did not fly the flag of a paying vessel.

SELF-TEST

1. Why does the market fail to produce nonexcludable public goods?

2. Identify each of the following goods as a nonexcludable public good, an excludable public good, or a private good:

   a. Composition notebook used for writing

   b. Shakespearean play performed in a summer theater

   c. An apple

   d. A telephone in service

   e. Sunshine

3. Give an example, other than a movie in a movie theater or a play in a theater, of a good that is nonrivalrous and excludable.

ASYMMETRIC INFORMATION

In market failure, the market does not provide the efficient or optimal amount of a good. This chapter has shown that both externalities and nonexcludable public goods can lead to market failure. Specifically, in the presence of externalities, the market output is different from the socially optimal output. In the case of negative externalities, the market produces too much; in the case of positive externalities, the market produces too little. In the case of nonexcludable public goods, some economists maintain that the market produces zero output. Assuming that there is a demand for the nonexcludable public good, zero output is definitely too little.

This section looks at another possible cause of market failure: asymmetric information. Asymmetric information is information that either the buyer or the seller in a market exchange has and that the other does not have. In other words, some information is hidden. For example, the seller of a house may have information about the house that the buyer does not have, such as that the roof leaks during a heavy rainfall.

Analyzing the effects of asymmetric information is similar to analyzing externalities—with one important difference. Externalities involves buyers, sellers, and third parties; this discussion considers only buyers and sellers.

Asymmetric Information
Information that either the buyer or the seller in a market exchange has and that the other does not have.

Asymmetric Information in a Product Market

In the discussion of externalities, the demand for a good represents marginal private benefits, and the supply of a good represents marginal private costs. This is also the case for the asymmetric information situation shown in Exhibit 6; that is, the demand curve, D_1, represents marginal private benefits (MPB) and the supply curve, S_1, represents marginal private costs (MPC). In the exhibit, D_1 and S_1 are the relevant curves when the seller has some information that the buyer does not have. Therefore, Q_1 is the market output when there is asymmetric information.

Suppose the buyer acquires the information that she previously did not have (but that the seller did have). With the new information, buying this particular good does not seem as appealing. The acquired information causes the buyer to lower her demand for the good.

EXHIBIT 6

Asymmetric Information in a Product Market

Initially, the seller has some information that the buyer does not have; there is asymmetric information. As a result, D_1 represents the demand for the good and Q_1 is the equilibrium quantity. Then the buyer acquires the information that she did not have earlier, and there is symmetric information. The information causes the buyer to lower her demand for the good so that now D_2 is the relevant demand curve and Q_2 is the equilibrium quantity. Conclusion: Fewer units of the good are bought and sold when there is symmetric information than when there is asymmetric information.

The relevant demand curve is now D_2. With symmetric information, the market output will be Q_2, which is less than Q_1.

As an example, the suppliers of cigarettes know that cigarette consumption can cause cancer but do not release this information to potential buyers. Under this condition, suppliers of cigarettes have certain information about cigarettes that buyers don't have; there is asymmetric information. If buyers do not have this information, the demand for cigarettes may be higher than it would be if buyers had it. In Exhibit 6, demand is D_1 instead of D_2. So more cigarettes will be purchased and consumed (Q_1) when there is asymmetric information than when there is symmetric information (Q_2).

Asymmetric Information in a Factor Market

Suppose in a resource or factor market, such as the labor market shown in Exhibit 7, the buyer has information that the seller does not have. The employing firm knows that its workers will be using a possibly toxic substance that may cause health problems in 20 to 30 years. Further, the company does not release this information to workers but hides it from them. Without this information, the supply curve of labor is represented by S_1, and the quantity of labor will be Q_1 at a wage rate of W_1. With the information, though, not as many people will be willing to work at the firm at the current wage. The supply curve of labor shifts left to S_2. The new equilibrium position shows that the quantity of labor falls to Q_2, and the wage rate rises to W_2.

Is There Market Failure?

Does asymmetric information cause markets to fail? In other words, does it create a situation in which the market does not provide the optimal output of a particular good? Certainly, in our examples, the output level of a good and the quantity of labor were lower with symmetric information than with asymmetric information. Stated differently, asymmetric

---

EXHIBIT 7

Asymmetric Information in a Factor Market

Initially, the buyer (of the factor labor), or the firm, has some information that the seller (of the factor) does not have; there is asymmetric information. Consequently, S_1 is the relevant supply curve, W_1 is the equilibrium wage, and Q_1 is the equilibrium quantity of labor. Then sellers acquire information that they did not have earlier, and there is symmetric information. The information causes the sellers to reduce their supply of the factor so that now S_2 is the relevant supply curve, W_2 is the equilibrium wage, and Q_2 is the equilibrium quantity of labor. Conclusion: Fewer factor units are bought and sold and wages are higher when there is symmetric information than when there is asymmetric information.

information seemingly resulted in too much or too many of something—either too much of a good being consumed or too many workers for a particular firm.

Some people argue that asymmetric information exists in nearly all exchanges. Rarely do buyers and sellers have the same information; each usually knows something the other doesn't. However, this argument misses the point, which is whether the asymmetric information fundamentally changes the outcome from what it would be if there were symmetric information. For example, a seller may know something that a buyer doesn't know, but even if the buyer knew what the seller knows, the outcome would be the same.

To illustrate, suppose a person buys a medication to relieve a severe headache. The person does not know that one side effect of the medication is sleepiness. In this case, asymmetric information may not matter. Possibly the buyer would not have changed her behavior even if she had known the medication caused sleepiness. So there is asymmetric information, but it may not change the outcome.

Of course, in another setting, the result may be different. Suppose the seller of a used car knows the car is a lemon, but the buyer doesn't know this. The person buys the car because he doesn't have the information the seller has. Asymmetric information matters in that the buyer would not have bought the car—or would not have bought the car at a given price—had he known what the seller knew. In this setting, asymmetric information changes the outcome.

Therefore, the presence of asymmetric information does not guarantee that the market fails. What matters is that if the asymmetric information brings about a different outcome than if there were symmetric information, then the case for market failure can be made.

Adverse Selection

Some economists argue that under certain conditions, information problems can eliminate markets (i.e., create *missing markets*) or change the composition of markets (i.e., bring about *incomplete markets*). In the used car market of our example,[3] sellers know more than buyers about the cars they are offering to sell; there is asymmetric information. For example, a seller knows whether the car requires a lot of maintenance. Because most buyers find it difficult to tell the difference between good used cars and lemons, suppose a single used car price emerges for a given model-make-year car that reflects both lemons and good cars.

Suppose this price is $10,000. A lemon owner will think this is a good price because she will receive an average price for a below-average car. On the other hand, a person who owns an above-average car will find this price too low; he won't want to sell it for an average price. As a result of lemon owners' liking the price and good car owners' not liking it, lemon owners will offer their cars for sale (the price is great), and the owners of good used cars will not (the price is too low).

This situation is called the problem of adverse selection. Adverse selection exists when the parties on one side of the market, who have information not known to others, self-select in a way that adversely affects the parties on the other side of the market. In the example, the owners of lemons offer their cars for sale; they select to sell their cars because they know (and only they know) that the average price they are being offered for their below-average cars is a good deal.

Through adverse selection, the supply of lemons on the market will rise, and the supply of high-quality, or good, used cars will fall. The relatively greater number of lemons will lower the average quality of a used car. As a result, for a given make-model-year used car, a new average price will emerge that is lower than it was before.

Let's say the new price is $8,000. The process repeats itself: people with above-average cars will think the average price of $8,000 is too low, and people with below-average cars will think this is a good price. The people with above-average cars will drop out of the used car

Adverse Selection
A phenomenon in which the parties on one side of the market, who have information not known to others, self-select in a way that adversely affects the parties on the other side of the market.

---

3. This material is based on the classic article by George Akerlof, "The Market for Lemons," *Quarterly Journal of Economics* (August 1970): 488–500.

Arriving Late to Class, Grading on a Curve, and Studying Together for the Midterm

A series of young children's books titled *Where's Waldo?* present the character Waldo drawn among hundreds of people and things. Although the objective, finding Waldo, may seem easy, finding him is roughly similar to finding a needle in a haystack. If you look long and hard, you'll eventually find him; if you simply glance at the page, you won't.

Finding economics is like finding Waldo. If you simply glance at your daily life, you will miss the economics; if you look long and hard, you will often find it. With this in mind, consider your life as a college student. On a typical day, you walk into a college classroom, sit down, listen to a lecture and take notes, enter into discussions, ask questions, answer questions, and then leave. Can you find the economics in this daily experience? Here are some places you might find economics lurking.

Arriving Late to Class

Class started five minutes ago. You are sitting at your desk, listening to the professor, and taking notes. The professor is discussing an unusually challenging topic today, and you are listening attentively. Then the classroom door opens. You turn at the sound and see two of your classmates arriving late to class. For a few seconds, your attention is diverted from the lecture. When you refocus your attention on the professor, you realize that you have missed an essential point, and you become mildly frustrated.

This scenario illustrates a negative externality. Your two classmates undertook an action—arriving late—and you incurred a cost because of their action. Your two classmates considered only their private benefits and costs of arriving to class late. They did not consider your cost—the external cost—of their action.

To get students to internalize the cost to others of their being late, the professor could try to persuade students not to be late. She could say that lateness imposes a cost on those who arrive on time and who are attentively listening to the lecture.

market, leaving only those with below-average used cars. Again, this will lead to a decline in the average quality of a used car, and eventually the average price of a used car will drop again.

Thus, asymmetric information leads to adverse selection, which in the used car market example, brings about a steady decline in the quality of used cars offered for sale. Theoretically, the adverse selection problem could lead to the total elimination of the good used car market. In other words, the lemons will drive all the good cars out of the market.

This ultimate adverse selection would not happen in the used car market for several possible reasons. For example, a buyer could hire his own mechanic to check the car he is thinking about buying. By doing so, he would acquire almost as much, if not as much, information about the car as the seller has. Thus, there would no longer be asymmetric information. Or the seller of a high-quality used car could offer a warranty on her car. Essentially, she could offer to fix any problems with the used car for a period of time after she sells it. The warranty offer would likely increase both the demand for the car and its price. (Lemon owners would not be likely to offer warranties; so their cars would sell for less than cars with warranties.)

In some cases, government has played a role in dealing with adverse selection problems. State governments can pass, and in some situations have passed, lemon laws, stating that car dealers must take back any defective cars. In addition, many states now require car dealers to openly state on used cars whether a car is offered with a warranty or as is.

Moral Hazard

Moral Hazard
A condition that exists when one party to a transaction changes his or her behavior in a way that is hidden from and costly to the other party.

In the used car example illustrating adverse selection, asymmetric information existed *prior* to an exchange. Before dollars changed hands, the seller of the used car had information about the car that the potential buyer did not have.

Asymmetric information can also exist *after* a transaction has been made. If it does, it can cause a moral hazard problem. Moral hazard occurs when one party to a transaction

Alternatively, the professor could impose a corrective tax on tardy students. In other words, she could set a tax equal to the external cost, perhaps taking one-half to one point off a student's test grade for each lateness.

Grading on a Curve

Alex is currently taking a sociology course. He would like to get an A or a B in the class but believes he is likely to receive a C or a D. Alex's situation is similar to that of a person who would like to be healthy every day for the rest of his life but who knows that he probably won't be. When a person knows he probably won't be healthy for his entire life, he buys health insurance. And, as explained in this chapter, after a person purchases health insurance, a moral hazard problem may arise. The person may not have so strong an incentive to remain healthy when he has health insurance as when he doesn't.

Would Alex react the same way if he could buy grade insurance? Suppose his sociology professor promises Alex that she will grade on a curve and that no one in the class will receive a grade lower than a C. With this assurance from his professor, will Alex have as strong an incentive to work hard to learn sociology? Does a moral hazard now arise? An economist is likely to answer the first question no and the second question yes.

Studying Together for the Midterm

Students usually study together if they think doing so will be mutually beneficial. That is, when two people agree to study together (say, for a midterm), they are usually entering into an exchange: "I will help you learn more of the material so that you can get a better grade if you do the same for me."

Consider two types of colleges: (1) a dormitory-based college in which many of the students live on campus in dormitories and (2) a commuter college in which the entire student body lives off campus. Students tend to study together more on dormitory-based campuses than on commuter campuses because the transaction costs of studying together—of entering into the exchange—are lower on a dormitory-based campus. If you live in a dormitory on campus, you incur relatively low transaction costs by studying with someone who also lives on campus (maybe a person living down the hall from you). But if everyone lives off campus, you incur relatively high transaction costs by studying with a fellow student. One of you has to drive to the other's house or apartment, or you have to meet at a local coffee bar.

changes his behavior in a way that is hidden from and costly to the other party. For example, suppose Smith buys a health insurance policy. After she has the insurance, she may be less careful to maintain good health because the cost to her of future health problems is not as high as it would have been without the insurance. Smith does not set out to make herself ill so that she can collect on the insurance, but her incentive to be as careful about her health and physical well-being is not as strong as it once was. As another example, a person with automobile collision insurance may be more likely to drive on an icy road in December in Minneapolis than if he didn't have the insurance. Or a person who has earthquake insurance may be more likely to forget to do a few things that will minimize damage during an earthquake, such as attaching bookcases to the walls. In these examples, the moral hazard problem causes people to take too few precautionary actions.

Insurance companies try to control for moral hazard in different ways. One way is by specifying certain precautions that an insured person must take. For example, a company that insures your house from fire may require you to have smoke detectors and a fire extinguisher. The insurance company may also set a deductible so that you pay part of the loss in case of a fire, thereby increasing your cost in the event of a fire and providing you with an added incentive to be careful.

SELF-TEST

1. Give an example that illustrates how asymmetric information can lead to more of a good being consumed than if there is symmetric information.

2. Adverse selection has the potential to eliminate some markets. How is this possible?

3. Give an example of moral hazard that is not used in the text.

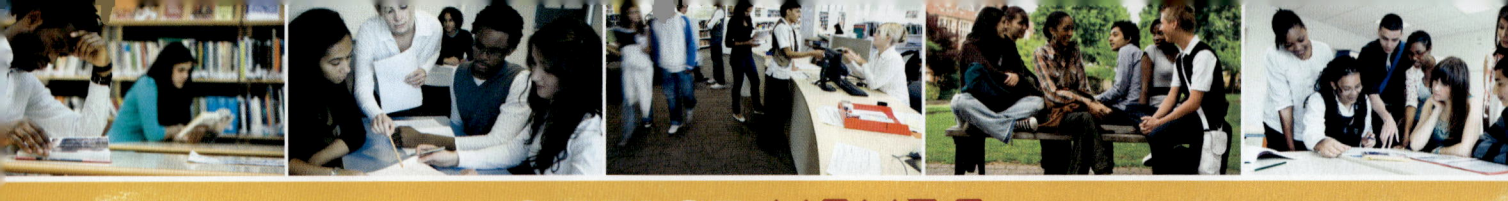
"Doesn't It Seem Wrong to Let Some Business Firms Pay to Pollute?"

STUDENT:

In our discussion, I know that pollution permits proved to be less costly at reducing pollution than setting pollution standards, but letting a business firm get away with polluting if it can pay enough money seems wrong. It seems as if it is paying to do something wrong.

INSTRUCTOR:

There's a different way to look at things. The firm is not paying to pollute; it is paying to have some other business firm reduce its pollution. Suppose firm A can eliminate its pollution at a lower cost than firm B. Firm B now pays firm A to eliminate its own (firm A's) pollution. Instead of saying that firm B is "paying to pollute," why not say that "firm B is paying firm A not to pollute."

STUDENT:

Putting it that way makes firm B sound like the good guy—the firm that pays other firms not to pollute.

INSTRUCTOR:

My point is that you cast firm B as the bad guy—the firm that pays to pollute. What I did was simply bring out another aspect of what

is happening. Firm B *pays firm A not to pollute* (that is my part of the story) so that in turn *it can pollute* (that is your part of the story). Also keep in mind that at the end of process, pollution is reduced, not increased. Instead of having the pollution from firms A and B, we have less (or no) pollution from firm A and perhaps the same amount of pollution from firm B.

STUDENT:

I see your point, but wouldn't it still be fairer if no money changed hands and both firms A and B were told that they had to eliminate *x* amount of pollution? In other words, wouldn't it be fairer to treat each firm the same way?

INSTRUCTOR:

Let's divide the world up into the two firms, A and B, and everyone else. Now as far as A and B are concerned, each of these two firms would prefer a system of pollution permits to a system of standards. We know this because a pollution permits program can always be turned into a standards program if doing so is preferable to buying and selling permits. To illustrate, suppose firms A and B are each emitting 3 units of pollution. Government now gives each firm 1 pollution permit, allowing it to emit 1 unit of pollution. If neither

---

CHAPTER SUMMARY

EXTERNALITIES

- An externality is a side effect of an action that affects the well-being of third parties. There are two types of externalities: negative and positive. A negative externality exists when an individual's or group's actions impose a cost (an adverse side effect) on others. A positive externality exists when an individual's or group's actions cause a benefit (a beneficial side effect) for others.

- When either negative or positive externalities exist, the market output is different from the socially optimal output. In the case of a negative externality, the market is said to overproduce the good connected with the negative externality (the socially optimal output is less than the market output). In the case of a

positive externality, the market is said to underproduce the good connected with the positive externality (the socially optimal output is greater than the market output). See Exhibits 1 and 3.

- Negative and positive externalities can be internalized or adjusted for in a number of different ways, including persuasion, the assignment of property rights, voluntary agreements, and taxes and subsidies. Also, regulations may be used to adjust for externalities directly.

THE COASE THEOREM

- The Coase theorem holds that when transaction costs are trivial or zero, the property rights assignment does not matter to the firm buys or sells its 1 permit, then what we essentially have is a standards system for eliminating (some) pollution. Each firm reduces its pollution from 3 units to 1 unit. End of story. But if the two firms start trading permits for money, we can conclude that each firm is better off with a pollution permits system than with a standards system. And this is what we usually see: firms buying and selling permits.

> ### STUDENT:
>
> So the point is that firms A and B prefer a pollution permits system to a standards system?

> ### INSTRUCTOR:
>
> Yes. But now we are left with what we call an "everyone else": Is everyone else better off with a pollution permits system than with a standards system? The answer is yes because it is less costly to eliminate a given amount of pollution with a pollution permits system than with standards. "Less costly" here means "fewer resources used." If fewer resources are used to eliminate pollution, then more resources are left over for other things. As a member of the Everyone Else Group, I am better off with more resources left over than with fewer resources to produce things that I want to buy.
>
> So let's now return to your original question: Wouldn't it be fairer if no money changed hands and both firms A and B were told that they had to eliminate *x* amount of pollution? To whom would that be fairer? It's not fairer to firms A and B because they prefer pollution permits to standards. And it's not really fairer to everyone else, because we suspect that everyone else prefers to have more instead of fewer resources left over after *x* amount of pollution has been emitted.

POINTS TO REMEMBER

1. Saying that "firms are paying to pollute" leaves out some of what is happening with a pollution permits system. Some firms are paying other firms not to pollute so that they can pollute. Firm B is paying firm A to not to pollute so that it (firm B) can pollute.
2. Pollution permits (that can be bought and sold) can eliminate a given amount of pollution with a lower resource cost than can a standards system.

resource allocative outcome. To put it differently, a property rights assignment will be undone if it benefits the relevant parties to undo it. The Coase theorem is significant for two reasons: (1) It shows that under certain conditions, the market can internalize externalities. (2) It provides a benchmark for analyzing externality problems; that is, it shows what would happen if transaction costs are trivial or zero.

THE ENVIRONMENT

- Some pollution is likely to be better than none because people derive utility from things that cause pollution, such as driving cars.
- Environmental problems can be tackled in more than one way. For example, both setting standards and selling pollution permits can be employed to deal with pollution. The economist is

interested in finding the cheapest way to solve environmental problems. Often, the solution tends to be through some measure of market environmentalism.

PUBLIC GOODS

- A public good is a good characterized by nonrivalry in consumption.
- A public good can be excludable or nonexcludable. Excludable public goods are goods that, while nonrivalrous in consumption, can be denied to people if they do not pay for them. Nonexcludable public goods are goods that are nonrivalrous in consumption and cannot be denied to people who do not pay for them.
- The market is said to fail in the provision of nonexcludable public goods because of the free-rider problem; that is, a supplier of

the good is not able to extract payment for the good because its benefits can be received without making payment.

ASYMMETRIC INFORMATION

• Asymmetric information exists when either the buyer or the seller in a market exchange has some information that the other does not have. Outcomes based on asymmetric information may be different from outcomes based on symmetric information.

• Adverse selection exists when the parties on one side of the market, who have information not known to others, self-select in a way that adversely affects the parties on the other side of the market. Adverse selection can lead to missing or incomplete markets.

• Moral hazard occurs when one party to a transaction changes his or her behavior in a way that is hidden from and costly to the other party.

KEY TERMS AND CONCEPTS

Market Failure
Externality
Negative Externality
Positive Externality
Marginal Social Costs (*MSC*)
Marginal Social Benefits (*MSB*)

Socially Optimal Amount
  (Output)
Internalizing Externalities
Coase Theorem
Rivalrous in Consumption
Public Good

Nonrivalrous in
  Consumption
Excludable
Nonexcludable
Free Rider

Asymmetric Information
Adverse Selection
Moral Hazard

QUESTIONS AND PROBLEMS

1. Identify each of the following as an adverse selection or a moral hazard problem.

   a. A person with car insurance fails to lock his car doors when he shops at a mall.

   b. A person with a family history of cancer purchases the most complete health coverage available.

   c. A person with health insurance takes more risks on the ski slopes of Aspen than he would otherwise.

   d. A college professor receives tenure (assurance of permanent employment) from her employer.

   e. A patient pays his surgeon before she performs the surgery.

2. People have a demand for sweaters, and the market provides sweaters. There is evidence that people also have a demand for national defense, but the market does not provide it. Why doesn't the market provide national defense? Is it because government is providing national defense, and therefore there is no need for the market to do so? Or is it because the market can't provide it?

3. Why is it cheaper to reduce, say, air pollution through market environmentalism (pollution permits that can be bought and sold) than through government standards and regulations?

4. Consider two types of divorce laws. Law A allows either the husband or the wife to obtain a divorce without the other person's consent. Law B permits a divorce only if both parties agree to it. Will there be more divorces under law A or law B, or will there be the same number of divorces under both laws? Why?

5. Economists sometimes shock noneconomists by stating that they do not favor the complete elimination of pollution. Explain the rationale for this position.

6. Give an example that illustrates the difference between private costs and social costs.

7. One view is that life is one big externality: just about everything someone does affects someone else either positively or negatively. To permit government to deal with externality problems is to permit government to tamper with everything in life. No clear line divides externalities in which government should become involved from those it should not. Do you support this position? Why or why not?

8. When will asymmetric information in a product market not cause market failure?

9. Name at least five government-provided goods that are not nonexcludable public goods.

10. In Exhibit 3, explain why the shaded triangle is representative of a market failure.

11. Some individuals argue that with increased population growth, negative externalities will become more common and that there will be more instances of market failure and more need for government to solve externality problems. Other individuals believe that as time passes technological advances will be used to solve negative externality problems and that there will be fewer instances of market failure and less need for government to deal with externality problems. What do you believe will happen? Give reasons to support your position.

12. Suppose there is a negative externality. If a tax is used to correct for the negative externality, what condition must be satisfied? (What must the tax equal?)

13. Give an example of each of the following:
    a. A good rivalrous in consumption and excludable
    b. A good nonrivalrous in consumption and excludable
    c. A good rivalrous in consumption and nonexcludable
    d. A good nonrivalrous in consumption and nonexcludable

14. Under what condition will $MSC = MPC$? When will $MSB = MPB$?

15. Identify three activities that generate negative externalities and three activities that generate positive externalities. Explain why each activity you identified generates the type of externality you specified.

WORKING WITH NUMBERS AND GRAPHS

1. Graphically portray:
    a. A negative externality
    b. A positive externality

2. Graphically represent:
    a. A corrective tax that achieves the socially optimal output
    b. A corrective tax that moves the market output farther away from the socially optimal output than was the case before the tax was applied

3. Using the following data, prove that pollution permits that can be bought and sold can reduce pollution from 12 units to 6 units at lower cost than a regulation that specifies each of the three firms must cut its pollution in half.

	Firm X	Firm Y	Firm Z
Cost of eliminating:			
First unit of pollution	$200	$500	$1,000
Second unit of pollution	300	700	2,000
Third unit of pollution	400	800	2,900
Fourth unit of pollution	500	900	3,400

32

AP PHOTO/PABLO MARTINEZ MONSIVAIS

PUBLIC CHOICE AND SPECIAL-INTEREST-GROUP POLITICS

Introduction Economics is a powerful analytical tool. As·you have seen, it can be used to analyze how markets and the economy work. In this chapter we use economics to analyze the behavior of politicians, voters, and members of special interest groups.

Specifically, we analyze public choice, the branch of economics in which economic principles and tools are applied to public sector decision making. Public choice is, in a sense, economics applied to politics.

Public Choice
The branch of economics in which economic principles and tools are applied to public sector decision making.

PUBLIC CHOICE THEORY

Public choice theorists reject the notion that people are like Dr. Jekyll and Mr. Hyde: that is, exhibiting greed and selfishness in their transactions in the private (market) sector and altruism and public spirit in their actions in the public sector. The same people who are the employers, employees, and consumers in the market sector are the politicians, bureaucrats, members of special interest groups, and voters in the public sector. According to public choice theorists, people in the market sector and people in the public sector behave differently not because they have different motives (or are different types of people) but because the two sectors have different institutional arrangements.

As a simple example, Erin Bloom works for a private, profit-seeking firm that makes radio components. Erin is cost conscious, does her work on time, and generally works hard. She knows that she must exhibit this type of work behavior if she wants to keep her job, get a raise, and be promoted. Erin leaves her job at the radio components company and takes a job with the Department of Health and Human Services (HHS) in Washington, D.C. Public choice theorists maintain that Erin is the same person (with different motives) whether working for HHS or for the radio components company.

However, even though Erin is the same person in and out of government, she will not necessarily exhibit the same work behavior. The costs and benefits of certain actions may be substantially different at HHS than at the radio components company. For example, perhaps the cost of being late for work is less in Erin's new job at HHS than it was at her old job. In her former job, she had to work overtime if she came in late; in her new job, her boss doesn't say anything. Erin is therefore more likely to be late in her new job than she was in her old one. She is simply responding to costs and benefits as they exist in her new work environment.

THE POLITICAL MARKET

Economists who practice positive economics want to understand their world. They want to understand not only the production and pricing of goods, unemployment, inflation, and the firm, but also political outcomes and political behavior. This section is an introduction to the political market.

Moving Toward the Middle: The Median Voter Model

During political elections, voters often complain that the candidates for office are too much alike. Some find the similarities frustrating, saying they would prefer to have more choice. However, as you will see, two candidates running for the same office often sound alike because they are competing for votes.

In Exhibit 1, parts (a), (b), and (c) all show a distribution of voters in which the political spectrum goes from the Far Left to the Far Right. Relatively few voters hold positions in either of the two extreme wings. Assuming that voters will vote for the candidate who comes closest to matching their ideological or political views, then people whose views are in the Far Left of the political spectrum will vote for the candidate closest to the Far Left, and so on.

Our election process begins with two candidates, a Democrat and a Republican, occupying the positions D_1 and R_1 in part (a), respectively. If the election were held today, the Republican would receive more votes than his Democrat opponent. The Republican would receive all the votes of the voters who position themselves to the right of R_1, the Democrat would receive all the votes of the voters who position themselves to the left of D_1, and the voters between R_1 and D_1 would divide their votes between the two candidates. The Republican would thus receive more votes than the Democrat.

EXHIBIT 1

The Move Toward the Middle

Political candidates tend to move toward the middle of the political spectrum. Starting with (a), the Republican receives more votes than the Democrat and would win the election if it were held today. To offset this, as shown in (b), the Democrat moves inward toward the middle of the political spectrum. The Republican tries to offset the Democrat's movement inward by also moving inward. As a result, both candidates move toward the political middle, getting closer to each other over time.

(a)

(b)

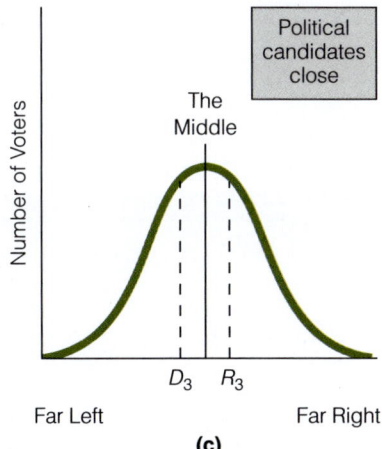

(c)

If, however, the election were not held today, the Democrat would likely notice (through polls and other sources) that her opponent was doing better than she was. To offset this, she would move toward the center, or middle, of the political spectrum to pick up some votes. Part (b) in Exhibit 1 illustrates this move by the Democrat. Relative to her position in part (a), the Democrat is closer to the middle of the political spectrum, and as a result she picks up votes. Voters to the left of D_2 would vote for the Democrat, voters to the right of R_2 would vote for the Republican, and the voters between the two positions would divide their votes between the two candidates. If the election were held now, the Democrat would win.

In part (c), each candidate, in an attempt to get more votes than the opponent, has moved closer to The Middle (D_3 and R_3). At election time, the two candidates are likely to be positioned side by side at the political center, or middle. In part (c), both candidates have become middle-of-the-roaders in their attempt to pick up votes.

The tendency of political candidates to move toward the center of the voter distribution—captured in the median voter model—is what causes many voters to complain that there is not much difference between candidates.

What Does the Theory Predict?

Although the median voter model explains why politicians running for the same office often sound alike, what does the model predict? Here are a few of the theory's predictions:

1. *Candidates will label their opponent as being either too far to the right or too far to the left.* The candidates know that whoever is closer to the middle of the political spectrum (in a two-person race) will win more votes and thus the election. To win, they will move toward the political middle, at the same time saying that their opponent is a member of the political fringe (i.e., a person far from the center). A Democrat may argue that his Republican opponent is too conservative; a Republican may argue that her Democrat opponent is too liberal.

2. *Candidates will call themselves middle-of-the-roaders, not right- or left-wingers.* In their move toward the political middle, candidates will try to portray themselves as moderates. In their speeches, they will assert that they represent the majority of voters and that they are practical, not ideological. They will not be likely to refer to themselves as ultraliberal or ultraconservative or as right- or left-wingers because to do so would send a self-defeating message to the voters.

3. *Candidates will take polls, and, if they are not doing well in the polls and their opponents are, they will modify their positions to become more like their opponents.* Polls tell candidates who the likely winner of the election will be. A candidate who finds out that she will lose the election (she is "down in the polls") is not likely to sit back and do nothing. The candidate will change her positions. Often, she will become more like the winner of the poll—that is, more like her political opponent.

4. *Candidates will speak in general, instead of specific, terms.* Voters agree more on ends than on the means of accomplishing those ends. For example, voters of the left, right, and middle believe that a strong economy is better than a weak economy. However, they do not all agree on the best way to make the economy strong. The person on the right might advocate less government intervention as one way, whereas the person on the left might advocate more government intervention. Most political candidates soon learn that addressing the issues specifically requires them to discuss means and that doing so increases the probability of their having an extreme-wing label attached to them. For example, a candidate who advocates more government intervention in the economy is more likely to be labeled "too far left" than a candidate who simply calls for a stronger national economy without discussing any specific means. In the candidate's desire to be perceived as a middle-of-the-roader, he is much more likely to talk about ends, on which voters agree, than about means, on which voters disagree.

Median Voter Model

A model suggesting that candidates in a two-person political race will attempt to match the preferences of the median voter (i.e., the person whose preferences are at the center, or in the middle, of the political spectrum).

A Simple Majority Voting Rule: The Case of the Statue in the Public Square

Public questions are often decided by the simple majority decision rule. Although most people think this is the fair and democratic way to do things, in certain instances a simple majority vote leads to undertaking a project whose costs are greater than its benefits.

Consider a community of 10 people, whose names are listed in column 1 of Exhibit 2. The community is considering whether to purchase a statue to put in the center of the public square. The cost of the statue is $1,000, and the community has previously agreed that if the statue is purchased, the 10 individuals will share the cost equally—that is, each will pay $100 in taxes (see column 3).

Column 2 shows the dollar value of the benefits that each individual will receive from the statue. For example, Applebaum places a dollar value of $150 on the statue, Browning places a dollar value of $140 on the statue, and so on. Column 4 notes the net benefit (+) or net cost (–) of the statue to each individual. A net benefit occurs if the dollar value an individual places on the statue is greater than the tax (cost) incurred. A net cost results if the reverse is true. Finally, column 5 indicates how

each member of the community would vote. An individual who believes the statue has a net benefit will vote for it, and an individual who believes the statue has a net cost will vote against it. Six individuals vote for the statue, and four individuals vote against it. The majority rules, and the statue is purchased and placed in the center of the public square.

However, the total dollar value of benefits to the community ($812) is less than the total tax cost to the community ($1,000). Using the simple majority decision rule has resulted in the purchase of the statue even though the benefits of the statue to the community are less than its costs.

This outcome is not surprising when you understand that the simple majority decision rule does not take into account the intensity of individuals' preferences. No matter how strongly a person feels about an issue, he or she registers only one vote. For example, even though Emerson places a net benefit of $1 on the statue and Isley places a net cost of $90 on the statue, each individual has only one vote. Isley has no way to register that he does not want the statue more than Emerson wants it.

EXHIBIT 2

Simple Majority Voting and Inefficiency The simple majority decision rule sometimes generates inefficient results. Here the statue is purchased even though the total dollar value of the benefits of the statue is less than the total dollar costs.

(1) Individuals	(2) Dollar Value of Benefits to Individual	(3) Tax Levied on Individual	(4) Net Benefit (+) or Net Cost (−)	(5) Vote For or Against
Applebaum	$150	$ 100	+$50	For
Browning	140	100	+ 40	For
Carson	130	100	+ 30	For
Davidson	110	100	+ 10	For
Emerson	101	100	+ 1	For
Finley	101	100	+ 1	For
Gunter	50	100	− 50	Against
Harris	10	100	− 90	Against
Isley	10	100	− 90	Against
Janowitz	10	100	− 90	Against
Total	$812	$1,000		

finding ECONOMICS

In a Presidential Election Debate During a presidential election debate, one candidate is asked what his plan is for health care in the country. He says that his plan would make health care more afford-able and responsive to peoples' needs. He then goes on to say that health care has been a problem in the United States for a long time and that it is about time for a solution. Where is the economics?

The median voter model predicts that candidates will speak in general, not specific, terms. This is what we have just heard one of the candidates do. He did not get into any specifics about his plan. For example, he probably will not specifically address how much the health care plan will cost, whom it will serve, and so on. ▲ ▲ ▲

thinking Like AN ECONOMIST

Testing Theories An economist thinks about theories and then tests them. She is not content to accept a theory—such as the one that says candidates in a two-person political race will gravitate toward the center of the political distribution—simply because it sounds right. The economist asks, "If the theory is right, what should I expect to see in the real world? If the theory is wrong, what should I expect to see in the real world?" Such questions direct the economist to look at effects to see whether the theory has explanatory and predictive power. If the four predictions of the median voter theory occur in the real world—candidates labeling themselves one way, speaking in general terms, and so on—then the economist can conclude that the evidence supports the theory. But if candidates en masse do not behave as the model predicts, then the economist must reject the theory. ■ ■ ■

VOTERS AND RATIONAL IGNORANCE

The preceding section explains something about the behavior of politicians, especially near or at election time. We turn now to voters.

The Costs and Benefits of Voting

Political commentators often remark that the voter turnout for this or that election was low: "Only 54 percent of registered voters actually voted." Are voter turnouts low because Americans are apathetic? Are they uninterested in political issues?

Public choice economists often explain low voter turnouts in terms of the costs and benefits of voting. As an example, Mark Quincy is thinking about voting in a presidential election. Mark may receive many benefits from voting: he may feel more involved in public affairs or think that he has met his civic responsibility. He may see himself as patriotic, or he may believe he has a greater right to criticize government if he takes an active part in it. In short, he may benefit by seeing himself as a doer instead of a talker. Ultimately, however, he will weigh these positive benefits against the costs of voting, which include driving to the polls, standing in line, and so on. If, in the end, Mark perceives the benefits of voting as greater than the costs, he will vote.

But suppose Mark believes he receives only one benefit from voting: determining the election outcome. His benefits-of-voting equation may look like this:

Mark's benefits of voting = Probability of Mark's vote determining the election outcome
× Additional benefits Mark receives if his candidate wins

Suppose two candidates, A and B, are running for office. If Mark votes, he will vote for A because he estimates that he benefits $100 if A is elected but only $40 if B is elected. The difference, $60, represents the additional benefits Mark receives if his candidate wins.

However, the probability of Mark's vote determining the outcome is questionable. With many potential voters, such as in a presidential election, the probability that one person's vote will determine the outcome is close to 0. To recognize this fact on an intuitive level, suppose A and B are the two major candidates in a presidential campaign. If you, as an individual voter, vote for A, the outcome of the election is likely to be the same as if you had voted for B or not voted at all. In other words, whether you vote, vote for A, or vote for B, the outcome is likely to be the same. In short, given many potential voters, the probability of one person's vote changing the outcome of an election is close to zero. In Mark's benefits-of-voting equation, $60 is multiplied by a probability so small that it might as well be 0. So $60 times 0 is 0. In short, Mark receives no benefits from voting.

But Mark may face certain costs. His costs-of-voting equation may look like this:

$$\text{Mark's cost of voting} = \text{Cost of driving to the polls}$$
$$+ \text{Cost of standing in line}$$
$$+ \text{Cost of filling out the ballot}$$

Obviously, Mark faces some positive costs of voting. Because his benefits of voting are 0 and his costs of voting are positive, Mark makes the rational choice if he decides not to vote.

Clearly, not everyone behaves this way, that is, chooses not to vote. Many people do vote in elections. Probably what separates the Marks in the world from the people who vote is that the voters receive some benefits that Mark does not. They might receive benefits simply by being part of the excitement of election day, by doing what they perceive as their civic duty, or for some other reason.

The point that public choice economists make is that if many individual voters will vote only if they perceive their vote as making a difference, then they probably will not vote because their vote is unlikely to make a difference. The low turnouts that appear to be a result of voter apathy may instead be a result of cost-benefit calculations.

Rational Ignorance

How often have you heard an opinion like this one? "Democracy would be better served if voters would take more of an interest in and become better informed about politics and government. Voters don't know much about the issues."

The problem is not that voters are too stupid to learn about the issues. Many voter-citizens who know little about politics and government are quite capable of learning about both, but they choose not to make the effort. The reason is perhaps predictable: the costs of becoming informed often outweigh the benefits. In short, many persons believe that becoming informed is simply not worth the effort. Hence, on an individual basis, it makes sense to be uninformed about politics and government, that is, to be in a state of rational ignorance.

As an example, Shonia Tyler has many things she can do with her leisure time. She could read a good novel, watch a television program, go out with friends, or become better informed about the candidates and the issues in the upcoming U.S. Senate race. Becoming informed, however, has costs. If Shonia stays home and reads about the issues, she can't go out with her friends. If she stays up late to watch a news program, she might be too tired to work efficiently the next day. These costs have to be weighed against the benefits of becoming better informed about the candidates and the issues. For Shonia, as for many people, the benefits are unlikely to be greater than the costs.

Many people see little personal benefit in becoming more knowledgeable about political candidates and issues. As with voting, the decision to remain uninformed may be linked to the small impact any single individual can have in a large-numbers setting.

Rational Ignorance
The state of not acquiring information because the costs of acquiring it are greater than the benefits.

Economic Illiteracy and Democracy

Citizens can vote even if they have no idea what they are doing. If enough voters fit that description, democratic governments are bound to make foolish decisions.

—Bryan Caplan, *Straight Talk About Economic Literacy*

Economist Bryan Caplan argues that a large percentage of the American public is economically illiterate. The result is a lot of foolishness gets turned into national economic policy.[1]

Although determining whether someone is illiterate may be easy, not so easy is ascertaining whether someone is economically illiterate. To determine illiteracy, you can just ask people to read or write something. If they can read and write, they are not illiterate. If they can't read and write, they are illiterate.

Unfortunately, there is no such simple test to determine economically illiteracy. Instead Caplan points to a survey that compared the responses of average Americans (1,510 of them) and professional economists (250 of them) to the same set of questions concerning economics and the economy. Here is one question from the survey: "Which do you think is more responsible for the recent increase in gasoline prices: the normal law of supply and demand, oil companies are trying to increase profits, both, or neither?" Although only 8 percent of economists said recent increases in gas prices were due to oil companies trying to increase profits, 78 percent of the noneconomists polled explained high gas prices this way. The explanation for high gas prices chosen by 83 percent of economists was supply and demand.

Indirectly, Caplan uses the economists' overwhelming response to the question as a benchmark by which to measure the economic illiteracy of the public. The closer the public responses are to the economists' responses, the less economically illiterate the public is; the farther away the public responses are from the economists' responses, the more economically illiterate the public is.

According to Caplan, looking at responses to numerous questions, the American public is largely economically illiterate. Caplan argues that such a great degree of economic illiteracy has to do with the price one pays for it. In fact, the price is rather low, and when the price is low, you would expect a higher degree of economic illiteracy than

when the price is high. In a phrase: False beliefs about economics are cheap. According to Caplan, if you underestimate the costs of excessive drinking, you can ruin your life. But if you underestimate the economic benefits of, say, free international trade, nothing really bad happens to you. Whatever happens to you is what would have happened if you didn't underestimate the economic benefits of free international trade. In other words, when being wrong really has no cost, a lot of people will be wrong—especially if one receives a personal psychological lift from holding an erroneous belief or position. Caplan puts it succinctly: "In a sense, then, there is a method to the average voter's madness. Even when his views are completely wrong, he gets the psychological benefit of emotionally appealing political beliefs at a bargain price. No wonder he buys in bulk."[2] In other words, x might be the wrong answer to the question, but if x is emotionally appealing to the respondent, and if having the wrong answer doesn't adversely affect the respondent, then x it is.

But if many people choose x, perhaps at a national level x gets turned into policy. In other words, if the majority of voting Americans believe that placing tariffs on foreign imports is desirable (when economists largely disagree), then, in a political system where politicians compete for votes, the public's erroneous belief is likely to find its way into international trade policy.

If one person's erroneous belief adversely affects only him, that is one thing. But it is quite another thing, Caplan argues, when the erroneous beliefs of many people adversely affect those who do not hold that belief. Yet this is what we often get in a representative democracy. Economically erroneous beliefs, chosen on an individual level because they are cheap to choose, often add up to democracies' choosing bad economic policies.

---

1. See Bryan Caplan's book, *The Myth of the Rational Voter: Why Democracies Choose Bad Policies* (Princeton, NJ: Princeton University Press, 2007).
2. See "The Myth of the Rational Voter," in *Cato Unbound*, November 6, 2006, at http://www.cato-unbound.org/2006/11/06/bryan-caplan/the-myth-of-the-rational-voter/ http://www.cato-unbound.org/2006/11/06/bryan-caplan/the-myth-of-the-rational-voter/

(Answers to Self-Test questions are in Answers to Self-Test Questions at the back of the book.)

1. If a politician running for office does not speak in general terms, does not try to move to the middle of the political spectrum, and does not take polls, is the median voter model therefore wrong?

2. Voters often criticize politicians running for office who do not speak in specific terms (that is, do not specify which spending programs will be cut, whose taxes will be raised, etc.). If voters want politicians running for office to speak in specific terms, why don't politicians do so?

3. Would bad weather be something that could affect the voter turnout? Explain your answer.

MORE ABOUT VOTING

Voting is often the method used to make decisions in the public sector. In this section, we discuss two examples to describe some of the effects (some might say problems) of voting as a decision-making method.

Example 1: Voting for a Nonexcludable Public Good

Suppose a community of 7 persons, A–G, wants to produce or purchase nonexcludable public good X. Each person in the community wants a different number of units of X, as shown in the following table:

Person	Number of Units of X Desired
A	1
B	2
C	3
D	4
E	5
F	6
G	7

   If the community of 7 persons holds a simple majority vote, then all 7 will vote to produce or purchase at least 1 unit of X. Six people (B–G) will vote for at least 2 units; five people (C–G), for at least 3 units; four people (D–G), for at least 4 units; three people (E–G), for at least 5 units; and two people (F–G), for at least 6 units. Only one person (G) will vote for 7 units.

   The largest number of units that receives a simple majority vote (half the total number of voters plus 1, or 4 votes) is 4 units. In other words, the community will vote to produce or purchase 4 units of X. Interestingly, 4 units is the most preferred outcome of only one of the seven members of the community, person D, who is the median voter. Half the voters (A, B, and C) prefer fewer than 4 units, and half the voters (E, F, and G) prefer more. Thus, our voting process has resulted in only the median voter obtaining his most preferred outcome.

   The outcome would have been the same even if the numbers had looked as they do in the following table:

Person	Number of Units of X Desired
A	0
B	0
C	0
D	4
E	7
F	7
G	7

In this case, four people (D–G) would have voted for at least 4 units, and only three people would have voted for anything less than 4 units. Again, 4 units would have been the outcome of the vote, and only the median voter would have obtained his most preferred outcome.

Example 2: Voting and Efficiency

Suppose three individuals have the marginal private benefits (*MPB*) shown in the following table for various units of nonexcludable public good Y:

Person	MPB of First Unit of Y	MPB of Second Unit of Y	MPB of Third Unit of Y
A	$400	$380	$190
B	150	110	90
C	100	90	80

If the cost of providing a unit of good Y is $360, what is the socially optimal, or efficient, amount of good Y? To answer this question, recall a few of the relationships from the last chapter:

1. The socially optimal, or efficient, amount of anything is the amount at which the marginal social benefits (*MSB*) equal the marginal social costs (*MSC*).

2. The sum of the marginal private benefits (*MPB*) and the marginal external benefits (*MEB*) equals the marginal social benefits (*MSB*): $MPB + MEB = MSB$.

3. The sum of the marginal private costs (*MPC*) and the marginal external costs (*MEC*) equals the marginal social costs (*MSC*): $MPC + MEC = MSC$.

In our example, the *MSC* for each unit is given as $360. We calculate the *MSB* for each unit by summing its *MPB*. For the first unit, the *MSB* is $650 ($400 + $150 + $100); for the second unit, it is $580; and for the third unit, it is $360. The socially optimal, or efficient, amount of good Y is 3 units because at this amount $MSB = MSC$.

Whether voting will give us efficiency largely depends on what tax each person, A–C, expects to pay. Suppose each person must pay an equal share of the price of a unit of good Y. In other words, the tax for each person is $120 ($360 per unit ÷ 3 persons = $120 per person per unit).

Person A will vote for 3 units because his *MPB* for each unit is greater than his tax of $120 per unit. Person B will vote for only 1 unit because his *MPB* for the first unit is greater than his tax of $120 per unit, but his *MPB* is not greater for the second or third unit. Person C will not vote for any units because his *MPB* for each unit is less than his tax of $120 per unit. The outcome, using a simple majority vote, is only 1 unit. A process of voting in which each voter pays an equal tax results in an inefficient outcome.

Now suppose, instead of paying an equal tax (of $120), each person pays a tax equal to his *MPB* at the socially optimal, or efficient, outcome. The socially optimal, or efficient, outcome is 3 units of good Y. So person A would pay a tax of $190 (his *MPB* for the third unit is $190). Person B would pay a tax of $90, and person C would pay a tax of $80. (The sum of the taxes paid is equal to the cost of the unit, or $360.)

With this different tax structure, will voting generate efficiency? If each person casts a truthful vote, the answer is yes. Each person will vote for 3 units.[3] In other words, if every-

---

3. Look at the situation for person A: His *MPB* for the first unit is $400 and his tax is $190; so he votes for the first unit. His *MPB* for the second unit is $380 and his tax is $190; so he votes for the second unit. His *MPB* for the third unit is $190 and his tax is $190; so he votes for the third unit. With respect to the last unit for person A, we are assuming that if his *MPB* is equal to the tax, he will vote in favor of the unit. The same holds for the analysis of voting for persons B and C.

one casts a truthful vote and everyone pays a tax equal to his or her *MPB* at the efficient outcome, then voting will generate efficiency.

Comparing the two tax structures—one where each person pays an equal tax and one where each person pays a tax equal to his *MPB*—we see that the tax structure makes the difference. In the case of equal tax shares, voting did not lead to efficiency; in the case of unequal tax shares, it did.

1. If the *MSC* in Example 2 had been $580 instead of $360, what would the socially optimal, or efficient, outcome have been?

2. In Example 2 with equal taxes, did the outcome of the vote make anyone worse off? If so, who and by how much?

SPECIAL INTEREST GROUPS

Special interest groups are subsets of the general population that hold (usually) intense preferences for or against a particular government service, activity, or policy. Often, special interest groups gain from public policies that may not be in accord with the interests of the general public. In recent decades, they have played a major role in government.

Information and Lobbying Efforts

Whereas the general voter is usually uninformed about issues, members of a special interest group are very well informed. For example, teachers are likely to know a lot about government education policies, farmers about government agriculture policies, and union members about government union policies. When it comes to their issues of interest, the special interest group members know much more than the general voter. The reason is simple: The more directly and intensely issues affect them, the greater the incentive is for individuals to become informed about them.

Given an electorate composed of uninformed general voters and informed members of special interest groups, the groups are often able to sway politicians in their favor. This effect occurs even when the general public is made worse off by such actions (which, of course, is not always the case).

Suppose special interest group A, composed of 5,000 individuals, favors a policy that will result in the redistribution of $50 million from 100 million general taxpayers to the group. The dollar benefit for each member of the special interest group is $10,000. Given this substantial dollar amount, members of the special interest group are likely to (1) sponsor or propose the legislation and (2) lobby the politicians who will decide the issue.

Further, the politicians will probably not hear from the general voter (i.e., general taxpayer). The general voter/taxpayer will be less informed about the legislation than the members of the special interest group, and, even if adequately informed, each person would have to calculate the benefits and the costs of lobbying against the proposed legislation. If the legislation passes, the average taxpayer will pay approximately 50¢, and the benefits of lobbying against the legislation are probably not greater than 50¢. Therefore, even if informed about the legislation, the general taxpayer would not be likely to argue against it. The benefits just wouldn't be worth the time and effort. Special interest bills therefore have a good chance of being passed in our legislatures.

Congressional Districts as Special Interest Groups

Most people do not ordinarily think of congressional districts as special interest groups. Special interest groups are commonly thought to include the ranks of public school

Special Interest Groups
Subsets of the general population that hold (usually) intense preferences for or against a particular government service, activity, or policy and that often gain from public policies that may not be in accord with the interests of the general public.

teachers, steel manufacturers, automobile manufacturers, farmers, environmentalists, bankers, truck drivers, doctors, and the like. For some issues, however, a congressional district may be a special interest group.

Suppose an air force base is located in a Texas congressional district. Then a Pentagon study determines that the base is not needed and that Congress should shut it down. The Pentagon study demonstrates that the cost to the taxpayers of keeping the base open is greater than the benefits to the country of maintaining it. But closing the air force base will hurt the pocketbooks of the people in the congressional district housing the base. Their congressional representative knows not only as much, but also that if she can't keep the base open, she isn't as likely to be reelected to office.

Therefore, she speaks to other members of Congress about the proposed closing. In a way, she acts as a lobbyist for her congressional district. Most members of Congress are probably willing to go along with the Texas representative, even though they know that their constituents will be paying more in taxes than, according to the Pentagon, is necessary to assure the national security of the country. If they don't go along with her, when they need a vote on one of their own special interest projects (sometimes the term "pork barrel" is used), the representative from Texas may not be so cooperative. In short, members of Congress sometimes trade votes: my vote on your air force base for your vote on subsidies to dairy farmers in my district. This type of vote trading—the exchange of votes to gain support for legislation—is commonly referred to as logrolling.

Logrolling
The exchange of votes to gain support for legislation.

Public Interest Talk, Special Interest Legislation

Special interest groups lobbying for special interest legislation usually don't use that phrase, but rather something like "legislation in the best interest of the general public." A couple of examples, both past and present, come to mind.

In the early nineteenth century, the British Parliament passed the Factory Acts, which put restrictions on women and children working. Those who lobbied for the restrictions said they did so for humanitarian reasons, that is, to protect young children and women from difficult and hazardous work in the cotton mills. There is evidence, however, that the men working in the factories were the main lobbyists for the Factory Acts and that a reduced supply of women and children directly benefited them by raising their wages. The male factory workers appealed to individuals' higher sensibilities instead of letting it be known that they would benefit at the expense of others.

Today, people calling for, say, economic protection from foreign competitors or greater federal subsidies rarely explain that they favor the measure because the legislation will make them better off while someone else pays the bill. Instead, they usually voice the public interest argument. Economic protectionism isn't necessary to protect industry X, but it is necessary to protect American jobs and the domestic economy. The special interest message often is, "Help yourself by helping us."

Sometimes this message is sincere, but other times it is not. In either case, it is likely to be as forcefully voiced.

Rent Seeking

Rent Seeking
Actions of individuals and groups who spend resources to influence public policy in the hope of redistributing (transferring) income to themselves from others.

Rent seeking consists of the actions of individuals and groups who spend resources to influence public policy in the hope of redistributing (transferring) income to themselves from others. To illustrate, suppose Smith is one of many producers of shoes and that he realizes he would be better off if he were the only one who produces shoes. With less competition from other shoe producers, the supply of shoes would fall, and the price would rise. Smith then would end up selling shoes at $100 a pair instead of $30 a pair.

Smith hires a law firm that specializes in lobbying government for its clients. Members of the law firm go to members of Congress and ask them to pass a law prohibiting all companies other than the Smith Shoe Company from producing shoes. The attorneys representing Smith promise to donate money to the political campaigns of the Congressional members with whom they speak. They also promise that Smith of Smith Shoe Company will try to persuade his workers that their work interests are best served by voting for specific members of Congress.

Smith is using resources to effect a transfer. Smith has spent money to influence Congress to give him a special privilege; specifically, he is asking for the right to be the only producer of shoes. Essentially, Smith is trying to bring about a transfer from shoe consumers to himself. He wants consumers to end up paying more for shoes so that he earns more from producing them. He is spending money to try to bring about this transfer from others to him. Smith is a *rent seeker*. Specifically, he is using resources (the money he spends goes for resources) in order to bring about a transfer from others to him.

Let's say that Smith spends a total of $100,000 to bring about the transfer. This is the cost of his rent seeking. From Smith's perspective, the decision to spend $100,000 to bring about a transfer, of, say $1 million is rational. But from society's perspective, all the resources that Smith uses to effect a transfer are wasted. The $100,000 is wasted because money spent trying to effect a transfer cannot be used to produce goods and services.

To see the negative effects rent-seeking has on society even more clearly, consider an extreme example. Let's say that today 1,000 individuals are all producing goods and services. Together they produce about $2 million worth of output a day. Tomorrow, all 1,000 individuals decide to spend their time and money trying to bring about a transfer. In other words, instead of producing, they spend their time rent seeking. At the end of the day, the cost to society of these 1,000 individuals' rent seeking instead of producing is obviously $2 million worth of output. Society is poorer by $2 million because the 1,000 individuals turned away from producing and toward rent seeking. In short, rent seeking is a socially wasteful activity.

Bringing About Transfers

In Exhibit 3, the market equilibrium price of the good is P_1. At this price, identifying both consumers' surplus and producers' surplus is easy. Consumers' surplus is the area under the demand curve and above the equilibrium price out to the equilibrium quantity, Q_1: areas $A + B + C$. Producers' surplus is the area under the equilibrium price and above the supply curve out to the equilibrium quantity, Q_1: $D + E$.

Now suppose the producers of the good lobby government for a price floor, P_2. If government grants this price floor, then the new price in the market is P_2 and consumers' surplus ends up being only area A. Consumers lose areas $B + C$ in consumers' surplus. At the new price of P_2, producers lose area E in

EXHIBIT 3

A Price Floor and a Transfer from Consumers to Producers

Market equilibrium price of the good is P_1. Consumers' surplus is the area $A + B + C$. Producers' surplus is the area $D + E$. If producers of the good lobby for and receive a price floor of P_2, then consumers' surplus ends up being only area A. Consumers lose areas $B + C$ in consumers' surplus, and producers gain area B in producers' surplus. By obtaining the price floor through government, producers of the good were able to take some consumers' surplus away from consumers and turn it into producers' surplus for themselves.

producers' surplus, and they gain area *B*. As long as area *E* (what they lose) is smaller than area *B* (what they gain), producers are better off selling at price P_2 than P_1. In Exhibit 3, area *E* is clearly smaller than *B*; so producers are better off.

The price floor has thus created a transfer. Area *B*, which was once consumers' surplus, is now producers' surplus. By getting the price floor, the producers of the good were able to take some consumers' surplus away from consumers and turn it into producers' surplus. If area *B* is equivalent to, say, $1,000, then producers have been able to transfer $1,000 from consumers to themselves. All the resources that the producers expended to get that transfer of $1,000 are referred to as the *rent seeking costs*, that is, the costs of trying to bring about the transfer. Again, from society's perspective, the resources expended to effect the transfer are wasted in that they cannot be used to produce goods and services. Society as a whole is a just a little bit poorer because of the rent seeking behavior of the producers.

Information, Rational Ignorance, and Seeking Transfers

Will rent seekers tell the truth about their rent seeking efforts (assuming they know the truth). Suppose Smith knows that his rent seeking will lead to greater producers' surplus for him and less consumers' surplus and that the losses to consumers will be greater than his gains. (If you look back at Exhibit 3, you will notice that the losses to consumers from the price floor—areas *B* + *C*—are greater than the gain of area B to the producer.) Will he advertise this information? Will he, for instance, lobby government by saying: "I would like a price floor for what I sell. I know that this will end up hurting consumers more than it benefits me, but so be it. As long as I am made better off, I don't really care how much consumers are made worse off. Can I have the transfer?"

He is unlikely to say this. For one thing, making such a barefaced request draws attention to the facts that he gains at consumers' expense and that his gain is smaller than what consumers lose. Smith wouldn't draw attention to this fact. Instead, he might try to argue that what is good for him is good (not bad) for others.

Can such rent-seeking efforts be successful? Won't the politicians turn Smith down because moving from an equilibrium price to a price floor hurts consumers more than it helps producers? (Yet there are price floors in the real world.) Won't the consumers rally against Smith because they know they are being hurt by his actions? And aren't the consumers greater in number than Smith (who is only one), and don't politicians care about votes (which means they must then care about the number of voters)?

First, consumers may not rally against Smith because they may not even know that he is lobbying government for a price floor. Recall the issue of rational ignorance, that is, not acquiring information because the costs of acquiring it are greater than the benefits.

Most individuals are rationally ignorant of many issues. If you know less about French literature than you could possibly know, then you are rationally ignorant of the subject. If you know less about computers than you could possibly know, then you are rationally ignorant of computers.

Similarly, many people are rationally ignorant of politics and government; that is, they know less than they could know largely because the marginal benefits of acquiring this kind of information are so low. And the benefits are low because an individual's one vote matters so little in the determination of an election, as we discussed earlier. In other words, the probability that your one vote will break a tie and decide who wins and who loses in an election—especially when millions of people are eligible to vote—is infinitesimally small.

So, if your vote is not going to determine an election outcome, what does it matter how much or how little information you have about the candidates, the issues, and events?

The answer to that question is perhaps best framed in terms of your options. Let's say two major candidates, A and B, are running for U.S. Senator from your state. You have the following options:

- *Option 1:* Be fully informed (on the Senate election issues) and vote for A.
- *Option 2:* Be fully informed and vote for B.
- *Option 3:* Be rationally ignorant and vote for A.
- *Option 4:* Be rationally ignorant and vote for B.
- *Option 5:* Be fully informed and not vote.
- *Option 6:* Be rationally ignorant and not vote.

No matter which option you choose, the outcome of the election will be what it will be. Your vote will likely not break a tie; your vote will not determine the election outcome. Therefore, the least-cost option is obviously option 6, to be rationally ignorant and not vote.

Of course, not everyone chooses this option. In the last presidential election, approximately 130 million persons voted, although millions of other eligible voters chose not to vote. Of the approximately 130 million who did vote, probably very many were rationally ignorant. Being otherwise would have been just too costly for them, especially given the fact that very few of them were under the delusion that their single vote would determine the election outcome.

Given that fact, if producers seek a transfer that ends up hurting consumers, consumers are not likely to know about it if they are rationally ignorant, and the incentive for them to be rationally ignorant is huge. So, when the producer lobbies the members of Congress for a price floor that helps him and hurts consumers, the consumers may not even know about the rent seeking. And even if they do, do they also know that a price floor leads to a greater loss in consumers' surplus than an increase in producers' surplus, especially when the producer has an incentive not to state the details of the transfer? Instead, the producer will probably wrap his special interest legislation in "public interest talk." Perhaps he will argue that without a price floor for his good, few producers will produce it, and that if few producers produce the good, people will lose their jobs, communities will lose tax revenue, and so forth. None of this has to be true, of course, but trying to figure out whether it might be true may be too costly an effort for most individuals to undertake.

On the other hand, let's say that rational ignorance does not exist. Everyone knows everything about everything. So, when the producer lobbies government for a price floor, the consumers immediately know about his activities; furthermore, they know that the loss of consumers' surplus (as a result of the price floor) will be greater than the gain in producers' surplus. Even so, consumers may still not fight the producers because, simply put, the loss to each individual consumer might be so small that it is not worth fighting to stop the price floor.

As an example, suppose 100 producers will benefit a total of $10 million if the price floor replaces the equilibrium price in the market. That is an average of $100,000 per producer. But suppose consumers will lose $15 million as a result of the price floor. If there are 100 million consumers, the average consumer loses only 15¢. A consumer will probably not spend $1 to fight a policy that costs him or her only 15¢.

The key in seeking transfers is to spread the loss from the transfer over as many people as possible so that on a per-person basis the loss is very small. The loss should be small enough that the individual will have little reason to argue against the policy that inflicts the loss.

Inheritance, Heirs, and Why the Firstborn Became King or Queen

Some economists have said that rent seeking often goes on within families, especially when an inheritance is involved. We present their argument in the form of a short story.

An elderly widow with three children has an estate worth $10 million, which she will leave to her children upon her death. But, of course, $10 million can be left to three adult children in a number of ways.

- She can split the $10 million into three equal parts, leaving $3.333 million to each.
- She can divide the $10 million unequally, perhaps leaving $9 million to A, $500,000 to B, and $500,000 to C.
- She can either tell each child how much he or she will inherit, or she can keep the dollar amount secret (until after her death).

©YALE CENTER FOR BRITISH ART, PAUL MELLON COLLECTION, USA/THE BRIDGEMAN ART LIBRARY

In other words, the elderly woman has two major decisions to make: how much money she will give each child and whether to tell them what they will receive upon her death.

If the woman is the type of person who craves attention and wants her children to fawn over her, she can use her inheritance to get them to do that. All she has to do is tell her children (1) that she will not divide her estate equally among the three of them and (2) that she hasn't yet decided on the amount each will receive. If she promises unequal inheritances that are yet to be determined, she almost guarantees that her children will engage in a rent-seeking battle for the bulk of her inheritance. The resultant battle is likely to take the form of each child fawning over the mother to curry favor.

The siblings know that the amount of the inheritance is fixed at $10 million and that whatever goes to one sibling will not go to the others. For example, if $3 million goes to sibling B or C, then A gets $3 million less. The widow has effectively put her three children in a situation in which they will invest resources (fawn over her) to effect a pure transfer. This is rent seeking.

The situation is different if the woman tells her children what she plans to leave each and then guarantees that under no circumstances will she change her mind. For example, she tells child A that he will receive $2 million, child B that she will receive $7 million, and child C that he will receive $1 million. The siblings now have no reason to invest resources in rent seeking. The $10 million has already been split up.

Alternatively, the mother can tell her children that she plans to divide her inheritance equally and nothing on earth can get her to do differently. Once again, if the children know how things are guaranteed to turn out and that any resources they use to change the results will be wasted, they will decide against trying to change the outcome. In other words, no child will seek rent.

Rent seeking used to be common in a slightly different context. In the days when kings and queens ruled, the royal firstborn usually inherited the throne. But why the first child? The third child could be a more capable king or queen than the first. Surely not every firstborn was more capable of being king or queen than every second, third, or fourth child.

If the firstborn were not predetermined to inherit the throne, the royal children would have engaged in a rent-seeking battle for it. In and of itself, the queen or king may not have had anything against this outcome, and, in fact, they may have liked it.

But they might not have liked it if their children engaged in such an intense rent-seeking battle that they tried to kill each other. If you were one of the siblings, you could get to the throne in two ways: (1) have the queen or king choose you as heir from among all your brothers and sisters; (2) kill your brothers and sisters so that you were the only one left. One way to cut down on the bloodshed was to simply have a rule stating that the firstborn would become king or queen. This rule didn't eliminate sibling murders completely—the second child might try to kill the first and therefore inherit the throne—but it certainly kept the number of sibling murders lower than what it might have been if any of the children could ascend to the throne.

1. The average farmer is likely to be better informed about federal agricultural policy than the average food consumer is. Why?

2. Consider special interest legislation that will transfer $40 million from group A to group B, where group B includes 10,000 persons. Is this special interest legislation more likely to pass when group A includes (a) 10,000 persons or (b) 10 million persons? Explain your answer.

3. Give an example of public interest talk spoken by a special interest group.

4. Why is rent-seeking activity socially wasteful?

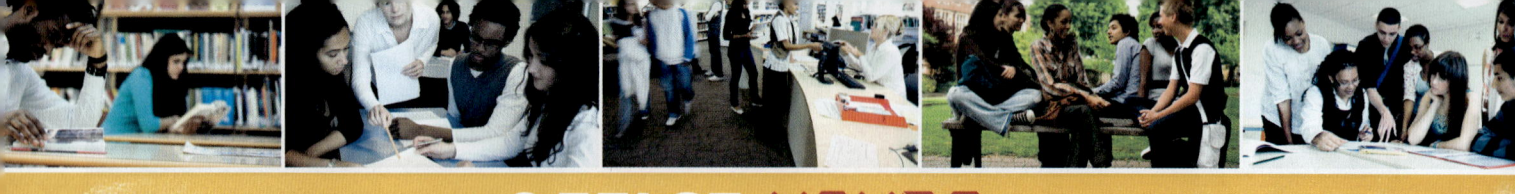

OFFICE HOURS

"Doesn't Public Choice Paint a Bleak Picture of Politics and Government?"

STUDENT:

In a way, public choice paints a rather bleak picture of politics and government.

INSTRUCTOR:

How so?

STUDENT:

Politicians don't seem to care about what is right or wrong. They just move to the middle of the voter distribution. People don't always vote because voting is sometimes too costly. People aren't always well informed on issues because accessing the information is too costly. And to top it off, special interests are engaged in rent seeking. Doesn't all this sound dismal to you?

INSTRUCTOR:

It sounds as if you want things to work differently. Unfortunately, we don't always get the results we want.

STUDENT:

I have to confess that I do. I want politicians to do the right thing, and I want people to be informed on issues and to cast intelligent votes.

INSTRUCTOR:

Probably many people want the same thing. My guess is that public choice economists want the same thing. But we can't let what we want color how we see the world.

STUDENT:

But who is to say that public choice economists analyze the world the right way? Maybe they are an overly cynical bunch of economists.

INSTRUCTOR:

What they are doesn't matter. What matters is what they say and what they predict. We don't judge an economic theory by how it sounds to us or by how we feel about it; we judge it by how well it explains and predicts what we see in the world.

CHAPTER SUMMARY

POLITICIANS AND THE MIDDLE: THE MEDIAN VOTER MODEL

- In a two-person race, candidates for the same office will gravitate toward the middle of the political spectrum to pick up votes. If a candidate does not do so and her opponent does, the opponent will win the election.
- Candidates do a number of things during campaigns that indicate they understand where they are headed—toward the middle. For example, candidates attempt to label their opponents as too far either right or left.
- Candidates usually pick labels for themselves that represent the middle of the political spectrum, they speak in general terms, and they take polls and adjust their positions accordingly.

VOTING AND RATIONAL IGNORANCE

- Voting has both costs and benefits. Many potential voters will not vote because the costs of voting—in terms of time spent going to the polls and so on—outweigh the benefits of voting, measured as the probability of their single vote determining the election outcome.
- Being unable to learn certain information is different from choosing not to learn it. Most voters choose not to be informed about political and government issues because the costs of becoming informed outweigh the benefits of becoming informed. They choose to be rationally ignorant.

If politicians move to the center of the voter distribution, if people are rationally ignorant, and if special interests sometimes engage in rent seeking, then that's the way things are whether we like it or not.

STUDENT:

But aren't economists supposed to be trying to make the world better?

INSTRUCTOR:

Let's assume that they are. Then isn't a good understanding of the world critical to doing this? For example, if the world is X, and I think it is Y, then I might make mistakes when I try to make the world a better place. Basing what I do on how things are has to be better than basing them on how I might want them to be.

STUDENT:

I can see your point. It's sort of like a doctor who wants to know your true condition before she prescribes any therapy. She may not like the fact that you have a particular disease, but it's important that she know about it so that she can prescribe the right medicine.

INSTRUCTOR:

I think that captures the spirit of what I'm talking about.

STUDENT:

Does it follow, then, that everything in public choice theory is right?

INSTRUCTOR:

No, it doesn't follow. Public choice theory—just like any theory in economics—has to be judged on how well it explains and predicts.

POINTS TO REMEMBER

1. Theories should be judged on how well they explain and predict (not how how they sound or feel).
2. Good economics seeks to know what exists, no matter how pleasant or unpleasant that is.

MORE ABOUT VOTING

- In a simple majority vote, given several options to choose from, the voting outcome is the same as the most preferred outcome of the median voter.
- Simple majority voting and equal tax shares can generate a different result from simple majority voting and unequal tax shares.

SPECIAL INTEREST GROUPS

- Special interest groups are usually well informed about their issues. Individuals have a greater incentive to become informed about issues that directly and intensely affect them.

- Legislation that concentrates the benefits on a few and disperses the costs over many is likely to pass because the beneficiaries will have an incentive to lobby for it, whereas those who pay the bill will not lobby against it because each of them pays such a small part of the bill.
- Special interest groups often engage in rent seeking, which is the expenditure of scarce resources to capture a pure transfer. Rent seeking is a socially wasteful activity because the resources used to effect transfers are not used to produce goods and services.

Public Choice

Median Voter Model

Rational Ignorance

Special Interest Groups

Logrolling

Rent Seeking

QUESTIONS AND PROBLEMS

1. Many individuals learn more about the car they are thinking of buying than about the candidates running for president of the United States. Explain why.

2. Would voters have a greater incentive to vote in an election involving only a few registered voters or in one that has many? Why? Why might a Republican label her opponent too far left and a Democrat label his opponent too far right?

3. If the model of politics and government presented in this chapter is true, what are some of the things we would expect to see?

4. The economist James Buchanan said, "If men should cease and desist from their talk about and their search for evil men and commence to look instead at the institutions manned by ordinary people, wide avenues for genuine social reform might appear." What did he mean?

5. It has often been said that Democrat candidates are more liberal in Democrat primaries and Republican candidates are more conservative in Republican primaries than either is in the general election, respectively. Explain why.

6. Some observers maintain that not all politicians move toward the middle of the political spectrum to obtain votes. They often cite Barry Goldwater in the 1964 presidential election and George McGovern in the 1972 presidential election as examples. Goldwater was viewed as occupying the right end of the political spectrum and McGovern the left end. Would this necessarily be evidence that does not support the median voter model? Are the exceptions to the theory explained in this chapter?

7. "Rent seeking may be rational from the individual's perspective, but it is not rational from society's perspective." Do you agree or disagree? Explain your answer.

8. John chooses not to vote in the presidential election. Does it follow that he is apathetic when it comes to presidential politics? Explain your answer.

9. Evaluate each of the following proposals for reform in terms of the material discussed in this chapter:

   a. Linking all spending programs to visible tax hikes

   b. A balanced budget amendment stipulating that Congress cannot spend more than total tax revenues

   c. A budgetary referenda process whereby the voters actually vote on the distribution of federal dollars to the different categories of spending (x percentage to agriculture, y percentage to national defense, etc.) instead of letting elected representatives decide.

10. Provide a numerical example that shows simple majority voting may be consistent with efficiency. Next, provide a numerical example that shows simple majority voting may be inconsistent with efficiency.

11. Some individuals see national defense spending as benefiting special interests—in particular, the defense industry. Others see it as directly benefiting not only the defense industry but the general public as well. Does this same difference between viewpoints apply to issues other than national defense? Name a few.

12. What are some ways of reducing the cost of voting to voters?

WORKING WITH NUMBERS AND GRAPHS

1. Suppose that three major candidates, A, B, and C, are running for president of the United States and that the distribution of voters is the same as shown in Exhibit 1. Two of the candidates, A and B, are currently viewed as right of the median, and C is viewed as left of the median. Is it possible to predict which candidate is the most likely to win?

2. Look back at Exhibit 2. Suppose that the net benefits and net costs for each person are known a week before election day and that it is legal to buy and sell votes. Furthermore, suppose that either buying or selling votes has no conscience cost. Would the outcome of the election be the same? Explain your answer.

3. In part (a) of the following figure, the distribution of voters is skewed to the left; in part (b), the distribution is skewed neither left nor right; and in part (c), it is skewed right. Assuming a two-person race for each distribution, will the candidate who wins the election in (a) hold different positions from the candidates who win the elections in (b) and (c)? Explain your answer.

(a)

(b)

(c)

CHAPTER 33

© KEITH MORRIS / ALAMY

THE ECONOMIC CASE FOR AND AGAINST GOVERNMENT: FIVE TOPICS CONSIDERED

Introduction Most of this book has been about economics, with government mentioned here and there in our discussions. This chapter presents some of the things that economists have to say about government, especially with respect to the role and effects of government in markets and in the economy.

ECONOMICS AND GOVERNMENT

Studying economics is difficult without hearing about government. Think back over what you have read in this textbook so far and count the number of times government was mentioned. Government came up in relation to minimum wage legislation, price floors, antitrust, monopoly, medical care, the distribution of income, poverty, regulation, natural monopoly, externalities, nonexcludable public goods, taxes, and other issues.

Not all economists agree on government's role in and effects on markets. For example, some economists believe government should play a big role in markets, others think it should play a small role, and still others believe it should play almost no role at all. In short, all economists might agree that market demand curves slope downward, but not all economists agree on the role of government in markets.

This chapter does not purport to identify all the intellectual differences among economists when they talk about government and markets. Its objective is much simpler and straightforward: to present you with some of what you will hear economists say when they are arguing the case for and against government. Specifically, it discusses five topics: (1) prisoner's dilemma settings, (2) externalities, (3) nonexcludable public goods, (4) the unintended effects of government actions, and (5) special interest groups and transfers. The first three are usually discussed in the context of the case *for* government; the last two are usually discussed in the context of the economic case *against* government.

THE ECONOMIC CASE FOR GOVERNMENT

Suppose that a society is comprised of 10 individuals and that all 10 individuals want X, which is a particular good or outcome. Together, these individuals work to get X, but no matter what they do, they cannot get it. The individuals are inept at bringing about X.

At the snap of our fingers, government appears with the ability to punish people if they do not follow certain laws and with the power to tax. This government now uses its powers to bring about X. Are the 10 individuals better off (1) with government and X than they were (2) without government and without X? Under certain conditions, the answer is yes.

This, in a nutshell, is part of the case for government. Government's raison d'être is that it can give individuals what they want when they don't seem capable of getting it on their own (i.e., without government). This theme plays out in three cases:

- Removal from the prisoner's dilemma
- Externalities
- Nonexcludable public goods

Government Can Remove Individuals from a Prisoner's Dilemma Setting

In this section we discuss how government can take individuals out of the prisoner's dilemma.

PRODUCING AND STEALING Consider two individuals, Jack and Jill, who live alone on an island. Both Jack and Jill can engage in two activities: each can produce some good, and each can steal from the other. In other words, both Jack and Jill are capable of being producers and thieves.

How much time each will devote to producing and stealing depends on the ratio of marginal benefits to marginal cost of each activity: Both producing and stealing come with benefits and costs. Suppose the marginal benefits and costs (expressed in dollars) of producing are currently as follows:

$$MB \text{ of producing} = \$40$$
$$MC \text{ of producing} = \$10$$

The MB/MC ratio for producing is therefore 4 ($40 ÷ $10 = 4). Now suppose the marginal benefits and costs of stealing are (again in dollars):

$$MB \text{ of stealing} = \$30$$
$$MC \text{ of stealing} = \$10$$

The MB/MC ratio of stealing is 3. Using these dollar amounts, the payoff from producing is currently higher than the payoff from stealing. For every $1 of cost devoted to producing, the return is $4, whereas, for every $1 of cost devoted to stealing, the return is $3. Faced with these payoffs, devoting the next hour to producing is better than devoting it to stealing.

Now suppose producing comes with declining marginal benefits; that is, as one produces more, the marginal benefits decline. Specifically, the marginal benefits of producing might decline from, say, $40 to $35, as someone spends an additional hour producing. So, a point will come when the MB/MC ratios for the two activities (producing and stealing) are the same.

$$\frac{MB}{MC} \text{ ratio for producing } = \frac{MB}{MC} \text{ ratio for stealing}$$

This is an equilibrium condition at which the individual has maximized utility. For Jack, this might come when he spends 7 hours a day producing and 1 hour stealing. For Jill, it might come when she spends 6 hours a day producing and 2 hours stealing.

BOTH JACK AND JILL REALIZE AN IMPORTANT POINT A day comes when both Jack and Jill realize that they would be better off if both of them stopped stealing: With no stealing, all of one's resources can go into production. But as long as stealing continues, some of one's resources will go for protection (protecting what one has produced from being stolen by the other). In terms of numbers, suppose 10 units of resources can be used for production, protection, or some combination of the two. When no one steals, all the resources can be used to produce goods. But when individuals steal, some of the 10 resource units must be used for protection against theft; so fewer than 10 units will be used to produce goods.

Realizing this very important point, Jack and Jill meet one day to discuss their situation. Both realize they would be better off if neither steals from the other. Seeing where their best interests lie, they agree not to steal from each other. In other words, they agree to a set of property rights that specifies what each produces is his or hers alone.

But the problem of theft is solved only if both Jack and Jill, having agreed not to steal, abide by their agreement. If Jack and Jill are in a prisoner's dilemma setting, their agreement to not steal is likely soon to be broken. Look at Exhibit 1, which shows the two options that each individual holds once he or she has entered into the agreement not to steal from the other. Each person can either (1) hold to the agreement or (2) break it. Holding to the agreement means that the person *does not steal* from the other, and breaking the agreement means that the person *does steal* from the other.

EXHIBIT 1

To Hold to the Agreement (Not to Steal) or to Break the Agreement

Each of two persons, Jack and Jill, has two options: (1) to hold to the agreement not to steal; (2) to break the agreement. Starting in box 4, both persons have chosen to break the agreement and to steal from the other. Jack and Jill realize that box 1 is better for each of them than box 4. Thus, they enter into an agreement not to steal so that they can reach box 1. But once in box 1, each person prefers a superior box. Box 2 is superior for Jack, and Box 3 is superior for Jill. Jack realizes that, no matter what Jill does, he is always better off breaking the agreement than holding to it. Jill realizes that, no matter what Jack does, she is always better off breaking the agreement than holding to it. The result is that both Jack and Jill choose to break the agreement, and thus both end up in box 4. Jack and Jill are in a prisoner's dilemma setting.

The numbers represent the various outcomes for each person, given his or her actions and the other person's actions. The higher the number is, the better off the person will be. For example, if both Jack and Jill break the agreement, the outcome is shown in box 4, with Jack receiving an 8 and Jill receiving an 8. If both hold to the agreement, the outcome is shown in box 1, where each person receives a 10. Jack and Jill entered into an agreement in the first place to make themselves better off; they instinctively knew that they were in box 4 (where each stole from the other) and that they could both be made better off if they agreed not to steal (thus moving from box 4 to box 1).

The problem is that once Jack and Jill move from box 4 to 1, a superior box exists for each. Box 2 is better than box 1 for Jack. He receives a 12 in box 2 and only a 10 in box 1. Box 3 is better Jill. She receives a 12 in box 3 and only a 10 in box 1. Will Jack and Jill be able to hold to the agreement or break it?

Jack realizes that if Jill holds to the agreement, he has two options: He can hold to the agreement and end up in box 1 with a 10, or he can break the agreement and end up in box 2 with a 12. His choice is to break the agreement.

But if Jack thinks Jill will break the agreement, what, then, is his best course of action? He realizes he can hold to the agreement and end up in box 3, receiving a 6, or break the agreement and end up in box 4, receiving an 8. His choice is to break the agreement.

So, no matter which option Jack thinks Jill will take (hold to the agreement or break the agreement), breaking the agreement is always better than holding to it.

The same logic holds for Jill. No matter which option Jill thinks Jack will take, breaking the agreement is always better for her.

The outcome, then, will be that both Jack and Jill break the agreement and end up in box 4. In other words, they end up right where they started before they entered into the agreement not to steal from each other. This setting is a prisoner's dilemma setting (as discussed in an earlier chapter).

Government can remove individuals from a prisoner's dilemma setting by changing the payoff matrix. Suppose government magically appears on the island and tells both Jack and Jill that if one steals from the other—that is, if either breaks the agreement not to steal—that person will pay a fine large enough to reduce his or her payoff number by 4. The penalty can be in the form of a monetary fine or imprisonment or both. The presence of government changes the payoff matrix.

In Exhibit 2, 4 is subtracted from the various payoff numbers: 4 is subtracted from 12 in box 2, 4 from 12 in box 3, and 4 from both numbers in box 4. Striking through various numbers in those three boxes shows us how things change for both Jack and Jill if government sets fines for stealing.

EXHIBIT 2

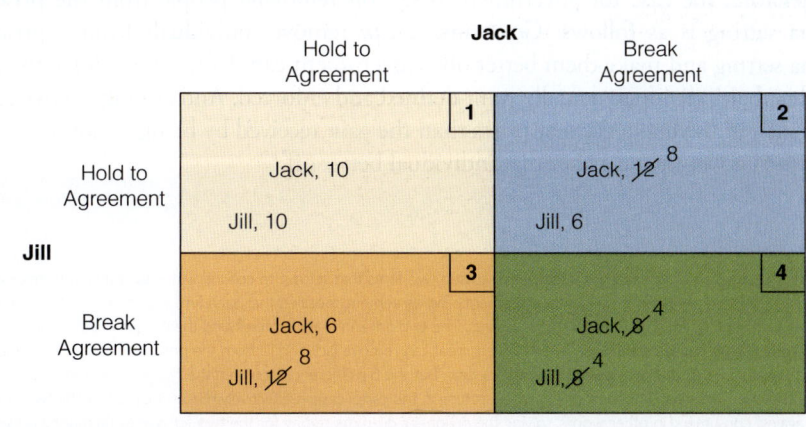

Government Removes Two Persons from a Prisoner's Dilemma Setting

Government changes the payoffs in the matrix by fining each person 4 if he or she breaks the agreement not to steal. As a result, now both Jack and Jill find it best to hold to the agreement. Government removes both Jack and Jill from box 4 in the prisoner's dilemma setting.

With the fine-adjusted payoff numbers in the payoff matrix, what will Jack and Jill decide to do now? If each believes that government will not only apprehend them if they steal and fine them accordingly, then Jack will decide to hold to the agreement and not steal from Jill. The reasoning is easy to see. Let's say Jill holds to the agreement. In that case, if Jack holds to the agreement too, he ends up in box 1 with a 10, but if he breaks the agreement, he ends up in box 2 with an 8. The better course of action is to hold to the agreement and not steal.

But, if Jack believes Jill will break the agreement, it is still better for him to hold to the agreement. If Jill breaks the agreement, then Jack has to decide whether it is better for him to end up in box 3 or 4. In box 3 he receives a 6; in box 4 he receives a 4. Thus, it is better for Jack to hold to the agreement (and not steal) and end up in box 3.

So, with the new payoff matrix shown in Exhibit 2, no matter what Jill chooses to do, Jack is always better off holding to the agreement than breaking it.

Of course, the same holds for Jill. No matter what Jill believes Jack will do (break the agreement or hold to it), it is always better for her to hold to the agreement. As a result of both Jack and Jill holding to the agreement, the outcome is in box 1, where both individuals receive a 10.

Thus government has been able to move both Jack and Jill out of box 4 and into box 1, the result that both Jack and Jill wanted. In short, government has been able to do for both Jack and Jill what they couldn't do—but wanted to do—for themselves. In this case, government effectively defines and enforces the property rights that both Jack and Jill want defined and enforced.

HAS GOVERNMENT MADE BOTH JACK AND JILL BETTER OFF? If government is costless, then government has undoubtedly made both Jack and Jill better off. But government isn't costless. Government needs taxes to support itself, and Jack and Jill have to pay taxes. How much they pay determines whether they are clearly better off with government than without it.

In Exhibit 1, box 4 is the box that both Jack and Jill would prefer *not* to be in. They prefer to be in box 1. The difference between the two boxes for each person is 2. The payoff for Jack and Jill in box 1 is 10, and the payoff for each of them in box 4 is 8—a difference of 2. In other words, Jack and Jill are each better off by 2 when they move from box 4 to box 1.

So, as long as each pays a tax to government that is less than 2, each is better off with government than without it. Although a move from box 4 to box 1 makes both Jack and Jill better off by 2, if each has to pay 1 to enable government do what it does, then the overall increase of moving from box 4 to box 1 is reduced to 1. The gain of 2 minus the tax of 1 equals 1. A tax of 2 would make both Jack and Jill no better or worse off with government than without it. A tax of 3 would make both of them worse off with government.

Therefore, the case for government based on removing people from the prisoner's dilemma setting is as follows: Government *can* remove individuals from a prisoner's dilemma setting and make them better off. Government can define and enforce the property rights that individuals actually want defined and enforced. And as long as government charges each individual a tax that is less than the gain received by being removed from the setting, then government makes that individual better off.[1]

---

1. In an earlier chapter on oligopoly and cartels, we discussed two firms that set out to collude with each other with respect to prices. Specifically, they entered into a cartel agreement. The agreement specified that each firm would raise prices and then not undercut the other firm (i.e., break the agreement). The two firms in that chapter found themselves in a prisoner's dilemma setting, similar to the one just described. Just as government can remove Jack and Jill from the prisoner's dilemma setting, it can remove the two firms from the prisoner's dilemma setting. But the big difference between the two cases is that if government removes the two firms from the prisoner's dilemma setting in the cartel case, it effectively makes it easier for the two firms to collude against consumers. In other words, solving the prisoner's dilemma setting for the two firms ends up making prices higher for consumers. In the case of Jack and Jill, no third party is adversely affected.

CAN GOVERNMENT ABUSE ITS POWERS? If both Jack and Jill opt for government in order to get out of the prisoner's dilemma setting, they automatically turn over certain powers to government. After all, government must have the power to apprehend and punish Jack and Jill if it is to be effective at removing them from the prisoner's dilemma setting. But once government has the power to apprehend and fine (which could constitute imprisonment), in addition to the power to tax, it could abuse those powers. For example, government has the power to make both Jack and Jill worse off or to make one of them better off and the other worse off. To illustrate, suppose government imposes a tax of 3 instead of 1 on each person. With a tax of 1, both Jack and Jill are made better off with government. But with a tax of 3, both are made worse off. The tax of 3 more than offsets the gains they receive from having government move them from box 4 to box 1 in Exhibit 1. Gaining 2 and losing 3 leaves both Jack and Jill with a –1.

Government could, however, tax Jill by 3 and not tax Jack at all. In this case, Jack will clearly benefit from government, but Jill won't. Jack ends up with the full gain of moving from box 4 to box 1 in Exhibit 1 (a gain of 2), but Jill doesn't. She gains 2, but then pays a tax of 3, leaving her with a –1 due to government.

Therefore, government can remove both Jack and Jill from a prisoner's dilemma setting that each wants to be removed from. However, Jack and Jill are not necessarily better off with than without government. Their status depends on what government charges in taxes. Depending on the amount of taxes and on who pays what tax, government can (1) make both persons better off, (2) make both persons worse off, (3) make one person better off and the other person worse off. The strongest case that can be made for government with reference to the prisoner's dilemma setting is that taxes need to be low enough to make both individuals better off with government than without it.

SELF-TEST

(Answers to Self-Test questions are in Answers to Self-Test Questions at the back of the book.)

1. How does a person go about deciding how much time and effort to devote to productive activities as opposed to stealing?

2. Explain why Jack and Jill can't move themselves from box 4 to box 1 in Exhibit 1.

3. "Government always makes parties in a prisoner's dilemma setting better off by removing them from the setting." Do you agree or disagree? Explain your answer.

Externalities

Just as a case can be made for government removing individuals from prisoner's dilemma settings, a case can be made for government with respect to externalities. This case was made in a previous chapter; so we need only to summarize it here.

Essentially, when both marginal external costs (*MEC*) and marginal external benefits (*MEB*) exist, the market—as evidenced by simple supply and demand—generates an inefficient equilibrium outcome. For example, in the case of a negative externality (and no positive externality):

$$MSC > MPC$$

where MSC = marginal social costs and MPC = marginal private costs. Also:

$$MSB = MPB$$

where MSB = marginal social benefits and MPB = marginal private benefits.

Efficiency requires that marginal social benefits (*MSB*) equal marginal social costs (*MSC*): $MSB = MSC$. But in the case of a negative externality (and no positive externality), the market achieves equilibrium where $MPB = MPC$. In other words, the market outcome is inefficient.

Can government change things so that the market outcome becomes the efficient outcome? As explained in a previous chapter, government could apply a tax to the activity that generates the negative externality. If it sets the tax equal to the marginal external cost (*MEC*) that the negative externality generates, then *MPC* plus the tax will be equal to *MSC*, and the market outcome will be the efficient outcome.

The strongest case for government with respect to a negative externality is that it needs to set the tax equal to the marginal external cost: $Tax = MEC$. A tax either greater or less than *MEC* does not achieve efficiency.

The same holds with respect to government and a positive externality, except that with a positive externality the government creates a subsidy instead of imposing a tax. In the case of a positive externality, the strong case for government holds when it sets the subsidy equal to the marginal external benefit (*MEB*) generated by the positive externality: $Subsidy = MEB$.

Therefore, a strong case can be made for government with respect to externalities. Government can use taxes and subsidies to turn an inefficient outcome into an efficient one. But doing so requires that certain conditions be met. Specifically, in the case of the tax and a negative externality, the tax must be equal to the marginal external cost (*MEC*). In the case of the subsidy and a positive externality, the subsidy must be equal to the marginal external benefit (*MEB*).

Nonexcludable Public Goods

A case for government can be made with respect to nonexcludable public goods, which were also discussed in a previous chapter; so, again, we will summarize.

The case for government with respect to nonexcludable public goods is that individuals may want certain goods—nonexcludable public goods—that the market will not produce. The market won't produce these goods because of the free rider problem. To illustrate, if good X is a nonexcludable public good, it is nonrivalrous in consumption (i.e., one person's consumption of the good doesn't take away from another person's consumption of it) and nonexcludable (i.e., excluding people from consuming it is impossible or prohibitively costly). Given nonrivalry and nonexcludability, individuals will choose not to pay for the good if it is produced. Why pay for a good that you cannot be prevented from consuming once it is produced? In short, individuals will choose to become *free riders* in consuming nonexcludable public goods. As a result, no producer will have an incentive to provide the good.

A government with the power to tax can overcome the free rider problem by forcing people to pay for the nonexcludable public good. In other words, government can tax individuals and then use the tax money either to produce the nonexcludable public good or to pay a private party to produce it. This is the case for government: government can overcome the free rider problem and provide individuals with nonexcludable public goods that they want but can't get through the market.

As with both prisoner's dilemma settings and externalities, the case for government with respect to nonexcludable public goods is not without a necessary condition: individuals must actually want the specific nonexcludable public good that government provides.

economics 24/7

Culture as a Public Good

Pizza is a private good, and national defense is a nonexcludable public good. Almost no one argues about pizza, but a lot of people argue about national defense. The difference has to do with the fact that there are all kinds of pizza. No matter what kind of pizza you like, you can buy it. Others don't have to eat the pizza you order if they don't want to. They can order their own.

© IMAGE COPYRIGHT MONKEY BUSINESS IMAGES, 2009. USED UNDER LICENSE FROM SHUTTERSTOCK.COM

But the same doesn't hold for national defense. Once the United States has a particular quality and quantity of national defense, everyone in the United States "consumes" the same national defense—the same "national defense pizza." No wonder people argue over national defense. One size and quality does not fit all.

Given that difference, consider culture. Is culture more like pizza or national defense? The dictionary definition of *culture* is "the totality of socially transmitted behavior patterns, arts, beliefs, institutions, and all other products of human work and thought." Apparently, a lot of different things—institutions, behavior patterns, beliefs—constitute a culture.

Not all people have the same culture. The culture of one group, or nation, of people, might be different from the culture of another. The American culture is different from the Brazilian culture, and so on. Differences are perhaps the most noticeable when people move to a place where the culture is very different from their own.

The culture of a place or a people is usually strong enough to be easily recognized. It is not usually something that goes without notice. In that it is easily recognizable and ever present, culture can be considered a nonexcludable public good. All public goods (whether excludable or nonexcludable) are nonrivalrous in consumption—that is, one person's consumption does not detract from another person's consumption. Culture has this characteristic. And any given culture is

also nonexcludable, in that people can neither be excluded from it by others nor very easily exclude themselves from it—unless, of course, one chooses to become a hermit. For better or worse, a specific culture is what it is, and it is a nonexcludable public good.

Cultures sometimes change. For example, it's been said that the culture in the United States in the 1950s was different from today's U.S. culture. When people make this statement, they often specify some way in which the culture today is different. They may speak about social mores, family relationships, music, politics, and so on.

Now think of cultures as you would think of items on a restaurant menu. Just as you can choose chicken, pasta, fish, or steak from a menu, suppose you could pick cultures from a menu. What would your preferred culture look like? What would it consist of? If you have a preferred culture, it tells you something about yourself and others. Maybe everyone has a preferred culture—where some things are spoken of and others things are not, where some things are acceptable and other things are not, and so on.

Now ask yourself whether many political arguments today aren't, at some deep level, about the culture. Think about the following topics with the phrase "the culture" in mind: immigration; pro-choice/pro-life; liberal and conservative movements; arguments over capitalism and socialism; financial bailouts; and the kind, level, and scope of taxes and of federal spending.

We are not sure how to specify the production function for a culture (what are the inputs?), nor are we sure how cultures get produced or how and why they sometimes change. Still, in that a given culture is an example of a nonexcludable public good, it is easy to understand why people would disagree over its makeup. After all, it's not pizza.

Also, a problem arises anytime government gets involved in providing nonexcludable public goods. Not everyone will want the specific quality or quantity of the good. To illustrate, most economists identify *national defense* as a nonexcludable public good. But not everyone who wants national defense wants the specific quality and quantity of national defense that the government provides. Some people prefer less national defense to more; others prefer more to less. Some people want their national defense to consist of many nuclear weapons; others prefer their national defense to consist of standard, nonnuclear weapons.

The Case for Smaller or Larger Government

According to most economists, a case can be made for government. The case, so far, is based on a government that removes individuals from prisoner's dilemma settings that they want to be removed from, that adjusts for negative and positive externalities, and that provides nonexcludable public goods to the public that the public demands. Based on these three factors, the case for government requires specific conditions to be satisfied, as noted.

Not all economists accept this case for government. Some economists would argue that the optimum size of government is much smaller than the government that would grow out of having to deal with prisoner's dilemma settings, adjust for externalities, and provide nonexcludable public goods. Other economists would argue that the optimum size of government is much larger and that government has an important role to play in other areas, such as income distribution, macroeconomic management of the economy, safety regulation, financial regulation, and so on. But the objective in this chapter is not to identify the optimum size and scope of government for the thousands of working economies, but rather to introduce some of the arguments for government's role in, and effects on, markets and the economy (with conditions identified). The next section presents some of the arguments voiced by economists in making the case against government.

SELF-TEST

1. What is the case for government with respect to externalities?

2. What is the case for government with respect to nonexcludable public goods?

THE ECONOMIC CASE AGAINST GOVERNMENT

The economic case against government is based on the unintended effects of government actions, government as a transfer mechanism, and special interest groups.

Unintended Effects of Government Actions

Sometimes government undertakes an action that has unintended and undesirable effects. To illustrate, consider one provision of the health-care bill passed in Congress in March 2010. The specifics are these: The Health Care and Education Reconciliation Act of 2010 is a reconciliation bill that was passed by the 111th United States Congress on March 21, 2010, to make changes to the Patient Protection and Affordable Care Act. The act was signed into law on March 30, 2010, by President Barack Obama. Together, the two acts (reconciliation, and patient protection and affordable care) are popularly often referred to as "health-care reform." One of the stated objectives of the proponents of health-care reform was to bring down health insurance costs, to lower medical and hospital costs, and to insure many of the millions of uninsured persons in the country.

Two provisions of health-care reform included making it unlawful for insurance companies to deny insurance to persons with a preexisting disease. In other words, a person who learns he has diabetes on, say, day 1, could not be denied insurance if he sought it on day 10. A second provision mandated a fine for those persons who chose not to buy insurance. In other words, if Jack, 29 years old, chose not to buy health insurance, he would pay a fine.

Now if we take these two provisions together—a fine for not buying insurance and prohibiting insurance firms from turning down a person with a preexisting disease—it is easy to see how some individuals will gain more by waiting until they become ill to buy insurance than they will lose by paying the fine for not buying insurance. At the time of writing, the fine for not buying insurance is $695. A person will have to weigh the cost of incurring the fine against what he saves in insurance premiums. No doubt some people will choose not to buy insurance (while they are healthy) if they can save more in insurance premiums than they will incur in fines.

The unintended effect of the two provisions, then, is that some people who had health insurance before health-care reform will choose to remain uninsured after health-care reform. However, this was not the stated intent of health-care reform. The intent was for those people with insurance to keep their insurance and for those persons without insurance to become insured.

Of course, if some healthy individuals choose to give up their insurance after health-care reform and wait until they become sick to buy insurance, then the pool of insured persons changes after health-care reform relative to what it was before the reform. Specifically, if the some of the healthy persons leave the pool of insured persons, the pool remaining contains a higher percentage of ill persons or likely-to-become-ill persons. This pool of persons is more costly to insure than the previous pool. As an example, suppose that the pool of insured persons before health-care reform consisted of 100 persons; 75 are healthy and won't get sick soon, and 25 are sick or will get sick soon. So 75 people are paying premiums and not obtaining insurance payouts, and 25 people are paying premiums and receiving insurance payouts. Then health-care is reformed, and 25 of the 75 healthy persons leave the pool. Now only 75 persons are in the pool of insured persons; 25 of them are sick, paying premiums, and receiving insurance payouts, and only 50 persons are healthy, paying premiums, and not receiving insurance payouts. Now the average cost of an insurance policy will be higher than it would have been had everyone stayed in the insurance pool.[2]

In fact, one of the objectives of health-care reform was to bring more people into the pool of insured persons so that insurance policies would become cheaper. In other words, increase the pool in our example from 100 persons to, say, 150 persons and hope that the percentage rise in the number of healthy persons is greater than the percentage rise in the number of sick persons. But by setting the fine for not buying insurance at a low enough level so that healthy individuals gain more by dropping their insurance and paying the fine than keeping their insurance and not paying the fine, Congress failed to enhance the incentive to buy health insurance, especially when it prohibited insurance companies from denying coverage based on preexisting conditions.

There are other examples of the unintended and undesirable effects of some government actions. For example, consider the minimum wage law (discussed in an earlier chapter). The stated objective of raising the minimum wage is to increase the incomes of the working poor. But because demand curves slope downward—that is, the demand curve for

2. "Thousands of consumers are gaming Massachusetts' 2006 health insurance law [similar in some provisions to national health-care reform] by buying insurance when they need to cover pricey medical care, such as fertility treatments and knee surgery, and then swiftly dropping coverage, a practice that insurance executives say is driving up costs for other people and small businesses. . . The problem is, it is less expensive for consumers—especially young and healthy people—to pay the monthly penalty of as much as $93 imposed under the state law for not having insurance, than to buy the coverage year-round. This is also the case under the federal health-care overhaul legislation signed by the president, insurers say." (Kay Lazar, "Short-Term Customers Boosting Health Care Costs," *The Boston Globe*, April 4, 2010.)

unskilled labor is downward sloping—firms hire fewer workers at a higher wage than at a lower wage. An unintended effect of raising the minimum wage, then, is that some people who worked at the lower wage lose their jobs at the higher wage. How many lose their jobs is an empirical issue: only a few, hundreds, or thousands?

Finally, consider a tax that government might place on a firm. Suppose government places a tax on the production of good X, produced by firm X. Government taxes the firm $1 for every unit of good X the firm produces. The intent of the tax is two-fold: to raise tax revenue and to get the firm to reduce the production of good X (perhaps because the production of good X generates a negative externality). The tax achieves its intended effects: it does raise tax revenue, and firm X does produce fewer units of good X. But the tax has other effects. By reducing the supply of good X, it indirectly leads to a higher prices for good X. Now consumers will pay higher prices for good X than they paid before. (In other words, they pay some of the tax that government placed on firm X). The higher price means that consumers' surplus declines. Also, because fewer units of good X are produced, firm X needs fewer workers. Higher prices, less consumers' surplus, and fewer workers working for firm X—these may all be considered the unintended effects of the government action in that some or all of the legislators who voted for the tax did not intend to create these effects.

Finally, consider what the federal government and many state governments were doing in 2009 and 2010: giving tax credits to first-time home buyers. For example, in 2009, Congress passed the Worker, Homeownership and Business Assistance Act. It gave up to an $8,000 tax credit to first-time home buyers who purchased a home to use as their principal residence. (A tax credit reduces one's taxes by the amount of the credit. For example, if you owe $30,000 in taxes and you receive a tax credit of $8,000, your tax obligation declines to $22,000.) In California in March 2010, Governor Arnold Schwarzenegger of California signed AB 183 into law. AB 183 provided a tax credit of up to $10,000 to Californians buying their first home or a brand new home. According to the governor, AB 183 would encourage home ownership, help the failing real estate market in California (prices and sales were declining at the time), and create jobs (in the home construction and related industries). These were the intended effects.

But there was an unintended effect. Because a tax credit reduces individual taxes if a person buys a house, some people will buy a house that they might not have bought without the tax credit. These additional buyers add demand to the housing market, and as demand for houses rises, so do prices. In other words, what the tax credit gives with one hand (lower taxes), it indirectly takes away with the other (higher house prices). Whether the tax credit really does encourage home ownership is unclear. It encourages home ownership through lowering taxes, but then discourages it through higher house prices.

SELF-TEST

1. "Proposed: Insurance companies cannot deny insurance coverage to persons with preexisting conditions, and anyone who chooses not to buy health insurance must pay a fine." Under what condition will healthy individuals who currently have health insurance choose not to drop their insurance?

2. How can a tax credit for first-time home buyers lead to higher house prices?

3. Is there a difference between a lower overall cost of buying a house and a lower house price? Explain your answer.

Government as Transfer Mechanism

In the first part of this chapter, the case for government was built largely on its providing certain goods, services, and outcomes that its citizens demanded. This function is clearly seen in government's role in removing individuals from prisoner's dilemma settings and in providing nonexcludable public goods. In both cases, government produces something of worth to the citizenry. Even when government adjusts for externalities, it can be said to have made an improvement. Given certain conditions, it takes an inefficient market outcome and turns it into an efficient one. Because efficiency is equivalent to maximizing net gains, government moves things from a position where net gains are not maximized (inefficiency) to a place where they are maximized (efficiency). In all three roles, government is productive: it produces something of worth to its citizens.

But government isn't only productive. Sometimes it involves itself in actions that transfer monies from one group of persons to another. In other words, sometimes government functions as a *transfer mechanism*, taking from X and giving to Y. For example, when government imposes tariffs (a tax) on imported goods (as shown in a later chapter), it essentially raises prices for domestic consumers, thus lowering consumers' surplus and raising the producer's surplus for domestic producers. In other words, a government that places a tariff on foreign imported cars essentially takes from domestic car consumers and gives to domestic car producers. It takes from one group of persons to give to another.

As another example, think of what government does when it passes a law stating that it will pay farmers the difference between the market price for their goods and a target price (above the market price). It takes from taxpayers and gives to farmers.

In the two preceding cases, government takes from one group and gives to another. Sometimes, though, government ends up giving to a group with one hand and then taking back with the other. Once again consider what happened when the California law AB 183 offered the $10,000 tax credit to first-time home buyers. Giving people a tax credit to buy a house increased the demand for houses, thus raising house prices. Government gave with one hand (by lowering taxes if you buy a house) but indirectly took away with the other hand (by undertaking an action that results in higher house prices).

TYPES OF TRANSFERS Not all transfers are the same. In fact, there are three different transfers. The first is a *voluntary transfer*. To illustrate, Smith giving Jones $100 for his birthday is a voluntary transfer. Smith willingly transfers $100 from himself to Jones. This kind of voluntary transfer is essentially a gift. As with any gift, both the gift giver and gift recipient benefit.

A second type of transfer is an *involuntary transfer*. This kind of transfer takes place when, say, an armed thief says to you, "Your money or your life." You transfer the money in your wallet to the thief with the gun, but you do so under coercion.

An involuntary transfer can also occur in a less violent—sometimes even legal—setting. To illustrate, we know that government sometimes pays farmers the difference between the market price for the good they sell and a higher target price. Suppose the price of good X is $4 and the target price is $6. Government uses tax monies to pay the producer of good X the $2 difference.

Possibly, if we asked all taxpayers whether they agreed to spending tax monies that way, at least some of them would say no. A sandwich restaurant owner might argue this way: "The market price for a sandwich I make and sell is $3. I wish there were a target price of $5 for the sandwich, and the government paid me the difference of $2 for every sandwich. But it doesn't. So why are farmers different from the restaurateurs?" For this taxpayer, the transfer—from him to others—is something he neither agreed to nor agrees with. He could very well consider this transfer involuntary (for him).

A third type of transfer, on the surface, appears to be involuntary, but it isn't. To differentiate this transfer from the voluntary and involuntary types, we call it the *involuntary-voluntary transfer*. That sounds like an oxymoron, and it needs to be explained.

Suppose a community of 100,000 persons wants to redistribute some income from themselves to persons they consider to be deserving of assistance. The group of 100,000 people identify 2,000 persons among them whom they desire to assist. One suggestion is for everyone simply to give the group of 2,000 persons what he or she wants to give. In other words, make voluntary contributions. A possible problem, though, is that some may choose to be free riders in much the same way that some choose to be free riders when it comes to paying for nonexcludable public goods. (Each person may think: "As long as everyone else contributes, I don't need to contribute, for two reasons. First, my contribution is a very small percentage of the total potential contributions. My small contribution isn't enough to make a significant difference in the lives of the 2,000 persons. Second, if others contribute, I can gain utility from their contributions—I feel better seeing the 2,000 persons helped—without incurring any of the costs. So why contribute?") Of course, if everyone chooses to be a free rider, the 2,000 persons will get no assistance.

Given this type of situation, the economic argument for government is the same as that for the provision of nonexcludable public goods. Specifically, government can overcome the free-rider problem by taxing individuals to pay for something they already want. So, from one perspective, the transfer from some persons to others looks involuntary because taxes are imposed. But *if* the community of 100,000 persons actually wants to assist the group of 2,000 persons—and can only accomplish this with government—*then* the transfer is voluntary. Hence this type of transfer is an *involuntary–voluntary transfer*. On the surface, the transfer looks involuntary; below the surface, it looks voluntary.[3]

Of the three types of transfers, involuntary transfers are the kind of transfers used in the case *against* government, that is, those involved with special interest groups and transfers.

SPECIAL INTEREST GROUPS AND TRANSFERS As discussed in the last chapter, special interest groups often seek transfers from others to themselves. In other words, they engage in rent-seeking activities. Special interest groups are often successful because of a combination of forces working in their favor and against the public interest. Two of these forces are rational ignorance (on the part of the public) and transfers that concentrate the benefits on a relatively few and disperse the costs over relatively many. If the costs of the transfers are spread over millions of individuals, so that no one individual incurs much of the cost, then no one has much of an incentive to lobby against the transfer. A transfer is like a tug of war. At one end of the rope, special interest groups are pulling in their direction; at the other end are the persons who end up paying for the benefits that the special interest group receives. Maybe only 10 members of the special interest group are at one end of the rope and 100 members of the public at the other end. But if the 100 members of the public aren't pulling and the 10 members of the special interest group are, then the special interest group wins, and the members of the public lose.

The case against government often makes two points about special interest groups. First, much of the legislation that looks like public interest legislation (which is supposed to benefit the public at large) is really no more than a hodge-podge of special interest legislation tied up together with a public interest bow. Again consider the tax credit policy for new home buyers, one objective of whose was to increase home ownership. Two of the groups that lobbied hard for the legislation were the building industry and realtors. An increase in demand for homes helps both groups. Or consider a tariff that is said to "strengthen American industry and save jobs." Often domestic producer interests lobby for the tariffs because tariffs benefit them at the expense of domestic consumers.

Second, special interest groups are often more inclined to press government for transfers instead of economic growth. In other words, in the battle between economic growth (increasing the size of the economic pie) and transfers (cutting a bigger slice of the pie for one group and a smaller slice for another group), transfers win out. We discuss this point next.

---

3. Be careful. Although some true involuntary–voluntary transfers exist in the world, not everything that someone claims is an involuntary–voluntary transfer, is.

Economic Growth Versus Transfers

The critics of government often point out that special interest groups favor transfer policies over economic growth policies. For example, special interest group A currently receives 1/100 of the country's economic pie, or Real GDP, which is the value of the entire output produced annually within a country's borders, adjusted for price changes. In other words, if the economic pie, or **Real GDP**, consists of $1 billion, then special interest group A receives 1/100 of the $1 billion.

Special interest group A can lobby for various types of policies.

- With one type of policy, the special interest group leaves the size of the economic pie constant and simply slices off a bigger piece of the pie for itself. Instead of receiving a 1/100 slice, it receives a 1/70 slice.

- A second type of policy increases the slice of the pie for the special interest group but decreases the size of the pie.

- A third type of policy increases the size of the pie but leaves the percentage that the special interest group receives constant.

In the real world, special interest groups tend to favor a transfer (the bigger-slice policy) over the economic growth policy (the bigger-pie policy). To understand why, consider three different cases.

CASE 1. SAME SLICE–BIGGER ECONOMIC PIE (ECONOMIC GROWTH) In this case, group A lobbies for a policy that will increase the size of the economic pie. The group incurs a cost of $100 to increase the size of the pie by $100,000. If we assume the group gets a 1/100 slice of the pie, then group A gets $1,000 of the $100,000 bigger pie. If we subtract what the group paid to lobby for the policy, $100, the group is left with a net benefit of $900.

CASE 2. BIGGER SLICE–SAME SIZE ECONOMIC PIE (TRANSFER) Group A lobbies for a policy that increases its slice of a given-size pie. The group incurs the same lobbying cost as in case 1, $100. As a result of the policy, group A gets $1,000, so that its net benefit in this case is the same as in case 1: $900.

Since the net benefits in the two cases are the same ($900), we could conclude that group A will be indifferent between the two cases. In other words, it should be indifferent between lobbying for a policy that results in a bigger pie and a policy that results in a bigger slice of a given size pie. But *before* group A would be indifferent, the size of the pie in case 1 had to grow by *100 times* more than the simple ($1,000) transfer in case 2 before group A became indifferent between the two cases. (The economic pie "had to grow by 100 times more . . ." because group A received a 1/100 slice of the pie.)

In fact, 1/100 of the U.S. economic pie would be a fairly large slice for any special interest group. A 1/100 slice of the U.S. Real GDP at $14 trillion amounts to $140 billion. For real-world special interest groups, the slice would be much smaller than 1/100. If group A's slice were, say, 1/10,000, the economic pie in case 1 would have to grow by 10,000 times the size of the transfer in case 2 before group A would be indifferent. It is just not realistic to expect the economic pie to grow by 10,000 times more than the amount of a reasonably sized transfer.

Therefore, because it takes such enormous growth in the size of the economic pie before group A would be indifferent between lobbying for a growth policy and a transfer policy, and because expecting this kind of growth is unrealistic, special interest groups will almost always prefer to lobby for transfer policies rather than economic growth policies.

CASE 3. BIGGER SLICE–SHRINKING ECONOMIC PIE (TRANSFER) In case 1 the economic pie grew, and in case 2 its size remained constant. Now suppose group A

Real GDP
The value of the entire output produced annually within a country's borders, adjusted for price changes.

lobbies for a policy that will increase its slice of a smaller pie, but this time, as a result of the policy, the pie will shrink in size.

Suppose that the lobbying costs of the policy are $100 and that, as a result, group A receives an extra $1,000, just as it did in cases 1 and 2. But this time, the economic pie shrinks by $500. If the group receives a 1/100 slice of the pie, then, because the pie shrinks by $500, group A loses 1/100 of $500, or $5. The group's net benefit is $895: an extra $1,000 (bigger slice) – $5 (due to the shrinking pie) – $100 (lobbying costs).

How much does the economic pie have to shrink before group A would not lobby for the policy in case 3? The answer is –$90,000 because –$90,000 times 1/100 is –$900. And $1,000 (bigger slice) – $900 (due to shrinking pie) – $100 (lobbying costs) is zero. If only money matters (and there is no conscience cost suffered by group A as a result of pushing for policies that shrink the economic pie), then group A would be fine with the pie shrinking by a total of –$89,900 as long as it could gain $1. [$1,000 (bigger slice) – $899 (due to the shrinking pie) – $100 (lobbying costs) = $1.].

The overall conclusion, based on all three cases, is that special interest groups are more likely to push for policies that increase the size of their slice of the economic pie than for ones that increase the size of the pie. In fact, they are likely to push for policies that increase the size of their slice even if it means that the economic pie will shrink.

To the degree, then, that government often responds to special interests, much legislation is therefore special interest legislation, much of which will be transfer legislation instead of growth legislation. Government may be involved in productive activities—providing nonexcludable public goods, and so on—but no doubt many of its activities will be geared toward effecting transfers among various groups of people.

Following the Leader in Pushing for Transfers

Suppose each of five special interest groups, A–E, has $100:

$$A = \$100$$
$$B = \$100$$
$$C = \$100$$
$$D = \$100$$
$$E = \$100$$

Now suppose group E lobbies government for a policy that will transfer $10 away from each of the groups A–D and to it. If the policy becomes law, then the distribution looks like this:

$$A = \$90$$
$$B = \$90$$
$$C = \$90$$
$$D = \$90$$
$$E = \$140$$

The members of group A realize that their relative position has declined as a result of the transfer. To try to reestablish its relative position, group A lobbies government for a policy that will take $10 away from each of the groups B–E and transfer that money to it. If the policy becomes law, then the distribution looks like this:

$$A = \$130$$
$$B = \$80$$

$$C = \$80$$
$$D = \$80$$
$$E = \$130$$

Now group A is on par with group E, but groups B–D fall farther behind in their relative position. As a result, each of these groups attempts to do what groups A and E did: lobby government to effect a transfer from others to it. If each group is successful, you would think that the outcome will be the same as at the starting point: Each group has $100. But that doesn't take into account the lobbying costs and perhaps the decline in economic growth that are part of the groups' transfer-seeking activities. In other words, instead of each group having $100 after seeking and receiving a $10 transfer, each group might end up with only $90. Although seeking transfers might have been rational for any one group, when the others followed suit, the aggregate outcome was an inferior position to the one occupied before the groups all sought transfers. In the end, all that seeking transfers did was to make everyone poorer.

Even if the groups realize that they are being self-defeating, they still might find it hard, if not impossible, to stop seeking transfers. In fact, they might be in a prisoner's dilemma setting, as shown in Exhibit 3, which identifies two groups, A and B. Each group has two options: seek transfers and do not seek transfers. The number in each box of the matrix represents how well off each group is: the higher the number, the better off the group.

Suppose both groups have chosen to seek transfers. The outcome is in box 4, where each group receives a 10. Box 1 is a superior box for both groups, because in box 1 each group receives 12. But even if the two groups agree not to seek transfers, they are not likely to hold to the agreement because each group has a box that is superior for it to box 1. Group A is better off in box 2, where it seeks a transfer and group B does not. Group B is better off in box 3, where it seeks a transfer and group A does not. In fact, no matter what group B does, seeking a transfer is always better for group A. Similarly, no matter what group A does, seeking a transfer is always better for group B. The result is that both groups end up in box 4.

The two groups are in a prisoner's dilemma setting, and they may want to get out of that setting but can't. Government could remove them from the setting by changing the payoff matrix, but it would have to say no to all special interest legislation. Some economists have argued that the current incentive structure for elected representatives isn't likely to get them to say no anytime soon.

Divisive Society: A NonExcludable Public Bad

Economist Mancur Olson has written:

This focus on distribution makes the significance of distributional issues [transfer issues] in political life relatively greater and the significance of widespread common interest in political life relatively smaller.

In other words, once the focus is on transfer issues or slicing-up-the-pie issues, the common interest in society begins to take a back seat.

EXHIBIT 3

Special Interest Groups in a Prisoner's Dilemma Setting

Special interest groups A and B are in a prisoner's dilemma setting. If both groups seek transfers, they end up in box 4. Box 1 is a better box for both groups, but to reach box 1, each group must choose not to seek a transfer from the other. However, from each group's perspective, no matter what the other group does, seeking a transfer is always better. The result is that both groups end up in box 4.

A possible unintended effect of this focus is that individuals begin to see their government as more heavily involved in taking sides than in serving the common interest. This perception creates a divisive society, where the members of groups see themselves as pitted against other groups, as were the groups A–E in the previous example. Each group starts to see the others as either (1) groups that have taken from us or (2) groups that we can take from. A divisive society is a *nonexcludable public bad*. It is a "bad" because it comes with disutility. It is "nonexcludable public" because, once it exists, no one remains unaffected. It is a little like the air we breathe, except now the air is polluted.

The cases for and against government have a certain kind of symmetry. The case for government was built on, among other things, its providing *nonexcludable public goods*. The case against government is built on, among other things, its being part of process that creates a *nonexcludable public bad*.

SELF-TEST

1. The net benefit for a special interest group from both a transfer policy and an economic growth policy is $1,000. If the group's slice of the pie is 1/1,000, how much larger than $1,000 does that increase in the size of the pie have to be before the group is indifferent between the two policies?

2. Group A receives a 1/100 slice of the economic pie, and group B receives a 1/10,000 slice. Which group would be less willing to advocate economic growth policies over transfer policies and why?

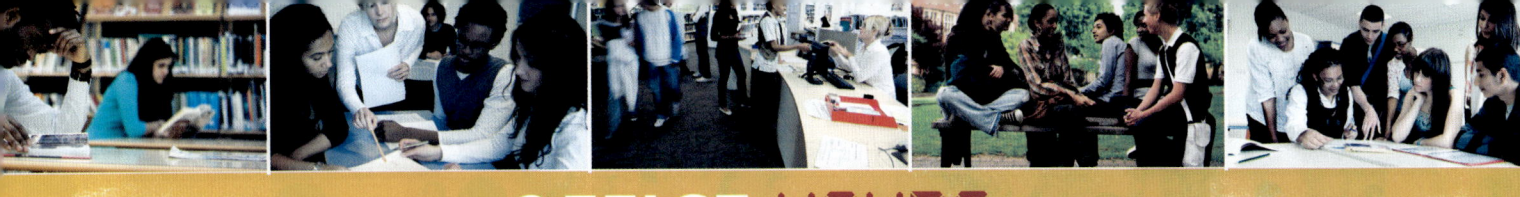

OFFICE HOURS

"I'm No Longer Sure What I Think."

STUDENT:

When I read the first part of this chapter, I see government in a very positive light. When I read the second part, I see government in a very negative light. I'm not sure that I know what I think about government anymore. Am I pro- or antigovernment when it comes to economic issues?

INSTRUCTOR:

You may be forcing things into an unwarranted *either–or* situation. The choice may not be between either *all* progovernment or *all* antigovernment. It could very well be that government does X well but Y poorly, so that you favor government doing X but not Y.

STUDENT:

Is this the way most economists look at things?

INSTRUCTOR:

To answer that question, let me first mention two terms—"market failure" and "government failure." In a previous chapter, we discussed market failure—that is, the market doesn't provide the ideal or optimal (or efficient) amount of a good. I'd say that most economists believe that there are examples of market failure, although not all economists agree on the degree of market failure that exists. Some economists seem to think that there are many examples of market failure, and some think there are very few.

Government failure is the public sector analogy to market failure. It is the situation where government's intervention in a market or in the economy leads to greater inefficiency or, simply put, makes things worse. I'd say that most economists believe that there are examples of government failure, but here again, not all economists agree on the degree of government failure that exists. Some economists seem to think that there are many examples of government failure, and some think there are very few.

STUDENT:

In other words, most economists think there is both market failure and government failure in the real world, but they do not all agree on the degree of each.

INSTRUCTOR:

Yes, I believe that's a fairly accurate representation of the current state of affairs. Remember, there are debates in economics. Sometimes these debates focus on narrowly defined economic issues (which often occur more in macroeconomics than in microeconomics), and sometimes they focus on the role and effects of government in markets and in the economy.

POINTS TO REMEMBER

1. Most economists believe that both market failure and government failure exist, but they often disagree on the degree of each.
2. Debates in economics focus on narrowly defined economic issues and on the role and effects of government in markets and in the economy.

GOVERNMENT AND PRISONER'S DILEMMA SETTINGS

- Two or more individuals may find themselves in a prisoner's dilemma setting from which they would like to remove themselves, but can't. Exhibit 1 shows this explicitly. Both individuals are in box 4 but would like to move to box 1. They make an agreement that will move them to box 1, but they aren't capable of keeping to the agreement. Their repeated actions lead them to box 4. Government can change the payoff matrix by fining each individual for taking a particular course of action and thus move the individuals out of box 4 to box 1.

EXTERNALITIES

- Given either negative or positive externalities, the market outcome is the inefficient outcome. Government can adjust for negative and positive externalities and thus move from the inefficient market outcome to the efficient outcome, where $MSB = MSC$. One way to do this is by applying taxes to the activity generating the negative externality and subsidies to the activity generating the positive externality. In both cases, to move from inefficiency to efficiency, the tax must be equal to the MEC in the negative externality case and the subsidy must be equal to the MEB in the positive externality case.

NONEXCLUDABLE PUBLIC GOODS

- A case can be made for government with respect to the provision of nonexcludable public goods that the market may not provide because of the free-rider problem. Government can overcome the free-rider problem by taxing individuals and then using the tax monies either to provide the nonexcludable public good itself or to pay a private party to produce and provide the nonexcludable public good.

UNINTENDED EFFECTS OF GOVERNMENT ACTIONS

- Government actions sometimes produce adverse unintended effects. In the text we identified some of the unintended effects of health-care reform, the minimum wage, and a tax credit policy for new home buyers.

SPECIAL INTEREST GROUPS, TRANSFERS, AND ECONOMIC GROWTH

- Special interest groups can seek policies that transfer income from others to themselves or that promote economic growth. Transfer-seeking policies are aimed at increasing the size of the economic pie received by the special interest group. The economic growth policies are intended to increase the size of the economic pie (without changing the slice of the pie received by the economic growth). Unless the special interest group receives a large slice of the economic pie, generally transfer policies, not economic growth policies, better serve the special interest groups.

- Two forces operate in favor of special interest group: rational ignorance on the part of the public and the fact that special interest legislation has a higher chance of passage if the benefits are concentrated on a relatively few and the costs are concentrated over relatively many.

THE ECONOMIC CASE FOR AND AGAINST GOVERNMENT

- Economic cases can be made for and against government. The case for government stresses the productive nature of some government actions: removing individuals from prisoner's dilemma settings that they want to be removed from, adjusting for externalities, and providing nonexcludable public goods. The case against government stresses the fact that government can act as an agent—a transfer mechanism—that makes it possible for one group to take from another and give to itself. This type of activity often creates a divisive society, wherein individuals and groups are pitted against each other. Also, the case against government is based on government actions sometimes producing adverse unintended effects.

Real GDP

1. Government can remove individuals from a prisoner's dilemma setting by changing the payoffs from various actions. Explain.

2. Under what condition would an individual choose to spend additional time producing instead of stealing? Under what condition would an individual choose to spend additional time stealing instead of producing?

3. Government can remove two individuals from a prisoner's dilemma setting and end up making one individual better off and the other individual worse off. Do you agree or disagree? Explain your answer. (*Hint:* Think taxes.)

4. What is the relationship between *MPC* and *MSC* if a negative externality exists? What is the relationship between *MPB* and *MSB* if a positive externality exists?

5. Government may provide, or be part of a process that generates, both nonexcludable public goods and bads. Do you agree or disagree? Explain your answer.

6. What is the case for government with respect to nonexcludable public goods?

7. Individuals sometimes disagree over the preferred quality and quantity of a nonexcludable public good. Why?

8. Special interest group A receives a 1/1,000 slice of the economic pie. Its net benefits from an economic growth policy are $3,000, which are the same as its net benefits from a transfer policy. What (absolute) change in the size of the economic pie is required to bring this result about?

9. Special interest groups that seek transfers may find themselves in a prisoner's dilemma setting. Do you agree or disagree? Explain your answer.

10. As presented in this chapter, what is the case for government? What is the case against government?

11. Explain how a tax credit policy for first-time home buyers can raise the demand for, and price of, houses.

12. In this chapter we discussed three types of transfers. Identify and explain each.

13. Even if government uses taxes to deal with a negative externality, an inefficient market outcome will not necessarily change into an efficient one. Do you agree or disagree? Explain your answer.

14. Government can use taxes and subsidies to change an inefficient market outcome into an efficient outcome. Do you agree or disagree? Explain your answer.

15. Does government always make individuals better off if it removes them from a prisoner's dilemma setting? Explain your answer.

16. In our story of Jack and Jill in the chapter, why couldn't they successfully remove themselves from box 4 in Exhibit 1?

CHAPTER 34

© BILLY E. BARNES / PHOTO EDIT

INTERNATIONAL TRADE

Introduction Economics is about trade, and trade crosses boundaries. People trade not only with people who live in their city, state, or country, but also with people in other countries. Many of the goods you consume are undoubtedly produced in other countries. This chapter examines international trade and the prohibitions sometimes placed on it.

INTERNATIONAL TRADE THEORY

International trade takes place for the same reasons that trade at any level exists. Individuals trade to make themselves better off. Pat and Zach, both of whom live in Cincinnati, Ohio, trade because they both value something the other has more than they value some of their own possessions. On an international scale, Elaine in the United States trades with Cho in China because Cho has something that Elaine wants and Elaine has something that Cho wants.

Obviously, the countries of the world have different terrains, climates, resources, worker skills, and so on. Therefore, some countries will be able to produce goods that other countries cannot produce or can produce only at extremely high costs. For example, Hong Kong has no oil, and Saudi Arabia has a large supply of it. Bananas do not grow easily in the United States, but they flourish in Honduras. Americans could grow bananas if they used hothouses, but it is cheaper for Americans to buy bananas from Hondurans than to produce bananas themselves.

Major U.S. exports include automobiles, computers, aircraft, corn, wheat, soybeans, scientific instruments, coal, and plastic materials. Major imports include petroleum, automobiles, clothing, iron and steel, office machines, footwear, fish, coffee, and diamonds. Some of the major exporting countries of the world are the United States, Germany, Japan, France, and the United Kingdom. These same countries are also among the major importers in the world.

How Countries Know What to Trade

Recall the concept of *comparative advantage,* an economic concept first discussed in Chapter 2. In this section, we discuss comparative advantage in terms of countries rather than in terms of individuals.

COMPARATIVE ADVANTAGE Assume a two-country/two-good world. The countries are the United States and Japan, and the goods are food and clothing. Both countries can produce the two goods in the four different combinations listed in Exhibit 1. For example, the United States can produce 90 units of food and 0 units of clothing, 60 units of food and 10 units of clothing, or other combinations. Japan can produce 15 units of food and 0 units of clothing, 10 units of food and 5 units of clothing, or other combinations.

Suppose the United States is producing and consuming the two goods in the combination represented by point *B* on its production possibilities frontier (PPF), and Japan is producing and consuming the combination of the two goods represented by point *F* on its PPF. In this case, neither of the two countries is specializing in the production of one of the two goods, nor are the two countries trading with each other. We call this the *no-specialization–no-trade (NS–NT) case* (see column 1 in Exhibit 2).

Now suppose the United States and Japan decide to specialize in the production of a specific good and to trade with each other, in what is called the *specialization–trade (S–T) case*. Whether the two countries will be better off through specialization and trade is best explained by means of a numerical example, but first we need to find the answers to two other questions: What good should the United States specialize in producing? What good should Japan specialize in producing? The general answer to both questions is the same: *Countries specialize in the production of the good in which they have a comparative advantage.* A country has a comparative advantage in the production of a good when it can produce the good at lower opportunity cost than another country can.

For example, in the United States, the opportunity cost of producing 1 unit of clothing (*C*) is 3 units of food (*F*); for every 10 units of clothing it produces, it forfeits 30 units of food. So the opportunity cost of producing 1 unit of food is 1/3 unit of clothing. In Japan, the opportunity cost of producing 1 unit of clothing is 1 unit of food (for every 5 units of clothing it produces, it forfeits 5 units of food). So, in the United States, the

Comparative Advantage
The advantage a country has when it can produce a good at lower opportunity cost than another country can.

| | **EXHIBIT 1** |

Production Possibilities in Two Countries

The United States and Japan can produce the two goods in the combinations shown. Initially, the United States is at point B on its PPF and Japan is at point F on its PPF. Both countries can be made better off by specializing in and trading the good in which each has a comparative advantage.

United States				**Japan**		
Points on Production Possibilities Frontier	**Food**	**Clothing**		**Points on Production Possibilities Frontier**	**Food**	**Clothing**
A	90	0		E	15	0
B	60	10		F	10	5
C	30	20		G	5	10
D	0	30		H	0	15

EXHIBIT 2

Both Countries Gain from Specialization and Trade

Column 1: Both the United States and Japan operate independently of each other. The United States produces and consumes 60 units of food and 10 units of clothing. Japan produces and consumes 10 units of food and 5 units of

clothing. Column 2: The United States specializes in the production of food; Japan specializes in the production of clothing. Column 3: The United States and Japan agree to the terms of trade of 2 units of food for 1 unit of clothing. They actually trade 20 units of food for 10 units of clothing. Column 4: Overall, the United

States consumes 70 units of food and 10 units of clothing. Japan consumes 20 units of food and 5 units of clothing. Column 5: Consumption levels are higher for both the United States and Japan in the S–T case than in the NS–NT case.

	No Specialization-No Trade (NS–NT) Case	Specialization-Trade (S–T) Case			
Country	(1) Production and Consumption in the NS–NT Case	(2) Production in the S–T Case	(3) Exports (−) Imports (+) Terms of Trade Are 2F = 1C	(4) Consumption in the S–T Case (2) + (3)	(5) Gains from Specialization and Trade (4) − (1)
United States					
Food	60 } Point B in	90 } Point A in	−20	70	10
Clothing	10 } Exhibit 1	0 } Exhibit 1	+10	10	0
Japan					
Food	10 } Point F in	0 } Point H in	+20	20	10
Clothing	5 } Exhibit 1	15 } Exhibit 1	−10	5	0

situation is $1C = 3F$, or $1F = 1/3C$; in Japan the situation is $1C = 1F$, or $1F = 1C$. The United States can produce food at a lower opportunity cost ($1/3C$, as opposed to $1C$ in Japan), whereas Japan can produce clothing at a lower opportunity cost ($1F$, as opposed to $3F$ in the United States). Thus, the United States has a comparative advantage in food, and Japan has a comparative advantage in clothing.

Suppose the two countries specialize in the production of the goods in which they have a comparative advantage. The United States specializes in the production of food (producing 90 units), and Japan specializes in the production of clothing (producing 15 units). In Exhibit 1, the United States locates at point A on its PPF, and Japan locates at point H on its PPF (see column 2 in Exhibit 2).

SETTLING ON THE TERMS OF TRADE After they have determined the goods to specialize in producing, the two countries must settle on the terms of trade, that is, how much food to trade for how much clothing. The United States faces the following situation: for every 30 units of food it does not produce, it can produce 10 units of clothing, as shown in Exhibit 1. Thus, 3 units of food have an opportunity cost of 1 unit of clothing ($3F = 1C$), or 1 unit of food has a cost of 1/3 unit of clothing ($1F = 1/3C$). Japan faces the following situation: for every 5 units of food it does not produce, it can produce 5 units of clothing. Thus, 1 unit of food has an opportunity cost of 1 unit of clothing ($1F = 1C$). For the United States, $3F = 1C$, and for Japan, $1F = 1C$.

With these cost ratios, both countries should be able to agree on terms of trade that specify $2F = 1C$. The United States would benefit by giving up 2 units of food instead of 3 units for 1 unit of clothing, whereas Japan would benefit by getting 2 units of food instead of only 1 unit for 1 unit of clothing. Suppose the two countries agree to the terms of trade of $2F = 1C$ and trade—in absolute amounts, 20 units of food for 10 units of clothing (see column 3 in Exhibit 2). Will they make themselves better off? We'll soon see that they do.

Dividing the Work

John and Veronica, husband and wife, have divided their household tasks: John usually does all the lawn work, fixes the cars, and does the dinner dishes, and Veronica cleans the house, cooks the meals, and does the laundry. Some sociologists might suggest that John and Veronica divided the household tasks along gender lines: men have for years done the lawn work, fixed the cars, and so on, and women have for years cleaned the house, cooked the meals, and so on. In other words, John is doing man's work, and Veronica is doing woman's work.

© COMSTOCK IMAGES/JUPITER IMAGES

Maybe they have followed gender lines, but the question remains why certain tasks became man's work and others became woman's work. Moreover, their arrangement doesn't explain why John and Veronica don't split every task evenly. In other words, why doesn't John clean half the house and Veronica clean half the house? Why doesn't Veronica mow the lawn on the second and fourth week of every month and John mow the lawn every first and third week of the month?

The law of comparative advantage may be the answer to all these questions. Consider two tasks: cleaning the house and mowing the lawn. The following table shows how long John and Veronica take to complete the two tasks individually.

	Time to Clean the House	Time to Mow the Lawn
John	120 minutes	50 minutes
Veronica	60 minutes	100 minutes

Here is the opportunity cost of each task for each person.

	Opportunity Cost of Cleaning the House	Opportunity Cost of Mowing the Lawn
John	2.40 mowed lawns	0.42 clean houses
Veronica	0.60 mowed lawns	1.67 clean houses

In other words, John has a comparative advantage in mowing the lawn, and Veronica has a comparative advantage in cleaning the house.

Now let's compare two settings. In setting 1, John and Veronica each do half of each task. In setting 2, John only mows the lawn and Veronica only cleans the house.

In setting 1, John spends 60 minutes cleaning half of the house and 25 minutes mowing half of the lawn, for a total of 85 minutes; Veronica spends 30 minutes cleaning half of the house and 50 minutes mowing half of the lawn, for a total of 80 minutes. The total time spent by Veronica and John cleaning the house and mowing the lawn is 165 minutes.

In setting 2, John spends 50 minutes mowing the lawn, and Veronica spends 60 minutes cleaning the house. The total time spent by Veronica and John cleaning the house and mowing the lawn is 110 minutes.

In which setting are Veronica and John better off? John works 85 minutes in setting 1 and 50 minutes in setting 2; so he is better off in setting 2. Veronica works 80 minutes in setting 1 and 60 minutes in setting 2; so Veronica is also better off in setting 2. Together, John and Veronica spend 55 fewer minutes in setting 2 than in setting 1. Getting the job done in 55 fewer minutes is the benefit of specializing in various duties around the house. Given those numbers, we would expect that John will mow the lawn (and do nothing else) and Veronica will clean the house (and do nothing else).

RESULTS OF THE SPECIALIZATION–TRADE (S–T) CASE Now the United States produces 90 units of food and trades 20 units to Japan, receiving 10 units of clothing in exchange. It consumes 70 units of food and 10 units of clothing. Japan produces 15 units of clothing and trades 10 to the United States, receiving 20 units of food in exchange. It consumes 5 units of clothing and 20 units of food (see column 4 in Exhibit 2).

Comparing the consumption levels in both countries in the two cases, the United States and Japan each consume 10 more units of food and no less clothing in the specialization–trade case than in the no-specialization–no-trade case (column 5 in Exhibit 2). Therefore, a country gains by specializing in producing and trading the good in which it has a comparative advantage.

Common Misconception About How Much We Can Consume

No country can consume beyond its PPF if it doesn't specialize and trade with other countries. But, as we have just seen, it can do so when there is specialization and trade. Look at the PPF for the United States in Exhibit 1. In the NS–NT case, the United States consumes 60 units of food and 10 units of clothing; that is, the United States consumes at point *B* on its PPF. In the S–T case, however, it consumes 70 units of food and 10 units of clothing. A point that represents this combination of the two goods is beyond the country's PPF.

How Countries Know When They Have a Comparative Advantage

Government officials of a country do not analyze pages of cost data to determine what their country should specialize in producing and then trade. Bureaucrats do not plot production possibilities frontiers on graph paper or calculate opportunity costs. Instead, the individual's desire to earn a dollar, a peso, or a euro determines the pattern of international trade. The desire to earn a profit determines what a country specializes in and trades.

To illustrate, Henri, an enterprising Frenchman, visits the United States and observes that beef is relatively cheap (compared with the price in France) and that perfume is relatively expensive. Noticing the price differences for beef and perfume between his country and the United States, he decides to buy some perfume in France, bring it to the United States, and sell it for the relatively higher U.S. price. With his profits from the perfume transaction, he buys beef in the United States, ships it to France, and sells it for the relatively higher French price. Obviously, Henri is buying low and selling high. He buys a good in the country where it is cheap and sells it in the country where it is expensive.

Henri's activities have a couple of consequences. First, he is earning a profit. The larger the price differences are between the two countries and the more he shuffles goods between countries, the more profit Henri earns.

Second, Henri's activities are moving each country toward its comparative advantage. The United States ends up exporting beef to France, and France ends up exporting perfume to the United States. Just as the pure theory predicts, individuals in the two countries specialize in and trade the good in which they have a comparative advantage. The outcome is brought about spontaneously through the actions of individuals trying to make themselves better off; they are simply trying to gain through trade.

ⓣhinking Like AN ECONOMIST

The Benefits of Searching for Profit Is the desire to earn profit useful to society at large? Henri's desire for profit moved both the United States and France toward specializing in and trading the good in which they had a comparative advantage. And when countries specialize and trade, they are better off than when they do neither. ●●●

You're Getting Better Because Others Are Getting Better

Smith can produce X in 30 minutes, and Y in 60 minutes. Jones can produce X in 2 hours and Y in 3 hours. Initially:

- Smith can produce X in 30 minutes and Y in 60 minutes.
- Jones can produce X in 2 hours and Y in 3 hours.

Smith is better at producing X and Y than Jones. Suppose that Smith gets even better at producing X. He can produce X in 15 minutes as opposed to 30 minutes.

- Smith can produce X in 15 minutes and Y in 60 minutes.
- Jones can produce X in 2 hours and Y in 3 hours.

Will Smith's getting better at producing X cause Jones to get better at producing Y? The quick and obvious answer is no. Smith's ability to produce X more quickly doesn't change the time it takes Jones to produce X and Y. It still takes Jones 2 hours to produce X and 3 hours to produce Y.

But look at things in terms of opportunity cost. Initially the opportunity cost for Smith of producing 1X is 1/2Y and the opportunity cost of producing 1Y is 2X. For Jones, the opportunity cost of producing 1X is 2/3Y and the opportunity cost of producing 1Y is 1½X. Given these opportunity costs, Smith has a comparative advantage in producing X, and Jones has a comparative advantage in producing Y.

When Smith gets better at doing X, his opportunity cost of producing 1X now *falls* to 1/4Y and his opportunity cost of doing 1Y *rises* to 4X. In other words, Smith's becoming better at producing X makes him relatively worse at producing Y.

As for Jones, because Smith has become relatively better at producing X, Jones has becoming relatively better at producing Y. We reach this conclusion by comparing Jones's opportunity cost of producing Y *before* and *after* Smith gets better at producing X. Before Smith gets better at producing X, Jones gives up 1½X to get 1Y, whereas Smith has to give up 2X to get 1Y.

- Jones gives up 1½X to get 1Y.
- Smith gives up 2X to get 1Y.

We might say that Jones has only a *slight* comparative advantage over Smith when it comes to producing Y. But after Smith gets better at producing X, Jones gives up 1½X to get 1Y, whereas Smith gives up 4X to get 1Y.

- Jones gives up 1½X to get 1Y.
- Smith gives up 4X to get 1Y.

Jones now has a *substantial* comparative advantage over Smith when it comes to producing Y.

Suppose X is being a lawyer and Y is being a farmer. When Smith becomes better as a lawyer, Jones automatically becomes a better farmer (or a relatively lower low-cost farmer). If we change things and say that X is being an accountant and Y is driving a truck, then as Smith becomes a better accountant, Jones automatically becomes a better trucker.

Looking at things in terms of opportunity cost provides us with an insight into our world. Namely, as some people become better at what they do, they naturally make other people better at what they do. Become a better mathematician, singer, or teacher, and you naturally make others better (a lower low-cost producer) at what they do.

SELF-TEST

(Answers to Self-Test questions are in Answers to Self-Test Questions at the back of the book.)

1. Suppose the United States can produce 120 units of X at an opportunity cost of 20 units of Y, and Great Britain can produce 40 units of X at an opportunity cost of 80 units of Y. Identify favorable terms of trade for the two countries.

2. If a country can produce more of all of its goods than any other country, would it benefit from specializing and trading? Explain your answer.

3. Do government officials analyze data to determine what their country can produce at a comparative advantage?

TRADE RESTRICTIONS

International trade theory shows that countries gain from free international trade, that is, from specializing in the production of the goods in which they have a comparative advantage and trading them for other goods. In the real world, however, the numerous types of trade restrictions give rise to the question: If countries gain from international trade, why are there trade restrictions? The answer requires an analysis of costs and benefits; specifically, we need to determine who benefits and who loses when trade is restricted. First, we need to explain some pertinent background information.

The Distributional Effects of International Trade

The previous section explained that specialization and international trade benefit individuals in different countries, but this is a net benefit. Not every individual person may gain.

To illustrate, Pam Dickson lives and works in the United States making clock radios. She produces and sells 12,000 clock radios per year at a price of $40 each. Currently, clock radios are not traded internationally. Individuals in other countries who make clock radios do not sell them in the United States.

Then one day, the U.S. market is opened to clock radios from China. Chinese manufacturers seem to have a comparative advantage in the production of clock radios because they sell theirs in the United States for $25 each. Pam realizes that she cannot compete at this price. Her sales drop to such a degree that she goes out of business. Thus, the introduction of international trade in this instance has harmed Pam personally.

Consumers' and Producers' Surpluses

The preceding example raises the issue of the distributional effects of free trade. The benefits of international trade are not equally distributed to all individuals in the population. Therefore, the topics of consumers' and producers' surpluses (Chapter 3) are relevant to our discussion of international trade:

Consumers' surplus is the difference between the maximum price a buyer is willing and able to pay for a good or service and the price actually paid.

Consumers' surplus = Maximum buying price − Price paid

Consumers' surplus is a dollar measure of the benefit gained by being able to purchase a unit of a good for less than one is willing to pay for it. For example, if Yakov would have paid $10 to see the movie at the Cinemax but paid only $4, his consumer surplus is $6. Consumers' surplus is the consumers' net gain from trade.

Producers' surplus (or sellers' surplus) is the difference between the price sellers receive for a good and the minimum or lowest price for which they would have sold the good.

Producers' surplus = Price received − Minimum selling price

Producers' surplus is a dollar measure of the benefit gained by being able to sell a unit of output for more than one is willing to sell it. For example, if Joan sold her knit sweaters for $24 each but would have sold them for as low as (but no lower than) $14 each, her producer surplus is $10 per sweater. Producers' surplus is the producers' net gain from trade.

Both consumers' and producers' surplus are represented in Exhibit 3. In part (a), the shaded triangle represents consumers' surplus. This triangle includes the area under the demand curve and above the equilibrium price. In part (b), the shaded triangle represents producers' surplus. This triangle includes the area above the supply curve and under the equilibrium price.

EXHIBIT 3

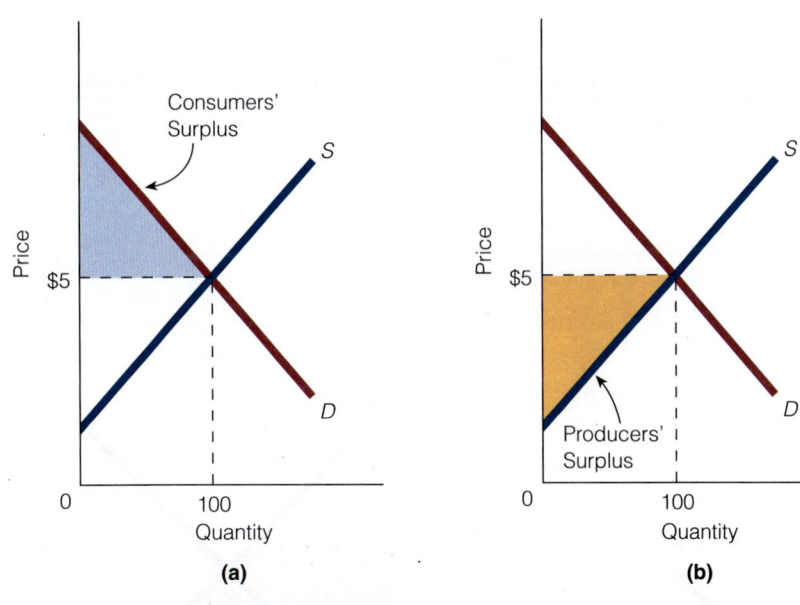

(a) **(b)**

Consumers' and Producers' Surplus

(a) Consumers' surplus. As the shaded area indicates, the difference between the maximum or highest amount consumers would be willing to pay and the price they actually pay is consumers' surplus. (b) Producers' surplus. As the shaded area indicates, the difference between the price sellers receive for the good and the minimum or lowest price they would be willing to sell the good for is producers' surplus.

finding ECONOMICS

While Negotiating the Price of a House Robin is negotiating the price of the house she wants to buy from Yakov. Her last offer for the house was $478,000, and he countered with $485,000. She is thinking about offering $481,000. Where is the economics?

Obviously, in this negotiation each person is trying to increase his or her surplus at the expense of the other. Specifically, the lower the price Robin pays, the higher her consumers' surplus will be and the lower Yakov's producers' surplus. Alternatively, the higher the price Yakov receives, the higher his producers' surplus will be and the lower Robin's consumers' surplus. ▲ ▲ ▲

The Benefits and Costs of Trade Restrictions

Of the numerous ways to restrict international trade, tariffs and quotas are two of the more common. We discuss these two methods using the tools of supply and demand, concentrating on two groups: U.S. consumers and U.S. producers.

TARIFFS A tariff is a tax on imports. The primary effect of a tariff is to raise the price of the imported good for the domestic consumer. Exhibit 4 illustrates the effects of a tariff on cars imported into the United States. The world price for cars is P_W, as shown in Exhibit 4(a). At this price in the domestic U.S. market, U.S. consumers buy Q_2 cars, as shown in part (b). They buy Q_1 from U.S. producers and the difference between Q_2 and Q_1 ($Q_2 - Q_1$) from foreign producers. In other words, U.S. imports at P_W are $Q_2 - Q_1$.

In this situation, consumers' surplus is the area under the demand curve and above the world price, P_W. This is the sum of the areas 1, 2, 3, 4, 5, and 6 [see Exhibit 4(b)]. Producers' surplus is the area above the supply curve and below the world price, P_W. This is area 7.

Now suppose a tariff is imposed. The price for imported cars in the U.S. market rises to $P_W + T$ (the world price plus the tariff). At this price, U.S. consumers buy Q_4 cars: Q_3 from U.S. producers and $Q_4 - Q_3$ from foreign producers. U.S. imports are $Q_4 - Q_3$, which is a smaller number of imports than at the pretariff price. An effect of tariffs, then, is to

Tariff
A tax on imports.

EXHIBIT 4

The Effects of a Tariff

A tariff raises the price of cars from P_W to $P_W + T$, decreases consumers' surplus, increases producers' surplus, and generates tariff revenue. Because consumers lose more than producers and government gain, there is a net loss due to the tariff.

	Consumers' Surplus	Producers' Surplus	Government Tariff Revenue
Free trade (No tariff)	$1 + 2 + 3 + 4 + 5 + 6$	7	None
Tariff	$1 + 2$	$3 + 7$	5
Loss or Gain	$- (3 + 4 + 5 + 6)$	$+3$	$+5$

Result of Tariff = Loss to consumers + Gain to producers + Tariff revenue
$$= -(3 + 4 + 5 + 6) \quad\quad +3 \quad\quad\quad +5$$
$$= -(4 + 6)$$

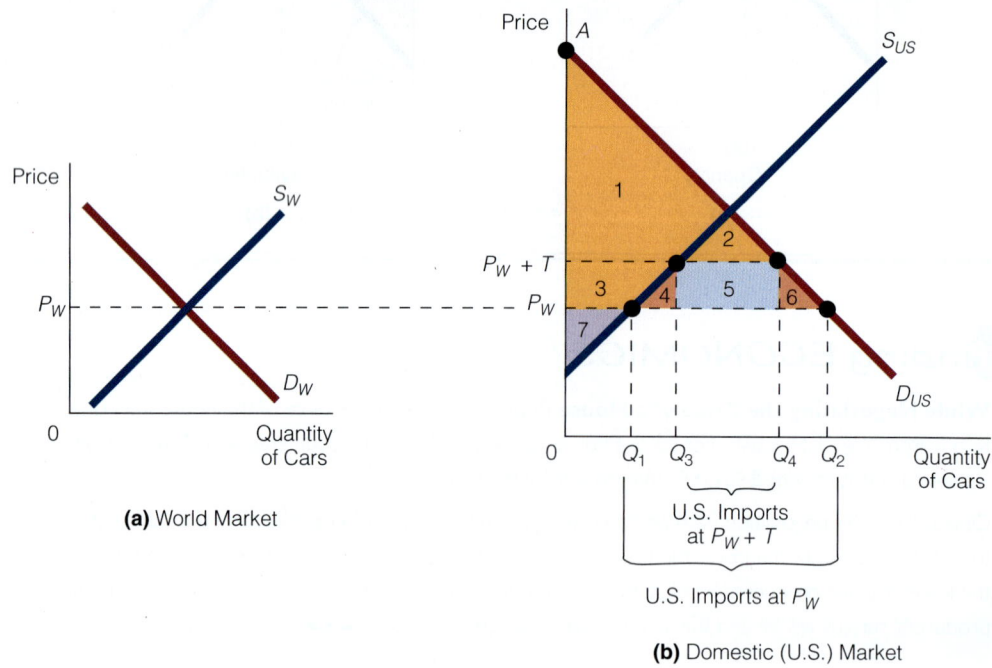

(a) World Market

(b) Domestic (U.S.) Market

reduce imports. After the tariff has been imposed, at price $P_W + T$, consumers' surplus consists of areas 1 and 2, and producers' surplus consists of areas 3 and 7.

Thus consumers receive more consumers' surplus when tariffs do not exist and less when they do exist. In our example, consumers received areas 1 through 6 in consumers' surplus when the tariff did not exist but only areas 1 and 2 when the tariff did exist. Because of the tariff, consumers' surplus was reduced by an amount equal to areas 3, 4, 5, and 6.

Producers, though, receive less producers' surplus when tariffs do not exist and more when they do exist. In our example, producers received producers' surplus equal to area 7 when the tariff did not exist, but they received producers' surplus equal to areas 3 and 7 with the tariff. Because of the tariff, producers' surplus increased by an amount equal to area 3.

The government collects tariff revenue equal to area 5. This area is obtained by multiplying the number of imports ($Q_4 - Q_3$) by the tariff, which is the difference between $P_W + T$ and P_W.[1]

---

1. For example, if the tariff is $100 and the number of imports is 50,000, then the tariff is $5 million.

In conclusion, the effects of the tariff are a decrease in consumers' surplus, an increase in producers' surplus, and tariff revenue for government. Because the loss to consumers (areas 3, 4, 5, 6) is greater than the gain to producers (area 3) plus the gain to government (area 5), *a tariff results in a net loss.* The net loss is areas 4 and 6.

QUOTAS A quota is a legal limit imposed on the amount of a good that may be imported. For example, the government may decide to allow no more than 100,000 foreign cars to be imported, or 10 million barrels of OPEC oil, or 30,000 Japanese television sets. A quota reduces the supply of a good and raises the price of imported goods for domestic consumers (Exhibit 5).

Once again, we consider the situation in the U.S. car market. At a price of P_W (established in the world market for cars), U.S. consumers buy Q_1 cars from U.S. producers and $Q_2 - Q_1$ cars from foreign producers. Consumers' surplus is equal to areas 1, 2, 3, 4, 5, and 6. Producers' surplus is equal to area 7.

Suppose now that the U.S. government sets a quota equal to $Q_4 - Q_3$. Because this is the number of foreign cars U.S. consumers imported when the tariff was imposed (see

Quota

A legal limit imposed on the amount of a good that may be imported.

EXHIBIT 5

	Consumers' Surplus	Producers' Surplus	Revenue of Importers
Free trade (No quota)	1 + 2 + 3 + 4 + 5 + 6	7	8
Quota	1 + 2	3 + 7	5 + 8
Loss or Gain	− (3 + 4 + 5 + 6)	+3	+5

Result of Quota = Loss to consumers + Gain to producers + Gain to importers
= − (3 + 4 + 5 + 6)   +3   +5
= − (4 + 6)

The Effects of a Quota

A quota that sets the legal limit of imports at $Q_4 - Q_3$ causes the price of cars to increase from P_W to P_Q. A quota raises price, decreases consumers' surplus, increases producers' surplus, and increases the total revenue importers earn. Because consumers lose more than producers and importers gain, there is a net loss due to the quota.

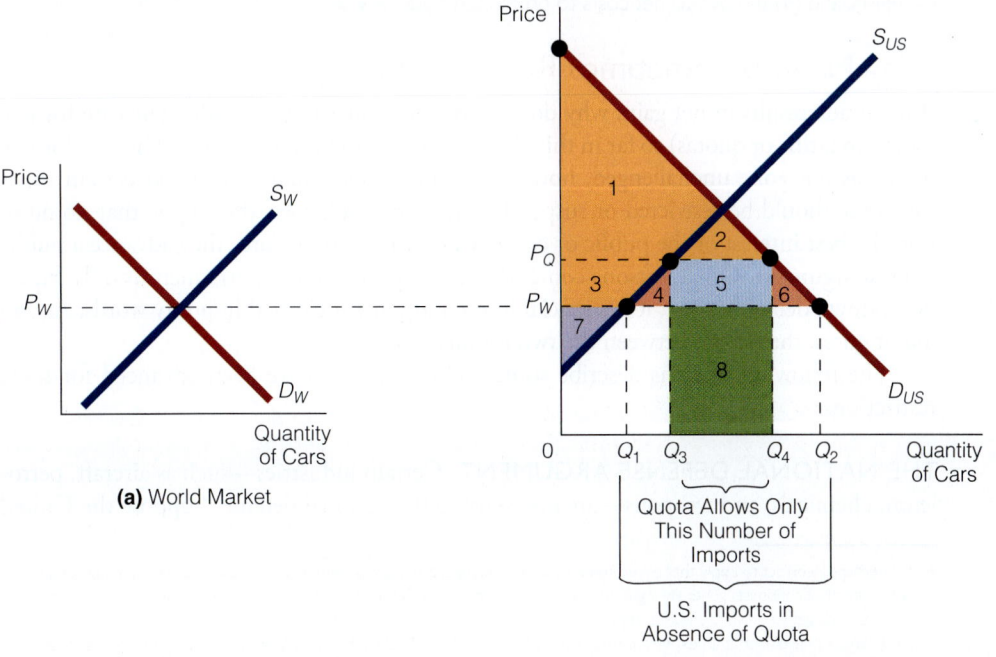

(a) World Market

(b) Domestic (U.S.) Market

Quota Allows Only This Number of Imports

U.S. Imports in Absence of Quota

Exhibit 4), the price of cars rises to P_Q in Exhibit 5 (which is equal to $P_W + T$ in Exhibit 4). At P_Q, consumers' surplus is equal to areas 1 and 2, and producers' surplus consists of areas 3 and 7. The decrease in consumers' surplus due to the quota is equal to areas 3, 4, 5, and 6; the increase in producers' surplus is equal to area 3.

However, area 5 is not transferred to government, as was the case when a tariff was imposed. Rather, it represents the additional revenue earned by the importers (and sellers) of $Q_4 - Q_3$. Before the quota, importers were importing $Q_2 - Q_1$, but only part of this total amount ($Q_4 - Q_3$) is relevant because this is the amount of imports now that the quota has been established. Before the quota was established, the dollar amount that the importers received for $Q_4 - Q_3$ was $P_W \times (Q_4 - Q_3)$, or area 8. Because of the quota, the price rises to P_Q, and they now receive $P_Q \times (Q_4 - Q_3)$, or areas 5 and 8. The difference between the total revenues on $Q_4 - Q_3$ with a quota and without a quota is area 5.

In conclusion, the effects of a quota are a decrease in consumers' surplus, an increase in producers' surplus, and an increase in total revenue for the importers who sell the allowed number of imported units. Because the loss to consumers (areas 3, 4, 5, 6) is greater than the increase in producers' surplus (area 3) plus the gain to importers (area 5), there is a *net loss as a result of the quota*. The net loss is equal to areas 4 and 6.[2]

finding ECONOMICS

In a Policy Debate There is a debate tonight at the college Irina attends, with four people on either side of the issue: Should the United States practice free trade? Irina attends the debate and comes away thinking that both sides made good points. The no-free-trade side argued that because other countries do not always practice free trade, neither should the United States. The pro-free-trade side argued that free trade leads to lower prices for U.S. consumers. Where is the economics?

Most of the debate, we believe, will fit into our discussion of Exhibits 4 and 5. These two exhibits show what happens to consumers and producers, and to society as a whole, as the result of both free and prohibited trade. The diagrams show (1) the benefits of prohibited free trade to domestic producers, (2) the costs of prohibited trade to domestic consumers, (3) tariff revenue to government, if it exists, and (4) the overall net costs to prohibited trade. ▲ ▲ ▲

Why Nations Sometimes Restrict Trade

If free trade results in net gain, why do nations sometimes restrict trade? The case for free trade (no tariffs or quotas) so far in this chapter appears to be a strong one. The case for free trade has not gone unchallenged, however. Some persons maintain that at certain times free trade should be restricted or suspended. In almost all cases, they argue that doing so is in the best interest of the public or country as a whole. In a word, they advance a public interest argument. Other persons contend that the public interest argument is only superficial; down deep, they say, it is a special interest argument clothed in pretty words. As you might guess, the debate between the two groups is often heated.

The following sections describe some arguments that have been advanced for trade restrictions.

THE NATIONAL DEFENSE ARGUMENT Certain industries—such as aircraft, petroleum, chemicals, and weapons—are necessary to the national defense. Suppose the United

---

2. It is perhaps incorrect to imply that government receives nothing from a quota. Although it receives nothing directly, it may gain indirectly. Economists generally argue that because government officials are likely to be the persons who decide which importers will get to satisfy the quota, importers will naturally lobby them. Thus, government officials will likely receive something, if only dinner at an expensive restaurant, while the lobbyist makes the pitch. In short, in the course of the lobbying, resources will be spent by lobbyists as they curry favor with government officials or politicians who have the power to decide who gets to sell the limited number of imported goods. In economics, lobbyists' activities geared toward obtaining special privileges are referred to as rent seeking.

Offshore Outsourcing, or Offshoring

Outsourcing is the term used to describe work done for a company by another company or by people other than the originating company's employees. Outsourcing entails purchasing a product or process from an outside supplier rather than producing it in-house. To illustrate, company X has, in the past, hired employees for personnel, accounting, and payroll services, but now a company in another state performs these duties. Company X has outsourced these work activities.

STR/AFP/GETTY IMAGES

When a company outsources certain work activities to individuals in another country, it is said to be engaged in offshore outsourcing, or offshoring. Consider a few examples. A New York securities firm replaces 800 software engineering employees with a team of software engineers in India. A computer company replaces 200 on-call technicians in its headquarters in Texas with 150 on-call technicians in India.

The benefits of offshoring for a U.S. firm are obvious; it pays lower wages to individuals in other countries for the same work that U.S. employees do for higher wages. Benefits also flow to the employees hired in the foreign countries. The costs of offshoring are said to fall on persons who lose their jobs as a result, such as the software engineer in New York or the on-call computer technician in Texas. Some have argued that offshoring will soon become a major political issue and that it could bring with it a wave of protectionism.

Offshoring will undoubtedly have both proponents and opponents. On a net basis, however, are there more benefits than costs or more costs than benefits? Consider a U.S. company that currently employs Jones as a software engineer, paying her x a year. Then, one day, the company tells Jones that it has to let her go; it is replacing her with a software engineer in India who will work for z a year (and, yes, $z < x$).

Why doesn't Jones simply agree to work for z, the same wage as that agreed to by the Indian software engineer? Obviously, Jones can work elsewhere for some wage between x and z. Assume this wage is y. So, even though offshoring has moved Jones from earning x to earning y, y is still more than z.

In short, the U.S. company is able to lower its costs from x to z, and Jones's income falls from x to y. The U.S. company lowers its costs more than Jones's income falls because the difference between x and z is greater than the difference between x and y.

If the U.S. company operates in a competitive environment, its lower costs will shift its supply curve to the right and lower prices. In other words, offshoring can reduce prices for U.S. consumers. The political fallout from offshoring might, in the end, depend on how visible, to the average American, the employment effects of offshoring are relative to the price reduction effect.

States has a comparative advantage in the production of wheat and country X has a comparative advantage in the production of weapons. Many Americans feel that the United States should not specialize in the production of wheat and then trade wheat to country X in exchange for weapons. Leaving weapons production to another country, they maintain, is too dangerous.

The national defense argument may have some validity, but even valid arguments may be abused. Industries that are not really necessary to the national defense may maintain otherwise. In the past, the national defense argument has been used by some firms in the following industries: pens, pottery, peanuts, papers, candles, thumbtacks, tuna fishing, and pencils.

THE INFANT INDUSTRY ARGUMENT Alexander Hamilton, the first U.S. secretary of the treasury, argued that so-called infant, or new, industries often need protection from older, established foreign competitors until they are mature enough to compete on an equal basis. Today, some persons voice the same argument. The infant industry argument is clearly an argument for temporary protection. Critics charge, however, that after an industry is protected from foreign competition, removing the protection is almost impossible; the once infant industry will continue to maintain that it isn't old enough to go it alone. Critics of the infant industry argument say that political realities make it unlikely that a benefit, once bestowed, will be removed.

Finally, the infant industry argument, like the national defense argument, may be abused. All new industries, whether they could currently compete successfully with foreign producers or not, would argue for protection on infant industry grounds.

Dumping
The sale of goods abroad at a price below their cost and below the price charged in the domestic market.

THE ANTIDUMPING ARGUMENT Dumping is the sale of goods abroad at a price below their cost and below the price charged in the domestic market. If a French firm sells wine in the United States for a price below the cost of producing the wine and below the price charged in France, it is dumping wine in the United States. Critics of dumping maintain that it is an unfair trade practice that puts domestic producers of substitute goods at a disadvantage.

In addition, critics charge that dumpers seek only to penetrate a market and drive out domestic competitors, only to raise prices. However, some economists point to the infeasibility of this strategy. After the dumpers have driven out their competition and raised prices, their competition is likely to return. For their efforts, the dumpers, in turn, would have incurred only a string of losses (owing to their selling below cost). Opponents of the antidumping argument also point out that domestic consumers benefit from dumping because they pay lower prices.

THE FOREIGN EXPORT SUBSIDIES ARGUMENT Some governments subsidize firms that export goods. If a country offers a below-market (interest rate) loan to a company, it is often argued, the government subsidizes the production of the good the firm produces. If, in turn, the firm exports the good to a foreign country, that country's producers of substitute goods call foul. They complain that the foreign firm has been given an unfair advantage that they should be protected against.[3]

Others say that consumers should not turn their backs on a gift (in the form of lower prices). If foreign governments want to subsidize their exports and thus give a gift to foreign consumers at the expense of their own taxpayers, then the recipients should not complain. Of course, the recipients are usually not the ones who are complaining. Usually, the complainers are the domestic producers who can't sell their goods at as high a price because of the so-called gift domestic consumers are receiving from foreign governments.

THE LOW FOREIGN WAGES ARGUMENT Some argue that American producers can't compete with foreign producers because American producers have to pay high wages to their workers and foreign producers pay low wages. The American producers insist that international trade must be restricted, or they will be ruined. However, the argument overlooks why American wages are high and foreign wages are low in the first place: productivity. High productivity and high wages are usually linked, as are low productivity and low wages. If an American worker, who receives $20 per hour, can produce (on average) 100 units of good X per hour, working with numerous capital goods, then the cost per unit may be lower than when a foreign worker, who receives $2 per hour, produces (on average) 5 units of X per hour, working by hand. In short, a country's high-wage disadvantage may be offset by its productivity advantage, and a country's low-wage advantage may be offset by its productivity disadvantage. High wages do not necessarily mean high costs when productivity and the costs of nonlabor resources are included.

---

3. Words are important in this debate. For example, domestic producers who claim that foreign governments have subsidized foreign firms say that they are not asking for economic protectionism, but only retaliation, or reciprocity, or simply tit for tat—words that have less negative connotation than those their opponents use.

THE SAVING DOMESTIC JOBS ARGUMENT Sometimes, the argument against completely free trade is made in terms of saving domestic jobs. Actually, this argument has cropped up before in its different guises. For example, the low foreign wages argument is one form of it: if domestic producers cannot compete with foreign producers because foreign producers pay low wages and domestic producers pay high wages, domestic producers will go out of business and domestic jobs will be lost. The foreign export subsidies argument is another version: if foreign government subsidies give a competitive edge to foreign producers, not only will domestic producers fail, but as a result of their failure, domestic jobs will be lost.

Critics of the saving domestic jobs argument (in all its guises) counterargue as follows: if a domestic producer is being outcompeted by foreign producers and if domestic jobs in an industry are being lost as a result, the world market is signaling that those labor resources could be put to better use in an industry in which the country holds a comparative advantage.

ⓣhinking Like AN ECONOMIST

Economics Versus Politics International trade often becomes a battleground between economics and politics. The simple tools of supply and demand and of consumers' and producers' surpluses show that free trade leads to net gains. On the whole, tariffs and quotas make living standards lower than they would be if free trade were permitted. On the other side, though, are the realities of business and politics. Domestic producers may advocate quotas and tariffs to make themselves better off, giving little thought to the negative effects on foreign producers or domestic consumers.

Perhaps the battle over international trade comes down to this: policies are largely advocated, argued, and lobbied for based more on their distributional effects than on their aggregate or overall effects. On an aggregate level, free trade produces a net gain for society, whereas restricted trade produces a net loss. But economists understand that even if free trade in the aggregate produces a net gain, not every single person will benefit more from free trade than from restricted trade. An example in this chapter showed how a subset of the population (producers) gains more, in a particular instance, from restricted trade than from free trade. In short, economists realize that the crucial question in determining real-world policies is more often, "How does it affect me?" than "How does it affect us?" ▲▲▲

SELF-TEST

1. Who benefits and who loses from tariffs? Explain your answer.

2. Identify the directional change in consumers' surplus and producers' surplus when we move from free trade to tariffs. Is the change in consumers' surplus greater than, less than, or equal to the change in producers' surplus?

3. What is a major difference between the effects of a quota and the effects of a tariff?

4. Outline the details of the infant industry argument for trade restriction.

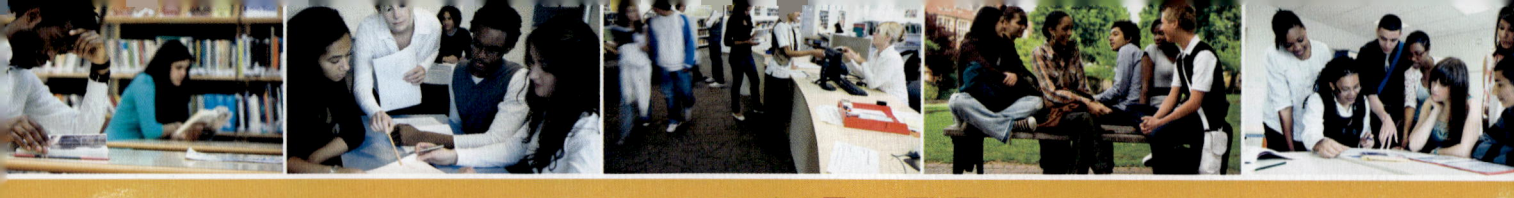

OFFICE HOURS

"Should We Impose Tariffs If They Impose Tariffs?"

STUDENT:

Here is a problem I have with our discussion of free and prohibited trade. Essentially, I am in favor of free international trade, but I think the United States should have free trade with countries that practice free trade with us. In other words, if country X practices free trade with the United States, then the United States should practice free trade with it. But if country Y places tariffs on U.S. goods entering the country, then the United States ought to place tariffs on country Y's goods entering this country.

INSTRUCTOR:

Many people feel the same way you do, but this opinion overlooks something that we showed in Exhibits 4 and 5: the losses of moving from free trade to prohibited trade (where either tariffs or quotas exist) are greater than the gains. Remember? There is a net loss to society in that move.

STUDENT:

I just think it is only fair that other countries get what they give. If they give free trade to us, then we ought to give free trade back to them. If they place tariffs and quotas on our goods, then we ought to do the same to their goods.

INSTRUCTOR:

You need to keep in mind the price the United States has to pay for this policy of tit for tat.

STUDENT:

What do you mean? What price does the United States have to pay?

INSTRUCTOR:

It has to incur the net loss illustrated in Exhibits 4 and 5. If you look back at Exhibit 4, for example, you'll notice that moving from free trade to prohibited trade (1) decreases consumers' surplus, (2) increases producers' surplus, and (3) raises tariff revenue. But when we count up all the gains of prohibited trade and compare them with all the losses, we conclude that the losses are greater than the gains. In other words, prohibited trade leads to a net loss.

STUDENT:

But suppose our practicing tit for tat (giving free trade for free trade and prohibited trade for prohibited trade) forces other countries to move away from prohibited trade. In other words, what I am saying is this: we need to look at this issue of free versus prohibited trade

---

CHAPTER SUMMARY

SPECIALIZATION AND TRADE

- A country has a comparative advantage in the production of a good if it can produce the good at a lower opportunity cost than another country can.
- Individuals in countries that specialize and trade have a higher standard of living than would be the case if their countries did not specialize and trade.
- Government officials do not analyze cost data to determine what their country should specialize in and trade. Instead, the desire to earn a dollar, peso, or euro guides individuals' actions and produces the unintended consequence that countries specialize in and trade the good(s) in which they have a

comparative advantage. However, trade restrictions can change this outcome.

TARIFFS AND QUOTAS

- A tariff is a tax on imports. A quota is a legal limit on the amount of a good that may be imported.
- Both tariffs and quotas raise the price of imports.
- Tariffs lead to a decrease in consumers' surplus, an increase in producers' surplus, and tariff revenue for the government. Consumers lose more through tariffs than producers and government (together) gain.

over time. Maybe the United States has to practice prohibited trade today (with those countries that impose tariffs or quotas on the United States) in order to force those countries to practice free trade tomorrow. Couldn't it work out that way?

INSTRUCTOR:

It could work out that way. Or, then, things could escalate toward greater prohibited trade. In other words, country A imposes tariffs and quotas on country B, and then country B raises its tariffs and quotas even higher on country A. So country A retaliates and raises its tariffs and quotas on country B, and so on.

STUDENT:

So what is your point? Is it that free trade is the best policy to practice no matter what other countries do.

INSTRUCTOR:

That is what many economists would say, but that is not really the point I am making here. I am rather making two points with respect to the discussion. First, in response to your position that the United States ought to practice tit for tat (give free trade for free trade, tariffs for tariffs, quotas for quotas), I am simply drawing your attention to the net loss Americans incur if they practice prohibited trade—no matter what other countries are doing. In other words, there is a net loss for Americans even if other countries are practicing free or prohibited trade. Second, with respect to your second point, about prohibited trade leading to free trade tomorrow, I am saying that we can't be sure that prohibited trade today won't lead to greater prohibitions on trade tomorrow. This is not to say you can't be right: it is possible for prohibited trade today to lead to less prohibited trade tomorrow.

POINTS TO REMEMBER

1. A country that imposes tariffs or quotas on imported goods incurs a net loss no matter what another country is doing—whether it is practicing free or prohibited trade.
2. We cannot easily predict the outcome of the United States' practicing tit for tat in international trade.

- Quotas lead to a decrease in consumers' surplus, an increase in producers' surplus, and additional revenue for the importers who sell the amount specified by the quota. Consumers lose more through quotas than producers and importers (together) gain.

ARGUMENTS FOR TRADE RESTRICTIONS

- The national defense argument states that certain goods—such as aircraft, petroleum, chemicals, and weapons—are necessary to the national defense and should be produced domestically whether the country has a comparative advantage in their production or not.
- The infant industry argument states that infant, or new, industries should be protected from free (foreign) trade so that they have time to develop and compete on an equal basis with older, more established foreign industries.

- The antidumping argument states that domestic producers should not have to compete (on an unequal basis) with foreign producers that sell products below cost and below the prices they charge in their domestic markets.
- The foreign export subsidies argument states that domestic producers should not have to compete (on an unequal basis) with foreign producers that have been subsidized by their governments.
- The low foreign wages argument states that domestic producers cannot compete with foreign producers that pay low wages to their employees when domestic producers pay high wages to their employees. For high-paying domestic firms to survive, limits on free trade are proposed.
- The saving domestic jobs argument states that through low foreign wages or government subsidies (or dumping and similar practices), foreign producers will be able to outcompete

domestic producers and that therefore domestic jobs will be lost. For domestic firms to survive and domestic jobs not to be lost, limits on free trade are proposed.

- Everyone does not accept the arguments for trade restrictions as valid. Critics often maintain that the arguments can be and are abused and that in most cases they are motivated by self-interest.

KEY TERMS AND CONCEPTS

Comparative Advantage   Tariff   Quota   Dumping

QUESTIONS AND PROBLEMS

1. If there is a net loss to society from tariffs, why do tariffs exist?

2. Consider two groups of domestic producers: those that compete with imports and those that export goods. Suppose the domestic producers that compete with imports convince the legislature to impose a high tariff on imports—so high, in fact, that almost all imports are eliminated. Does this policy in any way adversely affect domestic producers that export goods? If so, how?

3. Some economists have argued that because domestic consumers gain more from free trade than domestic producers gain from (import) tariffs and quotas, consumers should buy out domestic producers and rid themselves of costly tariffs and quotas. For example, if consumers save $400 million from free trade (through paying lower prices) and producers gain $100 million from tariffs and quotas, consumers can pay producers something more than $100 million but less than $400 million and get producers to favor free trade too. Assuming this scheme were feasible, what do you think of it?

4. Neither free trade nor prohibited trade comes with just benefits. Both come with benefits and costs. Therefore, free trade is no better or worse than prohibited trade. Comment.

5. Suppose that a constitutional convention is called tomorrow and that you are chosen as one of the delegates from your state. You and the other delegates must decide whether it will be constitutional or unconstitutional for the federal government to impose tariffs and quotas or to restrict international trade in any way. What would be your position?

6. "Whatever can be done by a tariff can be done by a quota." Discuss.

7. Even though Jeremy is a better gardener and novelist than Bill, Jeremy still hires Bill as his gardener. Why?

8. "The desire for profit can end up pushing countries toward producing goods in which they have a comparative advantage." Do you agree or disagree? Explain your answer.

9. Suppose the landmass known to you as the United States of America had been composed, since the nation's founding, of separate countries instead of separate states. Would you expect the standard of living of the people who inhabit this landmass to be higher, lower, or equal to what it is today? Why?

10. If country A is better than country B at producing all goods, will country A still be made better off by specializing and trading? Explain your answer. (*Hint:* Look at Exhibit 1.)

11. Suppose the U.S. government wants to curtail imports. Would it be likely to favor a tariff or a quota to accomplish its objective? Why?

12. Although a production possibilities frontier is usually drawn for a country, one could be drawn for the world. Picture the world's production possibilities frontier. Is the world positioned at a point on the PPF or below it? Give a reason for your answer.

WORKING WITH NUMBERS AND GRAPHS

1. Using the data in the table, answer the following questions:

   a. For which good does Canada have a comparative advantage?

   b. For which good does Italy have a comparative advantage?

   c. What might be a set of favorable terms of trade for the two countries?

   d. Prove that both countries would be better off in the specialization–trade case than in the no-specialization–no-trade case.

Points on Production Possibilities Frontier	Canada		Italy	
	Good X	Good Y	Good X	Good Y
A	150	0	90	0
B	100	25	60	60
C	50	50	30	120
D	0	75	0	180

2. In the following figure, P_W is the world price and $P_W + T$ is the world price plus a tariff. Identify the following:

a. The level of imports at P_W

b. The level of imports at $P_W + T$

c. The loss in consumers' surplus as a result of a tariff

d. The gain in producers' surplus as a result of a tariff

e. The tariff revenue as the result of a tariff

f. The net loss to society as a result of a tariff

g. The net benefit to society of moving from a tariff situation to a no-tariff situation

CHAPTER 35

PETER MENZEL / PHOTO RESEARCHERS, INC.

INTERNATIONAL FINANCE

Introduction When people travel to a foreign country, they buy goods and services in the country, whose prices are quoted in yen, pounds, euros, pesos, or some other currency. For example, a U.S. tourist in Germany might want to buy a good priced in euros and to know what the good costs in dollars and cents. The answer depends on the current exchange rate between the dollar and the euro, but what determines the exchange rate? This is just one of the many questions answered in this chapter.

THE BALANCE OF PAYMENTS

Balance of Payments

A periodic (usually annual) statement of the money value of all transactions between residents of one country and the residents of all other countries.

Debit

In the balance of payments, any transaction that supplies the country's currency in the foreign exchange market.

Foreign Exchange Market

The market in which currencies of different countries are exchanged.

Credit

In the balance of payments, any transaction that creates a demand for the country's currency in the foreign exchange market.

Countries keep track of their domestic level of production by calculating their gross domestic product (GDP). Similarly, they keep track of the flow of their international trade (receipts and expenditures) by calculating their balance of payments. The balance of payments is a periodic (usually annual) statement of the money value of all transactions between residents of one country and residents of all other countries. The balance of payments provides information about a nation's imports and exports, domestic residents' earnings on assets located abroad, foreign earnings on domestic assets, gifts to and from foreign countries (including foreign aid), the exchange of assets, and official transactions by governments and central banks.

Balance of payments accounts record both debits and credits. A debit is indicated by a minus (−) sign, and a credit is indicated by a plus (+) sign. *Any transaction that supplies the country's currency in the foreign exchange market is recorded as a debit.* (The foreign exchange market is the market in which currencies of different countries are exchanged.) For example, a U.S. retailer wants to buy Japanese television sets so that he can sell them in his stores in the United States. To buy the TV sets from the Japanese, the retailer first has to supply U.S. dollars (in the foreign exchange market) in return for Japanese yen. Then he will turn over the yen to the Japanese in exchange for the television sets.

Any transaction that creates a demand for the country's currency in the foreign exchange market is recorded as a credit. For example, a Russian retailer wants to buy computers from U.S. computer producers. To pay the U.S. producers, who want U.S. dollars,

EXHIBIT 1

Item	Definition	Example	Debits and Credits
Debit (−)	Any transaction that supplies the country's currency.	Jim, an American, supplies dollars in exchange for yen so that he can use the yen to buy Japanese goods.	
Credit (+)	Any transaction that creates a demand for the country's currency.	Svetlana, who is Russian and living in Russia, supplies rubles in order to demand dollars so that she can use the dollars to buy U.S. goods.	

the Russian retailer must supply rubles (in the foreign exchange market) in return for dollars. Then she will turn over the dollars to the U.S. producers in exchange for the computers.

The international transactions that are summarized in the balance of payments can be grouped into three categories, or three accounts—the current account, the capital account, and the official reserve account—and a statistical discrepancy. Exhibit 2 illustrates a U.S. balance of payments account for year Z. The data in the exhibit are hypothetical (to make the calculations simpler), but not unrealistic. In this section, we describe and explain each of the items in the balance of payments using the data in Exhibit 2 for our calculations.

Current Account

The current account includes all payments related to the purchase and sale of goods and services. The current account has three major components: exports of goods and services, imports of goods and services, and net unilateral transfers abroad.

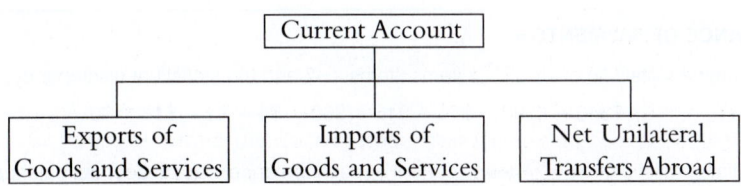

Current Account
The account in the balance of payments that includes all payments related to the purchase and sale of goods and services; components of the account include exports, imports, and net unilateral transfers abroad.

EXPORTS OF GOODS AND SERVICES Americans export goods (e.g., cars), they export services (e.g., insurance, banking, transportation, and tourism), and they receive income on assets they own abroad. All three activities increase the demand for U.S. dollars while increasing the supply of foreign currencies in the foreign exchange market; thus, they are recorded as credits (+). For example, if a foreigner buys a U.S. computer, payment must ultimately be made in U.S. dollars. Thus, she is required to supply her country's currency when she demands U.S. dollars. (We use "foreigner" in this chapter to refer to a resident of a foreign country.)

IMPORTS OF GOODS AND SERVICES Americans import goods and services, and foreigners receive income on assets they own in the United States. These activities increase the demand for foreign currencies while increasing the supply of U.S. dollars to the foreign exchange market; thus, they are recorded as debits (−). For example, if an American buys a Japanese car, payment must ultimately be made in Japanese yen. Thus, he is required to supply U.S. dollars when he demands Japanese yen.

EXHIBIT 2

U.S. Balance of Payments, Year Z

The data in this exhibit are hypothetical, but not unrealistic. All numbers are in billions of dollars. The plus and minus signs in the exhibit should be viewed as operational signs.

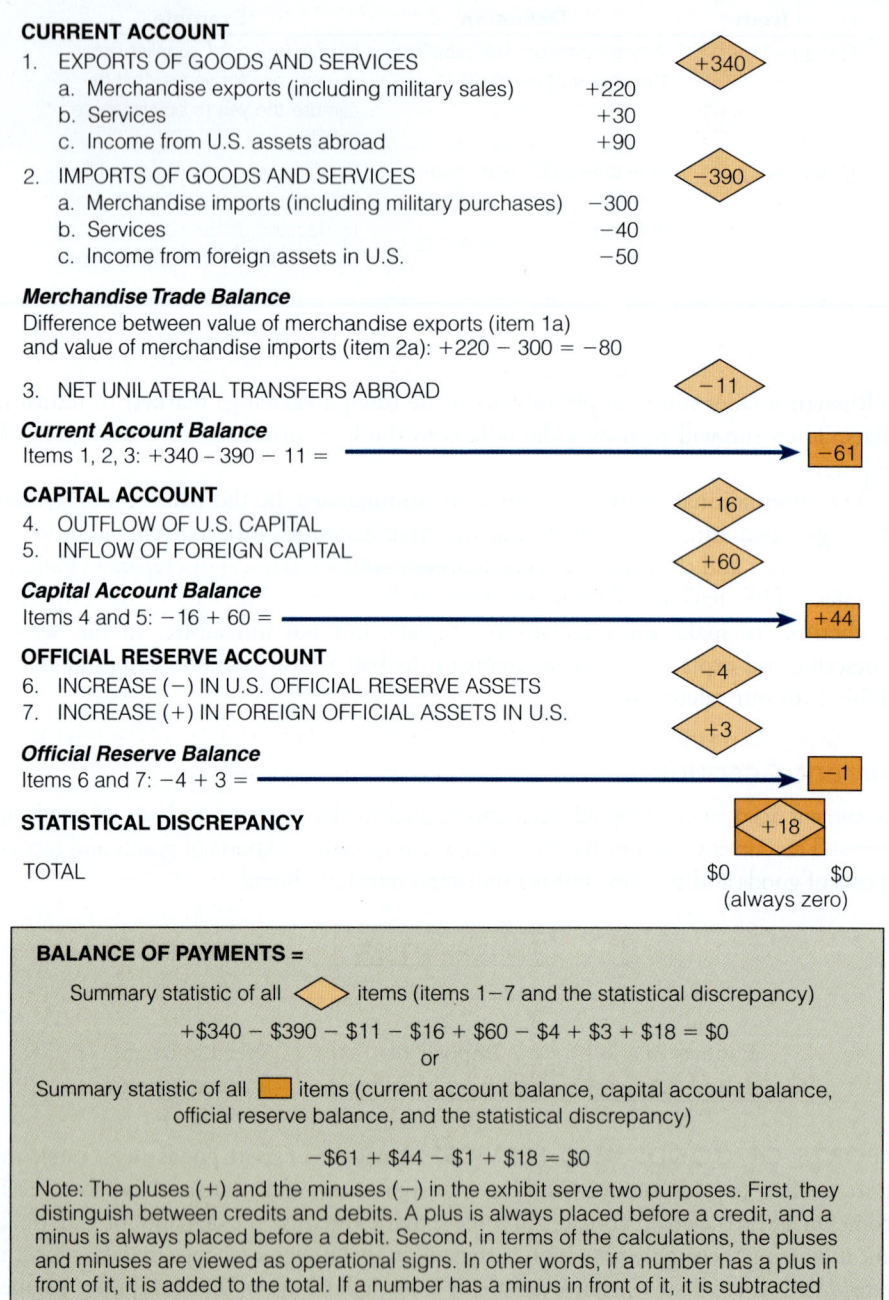

CURRENT ACCOUNT

1. EXPORTS OF GOODS AND SERVICES   +340
   a. Merchandise exports (including military sales)   +220
   b. Services   +30
   c. Income from U.S. assets abroad   +90
2. IMPORTS OF GOODS AND SERVICES   −390
   a. Merchandise imports (including military purchases) −300
   b. Services   −40
   c. Income from foreign assets in U.S.   −50

Merchandise Trade Balance
Difference between value of merchandise exports (item 1a) and value of merchandise imports (item 2a): +220 − 300 = −80

3. NET UNILATERAL TRANSFERS ABROAD   −11

Current Account Balance
Items 1, 2, 3: +340 − 390 − 11 = ⟶   −61

CAPITAL ACCOUNT

4. OUTFLOW OF U.S. CAPITAL   −16
5. INFLOW OF FOREIGN CAPITAL   +60

Capital Account Balance
Items 4 and 5: −16 + 60 = ⟶   +44

OFFICIAL RESERVE ACCOUNT

6. INCREASE (−) IN U.S. OFFICIAL RESERVE ASSETS   −4
7. INCREASE (+) IN FOREIGN OFFICIAL ASSETS IN U.S.   +3

Official Reserve Balance
Items 6 and 7: −4 + 3 = ⟶   −1

STATISTICAL DISCREPANCY   +18

TOTAL $0 $0
                                                             (always zero)

BALANCE OF PAYMENTS =

Summary statistic of all ⬦ items (items 1–7 and the statistical discrepancy)

+$340 − $390 − $11 − $16 + $60 − $4 + $3 + $18 = $0

or

Summary statistic of all ▪ items (current account balance, capital account balance, official reserve balance, and the statistical discrepancy)

−$61 + $44 − $1 + $18 = $0

Note: The pluses (+) and the minuses (−) in the exhibit serve two purposes. First, they distinguish between credits and debits. A plus is always placed before a credit, and a minus is always placed before a debit. Second, in terms of the calculations, the pluses and minuses are viewed as operational signs. In other words, if a number has a plus in front of it, it is added to the total. If a number has a minus in front of it, it is subtracted from the total.

In Exhibit 2, exports of goods and services total +$340 billion in year Z, and imports of goods and services total −$390 billion.[1] Before discussing the third component of the

---

1. In everyday language, people do not say, "Exports are a positive $x billion and imports are a negative $y billion." Placing a plus sign (+) in front of exports and a minus sign (−) in front of imports simply reinforces the essential point that exports are credits and imports are debits. This will be useful later when we calculate certain account balances.

current account—net unilateral transfers abroad—we define some important relationships between exports and imports.

Look at the difference between the *value of merchandise exports* (item 1a in Exhibit 2) and the *value of merchandise imports* (item 2a in the exhibit). This difference is the merchandise trade balance, or the balance of trade. Specifically, the merchandise trade balance is the difference between the value of merchandise exported and the value of merchandise imported. In year Z, the merchandise trade balance is $220 billion − $300 billion = −$80 billion.

Merchandise trade balance = Value of merchandise exports
− Value of merchandise imports

Merchandise Trade Balance
The difference between the value of merchandise exports and the value of merchandise imports.

If the value of a country's merchandise exports is less than the value of its merchandise imports, it is said to have a merchandise trade deficit.

Merchandise trade deficit = Value of merchandise exports
< Value of merchandise imports

Merchandise Trade Deficit
The situation when the value of merchandise exports is less than the value of merchandise imports.

If the value of a country's merchandise exports is greater than the value of its merchandise imports, it is said to have a merchandise trade surplus.

Merchandise trade surplus = Value of merchandise exports
> Value of merchandise imports

Merchandise Trade Surplus
The situation when the value of merchandise exports is greater than the value of merchandise imports.

Exhibit 3 shows the U.S. merchandise trade balance from 1997 to 2009. Notice that there has been a merchandise trade deficit in each of these years.

NET UNILATERAL TRANSFERS ABROAD Unilateral transfers are one-way money payments. They can go from Americans or the U.S. government to foreigners or foreign governments. If an American sends money to a relative in a foreign country, if the U.S. government gives money to a foreign country as a gift or grant, or if an American retires in a foreign country and receives Social Security checks there, all these transactions are referred to as unilateral transfers. If an American or the U.S. government makes a unilateral transfer abroad, this gives rise to a demand for foreign currency and a supply of U.S. dollars; thus, it is entered as a debit item in the U.S. balance of payments accounts.

Unilateral transfers can also go from foreigners or foreign governments to Americans or to the U.S. government. A foreign citizen sending money to a relative living in the United States is a unilateral transfer. A foreigner making a unilateral transfer to an American gives rise to a supply of foreign currency and a demand for U.S. dollars; thus, it is entered as a credit item in the U.S. balance of payments accounts.

Net unilateral transfers abroad include both types of transfers—from the United States to foreign countries and from foreign countries to the United States. The dollar amount of net unilateral transfers is negative if U.S. transfers are greater than foreign transfers. It is positive if foreign transfers are greater than U.S. transfers.

For year Z in Exhibit 2, we have assumed that the unilateral transfers made by Americans to foreign citizens are greater than the unilateral transfers made by foreign citizens to Americans. Thus, there is a *negative* net dollar amount, −$11 billion.

Items 1, 2, and 3 in Exhibit 2—exports of goods and services, imports of goods and services, and net unilateral transfers abroad—comprise the current account. The current account balance is the summary statistic for these three items. In year Z, it is −$61 billion. The news media sometimes call the current account balance the balance of payments. To an economist, this reference is incorrect; the balance of payments includes several more items.

Current Account Balance
In the balance of payments, the summary statistic for exports of goods and services, imports of goods and services, and net unilateral transfers abroad.

EXHIBIT 3

U.S. Merchandise Trade Balance

In each of the years shown, 1997–2009, a merchandise trade deficit has existed.

Source: U.S. Department of Commerce, Bureau of Economic Analysis.

Capital Account

The capital account includes all payments related to the purchase and sale of assets and to borrowing and lending activities. Its major components are the outflow of U.S. capital and the inflow of foreign capital.

Capital Account
The account in the balance of payments that includes all payments related to the purchase and sale of assets and to borrowing and lending activities. Components include outflow of U.S. capital and inflow of foreign capital.

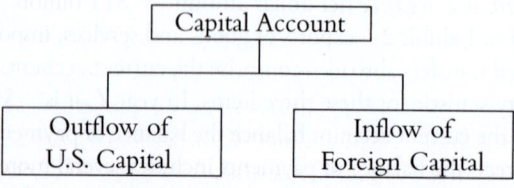

OUTFLOW OF U.S. CAPITAL American purchases of foreign assets and U.S. loans to foreigners are outflows of U.S. capital. As such, they give rise to a demand for foreign currency and a supply of U.S. dollars on the foreign exchange market. Hence, they are considered a debit. For example, if an American wants to buy land in Japan, U.S. dollars must be supplied to purchase (demand) Japanese yen.

INFLOW OF FOREIGN CAPITAL Foreign purchases of U.S. assets and foreign loans to Americans are inflows of foreign capital. As such, they give rise to a demand for U.S. dollars and to a supply of foreign currency on the foreign exchange market. Hence, they are considered a credit. For example, if a Japanese citizen buys a U.S. Treasury bill, Japanese yen must be supplied to purchase (demand) U.S. dollars.

Items 4 and 5 in Exhibit 2—outflow of U.S. capital and inflow of foreign capital—comprise the capital account. The capital account balance is the summary statistic for these two items. It is equal to the difference between the outflow of U.S. capital and the inflow of foreign capital. In year Z, it is $44 billion.

Official Reserve Account

A government possesses official reserve balances in the form of:

- Foreign currencies.
- Gold.
- Its reserve position in the International Monetary Fund (IMF, an international organization created to oversee the international monetary system).
- Special drawing rights (SDRs, an international money, created by the IMF, in the form of bookkeeping entries, like gold and currencies, which nations can use to settle international accounts).

Countries with a deficit in their combined current and capital accounts can draw on their reserves. For example, if the United States has a deficit in its combined current and capital accounts of $5 billion, it can draw down its official reserves to meet this deficit.

Item 6 in Exhibit 2 shows that the United States increased its reserve assets by $4 billion in year Z. This is a debit item because if the United States acquires official reserves (say, through the purchase of a foreign currency), it has increased the demand for the foreign currency and supplied dollars. Thus, an increase in official reserves is like an outflow of capital in the capital account and appears as a payment with a negative sign. Therefore, an increase in foreign official assets in the United States is a credit item.

Statistical Discrepancy

If someone buys a U.S. dollar with, say, Japanese yen, someone must sell a U.S. dollar. Thus, dollars purchased equal dollars sold.

In all the transactions discussed so far—exporting goods, importing goods, sending money to relatives in foreign countries, buying land in foreign countries—dollars were bought and sold. The total number of dollars sold must always equal the total number of dollars purchased. However, balance of payments accountants do not have complete information; they can record only the credits and debits they observe. There may be more debits or credits than those observed in a given year.

Suppose in year Z, all debits are observed and recorded, but not all credits, perhaps because of smuggling activities, secret bank accounts, people living in more than one country, and so on. To adjust for this lack of information, balance of payments accountants use the *statistical discrepancy,* which is the part of the balance of payments that adjusts for missing information. In Exhibit 2, the statistical discrepancy is +$18 billion. This means that

Capital Account Balance
The summary statistic for the outflow of U.S. capital, equal to the difference between the outflow of U.S. capital and the inflow of foreign capital.

International Monetary Fund (IMF)
An international organization created to oversee the international monetary system. The IMF does not control the world's money supply, but it does hold currency reserves for member nations and make loans to central banks.

Special Drawing Right (SDR)
An international money, created by the IMF, in the form of bookkeeping entries; like gold and currencies, it can be used by nations to settle international accounts.

economics 24/7

Merchandise Trade Deficit, We Thought We Knew Thee

You read in the newspaper that the United States has a merchandise trade deficit, that is, the value of merchandise exports for the United States is *less than* the value of merchandise imports. In terms of Exhibit 2, item 1a is less than item 2a. For example, Americans exported $600 billion worth of goods and imported $800 billion worth of goods. The merchandise trade deficit is $200 billion.

The word *deficit* has a negative connotation to many people, who think of a trade deficit as something bad. It's bad, some people say, "Because it means Americans owe money to foreigners. Specifically, Americans are 'in debt' to foreigners to the tune of $200 billion." Other people say that because Americans are increasing demand for foreign-produced goods by more [$200 billion more, to be exact] than foreigners are increasing demand for U.S.-produced goods, demand is "leaving the country."

However, neither sentiment is correct. Americans do not owe foreigners anything, and demand is not leaving the country. The reason is obvious: Americans have already paid this $200 billion to foreigners. The $200 billion is part of the overall $800 billion that Americans spent on imported goods.

Still, even if Americans don't owe $200 billion to foreigners, the $200 billion is not gone forever, never to return to the United States. Foreigners may have those dollars now, but they're not going to burn them, they're not going to eat them, and they're not going to give them away. What they are going to do with those dollars—in fact, the only thing they can do with those dollars—is use them to buy "something American."[2] They could buy real estate in the United States. For example, a Brazilian man with dollars might end up buying an apartment in downtown Manhattan. In other words, the dollars that we thought would leave the country for good are eventually coming back home.

A foreign firm with U.S. dollars could hire a construction company to build a factory in the United States—Tennessee, Virginia, or South Dakota—so that it can produce some of its goods in the United States and thus lower its transportation costs. An American might end up working at that factory and thus be paid with some of the dollars that once were held by foreigners. (And the American worker is likely to spend those dollars to buy U.S. goods and services.)

The main point is simple: the dollars that foreigners initially hold because of the merchandise trade deficit will begin to return to the United States. They are not gone forever.

_____

2. If you are thinking that the foreigners who have the $200 billion can trade those dollars for other currencies, you are right. A Frenchman might trade some of his dollars for pesos, euros, or yen, but now someone else has the dollars the Frenchman once had, and we then have to ask what this new person will do with the dollars.

$18 billion worth of credits (+) went unobserved in year Z. There may have been some hidden exports and unrecorded capital inflows that year.

What the Balance of Payments Equals

The balance of payments is the summary statistic for:

- Exports of goods and services (item 1 in Exhibit 2).
- Imports of goods and services (item 2).
- Net unilateral transfers abroad (item 3).
- Outflow of U.S. capital (item 4).
- Inflow of foreign capital (item 5).
- Increase in U.S. official reserve assets (item 6).
- Increase in foreign official assets in the United States (item 7).
- Statistical discrepancy.

Calculating the balance of payments in year Z using these items, we have (in billions of dollars) $+340 - 390 - 11 - 16 + 60 - 4 + 3 + 18 = 0$.

Alternatively, the balance of payments is the summary statistic for the following:

- Current account balance
- Capital account balance
- Official reserve balance
- Statistical discrepancy

Calculating the balance of payments in year Z using these items, we have (in billions of dollars) $-61 + 44 - 1 + 18 = 0$. The balance of payments for the United States in year Z equals zero.

SELF-TEST

(Answers to Self-Test questions are in Answers to Self-Test Questions at the back of the book.)

1. If an American retailer buys cars from a Japanese manufacturer, is this transaction recorded as a debit or a credit? Explain your answer.

2. Exports of goods and services equal $200 billion, and imports of goods and services equal $300 billion. What is the merchandise trade balance?

3. What is the difference between the merchandise trade balance and the current account balance?

THE FOREIGN EXCHANGE MARKET

If a U.S. buyer wants to purchase a good from a U.S. seller, the buyer simply gives the required number of U.S. dollars to the seller. If, however, a U.S. buyer wants to purchase a good from a seller in Mexico, the U.S. buyer must first exchange her U.S. dollars for Mexican pesos. Then, with the pesos, she buys the good from the Mexican seller. As explained, currencies of different countries are exchanged in the foreign exchange market. In this market, currencies are bought and sold for a price—the exchange rate. For instance, it might take $1.23 to buy a euro, 10¢ to buy a Mexican peso, and 13¢ to buy a Danish krone.

In this section, we explain why currencies are demanded and supplied in the foreign exchange market. Then we discuss how the exchange rate expresses the relationship between the demand for and the supply of currencies.

Exchange Rate
The price of one currency in terms of another currency.

The Demand for Goods

To simplify our analysis, we assume that there are only two countries in the world: the United States and Mexico. Thus there are only two currencies in the world: the U.S. dollar (USD) and the Mexican peso (MXN). We want to answer the following two questions:

1. What creates the demand for and the supply of dollars on the foreign exchange market?

2. What creates the demand for and the supply of pesos on the foreign exchange market?

Suppose an American wants to buy a couch from a Mexican producer. Before he can purchase the couch, the American must buy Mexican pesos; hence, Mexican pesos are demanded. The American buys Mexican pesos with U.S. dollars; that is, he supplies U.S. dollars to the foreign exchange market to demand Mexican pesos. *The U.S. demand for Mexican goods leads to (1) a demand for Mexican pesos and (2) a supply of U.S. dollars on the foreign exchange market* [see Exhibit 4(a)]. Thus, the demand for pesos and the supply of dollars are linked:

Demand for pesos ↔ Supply of dollars

The result is similar for a Mexican who wants to buy a computer from a U.S. producer. Before she can purchase the computer, the Mexican must buy U.S. dollars; hence, U.S. dollars are demanded. The Mexican buys the U.S. dollars with Mexican pesos. *The Mexican demand for U.S. goods leads to (1) a demand for U.S. dollars and (2) a supply of Mexican pesos on the foreign exchange market* [see Exhibit 4(b)]. Thus, the demand for dollars and the supply of pesos are linked:

Demand for dollars ↔ Supply of pesos

The Demand for and Supply of Currencies

Exhibit 5 shows the markets for pesos and dollars. Part (a) shows the market for Mexican pesos. The quantity of pesos is on the horizontal axis, and the exchange rate—stated in terms of the dollar price per peso—is on the vertical axis. Exhibit 5(b) shows the market for U.S. dollars, which mirrors what is happening in the market for Mexican pesos. Notice that the exchange rates in (a) and (b) are reciprocals of each other. If 0.10 USD = 1 MXN, then 10 MXN = 1 USD.

In Exhibit 5(a), the demand curve for pesos is downward-sloping, indicating that as the dollar price per peso increases, Americans buy fewer pesos and that as the dollar price per peso decreases, Americans buy more pesos.

Dollar price per peso ↑   Americans buy fewer pesos.
Dollar price per peso ↓   Americans buy more pesos.

For example, if it takes $0.10 to buy a peso, Americans will buy more pesos than they would if it takes $0.20 to buy a peso. (It is analogous to buyers purchasing more soft drinks at $3 a six-pack than at $5 a six-pack.) Simply put, the higher the dollar price per peso, the more expensive Mexican goods are for Americans and the fewer Mexican goods Americans will buy. Thus, a smaller quantity of pesos is demanded.

The supply curve for pesos in Exhibit 5(a) is upward sloping. The supply of Mexican pesos is linked to the Mexican demand for U.S. goods and U.S. dollars. Consider a price

---

The Demand for Goods and the Supply of Currencies

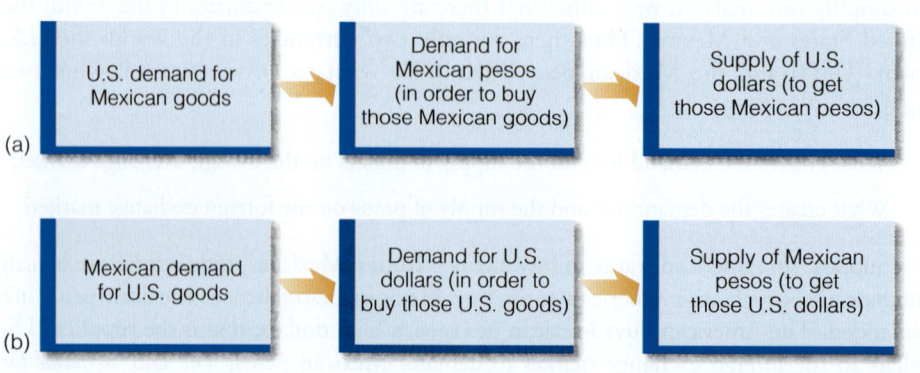

EXHIBIT 5

Translating U.S. Demand for Pesos into U.S. Supply of Dollars and Mexican Demand for Dollars into Mexican Supply of Pesos

(a) The market for pesos. (b) The market for dollars. The demand for pesos in (a) is linked to the supply of dollars in (b): when Americans demand pesos, they supply dollars. The supply of pesos in (a) is linked to the demand for dollars in (b): when Mexicans demand dollars, they supply pesos. In (a), the exchange rate is 0.10 USD = 1 MXN, which is equal to 10 MXN = 1 USD in (b). Exchange rates are reciprocals of each other.

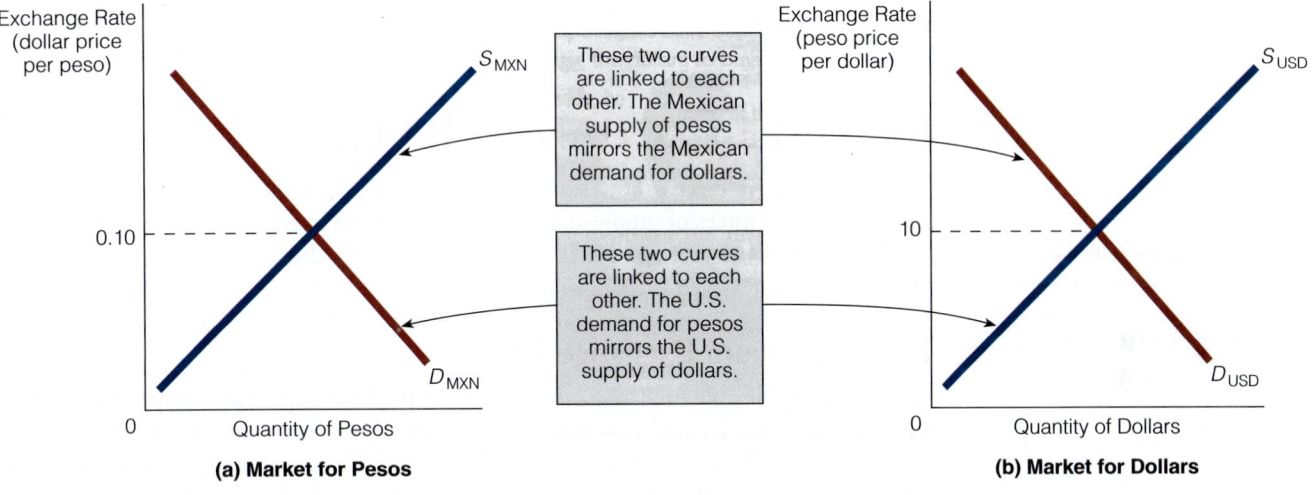

(a) Market for Pesos

(b) Market for Dollars

of $0.20 for 1 peso compared with a price of $0.10. At 0.10 USD = 1 MXN, a Mexican buyer gives up 1 peso and receives 10¢ in return. But at 0.20 USD = 1 MXN, a Mexican buyer gives up 1 peso and receives 20¢ in return. Thus, U.S. goods are cheaper for Mexicans at the exchange rate of 0.20 USD = 1 MXN.

To illustrate, suppose a U.S. computer has a price tag of $1,000. At an exchange rate of 0.20 USD = 1 MXN, a Mexican will have to pay 5,000 pesos to buy the American computer; but at an exchange rate of 0.10 USD = 1 MXN, a Mexican will have to pay 10,000 pesos for the computer:

$$0.20 \text{ USD} = 1 \text{ MXN}$$
$$1 \text{ USD} = (1 \div 0.20) \text{ MXN}$$
$$1,000 \text{ USD} = (1,000 \div 0.20) \text{ MXN}$$
$$= 5,000 \text{ MXN}$$

$$0.10 \text{ USD} = 1 \text{ MXN}$$
$$1 \text{ USD} = (1 \div 0.10) \text{ MXN}$$
$$1,000 \text{ USD} = (1,000 \div 0.10) \text{ MXN}$$
$$= 10,000 \text{ MXN}$$

To a Mexican buyer, the American computer is cheaper at the exchange rate of $0.20 per peso than at $0.10 per peso.

Exchange Rate	Dollar Price	Peso Price
0.20 USD = 1 MXN	1,000 USD	5,000 MXN [(1,000 ÷ 0.20) MXN]
0.10 USD = 1 MXN	1,000 USD	10,000 MXN [(1,000 ÷ 0.10) MXN]

Therefore, the higher the dollar price is per peso, the greater will be the quantity demanded of dollars by Mexicans (because U.S. goods will be cheaper) and hence the greater the quantity supplied of pesos to the foreign exchange market. The upward-sloping supply curve for pesos illustrates this relationship.

⊕hinking Like AN ECONOMIST

Linkages The demand for dollars is linked to the supply of pesos, and the demand for pesos is linked to the supply of dollars. Economists often think in terms of one activity being linked to another because economics, after all, is about exchange. In an exchange, one gives (supply) and gets (demand): John supplies $25 to demand the new book from the shopkeeper; the shopkeeper supplies the new book so that he may demand the $25. The diagram for such a transaction usually represents the demand for and supply of the new book, but it could also represent the demand for and supply of the money. Of course, in international exchange, where monies are bought and sold before goods are bought and sold, the diagrams reflect both. ●●●

FLEXIBLE EXCHANGE RATES

In this section, we discuss how exchange rates are determined in the foreign exchange market when the forces of supply and demand are allowed to rule. Economists refer to this as a **flexible exchange rate system**. In the next section, we discuss how exchange rates are determined under a fixed exchange rate system.

Flexible Exchange Rate System
The system whereby exchange rates are determined by the forces of supply and demand for a currency.

The Equilibrium Exchange Rate

In a completely flexible exchange rate system, the forces of supply and demand determine the exchange rate. In our two-country–two-currency world, suppose the equilibrium exchange rate (dollar price per peso) is 0.10 USD = 1 MXN, as shown in Exhibit 6. At this dollar price per peso, the quantity demanded of pesos equals the quantity supplied. There are no shortages or surpluses of pesos. At any other exchange rate, however, either an excess demand for pesos or an excess supply of pesos exists.

At the exchange rate of 0.12 USD = 1 MXN, a surplus of pesos exists. As a result, downward pressure will be placed on the dollar price of a peso (just as downward pressure will be placed on the dollar price of an apple if there is a surplus of apples). At the exchange rate of 0.08 USD = 1 MXN, there is a shortage of pesos, and upward pressure will be placed on the dollar price of a peso.

EXHIBIT 6

A Flexible Exchange Rate System

The demand curve for pesos is downward sloping. The higher the dollar price for pesos, the fewer pesos will be demanded; the lower the dollar price for pesos, the more pesos will be demanded. At 0.12 USD = 1 MXN, there is a surplus of pesos, placing downward pressure on the exchange rate. At 0.08 USD = 1 MXN, there is a shortage of pesos, placing upward pressure on the exchange rate. At the equilibrium exchange rate, 0.10 USD = 1 MXN, the quantity demanded of pesos equals the quantity supplied of pesos.

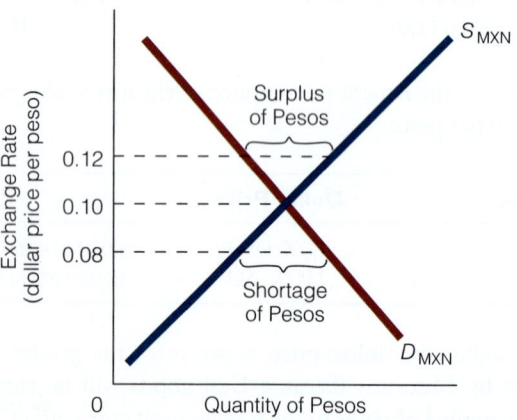

Changes in the Equilibrium Exchange Rate

Chapter 3 explains that a change in the demand for a good, in the supply of a good, or in both will change the good's equilibrium price. The same holds true for the price of currencies. A change in the demand for pesos, in the supply of pesos, or in both will change the equilibrium dollar price per peso. If the dollar price per peso rises—say, from 0.10 USD = 1 MXN to 0.12 USD = 1 MXN—the peso is said to have appreciated and the dollar to have depreciated. A currency has appreciated in value if it takes more of a foreign currency to buy it. A currency has depreciated in value if it takes more of it to buy a foreign currency.

For example, a movement in the exchange rate from 0.10 USD = 1 MXN to 0.12 USD = 1 MXN means that it now takes 12¢ instead of 10¢ to buy a peso, so the dollar has depreciated. The other side of the coin, so to speak, is that it takes fewer pesos to buy a dollar; so the peso has appreciated. That is, at an exchange rate of 0.10 USD = 1 MXN, it takes 10 pesos to buy \$1, but at an exchange rate of 0.12 USD = 1 MXN, it takes only 8.33 pesos to buy \$1.

Appreciation
An increase in the value of one currency relative to other currencies.

Depreciation
A decrease in the value of one currency relative to other currencies.

Factors That Affect the Equilibrium Exchange Rate

If the equilibrium exchange rate can change owing to a change in the demand for and supply of a currency, then understanding what factors can change demand and supply is important. This section presents three.

A DIFFERENCE IN INCOME GROWTH RATES An increase in a nation's income will usually cause the nation's residents to buy more of both domestic and foreign goods. The increased demand for imports will result in an increased demand for foreign currency.

Suppose U.S. residents experience an increase in income, but Mexican residents do not. As a result, the demand curve for pesos shifts rightward, as illustrated in Exhibit 7. This causes the equilibrium exchange rate to rise from 0.10 USD = 1 MXN to 0.12 USD = 1 MXN. *Ceteris paribus,* if one nation's income grows and another's lags behind, the currency of the higher-growth-rate country *depreciates,* and the currency of the lower-growth-rate country *appreciates.* To many persons, this effect seems paradoxical; nevertheless, it is true.

DIFFERENCES IN RELATIVE INFLATION RATES Suppose the U.S. price level rises 10 percent at a time when Mexico experiences stable prices. An increase in the U.S. price level will make Mexican goods relatively less expensive for Americans and U.S. goods relatively more expensive for Mexicans. As a result, the U.S. demand for Mexican goods will increase, and the Mexican demand for U.S. goods will decrease.

In turn, the demand for and the supply of Mexican pesos are affected. As shown in Exhibit 8, the demand for Mexican pesos will

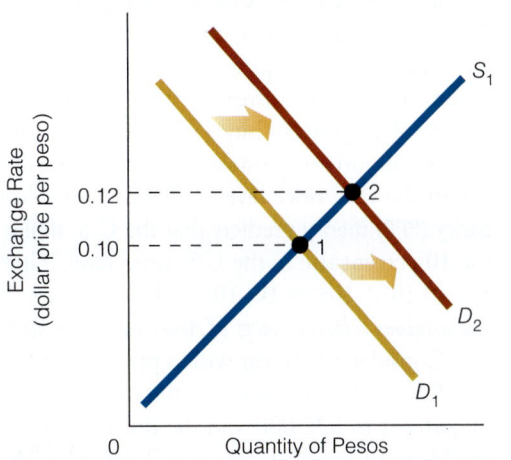

EXHIBIT 7

The Growth Rate of Income and the Exchange Rate

If U.S. residents experience a growth in income but Mexican residents do not, U.S. demand for Mexican goods will increase, and with it, the demand for pesos. As a result, the exchange rate will change; the dollar price of pesos will rise. The dollar depreciates, the peso appreciates.

Back to the Futures

Bill Whatley is the (fictional) owner of a Toyota dealership in Tulsa, Oklahoma. It is May, and Bill is thinking about a shipment of Toyotas he plans to buy in August. He knows that he must buy the Toyotas from Japan with yen, but he has a problem. The current price of ¥1 is $0.008. Bill wonders what the dollar price of a yen will be in August when he plans to make his purchase. If the price of ¥1 rises to $0.010, then, instead of paying $20,000 for a Toyota priced at ¥2.5 million, he will have to pay $25,000.[3] This difference of $5,000 may be enough to erase his profit on the sale of the cars.

Bill can, however, purchase a futures contract today for the needed quantity of yen in August. A futures contract is a contract in which the seller agrees to provide a good (in this example, a currency) to the buyer on a specified future date at an agreed-on price. In short, Bill can buy yen today at a specified dollar price and take delivery of the yen at a later date (in August). Problem solved.

But if the price of ¥1 falls to $0.007 in August, Bill would have to pay only $17,500 (instead of $20,000) for a Toyota priced at ¥2.5 million. Although he could increase his profit in this case, Bill, like other car dealers, might not be interested in assuming the risk associated with changes in exchange rates. He may prefer to lock in a sure thing.

Who would sell yen to Bill? The answer is someone who is willing to assume the risk of changes in the value of currencies. For example, Julie Jackson thinks that the dollar price of a yen will go down between now and August. Therefore, she'll enter into a contract with Bill requiring her to give him ¥2.5 million in August for $20,000—the exchange rate specified in the contract being 1 JPY = 0.008 USD. If she's right and the actual exchange rate in August is 1 JPY = 0.007 USD, then she can purchase the ¥2.5 million for $17,500 and fulfill the contract with Bill by turning the yen over to him for $20,000. She walks away with $2,500 in profit.

Many economists argue that futures contracts offer people a way of dealing with the risk associated with a flexible exchange rate system. If a person doesn't know what next month's exchange rate will be and doesn't want to take the risk of waiting to see, then he can enter into a futures contract and effectively shift the risk to someone who voluntarily assumes it.

---

3. If ¥1 equals $0.008, then a Toyota with a price of ¥2.5 million costs $20,000 because ¥2.5 million × $0.008 = $20,000. If ¥1 equals $0.010, then a Toyota with a price of ¥2.5 million costs $25,000 dollars because ¥2.5 million × $0.010 equals $25,000.

---

increase; Mexican goods are relatively cheaper than they were before the U.S. price level rose. The supply of Mexican pesos will decrease; American goods are relatively more expensive, and so Mexicans will buy fewer American goods; thus, they demand fewer U.S. dollars and supply fewer Mexican pesos.

As Exhibit 8 shows, the result of an increase in the demand for Mexican pesos and a decrease in their supply constitutes an *appreciation* in the peso and a *depreciation* in the dollar. It takes 11¢ instead of 10¢ to buy 1 peso (dollar depreciation); it takes 9.09 pesos instead of 10 pesos to buy $1 (peso appreciation).

An important question is how much will the U.S. dollar depreciate as a result of the rise in the U.S. price level? (Mexico's price level does not change.) The purchasing power parity (PPP) theory predicts that the U.S. dollar will depreciate by 10 percent as a result of the 10 percent rise in the U.S. price level. This requires the dollar price of a peso to rise to 11¢ (0.10 × 10¢ = 1¢, 10¢ + 1¢ = 11¢). A 10 percent depreciation in the dollar restores the *original relative prices of American goods to Mexican customers.*

Consider a U.S. car with a price tag of $20,000. If the exchange rate is 0.10 USD = 1 MXN, a Mexican buyer of the car will pay 200,000 pesos. If the car price increases by 10 percent to $22,000 and the dollar depreciates 10 percent (to 0.11 USD = 1 MXN), the Mexican buyer of the car will still pay only 200,000 pesos.

Purchasing Power Parity (PPP) Theory
Theory stating that exchange rates between any two currencies will adjust to reflect changes in the relative price levels of the two countries.

EXHIBIT 8

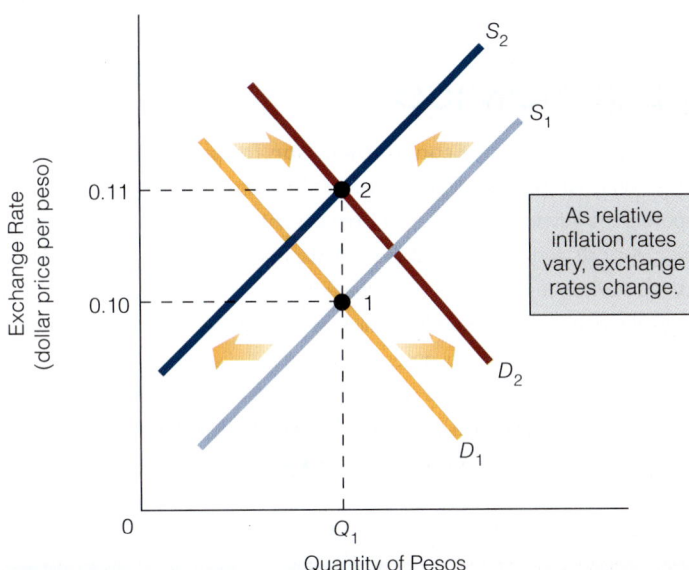

As relative inflation rates vary, exchange rates change.

Inflation, Exchange Rates, and Purchasing Power Parity (PPP)

If the price level in the United States increases by 10 percent while the price level in Mexico remains constant, then the U.S. demand for Mexican goods (and therefore pesos) will increase and the supply of pesos will decrease. As a result, the exchange rate will change; the dollar price of pesos will rise. The dollar depreciates, and the peso appreciates. PPP theory predicts that the dollar will depreciate in the foreign exchange market until the original price (in pesos) of American goods to Mexican customers is restored. In this example, this requires the dollar to depreciate 10 percent.

Exchange Rate	Dollar Price	Peso Price
0.10 USD = 1 MXN	20,000 USD	200,000 MXN [(20,000 ÷ 0.10) MXN]
0.11 USD = 1 MXN	22,000 USD	200,000 MXN [(22,000 ÷ 0.11) MXN]

In short, the PPP theory predicts that *changes in the relative price levels of two countries will affect the exchange rate in such a way that 1 unit of a country's currency will continue to buy the same amount of foreign goods* as it did before the change in the relative price levels. In our example, the higher U.S. inflation rate causes a change in the equilibrium exchange rate and leads to a depreciated dollar, but 1 peso continues to have the same purchasing power it previously did.

On some occasions, the PPP theory of exchange rates has predicted accurately, but not on others. Many economists suggest that the theory does not always predict accurately because the demand for and the supply of a currency are affected *by more than the difference in inflation rates between countries.* For example, as noted, different income growth rates affect the demand for a currency and therefore the exchange rate. In the *long run,* however, and particularly when the *difference in inflation rates across countries is large,* the PPP theory does predict exchange rates accurately.

CHANGES IN REAL INTEREST RATES As shown in the U.S. balance of payments in Exhibit 2, more than goods flow between countries. Financial capital also moves between countries. The flow of financial capital depends on different countries' *real interest rates—* interest rates adjusted for inflation.

To illustrate, suppose initially that the real interest rate is 3 percent in both the United States and Mexico. Then the real interest rate in the United States increases to 4.5 percent. As a result, Mexicans will want to purchase financial assets in the United States that pay a higher real interest rate than do financial assets in Mexico. The Mexican demand for dollars will increase, and therefore Mexicans will supply more pesos. As the supply of pesos increases on the foreign exchange market, the exchange rate (the dollar price per peso) will change; fewer dollars will be needed to buy pesos. In short, the dollar will appreciate, and the peso will depreciate.

🄵inding ECONOMICS

In the President Speaking to an Economic Advisor The president of the United States is speaking to an economic advisor. The president asks, "What are the effects of the rather large budget deficits?" In response, the advisor might say that large budget deficits can affect interest rates, the value of the dollar, exports and imports, and the merchandise trade balance. "How so?" the president asks. Big deficits, the advisor answers, mean that the federal government will have to borrow funds, which will increase the demand for credit. This will push up the interest rate. As the U.S. interest rate rises relative to interest rates in other countries, foreigners will want to purchase financial assets in the United States that pay a higher return. This will increase the demand for dollars, the dollar will appreciate, and foreign currencies will depreciate. In turn, this will affect both import and export spending, and thus it will affect the merchandise trade balance. ▲ ▲ ▲

SELF-TEST

1. In the foreign exchange market, how is the demand for dollars linked to the supply of pesos?

2. What could cause the U.S. dollar to appreciate against the Mexican peso on the foreign exchange market?

3. Suppose that the U.S. economy grows and that the Swiss economy does not. How will this affect the exchange rate between the dollar and the Swiss franc? Why?

4. What does the purchasing power parity theory say? Give an example to illustrate your answer.

FIXED EXCHANGE RATES

Fixed Exchange Rate System
The system whereby a nation's currency is set at a fixed rate relative to all other currencies, and central banks intervene in the foreign exchange market to maintain the fixed rate.

The major alternative to the flexible exchange rate system is the fixed exchange rate system, which works the way it sounds. Exchange rates are fixed; they are not allowed to fluctuate freely in response to the forces of supply and demand. Central banks buy and sell currencies to maintain agreed-on exchange rates. The workings of the fixed exchange rate system are described in this section.

Fixed Exchange Rates and Overvalued/Undervalued Currency

Once again, we assume a two-country–two-currency world, but this time the United States and Mexico agree to fix the exchange rate of their currencies. Instead of letting the dollar depreciate or appreciate relative to the peso, the two countries agree to set the price of 1 peso at $0.12; that is, they agree to the exchange rate of 0.12 USD = 1 MXN. Generally, we call this the fixed exchange rate or the *official price* of a peso.[4] Since we will include more than one official price in our discussion, 0.12 USD = 1 MXN is official price 1 (Exhibit 9).

Overvalued
A currency is overvalued if its price in terms of other currencies is above the equilibrium price.

If the dollar price of pesos is above its equilibrium level (which is the case at official price 1), a surplus of pesos exists, and the peso is said to be overvalued. In other words, the peso is fetching more dollars than it would at equilibrium. For example, if in equilibrium, 1 peso trades for $0.10, but at the official exchange rate 1 peso trades for $0.12, then the peso is said to be overvalued.

---

4. If the price of 1 peso is $0.12, the price of $1 is approximately 8.33 pesos. Thus, setting the official price of a peso in terms of dollars automatically sets the official price of a dollar in terms of pesos.

EXHIBIT 9

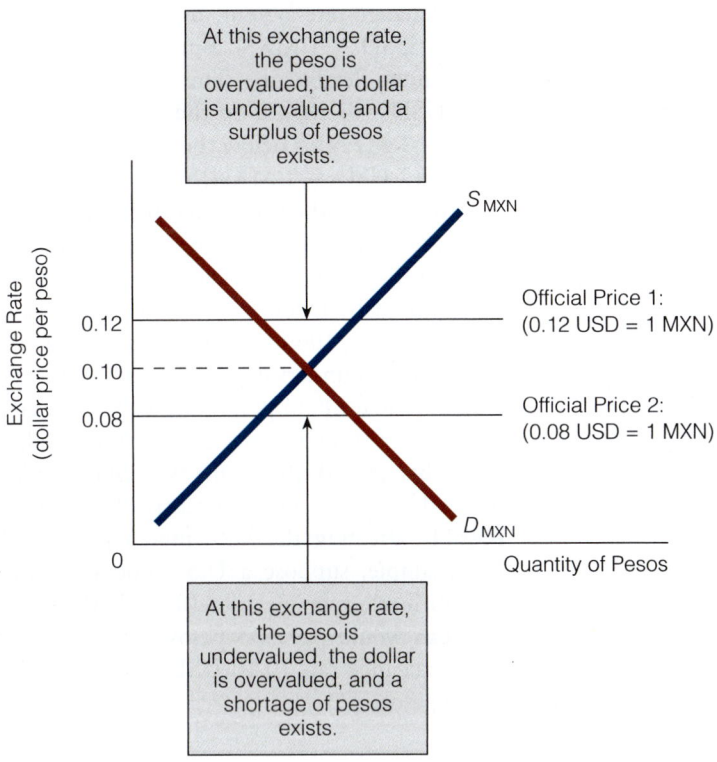

At this exchange rate, the peso is overvalued, the dollar is undervalued, and a surplus of pesos exists.

S_{MXN}

Official Price 1:
(0.12 USD = 1 MXN)

Official Price 2:
(0.08 USD = 1 MXN)

D_{MXN}

Quantity of Pesos

At this exchange rate, the peso is undervalued, the dollar is overvalued, and a shortage of pesos exists.

Exchange Rate (dollar price per peso)

0.12
0.10
0.08

0

A Fixed Exchange Rate System

In a fixed exchange rate system, the exchange rate is fixed—and it may not be fixed at the equilibrium exchange rate. The exhibit shows two cases. (1) If the exchange rate is fixed at official price 1, the peso is overvalued, the dollar is undervalued, and a surplus of pesos exists. (2) If the exchange rate is fixed at official price 2, the peso is undervalued, the dollar is overvalued, and a shortage of pesos exists.

Therefore, if the peso is overvalued, the dollar is undervalued; that is, it is fetching fewer pesos than it would at equilibrium. For example, if in equilibrium, $1 trades for 10 pesos, but at the official exchange rate, $1 trades for 8.33 pesos, then the dollar is undervalued.

Similarly, if the dollar price of pesos is below its equilibrium level (which is the case at official price 2 in Exhibit 9), a shortage of pesos exists, and the peso is undervalued; the peso is not fetching as many dollars as it would at equilibrium. Therefore, if the peso is undervalued, the dollar must be overvalued.

Overvalued peso ↔ Undervalued dollar
Undervalued peso ↔ Overvalued dollar

Undervalued

A currency is undervalued if its price in terms of other currencies is below the equilibrium price.

What Is So Bad About an Overvalued Dollar?

You read in the newspaper that the dollar is overvalued and that economists are concerned about the overvalued dollar. They are concerned because the exchange rate and hence the value of the dollar in terms of other currencies affects the amount of U.S. exports and imports. Because it affects exports and imports, it naturally affects the merchandise trade balance.

To illustrate, suppose the demand for and supply of pesos are represented by D_1 and S_1 in Exhibit 10. With this demand curve and supply curve, the equilibrium exchange rate is 0.10 USD = 1 MXN. Let's also suppose the exchange rate is fixed at this exchange rate. In other words, the equilibrium exchange rate and the fixed exchange rate are initially the same.

EXHIBIT 10

Fixed Exchange Rates and an Overvalued Dollar

Initially, the demand for and supply of pesos are represented by D_1 and S_1, respectively. The equilibrium exchange rate is 0.10 USD = 1 MXN, which also happens to be the official

(fixed) exchange rate. In time, the demand for pesos rises to D_2, and the equilibrium exchange rate rises to 0.12 USD = 1 MXN. The official exchange rate is fixed, however, so the dollar will be overvalued. As explained in the text, this can lead to a trade deficit.

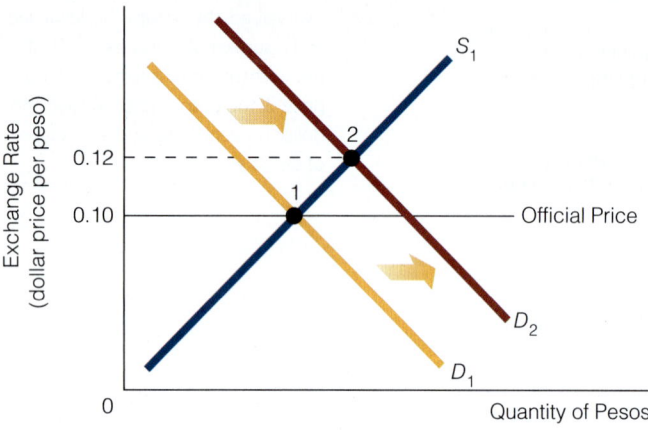

Time passes and eventually the demand curve for pesos shifts to the right, from D_1 to D_2. Under a flexible exchange rate system, the exchange rate would rise to 0.12 USD = 1 MXN. But a fixed exchange rate is in effect, not a flexible one. The exchange rate stays fixed at 0.10 USD = 1 MXN. So the fixed exchange rate (0.10 USD = 1 MXN) is below the new equilibrium exchange rate (0.12 USD = 1 MXN).

Recall that when the dollar price per peso is below its equilibrium level (which is the case), the peso is undervalued and the dollar is overvalued. At equilibrium (point 2 in Exhibit 10), 1 peso would trade for 0.12 dollars, but at its fixed rate (point 1), it trades for only 0.10 dollars; so the peso is undervalued. At equilibrium (point 2), $1 would trade for 8.33 pesos, but at its fixed rate (point 1), it trades for 10 pesos; so the dollar is overvalued.

What is bad about an overvalued dollar is that it makes U.S. goods more expensive for foreigners to buy, possibly affecting the U.S. merchandise trade balance. For example, suppose a U.S. good costs $100. At the equilibrium exchange rate (0.12 USD = 1 MXN), a Mexican would pay 833 pesos for the good, but at the fixed exchange rate (0.10 USD = 1 MXN), he will pay 1,000 pesos.

Exchange Rate	Dollar Price	Peso Price
0.12 USD = 1 MXN (equilibrium)	100 USD	833 MXN [(100 ÷ 0.12) MXN]
0.10 USD = 1 MXN (fixed)	100 USD	1,000 MXN [(100 ÷ 0.10) MXN]

The higher the prices are of U.S. goods (exports), the fewer of those goods Mexicans will buy, and, as just shown, an overvalued dollar makes U.S. export goods higher in price.

Ultimately, an overvalued dollar can affect the U.S. merchandise trade balance. As U.S. exports become more expensive for Mexicans, they buy fewer U.S. exports. If exports fall below imports, the result is a U.S. trade deficit.[5]

Government Involvement in a Fixed Exchange Rate System

In Exhibit 9, suppose the governments of Mexico and the United States agree to fix the exchange rate at 0.12 USD = 1 MXN. At this exchange rate, a surplus of pesos exists. To maintain the exchange rate at 0.12 USD = 1 MXN, the Federal Reserve System (the Fed) could buy the surplus of pesos with dollars. Consequently, the demand for pesos will increase, and the demand curve will shift to the right, ideally, by enough to raise the equilibrium rate to the current fixed exchange rate.

Alternatively, instead of the Fed's buying pesos (to mop up the excess supply of pesos), the Banco de Mexico (the central bank of Mexico) could buy pesos with some of its reserve dollars. (It doesn't buy pesos with pesos because using pesos would not reduce the surplus of pesos on the market.) This action by the Banco de Mexico will also increase the demand for pesos and raise the equilibrium rate.

5. The other side of the coin, so to speak, is that if the dollar is overvalued, the peso must be undervalued. An undervalued peso makes Mexican goods cheaper for Americans. So while the overvalued dollar is causing Mexicans to buy fewer U.S. exports, the undervalued peso is causing Americans to import more goods from Mexico. In conclusion, U.S. exports fall, U.S. imports rise, and we move closer to a trade deficit, or, if one already exists, it becomes larger.

Big Mac Economics

In an earlier chapter we explained why goods that can be easily transported from one location to another usually sell for the same price in all locations. For example, if a candy bar can be moved from Atlanta to Seattle, we would expect the candy bar to sell for the same price in both locations. The reason is that if the candy bar is priced higher in Seattle than Atlanta, people will move candy bars from Atlanta (where the price is relatively low) to Seattle to fetch the higher price. In other words, the supply of candy bars will rise in Seattle and fall in Atlanta. These changes in supply in the two locations affect the prices of the candy bars in the two locations. In Seattle the price will fall, and in Atlanta the price will rise. This price movement will stop when the prices of a candy bar are the same in the two locations.

CHARLES PERTWEE/BLOOMBERG VIA GETTY IMAGES NEWS

Now consider a good that is sold all over the world: McDonald's Big Mac. Suppose the exchange rate between the dollar and the yen is $1 = ¥100 and the price of a Big Mac in New York City is $3 and ¥400 in Tokyo. Given the exchange rate, a Big Mac is not selling for the same price in the two cities. In New York, it is $3, but in Tokyo it is $4 (the price in Tokyo is ¥400, and $1 = ¥100). Stated differently, in New York, $1 buys one-third of a Big Mac, but in Tokyo, $1 buys only one-fourth of a Big Mac. However, Big Macs won't be shipped from New York to Tokyo to fetch the higher price. Instead, the exchange rate is likely to adjust in such a way that the prices of a Big Mac are the same in both cities.

Now ask yourself what the exchange rate has to be between the dollar and yen before the Big Mac is the same dollar price in

New York and Tokyo. Of the following three exchange rates, pick the correct one:

1. $1 = ¥133.33
2. $1 = ¥150.00
3. $1 = ¥89.00

The answer is the first one: $1 = ¥133.33. At this exchange rate, a Big Mac in New York is $3, and a Big Mac in Tokyo that is ¥400 is $3 (once we have computed its price in dollars). At the exchange rate of $1 = ¥133.33, then ¥1 = $0.0075, and

$$\$0.0075 \times ¥400 = \$3.$$

The *purchasing power parity theory* in economics predicts that the exchange rate between two currencies will adjust so that, in the end, $1 buys the same amount of a given good in all places around the world. Thus, if the exchange rate is initially $1 = ¥100 when a Big Mac is $3 in New York and ¥400 in Tokyo, it will change to become $1 = ¥133.33. That is, the dollar will soon appreciate relative to the yen.

The Economist, a well-known economics magazine, publishes what it calls the Big Mac index each year. It shows current exchange rates and the cost of a Big Mac in different countries (just as we did here). Then it predicts which currencies will appreciate and depreciate based on this information. *The Economist* does not always predict accurately, but it does do so in many cases.

If you want to predict whether the euro, pound, or peso is going to appreciate or depreciate in the next few months, looking at exchange rates in terms of the price of Big Mac is a useful approach.

Finally, the two actions could be combined; that is, both the Fed and the Banco de Mexico could buy pesos.

Options Under a Fixed Exchange Rate System

Suppose there is a surplus of pesos in the foreign exchange market, indicating that the peso is overvalued and the dollar is undervalued. Suppose also that although the Fed and the Banco de Mexico each attempt to rectify this situation by buying pesos, this combined action is not successful. The surplus of pesos persists for weeks, along with an overvalued peso and an undervalued dollar. A few options are available.

Devaluation
A government action that changes the exchange rate by lowering the official price of a currency.

Revaluation
A government act that changes the exchange rate by raising the official price of a currency.

DEVALUATION AND REVALUATION Mexico and the United States could agree to reset the official price of the dollar and the peso. Doing so entails *devaluation* and *revaluation*. A devaluation occurs when the official price of a currency is lowered. A revaluation occurs when the official price of a currency is raised.

For example, suppose the first official price of a peso is 0.10 USD = 1 MXN, and the first official price of $1 is 10 pesos. Mexico and the United States agree to change the official price of their currencies. The second official price is 0.12 USD = 1 MXN, and the second official price of $1 is 8.33 pesos.

Moving from the first official price to the second, the peso has been revalued because it takes *more dollars to buy a peso* (12¢ instead of 10¢). Of course, moving from the first official price to the second means the dollar has been devalued because it takes *fewer pesos to buy a dollar* (8.33 pesos instead of 10).

One country might want to devalue its currency, but another country might not want to revalue its currency. For example, if Mexico wants to devalue its currency relative to the U.S. dollar, U.S. authorities might not always willingly comply because, if they do, the United States will not sell as many goods to Mexico. As explained earlier, revaluing the dollar means Mexicans have to pay more for it; instead of paying, say, 8.33 pesos for $1, Mexicans might have to pay 10 pesos. At a revalued dollar (a higher peso price for a dollar), Mexicans will find U.S. goods more expensive and not want to buy as many. Americans who produce goods to sell to Mexico may see that a revalued dollar will hurt their pocketbooks, and so they will argue against it.

PROTECTIONIST TRADE POLICY (QUOTAS AND TARIFFS) Recall that an overvalued dollar can bring on or widen a trade deficit. To deal with both the trade deficit and the overvalued dollar at the same time, some say a country can impose quotas and tariffs to reduce domestic consumption of foreign goods. (An earlier chapter explains how both tariffs and quotas meet this objective.) A drop in the domestic consumption of foreign goods goes hand in hand with a decrease in the demand for foreign currencies. In turn, this decrease can affect the value of the country's currency on the foreign exchange market. In this case, it can get rid of an overvalued dollar.

Economists are quick to point out, though, that trade deficits and overvalued currencies are sometimes used as an excuse to promote trade restrictions, many of which simply benefit special interests (e.g., U.S. producers that compete for sales with foreign producers in the U.S. market).

CHANGES IN MONETARY POLICY Sometimes, a nation can use monetary policy to support the exchange rate or the official price of its currency. Suppose the United States is continually running a merchandise trade deficit; year after year, imports are outstripping exports. To remedy this, the United States might enact a tight monetary policy to retard inflation and drive up interest rates (at least in the short run). The tight monetary policy will reduce the U.S. rate of inflation and thereby lower U.S. prices relative to prices in other nations. This effect will make U.S. goods relatively cheaper than they were before (assuming other nations don't also enact a tight monetary policy) promoting U.S. exports and discouraging foreign imports. It will also generate a flow of investment funds into the United States in search of higher real interest rates.

Some economists argue against fixed exchange rates because they think it unwise for a nation to adopt a particular monetary policy simply to maintain an international exchange rate. Instead, they believe domestic monetary policies should be used to meet domestic economic goals, such as price stability, low unemployment, low and stable interest rates, and so forth.

The Gold Standard

If nations adopt the gold standard, they *automatically fix* their exchange rates. Suppose the United States defines a dollar as equal to 1/10 of an ounce of gold and Mexico defines a peso as equal to 1/100 of an ounce of gold. Therefore, 1 ounce of gold could be bought with either $10 or 100 pesos. The fixed exchange rate between dollars and pesos is 10 MXN = 1 USD or 0.10 USD = 1 MXN.

To have an international gold standard, countries must do the following:

1. Define their currencies in terms of gold.

2. Stand ready and willing to convert gold into paper money and paper money into gold at the rate specified.

3. Link their money supplies to their holdings of gold.

With this last point in mind, consider how a gold standard would work. Initially assume that the gold standard (fixed) exchange rate of 0.10 USD = 1 MXN is the equilibrium exchange rate. Then, a change occurs: inflation in Mexico raises prices there by 100 percent. A Mexican table that was priced at 2,000 pesos before the inflation is now priced at 4,000 pesos. At the gold standard (fixed) exchange rate, Americans now have to pay $400 (4,000 pesos ÷ 10 pesos per dollar) to buy the table, whereas before the inflation Americans had to pay only $200 (2,000 pesos ÷ 10 pesos per dollar) for the table. As a result, Americans buy fewer Mexican tables; Americans import less from Mexico.

At the same time, Mexicans import more from the United States because American prices are now relatively lower than before inflation hit Mexico. As a quick example, suppose that before the inflation, an American pair of shoes cost $200 and that, as before, a Mexican table cost 2,000 pesos. At 0.10 USD = 1 MXN, the $200 American shoes cost 2,000 pesos and the 2,000-peso Mexican table cost $200. In other words, 1 pair of American shoes traded for (or equaled) 1 Mexican table.

Then inflation raised the price of the Mexican table to 4,000 pesos, or $400. Because the American shoes are still $200 (there has been no inflation in the United States) and the exchange rate is still fixed at 0.10 USD = 1 MXN, 1 pair of American shoes no longer equals 1 Mexican table; instead, it equals 1/2 of a Mexican table. In short, the inflation in Mexico has made U.S. goods *relatively cheaper* for Mexicans. As a result, Mexicans buy more U.S. goods; they import more from the United States.

To summarize, the inflation in Mexico causes Americans to buy fewer goods from Mexico and Mexicans to buy more goods from the United States. In terms of the merchandise trade balance for each country, in the United States, imports decline (Americans are buying less from Mexico) and exports rise (Mexicans are buying more from the United States); so the U.S. trade balance is likely to move into surplus. Contrarily, in Mexico, exports decline (Americans are buying less from Mexico) and imports rise (Mexicans are buying more from the United States); so Mexico's trade balance is likely to move into deficit.

On a gold standard, Mexicans have to pay for the difference between their imports and exports with gold. Gold is therefore shipped to the United States. An increase in the supply of gold in the United States expands the U.S. money supply. A decrease in the supply of gold in Mexico contracts the Mexican money supply. Prices are affected in both countries. In the United States, prices begin to rise; in Mexico, they begin to fall.

As U.S. prices go up and Mexican prices go down, the earlier situation begins to reverse itself. American goods look more expensive to Mexicans, and they begin to buy less, whereas Mexican goods look cheaper to Americans, and they begin to buy more. Consequently, American imports begin to rise and exports begin to fall; Mexican imports begin to fall and exports begin to rise. Thus, by changing domestic money supplies and price levels, the gold standard begins to correct the initial trade balance disequilibrium.

The change in the money supply that the gold standard sometimes requires has prompted some economists to voice the same charge against the gold standard that is often heard against the fixed exchange rate system: it subjects domestic monetary policy to international instead of domestic considerations. In fact, many economists cite this as part of the reason many nations abandoned the gold standard in the 1930s. At a time when unemployment was unusually high, many nations with trade deficits felt that matters would only get worse if they contracted their money supplies to live by the edicts of the gold standard.

1. Under a fixed exchange rate system, if one currency is overvalued, then another currency must be undervalued. Explain why this statement is true.

2. How does an overvalued dollar affect U.S. exports and imports?

3. In each of the following cases, identify whether the U.S. dollar is overvalued or undervalued:

   a. The fixed exchange rate is $2 = £1, and the equilibrium exchange rate is $3 = £1.

   b. The fixed exchange rate is $1.25 = €1, and the equilibrium exchange rate is $1.10 = €1.

   c. The fixed exchange rate is $1 = 10 pesos, and the equilibrium exchange rate is $1 = 14 pesos.

4. Under a fixed exchange rate system, why might the United States want to devalue its currency?

FIXED EXCHANGE RATES VERSUS FLEXIBLE EXCHANGE RATES

As in many economic situations, any exchange rate system has both its costs and its benefits. This section discusses some of the arguments and issues surrounding fixed exchange rates and flexible exchange rates.

Promoting International Trade

Which are better at promoting international trade: fixed or flexible exchange rates? This section presents the case for each.

THE CASE FOR FIXED EXCHANGE RATES Proponents of a fixed exchange rate system often argue that fixed exchange rates promote international trade, whereas flexible exchange rates stifle it. A major advantage of fixed exchange rates is certainty. Individuals in different countries know from day to day the value of their nation's currency. With flexible exchange rates, individuals are less likely to engage in international trade because of the added risk of not knowing from one day to the next how many dollars, euros, or yen they will have to trade for other currencies. Certainty is a necessary ingredient in international trade; flexible exchange rates promote uncertainty, which hampers international trade.

Economist Charles Kindleberger, a proponent of fixed exchange rates, believes that having fixed exchange rates is analogous to having a single currency for the entire United States instead of having a different currency for each of the 50 states. One currency in the United States promotes trade, whereas 50 different currencies would hamper it. In Kindleberger's view:

> *The main case against flexible exchange rates is that they break up the world market.... Imagine trying to conduct interstate trade in the USA if there were fifty different state monies, none of which was dominant. This is akin to barter, the inefficiency of which is explained time and again by textbooks.*[6]

THE CASE FOR FLEXIBLE EXCHANGE RATES Advocates of flexible exchange rates, as noted, maintain that it is better for a nation to adopt policies to meet domestic economic goals than to sacrifice domestic economic goals to maintain an exchange rate. Also, the chance is too great that the fixed exchange rate will diverge greatly from the equilibrium exchange rate, creating persistent balance of trade problems leading deficit nations to impose trade restrictions (tariffs and quotas) that hinder international trade.

---

6. Charles Kindleberger, *International Money* (London: Allen and Unwin, 1981), p. 174.

Optimal Currency Areas

As of 2010, the European Union (EU) consisted of 27 member states. According to the European Union, its ultimate goal is "an ever closer union among the peoples of Europe, in which decisions are taken as closely as possible to the citizen." As part of meeting this goal, the EU established its own currency—the euro—on January 1, 1999.[7] Although euro notes and coins were not issued until January 1, 2002, certain business transactions were made in euros beginning January 1, 1999.

The European Union and the euro are relevant to a discussion of an *optimal currency area.* An optimal currency area is a geographic area in which exchange rates can be fixed or a *common currency* used without sacrificing domestic economic goals, such as low unemployment. The concept of an optimal currency area originated in the debate over whether fixed or flexible exchange rates are better. Most of the pioneering work on optimal currency areas was done by Robert Mundell, the winner of the 1999 Nobel Prize in Economics.

Before discussing an optimal currency area, we need to look at the relationships among labor mobility, trade, and exchange rates. *Labor mobility* means that the residents of one country can move easily to another country.

Optimal Currency Area
A geographic area in which exchange rates can be fixed or a common currency used without sacrificing domestic economic goals, such as low unemployment.

TRADE AND LABOR MOBILITY Suppose there are only two countries: the United States and Canada. The United States produces calculators and soft drinks, and Canada produces bread and muffins. Currently, the two countries trade with each other, and there is complete labor mobility between them.

One day, the residents of both countries reduce their demand for bread and muffins and increase their demand for calculators and soft drinks. In other words, relative demand changes. Demand increases for U.S. goods and falls for Canadian goods. Business firms in Canada lay off employees because their sales have plummeted. Incomes in Canada begin to fall, and the unemployment rate begins to rise. In the United States, prices initially rise because of the increased demand for calculators and soft drinks. In response to the higher demand for their products, U.S. business firms begin to hire more workers and increase their production. Their efforts to hire more workers drive wages up and reduce the unemployment rate.

Because labor is mobile, some of the newly unemployed Canadian workers move to the United States to find work, easing the economic situation in both countries. The movement of labor will reduce some of the unemployment problems in Canada, and, with more workers in the United States, more output will be produced, thus dampening upward price pressures on calculators and soft drinks. Thus, changes in relative demand pose no major economic problems for either country if labor is mobile.

TRADE AND LABOR IMMOBILITY Now let's suppose that relative demand has changed but that labor is *not* mobile between the United States and Canada, perhaps due to either political or cultural barriers. If people cannot move, what happens in the economies of the two countries depends largely on whether exchange rates are fixed or flexible.

If exchange rates are flexible, the value of the U.S. currency changes vis-à-vis the Canadian currency. If Canadians want to buy more U.S. goods, they will have to exchange their domestic currency for U.S. currency. The demand for U.S. currency on the foreign exchange market increases at the same time that the supply of Canadian currency increases. Consequently, U.S. currency appreciates, and Canadian currency depreciates. Because Canadian currency depreciates, U.S. goods become relatively more expensive for Canadians; so they buy fewer. And because U.S. currency appreciates, Canadian goods become relatively cheaper for Americans; so they buy more. Canadian business firms begin to sell more goods; so they hire more workers, the unemployment rate drops, and the bad economic times in Canada begin to disappear.

---

7. As of 2010, 16 of the 27 member states have adopted the euro as their official currency.

If exchange rates are fixed, however, U.S. goods will not become relatively more expensive for Canadians, and Canadian goods will not become relatively cheaper for Americans. Consequently, the bad economic times in Canada (high unemployment) might last for a long time indeed instead of beginning to reverse. Thus, if labor is immobile, changes in relative demand may pose major economic problems when exchange rates are fixed but not when they are flexible.

COSTS, BENEFITS, AND OPTIMAL CURRENCY AREAS In addition to benefits, flexible exchange rates have costs. Exchanging one currency for another (say, U.S. dollars for Canadian dollars or U.S. dollars for Japanese yen) incurs a charge, and the risk is greater of not knowing what the value of one's currency will be on the foreign exchange market on any given day. For many countries, the benefits outweigh the costs, and so they have flexible exchange rate systems.

Suppose some of the costs of flexible exchange rates could be eliminated, while maintaining the benefits. When labor is mobile between the two countries, they could have a fixed exchange rate or adopt a common currency and retain the benefits of flexible exchange rates. Then they do not have to have separate currencies that float against each other because resources (labor) can move easily and quickly in response to changes in relative demand. The two countries can either fix exchange rates or adopt the same currency.

When labor in countries within a geographic area is mobile enough to move easily and quickly in response to changes in relative demand, the countries are said to constitute an *optimal currency area.* Countries in such an area can either fix their currencies or adopt the same currency and thus keep all the benefits of flexible exchange rates without incurring any of the costs.

The states within the United States are commonly said to constitute an optimal currency area. Labor can move easily and quickly between, say, North Carolina and South Carolina in response to relative demand changes. Some economists argue that the countries that compose the European Union make up an optimal currency area and that adopting a common currency—the euro—will benefit these countries. Other economists disagree. They argue that, although labor is somewhat more mobile in Europe today than in the past, certain language and cultural differences make labor mobility less than sufficient to constitute a true optimal currency area.

THE CURRENT INTERNATIONAL MONETARY SYSTEM

Managed Float

A managed flexible exchange rate system, under which nations now and then intervene to adjust their official reserve holdings to moderate major swings in exchange rates.

Today's international monetary system is best described as a managed flexible exchange rate system, sometimes referred to more casually as a managed float. In a way, this system is a rough compromise between the fixed and flexible exchange rate systems. The current system operates under flexible exchange rates, but not completely. Nations now and then intervene to adjust their official reserve holdings to moderate major swings in exchange rates.

Proponents of the managed float system stress the following advantages:

1. *It allows nations to pursue independent monetary policies.* Under a (strictly) fixed exchange rate system, fixed either by agreement or by gold, a nation with a merchandise trade deficit might have to enact a tight monetary policy to retard inflation and to promote its exports. This type of action is not needed with the managed float, whose proponents argue that solving trade imbalances by adjusting one price—the exchange rate—is better than adjusting the price level.

2. *It solves trade problems without trade restrictions.* As stated earlier, under a fixed exchange rate system, nations sometimes impose tariffs and quotas to solve trade imbalances. For example, a deficit nation might impose import quotas so that exports and imports of goods will be more in line. Under the current system, trade imbalances are usually solved through changes in exchange rates.

3. *It is flexible and therefore can easily adjust to shocks.* In 1973–1974, the OPEC nations dramatically raised the price of oil, resulting in trade deficits for many oil-importing

nations. A fixed exchange rate system would have had a hard time accommodating such a major change in oil prices, but the current system had little trouble. Exchange rates took much of the shock (with large changes in exchange rates), thus allowing most nations' economies to weather the storm with a minimum of difficulty.

Opponents of the current international monetary system stress the following disadvantages:

1. *It promotes exchange rate volatility and uncertainty and results in less international trade than would be the case under fixed exchange rates.* Under a flexible exchange rate system, volatile exchange rates make conducting business riskier for importers and exporters. As a result, there is less international trade than there would be under a fixed exchange rate system. Proponents respond that the futures market in currencies allows importers and exporters to shift the risk of fluctuations in exchange rates to others. For example, if an American company wants to buy a quantity of a good from a Japanese company three months from today, it can contract today for the desired quantity of yen that it will need at a specified price. It will not have to worry about a change in the dollar price of yen during the next three months. Purchasing a futures contract has a cost, but it is usually modest.

2. *It promotes inflation.* As we have seen, the monetary policies of different nations are not independent of one another under a fixed exchange rate system. For example, a nation with a merchandise trade deficit is somewhat restrained from inflating its currency because this will worsen the deficit problem. The deficit will make the nation's goods more expensive relative to foreign goods and promote the purchase of imports. In its attempt to maintain the exchange rate, a nation with a merchandise trade deficit would have to enact a tight monetary policy. Under the current system, a nation with a merchandise trade deficit does not have to maintain exchange rates or try to solve its deficit problem through changes in its money supply. Opponents of the current system argue that this frees nations to inflate, predicting that more inflation will result than would occur under a fixed exchange rate system.

3. *Changes in exchange rates alter trade balances in the desired direction only after a long time; in the short run, a depreciation in a currency can make the situation worse instead of better.* Soon after a depreciation in a trade-deficit nation's currency, the trade deficit, it is often argued, will increase (not decrease, as hoped) because import demand is inelastic in the short run: imports are not very responsive to a change in price. For example, suppose Mexico is running a trade deficit with the United States at the present exchange rate of 0.12 USD = 1 MXN. At this exchange rate, the peso is overvalued. Mexico buys 2,000 television sets from the United States, each with a price tag of $500. Assume Mexico therefore spends 8.33 million pesos on imports of American television sets. Now suppose that the overvalued peso begins to depreciate, say, to 0.11 USD = 1 MXN and that, in the short run, Mexican customers buy only 100 fewer American television sets (1,900). At a price of $500 each and an exchange rate of 0.11 USD = 1 MXN, Mexicans now spend 8.63 million pesos on imports of American television sets. In the short run, then, a depreciation in the peso has widened the trade deficit because the number of American television sets imported by Mexicans fell by less than the price of these television sets (in terms of pesos) increased. As time passes, imports will fall off more (it takes time for Mexican buyers to shift from higher-priced American goods to lower-priced Mexican goods), and the deficit will shrink.

SELF-TEST

1. What is an optimal currency area?

2. Country 1 produces good X, and country 2 produces good Y. People in both countries begin to demand more of good X and less of good Y. Assume that there is no labor mobility between the two countries and that a flexible exchange rate system exists. What will happen to the unemployment rate in country 2? Explain your answer.

3. How important is labor mobility in determining whether an area is an optimal currency area?

OFFICE HOURS

"Why Is the Depreciation of One Currency Tied to the Appreciation of Another Currency?"

STUDENT:

I know that when the dollar depreciates, some other currency appreciates. Is this just the way it is? For example, if $1 dollar equals €1 euro, and then $1.25 equals €1, the arithmetic of exchange rates tells me that now $1 will only fetch €0.8. Is that all there is to it?

INSTRUCTOR:

Not exactly. You're focusing on the arithmetic (of exchange rates) to the exclusion of the economics. There is an economic reason why dollar appreciation is linked to euro appreciation.

STUDENT:

What is that economic reason?

INSTRUCTOR:

Think of what can lead to the dollar's depreciating. Suppose you want to travel to Germany, where the euro is used. You take your dollars and buy euros with them. In other words, you do two things: You (1) buy euros by (2) supplying dollars.

Now think of how you are affecting the market for euros and the market for dollars. You are increasing the *demand for euros* in the market for euros, and you are increasing the *supply of dollars* in the market for dollars. Remember in Exhibit 5 how we linked the demand for one currency with the supply of another? That is happening here: Your demand for euros is linked to your supply of dollars. So, if you increase the demand for euros, you are automatically increasing the supply of dollars.

STUDENT:

I'm used to thinking that my buying something affects only one market. For instance, when I buy more books, the purchase affects only the market for books. You seem to be telling me that this is not the case when I buy a currency, such as the euro. To buy euros is to supply dollars.

INSTRUCTOR:

That's right. So when you increase the demand for euros, you automatically increase the supply of dollars. And then we have to ask ourselves what happens in each of the two markets: the market for euros and the market for dollars.

CHAPTER SUMMARY

BALANCE OF PAYMENTS

- The balance of payments provides information about a nation's imports and exports, domestic residents' earnings on assets located abroad, foreign earnings on domestic assets, gifts to and from foreign countries, and official transactions by governments and central banks.
- In a nation's balance of payments, any transaction that supplies the country's currency in the foreign exchange market is recorded as a debit (−). Any transaction that creates a demand for the country's currency is recorded as a credit (+).
- The three main accounts of the balance of payments are the current account, the capital account, and the official reserve account.

- The current account includes all payments related to the purchase and sale of goods and services. The three major components of the account are exports of goods and services, imports of goods and services, and net unilateral transfers abroad.
- The capital account includes all payments related to the purchase and sale of assets and to borrowing and lending activities. The major components are outflow of U.S. capital and inflow of foreign capital.
- The official reserve account includes transactions by the central banks of various countries.
- The merchandise trade balance is the difference between the value of merchandise exports and the value of merchandise

Well, if I increase the demand for euros, the price of a euro in terms of dollars will rise. Also, if I increase the supply of dollars, the price of a dollar in terms of euros will fall.

And what do you call it when the price of a euro has risen in terms of dollars?

We say the dollar has depreciated because it now takes more dollars and cents to buy a euro.

And what do you call it when the price of a dollar has fallen in terms of euros?

We say the euro has appreciated because it now takes fewer euros to buy a dollar.

So let's go back to your original query. You wondered whether the dollar's depreciating and the euro's appreciating were just matters of arithmetic. Now we know that they aren't. They are a matter of curves shifting in different markets.

POINTS TO REMEMBER

1. To buy a currency is to affect two markets, not just one. If you buy euros, you affect the euro market. But by selling dollars to buy euros, you also affect the dollar market.

2. The fact that when one currency depreciates another appreciates is a matter of curves shifting in two currency markets.

imports. If exports are greater than imports, a nation has a trade surplus; if imports are greater than exports, a nation has a trade deficit.

• The balance of payments equals Current account balance + Capital account balance + Official reserve balance + Statistical discrepancy.

THE FOREIGN EXCHANGE MARKET

• The market in which currencies of different countries are exchanged is called the foreign exchange market. In this market, currencies are bought and sold for a price: the exchange rate.

• When the residents of a nation demand a foreign currency, they must supply their own currency. For example, if Americans demand Mexican goods, they also demand Mexican pesos and supply U.S. dollars. If Mexicans demand American goods, they also demand U.S. dollars and supply Mexican pesos.

FLEXIBLE EXCHANGE RATES

• Under flexible exchange rates, the foreign exchange market will equilibrate at the exchange rate where the quantity demanded of a currency equals the quantity supplied of the currency; for example, the quantity demanded of U.S. dollars equals the quantity supplied of U.S. dollars.

• If the price of a nation's currency increases relative to a foreign currency, the nation's currency is said to have appreciated. For example, if the price of a peso rises from 0.10 USD = 1 MXN to 0.15 USD = 1 MXN, the peso has appreciated. If the price of a nation's currency decreases relative to a foreign currency, the nation's currency is said to have depreciated. For example, if the price of a dollar falls from 10 MXN = 1 USD to 8 MXN = 1 USD, the dollar has depreciated.

• Under a flexible exchange rate system, the equilibrium exchange rate is affected by a difference in income growth rates between countries, a difference in inflation rates between countries, and a change in (real) interest rates between countries.

FIXED EXCHANGE RATES

- Under a fixed exchange rate system, countries agree to fix the price of their currencies. The central banks of the countries must then buy and sell currencies to maintain the agreed-on exchange rate.

- If a persistent deficit or surplus in a nation's combined current and capital account exists at a fixed exchange rate, the nation has a few options to deal with the problem: devalue or revalue its currency, enact protectionist trade policies (in the case of a deficit), or change its monetary policy.

- A gold standard automatically fixes exchange rates. To have an international gold standard, nations must do the following: (1) define their currencies in terms of gold; (2) stand ready and willing to convert gold into paper money and paper money into gold at a specified rate; and (3) link their money supplies to their holdings of gold. The change in the money supply that the gold standard sometimes requires has prompted some economists to voice the same charge against the gold standard that is often heard against the fixed exchange rate system: it subjects domestic monetary policy to international instead of domestic considerations.

THE CURRENT INTERNATIONAL MONETARY SYSTEM

- Today's international monetary system is described as a managed flexible exchange rate system, or managed float. For the most part, the exchange rate system is flexible, although nations periodically intervene in the foreign exchange market to adjust rates. Because it is a managed float system, it is difficult to tell whether nations will emphasize the float part or the managed part in the future.

- Proponents of the managed flexible exchange rate system believe it offers several advantages: (1) It allows nations to pursue independent monetary policies. (2) It solves trade problems without trade restrictions. (3) It is flexible and therefore can easily adjust to shocks.

- Opponents of the managed flexible exchange rate system believe it has several disadvantages: (1) It promotes exchange rate volatility and uncertainty and results in less international trade than would be the case under fixed exchange rates. (2) It promotes inflation. (3) It corrects trade deficits only a long time after a depreciation in the currency; in the interim, it can make matters worse.

KEY TERMS AND CONCEPTS

Balance of Payments
Debit
Foreign Exchange Market
Credit
Current Account
Merchandise Trade Balance
Merchandise Trade Deficit

Merchandise Trade Surplus
Current Account Balance
Capital Account
Capital Account Balance
International Monetary Fund (IMF)
Special Drawing Right (SDR)

Exchange Rate
Flexible Exchange Rate System
Appreciation
Depreciation
Purchasing Power Parity (PPP) Theory

Fixed Exchange Rate System
Overvalued
Undervalued
Devaluation
Revaluation
Optimal Currency Area
Managed Float

QUESTIONS AND PROBLEMS

1. Suppose Canada has a merchandise trade deficit and Mexico has a merchandise trade surplus. The two countries have a flexible exchange rate system; so the Mexican peso appreciates and the Canadian dollar depreciates. However, soon after the depreciation of the Canadian dollar, Canada's trade deficit grows instead of shrinks. Why might this occur?

2. What are the strong and weak points of the flexible exchange rate system? What are the strong and weak points of the fixed exchange rate system?

3. Individuals do not keep a written account of their balance of trade with other individuals. For example, John doesn't keep an account of how much he sells to Alice and how much he buys from her. In addition, neither cities nor any of the 50 states calculate their balance of trade with all other cities and states. However, nations do calculate their

merchandise trade balance with other nations. If nations do so, should individuals, cities, and states do so? Why or why not?

4. Suppose the media report that the United States has a deficit in its current account. What does this imply about the U.S. capital account balance and official reserve account balance?

5. Give an example that illustrates how a change in the exchange rate changes the relative price of domestic goods in terms of foreign goods.

6. Suppose the United States and Japan have a flexible exchange rate system. Explain whether each of the following events will lead to an appreciation or depreciation in the U.S. dollar and Japanese yen.

   a. U.S. real interest rates rise above Japanese real interest rates.

b. The Japanese inflation rate rises relative to the U.S. inflation rate.

c. Japan imposes a quota on imports of American radios.

7. If everyone in the world spoke the same language, would the world be closer to or further from being an optimal currency area? Explain your answer.

8. Suppose the price of a Big Mac always rises by the percentage rise in the price level of the country in which it is sold. According to the purchasing power parity (PPP) theory, we would expect the price of a Big Mac to be the same everywhere in the world. Why?

9. Suppose your objective is to predict whether the euro (the currency of the European Union) and the U.S. dollar will appreciate or depreciate on the foreign exchange market in the next two months. What information would you need to help make your prediction? Specifically, how would this information help you predict the direction of the foreign exchange value of the euro and dollar? Next, explain how a person who could accurately predict exchange rates could become extremely rich in a short time.

10. Every nation's balance of payments equals zero. Therefore, is each nation on an equal footing in international trade and finance with every other nation? Explain your answer.

WORKING WITH NUMBERS AND GRAPHS

1. Use the following information to answer questions.

	U.S. Dollar Equivalent		Currency per U.S. Dollar	
	Thurs.	**Fri.**	**Thurs.**	**Fri.**
Russia (ruble)	0.0318	0.0317	31.4190	31.5290
Brazil (real)	0.3569	0.3623	2.8020	2.7601
India (rupee)	0.0204	0.0208	48.9100	47.8521

a. Between Thursday and Friday, did the U.S. dollar appreciate or depreciate against the Russian ruble?

b. Between Thursday and Friday, did the U.S. dollar appreciate or depreciate against the Brazilian real?

c. Between Thursday and Friday, did the U.S. dollar appreciate or depreciate against the Indian rupee?

2. If $1 equals ¥0.0093, what does ¥1 equal?

3. If $1 equals 7.7 krone (Danish), what does 1 krone equal?

4. If $1 equals 31 rubles, what does 1 ruble equal?

5. If the current account is –$45 billion, the capital account is +$55 billion, and the official reserve balance is –$1 billion, what does the statistical discrepancy equal?

6. Why does the balance of payments always equal zero?

GLOBALIZATION AND INTERNATIONAL IMPACTS ON THE ECONOMY

Introduction In the world in which we live, we hear much of *globalization*. In this chapter we discuss what globalization is, the causes of it, the costs and benefits of it, and its future. We then return to a framework of analysis we first used in the macroeconomics part of this text—aggregate demand and aggregate supply (*AD–AS*)—and we use *AD–AS* to discuss some of the effects of globalization on a national economy.

WHAT IS GLOBALIZATION?

Many economists define globalization as one of two things:

1. A phenomenon by which individuals and businesses in any part of the world are much more affected by events elsewhere in the world than before.

2. The growing integration of the national economies of the world to the degree that we may be witnessing the emergence and operation of a single worldwide economy.

These factors—people and businesses across the world having a greater impact on each other, creating a smaller world, and the movement toward a worldwide economy—are repeated in the many different definitions of globalization. Let's take a closer look at these key features.

A Smaller World

The first definition emphasizes that economic agents in any given part of the world are affected by events elsewhere in the world. If you live in the United States, you are affected not only by what happens in the United States but also by what happens in Brazil, Russia, and China. For example, in recent years, the Chinese government was using much of the money it earned in trade with the United States to buy bonds issued by the U.S. government. As a result of these Chinese purchases, interest rates in the United States ended up being lower than they would have been. Because of lowered interest rates, some people were able to take out mortgage loans to buy houses that they would not be eligible for otherwise. Some people took out car loans to buy cars that they otherwise would not have been able to buy.

Globalization
A phenomenon by which economic agents in any given part of the world are more affected by events elsewhere in the world than before; the growing integration of the national economies of the world to the degree that we may be witnessing the emergence and operation of a single worldwide economy.

So, in a sense, globalization makes the world smaller. China has not moved physically; it is no closer to the United States (in terms of distance) than it was 100 years ago. Still, because of globalization, what happens in distant China today has an effect on you, just as, in the past, what happened in locations only 10 miles or 100 miles away would affect you. For all practical purposes, we live in a smaller world today than people did 100 years ago.

finding ECONOMICS

In a Clothing Store Brandon is at a clothing store buying a number of items—shirts, sweaters, trousers, etc. He doesn't check to see in which country each of these items was produced. Instead, he just checks out the item and its price, and he decides whether to buy it. Where is the economics?

Many of the items Brandon buys were very likely produced in other countries. To Brandon, buying an item of clothing produced in China, Brazil, or India is really no different from buying an item of clothing in a factory 10 miles away. For Brandon, China, Brazil, or India might as well be down the street. In some ways, the world Brandon lives in is a small world, one in which distance doesn't matter as much as it used to; it is one in which trades between people living in different countries are becoming increasingly more common. ▲ ▲ ▲

A World Economy

Globalization is closely aligned with a movement toward more free enterprise, freer markets, and more freedom of movement for people and goods. Thomas Friedman, author of several books on globalization, states that "globalization means the spread of free-market capitalism in the world." Economic globalization is essentially a free enterprise activity, and, to the degree that many countries are globalizing, they are moving toward greater free enterprise practices. Much of this globalization and much of the movement toward freer markets are occurring in the world today.

With globalization, the world is moving from hundreds of national economies toward *one large world economy.* In this world economy, speaking about *different* economic systems does not make as much sense as it once did. Speaking about *the* economic system for that one world economy does make sense. And, as explained, the economic system that best describes what is happening in the world economy is free enterprise, or capitalism.

finding ECONOMICS

In *The Economist* "Mr. Bhattacharjee is not the first leader to preach socialism while practising capitalism." Mr. Bhattacharjee is the chief minister of the Indian state, West Bengal. The statement about him was made in *The Economist* (a news magazine that covers economic issues in particular) in November 2007. Where is the economics?

The statement gives us a glimpse into what is happening in the world today with respect to the adoption of economic systems—specifically, the movement toward capitalism. ▲ ▲ ▲

TWO WAYS TO SEE GLOBALIZATION

Sometimes, a definition is not as good a description or explanation as a picture. Let's create two mental pictures that should give you a good idea of what globalization is about. The first picture is of a world without any barriers to trade, where the cost of dealing with anyone in the world is essentially the same.

economics 24/7

Should You Leave a Tip?

In the United States, tipping in restaurants is common, amounting to $16 billion a year. Yet 24 percent of the individuals in one study said that they thought tipping was unfair to customers. In the past, some states prohibited tipping. For example, in the early 1900s, Arkansas, Mississippi, Iowa, South Carolina, Tennessee, and Washington passed laws to prohibit tipping.

Of all the people in the rest of the world, some have the same tipping practices as Americans, but certainly not all. For example, adding an automatic service charge to a restaurant bill is increasingly customary in European restaurants, rather than tipping the server. Little tipping of any sort goes on in Argentina and Vietnam. Much less tipping occurs (i.e., fewer service providers expect tips) in Australia, New Zealand, and Italy than in the United States, and more tipping goes on in Mexico and Egypt than in the United States.

© MOODBOARD/ALAMY

In several studies, researchers looked at the number of different service providers (out of a total of 33) for which tipping is customary in a given country: the more service providers it was customary to tip in a country, the higher the country's so-called prevalence of tipping. For example, if it was customary to tip 31 different service providers in country A but only 15 in country B, then country A would have a higher prevalence of tipping than country B.

The conclusion of these studies is that countries where success and materialism were highly valued had a higher prevalence to tip than countries where caring and personal relationships were highly valued. In addition, the prevalence of tipping increased as the national need for achievement and recognition rose. In one study, tipping was more prevalent in countries with lower taxes than in countries with higher taxes.

If speaking in terms of a world economy instead of hundreds of national economies is becoming increasingly relevant, will tipping practices around the world become more uniform? If they do, toward what degree of tipping will they gravitate? Even if we do not know the answers, these questions get us to do two things: first, they get us to think about what changes we are likely to see in our everyday lives as globalization continues, whether the changes will be only in the economic realm (e.g., we can buy more clothes from China), or whether they will disperse outward into the social and cultural realms. Second, the questions force us to separate into categories things that are so deeply embedded in the character of a people (and therefore unlikely to change) from things that are somewhat superficial (and therefore more likely to change). Which is a rock (incapable of absorbing), and which is a sponge (capable of absorbing)?

No Barriers

Suppose land were not divided into nation states—no United States, no China, no Russia. Also suppose physical, economic, or political barriers to trade did not exist. Essentially, then, you could trade with anyone, no matter where in the world this person lived. You could trade with a person living 5,000 miles away as easily as you could trade with your next-door neighbor.

In this pretend world, businesses could hire workers and set up factories anywhere in the world. People could open savings accounts in banks 7,000 miles away or buy stock in companies located on the other side of the globe.

In a sense, our world—the world that we live in today—is moving in this direction. As it does, a nation's economy (e.g., the U.S. economy) becomes more and more a part of the world economy. Consequently, speaking about a world or global economy, rather than about the Russian, U.S., or Chinese economy, becomes increasingly relevant.

A Union of States

The second way to see globalization is familiar to people who reside in the United States, made up as it is of 50 states. Today, moving goods and services among these states is easy. A person can produce goods in, say, North Carolina and then transport them (with only a few exceptions) for sale to every state in the country. In addition, a person living anywhere in the United States can move to any state and work, save, purchase, sell, and so on. In other words, within the United States, the free movement of people and goods is possible.

Some people will argue today that economic globalization is, in a way, similar to changing countries (of the world) into states of one country. It is similar to making independent countries such as the United States, Russia, China, Brazil, and Japan into the United States of the World.

GLOBALIZATION FACTS

You know globalization is occurring, when you see certain things happening in the world:

- Countries in the world opening up to more trade with each other
- People in one country investing some of their money in other countries
- Companies in one country hiring people in other countries

Essentially, you need to see people in the world acting more as they once acted only within their individual countries. Some evidence suggests that all these things are happening.

International Trade

Tariff
A tax on imports.

The average tariff rate in the United States was 40 percent in 1946. The average tariff today is about 1.6 percent. Also, the federal government's revenue from tariffs in the early 1900s accounted for half of all its revenues, whereas today tariffs account for less than 2 percent. Exhibit 1 presents average tariff rates in the United States during the period 1930–2010.

The decline in tariff rates in the United States mirrors similar declines in countries such as India, China, Brazil, and many others. For example, in 2000, the average tariff rate in China was 18.7 percent; one year later, it was 12.8 percent. In 2000, the average tariff rate in India was 30.2 percent; one year later, it was 21 percent. Furthermore, both India and China are trading more with other countries. For example, 15 years ago, China did not

---

EXHIBIT 1

Average U.S. Tariff Rates, 1930–2010

trade much with the countries of Europe. Today, for most European countries, China is one of their top five trading partners.

As further evidence of globalization, between 1973 and 2010, countries exported and imported more goods. Exports became a larger percentage of a country's total output. On an individual level, suppose you produce computers. Last year, all the computers you produced were purchased by residents of the country in which you live. This year, residents of your country purchase half of your computers, and persons who live in foreign countries purchased the other half. In 2010, U.S. exports and imports were more like the second scenario; in 1973, things were closer to the first scenario.

Foreign Exchange Trading

When people of one country want to trade with people of another country or invest in a foreign company, they have to buy the currency used in the other country. So if globalization is occurring, we would expect a lot more currency exchanges to take place. In economics, *foreign exchange trading* is the buying and selling of foreign currencies. In 1995, daily foreign exchange trading was 60 times higher than it was in 1977. In 1992, daily foreign exchange trading amounted to $820 billion. In 1998, this amount had risen to $1.5 trillion, close to doubling in just six years. In 2007, foreign exchange trading had risen to over $3 trillion.

Foreign Direct Investment

If a U.S. company wants to invest in a company in, say, Russia, it undertakes what is called *foreign direct investment.* The more foreign direct investment there is, the more likely it is that the process of globalization is at work. In 1975, foreign direct investment amounted to $23 billion. In 1997, it had risen to $644 billion, a 30-fold increase. In 1980, 6.2 percent of the U.S. population was foreign born; in 2005, it was 12 percent. Between 1984 and 2003, U.S. investment holdings in foreign companies tripled, and foreign investment in the United States increased six-fold.

Personal Investments

Many people in the United States own stocks, and if you own a number of stocks, you are said to have a stock portfolio. In 1980, these stock portfolios were comprised of no more than 2 percent of foreign stocks. Today, it is 14 percent. Thus, Americans are increasingly buying stock in foreign companies.

finding ECONOMICS

In a Foreign Stock Transaction Two years ago Jake bought a few foreign stocks. Specifically, he bought 1,000 shares of an Irish firm's stock and 400 shares of a French firm's stock. In both Ireland and France the currency used is the euro. In recent months, the value of the dollar in relationship to the euro has been falling. In other words, it now takes more dollars and cents to buy a euro than it did when Jake bought the stock. Where is the economics?

The economics appears in two places. First, buying foreign stocks is part of the overall globalization picture. Second, Jake's return for buying the foreign stocks is rising as the dollar falls. When Jake sells the foreign stock, he will be paid in euros, and euros are rising in value relative to the dollar. So, when he exchanges the euros for dollars, he will get more dollars now than he would have before the dollar fell in value (in relation to the euro). ▲▲▲

The World Trade Organization

The World Trade Organization (WTO) is an international organization whose mission is to promote international free trade (trade between countries). In 1948, only 23 countries of the world chose to be members of the precursor to the WTO, GATT (General Agreement on Tariffs and Trade); in mid-2010, that number had risen to 153 countries.

Business Practices

More and more, Americans are working for foreign companies with offices in the United States. For example, the number of Americans working for foreign companies (with offices in the United States) grew from 4.9 million in 1991 to 6.5 million in 2001, an increase of 1.6 million.

THE MOVEMENT TOWARD GLOBALIZATION

How did we come to live in a global economy? How and when did the process start? Globalization has been on the world stage for over two decades. In fact, the world has gone through different globalization periods. For example, globalization was occurring during the period from the mid-1800s to the late 1920s, and some people today refer to it as the First Era of Globalization. In some ways, when it came to the movement of people, the world then was freer than the world today, as evidenced by the fact that many people moved from country to country without a passport, which was not required.

The First Era of Globalization was largely ended by World Wars I and II and by the Great Depression. Even though the Great Depression and the world wars were over by 1945, globalization did not start anew right away. The Cold War essentially divided the world into different camps (free versus unfree, capitalist versus communist), which led to relatively high political and economic barriers. The visible symbol of these barriers—the Berlin Wall—separated not only East from West Germany but one group of countries living under one political and economic system from another group of countries living under a different political and economic system.

Today's more recent period of globalization has several causal factors. Not everyone agrees on all of them, and not everyone agrees on the weight one assigns to each. For example, some people will argue that one factor means more to globalization than another. Still, you should be aware of the causal factors of globalization most often mentioned.

The End of the Cold War

The Cold War intensified after World War II and, most agree, ended with the visible fall of the Berlin Wall in 1989. This event, although historic in and of itself, occurred at the time when the Soviet empire was beginning to crumble, and many of the communist East European countries were breaking away from the Soviet Union. As some explain the event, the end of the Cold War resulted in turning two different worlds (the capitalist and communist worlds) into one. It resulted in a thawing of not only political but economic relations between former enemies. You might not trade with your enemy, but once that person or country is no longer your enemy, you don't feel the same need to exclude him or it from your political and economic life.

At the beginning of this section, we asked you to imagine a world where no barriers affected your trading with anyone in the world. The barriers might be distance, culture, politics, or anything else. The Cold War acted as a political barrier between certain groups of countries; once it ended, one barrier standing in the way of trade disappeared. In fact, if United States and the Soviet Union were still engaged in the Cold War, the current period of economic liberalization (freer markets, lower tariffs) and globalization might not be taking place. Even though the end of the Cold War might not be the full and only cause for the current period of globalization, if it had not ended, globalization would probably not be accelerating at the pace it is today.

economics 24/7

Proper Business Etiquette Around the World

Customs and traditions differ among countries, sometimes when it comes to conducting business. Not knowing how business is done in a country can act as a stumbling block to getting it done. What follows is a list of countries and certain rules of business etiquette in the different countries.[1]

Beijing, China
- If someone offers you his or her business card, accept with both hands, read it immediately, and then present your business card to the person.
- In business, men normally wear a suit and tie.

Berlin, Germany
- When out with German business associates, try not to talk about sports. Many businesspeople believe that sports talk is the domain of the uneducated.
- Drinking before all have raised their glasses together is considered impolite.

Dubai, United Arab Emirates
- Do not arrange appointments on Friday because it is Dubai's day of prayer and rest.
- Business slows down during the month of Ramadan (when Muslims fast). Foreign businesspeople are expected to observe the slower pace.

Hong Kong
- Running out of business cards is considered impolite.

Mexico City
- Having business cards printed in English on one side and in Spanish on the other is considered good form.
- Business clothing is fairly formal.

Sydney, Australia
- Knowing about the latest sports matches is important.
- Don't take yourself too seriously.

Tokyo, Japan
- Remove your shoes when entering a Japanese home.

Zurich, Switzerland
- People often greet each other when entering an office or shop. Try to do the same, even if your greeting is in your own language.
- Talking about money or personal wealth is frowned upon.

---

1. The reference guide is *The Economist*'s City Guide.

Advancing Technology

In the past, innovations such as the internal combustion engine, steamship, telephone, and telegraph led to increased trade between people in different countries. All of these inventions led to lower transportation or communication costs, and lower costs mean fewer barriers to trade. What technology often does is lower the hindrances (of physical distance) that act as stumbling blocks to trade. For example, the cost of a 3-minute telephone call from New York to London in 1930 was $250. In 1960, it was $60.42; in 1980, it was $6.32; and in 2000, it was 40¢. Today, the cost is even less. As the costs of communicating continue to fall, in some sense, the hindrance to trade imposed by physical distance is overcome. Businesspeople in the United States, for example, can more cheaply talk with businesspeople in China.

Also consider the price of a computer over the years. In 1960, the cost of a computer—one comparable to the desktop computer that many people today have on their desks at home—was $1.8 million. That computer was $199,983 in 1970, $27,938 in 1980, $7,275 in 1990, $1,000 in 2000, and $500 in 2010. People today not only use computers for their work, but they communicate with others via the Internet. The personal computer and Internet technology enable people to communicate with others over long distances, thus increasing the probability that they will trade with one other.

Today, even farmers in poor developing countries can have access to people and to information that they didn't have access to only a few years ago. A farmer in the Ivory Coast can check agricultural prices in the world with a cell phone—something that was unheard of a decade ago. Or consider such innovations as online banking. Years ago, it was common to have your bank just down the road from you. Today, you can open up an account with an online bank, many of which are located nowhere near you.

Policy Changes

Governments have the power to slow down the process of globalization if they want. Suppose two countries, A and B, have free economic relations with each other. Neither country imposes tariffs on the goods of the other. Neither country prevents its citizens from going to the other country to live and work. Neither country hampers its citizens from investing in the other country. Then, one day, for whatever reason, the government of country A decides to impose tariffs on the goods of country B and to limit its citizens from traveling to and investing in country B. In other words, the government of country A decides to close its political and economic doors.

Just as a government of one country can close the door on another, it can open the door too, and it can do so a little, more than a little, or a lot. In recent decades, governments of many countries have been opening their doors to other countries. China has opened its door, India has opened its door, and Russia has opened its door.

The driving forces of this most recent period of globalization have been (1) the end of the Cold War, (2) technological changes that lower the costs of transporting goods and communicating with people, and (3) government policy changes that express an openness toward freer markets and long-distance trade.

SELF-TEST

(Answers to Self-Test questions are in Answers to Self-Test Questions at the back of the book.)

1. Some have said that the end of the Cold War has led to greater globalization. Explain the reasoning.

2. What is globalization?

3. How might advancing technology lead to increased globalization?

BENEFITS AND COSTS OF GLOBALIZATION

Some people believe that globalization is, in general, a good thing and that its benefits outweigh its costs. Other people take the opposite view that the costs of globalization are greater than the benefits. Let's look at what supporters say are its benefits and what opponents say are its costs. As you read, you will probably begin to form your own opinion.

The Benefits

TRADE To say that the world is undergoing globalization is really no more than saying that people are trading with more people, at greater distances, than they once did. They are trading different things: money for goods, their labor services for money, their savings for expected returns, and so on. Expanding trade—which is what globalization is about—is no more than extending the benefits of trading to people you might not have traded with earlier.

Economist David Friedman compared free international trade to a technology. He says that you can produce, say, cars in two ways. You can set up factories in Detroit,

Michigan, and produce them. Or you can harvest wheat in the Midwest, load it on ships and send it to Japan, and then wait for the ships to return with cars. Looking at things the second way sometimes brings out the magic of trade. After all, with free trade across countries, wheat gets turned into cars, an accomplishment that really is magical. The lesson Friedman is trying to communicate is that we all think a technological improvement is a good thing because it often leads to a higher standard of living. So, trading with people across the world really is nothing more than a technology of sorts; it is a way to turn wheat into cars. The more we trade with others, the more magic we witness.

INCOME PER PERSON The benefits of globalization can be seen in a slightly more concrete way. As both India and China opened up their economies to globalization in recent decades, they experienced increases in income per person. For example, between 1980 and 2000, income per person doubled in India. Between 1940 and 2000, income per person increased by 400 percent in China, with much of the increase coming in recent years. According to the International Monetary Fund, these dramatic increases in income per person accompanied the expansion of free international trade (a key component of globalization).

PRICES Numerous studies have established a link between lower prices and the degree of international trade and globalization. Simply put, free international trade lowers prices. For example, Exhibit 2 shows the CPI (consumer price index) and an import price index for the period 1990–2004. The CPI (which contains domestic goods and imported goods) rose faster than the import price index (which contains only imported goods). Also, between 1977 and 2004, the inflation-adjusted prices for an array of goods traded between countries fell, whereas the inflation-adjusted prices for an array of goods not traded between countries actually increased. Some of the traded goods whose prices fell are audio equipment (26 percent), TV sets (51 percent), toys (34 percent), and clothing (9 percent); some of the nontraded goods whose prices increased are whole milk (28 percent), butter (23 percent), ice cream (18 percent), and peanut butter (9 percent).

PRODUCTIVITY AND INNOVATION Firms that face global competition are often pushed to increase their productivity and to innovate more. According to the 2006 *Economic Report of the President,* "Studies show that firms exposed to the world's best practices demonstrate higher productivity through many channels, such as learning from these best practices, and also creating new products and processes in response to this exposure." For example, one study from the United Kingdom showed that the number of firms

EXHIBIT 2

CPI and Import Price Index, 1990–2004
The CPI increased at a faster rate during the period 1990–2004 than the import price index (which both increased and decreased during the period).

Source: Bureau of Labor Statistics.

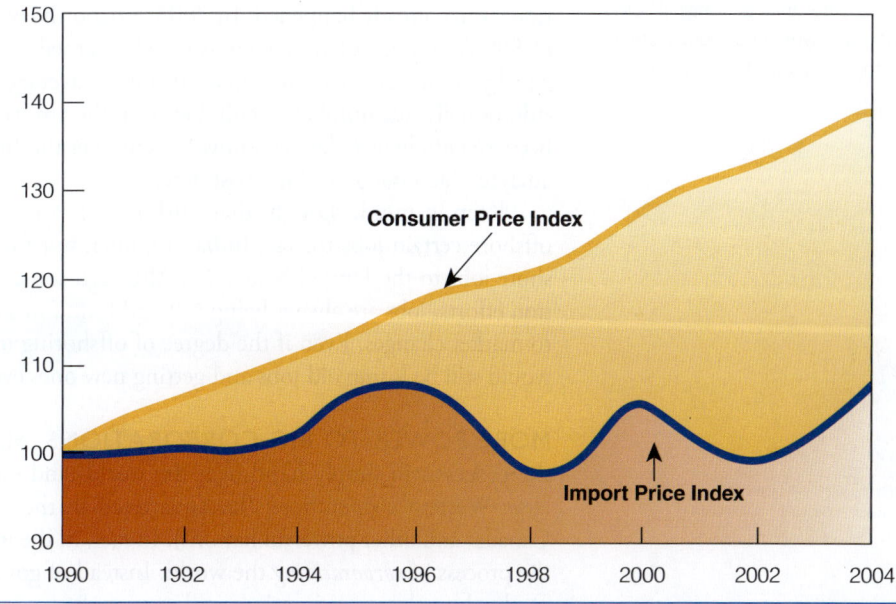

that faced global competition and reported product or process innovations was almost three times the number of firms that did not face global competition.

Or consider the extreme case of North and South Korea. The two countries share a people and a culture, but North Korea avoided the process of globalization during the period in which South Korea embraced it. South Koreans currently enjoy a much higher standard of living than North Koreans.

The Costs

INCREASED INCOME INEQUALITY Globalization's critics often point out that globalization seems to go hand in hand with increased income inequality between rich and poor countries in the world. In fact, income inequality has increased. For example, 100 years ago, people in rich countries had about 10 times more income than people in poor countries. Today, they have about 75 times more income. Without a doubt, globalization and income inequality are strongly correlated. The question, though, is whether globalization causes the inequality. The critics of globalization say it does, whereas the supporters say it does not.

The supporters of globalization liken it to a train. Economic systems that get on the train will benefit and reach their economic destinies faster, but those that do not will get left farther and farther behind. In other words, globalization does not increase income inequality; rather, some other combination of circumstances—of some countries globalizing while others are not—is the cause. In simple terms, if everyone is walking, some faster than others, then some will always be in front. If the fast walkers start to run while the others continue their slow walking pace, the gap between the ones in front and the ones in back will grow.

Of course, getting on the globalization train is not always a matter of choice. The conductor does not always let some people on. Some rich countries work against certain poor countries to counter their globalization efforts. For example, tariffs on goods imported from the poor, developing world are 30 percent above the global average for all tariffs.

LOSING AMERICAN JOBS Many critics of globalization argue that it can result in Americans losing certain jobs. Suppose a U.S. company hires engineers in India to do jobs once done by Americans. This practice of hiring people in other countries is often called offshoring.

Some Americans may lose their jobs to workers in other countries due to globalization. It has already happened. In 2003, a major New York securities firm replaced its team of 800 American software engineers, who earned about $150,000 per year each, with an equally competent team in India earning an average of about $20,000 a year per person. Additionally, the number of radiologists in the United States is expected to fall significantly because radiological data can now be sent over the Internet to Asian radiologists, who can analyze it at a fraction of the cost here.

Keep in mind, though, that offshoring is a two-way street: the United States might offshore certain jobs to, say, India or China, but foreign countries around the world offshore jobs to the United States too. Although some Americans lose jobs due to globalization efforts, jobs are always being lost and found in a dynamic economy that is responding to market changes. Even if the degree of offshoring in the United States were zero, people would still be losing old jobs and getting new ones every day.

MORE POWER TO BIG CORPORATIONS Many critics of globalization argue that the process will simply hand over the world (and especially the developing countries) to large Western corporations (headquartered in the United States, the United Kingdom, Canada, and other powerful nations). In fact, in the minds of many people, globalization is the process of *corporatizing* the world. Instead of governments deciding what will and will not be done, large corporations will assume the responsibility.

Offshoring
Work done for a company by persons other than the original company's employees in a country other than the company's home country.

Will Globalization Change the Sound of Music?

Suppose you had only 100 people to whom you could sell a good. Given this small number, you had better sell something that at least some of the 100 people want to buy. For example, if the 100 people don't like fruit salad, then you better not produce and offer to sell fruit salad; if some of them like bread, then perhaps you should produce and offer to sell bread.

Now increase the number of people from 100 to 1 million. A group of 1 million is much more likely than a group of 100 to contain people who like fruit salad. In other words, as the size of the potential customer base increases, the number of things you can sell increases too. In a world of 100 people, you can sell only bread, but in a world of 1 million people, you can sell fruit salad or bread.

So the larger the size is of the potential customer base (the more people you can possibly sell to), the greater the variety of goods for sale is likely to be. Globalization is, to a large degree, expanding everyone's ability to potentially sell to more people. American companies aren't limited to selling only to Americans; they can sell to others in the world too. Chinese firms aren't limited to selling only to Chinese; they can sell to others around the world.

As a musician, you can play different styles of music: jazz, pop, classical, hard rock, metal, hip-hop, and so on. If you are limited to selling your music to the people of a single state in the United States, you can offer to sell fewer styles of music than if you could sell your music to the people who reside throughout the United States.

More specifically, consider the musician in the United States who is experimenting with a new style of music. With a population of only the United States (310 million) as a potential customer base, the musician might not yet have enough actual customers to make it worth producing and offering to sell this particular, unique, and narrowly defined music. However, if the musician can draw on the population of the world (6.8 billion), then she might be able to find enough people who are willing to buy her new type of music.

As we move toward a world economy, we see a greater variety within almost every category of goods: a greater variety of music to listen to, books to read, types of television shows to watch, and so on. Today, the greater variety of goods you see in your world is an effect of globalization.

The proponents of globalization often point out a major difference between a corporation and a government. First, a government can force people to do certain things (such as pay taxes or join the military). No corporation can coerce people; instead, corporations can simply produce goods that they hope customers will buy. Additionally, the proponents of globalization often argue that the critics overestimate the influence and reach of large transnational companies. For example, in 2000, the top 100 transnational companies produced only 4.3 percent of the entire world's output, which is about as much as what one country, the United Kingdom, produced in 2000.

THE CONTINUING GLOBALIZATION DEBATE

Many (but certainly not all) economists argue that the worldwide benefits of globalization are likely to be greater than the worldwide costs. Of course, not everyone is going to see the beneficial side of globalization. To a large degree, whether people support or criticize globalization seems to depend on where they are sitting. Globalization does not affect everyone in the same way, and often *how* it affects *you* determines how you feel about it. For example, suppose Sanders, an American worker residing in New York, loses his job to an Indian worker in New Delhi, India, who will do Sanders' job for less pay. In this case, Sanders incurs real costs, but for Sanders' company, the change means lower costs and higher profits. For the company's customers, the change might mean lower prices. So in this case, Sanders is probably a strong opponent of offshoring, but his company and its customers are probably supporters.

Seeing the benefits of globalization is often much more difficult than seeing its costs. For example, the supporters of globalization argue that it brings greater economic wealth, lower prices, more innovation, less poverty, and so on. Yet seeing all these benefits is sometimes difficult. When you buy cheaper or different goods because of globalization, you probably never say, "Wow, I can't believe all the benefits I get from globalization!" In fact, you might not even connect the lower-priced goods with globalization at all. The benefits of globalization tend to be difficult to perceive, partly because they are so widely dispersed.

The costs of globalization, in contrast, are more visible, often because they are so concentrated. A person who loses a job because of freer international trade in the world knows exactly what is to blame for his predicament. He surely could receive some benefits from globalization (as a consumer), but he also could, for a time, incur some rather high costs (as an unemployed worker). This person is likely to know of the costs but be unaware of the benefits.

In the end, the people who receive only benefits from globalization might not be able to see them or to connect them with globalization. The people who receive benefits and costs from globalization may be aware only of the costs. This one-sided view could create strong antiglobalization sentiment in a country.

MORE OR LESS GLOBALIZATION: A TUG OF WAR?

Is increased globalization inevitable? Will the day come when all countries in the world are like the 50 states in the United States—part of one global economy with easy movement of people, resources, financial capital, goods, and services among the countries? Or will the conditions that prevented globalization reappear and reverse the trend?

This struggle is like a tug of war. The forces of globalization pull in one direction, and the forces of antiglobalization pull in the other. As of today, the forces of globalization are moving things in their direction, but the trend may not continue uninterrupted. Surely, at any time, the forces of antiglobalization could put on a burst of energy and give an extra strong tug on the rope.

To help answer the question about the future of globalization, recall what we said about the driving forces of the most recent era of globalization: the end of the Cold War, changes in technology (which lowered the costs of transportation and communication), and policy changes that opened up countries' economies to each other.

Less Globalization

INCREASED POLITICAL TENSION The end of the Cold War is a historical fact that we cannot undo, but we could enter a period when political tensions among countries or among groups of countries emerge. We are not suggesting that such a period of tension will happen, only that it could. If it did, it could slow down globalization or, depending on the severity of the tension, even reverse it.

TERRORISM Another inhibiting factor to globalization is global terrorism. Global terrorism tends to motivate certain countries into closing borders and into being much more careful about the people and goods crossing their borders.

TECHNOLOGY We cannot undo our technology. We cannot go from a world with the Internet to one without it. So it is unlikely that anything technological will slow down or reverse globalization.

GOVERNMENT POLICIES Policy changes can slow down or reverse globalization. Governments of countries that opened up their economies to others could reverse their course; doors that opened to other nations can be closed. Whether this sort of isolationism will happen in the future is an unknown.

More Globalization

Some still argue that even with the forces of antiglobalization looming on the horizon, the forces of globalization are stronger. In the end, these individuals say, the forces of globalization will win the tug of war. They believe that, in the long run, economics influences politics, not the other way around. As some proof of that assertion, they often point to the former Soviet Union and to China, both entrenched communist countries. Both countries saw, in the end, that they were worse off by holding themselves outside the orbit of free market forces. You might say that they found themselves outside the theater where economic forces were playing major roles on the world stage.

Many economists argue that globalization is not just a passing trend. They argue that the basic globalization force that will probably not be overcome—no matter how strong the political forces may be against it—is the human inclination that the founder of modern economics, Adam Smith, noticed more than 200 years ago: human beings want to trade with each other. In fact, the desire to trade separates us from all other species, Smith said. In his words, "Man is an animal that makes bargains: no other animal does this—no dog exchanges bones with another."

We want to trade with people: our next-door neighbor, the person down the street, the person on the other side of town, the person in the next state, the person on the other side of the country, and ultimately the person on the other side of the world. Some economists go on to suggest that our trading inclination is a good thing in that when we trade with people, we not only tolerate them but we have much less reason to fight with them. Robert Wright, a journalist and scholar, argues that it is not a coincidence that religious toleration is high in the United States, a country that is open to trade and globalization. We often see, he argues, that people who live in countries that trade with other people—people who live in countries that are open to other people—are people who tolerate others.

In a similar vein, Thomas Friedman advanced his "Golden Arches theory of conflict prevention," which states that "no two countries that both had McDonald's had fought a war against each other since each got its McDonald's." The United States will not fight Germany because both countries have McDonald's. France won't fight Mexico because both countries have McDonald's. Certainly, the mere presence of a McDonald's does not prevent people from fighting with other people. McDonald's is symbolic of certain forces at work in the country. For Friedman, the franchise is a symbol of a certain degree of economic globalization and a level of economic development sufficient enough to support a large middle class.

SELF-TEST

1. Identify some of the benefits of globalization.

2. Identify some of the costs of globalization.

INTERNATIONAL FACTORS AND AGGREGATE DEMAND

Preceding chapters have described domestic factors that can change aggregate demand and thus affect the U.S. economy. Changes that occur in other countries can also influence the U.S. economy. This section discusses two key international factors that can affect the U.S. economy by first affecting U.S. aggregate demand: net exports and the J-curve.

Net Exports

In an earlier chapter, net exports are defined as the difference between exports (*EX*) and imports (*IM*). For example, if exports are $80 billion and imports are $60 billion, then net exports are $20 billion. Also, recall that if net exports rise, the *AD* curve shifts to the right; if net exports fall, the *AD* curve shifts to the left.

Two factors can change net exports: (1) foreign Real GDP and (2) the exchange rate. To simplify matters, we assume there are only two countries in the world: the United States and Japan.

FOREIGN REAL GDP (OR FOREIGN REAL NATIONAL INCOME) As Japan's Real GDP (or real national income) rises, the Japanese buy more U.S. goods. As a result, U.S. net exports rise, and the *AD* curve shifts to the right. As Japan's Real GDP falls, the Japanese buy fewer U.S. goods. As a result, U.S. net exports fall, and the *AD* curve shifts to the left.

Thus economic expansions and contractions in other countries are felt in the United States. Given a contraction in Japan, with a lower Real GDP in Japan, the Japanese buy fewer U.S. goods. U.S. exports fall, and so do net exports. As a result, the *AD* curve in the United States shifts to the left. Because the *AD* curve shifts to the left, Real GDP in the United States falls.

EXCHANGE RATE Recall that the exchange rate is the price of one country's currency expressed in terms of another country's currency. If a country's currency *appreciates*, it takes less of that country's currency to buy the other. On the other hand, if a country's currency *depreciates*, it takes more of that country's country to buy the other.

Appreciation and depreciation affect the prices of a country's goods. If, say, the U.S. dollar depreciates relative to the Japanese yen, U.S. residents have to pay more dollars to buy Japanese goods. To illustrate, suppose the dollar price of a yen is $0.012 and that a Toyota is priced at ¥2 million. At this exchange rate, a U.S. resident pays $24,000 for a Toyota ($0.012 × ¥2 million = $24,000). If the dollar depreciates to $0.018 for ¥1, then the U.S. resident will have to pay $36,000 for a Toyota.

As the dollar depreciates, Japanese goods become more expensive for U.S. residents. So they buy fewer Japanese goods, and U.S. imports decline.[2] The other side of the coin is that as the dollar depreciates relative to the yen, the yen appreciates relative to the dollar. Thus U.S. goods become less expensive for the Japanese, and they buy more U.S. goods. So U.S. exports rise.

In summary, a depreciation in the dollar and an appreciation in the yen will raise U.S. exports, lower U.S. imports, and therefore raise U.S. net exports. This shifts the U.S. *AD* curve to the right, leading to a rise in the U.S. Real GDP level.

The series of events are symmetrical if the U.S. dollar appreciates relative to the Japanese yen. In this case, U.S. goods become more expensive for the Japanese, causing them to buy fewer U.S. goods; so U.S. exports fall. And Japanese goods become cheaper for U.S. residents, causing them to buy more Japanese goods; so U.S. imports rise. A decline in U.S. exports, along with a rise in U.S. imports, will cause U.S. net exports to fall. The U.S. *AD* curve shifts to the left, leading to a decline in U.S. Real GDP.

For a quick review of the international factors that can shift the U.S. *AD* curve, see Exhibit 3.

---

2. Throughout this chapter, unless otherwise explicitly stated, we assume that if the physical quantity of exports rises (falls), the total spending on exports rises (falls). Also, if the physical quantity of imports rises (falls), the total spending on imports rises (falls). Because of this assumption, it is not necessary to differentiate constantly between the physical quantity of imports and the total spending on imports. Given our assumption, they go up and down together. One place we explicitly drop this assumption is in the discussion of the J-curve.

EXHIBIT 3

International Impacts on the U.S. AD Curve

Anything that increases U.S. net exports shifts the U.S. AD curve to the right. This includes an increase in Japan's Real GDP (in a two-country world, where the two countries are Japan and the United States) and a depreciation in the dollar. Anything that decreases U.S. net exports shifts the U.S. AD curve to the left. This includes a decrease in Japan's Real GDP and an appreciation in the dollar.

The J-Curve

So far, we have assumed that if the dollar depreciates relative to the Japanese yen, U.S. residents and the Japanese will buy more U.S. goods and fewer Japanese goods. Thus, U.S. exports rise, U.S. imports fall, and U.S. net exports rise.

But this scenario may not happen initially. There may be a difference between what *initially* happens and what *ultimately* happens. To illustrate, suppose U.S. residents are currently buying 100,000 cars from the Japanese, the average Japanese car sells for ¥2 million, and the exchange rate is currently $0.012 per yen. This means U.S. residents are spending an average of $24,000 a car for 100,000 cars. Thus, a total of $2.4 billion is spent on imported Japanese cars.

Then the exchange rate changes, and the dollar depreciates to $0.018 per yen, causing the average price of a Japanese car to jump to $36,000. At this higher price, U.S. residents buy fewer Japanese cars, but they don't buy that many fewer right away. Instead of buying 100,000 cars, they initially buy 90,000 cars. Now a total of $3.24 billion is spent on imported Japanese cars. Instead of declining after a depreciation in the dollar, U.S. spending on imports initially rises. If we assume U.S. exports have not changed yet, a rise in U.S. imports will lead to a fall in U.S. net exports and cause the U.S. AD curve to shift to the left.

But this situation is not likely to last. In time, U.S. residents will switch from the higher-priced Japanese goods to lower-priced U.S. goods. For example, after a while, U.S. residents purchase only 60,000 Japanese cars. At this number, with the exchange rate of $0.018 per yen, U.S. spending on imported Japanese cars is $2.16 billion. In time, too, U.S. exports will rise, and the combination of rising exports and falling imports will lead to an increase in net exports. The U.S. AD curve will shift to the right.

This phenomenon, in which import spending initially rises after a depreciation and then later falls, is summarized in the **J-curve**, so-called because the curve showing the change in net exports due to a currency depreciation has the shape of a J. In Exhibit 4, the United States initially has negative net exports of –$40 billion (its imports of $130 billion are greater than its exports of $90 billion). This position is represented by point *A* in the exhibit.

Next, the dollar depreciates relative to the yen. Total spending on imports rises to, say, $150 billion; so net exports rise to –$60 billion, as represented by point *B*.

In time, though, exports rise to, say, $100 billion and imports fall to, say, $100 billion, making net exports equal to zero. This is represented by point *C*.

If we start at point *A* and draw a line to point *B* and then to point *C*, we have a J-curve. This is the route that net exports may take after a depreciation in a country's currency.

J-Curve

The curve that shows a short-run worsening in net exports after a currency depreciation, followed by an improvement.

How Hard Will It Be to Get into Harvard in 2025?

The Indian Institute of Technology (in India) is one of the hardest universities in the world to be admitted to, largely because of its reputation. It has been compared to putting Harvard, MIT (Massachusetts Institute of Technology), and Princeton together.

In an average year, about 178,000 high school seniors in India take the exam necessary to apply to the Indian Institute of Technology. Just over 3,500 students (only 1.96 percent of all applicants) are admitted. In comparison, the admission rate of Harvard University is nearly 10 percent. Often, students from India who are admitted to MIT, Princeton, and Cal Tech (all of which are listed in the top 10 of U.S. colleges and universities) cannot gain admission to the Indian Institute of Technology.

Other highly prestigious U.S. universities and colleges—such as Brown, Columbia, Cornell, Dartmouth, Harvard, the University of Pennsylvania, Princeton, Yale, Stanford, Northwestern, and Duke—have some of the most selective admission criteria of all colleges and universities in the country. Each year, students who have the grade point average and standardized test scores to be considered for admission are turned away. This phenomenon has been occurring at the same time that college tuition in this country has been increasing rapidly. For example, during the period 1990–2003, college tuition went up by 130 percent, considerably more than medical care costs, the price of housing, food, gasoline, cars, and so on. If we look around the world at other prestigious institutions of higher learning, we see the same characteristics: The admission rate is usually low, and the cost is usually high.

Consider how grades (one major criterion) and money actually function in admissions: They are both rationing devices. We know that because of scarcity, some mechanism has to ration the available resources, goods, and services. Still we have to ask why these two rationing devices—grades and money—have become stiffer when it comes to being admitted to the top universities in the world? Why must grades and tuitions be ever higher?

The answer is twofold. First, the population of the world increased while the number of Harvards did not. Harvard cannot clone itself; nor can Yale, the Indian Institute of Technology, or MIT. To a large degree, the world has only one Harvard, Oxford (in the United Kingdom), and Indian Institute of Technology. We can produce more computers, houses, and dining room chairs as the population of the world increases, but producing more Harvards seems to be much more difficult. So, over time, top-notch, one-of-a-kind educational institutions become relatively more scarce. As a result, the rationing devices for such institutions must work harder, and getting admitted to such places will become harder and more expensive.

The second reason involves globalization. One of things that pays a high dividend in a global economy is education. Brains seem to matter more than brawn, increasing the overall demand for a college education—not just at Harvard, but at all levels of higher education (from community colleges to four-year state and private universities). So, will the premium placed on education in a global economy cause the demand at the most prestigious educational establishments to rise at a faster rate than at other colleges? That question is like asking, "If the premium for playing music were to rise, would the demand to be at Juilliard (one of the premier music institutions in the world) rise faster than the demand to study with the local piano teacher down the street?" The likely answer is yes. With a growing world population, and with the global economy paying a high premium to those who are educated (compared to those who are not), we can expect it to get increasingly difficult and more expensive to be admitted to the world's best institutions of higher learning.

thinking Like AN ECONOMIST

Short Run and Long Run The discussion of the J-curve points out that economists sometimes think in terms of both the short run and the long run. Does the depreciation of a country's currency lead to an increase or a decrease in import spending? According to the J-curve theory, both an increase and a decrease result. Import spending may initially increase, but in the long run it decreases. An economist's answers may differ depending on the time horizon under consideration. ● ● ●

EXHIBIT 4

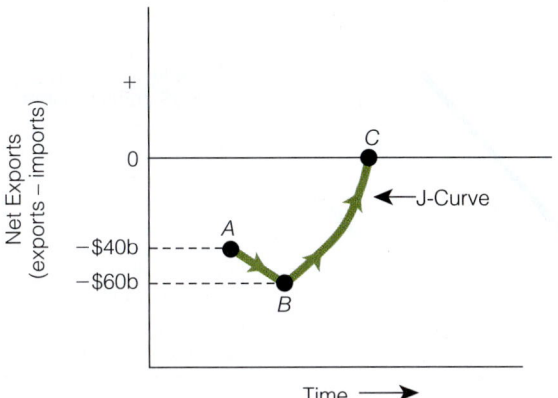

The J-Curve

The United States starts with net exports of –$40 billion. As the dollar depreciates, net exports increase to –$60 billion. With time, net exports become $0. If we follow the course of net exports, we map out a J. This is called the J-curve.

SELF-TEST

1. Explain how an economic boom in one country can be felt in another country.

2. Predict and explain what will happen to U.S. Real GDP if the dollar appreciates relative to the Japanese yen.

INTERNATIONAL FACTORS AND AGGREGATE SUPPLY

Just as international factors can affect the demand side of the U.S. economy, certain international factors can affect the supply side. This section discusses a few international factors that can shift the U.S. aggregate supply curve.

Foreign Input Prices

We know that a change in the price of inputs will shift the short-run aggregate supply (*SRAS*) curve. For example, if the price of labor (wage rate) rises, the *SRAS* curve shifts leftward.

American producers buy inputs not only from other Americans but also from foreigners. A rise in the price of foreign inputs leads to a leftward shift in the U.S. *SRAS* curve. A fall in the price of foreign inputs leads to a rightward shift in the U.S. *SRAS* curve.

Why Foreign Input Prices Change

Supply and demand in the input market in the foreign country could change, possibly causing a rise in the price of foreign inputs. For example, suppose U.S. producers buy input X from Japan. The supply of X in Japan could fall, or the demand for X in Japan could rise. Either or both changes would increase the price of X for U.S. producers.

THE EXCHANGE RATE A change in the exchange rate between the dollar and the yen could change the price of a foreign input. For example, a depreciation in the dollar relative to the yen would make input X more expensive for U.S. producers. An appreciation in the dollar would make input X less expensive for U.S. producers. Exhibit 5 presents a summary of the points in this section.

EXHIBIT 5

International Impacts on the U.S. *SRAS* Curve

The U.S. *SRAS* curve shifts if foreign input prices change. If foreign input prices rise, the U.S. *SRAS* curve shifts leftward; if foreign input prices fall, the *SRAS* curve shifts rightward. Similarly, if the dollar depreciates, foreign inputs become more expensive and the *SRAS* curve shifts leftward. If the dollar appreciates, foreign inputs become cheaper and the *SRAS* curve shifts rightward.

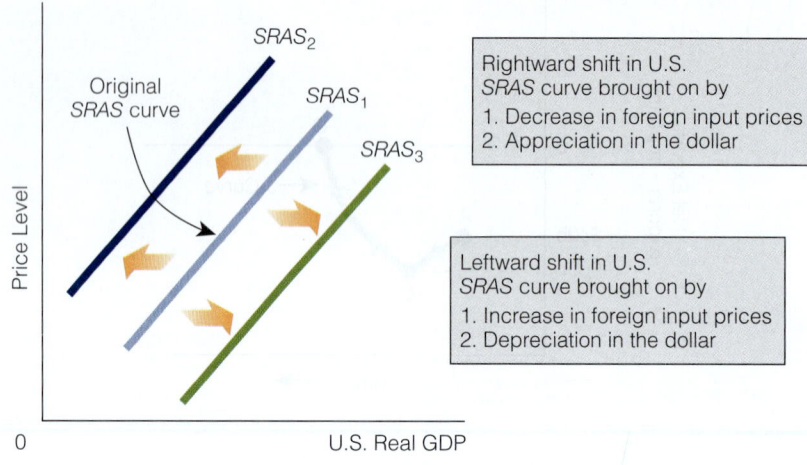

FACTORS THAT AFFECT BOTH AGGREGATE DEMAND AND AGGREGATE SUPPLY

Changes in some international factors can affect both aggregate demand and short-run aggregate supply in the United States. Two of these factors are the exchange rate and relative interest rates.

The Exchange Rate

As explained, changes in exchange rates affect both the *AD* and *SRAS* curves. The overall, or net, effect on Real GDP depends on how much the *AD* curve shifts relative to the shift in the *SRAS* curve. We consider two cases: dollar depreciation and dollar appreciation.

DOLLAR DEPRECIATION As the dollar depreciates, the *AD* curve shifts rightward and the *SRAS* curve leftward.

- If the AD curve shifts rightward by more than the SRAS curve shifts leftward, Real GDP rises [see Exhibit 6(a)].

- If the *AD* curve shifts rightward by less than the SRAS curve shifts leftward, Real GDP falls [see Exhibit 6(b)].

- If the *AD* curve shifts rightward by the same amount that the *SRAS* curve shifts leftward, Real GDP does not change [see Exhibit 6(c)].

    In each of these three cases, the price level rises. In summary, dollar depreciation raises the price level and may accompany an increasing, decreasing, or constant Real GDP.

DOLLAR APPRECIATION As the dollar appreciates, the *AD* curve shifts leftward and the *SRAS* curve rightward. Once again, what happens to Real GDP depends on the relative shifts of the two curves.

- If the *AD* curve shifts leftward by more than the *SRAS* curve shifts rightward, Real GDP falls.

EXHIBIT 6

Depreciation in the Dollar: Effects on the Price Level and Real GDP

A change in exchange rates affects both aggregate demand and short-run aggregate supply.

If the dollar depreciates, the AD curve shifts rightward and the SRAS curve shifts leftward. The overall impact on Real GDP—up, down, or unchanged—depends on whether the AD curve

shifts rightward by (a) more, (b) less, or (c) an amount equal to the leftward shift in the SRAS curve. In all three cases, dollar depreciation leads to a higher price level.

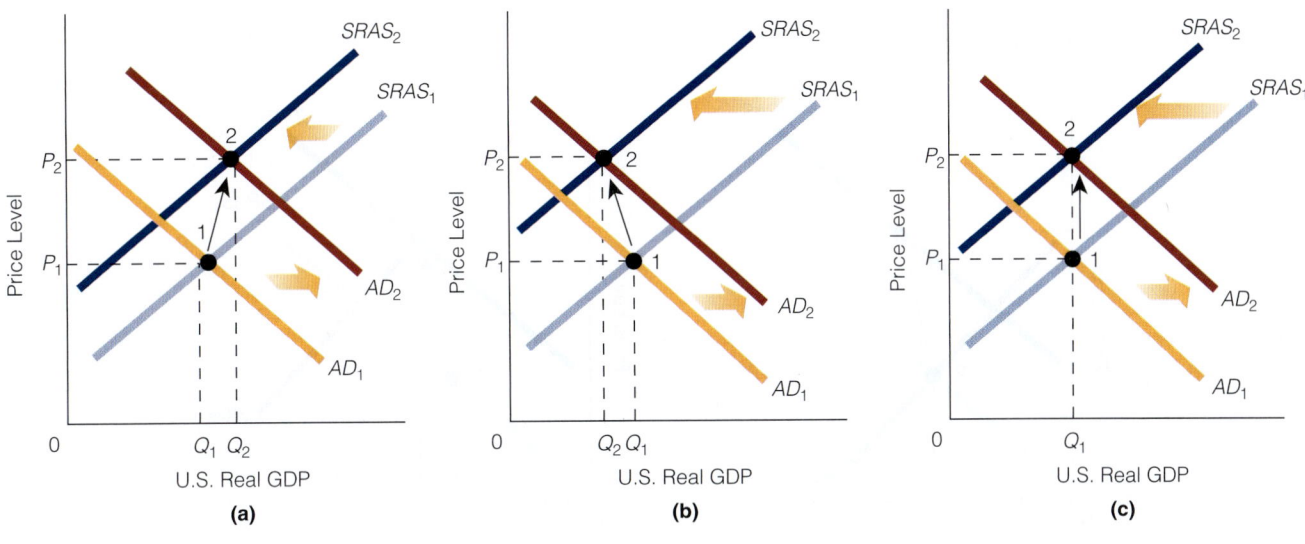

(a)   (b)   (c)

- If the AD curve shifts leftward by less than the $SRAS$ curve shifts rightward, Real GDP rises.
- If the AD curve shifts leftward by the same amount that the $SRAS$ curve shifts rightward, Real GDP does not change.

In each case, though, the price level falls. In summary, dollar appreciation lowers the price level and may accompany an increasing, decreasing, or constant Real GDP.

The Role That Interest Rates Play

In a two-country world with only the United States and Japan, real interest rates rise in the United States and remain constant in Japan. The higher real interest rates in the United States will attract foreign capital (in search of the highest return possible). Because foreigners will be interested in dollar-denominated assets that pay interest, they will have to exchange their country's currency for U.S. dollars. This need will increase the demand for U.S. dollars and lead to an appreciation in the dollar.

Then, if the dollar appreciates, we know that both the U.S. AD and $SRAS$ curves are affected. The AD curve shifts leftward, and the $SRAS$ curve shifts rightward. As explained, the effect on Real GDP depends on the relative shifts in the two curves. Many economists argue, however, that given the interest rate differential between the two countries, the AD curve typically tends to shift leftward by more than the $SRAS$ curve shifts rightward, and thus Real GDP falls [see Exhibit 7(a)]. In summary, typically, a rise in real interest rates in the United States relative to foreign interest rates tends to decrease U.S. Real GDP.

Now suppose real interest rates fall in the United States relative to interest rates in Japan. The higher real interest rate in Japan attracts capital to Japan. The demand for yen

EXHIBIT 7

International Interest Rates, Exchange Rates, and Real GDP

(a) If the U.S. real interest rate is higher than the Japanese real interest rate, capital will flow from Japan to the United States. In the process, the demand for the dollar rises, and the dollar appreciates. Dollar appreciation causes the AD curve to shift leftward by more than the SRAS curve shifts rightward, which is typical given the initial event. As a result, U.S. Real GDP falls. (b) If the U.S. real interest rate is lower than the Japanese real interest rate, capital will flow from the United States to Japan. In the process, the demand for yen rises, the supply of dollars rises, and the yen appreciates and the dollar depreciates. Dollar depreciation causes the AD curve to shift rightward and the SRAS curve to shift leftward. We have drawn the AD curve shifting rightward by more than the SRAS curve shifts leftward, which is typical given the initial event. As a result, U.S. Real GDP rises.

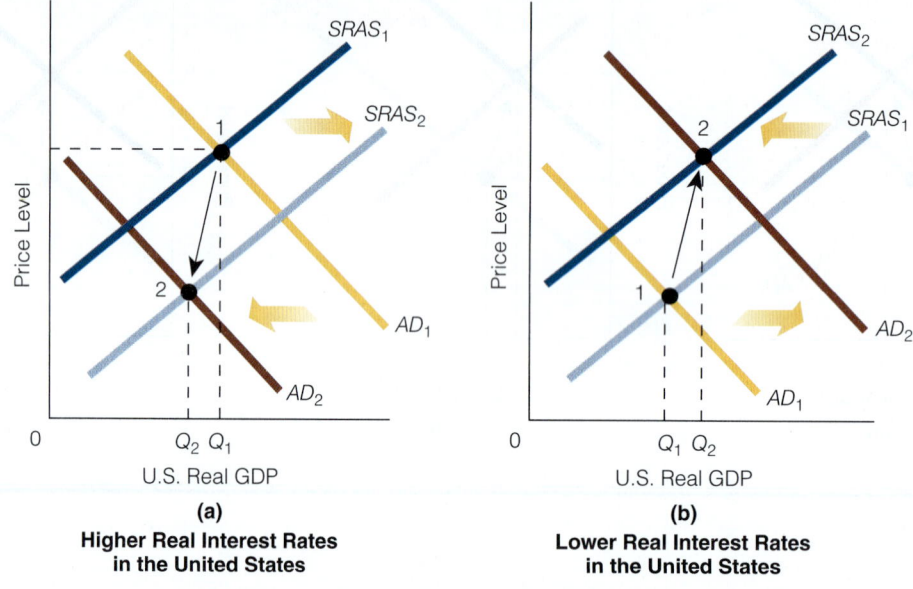

(a)
Higher Real Interest Rates in the United States

(b)
Lower Real Interest Rates in the United States

rises, and as a result the yen appreciates and the dollar depreciates. A depreciated dollar shifts the U.S. AD curve rightward and the SRAS curve leftward [see Exhibit 7(b)]. Many economists argue that given the interest rate differential, the AD curve typically tends to shift rightward by more than the SRAS curve shifts leftward, and thus Real GDP rises. In summary, typically, a fall in real interest rates in the United States relative to foreign interest rates tends to increase U.S. Real GDP.

1. How do foreign input prices affect the U.S. SRAS curve?

2. What is the effect on the U.S. price level of Japan's having lower real interest rates than the United States? Explain your answer.

DEFICITS: INTERNATIONAL EFFECTS AND DOMESTIC FEEDBACK

Deficits in the United States—both budget and trade deficits—affect the U.S. economy. We know how the budget deficit can directly affect the U.S. economy. However, the budget deficit can also have international effects, which can then feed back into the U.S. economy. This section looks at the possibilities of feedback effects and the relationship between the budget deficit and the trade deficit.

The Budget Deficit and Expansionary Fiscal Policy

Suppose that North Dakotans want their elected representatives in Congress to push for a spending program that will assist them and no one else and that their elected representatives oblige them. Congress passes the spending program but does not raise the taxes necessary to pay for it. This domestic action can affect the international economic scene, and here's how.

Even with a budget deficit, Congress passes the spending program to help North Dakotans but neither raises taxes to finance the program nor cuts any other spending programs on the books. As a result of these actions—one more spending program, no fewer spending programs, and no more taxes—the budget deficit grows. To finance the growing budget deficit, the U.S. Treasury borrows more funds in the credit (or loanable funds) market than it would have borrowed if the North Dakotan spending program had not been passed. The increased demand for credit raises the real interest rate. The higher U.S. interest rate attracts foreign capital. The demand for dollars in the foreign exchange market rises, and the dollar appreciates.

As this happens, the U.S. *AD* curve shifts leftward, and the *SRAS* curve shifts rightward. The *AD* curve shifts leftward by more than the *SRAS* curve shifts rightward, putting downward pressure on Real GDP.

But Real GDP might not *actually* decrease. That's because we have discussed only how a rising budget deficit affects the exchange rate (via the interest rate) and feeds back into the domestic economy. We also need to consider the direct effect of the rising budget deficit on the domestic economy. Under certain conditions (e.g., zero crowding out), expansionary fiscal policy can raise aggregate demand and is effective at raising Real GDP. So:

1. The rising budget deficit affects the domestic economy directly and pushes *Real GDP upward*.

2. But increased deficit financing raises U.S. interest rates and prompts increased foreign capital inflows, an increased demand for dollars, and dollar appreciation. Under typical conditions, an appreciated dollar feeds back into the domestic economy and pushes *Real GDP downward*.

Obviously, what happens on a net basis depends on how strong the international feedback effects are on the domestic economy. Are they strong enough to offset the initial expansionary push (upward) in Real GDP? Even if not and Real GDP rises on net, we can still conclude that expansionary fiscal policy raises Real GDP more in a closed economy (which does not trade goods and services with other countries) than in an open economy (which trades goods and services with other countries). The reason is that in a closed economy the international feedback effects that reduce Real GDP are absent (see the second point in the preceding list).

Exhibit 8(a) illustrates the point. With zero crowding out, expansionary fiscal policy shifts the aggregate demand curve from AD_1 to AD_2. But because of the higher interest rates, increased foreign capital inflows, and dollar appreciation, the *AD* curve shifts leftward from AD_2 to AD_3, and the *SRAS* curve shifts rightward from $SRAS_1$ to $SRAS_2$. In a closed economy, Real GDP rises from Q_1 to Q_2. In an open economy, where international feedback effects play a role, Real GDP ends up at a lower level, Q_3.

The Budget Deficit and Contractionary Fiscal Policy

If expansionary fiscal policy raises Real GDP more in a closed economy than in an open economy, what are the effects of contractionary fiscal policy in the two types of economies? Suppose reduced government spending decreases the budget deficit. With a diminished budget deficit, the U.S. Treasury borrows fewer funds in the credit market than it would have if government spending had not been reduced. The decreased demand for loanable funds lowers the real interest rate (relative to foreign interest rates), making foreign assets seem more desirable. The demand for foreign currencies increases, and the dollar depreciates in value.

Closed Economy
An economy that does not trade goods and services with other countries.

Open Economy
An economy that trades goods and services with other countries.

EXHIBIT 8

Expansionary and Contractionary Fiscal Policy in Open and Closed Economies

(a) The consequences of expansionary fiscal policy for both open and closed economies. Congress passes a spending program without raising taxes, and the AD curve shifts from AD_1

to AD_2. To finance the growing budget deficit, the Treasury borrows more funds in the loan-able funds market, and the interest rate rises. The higher interest rate attracts foreign capital and causes the dollar to appreciate. As the dollar appreciates, the AD curve shifts from AD_2 to AD_3, and the SRAS curve shifts from $SRAS_1$

to $SRAS_2$. Real GDP goes from Q_1 to Q_2 in a closed economy, and from Q_1 to Q_3 in an open economy. Expansionary fiscal policy raises Real GDP more in a closed economy than in an open economy. (b) Contractionary fiscal policy lowers Real GDP more in a closed economy than in an open economy.

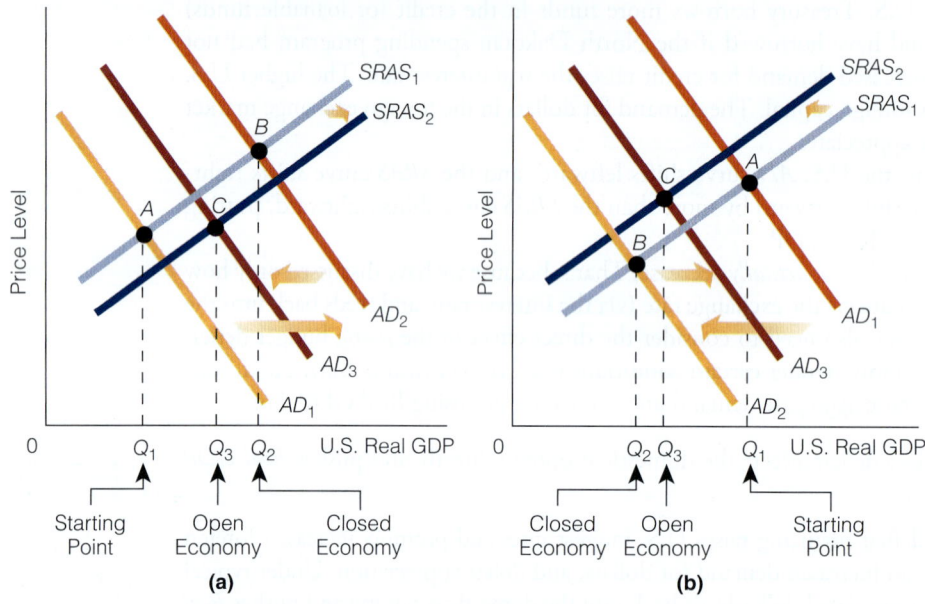

(a)   (b)

At the same time, the U.S. AD curve shifts to the right, and the SRAS curve shifts to the left. The AD curve shifts rightward by more than the SRAS curve shifts leftward, putting upward pressure on Real GDP. However, Real GDP might not *actually* increase. Under certain conditions, the lower budged deficit due to a cut in government spending reduces aggregate demand and therefore reduces Real GDP. So:

1. The cut in government spending reduces the budget deficit and affects the domestic economy directly, pushing *Real GDP downward.*

2. But reduced deficit financing lowers U.S. interest rates and prompts increased capital outflows, increased demand for foreign currencies, and dollar depreciation. Under typi-cal conditions, a depreciated dollar feeds back into the domestic economy and pushes *Real GDP upward.*

What happens *on a net basis* depends on whether the international feedback effects on the domestic economy are strong enough to offset the initial contractionary push in Real GDP.

Even if the international feedback effects on the domestic economy do not outweigh the initial contractionary push (downward) in Real GDP, and even if Real GDP falls on net, we can still conclude that contractionary fiscal policy lowers Real GDP more in a closed economy than in an open economy.

Exhibit 8(b) illustrates our point. The cut in government spending shifts the AD curve from AD_1 to AD_2. But because of the lower interest rates, increased capital outflows, and dollar depreciation, the *AD* curve shifts rightward from AD_2 to AD_3, and the *SRAS* curve shifts leftward from $SRAS_1$ to $SRAS_2$. In a closed economy, Real GDP falls from Q_1 to Q_2. In an open economy, where international feedback effects play a role, Real GDP ends up at Q_3.

The Effects of Monetary Policy

Monetary policy certainly affects international economic factors that feed back to the United States. Here we consider both expansionary and contractionary monetary policy.

EXPANSIONARY MONETARY POLICY Suppose the Federal Reserve increases the money supply. In Exhibit 9(a), the increase causes the *AD* curve to shift rightward from AD_1 to AD_2 and Real GDP to rise from Q_1 to Q_2.

An increase in the money supply also has international effects. Expansionary monetary policy causes interest rates to fall in the short run (the liquidity effect), leading to an outflow of capital from the United States. Americans begin to supply more dollars on the foreign exchange market so that they can purchase foreign assets. As the supply of dollars rises, the dollar depreciates.

Dollar depreciation affects both U.S. aggregate demand and U.S. short-run aggregate supply. As noted, it shifts the *AD* curve to the right and the *SRAS* curve to the left. In Exhibit 9(a), the *AD* curve shifts to the right (from AD_2 to AD_3), and the *SRAS* curve shifts to the left (from $SRAS_1$ to $SRAS_2$). Consequently, Real GDP rises from Q_2 to Q_3.

Expansionary and Contractionary Monetary Policy in Open and Closed Economies

(a) The consequences of expansionary monetary policy for both open and closed economies. The Fed increases the money supply, and the *AD* curve shifts from AD_1 to AD_2.

Real GDP rises from Q_1 to Q_2. The increased money supply leads to lower interest rates in the short run, promoting U.S. capital outflow and a depreciated dollar, which raises U.S. exports, lowers U.S. imports, and raises U.S. net exports. Higher net exports shift the *AD* curve rightward from AD_2 to AD_3. The depreciated

dollar shifts the *SRAS* curve leftward from $SRAS_1$ to $SRAS_2$. Real GDP ends up at Q_3. Expansionary monetary policy raises Real GDP more in an open economy than in a closed economy. (b) Contractionary monetary policy lowers Real GDP more in an open economy than in a closed economy.

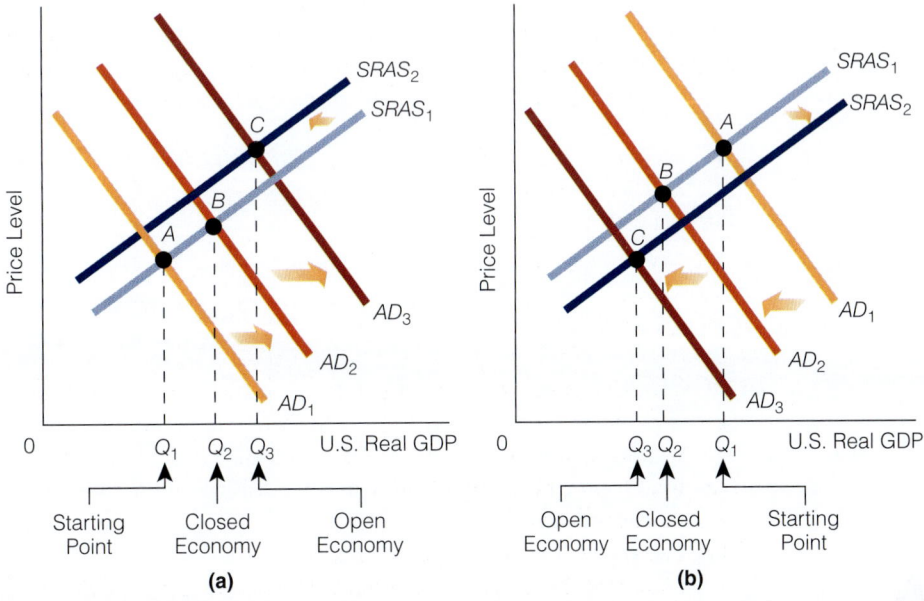

(a)

(b)

Therefore, expansionary monetary policy raises Real GDP more in an open economy than in a closed economy.

CONTRACTIONARY MONETARY POLICY If the Federal Reserve contracts the money supply, the AD curve shifts leftward from AD_1 to AD_2, and Real GDP falls from Q_1 to Q_2 [see Exhibit 9(b)].

A decrease in the money supply also has international effects. Contractionary monetary policy causes interest rates to rise, leading to an inflow of foreign capital into the United States. The demand for dollars rises on the foreign exchange market, and the dollar appreciates. Dollar appreciation affects both U.S. aggregate demand and U.S. short-run aggregate supply. As we know, dollar appreciation shifts the AD curve to the left and the $SRAS$ curve to the right. In Exhibit 9(b), the AD curve shifts from AD_2 to AD_3, and the $SRAS$ curve shifts from $SRAS_1$ to $SRAS_2$. Consequently, Real GDP falls from Q_2 to Q_3.

Therefore, contractionary monetary policy lowers Real GDP more in an open economy than in a closed economy.

SELF-TEST

1. Explain how expansionary monetary policy works in an open economy.

2. Explain how expansionary fiscal policy works in an open economy.

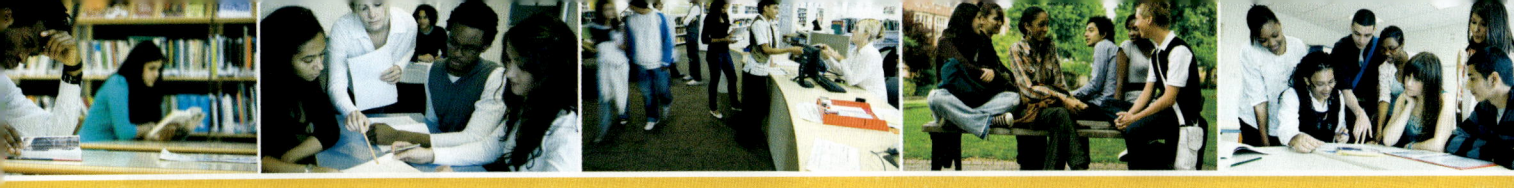

OFFICE HOURS

"Why Do Some People Favor Globalization and Others Do Not?"

STUDENT:

One of the things I have noticed about globalization is that some people in the United States seem to be in favor of it and others seem to be against it. Why is this?

INSTRUCTOR:

It probably has much to do with how the benefits and costs of globalization are distributed across the population. People in one location might receive mainly the benefits, and people in some other location might incur mostly the costs.

STUDENT:

Can you give a real-world example?

INSTRUCTOR:

A while back, *The New York Times* reported about two cities in Michigan: Holland and Greenville.[3] In Holland, a factory was losing business and firing workers. Then a German company bought it. Today the factory is shipping wastewater treatment equipment to countries in the Middle East and Asia. Also, it is operating with twice as many workers as it did before the German company bought it. The people in Holland, Michigan, see this as a benefit of globalization.

Only 60 miles away from Holland, in Greenville, Michigan, the story is different. In Greenville, a Swedish company shut down what had been the largest refrigerator factory in the country and eliminated about 2,700 jobs in the town. For the people of Greenville, globalization came with costs.

STUDENT:

What do most economists say about globalization? Do they think that, for the country as a whole, globalization comes with net benefits (more benefits than costs) or net costs (more costs than benefits)?

3. See Peter S. Goodman, "2 Outcomes When Foreigners Buy Factories," *New York Times*, April 7, 2008.

INSTRUCTOR:

Most economists seem to think that globalization comes with net benefits.

STUDENT:

But economic policy isn't always determined by what economists think, is it?

INSTRUCTOR:

You're right about that. Economic policy doesn't get made in a political vacuum. Politics plays a role in deciding which economic policies get adopted and implemented. Think about this in terms of our Michigan cities example. Suppose we went to Greenville, where jobs had been lost, and tell the residents of the city that globalization, on net, is good for the country. Suppose we said that, for the country as a whole, benefits from globalization outweigh the costs. The residents of Greenville might say that is all well and good, but globalization hasn't been that good to them and that is all they care about. As a result, their vote, to the extent that they have one on the issue, is *against* globalization.

STUDENT:

I see. In other words, sometimes what might be beneficial for the country (as a whole) is not beneficial for some part of it.

INSTRUCTOR:

That is the way some things turn out.

POINTS TO REMEMBER

1. Globalization can come with net benefits for a country, but not everyone in the country necessarily benefits from globalization.
2. The benefits and costs of globalization are not evenly spread throughout a country. The benefits may fall on some people and the costs on others.

CHAPTER SUMMARY

WHAT IS GLOBALIZATION?

- Globalization is a phenomenon by which individuals and businesses in any part of the world are much more affected by events elsewhere in the world than before; it is the growing integration of national economies of the world to the degree that we may be witnessing the emergence and operation of a single worldwide economy.

- Certain facts provide evidence that globalization is occurring. Some of these facts are (1) lower tariff rates in many countries, (2) many countries exporting and importing more goods than in the past, (3) greater foreign exchange trading, (4) more foreign direct investment, (5) many more people owning foreign stocks, (6) many more countries having joined the WTO in recent years, and (7) a greater number of Americans working for foreign companies with offices in the United States.

MOVEMENT TOWARD GLOBALIZATION

- What has caused this most recent push toward globalization? In the chapter we identified (1) the end of the Cold War, (2) advancing technology, and (3) policy changes as causal factors.

BENEFITS AND COSTS OF GLOBALIZATION

- Some of the benefits of globalization include (1) benefits from increased international trade, (2) greater income per person, (3) lower prices for goods, (4) greater product variety, and (5) increased productivity and innovation.

- Some of the costs of globalization include (1) increased income inequality (although there is some debate here), (2) offshoring, and (3) increased economic power for large corporations (although there is some debate here too).

- Seeing the benefits of globalization is often much more difficult than seeing the costs. The benefits are largely dispersed over a large population, but the costs (e.g., offshoring) might be concentrated on relatively few.

THE FUTURE OF GLOBALIZATION

- The future of globalization is under debate. Some persons argue that globalization will continue; others say it will stall and (perhaps) backtrack.

NET EXPORTS AND AGGREGATE DEMAND

- An increase in net exports will shift the *AD* curve to the right. A decrease in net exports will shift the *AD* curve to the left.

- Two factors can change net exports: foreign Real GDP (or real national income) and exchange rates. For example, in a two-country world (Japan and the United States), an increase in Japan's Real GDP and a depreciation in the dollar will increase

U.S. net exports and shift the U.S. *AD* curve to the right. Alternatively, a decrease in Japan's Real GDP and an appreciation in the dollar will decrease U.S. net exports and shift the U.S. *AD* curve to the left.

THE AGGREGATE SUPPLY CURVE AND INTERNATIONAL FACTORS

- A change in foreign input prices will impact the U.S. *SRAS* curve. For example, an increase in foreign input prices will shift the U.S. *SRAS* curve to the left. A decrease in foreign input prices will shift the U.S. *SRAS* curve to the right.

- A change in foreign input prices can be the result of changes in the input market in the foreign country.

- A change in foreign input prices (paid by U.S. producers) can be the result of a change in the exchange rate. For example, if the dollar depreciates, U.S. producers will pay higher prices for foreign inputs. If the dollar appreciates, U.S. producers will pay lower prices for foreign inputs.

INTERNATIONAL FACTORS AND AGGREGATE DEMAND AND SHORT-RUN AGGREGATE SUPPLY

- A change in the exchange rate will affect both the U.S. *AD* curve and the U.S. *SRAS* curve. For example, if the dollar depreciates, the *AD* curve will shift to the right, and the *SRAS* curve will shift to the left.

- A change in real interest rates will affect both the U.S. *AD* curve and the U.S. *SRAS* curve. To illustrate, suppose the U.S. real interest rate rises relative to the Japanese interest rate. Higher real interest rates in the United States will attract foreign capital. Foreigners, in search of U.S. assets that pay interest, will bid up the price of a dollar; thus, the dollar appreciates. If the dollar appreciates, the *AD* curve will shift to the left, and the *SRAS* curve will shift to the right. The U.S. price level will fall. What happens to the U.S. Real GDP depends on the relative shifts in the *AD* and *SRAS* curves. Typically, the *AD* curve shifts leftward by more than the *SRAS* curve shifts rightward, and so Real GDP falls.

FISCAL AND MONETARY POLICY IN CLOSED AND OPEN ECONOMIES

- Expansionary fiscal policy raises Real GDP more in a closed economy than in an open economy.

- Contractionary fiscal policy lowers Real GDP more in a closed economy than in an open economy.

- Expansionary monetary policy raises Real GDP more in an open economy than in a closed economy.

- Contractionary monetary policy lowers Real GDP more in an open economy than in a closed economy.

KEY TERMS AND CONCEPTS

Globalization

Tariff

Offshoring

J-Curve

Closed Economy

Open Economy

QUESTIONS AND PROBLEMS

1. Assume a two-country world where the two countries are the United States and Japan. Note the impact on U.S. Real GDP of each of the following:

   a. A fall in the real interest rate in the United States relative to the real interest rate in Japan

   b. An economic expansion in Japan

2. How do tariff rates in the United States today compare with 1946?

3. Give a numerical example to illustrate what the depreciation (of a country's currency) does to the prices of its imports.

4. Will globalization lead to some people losing jobs? Explain your answer.

5. If Americans buy fewer units of good X, which is produced in Japan, will they necessarily spend less money overall on good X? Explain your answer.

6. David Friedman said that free (international) trade is a technology. Explain what he means.

7. "The discussion of the J-curve points out that economists sometimes think in terms of both the short run and the long run." Do you agree or disagree? Explain your answer.

8. What is Thomas Friedman's Golden Arches theory of conflict prevention?

9. Explain how a change in the exchange rate can change both the U.S. *AD* and *SRAS* curves.

10. Some have argued that the end of the Cold War acted as a catalyst toward greater globalization. How so?

11. Suppose country A undertakes a policy mix of contractionary fiscal policy and expansionary monetary policy. What do you predict would happen to real interest rates, the value of country A's currency, and net exports? Explain your answer.

12. What effect might advancing technology have on globalization?

13. Why might import spending rise in a country soon after a depreciation of its currency? Is import spending likely to fall over time? Explain your answers.

14. Identify and explain two of the benefits and two of the costs of globalization.

15. Explain why expansionary monetary policy is more likely to increase Real GDP in an open economy than in a closed economy.

16. How might governments impact globalization?

17. Explain why contractionary fiscal policy is more likely to decrease Real GDP in a closed economy than in an open economy.

18. If globalization continues over the next few decades, how might your life be different?

19. Explain why contractionary monetary policy lowers Real GDP more in an open economy than in a closed economy.

20. Why might it be easier to recognize the costs of globalization than the benefits?

WORKING WITH NUMBERS AND GRAPHS

1. Starting with an exchange rate of $1 = ¥114 and a price tag of ¥10,000 for a Japanese item, show what happens to the price of the Japanese item if the yen depreciates by 5 percent.

2. Graphically show and explain the domestic and feedback effects on Real GDP in the United States as a result of contractionary fiscal policy.

3. Graphically show and explain the domestic and feedback effects on Real GDP in the United States as a result of contractionary monetary policy.

CHAPTER **37**

© IMAGE COPYRIGHT IOANA DRUTU, 2009. USED UNDER LICENSE FROM SHUTTERSTOCK.COM

STOCKS, BONDS, FUTURES, AND OPTIONS

Introduction

Economic and financial news is all around us. "The economy is headed toward recession." "The value of the dollar is falling." "The budget deficit is growing." "The stock market took a loss today." "Bonds are strong."

Much of this book has dealt with economic news items. In this chapter we turn to the part of economics that relates to financial matters: stocks, bonds, futures, and options.

FINANCIAL MARKETS

Everyone has heard of stocks and bonds, and everyone knows that stocks and bonds can be sold and purchased. But not everyone knows the economic purpose that stocks and bonds serve.

Buying and selling stocks and bonds take place in financial markets, which channel money from some people to other people. To illustrate, Jones has saved $10,000 over two years, and Smith is just starting a new company. Smith needs money to get the new company up and running. Jones would like to invest the savings and receive a return. Jones and Smith may not know each other; in fact, they may live on opposite ends of the country. A financial market, however, can bring these two people together, allowing Jones either to invest in Smith's company or to lend Smith some money. For example, Jones might either buy stock in Smith's company or buy a bond that Smith's company issues. In this chapter we discuss more about how people like Smith and Jones help each other through a financial market. In this section, we discuss stocks; in the next section, bonds.

STOCKS

Stock
A claim on the assets of a corporation that gives the purchaser a share of ownership in the corporation.

What does it mean when someone tells you that she owns 100 shares of a stock? If Jane owns 100 shares of Yahoo! stock, she is a part owner in Yahoo!, Inc., a global Internet media company that offers a network of World Wide Web programming. A stock is a claim on the assets of a corporation that gives the purchaser a share of ownership in the corporation.

Jane is not an owner in the sense that she can walk into Yahoo! headquarters (in Santa Clara, California) and start issuing orders. She cannot hire or fire anyone, and she cannot decide what the company will or will not do over the next few months or years. But still she is an owner, and as an owner she can, if she wants, sell her ownership rights in Yahoo! All she has to do is find a buyer for her 100 shares of stock. Most likely, she could do so in a matter of minutes, if not seconds.

ⓕinding ECONOMICS

At an Online Brokerage Website Frank has an account with TD Ameritrade. He goes online one morning to see at what price Yahoo! stock (symbol YHOO) is selling. At 10:45 a.m. EDT, the stock is selling at $29.74 a share. One minute later it is selling for one cent less at $29.73. Where is the economics?

Supply and demand are at work with respect to the Yahoo stock price. The equilibrium price is changing fairly fast in this market. At 10:45 a.m. EDT, the equilibrium price is $29.74. One minute later it has fallen to $29.73. Ten minutes later it has risen to $27.99. Think of how fast the market for Yahoo! stock equilibrates compared to some other markets (such as the housing market). ▲ ▲ ▲

Where Are Stocks Bought and Sold?

Groceries are bought and sold at the grocery store. Clothes are bought and sold at the clothing store. But where are stocks bought and sold?

To answer that question, let's go back to 1792, when 24 men met under a buttonwood tree on what is now Wall Street in New York City. These men essentially bought and sold stock (for themselves and their customers) at this location. Someone might have said, "I want to sell 20 shares in company X. Are you willing to buy them for $2 a share?"

From this humble beginning came the New York Stock Exchange (NYSE). Every weekday (excluding holidays), men and women meet at the NYSE in New York City and buy and sell stock. For example, suppose you own 100 shares of a stock that is listed on the NYSE. You do not have to travel to the exchange to sell it. You simply contact a stockbroker (either over the phone, in person, or online), who conveys your wishes to sell the stock to a person at the NYSE itself. That person at the NYSE then executes your order.

The NYSE is not the only exchange where stocks are bought and sold. They are also traded on the American Stock Exchange (AMEX) and the NASDAQ stock market (pronounced "NAS-dak"; National Association of Securities Dealers Automated Quotations). Buying and selling stock on the NASDAQ do not take place in the same way as on the NYSE. Instead of taking place in a central location, trades on the NASDAQ, an electronic stock market, are executed through a sophisticated computer and telecommunications network. The NYSE might in fact change to this kind of market in the near future; instead of people meeting in one location to buy and sell stock, they could do it electronically.

Increasingly, Americans are buying and selling stocks not only on the U.S. stock exchanges and markets, but on foreign stock exchanges and markets too. For example, an American might buy a stock listed on the German Stock Exchange, the Montreal Stock Exchange, or the Swiss Exchange.

The Dow Jones Industrial Average (DJIA)

You may have heard news commentators say, "The Dow fell 302 points on heavy trading." They are talking about the **Dow Jones Industrial Average (DJIA)**, which first appeared on the scene more than 100 years ago, on May 26, 1896, and was devised by Charles H. Dow. Dow took 11 stocks, summed their prices on a particular day, and then divided by 11. The average price was the DJIA. (Some of the original companies included American Cotton Oil, Chicago Gas, National Lead, and U.S. Rubber.)

Dow Jones Industrial Average (DJIA)
The most popular, widely cited indicator of day-to-day stock market activity; a weighted average of 30 widely traded stocks on the New York Stock Exchange.

When Charles Dow first computed the DJIA, the stock market was not highly regarded in the United States. Prudent investors bought bonds, not stocks. Stocks were thought to be the arena for speculators and conniving Wall Street operators. Back then, Wall Streeters were seen as managing stock prices to make themselves better off at the expense of others. A lot of gossip went around about what was and was not happening in the stock market.

Dow devised the DJIA to convey information about what was really happening in the stock market. Before the DJIA, people had a hard time figuring out whether the stock market, on average, was rising or falling. Instead, they knew only that a particular stock went up or down by so many cents or dollars. The average price of a certain number of stocks, Dow thought, would largely mirror what was happening in the stock market as a whole. With this number, people could then gain some sense of what the stock market was doing on any given day.

Today, the DJIA consists of 30 stocks that are widely held by individuals and institutional investors (see Exhibit 1, which shows the 30 stocks in the Dow Industrial Average as of August 9, 2010). The list can and does change from time to time, as determined by the editors of *The Wall Street Journal*. And the DJIA is no longer computed simply by summing the prices of stocks and dividing by 30. A special divisor is used to avoid distortions that can occur, such as companies splitting their stock shares. Exhibit 2 shows the Dow Jones Industrial Average during the period of January 1, 2006–April 13, 2010.

In addition to the DJIA, other prominent stock indexes are cited in the United States. A few include the NASDAQ Composite, the Standard & Poor's 500, the Russell 2000, and the Wilshire 5000. There are also prominent stock indexes around the world, such as the Hang Seng (in Hong Kong), the Bovespa (Brazil), IPC (Mexico), BSE 30 (India), CAC 40 (France), and others.

What causes the DJIA to go up or down? Economic consulting firms have attempted to find out what influences the Dow. According to many economists, the Dow is closely connected to changes in such things as consumer credit, business expectations, exports and imports, personal income, and the money supply. For example, increases in consumer credit are expected to push the Dow up, the connection being that when consumer credit rises, people will buy more goods and services, and this is good for the companies that sell goods and services. When consumer credit falls, the opposite effect occurs.

EXHIBIT 1

The 30 Stocks of the Dow Jones Industrial Average (DJIA)

Here are the 30 stocks that comprise the Dow Jones Industrial Average.

3M Co.	Intel Corp.
Alcoa Inc.	International Business Machines Corp.
American Express Co.	Johnson & Johnson
AT&T Inc.	JPMorgan Chase & Co.
Bank of America	Kraft Foods, Inc.
Boeing Co.	McDonald's Corp.
Caterpillar Inc.	Merck & Co. Inc.
Chevron	Microsoft Corp.
Cisco Systems	Pfizer Inc.
Coca-Cola Co.	Procter & Gamble Co.
E.I. DuPont de Nemours & Co.	Travelers Companies Inc.
ExxonMobil Corp.	United Technologies Corp.
General Electric Co.	Verizon Communications Inc.
Hewlett-Packard Co.	Wal-Mart Stores Inc.
Home Depot Inc.	Walt Disney Co.

EXHIBIT 2

DJIA, January 1, 2006–April 13, 2010

Here we show the ups and downs of the DJIA from January 2006 to April 13, 2010.

How the Stock Market Works

To raise money for investment in a new product or a new manufacturing technique, a company can do one of three things. First, it can go to a bank and borrow the money. Second, it can borrow the money by issuing a bond (a promise to repay the borrowed money with interest; you will learn more about bonds later in the chapter). Third, it can sell or issue stock in the company; that is, it can sell part of the company. Stocks are also called *equity* because the buyer of the stock has part ownership of the company.

When a company is initially formed, the owners set up a certain amount of stock, which is often worth very little. The owners of the company try to find people (usually friends and associates) who would be willing to buy the stock (in the hopes that one day it will be worth something). In these early days of the company, anyone who owns stock would find it nearly impossible to sell it. For example, if Jones owns 100 shares of a new company that almost no one had heard of, hardly anyone would be willing to pay any money to buy the stock.

As the company grows and needs more money, it may decide to offer its stock on the open market, that is, offer it to anyone who wants to buy it. By this time, the company may be known well enough that some people are willing to buy it. The company makes what is called an initial public offering (IPO) of its stock. The process is quite simple. Usually, an investment bank sells the stock for the company for an initial price—say, $10 a share. Investors find out about IPOs because they are announced in *The Wall Street Journal*.

For example, suppose that William Welch started a company in 1895 and that, through the years, the company was passed down to family members. In 2011, the family members running the company want to expand it to two, three, or four times its current size. To get the money to do this, one way is to sell shares in the company—that is, by issuing stock. Once they have issued shares in the company to the public, the company is no longer solely family owned. Now many of the public own part of it too.

After the IPO, the stock is usually traded on a stock exchange or in an electronic stock market. Sometimes, the stock that initially sold for $10 will rise in price, and sometimes it will fall like a rock. Its success or failure all depends on what people in the stock market think the issuing company will do in the future. If they think the company is destined for big earnings, the stock will likely rise in price. If they think the company is destined for losses or only marginal earnings, the stock will likely fall in price.

In a way, trading stock is much like trading baseball cards, paintings, or anything else. The price depends on the forces of supply and demand. If demand rises and supply is constant, then the price of the stock will rise. If demand falls and supply is constant, then the price of the stock will fall.

Initial Public Offering (IPO)
A company's first offering of stock to the public.

Investment Bank
A firm that acts as an intermediary between the company that issues the stock and the public that wishes to buy it.

economics 24/7

Are Some Economists Poor Investors?

You might think that economists would do pretty well in the stock market compared to the average person. After all, the job of economists is to understand how markets work and to study key economic indicators.

So how do you explain a May 11, 2005, article in the *Los Angeles Times* titled "Experts Are at a Loss on Investing"? The article looked at the investments of four economists—all Nobel Prize winners in economics. Not one of them said that he invests the way he should invest, and none of them seemed to be getting rich through their investments. Often, there seems to be a big difference between knowing what to do and doing it.

Harry M. Markowitz won the Nobel Prize in Economics in 1990 for his work in financial economics. He is known as the father of modern portfolio theory, the main idea being that people should diversify their investments. Markowitz, however, did not follow his own advice. Most of his life, he put half of his money in a stock fund and the other half in a conservative, low-interest investment. Markowitz, age 77 at the time, says, "In retrospect, it would have been better to have been more in stocks when I was younger."

George Akerlof, who won the Nobel Prize in Economics in 2001, had invested most of his money in money market accounts, which tend to have relatively low interest rate returns but are safe. Akerlof, when confronted with this fact, said, "I know it's utterly stupid."

Clive Granger, who won the Nobel Prize in Economics in 2003, was asked about his investments. He said, "I would rather spend my time enjoying my income than bothering about investments."

Daniel Kahneman, who won the Nobel Prize in Economics in 2002, had this to say about his investments: "I think very little about my retirement savings, because I know that thinking could make me poorer or more miserable or both."

Almost every activity comes with both benefits and costs. Investing wisely certainly has its benefits, but it has its costs too. Finding out about various investments, researching them, and keeping informed on how they are doing all take time.

The investment behaviors of our four Nobel Prize winners also point out something else. Many people think that economics is simply about money and money matters, but it is not. It is about utility and happiness and making oneself better off. Each of our four Nobel Prize winners might not have been doing the best thing for his wallet, but certainly each knew this and continued on the same path anyway. Each was willing to sacrifice some money to live a preferred lifestyle.

What is the lesson for you? You might care nothing about your investments and simply hope that your financial future will take care of itself. Or you could spend all of your time regularly watching, researching, and evaluating various investments that either you have made or plan to make. But neither extreme is sensible. You can learn enough about investments to protect yourself from the financial uncertainties of the future but not spend so much time worrying about the future that you don't enjoy the present.

Why Do People Buy Stock?

Millions of people in the United States and in countries all over the world buy stock every day. Sometimes, people buy a stock because they hear that others are buying it and because they think the stock is hot. In other words, the stock is very popular and everyone wants it. In the 1990s, some of the Internet stocks fit this description. People bought stocks such as Yahoo!, Amazon.com, and eBay just because they thought the Internet was the wave of the future and almost anything connected with the Internet was destined for great profit.

More often, though, people buy a stock because they think the earnings of the company that initially issued the stock are likely to rise. (Remember that a share of stock represents ownership in a company.) The more profitable that company is expected to be, the more likely people are going to want to own that company, and therefore the greater the demand will be for the company's stock.

Most people therefore buy stock for a couple of typical reasons. Some buy stocks for the dividends, which are payments made to stockholders based on a company's profits. For example, suppose company X has issued one million shares of stock that are owned by

Dividend
A share of the profits of a corporation distributed to stockholders.

investors. Each year, if the company's profit and loss statement shows a profit, it distributes some of the profit among the owners of the company as dividends. This year's dividend might be $1 for each share of stock a person owns. So if Jones owns 50,000 shares of stock, she will receive a dividend check for $50,000.

The other reason to buy stock is for the expected gain in its price. Stockholders can make money if they buy shares at a lower price and sell at a higher price. For example, Smith buys 100 shares of Microsoft stock today. He thinks that the company is going to do well and that a year from now he can sell it for as much as $50 more a share than his purchase price. In other words, he hopes to earn $5,000 on his stock purchase.

People also sell stock for many reasons. Smith might sell his 100 shares of IBM because he needs the money, perhaps to help his son pay for college or to put together a down payment for a house. Another common reason for selling stock is that the stockholder thinks the stock is likely to go down in price soon. Selling today at $25 a share is better than selling one week from now at $18 a share.

How to Buy and Sell Stock

Buying and selling stock are relatively easy. You can buy or sell stock through a full-service stockbrokerage firm, a discount broker, or an online broker. With all varieties of brokers, you usually open an account by depositing a certain dollar amount, commonly between $1,000 and $2,500. Once you have opened an account, you can begin to trade (i.e., buy and sell stock).

With a full-service broker, you may call up on the phone and ask your broker to recommend a good stock. Your broker, usually called an *account representative,* might say that you should buy X, Y, or Z stock. When you ask why these are good stocks to buy, the representative may say that the firm's research department has looked closely at them and believes they are headed for good times based on the current economic situation in the country, the level of exports, the new technology that is coming to market, and other factors.

If you do not need help selecting stocks, you can go either to a discount broker or to an online broker. You can call up a discount broker, as you did a full-service broker, and say you want to buy or sell so many shares of a given stock. The broker will execute the trade for you but not offer any advice.

You can do the same thing online. You go to your broker's website, log in, enter your username and password, and then buy or sell stock. You may, for example, submit an order to buy 100 shares of stock X. Your online broker will register your buy request and then advise you when it has been executed. Your account, easily visible online, will show how much cash you have in it, how many shares of a stock you hold, and so on.

Buying Stocks or Buying the Market

You can use various methods to decide which stocks to purchase. The first way is to buy shares of stock that you think are going to rise in price. So you might buy 50 shares of Microsoft, 100 shares of General Electric, and 500 shares of Amazon.com.

Another way is to invest in a stock mutual fund, which is a collection of stocks that is managed by a fund manager who works for a mutual fund company. For example, Smith may operate Mutual Fund Z at Mutual Fund Company Z. If you put, say, $10,000 into Mutual Fund Z, you are in effect buying stocks in that fund. If the fund consists of stocks A, B, C, W, and X, the fund manager may, on any given day, buy more of A and sell some of B or sell all of C and add stock D to the fund portfolio. Thus, as a buyer of the fund, you put your money into the manager's hands, and the fund manager does what he or she thinks is best to maximize the overall returns from the fund.

Mutual fund companies often advertise the records of their fund managers. They might say, "Our fund managers have the best record on Wall Street. Invest with us and get the highest returns you can." You may be prompted to put your money in the hands of the experts because you feel they know better than you which stocks to buy and sell and when to do either.

You could use another strategy, though, and buy the stocks that make up a stock index. For example, the DJIA, a stock index, gives us information on the performance of the 30 stocks that make up the Dow. Other indexes are made up differently. The Standard & Poor's 500 index is a broad index of stock market activity because it is made up of 500 of the largest U.S. companies. Another broad-based stock index is the Wilshire 5000, which consists of the stocks of about 6,500 firms. (Yes, even though it consists of more than 5,000 firms, it is still called the Wilshire 5000.) So, instead of buying a mutual fund that consists of various stocks picked by the so-called experts, you can buy a mutual fund that consists of the stocks that make up a particular index.

An easy way to do this is to buy what are called Spyders. The term "Spyders" comes from SPDRs, which stands for Standard & Poor's Depository Receipts. Spyders are securities that represent ownership in the SPDR Trust, which buys the stocks that make up the Standard & Poor's (S&P) 500 index and that are traded under the symbol SPY. At the time of writing, Spyders were selling for about $135 a share. Spyders cost one-tenth of the S&P index (the total of the share prices of the stocks in the S&P). For example, if the S&P index is 1,350 , then a Spyder will sell for $135.

When you buy Spyders, you are buying the stock of 500 companies. Because you are buying the stock of so many companies, you are said to be *buying the market*. For example, suppose Jack decides to buy the market instead of buying a few individual stocks. He opens an account with an online broker; that is, he goes online, opens an account, and sends the broker a check so that he can start trading (buying and selling stock). He then checks (at the online broker web site) on the current price of Spyders, which is, say, $135 per share. He decides to buy 100 shares, for a total price of $13,500. (His online broker charges him a small commission for this stock purchase.) In a minute or less, he sees that he has purchased the 100 shares. That's all there is to it.

How to Read the Stock Market Page

Once you have purchased some stock, you will want to know how it is doing. Is it rising or falling in price? Is it paying a dividend? How many shares were traded today?

One of the places with the answers to these questions, as well as other information, is the newspaper (many of which, of course, are online). On the stock market page, you will see something similar to what you see in Exhibit 3. Let's look at each item in each column of the bottom line (set in **boldface**).

EXHIBIT 3

How to Read the Stock Market Page of a Newspaper   This is part of the stock market page of a newspaper. We   explain how to read the page in the text.

(1)	(2)	(3)	(4)	(5)	(6)	(7)	(8)	(9)	(10)	(11)	(12)
52W high	52W low	Stock	Ticker	Div	Yield %	P/E	Vol 00s	High	Low	Close	Net chg
45.39	19.75	ResMed	RMD			57.5	3831	42.00	39.51	41.50	−1.90
11.63	3.55	Revlon A	REV				162	6.09	5.90	6.09	+0.12
77.25	55.13	RioTinto	RTP	2.30	3.2		168	72.75	71.84	72.74	+0.03
31.31	16.63	RitchieBr	RBA			20.9	15	24.49	24.29	24.49	-0.01
8.44	1.75	RiteAid	RAD				31028	4.50	4.20	4.31	+0.21
38.63	18.81	RobtHall	RHI			26.5	6517	27.15	26.50	26.50	+0.14
51.25	**27.69**	**Rockwell**	**ROK**	**1.02**	**2.1**	**14.5**	**6412**	**47.99**	**47.00**	**47.54**	**+0.24**

1. *52W high.* This stands for the high price of the stock over the past 52 weeks. For this stock, you see the number 51.25, which is $51.25.

2. *52W low.* This stands for the low price of the stock over the past 52 weeks. For this stock, you see the number 27.69, or $27.69.

3. *Stock.* In this column, you see Rockwell. This is either an abbreviation of the name or the full name of the company that issued the stock. The company here is Rockwell Automation Incorporated.

4. *Ticker.* ROK is the stock or ticker symbol for Rockwell Automation Incorporated.

5. *Div.* This stands for dividend. You see the number 1.02 on the bottom line, which means that the last annual dividend per share of stock was $1.02. For example, a person who owned 5,000 shares of Rockwell Automation stock would have received $1.02· per share, or $5,100 in dividends. (A blank, as in the line above in the exhibit, means the company does not currently pay out dividends.)

6. *Yield %.* The yield of a stock is the dividend divided by the closing price.

$$\text{Yield} = \frac{\text{Dividend per share}}{\text{Closing price per share}}$$

The closing price of the stock (shown in column 11) is 47.54 ($47.54). If we divide the dividend ($1.02) by the closing price ($47.54), we get a yield of 2.1 percent. The higher the yield, the better the prospects are for the stock, *ceteris paribus*. For example, a stock that yields 5 percent is better than a stock that yields 3 percent, if all other things between the two stocks are the same.

7. *P/E.* This stands for P/E ratio, or price-earnings ratio. The number here, 14.5, is obtained by taking the latest closing price per share and dividing it by the latest available net earnings per share.

$$\frac{P}{E} = \frac{\text{Closing price per share}}{\text{Net earnings per share}}$$

A stock with a P/E ratio of 14.5 means that it is selling for a share price that is 14.5 times its earnings per share.

A high P/E ratio usually indicates that people expect higher-than-average growth in earnings. Suppose that most stocks have a P/E ratio of 14.5, that is, they sell for a share price that is 14.5 times their earnings per share. Also suppose that stock X has a P/E ratio of, say, 50. What would make stock X have a P/E ratio so much higher than most stocks? Obviously, the people buying stock X expect that its future earnings will somehow warrant the higher prices they are paying for the stock today. Whether they are right remains to be seen.

8. *Vol 00s.* This stands for volume in the hundreds. The number 6412 translates to 641,200. It means that 641,200 shares of this stock were traded (bought and sold) on this day.

9. *High.* This stands for the high price the stock traded for on this day. The number is 47.99 ($47.99).

10. *Low.* This stands for the low price the stock traded for on this day. The number is 47.00 ($47.00).

11. *Close.* This is the share price of the stock when trading stopped on this day: 47.54 ($47.54).

12. *Net chg.* This stands for net change: +0.24 (+$0.24). The price of the stock on this day closed 24¢ higher than it did the day before.

(Answers to Self-Test questions are in Answers to Self-Test Questions at the back of the book.)

1. How many stocks does the DJIA consist of?

2. Why do people buy stocks?

3. What does the yield of a stock equal?

4. What does a P/E ratio of 23 mean?

BONDS

If a company in St. Louis wants to build a new factory, how can it get the necessary money? Issuing bonds is the third way that companies raise money (besides borrowing from a bank and issuing stock). A bond is simply an IOU, or a promise to pay. Typically, companies, governments, or government agencies issue bonds, in each case, the purpose being to borrow money. The issuer of a bond is a borrower, and the person who buys the bond is a lender.

Bond
An IOU, or a promise to pay.

The Components of a Bond

A bond has three major components: face (par) value, maturity date, and coupon rate.

Face Value (Par Value)
Dollar amount specified on a bond, the total amount the issuer of the bond will repay to the buyer of the bond.

FACE VALUE The face value, or par value, of a bond is the total amount the issuer of the bond will repay to the buyer of the bond. For example, suppose Smith buys a bond from Company Z, and the face value is $10,000. Company Z promises to pay Smith $10,000 at some point in the future.

MATURITY DATE The maturity date is the day that the issuer of the bond must pay the buyer the face value; it is the date the bond is said to come due. For example, suppose Smith buys a bond with a face value of $10,000 that matures on December 31, 2015. On December 31, 2015, he receives $10,000 from the issuer of the bond.

COUPON RATE The coupon rate is the percentage of the face value that the bond-holder receives each year until the bond matures. For example, suppose Smith buys a bond with a face value of $10,000 that matures in 5 years and has a coupon rate of 10 percent. He receives a coupon payment of $1,000 each year for 5 years.

To illustrate, Jorge buys a bond with a face value of $100,000 and a coupon rate of 7 percent. The maturity date of the bond is 10 years from today. Each year, for the next 10 years, Jorge receives 7 percent of $100,000 from the issuer, which amounts to $7,000 a year for each of the 10 years. In the 10th year, he also receives $100,000 from the bond issuer. This bond has a maturity date in 10 years, a coupon rate of 7 percent, and a face value of $100,000.

Bond Ratings

Bonds are rated, or evaluated. The more likely the bond issuer is to pay the face value of the bond at maturity and meet all scheduled coupon payments, the higher the bond's rating will be. Two of the best-known ratings are Standard & Poor's and Moody's. If a bond gets a rating of AAA from Standard & Poor's or a rating of Aaa from Moody's, it has received the highest rating possible. You can be sure that it is one of the securest bonds you can buy; there is little doubt that the bond issuer will pay the face value of the bond at maturity and meet all scheduled coupon payments.

Bonds rated in the B to D category are of lower quality than those in the A category. A bond in the C category may be in default (the issuer of the bond cannot pay off the bond), and those in the D category are definitely in default.

economics 24/7

$1.3 Quadrillion

At the close of the twentieth century, the editors of the financial magazine *The Economist* identified the highest-returning investments for each year, beginning in 1900 and ending in 1999. For example, the highest-returning investment in 1974 was gold, in 1902 it was U.S. Treasury bills, and in 1979 it was silver.

The editors then asked how much income a person would have earned by the end of 1999, if she had invested $1 in the highest-returning investment in 1900, and then taken the returns from that investment and invested it in the highest-returning investment in 1901, and so on for each year during the century. After taxes and dealer costs, she would have earned $1.3 quadrillion. (Quadrillion comes after trillion. In 2009, Bill Gates, the richest person in the world, had $40 billion; so $1.3 quadrillion is 32,500 times what Bill Gates had at the time.) So, with perfect foresight (or a crystal ball that always correctly tells you what the highest-returning investment of the year will be), you could be rich beyond your imagination.

After the editors ran their experiment, they changed it. They went back and asked themselves what one would have earned over the twentieth century if, instead of investing in the highest returning investment in a given year, she invested in it one year later. For example, if X was the best investment in 1956, she invested in it in 1957.

The editors made this change in the belief that many people invest in a hot investment only when it is too late. By the time they hear about it, investing in it then is usually too late. (Think of an investment as a mountain: going up the mountain is comparable to increasing returns on the investment, and going down the mountain is comparable to decreasing returns. Only when the investment is near its peak do many people hear about it. But then it's too late. The only way to go is down.)

To put this into context, the person with the crystal ball or with perfect foresight would have invested in the Polish stock market in 1993, when no one was talking about it, and he would have reaped a 754 percent gain. The typical investor would have invested in it one year later, in 1994, when everyone was talking about it. The problem is that the Polish stock market fell by 55 percent in 1994.

So the person who invested always one year late over the twentieth century would have earned, after taxes and dealer costs, $290!

What are the economic lessons? First, the best investments are often the ones that you don't hear about until it is too late. Second, ignoring the first lesson—thinking that a popular investment is necessarily a good investment—is often the way to low returns.

© NONSTOCK/JUPITER IMAGES

Bond Prices and Yields (or Interest Rates)

The price that a person pays for a bond depends on market conditions. The greater the demand is for the bond relative to the supply, the higher the price will be. The price is important because it determines the yield, or interest rate, that the bondholder receives on the bond. (In everyday language, the yield is referred to as the interest rate on the bond. For example, someone might ask what interest rate is that bond paying? We could easily substitute the term "yield" for the term "interest rate," and the answer might be something like "5.26 percent.")

Let's suppose that Gupta is the owner of a bond with a face value of $1,000 and a coupon rate of 5 percent. He decides to sell this bond to Jones for $950. If the coupon payment on this bond is 5 percent of $1,000 each year, or $50, Jones can expect to receive $50 each year. But the yield (sometimes called the *current yield*) on the bond is the coupon payment divided by the price paid for the bond.

$$\text{Yield (or interest rate)} = \frac{\text{Annual coupon payment}}{\text{Price paid for the bond}}$$

Yield
The amount equal to the annual coupon payment divided by the price paid for the bond.

In this example, the yield is $50 ÷ $950 = 5.26 percent. For the bond buyer, the higher the yield is, the better the deal is.

Now suppose Jones paid $1,100 for the bond instead of $950. In this case, the yield would be $50 ÷ $1,100 = 4.54 percent. In other words, as the price paid for the bond rises, the yield declines.

The coupon rate and the yield are the same when the price paid for the bond equals the face value. For example, a bond with a face value of $1,000 and a coupon rate of 5 percent is purchased for $1,000. The yield ($50 ÷ $1,000) is 5 percent, which is equal to the coupon rate.

Common Misconceptions About the Coupon Rate and Yield (Interest Rate)

Many people seem to think that the coupon rate of a bond is the yield that the bond earns. This is not true, as you now know. The yield (or interest rate) and the coupon rate are two different things.

- Only when the price of the bond equals the face value of the bond does the yield (interest rate) equal the coupon rate.
- When the price of the bond is lower than the face value of the bond, the yield will be greater than the coupon rate.
- When the price of the bond is greater than the face value of the bond, the yield will be lower than the coupon rate.

Types of Bonds

This section briefly describes some of the many types of bonds that companies, governments, and government agencies issue.

CORPORATE BONDS   A corporate bond is issued by a private corporation. Typically, a corporate bond has a $10,000 face value. Corporate bonds may sell for a price above or below face value depending on current supply-and-demand conditions. The interest that corporate bonds pay is fully taxable.

MUNICIPAL BONDS   Municipal bonds are issued by state and local governments. States may issue bonds to help pay for, say, a new highway. Local governments may issue bonds to finance a civic auditorium or a sports stadium. Many people purchase municipal bonds because the interest paid on them is not subject to federal taxes.

TREASURY BILLS, NOTES, AND BONDS   When the federal government wants to borrow funds, it can issue Treasury bills (T-bills), notes, or bonds. These securities differ only in their time to maturity. Although called by different names, all are bonds. Treasury bills mature in 13, 26, or 52 weeks. Treasury notes mature in 2 to 10 years, and Treasury bonds mature in 10 to 30 years. Treasury bills, notes, and bonds are considered very safe investments because it is unlikely the federal government will default on its bond obligations. The federal government has the power to tax to pay off bondholders.

INFLATION-INDEXED TREASURY BONDS   In 1997, the federal government began to issue inflation-indexed bonds. The first indexed Treasury bonds that were issued mature in 10 years and were available at face values as small as $1,000.

An inflation-indexed Treasury bond differs from a nonindexed Treasury bond in that an inflation-indexed Treasury bond guarantees the purchaser a certain real rate of return; a nonindexed Treasury bond does not. For example, suppose you purchase an inflation-indexed, 10-year, $1,000 bond that pays a 4 percent coupon rate. If there is no inflation, the annual interest payment will be $40. But if the inflation rate is, say, 3 percent, the government will mark up the value of the bond by 3 percent—from $1,000 to $1,030. Then it will pay 4 percent on this higher dollar amount. So instead of paying $40 each year, it pays $41.20. By increasing the monetary value of the security by the rate of inflation, the government guarantees the bondholder a real return of 4 percent.

How to Read the Bond Market Page

On the bond market page of the newspaper, you can find information about the different types of bonds. Here we discuss how to read the information that relates to both corporate bonds and Treasury bonds. First, let's look at corporate bonds.

CORPORATE BONDS Not all publications will present corporate bond information in exactly the same format. The format in Exhibit 4 is common, though.

1. *Bonds.* This column presents three pieces of information: (1) the abbreviation for the company that issued the bond—AT&T, a telecommunications company; (2) the coupon rate of the bond, 6 5/8; (3) the year the bond matures, 2034.

2. *Cur Yld.* In this column is the current yield. (We showed how to compute the yield on a bond.) If the bond is purchased today (hence the word "current"), it will provide a yield of 6.7 percent.

3. *Vol.* In this column is the volume, 115. The dollar volume today is $115,000.

4. *Close.* In this column, you find the closing price for the bond on this day, 99 1/2. Bond prices are quoted in points and fractions, and each point is $10. Thus, 99 1/2 is $995.00: 99.5 × 10 = $995.00.

5. *Net Chg.* This column shows the net change for the day. Here, it is –3/4, which means that the price on this day was $7.50 lower than it was the previous day.

TREASURY BONDS Not all publications will present Treasury bond information in exactly the same format. The format in Exhibit 5 is common, though.

1. *Rate.* In this column, you find the coupon rate of the bond. This Treasury bond pays 7 3/4 percent of the face value of the bond in annual interest payments.

2. *Maturity.* In this column, you find when the bond matures. This Treasury bond matures in February 2012.

3. *Bid.* In this column, you find how much the buyer is willing to pay for the bond (or the price you will receive if you sell the bond): 105:12. The number after the colon stands for 32nds of $10. Therefore, 105:12 is $1,053.75. First, multiply 105 × $10 = $1,050. Second, turn 12/32 into 0.375, and multiply by $10, giving you $3.75. Then add $3.75 to $1,050 to get $1,053.75.

4. *Ask.* In this column, you find how much the seller is asking for to sell the bond. This is the price you will pay if you buy the bond: $1,054.37.

(1) Bonds	(2) Cur Yld	(3) Vol	(4) Close	(5) Net Chg
AT&T 6 5/8 34	6.7	115	99 1/2	−3/4

How to Read Corporate Bond Information

This is a common format for corporate bond information.

EXHIBIT 5

How to Read Treasury Bond Information

This is a common format for treasury bond information.

(1) Rate	(2) Maturity	(3) Bid	(4) Ask	(5) Chg	(6) Yield
7 3/4	Feb. 12	105:12	105:14	−1	5.50

5. ***Chg.*** In this column, you find the change in the price of the bond from the previous trading day, expressed in 32nds. Therefore, −1 means that the price of the bond fell by 1/32nd of $10, or approximately 32¢ from the previous day.

6. ***Yield.*** In this column, you find the yield, which is based on the ask price. Someone who buys the bond today (at the ask price) and holds it to maturity will reap a return of 5.50 percent.

Risk and Return

Whether buying stocks or bonds, the common denominator is that people buy them for the return. Simply stated, they hope to make money. How much money people can hope to make is tied directly to the different risk and return factors of stocks and bonds. For example, buying stock in a new company might be much riskier than buying a bond issued by the U.S. Treasury. You can be fairly sure that the U.S. Treasury is going to pay off that bond because the U.S. government has the ability to tax people. But you cannot be so sure of a positive return on the stock you buy in the new company. You might buy the stock for $10 one day, and three days later it falls to $1 and stays at that price (or thereabouts) for 10 years.

In Chapter 1, we said that a well-known principle in economics is that there is no free lunch. Applied to stocks and bonds (or any investment), that principle means you never get something for nothing. In short, higher returns come with higher risks, and lower returns come with lower risks. Treasury bonds, for example, will often pay (relatively) low returns because they are safe (risk-free).

SELF-TEST

1. What is a bond?

2. If the coupon payment on a bond is $400 a year and the coupon rate is 7 percent, what is the face value?

3. If the annual coupon payment for a bond is $1,000 and the price paid for the bond is $9,500, what is the yield or interest rate?

4. What is the difference between a municipal bond and a Treasury bond?

FUTURES AND OPTIONS

In this section, we discuss both futures and options.

Futures

Myers is a miller. He buys wheat from the wheat farmer, turns the wheat into flour, and then sells the flour to the baker. Obviously, he wants to earn a profit for what he does. How much, if any, profit he earns depends on the price at which he can buy the wheat and the price at which he can sell the flour.

economics 24/7

What Do Private Equity Firms Do?

Suppose a large corporation is full of top-level managers who are not carefully looking out for the company's shareholders. Maybe the corporation has a few losing operations that it should have shut down, or it has purchased too many corporate jets for use by top managers.

Enter the private equity firm. A private equity firm is a group of investors that seeks to buy up the publicly traded stock of the large corporation and then take the corporation private. Often, the private equity firm uses debt to buy the publicly traded stock. In other words, the private equity firm borrows much of the money needed to buy the public corporation.

As an example, Company X is a corporation that in the past few years has earned $20 million a year in profits. The private equity firm buys the stock of the corporation for 10 times the annual profits, or $200 million. The private equity firm itself puts up $60 million and borrows $140 million.

Once the private equity firm owns the corporation, it begins to cut costs and enhance efficiency. Maybe it gets rid of a few of the corporate jets, cuts a few losing operations, gets rid of some management that it feels is unnecessary, and invests in new products.

Now suppose profits rise to $22 million a year. The equity firm then pays $22 million for each of five years to repay $110 million of its $140 million debt, and then it sells the company for 10 times its annual earnings of $22 million, or $220 million. Out of the $220 million it repays the remainder of its debt ($30 million) and walks away with $190 million profit.

Of course, the firm is not guaranteed to generate greater profits. Even if the company only continued to earn $20 million in profits a year, the equity firm could use the $20 million in profits for, say, five years to pay off $100 million (of the $140 million debt) and then sell the company for what it purchased it for: $200 million. Out of the $200 million sales proceeds, the private equity firm would retire the remainder of the debt ($40 million), leaving it with $160 million in profit.

Is the existence of private equity firms a good thing? Some people will argue that private equity firms cut costs and enhance efficiency. Simply put, they increase the value of the firms in which they invest. Others argue that private equity firms exploit firms filled with managers who are averse to debt. They say that companies with too much cash and too little debt become targets for private equity firms to buy. The result, critics argue, is that ordinary shareholders are often hurt because buyout prices are often too low.

Myers decides to buy a futures contract in wheat. A futures contract is a contract in which the seller agrees to provide a good (in this case, wheat) to the buyer on a specified future date at an agreed-on price. For example, Myers might buy bushels of wheat now, for a price of $3 a bushel, to be delivered to him in six months.

But who would sell him the futures contract? A likely possibility is a *speculator*, someone who buys and sells commodities to profit from changes in the market. A speculator assumes risk in the hope of making a gain.

Suppose Smith, a speculator, believes that the price of wheat six months from now is going to be lower than it is today. She may look at things this way: "The price of wheat today is $3 a bushel. I think the price of wheat in six months will be close to $2 a bushel. I will promise the miller that I will deliver him as much wheat as he wants in six months if, in return, he agrees today to pay me $3 a bushel for it. Then, in six months, I will buy the wheat for $2 a bushel, sell it to the miller for $3 a bushel, and earn myself $1 profit on each bushel." So Myers, the miller, and Smith, the speculator, enter into a futures contract. Myers buys 200 bushels of wheat for delivery in six months; Smith sells 200 bushels of wheat for delivery in six months.

Each party gets something out of the deal. Myers, the miller, gets peace of mind. He knows that he will be able to buy the wheat at a price that will let him earn a profit on his deal with the baker. Smith takes a chance, which she is willing to take, for the chance of earning a profit.

Futures Contract
An agreement to buy or sell a specific amount of something (a commodity, a currency, a financial instrument) at an agreed-on price on a stipulated future date.

As another example, Wilson is a farmer who grows primarily corn. The current price of corn is $3.34 a bushel. Wilson doesn't have any corn to sell right now, but he will in two months. He hopes that over the next two months the price of corn won't fall to, say, something under $3. He decides to enter into a futures contract in corn. He promises to deliver 5,000 bushels of corn two months from now for $3.34 a bushel. Leung, a speculator in corn, decides that this is a good deal for him because he believes that in two months the price of a bushel of corn will have risen to $3.94. So Wilson and Leung enter into a futures contract. Two months pass and the price of corn has dropped to $3.10. Leung turned out to be wrong about the price rising. So farmer Wilson delivers 5,000 bushels of corn to speculator Leung, for which Leung pays Wilson $3.34 a bushel (for a total of $16,700), as agreed. Then Leung turns around and sells the corn for $3.10 a bushel (receiving $15,500), losing $1,200 on the deal.

CURRENCY FUTURES A futures contract can be written for wheat, as we have seen, or for a currency, a stock index, or even bonds. Here is how a currency futures contract works.

You check the dollar price of a euro today and find that it is $1.20. Thus, for every $1.20, you get 1 euro in return. You expect that in three months you will have to pay $1.50 to buy a euro. With this in mind, you enter into a futures contract. Essentially, you say that you are willing to buy $10 million worth of euros three months from now for $1.20 a euro. Anyone who thinks the dollar price of a euro will be lower (not higher) in three months might be willing to enter into this contract with you. Suppose you and Werner enter a contract. You promise to buy $10 million worth of euros in three months (at $1.20 a euro), and Werner promises to sell you $10 million worth of euros in three months at that price.

Three months pass, and it now takes $1.30 to buy a euro. Werner has to buy $10 million worth of euros at an exchange rate of $1.30 per euro. For $10 million, he gets 7,692,307 euros, which he turns over to you for $1.20 each, leaving him with $9,230,768. Obviously, Werner has taken a loss; he spent $10 million to get $9,230,768 in return, for a loss of $769,232.

On the other side of the deal, you now have 7,692,307 euros, for which you paid $9,230,768. If you sell them all, because you get $1.30 for every euro, you will get approximately $10 million. You are better off by $769,232.

Options

Option

A contract that gives the owner the right, but not the obligation, to buy or sell shares of a stock at a specified price on or before a specified date.

An **option** is a contract that gives the owner of the option the right, but not the obligation, to buy or sell shares of a stock at a specified price on or before a specified date. There are two types of options: calls and puts.

CALL OPTION *Call* options give the owner of the option the right to *buy* shares of a stock at a specified price within the time limits of the contract. The specified price at which the buyer can buy shares of a stock is called the *strike price*. For example, Brown buys a call option for $20. The call option specifies that he can buy 100 shares of IBM stock at a strike price of $150 within the next month. If the price of IBM stocks falls below $150, Brown will not exercise his call option. He simply tears it up and accepts the fact that he has lost $20. If he still wants to buy IBM stock, he can do so through his stockbroker as he normally does and pay the going price, which is lower than $150. But if the price rises above $150, he exercises the call option, buys the stock at $150 a share, and then sells it for the higher market price. He has made a profit.

If Brown buys a call option, someone has to sell it to him. Anyone who would sell Brown a call option is a person who thought the option wouldn't be exercised. For example, if Jones believed that the price of IBM was going to fall below $150, then he would gladly sell a call option to Brown for $20, thinking that the option would never be exercised. That's $20 in his pocket.

PUT OPTIONS *Put* options give the owner the right, but not the obligation, to *sell* (rather than buy, as in a call option) shares of a stock at a strike price during some period of time. For example, suppose Martin buys a put option to sell 100 shares of IBM stock at $130 during the next month. If the share price rises above $130, Martin will not exercise his put option. He will simply tear it up and sell the stock for more than $130. On the other hand, if the price drops below $130, then he will exercise his option to sell the stock for $130 a share.

So, people who think the price of the stock is going to decline buy put options. Obviously, the people who think the price of the stock is going to rise sell put options. Why not sell a put option for, say, $20, if you expect the price of the stock to rise? The buyer is not going to exercise the option.

HOW YOU CAN USE CALL AND PUT OPTIONS You can use call and put options in a number of ways. Suppose you think a stock, currently selling for $250 a share, is going to rise in price during the next few months. You don't have enough money to buy many shares of stock, but you would like to benefit from the rise in the price of the stock. In such a case, you can buy a call option, which will sell for a fraction of the cost of the stock. So with limited resources, you decide to buy the call option, which gives you the right to buy, say, 100 shares of the stock at $250 anytime during the next three months.

A natural question is, if you don't have the money to buy the stock at $250 a share now, how are you going to buy it at $250 in a few months? You don't have to buy the stock. If you are right that the price of the stock will rise, then your call option will become worth more to people. In other words, if you bought the option when the price of the stock was $250 and the stock rises to $300, then your call option has become more valuable. You can sell it and benefit from the uptick in the price of the stock.

Alternatively, let's say you expect the price of the stock to fall. Then you can buy a put option. In other words, you buy the right to sell the stock for $250 anytime during the next three months. If the price does fall, your option becomes more valuable. In fact, the farther the price falls, the more valuable your put option becomes. People who have the stock and want to sell it for a price higher than it currently fetches on the market will be willing to buy your put option from you for some price higher than the price you paid.

As an example, the current price of a call option for AT&T stock is $10, and the current price of AT&T stock is $100. Ginny decides to buy a call option for $10, giving her the right to buy AT&T at a price of $100. Five months pass, and the price of AT&T shares has risen to $150. If Ginny wants, she can exercise her call option to buy AT&T stock at $100 (which is $50 less than the current price of $150). In other words, she can spend $100 to buy a share of stock, which she can turn around and immediately sell for $150, making a profit of $50 per share.

SELF-TEST

1. What is a futures contract?

2. You expect that a stock will rise in the next few months, but you do not have enough money to buy many shares of the stock. What can you do instead?

3. What is a put option?

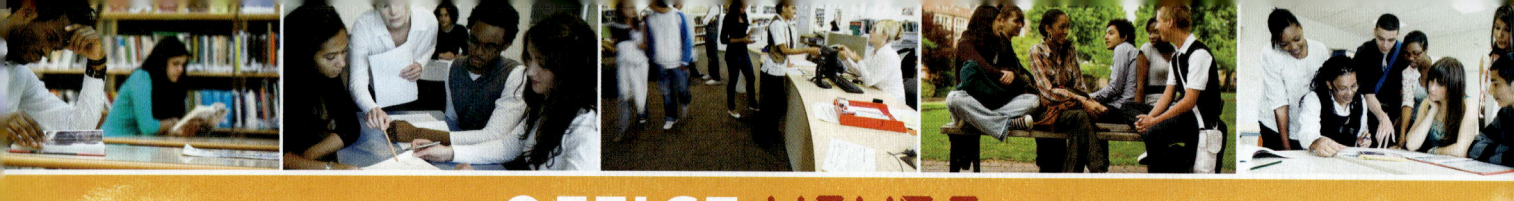

OFFICE HOURS

"I Have Three Questions."

STUDENT:

Can a firm that issues a bond set the coupon rate at any rate it wants?

INSTRUCTOR:

No. To illustrate, suppose company A needs to borrow $10 million and decides to issue $10,000 bonds. The only way anyone would be willing to buy one of these bonds (that is, lend the company $10,000) is if the company promises the buyers a rate of return comparable to the interest rate they could get if they simply put the money in a savings account. The company has to set the coupon rate in such a way that it attracts people to its bonds. If people are earning, say, 5 percent on their savings accounts, they will not lend money to the company unless the company pays a coupon rate of at least 5 percent. In short, the coupon rate is set at a competitive level—not just any level the company chooses.

STUDENT:

Is it a good idea to buy stock?

INSTRUCTOR:

A lot depends on such factors as your age (are you at the beginning of your work career or near the end), your income, and how much you can afford to invest in the stock market. Stock is not guaranteed to go up in price. For example, consider what happened to the DJIA in the 1930s. At the beginning of 1930, the Dow stood around 250, but at the end of 1939, it was around 150. Over the decade of the 1930s, the Dow went down by 40 percent.

However, having said this, stock prices have gone up over the long run. For example, suppose we look at the S&P Index during the period 1926–2004. The data show that you would have had a 70 percent likelihood of earning a positive investment return over a one-year period, but that would have risen to an 86.5 percent chance of a positive investment return if you had held the stocks in the index over a five-year period. The probability of a positive return goes up to 97.1 percent if you had held the stocks for 10 years. The longer you hold stocks in the stock market, the more likely it is that you will earn a positive return.

STUDENT:

Last question: Suppose I buy 100 shares of stock at a price of, say, $40 a share. The stock goes down in price to $32. Shouldn't I wait until the share price rises to $40 or higher before I sell it?

INSTRUCTOR:

When it comes to stock, what goes down is not guaranteed to go up. Even if the stock's price has gone down by $8, it might go down more. You want always to look forward, to the future (not backward, to the past), when deciding whether to sell a stock. If you think the price may fall even farther, selling at $32 (taking an $8 per share loss) is better than selling at $25 and taking a bigger loss. If you think there is a reason for the price to rise, then hold on to the stock.

POINTS TO REMEMBER

1. A company that issues bonds cannot set the coupon rate at whatever rate it wants.
2. Based on the period 1926–2004, the longer a person would have held stocks, the higher the probability is that he or she would have received a positive return.
3. Stocks that go down in price are not guaranteed to go back up.

CHAPTER SUMMARY

STOCKS

- A stock is a claim on the assets of a corporation that gives the purchaser a share (ownership) in the corporation. Stocks are sometimes called "equity" because the buyer of the stock has part ownership of the company that initially issued the stock.
- Stocks are bought and sold on exchanges and markets, such as the New York Stock Exchange.
- Some people buy stocks for the dividends, which are payments made to stockholders based on a company's profits; others attempt to make money by buying shares at a lower price and selling at a higher price.
- Today, 30 stocks make up the Dow Jones Industrial Average (DJIA). The DJIA was devised by Charles Dow to convey information about what was happening in the stock market.
- A stock index fund consists of the stocks that make up an index.
- The yield (or interest rate) of a stock is equal to the dividend divided by the closing price of the stock.
- The P/E ratio for a stock is equal to the closing price per share (of the stock) divided by the net earnings per share. A stock with a P/E ratio of, say, 15 means that the stock is selling for a share price that is 15 times its earnings per share.

BONDS

- A bond is an IOU, or a promise to pay, typically issued by companies, governments, or government agencies.
- The three major components of a bond are face (par) value, maturity date, and coupon rate.
- The price that a person pays for a bond depends on market conditions: the greater the demand is for the bond relative to the supply, the higher the price will be.
- The (current) yield on the bond is the coupon payment divided by the price paid for the bond.
- Bonds are rated or evaluated. The more likely the bond issuer is to pay the face value of the bond at maturity and meet all scheduled coupon payments, the higher the bond's rating will be.
- The price of a bond and its yield (or interest rate) are inversely related.

FUTURES AND OPTIONS

- In a futures contract, a seller agrees to provide a good to the buyer on a specified future date at an agreed-on price.
- An option is a contract giving the owner the right, but not the obligation, to buy or sell a good at a specified price on or before a specified date.

KEY TERMS AND CONCEPTS

Stock
Dow Jones Industrial
  Average (DJIA)

Initial Public Offering
  (IPO)
Investment Bank

Dividend
Bond
Face Value (Par Value)

Yield
Futures Contract
Option

QUESTIONS AND PROBLEMS

1. If the face value of a bond is $10,900 and the annual coupon payment is $600, what is the coupon rate?
2. Why might a person purchase an inflation-indexed Treasury bond?
3. "If you can predict interest rates, then you can earn a fortune buying and selling bonds." Do you agree or disagree? Explain your answer.
4. Why might a person buy a futures contract?
5. Why might a person buy a call option?
6. "The currency speculator who sells futures contracts assumes the risk that someone else doesn't want to assume." Do you agree or disagree? Explain your answer.
7. If you thought the share price of a stock was going to fall, would you buy a call option or a put option?
8. "An issuer of a bond is a borrower." Do you agree or disagree? Explain your answer.
9. Which of the two stocks has a bigger gap between its closing price and net earnings per share: Stock A with a P/E ratio of 15 or Stock B with a P/E ratio of 44? Explain your answer.
10. If the share price of each of 500 stocks rises on Monday, does everyone in the stock market believe that stocks are headed even higher? (No one will buy a stock if he or she thinks share prices are headed lower.)
11. What does it mean if someone invests in a mutual fund? In a stock market fund?
12. What does it mean to buy the market?
13. What does it mean if the Dow Jones Industrial Average rises by, say, 100 points in a day?
14. What is the purpose of financial markets?

WORKING WITH NUMBERS AND GRAPHS

1. You own 1,250 shares of stock X, and you read in the newspaper that the dividend for the stock is 3.88. What did you earn in dividends?

2. The closing price of a stock is $90.25, and the dividend is $3.50. What is the yield of the stock?

3. The closing price of the stock is $66.40, and the net earnings per share are $2.50. What is the stock's P/E ratio?

4. The face value of a bond is $10,000, and the annual coupon payment is $850. What is the coupon rate?

5. A person buys a bond that matures in 10 years and pays a coupon rate of 10 percent. The face value of the bond is $10,000. How much money will the bondholder receive in the tenth year?

Chapter 1

CHAPTER 1, PAGE 3

1. False. It takes two things for scarcity to exist: finite resources and infinite wants. If people's wants were equal to or less than the finite resources available to satisfy their wants, scarcity would not exist. Scarcity exists only because people's wants are greater than the resources available to satisfy their wants. Scarcity is the condition resulting from infinite wants clashing with finite resources.

2. Because of scarcity, there is a need for a rationing device. People will compete for the rationing device. For example, if dollar price is the rationing device, people will compete for dollars.

3. Because our unlimited wants are greater than our limited resources—that is, because scarcity exists—some wants must go unsatisfied. We must choose which wants we will satisfy and which we will not.

CHAPTER 1, PAGE 12

1. Everytime a student is late to history class, the instructor subtracts one-tenth of a point from the person's final grade. If the instructor raises the opportunity cost of being late to class by subtracting one point from the final grade, economists predict that fewer students would be late to class. In summary, the higher the opportunity cost is of being late to class, the less likely people will be late to class.

2. Yes. To illustrate, suppose the marginal benefits and marginal costs (in dollars) are as follows for various hours of studying:

Hour	Marginal Benefits	Marginal Costs
First hour	$20.00	$10.00
Second hour	$14.00	$11.00
Third hour	$13.00	$12.00
Fourth hour	$12.10	$12.09
Fifth hour	$11.00	$13.00

Clearly, you will study the first hour because the marginal benefits are greater than the marginal costs. Stated differently, studying the first hour has a net benefit of $10 (the difference between the marginal benefits of $20 and the marginal costs of $10). If you stop studying after the first hour and do not proceed to the second, then you forfeit the net benefit of $3 for the second hour. To maximize your net benefits of studying, you must proceed until the marginal benefits and the marginal costs are as close to equal as possible. (In the extreme, this is an epsilon away from equality. However, economists simply speak of the "equality" of the two for convenience.) In this case, you

study through the fourth hour. You do not study the fifth hour because it is not worth it; the marginal benefits of studying the fifth hour are less than the marginal costs. In short, studying the fifth hour has a net cost.

3. You might feel sleepy the next day, you might be less alert while driving, and so on.

CHAPTER 1, PAGE 17

1. The purpose of building a theory is to explain something that is not obvious. For example, the cause of changes in the unemployment rate is not obvious, and so the economist would build a theory to explain changes in the unemployment rate.

2. A theory of the economy seeks to explain why certain things in the economy happen. For example, a theory of the economy might try to explain why prices rise or why output falls. A description of the economy is simply a statement of what exists in the economy. For example, we could say that the economy is growing or contracting or that more jobs are available this month than last month. A description doesn't answer questions; it simply tells us what is. A theory tries to answer a why question, such as, "Why are more jobs available this month than last month?"

3. If you do not test a theory, you will never know whether you have accomplished your objective in building the theory in the first place. In other words, you will not know if you have accurately explained something. We do not simply accept a theory if it sounds right, because what sounds right may actually be wrong. For example, no doubt during the time of Columbus, the theory that the earth was flat sounded right to many people and the theory that the earth was round sounded ridiculous. The right-sounding theory turned out to be wrong, though, and the ridiculous-sounding theory turned out to be right.

4. Unless stated otherwise, when economics instructors identify the relationship between two variables, they implicitly make the *ceteris paribus* assumption. In other words, the instructor is really saying, "If the price of going to the movies goes down, people will go to the movies more often—assuming that nothing else changes, such as the quality of movies, and so on." Instructors don't always state *"ceteris paribus"* because if they did, they would be using the term every minute of a lecture. So the instructor is right, although a student new to economics might not know what the instructor is assuming but not saying.

Chapter 2

CHAPTER 2, PAGE 46

1. A straight-line PPF represents constant opportunity costs between two goods. For example, for every unit of X produced, one unit of Y is forfeited. A bowed-outward PPF represents increasing opportunity costs. For example, we may have to forfeit one unit of X to produce the eleventh unit of

Y, but we have to forfeit two units of X_1 to produce the one-hundredth unit of Y.

2. A bowed-outward PPF is representative of increasing costs. In short, the PPF would not be bowed outward if increasing costs did not exist. To prove this, look back at Exhibits 1 and 2. In Exhibit 1, costs are constant (not increasing), and the PPF is a straight line. In Exhibit 2, costs are increasing, and the PPF is bowed outward.

3. The first condition is that the economy is currently operating *below* its PPF. It is possible to move from a point below the PPF to a point on the PPF and get more of all goods. The second condition is that the economy's PPF shifts outward.

4. False. Take a look at Exhibit 5. All of the numerous productive efficient points lie on the PPF.

Chapter 3
CHAPTER 3, PAGE 65

1. Popcorn is a normal good for Sandi. Prepaid telephone cards are an inferior good for Mark.

2. Asking why demand curves are downward sloping is the same as asking why price and quantity demanded are inversely related (as one rises, the other falls). Two reasons for this are mentioned in this section: (1) As price rises, people substitute lower-priced goods for higher-priced goods. (2) Because individuals receive less utility from an additional unit of a good they consume, they are only willing to pay less for the additional unit. The second reason is a reflection of the law of diminishing marginal utility.

3. Suppose only two people, Bob and Alice, have a demand for good X. At a price of $7, Bob buys 10 units and Alice buys 3 units; at a price of $6, Bob buys 12 units and Alice buys 5 units. One point on the market demand curve represents a price of $7 and a quantity demanded of 13 units; another point represents $6 and 17 units. A market demand curve is derived by adding the quantities demanded at each price.

4. A change in income, preferences, prices of related goods, the number of buyers, and expectations of future price can change demand. A change in the price of the good changes the quantity demanded of it. For example, a change in *income* can change the *demand* for oranges, but only a change in the *price* of oranges can directly change the *quantity demanded* of oranges.

CHAPTER 3, PAGE 70

1. Increasing the quantity supplied of houses over the next ten hours would be difficult; so the supply curve in (a) is vertical, as in Exhibit 8. Increasing the quantity supplied of houses over the next three months is possible; so the supply curve in (b) is upward sloping.

2. a. The supply curve shifts to the left.

   b. The supply curve shifts to the left.

   c. The supply curve shifts to the right.

3. False. If the price of apples rises, the *quantity supplied* of apples will rise—not the *supply*. We are talking about a *movement* from one point on a supply curve to a point higher up on the supply curve, not about a shift in the supply curve.

CHAPTER 3, PAGE 80

1. Disagree. In the text, we plainly saw how supply and demand work at an auction. Supply and demand are at work in the grocery store too, even though no auctioneer is present. The essence of the auction example is the auctioneer's raising the price when there was a shortage and lowering the price when there was a surplus. The same thing happens at the grocery store. For example, given a surplus of corn flakes, the manager of the store is likely to run a sale (lower prices) on them. Many markets without auctioneers act *as if* auctioneers were raising and lowering prices in response to shortages and surpluses.

2. No. It could be the result of a higher supply of computers. Either a decrease in demand or an increase in supply will lower price.

3. a. Lower price and quantity

   b. Lower price and higher quantity

   c. Higher price and lower quantity

   d. Lower price and quantity

4. At equilibrium quantity, the maximum buying price and the minimum selling price are the same. For example, in Exhibit 15, both prices are $40 at the equilibrium quantity of 4. The equilibrium quantity is the only quantity at which the maximum buying price and the minimum selling price are the same.

5. $44; $34

Chapter 4
CHAPTER 4, PAGE 87

1. A rationing device is necessary because scarcity exists. If scarcity did not exist, a rationing device would not be needed.

2. If (dollar) price is the rationing device used, then individuals have an incentive to produce goods and services, sell them for money (for the dollar price), and then use the money to buy what they want. If another rationing device were used (say, first-come-first-service, or "need," etc.), then the incentive to produce would be dramatically dampened. Why produce a good if the only way you can "sell" it (i.e., ration the good) is by way of first-come-first-served.

3. Price conveys information about the relative scarcity of a good. In the orange juice example, a rise in the price of orange juice transmitted information relating to the increased relative scarcity of orange juice due to a cold spell in Florida.

CHAPTER 4, PAGE 94

1. Yes, if nothing else changes—that is, yes, *ceteris paribus*. If other things change, though, they may not. For example, if the government imposes an effective price ceiling on gasoline, Jamie may pay lower gas prices at the pump but have to wait in line to buy the gas (due to first-come-first-served rationing of the shortage). Whether Jamie is better off paying a higher price and not waiting in line or paying a lower price and waiting in line is not clear. The point, however, is that buyers don't necessarily prefer lower prices to higher prices unless everything else (quality, wait, service, etc.) stays the same.

2. Disagree. Both long-lasting shortages and long lines are caused by price ceilings. First, the price ceiling is imposed, creating the shortage; then the rationing device of first-come-first-served

emerges because price isn't permitted to fully ration the good. Every day, shortages occur that don't cause long lines to form. Instead, buyers bid up price, output and price move to equilibrium, and there is no shortage.

3. Buyers might argue for price ceilings on the goods they buy, especially if they don't know that price ceilings have some effects they may not like (e.g., fewer exchanges, first-come-first-served rationing devices, etc.). Sellers might argue for price floors on the goods they sell, especially if they expect their profits to rise. Employees might argue for a wage floor on the labor services they sell, especially if they don't know that they may lose their jobs or have their hours cut back as a result.

CHAPTER 4, PAGE 96

1. $1A = \frac{2}{3}B$ and $1B = 1.5A$

2. The statement is correct in the sense that good X has a higher money price than it used to have. It is misleading because a higher money price doesn't necessarily mean a higher relative price. For example, if the absolute (money) price of good X is $10 and the absolute price of good Y is $20, then the relative price of X is ½ units of Y. Now suppose the absolute price of X rises to $15 while the absolute price of Y rises to $60. The new relative price of X is now ¼ units of Y. In other words, the absolute price of X rises (from $10 to $15) while its relative price falls (from ½Y to ¼Y). Good X can become more expensive in money terms as it becomes cheaper in terms of other goods.

Chapter 5

CHAPTER 5, PAGE 101

1. The more requests for tickets and the faster the tickets sell out, the more popular the show.

2. They could charge a positive ticket price for shows in which the quantity demanded of seats equaled the quantity supplied of seats at a positive price. This may not always be the case, though, as shown in Exhibit 2.

CHAPTER 5, PAGE 102

1. Yes. For example, suppose a 30 percent down payment was needed to obtain a mortgage loan instead of a 10 percent down payment. Fewer individuals would be able to obtain a loan to buy a house, lowering the demand for houses and thus lowering house prices.

2. Yes. Reducing one's taxes because he or she has purchased a house makes buying a house more attractive, which leads to a higher demand for houses. The higher demand for houses raises the equilibrium price of houses.

CHAPTER 5, PAGE 103

1. The airlines company will likely use the rationing device of first-come/first-served. The people who book their reservations early get their pick of seats; those who do not book early have to take the left over seats.

2. The equilibrium price of the window seat is less than the equilibrium price of the aisle seat; the equilibrium price of the middle seat is lower than the equilibrium price of the window seat. For example, if the equilibrium price of the aisle seat is

$300, then the equilibrium price of the window seat might be $280, with the equilibrium price of the aisle seat even lower at, say, $250.

CHAPTER 5, PAGE 105

1. The price of food will rise along with the premium for food insurance.

2. The new demand curve would be between D_1 and D_2.

CHAPTER 5, PAGE 106

1. If supply and tuition are constant and demand rises, the shortage of openings at the university will become greater. The university will continue to use its nonprice-rationing devices (GPA, SAT scores, ACT scores) but will have to raise the standards of admission. Instead of requiring a GPA of, say, 3.5 for admission, it may raise the requirement to 3.8.

2. Not likely. A university that didn't make admission easier in the face of a surplus of openings might not be around much longer. When tuition cannot be adjusted directly—in other words, when the rationing device of price cannot be adjusted—it is likely that the nonprice-rationing device (standards) will be.

CHAPTER 5, PAGE 108

1. Any price above 70¢.

2. Assuming that tolls are not used, freeway congestion will worsen. An increase in driving population simply shifts the demand curve for driving to the right.

CHAPTER 5, PAGE 109

1. Moving from a system where patients cannot sue their HMOs to one where they can gives patients something they didn't have before (the right to sue) at a higher price (higher charges for healthcare coverage). The "free lunch"—the right to sue—isn't free after all.

2. If the students get the extra week and nothing else changes, then the students will probably say they are better off. In other words, more of one thing (time) and no less of anything else makes one better off. But if because of the extra week, the professor grades their papers harder than she would have otherwise, then some or all of the students may say that they weren't made better off by the extra week.

CHAPTER 5, PAGE 110

1. A possible answer: Of two cities, one has clean air and the other has dirty air. The demand to live in the clean-air city is higher than the demand to live in the dirty-air city. As a result, housing prices are higher in the clean-air city.

2. Ultimately, the person who owns the land in the good-weather city receives the payment. Look at it this way: People have a higher demand for houses in good-weather cities than they do for houses in bad-weather cities. As a result, house builders receive higher prices for houses built and sold in good-weather cities. Because of the higher house prices, builders have a higher demand for land in good-weather cities. In the end, higher demand for land translates into higher land prices or land rents for landowners.

CHAPTER 5, PAGE 111

1. Suppose University X gives a full scholarship to every one of its football players (all of whom are superathletes). In addition, suppose that the full scholarship (translated into wages) is far below the equilibrium wage of each of the football players. (Think of it this way: Each football player gets a wage, or full scholarship, of $10,000 a year, when his equilibrium wage is $40,000 a year.) Paying lower than the equilibrium wage will end up transferring dollars and other benefits from the football players to the university, to the new field house and track, and perhaps to you if you use the track for exercise.

2. If paying student athletes (a wage above the full scholarship) lowers consumers' demand for college athletics, then the equilibrium wage for college athletes is not as high as shown in Exhibit 9.

CHAPTER 5, PAGE 112

1. Answers will vary. Students sometimes say that it is "fairer" if everyone is charged the same price. Is it unfair then that moviegoers pay less if they go to the 2 p.m. movie than if they go to the 8 p.m. movie?

2. We learned about price ceilings in the previous chapter. Specifically, we learned that a price ceiling creates a shortage. In the application dealing with the 10:00 a.m. class, the university charged a below-equilibrium price for the 10:00 a.m. class, leading to a shortage of such classes.

CHAPTER 5, PAGE 113

1. Price will fall.
2. Quantity will rise.

Chapter 6

CHAPTER 6, PAGE 123

1. The CPI is calculated as follows: (1) Define a market basket; (2) determine how much it would cost to purchase the market basket in the current year and in the base year; (3) divide the dollar cost of purchasing the market basket in the current year by the dollar cost of purchasing the market basket in the base year; (4) multiply the quotient by 100. For a review of this process, see Exhibit 1.

2. It is a year that is used for comparison purposes with other years.

3. Annual nominal income has risen by 13.85 percent , and prices have risen by 4.94 percent. We conclude that because nominal income has risen more than prices, real income has increased. Alternatively, you can look at it this way: Real income in year 1 is $31,337, and real income in year 2 is $33,996.

CHAPTER 6, PAGE 129

1. The frictionally unemployed person has readily transferable skills, and the structurally unemployed person does not.

2. It implies that the (actual, measured) unemployment rate in the economy is greater than the natural unemployment rate. For example, if the unemployment rate is 8 percent and the natural unemployment rate is 6 percent, the cyclical unemployment rate is 2 percent.

Chapter 7

CHAPTER 7, PAGE 136

1. GDP is a measure of production in a country. When stocks are purchased and sold, no production occurs. A stock purchase and sale simply represent the trading of existing assets. Specifically, if person A owns 100 shares of stock X and then sells the shares to person B, all that has happened is that person B owns something that person A once owned. No more goods and services have been produced.

2. No. GDP doesn't account for all productive activity (e.g., it omits the production of nonmarket goods and services). A GDP of $0 doesn't necessarily mean that there was no production in the country.

CHAPTER 7, PAGE 139

1. In the expenditure approach, GDP is computed by finding the sum of consumption, investment, government purchases, and net exports. (Net exports are equal to exports minus imports.)

2. Yes. To illustrate, suppose consumption is $200, investment is $80, and government purchases are $70. The sum of these three spending components of GDP is $350. Now suppose exports are $0 but imports are $100, which means that net exports are −$100. Since $GDP = C + I + G + (EX − IM)$, GDP is $250.

3. No. Each individual would have $40,000 worth of goods and services only if the entire GDP were equally distributed across the country. There is no indication that this is the case. The $40,000 (per capita GDP) says that the "average" person in the country has access to $40,000 worth of goods and services, but in reality the average person may not exist. For example, if Smith earns $10,000 and Jones earns $20,000, then the average person earns $15,000. But neither Smith nor Jones earns $15,000; so neither is average.

CHAPTER 7, PAGE 149

1. We can't know for sure; we can only say what might have caused the rise in GDP. It could be (a) a rise in prices with no change in output, (b) a rise in output with no change in prices, (c) rises in both prices and output, or (d) a percentage increase in prices that is greater than the percentage decrease in output . . . or some other situation.

2. More output was produced in year 2 than in year 1.

3. Yes. Business cycles—ups and downs in Real GDP—don't prevent Real GDP from growing over time. Exhibit 6 shows Real GDP higher at the second peak than at the first, even though there is a business cycle between the peaks.

Chapter 8

CHAPTER 8, PAGE 166

1. In the real balance effect, a rise (fall) in the price level causes purchasing power to fall (rise), thereby decreasing (increasing) a person's monetary wealth. As people become less (more) wealthy, the quantity demanded of Real GDP falls (rises).

2. If the dollar appreciates, it takes more foreign currency to buy a dollar and fewer dollars to buy foreign currency. U.S. goods

(denominated in dollars) become more expensive for foreigners, and foreign goods become cheaper for Americans. In turn, foreigners buy fewer U.S. exports, and Americans buy more foreign imports. As exports fall and imports rise, net exports fall. If net exports fall, total expenditures fall, *ceteris paribus*. As total expenditures fall, the *AD* curve shifts to the left.

3. Total spending is the product of the money supply times velocity. Let the money supply be $400 and velocity 3. Then total spending is $1,200. Now suppose that the money supply rises to $500 but that velocity declines to 2. Total spending has fallen to $1,000 even though the money supply has increased. So, yes, the money supply can rise while total spending declines.

CHAPTER 8, PAGE 171

1. As wage rates decline, the cost per unit of production falls. In the short run (assuming prices are constant), profit per unit rises. Higher profit causes producers to produce more units of their goods and services. In short, the *SRAS* curve shifts to the right.

2. Last year, 10 workers produced 100 units of good X in 1 hour. This year, 10 workers produced 120 units of good X in 1 hour.

3. Workers initially misperceive the change in their real wage due to a change in the price level. For example, the nominal wage is $30, and the price level is 1.50; the real wage is therefore $20. Then the nominal wage falls to $25, and the price level falls to 1.10. The real wage is now $22.72. But suppose workers misperceive the decline in the price level and mistakenly believe it has fallen to 1.40. They will now perceive their real wage as $17.85 ($25 ÷ 1.40). In other words, they will misperceive their real wage as falling when it has actually increased. How will workers react if they believe their real wage has fallen? They will cut back on the quantity supplied of labor, reducing output (or Real GDP). This process is consistent with an upward-sloping *SRAS* curve: A decline in the price level leads to a reduction in output.

CHAPTER 8, PAGE 177

1. In long-run equilibrium, the economy is producing Natural Real GDP. In short-run equilibrium, the economy is not producing Natural Real GDP, although the quantity demanded of Real GDP equals the quantity supplied of Real GDP.

2. The diagram should show the price level in the economy at P_1 and Real GDP at Q_1, but the intersection of the *AD* curve and the *SRAS* curve is at some point other than (P_1, Q_1). In addition, the *LRAS* curve should not be at Q_1 or at the intersection of the *AD* and *SRAS* curves.

Chapter 9

CHAPTER 9, PAGE 185

1. Say's law states that supply creates its own demand. In a barter economy, Jones supplies good X so that she can use it to demand some other good (e.g., good Y). The act of supplying is motivated by the desire to demand. Supply and demand are opposite sides of the same coin.

2. No, total spending will not decrease. For classical economists, an increase in saving (reflected in a decrease in consumption) will lower the interest rate and stimulate investment spending. So one spending component (consumption) goes down, and

another (investment) goes up. Moreover, according to classical economists, the decrease in one spending component will be completely offset by an increase in another spending component so that overall spending does not change.

3. Prices and wages are flexible; they move up and down in response to market conditions.

CHAPTER 9, PAGE 190

1. A recessionary gap exists if the economy is producing a Real GDP level that is less than Natural Real GDP. An inflationary gap exists if the economy is producing a Real GDP level that is more than Natural Real GDP.

2. When the economy is in a recessionary gap, the labor market has a surplus. When the economy is in an inflationary gap, the labor market has a shortage.

3. The economy is somewhere above the institutional PPF and below the physical PPF.

CHAPTER 9, PAGE 199

1. In a recessionary gap, the existing unemployment rate is greater than the natural unemployment rate, implying that unemployment is relatively high. As wage contracts expire, business firms negotiate new ones that pay workers lower wage rates. As a result, the *SRAS* curve shifts rightward. At the same time, the price level begins to fall. The economy moves down the *AD* curve—eventually to the point where it intersects the *LRAS* curve. At this point, the economy is in long-run equilibrium.

2. In an inflationary gap, the existing unemployment rate is less than the natural unemployment rate, implying that unemployment is relatively low. As wage contracts expire, business firms negotiate contracts that pay workers higher wage rates. As a result, the *SRAS* curve shifts leftward. At the same time, the price level begins to rise. The economy moves up the *AD* curve—eventually to the point where it intersects the *LRAS* curve. At this point, the economy is in long-run equilibrium.

3. Any changes in aggregate demand affect—in the long run—only the price level, not the Real GDP level or the unemployment rate. Stated differently, changes in *AD* in an economy have no long-run effect on the Real GDP that a country produces or on its unemployment rate; changes in *AD* change only the price level in the long run.

Chapter 10

CHAPTER 10, PAGE 212

1. They mean that an economy may not self-regulate at Natural Real GDP (Q_N). Instead, an economy can get stuck in a recessionary gap.

2. To say that the economy is self-regulating is the same as saying that prices and wages are flexible and adjust quickly. They are just two ways of describing the same thing.

3. Aggregate demand may be too low mainly because Say's law may not hold in a money economy. This raises the question: Why *doesn't* Say's law hold in a money economy? Keynes argued that an increase in saving (which leads to a decline in demand) does not necessarily bring about an equal amount of additional investment (which would lead to an increase in

demand) because neither saving nor investment is exclusively affected by changes in the interest rate. See Exhibit 1 for the way Keynes might have used numbers to explain his position.

CHAPTER 10, PAGE 217

1. Autonomous consumption is one of the components of overall consumption. To illustrate, look at the consumption function: $C = C_0 + (MPC \times Y_d)$. The part of overall consumption (C) that is autonomous is C_0, and this part does not depend on disposable income. The part of consumption that does depend on disposable income (i.e., that changes as disposable income changes) is the ($MPC \times Y_d$) part. For example, assume the $MPC = 0.80$. If Y_d rises by $1,000, then consumption goes up by $800.

2. $\dfrac{1}{1 - 0.70} = \dfrac{1}{0.30} = 3.33$

3. The multiplier falls. For example, if $MPC = 0.20$, then the multiplier is 1.25, but if $MPC = 0.80$, then the multiplier is 5.

CHAPTER 10, PAGE 221

1. Keynes believed that the economy may not always self-regulate itself at Natural Real GDP. In other words, households and businesses (the private sector of the economy) are not always capable of generating enough aggregate demand in the economy so that the economy equilibrates at Natural Real GDP.

2. The increase in autonomous spending will lead to a greater increase in total spending and to a shift rightward in the AD curve. If the economy is operating in the horizontal section of the Keynesian AS curve, Real GDP will rise and there will be no change in prices.

3. Agree. The economist who believes the economy is inherently unstable sees a role for government, which is supposed to stabilize the economy at Natural Real GDP. The economist who believes the economy is self-regulating (capable of moving itself to Natural Real GDP) sees little if any role for government in the economy because the economy is already doing the job government would supposedly do.

CHAPTER 10, PAGE 227

1. When $TP > TE$, firms are producing and offering for sale more units of goods and services than consumers want to buy. As a result, business inventories rise above optimal levels. In reaction, firms cut back on their production of goods and services. This leads to a decline in Real GDP. Real GDP stops falling when $TP = TE$.

2. When $TE > TP$, consumers want to buy more than firms are producing and offering for sale. As a result, business inventories fall below optimal levels. In reaction, firms increase the production of goods and services. This leads to a rise in Real GDP. Real GDP stops rising when $TP = TE$.

Chapter 11

CHAPTER 11, PAGE 239

1. With a proportional income tax, the tax rate is constant as one's income rises. With a progressive income tax, the tax rate rises as one's income rises (up to some point). With a regressive income tax, the tax rate falls as one's income rises.

2. In 2007, the top 5 percent of income earners received 37.44 percent of all income and paid 60.63 percent of all income taxes.

3. Individual income tax, corporate income tax, and Social Security taxes.

4. The cyclical budget deficit is the part of the budget deficit that is the result of a downturn in economic activity.

CHAPTER 11, PAGE 245

1. If crowding out does not occur, expansionary fiscal policy is predicted to increase aggregate demand, and if the economy is in a recessionary gap, either reduce or eliminate the gap. However, if the crowding out is, say, complete, then expansionary fiscal policy will not meet its objective. For example, suppose government purchases rise by $100 million, and private spending decreases by $100 million. There is no net effect on aggregate demand.

2. Suppose the economy is currently in a recessionary gap in time period 1. Expansionary fiscal policy is needed to remove the economy out of its recessionary gap, but the fiscal policy lags (data lag, wait-and-see lag, etc.) may be so long that by the time the fiscal policy is implemented, the economy has moved itself out of the recessionary gap, making the expansionary fiscal policy not only unnecessary but potentially capable of moving the economy into an inflationary gap. Exhibit 5 depicts the process.

3. The federal government spends more on a particular program. As a result, the budget deficit grows, and the federal government increases its demand for loanable funds (or credit) to finance the larger deficit. Because of the heightened demand for loanable funds, the interest rate rises; and in response to the higher interest rate, business firms cut back on investment. An increase in government spending thus has indirectly led to a decline in investment spending.

CHAPTER 11, PAGE 249

1. Suppose that a person's taxable income rises by $1,000 to $45,000 and that her taxes rise from $10,000 to $10,390 as a result. Her marginal tax rate—the percentage of additional taxable income paid in taxes—is 39 percent. Her average tax rate—the percentage of her (total) income paid in taxes—is 23 percent.

2. Not necessarily. A rise in revenues depends on whether the percentage rise in tax rates is greater than or less than the percentage fall in the tax base. Here's a simple example: Suppose the average tax rate is 10 percent and the tax base is $100. Tax revenues equal $10. If the tax rate rises to 12 percent (a 20 percent rise) and the tax base falls to $90 (a 10 percent fall), tax revenues rise to $10.80. In other words, if the tax rate rises by a greater percentage than the tax base falls, tax revenues rise. Now suppose that the tax base falls to $70 (a 30 percent fall) instead of to $90. Now tax revenues are $8.40. In other words, if the tax rate rises by a smaller percentage than the tax base falls, tax revenues fall.

Chapter 12

CHAPTER 12, PAGE 258

1. Money evolved because individuals wanted to make trading easier (less time-consuming). This desire motivated individuals to accept the good (in a barter economy) that had greater acceptability than all other goods. In time, the effect

snowballed, and finally the good that initially had greater acceptability became widely accepted for purposes of exchange. At this point, the good became money.

2. No. M1 will fall, but M2 will not rise; it will remain constant. To illustrate, suppose M1 = $400 and M2 = $600. If people remove $100 from checkable deposits, M1 will decline to $300. For purposes of illustration, think of M2 as equal to M1 + money market accounts. The M1 component of M2 falls by $100, but the money market accounts component rises by $100; so there is no net effect on M2. In conclusion, M1 falls and M2 remains constant.

3. In a barter (moneyless) economy, a double coincidence of wants will not occur for every transaction. When it does not occur, the cost of the transaction increases because more time must be spent to complete the trade. In a money economy, money is acceptable for every transaction; so a double coincidence of wants is not necessary. All buyers offer money for what they want to buy, and all sellers accept money for what they want to sell.

CHAPTER 12, PAGE 260

1. The bank's reserves remain constant. Since reserves equal bank deposits at the Fed plus vault cash, removing $5 million from bank deposits at the Fed and adding the $5 million to vault cash keeps the total dollar amount of reserves constant.

2. Required reserves = r × Checkable deposits, where r = required reserve ratio. If checkable deposits equal $87 million and required reserves equal 6 million, then r equals the required reserves divided by checkable deposits: $6 million ÷ $87 million = a required reserve ratio of 6.89.

3. Reserves = Required reserves + Excess reserves. If reserves are $6 million and excess reserves are $4 million, then required reserves are $2 million. Required reserves = r × Checkable deposits, where r = required reserve ratio. If required reserves are $2 million and r = 8 percent, then checkable deposits must equal $25 million; 8 percent of $25 million is $2 million.

CHAPTER 12, PAGE 265

1. It is a moral hazard problem. A moral hazard problem exists when one party to a transaction changes his or her behavior in a way that is hidden from and costly to the other party. By promising to pay Samantha's expenses over $1,000, Jack provides Samantha with an incentive to push her expenses beyond $1,000, especially if she thinks her expenses will be close to $1,000. Simply put, Samantha has an incentive to act in a way that is hidden from and potentially costly to Jack. How might Jack lessen the moral hazard problem? Perhaps he could promise to pay a certain percentage of each dollar of Samantha's expenses over $1,000 instead of promising to pay every dollar of them.

2. A bank's capital or net worth is equal to the difference between its assets and liabilities. As bank A's assets decline in value (because some loans are not being repaid), the difference between its assets and liabilities diminishes; so its bank capital diminishes. If assets fall below liabilities, the bank will end up with negative bank capital or net worth.

3. Financial intermediaries essentially bring lenders and borrowers together. For example, Smith wants to lend $100 and Jones wants to borrow $100, but neither Smith nor Jones is in contact with the other. Instead of dealing with each other directly, both Smith and Jones go to a bank. Smith deposits $100 into the bank, and then the bank lends some or all of the $100 to Jones.

Chapter 13
CHAPTER 13, PAGE 274

1. Federal Reserve Bank of New York.

2. To control the money supply.

3. It means the Fed stands ready to lend funds to banks that are suffering cash management, or liquidity, problems.

CHAPTER 13, PAGE 281

1. a. Money supply falls.

   b. Money supply rises.

   c. Money supply falls.

2. The federal funds rate is the interest rate one bank charges another bank for a loan. The discount rate is the interest rate the Fed charges a bank for a loan.

3. Reserves in bank A rise; reserves in the banking system remain the same (bank B loses the reserves that bank A borrowed).

4. Reserves in bank A rise; reserves in the banking system rise because there is no offset in reserves for any other bank.

Chapter 14
CHAPTER 14, PAGE 295

1. If $M × V$ increases, total expenditures increase. In other words, people spend more. For example, instead of spending $3 billion on goods and services, they spend $4 billion. But more spending (greater total expenditures) means that there must be greater total sales. $P × Q$ represents this total dollar value of sales.

2. The equation of exchange is a truism: MV necessarily equals PQ. This is similar to saying that $2 + 2$ necessarily equals 4. It cannot be otherwise. The simple quantity theory of money, which is built on the equation of exchange, can be tested against real-world events. The simple quantity theory of money assumes that both velocity and Real GDP are constant and then, based on these assumptions, predicts that changes in the money supply will be strictly proportional to changes in the price level. This prediction can be measured against real-world data. So the simple quantity theory of money may offer insights into how the economy works. The equation of exchange does not do this.

3. a. The AD curve shifts rightward.

   b. The AD curve shifts leftward.

   c. The AD curve shifts rightward.

   d. The AD curve shifts leftward.

CHAPTER 14, PAGE 298

1. a. As velocity rises, the AD curve shifts to the right. In the short run, P rises and Q rises. In the long run, Q will return to its original level, and P will be higher than it was in the short run.

b. As velocity falls, the *AD* curve shifts to the left. In the short run, *P* falls and *Q* falls. In the long run, *Q* will return to its original level, and *P* will be lower than it was in the short run.

c. As the money supply rises, the *AD* curve shifts to the right. In the short run, *P* rises and *Q* rises. In the long run, *Q* will return to its original level, and *P* will be higher than it was in the short run.

d. As the money supply falls, the *AD* curve shifts to the left. In the short run, *P* falls and *Q* falls. In the long run, *Q* will return to its original level, and *P* will be lower than it was in the short run.

2. Yes, a change in velocity can offset a change in the money supply (on aggregate demand). Suppose that the money supply rises and velocity falls. A rise in the money supply shifts the *AD* curve to the right, and a fall in velocity shifts the *AD* curve to the left. If the strength of each change is the same, *AD* does not change.

CHAPTER 14, PAGE 304

1. This question cannot be answered based on the information given. We know only that three prices have gone up; we don't know if other prices (in the economy) have gone up, if other prices have gone down, or if some have gone up and others have gone down. To determine whether inflation has occurred, we have to know what has happened to the price level, not simply to three prices.

2. No. For continued inflation (continued increases in the price level) to be the result of continued decreases in *SRAS,* workers would have to continually ask for and receive higher wages while output was dropping and the unemployment rate rising. This combination of circumstances is not likely.

3. Continued inflation.

CHAPTER 14, PAGE 310

1. 3 percent.

2. Yes, it is possible. This would occur if the expectations effect immediately set in and outweighed the liquidity effect.

3. Certainly, the Fed directly affects the supply of loanable funds and the interest rate through an open market operation. But it works as a catalyst to indirectly affect the loanable funds market and the interest rate via the changes in Real GDP, the price level, and the expected inflation rate. We can say this: The Fed directly affects the interest rate via the liquidity effect, and it indirectly affects the interest rate via the income, price-level, and expectations effects.

Chapter 15

CHAPTER 15, PAGE 320

1. Smith buys a bond for a face value of $10,000 that promises to pay a 10 percent interest rate each year for 10 years. In one year, though, bonds are offered for a face value of $10,000 that pay an 11 percent interest rate each year for 10 years. If Smith wants to sell his bond, he won't be able to sell it for $10,000. No one today will pay $10,000 for a bond that pays a 10 percent interest rate when a new $10,000 bond pays an 11 percent interest rate. Smith will have to lower the price of his bond if he wants to sell it. Thus, as interest rates rise, the bond prices of old or existing bonds decrease.

2. We disagree for two reasons. First, if the money market is in the liquidity trap, a rise in the money supply will not affect interest rates and therefore will not affect investment or the goods and services market. Second, even if the money market is not in the liquidity trap, a rise in the money supply affects the goods and services market not directly but indirectly: The rise in the money supply lowers the interest rate, causing investment to rise (assuming investment is not interest insensitive). As investment rises, the *AD* curve shifts rightward, affecting the goods and services market. In the Keynesian transmission mechanism, an important intermediate market lies between the money market and the goods and services market. Thus, the money market can affect the goods and services market only indirectly.

3. A rise in the money supply brings about an excess supply of money in the money market that flows to the goods and services market, stimulating aggregate demand.

CHAPTER 15, PAGE 325

1. Keynesians believe that prices and wages are inflexible downward but not upward. They believe it is more likely that natural forces will move an economy out of an inflationary gap than out of a recessionary gap.

2. Suppose the economy is regulating itself out of a recessionary gap, but Fed officials don't know it. Thinking that the economy is stuck in a recessionary gap, the Fed increases the money supply. When the money supply is felt in the goods and services market, the *AD* curve intersects the *SRAS* curve (which has been moving rightward, unbeknownst to officials) at a point that represents an inflationary gap. In other words, the Fed has moved the economy from a recessionary gap to an inflationary gap instead of from a recessionary gap to long-run equilibrium at the Natural Real GDP level.

3. It makes it stronger, *ceteris paribus.* If the economy can't get itself out of a recessionary gap, then the case is stronger that the Fed should. However, expansionary monetary policy may still not work ideally; the correct implementation of the policy may meet with problems.

CHAPTER 15, PAGE 329

1. This is an open-ended question whose answer depends on many factors. First, what does the rule specify? Not all rules are alike. Second, the answer depends on the stability and predictability of velocity. For example, suppose the rule specifies that each year the money supply will rise by the average annual growth rate in Real GDP. If velocity is constant, this will produce price stability. But if velocity is extremely volatile, changes in velocity might offset changes in the money supply, leading to deflation instead of price stability. For example, suppose Real GDP rises by 3 percent and the money supply increases by 3 percent, but velocity decreases by 3 percent. The change in velocity offsets the change in the money supply, leaving a net effect of a 3 percent rise in Real GDP. This, then, would lead to a 3 percent decline in the price level.

2. Here is the Taylor rule specification: Federal funds rate target = 1.5 (4 percent) + 0.5 (5 percent) + 1 = 9.5 percent.

Chapter 16

CHAPTER 16, PAGE 341

1. A given Phillips curve identifies different combinations of inflation and unemployment; for example, 4 percent inflation with 5 percent unemployment and 2 percent inflation with 7 percent unemployment. For these combinations of inflation and unemployment to be permanent, there must be only one (downward-sloping) Phillips curve that never changes.

2. Sometimes there is and sometimes there isn't. Look at Exhibit 3. Unemployment is higher and inflation is lower in 1964 than in 1965; so there is a tradeoff between these two years. But both unemployment and inflation are higher in 1980 than in 1979; between these two years, there is no tradeoff between inflation and unemployment.

3. Workers are fooled into thinking that the inflation rate is lower than it is. In other words, they underestimate the inflation rate and therefore overestimate the purchasing power of their wages.

CHAPTER 16, PAGE 351

1. No. PIP says that, under certain conditions, neither expansionary fiscal policy nor expansionary monetary policy will be able to increase Real GDP and lower the unemployment rate in the short run. The conditions are that the policy change is anticipated correctly, individuals form their expectations rationally, and wages and prices are flexible.

2. None. Given an unanticipated increase in aggregate demand, the economy moves from point 1 to 2 (in Exhibit 10) in the short run and then to point 3. This occurs whether people are holding rational or adaptive expectations.

3. In the short run, the price level rises and Real GDP declines. In the long run, the price level rises and Real GDP is constant.

CHAPTER 16, PAGE 353

1. Both. The relevant question is whether the decline in the money supply was caused by a change on the supply side of the economy. If the answer is no, then the decline in the money supply is consistent with a demand-induced business cycle. If the answer is yes, then it is consistent with a supply-induced (real) business cycle.

2. New Keynesians believe that prices and wages are somewhat inflexible; new classical economists believe that prices and wages are flexible.

Chapter 17

CHAPTER 17, PAGE 371

1. This is shown in Exhibit 4. A decline in taxes shifts the labor supply curve to the right, which increases the equilibrium level of labor in the labor market. More labor generates more output (Real GDP), as shown in Exhibit 4(b). And more Real GDP is consistent with the *LRAS* curve having shifted to the right.

2. Physical capital consists of the produced goods that are used as inputs for further production, such as factories, machinery, tools, computers, and buildings. Human capital refers to the knowledge and skills individuals acquire through education, training, and experience.

3. In neoclassical growth theory, technology was, in a sense, "just there." Technological advances just happened, but how these advances happened was not fully understood. Technology was something that was exogenous—outside the economic system and outside of our control. In new growth theory, technology is said to be endogenous. It can be increased or decreased by the amount of resources devoted to it. Also, technology is viewed as being related to ideas.

4. Labor is the movement factor, and both capital and the technology coefficient are shift factors.

Chapter 18

CHAPTER 18, PAGE 378

1. If a bank has assets of $100 and liabilities of $80, it has a net worth or capital of $20. If its assets decline in value from $100 to $90, the bank's net worth falls from $20 to $10, but the bank is still solvent. In other words, the bank's net worth or capital stood between the bank and insolvency. The bigger the net worth or capital is, the bigger the buffer will be between declining asset values and insolvency. This bank can withstand a $20 decline in assets before becoming insolvent. A bank with a bigger net worth or capital could withstand a greater decline in assets before becoming insolvent.

2. If a bank has assets of $100 and liabilities of $80, it has a net worth or capital of $20. If the bank's assets decline in value by $30, the bank now has a negative net worth or capital of −$10. As a result, the bank may go out of business or pull back on its lending activities. Either way, there is less lending activity.

3. A financial crisis occurs when financial firms and markets have problems that make it difficult for people to obtain loans from banks and other financial institutions.

CHAPTER 18, PAGE 383

1. The global-savings-glut explanation is that in some countries saving was greater than investment; so the excess savings flowed into the United States and lowered interest rates (including mortgage interest rates). The low mortgage rates fueled house buying, which pushed up house prices. The Fed-low-interest-rate explanation is that the Fed kept the federal funds rate low, which kept mortgage interest rates low. The low mortgage interest rates fueled house buying, which pushed up house prices.

2. Taylor concludes that when we compare actual Fed monetary policy with the Taylor rule monetary policy, monetary policy was "too expansionary" during the early 2000s. John Taylor believes that this deviation from the rule brought about the "too low" interest rates that led to rising house prices in the United States. One piece of evidence in his favor is that there is a strong correlation between a housing boom in different countries (where housing boom is defined in terms of housing investment as a percentage of GDP) and deviations from the Taylor rule. For example, within OECD countries, the countries whose monetary policies deviated most from the Taylor Rule had bigger housing booms than those whose monetary policies deviated less.

CHAPTER 18, PAGE 391

1. Suppose a bank has $100 in assets and $97 in liabilities. The bank therefore has $3 in capital. Its leverage ratio rises to 100 to 3 or 331/3 to 1. If the assets of the bank decline by 4 percent to $96, the bank is now insolvent with negative capital of −$1. Contrast this with a bank that has $100 in assets and $90 in assets. The bank has $10 in capital, and its leverage ratio is 10 to 1. If the assets of the bank decline by 4 percent to $96, the bank remains solvent with capital of $6. The lesson: The greater the leverage ratio is, the more likely it is that a decline in asset values will result in insolvency.

2. We agree. Suppose the assets held by banks begin to decline in value, and, as a result, the banks end up lending less. Reduced bank lending reduces economic activity, resulting in less production, a decline in sales, and rising unemployment in the real sector. Because of these problems, some people in the real sector, who earlier took out loans from banks, are unable to repay their loans, thus exacerbating the problems that already exist in the financial sector.

3. Regulatory capital arbitrage is a means of changing the composition of assets in such a way as to lower the overall amount of capital a financial institution holds for a given level of assets.

Chapter 19

CHAPTER 19, PAGE 406

1. Economist A believes that the percentage change in the tax rate will be smaller than the percentage change in the tax base. Economist B believes the percentage change in the tax rate will be larger than the percentage change in the tax base.

2. When government spends $1, the entire $1 enters the spending stream, but when government cuts taxes by $1, individuals spend some of the dollar they now get to keep and save some of it. For example, they might spend 60¢ of the dollar and save 40¢.

3. Agree. At any given point in time, government has a specific size and scope. If economist A believes the optimal size and scope of government is greater than the current size and scope, then she is more likely to recommend increased government purchases over tax cuts if she deems an expansionary fiscal policy measure is needed to sti mulate the economy (holding all other things equal, such as the size of the government spending multiplier and the tax multiplier, etc.). If economist B believes the optimal size and scope of government is less than the current scope, then he is more likely to recommend tax cuts over increased government purchases if he deems an expansionary fiscal policy measure is needed to stimulate the economy.

Chapter 20

CHAPTER 20, PAGE 418

1. $E_d = 1.44$

2. If there is a change in price, the quantity demanded will change (in the opposite direction) by 0.39 times the percentage change in price. For example, if price rises 10 percent, then the quantity demanded will fall 3.9 percent. If price rises 20 percent, then the quantity demanded will fall 7.8 percent.

3. a. Total revenue falls.
   b. Total revenue falls.
   c. Total revenue remains constant.
   d. Total revenue rises.
   e. Total revenue rises.

4. Alexi is implicitly assuming that demand is inelastic. If, however, she is wrong and demand is elastic, then a rise in price will actually lower total revenue.

CHAPTER 20, PAGE 421

1. No. Moving from 7 to 9 substitutes doesn't necessarily change demand from being inelastic to elastic. It simply leads to a rise in price elasticity of demand, *ceteris paribus*. For example, if price elasticity of demand is 0.45 when good X has 7 substitutes, it will be higher when there are 9 substitutes, *ceteris paribus*. Higher could be 0.67. If this is the case, demand is still inelastic (but less so than before).

2. a. Dell computers
   b. Heinz ketchup
   c. Perrier water

   In all three cases, the good with the higher price elasticity of demand is the more specific of the two goods; therefore, it has more substitutes.

CHAPTER 20, PAGE 432

1. An income elasticity of demand of 1.33 means that the good (in question) is a normal good and that it is income elastic; that is, as income rises, the quantity demanded rises by a greater percentage. In this case, quantity demanded rises by 1.33 times the percentage change in income. If income rises by 10 percent, the quantity demanded of the good will rise by 13.3 percent.

2. A change in price does not change quantity supplied.

3. Tax revenue is equal to the tax times the quantity sold. If demand is inelastic, there will be a smaller cutback in quantity sold due to the higher price brought about by the tax.

4. Under the condition that the demand for computers is perfectly inelastic or that the supply of computers is perfectly elastic.

Chapter 21

CHAPTER 21, PAGE 441

1. The paradox is that water, which is essential to life, is cheap, and diamonds, which are not essential to life, are expensive. The solution to the paradox depends on knowing the difference between total and marginal utility and the law of diminishing marginal utility. By saying that water is essential to life and diamonds are not essential to life, we signify that water gives us high total utility relative to diamonds. But then someone asks, "Well, if water gives us greater total utility than diamonds do, why isn't the price of water greater than the price of diamonds?" The answer is, "Price isn't a reflection of total utility; it is a reflection of marginal utility. The marginal utility of water is less than that of diamonds." This answer raises another question, "How can the total utility of water be

greater than that of diamonds, but the marginal utility of water be less than that of diamonds?" The answer is based on the fact that water is plentiful and diamonds are not and on the law of diminishing marginal utility. There is so much more water relative to diamonds that the next (additional) unit of water gives us less utility (lower marginal utility) than the next unit of diamonds.

2. If total utility declines, marginal utility must be negative. For example, if total utility is 30 utils when Lydia consumes 3 apples and 25 utils when she consumes 4 apples, the fourth apple must have a marginal utility of −5 utils. Chapter 1 explains that something that takes utility away from us (or gives us disutility) is called a *bad*. For Lydia, the fourth apple is a bad, not a good.

3. The total and marginal utilities of a good are the same for the first unit of the good consumed. For example, before Tomas eats his first apple, he receives no utility or disutility from apples. Eating the first apple, he receives 15 utils. So the total utility (TU) for 1 apple is 15 utils, and the marginal utility (MU) for the first apple is 15 utils. Exhibit 1 shows that TU and MU are the same for the first unit of good X.

CHAPTER 21, PAGE 446

1. Alesandro is not in consumer equilibrium because the marginal utility per dollar of X is 16 utils and the marginal utility per dollar of Y is 13.14 utils. To be in equilibrium, a consumer has to receive the same marginal utility per dollar for each good consumed.

2, It means the marginal utility–price ratio for one of the goods is higher than the ratio for the other good.

CHAPTER 21, PAGE 450

1. Yes, Brandon is compartmentalizing. He is treating the $100 that comes from his grandmother differently from the $100 that comes from his father.

2. The endowment effect relates to individuals valuing X more highly when they possess it than when they don't but are thinking of acquiring it. Friedman argues that if we were to go back in time to a hunter-gatherer society when there were no well-established property rights (no rules as to what is mine and thine), we would find individuals who would fight hard to keep what they possessed but would not fight as hard to acquire what they did not possess. These individuals would have a higher probability of surviving than those who would fight hard in both cases. Thus, those who would fight hard only to keep what they possessed would have a higher probability of reproductive success. The characteristic of holding on to what you have has been passed down from generation to generation, and, although it may not be as important today as it was in a hunter-gatherer society, it still influences behavior.

Chapter 22

CHAPTER 22, PAGE 467

1. No. Individuals will form teams or firms only when the sum of what they can produce as a team (or firm) is greater than the sum of what they can produce working alone.

2. The person earning the low salary has lower implicit costs and so is more likely to start a business. She gives up less to start a business.

3. Accounting profit is larger. Only explicit costs are subtracted from total revenue in computing accounting profit, but both explicit and implicit costs are subtracted from total revenue in computing economic profit. If implicit costs are zero, then accounting profit and economic profit are the same. Economic profit is never greater than accounting profit.

4. A business owner can be earning a profit but not covering costs when he is earning (positive) accounting profit but his total revenue does not cover the sum of his explicit and implicit costs. For example, suppose Brad earns total revenue of $100,000 and has explicit costs of $40,000 and implicit costs of $70,000. His accounting profit is $60,000, but his total revenue of $100,000 is not large enough to cover the sum of his explicit and implicit costs ($110,000). Brad's economic profit is a negative $10,000. In other words, although Brad earns an accounting profit, he takes an economic loss.

CHAPTER 22, PAGE 474

1. No. The short run and the long run are not lengths of time. The short run is that period of time when some inputs are fixed and therefore the firm has fixed costs. The long run is any period of time when no inputs are fixed (i.e., all inputs are variable) and thus all costs are variable costs. The short run can be, say, six months, and the long run can be a much shorter period of time. In other words, the time period when there are no fixed inputs can be shorter than the time period when there are fixed inputs.

2. The law of diminishing marginal returns holds only when we add more of one input to a given (fixed) quantity of another input. The statement does not identify one input as fixed (it says that both increase), and so the law of diminishing marginal returns is not relevant in this situation.

3. When MC is declining, MPP is rising; when MC is constant, MPP is constant; and when MC is rising, MPP is falling.

CHAPTER 22, PAGE 485

1. $ATC = TC/Q$ and $ATC = AFC + AVC$.

2. Yes. Suppose a business incurs a cost of $10 to make a product. Before it can sell the product, though, the demand for it falls and moves the market price from $15 to $6. Does the owner of the business say, "I can't sell the product for $6 because I'd be taking a loss"? If she does, she chooses to let a sunk cost affect her current decision. Instead, she should ask herself, "Do I think the market price of the product will rise or fall?" If she thinks it will fall, she should sell the product today for $6.

3. Unit costs are another name for average total costs (ATC); so the question is what happens to ATC as MC rises? You might be inclined to say that as MC rises, so does ATC, but this is not necessarily so [see region 1 in Exhibit 6(b)]. What matters is whether MC is greater than ATC. If it is, then ATC will rise. If it is not, then ATC will decline. This is a trick question of sorts. There is a tendency to misinterpret the average-marginal rule and to believe that as marginal cost rises, average total cost rises and that as marginal cost falls, average total cost falls. But

the average-marginal rule actually says that when *MC* is above *ATC*, *ATC* rises, and when *MC* is below *ATC*, *ATC* falls.

4 Yes. As marginal physical product (*MPP*) rises, marginal cost (*MC*) falls. If *MC* falls enough to move below unit cost (which is the same as average total cost), then unit cost declines. Similarly, as *MPP* falls, *MC* rises. If *MC* rises enough to move above unit cost, then unit cost rises.

CHAPTER 22, PAGE 489

1. It currently takes 10 units of X and 10 units of Y to produce 50 units of good Z. Let both X and Y double to 20 units each. As a result, the output of Z more than doubles—say, to 150 units. When inputs are increased by some percentage and output increases by a greater percentage, then economies of scale are said to exist. When economies of scale exist, unit costs fall, and another name for unit costs is average total costs.

2. The *LRATC* curve would be horizontal. When there are constant returns to scale, output doubles if inputs double. If this happens, unit costs stay constant. In other words, they don't rise and they don't fall; so the *LRATC* curve is horizontal.

3. Unit costs must have been lower when it produced 200 units than when it produced 100 units. That is, there were economies of scale between 100 units and 200 units. To explain further, profit per unit is the difference between price per unit and cost per unit (or unit costs): Profit per unit = Price per unit − Cost per unit. Suppose the unit cost is $3 when the price is $4—giving a profit per unit of $1. Next, there are economies of scale as the firm raises output from 100 units to 200 units. Unit costs must fall—let's say to $2 per unit. If price is $3, then there is still a $1 per-unit profit.

Chapter 23

CHAPTER 23, PAGE 498

1. It means the firm cannot change the price of the product it sells by its actions. For example, if firm A cuts back on the supply of what it produces and the price of its product does not change, then firm A cannot control the price of the product it sells. In other words, if price is independent of a firm's actions, that firm does not have any control over price.

2. The easy, and incomplete, answer is that a perfectly competitive firm is a price taker because it is in a market where it cannot control the price of the product it sells. But this simply leads to the question: Why not? The answer is that it is in a market where its supply is small relative to the total market supply, it sells a homogeneous good, and all buyers and sellers have all relevant information.

3. If a perfectly competitive firm tries to charge a price higher than the equilibrium price, all buyers will know this (assumption 3). These buyers will then simply buy from another firm that sells the same (homogeneous) product (assumption 2).

4. No. A market doesn't have to perfectly match all assumptions of the theory of perfect competition for it to be labeled a perfectly competitive market. What is important is whether it acts *as if* it is perfectly competitive. "If it walks like a duck and it quacks like a duck, it's a duck." If it acts like a perfectly competitive market, it's a perfectly competitive market.

CHAPTER 23, PAGE 506

1. No. Whether a firm earns profits depends on the relationship between price (*P*) and average total cost (*ATC*). If *P* > *ATC*, then the firm earns profits. To understand this, remember that profits exist when total revenue (*TR*) minus total cost (*TC*) is a positive number. Total revenue is simply price times quantity (*TR* = *P* × *Q*), and total cost is average total cost times quantity (*TC* = *ATC* × *Q*). Because quantity (*Q*) is common to both *TR* and *TC*, if *P* > *ATC*, then *TR* > *TC*, and the firm earns profits.

2. In the short run, whether a firm should shut down depends on the relationship between price and average variable cost (*AVC*), not between price and *ATC*. It depends on whether price is greater or less than average variable cost. If *P* > *AVC*, the firm should continue to produce; if *P* < *AVC*, it should shut down.

3. As long as *MR* > *MC*—for example, *MR* = $6 and *MC* = $4—the firm should produce and sell additional units of a good because this adds more to *TR* than it does to *TC*. It is adding $6 to *TR* and $4 to *TC*. Whenever you add more to *TR* than you do to *TC*, the gap between the two becomes larger.

4. We start with the upward sloping market supply curve and work backward. First, market supply curves are upward sloping because they are the "addition" of individual firms' supply curves, which are upward sloping. Second, individual firms' supply curves are upward sloping because they are the portion of their marginal cost curves above their average variable cost curves, and this portion of the *MC* curve is upward sloping. Third, marginal cost curves have upward sloping portions because of the law of diminishing marginal returns. In conclusion, market supply curves are upward sloping because of the law of diminishing marginal returns.

CHAPTER 23, PAGE 515

1. According to the theory of perfect competition, the profits will draw new firms into the market. As these new firms enter the market, the market supply curve will shift to the right. As a result of a larger supply, price will fall. As price declines, profit will decline until firms in the market are earning (only) normal (or zero economic) profit. When there is zero economic profit, firms no longer have an incentive to enter the market.

2. No. The market is only in long-run competitive equilibrium when firms have no incentive to (1) enter or exit the industry, (2) produce more or less output, and (3) change their plant size. If any of these conditions is not met, then the market is not in long-run equilibrium.

3. Initially, price will rise. Recall from Chapter 3 that when demand increases, *ceteris paribus,* price rises. In time, though, price will drop because new firms will enter the industry due to the positive economic profits generated by the higher price. How far the price drops depends on whether the firms are in a constant-cost, an increasing-cost, or a decreasing-cost industry. In a constant-cost industry, price will return to its original level; in an increasing-cost industry, price will return to a level above its original level; and in a decreasing-cost industry, price will return to a level below its original level.

4. Maybe initially, but probably not after certain adjustments are made. If firm A really has a genius on its payroll and, as a result, earns higher profits than firm B, then firm B might try

to hire the genius away from firm A by offering the genius a higher income. To keep the genius, firm A will have to match the offer. As a result, the costs of firm A will rise, and if nothing else changes, its profits will decline.

CHAPTER 23, PAGE 517

1. It depends on how many firms in the market witness higher costs. If it is only one, then the market supply curve is not likely to shift enough to bring about a higher price. If, however, many firms in the market witness higher costs, then the market supply curve will shift left, and price will rise.

2. No. Perfectly competitive firms that sell homogeneous products will not advertise individually, but the industry might advertise in the hope of pushing the market (industry) demand curve (for their product) to the right.

Chapter 24
CHAPTER 24, PAGE 524

1. Let's assume that any product a firm sells has some close substitutes. The question, however, is how close the substitute has to be before the theory of monopoly is not useful. For example, a "slightly close" substitute for a seller's product may not be close enough to matter. The theory of monopoly may still be useful in predicting a firm's behavior.

2. Economies of scale exist when a firm, say, doubles inputs and its output more than doubles, lowering its unit costs (average total costs) in the process. If economies of scale exist only when a firm produces a large quantity of output and one firm is already producing this output, then new firms (that start off producing less output) will have higher unit costs than those of the established firm. Some economists argue that this will make the new firms uncompetitive compared to the established firm. In other words, economies of scale will act as a barrier to entry, effectively preventing firms from entering the industry and competing with the established firm.

3. In a monopoly, there is a single seller of a good that has no close substitutes, and the barriers to entry are extremely high barriers. If a movie superstar has so much talent that the moviegoing public puts her in a class by herself, she might be considered a monopolist. Anyone can try to compete with her, but she may have such great talent (relative to everyone else) that no one will be able to effectively compete. Her immense talent acts as a barrier to entry in the sense that even if others try to compete with her, they won't be a close substitute for her.

CHAPTER 24, PAGE 531

1, The single-price monopolist has to lower price to sell an additional unit of its good (this is what a downward-sloping demand curve necessitates). As long as it has to lower price to sell an additional unit, its marginal revenue will be below its price. A demand curve plots price (P) and quantity (Q), and a marginal revenue curve plots marginal revenue (MR) and quantity (Q). Because $P > MR$ for a monopolist, its demand curve will lie above its marginal revenue curve.

2. No. Profit depends on whether price is greater than average total cost. A monopolist could produce the quantity of output at which $MR = MC$, charge the highest price per unit possible for the output, and still have its unit costs (ATC) greater than price. In this case, the monopolist incurs losses; it does not earn profits.

3. No. The last chapter explains that a firm is resource allocative efficient when it charges a price equal to its marginal cost ($P = MC$). The monopolist does not do this; it charges a price above marginal cost. Profit maximization ($MR = MC$) does not lead to resource allocative efficiency ($P = MC$) because for the monopolist, $P > MR$. This is not the case for the perfectly competitive firm, where $P = MR$.

4. A monopolist is searching for the highest price at which it can sell its product. In contrast, the perfectly competitive firm doesn't have to search; it simply takes the equilibrium price established in the market. For example, suppose Nancy is a wheat farmer. She gets up one morning and wants to know at what price she should sell her wheat. She simply turns on the radio, listens to the farm report, and finds out that the equilibrium price per bushel of wheat is, say, $5. Being a price taker, she knows she can't sell her wheat for a penny more than this ($5 is the highest price), and she won't want to sell her wheat for a penny less either. The monopoly firm doesn't know what the highest price is for the product it sells. It has to search for it; it has to experiment with different prices before it finds the "highest" price.

CHAPTER 24, PAGE 539

1. a. A monopoly firm produces too little output relative to a perfectly competitive firm; this causes the deadweight loss of monopoly.

   b. The profits of the monopoly are sometimes subject to rent-seeking behavior. Rent seeking, while rational for an individual firm, wastes society's resources. Society receives no benefit if one firm expends resources to take over the monopoly position of another firm. Resources that could have been used to produce goods (e.g., computers, software, shoes, houses, etc.) are instead used to transfer profits from one firm to another.

   c. A monopolist may not produce its products at the lowest possible cost. Again, failure to do so wastes society's resources.

2. An example helps to illustrate this concept. Suppose a perfectly competitive firm would produce 100 units of good X, but a monopoly firm would produce only 70 units, for a difference of 30 units. Buyers value these 30 units by more than it would cost the monopoly firm to produce them, yet the monopoly firm chooses not to produce the units. The net benefit (benefits to buyers minus costs to the monopolist) of producing these 30 units is said to be the deadweight loss of monopoly. It represents how much buyers lose because the monopolist chooses to produce less than the perfectly competitive firm.

3. If a seller is not a price searcher, then it is a price taker. A price taker can sell its product at only one price, the market equilibrium price.

Chapter 25
CHAPTER 25, PAGE 547

1. A monopolistic competitor is like a monopolist in that it faces a downward-sloping demand curve; it is a price searcher, $P > MR$; and it is not resource allocative efficient. It is like

a perfect competitor in that it sells to many buyers and competes with many sellers, and entry into and exit from the market are easy.

2. Essentially, they face downward sloping demand curves. Because the demand curve is downward sloping, it cannot be tangent to the lowest point on a U-shaped ATC curve (see Exhibit 3).

CHAPTER 25, PAGE 550

1. The incentive in both cases is the same: profit. Firms have an incentive to form a cartel to increase their profits. After the cartel is formed, however, each firm has an incentive to break the cartel to increase its profits even further (see Exhibit 5). If there is no cartel agreement, the firm is earning zero profits by producing q_1. After the cartel is formed, it earns $CP_C AB$ in profits by producing q_C. But it can earn even higher profits ($FP_C DE$) by cheating on the cartel and producing q_{CC}.

2. An oligopolistic firm is a price searcher. A price searcher faces a downward-sloping demand curve, which an oligopolistic firm faces. Also, an oligopolistic firm has some control over the price it charges, which is the hallmark of a price searcher.

Chapter 26

CHAPTER 26, PAGE 572

1. How a market is defined will help determine whether a firm is considered a monopoly. If a market is defined broadly, it will include more substitute goods, and so the firm is less likely to be considered a monopolist. If a market is defined narrowly, it will include fewer substitute goods, and so the firm is more likely to be considered a monopolist.

2. The four-firm concentration ratio is 20 percent; the Herfindahl index is 500. The formulas in Exhibit 1 show how each is computed.

3. The Herfindahl index provides information about the dispersion of firm size in an industry. For example, suppose the top four firms in an industry have 15 percent, 10 percent, 9 percent, and 8 percent market shares. The four-firm concentration ratio will be the same for an industry with 15 firms as it is for an industry with 150 firms. The Herfindahl index will be different in the two situations.

CHAPTER 26, PAGE 579

1. Average cost pricing is the same as profit regulation. The regulators state that the natural monopolist must charge a price equal to its average total costs ($P = ATC$). Under this pricing policy, there is no incentive for the natural monopolist to keep costs down. In fact, there may be an incentive to deliberately push costs up. Higher costs—in the form of higher salaries or more luxurious offices—simply mean higher prices to cover the higher costs.

2. No matter what the motive for initially regulating an industry, eventually, the regulating agency will be "captured" by the special interests (the firms) in the industry. In the end, the regulatory body will not so much regulate the industry as serve the interests of the firms in it.

3. According to the capture theory, the outcomes of the regulatory process will favor the regulated firms. According to the

public choice theory, the outcomes of the regulatory process will favor the regulators.

4. Sometimes, they favor regulation, and at other times, they do not. Economists make the point that regulation involves both costs and benefits, and whether the particular regulation in question is worthwhile depends on whether the costs are greater or less than the benefits.

Chapter 27

CHAPTER 27, PAGE 589

1. $MRP = MR \times MPP$. For a perfectly competitive firm, $MR = P$, so MR is $10. MPP in this case is 19 units. It follows that $MRP = 190.

2. There is no difference between MRP and VMP if the firm is perfectly competitive. In this situation, $P = MR$, and because $MRP = MR \times MPP$ and $VMP = P \times MPP$, the two are the same. If the firm is a price searcher—monopolist, monopolistic competitor, or oligopolist—$P > MR$; therefore, $VMP > MRP$.

3. A factor price taker can buy all it wants of a factor at the equilibrium price, and it will not cause factor price to rise. For example, if firm X is a factor price taker in the labor market, it can buy all the labor it wants at the equilibrium wage, and it will not cause this wage to rise.

4. It should buy the quantity at which MRP of labor equals MFC of labor.

CHAPTER 27, PAGE 600

1. The MRP curve is the firm's factor demand curve. $MRP = P \times MPP$ for a perfectly competitive firm; so if either the price of the product that labor produces rises or the MPP of labor rises (reflected in a shift in the MPP curve), the factor demand curve shifts rightward.

2. It means that for every 1 percent change in the wage rate, the quantity demanded of labor changes by 3 times this percentage. For example, if wage rates rise 10 percent, then the quantity demanded of labor falls 30 percent.

3. The short answer is because supply-and-demand conditions differ among markets. The question of why supply-and-demand conditions differ is answered in Exhibit 11.

4. We can't answer this question specifically without more information. We know that under four conditions, wage rates would not differ: (1) The demand for every type of labor is the same; (2) the jobs have no special nonpecuniary aspects; (3) all labor is ultimately homogeneous and can costlessly be trained for different types of employment; and (4) all labor is mobile at zero cost. For wage rates to differ, one or more of these conditions is not being met. For example, perhaps labor is not mobile at zero cost.

Chapter 28

CHAPTER 28, PAGE 612

1. The demand for union labor is lowered by a decline in (a) the demand for the product union labor produces, (b) the price of substitute factors, and (c) the marginal physical product of union labor.

2. A closed shop requires an employee to be a member of the union before being hired; a union shop does not. The union shop requires employees to join the union within a certain period of time after becoming employed.

3. The purpose of a strike is to prove to management that union members will not work for a wage rate that is lower than the rate specified by the union. In terms of Exhibit 3, it is to prove that union members will not work for less than W_2.

CHAPTER 28, PAGE 618

1. A monopsonist cannot buy additional units of a factor without increasing the price it pays for the factor. A factor price taker can.

2. The minimum wage can increase the number of people working under the following conditions: (1) The firm hiring the labor is a monopsonist, and (2) the minimum wage is above the wage it is already paying and below the wage that corresponds to the point where $MFC = MRP$. In Exhibit 4(c), suppose the firm is currently purchasing Q_1 labor and paying W_1. Then W_2 becomes the minimum wage the monopsonist can pay to workers. Now it hires Q_2 workers. Notice, however, that if the monopsonist had to pay a wage higher than the wage that equates MFC and MRP, it would employ fewer workers than Q_1.

3. If the higher wage rate reduces the number of people working in the unionized sector and the people who lose their jobs in the unionized sector move to the nonunionized sector, then the supply of labor will increase in the nonunionized sector and wage rates will fall. See Exhibit 6.

Chapter 29

CHAPTER 29, PAGE 625

1. Government can change the distribution of income through transfer payments and taxes. Look at this equation: Individual income = Labor income + Asset income + Transfer payments − Taxes. By increasing one person's taxes and increasing another person's transfer payments, government can change people's incomes.

2. The statement is true. For example, two people can have unequal incomes at any one point in time and still earn the same total incomes over time. For example, in year 1, Patrick earns $40,000 and Francine earns $20,000. In year 2, Francine earns $40,000 and Patrick earns $20,000. In each year, there is income inequality, but over the 2 years, Patrick and Francine earn the same income ($60,000).

3. No. Individual income = Labor income + Asset income + Transfer payments − Taxes. Smith's income could come entirely from labor income, and Jones's income could come entirely from asset income. The same dollar income does not necessitate the same source of income.

CHAPTER 29, PAGE 630

1. No. The income shares total 105 percent.

2. A Gini coefficient of 0 represents perfect income equality, and a Gini coefficient of 1 represents complete income inequality. So we are sure that country A has neither perfect income equality nor complete income inequality. Saying anything further is difficult. Usually, the Gini coefficient is used as a comparative measure. For example, if country A's Gini

coefficient is 0.45 and country B's is 0.60, we could say that country A has a more equal (less unequal) distribution of income than country B.

CHAPTER 29, PAGE 633

1. The simple fact that Jack earns more than Harry is not evidence of wage discrimination. We do not know whether wage discrimination exists. For example, we do not know whether Jack and Harry work the same job, how productive each is, and so on.

2. It could affect it negatively or positively. The probability of both higher and lower incomes is greater if a person assumes a lot of risk than if a person plays it safe. Suppose Nancy has decided she wants to be an actress, although her parents want her to be an accountant. The chances of her being successful in acting are small, but if she is successful, she will earn a much higher income than if she had been an accountant (a top actress earns more than a top accountant). Of course, if she isn't successful, she will earn less income as an actress than she would have as an accountant (the average actress earns less than the average accountant).

CHAPTER 29, PAGE 635

1. Whether poor people always exist depends on how we define poverty. If we define it in relative terms and we assume no absolute income equality, then some people must fall into, say, the lowest 10 percent of income earners. We could refer to these persons as poor. Remember, though, that these persons are relatively poor—they earn less than a large percentage of the income earners in the country—but we do not know anything about their absolute incomes. In a world of multi-million-dollar income earners, a person who earns $100,000 might be considered poor.

2. 13 percent

3. An African American or Hispanic female who is the head of a large family and who is young and has little education.

Chapter 30

CHAPTER 30, PAGE 645

1. Because there is a monetary incentive for them to be equal. Suppose the return on capital is 12 percent, and the price for loanable funds is 10 percent. In this case, a person could borrow loanable funds at 10 percent and invest in capital goods to earn the 12 percent return. In the meantime, though, the amount of capital increases and its return falls. If the interest rates are reversed and the return on capital is lower than the price for a loanable fund, no one will borrow to invest in capital goods. Over time, then, the stock of capital will diminish and its return will rise.

2. Because the real interest rate is the rate paid by borrowers and received by lenders. For example, a person who borrows funds at a 12 percent interest rate when the inflation rate is 4 percent will be paying only an 8 percent (real) interest rate to the lender. Stated differently, the lender has 8 percent, not 12 percent, more buying power by making the loan.

3. $907.03. The formula is $PV = \$1,000/(1 + 0.05)^2$.

4. No. The present value of $2,000 a year for 4 years at an 8 percent interest rate is $6,624.25. $[PV = \$2,000/(1 + 0.08)^1 + \$2,000/(1 + 0.08)^2 + \$2,000/(1 + 0.08)^3 + \$2,000/(1 + 0.08)^4]$. The present value is less than the cost of the capital good; so the purchase is not worthwhile.

CHAPTER 30, PAGE 650

1. Jones earns $2 million a year as a news anchor for KNBC. His next best alternative in the news industry is earning $1.9 million a year as a news anchor for KABC. If Jones were not working in the news industry, his next best alternative would be as a journalism professor earning $100,000 a year. Within the news industry, Jones earns $100,000 economic rent (the difference between $2 million and $1.9 million). Outside the news industry, Jones earns $1.9 million in economic rent (the difference between $2 million and $100,000).

2. It is $0.

3. When a firm competes for artificial rents, it expends resources to transfer economic rent from another firm to itself. In other words, resources are used to bring about a transfer. No additional goods and services are produced as a part of the process. But when a firm competes for real rents, resources are used to produce additional goods and services.

CHAPTER 30, PAGE 653

1. A probability cannot be assigned to uncertainty; a probability can be assigned to risk.

2. Many theories purport to explain profit. One theory states that profit exists because uncertainty exists: no uncertainty, no profit. Another states that profit exists because of arbitrage opportunities (the opportunities to buy low and sell high), to which some people are alert. Still another theory states that profit exists because some people (entrepreneurs) are capable of creating profit opportunities by devising a new product, production process, or marketing strategy.

3. Profit can be a signal, especially if it is earned in a competitive market. Specifically, profit signals that buyers value a good (as evidenced by the price they are willing and able to pay for the good) more than the factors that go into making the good.

Chapter 31

CHAPTER 31, PAGE 663

1. The market output does not reflect or adjust for either external costs (in the case of a negative externality) or external benefits (in the case of a positive externality). The socially optimal output does.

2. Certainly, if no costs are incurred by moving from the market output to the socially optimal output, the answer is yes. But this isn't likely to be the case. The economist considers whether the benefits of moving to the socially optimal output are greater than or less than the costs of moving to the socially optimal output. If the benefits are greater than the costs, then yes; if the benefits are less than the costs, then no.

CHAPTER 31, PAGE 667

1. Internalizing an externality means adjusting the private cost by the external cost. To illustrate, suppose someone's private cost is $10 and the external cost is $2. If the person internalizes the externality, the external cost becomes his cost, which is now $12.

2. Transaction costs are associated with the time and effort needed to search out, negotiate, and consummate an exchange. These costs are higher for buying a house than for buying a hamburger. It takes more time and effort to search out a house to buy, negotiate a price, and consummate the deal than it takes to search out and buy a hamburger.

3. Under certain conditions, no. Specifically, if transaction costs are zero or trivial, the property rights assignment that a court makes is irrelevant to the resource allocative outcome. Of course, if transaction costs are not zero or trivial, then the property rights assignment a court makes does matter.

4. Given a negative externality, there is a marginal external cost. The marginal external cost (MEC) plus the marginal private cost (MPC) equals the marginal social cost (MSC): $MSC = MPC + MEC$. If a corrective tax (t) is to adjust correctly for the marginal external cost associated with the negative externality, it must be equal to the marginal external cost—in other words, tax = MEC. With this condition fulfilled, $MPC + \text{tax} = MSC = MPC + MEC$.

CHAPTER 31, PAGE 669

1. All other things held constant, less pollution is preferable to more pollution. Zero pollution is the least amount of pollution possible; therefore, zero pollution is best. But in reality, all other things are not held constant. Sometimes, when we reduce pollution, we also eliminate some of the things we want. The economist wants to eliminate pollution as long as the benefits of eliminating pollution are greater than the costs. When the benefits equal the costs, the economist would stop eliminating pollution. If society has eliminated so much pollution that the costs of eliminating it are greater than the benefits, then society has gone too far. It has eliminated too much pollution. Some units of pollution are simply not worth eliminating.

2. Under market environmentalism, the entities that can eliminate pollution at the least cost are the ones that eliminate the pollution. This is not the case under standards, where both the low-cost and high-cost eliminators of pollution must reduce pollution.

3. The dollar price of the pollution permits is a cost for firm Z, but not a cost to society. As far as society is concerned, firm Z simply paid $660 to firms X and Y. Firm Z ended up with $660 less, and firms X and Y ended up with $660 more; the amounts offset. Only when resources are used in eliminating pollution is the dollar cost of those resources counted as a cost to society of eliminating pollution.

CHAPTER 31, PAGE 672

1. After a nonexcludable public good is produced, the individual or firm that produced it wouldn't be able to collect payment for it. When a nonexcludable public good is provided to one person, it is provided to everyone. Because an individual can consume the good without paying for it, he is likely to take a free ride. Another way of answering this question is simply to say, "The market fails to produce nonexcludable public goods because of the free-rider problem."

2. (a) A composition notebook is a private good. It is rivalrous in consumption; if one person is using it, someone else cannot. (b) A Shakespearean play performed in a summer theater is an excludable public good. It is nonrivalrous in consumption (everyone in the theater can see the play) but excludable (a person must pay to get into the theater). (c) An apple is a private good. It is rivalrous in consumption; if one person eats it, someone else cannot. (d) A telephone in service is a private good. One person using the phone (e.g., in your house) prevents someone else from using it. (e) Sunshine is a nonexcludable public good. It is nonrivalrous in consumption (one person's consumption of it doesn't reduce its consumption by others) and nonexcludable (people cannot be excluded from consuming the sunshine).

3. A concert is an example. If one person consumes the concert, this does not take away from others consuming it to the same degree. However, people can be excluded from consuming it.

CHAPTER 31, PAGE 677

1. The sellers of a fictional product X know that the good could, under certain conditions, cause health problems, but they do not release this information to the buyers. Consequently, the demand for good X is likely to be greater than it would be if there were symmetric information. The quantity consumed of good X is likely to be higher when there is asymmetric information than when there is symmetric information.

2. In the used car market discussed in the text, if there are two types of used cars— good used cars and lemons—and asymmetric information, the market price for a used car may understate the value of a good used car and overstate the value of a lemon. This will induce sellers of lemons to enter the market and sellers of good cars to leave it. (The owners of good used cars will not want to sell their cars for less than their cars are worth.) In theory, the used car market may eventually consist of nothing but lemons. In other words, a used car market for good cars no longer exists.

3. A college professor tells her students that she does not believe in giving grades of D or F. As a result, her students do not take as many "precautionary" measures to guard against receiving low grades. Does your example have the characteristic of this example—namely, one person's assurance affecting another person's incentive?

Chapter 32
CHAPTER 32, PAGE 689

1. No. The model doesn't say every politician has to do these things; it simply predicts that politicians who do these things have an increased chance of winning the election in a two-person race.

2. Voters may want more information from politicians, but supplying that information is not always in the best interests of political candidates. When they speak in specific terms, politicians are often labeled as being at one end or the other of the political spectrum. But politicians don't win elections by being in the right wing or left wing; they win elections by being in the middle.

3. Yes. In the cost equation of voting, we included (1) the cost of driving to the polls, (2) the cost of standing in line, and (3) the cost of filling out the ballot. Bad weather (heavy rain, snow, ice) would likely raise the cost of driving to the polls and standing in line, therefore raising the cost of voting. The higher the cost of voting is, the less likely it is that people will vote, *ceteris paribus*.

CHAPTER 32, PAGE 691

1. 2 units

2. In Example 2 with equal taxes, 1 unit received a simple majority of the votes. Person C was made worse off because his *MPB* for the first unit of good Y was $100, but he ended up paying a tax of $120 and was worse off by $20.

CHAPTER 32, PAGE 697

1. Both farmers and consumers are affected by federal agricultural policy, but not in the same way and not to the same degree. Federal agricultural policy directly affects farmers' incomes, usually by a large amount. It indirectly affects consumers' costs, but not as much as it affects farmers' incomes. Simply put, farmers have more at stake than consumers when it comes to federal agricultural policy. People tend to be better informed about matters that mean more to them.

2. The legislation is more likely to pass when group A includes 10 million persons because the wider the dispersal of the costs of the legislation, the greater the likelihood is of passage. When costs are widely dispersed, the cost to any one individual is so small that she or he is unlikely to lobby against the legislation.

3. Examples include teachers saying that more money for education will help the country compete in the global marketplace; domestic car manufacturers saying that tariffs on foreign imports will save American jobs and U.S. manufacturing; farmers saying that subsidies to farmers will preserve the "American" farm and a way of life that Americans cherish. Whether any of these groups is right or wrong is not the point. The point is that special interest groups are likely to advance their arguments (good or bad) with public interest talk.

4. Rent seeking is socially wasteful because the resources that are used to seek rent could instead be used to produce goods and services.

Chapter 33
CHAPTER 33, PAGE 707

1. He calculates the MB/MC ratio of producing and the MB/MC ratio of stealing. If the first ratio is greater than the second, then he devotes the next hour to producing rather than stealing because the return from producing is greater than the return from stealing. He continues to devote more time to producing until the two ratios are the same.

2. Once Jack and Jill have agreed to stop stealing, each has an incentive to steal from the other. In terms of the payoff matrix in Exhibit 1, Jack and Jill may initially be in box 4. They make an agreement to stop stealing so that they can move to box 1. But once in box 1, each person can make himself or herself better off by moving to a different box. Jack is better off moving from box 1 to box 2, and Jill is better off moving from box 1 to box 3. They are likely, then, to break the agreement (not to steal) and try to move to their respective superior boxes, especially when no one can punish them for making the move. To explain why Jack and Jill can't move themselves

from box 4 to box 1 in Exhibit 1, the short answer is because there is no enforcer of the agreement. Government may later come along to fill the role of the enforcer of the agreement between Jack and Jill.

3. Disagree. Whether it makes parties in a prisoner's dilemma setting better off by removing them from the setting depends on how much each party gains by being removed compared with how much each party pays in tax to government. If the gain from being removed from the setting is 2, and the tax is 3, then a person is made worse off with government than without. If the gain is 2 and the tax is 1, then the person is made better off. If the gain is 2 and the tax is 2, then the person is made neither better off nor worse off.

CHAPTER 33, PAGE 710

1. With respect to a negative externality, if government can set the tax equal to the marginal external cost, then it can change an inefficient market outcome into an efficient one. With respect to a positive externality, if government can set the subsidy equal to the marginal external benefit, then it can change an inefficient market outcome into an efficient one.

2. Individuals might want certain nonexcludable public goods that the market will not produce. The market won't produce these goods because it cannot overcome the free-rider problem. Specifically, because nonexcludable public goods, once produced, cannot be denied to anyone, no one will have an incentive to pay for the good. Instead, individuals will choose to be free riders. Knowing this, no market participant will produce the good. Government can overcome the free-rider problem by taxing individuals, then using the tax monies either to produce the nonexcludable public good itself or to pay someone else to produce it.

CHAPTER 33, PAGE 712

1. Under the condition that the fine is greater than what people could save in monthly premiums by dropping their insurance.

2. The tax credit lowers the overall cost of buying a house; that is, a person who buys a house finds that his or her taxes are lowered. As a result, the demand to buy a house rises. As house demand rises, so do house prices.

3. Yes. When buying a house, the purchaser has to consider many factors: the interest rate on a mortgage loan, the taxes paid as a result of buying the house, the price of the house, and so on. In the tax credit policy example in this section, the tax credit initially lowered the overall cost of buying a house because it reduced the taxes a person would pay as a result of buying a house. But because it made buying a house less expensive, more people became homebuyers. In other words, the demand for houses increased. Because the demand for houses increased, house prices increased, all other things remaining constant.

CHAPTER 33, PAGE 718

1. 1,000 times larger

2. Group B would be less willing to advocate growth policies over transfer policies. The smaller the slice of the economic pie the group receives, the less they receive from any economic growth, thus the less willing they would be to advocate growth over transfers.

Chapter 34

CHAPTER 34, PAGE 727

1. For the United States, $1X = 1/6Y$ or $1Y = 6X$. For England, $1X = 2Y$ or $1Y = 1/2X$. Let's focus on the opportunity cost of $1X$ in each country. In the United States, $1X = 1/6Y$, and in Great Britain, $1X = 2Y$. Terms of trade that are between these two endpoints would be favorable for the two countries. For example, suppose we choose $1X = 1Y$. This is good for the United States because it would prefer to give up $1X$ and get $1Y$ in trade than to give up $1X$ and get only $1/6Y$ (without trade). Similarly, Great Britain would prefer to give up $1Y$ and get $1X$ in trade than to give up $1Y$ and get only $1/2X$ (without trade). Any terms of trade between $1X = 1/6Y$ and $1X = 2Y$ will be favorable to the two countries.

2. Yes. This is what the theory of comparative advantage shows. Exhibit 1 shows that the United States could produce more of both food and clothing than Japan. Still, the United States benefits from specialization and trade, as shown in Exhibit 2. In column 5 of this exhibit, the United States can consume 10 more units of food by specializing and trading.

3. No. It is the desire to buy low and sell high (earn a profit) that pushes countries into producing and trading at a comparative advantage. Government officials do not collect cost data and then issue orders to firms in the country to produce X, Y, or Z. We have not drawn the PPFs in this chapter and identified the cost differences between countries to show what countries actually do in the real world. We described things technically simply to show how countries benefit from specialization and trade.

CHAPTER 34, PAGE 735

1. Domestic producers benefit because producers' surplus rises; domestic consumers lose because consumers' surplus falls. Also, government benefits in that it receives the tariff revenue. Moreover, consumers lose more than producers and government gains; so tariffs result in a net loss.

2. Consumers' surplus falls by more than producers' surplus rises.

3. With a tariff, the government receives tariff revenue. With a quota, it does not. In the latter case, the revenue that would have gone to government goes, instead, to the importers who get to satisfy the quota.

4. Infant or new domestic industries need to be protected from older, more established competitors until they are mature enough to compete on an equal basis. Tariffs and quotas provide these infant industries the time they need.

Chapter 35

CHAPTER 35, PAGE 747

1. A debit. When an American enters into a transaction in which he has to supply U.S. dollars in the foreign exchange market (to demand a foreign currency), the transaction is recorded as a debit.

2. We do not have enough information to answer this question. The merchandise trade balance is the difference between the value of *merchandise* exports and *merchandise* imports. The question gives only the value of exports and imports. "Exports" is a more inclusive term than merchandise exports. Exports

include (a) merchandise exports, (b) services, and (c) income from U.S. assets abroad (see Exhibit 2). Similarly, "imports" is a more inclusive term than merchandise imports. It includes (a) merchandise imports, (b) services, and (c) income from foreign assets in the United States.

3. The merchandise trade balance includes fewer transactions than are included in the current account balance. The merchandise trade balance is the summary statistic for merchandise exports and merchandise imports. The current account balance is the summary statistic for exports of goods and services (which include merchandise exports), imports of goods and services (which include merchandise imports), and net unilateral transfers abroad (see Exhibit 2).

CHAPTER 35, PAGE 754

1. As the demand for dollars increases, the supply of pesos increases. For example, suppose someone in Mexico wants to buy something produced in the United States. The American wants to be paid in dollars, but the Mexican has pesos, not dollars. So she has to buy dollars with pesos; in other words, she has to supply pesos to buy dollars. Thus, as she demands more dollars, she will necessarily have to supply more pesos.

2. The dollar is said to have appreciated (against the peso) when it takes more pesos to buy a dollar and fewer dollars to buy a peso. For this to occur, either the demand for dollars must increase (which means the supply of pesos increases) or the supply of dollars must decrease (which means the demand for pesos decreases). To see this graphically, look at Exhibit 5(b). The only way for the peso price per dollar to rise (on the vertical axis) is for either the demand curve for dollars to shift to the right or the supply curve of dollars to shift to the left. Each of these occurrences is mirrored in the market for pesos in part (a) of the exhibit.

3. *Ceteris paribus,* the dollar will depreciate relative to the franc. As incomes for Americans rise, the demand for Swiss goods rises. This increases the demand for francs and the supply of dollars on the foreign exchange market. In turn, this leads to a depreciated dollar and an appreciated franc.

4. The theory states that the exchange rate between any two currencies will adjust to reflect changes in the relative price levels of the two countries. For example, suppose the U.S. price level rises 5 percent and Mexico's price level remains constant. According to the PPP theory, the U.S. dollar will depreciate 5 percent relative to the Mexican peso.

CHAPTER 35, PAGE 760

1. The terms *overvalued* and *undervalued* refer to the equilibrium exchange rate: the exchange rate at which the quantity demanded and the quantity supplied of a currency are the same in the foreign exchange market. Let's suppose the equilibrium exchange rate is 0.10 USD = 1 MXN. This is the same as saying that 10 pesos = $1 If the exchange rate is fixed at 0.12 USD = 1 MXN (which is the same as 8.33 pesos = $1), the peso is overvalued and the dollar is undervalued. Specifically, a currency is overvalued if 1 unit of it fetches more of another currency than it would in equilibrium; a currency is undervalued if 1 unit of it fetches less of another currency than it would in equilibrium. In equilibrium, 1 peso would fetch $0.10, and at the current exchange rate it fetches $0.12; so the

peso is overvalued. In equilibrium, $1 would fetch 10 pesos, and at the current exchange rate, it fetches only 8.33 pesos; so the dollar is undervalued.

2. An overvalued dollar means some other currency—let's say it is the Japanese yen—is undervalued. An overvalued dollar makes U.S. goods more expensive for the Japanese; so they buy fewer U.S. goods. This reduces U.S. exports. On the other hand, an undervalued yen makes Japanese goods cheaper for Americans; so they buy more Japanese goods, and the United States imports more. Thus, an overvalued dollar reduces U.S. exports and raises U.S. imports.

3. a. Dollar is overvalued.

   b. Dollar is undervalued.

   c. Dollar is undervalued.

4. When a country devalues its currency, it makes it cheaper for foreigners to buy its products.

CHAPTER 35, PAGE 763

1. An optimal currency area is a geographic area in which exchange rates can be fixed or a common currency used without sacrificing any domestic economic goals.

2. As the demand for good Y falls, the unemployment rate in country 2 will rise, but the increase is likely to be temporary. The increased demand for good X (produced by country 1) will increase the demand for country 1's currency, leading to an appreciation in country 1's currency and a depreciation in country 2's currency. Country 1's good X will become more expensive for the residents of country 2, and they will buy less. Country 2's good Y will become less expensive for the residents of country 1, and they will buy more. As a result of the additional purchases of good Y, country 2's unemployment rate will begin to decline.

3. Labor mobility is very important in determining whether an area is an optimal currency area. Given little or no labor mobility, an area is not likely to be an optimal currency area. If there is labor mobility, an area is likely to be an optimal currency area.

Chapter 36

CHAPTER 36, PAGE 776

1. As some explain it, the end of the Cold War resulted in turning two different worlds (the capitalist and communist worlds) into one world. It resulted in a thawing of not only political but also economic relations between former enemies. You might not trade with your enemy, but, once that person or country is no longer your enemy, you do not feel the same need to cut him or it out of your political and economic life.

2. Globalization is the phenomenon by which individuals and businesses in any part of the world are much more affected by events elsewhere in the world than before; it is the growing integration of the national economies of the world to the degree that we may be witnessing the emergence and operation of a single worldwide economy.

3. Advancing technology can reduce both transportation and communication costs, thus making it less costly to trade with people around the world.

CHAPTER 36, PAGE 781

1. The benefits identified in the section include (a) benefits from increased international trade, (b) greater income per person, (c) lower prices for goods, (d) greater product variety, and (e) increased productivity and innovation.

2. The costs identified in the section include (a) increased income inequality, (b) offshoring, and (c) more power for big corporations.

CHAPTER 36, PAGE 785

1. In country A, there is an economic expansion, and real income rises. As a result, residents of the country buy more imports from country B. In country B, exports rise relative to imports, thus increasing net exports. As net exports in country B rise, the *AD* curve for country B shifts to the right, increasing Real GDP.

2. If the dollar appreciates, the Japanese yen depreciates. U.S. products become more expensive for the Japanese, and Japanese products become cheaper for Americans. U.S. imports will rise, U.S. exports will fall, and consequently U.S. net exports will fall. As a result, the *AD* curve in the United States will shift leftward, pushing down Real GDP.

CHAPTER 36, PAGE 788

1. Foreign input prices can change directly as a result of supply conditions in the foreign country, or they can change indirectly as a result of a change in the exchange rate. In either case, as foreign input prices rise—either directly or as a result of a depreciated dollar—the U.S. *SRAS* curve shifts leftward. If foreign input prices fall—either directly or as a result of an appreciated dollar—the *SRAS* curve shifts rightward.

2. The higher real interest rates in the United States attract capital to the United States, increasing the demand for the dollar. As a result, the dollar appreciates and the yen depreciates. An appreciated dollar shifts the U.S. *AD* curve leftward and the U.S. *SRAS* curve rightward. The *AD* curve shifts leftward by more than the *SRAS* curve shifts rightward; so the price level falls.

CHAPTER 36, PAGE 792

1. When the money supply is raised, the *AD* curve shifts rightward, pushing up Real GDP. Also, as a result of the increased money supply, interest rates may decline in the short run, promoting U.S. capital outflow and a depreciated dollar. As a result of the depreciated dollar, imports become more expensive for Americans, and U.S. exports become cheaper for foreigners. Imports fall and exports rise, thereby increasing net exports and *again* shifting the *AD* curve to the right. Real GDP rises.

2. Expansionary fiscal policy pushes the *AD* curve rightward and (under certain conditions) raises Real GDP. If the expansionary fiscal policy causes a deficit, then the government will have to borrow to finance the deficit, and interest rates will be pushed upward. As a result of the higher interest rates, foreign capital inflows and dollar appreciation increase, thus pushing the *AD* curve leftward and the *SRAS* curve rightward.

Chapter 37

CHAPTER 37, PAGE 804

1. 30

2. Stocks are purchased either for the dividends that the stocks may pay, the expected gain in price (of the stock), or both.

3. Yield equals the dividend per share (of the stock) divided by the closing price per share.

4. A P/E ratio of 23 means that the stock is selling for a share price that is 23 times its earnings per share.

CHAPTER 37, PAGE 808

1. A bond is an IOU or a promise to pay. The issuer of a bond is borrowing funds and promising to pay back those funds (with interest) at a later date.

2. $0.07x = \$400$, so $x = \$400 \div 0.07$, or $\$5,714.29$.

3. $\$1,000/\$9,500 = 10.53$ percent

4. A municipal bond is issued by a state or local government, and a Treasury bond is issued by the federal government.

CHAPTER 37, PAGE 811

1. A futures contract is a contract in which the seller agrees to provide a good to the buyer on a specified future date at an agreed-upon price.

2. You can buy a call option, which sells for a fraction of the cost of the stock. A call option gives the owner of the option the right to buy shares of a stock at a specified price within the time limits of the contract.

3. A put option gives the owner the right, but not the obligation, to *sell* (rather than buy, as in a call option) shares of a stock at a strike price during some period of time.

Web Chapter 38

CHAPTER 38, PAGE 819

1. The farmer does so through the futures market. Specifically, she enters into a futures contract with someone who will guarantee to take delivery of her foodstuff (in the future) for a stated price. Then, if the price goes up or down between the present and the future, the farmer does not have to worry. She has locked in the price of her foodstuff.

2. If the farmer faces an inelastic demand curve, the order of preference would be (b)−(a)−(c); that is, he prefers (b) to (a) and (a) to (c). If all farmers except himself have bad weather (b), then the market supply curve of the individual farmer's product shifts to the left, bringing about a higher price. But the individual farmer's supply curve doesn't shift to the left; it stays where it is. Thus, the individual farmer sells the same amount of output at the higher price. Consequently, his total revenue rises. In (a), both the market supply curve and the individual farmer's supply curve shift left; so the farmer has less to sell at a higher price. Again, if the demand is inelastic, the individual farmer will increase his total revenue but not as much as in (b) where the individual farmer's output does not fall. Finally, in (c), the market supply curve shifts to the right, lowering price. If demand is inelastic, this lowers total revenue.

3. Increased productivity will lead to higher total revenue when demand is elastic. To illustrate, increased productivity shifts the supply curve to the right, lowering price. If demand is elastic, then the percentage rise in quantity sold is greater than the percentage fall in price; therefore, total revenue rises. In summary, increased productivity leads to higher total revenue when demand is elastic.

CHAPTER 38, PAGE 823

1. Because the deficiency payment is the difference between the target price and the market price, the answer depends on the market price. If the market price is, say, $4, and the target price is $7, then the deficiency payment is $3.

2. A farmer pledges a certain number of bushels of foodstuff to obtain a loan—say, 500 bushels. He receives a loan equal to the number of bushels times the designated loan rate per bushel. If the loan rate is $2 per bushel and 500 bushels are pledged, then the loan is $1,000. The farmer ends up paying back the loan with interest or keeping the loan and forfeiting the bushels of the crop. Which course of action the farmer takes depends on the market price of the crop. If the market price of the crop is higher than the loan rate, he pays back the loan and sells the crop. If the market price is less than the loan rate, he forfeits the crop. A nonrecourse loan guarantees that the farmer will not receive less than the loan rate for each bushel of his crop.

3. The effects of a price support are (a) a surplus, (b) fewer exchanges (less bought by private citizens), (c) higher prices paid by consumers of the crop (on which the support exists), and (d) government purchase and storage of the surplus crop (for which taxpayers pay).

GLOSSARY

A

Absolute (Money) Price The price of a good in money terms.

Absolute Real Economic Growth An increase in Real GDP from one period to the next.

Abstract The process (used in building a theory) of focusing on a limited number of variables to explain or predict an event.

Accounting Profit The difference between total revenue and explicit costs.

Activists Persons who argue that monetary and fiscal policies should be deliberately used to smooth out the business cycle.

Adaptive Expectations Expectations that individuals form from past experience and modify slowly as the present and the future become the past (i.e., as time passes).

Adjustable Rate Mortgage A mortgage loan where the interest rate on the loan is adjusted periodically depending on various factors.

Adverse Selection A phenomenon that occurs when the parties on one side of the market, who have information not known to others, self-select in a way that adversely affects the parties on the other side of the market.

Aggregate Demand The quantity demanded of all goods and services (Real GDP) at different price levels, *ceteris paribus*.

Aggregate Demand (AD) Curve The quantity demanded of all goods and services (Real GDP) at different price levels, *ceteris paribus*. A curve that shows the quantity demanded of all goods and services (Real GDP) at different price levels, *ceteris paribus*.

Aggregate Supply The quantity supplied of all goods and services (Real GDP) at different price levels, *ceteris paribus*.

Antitrust Law Legislation passed for the stated purpose of controlling monopoly power and preserving and promoting competition.

Appreciation An increase in the value of one currency relative to other currencies.

Arbitrage Buying a good at a low price and selling it for a higher price.

Asset Anything of value that is owned or that one has claim to and that has value.

Asymmetric Information Information that either the buyer or the seller in a market exchange has and that the other does not have.

Automatic Fiscal Policy Changes in government expenditures and/or taxes that occur automatically without (additional) congressional action.

Autonomous Consumption The part of consumption that is independent of disposable income.

Average Fixed Cost (AFC) Total fixed cost divided by quantity of output: $AFC = TFC/Q$.

Average Total Cost (ATC), or Unit Cost Total cost divided by quantity of output: $ATC = TC/Q$.

Average Variable Cost (AVC) Total variable cost divided by quantity of output: $AVC = TVC/Q$.

Average-Marginal Rule When the marginal magnitude is above the average magnitude, the average magnitude rises; when the marginal magnitude is below the average magnitude, the average magnitude falls.

B

Bad Anything from which individuals receive disutility or dissatisfaction.

Balance of Payments A periodic (usually annual) statement of the money value of all transactions between residents of one country and the residents of all other countries.

Balanced Budget The budget when government expenditures equal tax revenues.

Balance Sheet A record of the assets and liabilities of a bank.

Barter Exchanging goods and services for other goods and services without the use of money.

Base Year The year chosen as a point of reference or basis of comparison for prices in other years; a benchmark year.

Board of Governors The governing body of the Federal Reserve System.

Bond An IOU, or promise to pay.

Budget Constraint All the combinations or bundles of two goods a person can purchase, given a certain money income and prices for the two goods.

Budget Deficit The deficit when government expenditures are greater than tax revenues.

Budget Surplus The surplus when tax revenues are greater than government expenditures.

Business Firm An entity that employs factors of production (resources) to produce goods and services to be sold to consumers, other firms, or the government.

C

Capital Produced goods that can be used as inputs for further production, such as factories, machinery, tools, computers, and buildings.

Capital Account The account in the balance of payments that includes all payments related to the purchase and sale of assets and to borrowing and lending activities. Components include outflow of U.S. capital and inflow of foreign capital.

Capital Account Balance The summary statistic for the outflow of U.S. capital equal to the difference between the outflow of U.S. capital and the inflow of foreign capital.

Capital Consumption Allowance (Depreciation) The estimated amount of capital goods used up in production through natural wear, obsolescence, and accidental destruction.

Capture Theory of Regulation A theory holding that no matter what the motive is for the initial regulation and the establishment of the regulatory agency, eventually the agency will be captured (controlled) by the special interests of the industry being regulated.

Cartel An organization of firms that reduces output and increases price in an effort to increase joint profits.

Cartel Theory A theory of oligopoly in which oligopolistic firms act as if there were only one firm in the industry.

Cash Leakage Occurs when funds are held as currency instead of deposited into a checking account.

Ceteris Paribus A Latin term meaning "all other things constant" or "nothing else changes."

Checkable Deposits Deposits on which checks can be written.

Closed Economy An economy that does not trade goods and services with other countries.

Closed Shop An organization in which an employee must belong to the union before he or she can be hired.

Coase Theorem In the case of trivial or zero transaction costs, the property rights assignment does not matter to the resource allocative outcome.

Collective Bargaining The process whereby wage rates and other issues are determined by a union bargaining with management on behalf of all union members.

Comparative Advantage The advantage a country has when it can produce a good at lower opportunity cost than someone else or than another country can.

Complements Two goods that are used jointly in consumption. If two goods are complements, the demand for one rises as the price of the other falls (or the demand for one falls as the price of the other rises).

Complete Crowding Out A decrease in one or more components of private spending that completely offsets the increase in government spending.

Concentration Ratio The percentage of industry sales (or assets, output, labor force, or some other factor) accounted for by x number of firms in the industry.

Conglomerate Merger A merger between companies in different industries.

Constant Returns to Scale The condition when inputs are increased by some percentage and output increases by an equal percentage, causing unit costs to remain constant.

Constant-Cost Industry An industry in which average total costs do not change as (industry) output increases or decreases when firms enter or exit the industry, respectively.

Consumer Equilibrium Equilibrium that occurs when the consumer has spent all income and the marginal utilities per dollar spent on each good purchased are equal:

$MU_A/P_A = MU_B/P_B = \ldots = MU_Z/P_Z$, where the letters A–Z represent all the goods a person buys.

Consumer Price Index (CPI) A widely cited index number for the price level; the weighted average of prices of a specific set of goods and services purchased by a typical household; a widely cited index number for the price level.

Consumers' Surplus (CS) The difference between the maximum price a buyer is willing and able to pay for a good or service and the price actually paid: $CS =$ Maximum buying price $-$ Price paid.

Consumption The sum of spending on durable goods, nondurable goods, and services.

Consumption Function The relationship between consumption and disposable income. In the consumption function used in this text, consumption is directly related to disposable income and is positive even at zero disposable income: $C = C_0 + (MPC)(Y_d)$.

Contestable Market A market in which entry is easy and exit is costless, new firms can produce the product at the same cost as current firms, and exiting firms can easily dispose of their fixed assets by selling them.

Continued Inflation A continued increase in the price level.

Contractionary Fiscal Policy Decreases in government expenditures and/or increases in taxes to achieve economic goals.

Contractionary Monetary Policy The policy by which the Fed decreases the money supply.

Credit In the balance of payments, any transaction that creates a demand for the country's currency in the foreign exchange market.

Cross Elasticity of Demand A measure of the responsiveness in quantity demanded of one good to changes in the price of another good.

Crowding Out The decrease in private expenditures that occurs as a consequence of increased government spending or the financing needs of a budget deficit.

Currency Coins and paper money.

Current Account The account in the balance of payments that includes all payments related to the purchase and sale of goods and services; components of the account include exports, imports, and net unilateral transfers abroad.

Current Account Balance In the balance of payments, the summary statistic for exports of goods and services, imports of goods and services, and net unilateral transfers abroad.

Cyclical Deficit The part of the budget deficit that is a result of a downturn in economic activity.

Cyclical Unemployment Rate The difference between the unemployment rate and the natural unemployment rate.

D

Deadweight Loss The loss to society of not producing the competitive, or supply-and-demand-determined, level of output.

Deadweight Loss of Monopoly The net value (value to buyers over and above costs to suppliers) of the difference between the competitive quantity of output (where $P = MC$) and the monopoly quantity of output (where $P > MC$); the loss of not producing the competitive quantity of output.

Debit In the balance of payments, any transaction that supplies the country's currency in the foreign exchange market.

Decisions at the Margin Decision making characterized by weighing the additional (marginal) benefits of a change against the additional (marginal) costs of a change with respect to current conditions.

Decreasing-Cost Industry An industry in which average total costs decrease as output increases and increase as output decreases when firms enter and exit the industry, respectively.

Demand The willingness and ability of buyers to purchase different quantities of a good at different prices during a specific time period.

Demand Curve The graphical representation of the law of demand.

Demand for Money (Balances) The inverse relationship between the quantity demanded of money balances and the price of holding money balances.

Demand Schedule The numerical tabulation of the quantity demanded of a good at different prices. A demand schedule is the numerical representation of the law of demand.

Depreciation A decrease in the value of one currency relative to other currencies.

Derived Demand Demand that is the result of some other demand. For example, factor demand is the result of the demand for the products that the factors go to produce.

Devaluation A government action that changes the exchange rate by lowering the official price of a currency.

Diamond-Water Paradox The observation that things with the greatest value in use sometimes have little value in exchange and things with little value in use sometimes have the greatest value in exchange.

Direct Finance Borrowers and lenders come together in a market setting, such as in the bond market.

Directly Related Two variables are directly related if they change in the same way.

Discount Loan A loan the Fed makes to a commerical bank.

Discount Rate The interest rate the Fed charges depository institutions that borrow reserves from it.

Discretionary Fiscal Policy Deliberate changes of government expenditures and/or taxes to achieve economic goals.

Diseconomies of Scale The condition when inputs are increased by some percentage and output increases by a smaller percentage, causing unit costs to rise.

Disequilibrium A state of either surplus or shortage in a market.

Disequilibrium Price A price other than equilibrium price; a price at which quantity demanded does not equal quantity supplied.

Disposable Income The portion of personal income that can be used for consumption or saving. It is equal to personal income minus personal taxes (especially income taxes).

Disutility The dissatisfaction one receives from a bad.

Dividend A share of the profits of a corporation distributed to stockholders.

Double Coincidence of Wants In a barter economy, a requirement, which must be met before a trade can be made, that a trader must find another trader who is willing to trade what the first trader wants and at the same time wants what the first trader has.

Double Counting Counting a good more than once when computing GDP.

Dow Jones Industrial Average (DJIA) The most popular, widely cited indicator of day-to-day stock market activity. The DJIA is a weighted average of 30 widely traded stocks on the New York Stock Exchange.

Dumping The sale of goods abroad at a price below their cost and below the price charged in the domestic market.

E

Economic Growth Increases in Real GDP.

Economic Profit The difference between total revenue and total cost, including both explicit and implicit costs.

Economic Rent Payment in excess of opportunity costs.

Economics The science of scarcity; the science of how individuals and societies deal with the fact that wants are greater than the limited resources available to satisfy those wants.

Economies of Scale Economies that exist when inputs are increased by some percentage and output increases by a greater percentage, causing unit costs to fall.

Efficiency Exists when marginal benefits equal marginal costs.

Efficiency Wage Models These models hold that it is sometimes in the best interest of business firms to pay their employees higher-than-equilibrium wage rates.

Elastic Demand The demand when the percentage change in quantity demanded is greater than the percentage change in price. Quantity demanded changes proportionately more than price changes.

Elasticity of Demand for Labor The percentage change in the quantity demanded of labor divided by the percentage change in the wage rate.

Elasticity of Investment A measure of the responsiveness of investment to changes in the interest rate.

Employee Association An organization whose members belong to a particular profession.

Employment Rate The percentage of the civilian noninstitutional population that is employed: Employment rate = Number of employed persons/Civilian noninstitutional population.

Entrepreneurship The talent that some people have for organizing the resources of land, labor, and capital to produce goods, seek new business opportunities, and develop new ways of doing things.

Equation of Exchange An identity stating that the money supply (M) times velocity (V) must be equal to the price level (P) times Real GDP (Q): $MV = PQ$.

Equilibrium Equilibrium means "at rest." Equilibrium in a market is the price–quantity combination from which there is no tendency for buyers or sellers to move away. Graphically, equilibrium is the intersection point of the supply and demand curves.

Equilibrium Price (Market-Clearing Price) The price at which quantity demanded of the good equals quantity supplied.

Equilibrium Quantity The quantity that corresponds to equilibrium price. The quantity at which the amount of the good that buyers are willing and able to buy equals the amount that sellers are willing and able to sell, and both equal the amount actually bought and sold.

Equity (in a Home) The difference between what one owes on a home and the price at which the house can be sold.

Excess Capacity Theorem Theorem that a monopolistic competitor in equilibrium produces an output smaller than the one that would minimize its costs of production.

Excess Reserves Any reserves held beyond the required amount; the difference between (total) reserves and required reserves.

Exchange (Trade) The process of giving up one thing for something else.

Exchange Rate The price of one currency in terms of another currency.

Excludable A characteristic of a good whereby it is possible, or not prohibitively costly, to exclude someone from receiving the benefits of the good after it has been produced.

Expansionary Fiscal Policy Increases in government expenditures and/or decreases in taxes to achieve particular economic goals.

Expansionary Monetary Policy The policy by which the Fed increases the money supply.

Expectations Effect The change in the interest rate due to a change in the expected inflation rate.

Explicit Cost A cost incurred when an actual (monetary) payment is made.

Exports Total foreign spending on domestic (U.S.) goods.

Externality A side effect of an action that affects the well-being of third parties.

F

Face Value (Par Value) Dollar amount specified on a bond, the total amount the issuer of the bond will repay to the buyer of the bond.

Factor Price Taker A firm that can buy all of a factor it wants at the equilibrium price. It faces a horizontal (flat, perfectly elastic) supply curve of factors.

Federal Funds Market A market where banks lend reserves to one another, usually for short periods.

Federal Funds Rate The interest rate in the federal funds market; the interest rate banks charge one another to borrow reserves.

Federal Funds Target Rate The interest rate that the Fed wants the federal funds market rate to be.

Federal Open Market Committee (FOMC) The 12-member policy-making group within the Fed. The committee has the authority to conduct open market operations.

Federal Reserve Notes Paper money issued by the Fed.

Federal Reserve System (the Fed) The central bank of the United States.

Final Good A good in the hands of its final user.

Financial Intermediary A financial intermediary transfers funds from those who want to lend funds to those who want to borrow them.

Fine-Tuning The (usually frequent) use of monetary and fiscal policies to counteract even small undesirable movements in economic activity.

Fiscal Policy Changes in government expenditures and/or taxes to achieve macroeconomic goals, such as low unemployment, stable prices, and economic growth.

Fixed Costs Costs that do not vary with output; the costs associated with fixed inputs.

Fixed Exchange Rate System The system whereby a nation's currency is set at a fixed rate relative to all other currencies, and central banks intervene in the foreign exchange market to maintain the fixed rate.

Fixed Input An input whose quantity cannot be changed as output changes.

Fixed Investment Business purchases of capital goods, such as machinery and factories, and purchases of new residential housing.

Flexible Exchange Rate System The system whereby exchange rates are determined by the forces of supply and demand for a currency.

Foreign Exchange Market The market in which currencies of different countries are exchanged.

Fractional Reserve Banking A banking arrangement that allows banks to hold reserves equal to only a fraction of their deposit liabilities.

Free Rider Anyone who receives the benefits of a good without paying for it.

Frictional Unemployment Unemployment due to the natural "frictions" of the economy, which is caused by changing market conditions and is represented by qualified individuals with transferable skills who change jobs.

Friedman Natural Rate Theory The idea that, in the long run, unemployment is at its natural rate. Within the Phillips curve framework, the natural rate theory specifies that there is a long-run Phillips curve, which is vertical at the natural rate of unemployment.

Full Employment The condition that exists when the unemployment rate is equal to the natural unemployment rate.

Futures Contract An agreement to buy or sell a specific amount of something (commodity, currency, financial instrument) at an agreed-on price on a stipulated future date.

G

Game Theory A mathematical technique used to analyze the behavior of decision makers who try to reach an optimal position for themselves through game playing or the use of strategic behavior, who are fully aware of the interactive nature of the process at hand, and who anticipate the moves of other decision makers.

Gini Coefficient A measure of the degree of inequality in the income distribution.

Globalization A phenomenon by which economic agents in any given part of the world are more affected by events elsewhere in the world than before; the growing integration of the national economies of the world to the degree that we may be witnessing the emergence and operation of a single worldwide economy.

Good Anything from which individuals receive utility or satisfaction.

Government Bureaucrat An unelected person who works in a government bureau and who is assigned a special task relating to a law or program passed by the legislature.

Government Spending Multiplier The number that, when multiplied by the change in government spending, gives us the change in total spending (and, if prices are constant, the change in Real GDP).

Government Purchases Federal, state, and local government purchases of goods and services and gross investment in highways, bridges, and so on.

Government Transfer Payments Payments to persons that are not made in return for goods and services currently supplied.

Gross Domestic Product (GDP) The total market value of all final goods and services produced annually within a country's borders.

H

Herfindahl Index Index that measures the degree of concentration in an industry, equal to the sum of the squares of the market shares of each firm in the industry.

Horizontal Merger A merger between firms that are selling similar products in the same market.

Human Capital Education, development of skills, and anything else that is particular to the individual and that increases personal productivity.

I

Implicit Cost A cost that represents the value of resources used in production for which no actual (monetary) payment is made.

Imports Total domestic (U.S.) spending on foreign goods.

Incentive Something that encourages or motivates a person to undertake an action.

Income Effect The change in the interest rate due to a change in Real GDP.

Income Elastic The condition when the percentage change in quantity demanded of a good is greater than the percentage change in income.

Income Elasticity of Demand A measure of the responsiveness of quantity demanded to changes in income.

Income Inelastic The condition when the percentage change in quantity demanded of a good is less than the percentage change in income.

Income Unit Elastic The condition when the percentage change in quantity demanded of a good is equal to the percentage change in income.

Incomplete Crowding Out The decrease in one or more components of private spending that only partially offsets the increase in government spending.

Increasing-Cost Industry An industry in which average total costs increase as output increases and decrease as output decreases when firms enter and exit the industry, respectively.

Independent Two variables are independent if, as one changes, the other does not.

Indifference Curve The curve that represents an indifference set and that shows all the bundles of two goods giving an individual equal total utility.

Indifference Curve Map Represents a number of indifference curves for a given individual with reference to two goods.

Indifference Set Group of bundles of two goods that give an individual equal total utility.

Indirect Finance Funds are loaned and borrowed through a financial intermediary.

Industrial Policy A deliberate policy by which government aids industries that are the most likely to be successful in the world marketplace—that is, waters the green spots.

Inelastic Demand The demand when the percentage change in quantity demanded is less than the percentage change in price. Quantity demanded changes proportionately less than price changes.

Inferior Good A good the demand for which falls (rises) as income rises (falls).

Inflation An increase in the price level.

Inflationary Gap The condition in which the Real GDP that the economy is producing is greater than the Natural Real GDP and the unemployment rate is less than the natural unemployment rate.

Inflation Targeting Targeting that requires the Fed to keep the inflation rate near a predetermined level.

Initial Public Offering (IPO) A company's first offering of stock to the public.

In-Kind Transfer Payments Transfer payments, such as food stamps, medical assistance, and subsidized housing, that are made in a specific good or service rather than in cash.

Insolvency The condition when liabilities are greater than assets.

Institution The rules of the game in a society or, more formally, the humanly devised constraints that shape human interaction; the rules and regulations, laws, customs, and business practices of a country.

Interest Rate Effect The changes in household and business buying as the interest rate changes (which, in turn, is a reflection of a change in the demand for or supply of credit brought on by price level changes).

Intermediate Good A good that is an input in the production of a final good.

Internalizing Externalities An externality is internalized if the persons or group that generated the externality incorporate into their own private or internal cost-benefit calculations the external benefits (in the case of a positive externality) or the external costs (in the case of a negative externality) that third parties bear.

International Monetary Fund (IMF) An international organization created to oversee the international monetary system. The IMF does not control the world's money supply, but it does hold currency reserves for member nations and make loans to central banks.

International Trade Effect The change in foreign sector spending as the price level changes.

Interpersonal Utility Comparison Comparing the utility one person receives from a good, service, or activity with the utility another person receives from the same good, service, or activity.

Inventory Investment Changes in the stock of unsold goods.

Inversely Related Two variables are inversely related if they change in opposite ways.

Investment The sum of all purchases of newly produced capital goods, changes in business inventories, and purchases of new residential housing.

Investment Bank A firm that acts as an intermediary between the company that issues the stock and the public that wishes to buy the stock.

J

J-Curve The curve that shows a short-run worsening in net exports after a currency depreciation, followed by an improvement.

L

Labor The physical and mental talents people contribute to the production process.

Labor Force Participation Rate The percentage of the civilian noninstitutional population that is in the civilian labor force. Labor force participation rate = Civilian labor force/Civilian noninstitutional population.

Laffer Curve The curve, named after Arthur Laffer, that shows the relationship between tax rates and tax revenues. According to the Laffer curve, as tax rates rise from zero, tax revenues rise, reach a maximum at some point, and then fall with further increases in tax rates.

Laissez-Faire A public policy of not interfering with market activities in the economy.

Land All natural resources, such as minerals, forests, water, and unimproved land.

Law of Demand As the price of a good rises, the quantity demanded of the good falls, and as the price of a good falls, the quantity demanded of the good rises, *ceteris paribus*.

Law of Diminishing Marginal Returns As ever larger amounts of a variable input are combined with fixed inputs, eventually the marginal physical product of the variable input will decline.

Law of Diminishing Marginal Utility For a given time period, the marginal (additional) utility or satisfaction gained by consuming equal successive units of a good will decline as the amount consumed increases.

Law of Increasing Opportunity Costs As more of a good is produced, the opportunity costs of producing that good increase.

Law of Supply As the price of a good rises, the quantity supplied of the good rises, and as the price of a good falls, the quantity supplied of the good falls, *ceteris paribus*.

Least-Cost Rule Rule that specifies the combination of factors that minimizes costs. This requires that the following condition be met: $MPP_1/P_1 = MPP_2/P_2 = \ldots = MPP_N/P_N$, where the numbers stand for the different factors.

Leverage The use of borrowed funds to increase the returns that can be earned with a given amount of capital.

Liability Anything that is owed to someone else.

Liquidity Effect The change in the interest rate due to a change in the supply of loanable funds.

Liquidity Trap The horizontal portion of the demand curve for money.

Loanable Funds Funds that someone borrows and another person lends, for which the borrower pays an interest rate to the lender.

Lock-In Effect The situation when a particular product or technology becomes the standard and is difficult or impossible to dislodge as the standard.

Logrolling The exchange of votes to gain support for legislation.

Long Run A period of time in which all inputs in the production process can be varied (no inputs are fixed).

Long-Run Aggregate Supply (LRAS) Curve The *LRAS* curve is a vertical line at the level of Natural Real GDP. It represents the output the economy produces when wages and prices have adjusted to their (final) equilibrium levels and neither producers nor workers have any relevant misperceptions.

Long-Run Average Total Cost (LRATC) Curve A curve that shows the lowest (unit) cost at which the firm can produce any given level of output.

Long-Run Competitive Equilibrium The condition where $P = MC = SRATC = LRATC$. There are zero economic profits, firms are producing the quantity of output at which price is equal to marginal cost, and no firm has an incentive to change its plant size.

Long-Run Equilibrium The condition that exists in the economy when wages and prices have adjusted to their (final) equilibrium levels and workers do not have any relevant misperceptions. Graphically, long-run equilibrium occurs at the intersection of the *AD* and *LRAS* curves.

Long-Run (Industry) Supply (LRS) Curve Graphic representation of the quantities of output that the industry is prepared to supply at different prices after the entry and exit of firms are completed.

Lorenz Curve A graph of the income distribution that expresses the relationship between the cumulative percentage of households and the cumulative percentage of income.

M

M1 Currency held outside banks plus checkable deposits plus traveler's checks.

M2 M1 plus savings deposits (including money market deposit accounts) plus small-denomination time deposits plus (retail) money market mutual funds.

Macroeconomics The branch of economics that deals with human behavior and choices as they relate to highly aggregate markets (e.g., the goods and services market) or the entire economy.

Managed Float A managed flexible exchange rate system, under which nations now and then intervene to adjust their official reserve holdings to moderate major swings in exchange rates.

Managerial Coordination The process in which managers direct employees to perform certain tasks.

Marginal Benefits Additional benefits. The benefits connected to consuming an additional unit of a good or undertaking one more unit of an activity.

Marginal Cost (MC) The change in total cost that results from a change in output: $MC = \Delta TC/\Delta Q$.

Marginal Costs Additional costs; the costs connected to consuming an additional unit of a good or undertaking one more unit of an activity.

Marginal Factor Cost (MFC) The additional cost incurred by employing an additional factor unit.

Marginal (Income) Tax Rate The change in a person's tax payment divided by the change in his or her taxable income: ΔTax payment/ΔTaxable income.

Marginal Physical Product (MPP) The change in output that results from changing the variable input by one unit, holding all other inputs fixed.

Marginal Productivity Theory Theory stating that firms in competitive or perfect product and factor markets pay factors their marginal revenue products.

Marginal Propensity to Consume (MPC) The ratio of the change in consumption to the change in disposable income: $MPC = \Delta C/\Delta Y_d$.

Marginal Propensity to Save (MPS) The ratio of the change in saving to the change in disposable income: $MPS = \Delta S/\Delta Y_d$.

Marginal Rate of Substitution The amount of one good an individual is willing to give up to obtain an additional unit of another good and maintain equal total utility.

Marginal Revenue (MR) The change in total revenue that results from selling one additional unit of output.

Marginal Revenue Product (MRP) The additional revenue generated by employing an additional factor unit.

Marginal Social Benefits (MSB) The sum of marginal private benefits (*MPB*) and marginal external benefits (*MEB*): $MSB = MPB + MEB$.

Marginal Social Costs (MSC) The sum of marginal private costs (*MPC*) and marginal external costs (*MEC*): $MSC = MPC + MEC$.

Marginal Utility The additional utility a person receives from consuming an additional unit of a good.

Market Any place people come together to trade.

Market Coordination The process in which individuals perform tasks, such as producing certain quantities of goods, based on changes in market forces, such as supply, demand, and price.

Market Failure A situation in which the market does not provide the ideal or optimal amount of a good.

Market Structure The particular environment of a firm, the characteristics of which influence the firm's pricing and output decisions.

Median Voter Model A model suggesting that candidates in a two-person political race will move toward matching the preferences of the median voter (i.e., the person whose preferences are at the center, or in the middle, of the political spectrum).

Medium of Exchange A function of money, anything that is generally acceptable in exchange for goods and services.

Merchandise Trade Balance The difference between the value of merchandise exports and the value of merchandise imports.

Merchandise Trade Deficit The situation when the value of merchandise exports is less than the value of merchandise imports.

Merchandise Trade Surplus The situation when the value of merchandise exports is greater than the value of merchandise imports.

Microeconomics The branch of economics that deals with human behavior and choices as they relate to relatively small units—an individual, a firm, an industry, a single market.

Minimum Efficient Scale The lowest output level at which average total costs are minimized.

Monetary Policy Changes in the money supply, or in the rate of change of the money supply, to achieve particular macroeconomic goals.

Monetary Wealth The value of a person's monetary assets. Wealth, as distinguished from monetary wealth, refers to the value of all assets owned, both monetary and nonmonetary. In short, a person's wealth equals his or her monetary wealth (e.g., $1,000 cash) plus nonmonetary wealth (e.g., a car or a house).

Money Any good that is widely accepted for purposes of exchange and in the repayment of debt.

Money Market Deposit Account (MMDA) An interest-earning account at a bank or thrift institution. Usually, a minimum balance is required for an MMDA, and most offer limited check-writing privileges.

Money Market Mutual Fund (MMMF) An interest-earning account at a mutual fund company. Usually, a minimum balance is required for an MMMF account. Most MMMF accounts offer limited check-writing privileges. Only retail MMMFs are part of M2.

Monitor A person in a business firm who coordinates team production and reduces shirking.

Monopolistic Competition A theory of market structure based on three assumptions: many sellers and buyers, firms producing and selling slightly differentiated products, and easy entry and exit.

Monopoly A theory of market structure based on three assumptions: There is one seller, it sells a product for which no close substitutes exist, and there are extremely high barriers to entry.

Monopsony A single buyer in a factor market.

Moral Hazard A condition that exists when one party to a transaction changes his or her behavior in a way that is hidden from and costly to the other party.

Mortgage-Backed Securities (MBS) A type of asset-backed security that is secured by a mortgage or collection of mortgages.

Multiplier The number that is multiplied by the change in autonomous spending to obtain the overall change in total spending. The multiplier (m) is equal to $1/(1 - MPC)$. If the economy is operating below Natural Real GDP, then the multiplier turns out to be the number that is multiplied by the change in autonomous spending to obtain the change in Real GDP.

N

National Income Total income earned by U.S. citizens and businesses, no matter where they reside or are located. National income is the sum of the payments to resources (land, labor, capital, and entrepreneurship). National income = Compensation of employees + Proprietors' income + Corporate profits + Rental income of persons + Net interest.

Natural Monopoly The condition where economies of scale are so pronounced that only one firm can survive.

Natural Real GDP The Real GDP that is produced at the natural unemployment rate. The Real GDP that is produced when the economy is in long-run equilibrium.

Natural Unemployment Unemployment caused by frictional and structural factors in the economy. Natural unemployment rate = Frictional unemployment rate + Structural unemployment rate.

Negative Externality The condition that exists when a person's or group's actions cause a cost (adverse side effect) to be felt by others.

Negative Sum Game A game in which losses are greater than gains so that the sum of losses and gains is negative.

Net Domestic Product (NDP) GDP minus the capital consumption allowance.

Net Exports Exports minus imports.

Net Worth (or Capital) The difference between assets and liabilities. For example, if assets are $100 and liabilities are $80, net worth, or capital, is $20.

Network Good A good whose value increases as the expected number of units sold increases.

Neutral Good A good the demand for which does not change as income rises or falls.

Nominal Income The current-dollar amount of a person's income.

Nominal Interest Rate The interest rate determined by the forces of supply and demand in the loanable funds market. The interest rate actually charged (or paid) in the market; the market interest rate. Nominal interest rate = Real interest rate + Expected inflation rate.

Nonactivists Persons who argue against the deliberate use of discretionary fiscal and monetary policies. They believe in a permanent, stable, rule-oriented monetary and fiscal framework.

Nonexcludable A characteristic of a good whereby it is impossible, or prohibitively

costly, to exclude someone from receiving the benefits of the good after it has been produced.

Nonrivalrous in Consumption A good is nonrivalrous in consumption if its consumption by one person does not reduce its consumption by others.

Normal Good A good the demand for which rises (falls) as income rises (falls).

Normal Profit (Zero Economic Profit) A firm that earns normal profit is earning revenue equal to its total costs (explicit plus implicit costs); the level of profit necessary to keep resources employed in the firm.

Normative Economics The study of "what should be" in economic matters.

O

Offshoring Work done for a company by persons other than the original company's employees in a country other than the one in which the company is located.

Oligopoly A theory of market structure based on three assumptions: few sellers and many buyers, firms producing either homogeneous or differentiated products, and significant barriers to entry.

One-Shot Inflation A one-time increase in the price level. An increase in the price level that does not continue.

Open Economy An economy that trades goods and services with other countries.

Open Market Operations The buying and selling of government securities by the Fed.

Open Market Purchase The buying of government securities by the Fed.

Open Market Sale The selling of government securities by the Fed.

Opportunity Cost The most highly valued opportunity or alternative forfeited when a choice is made.

Optimal Currency Area A geographic area in which exchange rates can be fixed or a common currency used without sacrificing domestic economic goals, such as low unemployment.

Option A contract that gives the owner the right, but not the obligation, to buy or sell shares of a stock at a specified price on or before a specified date.

Overvalued A currency is overvalued if its price in terms of other currencies is above the equilibrium price.

Own Price The price of a good. For example, if the price of oranges is $1, this is its own price.

P

Per-Capita Real Economic Growth An increase from one period to the next in per-capita Real GDP, which is Real GDP divided by population.

Perfect Competition A theory of market structure based on four assumptions: (1) There are many sellers and buyers, (2) sellers sell a homogeneous good, (3) buyers and sellers have all relevant information, and (4) entry into or exit from the market is easy.

Perfect Price Discrimination A price structure in which the seller charges the highest price that each consumer is willing to pay for the product rather than go without it.

Perfectly Elastic Demand The demand when a small percentage change in price causes an extremely large percentage change in quantity demanded (from buying all to buying nothing).

Perfectly Inelastic Demand The demand when the quantity demanded does not change as price changes.

Personal Income The amount of income that individuals actually receive. It is equal to national income minus undistributed corporate profits, social insurance taxes, and corporate profits taxes, plus transfer payments.

Phillips Curve A curve that originally showed the relationship between wage inflation and unemployment and that now more often shows the relationship between price inflation and unemployment.

Policy Ineffectiveness Proposition (PIP) If (1) a policy change is correctly anticipated, (2) individuals form their expectations rationally, and (3) wages and prices are flexible, then neither fiscal policy nor monetary policy is effective at meeting macroeconomic goals.

Positive Economics The study of "what is" in economic matters.

Positive Externality The condition that exists when a person's or group's actions cause a benefit (beneficial side effect) for others.

Positive Rate of Time Preference Preference for earlier over later availability of goods.

Positive Sum Game A setting in which an activity takes place. A positive game generates only winners (or gains).

Poverty Income Threshold (Poverty Line) Income level below which people are considered to be living in poverty.

Present Value The current worth of some future dollar amount of income or receipts.

Price Ceiling A government-mandated maximum price above which legal trades cannot be made.

Price Discrimination A price structure in which the seller charges different prices for the product it sells and the price differences do not reflect cost differences.

Price Elasticity of Demand A measure of the responsiveness of quantity demanded to changes in price.

Price Elasticity of Supply A measure of the responsiveness of quantity supplied to changes in price.

Price Floor A government-mandated minimum price below which legal trades cannot be made.

Price Index A measure of the price level.

Price Leadership Theory A theory of oligopoly in which the dominant firm in the industry determines price, and all other firms take their price as given.

Price Level A weighted average of the prices of all good and services.

Price Searcher A seller that has the ability to control to some degree the price of the product it sells.

Price Support A government-mandated minimum price for agricultural products; an example of a price floor.

Price Taker A seller that does not have the ability to control the price of the product it sells; the seller takes the price determined in the market.

Price-Level Effect The change in the interest rate due to a change in the price level.

Producers' (Sellers') Surplus (PS) The difference between the price sellers receive for a good and the minimum or lowest price for which they would have sold the good: PS = Price received – Minimum selling price.

Production Function A function that specifies the relation between technology and the quantity of factor inputs to output or Real GDP.

Production Possibilities Frontier (PPF) Represents the possible combinations of two goods that can be produced in a certain period of time under the conditions of a given state of technology and fully employed resources.

Productive Efficiency The situation that exists when a firm produces its output at the lowest possible per-unit cost (lowest ATC).

Productive Efficient The condition where the maximum output is produced with the given resources and technology.

Productive Inefficiency The condition where less than the maximum output is produced with given resources and technology. Productive inefficiency implies that more of one good can be produced without any less of another good being produced.

Productive Inefficient The condition where less than the maximum output is produced with the given resources and technology. Productive inefficiency implies that more of one good can be produced without any less of another being produced.

Profit The difference between total revenue and total cost.

Profit-Maximization Rule The rule that profit is maximized by producing the quantity of output at which $MR = MC$.

Progressive Income Tax An income tax system in which one's tax rate rises as one's taxable income rises (up to some point).

Proportional Income Tax An income tax system in which a person's tax rate is the same no matter what his or her taxable income is.

Public Choice The branch of economics that deals with the application of economic principles and tools to public sector decision making.

Public Choice Theory of Regulation A theory holding that regulators are seeking to do—and will do through regulation—what is in their best interest (specifically to enhance their power and the size and budget of their regulatory agencies).

Public Debt The total amount that the federal government owes its creditors.

Public Employee Union A union whose membership is made up of individuals who work for the local, state, or federal government.

Public Franchise A right granted to a firm by government that permits the firm to provide a particular good or service and that excludes all others from doing the same.

Public Good A good the consumption of which by one person does not reduce the consumption by another person—that is, it is nonrivalrous in consumption. There are both excludable and nonexcludable public goods. An excludable public good, while nonrivalrous in consumption, can be denied to a person who does not pay for it. A nonexcludable public good is nonrivalrous in consumption and cannot be denied to a person who does not pay for it.

Public Interest Theory of Regulation A theory holding that regulators are seeking to do—and will do through regulation—what is in the best interest of the public or society at large.

Purchasing Power The quantity of goods and services that can be purchased with a unit of money. Purchasing power and the price level are inversely related: As the price level goes up (down), purchasing power goes down (up).

Purchasing Power Parity (PPP) Theory Theory stating that exchange rates between any two currencies will adjust to reflect changes in the relative price levels of the two countries.

Pure Economic Rent A category of economic rent where the payment is to a factor that is in fixed supply, implying that it has zero opportunity costs.

Q

Quota A legal limit on the amount of a good that may be imported.

R

Rational Expectations Expectations that individuals form based on past experience and on their predictions about the effects of present and future policy actions and events.

Rational Ignorance The state of not acquiring information because the costs of acquiring it are greater than the benefits.

Rationing Device A means for deciding who gets what of available resources and goods.

Real Balance Effect The change in the purchasing power of dollar-denominated assets that results from a change in the price level.

Real GDP The value of the entire output produced annually within a country's borders, adjusted for price changes.

Real Income Nominal income adjusted for price changes.

Real Interest Rate The nominal interest rate adjusted for expected inflation, that is, the nominal interest rate minus the expected inflation rate. When the expected inflation rate is zero, the real interest rate equals the nominal interest rate.

Recessionary Gap The condition in which the Real GDP that the economy is producing is less than the Natural Real GDP and the unemployment rate is greater than the natural unemployment rate.

Regressive Income Tax An income tax system in which a person's tax rate declines as his or her taxable income rises.

Regulatory Capital The amount of capital that a financial institution must hold because of regulatory requirements.

Regulatory Capital Arbitrage A means of changing the composition of assets in such a way as to lower the overall amount of capital a financial institution holds for a given level of assets.

Regulatory Lag The time period between when a natural monopoly's costs change and when the regulatory agency adjusts prices for it.

Relative Price The price of a good in terms of another good.

Rent Seeking Actions of individuals and groups who spend resources to influence public policy in the hope of redistributing (transferring) income to themselves from others.

Required Reserve Ratio (r) A percentage of each dollar deposited that must be held on reserve (at the Fed or in the bank's vault).

Required Reserves The minimum amount of reserves a bank must hold against its checkable deposits as mandated by the Fed.

Reserve Deficient The situation that exists when a bank holds fewer reserves than specified by the required reserve ratio.

Reserve Requirement The rule that specifies the amount of reserves a bank must hold to back up deposits.

Reserves The sum of bank deposits at the Fed and vault cash.

Residual Claimants Persons who share in the profits of a business firm.

Resource Allocative Efficiency The situation when firms produce the quantity of output at which price equals marginal cost: $P = MC$.

Revaluation A government action that changes the exchange rate by raising the official price of a currency.

Rivalrous in Consumption A good whose consumption by one person reduces its consumption by others.

Roundabout Method of Production The production of capital goods that enhance productive capabilities to ultimately bring about increased consumption.

S

Savings Deposit An interest-earning account at a commercial bank or thrift institution. Normally, checks cannot be written on savings deposits, and the funds in a savings deposit can be withdrawn (at any time) without a penalty payment.

Say's Law Supply creates its own demand. Production creates demand sufficient to purchase all the goods and services produced.

Scarcity The condition in which our wants are greater than the limited resources available to satisfy those wants.

Screening The process employers use to increase the probability of choosing good employees based on certain criteria.

Second-Degree Price Discrimination A price structure in which the seller charges a uniform price per unit for one specific quantity, a lower price for an additional quantity, and so on.

Securitization The process by which financial institutions aggregate debt (such as loans) in a pool and then issues securities backed by the pool.

Shirking The behavior of a worker who is putting forth less than the agreed-to effort.

Short Run A period of time in which some inputs in the production process are fixed.

Shortage (Excess Demand) A condition in which quantity demanded is greater than quantity supplied. Shortages occur only at prices below equilibrium price.

Short-Run Aggregate Supply (SRAS) Curve A curve that shows the quantity supplied of all goods and services (Real GDP) at different price levels, *ceteris paribus*.

Short-Run Equilibrium The condition that exists in the economy when the quantity demanded of Real GDP equals the (short-run) quantity supplied of Real GDP. This condition is met where the aggregate demand curve intersects the short-run aggregate supply curve.

Short-Run (Firm) Supply Curve The portion of the firm's marginal cost curve that lies above the average variable cost curve.

Short-Run Market (Industry) Supply Curve The horizontal addition of all existing firms' short-run supply curves.

Simple Deposit Multiplier The reciprocal of the required reserve ratio, $1/r$.

Simple Quantity Theory of Money The theory assuming that velocity (V) and Real

GDP (*Q*) are constant and predicting that changes in the money supply (*M*) lead to strictly proportional changes in the price level (*P*).

Slope The ratio of the change in the variable on the vertical axis to the change in the variable on the horizontal axis.

Socially Optimal Amount (Output) An amount that takes into account and adjusts for all benefits (external and private) and all costs (external and private). The socially optimal amount is the amount at which $MSB = MSC$. Sometimes, the socially optimal amount is referred to as the efficient amount.

Special Drawing Right (SDR) An international money, created by the IMF, in the form of bookkeeping entries; like gold and currencies, it can be used by nations to settle international accounts.

Special Interest Groups Subsets of the general population that hold (usually) intense preferences for or against a particular government service, activity, or policy and that often, special interest groups gain from public policies that may not be in accord with the interests of the general public.

Special-Purpose Vehicle (SPV) A legal entity created to fulfill narrow, specific, or temporary objectives.

Stagflation The simultaneous occurrence of high rates of inflation and unemployment.

Stock A claim on the assets of a corporation that gives the purchaser a share of the corporation.

Store of Value A function of money; the ability of an item to hold value over time.

Strike The situation in which union employees refuse to work at a certain wage or under certain conditions.

Structural Deficit The part of the budget deficit that would exist even if the economy were operating at full employment.

Structural Unemployment Unemployment due to structural changes in the economy that eliminate some jobs and create other jobs for which the unemployed are unqualified.

Subprime Mortgage Loan A nontraditional mortgage loan granted to persons who might have low credit ratings or some other factors that suggest they could default on the debt repayment.

Subsidy A monetary payment by government to a producer of a good or service.

Substitutes Two goods that satisfy similar needs or desires. If two goods are substitutes,

the demand for one rises as the price of the other rises (or the demand for one falls as the price of the other falls).

Sunk Cost A cost incurred in the past that cannot be changed by current decisions and therefore cannot be recovered.

Supply The willingness and ability of sellers to produce and offer to sell different quantities of a good at different prices during a specific time period.

Supply Curve The graphical representation of the law of supply.

Supply Schedule The numerical tabulation of the quantity supplied of a good at different prices. A supply schedule is the numerical representation of the law of supply.

Surplus (Excess Supply) A condition in which quantity supplied is greater than quantity demanded. Surpluses occur only at prices above equilibrium price.

T

T-Account A simplified balance sheet that shows the changes in a bank's assets and liabilities.

Target Price A guaranteed price; if the market price is below the target price, the farmer receives a deficiency payment equal to the difference between the target price and the market price.

Tariff A tax on imports.

Tax Base In terms of income taxes, the total amount of taxable income. Tax revenue = Tax base × (average) Tax rate.

Tax Multiplier The number that, when multiplied by the change in taxes, gives us the change in total spending (and if prices are constant, the change in Real GDP).

Technology The body of skills and knowledge involved in the use of resources in production. An advance in technology commonly refers to the ability to produce more output with a fixed amount of resources or the ability to produce the same output with fewer resources.

Term Auction Facility (TAF) Program A program under which the Fed auctions funds to depository institutions. Each TAF auction is for a fixed amount, with the TAF rate determined by the auction process (subject to a minimum bid rate).

Terms of Trade How much of one thing is given up for how much of something else.

Theory An abstract representation of the real world designed with the intent to better understand it.

Third-Degree Price Discrimination A price structure in which the seller charges different prices in different markets or charges a different price to different segments of the buying population.

Tie-In Sale A sale whereby one good can be purchased only if another good is also purchased.

Time Deposit An interest-earning deposit with a specified maturity date. Time deposits are subject to penalties for early withdrawal. Small-denomination time deposits are deposits of less than $100,000.

Total Cost (TC) The sum of fixed and variable costs.

Total Revenue (TR) Price times quantity sold.

Total Surplus (TS) The sum of consumers' surplus and producers' surplus: $TS = CS + PS$.

Total Utility The total satisfaction a person receives from consuming a particular quantity of a good.

Transaction Costs The costs associated with the time and effort needed to search out, negotiate, and consummate an exchange.

Transfer Payment A payment to persons that is not made in return for goods and services currently supplied.

Transitivity The principle whereby if A is preferred to B, and B is preferred to C, then A is preferred to C.

Transmission Mechanism The routes, or channels, traveled by the ripple effects that the money market creates and that affect the goods and services market (represented by the aggregate demand and aggregate supply curves in the *AD–AS* framework).

Trust A combination of firms that come together to act as a monopolist.

U

U.S. Treasury Securities Bonds and bond-like securities issued by the U.S. Treasury when it borrows.

Undervalued A currency is undervalued if its price in terms of other currencies is below the equilibrium price.

Unemployment Rate The percentage of the civilian force that is unemployed: Unemployment rate = Number of unemployed persons ÷ Civilian labor force.

Unit Elastic Demand The demand when the percentage change in quantity demanded is equal to the percentage change in price. The quantity demanded changes proportionately to price changes.

Unit of Account A function of money, a common measure in which relative values are expressed.

Util An artificial construct used to measure utility.

Utility A measure of the satisfaction, happiness, or benefit that results from the consumption of a good.

V

Value Added The dollar value contributed to a final good at each stage of production.

Value Marginal Product (VMP) The price of the good multiplied by the marginal physical product of the factor: $VMP = P \times MPP$.

Variable Costs Costs that vary with output; the costs associated with variable inputs.

Variable Input An input whose quantity can be changed as output changes.

Veil of Ignorance The imaginary veil or curtain behind which a person does not know his or her position in the income distribution.

Velocity The average number of times a dollar is spent to buy final goods and services in a year.

Vertical Merger A merger between companies in the same industry but at different stages of the production process.

W

Wage Discrimination The situation in which individuals of equal ability

and productivity (as measured by their contribution to output) are paid different wage rates.

Wealth The value of all assets owned, both monetary and nonmonetary.

X

X-Inefficiency The increase in costs and organizational slack in a monopoly resulting from the lack of competitive pressure to push costs down to their lowest possible level.

Y

Yield The annual coupon payment divided by the price paid for the bond.

Note: Locators followed by an n indicate notes and by an ex indicate examples.